1949 Lithium salts first used for bipolar disorder. *p. 244*

1951 Chlorpromazine, first antipsychotic drug, tested. *p. 456*

1951 Carl Rogers publishes *Client-Centered Therapy. p. 68*

1952 First edition of DSM published by the American Psychiatric Association. *p. 103*

1952 Sex-change operation performed on Christine Jorgensen. *p. 418*

1953 Alfred Kinsey reports on sexual behavior of women. *p. 418*

1953 Samaritans, first suicide prevention center, founded in England. *p. 277*

1955 The Los Angeles Suicide Prevention Center founded. *p. 277*

1956 Family systems theory and therapy launched. *p. 72*

1958 Joseph Wolpe develops desensitization. *p. 146*

1961 Thomas Szasz publishes *The Myth of Mental Illness. p. 4*

1962 Albert Ellis proposes rational-emotive therapy. *p. 131*

1963 The Community Mental Health Act helps trigger deinstitutionalization in the United States. *p. 465*

1963 Antianxiety drug Valium introduced in the United States. *p. 135*

1964 U.S. Surgeon General warns that smoking can be dangerous to human health. *p. 364*

1965 Norepinephrine and serotonin theories of depression proposed. *p. 199*

1967 Aaron Beck publishes cognitive theory and therapy for depression. *pp. 205, 228*

1967 Methadone maintenance treatment begins. *p. 380*

1967 Holmes and Rahe develop Social Adjustment Rating Scale to measure life stress. *p. 306*

1969 Elisabeth Kübler Ross publishes *On Death and Dying. p. 266*

1970 Masters and Johnson publish *Human Sexual Inadequacy* and launch sex therapy. *p. 400*

1972 CAT scan introduced. *p. 96*

1973 DSM stops listing homosexuality as a mental disorder. *p. 418*

1973 David Rosenhan conducts study *On Being Sane in Insane Places. pp. 73, 445*

1975 Endorphins — natural opioids — discovered in human brain. *p. 359*

1975 Martin Seligman publishes *Helplessness. p. 208*

1975 U.S. Supreme Court declares that patients in institutions have right to adequate treatment. *p. 596*

1981 MRI first used as diagnostic tool. *p. 96*

1981 Researchers discover that Ritalin helps persons with ADHD. *p. 555*

1982 John Hinckley found not guilty by reason of insanity of the attempted murder of President Reagan. *p. 582*

1987 Antidepressant Prozac approved in the United States. *p. 238*

1988 American Psychological Society founded. *p. 21*

1990 Human Genome Project launched. *p. 49*

1990 Dr. Jack Kevorkian performs his first assisted suicide. *p. 276*

1993 Annual Prozac sales reach $1.2 billion. *p. 238*

1994 DSM-IV published. *p. 103*

1998 Annual Prozac sales reach $3 billion. *p. 238*

1998 Viagra goes on sale in the United States. *p. 404*

1999 Killing rampage at Columbine High School stirs public concern about identifying and treating dangerousness in children. *p. 594*

1999 U.S. Supreme Court rules that mental patients have a right to treatment in the community rather than in institutions when it is available. *p. 598*

abnormal*psychology*

abnormal *psychology*

FOURTH EDITION

Ronald J. Comer
Princeton University

Worth Publishers
New York

Abnormal Psychology, Fourth Edition
© 2001, 1998, 1995, 1992 by Worth Publishers and W. H. Freeman and Company
All rights reserved.
Printed in the United States of America

Printing: 5 4 3 2 1
Year: 03 02 01 00

Publisher: Catherine Woods
Sponsoring Editor: Marjorie Byers
Development Editor: Moira Lerner
Senior Marketing Manager: Renee Ortbals
Project Editor: Jane O'Neill
Art Director and Cover/Text Design: Barbara Reingold
Production Manager: Sarah Segal
New Media and Supplements Editor: Graig Donini
Layout Design: Paul Lacy
Illustration Coordinator: Lou Capaldo
Photo Researcher: Deborah Goodsite
Cover and Chapter Opening Illustrations: Wiktor Sadowski
Composition: Compset, Inc.
Manufacturing: Von Hoffmann Press
Cover Printer: Coral Graphic Services, Inc.

Library of Congress Cataloging-in-Publication Data
Comer, Ronald J.
    Abnormal psychology / Ronald J. Comer.--4th ed.
        p. cm.
    Includes bibliographical references and index.
    ISBN 0-7167-3852-X
    1. Psychology, Pathological. I. Title.

    RC454.C634 2000
    616.89--dc21   00-034734

Worth Publishers
41 Madison Avenue
New York, NY 10010
www.worthpublishers.com

To Catherine Woods,
whose vision, wisdom, and grace
guided this book

Ronald J. Comer has been a professor in Princeton University's Department of Psychology for the past 26 years and has served as director of clinical psychology studies for most of that time. He is also currently the director of the department's undergraduate program.

Professor Comer has received the President's Award for Distinguished Teaching at the university. His course "Abnormal Psychology" is one of the university's most popular, and he has offered it almost every year since his arrival at Princeton.

He is also a practicing clinical psychologist and serves as a consultant to the Eden Institute for Persons with Autism and to hospitals and family practice residency programs throughout New Jersey. Additionally, he holds an adjunct position as Clinical Associate Professor of Family Medicine at the UMDNJ-Robert Wood Johnson Medical School.

In addition to writing *Abnormal Psychology*, Professor Comer is the author of the textbook *Fundamentals of Abnormal Psychology*, now in its second edition. He has also published a number of journal articles in clinical psychology, social psychology, and family medicine.

Professor Comer was an undergraduate at the University of Pennsylvania and a graduate student at Clark University. He currently lives in Lawrenceville, New Jersey, with his wife, Marlene, and their dog, Annie. From there, he can keep an eye on his New York–residing sons, Greg and Jon, and on the Philadelphia sports teams with which he grew up.

contents in brief

Contents

CHAPTER ⑪

Eating Disorders   321

CHAPTER ⑫

Substance-Related Disorders   349

CHAPTER (16)

CHAPTER (17)

CHAPTER (18)

$\mathcal{I}$have always believed that the task of writing a textbook on abnormal psychology is similar to that of developing a course on the subject. In each undertaking, my goal is to open the doors of this important field for students in an enlightening, provocative, and engaging way—one that conveys my passion for the field and for those people who are faced with psychological problems and my deep respect for the clinical field's practitioners and researchers.

There are also parallels between writing a new edition of a textbook and revising a course. In each case, one is trying to update the material thoroughly, retain techniques that have been successful previously, eliminate or change what has been unsuccessful, and develop new forms of presentation that can better enlighten and excite students. Although I am deeply gratified by the very positive responses of professors and students to the past editions of *Abnormal Psychology*, I have thought long and hard about how to keep improving this text for a new generation of students. Similarly, I have listened carefully to my colleagues in this enterprise—the professors and students who have used the textbook over the past nine years—and I have sought to incorporate their ideas into *Abnormal Psychology,* Fourth Edition. The result, I believe, is a book that will greatly please both professors and readers. At the risk of seeming shamelessly immodest, I would like to describe what I believe to be special about this book.

Continuing Strengths

In this edition, I have been careful to retain the goals, themes, material, and techniques that have worked successfully and been embraced enthusiastically by past readers.

BREADTH AND BALANCE The field's many theories, studies, disorders, and treatments are presented completely and accurately. *All* major models—psychological, biological, and sociocultural—receive objective, balanced, up-to-date coverage, without bias toward any single approach.

HUMANITY The subject of abnormal psychology is people—very often people in great pain. I have therefore tried to write always with humanity and to impart this awareness to students. The book also speaks with a single voice, in clear and straightforward language—the main advantage of a single-author book.

INTEGRATED COVERAGE OF TREATMENT Discussions of treatment are presented throughout the book. In addition to a complete overview of treatment in the opening chapters, each of the pathology chapters includes a full discussion of relevant treatment approaches.

RICH CASE MATERIAL I integrate numerous clinical examples, to bring theoretical and clinical issues to life.

CROSS-CULTURAL AND GENDER COVERAGE Issues raised by ethnic and gender differences, as well as related problems of bias, are given constant consideration, and, in fact, the sociocultural model is presented on an equal footing with the other models of psychological abnormality. Coverage includes such topics as gender and depression, the historical use of labeling to suppress certain groups of individuals, and race differences in body image and eating behavior.

TOPICS OF SPECIAL INTEREST I devote full chapters to important subjects that are of special interest to college-age readers, such as eating disorders and suicide, and I also cover controversial issues that are currently being spotlighted by the news media, including the rise in Ritalin use, treatment over the Internet, the right to commit suicide, and the use of St. John's wort and other "natural" treatments.

A FOCUS ON CRITICAL THINKING The book provides tools for thinking critically about abnormal psychology. Readers acquire an ability to assess and question current beliefs.

"CROSSROADS" The concluding section in each chapter, *Crossroads*, brings together the principles and findings of the various models of abnormality. Each *Crossroads* section asks whether competing models can work together in a more integrated approach and describes growing efforts of this kind. It also summarizes where the field now stands and where it may be going.

STIMULATING ILLUSTRATIONS Chapters illustrate concepts, disorders, treatments, and applications with stunning photographs, diagrams, and graphs. All graphs and tables, many new to this edition, reflect the most up-to-date data available.

ADAPTABILITY Chapters are self-contained, so they can be assigned in whatever order makes sense to the professor.

Changes and Features New to This Edition

The study of abnormal psychology continues to grow steadily. Similarly, the field of undergraduate education is in constant motion, with new pedagogical techniques and insights emerging each day. Such developments have spurred me to include a variety of important changes and new features in the current edition.

THOROUGH UPDATE I have presented recent theories, research, and events—including more than 1,500 new references from the years 1998–2000, 45 new tables and figures, and close to 200 new photos.

DSM-IV UPDATE All DSM-IV information reflects changes found in the newly published *DSM-IV Text Revision*.

ENHANCED INTEGRATION OF MODELS Discussions throughout the text, and particularly the revised *Crossroads* discussions, help students better understand where and how the various models work together, along with clarifying how the models differ.

MORE EFFICIENT OVERVIEW OF MODELS In this edition I have combined the introductory coverage of the various models—biological, psychodynamic, behavioral, cognitive, humanistic-existential, and sociocultural—into one chapter instead of two.

INNOVATIVE DESIGN In an outstanding lecture, a variety of stimulating elements merge with the basic presentation to captivate the audience—anecdotes, interesting side points, provocative questions, slides, video, and the like. Shouldn't textbook discussions offer the same exciting blend? This edition offers a unique and accessible design—a single text column adjoined by a large margin space—that allows precise intersections between text discussions and perfectly placed side views, quotes, critical thinking questions, key definitions, DSM-IV criteria, special photos and illustrations, and more. Trial runs reveal that readers love the stimulating blend offered by this design and that it helps them better understand and retain the material.

NEW FEATURE: "SIDE VIEWS" I have strategically placed interesting psychology facts, findings, tidbits, and quotes in margins throughout the text to engage students and make the material more accessible. Topics include Freud's fee for therapy, famous movie therapists, and the cost of developing a psychotropic drug. There are more than 500 side views in all.

NEW FEATURE: "CONSIDER THIS" Every chapter includes numerous critical thought questions, under the rubric *Consider This*, located in margins and at the end of boxed material. More than 200 such questions are offered.

NEW FEATURE: MARGIN GLOSSARY About 500 key words are defined in the margins of pages on which the words appear. In addition, a traditional glossary is available at the back of the book.

NEW FEATURE: DSM-IV CHECKLISTS The discussion of each disorder is accompanied by a detailed checklist of the DSM-IV criteria used to diagnose the disorder.

NUMEROUS NEW BOXES: A variety of new boxes have been added, covering topics such as the Y2K scare, questionable ethics in drug therapy research, books recommended by therapists, and computer therapy.

NEW FEATURE: "CYBERSTUDY" Each chapter ends with a *CyberStudy* section—a guide for integrating the chapter material with videos and other features found on the *Student CD-ROM*.

MORE DETAILED CHAPTER OVERVIEWS AND OUTLINES appear at the beginning of each chapter.

CASE STUDIES OPEN EVERY CHAPTER to immediately engage the reader and bring the material to life.

ENHANCED CHAPTER SUMMARIES help students better review and retain chapter material by highlighting key words and citing appropriate text pages.

Supplements

The very enthusiastic response to supplements accompanying previous editions has been gratifying. This edition is able to retain those supplements and to enhance them.

ENHANCED: VIDEO SEGMENTS FOR *ABNORMAL PSYCHOLOGY* Designed to bring an added dimension to lectures, this set of four videotapes (ISBNs 0–7167–5121–6; 0–7167–5157–7) contains more than 80 one- to eight-minute clips that depict disorders, show historical footage, and illustrate clinical topics, pathologies, treatments, laboratory experiments, and clinical dilemmas. A new fourth tape (ISBN 0–7167–5157–7) adds more than one-and-a-half hours of excerpts taken from the outstanding series *The Mind*, Second Edition; *The Brain*, Second Edition; and *The World of Abnormal Psychology*.

ENHANCED: STUDENT CD-ROM This interactive CD-ROM, which accompanies each textbook, offers students numerous intriguing videos running three to five minutes each. Videos usually center on a person with a disorder discussed in the text. The students first view the video and then answer a series of thought-provoking questions about it. Their answers can be entered directly on the screen and then saved to a disk or printed out to be handed in. Additionally, the CD contains multiple-choice practice test questions, with built-in instructional feedback for every answer. The *CyberStudy* section at the end of each chapter directly ties chapter material to the CD. Sixteen new videos have been added to this edition's CD-ROM, along with new questions and practice tests.

NEW: *ABNORMAL PSYCHOLOGY* WEB COMPANION, INCLUDING ON-LINE QUIZZING, AT WWW.WORTHPUBLISHERS.COM/COMERABNORMALPSYCHOLOGY4E This Web site offers an ever-expanding set of resources for both students and instructors. Features include flashcards for learning key vocabulary, multiple-choice practice tests for every chapter with built-in instructional feedback, Web links, and periodic *newsletters* that inform students of new research in the context of the book's coverage. The Web site is also the access point for *on-line quizzing*. Instructors can easily and securely quiz students on-line using prewritten, multiple-choice questions for each text chapter (not from the *Test Bank*). Students receive instant feedback and can take the quizzes many times. Instructors can view results by quiz, student, or question or can get weekly results via e-mail.

ENHANCED: INSTRUCTOR'S TRANSPARENCY SET Fifty full-color images, charts, photos, and graphs from the text are available for use in lectures (ISBN 0–7167–3858–9). Additionally, there are many transparency masters of text tables and DSM-IV criteria listings available in the *Instructor's Manual*.

ENHANCED: STUDENT WORKBOOK The *Student Workbook and Study Guide* (ISBN 0–7167–3853–8), by Katherine M. Nicolai of Rockhurst College, actively involves students in the text material, using a variety of engaging exercises. Students who complete the exercises can better organize and apply what they have studied.

ENHANCED: INSTRUCTOR'S TEST BANK (PRINTED AND CD-ROM) This enhanced and greatly improved *Test Bank,* by Debra and John Hull of Wheeling Jesuit University (ISBN 0–7167–3856–2), offers more than 2,000 multiple-choice, fill-in-the-blank, and essay questions. Each question is assessed according to difficulty, identified as factual or applied, and keyed to the page in the text where the source information appears. The electronic version on a dual-platform CD-ROM (ISBN 0–7167–3857–0) allows you to add, edit, and resequence questions. The CD is also the access point for *on-line testing*. With Diploma (from Brownstone Research Group), instructors can now create and administer secure exams over a network and over the Internet, with questions that incorporate multimedia and interactive exercises. The program lets you restrict tests to specific computers or time blocks and includes an impressive suite of gradebook and result-analysis features.

ENHANCED: INSTRUCTOR'S RESOURCE MANUAL This extensive teaching resource (ISBN 0–7167–3855–4), by Stephen M. Saunders of Marquette University, with added material and a video guide by me, ties together the supplements package for instructors and teaching assistants. The *Resource Manual* offers strategies for using the *Video Segments*, *Student CD-ROM*, Web site, and transparencies. It further includes detailed chapter outlines, lists of learning objectives, and many new ideas for lectures and for launching class discussions. It also lays out precise DSM-IV criteria for each of the disorders and offers most of this material in transparency masters.

Acknowledgments

I am enormously grateful to the many people who have contributed to writing and producing this book. I particularly thank Marlene Comer for her superb, never-ending work on every aspect of the manuscript, from making editorial judgments to typing.

In addition, I am greatly indebted to Marion Kowalewski for her outstanding work on the manuscript, to Marlene Catania, for her fine work on the references, as well as to the wonderful help of Arlene Kerch, Vera Sohl, Bernie VanUiter, and Carole Zaffarese. And I sincerely appreciate the superb work of the book's research assistants, including Linda Chamberlin, Jon Comer, and Greg Comer.

Throughout four editions, I have received valuable feedback from academicians and clinicians who have reviewed portions of the manuscript and commented on its clarity, accuracy, and completeness. Their collective knowledge, and their willingness to share it with me, have in large part shaped the fourth edition. I am of course indebted to those who reviewed the manuscript of the new edition: Greg Bolich, Cleveland Community College; Loretta Butehorn, Boston College; David N. Carpenter, Southwest Texas State University; John Forsyth, University at Albany, State University of New York; Mary W. Meagher, Texas A&M University; Sandy Naumann, Delaware Technical & Community College; Randall Salekin, Florida International University; John Suler, Rider University; Lance L. Weinmann, Canyon College; and Doug Wessel, Black Hills State University.

I also wish to thank the many professors and clinicians around the country who offered special counsel on the fourth edition, through personal communication with me during the writing of the text: Joni L. Mihura, University of Toledo; Mary Ann M. Pagaduan, American Osteopathic Association; Harold A. Pincus, Chair, DSM-IV, University of Pittsburgh, Western Psychiatric Institute and Clinic; Chris Piotrowski, University of West Florida; R. W. Rieber, John Jay College, CUNY; and James M. Wood, University of Texas at El Paso.

I acknowledge once again the reviewers of earlier editions. Their contributions remain integral to the quality of the revision: Kent G. Bailey, Virginia Commonwealth University; Marna S. Barnett, Indiana University of Pennsylvania; Otto A. Berliner, Alfred State College; Allan Berman, University of Rhode Island; Douglas Bernstein, University of Toronto, Mississauga; Sarah Cirese, College of Marin; Victor B. Cline, University of Utah; E. M. Coles, Simon Fraser University; Frederick L. Coolidge, University of Colorado, Colorado Springs; Mary Dozier, University of Delaware; S. Wayne Duncan, University of Washington, Seattle; Morris N. Eagle, York University; Alan Fridlund, University of California, Santa Barbara; Stan Friedman, Southwest Texas State University; Lawrence L. Galant, Gaston College; Morton G. Harmatz, University of Massachusetts; David A. Hoffman, University of California, Santa Cruz; William G. Iacono, University of Minnesota; Bernard Kleinman, University of Missouri, Kansas City; Alan G. Krasnoff, University of Missouri, St. Louis; Robert D. Langston, University of Texas, Austin; Kimberlyn Leary, University of Michigan; Harvey R. Lerner, Kaiser-Permanente Medical Group; Arnold D. LeUnes, Texas A&M University; Michael P. Levin, Kenyon College; Mary Margaret Livingston, Louisiana Technical University; Joseph LoPiccolo, University of Missouri, Columbia; Jerald J. Marshall, University of Central Florida; Janet R. Matthews, Loyola University; Robert J. McCaffrey, State University of New York, Albany; F. Dudley McGlynn, Auburn University; Lily D. McNair, University of Georgia; Katherina M. Nicolai, Iowa State University; Daniel Paulson, Carthage College; Paul A. Payne, University of Cincinnati; David V. Perkins, Ball State University; Norman Poppel, Middlesex County College; David E. Powley, University of Mobile; Max W. Rardin, University of Wyoming, Laramie; Lynn P. Rehm, University of Houston; Leslie A. Rescorla, Bryn Mawr College; Vic Ryan, University of Colorado, Boulder; A. A. Sappington, University of Alabama, Birmingham; Roberta S. Sherman, Bloomington Center for Counseling and Human Development; Sandra T. Sigmon, University of Maine, Orono; Janet A. Simons, Central Iowa Psychological Services; Jay R. Skidmore, Utah State

University; John M. Spores, Purdue University, South Central; Thomas A. Tutko, San Jose State University; Norris D. Vestre, Arizona State University; Joseph L. White, University of California, Irvine; and Amy C. Willis, Washington, DC, Veterans Administration Medical Center.

The authors of the book's supplements package have my thanks for again doing splendid jobs with their respective supplements: Debra B. Hull and John H. Hull, Wheeling Jesuit University (*Test Bank*); Stephen M. Saunders, Marquette University (*Instructor's Manual*), Katherine M. Nicolai, Rockhurst College (*Study Guide*), Elaine Cassel, Lord Fairfax Community College and Marymount University (*CD-ROM*).

I wish to also extend my deep appreciation to the core team of professionals at Worth Publishers and W. H. Freeman and Company who have worked so closely with me to produce this edition. Although the author gets most of the credit, the production of a textbook represents a collaboration by more people than one can possibly imagine. Ultimately, the book's quality reflects the ability, judgment, and dedication of these people. In my case, I was blessed with a core team of extraordinary people—each extremely talented, each committed to excellence, each dedicated to the education of readers, each bound by a remarkable work ethic, and each a wonderful person. It is accurate to say that these people were my co-authors and co-teachers in this enterprise, and I am forever in their debt. They are, in alphabetical order: Marge Byers, sponsoring editor; Mark Cajigao, former sponsoring editor; Deborah Goodsite, photo researcher; Paul Lacy, page layout artist; Moira Lerner, development editor; Jane O'Neill, project editor; Barbara Reingold, art director; Sarah Segal, production manager; and Catherine Woods, publisher. I should note that it was Catherine who first proposed the idea of a textbook format that would parallel the elements of a successful lecture and who then assembled and oversaw the perfect team to accomplish this ambitious goal. Throughout this undertaking, as always, she has been an individual of great vision, a wise and caring leader, and a person of the highest character and warmth.

In addition to this core team, there are a number of other people at Worth and at Freeman to whom I am indebted. Elizabeth Widdicombe, president of Worth and Freeman, has continued to lead the companies courageously, to create a very supportive environment for my books, and to be a good friend. I am also indebted to Graig Donini, Worth new media and supplements editor, who has so skillfully developed and guided the production of the extraordinary and innovative supplements package that accompanies the text. Still other professionals from Worth and Freeman to whom I am indebted are: Todd Elder, director of advertising; Tracey Kuehn, associate managing editor; Lou Capaldo, illustration coordinator; Wiktor Sadowski, cover and chapter opening illustrator; Barbara Salazar, copy editor; Ann-Marie WongSam and Karen Osborne, proofreaders; Ellen Brennan, indexer; Michele Kornegay, free-lance project editor; Megan Burns, editorial assistant; Vickii Wong, photo research assistant; Nancy Giraldo Walker, rights and permissions manager; and John Philp, for his help with *CyberStudy* images.

Finally, not to be overlooked are the superb professionals at Worth and at Freeman who continuously work with remarkable energy, skill, and judgment to bring my books to the attention of professors across the world: Renee Ortbals, senior marketing manager; Marie Schappert, vice-president and director of sales; and the company's wonderful sales representatives. Thank you.

Like all previous editions, a project of this scope would not be possible without a loving and supportive family, and I am truly grateful to mine. As time moves on, I am particularly grateful that all those whom I cited and thanked three years ago are still here, sharing with me the adventures of life—Claire Comer, Herman Kramer, Pam Weinstein, Steve Comer, Dave Slotkin, Hadaso Slotkin, Sharon Hardy, Chuck Hardy, Alan Hershman, and Annie Comer (the four-legged Comer). As in the past, I offer a special thanks and word of love to my wife, Marlene, who makes my life so rich and complete and joyful. And, finally, I'd like to mention and acknowledge my sons, Greg and Jon. I know that I have many things to be grateful for in life, but at the top of the list is the opportunity to be a part of their lives and to have seen them develop from precious infants into such accomplished, good, and caring adults. They fill my life with pride and meaning and love, and I thank them for being the wonderful people, and sons, that they are.

Ronald J. Comer
Princeton University
July 2000

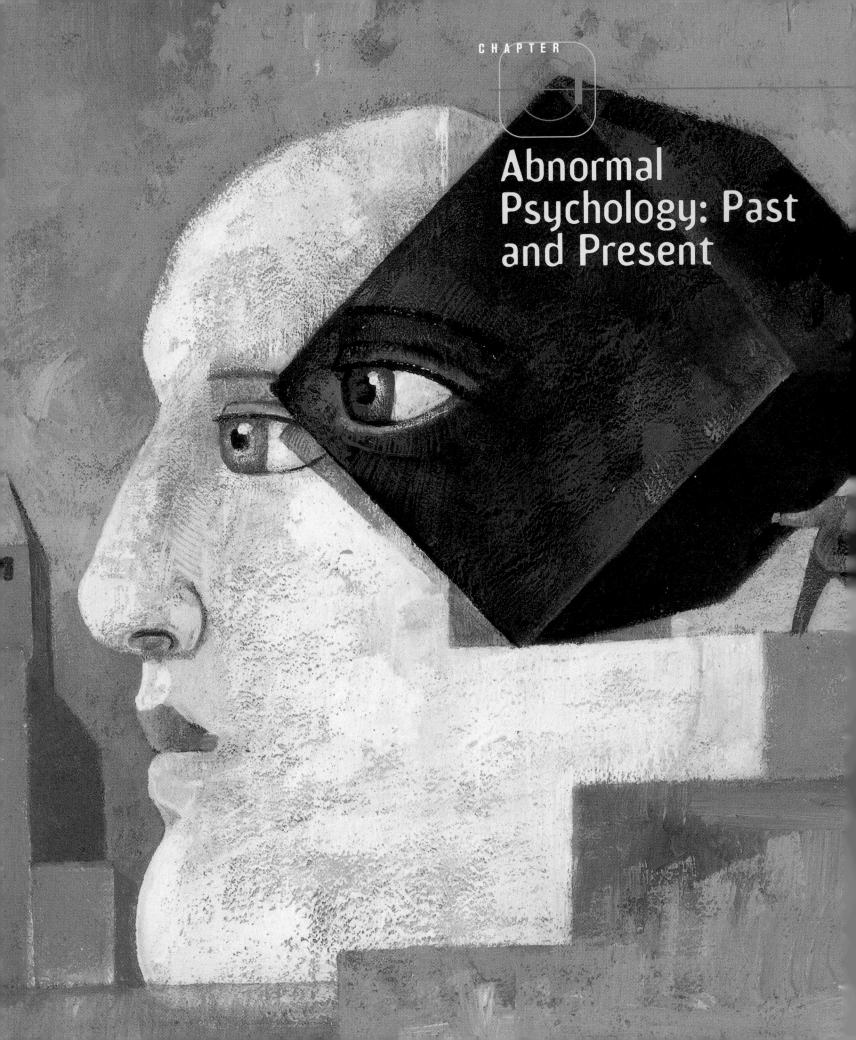

Abnormal Psychology: Past and Present

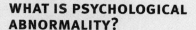 Alexandra cries herself to sleep every night. She is certain that the future holds nothing but misery. Indeed, this is the only thing she does feel certain about. "I'm going to die and my daughters are going to die. We're doomed. The world is ugly. I detest every moment of this life." She has great trouble sleeping. She is afraid to close her eyes, afraid that she will never wake up, and what will happen to her daughters then? When she does drift off to sleep, her dreams are nightmares filled with blood, dismembered bodies, thunder, decay, death, destruction.

One morning Alexandra has trouble getting out of bed. The thought of facing another day overwhelms her. Again she wishes she were dead, and she wishes her daughters were dead. "We'd all be better off." She feels paralyzed by her depression and anxiety, too tired to move and too afraid to leave her house. She decides once again to stay home and to keep her daughters with her. She makes sure that all shades are drawn and that every conceivable entrance to the house is secured. She is afraid of the world and afraid of life. Every day is the same, filled with depression, fear, immobility, and withdrawal. Every day is a nightmare.

During the past year Brad has been hearing mysterious voices that tell him to quit his job, leave his family, and prepare for the coming invasion. These voices have brought tremendous confusion and emotional turmoil to Brad's life. He believes that they come from beings in distant parts of the universe who are somehow wired to him. Although it gives him a sense of purpose and specialness to be the chosen target of their communications, they also make him tense and anxious. He dreads the coming invasion. When he refuses an order, the voices insult and threaten him and turn his days into a waking nightmare.

Brad has put himself on a sparse diet against the possibility that his enemies may be contaminating his food. He has found a quiet apartment far from his old haunts where he has laid in a good stock of arms and ammunition. His family and friends have tried to reach out to Brad, to understand his problems, and to dissuade him from the disturbing course he is taking. Every day, however, he retreats further into his world of mysterious voices and imagined dangers.

Most of us would probably consider Alexandra's and Brad's emotions, thoughts, and behavior psychologically abnormal, the result of a state sometimes called *psychopathology*, *maladjustment*, *emotional disturbance*, or *mental illness*. These terms have been applied to the many problems that seem closely tied to the human brain or mind. Psychological abnormality affects the famous and the obscure, the rich and the poor, the upright and the perverse. Politicians, actors, writers, and other public figures of the present and the past have struggled with it. Psychological problems can bring great suffering, but they can also be the source of inspiration and energy.

Because they are so common and so personal, these problems capture the interest of us all. Hundreds of novels, plays, films, and television programs have explored what many people see as the dark side of human nature, and self-help books flood the market (see Box 1-1). Mental health experts are popular guests on both television and radio, and some even have their own shows.

The field devoted to the scientific study of the problems we find so fascinating is usually called **abnormal psychology**. As in any science, workers in this field, called *clinical scientists*, gather information systematically so that they may describe, predict, and explain the phenomena they study. The knowledge that they acquire is then used by *clinical practitioners*, whose role is to detect, assess, and treat abnormal patterns of functioning.

What Is Psychological Abnormality?

Although their general goals are similar to those of other scientific professionals, clinical scientists and practitioners face problems that make their work especially difficult. One of the most troubling is that psychological abnormality is very hard to define. Consider once again Alexandra and Brad. Why are we so ready to call their responses abnormal?

Although many definitions of abnormality have been proposed over the years, none is universally accepted (Mechanic, 1999). Still, most of the definitions have certain features in common, often called "the four D's": deviance, distress, dysfunction, and danger. That is, patterns of psychological abnormality are typically *deviant* (different, extreme, unusual, perhaps even bizarre); *distressing* (unpleasant and upsetting to the person); *dysfunctional* (interfering with the person's ability to conduct daily activities in a constructive way); and possibly *dangerous*. These criteria offer a useful starting point from which to explore the phenomena of psychological abnormality. As we shall see, however, they have key limitations.

Deviance

Abnormal psychological functioning is *deviant*, but deviant from what? Alexandra's and Brad's behaviors, thoughts, and emotions are different from those that are considered normal in our place

Deviance and abnormality *Along the Niger River, men of the Wodaabe tribe put on elaborate makeup and costumes to attract women. In Western society, the same behavior would break behavioral norms and probably be judged abnormal.*

and time. We do not expect people to cry themselves to sleep every night, wish themselves dead, or obey voices that no one else hears.

In short, behavior, thoughts, and emotions are deemed abnormal when they violate a society's ideas about proper functioning. Each society establishes **norms**—explicit and implicit rules for proper conduct. Behavior that violates *legal* norms is called criminal. Behavior, thoughts, and emotions that violate norms of psychological functioning are called abnormal.

Judgments of abnormality vary from society to society. A society's norms grow from its particular **culture**—its history, values, institutions, habits, skills, technology, and arts. A society whose culture places great value on competition and assertiveness may accept aggressive behavior, whereas one that emphasizes cooperation and gentleness may discourage aggressive behavior and even condemn it as abnormal. A society's values may also change over time, causing its views of what is psychologically abnormal to change as well. In Western society, for example, a woman's participation in the business world was widely considered inappropriate and strange a hundred years ago. Today the same behavior is usually admired.

Judgments of abnormality depend on *specific circumstances* as well as on cultural norms. What if, for example, we were to learn that the desperately unhappy Alexandra lives in Serbia, an area pulled apart by years of combat, and that the happiness she once knew vanished when her husband and son were killed. As year followed year with only temporary relief, Alexandra stopped expecting anything except more of the same. In this light, Alexandra's reactions do not seem so inappropriate. If anything is abnormal here, it is her situation. Many painful human experiences produce intense reactions—large-scale catastrophes and disasters, rape, child abuse, war, terminal illness, chronic pain (Ursano et al., 1999; Turner & Lloyd, 1995). Is there an "appropriate" way to react to such things? Should we ever call reactions to them abnormal?

NORM-BUSTERS

In 1971, women in English mental hospitals outnumbered men by 35 to 1. That ratio was reversed, however, in English prisons (Asimov, 1997). Might gender influence how a society interprets norm-breaking behavior?

Changing times *Two decades ago, a woman's love for bullfighting would have been considered strange, perhaps even abnormal. Today Cristina Sánchez is one of Spain's finest matadors and is considered a role model.*

Distress

Even functioning that is considered unusual does not necessarily qualify as abnormal. According to many clinical theorists, behavior, ideas, or emotions usually have to cause *distress* before they can be labeled abnormal. Consider the Ice Breakers, a group of people in Michigan who go swimming in lakes throughout the state every weekend from November through February. The colder the weather, the better they like it. One man, a member of the group for seventeen years, says he loves the challenge. Man against the elements. A 37-year-old lawyer believes that the weekly shock is good for her health. "It cleanses me," she says. "It perks me up and gives me strength." Another Ice Breaker likes the special bond the group members share. "When we get together, we know we've done something special, something no one else understands. I can't even tell most of the people I know that I'm an Ice Breaker."

Certainly these people are different from most of us, but is their behavior abnormal? Far from experiencing distress, they feel energized and challenged. Their positive feelings must cause us to hesitate before we decide that they are functioning abnormally.

Should we conclude, then, that feelings of distress must always be present before a person's functioning can be considered abnormal? Not necessarily. Some people who function abnormally maintain a positive frame of mind. What if this were the case with Brad, the young man who hears mysterious voices? Brad does experience severe distress over the coming invasion and the life changes he feels forced to make. But what if he enjoyed listening to the voices, felt honored to be chosen, and looked forward to saving the world? Shouldn't we still regard his

ABNORMAL PSYCHOLOGY The scientific study of abnormal behavior in order to describe, predict, explain, and change abnormal patterns of functioning.

NORMS A society's stated and unstated rules for proper conduct.

CULTURE A people's common history, values, institutions, habits, skills, technology, and arts.

DYSFUNCTION IN THE WORKPLACE
Stress and psychological issues are increasingly interfering with job attendance, according to recent surveys (Shellenbarger, 1998). Unscheduled absences from work have risen 11 to 25 percent since 1995, with stress and personal matters cited as the fastest-growing causes.

functioning as abnormal? As we shall discover in Chapter 7, people whose behaviors are described as manic often feel just wonderful, yet still they are diagnosed as psychologically disturbed. Indeed, in many cases it is their euphoria and disproportionate sense of well-being that make them candidates for this diagnosis.

Dysfunction

Abnormal behavior tends to be *dysfunctional;* that is, it interferes with daily functioning. It so upsets, distracts, or confuses people that they cannot care for themselves properly, participate in ordinary social interactions, or work productively. Brad, for example, has quit his job, left his family, and prepared to withdraw from the productive life he once led.

Here again one's culture plays a role in the definition of abnormality. Our society holds that it is important to carry out daily activities in an effective, self-enhancing manner. Thus Brad's behavior is likely to be regarded as abnormal and undesirable, whereas that of the Ice Breakers, who continue to perform well in their jobs and enjoy fulfilling relationships, would probably be considered simply unusual.

Then again, dysfunction alone does not necessarily indicate psychological abnormality. Some people (Gandhi, Dick Gregory, or César Chávez, for example) fast or in other ways deprive themselves of things they need as a means of protesting social injustice. Far from receiving a clinical label of some kind, they are widely viewed as admirable people—caring, sacrificing, even heroic.

Danger

Perhaps the ultimate in psychological dysfunctioning is behavior that becomes *dangerous* to oneself or others. Individuals whose behavior is consistently careless, hostile, or confused may be placing themselves or those around them at risk. Brad, for example, seems to be endangering himself by his diet and others by his buildup of arms and ammunition.

Although danger is often cited as a feature of abnormal psychological functioning, research suggests that it is actually the exception rather than the rule (Taylor & Gunn, 1999; Monahan, 1993, 1992). Despite popular misconceptions, most people struggling with anxiety, depression, and even bizarre thinking pose no immediate danger to themselves or to anyone else.

A spiritual experience *In the Val d' Isère, France, students bury themselves in snow up to their necks. Far from experiencing distress or displaying abnormality, they are engaging in a Japanese practice designed to open their hearts and enlarge their spirits.*

The Elusive Nature of Abnormality

If the concept of abnormality depends so heavily on social norms and values, it is no wonder that efforts to define psychological abnormality typically raise as many questions as they answer. Ultimately, each society selects general criteria for defining abnormality and then uses those criteria to judge particular cases.

Noting society's role in this process, one clinical theorist, Thomas Szasz (1997, 1987, 1961), argues that the whole concept of mental illness is invalid, a myth of sorts. According to Szasz, the deviations that society calls abnormal are simply "problems in living," not signs of something wrong within the person. Societies, he is convinced, invent the concept of mental illness so that they can better control or change people whose unusual patterns of functioning upset or threaten the social order.

Even if we assume that psychological abnormality is a valid concept and that it can indeed be defined, we may be unable to apply our definition consistently. If a behavior—excessive use of alcohol among college students, say—is familiar enough, the society may fail to recognize that it is deviant, distressful, dysfunctional, and dangerous. Thousands of college students throughout the United States are so dependent on alcohol that it interferes with their personal and aca-

TREATMENT A procedure designed to help change abnormal behavior into more normal behavior. Also called *therapy.*

demic lives, causes them great discomfort, jeopardizes their health, and often endangers them and the people around them. Yet their problem often goes unnoticed, certainly undiagnosed, by college administrators, other students, and health professionals. Alcohol is so much a part of the college subculture that it is easy to overlook drinking behavior that has become abnormal.

Conversely, a society may have trouble distinguishing between an abnormality that requires intervention and an *eccentricity*, or marked individuality, that others have no right to interfere with (see Box 1-2 on the next page). From time to time we see or hear about people who behave in ways we consider strange, such as a man who lives alone with a dozen cats and rarely talks to other people. The behavior of such people is deviant, and it may well be distressful and dysfunctional, yet many professionals think of it as eccentric rather than abnormal.

In short, while we may agree to define psychological abnormalities as patterns of functioning that are deviant, distressful, dysfunctional, and sometimes dangerous, we should be clear that these criteria are often vague and subjective. When is a pattern of behavior deviant, distressful, dysfunctional, and dangerous enough to be considered abnormal? The question may be impossible to answer. Few of the current categories of abnormality that we will meet in this book are as clear-cut as they may seem, and most continue to be debated by clinicians.

What Is Treatment?

Once clinicians decide that a person is indeed suffering from some form of psychological abnormality, they seek to treat it. **Treatment**, or *therapy*, is a procedure designed to change abnormal behavior into more normal behavior; it, too, requires careful definition (Brent & Kolko, 1998). For clinical scientists, the problem is closely related to defining abnormality. Consider the case of Bill:

> **February:** He cannot leave the house; Bill knows that for a fact. Home is the only place where he feels safe—safe from humiliation, danger, even ruin. If he were to go to work, his co-workers would somehow reveal their contempt for him. A pointed remark, a quizzical look—that's all it would take for him to get the message. If he were to go shopping at the store, before long everyone would be staring at him. Surely others would see his dark mood and thoughts; he wouldn't be able to hide them. He dare not even go for a walk alone in the woods—his heart would probably start racing again, bringing him to his knees and leaving him breathless, incoherent, and unable to get home. No, he's much better off staying in his room, trying to get through another evening of this curse called life.

> **July:** Bill's life revolves around his circle of friends: Bob and Jack, whom he knows from the office, where he was recently promoted to director of customer relations, and Frank and Tim, his weekend tennis partners. The gang meets for dinner every week at someone's house, and they chat about life, politics, and their jobs. Particularly special in Bill's life is Janice. They go to movies, restaurants, and shows together. She thinks Bill's just terrific, and Bill finds himself beaming whenever she's around. Bill looks forward to work each day and his one-on-one dealings with customers. He is enjoying life and basking in the glow of his many activities and relationships.

Bill's thoughts, feelings, and behavior were so debilitating in February that they affected all aspects of his life. Most of his symptoms had disappeared by July, and he returned to his previous level of functioning. All sorts of factors may have contributed to Bill's improvement. Friends and family members may have offered support or advice. A new job or vacation may have lifted his spirits. Perhaps he changed his diet or started to exercise. Any or all of these things may have been useful to Bill, but they could not be considered treatment, or therapy. Those

ANIMAL HOARDERS

Who collects large numbers of animals? Studies suggest that 75 percent of animal hoarders are women; 70 percent are single, divorced, or widowed; half are over 60 years old (Patronek, 1999). Most such individuals collect only one or two species, usually cats.

NORMAL DIFFERENCES?

In one survey, sizable numbers of people confessed to such deviant behaviors as snooping in their hosts' medicine cabinets (39 percent), not always flushing the toilet (23 percent), and believing that they have seen a ghost (10 percent) (Kanner, 1995). Should their behaviors be considered abnormal?

BOX 1-2

Marching to a Different Drummer: Eccentrics

Eccentricity takes a break *Gene Pool, a 37-year-old carpenter, journeys repeatedly around New York City wearing an outfit made of 500 empty cans. The reason? To make a statement about the need for recycling and to be noticed. Here he rests for a while on a city park bench.*

Gary Holloway, an environmental planner in San Francisco, keeps a veritable stable of hobbyhorses. He is also fascinated by Martin Van Buren. . . . He discovered that Van Buren was the only U.S. president not to have a society dedicated to his memory, so he promptly founded the Van Buren Fan Club. Holloway is a lifelong devotee of St. Francis of Assisi, and frequently dresses in the habit of a Franciscan monk. "It's comfortable, fun to wear, and I like the response I get when I wear it," he explains. "People always offer me a seat on the bus."

(WEEKS & JAMES, 1995, PP. 29, 36–37)

The dictionary defines an *eccentric* as a person who deviates from common behavior patterns or displays odd or whimsical behavior. But how can we separate a psychologically healthy person who has unusual habits from a person whose oddness is a symptom of psychopathology? Until recently, little research was done on eccentrics, but a lighthearted study may have started the ball rolling (Weeks & James, 1995).

The researcher David Weeks studied 1,000 eccentrics over a ten-year period and was able to pinpoint fifteen characteristics common to them. Altogether, he estimates that as many as 1 in 5,000 persons may be "classic, full-time eccentrics." Men and women seem equally prone to such patterns.

Weeks suggests that eccentrics do not typically suffer from mental disorders. Whereas the unusual behavior of persons with mental disorders is thrust upon them and usually causes them suffering, eccentricity is chosen freely and provides pleasure. In short, "Eccentrics know they're different and glory in it" (Weeks & James, 1995, p. 14). Similarly, the thought

---

terms are usually reserved for special, systematic procedures that are designed to help people overcome their psychological difficulties. According to the clinical theorist Jerome Frank, all forms of therapy have three essential features:

1. A *sufferer* who seeks relief from the healer.
2. A trained, socially accepted *healer,* whose expertise is accepted by the sufferer and his or her social group.
3. A *series of contacts* between the healer and the sufferer, through which the healer, often with the aid of a group, tries to produce certain changes in the sufferer's emotional state, attitudes, and behavior.

(Frank, 1973, pp. 2-3)

Frank's definition seems straightforward enough, yet clinicians argue about how to apply it. Carl Rogers, a pioneer in the modern clinical field whom we will meet in Chapter 3, noted that "therapists are not in agreement as to their goals or aims. . . . They are not in agreement as to what constitutes a successful outcome of their work. They cannot agree as to what constitutes a failure. It seems as though the field is completely chaotic and divided." Some clinicians view abnormality as an illness and so consider therapy a procedure that helps *cure* the illness. Others see abnormality as a problem in living and therapists as *teachers* of more functional behavior and thought. Clinicians even differ on what to call the person undergoing therapy: those who see abnormality as an illness speak of the "patient," while those who view it as a problem in living refer to the "client." Because both terms are so common, this book will use them interchangeably.

Despite their differences, most clinicians do agree that large numbers of people need therapy of one kind or another. Later, we shall encounter evidence that therapy is indeed often helpful (DeRubeis & Crits-Christoph, 1998).

COLLEGE COUNSELING
About 7 to 8 percent of all college students seek psychological counseling. The percentage is higher at small, private colleges and prestigious schools (Gallagher, 1998).

processes of eccentrics are not severely disrupted, and they do not leave the person dysfunctional.

In fact, Weeks found that eccentrics actually had fewer emotional problems than the general population. Perhaps being an "original" is good for mental health. The eccentrics in his study also seemed physically healthier than others, visiting a doctor only once every eight years on average. Weeks concludes that most eccentrics, despite their deviant behavior—perhaps even because of it—are happy, well-adjusted, and joyful people.

Are You Eccentric?

According to Weeks, the following 15 qualities (in descending order of importance) are characteristic of eccentrics. The first five are the most definitive, but possessing any ten may qualify a person as an eccentric.

- ⁜ Nonconforming
- ⁜ Creative
- ⁜ Strongly curious
- ⁜ Idealistic
- ⁜ Happily obsessed with a hobby (often more than one)
- ⁜ Aware from early childhood of being different from others
- ⁜ Intelligent
- ⁜ Opinionated and outspoken
- ⁜ Noncompetitive
- ⁜ Unusual eating or living habits
- ⁜ Not interested in the opinions or company of others
- ⁜ Mischievous sense of humor
- ⁜ Single
- ⁜ Eldest or only child
- ⁜ Bad speller

Famous Eccentrics

- ⁜ **James Joyce** always carried a tiny pair of lady's bloomers, which he waved in the air to show approval.
- ⁜ **Emily Dickinson** always wore white, never left her room, and hid her poems in tiny boxes.
- ⁜ **Benjamin Franklin** took "air baths" for his health, sitting naked in front of an open window.
- ⁜ **President John Quincy Adams** swam nude in the Potomac River each morning.
- ⁜ **Alexander Graham Bell** covered the windows of his house to keep out the rays of the full moon. He also tried to teach his dog how to talk.
- ⁜ The writer **D. H. Lawrence** enjoyed removing his clothes and climbing mulberry trees.

(ASIMOV, 1997; WEEKS & JAMES, 1995)

How Was Abnormality Viewed and Treated in the Past?

In any given year as many as 30 percent of the adults and 20 percent of the children and adolescents in the United States display serious psychological disturbances and are in need of clinical treatment (Kessler & Zhao, 1999; Kazdin, 1993; Regier et al., 1993). It is estimated that up to 19 of every hundred adults have a significant anxiety disorder, 10 suffer from profound depression, 5 display a personality disorder (inflexible and maladaptive personality traits), 1 has schizophrenia (loses touch with reality for an extended period of time), 1 experiences the brain deterioration of Alzheimer's disease, and 11 abuse alcohol or other drugs. Add to these figures as many as 600,000 suicide attempts, 500,000 rapes, and 3 million cases of child abuse each year, and it becomes apparent that abnormal psychological functioning is a pervasive problem in this country (Frankel, 1995; Koss, 1993; McCurdy & Daro, 1993). The numbers and rates in other countries are similarly high (Bijl, Ravelli, & van Zessen, 1998). Furthermore, most people go through periods of extreme tension, demoralization, or other forms of psychological discomfort in their lives and at such times experience at least some of the distress associated with psychological disorders.

It is tempting to conclude that unique characteristics of the modern world are responsible for these numerous emotional problems—rapid technological change, perhaps, or a decline in religious, family, or other support systems (see Box 1-3 on the next page). Although the special pressures of modern life probably do contribute to psychological dysfunctioning, they are hardly its primary cause. Historical records demonstrate that every society, past and present, has witnessed psychological abnormality. Perhaps, then, the proper place to begin our examination of abnormal behavior and treatment is in the past.

FINANCIAL TOLL

The total economic cost of psychological disorders, including substance abuse, in the United States—direct treatment costs, lost wages, and the like—is more than $400 billion each year (NIDA, 1998; Rice & Miller, 1998).

As we look back, we can see how each society has struggled to understand and treat psychological problems, and we can observe that many present-day ideas and treatments have roots in the past. A look backward makes it clear that progress in the understanding and treatment of mental disorders has hardly been a steady movement forward. In fact, many of the inadequacies and controversies that mark the clinical field today parallel those of the past. At the same time, looking back can help us to appreciate the significance of recent breakthroughs and the importance of the journey that lies ahead.

Ancient Views and Treatments

Most of our knowledge of prehistoric societies has been acquired indirectly and is based on inferences made from archaeological discoveries. Historians scrutinize the unearthed bones, artwork, and other remnants of ancient societies to find clues to people's customs and beliefs. Any conclusions are at best tentative and are always subject to revision in the face of new discoveries.

Thus our knowledge of how ancient societies viewed and treated people with mental disturbances is limited. Most historians believe that prehistoric societies

---

BOX **1-3**

A Century of Firsts

Some therapists believe that the dramatic technological, social, and political changes of recent times have contributed to the onslaught of psychological problems found in today's world. A quick look at some of the "firsts" occurring throughout the twentieth century reminds us of how much society has changed during the past 100 years.

1903	Electrocardiograph invented
	First airplane with motor
1904	First double-sided records
1906	First women allowed to vote in Finland
1907	Vacuum cleaner invented
1908	Cellophane invented
1911	First air conditioner
1914	First military tank
1917	First electric razor
1918	Automatic toaster invented
1920	First women allowed to vote in the United States
1925	First circuit breaker
1927	First talking movie
1928	Color television invented
1930	First jet engine
1941	First aerosol can
1945	First use of atomic bomb
1947	First LP record

1948	Velcro invented
1960	First oral contraceptive
1963	First audio cassette
1964	First successful coronary artery bypass surgery
1964	First synthesizer
1969	First video cassette

1969	First astronauts walk on moon
1971	First microprocessor
1972	First compact disc
1982	Artificial heart invented
1996	Dolly, a cloned sheep, is born

One plus zero equals two *This digital portrait of Dolly, the cloned sheep, reminds us that we can continue to expect dramatic changes and their aftereffects throughout the twenty-first century.*

regarded abnormal behavior as the work of evil spirits. These early societies apparently explained all phenomena as resulting from the actions of magical, sometimes sinister beings who controlled the world. In particular, they viewed the human body and mind as a battleground between external forces of good and evil. Abnormal behavior was typically interpreted as a victory by evil spirits, and the cure for such behavior was to force the demons from a victim's body.

This supernatural view of abnormality may have begun as far back as the Stone Age, a half-million years ago. Some skulls from that period recovered in Europe and South America show evidence of an operation called **trephination**, in which a stone instrument, or *trephine*, was used to cut away a circular section of the skull. Historians surmise that this operation was performed as a treatment for severe abnormal behavior—either hallucinations, in which people saw or heard things not actually present, or melancholia, characterized by extreme sadness and immobility. The purpose of opening the skull was to release the evil spirits that were supposedly causing the problem (Selling, 1940).

In recent years, some historians have questioned whether Stone Age people actually believed that evil spirits caused abnormal behavior. Trephination may instead have been used to remove bone splinters or blood clots caused by stone weapons during tribal warfare (Maher & Maher, 1985). Either way, later societies clearly did attribute abnormal behavior to possession by demons. Egyptian, Chinese, and Hebrew writings all account for psychological deviance this way. The Bible, for example, describes how an evil spirit from the Lord affected King Saul and how David feigned madness in order to convince his enemies that he was visited by divine forces.

The treatment for abnormality in these early societies was often **exorcism**, conducted by a *shaman*, or priest. The idea was to coax the evil spirits to leave or to make the person's body an uncomfortable place for them to live in. The shaman might recite prayers, plead with the evil spirits, insult them, perform magic, make loud noises, or have the person drink bitter potions. If these techniques failed, more extreme forms of exorcism, such as whipping or starvation, would be tried.

Greek and Roman Views and Treatments

In the years from roughly 500 B.C. to A.D. 500, in the flourishing Greek and Roman civilizations, philosophers and physicians identified a number of mental disorders. Heading the list were *melancholia*, a condition marked by unshakable sadness; *mania*, a state of euphoria and frenzied activity; *dementia*, a general intellectual decline; *hysteria*, the presence of a physical ailment with no apparent physical cause; *delusions*, blatantly false beliefs; and *hallucinations*, the experience of imagined sights or sounds as if they were real. Although demonological interpretations of mental and physical illness were still widespread, philosophers and physicians began to offer alternative explanations during this period.

Hippocrates (460–377 B.C.), often called the father of modern medicine, taught that illnesses had *natural* causes. He saw abnormal behavior as a disease arising from internal physical problems. Specifically, he believed that some form of brain pathology was the culprit, and that it resulted—like all other forms of disease, in his view—from an imbalance of four fluids, or **humors**, that flowed through the body: *yellow bile, black bile, blood,* and *phlegm*. An excess of yellow bile, for example, caused mania; an excess of black bile was the source of melancholia. To treat psychological dysfunctioning, Hippocrates sought to correct the underlying physical pathology. He believed, for instance, that the excess of black bile underlying melancholia could be reduced by a quiet life, a vegetable diet, temperance, exercise, celibacy, and even bleeding.

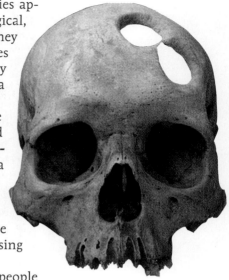

Expelling evil spirits *The two holes in this skull recovered from ancient times indicate that the person underwent trephination, possibly for the purpose of releasing evil spirits and curing mental dysfunctioning.*

ConsiderThis

● People of the Stone Age did not leave written records, so archaeologists cannot be certain that trephination was in fact an ancient treatment for mental dysfunctioning. How else might we explain the holes found in the skulls recovered from early times? • Why do you think historians have settled on mental illness as an explanation?

TREPHINATION An ancient operation in which a stone instrument was used to cut away a circular section of the skull, perhaps to treat abnormal behavior.

EXORCISM The practice in early societies of treating abnormality by coaxing evil spirits to leave the person's body.

HUMORS According to Greek and Roman physicians, bodily chemicals that influence mental and physical functioning.

Humors in action *Hippocrates believed that imbalances of the four humors affected personality. In these depictions of two of the humors, yellow bile (left) drives a husband to beat his wife, and black bile (right) leaves a man melancholic and sends him to bed.*

Hippocrates' focus on internal causes for abnormal behavior was shared by the great Greek philosophers Plato (427–347 B.C.) and Aristotle (384–322 B.C.) and later was amplified by influential Greek and Roman physicians. The physician Aretaeus (A.D. 50–130) suggested that abnormal behavior could also be caused by emotional problems, and Greek and Roman physicians came to treat mental illnesses with a mixture of medical and psychological techniques. Before resorting to such extreme methods as bleeding patients or restraining them with mechanical devices, many Greek physicians first prescribed a warm and supportive atmosphere, music, massage, exercise, and baths. Roman physicians were even more emphatic about the need to soothe and comfort patients who had mental disorders.

Europe in the Middle Ages: Demonology Returns

The enlightened views of noted physicians and scholars during the Greco-Roman period did not prevent less educated people from continuing to believe in demons. And with the decline of Rome, demonology enjoyed a strong resurgence, as a growing distrust of science spread throughout Europe.

From A.D. 500 to 1350, the period known as the Middle Ages, the power of the clergy increased greatly throughout Europe. In those days, the church rejected scientific forms of investigation, and it controlled all education. Religious beliefs, which were highly superstitious and demonological at this time, came to dominate all aspects of life. Once again behavior was usually interpreted as a conflict between good and evil, God and the devil. Deviant behavior, particularly psychological dysfunctioning, was seen as evidence of Satan's influence. Although some scientists and physicians still insisted on medical explanations and treatments, their views carried little weight in this atmosphere.

The Middle Ages were a time of great stress and anxiety, of war, urban uprisings, and plagues. People blamed the devil for these troubles and feared being possessed by him. The incidence of abnormal behavior apparently increased dramatically during this period. In addition, there were outbreaks of *mass madness,* in which large numbers of people apparently shared delusions and hallucinations (see Box 1-4). Two common forms were tarantism and lycanthropy.

Tarantism (also known as *St. Vitus's dance*) was a form of mania in which groups of people would suddenly start to jump, dance, and go into convulsions (Sigerist, 1943). Some dressed oddly; others tore off their clothing. All were convinced that they had been bitten and possessed by a wolf spider, now called a tarantula, and they sought to cure their disorder by performing a dance called a *tarantella.* People with *lycanthropy* thought they were possessed by wolves or other animals. They acted wolflike and imagined that fur was growing all over their bodies. Stories of lycanthropes, more popularly known as *werewolves,* have been passed down to us and continue to fire the imagination of writers, moviemakers, and their audiences.

Many earlier demonological treatments for psychological abnormality reemerged in the Middle Ages, and techniques of exorcism were revived. Clergymen were generally in charge of treatment during this period, and they would plead, chant, or pray to the devil or evil spirit to leave the body of a person behaving strangely. They might also administer holy water or bitter drinks. If these

CLERICAL INFLUENCE
During the Middle Ages, there was, on average, one church for every 200 people (Asimov, 1997).

techniques did not work, they might try to insult the devil and attack his pride (Satan's great weakness, they believed), or, in more extreme cases, starve, whip, scald, or stretch the individual.

It was not until the Middle Ages drew to a close that demonology and its methods began to lose favor (Magherini & Biotti, 1998). Cities throughout Europe grew larger, and municipal authorities gained more power. Increasingly they took over nonreligious activities, including the administration of hospitals and the care of people suffering from mental disorders. Medical views of abnormality gained favor once again. When lunacy trials were held in late thirteenth-century England to determine the sanity of certain persons, it was not unusual for natural causes, such as a "blow to the head" or "fear of one's father," to be held responsible for an individual's unusual behavior (Neugebauer, 1979, 1978). During these same years, many people with psychological disturbances received treatment in medical hospitals. The Trinity Hospital in England, for example, was established to treat "madness," among other kinds of illness, and to keep the mad "safe until they are restored to reason" (Allderidge, 1979, p. 322).

Bewitched or bewildered? *A great fear of witchcraft swept Europe even during the "enlightened" Renaissance. Tens of thousands of people, mostly women, were thought to have made a pact with the devil. Some appear to have had mental disorders, which caused them to act strangely (Zilboorg & Henry, 1941). This individual is being "dunked" repeatedly until she confesses to witchery.*

The Renaissance and the Rise of Asylums

During the early part of the Renaissance, a period of flourishing cultural and scientific activity (about 1400–1700), demonological views of abnormality continued to decline. The German physician Johann Weyer (1515–1588), the first medical practitioner to specialize in mental illness, believed that the mind was as susceptible to sickness as the body. He is now considered the founder of the modern study of psychopathology.

The care of people with mental disorders continued to improve in this atmosphere. In England such individuals might be kept at home and their families

---

B O X 1-4

Ascending to a Higher Kingdom

In 1997 the world was shocked to learn of the bizarre beliefs held by the Heaven's Gate cult when thirty-nine of its members committed suicide at an expensive house outside San Diego. Videotapes and writings left behind and postings on the Internet revealed that the members had believed that their bodies were mere "containers" for higher heavenly spirits and that a UFO was hiding in the slipstream of the comet Hale-Bopp, coming to take them home to "their world." Ultimately, they believed, their deaths would free them to enter a higher kingdom.

The public was particularly alarmed by the key role that the mass media and modern communication systems apparently played in the rise and spread of Heaven's Gate. In 1993, try-

ing to create interest in the group, its leader, Marshall Herff Applewhite (see photo), ran an ad in *USA Today* that described the cult's philosophical bonds with other millennial groups—groups that expected the world to end in the year 2000. Beyond this form of publicity, the cult members became experts on the Internet and used it to

learn about UFO sightings and other signs of "higher life." In addition, cult members apparently recruited new members by sending messages out to Internet newsgroups focused on suicide, depression, and substance abuse.

ConsiderThis

What features do the beliefs, behaviors, and circumstances of the Heaven's Gate cult share with past forms of "mass madness," such as tarantism and lycanthropy? • Does the Internet pose a special danger in the emergence and spread of new forms of mass madness?

Bedlam *In this eighteenth-century work from* The Rake's Progress, *William Hogarth depicted London's Bethlehem Hospital, or Bedlam, as a chaotic asylum where people of fashion came to marvel at the strange behavior of the inmates.*

The "crib" *Outrageous devices and techniques, such as the "crib," were used in asylums, and some continued to be used even during the reforms of the nineteenth century.*

THE BARD ON BEHAVIOR

Writing during the Renaissance, William Shakespeare (1564–1616) speculated on the nature and causes of abnormal behavior in 20 of his 38 plays and in many of his sonnets (Dalby, 1997).

BIAS IN THE ASYLUMS

Most of the patients in asylums, from all classes and circumstances, were women (Gold, 1998; Showalter, 1985).

aided financially by the local parish. Across Europe religious shrines were devoted to the humane and loving treatment of people with mental disorders. The best known of these shrines was actually established centuries earlier at Gheel in Belgium, but beginning in the fifteenth century, people came to it from all over the world for psychic healing. Local residents welcomed these pilgrims into their homes, and many stayed on to form the world's first "colony" of mental patients. Gheel was the forerunner of today's community mental health programs, and it continues to demonstrate that people with psychological disorders can respond to loving care and respectful treatment (Aring, 1975, 1974). Today, patients are still welcome to live in foster homes in this town, interacting with other residents, until they recover.

Unfortunately, these improvements in care began to fade by the mid-sixteenth century. By then municipal authorities had discovered that private homes and community residences could house only a small percentage of those with severe mental disorders and that medical hospitals were too few and too small. Increasingly, they converted hospitals and monasteries into **asylums**, institutions whose sole purpose was to care for people with mental illness. These institutions were founded with every intention of providing good care. Once the asylums started to overflow with patients, however, they instead became virtual prisons where patients were held in filthy conditions and treated with unspeakable cruelty.

The first asylum had been founded in Muslim Spain in the early fifteenth century, but the idea did not gain full momentum until the 1500s. In 1547, Bethlehem Hospital was given to the city of London by Henry VIII for the sole purpose of confining the mentally ill. In this asylum patients bound in chains cried out for all to hear. During certain phases of the moon in particular, they might be chained and whipped in order to prevent violence (Asimov, 1997). The hospital even became a popular tourist attraction; people were eager to pay to look at the howling and gibbering inmates. The hospital's name, pronounced "Bedlam" by the local people, has come to mean a chaotic uproar. Similarly, in the Lunatics'

Tower in Vienna, patients were herded into narrow hallways by the outer walls, so that tourists outside could look up and see them. In La Bicêtre in Paris, patients were shackled to the walls of cold, dark, dirty cells with iron collars and given spoiled food that could be sold nowhere else (Selling, 1940). Such asylums remained a popular form of "care" until the late 1700s.

The Nineteenth Century: Reform and Moral Treatment

As 1800 approached, the treatment of people with mental disorders began to change for the better once again. Historians usually point to La Bicêtre, an asylum in Paris for male patients, as the first site of asylum reform. In 1793, during the French Revolution, Philippe Pinel (1745–1826) was named the chief physician there. He argued that the patients were sick people whose illnesses should be treated with sympathy and kindness rather than chains and beatings. He unchained them and allowed them to move freely about the hospital grounds, replaced the dark dungeons with sunny, well-ventilated rooms, and offered support and advice. Pinel's approach proved remarkably successful. Patients who had been shut away for decades were now enjoying fresh air and sunlight and being treated with dignity. Many improved greatly over a short period of time and were released. Pinel later brought similar reforms to a mental hospital in Paris for female patients, La Salpetrière. Jean Esquirol (1772–1840), Pinel's student and successor, went on to help establish ten new mental hospitals that operated on the same principles.

Meanwhile an English Quaker named William Tuke (1732–1819) was bringing similar reforms to northern England. In 1796 he founded the York Retreat, a rural estate where about thirty mental patients were lodged as guests in quiet country houses and treated with a combination of rest, talk, prayer, and manual work.

THE SPREAD OF MORAL TREATMENT The methods of Pinel and Tuke, called **moral treatment** because they emphasized moral guidance and humane and respectful techniques, caught on throughout Europe and the United States. Patients with psychological disorders were increasingly perceived as potentially productive human beings whose mental functioning had broken down under stress. They were considered deserving of individualized care, including discussions of their problems, useful activities, work, companionship, and quiet.

The person most responsible for the early spread of moral treatment in the United States was Benjamin Rush (1745–1813), an eminent physician at Pennsylvania Hospital. Limiting his practice to mental illness, Rush developed innovative, humane approaches to treatment. For example, he required that the hospital hire intelligent and sensitive attendants to work closely with patients, reading and talking to them and taking them on regular walks. He also suggested that it would be therapeutic for doctors to give small gifts to their patients now and then. Rush, widely considered the father of American psychiatry, also wrote the first American treatise on mental illness and organized the first American course in psychiatry.

ASYLUM A type of institution that first became popular in the sixteenth century to provide care for persons with mental disorders. Most became virtual prisons.

MORAL TREATMENT A nineteenth-century approach to treating people with mental dysfunction which emphasized moral guidance and humane and respectful treatment.

Dance in a madhouse *A popular feature of moral treatment was the "lunatic ball." Hospital officials would bring patients together to dance and enjoy themselves. One such ball is shown in this painting,* Dance in a Madhouse, *by George Bellows.*

The advocate *From 1841 to 1881 the Boston schoolteacher Dorothea Dix tirelessly campaigned for more humane forms of treatment in mental hospitals throughout the United States.*

"I come as the advocate of helpless, forgotten, insane, idiotic men and women . . . of beings wretched in our prisons, and more wretched in our almshouses."

Dorothea Dix, 1843,
describing her mission to the
Massachusetts legislature

Rush's work was influential, but it was a Boston schoolteacher named Dorothea Dix (1802–1887) who made humane care a public and political concern in the United States. In 1841 Dix had gone to teach Sunday school at a local prison and been shocked by the conditions she saw there. Before long, her interest in prison conditions broadened to include the plight of poor and mentally ill people throughout the country. A powerful campaigner, Dix went from state legislature to state legislature speaking of the horrors she had observed and calling for reform. Similarly, she told the Congress of the United States that mentally ill people across the country were still being "bound with galling chains, bowed beneath fetters and heavy iron balls attached to drag chains, lacerated with ropes, scourged with rods and terrified beneath storms of execration and cruel blows" (Zilboorg & Henry, 1941, pp. 583–584).

From 1841 until 1881, Dix fought for new laws and greater government funding to improve the treatment of people with mental disorders. Each state was made responsible for developing effective public mental hospitals. Dix personally helped establish thirty-two of these **state hospitals**, all intended to offer moral treatment (Bickman & Dokecki, 1989). Similar hospitals were established throughout Europe.

THE DECLINE OF MORAL TREATMENT As we have observed, the treatment of abnormality has followed a crooked path (see Box 1-5). Over and over again, relative progress has been followed by serious decline. Viewed in this context, it is not surprising that the moral treatment movement began to decline toward the end of the nineteenth century.

Several factors were responsible (Bockoven, 1963). One was the reckless speed with which the moral movement had spread. As mental hospitals multiplied, severe money and staffing shortages developed, recovery rates declined, and overcrowding in the hospitals became a major problem. Under such conditions it was often impossible to provide individual care and genuine concern. Another factor was the assumption behind moral treatment that all patients could be cured if treated with humanity and dignity. For some, this was indeed sufficient. Others, however, needed more effective treatments than any that had yet been developed. Many of these people remained hospitalized till they died. An additional factor contributing to the decline of moral treatment was the emergence of a new wave of prejudice against people with mental disorders. As more and more patients disappeared into the large, distant mental hospitals, the public came to view them as strange and dangerous. In turn, people were less open-

handed when it came to making donations or allocating government funds. Moreover, many of the patients entering public mental hospitals in the United States in the late nineteenth century were impoverished foreign immigrants, whom the public had little interest in helping.

By the early years of the twentieth century, the moral treatment movement had ground to a halt in both the United States and Europe. Public mental hospitals were providing only custodial care and ineffective medical treatments and were becoming more overcrowded every year. Long-term hospitalization became the rule once again.

> **STATE HOSPITALS** State-run public mental institutions in the United States.
>
> **SOMATOGENIC PERSPECTIVE** The view that abnormal psychological functioning has physical causes.
>
> **PSYCHOGENIC PERSPECTIVE** The view that the chief causes of abnormal functioning are psychological.

The Early Twentieth Century: The Somatogenic and Psychogenic Perspectives

As the moral movement was declining in the late 1800s, two opposing perspectives emerged and began to vie for the attention of clinicians: the **somatogenic perspective**, the view that abnormal psychological functioning has physical causes, and the **psychogenic perspective**, the view that the chief causes of abnormal functioning are psychological. These perspectives came into full bloom during the twentieth century.

THE SOMATOGENIC PERSPECTIVE The somatogenic perspective has at least a 2,400-year history—remember Hippocrates' view that abnormal behavior resulted from brain disease and an imbalance of humors? Not until the late nineteenth century, however, did this perspective make a triumphant return and begin to gain wide acceptance.

Two factors were responsible for this resurgence. One was the work of an eminent German researcher, Emil Kraepelin (1856–1926). In 1883 Kraepelin published an influential textbook which argued that physical factors, such as fatigue, are responsible for mental dysfunction. In addition, as we shall see in Chapter 4, he also constructed the first modern system for classifying abnormal behavior (Hoff, 1998). He identified various *syndromes,* or clusters of symptoms, listed their physical causes, and discussed their expected course (Jablensky, 1995). Kraepelin also measured the effects of various drugs on abnormal behavior.

Back wards *Overcrowding, limited funding, and ineffective hospital treatments led to the creation of crowded, often appalling back wards in state hospitals across the United States, which continued well into the twentieth century.*

New biological discoveries also spurred the rise of the somatogenic perspective. One of the most important discoveries was that an organic disease, *syphilis*, led to *general paresis,* an irreversible disorder with both physical and mental symptoms, including paralysis and delusions of grandeur. In 1897 Richard von Krafft-Ebing (1840–1902), a German neurologist, injected matter from syphilis sores into patients suffering from general paresis and found that none of the patients developed symptoms of syphilis. Their immunity could have been caused only by an earlier case of syphilis. Since all patients with general paresis were now immune to syphilis, Krafft-Ebing theorized that syphilis had been the cause of their general paresis. Finally, in 1905, Fritz Schaudinn (1871–1906), a German zoologist, discovered that the microorganism *Treponema pallida* was responsible for syphilis, which in turn was responsible for general paresis.

The work of Kraepelin and the new understanding of general paresis led numerous researchers and practitioners to suspect that organic factors were responsible for many mental disorders, perhaps all of them. These theories and the possibility of quick and effective medical solutions for mental disorders were especially welcomed by those who worked in mental hospitals, where patient populations were now growing at an alarming rate.

Despite the general optimism, biological approaches yielded largely disappointing results throughout the first half of the twentieth century. Although many medical treatments were developed for patients in mental hospitals during that time, most of the techniques failed to work. Physicians tried tooth extraction, tonsillectomy, hydrotherapy (alternating hot and cold baths), and lobotomy, a surgical severing of certain nerve fibers in the brain. Not until the 1950s, when a number of effective medications were finally discovered, did the somatogenic perspective truly begin to pay off for patients.

THE PSYCHOGENIC PERSPECTIVE The late nineteenth century also saw the emergence of the psychogenic perspective, the view that the chief causes of abnormal functioning are often psychological. This perspective, too, has a long history. The Roman statesman and orator Cicero (106–43 B.C.) held that psychological disturbances could cause bodily ailments, and the Greek physician Galen believed that many mental disorders are caused by fear, disappointment in love, and other psychological events. However, the psychogenic perspective did not gain much of a following until studies of *hypnotism* demonstrated its potential.

Hypnotism is a procedure that places people in a trancelike mental state during which they become extremely suggestible. It was used to help treat psychological disorders as far back as 1778, when an Austrian physician named Friedrich Anton Mesmer (1734–1815) established a clinic in Paris. His patients suffered from *hysterical disorders*, mysterious bodily ailments that had no apparent physical basis. Mesmer had his patients sit in a darkened room filled with music; then he appeared, dressed in a flamboyant costume, and touched the troubled area of each patient's body with a special rod. A surprising number of patients seemed to be helped by this treatment, called *mesmerism*. Their pain, numbness, or paralysis disappeared. Several scientists believed that Mesmer was inducing a trancelike state in his patients and that this state was causing their symptoms to disappear. The treatment was so controversial, however, that eventually Mesmer was banished from Paris.

It was not until years after Mesmer died that many researchers had the courage to investigate his procedure, later called hypnotism (from *hypnos*, the Greek word for sleep), and its effects on hysterical disorders. By the late nineteenth century, two competing views had emerged. Because hypnosis—a technique relying on the power of suggestion—was able to alleviate hysterical ailments, some scientists concluded that hysterical disorders must be caused by the power of suggestion—that is, by the mind—in the first place. In contrast, other scientists believed that hysterical disorders had subtle physiological causes. For example, Jean Charcot (1825–1893), Paris's most eminent neurologist, argued that hysterical disorders were the result of degeneration in portions of the brain.

The experiments of two physicians practicing in the city of Nancy in France finally seemed to settle the matter. Hippolyte-Marie Bernheim (1840–1919) and Ambroise-Auguste Liébault (1823–1904) showed that hysterical disorders could actually be induced in otherwise normal subjects while they were under the influence of hypnosis. That is, the physicians could make normal people experience deafness, paralysis, blindness, or numbness by means of hypnotic suggestion—and they could remove these artificial symptoms by the same means. Thus, they established that a *mental* process—hypnotic suggestion—could both cause and cure even a physical dysfunction. Leading scientists, including Charcot, finally embraced the idea that hysterical disorders were largely psychological in origin, and the psychogenic perspective rose in popularity.

DR. DICKENS, I PRESUME
Although controversial in professional circles, Mesmer's treatment attracted many persons outside the clinical field. Charles Dickens, the nineteenth-century English novelist, so strongly believed in mesmerism that he considered himself to be a doctor in this method of healing the sick (Asimov, 1997).

The roots of psychogenic theory *The nineteenth century's leading neurologist, Jean Charcot, gives a clinical lecture in Paris on hypnotism and hysterical disorders.*

Among those who studied the effects of hypnotism on hysterical disorders was Josef Breuer (1842–1925) of Vienna. This physician discovered that his patients sometimes awoke free of hysterical symptoms after speaking candidly under hypnosis about past upsetting events. During the 1890s Breuer was joined in his work by another Viennese physician, Sigmund Freud (1856–1939). As we shall see in Chapter 3, Freud's work eventually led him to develop the theory of **psychoanalysis**, which holds that many forms of abnormal and normal psychological functioning are psychogenic. In particular, he believed that unconscious psychological processes are at the root of such functioning.

Freud also developed the *technique* of psychoanalysis, a form of discussion in which clinicians help troubled people acquire insight into their unconscious psychological processes. He believed that such insight, even without hypnotic procedures, would help the patients overcome their psychological problems. Freud and his followers applied the psychoanalytic treatment approach primarily to patients suffering from anxiety or depression, problems that did not typically require hospitalization. These patients visited therapists in their offices for sessions of approximately an hour and then went about their daily activities—a format of treatment now known as *outpatient therapy*. By the early twentieth century, psychoanalytic theory and treatment were widely accepted throughout the Western world.

The psychoanalytic approach had little effect on the treatment of severely disturbed patients in mental hospitals, however. This type of therapy requires levels of clarity, insight, and verbal skill beyond the capabilities of most such patients. Moreover, psychoanalysis often takes years to be effective, and the overcrowded and understaffed public mental hospitals could not accommodate such a leisurely pace.

Current Trends

It would hardly be accurate to say that we now live in a period of widespread enlightenment or dependable treatment (see Box 1-6 on the next page). In fact, one survey found that 43 percent of respondents currently believe that people bring on mental disorders themselves and 35 percent consider the disorders to be caused by sinful behavior (Murray, 1993). Nevertheless, the past 50 years have brought major changes in the ways clinicians understand and treat abnormal functioning. There are more theories and types of treatment, more research studies, more information, and, perhaps for these reasons, more disagreements about abnormal functioning today than at any time in the past. In some ways the study and treatment of psychological disorders have made great strides, but in other respects clinical scientists and practitioners are still struggling to make a difference.

How Are People with Severe Disturbances Cared For?

In the 1950s researchers discovered a number of new **psychotropic medications**—drugs that primarily affect the brain and alleviate many symptoms of mental dysfunctioning. They included the first *antipsychotic drugs*, to correct extremely confused and distorted thinking; *antidepressant drugs*, to lift the mood of depressed people; and *antianxiety drugs*, to reduce tension and worry.

With the discovery and application of these drugs, many patients who had spent years in mental hospitals began to show signs of improvement. Hospital administrators, encouraged by these results and pressured by a growing public outcry over the terrible conditions in public mental hospitals, began to discharge patients almost immediately.

Since the discovery of these medications, mental health professionals in most of the developed nations of the world have followed a policy of **deinstitutionalization**, releasing hundreds of thousands of patients from public mental hospitals. On any given day in 1955, close to 600,000 people were confined in public

PSYCHOANALYSIS Either the theory or the treatment of abnormal mental functioning that emphasizes unconscious psychological forces as the cause of psychopathology.

PSYCHOTROPIC MEDICATIONS Drugs that mainly affect the brain and reduce many symptoms of mental dysfunctioning.

DEINSTITUTIONALIZATION The practice, begun in the 1960s, of releasing hundreds of thousands of patients from public mental hospitals.

TOPS IN HIS FIELD

Sigmund Freud's fee for one session of therapy was $20—$160 in today's dollars. That is comparable to the fees of some higher-priced therapists in New York City and Los Angeles.

LINGERING BELIEFS

19 percent of Americans believe that people with psychological disorders have too little willpower or self-discipline to deal with their problems.

24 percent believe that persons will not develop psychological disorders if they keep busy and have good family relationships and close friends.

34 percent view clinical depression as a normal part of life that can be worked through without treatment.

(NMHA, 1999)

BOX 1-6

The Moon and the Mind

Primitive societies believed that the moon had magical, mystical powers and that its changes portended events of many kinds. The moon supposedly had the power to impregnate women, to make plants grow, and to drive people crazy. Later societies also credited the power of the moon to affect behavior, and they applied the terms "lunatic" and "lunacy" to the person and the behavior to capture their lunar, or moonlike, qualities. Even today many institutions and people believe that behavior is affected by the phases of the moon.

Anecdotal evidence abounds: police officers have sometimes noted more violent and bizarre crimes during the full moon, and certain hospitals have claimed to experience an increase in births. One hospital even linked the full moon to the onset of ulcers and heart attacks. A Wall Street broker for years used the schedule of the full moon as a guide in giving investment advice—successfully (Gardner, 1984).

A number of scientists have advanced theories to explain a lunar effect on human behavior. Some say that since the moon causes the tides of the oceans, it is reasonable to expect that it has a similar effect on the bodily fluids of human beings (whose composition is more than 80 percent water). The increase in births might therefore be explained by the force of the moon on the expectant mother's amniotic fluid. Similar tidal and gravitational effects have been used to explain the apparent increases in bizarre behavior during full moons. Other scientists argue that people's expectations may be the cause of such strange behavior. That is, because certain persons expect to be influenced by a full moon, they may be more attentive and responsive to their unusual ideas, desires, or sensations at that time.

Still other researchers, perhaps less moonstruck, have performed statistical analyses of the actual numbers of births, crimes, and incidents of unusual behavior that occur during the full moon. Only a few have found evidence supporting the influence of the moon on various scales of human behavior (Raison, Klein, & Steckler, 1999; de Castro & Pearcy, 1995; Byrnes & Kelly, 1992). In view of the weakness of support for the popular lunacy theory, some scientists have suggested that we drop the entire question. Others, undissuaded, claim that the lack of statistical evidence is not the problem—the problem has been the researchers' failure to look at the right variables, to use the appropriate measures, or to look at enough days both before and after the full moon. Perhaps, for example, studies of mental hospital admissions should take a lag time into account because the moon-induced behavior may not be identified or the individuals may not be admitted until a week or more after the full moon (Cyr & Kalpin, 1988). The debate continues to this day, as scientists and philosophers alike try to determine whether the cause of lunacy does indeed lie in the heavens or in our minds.

Lunar effect *Moonstruck maidens dance in the town square in this eighteenth-century French engraving.*

mental institutions across the United States (see Figure 1-1). Today the daily patient population in the same kinds of hospitals is around 70,000 (Lang, 1999; Torrey, 1997).

In short, outpatient care has now become the primary mode of treatment for people with severe psychological disturbances as well as for those with more moderate problems. Today when severely impaired people do need institutionalization, they are usually given *short-term* hospitalization (NAPHS, 1999; Thompson et al., 1995). Ideally, they are then given outpatient psychotherapy and medication in community programs and residences.

Chapters 3 and 15 will look more closely at this recent emphasis on community care for people with severe psychological disturbances—a philosophy called the *community mental health approach*. The approach has been helpful for many patients, but too few community programs are available to address current needs

PRIVATE PSYCHOTHERAPY An arrangement in which a person directly pays a therapist for counseling services.

in the United States. As a result, hundreds of thousands of persons with severe disturbances fail to make lasting recoveries, and they shuffle back and forth between the mental hospital and the community. After release from the hospital, they receive minimal care at best and often wind up living in decrepit rooming houses or on the streets. In fact, an estimated 150,000 or more persons with severe psychological disturbances are currently homeless on any given day; even more are inmates of jails and prisons (Lang, 1999; Torrey, 1997; Manderscheid & Rosenstein, 1992). Their abandonment is truly a national disgrace.

How Are People with Less Severe Disturbances Treated?

The treatment picture for people with moderate psychological disturbances has been more positive than that for people with severe disorders. Since the 1950s, outpatient care has continued to be the preferred mode of treatment for them, and the number and types of facilities that offer such care have expanded to meet the need (NAPHS, 1999; Redick et al., 1996).

Before the 1950s, almost all outpatient care took the form of **private psychotherapy**, an arrangement by which an individual directly pays a psychotherapist for counseling services. This tended to be an expensive form of treatment, available only to the wealthy. Since the 1950s, however, most health insurance plans have expanded coverage to include private psychotherapy, so that it is now also widely available to people with modest incomes (Levin, 1992). In addition, outpatient therapy is now offered at a number of less expensive settings, such as community mental health centers, crisis intervention centers, family service centers, and other social service agencies (Redick et al., 1996; Olfson, Pincus, & Dial, 1994). The new settings have spurred a dramatic increase in the number of persons seeking outpatient care for psychological problems.

Nationwide surveys suggest that between 16 and 22 million adults in the United States, one of every eight, now receive therapy for psychological problems in the course of a year (Kessler et al., 1994; Narrow et al., 1993). It has also become increasingly common for children to be treated for psychological problems (Kazdin, 1993).

Outpatient treatments are also becoming available for more and more kinds of problems. When Freud and his colleagues first began to practice, most of their patients suffered from anxiety or depression. These problems still dominate therapy today; almost half of all clients suffer from them. However, people with other kinds of disorders are also receiving therapy (Zarin et al., 1998; Narrow et al., 1993). In addition, at least 25 percent of clients enter therapy because of milder problems in living, problems with marital, family, job, peer, school, or community relationships.

In fact, so many persons now seek therapy that private insurance companies have recently changed their plans of coverage for mental health patients. Most companies have developed *managed care programs*, in which the insurance company determines such key issues as which therapists their clients may choose, the cost of sessions, and the number of sessions for which a client may be reimbursed (Manderscheid et al., 1999). As we shall discuss later in the text, therapists and clients typically dislike these programs. They fear that the programs inevitably shorten therapy (often for the worse),

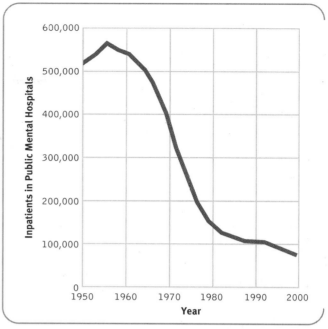

FIGURE 1-1 **The impact of deinstitutionalization** *The number of patients (70,000) now hospitalized in public mental hospitals in the United States is a small fraction of the number hospitalized in 1955. (Adapted from Lang, 1999; Torrey, 1997, 1988.)*

The availability of therapy *Therapy for people with mild to severe psychological disturbances is widely available today in individual, group, and family formats.*

unfairly favor treatments whose results are not always lasting (for example, drug therapy), and amount to regulation of therapy by insurance companies rather than by therapists.

Yet another change in outpatient care since the 1950s has been the development of programs devoted exclusively to one kind of psychological problem. We now have, for example, suicide prevention centers, substance abuse programs, eating disorder programs, phobia clinics, and sexual dysfunction programs. Clinicians in these programs have the kind of expertise that can be acquired only by concentration in a single area.

What Are Today's Leading Theories and Professions?

One of the most important developments in the modern understanding and treatment of abnormal psychological functioning has been the growth of numerous theoretical perspectives that now coexist in the clinical field. Before the 1950s, the *psychoanalytic perspective*, with its emphasis on unconscious psychological problems as the cause of abnormal behavior, was dominant. Then the discovery of effective psychotropic drugs inspired new respect for the somatogenic, or *biological*, view. As we shall see in Chapter 3, other influential perspectives that have emerged since the 1950s are the *behavioral*, *cognitive*, *humanistic-existential*, and *sociocultural* schools of thought. At present no single viewpoint dominates the clinical field as the psychoanalytic perspective once did. Today's many perspectives often seem to conflict and compete with one another; yet, as we shall observe, in some instances they complement each other and together provide more comprehensive explanations and treatments for psychological disorders than any one perspective can provide alone (Gabbard & Goodwin, 1996).

In addition to multiple viewpoints in the clinical field, there are now a variety of professional practitioners available to help people with psychological problems (Peterson et al., 1996; Murstein & Fontaine, 1993). Before the 1950s, psychotherapy was offered only by *psychiatrists,* physicians who complete three to four additional years of training after medical school (a *residency*) in the treatment of abnormal mental functioning. After World War II, however, the demand for mental health services expanded so rapidly that other professional groups stepped in to fill the need (Humphreys, 1996).

Among those other groups are *clinical psychologists*—professionals who earn a doctorate in clinical psychology by completing four years of graduate training in abnormal functioning and its treatment and also complete a one-year internship at a mental hospital or mental health agency. Before their professional responsibilities expanded into the area of treatment, clinical psychologists were principally assessors and researchers of abnormal functioning. Some of them still specialize in those activities.

Therapy in the cinema *The variety and impact of today's mental health professionals are reflected in the work of cinematic therapists such as Dr. Sean McGuire (*Good Will Hunting*), at left, and the late Dr. Malcolm Crowe (*The Sixth Sense*). Other notable film clinicians include Drs. Berger (*Ordinary People*), Lecter (*The Silence of the Lambs*), Sobel (*Analyze This*), and Petersen and Murchison (*Spellbound*), as well as Nurse Ratchet (*One Flew Over the Cuckoo's Nest*).*

Table 1-1

Profiles of Mental Health Professionals

	DEGREE	BEGAN TO PRACTICE	CURRENT NUMBER	MEDIAN AGE	PERCENT MALE
Psychiatrists	M.D., D.O.	1840s	33,486	52	75
Psychologists	Ph.D., Psy.D., Ed.D.	Late 1940s	69,817	48	52
Social workers	M.S.W., D.S.W.	Early 1950s	188,792	47	23
Marriage and family therapists	Various	1940s	46,227	52	45

Source: Barber, 1999; Zarin et al., 1988; Peterson et al., 1996; Knowlton, 1995.

Psychotherapy and related services are also provided by *counseling psychologists, educational and school psychologists, psychiatric nurses, marriage therapists, family therapists,* and—the largest group—*psychiatric social workers* (see Table 1-1). Each of these specialties has its own graduate training program (Neimeyer, 1996; Peterson et al., 1996). Theoretically, each conducts therapy in a distinctive way, but in reality clinicians from the different professions often use similar techniques. In fact, the individual differences within a professional group are sometimes much greater than the general differences between groups.

One final important development in the study and treatment of mental disorders since World War II has been a heightened appreciation of the need for effective research. As theories and forms of treatment have accumulated, *clinical researchers* have tried to discover which concepts provide the best explanations and predictions, which treatments are most effective, and what kinds of modifications may be required. Today well-trained clinical researchers conduct studies in universities, medical schools, laboratories, mental hospitals, mental health centers, and other clinical settings throughout the world. Their work has already produced important discoveries and changed many of our ideas about abnormal psychological functioning.

CROSSROADS:
A Work in Progress

Since ancient times, people have tried to explain, treat, and study abnormal behavior. By examining the responses of past societies to such behaviors, we can better understand the roots of our present views and treatments. In addition, a look backward helps us appreciate just how far we have come—how humane our present views, how impressive our recent discoveries, and how important our current emphasis on research.

At the same time we must recognize the many problems in abnormal psychology today. The field has yet to agree on one definition of abnormality. It is currently made up of conflicting schools of thought and treatment whose members are often unimpressed by the claims and accomplishments of the others'. And clinical practice is carried out by a variety of professionals trained in different ways.

As we proceed through the topics in this book and look at the nature, treatment, and study of abnormal functioning, we must keep in mind the field's current strengths and weaknesses, the progress that has been made, and the journey that lies ahead. Perhaps the most important lesson to be learned from our look at the history of this field is that our current understanding of abnormal behavior

PROFESSIONAL SHIFT

In 1978, only 28 percent of psychologists were female, compared to 37 percent in 1988 and 48 percent today. The rise in female professionals is likely to continue: women now earn 75 percent of the bachelor degrees in psychology and 66 percent of the advanced degrees (Barber, 1999).

PATIENT DUMPING

According to a recent study, at least two-thirds of mental hospitals in the United States currently engage in the practice of "patient dumping" (Grinfeld, 1998; Schlesinger et al., 1997). They periodically deny care to patients or transfer them to other facilities, largely because the individuals require costly care or are underinsured.

represents a work in progress. The clinical field stands at a *crossroads*, with some of the most important insights, investigations, and changes yet to come.

How, then, should we proceed in our examination of abnormal psychology? To begin with, we need to learn about the basic tools and perspectives that today's scientists and practitioners find most useful. This is the task we turn to in the next several chapters. Chapter 2 describes the research strategies that are currently adding to our knowledge of abnormal functioning. Chapter 3 then examines the range of views that influence today's clinical theorists and practitioners. Finally, Chapter 4 examines how abnormal behaviors are currently being assessed, diagnosed, and treated. Later chapters present the major categories of psychological abnormality as well as the leading explanations and treatments for each of them. In the final chapter we shall see how the science of abnormal psychology and its professionals address current social issues and interact with legal, social, and other institutions in our world.

SUMMARY AND REVIEW

■ **What is psychological abnormality?** Abnormal functioning is generally considered to be deviant, distressful, dysfunctional, and dangerous. Behavior must also be considered in the context in which it occurs, however, and the concept of abnormality depends on the norms and values of the society in question. *pp. 2–5*

■ **What is treatment?** Therapy is a systematic process for helping people overcome their psychological difficulties. It typically requires a patient, a therapist, and a series of therapeutic contacts. *pp. 5–6*

■ **How was abnormality viewed and treated in the past?** The history of psychological disorders stretches back to ancient times.

PREHISTORIC SOCIETIES Prehistoric societies apparently viewed abnormal behavior as the work of evil spirits. There is evidence that Stone Age cultures used trephination, a primitive form of brain surgery, to treat abnormal behavior. People of early societies also sought to drive out evil spirits by exorcism. *pp. 8–9*

GREEKS AND ROMANS Physicians of the Greek and Roman empires offered more enlightened explanations of mental disorders. Hippocrates believed that abnormal behavior was due to an imbalance of the four bodily fluids, or humors: black bile, yellow bile, blood, and phlegm. Treatment consisted of correcting the underlying physical pathology through diet and lifestyle. *pp. 9–10*

THE MIDDLE AGES In the Middle Ages, Europeans returned to demonological explanations of abnormal behavior. The clergy was very influential and held that mental disorders were the work of the devil. As the Middle Ages drew to a close, such explanations and treatments began to decline, and people with mental disorders were increasingly treated in hospitals instead of by the clergy. *pp. 10–11*

THE RENAISSANCE Care of people with mental disorders continued to improve during the early part of the Renaissance. Certain religious shrines became dedicated to the humane treatment of such individuals. By the middle of the sixteenth century, however, persons with mental disorders were being warehoused in asylums. *pp. 11–13*

THE NINETEENTH CENTURY Care of those with mental disorders started to improve again in the nineteenth century. In Paris, Philippe Pinel started the movement toward moral treatment. Similar reforms were brought to England by William Tuke. Similarly, Dorothea Dix spearheaded a movement in the United States to ensure legal rights and protection for people with mental disorders and to establish state hospitals for their care. Unfortunately, the moral treatment movement disintegrated by the late nineteenth century, and men-

PSYCHOLOGICALLY INCORRECT

Some past terms for abnormal behavior are considered unacceptable today. "Lunacy" was used before the twentieth century because phases of the moon (lunar phases) were thought to produce such behavior. Similarly, the term "deranged"—first used in the case of a very orderly man who suddenly became "disarranged"—is now obsolete.

tal hospitals again became warehouses where the inmates received minimal care. *pp. 13–15*

THE EARLY TWENTIETH CENTURY The turn of the twentieth century saw the return of the somatogenic perspective, the view that abnormal psychological functioning is caused primarily by physical factors. Key to this development were the work of Emil Kraepelin in the late 1800s and the finding that general paresis was caused by the organic disease syphilis. The same period saw the rise of the psychogenic perspective, the view that the chief causes of abnormal functioning are psychological. An important factor in its rise was the use of hypnotism to treat patients with hysterical disorders. Sigmund Freud's psychogenic approach, psychoanalysis, eventually gained wide acceptance and influenced future generations of clinicians. *pp. 15–17*

■ **Current trends** The past 50 years have brought significant changes in the understanding and treatment of abnormal functioning. In the 1950s, researchers discovered a number of new psychotropic medications, drugs that mainly affect the brain and reduce many symptoms of mental dysfunctioning. Their success contributed to a policy of deinstitutionalization, under which hundreds of thousands of patients were released from public mental hospitals. In addition, outpatient treatment has become the primary approach for most persons with mental disorders, both mild and severe. Finally, a variety of perspectives and professionals have come to operate in the field of abnormal psychology, and many well-trained clinical researchers now investigate the field's theories and treatments. *pp. 17–21*

THE HARD SELL

Freud's breakthrough book *The Interpretation of Dreams* (1900) brought him rapid fame and was later viewed as a masterpiece, but it sold very poorly in its initial release (Gay, 1999).

CYBER **STUDY**

▲ *What did past hospital treatments for severe mental disorders look like?* ▲ *How might it have felt to receive or administer these treatments?* ▲ *Observe the predecessors of modern electroconvulsive therapy.* ▲ *Are the early treatments behind us?*

SEARCH THE *ABNORMAL PSYCHOLOGY* CD-ROM FOR

▲ Chapter 1 video case and discussion
   Early Procedures in Mental Hospitals

▲ Chapter 1 practice test and feedback

▲ Additional video case and discussion
   Early Electroconvulsive Therapy

LOG ON TO THE COMER WEB PAGE

[www.worthpublishers.com/comerabnormalpsychology4e] **FOR**

▲ Suggested Web links, research exercises, FAQ page, additional Chapter 1 practice test questions

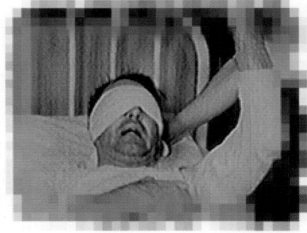

Research in Abnormal Psychology

"The brain is an organ of minor importance."

Aristotle, Greek philosopher, fourth century B.C.

"Woman may be said to be an inferior man."

Aristotle

"[Louis Pasteur's] theory of germs is a ridiculous fiction."

Pierre Pochet, professor of physiology, 1872

"Everything that can be invented has been invented."

Charles Duell, U.S. Patent Office, 1899

"The theory of relativity [is] worthless and misleading."

T. J. J. See, U.S. Government Observatory, 1924

"If excessive smoking actually plays a role in the production of lung cancer, it seems to be a minor one."

W. C. Heuper, National Cancer Institute, 1954

"Space travel is utter bilge."

Richard van der Riet Wooley, British Astronomer Royal, 1956

"There is no reason for any individual to have a computer in their home."

Ken Olson, Digital Equipment Corp., 1977

"The cloning of mammals . . . is biologically impossible."

James McGrath and Davor Solter, genetic researchers, 1984

Each of these statements was once accepted as gospel. Had their validity not been tested, had they been judged on the basis of conventional wisdom alone, had new ideas not been proposed and investigated, human knowledge and progress would have been severely limited. What enabled thinkers to move beyond such misperceptions? The answer, quite simply, is *research,* the systematic search for facts through the use of careful observations and investigations.

Research is as important to the field of abnormal psychology as to any other field of study. Consider, for example, *schizophrenia* and the treatment procedure known as the *lobotomy.* Schizophrenia is a severe disorder that causes people to lose contact with reality. Their thoughts, perceptions, and emotions become distorted and disorganized, and their behavior may be bizarre and withdrawn. For the first half of the twentieth century, this condition was attributed to inappropriate parenting. Clinicians blamed *schizophrenogenic* ("schizophrenia-causing") *mothers* for the disorder—women they described as cold and domineering, and impervious to their children's needs. As we will see in Chapter 14, this widely held belief turned out to be wrong.

During the same era, practitioners developed a surgical procedure that supposedly cured schizophrenia. In this procedure, called a lobotomy, a pointed instrument was inserted into the frontal lobe of the brain and rotated, destroying a considerable amount of brain tissue. Early reports described lobotomized patients as showing near-miraculous improvement. This impression, too, turned out to be wrong, though the mistake wasn't discovered until tens of thousands of persons had been lobotomized. Far from curing schizophrenia, lobotomies caused irreversible brain damage that left many patients withdrawn and even stuporous.

These errors underscore the importance of sound research in abnormal psychology. Theories and treatments that seem reasonable and effective in individual instances may prove disastrous when applied to various people or situations. Only by rigorously testing a theory or technique on representative groups of subjects can clinicians evaluate the accuracy and usefulness of their ideas and techniques. Until clinical researchers conducted relevant studies, millions of parents, already heartbroken by their children's schizophrenia, were additionally stigmatized as the primary cause of the disorder; and countless people with schizophrenia, already debilitated by their symptoms, were made permanently apathetic and spiritless by a lobotomy.

Clinical researchers face certain challenges that make their investigations particularly difficult. They must, for example, figure out how to measure such elusive concepts as unconscious motives, private thoughts, mood change, and human potential (Schwarz, 1999). They must consider the different cultural backgrounds, races, and genders of the people they select as research subjects (Rogler, 1999). And, as we are reminded in Box 2-1, they must always ensure that the rights of their subjects, both human and animal, are not violated (Bersoff & Bersoff, 1999). Despite such difficulties, research in this field has taken giant steps forward, especially during the last thirty-five years. In the past, most clinical researchers were limited by lack of training and a paucity of useful techniques. Now graduate clinical programs train large numbers of students to conduct appropriate studies on clinical topics. Moreover, the development of

BOX 2-1

Animals Have Rights

For years researchers have learned about abnormal human behavior from experiments with animals. Animals have sometimes been shocked, prematurely separated from their parents, and starved; they have had their brains surgically changed and even been killed, or "sacrificed," so that researchers could autopsy them. Are such actions always ethically acceptable?

Animal rights activists say no. They have called the undertakings cruel and unnecessary and have fought many forms of animal research with legal protests and demonstrations. Some have even harassed scientists and vandalized their labs. In turn, some researchers accuse the activists of caring more about animals than about human beings.

In response to this controversy, a number of state courts have ruled that university researchers must publicly disclose their research proposals to help ensure the well-being of animal subjects. Similarly, government agencies and the American Psychological

Association have issued rules and guidelines for animal research. Still the battle goes on.

Where does the public stand on the issue? In a recent survey of British citizens, 64 percent of the respondents

said that they disagree with animal research—71 percent of the women and 57 percent of the men (MORI, 1999). But such public disapproval appears tenuous. In the same survey, a mere reminder that animal research can hasten clinical progress led to expressions of approval by a slim majority of the respondents. People in animal rights surveys tend to approve of experiments that use mice or rats more than those that use monkeys. Most of them disapprove of experiments that bring pain to animals, except when the investigations are seeking a cure for childhood leukemia, AIDS, or other life-threatening problems.

ConsiderThis

⊙ Do restrictions on animal research interfere with necessary investigations and thus limit potential gains for human beings? • Is there a way to address the concerns of both activists and scientists?

new research methods has greatly improved our understanding of psychological dysfunction.

What Do Clinical Researchers Do?

Clinical researchers, also called clinical scientists, try to discover universal laws, or principles, of abnormal psychological functioning. They search for general, or **nomothetic**, truths about the nature, causes, and treatments of abnormality ("nomothetic" is derived from the Greek *nomothetis,* "lawgiver"). They do not typically assess, diagnose, or treat individual clients; that is the job of clinical practitioners, who seek an *idiographic,* or individualistic, understanding of abnormal behavior (Stricker & Trierweiler, 1995). We shall explore the work of practitioners in later chapters.

To gain a nomothetic understanding of abnormal psychology, clinical researchers, like scientists in other fields, rely primarily on the **scientific method**—that is, they systematically collect and evaluate information through careful observations (Beutler et al., 1995). These observations in turn enable them to pinpoint and explain relationships between variables. Simply stated, a *variable* is any characteristic or event that can vary, whether from time to time, from place to place, or from person to person. Age, sex, and race are human variables. So are eye color, occupation, and social status. Clinical researchers are interested in variables such as childhood upsets, present life experiences, moods, social and occupational functioning, and responses to treatment. They try to determine whether two or more such variables change together and whether a change in one variable causes a change in another. Will the death of a parent cause a child to become depressed? If so, will a given treatment reduce that depression?

Such questions cannot be answered by logic alone, because scientists, like all human beings, make frequent errors in thinking (NAMHC, 1996). Thus clinical researchers must depend mainly on three methods of investigation: the *case study,* which typically focuses on but one individual, and the *correlational method* and *experimental method,* approaches that usually gather information about many individuals. Each is best suited to certain kinds of circumstances and questions (Beutler et al., 1995). Collectively, these methods enable scientists to form and test *hypotheses,* or hunches, that certain variables are related in certain ways—and to draw broad conclusions as to why. More properly, a hypothesis is a tentative explanation offered to provide a basis for an investigation.

The Case Study

A **case study** is a detailed and often interpretive description of a person's life and psychological problems. It describes the person's history, present circumstances, and symptoms. It may also speculate about why the problems developed and it may describe the application and results of a particular treatment.

In his famous case study of Little Hans (1909), Sigmund Freud discusses a 4-year-old boy who has developed a fear of horses. Freud gathered his material from detailed letters sent him by Hans's father, a physician who had attended lectures on psychoanalysis, and from his own limited interviews with the child. Freud's study runs 140 pages in his *Collected Papers,* so only key excerpts are presented here.

> One day while Hans was in the street he was seized with an attack of morbid anxiety. . . . [Hans's father wrote:] "He began to cry and asked to be taken home. . . . In the evening he grew visibly frightened; he cried and could not be separated from his mother. . . . [When taken for a walk the next day], again he began to cry,

"*Sure, we need more research in alchemy, necromancy, and sorcery, but where is the money going to come from?*"

A GROWTH PROFESSION

Ninety percent of all scientists who have ever lived are alive today. More scientific papers have been published in the past 40 years than were published in all the years before (Asimov, 1997).

NOMOTHETIC UNDERSTANDING A general understanding of the nature, causes, and treatments of abnormal psychological functioning in the form of laws or principles.

SCIENTIFIC METHOD The process of systematically gathering and evaluating information through careful observations to gain an understanding of a phenomenon.

CASE STUDY A detailed account of a person's life and psychological problems.

did not want to start, and was frightened. . . . On the way back from Schönbrunn he said to his mother, after much internal struggling: 'I was afraid a horse would bite me.' . . . In the evening he . . . had another attack similar to that of the previous evening. . . ."

But the beginnings of this psychological situation go back further still. . . . The first reports of Hans date from a period when he was not quite three years old. At that time, by means of various remarks and questions, he was showing a quite peculiarly lively interest in that portion of his body which he used to describe as his 'widdler' [his word for penis]. . . .

When he was three and a half his mother found him with his hand to his penis. She threatened him in these words: 'If you do that, I shall send for Dr. A. to cut off your widdler. And then what'll you widdle with?' . . . This was the occasion of his acquiring [a] 'castration complex.' . . .

[At the age of four, Hans entered] a state of intensified sexual excitement, the object of which was his mother. The intensity of this excitement was shown by . . . two attempts at seducing his mother. [One such attempt, occurring just before the outbreak of his anxiety, was described by his father:] "This morning Hans was given his usual daily bath by his mother and afterwards dried and powdered. As his mother was powdering round his penis and taking care not to touch it, Hans said: 'Why don't you put your finger there? . . .'"

. . . The father and son visited me during my consulting hours. . . . Certain details which I now learnt—to the effect that [Hans] was particularly bothered by what horses wear in front of their eyes and by the black round their mouths—were certainly not to be explained from what we knew. But as I saw the two of them sitting in front of me and at the same time heard Hans's description of his anxiety-horses, a further piece of the solution shot through my mind. . . . I asked Hans jokingly whether his horses wore eyeglasses, to which he replied that they did not. I then asked him whether his father wore eyeglasses, to which, against all the evidence, he once more said no. Finally I asked him whether by 'the black round the mouth' he meant a moustache; and I then disclosed to him that he was afraid of his father, precisely because he was so fond of his mother. It must be, I told him, that he thought his father was angry with him on that account; but this was not so, his father was fond of him in spite of it, and he might admit everything to him without any fear. Long before he was in the world, I went on, I had known that a little Hans would come who would be so fond of his mother that he would be bound to feel afraid of his father because of it. . . .

By enlightening Hans on this subject I had cleared away his most powerful resistance. . . . [T]he little patient summoned up courage to describe the details of his phobia, and soon began to take an active share in the conduct of the analysis.

. . . It was only then that we learnt [that Hans] was not only afraid of horses biting him—he was soon silent upon that point—but also of carts, of furniture-vans, and of buses . . . , of horses that started moving, of horses that looked big and heavy, and of horses that drove quickly. The meaning of these specifications was explained by Hans himself: he was afraid of horses falling down, and consequently incorporated in his phobia everything that seemed likely to facilitate their falling down.

It was at this stage of the analysis that he recalled the event, insignificant in itself, which immediately preceded the outbreak of the illness and may no doubt be regarded as the exciting cause of the outbreak. He went for a walk with his mother, and saw a bus-horse fall down and kick about with its feet. This made a great impression on him. He was terrified, and thought the horse was dead; and from that time on he thought that all horses would fall down. His father pointed out to him that when he saw the horse fall down he must have thought of him, his father, and have wished that he might fall down in the same way and be dead. Hans did not dispute this interpretation. . . . From that time forward his behavior to his father was unconstrained and fearless, and in fact a trifle overbearing.

FREUD AT WORK

For almost 40 years Freud treated patients 10 hours per day, five or six days per week (Schwartz, 1993).

BIASED EVIDENCE

Hans's father, the primary source of information in the case of Little Hans, was a great admirer of Freud and not entirely objective. Of all the household events that might have affected Hans, he communicated to Freud only those he knew would interest the founder of psychoanalysis and support his theory (Schwartz, 1993).

It is especially interesting . . . to observe the way in which the transformation of Hans's libido into anxiety was projected on to the principal object of his phobia, on to horses. Horses interested him the most of all the large animals; playing at horses was his favorite game with the older children. I had a suspicion— and this was confirmed by Hans's father when I asked him—that the first person who had served Hans as a horse must have been his father. . . . When repression had set in and brought a revulsion of feeling along with it, horses, which had till then been associated with so much pleasure, were necessarily turned into objects of fear.

[Hans later reported] two concluding phantasies, with which his recovery was rounded off. One of them, that of [a] plumber giving him a new and . . . bigger widdler, was . . . a triumphant wish-phantasy, and with it he overcame his fear of castration. . . . His other phantasy, which confessed to the wish to be married to his mother and to have many children by her . . . corrected that portion of those thoughts which was entirely unacceptable; for, instead of killing his father, it made him innocuous by promoting him to a marriage with Hans's grandmother. With this phantasy both the illness and the analysis came to an appropriate end.

(Freud, 1909)

Most clinicians take notes and keep records in the course of treating their patients, and some, like Freud, further organize such notes into a formal case study to be shared with other professionals. The clues offered by a case study may help a clinician better understand or treat the person under discussion (Stricker & Trierweiler, 1995). In addition, case studies may play nomothetic roles that go far beyond the individual clinical case (Beutler et al., 1995; Smith, 1988).

"Modern medicine . . . does reasonably well at measuring disease, but not that well at measuring health."

James Neel, geneticist, 1994

How Are Case Studies Helpful?

Case studies can be a *source of new ideas* about behavior and "open the way for discoveries" (Bolgar, 1965). Freud's own theory of psychoanalysis was based mainly on the patients he saw in private practice. He pored over their case studies, such as the one he wrote about Little Hans, to find what he believed to be universal psychological processes and principles of development. In addition, a case study may offer *tentative support* for a theory. Freud used case studies in this way, as well, regarding them as evidence for the accuracy of his ideas. Conversely, case studies may serve to *challenge a theory's assumptions* (Kratochwill, 1992).

Case studies may also inspire *new therapeutic techniques* or describe unique applications of existing techniques. The psychoanalytic principle that says patients may benefit from discussing their problems and discovering underlying psychological causes, for example, has roots in the famous case study of Anna O., presented by Freud's collaborator Josef Breuer, a case we shall explore in Chapter 3. Similarly, Freud believed that the case study of Little Hans demonstrated the therapeutic potential of a verbal approach for children as well as for adults.

Finally, case studies may offer opportunities to study *unusual problems* that do not occur often enough to permit a large number of observations (Lehman, 1991). For years information about multiple personality disorders was based almost exclusively on case studies, such as the famous *The Three Faces of Eve,* a clinical account of a woman who displayed three alternating personalities, each having a distinct set of memories, preferences, and personal habits (Thigpen & Cleckley, 1957).

Does mental dysfunctioning run in families? *One of the most celebrated case studies in abnormal psychology is a study of identical quadruplets dubbed the "Genain" sisters by researchers (after the Greek words for "dire birth"). All the sisters developed schizophrenia in their twenties.*

Case study, Hollywood style *Case studies often find their way into the arts or media and capture the public's attention. Unfortunately, as this movie poster of* The Three Faces of Eve *illustrates, the studies may be trivialized or sensationalized in those venues.*

INTERNAL VALIDITY The accuracy with which a study can pinpoint one out of various possible factors as being the cause of a phenomenon.

EXTERNAL VALIDITY The degree to which the results of a study may be generalized beyond that study.

CORRELATION The degree to which events or characteristics vary along with each other.

CORRELATIONAL METHOD A research procedure used to determine how much events or characteristics vary along with each other.

What Are the Limitations of Case Studies?

Case studies, although useful in many ways, also have limitations. First, they are reported by *biased observers,* that is, by therapists who have a personal stake in seeing their treatments succeed (Stricker & Trierweiler, 1995; Lehman, 1991). These observers must choose what to include in a case study, and their choices may at times be self-serving. Second, case studies rely upon *subjective evidence.* Are a client's dysfunction and improvement really caused by the events that the therapist or client says are responsible? In fact, these are only a small subset of the events that may be contributing to the situation. When investigators are able to rule out all possible causes except one, a study is said to have internal accuracy, or **internal validity**. Obviously, case studies rate low on that score.

Another problem with case studies is that they provide *little basis for generalization.* Even if we agree that Little Hans developed a dread of horses because he was terrified of castration and feared his father, how can we be confident that other people's phobias are rooted in the same kinds of causes? Events or treatments that seem important in one case may be of no help at all in efforts to understand or treat others. When the findings of an investigation can be generalized beyond the immediate study, the investigation is said to have external accuracy, or **external validity**. Case studies rate low on external validity, too (Lehman, 1991).

The limitations of the case study are largely addressed by two other methods of investigation: the correlational method and the experimental method. They do not offer the richness of detail that makes case studies so interesting, but they do help investigators draw broad conclusions about abnormality in the population at large. Thus they are now the preferred methods of clinical investigation (Pincus et al., 1993). Three features of these methods enable clinical investigators to gain nomothetic insights: (1) The researchers typically observe many individuals. That way, they can collect enough information, or *data,* to support a conclusion. (2) The researchers apply procedures uniformly. Therefore other researchers can repeat, or *replicate,* a particular study to see whether it consistently gives the same findings. (3) The researchers use *statistical tests* to analyze the results of a study. These tests can help indicate whether broad conclusions are justified.

The Correlational Method

Correlation is the degree to which events or characteristics vary with each other. The **correlational method** is a research procedure used to determine this "co-relationship" between variables. This method can, for example, answer the question "Is there a correlation between the amount of stress in people's lives and the degree of depression they experience?" That is, as people keep experiencing stressful events, are they increasingly likely to become depressed? To test this question, researchers have collected life stress scores (for example, the number of threatening events experienced during a certain period of time) and depression scores (for example, scores on a depression survey) from individuals, and have correlated these scores.

The people who are chosen for a study are its *subjects,* or *participants,* collectively called the *sample.* A sample must be representative of the larger population that the researchers wish to understand (Sandelowski, 1995). Otherwise the relationship found in the study may not apply elsewhere in the real world—may not have external validity (see Box 2-2 on page 32). If researchers were to find a correlation between life stress and depression in a sample consisting entirely of children, for example, they could not draw clear conclusions about what, if any, correlation exists among adults.

Describing a Correlation

Suppose we use the correlational method to conduct a study of depression. We collect life stress scores and depression scores for ten subjects, and we plot the scores on a graph, as shown in Figure 2-1. As you can see, the subject named Jim has a recent life stress score of 7, meaning seven threatening events over the past three months; he also has a depression score of 25. Thus he is "located" at the point on the graph where these two scores meet. The graph provides a visual representation of our data. Here, notice that the data points all fall roughly along a straight line that slopes upward. We draw the line so that the data points are as close to it as possible. This line is called the *line of best fit.*

The line of best fit in Figure 2-1 slopes upward and to the right, indicating that the variables under examination are increasing or decreasing together. That is, the greater someone's life stress score, the higher his or her score on the depression scale. When variables change the same way, their correlation is said to have a *positive direction* and is referred to as a *positive correlation.* Most studies of recent life stress and depression have indeed found a positive correlation between those two variables (Kendler, Karkowski, & Prescott, 1999; Stader & Hokanson, 1998; Paykel & Cooper, 1992).

Correlations can have a negative rather than a positive direction. In a *negative correlation,* the value of one variable increases as the value of the other variable decreases. Researchers have found, for example, a negative correlation between depression and activity level. The greater one's depression, the lower the number of one's activities. When the scores of a negative correlation are plotted, they produce a downward-sloping graph, like the one shown in Figure 2-2.

There is still a third possible outcome for a correlational study. The variables under study may be *unrelated,* meaning that there is no consistent relationship between them. As the measures of one variable increase, those of the other variable sometimes increase and sometimes decrease. The graph of this outcome looks like Figure 2-3. Here the line of best fit is horizontal, with no slope at all. Studies have found that depression and intelligence are unrelated, for example.

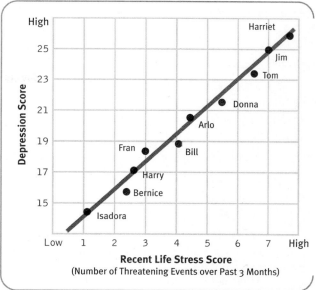

FIGURE 2-1 Positive correlation
The relationship between amount of recent stress and feelings of depression shown by this hypothetical sample of ten subjects is a near-perfect "positive" correlation.

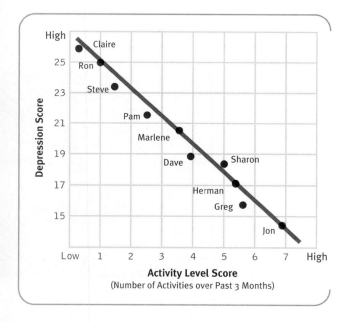

FIGURE 2-2 Negative correlation
The relationship between number of activities and feelings of depression shown by this hypothetical sample is a near-perfect "negative" correlation.

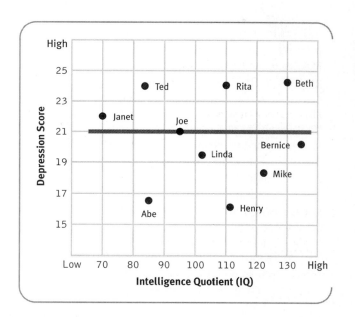

FIGURE 2-3 No correlation
The relationship between intelligence and feelings of depression shown by this hypothetical sample is a "near-zero" correlation.

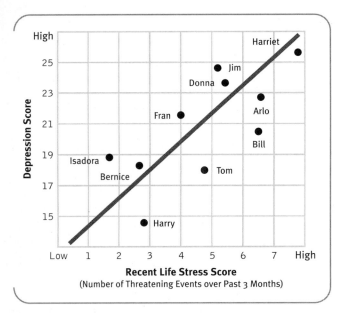

FIGURE 2-4 Magnitude of correlation
The relationship between amount of recent stress and feelings of depression shown by this hypothetical sample is a "moderately positive" correlation.

In addition to knowing the direction of a correlation, researchers need to know its *magnitude,* or strength. That is, how closely do the two variables correspond? Does one *always* vary along with the other, or is their relationship less exact? When two variables are found to vary together very closely in subject after subject, the correlation is said to be high, or strong.

Look again at Figure 2-1. In this graph of a positive correlation between depression and life stress, the data points all fall very close to the line of best fit. Researchers can predict each person's score on one variable with a high degree of confidence if they know his or her score on the other. But what if the graph of the correlation between depression and life stress looked more like Figure 2-4? Now the data points are loosely scattered around the line of best fit rather than hugging it closely. In this case, researchers could not predict with as much accuracy a subject's score on one variable from the score on the other variable. The correlation in Figure 2-1 is stronger, or greater in magnitude, than that in Figure 2-4.

The direction and magnitude of a correlation are often calculated numerically and expressed by a statistical term called the *correlation coefficient,* symbolized by the letter *r*. The correlation coefficient can vary from +1.00, which indicates a perfect positive correlation between two variables, down to −1.00, which represents a perfect negative correlation. The *sign* of the coefficient (+ or −) signifies the direction of the correlation; the *number* represents its magnitude. An *r* of .00 reflects a zero correlation, or no relationship between variables. The closer *r* is to .00, the weaker, or lower in magnitude, the correlation. Thus correlations of +.75 and −.75 are of equal magnitude and equally strong, whereas a correlation of +.25 is weaker than either.

B O X **2-2**

Research: A Man's World?

For many years scientists in Western society have favored the use of young white men as subjects for research on human functioning (Stark-Adamek, 1992; Gannon et al., 1992). Only recently have they come to appreciate that findings from studies using such subjects may not be relevant to persons of a different sex, race, or age (Roehrich & Wilsnack, 1998). This research bias may, we are now learning, lead to some mistaken beliefs about the symptoms, causes, course, and treatment of various mental disorders.

One review of the leading studies on schizophrenia, for example, has revealed that male subjects outnumber female subjects by more than 2 to 1 (Wahl & Hunter, 1992), despite the fact that this disorder is as common in women as in men. How can we be sure that the insights drawn from these studies are accurate for all per-

sons with schizophrenia rather than just for men with this disorder?

Similarly, medications for mental disorders have been tested on groups made up largely of young white male subjects and on that basis alone have been made available to all patients. Often, however, such medications have turned out to act differently, sometimes dangerously so, in elderly, female, or nonwhite populations (Cimons, 1999; Goodman, 1992; Wolfe et al., 1988).

Reviews show that researchers are doing better each year—becoming more aware of gender, race, and age, and designing more appropriate studies (Sue et al., 1994; Gannon et al., 1992). In fact, both the Canadian and American Psychological Associations now offer guidelines to enlighten their members (Stark-Adamek, 1992), and the U.S. Food and Drug Administration now requires pharmaceutical companies to test all drugs on both genders

(Cimons, 1999). They are aware that when research is biased in these ways, knowledge is limited, progress is stifled, and everyone loses.

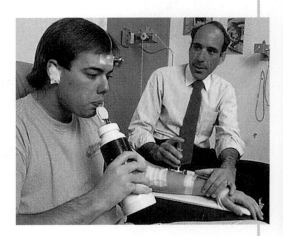

Overused and overstudied? *The majority of medical and psychological studies have used young white men as subjects. Here one such subject drinks various substances to help determine whether the effects of alcohol are linked to genetic factors.*

Everyone's behavior is changeable, and many human responses can be measured only approximately. Most correlations found in psychological research, therefore, fall short of a perfect positive or negative correlation. One study of life stress and depression, with a sample of 68 adults, found a correlation of +.53 (Miller, Ingraham, & Davidson, 1976). Although hardly perfect, a correlation of this magnitude is considered large in psychological research.

When Can Correlations Be Trusted?

Scientists must decide whether the correlation they find in a given sample of subjects accurately reflects a real correlation in the general population. Could the observed correlation have occurred by mere chance? They can never know for certain, but they can test their conclusions by a *statistical analysis* of their data, using principles of probability. In essence, they ask how likely it is that the study's particular findings have occurred by chance. If the statistical analysis indicates that chance is unlikely to account for the correlation they found, researchers may conclude that their findings reflect a real correlation in the general population.

A cutoff point helps researchers make this decision. By convention, if there is less than a 5 percent probability that a study's findings are due to chance (signified as $p < .05$), the findings are said to be *statistically significant* and are thought to reflect the larger population. In the life stress study described earlier, a statistical analysis indicated a probability of less than 5 percent that the +.53 correlation found in the sample was due to chance (Miller et al., 1976). Therefore, the researchers concluded with some confidence that among adults in general, depression does tend to rise along with the amount of recent stress in a person's life. Generally, our confidence increases with the size of the sample and the magnitude of the correlation. The larger they are, the more likely it is that a correlation will be statistically significant.

What Are the Merits of the Correlational Method?

The correlational method has certain advantages over the case study (see Table 2-1). First, it possesses high *external validity*. Because researchers measure their variables, observe large samples, and apply statistical analyses, they are in a better position to generalize their correlations to people beyond the ones they have studied. Furthermore, researchers can easily repeat correlational studies using new samples of subjects to check the results of earlier studies.

On the other hand, correlational studies, like case studies, lack *internal validity* (Goodwin, 1995). Although correlations allow researchers to describe the relationship between two variables, they do not *explain* the relationship. When we look at the positive correlation found in many life stress studies, we may be tempted to conclude that increases in recent life stress cause people to feel more depressed. In fact, however, the two variables may be correlated for any one of

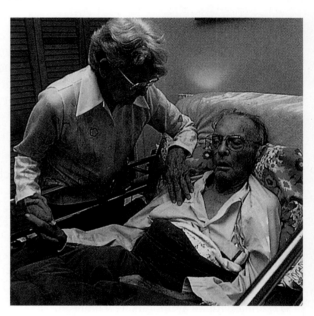

Life stress and depression *Numerous studies have found a correlation between life stress and depression. The pressures of caring for a chronically ill spouse, for example, have been linked to depression in caretakers (Given et al., 1999).*

Table 2-1

Relative Strengths and Weaknesses of Research Methods

	PROVIDES INDIVIDUAL INFORMATION (IDIOGRAPHIC)	PROVIDES GENERAL INFORMATION (NOMOTHETIC)	PROVIDES CAUSAL INFORMATION	STATISTICAL ANALYSIS IS POSSIBLE	REPLICABLE
Case study	Yes	No	No	No	No
Correlational method	No	Yes	No	Yes	Yes
Experimental method	No	Yes	Yes	Yes	Yes

ConsiderThis

⦿ How would you interpret the sizable correlation found between life stress and depression? • How would you decide which of various possible interpretations is the most accurate?

PSYCHOPATHOLOGY IN THE NEW MILLENNIUM

In 1999 the U.S. government granted $7.3 million for an ambitious new mental health epidemiology study. The five-year study will examine the prevalence of psychological problems among 10,000 adults (NIMH, 1999).

EPIDEMIOLOGICAL STUDY A study that measures the incidence and prevalence of a disorder in a given population.

INCIDENCE The number of new cases of a disorder occurring in a population over a specific period of time.

PREVALENCE The total number of cases of a disorder occurring in a population over a specific period of time.

LONGITUDINAL STUDY A study that observes the same subjects on many occasions over a long period of time.

three reasons: (1) Life stress may cause depression. (2) Depression may cause people to experience more life stress (for example, a depressive approach to life may cause people to mismanage their money or may interfere with social relationships). (3) Depression and life stress may each be caused by a third variable, such as poverty.

Although correlations say nothing about causation, they can still be of great use to clinicians. Clinicians know, for example, that suicide attempts increase as people become more depressed. Thus, when they work with severely depressed clients, they keep on the lookout for signs of suicidal thinking (Beck, 1993, 1967). Perhaps depression directly causes suicidal behavior, or perhaps a third variable, such as a sense of hopelessness, causes both depression and suicidal thoughts. Whatever the cause, just knowing that there is a correlation may enable clinicians to take measures (such as hospitalization) to help save lives.

Of course, in other instances, clinicians do need to know whether one variable causes another. Do parents' marital conflicts cause their children to be more anxious? Does job dissatisfaction lead to feelings of depression? Will a given treatment help people to cope more effectively in life? Questions about causality call for the experimental method, as we shall see later.

Special Forms of Correlational Research

Epidemiological studies and longitudinal studies are two kinds of correlational research used widely by clinical investigators. **Epidemiological studies** reveal the incidence and prevalence of a disorder in a particular population (Weissman, 1995). **Incidence** is the number of new cases that emerge during a given period of time. **Prevalence** is the *total* number of cases in the population during a given time period; prevalence includes both existing and new cases.

Over the past 25 years clinical researchers throughout the United States have worked on the largest epidemiological study ever conducted, called the Epidemiologic Catchment Area Study. They have interviewed more than 20,000 people in five cities to determine the prevalence of many psychological disorders and the treatment programs used (Regier et al., 1993). Another large-scale epidemiological study in the United States, the National Comorbidity Survey, has questioned more than 8,000 individuals (Kessler & Zhao, 1999; Anthony et al., 1995, 1994; Kessler et al., 1994). Both studies have been further compared with epidemiological studies in other countries, to see how rates of mental disorders and treatment programs vary around the world (Weissman, 1995).

Such epidemiological studies have helped researchers identify groups at risk for particular disorders. Women, it turns out, have a higher rate of anxiety disorders and depression than men, while men have a higher rate of alcoholism than women. Elderly people have a higher rate of suicide than younger people, African Americans have a higher rate of high blood pressure than white Americans, and the people in some non-Western countries (such as Taiwan) have a higher rate of mental disorders than those in Western countries. Such trends may lead researchers to suspect that something unique about certain groups or settings is helping to cause particular disorders (Rogers & Holloway, 1990). Declining health in elderly people, for example, may make them more likely to commit suicide; cultural pressures in a given country may be responsible for a higher rate of mental dysfunctioning there. Yet, like other forms of correlational research, epidemiological studies themselves cannot confirm such suspicions.

In **longitudinal studies** (also called **high-risk** or **developmental studies**), researchers observe the same subjects on many occasions over a long period of time. In one such study, investigators observed the progress over the years of normally functioning children whose mothers or fathers suffered from schizophrenia (Parnas, 1988; Mednick, 1971). The researchers found, among other things, that the children of the parents with the most severe cases of schizophrenia were more likely to develop a psychological disorder and to commit crimes later in their lives. Because longitudinal studies document the order of events, their correlations provide clues about which events are more likely to be causes and which to be the consequences. Certainly, for example, the children's problems did not cause their parents' schizophrenia. But longitudinal studies still cannot pinpoint causation. Did the children who developed psychological problems inherit a genetic factor? Or did their problems result from their parents' inadequate coping behaviors, their parents' long absences due to hospitalization, or some other factor? Again, only experimental studies can supply an answer.

The Experimental Method

An **experiment** is a research procedure in which a variable is manipulated and the manipulation's effect on another variable is observed. In fact, most of us perform experiments throughout our lives without knowing that we are behaving so scientifically.

Twins, correlation, and inheritance *Correlational studies of many pairs of twins have suggested a link between genetic factors and certain psychological disorders. Identical twins (who have identical genes) display a higher correlation for some disorders than do fraternal twins (whose genetic makeup is not identical).*

Suppose that we go to a party on campus to celebrate the end of midterm exams. As we mix with people at the party, we begin to notice many of them becoming quiet and depressed. It seems the more we talk, the more subdued the other guests become. As the party deteriorates before our eyes, we decide we have to do something, but what? Before we can eliminate the problem, we need to know what's causing it.

Our first hunch may be that something we're doing is responsible. Perhaps our remarks about academic pressures have been upsetting everyone. We decide to change the topic to skiing in the mountains of Colorado, and we watch for signs of depression in our next round of conversations. The problem seems to clear up; most people now smile and laugh as they chat with us. As a final check of our suspicions, we could go back to talking about school with the next several people we meet. Their dark and dismal reaction would probably convince us that our propensity to talk about school was indeed the cause of the problem.

We have just performed an experiment, testing our hypothesis about a causal relationship between our conversational gambits and the depressed mood of the people around us. We manipulated the variable that we suspected to be the cause (the topic of discussion) and then observed the effect of that manipulation on the other variable (the mood of the people around us). In scientific experiments, the manipulated variable is called the **independent variable** and the variable being observed is called the **dependent variable**.

To examine the experimental method more fully, let us consider a question that is often asked by clinicians: "Does a particular therapy relieve the symptoms of a particular disorder?" (Kendall, 1998; Lambert & Bergin, 1994). Because this question is about a causal relationship, it can be answered only by an experiment. That is, experimenters must give the therapy in question to people who are suffering from a disorder and then observe whether they improve. Here the therapy is the independent variable, and psychological improvement is the dependent variable.

The goal of an experiment is to isolate and identify a cause. If we cannot separate the true, or primary, cause from a host of other possible causes, then the experiment gives us very little information. Thus experimenters must try to eliminate all *confounds* from the study—variables other than the independent variable that may also be affecting the dependent variable. When there are confounds in an experiment, they, rather than the independent variable, may be causing the observed changes (Goodwin, 1995).

For example, situational variables, such as the location of the therapy office (say, a quiet country setting) or a soothing color scheme in the office, may have a

"Find out the cause of this effect,
Or rather say, the cause of this defect,
For this effect defective comes by cause."

William Shakespeare, *Hamlet*

EXPERIMENT A research procedure in which a variable is manipulated and the effect of the manipulation is observed.

INDEPENDENT VARIABLE The variable in an experiment that is manipulated to determine whether it has an effect on another variable.

DEPENDENT VARIABLE The variable in an experiment that is expected to change as the independent variable is manipulated.

therapeutic effect on participants in a therapy study. Or perhaps the participants are unusually motivated or have high expectations that the therapy will work, which thus accounts for their improvement. To guard against confounds, researchers include three important features in their experiments—a *control group*, *random assignment*, and a *blind design* (Goodwin, 1995).

The Control Group

A **control group** is a group of subjects who are *not* exposed to the independent variable under investigation but whose experience is similar to that of the **experimental group**, the subjects who *are* exposed to the independent variable. By comparing the two groups, an experimenter can better determine the effect of the independent variable.

To study the effectiveness of a particular therapy, for example, experimenters typically divide subjects into two groups after obtaining their consent to participate in the experiment (see Box 2-3). The experimental group may come into an office and receive the therapy for an hour, while the control group may simply come into the office for an hour. If the clients in the experimental group improve more than the clients in the control group, the experimenters may conclude that the therapy was effective, above and beyond the effects of time, the office setting, and any other confounds. To guard against confounds, experimenters try to provide all participants, both control and experimental, with experiences that are identical in every way—except for the independent variable.

Of course, it is possible that the differences observed between an experimental group and control group have occurred simply by chance. Thus, as with correlational studies, investigators who conduct experiments must do a statistical analysis on their data and find out how likely it is that the observed differences are due to chance. If the likelihood is very low—less than 5 percent ($p < .05$)—the differences between the two groups are considered to be statistically significant, and the experimenter may conclude with some confidence that they are due to the independent variable. As a general rule, if the sample of subjects is large, if the difference observed between groups is great, and if the range of scores within each group is small, the findings of an experiment are likely to be statistically significant.

Random Assignment

Researchers must also watch out for differences in the makeup of the experimental and control groups, since those differences may also confound a study's results. In a therapy study, for example, it may happen that the experimenter has unintentionally put wealthier subjects in the experimental group and poorer subjects in the control group. This difference, rather than their therapy, could be the cause of the greater improvement later found among the experimental subjects (Persons & Silberschatz, 1998). To reduce the effects of preexisting differences, experimenters typically use **random assignment**. This is the general term for any selection procedure that ensures that every subject in the experiment is as likely to be placed in one group as the other. We might, for example, try flipping a coin or picking names out of a hat.

Blind Design

A final confound problem is *bias*. Participants may bias an experiment's results by trying to please or help the experimenter (Kazdin, 1994). In a therapy experiment, for example, those who receive the treatment, knowing the purpose of the study and knowing which group they are in, might actually work harder to feel better or fulfill the experimenter's expectations. If so, *subject bias* rather than therapy could be causing their improvement.

To avoid this bias, experimenters can prevent participants from finding out which group they are in. This strategy is called a **blind**

STATISTICAL SIGNIFICANCE VS. CLINICAL SIGNIFICANCE

Even if subjects improve because of treatment, we do not know whether the amount of improvement is meaningful in their lives. For example, a subject who is less depressed than previously may still be too unhappy to enjoy life. Thus, although experimenters can determine *statistical significance*, only individuals and their clinicians can evaluate *clinical significance*.

What works? *As many as 400 different kinds of therapies are currently used for psychological problems. In one approach,* art therapy, *clients probe, express, and work out their feelings through drawings. An experimental design is needed to determine whether this or any other form of treatment actually causes clients to improve.*

BOX **2-3** | 37

design because subjects are blind as to their assigned group. In a therapy study, for example, control subjects could be given a *placebo* (Latin for "I shall please"), something that looks or tastes like real therapy but has none of its key ingredients (Streiner, 1999; Addington, 1995). This "imitation" therapy is called *placebo therapy*. If the experimental (true therapy) subjects then improve more than the control (placebo therapy) subjects, experimenters have more confidence that the true therapy has caused their improvement.

An experiment may also be confounded by *experimenter bias* (Margraf et al., 1991). That is, experimenters may have expectations that they unintentionally transmit to their subjects. This bias is sometimes referred to as the *Rosenthal effect*, after the psychologist who first identified it (Rosenthal, 1966). Experimenters can eliminate their own bias by arranging to be blind themselves. In a drug therapy study, for example, an aide could make sure that the real medication and the placebo drug look identical. The experimenter could then administer treatment without knowing which participants were receiving true medications and which were receiving false medications.

While the participants *or* the experimenter may be kept blind in an experiment, it is best that *both* be blind (a *double-blind design*). In fact, most experiments for testing the efficacy of promising drugs now use double-blind designs (Morin et al., 1995). Moreover, in many experiments, the patients' improvement is assessed by a group of independent judges, and the judges, too, are blind to group assignments—a *triple-blind design*.

Alternative Experimental Designs

It is not easy to devise an experiment that is both well controlled and enlightening. Control of every possible confound is rarely attained in practice. Moreover, because psychological experiments typically use living beings, ethical and practical considerations limit the kinds of manipulations one can do (Bersoff & Bersoff, 1999). Thus clinical researchers must often settle for less than perfect experimental designs. The most common such variations are the quasi-experimental design, the natural experiment, the analogue experiment, and the single-subject experiment.

Quasi-Experimental Design

In **quasi-experiments**, or **mixed designs**, investigators do not randomly assign subjects to control and experimental groups, but instead make use of groups that already exist in the world at large (Kazdin, 1994). For example, because investigators of child abuse cannot actually inflict abuse on a randomly chosen group of children, they must instead compare children who already have a history of abuse with children who do not. Of course, such a strategy violates the rule of random assignment, and so introduces possible confounds into the study. Children who receive physical punishment, for example, usually come from poorer and larger families than children who are punished verbally. Any differences found later in the moods or self-concepts of the two groups of children may be due to differences in wealth or family size rather than to the abuse.

ConsiderThis

In drug therapy studies, some control subjects who receive placebo pills actually show improvements. Why might sugar pills or other kinds of placebo treatments help people feel better?

CONTROL GROUP In an experiment, a group of subjects who are *not* exposed to the independent variable.

EXPERIMENTAL GROUP In an experiment, the subjects who *are* exposed to the independent variable under investigation.

RANDOM ASSIGNMENT A selection procedure that ensures that subjects are randomly placed either in the control group or in the experimental group.

BLIND DESIGN An experiment in which subjects do not know whether they are in the experimental or the control condition.

QUASI-EXPERIMENT An experiment in which investigators make use of control and experimental groups that already exist in the world at large. Also called a *mixed design*.

Child-abuse researchers often try to address the confound problems of quasi-experiments by assembling a *matched control group*. That is, they match the experimental subjects with control subjects who are similar in age, sex, race, number of children in the family, socioeconomic status, type of neighborhood, or other important characteristics (Kinard, 1982). For every abused child in the experimental group, they choose an unabused child with similar characteristics to be included in the control group. When the data from studies of this kind have shown that abused children are typically sadder and think less of themselves than matched control subjects who have not been abused, the investigators have been able to conclude with some confidence that abuse is causing the differences (Kinard, 1982).

Natural Experiment

In **natural experiments** nature itself manipulates the independent variable, while researchers systematically observe the effects. Natural experiments provide a means of studying the psychological effects of unusual and unpredictable events such as floods, earthquakes, plane crashes, and fires. Because their subjects are selected by an accident of fate rather than by conscious design, natural experiments are actually a kind of quasi-experiment.

On February 26, 1972, a dam gave way in the town of Buffalo Creek, West Virginia, releasing 132 million gallons of black slag, mud, and water into the valley below. The disaster killed 125 people, injured hundreds more, and left thousands homeless. Eighteen months later, the researcher Goldine Gleser and her colleagues (1981) collected data from 381 survivors and from a control group of people who lived elsewhere. The survivors of the flood scored significantly higher on anxiety and depression measures (dependent variables) than the controls did. The survivors also experienced more difficulty falling asleep or staying asleep and had more nightmares.

Natural experiments *A man surveys the damage wrought by a hurricane upon his home and belongings. Natural experiments conducted in the aftermath of such catastrophes have found that many survivors experience lingering feelings of anxiety and depression.*

Because natural experiments rely on unexpected occurrences in nature, they cannot be repeated at will. Also, because each natural event is unique in some ways, broad generalizations drawn from a single study could be incorrect. Nevertheless, catastrophes have provided opportunities for hundreds of natural experiments over the years, and certain findings have been obtained repeatedly. As a result, clinical scientists have identified patterns of reactions that often occur in such situations. We shall observe these patterns—acute stress disorders and posttraumatic stress disorders—in Chapter 6.

Analogue Experiment

There is one way in which investigators can manipulate independent variables relatively freely while avoiding many of the ethical and practical limitations of clinical research. They can induce laboratory subjects to behave in ways that seem to resemble real-life abnormal behavior and then conduct experiments on the laboratory-created, analogous form of abnormality, hoping to shed light on its real-life counterpart. This is called an **analogue experiment**.

Often analogue studies use animals as subjects. Animal subjects are easier to gather and manipulate than human subjects, and their use poses fewer ethical problems. While the needs and rights of animal subjects must be considered, most experimenters are willing to subject animals to more discomfort than human subjects. They believe that the insights gained from such experimentation outweigh the discomfort of the animals, as long as their distress is not excessive (Plous, 1996; Overmier, 1992). In addition, experimenters can, and often do, use human subjects in analogue experiments.

As we shall see in Chapter 7, the investigator Martin Seligman has used analogue studies with great success to investigate the causes of human depression.

"Ants are so much like human beings as to be an embarrassment. [They] launch armies into wars, use chemical sprays to alarm and confuse enemies, capture slaves, [and] engage in child labor. . . . They exchange information ceaselessly. They do everything but watch television."

Dr. Lewis Thomas, Memorial Sloan-Kettering Cancer Center

Seligman has theorized that depression results when people believe they no longer have any control over the good and bad things that happen in their lives. To test this theory, he has produced depression-like symptoms in laboratory subjects by repeatedly giving them negative reinforcements (shocks, loud noises, task failures) over which they have no control. In these "learned helplessness" studies, the participants seem to give up, lose their initiative, and become sad—suggesting to some clinicians that human depression itself may indeed be caused by loss of control over one's reinforcements in life.

It is important to remember that the laboratory-induced learned helplessness produced in Seligman's analogue experiments is not known with certainty to be analogous to human depression. If this laboratory phenomenon is actually only superficially similar to depression, then the clinical inferences drawn from such experiments may be wrong and misleading. This, in fact, is the major limitation of all analogue research (Vredenburg, Flett, & Krames, 1993): researchers can never be certain that the phenomena they see in the laboratory are the same as the psychological disorders they are investigating.

Similar enough? *Chimpanzees and human beings share more than 90 percent of their genetic material, but their brains and bodies are very different, as are their perceptions and experiences. Thus, abnormal-like behavior produced in animal analogue experiments may differ from the human abnormality under investigation.*

Single-Subject Experiment

Sometimes scientists do not have the luxury of experimenting on numerous subjects. They may, for example, be investigating a disorder so rare that few subjects are available. Experimentation is still possible, however, in the form of the **single-subject experimental design**. Here a single subject is observed both before and after the manipulation of an independent variable (Goodwin, 1995; Kazdin, 1994).

Researchers begin such experiments by collecting *baseline data*—information about a subject's behavior before any manipulations. These data set a standard with which later behavioral changes may be compared. The experimenters next introduce the independent variable and then again observe the subject's behavior. Any changes in behavior are attributed to the effects of the independent variable. Common single-subject experimental designs are the *ABAB* and *multiple-baseline designs* (Goodwin, 1995).

"Life is the art of drawing sufficient conclusions from insufficient premises."

Samuel Butler (1835–1902)

ABAB DESIGN In an *ABAB*, or *reversal, design,* a subject's behavior is measured and compared not only during a baseline period (condition A) and after the introduction of the independent variable (condition B) but also after the independent variable has been removed (condition A) and yet again after it has been reintroduced (condition B). If the subject's responses change back and forth along with changes in the independent variable, the experimenter may conclude that the independent variable is causing the shifting responses (Kratochwill, 1992). Essentially, in an ABAB design a subject is compared with himself or herself under different conditions rather than with control subjects. Subjects, therefore, serve as their own controls.

One clinical researcher used an ABAB design to test whether the systematic use of rewards was helping to reduce a teenage boy's habit of disrupting his special education class with loud talk (Deitz, 1977). The treatment program consisted of rewarding the boy, who suffered from mental retardation, with extra teacher time whenever he went 55 minutes without interrupting the class more than three times. When observed during a baseline period, the student was found to frequently disrupt the class with loud talk. Next the boy was given a series of teacher reward sessions (the independent variable); his loud talk decreased dramatically, as expected. Then the rewards from the teacher were stopped, and the student's loud talk increased once again. Apparently the independent variable had indeed been the cause of the improvement. To be still more confident about

NATURAL EXPERIMENT An experiment in which nature, rather than an experimenter, manipulates an independent variable.

ANALOGUE EXPERIMENT A research method in which the experimenter produces abnormal-like behavior in laboratory subjects and then conducts experiments on the subjects.

SINGLE-SUBJECT EXPERIMENT A research method in which a single subject is observed and measured both before and after the manipulation of an independent variable.

"*Oh, not bad. The light comes on, I press the bar, they write me a check. How about you?*"

this conclusion, the researcher had the teacher apply reward sessions yet again. Once again the subject's behavior improved.

MULTIPLE-BASELINE DESIGN A *multiple-baseline design* does not employ the reversals found in an ABAB design. Instead, the experimenter selects two or more behaviors (two dependent variables) displayed by a subject and observes the effect that the manipulation of an independent variable has on each behavior (Balk, 1995; Herz et al., 1992). Let us say that the teenage boy in the ABAB study displayed two kinds of inappropriate behavior—the disruptive talk during class and odd grimaces. In a multiple-baseline design, the experimenter would first collect baseline data on both the frequency of the boy's disruptive talk and the frequency of his facial grimaces during a 55-minute period. In the next phase of the experiment, the experimenter would reward the boy with extra teacher time whenever he cut down his verbalizations but not when he cut down his grimaces. The experimenter would then measure changes in the boy's verbal and grimacing behaviors, expecting the verbal interruptions to decrease but the grimacing to remain about the same as before. In the final phase of the experiment, the experimenter would also reward the boy with extra teacher attention whenever he reduced his grimacing, expecting that this manipulation would now reduce the grimacing as well. If the expected pattern of changes was observed, it would be reasonable to conclude that the manipulation

BOX 2-4

Human Subjects Have Rights, Too

In the 1950s and 1960s, almost 100 mental patients unknowingly became subjects in "depatterning" experiments designed to test the feasibility of *brainwashing*, or *mind control*. Most of the subjects emerged disabled from these studies, which were funded by both the Canadian government and the United States CIA. They retained only limited memories of the life they had lived before they entered the hospital.

One of the subjects, Linda Macdonald, checked into a Canadian institution in 1963 to be treated for fatigue and depression. Six months later, she couldn't read, write, cook a meal, or remember her husband, her five children, or any of the first 26 years of her life. During her stay, Ms. Macdonald was given massive doses of drugs, put into a drug-induced sleep for 86 days, given more than 100 electroconvulsive treatments, and exposed to "psychic driving," a technique in which repetitive taped messages were played for her 16 hours a day (Davis, 1992; Powis, 1990). Later Macdonald and other victims sued the Canadian and United States governments for subjecting

them to these experiments without their permission. They each received $100,000 to $200,000.

In response to such abuses, a number of regulations were established in the 1970s to ensure that the rights of all human subjects, particularly those with psychological disorders, were protected. In the United States, the Department of Health and Human Services insisted that potential human subjects be clearly informed that they are indeed participating in a study, what procedures will be used, any foreseeable risks, and other such matters. In addition, universities and other research institutions established committees to oversee the well-being of subjects in their facilities. Moreover, universities began to train ethicists, who conferred with philosophers, psychologists, physicians, civil rights experts, and people from all sectors of society in ongoing efforts to develop acceptable research guidelines.

These efforts have greatly improved the ethics of clinical research, but some problems remain. In fact, the clinical field has been rocked in recent years by a new series of reports that

reveal that during the past two decades, many patients with severe mental disorders have been harmed or placed at risk in clinical studies (Kong, 1998). The studies in question typically involve antipsychotic drug treatments for patients with psychosis (loss of contact with reality). It appears that many patients in these studies have agreed to receive drug treatments (or not to receive them) without fully understanding the risks involved. In addition, the drugs used in these studies have left some of the subjects with more intense psychotic symptoms. Four types of studies have been cited:

❖ **New Drug Studies** Patients are administered an experimental drug to see whether it reduces their symptoms. The new drug is being tested for effectiveness, safety, undesired effects, and dosage, meaning that the patients may be helped, unaffected, or damaged by the drugs.

❖ **Placebo Studies** When a new drug is being tested on a group of experimental subjects, researchers may administer a placebo drug to a group of control subjects (Quitkin, 1999). The improvement of the exof the independent variable (attention from the teacher), rather than some other factor, was responsible for the changes in the two behaviors.

Obviously, single-subject experiments—both ABAB and multiple-baseline designs—are similar to individual case studies in their focus on one subject. In single-subject experiments, however, the independent variable is manipulated systematically so that the investigator can confidently draw conclusions about the cause of an observed effect. The single-subject experiment therefore has greater internal validity than the case study (Lehman, 1991). At the same time, single-subject experiments, like case studies, have only limited external validity. Because only one subject is studied, the experimenter cannot be sure that the subject's reaction to the independent variable is typical of people in general.

> "Every individual is the exception to the rule."
>
> C. G. Jung, 1921

CROSSROADS:
The Use of Multiple Research Methods

As we noted at the beginning of this chapter, clinical scientists are always searching for general laws that will help explain, prevent, and treat psychological disorders. Various obstacles impede their progress, however (de Groot & Kennedy, 1995; Stricker & Trierweiler, 1995). We have already observed some of them. The most fundamental are summarized below.

1. *Clinical scientists must respect the rights of both human subjects and animal subjects* (see Box 2-4). Ethical considerations greatly limit the kinds of investigations that clinical scientists can conduct (Sigmon, 1995).

perimental subjects is then compared to that of the placebo control subjects to determine the new drug's effectiveness. Unfortunately, in such studies, the placebo control subjects—often people with severe disorders—are receiving no treatment at all. For this reason, a growing number of researchers believe it is better to administer an established medication, rather than a placebo drug, to subjects in control groups. Progress on the experimental drug can then be compared to progress on the established drug to determine the promise of the new drug.

❖ **Symptom-Exacerbation Studies**
Patients are given drugs designed to intensify their symptoms, so that researchers may learn more about the biology of their disorder. For example, people suffering from psychotic disorders have been given apomorphine, amphetamine, ketamine, and other drugs that lead to more delusions, hallucinations, and the like.

❖ **Medication-Withdrawal Studies**
Researchers prematurely stop medications for patients who have been symptom-free while taking the medications. The researchers then follow the patients as they relapse, in the hope of learning more about how and when patients can be taken off particular medications.

Each of these kinds of studies seeks to increase understanding of the biology of certain disorders and to improve treatment. Yet at what risk? When does the benefit to many outweigh the suffering of a few? As the clinical community and the public have grown more aware of the risks involved in these studies, they have called for better safeguards to protect research subjects with mental disorders. In 1999 the National Institute of Mental Health suspended some of its symptom-exacerbation studies, and the presidentially appointed National Bioethics Advisory Commission issued numerous recommendations, including the suggestion that a permanent federal panel be created to review high-risk and low-benefit clinical studies.

This important issue is far from being resolved. Some researchers believe that much more must be done to protect the rights of patients in research, while others worry that stringent new regulations may prevent the discovery of valuable clinical insights and treatments. In the meantime, the controversy itself reflects the value our society places on maintaining a balance between scientific advances and an individual's rights.

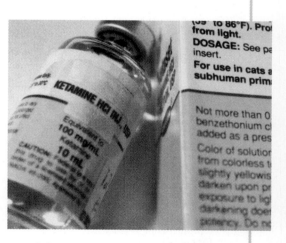

"Special K" *One of the most controversial lines of research in recent years has been the administration of ketamine to produce or intensify psychotic symptoms in subjects. This surgical anesthetic also produces powerful hallucinogenic symptoms, and is known on the street as "Special K" or the "date-rape drug."*

2. *The causes of human functioning are very complex.* Because human behavior generally results from multiple factors working together, it is difficult to pinpoint specific causes. So many factors can influence human functioning that it has actually been easier to unravel the complexities of energy and matter than to understand human sadness, stress, and anxiety.

3. *Human beings are changeable.* Moods, behaviors, and thoughts fluctuate. Is the person under study today truly the same as he or she was yesterday? Variability in a single person, let alone from person to person, limits the kinds of conclusions researchers can draw about abnormal functioning (Schwarz, 1999).

4. *Human self-awareness may influence the results of clinical investigations.* When human subjects know they are being studied, that knowledge influences their behavior. They may try to respond as they think researchers expect them to or to present themselves in a favorable light. Similarly, the attention they receive from investigators may itself increase their optimism and improve their mood. It is an axiom of science that the very act of measuring an object distorts the object to some degree. Nowhere is this more true than in the study of human beings.

5. *Clinical investigators have a special link to their subjects.* Clinical scientists, too, experience mood changes, troubling thoughts, and family problems. They may identify with the pain of their subjects or have personal opinions about their problems. These feelings can bias an investigator's attempts to understand abnormality (Rogler, 1999).

In short, human behavior is so complex that clinical scientists must use a variety of methods to study it. Each method addresses some of the inherent problems, but no one method overcomes them all. Case studies allow investigators to consider a broader range of causes, but experiments pinpoint causes more precisely. Similarly, correlational studies allow broad generalizations, but case studies are richer in detail. It is best to view the various methods of investigation as a collection of tools that together may build an understanding of abnormal human functioning.

Thus today's clinical researchers typically use multiple approaches to investigate the various pathologies and treatments that make up the clinical field. When more than one of these methods has been used to investigate a disorder and all the results point in the same direction, we are probably making progress toward understanding and treating that disorder. Conversely, if the methods produce conflicting results, we must admit that our knowledge in that particular area is still tentative.

Before accepting any research findings, however, students of the clinical field must review the details of the studies with a very critical eye. Were the variables properly controlled? Was the choice of subjects representative, was the sample large enough to be meaningful, and has bias been eliminated? Are the investigator's conclusions justified? How else might the results be interpreted? Only after painstaking scrutiny can we conclude that a truly informative investigation has taken place.

PLACES OF STUDY

Only about 25 percent of studies that measure the effectiveness of various drug treatments take place in academic settings or medical centers. The rest are conducted by independent researchers who contract with pharmaceutical companies (Whitaker, 1998).

IT'S OFFICIAL

The word "scientist" did not exist until it was coined by the nineteenth-century English scholar William Whewell (Asimov, 1997).

SUMMARY AND REVIEW

■ **What do clinical scientists do?** Researchers use the scientific method to uncover nomothetic principles of abnormal psychological functioning. They attempt to identify and examine relationships between variables, and depend primarily on three methods of investigation. *pp. 25–27*

■ **The case study** A case study is a detailed account of a person's life and psychological problems. It can serve as a source of ideas about behavior, provide support for theories, challenge theories, clarify new treatment techniques, or offer an opportunity to study an unusual problem. Yet case studies may be reported by biased observers and rely on subjective evidence. In addition, they tend to have low internal validity and low external validity. *pp. 27–30*

◼ **The correlational method** Correlational studies systematically observe the degree to which events or characteristics vary together. This method allows researchers to draw broad conclusions about abnormality in the population at large.

A correlation may have a positive or negative direction, and may be high or low in magnitude. It can be calculated numerically and expressed by the correlation coefficient (r). Researchers perform a statistical analysis to determine whether the correlation found in a study is truly characteristic of the larger population or due to chance. Correlational studies generally have high external validity but lack internal validity. Two widely used forms of the correlation method are epidemiological studies and longitudinal studies. *pp. 30–35*

◼ **The experimental method** In experiments, researchers manipulate suspected causes to see whether expected effects will result. The variable that is manipulated is called the independent variable and the variable that is expected to change as a result is called the dependent variable.

Confounds are variables other than the independent variable that are also acting on the dependent variable. To minimize their possible influence, experimenters use control groups, random assignment, and blind designs. The findings of experiments, like those of correlational studies, must be analyzed statistically. *pp. 35–37*

◼ **Alternative experimental designs** Clinical experimenters must often settle for experimental designs that are less than ideal, including the quasi-experiment, the natural experiment, the analogue experiment, and the single-subject experiment. *pp. 37–41*

◼ **The use of multiple research methods** Because human subjects have rights that must be respected, because the origins of behavior are complex, because behavior varies, and because the very act of observing a subject's behavior influences that behavior, it can be difficult to assess the findings of clinical research. Also, researchers must take into account their own biases and a study's unintended impact on subjects' usual behavior. To help address such obstacles, clinical investigators must use multiple research approaches. *pp. 41–42*

> "Nothing has such power to broaden the mind as the ability to investigate systematically and truly all that comes under thy observation in life."
>
> Marcus Aurelius Antoninus
> (A.D. 121–180)

◯ **CYBER STUDY**

▲ *Observe genetic research in action.* ▲ *How do researchers measure psychopathology?* ▲ *How do researchers observe brain activity?* ▲ *How can antisocial behavior be studied?*

SEARCH THE *ABNORMAL PSYCHOLOGY* CD-ROM FOR

▲ **Chapter 2 video case and discussion**
   Mood Disorders: Hereditary Factors

▲ **Chapter 2 practice test and feedback**

▲ **Additional video cases and discussions**
   "Derrick"—Hamilton Depression Scale
   "Al"—Alcoholic Disorders: Hereditary Factors
   The Mind of the Psychopath

LOG ON TO THE COMER WEB PAGE

[www.worthpublishers.com/comerabnormalpsychology4e] **FOR**

▲ **Suggested Web links, research exercises, FAQ page, additional Chapter 2 practice test questions**

 Philip Berman, a 25-year-old single unemployed former copy editor for a large publishing house, . . . had been hospitalized after a suicide attempt in which he deeply gashed his wrist with a razor blade. He described [to the therapist] how he had sat on the bathroom floor and watched the blood drip into the bathtub for some time before he telephoned his father at work for help. He and his father went to the hospital emergency room to have the gash stitched, but he convinced himself and the hospital physician that he did not need hospitalization. The next day when his father suggested he needed help, he knocked his dinner to the floor and angrily stormed to his room. When he was calm again, he allowed his father to take him back to the hospital.

The immediate precipitant for his suicide attempt was that he had run into one of his former girlfriends with her new boyfriend. The patient stated that they had a drink together, but all the while he was with them he could not help thinking that "they were dying to run off and jump in bed." He experienced jealous rage, got up from the table, and walked out of the restaurant. He began to think about how he could "pay her back."

Mr. Berman had felt frequently depressed for brief periods during the previous several years. He was especially critical of himself for his limited social life and his inability to have managed to have sexual intercourse with a woman even once in his life. As he related this to the therapist, he lifted his eyes from the floor and with a sarcastic smirk said, "I'm a 25-year-old virgin. Go ahead, you can laugh now." He has had several girlfriends to date, whom he described as very attractive, but who he said had lost interest in him. On further questioning, however, it became apparent that Mr. Berman soon became very critical of them and demanded that they always meet his every need, often to their own detriment. The women then found the relationship very unrewarding and would soon find someone else.

During the past two years Mr. Berman had seen three psychiatrists briefly, one of whom had given him a drug, the name of which he could not remember, but that had precipitated some sort of unusual reaction for which he had to stay in a hospital overnight. . . . Concerning his hospitalization, the patient said that "It was a dump," that the staff refused to listen to what he had to say or to respond to his needs, and that they, in fact, treated all the patients "sadistically." The referring doctor corroborated that Mr. Berman was a difficult patient who demanded that he be treated as special, and yet was hostile to most staff members throughout his stay. After one angry exchange with an aide, he left the hospital without leave, and subsequently signed out against medical advice.

Mr. Berman is one of two children of a middle-class family. His father is 55 years old and employed in a managerial position for an insurance company. He perceives his father as weak and ineffectual, completely dominated by the patient's overbearing and cruel mother. He states that he hates his mother with "a passion I can barely control." He claims that his mother used to call him names like "pervert" and "sissy" when he was growing up, and that in an argument she once "kicked me in the balls." Together, he sees his parents as rich, powerful, and selfish, and, in turn, thinks that they see him as lazy, irresponsible, and a behavior problem. When his parents called the therapist to discuss their son's treatment, they stated that his problem began with the birth of his younger brother, Arnold, when Philip was 10 years old. After Arnold's birth Philip apparently became an "ornery" child who cursed a lot and was difficult to discipline. Philip recalls this period only vaguely. He reports that his mother once was hospitalized for depression, but that now "she doesn't believe in psychiatry."

Mr. Berman had graduated from college with average grades. Since graduating he had worked at three different publishing houses, but at none of them for more than one year. He always found some justification for quitting. He usually sat around his house doing very little for two or three months after quitting a job, until his parents prodded him into getting a new one. He described innumerable interactions in his life with teachers, friends, and employers in which he felt offended or unfairly treated, . . . and frequent arguments that left him feeling bitter . . . and spent most of his time alone, "bored." He was unable to commit himself to any person, he held no strong convictions, and he felt no allegiance to any group.

The patient appeared as a very thin, bearded, and bespectacled young man with pale skin who maintained little eye contact with the therapist and who had an air of angry bitterness about him. Although he complained of depression, he denied other symptoms of the depressive syndrome. He seemed preoccupied with his rage at his parents, and seemed particularly invested in conveying a despicable image of himself. . . .

(Spitzer et al., 1983, pp. 59-61)

Philip Berman is clearly a troubled person, but how did he come to be that way? How do we explain and correct his many problems? In confronting these questions, we must first look at the wide range of complaints we are trying to understand: Philip's depression and anger, his social failures, his lack of employment, his distrust of those around him, and the problems within his family. Then we must sort through all kinds of potential causes, internal and external, biological and interpersonal, past and present. Which is having the biggest impact on his behavior?

"Men are apt to believe what they least understand."

Michel de Montaigne, 1533–1592

Although we may not realize it, we all use theoretical frameworks as we read about Philip. Over the course of our lives, each of us has developed a perspective that helps us make sense of the things other people say and do. In science, the perspectives used to explain phenomena are known as **models**, or **paradigms**. Each model spells out the scientist's basic assumptions, gives order to the field under study, and sets guidelines for its investigation (Kuhn, 1962). It influences what the investigators observe, as well as the questions they ask, the information they seek, and how they interpret this information (Plante, 1999; Nietzel et al., 1994). To understand how a clinician explains or treats a specific set of symptoms, such as Philip's, we must know which model shapes his or her view of abnormal functioning.

Until recently, clinical scientists of a given place and time tended to agree on a single model of abnormality—a model greatly influenced by the beliefs of their culture. The demonological model that was used to explain abnormal functioning during the Middle Ages, for example, borrowed heavily from medieval society's concerns with religion, superstition, and warfare. Medieval practitioners would have seen the devil's guiding hand in Philip Berman's efforts to commit suicide and his feelings of depression, rage, jealousy, and hatred. Similarly, their treatments for him—from prayers to whippings—would have sought to drive foreign spirits from his body.

MODEL A set of assumptions and concepts that help scientists explain and interpret observations. Also called a *paradigm*.

NEURON A nerve cell.

Today several models are used to explain and treat abnormal functioning. This variety has resulted from shifts in values and beliefs over the past half century, as well as improvements in clinical research. At one end of the spectrum is the *biological model,* which sees physical processes as the key to human behavior.

At the other end is the *sociocultural model,* which examines the effects of society and culture on individual behavior. In between are four models that focus on more psychological and personal aspects of human functioning: the *psychodynamic model* looks at people's unconscious internal processes and conflicts; the *behavioral model* emphasizes behavior and the ways in which it is learned; the *cognitive model* concentrates on the thinking that underlies behavior; and the *humanistic-existential model* stresses the role of values and choices in human functioning.

Given their different assumptions and concepts, the models are sometimes in conflict. Those who follow one perspective often scoff at the "naive" interpretations, investigations, and treatment efforts of the others. Yet none of the models is complete in itself. Each focuses mainly on one aspect of human functioning, and none can explain all aspects of abnormality.

The Biological Model

Philip Berman is a biological being. His thoughts and feelings are the results of biochemical and bioelectrical processes throughout his brain and body. Biological theorists believe that a full understanding of his thoughts, emotions, and behavior must therefore include an understanding of their biological basis. Not surprisingly, they believe that the most effective treatments for Philip's problems will then be biological ones.

How Do Biological Theorists Explain Abnormal Behavior?

Adopting a medical perspective, biological theorists view abnormal behavior as an illness brought about by malfunctioning parts of the organism. Typically, they point to a malfunctioning brain as the cause of abnormal behavior, focusing particularly on problems in brain anatomy, brain chemistry, or genetics (Mesulam et al., 1999; Schwartz, 1999).

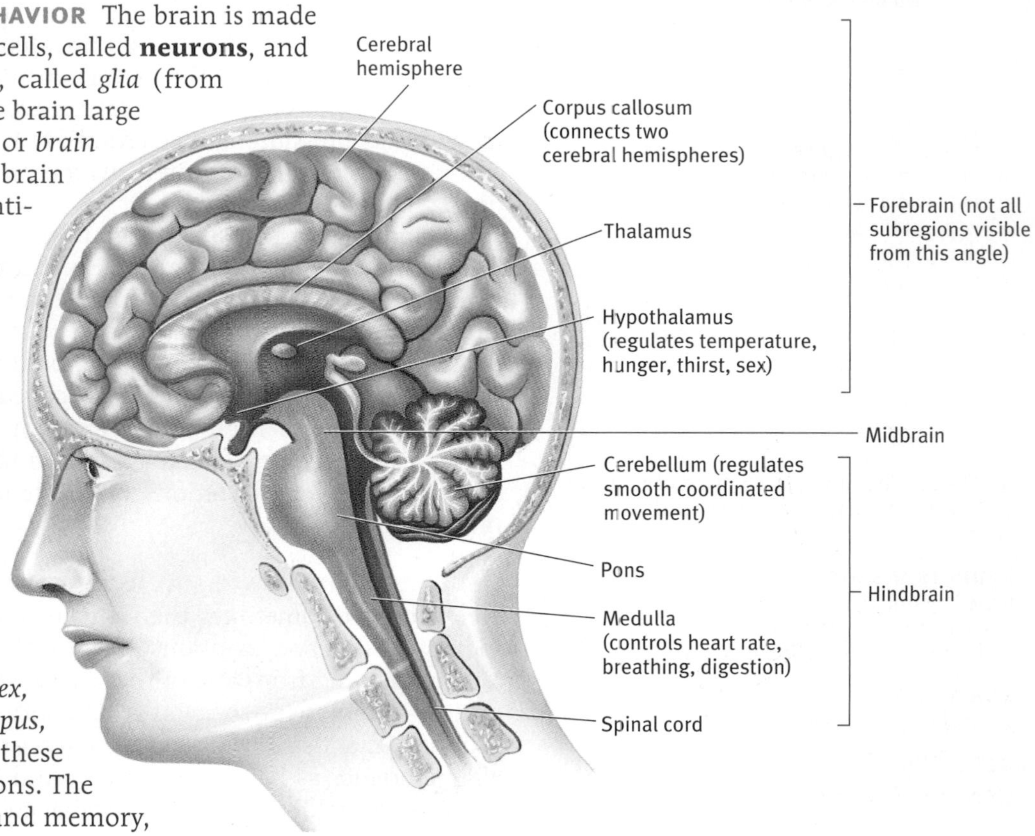

BRAIN ANATOMY AND ABNORMAL BEHAVIOR The brain is made up of approximately 100 billion nerve cells, called **neurons**, and thousands of billions of support cells, called *glia* (from the Greek meaning "glue"). Within the brain large groups of neurons form distinct areas, or *brain regions*. To identify the regions of the brain more easily, let us imagine them as continents, countries, and states.

At the bottom of the brain is the "continent" known as the *hindbrain,* which is in turn made up of countrylike regions called the *medulla, pons,* and *cerebellum* (see Figure 3-1). In the middle of the brain is the "continent" called the *midbrain.* And at the top is the "continent" called the *forebrain,* which is composed of countrylike regions called the *cerebrum* (the two cerebral hemispheres), the *thalamus,* and the *hypothalamus,* each in turn made up of statelike regions. The cerebrum, for instance, consists of the *cortex, corpus callosum, basal ganglia, hippocampus,* and *amygdala.* The neurons in each of these brain regions control important functions. The hippocampus helps control emotions and memory,

"I am a brain, Watson. The rest of me is a mere appendix."

Sherlock Holmes, in Arthur Conan Doyle's "Adventure of the Mazarin Stone"

FIGURE 3-1 **The human brain** *A slice through the center of the brain reveals its major divisions and regions. Each region, composed of numerous neurons, is responsible for certain functions.*

- Cerebral hemisphere
- Corpus callosum (connects two cerebral hemispheres)
- Thalamus
- Hypothalamus (regulates temperature, hunger, thirst, sex)
- Forebrain (not all subregions visible from this angle)
- Midbrain
- Cerebellum (regulates smooth coordinated movement)
- Pons
- Medulla (controls heart rate, breathing, digestion)
- Spinal cord
- Hindbrain

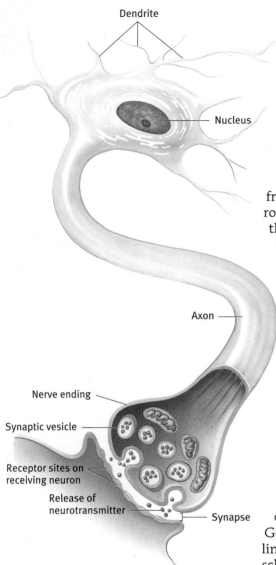

Dendrite

Nucleus

Axon

Nerve ending

Synaptic vesicle

Receptor sites on receiving neuron

Release of neurotransmitter

Synapse

FIGURE 3-2 **A typical neuron** *A message travels down the neuron's axon to the nerve ending, where neurotransmitters carry the message across the synaptic space to a receiving neuron. (Adapted from Bloom, Lazerson, & Hofstadter, 1985, p. 35.)*

SYNAPSE The tiny space between the nerve ending of one neuron and the dendrite of another.

NEUROTRANSMITTER A chemical that, released by one neuron, crosses the synaptic space to be received at receptors on the dendrites of neighboring neurons.

HORMONES The chemicals released by glands into the bloodstream.

GENE Chromosome segments that control the characteristics and traits we inherit.

for example. Using a variety of research techniques, clinicians have discovered connections between certain psychological disorders and problems in specific areas of the brain. One such disorder is *Huntington's disease,* a degenerative disorder marked by violent emotional outbursts, memory loss and other cognitive difficulties, suicidal thinking, involuntary body movements, and absurd beliefs. This disease has been traced to a loss of cells in the basal ganglia.

BRAIN CHEMISTRY AND ABNORMAL BEHAVIOR Biological researchers have also learned that psychological disorders can be related to problems in the transmission of messages from neuron to neuron. Information spreads throughout the brain in the form of electrical impulses that travel from one neuron to one or more others. An impulse is first received by a neuron's *dendrites,* antenna-like extensions located at one end of the neuron. From there it travels down the neuron's *axon,* a long fiber extending from the neuron body. Finally, it is transmitted to other neurons through the *nerve endings,* at the far end of the neuron (see Figure 3-2).

But how do messages get from the nerve endings of one neuron to the dendrites of another? After all, the neurons do not actually touch each other. A tiny space, called the **synapse**, separates one neuron from the next, and the message must somehow move across that space. When an electrical impulse reaches a neuron's ending, the nerve ending is stimulated to release a chemical, called a **neurotransmitter**, that travels across the synaptic space to *receptors* on the dendrites of the adjacent neurons. Upon reception, some neurotransmitters tell the receiving neurons to "fire," that is, to trigger their own electrical impulse. Other neurotransmitters carry an inhibitory message; they tell receiving neurons to stop all firing. Obviously, neurotransmitters play a key role in moving information through the brain (see Table 3-1).

Researchers have identified dozens of neurotransmitters in the brain, and they have learned that each neuron uses only certain kinds (Barondes, 1993). Studies indicate that abnormal activity by certain neurotransmitters can lead to specific mental disorders (Robert, Rubin-Brunet, & Darcourt, 1999; Gershon & Rieder, 1992). Certain anxiety disorders, for example, have been linked to low activity of the neurotransmitter *gamma-aminobutyric acid* (*GABA*), schizophrenia has been linked to excessive activity of the neurotransmitter *dopamine,* and depression has been linked to low activity of the neurotransmitter *serotonin.* Perhaps low serotonin activity is responsible for Philip Berman's pattern of depression and rage.

In addition to focusing on neurons and neurotransmitters, researchers have learned that mental disorders are sometimes related to abnormal chemical activity in the body's *endocrine system.* Endocrine glands, located throughout the body, work in association with neurons to control such vital activities as growth, reproduction, sexual activity, heart rate, body temperature, energy, and responses to stress. The glands release chemicals called **hormones** into the bloodstream, and these chemicals then propel body organs into action. During times of stress, for example, the *adrenal glands,* located on top of the kidneys, secrete the hormone *cortisol.* Abnormal secretions of this chemical have been tied to anxiety and mood disorders.

GENETICS AND ABNORMAL BEHAVIOR Abnormalities in brain anatomy or chemistry are sometimes the result of genetic inheritance. Each cell in the human brain and body contains 23 pairs of *chromosomes,* with each chromosome in a pair inherited from one of the person's parents. Every chromosome contains a multitude of **genes**—segments that control the characteristics and traits a person inherits. Scientists have known for years that genes help determine such physical characteristics as hair color, height, and eyesight. Genes can make people more prone to heart disease, cancer, or diabetes, and perhaps to possessing artistic or musical skill. In recent years, researchers have discovered that genes may also influence behavior, including abnormal behavior.

Studies suggest that inheritance plays a part in mood disorders, schizophrenia, mental retardation, Alzheimer's disease, and other mental disorders (Faraone, Tsuang, & Tsuang, 1999; Hyman, 1999). Yet, with few exceptions, researchers have not been able to identify the specific genes that are the culprits. Nor do they yet know the extent to which genetic factors contribute to various mental disorders. It appears that in most cases no single gene is responsible for a particular behavior or mental disorder. Instead, many genes combine to help produce our actions and reactions, both functional and dysfunctional.

More than coincidence? *Studies of twins suggest that some aspects of behavior and personality are influenced by genetic factors. Many identical twins, like these musicians, are found to have similar taste, behave in similar ways, and make similar life choices. Some even develop similar abnormal behaviors.*

Biological Treatments

Biological practitioners look for certain kinds of clues when they try to understand abnormal behavior. Does the person's family have a history of that behavior, and hence a possible genetic predisposition to it? (Philip Berman's case history mentions that his mother was once hospitalized for depression.) Does the disorder seem to follow its own course? (Philip's depressed feelings were described as periodic; they seemed to come and go over the course of several years.) Is the behavior aggravated by factors that could have had a physiological effect? (Philip was having a drink when he flew into a jealous rage at the restaurant.)

Once the clinicians have pinpointed physical sources of dysfunctioning, they are in a better position to apply a biological course of treatment. The three leading kinds of biological treatments used today are *drug therapy, electroconvulsive therapy,* and *psychosurgery.* Drug therapy is by far the most common of these approaches (see Box 3-1 on the next page); psychosurgery is infrequent.

THE HUMAN GENOME PROJECT

Scientists launched the *Human Genome Project* in 1990, designed to map *all* of the estimated 100,000 genes in the human body. The project, which is now on the verge of reaching its final goal, has already linked more than 3,200 kinds of gene defects to medical diseases and mental disorders (Cuticchia, 2000; NIH, 1998; Glausiusz, 1997, 1996).

Table 3-1

Facts about the Brain

- ❖ Around 95 percent of what is known about the brain has been learned in the past 10 years.
- ❖ A worm's brain has 23 neurons.
- ❖ An ostrich's brain is smaller than its eye.
- ❖ The average human brain weighs 3 pounds; the human liver weighs around $4\frac{1}{2}$ pounds.
- ❖ While the brain only accounts for about 2 percent of the total human body weight, it requires about 25 percent of the oxygen intake.
- ❖ Aristotle believed that the brain served merely as a cooling organ for the blood.
- ❖ 80 percent of the human brain is water.
- ❖ Messages travel to the brain at 224 miles per hour.
- ❖ One neuron may connect to as many as 25,000 others.
- ❖ The brain of the Neanderthal was *bigger* than that of the modern man.

Source: Ash, 1999; Jordon, 1998; Asimov, 1997; Roan, 1995.

BOX **3-1**

Nature's Way

In the United States today, 20 million baby boomers are taking to "herbal" supplements and "natural" hormones to combat ills ranging from arthritis to depression. Although such dietary supplements are experiencing a remarkable growth in popularity, they are hardly new. Chinese healers compiled the first of their 11,000 medicinal herb formulas as far back as 3000 B.C.

Herbal and hormone supplements are a $6.5 billion industry in the United States, and its sales increase by 20 percent each year (Wasik, 1999). This sales explosion can be traced to the 1994 passage of the Dietary Supplement Health and Education Act, which provides that dietary supplements are not bound by the same legal requirements as medicinal drugs. Drugs must be proved safe and effective by their manufacturers in order to receive approval—through a testing process that costs the manufacturers

hundreds of millions of dollars. In contrast, dietary supplements are assumed to be safe unless the U.S. Food and Drug Administration can prove them harmful. In the wake of this law, 4,000 manufacturers have rushed dietary supplements into the marketplace, typically without research and often with extraordinary claims about their healing powers (Musak, 1999).

Many other countries—including Canada, Germany, and China—regulate supplements more stringently, requiring prescriptions by physicians and encouraging ongoing research. In fact, most of the research on these supplements has been conducted outside the United States. Although such research is increasing, it is minimal in comparison with the extensive investigations conducted on medicinal drugs. There is a serious shortage of knowledge about the effectiveness of most supplements and about their proper dosages, unintended effects, and inter-

actions with other substances. Buyers must be vigilant, always operating by the principle of *caveat emptor*.

Melatonin supplements are a case in point. Melatonin is a hormone produced by the pineal gland in the brains of humans and other animals. Because this hormone controls our *circadian rhythm,* or "body clock," manufacturers of melatonin supplements claim that their product can lift depression, strengthen the immune system, lower cholesterol, extend the life span, increase energy, improve sleep, reduce stress, cure jet lag, and even increase sexual performance, while at the same time preventing cancer, heart disease, cataracts, ulcers, Parkinson's disease, Alzheimer's disease, and pregnancy. Small wonder that General Nutrition Centers, a nationwide retail chain, sells about 4,000 bottles of melatonin every day, even more than vitamin C (Bonn, 1996; deVita, 1996). But does the reality of this supplement

A Long Road

It takes an average of 15 years and $500 million for a pharmaceutical company in the United States to bring a newly discovered drug to market. First, the drug's safety and benefits must be tested in the laboratory for six years. Next, the drug must be tested on more than 3,000 human volunteers over a seven-year span. The Food and Drug Administration then takes an average of two years to decide on approval.

In the 1950s, researchers discovered several effective **psychotropic medications**, drugs that mainly affect emotions and thought processes. These drugs have greatly improved the outlook for a number of mental disorders and today are used widely, either alone or with other forms of therapy. However, the psychotropic drug revolution has also produced some major problems. Many believe,

Worldwide phenomenon *The psychotropic drug revolution has spread throughout the world. Here a nurse gives medications to patients at Cambodia's largest mental health facility.*

live up to the hype? Not according to a growing body of research.

On the positive side, small doses of melatonin may indeed produce restful sleep in some healthy adults (Wurtman, 1994). Small doses can also help reduce jet lag by resetting the body's internal clock, tricking the body into believing that it is still nighttime (Bonn, 1996). And melatonin can be useful for night-shift workers and the blind, whose circadian rhythms may be out of sync. On the other hand, melatonin supplements do not seem to be much of an aphrodisiac. Nor have studies established any effect of melatonin on heart disease or cholesterol levels. Overall, the interactions between the immune system and melatonin are not well understood. And no reliable evidence exists for melatonin as a fountain of youth (Turek, 1996; Ebihara et al., 1986). Some researchers even worry that melatonin supplements could damage a person's health. Its long-term actions have yet to be investigated, proper dosages are still undetermined, and its effects during pregnancy and puberty and its interactions with other drugs are unknown (Bonn, 1996; Chase, 1996).

In recent years, melatonin supplements have been joined in the marketplace by other mental health remedies such as the depression-fighters *St. John's wort* and *SAMe* and the memory enhancer *ginkgo biloba.* These dietary supplements too are enjoying enormous sales, yet research to determine their proper dosage, effectiveness, and safety—or lack thereof—is really in its infancy.

Before corn flakes *A highly esteemed pioneer in natural treatments, Dr. John Harvey Kellogg was known for using offbeat approaches at his Battle Creek Sanitarium during the late 1800s and early 1900s. Among his cures were high-bran diets and "cleansing enemas" for those who suffered from "ulcers, diabetes, schizophrenia, acne . . . and premature old age."*

for example, that the drugs are overused. Moreover, while drugs are effective in many cases, they do not help everyone.

Four major psychotropic drug groups are used in therapy: antianxiety, antidepressant, antibipolar, and antipsychotic drugs. **Antianxiety drugs**, also called *minor tranquilizers* or *anxiolytics,* help reduce tension and anxiety. These drugs include *alprazolam* (trade name Xanax) and *diazepam* (Valium). **Antidepressant drugs** help improve the mood of people who are depressed. These drugs, which include *fluoxetine* (Prozac) and *sertraline* (Zoloft), are able to help around 60 percent of those with depression (Einarson et al., 1999; Hirschfeld, 1999). **Antibipolar drugs** help stabilize the moods of those with a bipolar disorder, a condition marked by mood swings from mania to depression. The most widely used of these drugs is *lithium,* which, like the antidepressants, is helpful in approximately 60 percent of cases (Maj et al., 1998; Prien, 1992). Finally, **antipsychotic drugs** help reduce the confusion, hallucinations, and delusions of *psychotic disorders,* disorders marked by a loss of contact with reality. Common antipsychotic drugs are *haloperidol* (Haldol) and *risperidone* (Risperdal). Research has shown that these drugs are more effective than any other single form of treatment for schizophrenia and other psychotic disorders, reducing symptoms in at least 65 percent of patients (Lieberman et al., 1996).

The second form of biological treatment, used primarily on depressed patients, is **electroconvulsive therapy (ECT)**. Two electrodes are attached to a patient's forehead and an electrical current of 65 to 140 volts is passed briefly through the brain. The current causes a brain seizure that lasts up to a few minutes. After seven to nine ECT sessions, spaced two or three days apart, many patients feel considerably less depressed. The treatment is able to improve the

PSYCHOTROPIC MEDICATIONS Drugs that primarily affect the brain and reduce many symptoms of mental dysfunctioning.

ANTIANXIETY DRUGS Psychotropic drugs that help reduce tension and anxiety.

ANTIDEPRESSANT DRUGS Psychotropic drugs that improve the moods of people with depression.

ANTIBIPOLAR DRUGS Psychotropic drugs that help stabilize the moods of people suffering from a bipolar mood disorder.

ANTIPSYCHOTIC DRUGS Psychotropic drugs that help correct the confusion, hallucinations, and delusions found in psychotic disorders.

ELECTROCONVULSIVE THERAPY (ECT) A form of biological treatment, used primarily on depressed patients, in which a brain seizure is triggered as an electric current passes through electrodes attached to the patient's forehead.

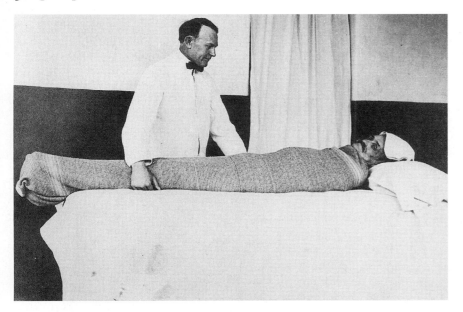

Not that long ago *Before effective psychotropic drugs were developed, clinicians in mental institutions used techniques such as the "wet pack," designed for calming excited patients.*

mood of approximately 60 percent of depressed subjects (Rey & Walters, 1997; Sackeim, 1990). It is used on tens of thousands of depressed persons annually, particularly those whose depression fails to respond to other treatments (Cauchon, 1995; Foderaero, 1993).

A third form of biological treatment is **psychosurgery**, brain surgery for mental disorders. It is thought to have roots as far back as trephining, the prehistoric practice of chipping a hole in the skull of a person who behaved strangely. Modern procedures are derived from a technique first developed in the late 1930s by a Portuguese neuropsychiatrist, Antonio de Egas Moniz. In this procedure, known as a *lobotomy,* a surgeon cuts the connections between the brain's frontal lobes and the lower centers of the brain.

Today's brain surgery procedures are much more precise than the lobotomies of the past (Weingarten, 1999). They have fewer unwanted effects and are apparently helpful in some cases of severe depression, anxiety, and obsessive-compulsive disorder. Even so, they are considered experimental and are used only after certain severe disorders have continued for years without responding to any other form of treatment (Goodman et al., 1992).

Assessing the Biological Model

Today the biological model commands considerable respect. Biological research is producing valuable new information at an accelerating pace. And biological treatments often bring great relief when other approaches have failed. At the same time, this model has its shortcomings. Some of its proponents seem to expect that all human behavior can be explained in biological terms and treated with biological methods. This view can limit rather than enhance our understanding of abnormal functioning (Anderson & Scott, 1999; Miller, 1999). Our mental life is an interplay of biological and nonbiological factors, and it is important to understand that interplay rather than to focus on biological variables alone.

A second shortcoming of this model is that much of the evidence for biological explanations is incomplete or inconclusive. Many brain studies, for example, are conducted on animals in whom symptoms of depression, anxiety, or some other abnormality have been produced by drugs, surgery, or experimental manipulation. Researchers can never be certain that the animals are experiencing the human disorder under investigation.

Finally, several of today's biological treatments are capable of producing significant undesirable effects. Antipsychotic drugs, for example, may produce *extrapyramidal effects* in some individuals, movement problems such as severe shaking, bizarre-looking contractions of the face and body, and extreme restlessness. Clearly such costs must be addressed and weighed against the drug's benefits.

ConsiderThis

⊙ The use of psychotropic medications is on the increase in our society. What might the enormous popularity of these drugs suggest about the needs and coping styles of individuals today, about the pace of modern life, and about problem solving in our technological society?

PSYCHOSURGERY Brain surgery for mental disorders.

ID According to Freud, the psychological force that produces instinctual needs, drives, and impulses.

EGO According to Freud, the psychological force that employs reason and operates in accordance with the reality principle.

The Psychodynamic Model

The *psychodynamic model* is the oldest and most famous of the modern psychological models. Psychodynamic theorists believe that a person's behavior, whether normal or abnormal, is determined largely by underlying psychological forces of which he or she is not consciously aware. These internal forces are described as *dynamic*—that is, they interact with one another; and their interaction gives rise to behavior, thoughts, and emotions. Abnormal symptoms are viewed as the result of *conflicts* between these forces.

Psychodynamic theorists would view Philip Berman as a person in conflict. They would want to explore his past experiences because, in their view, psychological conflicts are tied to early relationships and to traumatic experiences that occurred during childhood. Psychodynamic theories rest on the *deterministic* assumption that no symptom or behavior is "accidental": all behavior is determined by past experiences. Thus Philip's hatred for his mother, his memories of her as cruel and overbearing, the weakness and ineffectiveness of his father, and the birth of a younger brother when Philip was 10 may all be important to the understanding of his current problems.

The psychodynamic model was first formulated by the Viennese neurologist Sigmund Freud (1856–1939) at the turn of the twentieth century. First, Freud worked with the physician Josef Breuer (1842–1925), conducting experiments on hypnosis and hysterical illnesses—mysterious physical ailments with no apparent medical cause. In a famous case, Breuer had treated a woman he called "Anna O.," whose hysterical symptoms included paralysis of the legs and right arm, deafness, and disorganized speech. Breuer placed the woman under hypnosis, expecting that suggestions made to her in that state would help rid her of her hysterical symptoms. While she was under hypnosis, however, she began to talk about traumatic past events and to express deeply felt emotions. This venting of repressed memories seemed to enhance the effectiveness of the treatment. Anna referred to it as her "talking cure."

Freud and Freud *Anna Freud, the last of Sigmund Freud's six children, studied psychoanalysis with her father and then opened a practice next door to his. (They shared a waiting room.) Her work on defense mechanisms, other ego activities, and child development made her a major figure in her own right.*

Building on this early work, Freud developed the theory of *psychoanalysis* to explain both normal and abnormal psychological functioning, and a corresponding method of treatment, a conversational approach also called psychoanalysis. During the early 1900s, Freud and several of his colleagues in the Vienna Psychoanalytic Society—including Carl Gustav Jung (1875–1961) and Alfred Adler (1870–1937)—became the most influential clinical theorists in the Western world. Freud's 24 volumes on psychoanalytic theory and treatment are still widely studied today.

How Did Freud Explain Normal and Abnormal Functioning?

Freud believed that three central forces shape the personality—instinctual needs, rational thinking, and moral standards. All these forces, he believed, operate at the *unconscious* level, unavailable to immediate awareness; and he believed them to be dynamic, or interactive. Freud called the forces the *id, ego,* and *superego.*

THE ID Freud used the term **id** to denote instinctual needs, drives, and impulses. The id operates in accordance with the *pleasure principle;* that is, it always seeks gratification. Freud also believed that all id instincts tend to be sexual, noting that from the very earliest stages of life a child's pleasure is obtained from nursing, defecating, masturbating, and so on—all activities that he considered to have sexual overtones. He further suggested that a person's *libido*, or sexual energy, fuels the id.

THE EGO During our early years we come to recognize that our environment will not meet every instinctual need. Our mother, for example, is not always available to do our bidding. A part of the id separates off and becomes the **ego**. Like the id, the ego unconsciously seeks gratification, but it does so in accordance with the *reality principle,* the knowledge we acquire through experience that it

Table 3-2

Defense Mechanisms to the Rescue

DEFENSE	OPERATION	EXAMPLE
Repression	Person avoids anxiety by simply not allowing painful or dangerous thoughts to become conscious.	An executive's desire to run amok and attack his boss and colleagues at a board meeting is denied access to his awareness.
Denial	Person simply refuses to acknowledge the existence of an external source of anxiety.	You are not prepared for tomorrow's final exam, but you tell yourself that it's not actually an important exam and that there's no good reason not to go to a movie tonight.
Fantasy	Person imagines events as a means of satisfying unacceptable, anxiety-producing desires that would otherwise go unfulfilled.	An aggressive driver cuts in front of you and pulls into the last remaining parking space. You later fantasize about getting out of your car and beating the person to a pulp in front of admiring onlookers.
Projection	Person attributes own unacceptable impulses, motives, or desires to other individuals.	The executive who repressed his destructive desires may project his anger onto his boss and claim that it is actually the boss who is hostile.
Rationalization	Person creates a socially acceptable reason for an action that actually reflects unacceptable motives.	A student explains away poor grades by citing the importance of the "total experience" of going to college and claiming that too much emphasis on grades would actually interfere with a well-rounded education.
Reaction formation	Person adopts behavior that is the exact opposite of impulses he or she is afraid to acknowledge.	A man experiences homosexual feelings and responds by taking a strong antihomosexual stance.
Displacement	Person displaces hostility away from a dangerous object and onto a safer substitute.	After your parking spot was taken, you released your pent-up anger by starting a fight with your roommate.
Intellectualization (isolation)	Person represses emotional reactions in favor of overly logical response to a problem.	A woman who has been beaten and raped gives a detached, methodical description of the effects that such attacks may have on victims.
Undoing	Person tries to make up for unacceptable desires or acts, frequently through ritualistic behavior.	A woman who has aggressive feelings toward her husband dusts and straightens their wedding photograph every time such thoughts occur to her.
Regression	Person retreats from an upsetting conflict to an early developmental stage at which no one is expected to behave maturely or responsibly.	A boy who cannot cope with the anger he feels toward his rejecting mother regresses to infantile behavior, soiling his clothes and no longer taking care of his basic needs.
Overcompensation	Person tries to cover up a personal weakness by focusing on another, more desirable trait.	A very shy young woman overcompensates for her weak social skills by spending many hours in the gym trying to perfect her physical condition.
Sublimation	Person expresses sexual and aggressive energy in ways that are acceptable to society.	Athletes, artists, surgeons, and other highly dedicated and skilled people may be reaching their high levels of accomplishment by directing otherwise potentially harmful energies into their work.

can be unacceptable to express our id impulses outright. The ego, employing reason, guides us to know when we can and cannot express those impulses.

The ego develops basic strategies, called **ego defense mechanisms**, to control unacceptable id impulses and avoid or reduce the anxiety they arouse. The most basic defense mechanism, *repression*, prevents unacceptable impulses from ever reaching consciousness. There are many other ego defense mechanisms, and each of us tends to favor some over others (see Table 3-2).

THE SUPEREGO The **superego** grows from the ego, just as the ego grows out of the id. As we learn from our parents that many of our id impulses are unacceptable, we unconsciously adopt, or *introject*, our parents' values. We identify with our parents and judge ourselves by their standards. When we uphold their values, we feel good; when we go against them, we feel guilty. In short, we develop a *conscience*.

According to Freud, these three parts of the personality—the id, ego, and superego—are often in some degree of conflict. A healthy personality is one in which an effective working relationship, an acceptable compromise, has formed among the three forces. If the id, ego, and superego are in excessive conflict, the person's behavior may show signs of dysfunction.

Freudians would therefore view Philip Berman as someone whose personality forces have a poor working relationship. His ego and superego are unable to control his id impulses, which lead him repeatedly to act in impulsive and often dangerous ways—suicide gestures, jealous rages, job resignations, outbursts of temper, frequent arguments.

DEVELOPMENTAL STAGES Freud proposed that at each stage of development, from infancy to maturity, new events and pressures challenge individuals and require adjustments in their id, ego, and superego. If the adjustments are successful, they lead to personal growth. If not, the person may become **fixated**, or entrapped, at an early stage of development. Then all subsequent development suffers, and the individual may well be headed for abnormal functioning in the future. Because parents are the key environmental figures during the early years of life, they are often seen as the cause of improper development.

Freud named each stage of development after the body area, or *erogenous zone*, that he considered most important to the child at that time. For example, he referred to the first 18 months of life as the *oral stage*. During this stage, children fear that the mother who feeds and comforts them will disappear. Children whose mothers consistently fail to gratify their oral needs may become fixated at the oral stage and display an "oral character" throughout their lives, marked by extreme dependence or extreme mistrust. Such persons are particularly prone to develop depression. As we shall see in later chapters, Freud linked fixations at the other stages of development—*anal* (18 months to 3 years of age), *phallic* (3 to 5 years), *latency* (5 to 12 years), and *genital* (12 years to adulthood)—to yet other kinds of psychological dysfunction.

Critical training *Freud believed that toilet training is a critical developmental experience. Children whose training is too harsh may become "fixated" at the anal stage and develop an "anal character"—stubborn, contrary, stingy, or controlling.*

How Do Other Psychodynamic Explanations Differ from Freud's?

Personal and professional differences between Freud and his colleagues led to a split in the Vienna Psychoanalytic Society early in the twentieth century. Carl Jung, Alfred Adler, and others developed new theories. Although the new theories departed from Freud's ideas in important ways, each held on to Freud's belief that human functioning is shaped by dynamic (interacting) psychological forces. Thus all such theories, including Freud's, are referred to as *psychodynamic*.

Three of today's most influential psychodynamic theories are ego theory, self theory, and object relations theory. **Ego theorists** emphasize the role of the ego and consider it a more independent and powerful force than Freud did. **Self theorists**, in contrast, give greatest attention to the role of the *self*—the unified personality—rather than to any one component of the personality. They believe that the basic human motive is to save and strengthen the wholeness of the self (Dorpat, 1998; Lynch, 1998; Kohut, 1977). **Object relations theorists** propose that people are motivated mainly by a need to have relationships with others, and that severe problems in the relationships between children and their caregivers may lead to abnormal development and psychological difficulties (Fonagy, 1999; Kernberg, 1997; Grotstein, 1996, 1995).

EGO DEFENSE MECHANISMS According to psychoanalytic theory, strategies developed by the ego to control unacceptable id impulses and to avoid or reduce the anxiety they arouse.

SUPEREGO According to Freud, the psychological force that represents a person's values and ideals.

FIXATION According to Freud, a condition in which the id, ego, and superego do not mature properly and are frozen at an early stage of development.

EGO THEORY The psychodynamic theory that emphasizes the role of the ego and considers it an independent force.

SELF THEORY The psychodynamic theory that emphasizes the role of the self—our unified personality.

OBJECT RELATIONS THEORY The psychodynamic theory that views the desire for relationships as the key motivating force in human behavior.

Like mother, like daughter *According to Freud, boys become attracted to their mothers and girls to their fathers during the phallic stage. Children repress these taboo impulses and identify instead with the parent of the same sex, acting like that parent in every way.*

Psychodynamic Therapies

Psychodynamic therapies range from classical Freudian psychoanalysis to newer therapies based on self theory or object relations theory. All seek to uncover past traumas and the inner conflicts that have resulted from them. All try to help clients resolve, or settle, those conflicts and to resume personal development.

According to most psychodynamic therapists, the search for insight cannot be rushed or imposed. Therapists must subtly guide the explorations so that the patients discover their underlying problems for themselves. To aid in the process, the therapists rely on such techniques as *free association, therapist interpretation, catharsis,* and *working through* (Kernberg, 1997).

FREE ASSOCIATION In psychodynamic therapies, the patient is responsible for starting and leading each discussion. The therapist tells the patient to describe any thought, feeling, or image that comes to mind, even if it seems unimportant or irrelevant. This practice is known as **free association**. The therapist expects that the patient's associations will eventually uncover unconscious processes and underlying dynamics. Notice how free association helps this New Yorker to discover threatening impulses and conflicts within herself:

> *Patient:* So I started walking, and walking, and decided to go behind the museum and walk through Central Park. So I walked and went through a back field and felt very excited and wonderful. I saw a park bench next to a clump of bushes and sat down. There was a rustle behind me and I got frightened. I thought of men concealing themselves in the bushes. I thought of the sex perverts I read about in Central Park. I wondered if there was someone behind me exposing himself. The idea is repulsive, but exciting too. I think of father now and feel excited. I think of an erect penis. This is connected with my father. There is something about this pushing in my mind. I don't know what it is, like on the border of my memory. (*Pause*)
>
> *Therapist:* Mm-hmm. (*Pause*) On the border of your memory?
>
> *Patient:* (*The patient breathes rapidly and seems to be under great tension*) As a little girl, I slept with my father. I get a funny feeling. I get a funny feeling over my skin, tingly-like. It's a strange feeling, like a blindness, like not seeing something. My mind blurs and spreads over anything I look at. I've had this feeling off and on since I walked in the park. My mind seems to blank off like I can't think or absorb anything.
>
> (*Wolberg, 1967, p. 662*)

FREE ASSOCIATION A psychodynamic technique in which the patient describes any thought, feeling, or image that comes to mind, even if it seems unimportant.

RESISTANCE An unconscious refusal to participate fully in therapy.

TRANSFERENCE According to psychodynamic theorists, a process that occurs during psychotherapy, in which patients act toward the therapist as they did or do toward important figures in their lives.

DREAM A series of ideas and images that form during sleep.

CATHARSIS The reliving of past repressed feelings in order to settle internal conflicts and overcome problems.

WORKING THROUGH The psychoanalytic process of facing conflicts, reinterpreting feelings, and overcoming one's problems.

THERAPIST INTERPRETATION Psychodynamic therapists listen carefully as patients talk, looking for clues, drawing tentative conclusions, and sharing interpretations when they think the patient is ready to hear them. Interpretations of three phenomena are particularly important—*resistance, transference,* and *dreams.*

Patients are showing **resistance**, an unconscious refusal to participate fully in therapy, when they suddenly cannot free associate or when they change a subject to avoid a painful discussion. They demonstrate **transference** when they act and feel toward the therapist as they did or do toward important persons in their lives, especially their parents, siblings, and spouses. Consider again the woman who walked in Central Park. As she continues talking, the therapist helps her to explore her transference:

> *Patient:* I get so excited by what is happening here. I feel I'm being held back by needing to be nice. I'd like to blast loose sometimes, but I don't dare.
> *Therapist:* Because you fear my reaction?
> *Patient:* The worst thing would be that you wouldn't like me. You wouldn't speak to me friendly; you wouldn't smile; you'd feel you can't treat me and discharge me from treatment. But I know this isn't so, I know it.
> *Therapist:* Where do you think these attitudes come from?
> *Patient:* When I was nine years old, I read a lot about great men in history. I'd quote them and be dramatic. I'd want a sword at my side; I'd dress like an Indian. Mother would scold me. Don't frown, don't talk so much. Sit on your hands, over and over again. I did all kinds of things. I was a naughty child. She told me I'd be hurt. Then at fourteen I fell off a horse and broke my back. I had to be in bed. Mother then told me on the day I went riding not to, that I'd get hurt because the ground was frozen. I was a stubborn, self-willed child. Then I went against her will and suffered an accident that changed my life, a fractured back. Her attitude was, "I told you so." I was put in a cast and kept in bed for months.
>
> *(Wolberg, 1967, p. 662)*

"Don't worry. Fantasies about devouring the doctor are perfectly normal."

Finally, many psychodynamic therapists try to help patients interpret their **dreams**. Freud (1924) called dreams the "royal road to the unconscious." He believed that repression and other defense mechanisms operate less completely during sleep and that dreams, correctly interpreted, can reveal unconscious instincts, needs, and wishes (see Box 3-2 on the next page). Freud identified two kinds of dream content, manifest and latent. *Manifest content* is the consciously remembered dream, *latent content* its symbolic meaning. To interpret a dream, therapists must translate its manifest content into its latent content.

CATHARSIS Insight must be an emotional as well as intellectual process. Psychodynamic therapists believe that patients must experience **catharsis**, a reliving of past repressed feelings, if they are to settle internal conflicts and overcome their problems.

WORKING THROUGH A single episode of interpretation and catharsis will not change the way a person functions. The patient and therapist must examine the same issues over and over in the course of many sessions, each time with greater clarity. This process, called **working through**, usually takes a long time, often years. When psychodynamic treatment is scheduled once a week—as most forms of it now are—it is properly known as *psychodynamic,* or *psychoanalytic, therapy.* The term *psychoanalysis,* or simply *analysis,* is reserved for therapy given on a daily basis.

SHORT-TERM PSYCHODYNAMIC THERAPIES In several short versions of psychodynamic therapy, developed over the past few decades, patients choose a single problem—a *dynamic focus*—to work on, such as difficulty getting along with other people (Sifneos, 1992, 1987; Davanloo, 1980). The therapist and patient concentrate on this problem throughout the treatment and work only on the psychodynamic issues that relate to it (such as unresolved oral needs). Only a limited number of studies have tested the effectiveness of these short-term psychodynamic therapies, but their findings do suggest that the approaches are sometimes quite helpful to patients (Sigal et al., 1999; Messer et al., 1992; Crits-Christoph, 1992).

EARLY ROOTS

Freud himself tried short-term therapy with some of his patients and judged it to be effective "provided that one hits the right time at which to employ it." He is reported to have successfully treated the composer Gustav Mahler for his psychological difficulties during just two country walks (Johnston, 1999).

BOX **3-2**

Perchance to Dream

All people dream; so do dogs, and maybe even fish. In fact, although they may not remember them, people average close to 1,500 dreams per year. Some claim that dreams reveal the future; others see them as inner journeys or alternate realities. Sigmund Freud (1900) believed that we express and attempt to fulfill unsatisfied desires with our dreams. His colleague Alfred Adler believed that dreams prepare us for waking life by allowing us to rehearse new behav-

The Nightmare by Johann Heinrich Füssli

iors or alerting us to internal problems (Kramer, 1992).

Biological theorists offer a different, though not entirely incompatible, view. Some propose that random signals come from various areas of the brain as we sleep. The brain's cortex, the seat of higher cognitive functioning, attempts to make sense of this random bombardment of electrical activity. The result is a dream, often irrational or weird (Flanagan, 2000; Begley, 1989; Hobson & McCarley, 1977). Many biological theorists believe that the resulting dream may also be influenced by the person's drives, fears, and ambitions.

According to surveys and studies, two-thirds of people's dreams involve unpleasant material, such as aggression, threats, rejection, confusion, or an inability to communicate (Van de Castle, 1993). Commonly, a dreamer is chased or attacked by a threatening figure, suggesting to some theorists that the dreamer is running from real-life fears, unpleasant issues, or distrusted persons.

Eighty percent of college students report having had dreams of falling. Such dreams are thought to occur when our sense of security is threatened or when we are in fear of losing control. Many people say falling dreams are the first ones they can remember, although people can have them at any stage of life (Van de Castle, 1993; Cartwright & Lamberg, 1992).

Another common theme is public nudity. One study found that 43 percent of American college-age subjects reported having such dreams, compared to 18 percent of Japanese subjects (Vieira, 1993). Freud (1900) viewed dreams of nudity as an unconscious wish to exhibit oneself. Others argue that people who have these dreams may be afraid of being seen for who they really are (Van de Castle, 1993).

Dreams also may differ by gender. In a landmark study in 1951, the researcher Calvin Hall found that men dreamed twice as often about men as they did about women, whereas women dreamed about men and women in equal proportions. In addition, most male dreams took place outdoors, while female dreams were more often set in the home or elsewhere indoors. Men's sexual dreams were more likely to include women they did not know, whereas women dreamed more often about men they cared for. A later study in 1980 found no significant changes in these patterns (Van de Castle, 1993). However, more recent studies find that men's and women's dreams are becoming more androgynous, that women's dreams now take place outdoors more than they did in the past, and that women are now as likely as men to behave aggressively in their dreams (Kramer, 1989).

Assessing the Psychodynamic Model

Freud and his followers have brought great changes to the way abnormal functioning is understood (Nietzel et al., 1994). Largely because of their work, a wide range of theorists today look for answers and explanations outside biological processes. Psychodynamic theorists have also helped us to understand that abnormal functioning may be rooted in the same processes as normal functioning. Psychological conflict is a common experience; it leads to abnormal functioning only if the conflict becomes excessive.

Freud and his many followers have also had a monumental impact on treatment. They were the first to apply theory and techniques systematically to treatment. They were also the first to demonstrate the potential of psychological, as opposed to biological, treatment, and their ideas have served as starting points for many other psychological treatments.

The father factor *Because mothers provided almost all infant care in his day, Freud looked largely to maternal influences for explanations of personality development and psychological problems. Today many fathers also actively care for their young children, causing psychodynamic theorists to adapt their explanations accordingly. It turns out that fathers and mothers are more similar than different when it comes to nurturing.*

At the same time, the psychodynamic model has some key limitations. The concepts on which it is based are difficult to define and to research (Nietzel et al., 1994; Erdelyi, 1992, 1985). Because processes such as id drives, ego defenses, and fixation are abstract and supposedly operate at an unconscious level, there is no way of knowing for certain if they are occurring. Not surprisingly, then, psychodynamic explanations and treatments have garnered limited research support, and psychodynamic theorists and therapists have been forced to rely largely on evidence provided by individual case studies (Bein, 1998; Teller & Dahl, 1995; Prochaska & Norcross, 1994).

Partly in reaction to these problems, other models of abnormality have been developed over the past several decades. Nevertheless, as we can see in Figure 3-3, 11 percent of today's therapists identify themselves as Freudian therapists and 22 percent as contemporary psychodynamic therapists (Prochaska & Norcross, 1994). And, interestingly, many practitioners of other models report that when they seek help for their own problems, psychodynamic therapy is their choice (Norcross & Prochaska, 1984).

The Behavioral Model

Like psychodynamic theorists, behavioral theorists believe that our actions are determined largely by our experiences in life. However, the *behavioral model* concentrates wholly on *behaviors*, the responses an organism makes to its environment. Behaviors can be external (going to work, say) or internal (having a feeling or thought). In the behavioral view, people are the sum total of their learned behaviors. Behavioral theorists, therefore, base their explanations and treatments on *principles of learning,* the processes by which these behaviors change in response to the environment.

Many learned behaviors help people to cope with daily challenges and to lead happy, productive lives. However, abnormal behaviors also can be learned. Behaviorists who try to explain Philip Berman's problems might view him as a man who has received improper training: he has learned behaviors that offend others and repeatedly work against him.

Whereas the psychodynamic model had its beginnings in the clinical work of physicians, the behavioral model began in laboratories where psychologists were running experiments

FIGURE 3-3 **Theoretical orientations of today's clinicians** *In one survey, almost 40 percent of 818 psychologists, counselors, psychiatrists, and social workers labeled themselves as "eclectic." (Adapted from Prochaska & Norcross, 1994; Norcross et al., 1988; Norcross & Prochaska, 1986.)*

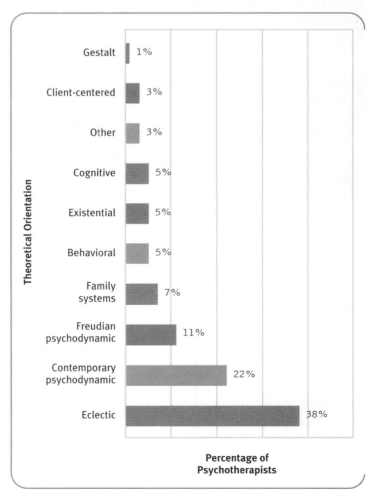

Theoretical Orientation	Percentage
Gestalt	1%
Client-centered	3%
Other	3%
Cognitive	5%
Existential	5%
Behavioral	5%
Family systems	7%
Freudian psychodynamic	11%
Contemporary psychodynamic	22%
Eclectic	38%

Percentage of Psychotherapists

See and do *Modeling may account for some forms of abnormal behavior. A well-known study by Albert Bandura and his colleagues (1963) demonstrated that children learned to abuse a doll by observing an adult hit it. Children who had not been exposed to the adult model did not mistreat the doll.*

on **conditioning**, simple forms of learning. The researchers manipulated *stimuli* and *rewards,* then observed how their manipulations affected their subjects' responses.

During the 1950s, many clinicians became frustrated with what they viewed as the vagueness and slowness of the psychodynamic model. Some of them began to apply the principles of learning to the study and treatment of psychological problems (Wolpe, 1997, 1987). Their efforts gave rise to the behavioral model of abnormality.

How Do Behaviorists Explain Abnormal Functioning?

Learning theorists have identified several different forms of conditioning, and each may produce abnormal behavior as well as normal behavior. In **operant conditioning**, for example, humans and animals learn to behave in certain ways as a result of receiving *rewards*—any satisfying consequences—whenever they do so. In **modeling**, individuals learn responses simply by observing other individuals and repeating their behaviors (see Box 3-3).

In a third form of conditioning, **classical conditioning**, learning occurs by *temporal association*. When two events repeatedly occur close together in time, they become fused in a person's mind, and before long the person responds in the same way to both events. If one event produces a response of joy, the other brings joy as well; if one event brings feelings of relief, so does the other. A closer look at this form of conditioning illustrates how the behavioral model can account for abnormal functioning.

Ivan Pavlov (1849–1936), a famous Russian physiologist, first demonstrated classical conditioning with animal studies. He placed a bowl of meat powder before a dog, producing the natural response that all dogs have to meat: they start to salivate (see Figure 3-4). Next Pavlov added a step: just before presenting the dog with meat powder, he sounded a metronome. After several such pairings of metronome tone and presentation of meat powder, Pavlov noted that the dog began to salivate as soon as it heard the metronome. The dog had learned to salivate in response to a sound.

In the vocabulary of classical conditioning, the meat in this demonstration is an *unconditioned stimulus (US)*. It elicits the *unconditioned response (UR)* of salivation, that is, a natural response with which the dog is born. The sound of the metronome is a *conditioned stimulus (CS)*, a previously neutral stimulus that comes to be linked with meat in the dog's mind. As such, it too produces a salivation response. When the salivation response is produced by the conditioned stimulus rather than by the unconditioned stimulus, it is called a *conditioned response (CR)*.

BEFORE CONDITIONING	AFTER CONDITIONING
CS: Tone → No response	CS: Tone → CR: Salivation
US: Meat → UR: Salivation	US: Meat → UR: Salivation

If, after conditioning, the conditioned stimulus is repeatedly presented alone, without being paired with the unconditioned stimulus, it will eventually stop eliciting the conditioned response. When Pavlov stopped pairing the metronome

CONDITIONING A simple form of learning.

OPERANT CONDITIONING A process of learning in which behavior that leads to satisfying consequences is likely to be repeated.

MODELING A process of learning in which an individual acquires responses by observing and imitating others.

CLASSICAL CONDITIONING A process of learning by temporal association in which two events that repeatedly occur close together in time become fused in a person's mind and produce the same response.

BOX 3-3

Maternal Instincts

On an August day in 1996, a 3-year-old boy climbed over a barrier at the Brookfield Zoo in Illinois and fell 24 feet onto the cement floor of the gorilla compound. An 8-year-old 160-pound gorilla named Binti-Jua picked up the child and cradled his limp body in her arms. The child's mother, fearing the worst, screamed out, "The gorilla's got my baby!" But Binti protected the boy as if he were her own. She held off the other gorillas, rocked him gently, and carried him to the entrance of the gorilla area, where rescue workers were waiting. Within hours, the incident was seen on videotape replays around the world, and Binti was being hailed for her maternal instincts.

When Binti was herself an infant, she had been removed from her mother, Lulu, who did not have enough milk. To make up for this loss, keepers at the zoo worked around the clock to nurture Binti; she was always being held in someone's arms. When Binti became pregnant at age 6, trainers were afraid that the early separation from her mother would leave her ill prepared to raise an infant of her own. So they gave her mothering lessons and taught her to nurse and carry around a stuffed doll.

ConsiderThis

What was responsible for the gorilla's surprisingly gentle and nurturing care for the hurt child? • Was it, as object relations theorists might hold, an expression of attachment and bonding, already experienced with her own 17-month-old daughter? • Was it the memory of the nurturing behavior she observed in human models during her own infancy, as behaviorists might claim? • Or might it have been the parenting training she received during her pregnancy?

---

tone and meat powder, for example, the dog salivated less and less in response to the tone. The conditioned response was undergoing *extinction.*

Classical conditioning explains many familiar behaviors. The romantic feelings a young man experiences when he smells his girlfriend's perfume, say, may represent a conditioned response. Initially this perfume may have had limited emotional effect on him, but because the fragrance was present during several romantic encounters, it too came to elicit a romantic response.

Abnormal behaviors, too, can be acquired by classical conditioning. Consider a young boy who is repeatedly frightened by a neighbor's large German shepherd dog. Whenever the child walks past the neighbor's front yard, the dog barks loudly and lunges at him, stopped only by a rope tied to the porch. In this unfortunate situation, the boy's parents are not surprised to discover that he develops a fear of dogs. They are stumped, however, by another intense fear the child displays, a fear of sand. They cannot understand why he cries whenever they take him to the beach and screams in fear if sand even touches his skin.

Where did this fear of sand come from? Classical conditioning. It turns out that a big sandbox is set up in the neighbor's front yard for the dog to play in. Every time the dog barks and lunges at the boy, the sandbox is there too. After repeated pairings of this kind, the child comes to fear sand as much as he fears the dog.

FIGURE 3-4 **Working for Pavlov** *In Ivan Pavlov's experimental device, the dog's saliva was collected in a tube as it was secreted, and the amount was recorded on a revolving cylinder called a kymograph. The experimenter observed the dog through a one-way glass window.*

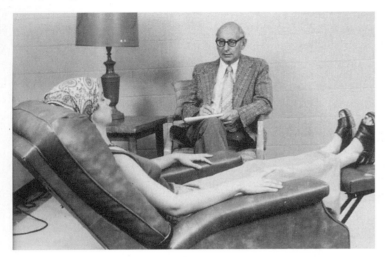

Desensitization *Joseph Wolpe, the psychiatrist who developed the behavioral treatment of systematic desensitization, first teaches a client to relax, then guides her to confront feared objects or situations, real or imagined, while she remains relaxed.*

Behavioral Therapies

Behavioral therapy aims to identify the behaviors that are causing a person's problems and then tries to replace them with more appropriate ones, by applying the principles of classical conditioning, operant conditioning, or modeling (Martin & Pear, 1999). The therapist's attitude toward the client is that of teacher rather than healer. A person's early life matters only for the clues it can provide to current conditioning processes.

Classical conditioning treatments, for example, may be used to change abnormal reactions to particular stimuli. **Systematic desensitization** is one such method, often applied in cases of *phobia*—a specific and unreasonable fear. In this step-by-step procedure, clients learn to react calmly instead of with intense fear to the objects or situations they dread (Wolpe, 1990, 1987, 1958). First, they are taught the skill of relaxation over the course of several sessions. Next, they construct a *fear hierarchy,* a list of feared objects or situations, starting with those that are least troublesome and ending with the ones that are most dreaded. Here is the hierarchy developed by a man who was afraid of criticism, especially about his mental stability:

1. Friend on the street: "Hi, how are you?"
2. Friend on the street: "How are you feeling these days?"
3. Sister: "You've got to be careful so they don't put you in the hospital."
4. Wife: "You shouldn't drink beer while you are taking medicine."
5. Mother: "What's the matter, don't you feel good?"
6. Wife: "It's just you yourself, it's all in your head."
7. Service station attendant: "What are you shaking for?"
8. Neighbor borrows rake: "Is there something wrong with your leg? Your knees are shaking."
9. Friend on the job: "Is your blood pressure okay?"
10. Service station attendant: "You are pretty shaky, are you crazy or something?"

(Marquis & Morgan, 1969, p. 28)

Conditioning for fun and profit *Pet owners have discovered that they can teach animals a wide assortment of tricks by using the principles of conditioning. Only 3 percent of all dogs have learned to "sing," while 21 percent know how to sit, the most common dog trick (Pet Food Institute).*

Desensitization therapists next have their clients either imagine or actually confront each item on the hierarchy while in a state of relaxation. In step-by-step pairings of feared items and relaxation, clients move up the hierarchy until at last they can face every one of the items without experiencing fear. As we shall see in Chapter 5, research has shown systematic desensitization and other classical conditioning techniques to be effective in treating phobias (Ollendick & King, 1998; Wolpe, 1997).

Assessing the Behavioral Model

The number of behavioral clinicians has grown steadily since the 1950s, and the behavioral model has become a powerful force in the clinical field. Various behavioral theories have been proposed over the years, and many treatment techniques have been developed. Approximately 5 percent of today's therapists report that their approach is mainly behavioral (Prochaska & Norcross, 1994).

Perhaps the greatest appeal of the behavioral model is that it can be tested in the laboratory, whereas psychodynamic theories generally cannot. The behaviorists' basic concepts—stimulus, response, and reward—can be observed and measured. Even more important, the results of research have lent considerable support to the behavioral model (Wolpe, 1997). Experimenters have successfully used the principles of learning to create clinical symptoms in laboratory subjects, suggesting that psychological disorders may indeed develop in the same way. In addition, research has found that behavioral treatments can be helpful to people with specific fears, social deficits, mental retardation, and other problems (DeRubeis & Crits-Christoph, 1998; Emmelkamp, 1994). Their effectiveness is, in fact, all the more impressive in view of their short duration and low overall cost.

At the same time, research has also revealed weaknesses in the model. Certainly behavioral researchers have produced specific symptoms in subjects. But are these symptoms *ordinarily* acquired in this way? There is still no indisputable evidence that most people with psychological disorders are victims of improper conditioning. Similarly, behavioral therapies have limitations. The improvements noted in the therapist's office do not always extend to real life. Nor do they necessarily last without continued therapy (Nietzel et al., 1994; Stokes & Osnes, 1989).

Finally, some critics hold that the behavioral view is too simplistic, that its concepts fail to account for the complexity of human behavior. In 1977 Albert Bandura, the behaviorist who earlier had identified modeling as a key conditioning process, argued that in order to feel happy and function effectively people must develop a positive sense of **self-efficacy**. That is, they must know that they can master and perform needed behaviors whenever necessary. Other behaviorists of the 1960s and 1970s similarly recognized that human beings engage in *cognitive behaviors,* such as anticipating or interpreting—ways of thinking that until then had been largely ignored in behavioral theory and therapy. These individuals developed *cognitive-behavioral theories* that took unseen cognitive behaviors into greater account (Meichenbaum, 1993; Goldiamond, 1965).

Cognitive-behavioral theorists bridge the behavioral model and the cognitive model, the theoretical approach we turn to next. On the one hand, their explanations are based squarely on learning principles. These theorists believe, for example, that cognitive processes are learned by classical conditioning, operant conditioning, and modeling. On the other hand, cognitive-behavioral theorists share with other kinds of cognitive theorists a belief that the ability to think is the most important aspect of human functioning (Dougher, 1997; Wilson, Hayes, & Gifford, 1997).

The Cognitive Model

Philip Berman, like the rest of us, has *cognitive* abilities—special intellectual capacities to think, remember, and anticipate. These abilities can help him accomplish a great deal in life. Yet they can also work against him. As he thinks about his experiences, Philip may develop false ideas. He may misinterpret experiences in ways that lead to poor decisions, maladaptive responses, and painful emotions.

In the early 1960s two clinicians, Albert Ellis (1962) and Aaron Beck (1967), proposed that cognitive processes are at the center of behavior, thought, and emotions and that we can best understand abnormal functioning by looking to cognition—a perspective known as the *cognitive model.* Building on earlier work from the experimental field of social psychology, Ellis and Beck claimed that clinicians must ask questions about the assumptions and attitudes that color a client's perceptions, the thoughts running through that person's mind, and the conclusions they are leading to. Other theorists and therapists soon embraced and expanded their ideas and techniques.

SYSTEMATIC DESENSITIZATION A behavioral treatment in which clients with phobias learn to react calmly instead of with intense fear to the objects or situations they dread.

SELF-EFFICACY The belief that one can master and perform needed behaviors whenever necessary.

"We are molded and remolded by those who have loved us."

François Mauriac

"Stimulus, response! Stimulus, response! Don't you ever think?*"*

A clinical pioneer *Aaron Beck proposes that many forms of abnormal behavior can be traced to cognitive factors, such as upsetting thoughts and illogical thinking.*

How Do Cognitive Theorists Explain Abnormal Functioning?

To cognitive theorists, we are all artists. We reproduce and create the world in our minds as we try to understand the events going on around us. If we are effective artists, our cognitions tend to be accurate (they agree with the perceptions of others) and useful. If we are ineffective artists, we may create a cognitive inner world that is painful and harmful to ourselves.

Abnormal functioning can result from several kinds of cognitive problems. Some people may make *assumptions* and adopt *attitudes* that are disturbing and inaccurate (Ellis, 1999, 1997, 1962). Philip Berman, for example, often seems to assume that his past history has condemned him to a situation that he cannot escape. He believes that he was victimized by his parents and that he is now forever doomed by his past. He seems to approach all new experiences and relationships with expectations of failure and disaster.

Illogical thinking processes are another source of abnormal functioning, according to cognitive theorists. Beck (1993, 1991, 1967), for example, has found that some people consistently and illogically arrive at self-defeating conclusions. As we shall see in Chapter 7, he has identified a number of illogical thought processes regularly found in depression, such as *overgeneralization*, the drawing of broad negative conclusions on the basis of a single insignificant event. One depressed student couldn't remember the date of Columbus's third voyage to America during a history class. Overgeneralizing, she spent the rest of the day in despair over her invincible ignorance.

Cognitive Therapies

According to cognitive therapists, people with psychological disorders can overcome their problems by developing new, more functional ways of thinking. Because different forms of abnormality may involve different kinds of cognitive dysfunctioning, cognitive therapists have developed a number of strategies. Beck (1997, 1996, 1967), for example, has developed an approach that is widely used in cases of depression.

In Beck's approach, called simply **cognitive therapy**, therapists help clients recognize the negative thoughts, biased interpretations, and errors in logic that dominate their thinking and, according to Beck, cause them to feel depressed. Therapists also guide clients to challenge their dysfunctional thoughts, try out new interpretations, and ultimately apply the new ways of thinking in their daily lives. As we shall see in Chapter 8, people with depression who are treated with Beck's approach improve much more than those who receive no treatment (Shaw & Segal, 1999; Hollon & Beck, 1994).

In the excerpt that follows, a cognitive therapist guides a depressed 26-year-old graduate student to recognize the connection between the way she interprets her experiences and the way she feels and to begin questioning the accuracy of her interpretations:

> *Therapist:* How do you understand it?
> *Patient:* I get depressed when things go wrong. Like when I fail a test.
> *Therapist:* How can failing a test make you depressed?
> *Patient:* Well, if I fail I'll never get into law school.
> *Therapist:* So failing the test means a lot to you. But if failing a test could drive people into clinical depression, wouldn't you expect everyone who failed the test to have a depression? . . . Did everyone who failed get depressed enough to require treatment?
> *Patient:* No, but it depends on how important the test was to the person.

> "It is the mark of an educated mind to be able to entertain a thought without accepting it."
>
> Aristotle

> *Therapist:* Right, and who decides the importance?
> *Patient:* I do.
> *Therapist:* And so, what we have to examine is your way of viewing the test (or the way that you think about the test) and how it affects your chances of getting into law school. Do you agree?
> *Patient:* Right. . . .
> *Therapist:* Now what did failing mean?
> *Patient:* (*Tearful*) That I couldn't get into law school.
> *Therapist:* And what does that mean to you?
> *Patient:* That I'm just not smart enough.
> *Therapist:* Anything else?
> *Patient:* That I can never be happy.
> *Therapist:* And how do these thoughts make you feel?
> *Patient:* Very unhappy.
> *Therapist:* So it is the meaning of failing a test that makes you very unhappy. In fact, believing that you can never be happy is a powerful factor in producing unhappiness. So, you get yourself into a trap—by definition, failure to get into law school equals "I can never be happy."
>
> (*Beck et al., 1979, pp. 145-146*)

Assessing the Cognitive Model

The cognitive model has had very broad appeal. In addition to the behaviorists who now include cognitive concepts in their theories about learning, there are a great many clinicians who believe that thinking processes are in fact much more than conditioned reactions. Cognitive theory, research, and treatments have developed in so many interesting ways that the model is now viewed as separate from the behavioral school that launched it.

Approximately 5 percent of today's therapists identify their approach as cognitive (Prochaska & Norcross, 1994). When examined more closely, this overall percentage actually reveals a split in the clinical community. A full 10 percent of psychologists and other counselors employ cognitive therapy primarily, compared to only 1 percent of psychiatrists and 4 percent of social workers (Prochaska & Norcross, 1994; Norcross, Prochaska, & Farber, 1993). In any case, the number of professionals using cognitive approaches appears to be rising.

There are several reasons for the model's popularity. First, it focuses on a process unique to human beings, the process of human thought. Just as our special cognitive abilities are responsible for so many human accomplishments, they may also be responsible for the special problems found in human functioning. Thus many theorists from varied backgrounds find themselves drawn to a model that sees thought as the primary cause of normal or abnormal behavior.

Cognitive theories also lend themselves to research. Investigators have found that many people with psychological disorders do indeed make the kinds of assumptions and errors in thinking the theorists claim (Clark, Beck, & Alford, 1999; Whisman & McGarvey, 1995). Yet another reason for the popularity of the cognitive model is the impressive performance of cognitive therapies. They have proved to be very effective for treating depression, panic disorder, and sexual dysfunctions, for example (Clark et al., 1999; DeRubeis & Crits-Christoph, 1998; Hollon & Beck, 1994). They also adapt well to new technologies (see Box 3-4 on the next page).

Nevertheless, the cognitive model, too, has its drawbacks (Beck, 1997, 1991; Meichenbaum, 1997, 1992). First, although disturbed cognitive processes are found in many forms of abnormality, their precise role has yet to be determined. The cognitions seen in psychologically troubled people could well be a result rather than a cause of their difficulties. Second, although cognitive therapies are clearly of help to many people, they do not help everyone. Research findings have

A CRISIS OF CONFIDENCE
People who generally lack confidence and doubt themselves cannot even take pleasure in their achievements. In a recent study at Ohio State University, self-doubting freshmen felt uncomfortable when asked to list successes in their lives. The more successes they were asked to list, the greater their drop in self-esteem. Confident freshmen, in contrast, welcomed the opportunity to make such a list—the more items requested, the better (Arkin et al., 1999).

COGNITIVE THERAPY A therapy developed by Aaron Beck that helps people recognize and change their faulty thinking processes.

BOX **3-4**

e-Therapy

In this age of the Internet, it is hardly surprising that a growing number of therapists are setting up on-line services, inviting persons with problems to e-mail their questions and concerns (Barak, 1999; Keilman, 1999). Such services have raised concerns about confidentiality and the quality of care provided (Gorman, 1998; Foderaro, 1994). In fact, the American Psychological Association has tried to formulate guidelines for psychologists who offer them (Sleek, 1995).

Similarly, there are now chat groups on the Internet for everything from depression to substance abuse, anxiety, and eating disorders. These groups provide opportunities for people with similar problems to communicate with each other, freely trading advice and empathy. Of course, people who choose "chat group therapy" do not know who is on the other end of the computer connection or whether the advice they receive is at all appropriate. Distasteful or insulting messages are not uncommon (Ehrman, 1995).

Another new computer-age development is software programs that profess to offer help for emotional distress (Oldenburg, 1995; Wiegner, 1995). Advocates suggest that people may find it easier to reveal sensitive personal information to a computer than to a therapist (Greist & Klein, 1980). The computer offers them the freedom to express their thoughts and emotions without fear of being judged (Lawrence, 1986). It is never tired, angry, or bored (Colby et al., 1979) and does not make grimaces, gestures, or harrumphing noises that signal surprise, disapproval, or dismay. Moreover, the computer therapist is always available, it can reach a large number of people, and its fees are modest. These are all attractive attributes in a therapist.

One computer program simulates a client-centered therapy session. The patient types in a response to a question, and the computer selects the next question on the basis of key words that appear in the response. Another helps people articulate their problems in "if–then" statements, a basic technique used by cognitive therapists (Binik et al., 1988). Still another program offers a form of cognitive therapy for depression, in the process quoting authors such as Leo Tolstoy and Bertrand Russell.

Research indicates that some of these programs are indeed helpful (Elias, 2000, 1995). Computers may never substitute fully for the judgment of a trained therapist. Yet, as more complex and humanlike computer programs are developed, Internet and computer services may indeed find a place as adjuncts to other forms of treatment.

begun to reveal limits to the effectiveness of these approaches. Is it enough to change the cognitive habits of a person with a serious psychological dysfunction? Can such specific changes make a general and lasting difference in the way the person feels and behaves?

Furthermore, like the other models we have examined, the cognitive model is narrow in certain ways. Although cognition is a very special human dimension, it is still only one part of human functioning. Aren't human beings more than the sum total of their thoughts, emotions, and behaviors? Shouldn't explanations of human functioning also consider broader issues such as how people approach life, what value they extract from it, and how they deal with the question of life's meaning? This is the position of the humanistic-existential perspective.

The Humanistic-Existential Model

Philip Berman is more than the sum of his psychological conflicts, learned behaviors, or cognitions. Being human, he also has the ability to pursue philosophical goals such as self-awareness, strong values, a sense of meaning in life, and freedom of choice. According to humanistic and existential theorists, Philip's problems can be understood only in the light of such complex goals. Humanistic and existential theorists are usually grouped together—in an approach known as the *humanistic-existential model*—because of their common focus on these broader dimensions of human existence. At the same time, there are important differences between them.

Humanists, the more optimistic of the two groups, believe that human beings are born with a natural tendency to be friendly, cooperative, and constructive. People, these theorists propose, are driven to **self-actualize**—that is, to fulfill this potential for goodness and growth. They can do so, however, only if they

SELF-ACTUALIZATION The humanistic process by which people fulfill their potential for goodness and growth.

honestly recognize and accept their weaknesses as well as their strengths and establish satisfying personal values to live by. Humanists further suggest that self-actualization leads naturally to a concern for the welfare of others and to behavior that is loving, courageous, spontaneous, and independent (Maslow, 1970).

Existentialists agree that human beings must have an accurate awareness of themselves and live meaningful—they say "authentic"—lives in order to be psychologically well adjusted. These theorists do not believe, however, that people are naturally inclined to live constructively. They believe that from birth we have total freedom, either to face up to our existence and give meaning to our lives or to shrink from that responsibility. Those who choose to "hide" from responsibility and choice will view themselves as helpless and weak and may live empty, inauthentic, and dysfunctional lives as a result.

The humanistic and existential views of abnormality both date back to the 1940s. At that time Carl Rogers (1902–1987), often considered the pioneer of the humanistic perspective, developed *client-centered therapy,* a warm and supportive approach that contrasted sharply with the psychodynamic techniques of the day. He also proposed a theory of personality that paid little attention to irrational instincts and conflicts. About the same time, other humanistic theories developed by Abraham Maslow (1908–1970) and Frederick (Fritz) Perls (1893–1970) also received widespread attention.

The existential view of personality and abnormality appeared during this same period. Many of its principles came from the ideas of nineteenth-century European existential philosophers who held that human beings are constantly defining and so giving meaning to their existence through their actions. In the late 1950s a book titled *Existence* described a number of major existential ideas and treatment approaches and helped them gain recognition (May, Angel, & Ellenberger, 1958).

The humanistic and existential theories, and their uplifting and sometimes spiritual implications, were extremely popular during the 1960s and 1970s, years of considerable soul-searching and social upheaval in Western society. They have since lost some of their popularity, but they continue to influence the ideas and work of many clinicians.

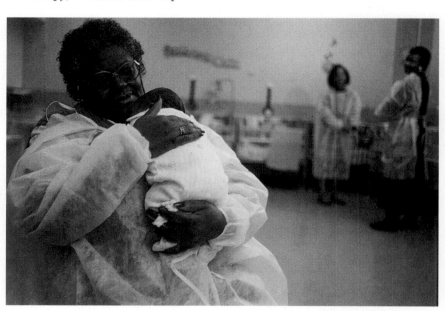

Actualizing the self *Humanists suggest that self-actualized people, such as this hospital volunteer who works with drug-addicted babies, show concern for the welfare of humanity. They are also thought to be highly creative, spontaneous, independent, and humorous.*

Rogers's Humanistic Theory and Therapy

According to Carl Rogers (1987, 1961, 1951), the road to dysfunction begins in infancy. We all have a basic need to receive *positive regard* from the important people in our lives (primarily our parents). Those who receive *unconditional* (nonjudgmental) *positive regard* early in life are likely to develop *unconditional self-regard.* That is, they come to recognize their worth as persons, even while recognizing that they are not perfect. Such people are in a good position to actualize their positive potential.

Unfortunately, some children are repeatedly made to feel that they are not worthy of positive regard. As a result, they acquire *conditions of worth,* standards that tell them they are lovable and acceptable only when they conform to certain guidelines. In order to maintain positive self-regard, these people have to look at themselves very selectively, denying or distorting thoughts and actions that do not measure up to their conditions of worth. They thus acquire a distorted view of themselves and their experiences.

The constant self-deception makes it impossible for these people to self-actualize. They do not know what they are truly feeling, what they genuinely need, or what values and goals would be meaningful for them. Moreover, they

CLIENT-CENTERED THERAPY The humanistic therapy developed by Carl Rogers in which clinicians try to help clients by conveying acceptance, accurate empathy, and genuineness.

GESTALT THERAPY The humanistic therapy developed by Fritz Perls in which clinicians actively move clients toward self-recognition and self-acceptance by using techniques such as role-playing and self-discovery exercises.

EXISTENTIAL THERAPY A therapy that encourages clients to accept responsibility for their lives and to live with greater meaning and values.

spend so much energy trying to protect their self-image that little is left for self-actualizing. Problems in functioning are then inevitable.

Rogers might view Philip Berman as a man who has gone astray. Rather than striving to fulfill his positive human potential, he drifts from job to job, relationship to relationship, and outburst to outburst. In every interaction he is defending himself, trying to interpret events in ways he can live with, usually blaming his problems on other people. Yet his constant efforts at self-defense and self-enhancement are only partly successful. His basic negative self-image continually reveals itself. Rogers would probably link this problem to the critical ways Philip was treated by his mother throughout his childhood.

Clinicians who practice Rogers's **client-centered therapy** try to create a supportive climate in which clients feel able to look at themselves honestly and acceptingly (Thorne & Lambers, 1998; Raskin & Rogers, 1995; Rogers, 1987, 1967, 1951). The therapist must display three important qualities throughout the therapy—unconditional positive regard for the client, accurate empathy, and genuineness.

Therapists show *unconditional positive regard* by conveying full and warm acceptance no matter what clients say, think, or feel. They show *accurate empathy* by accurately hearing what clients are saying and sensitively communicating it back to them. Finally, therapists must convey *genuineness,* also referred to as *congruence.* Unless therapists' communications are honest and genuine, clients may perceive them as mechanical and false. The following interaction shows the therapist using all these qualities to move the client toward greater self-awareness:

> *Client:* Yes, I know I shouldn't worry about it, but I do. Lots of things—money, people, clothes. In classes I feel that everyone's just waiting for a chance to jump on me. . . . When I meet somebody I wonder what he's actually thinking of me. Then later on I wonder how I match up to what he's come to think of me.
>
> *Therapist:* You feel that you're pretty responsive to the opinions of other people.
>
> *Client:* Yes, but it's things that shouldn't worry me.
>
> *Therapist:* You feel that it's the sort of thing that shouldn't be upsetting, but they do get you pretty much worried anyway.
>
> *Client:* Just some of them. Most of those things do worry me because they're true. The ones I told you, that is. But there are lots of little things that aren't true. . . . Things just seem to be piling up, piling up inside of me. . . . It's a feeling that things were crowding up and they were going to burst.
>
> *Therapist:* You feel that it's a sort of oppression with some frustration and that things are just unmanageable.
>
> *Client:* In a way, but some things just seem illogical. I'm afraid I'm not very clear here but that's the way it comes.
>
> *Therapist:* That's all right. You say just what you think.
>
> *(Snyder, 1947, pp. 2–24)*

MUSICAL INTERVENTION

Some therapists consider music therapy to be a form of humanistic treatment because of music's ability to inspire people, to arouse previously unavailable emotions, insights, and memories, and even to evoke spiritual feelings (Shultis, 1999; Steckler, 1998). The healing power of music has long been recognized; in Greek mythology, Apollo was the god of both music and medicine (Kahn & Fawcett, 1993).

In such an atmosphere, persons are expected to feel accepted by their therapists. They then may be able to look at themselves with honesty and acceptance—a process called *experiencing.* That is, they begin to value their own emotions, thoughts, and behaviors, and so they are freed from the insecurities and doubts that prevent self-actualization.

Client-centered therapy has not fared very well in research. Although some studies show that people who receive this therapy improve more than control subjects (Greenberg et al., 1998, 1994; Stuhr & Meyer, 1991), many other studies have failed to document any such advantage (Rudolph et al., 1980; Dircks et al., 1980). All the same, Rogers's therapy has had a positive influence on clinical practice. It was one of the first major alternatives to psychodynamic therapy, and it helped open up the field to new approaches. Rogers also helped pave the way for psychologists to practice psychotherapy; it had previously been considered the exclusive territory of psychiatrists. And his commitment to clinical research helped promote the systematic study of treatment (Lakin, 1998; Rogers & Sanford, 1989). Approximately 3 percent of today's therapists report that they employ the client-centered approach (Prochasca & Norcross, 1994).

Gestalt Theory and Therapy

Gestalt therapy, another humanistic approach, was developed in the 1950s by a charismatic clinician named Fritz Perls. Gestalt therapists, like client-centered therapists, guide their clients toward self-recognition and self-acceptance (Greenberg et al., 1998; Yontef, 1998). But unlike client-centered therapists, they often try to achieve this goal by challenging and even frustrating their clients. Gestalt techniques are also meant to shorten the therapy process. Some of Perls's favorite techniques were skillful frustration, role playing, and numerous rules and exercises.

In the technique of *skillful frustration,* gestalt therapists refuse to meet their clients' expectations or demands. This use of frustration is meant to help people see how they often try to manipulate others into meeting their needs. In the technique of *role playing,* the therapists instruct clients to act out various roles. A person may be told to be another person, an object, an alternative self, or even a part of the body (Polster, 1992). Role playing can become intense, as individuals are encouraged to fully express emotions. Many cry out, scream, kick, or pound. Through this experience they may come to "own" (accept) feelings that previously made them uncomfortable.

Perls also developed a list of *rules* to ensure that clients will look at themselves more closely. In some versions of gestalt therapy, for example, clients may be required to use "I" language rather than "it" language. They must say, "I am frightened" rather than "The situation is frightening." Yet another common rule requires clients to stay in the *here and now.* They have needs now, are hiding their needs now, and must observe them now.

Approximately 1 percent of clinicians describe themselves as gestalt therapists (Prochaska & Norcross, 1994). Because they believe that subjective experiences and self-awareness cannot be measured objectively, controlled research has rarely been done on the gestalt approach (Greenberg et al., 1998, 1994).

Techniques of gestalt therapy *Gestalt therapists may guide their clients to express their needs and feelings in their full intensity through role playing, banging on pillows, and other exercises. In a gestalt therapy group, members may help each other to "get in touch" with their needs and feelings.*

"Do not dwell in the past, do not dream of the future, concentrate the mind on the present moment."

Buddha

Existential Theories and Therapy

Like humanists, existentialists believe that psychological dysfunctioning is caused by self-deception; but existentialists are talking about a kind of self-deception in which people hide from life's responsibilities and fail to recognize that it is up to them to give meaning to their lives. According to existentialists, many people become overwhelmed by the pressures of present-day society and so look to others for explanations, guidance, and authority. They overlook their personal freedom of choice and avoid responsibility for their lives and decisions (May & Yalom, 1995, 1989; May, 1987, 1961). Such people are left with empty, inauthentic lives. Their dominant emotions are anxiety, frustration, boredom, alienation, and depression.

Existentialists might view Philip Berman as a man who feels overwhelmed by the forces of society. He sees his parents as "rich, powerful, and selfish," and he perceives teachers, acquaintances, and employers as abusive and oppressing. He fails to appreciate his choices in life and his capacity for finding meaning and direction. Quitting becomes a habit with him—he leaves job after job, ends every romantic relationship, flees difficult situations, and even attempts suicide.

In **existential therapy** people are encouraged to accept responsibility for their lives and for their problems. They are helped to recognize their freedom so that they may choose a different course and live with greater meaning and

THE TOLL OF BOREDOM

Twenty-one percent of Americans say they are regularly "bored out of their mind." Around 44 percent of all people eat when they are bored, 27 percent go for a drive, and 9 percent have a drink. The most boring time of the week is Sunday for 13 percent of people, weekday afternoons for 10 percent, and weeknights for 7 percent (Kanner, 1999).

Rejecting victimhood *Emphasizing the need to accept responsibility, recognize one's choices, and live a meaningful life, existential therapists guide clients to reject feelings of victimhood.* (Calvin and Hobbes © 1993 Watterson. Reprinted with permission of Universal Press Syndicate. All rights reserved.)

stronger values (May & Yalom, 1995, 1989). For the most part, existential therapists care more about the *goals* of therapy than the use of specific techniques; methods vary greatly from clinician to clinician (Greenberg et al., 1997; May & Yalom, 1995, 1989). At the same time, most do place great emphasis on the *relationship* between therapist and client and try to create an atmosphere of candor, hard work, and shared learning and growth (Schneider, 1998; Frankl, 1975, 1963).

> *Patient:* I don't know why I keep coming here. All I do is tell you the same thing over and over. I'm not getting anywhere.
> *Doctor:* I'm getting tired of hearing the same thing over and over, too.
> *Patient:* Maybe I'll stop coming.
> *Doctor:* It's certainly your choice.
> *Patient:* What do you think I should do?
> *Doctor:* What do you want to do?
> *Patient:* I want to get better.
> *Doctor:* I don't blame you.
> *Patient:* If you think I should stay, ok, I will.
> *Doctor:* You want me to tell you to stay?
> *Patient:* You know what's best; you're the doctor.
> *Doctor:* Do I act like a doctor?
>
> *(Keen, 1970, p. 200)*

Existential therapists do not believe that experimental methods can adequately test the effectiveness of their treatments (May & Yalom, 1995, 1989). They think of research as reducing individuals to test measures or scale scores, serving only to dehumanize them further. Not surprisingly, then, very little controlled research has been devoted to the effectiveness of this approach (Prochaska & Norcross, 1994). Nevertheless, as many as 5 percent of today's therapists use an approach that is primarily existential (Prochaska & Norcross, 1994).

Assessing the Humanistic-Existential Model

The humanistic-existential model appeals to many people in and out of the clinical field. In recognizing the special challenges of human existence, humanistic and existential theorists tap into an aspect of psychological life that is typically missing from the other models (Fuller, 1982) (see Box 3-5). Moreover, the factors that they say are essential to effective functioning—self-acceptance, personal values, personal meaning, and personal choice—are certainly lacking in many people with psychological disturbances.

The optimistic tone of the humanistic-existential model is also an attraction. Theorists who follow these principles offer great hope when they assert that de-

"The difficulty in life is the choice."

George Moore, *The Bending of the Bough*

spite the often overwhelming pressures of modern society, we can make our own choices, determine our own destiny, and accomplish much. Still another attractive feature of the model is its emphasis on health (Cowen, 1991). Unlike clinicians from some of the other models who see individuals as patients with psychological illnesses, humanists and existentialists view them simply as people whose special potential has yet to be fulfilled. Moreover, they believe that a person's behavior can be influenced by his or her own innate goodness and potential, and by a willingness to take responsibility, more than by any factor in the past.

At the same time, the humanistic-existential focus on abstract issues of human fulfillment gives rise to a major problem from a scientific point of view: these issues are resistant to research. In fact, with the notable exception of Rogers, who spent years investigating his clinical methods, humanists and existentialists tend to reject the research approaches that now dominate the field. They argue the merits of their views using logic, introspection, and individual case histories. In consequence, the model has received limited empirical examination or support.

ConsiderThis

◉ Many theorists worry about a growing trend toward "victimization" in our society, a tendency to portray undesirable behaviors as inevitable or uncontrollable consequences of early mistreatment or societal stress. What might be some of the dangers of overapplying the "victim" label?

BOX 3-5

Faith Linked to Mental Health

For years, many clinical theorists and practitioners have viewed religion as a negative factor in mental health (Theilman, 1998; Neeleman & Persaud, 1995). They have suspected that people with strong religious beliefs are more superstitious, irrational, guilt-ridden, and unstable than others, and less able to cope with life's difficulties. Recently, however, a growing body of research has indicated that these views are wrong. Religious faith and mental health can be closely linked (Elkins, 1999; Ellison & Levin, 1998; Koenig et al., 1998).

A number of studies have examined the mental health of people who view God as warm, caring, helpful, and dependable. Repeatedly, these individuals are found to be less lonely, depressed, or anxious than people who believe that God is cold and unresponsive or those without religious belief of any kind. They also seem to

cope better with major life stresses, from illness to war, and they are less likely to abuse drugs (Miller, 1998; Clay, 1996). Accordingly, a growing number of therapists are including a focus on spiritual and religious issues when treating religious clients (Razali et al., 1998).

ConsiderThis

◉ Why might positive religious beliefs be linked to mental health? • Why have so many clinicians been suspicious of religious beliefs for so long? • Are some models of abnormality more likely than others to present a negative view of religion?

The Sociocultural Model

Philip Berman is also a social being. He is surrounded by people and by institutions, he is a member of a family and a society, and he participates in both social and professional relationships. Thus social forces are always operating upon Philip, setting boundaries and expectations that guide and at times pressure him, helping to shape his behavior, thoughts, and emotions as surely as any internal mechanism.

According to the *sociocultural model,* abnormal behavior is best understood in light of the social and cultural forces that influence an individual (Kleinman & Cohen, 1997; NAMHC, 1996). What are the norms of the society? What roles does the person play in the social environment? What kind of family structure is the person a part of? And how do other people view and react to him or her? The model borrows concepts and principles from two fields: *sociology,* the study of human relationships and social groups, and *anthropology,* the study of human cultures and institutions.

How Do Sociocultural Theorists Explain Abnormal Functioning?

Because behavior is shaped by social forces, sociocultural theorists hold, we must examine a person's social surroundings if we are to understand abnormal behavior. Sociocultural explanations focus on *family structure and communication, social networks, societal conditions,* and *societal labels and roles.*

FAMILY STRUCTURE AND COMMUNICATION According to **family systems theory**, the family is a *system* of interacting parts—the family members—who interact with one another in consistent ways and conform to implicit rules unique to each family (McGoldrick, Gerson, & Shellenberger, 1999; Rolland & Walsh, 1994). The parts interact in ways that enable the system to maintain itself and survive—a state known as *homeostasis.* Family systems theorists believe that the structure and communication patterns of some families actually force individual members to behave in a way that otherwise seems abnormal. If the members were to behave normally, they would severely strain the family's homeostasis and customary manner of operation, and would actually increase their own and their family's turmoil. The natural responses by other family members would in fact tend to counteract such "normal" behavior.

Family systems theory holds that certain family systems are particularly likely to produce abnormal functioning in individual members (Becvar & Becvar, 1993; Nichols, 1992, 1984). Some families, for example, have an *enmeshed* structure in which the members are grossly overinvolved in each other's activities, thoughts, and feelings. Children from this kind of family may have great difficulty becoming independent in life. Some families display *disengagement,* which is marked by very rigid boundaries between the members. Children from these families may have difficulty functioning in a group or giving or requesting support.

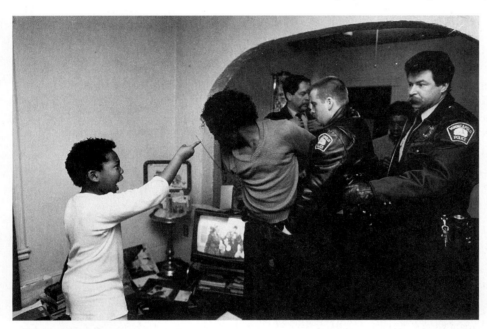

The dysfunctional family *People in dysfunctional families often face special pressures and in addition may be called upon to behave and think in ways that are personally maladaptive. This 8-year-old had to call the police when he saw his father attacking his mother with a knife. The child's rage, frustration, and emotional pain are apparent.*

In the sociocultural model, Philip Berman's angry and impulsive personal style might be seen as the product of a disturbed family structure. According to family systems theorists, the whole family—mother, father, Philip, and his brother Arnold—relate in such a way as to maintain Philip's behavior. Family theorists might be particularly interested in the conflict between Philip's mother and father and the imbalance between their parental roles. They might see Philip's behavior as both a reaction to and stimulus for his parents' behaviors. With Philip acting out the role of the misbehaving child, or scapegoat, his parents may have little need or time to question their own relationship.

Family systems theorists would also seek to clarify the precise nature of Philip's relationship with each parent. Is he enmeshed with his mother and/or disengaged from his father? They would look too at the rules governing the sibling relationship in the family, the relationship between the parents and Philip's brother, and the nature of parent-child relationships in previous generations of the family.

THE PERFECT SIZE

Today only 36 percent of people believe that the ideal family size is three or more children, compared to 66 percent in 1938 and 80 percent in 1962 (Kate, 1998).

SOCIAL NETWORKS AND SUPPORTS Socio-cultural theorists are also concerned with the broader social networks in which people operate, including their social and professional relationships. How well do they communicate with others? What kind of signals do they send to or receive from others? Researchers have often found ties between deficiencies in social networks and deficiencies in a person's functioning (Thoits, 1999). They have noted, for example, that people who are isolated and lack social support or intimacy in their lives are more likely to become depressed when under stress and to remain depressed longer than are people with supportive spouses or warm friendships (Husaini, 1997; Paykel & Cooper, 1992).

SOCIETAL CONDITIONS Wide-ranging societal conditions may create special stresses and increase the likelihood of abnormal functioning in some members (Thoits, 1999; Kleinman & Cohen, 1997). Researchers have learned, for example, that psychological abnormality, especially severe psychological abnormality, is more common in the lower socioeconomic classes than in the higher ones (Eaton & Muntaner, 1999; NAMHC, 1996). Perhaps the special pressures of lower-class life explain this relationship (Adler et al., 1994). That is, the higher rates of crime, unemployment, overcrowding, and homelessness, the inferior medical care, and the limited educational opportunities of lower-class life may place great stress on members of these groups (Zima et al., 1996; Ensminger, 1995). Conversely, it may be that people who suffer from severe mental disturbances are less effective at work and earn less money and, as a result, *drift downward* to a lower socioeconomic class.

Sociocultural researchers have noted that racial and sexual prejudice and discrimination may also contribute to certain forms of abnormal functioning (Clark et al., 1999). Women in Western society receive diagnoses of anxiety and depressive disorders at least twice as often as men (Gold, 1998; Culbertson et al., 1997). Similarly, African Americans experience unusually high rates of anxiety disorders (Blazer et al., 1991; Eaton, Dryman, & Weissman, 1991). Hispanic persons, particularly young men, have higher rates of alcoholism than members of most other ethnic groups (Helzer, Burnman, & McEvoy, 1991). And Native Americans display exceptionally high alcoholism and suicide rates (Kinzie et al., 1992). Although many factors may combine to produce these differences, racial and sexual prejudice and the problems they pose may contribute to abnormal patterns of tension, unhappiness, low self-esteem, and escape.

SOCIETAL LABELS AND ROLES Sociocultural theorists also believe that abnormal functioning is influenced greatly by the labels and roles assigned to troubled people (Scheff, 1999; Szasz, 1997, 1987, 1963). When people stray from the norms of their society, the society calls them deviant and, in many cases, "mentally ill." Such labels tend to stick. Moreover, when people are viewed in particular ways, reacted to as "crazy," and perhaps even encouraged to act sick, they gradually learn to accept and play the assigned role. Ultimately the label seems appropriate.

A famous study by the clinical investigator David Rosenhan (1973) supports this position. Eight normal people presented themselves at various mental hospitals, complaining that they had been hearing voices say the words "empty," "hollow," and "thud." On the basis of this complaint alone, each was diagnosed as having schizophrenia and admitted. As the sociocultural model would predict, the "pseudopatients" had a hard time convincing others that they were well once

The dysfunctional society *The pressures and uncertainty of living in a war-torn environment may contribute to the development of psychological problems. The environment's ongoing violence may leave some individuals feeling numb and confused. This child seems to hardly notice the burning bombed truck behind him as he bicycles through Northern Ireland.*

PRESSURES OF POVERTY

Each year around 90 of every 1,000 poor persons are victims of violent crime, compared to 50 of every 1,000 middle-income people and 40 of every 1,000 wealthy people (U.S. Bureau of Justice Statistics, 1996).

FAMILY SYSTEMS THEORY A theory that views the family as a system of interacting parts whose interactions exhibit consistent patterns and unstated rules.

THE POWER OF DIAGNOSIS
People who are diagnosed with a mental disorder report having twice as much difficulty obtaining and keeping medical insurance as do people with any other condition, including diabetes and hypertension (Druss & Rosenheck, 1998).

they had been given the diagnostic label. Their hospitalizations ranged from 7 to 52 days, even though they behaved normally as soon as they were admitted. In addition, the label kept influencing the way the staff viewed and dealt with them. For example, one pseudopatient who paced the corridor out of boredom was, in clinical notes, described as "nervous." Finally, the pseudopatients reported that the staff's behavior toward them and other patients was often authoritarian, limited, and counterproductive. Overall, the pseudopatients came to feel powerless, invisible, and bored.

Sociocultural Treatments

Although many clients meet alone with their therapists in *individual therapy,* sociocultural theories have helped spur the growth of other treatment formats and settings. In *group therapy,* therapists meet with a group of clients who all share similar problems. In *family* and *couple therapy,* the therapist and client are joined by other family members. In *community treatment,* the meetings take place in or near the client's everyday environment.

Therapists of any orientation may work with clients in these broad formats, applying the techniques and principles of their preferred models. In such instances the therapy is not purely sociocultural. However, more and more of the clinicians who use these formats believe that psychological problems emerge in a social setting and are best treated in such a setting. In addition, some of these clinicians have developed special sociocultural strategies for use in group, family, couple, and community treatments.

The self-help movement *Thousands of self-help groups around the world help people cope with a variety of problems. Here members of an AIDS support group participate in a group exercise.*

GROUP THERAPY Thousands of therapists specialize in **group therapy**, and countless others run therapy groups as part of a more varied practice. One survey of clinical psychologists, for example, revealed that almost one-third of them devoted some portion of their practice to group therapy (Norcross et al., 1993). Typically, members of a therapy group meet together with a therapist and discuss the problems of one or more of the people in the group. Together they develop important insights, build social skills, strengthen feelings of self-worth, and share useful information or advice (Vinogradov & Yalom, 1994; Yalom, 1985). Many groups are created with particular client populations in mind; for example, there are groups for people with alcoholism, for those who are physically handicapped, and for people who are divorced, abused, or bereaved (Bednar & Kaul, 1994; DeAngelis, 1992).

Research suggests that group therapy is of help to many clients, often as helpful as individual therapy (Bednar & Kaul, 1994; Vinogradov & Yalom, 1994). The group format has also been used for purposes that are educational rather than therapeutic, such as "consciousness raising" and spiritual inspiration.

A format similar to group therapy is the **self-help group** (or **mutual help group**). Here people who have similar problems (bereavement, substance abuse, illness, unemployment, divorce) come together to help and support one another without the direct leadership of a professional clinician (Fehre & White, 1996). These groups have become very popular since the 1970s. Today there are about 500,000 such groups attended by 15 million people in the United States alone. The groups tend to offer more direct advice than is provided in group therapy and to encourage more exchange of information or "tips" (Silverman, 1992).

Self-help groups are popular for several reasons. Some of the members are looking for inexpensive and interesting alternatives to traditional treatment. Others have simply lost confidence in the ability of clinicians to help with their problems (Silverman, 1992). Still other people find self-help groups less threatening than therapy groups. The rise of these groups may also be tied to the decline of family life and other traditional sources of emotional support in Western society (Bloch, Crouch, & Reibstein, 1982).

ConsiderThis

⦿ Interest in self-help groups has grown in recent years. What might be the advantages and disadvantages of these groups in comparison with professional treatment?

FAMILY THERAPY **Family therapy** was first introduced in the 1950s. A therapist meets with all members of a family, points out problem behaviors and interactions, and helps the whole family to change (Glick, 1999; Minuchin, 1997; Bowen, 1960). Here, the entire family is viewed as the unit under treatment, even if only one of the members receives a clinical diagnosis. The following is a typical interaction between family members and a therapist:

> Tommy sat motionless in a chair gazing out the window. He was fourteen and a bit small for his age. . . . Sissy was eleven. She was sitting on the couch between her Mom and Dad with a smile on her face. Across from them sat Ms. Fargo, the family therapist.
>
> Ms. Fargo spoke. "Could you be a little more specific about the changes you have seen in Tommy and when they came about?"
>
> Mrs. Davis answered first. "Well, I guess it was about two years ago. Tommy started getting in fights at school. When we talked to him at home he said it was none of our business. He became moody and disobedient. He wouldn't do anything that we wanted him to. He began to act mean to his sister and even hit her."
>
> "What about the fights at school?" Ms. Fargo asked.
>
> This time it was Mr. Davis who spoke first. "Ginny was more worried about them than I was. I used to fight a lot when I was in school and I think it is normal. . . . But I was very respectful to my parents, especially my Dad. If I ever got out of line he would smack me one."
>
> "Have you ever had to hit Tommy?" Ms. Fargo inquired softly.
>
> "Sure, a couple of times, but it didn't seem to do any good."
>
> All at once Tommy seemed to be paying attention, his eyes riveted on his father. "Yeah, he hit me a lot, for no reason at all!"
>
> "Now, that's not true, Thomas." Mrs. Davis has a scolding expression on her face. "If you behaved yourself a little better you wouldn't get hit. Ms. Fargo, I can't say that I am in favor of the hitting, but I understand sometimes how frustrating it may be for Bob."
>
> "You don't know how frustrating it is for me, honey." Bob seemed upset. "You don't have to work all day at the office and then come home to contend with all of this. Sometimes I feel like I don't even want to come home."
>
> Ginny gave him a hard stare. "You think things at home are easy all day? I could use some support from you. You think all you have to do is earn the money and I will do everything else. Well, I am not about to do that anymore." . . .
>
> Mrs. Davis began to cry. "I just don't know what to do anymore. Things just seem so hopeless. Why can't people be nice in this family anymore? I don't think I am asking too much, am I?"
>
> Ms. Fargo spoke thoughtfully. "I get the feeling that people in this family would like things to be different. Bob, I can see how frustrating it must be for you to work so hard and not be able to relax when you get home. And, Ginny, your job is not easy either. You have a lot to do at home and Bob can't be there to help because he has to earn a living. And you kids sound like you would like some things to be different too. It must be hard for you, Tommy, to be catching so much flack these days. I think this also makes it hard for you to have fun at home too, Sissy."
>
> She looked at each person briefly and was sure to make eye contact. "There seems to be a lot going on. . . . I think we are going to need to understand a lot of things to see why this is happening. . . ."
>
> *(Sheras & Worchel, 1979, pp. 108–110)*

Family therapists may follow any of the major theoretical models, but more and more of them are adopting the sociocultural principles of family systems theory. Today 7 percent of all therapists identify themselves mainly as *family systems therapists* (Prochaska & Norcross, 1994).

ConsiderThis

● In *Anna Karenina* the writer Leo Tolstoy wrote, "All happy families resemble one another; every unhappy family is unhappy in its own fashion." Would family systems theorists agree with Tolstoy? • Why are people so affected by their families?

CHANGING FAMILY, CHANGING PRESSURES

In 60 percent of American families, both spouses now work outside the house, more than double the percentage of several decades ago. Around 56 percent of them cite lack of time and 39 percent cite balancing their personal and professional lives as their biggest challenges (Kate, 1998).

GROUP THERAPY A therapy format in which a group of people with similar problems meet together with a therapist to work on those problems.

SELF-HELP GROUP A group made up of people with similar problems who help and support one another without the direct leadership of a clinician. Also called a *mutual help group*.

FAMILY THERAPY A therapy format in which the therapist meets with all members of a family and helps them to change in therapeutic ways.

As we observed earlier, family systems theory holds that each family has its own rules, structure, and communication patterns that shape the individual members' behavior. In one family systems approach, *structural family therapy*, therapists try to change the family power structure, the roles each person plays, and the alliances between members (Nichols & Minuchin, 1999; Minuchin, 1997, 1987, 1974). In another, *conjoint family therapy*, therapists try to help members recognize and change harmful patterns of communication (Satir, 1987, 1967, 1964).

Family therapies of various kinds can be quite helpful for certain persons and problems. Studies have found that the overall improvement rate for families that undergo such treatments is between 50 and 65 percent, compared to 35 percent for families in control groups (Gurman et al., 1986; Todd & Stanton, 1983). The involvement of the father seems greatly to increase the chances of success.

Shared responsibility *Regardless of the therapist's orientation, individuals in couple therapy are encouraged to recognize and address their own contributions to the relationship.*

COUPLE THERAPY In **couple therapy**, or **marital therapy**, the therapist works with two individuals who are in a long-term relationship. Often they are husband and wife, but the couple need not be married or even living together. Like family therapy, couple therapy often focuses on the structure and communication patterns occurring in the relationship (Nichols & Minuchin, 1999; Baucom et al., 1998). A couple approach may also be employed when a child's psychological problems are traced to problems that may exist between the parents (Fauber & Long, 1992).

Although some degree of conflict exists in any long-term relationship (see Table 3-3), many adults in our society experience serious marital discord (Bradbury & Karney, 1993; Markman & Hahlweg, 1993). The divorce rate in Canada, the United States, and Europe is now close to 50 percent of the marriage rate (NCHS, 2000, 1999). Many couples who live together without marrying apparently have similar levels of difficulty (Greeley, 1991).

Couple therapy, like family and group therapy, may follow the principles of any of the major therapy orientations. *Behavioral couple therapy,* for example, uses many techniques from the behavioral perspective (Cordova & Jacobson, 1993; Jacobson, 1989). Therapists help spouses recognize and change problem behaviors largely by teaching specific problem-solving and communication skills. A broader, more sociocultural version, called *integrative couple therapy*, additionally helps partners accept behaviors that they cannot change and embrace the whole relationship nevertheless (Lawrence et al., 1999; Cordova & Jacobson, 1993). Partners are asked to see such behaviors as an understandable result of basic differences between them.

Couples treated by couple therapy seem to show greater improvement in their relationships than couples with similar problems who fail to receive treatment, but no one form of couple therapy stands out as superior to others (Christensen & Heavy, 1999; Baucom et al., 1998). At the same time, only about half of all treated couples say they are "happily married" at the end of couple therapy. And, according to some studies, as many as 38 percent of successfully treated couples may relapse within two to four years after therapy (Snyder, Wills, & Grady-Fletcher, 1991). Couples who are younger, well adjusted, and less rigid in their gender roles tend to have the best results.

"I've been a cow all my life, honey. Don't ask me to change now."

Table 3-3

Facts about Couples

- ✤ Annual marriage rate in the United States: 51 per 1,000 unmarried women

- ✤ Annual divorce rate in the United States: 20 per 1,000 married women

- ✤ State with highest marriage rate: Nevada

- ✤ State with highest divorce rate: Nevada

- ✤ Countries with highest divorce rates: Maldives and Cuba

- ✤ Countries with lowest divorce rates: Guatemala and Macedonia

- ✤ Percentage of populace admitting to an adulterous relationship: Britons (42 percent), Italians (38 percent), North Americans (24 percent), and Spaniards (22 percent)

- ✤ Most common sources of marital bickering: money (29 percent), television selections (28 percent), time together (21 percent), child discipline (20 percent)

- ✤ Length of silent treatment after a spousal fight: one week (3 percent), one day (21 percent), one hour (31 percent), five minutes (19 percent)

- ✤ Winner of spousal disagreements: neither spouse (47 percent)

- ✤ Ideal marital partner as described by
    American teens: person who is fun, sexy, and rich
    Guatemalan teens: person who likes children

Source: Uretsky, 1999; Kanner, 1998, 1995; *Time*, 1998; *Roper Reports*, 1998; National Center for Health Statistics, 1998; United Nations, 1998; Janus & Janus, 1993.

Is Divorce Too Easy?

According to surveys, almost two-thirds of all adults believe that it should be harder than it is now for married couples with young children to get a divorce (Kirn, 1997).

Community Treatment Following sociocultural principles, **community mental health treatment** programs allow clients, particularly those with severe psychological difficulties, to receive treatment in familiar surroundings as they try to recover. In 1963 President Kennedy called for such a "bold new approach" to the treatment of mental disorders—a community approach that would enable most people with psychological problems to receive services from nearby agencies rather than distant facilities or institutions. Congress passed the Community Mental Health Act soon after, launching the *community mental health movement* across the United States. A number of other countries have launched similar movements.

A key principle of community treatment is *prevention* (Pentz, 1999; Lamb, 1994). Here clinicians actively reach out to clients rather than wait for them to seek treatment. Research suggests that prevention efforts are often very successful (Reppucci, Woolard, & Fried, 1999; Heller, 1996). Community workers recognize three types of prevention, which they call *primary, secondary,* and *tertiary.*

Primary prevention consists of efforts to improve community attitudes and policies. Its goal is to prevent psychological disorders altogether (Burnette, 1996; Martin, 1996). Community workers may lobby for better community recreational programs or child-care facilities, consult with a local school board to help develop a curriculum, or offer health fairs or public workshops on stress reduction.

Secondary prevention consists of identifying and treating psychological disorders in the early stages, before they become serious. Community workers may work with schoolteachers, ministers, or police to help

Community mental health *Hot-line operators at the Women's Crisis Center in Moscow receive calls from victims of domestic violence and set community programs in motion to help the victims and prevent further abuse.*

them recognize the early signs of psychological dysfunction and teach them how to help people find treatment (Newman et al., 1996; Zax & Cowen, 1976, 1969).

The goal of *tertiary prevention* is to provide effective treatment as soon as it is needed so that moderate or severe disorders do not become long-term problems. Today community agencies across the United States do successfully offer tertiary care for millions of people with moderate psychological problems, but, as we observed in Chapter 1, they often fail to provide the services needed by hundreds of thousands with severe disturbances.

Why has the community mental health approach fallen short for so many people with severe disturbances? As we shall see in later chapters, one of the major reasons is lack of funding. In 1981, when only 750 of the planned 2,000 community mental health centers were in place across the United States, almost all federal funding was withdrawn and replaced with smaller financial grants to the states (Humphreys & Rappaport, 1993). Whether or not this trend will continue in the twenty-first century depends on how health care is reformed (Kiesler, 1992) and on how states spend the hundreds of millions of dollars saved by the closing of large state hospitals (Torrey, 1997).

Assessing the Sociocultural Model

The sociocultural model has added greatly to the understanding and treatment of abnormal functioning. Today most clinicians take family, social, and societal issues into account, factors that were overlooked just 30 years ago (Tamplin, Goodyer, & Herbert, 1998; NAMHC, 1996). In addition, clinicians have become more aware of the impact of clinical and social labels. Finally, as we have just observed, sociocultural treatment formats sometimes succeed where traditional approaches have failed (Heller, 1996).

At the same time, the sociocultural model, like the other models, has certain problems. To begin with, sociocultural research findings are often difficult to interpret. Research may reveal a relationship between certain sociocultural factors and a particular disorder, yet fail to establish that they are its *cause*. Studies show a link between family conflict and schizophrenia, for example, but that finding does not necessarily mean that family dysfunction causes schizophrenia (Miklowitz et al., 1995; Velligan et al., 1995). It is equally possible that family functioning is disrupted by the tension and conflict created by the schizophrenic behavior of a family member (Eakes, 1995).

Another limitation of the model is its inability to predict abnormality in specific individuals (Reynolds, 1998). For example, if societal conditions such as prejudice and discrimination are key causes of anxiety and depression, why do only some of the people subjected to such forces experience psychological disorders? Are still other factors necessary for the development of the disorders?

Given these limitations, most clinicians view sociocultural explanations as operating in conjunction with biological or psychological explanations. They agree that sociocultural factors may create a climate favorable to the development of certain disorders. They believe, however, that biological or psychological conditions or both must also be present in order for the disorders to evolve.

Modern "mass madness"? *Some sociocultural theorists believe that intense social stressors may produce outbreaks of "mass madness" such as the Los Angeles riots of 1992. In a vicious cycle, the riots, which occurred against a backdrop of poverty, unemployment, and prejudice, produced further stress for members of the community, such as Joe and Joyce Wilson, who survey the damage to their business, Pop's Restaurant.*

> **ALTERNATIVE "TREATMENT"**
>
> It is estimated that jails across the United States admit 700,000 people with severe mental disorders each year. The daily cost of jail is $137 per inmate; the daily cost of community mental health treatment is $60 per patient (Treatment Advocacy Center, 1999; U.S. Public Health Service, 1999).

CROSSROADS:
Integration of the Models

Today's leading models vary widely (see Table 3-4). They look at behavior differently, begin with different assumptions, arrive at different conclusions, and apply different treatments. Yet none of the models has proved consistently superior. Each helps us appreciate a key aspect of human functioning, and each has important strengths as well as serious limitations.

Table 3-4

Comparing the Models

	BIOLOGICAL	PSYCHODYNAMIC	BEHAVIORAL	COGNITIVE	HUMANISTIC	EXISTENTIAL	SOCIO-CULTURAL
Cause of dysfunction	Biological malfunction	Underlying conflicts	Maladaptive learning	Maladaptive thinking	Self-deceit	Avoidance of responsibility	Family or social stress
Research support	Strong	Modest	Strong	Strong	Weak	Weak	Moderate
Consumer designation	Patient	Patient	Client	Client	Patient or client	Patient or client	Client
Therapist role	Doctor	Interpreter	Teacher	Persuader	Observer	Collaborator	Social facilitator
Key therapist technique	Biological intervention	Free association and interpretation	Conditioning	Reasoning	Reflection	Varied	Social inter-vention
Therapy goal	Biological repair	Broad psychological change	Functional behaviors	Adaptive thinking	Self-actualization	Authentic life	Effective family or social system

With all their differences, the conclusions and techniques of the different models are often compatible (Friman et al., 1993). Certainly our understanding and treatment of abnormal behavior are more complete if we appreciate the biological, psychological, *and* sociocultural aspects of a person's problem rather than only one of them (Sabo, 1999). Not surprisingly, then, a growing number of clinicians are formulating explanations of abnormal behavior that consider more than one kind of cause at a time. These explanations, sometimes called **biopsychosocial theories**, state that abnormality results from the interaction of genetic, biological, developmental, emotional, behavioral, cognitive, social, *and* societal influences. If so, the task facing researchers and clinicians is to identify the relative importance of each factor and learn how the factors work together to produce abnormal functioning. A case of depression, for example, might best be explained by pointing collectively to an individual's inheritance of unfavorable genes, traumatic losses during childhood, negative ways of thinking, and social isolation.

Some biopsychosocial theorists favor a **diathesis-stress explanation** of how the various factors work together to cause abnormal functioning ("diathesis" means a vulnerability or a predisposed tendency). According to this theory, people must first have a biological, psychological, or sociocultural predisposition to develop a disorder and must then be subjected to episodes of severe stress. In a case of depression, for example, we might find that unfavorable genes and related biochemical abnormalities predispose the individual to develop the disorder, while the loss of a loved one actually triggers its onset.

Other biopsychosocial theorists favor a **reciprocal effects explanation** of abnormal functioning. They believe that some key factors help produce abnormal functioning by influencing other key factors—that is, by increasing the likelihood or intensity of the other factors (Saudino et al., 1997; Kendler et al., 1995). Say, for example, a man inherits a genetic tendency to be timid and awkward. Because of his timidity and awkwardness, this individual may accept unpleasant partners in his life more readily than most other people would, thus increasing his chances of experiencing stressful relationships, breakups, or periods of isolation in his life—each a factor conducive to depression. In addition, his experiences of interpersonal stress may lower his serotonin activity, another factor conducive to

BIOPSYCHOSOCIAL THEORIES Explanations that explain abnormality as resulting from an interaction of genetic, biological, developmental, emotional, behavioral, cognitive, social, and societal influences.

DIATHESIS-STRESS EXPLANATION The view that a person must first have a predisposition to a disorder and then be subjected to episodes of severe stress in order to develop the disorder.

RECIPROCAL EFFECTS EXPLANATION The view that key factors produce abnormality by increasing the likelihood or intensity of other key factors.

depression. In short, by profoundly affecting each other, a variety of relevant factors may collectively drive an individual toward depression.

In a similar quest for integration, many therapists are now combining treatment techniques from several different models (Norcross, Beutler, & Clarkin, 1998). In fact, 38 percent of today's clinical practitioners describe their approach as "eclectic." Studies confirm that clinical problems often respond better to combined approaches than to any one therapy alone (Glass et al., 1998; Beitman, 1996, 1993; Seligman, 1994). For example, as we shall see, drug therapy combined with cognitive therapy is sometimes the most effective treatment for depression (Keller, 1999).

Given the recent rise in biopsychosocial theories and combination treatments, our examination of abnormal behavior throughout this book will take a particular direction. Of course, as different disorders are presented, we will look at how today's models explain each disorder, how clinicians who adhere to each model treat people with the disorder, and how well these explanations and treatments are supported by research. Just as important, however, we will also be observing how the explanations and treatments may build upon and strengthen each other, and, whenever relevant, we will examine current efforts toward integration of the models.

SUMMARY AND REVIEW

- **Models of psychological abnormality** Scientists and clinicians use models, or paradigms, to understand and treat abnormal behavior. The principles and techniques of treatment used by clinical practitioners correspond to their preferred models. *pp. 45–47*

- **The biological model** Biological theorists look at the biological processes of human functioning to explain abnormal behavior, pointing to anatomical or biochemical problems in the brain and body. Such abnormalities are sometimes the result of genetic inheritance. Biological therapists use physical and chemical methods to help people overcome their psychological problems. The leading ones are drug therapy, electroconvulsive therapy, and, on rare occasions, psychosurgery. *pp. 47–52*

- **The psychodynamic model** Psychodynamic theorists believe that an individual's behavior, whether normal or abnormal, is determined by underlying psychological forces. They consider psychological conflicts to be rooted in early parent-child relationships and traumatic experiences. The psychodynamic model was formulated by Sigmund Freud, who said that three dynamic forces—the id, ego, and superego—interact to produce thought, feeling, and behavior. Other psychodynamic theories are ego theory, self theory, and object relations theory. Psychodynamic therapists help people uncover past traumas and the inner conflicts that have resulted from them. They use a number of techniques, including free association and interpretations of psychological phenomena such as resistance, transference, and dreams. *pp. 52–59*

- **The behavioral model** Behaviorists concentrate on behaviors and propose that they develop in accordance with the principles of learning. These theorists hold that three types of conditioning—classical conditioning, operant conditioning, and modeling—account for all behavior, whether normal or dysfunctional. The goal of the behavioral therapies is to identify the client's problematic behaviors and replace them with more appropriate ones, using techniques based on one or more of the principles of learning. The classical conditioning approach of systematic desensitization, for example, has been effective in treating phobias. *pp. 59–63*

- **The cognitive model** According to the cognitive model, we must understand human thought to understand human behavior. When people display abnor-

Genetic vs. Congenital

The terms "genetic" and "congenital" both come from the Greek for "birth." Genetic defects are inherited, determined at the moment of conception, and can be passed down to other generations. Congenital defects—defects with which a child is born—are not inherited; they develop after conception, during the gestation period (Johnsen, 1994).

mal patterns of functioning, cognitive theorists point to cognitive problems, such as maladaptive assumptions and illogical thinking processes. Cognitive therapists try to help people recognize and change their faulty ideas and thinking processes. Among the most widely used cognitive treatments is Beck's cognitive therapy. *pp. 63–66*

■ **The humanistic-existential model** The humanistic-existential model focuses on the human need to successfully confront philosophical issues such as self-awareness, values, meaning, and choice in order to be satisfied in life.

Humanists believe that people are driven to self-actualize. When this drive is interfered with, abnormal behavior may result. One group of humanistic therapists, client-centered therapists, try to create a very supportive therapy climate in which people can look at themselves honestly and acceptingly, thus opening the door to self-actualization. Another group, gestalt therapists, use more active techniques to help people recognize and accept their needs.

According to existentialists, abnormal behavior is the result of a person's hiding from life's responsibilities. Existential therapists encourage people to accept responsibility for their lives, to recognize their freedom to choose a different course, and to choose to live with greater meaning. *pp. 66–71*

■ **The sociocultural model** The sociocultural model looks outward to the social forces that affect members of a society. Some sociocultural theorists emphasize the family system, believing that a family's structure or communication patterns may force members to behave in abnormal ways. Others look at social networks and support, and still others examine societal conditions to see what special stresses they may pose. Finally, some theorists focus on societal labels and roles; they hold that society calls certain people "mentally ill" and that the label itself may influence how a person behaves and is responded to.

Sociocultural principles are often applied in such therapy formats as group, family, and couple therapy. Research indicates that these formats are useful for some problems and under some circumstances. In community treatment, therapists try to work with people in settings close to home, school, and work. Their goal is either primary, secondary, or tertiary prevention. *pp. 71–78*

> "Creative minds always have been known to survive any kind of bad training."
>
> Anna Freud

A NEW FAMILY CONSTELLATION
Twenty-six percent of today's families are headed by a single parent, compared to 2 percent 50 years ago (Stacey, 1996; NCHS, 1995).

CYBER STUDY

▲ *Observe the biological, psychodynamic, and sociocultural models in action.* ▲ *See how treatments vary.* ▲ *How have biological treatments improved over the years?* ▲ *Are dreams the "royal road to the unconscious?"*

SEARCH THE *ABNORMAL PSYCHOLOGY* CD-ROM FOR

▲ Chapter 3 video cases and discussions
   Early Electroconvulsive Therapies
   "Larry"—Psychoanalytic Therapy Session
   "Jim"—Treating Drug Addiction: A Behavioral Approach

▲ Chapter 3 practice test and feedback

▲ Additional video cases and discussions
   "Meredith"—Mood Disorders: Medication and Talk Therapy
   "Walter"—Alzheimer's Disease

LOG ON TO THE COMER WEB PAGE

[www.worthpublishers.com/comerabnormalpsychology4e] **FOR**

▲ Suggested Web links, research exercises, FAQ page, additional Chapter 3 practice test questions

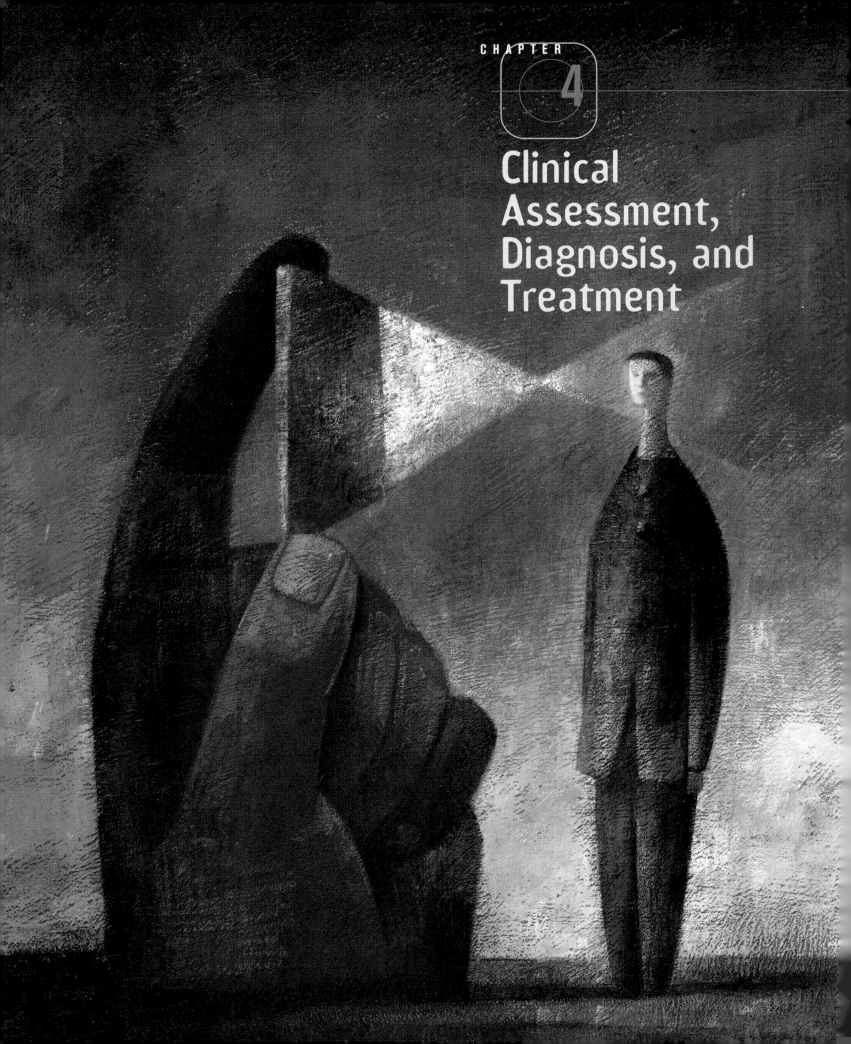

Clinical Assessment, Diagnosis, and Treatment

Angela Savanti was 22 years old, lived at home with her mother, and was employed as a secretary in a large insurance company. She . . . had had passing periods of "the blues" before, but her present feelings of despondency were of much greater proportion. She was troubled by a severe depression and frequent crying spells, which had not lessened over the past two months. Angela found it hard to concentrate on her job, had great difficulty falling asleep at night, and had a poor appetite. . . . Her depression had begun after she and her boyfriend Jerry broke up two months previously.

(Leon, 1984, p. 109)

Her feelings of despondency led Angela Savanti to make an appointment with a therapist at a local counseling center. The first step the clinician took was to learn as much as possible about Angela and her disturbance. Who is she, what is her life like, and what precisely are her symptoms? The answers might help to reveal the causes and probable course of her present dysfunction and suggest what kinds of strategies would be most likely to help her. Treatment could then be tailored to Angela's needs and particular pattern of abnormal functioning.

In Chapters 2 and 3 we saw how researchers in abnormal psychology build a *nomothetic*, or general, understanding of abnormal functioning. Clinical practitioners apply this general information in their work, but their main focus when faced with a new client is to compile **idiographic**, or individual, information about the person. To help a particular client overcome his or her problems, a practitioner must have the fullest possible understanding of that person and know the circumstances under which the problems arose (Tucker, 1998). Only after thoroughly examining the person can the therapist effectively apply relevant nomothetic information. Clinicians use the procedures of *assessment* and *diagnosis* to gather individual information about a client. Then they are in a position to apply *treatment*.

Clinical Assessment: How and Why Does the Client Behave Abnormally?

Assessment is simply the collecting of relevant information in an effort to reach a conclusion. It goes on in every realm of life. We make assessments when we decide what cereal to buy or which presidential candidate to vote for. College admissions officers, who have to select the "best" of the students applying to their college, depend on academic records, recommendations, achievement test scores, interviews, and application forms to help them decide. Employers, who have to predict which applicants are most likely to be effective workers, collect information from résumés, interviews, references, and perhaps on-the-job observations.

Clinical assessment is used to determine how and why a person is behaving abnormally and how that person may be helped (see Box 4-1 on the next page). It also enables clinicians to evaluate people's progress after they

ConsiderThis

◉ Many people argue for a "people-first" approach to clinical labeling, recommending, for example, the phrase "a person with schizophrenia" rather than "a schizophrenic" (Foderaro, 1995). Why might this approach to labeling be preferable?

have been in treatment for a while and decide whether the treatment should be changed. The specific tools that are used to do an assessment depend on the clinician's theoretical orientation (Needleman, 1999; Smith, 1998). Psychodynamic clinicians, for example, use methods that assess a client's personality and probe for any unconscious conflicts he or she may be experiencing. This kind of assessment, called a *personality assessment*, enables them to piece together a clinical picture in accordance with the principles of their model. Behavioral and cognitive clinicians are more likely to use assessment methods that reveal specific dysfunctional behaviors and cognitions. The goal of this kind of assessment, called a *behavioral assessment*, is to produce a *functional analysis* of the person's behaviors—an analysis of how the behaviors are learned and reinforced (Haynes & O'Brien, 2000).

The hundreds of clinical assessment techniques and tools that have been developed fall into three categories: *clinical interviews*, *tests*, and *observations*. To be useful, these tools must be *standardized* and have clear *reliability* and *validity*.

Characteristics of Assessment Tools

In order to get meaningful results, all clinicians must follow the same procedures when using a particular technique of assessment. To **standardize** a technique is to set up common steps to be followed whenever it is administered. Similarly, clinicians must standardize the way they interpret the results of an assessment tool in order to be able to understand what a particular score means. They may standardize the scores of a test, for example, by first administering it to a group of subjects whose performance will then serve as a common standard, or norm, against which later individual scores can be measured. The group that initially takes the test is called the *standardization sample*. This sample must be typical of

BOX **4-1**

Assessing Van Gogh

Vincent van Gogh, a self-portrait

Vincent van Gogh led a tortured and unhappy life. In a legendary incident the artist cut off one of his ears. Later he was admitted to a mental institution, and ultimately he committed suicide. Van Gogh wrote a great deal about his pain and anguish, describing mental and physical torment and hallucinations. For years clinicians have speculated that van Gogh suffered from a mood disorder, schizophrenia, or both (Hershman & Lieb, 1998). Recently, however, these assessments have been challenged (Rosenfeld, 1998).

ConsiderThis

◉ Would people react to van Gogh's work differently if they thought of him as having had an ear disorder rather than a psychological disorder? • Why do people find it fascinating to assess famous people, particularly those in the arts, long after their death?

A Harvard neurologist has suggested that van Gogh in fact suffered from *Geschwind's syndrome*, technically known as *interictal personality disorder*, caused by brain seizure disorder, or epilepsy. Van Gogh displayed many of its symptoms, including excessive drawing (hypergraphia), hyperreligiosity, and aggression (Trotter, 1985).

In contrast, medical specialists in Colorado have concluded that van Gogh suffered from an extreme form of *Menière's syndrome*, a disorder marked by an excessive buildup of fluid in the inner ear. The enormous pressure may produce nausea, dizziness, poor balance, pain, deafness, and constant buzzing or ringing sensations. Perhaps van Gogh cut off his ear in an effort to reduce the pain. And perhaps his other problems and pains arose from the severe secondary psychological problems that can accompany Menière's syndrome (Scott, 1990).

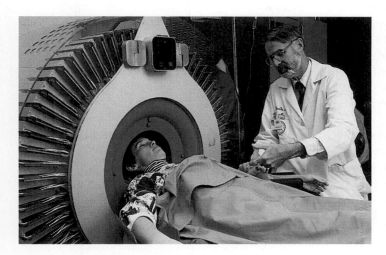

The PET scan *Elaborate biological tests such as positron emission tomography (PET) help detect abnormal brain activity that may be causing psychological problems.*

Oops! *These judges of a high school diving competition, actually coaches from the opposing teams, arrive at very different assessments of the same diver. The low interrater reliability may reflect evaluator bias or defects in the scoring procedure.*

the larger population the test is intended for. If an aggressiveness test meant for the public at large were standardized on a group of marines, for example, the resulting "norm" might turn out to be misleadingly high.

Reliability refers to the *consistency* of assessment measures. A good assessment tool will always yield the same results in the same situation (Exner, 1999; Kline, 1993). An assessment tool has high *test–retest reliability*, one kind of reliability, if it yields the same results every time it is given to the same people. If a woman's responses on a particular test indicate that she is generally a heavy drinker, the test should produce the same result when she takes it again a week later. To measure test–retest reliability, subjects are tested on two occasions and the two scores are correlated. The higher the correlation, the greater the test's reliability (see Chapter 2).

An assessment tool shows high *interrater* (or *interjudge*) *reliability*, another kind of reliability, if different judges independently agree on how to score and interpret it. True–false and multiple-choice tests yield consistent scores no matter who evaluates them, but other tests require that the evaluator make a judgment. Consider a test that requires the person to draw a copy of a picture, which a judge then rates for accuracy. Different judges may give different ratings to the same drawing.

Finally, an assessment tool must have **validity**: it must *accurately* measure what it is supposed to be measuring (Haynes, Nelson, & Blaine, 1999; Kline, 1993). Suppose a weight scale reads 12 pounds every time a 10-pound bag of sugar is placed on it. Although the scale is reliable because its readings are consistent, those readings are not valid, or accurate.

A given assessment tool may appear to be valid simply because it makes sense and seems reasonable. However, this sort of validity, called *face validity*, does not by itself mean that the instrument is trustworthy. A test for depression, for example, might include questions about how often a person cries. Because it makes sense that depressed people would cry, these test questions would have face validity. It turns out, however, that many people cry a great deal for reasons other than depression, and some extremely depressed people fail to cry at all. Thus an assessment tool should not be used unless it meets more exacting criteria of validity, such as high predictive or concurrent validity (Goodwin, 1995).

Predictive validity is a tool's ability to predict future characteristics or behavior. Let us say that a test has been developed to identify elementary school children who are likely to take up cigarette smoking in junior high school. The test gathers information about the children's parents—their personal characteristics, smoking habits, and attitudes toward smoking—and on that basis identifies high-risk children. To establish the test's predictive validity, we could administer it to a

IDIOGRAPHIC UNDERSTANDING An understanding of the behavior of a particular individual.

ASSESSMENT The process of collecting and interpreting relevant information about a client or subject.

STANDARDIZATION The process in which a test is administered to a large group of persons whose performance then serves as a common standard or norm against which any individual's score can be measured.

RELIABILITY A measure of the consistency of test or research results.

VALIDITY The accuracy of a test's or study's results; that is, the extent to which the test or study actually measures or shows what it claims.

group of elementary school students, wait until they were in junior high school, and then check to see which children actually did become smokers.

Concurrent validity is the degree to which the measures obtained from one tool agree with measures obtained from other assessment techniques. Subjects' scores on a new test designed to measure anxiety, for example, should correlate highly with their scores on other anxiety tests or with their behavior during clinical interviews.

Before any assessment technique can be fully useful, it must meet the requirements of standardization, reliability, and validity (Haynes et al., 1999). No matter how insightful or clever a technique may be, clinicians cannot profitably use its results if they are uninterpretable, inconsistent, or inaccurate. Unfortunately, more than a few clinical assessment tools fall short, suggesting that at least some clinical assessments, too, miss their mark.

Clinical Interviews

Most of us feel instinctively that the best way to get to know people is to meet with them face to face. Under these circumstances, we can see them react to what we do and say, observe as well as listen as they answer, watch them observing us, and generally get a sense of who they are. A **clinical interview** is just such a face-to-face encounter (Hersen & Van Hasselt, 1998). If during a clinical interview a man looks as happy as can be while describing his sadness over the recent death of his mother, the clinician may suspect that the man actually has conflicting emotions about this loss. Almost all practitioners use interviews as part of the assessment process.

CONDUCTING THE INTERVIEW The interview is often the first contact between client and clinician. Clinicians use it to collect detailed information about the person's problems and feelings, lifestyle and relationships, and personal history. They may also ask about the person's expectations of therapy and motives for seeking it. The clinician who worked with Angela Savanti began with a face-to-face interview:

> Angela was dressed neatly when she appeared for her first interview. She was attractive, but her eyes were puffy and ringed with dark circles. She answered questions and related information about her life history in a slow, flat tone of voice, which had an impersonal quality to it. She sat stiffly in her chair. . . .
>
> The client stated that the time period just before she and her boyfriend terminated their relationship had been one of extreme emotional turmoil. She was not sure whether she wanted to marry Jerry, and he began to demand that she decide either one way or the other. Mrs. Savanti [Angela's mother] did not seem to like Jerry and was very cold and aloof whenever he came to the house. Angela felt caught in the middle and unable to make a decision about her future. After several confrontations with Jerry over whether she would marry him or not, he told her he felt that she would never decide, so he was not going to see her anymore. . . .
>
> Angela stated that her childhood was a very unhappy period. Her father was seldom home, and when he was present, her parents fought constantly. . . . Sometimes after an argument, Mrs. Savanti told her daughters that she had ruined her life by marrying their father. . . .
>
> Angela recalled feeling very guilty when Mr. Savanti left. . . . She revealed that whenever she thought of her father, she always felt that she had been responsible in some way for his leaving the family. . . .
>
> Angela described her mother as the "long-suffering type" who said that she had sacrificed her life to make her children happy, and the only thing she ever got in return was grief and unhappiness. Angela related that her mother rarely smiled or laughed and did not converse very much with the girls. . . . When Angela and [her sister] began dating, Mrs. Savanti . . . commented on how tired she

CLINICAL INTERVIEW A face-to-face encounter in which clinicians ask questions of clients, weigh their responses and reactions, and learn about them and their psychological problems.

MENTAL STATUS EXAM A set of interview questions and observations designed to reveal the degree and nature of a client's abnormal functioning.

ConsiderThis

was because she had waited up for them. She would make disparaging remarks about the boys they had been with and about men in general. . . .

Angela revealed that she had often been troubled with depressed moods. During high school, if she got a lower grade in a subject than she had expected, her initial response was one of anger, followed by depression. She began to think that she was not smart enough to get good grades, and she blamed herself for studying too little. Angela also became despondent when she got into an argument with her mother or felt that she was being taken advantage of at work. . . .

The intensity and duration of the [mood change] that she experienced when she broke up with Jerry were much more severe. She was not sure why she was so depressed, but she began to feel it was an effort to walk around and go out to work. Talking with others became difficult. Angela found it hard to concentrate, and she began to forget things she was supposed to do. . . . She preferred to lie in bed rather than be with anyone, and she often cried when alone.

(Leon, 1984, pp. 110–115)

Beyond gathering basic background data of this kind, clinical interviewers give special attention to whatever topics they consider most important. Psychodynamic interviewers try to learn about the person's needs and memories of past events and relationships (Shea, 1990; Pope, 1983). Behavioral interviewers have an acronym, SORC, for the kinds of information they need to gather in order to do a functional analysis: relevant information about the *stimuli* that trigger the abnormal functioning; about the *organism*, or person; about the precise nature of the abnormal *responses*; and about the *consequences* of those responses (Reyna, 1989). Cognitive interviewers try to discover assumptions and interpretations that influence the person (Kendall, 1990). Humanistic clinicians ask about the person's self-evaluation and self-concept (Aiken, 1985; Brown, 1972). Biological clinicians look for signs of biochemical or neurological dysfunction. And sociocultural interviewers ask about the family, social, and cultural environments.

Interviews can have either an unstructured or a structured format (Plante, 1999; First et al., 1995). In an *unstructured interview*, the clinician asks open-ended questions, perhaps as simple as "Would you tell me about yourself?" The lack of structure allows the interviewer to follow interesting leads and explore relevant topics that could not be anticipated before the interview.

In a *structured interview*, clinicians ask prepared questions. Sometimes they use a published *interview schedule*—a standard set of questions designed for all interviews (Vacc & Juhnke, 1997). Many structured interviews include a **mental status exam**, a set of questions and observations that systematically evaluate the client's awareness, orientation with regard to time and place, attention span, memory, judgment and insight, thought content and processes, mood, and appearance (Nicholi, 1999). A structured format ensures that clinicians will cover the same kinds of important issues in all their interviews and enables them to compare the responses of different individuals.

Although most clinical interviews have both unstructured and structured portions, many clinicians favor one kind over the other (Nietzel et al., 1994). Unstructured interviews typically appeal to pschodynamic and humanistic clinicians (Pope, 1983). Structured formats are widely used by behavioral clinicians, who need to do a systematic review of a person's behaviors (Pope, 1983). They are also popular among cognitive interviewers, who need to pinpoint attitudes or thinking processes that may underlie abnormal behavior.

"So, Mr. Fenton, . . . Let's begin with your mother."

The structured interview *In a structured interview, clinicians gather information by asking a set of standard questions regardless of the client's particular symptoms.* (The Far Side © Farworks, Inc. Reprinted with permission of Universal Press Syndicate. All rights reserved.)

WHAT ARE THE LIMITATIONS OF CLINICAL INTERVIEWS? Although interviews often produce valuable information about people (Girón et al., 1998), there are limits to what they can accomplish. One problem is the potential lack of validity, or accuracy, of this assessment technique. Individuals may intentionally mislead in order to present themselves in a positive light or to avoid discussing embarrassing topics (Plante, 1999; Barker et al., 1994). Or they may be *unable* to give an accurate report. People who suffer from depression, for example, are unduly pessimistic in their judgments, often describing themselves as incompetent at work or inadequate as parents when that isn't the case at all (Beck, 1997, 1991, 1967).

Interviewers too may make mistakes in judgments that slant the information they gather. They usually rely too heavily on first impressions, for example, and give too much weight to unfavorable information about a client (Meehl, 1996, 1960; Aiken, 1985). Interviewer biases, including gender, race, and age biases, may also influence the interviewers' interpretations of what a client says (Plante, 1999; Edelstein & Semenchuk, 1996).

Interviews, particularly unstructured ones, may also lack reliability (Teare et al., 1999). People respond differently to different interviewers, providing less information to a cold interviewer than to a warm and supportive one (Eisenthal, Koopman, & Lazare, 1983). Similarly, a clinician's race, sex, age, and appearance may influence a client's responses (Paurohit, Dowd, & Cottingham, 1982).

Because different clinicians can obtain different answers and draw different conclusions, even when they ask the same questions of the same person (Langwieler & Linden, 1993), some researchers believe that interviewing should be discarded as a tool of clinical assessment. This might be a reasonable suggestion if there were any problem-free techniques to use instead. As we shall see, however, the two other kinds of clinical assessment methods also have serious limitations.

Clinical Tests

Tests are devices for gathering information about a few aspects of a person's psychological functioning, from which broader information about the person can be inferred (Watkins & Campbell, 2000; Goldstein & Hersen, 1990). This form of assessment can often reveal subtle information that might not become apparent during an interview or observation. On the surface, it may look easy to design an effective test. Every month, magazines and newspapers present new tests purporting to tell us about our personalities, our relationships, our sex lives, our reactions to stress, our ability to succeed. Such tests might sound convincing, but most of them lack reliability, validity, and standardization. That is, they do not yield consistent, accurate information or say anything meaningful about where we stand in comparison with others.

More than 500 different clinical tests are currently in use throughout the United States. The ones that clinicians find most useful and employ most frequently are of six kinds: *projective tests, personality inventories, response inventories, psychophysiological tests, neurological and neuropsychological tests,* and *intelligence tests.*

PROJECTIVE TESTS **Projective tests** require that subjects interpret vague stimuli, such as inkblots or ambiguous pictures, or follow open-ended instructions such as "Draw a person." Theoretically, when stimuli and instructions are so vague, subjects will "project" aspects of their personality into the task, responding in ways that reveal their inner needs and fears. Projective tests are used primarily by psychodynamic clinicians to help assess the unconscious drives and conflicts they believe to be at the root of abnormal functioning (Sugarman & Kanner, 2000; Lerner, 1998). The most widely used projective tests are the *Rorschach test*, the *Thematic Apperception Test*, *sentence-completion tests*, and *drawings*.

RORSCHACH TEST In 1911 Hermann Rorschach, a Swiss psychiatrist, experimented with the use of inkblots in his clinical work. He made thousands of blots by dropping ink on paper and then folding the paper in half to create a symmetrical but wholly accidental design, such as the one shown in Figure 4-1.

Rorschach found that everyone saw images in these blots. In addition, the images a viewer saw seemed to correspond in important ways with his or her psychological condition. People diagnosed with schizophrenia, for example, tended to see images that differed from those described by people with anxiety disorders.

Rorschach selected ten inkblots and published them in 1921 with instructions for their use in assessment. This set was called the *Rorschach Psychodynamic Inkblot Test*. Rorschach died just eight months later, at the age of 37, but his work was continued by others, and his inkblots took their place among the most widely used projective tests of the twentieth century.

Clinicians administer the "Rorschach," as it is commonly called, by presenting one inkblot card at a time and asking respondents what they see, what the inkblot seems to be, or what it reminds them of. In the following exchange, a tense 32-year-old woman who complains of feeling unworthy and lacking in confidence responds to one Rorschach inkblot:

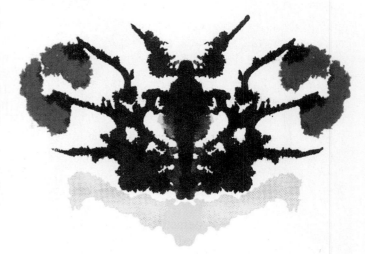

FIGURE 4-1 **An inkblot similar to those used in the Rorschach test**

> *Subject:* Oh, dear! My goodness! O.K. Just this [upper] part is a bug. Something like an ant—one of the social group which is a worker, trying to pull something. I think this is some kind of food for the rest of the ants. It's a bee because it has wings, a worker bee bringing up something edible for the rest of the clan. . . . Here is the bee, the mouth and the wings. I don't think bees eat leaves but it looks like a leaf or a piece of lettuce.
>
> *Clinician:* What makes it look like a piece of lettuce?
>
> *Subject:* Its shape and it has a vein up the middle. It is definitely a bee.
>
> *(Klopfer & Davidson, 1962, p. 164)*

In the early years, Rorschach testers paid special attention to the ideas and images that the inkblots evoked, called the *thematic content*. Testers now also pay attention to the *style* of the responses: Do the subjects view the design as a whole or see specific details? Do they focus on the blots or on the white spaces between them? Do they use or do they ignore the shadings and colors in several of the cards? Do they see human movement in the designs, or animal movement? Here is how the clinician interpreted the bug responses of the woman quoted above:

> The bee may reflect the image she has of herself as a hard worker (a fact noted by her supervisor). In addition, the "bee bringing up something edible for the rest of the clan" suggests that she feels an overwhelming sense of responsibility toward others.
>
> This card frequently evokes both masculine and feminine sexual associations, either in direct or symbolic form. Apparently [this woman] is not able to handle such material comfortably either overtly or in a more socialized manner, and so both sexual symbols are replaced by the oral symbolism of providing food.
>
> *(Klopfer & Davidson, 1962, pp. 182–183)*

BELIEVE IT OR NOT

By a strange coincidence, Hermann Rorschach's young schoolmates gave him the nickname Klex, a variant on the German *Klecks*, which means "inkblot" (Schwartz, 1993).

THEMATIC APPERCEPTION TEST The *Thematic Apperception Test (TAT)* is a pictorial projective test (Murray, 1938; Morgan & Murray, 1935). People who take the TAT are commonly shown thirty black-and-white pictures of individuals in unspecified situations and are asked to make up a dramatic story about each card. They must tell what is happening in the picture, what led up to it, what the characters are feeling and thinking, and what the outcome of the situation will be.

Clinicians who use the TAT believe that the respondents always identify with one of the characters on each card, called the *hero*. The stories are thought to reflect the respondents' own circumstances, needs, emotions, and sense of reality

TEST A device for gathering information about a few aspects of a person's psychological functioning from which broader information about the person can be inferred.

PROJECTIVE TEST A test consisting of ambiguous material that people interpret or respond to.

FIGURE 4-2 **A picture used in the Thematic Apperception Test**

and fantasy. For example, a female client seems to be revealing her own feelings in this story about the TAT picture shown in Figure 4-2, one of the few TAT pictures permitted for display in textbooks:

> This is a woman who has been quite troubled by memories of a mother she was resentful toward. She has feelings of sorrow for the way she treated her mother, her memories of her mother plague her. These feelings seem to be increasing as she grows older and sees her children treating her the same way that she treated her mother.
>
> *(Aiken, 1985, p. 372)*

SENTENCE-COMPLETION TEST The *sentence-completion test*, first developed in the 1920s (Payne, 1928), asks people to complete a series of unfinished sentences, such as "I wish _____" or "My father _____." The test is considered a good springboard for discussion and a quick and easy way to pinpoint topics to explore.

DRAWINGS On the assumption that a drawing tells us something about its creator, clinicians often ask clients to draw human figures and talk about them. Evaluations of these drawings are based on the details and shape of the drawing, solidity of the pencil line, location of the drawing on the paper, size of the figures, features of the figures, use of background, and comments made by the respondent during the drawing task.

The *Draw-a-Person (DAP) Test* is the most popular of the drawing tests (Machover, 1949). Subjects are first told to draw "a person"; that done, they are told to draw another person of the opposite sex. Some clinicians hold that a disproportionately large or small head may indicate problems in intellectual functioning, social behavior, or control of body impulses and that big eyes may indicate high levels of suspiciousness.

WHAT ARE THE MERITS OF PROJECTIVE TESTS? Until the 1950s, projective tests were the most common technique for assessing personality. In recent years, however, clinicians and researchers have relied on them largely to gain "supplementary" insights (Westen, Feit, & Zittel, 1999; Clark, 1995). One reason for this shift is that practitioners who follow the newer models have less use for the tests than psychodynamic clinicians do (Kline, 1993). Even more important, the tests have rarely demonstrated impressive reliability or validity (Halperin & McKay, 1998; Wood et al., 1996; Weiner, 1995).

In reliability studies, different clinicians have tended to score the same person's projective test quite differently (Plante, 1999; Little & Shneidman, 1959). Standardized procedures for administering and scoring the tests have been developed and might improve the consistency of the results if all practitioners used them (Weiner, 1999, 1998; Exner, 1997, 1993), but the procedures have been slow to gain universal acceptance.

Research has also challenged the validity of projective tests. When clinicians try to describe a client's personality and feelings on the basis of responses to projective tests, their conclusions often fail to match those of the client's psychotherapist or those gathered from an extensive case history (Golden, 1964; Sines, 1959). Another validity problem is that projective tests are sometimes biased against minority ethnic groups (Dana, 1999). For example, people are supposed to identify with the characters in the Thematic Apperception Test (TAT) when they make up stories about them, yet no members of minority groups are in the TAT pictures. In response to this problem, some clinicians have

Drawing test *Drawing tests are commonly used to assess the functioning of children. Two popular tests are the House-Tree-Person test, in which subjects draw a house, tree, and person; and the Kinetic Family Drawing test, in which subjects draw their household members performing some activity ("kinetic" means "active").*

The art of assessment *Clinicians often view works of art as informal projective tests in which artists reveal their conflicts and mental stability. The sometimes bizarre cat portraits of the early-twentieth-century artist Louis Wain, for example, have been interpreted as reflections of the psychosis with which he struggled for many years. Others believe such interpretations are incorrect, however, and note that the decorative patterns in some of his later paintings were actually based on textile designs.*

developed other TAT-like tests with African American or Hispanic figures (Flanagan & diGuiseppe, 1999; Costantino, 1986).

PERSONALITY INVENTORIES An alternative way to collect information about individuals is to ask them to assess themselves. The **personality inventory** asks respondents a wide range of questions about their behavior, beliefs, and feelings. In the typical personality inventory, individuals indicate whether or not each of a long list of statements applies to them. Clinicians then use the responses to draw conclusions about the person's personality and psychological functioning.

By far the most widely used personality inventory is the *Minnesota Multiphasic Personality Inventory (MMPI)* (Butcher, 1999). Two adult versions are available—the original test, published in 1945, and the *MMPI-2*, a 1989 revision. Currently these two versions are competing for clinicians' favor (Downey, Sinett, & Seeberger, 1998). A special version of the test for adolescents, the *MMPI-A*, is also used widely.

The traditional MMPI consists of 550 self-statements, to be labeled "true," "false," or "cannot say." The statements describe physical concerns; mood; morale; attitudes toward religion, sex, and social activities; and psychological symptoms, such as fears or hallucinations. The inventory was constructed by a method called *criterion keying*. The authors asked 724 "normal" people (hospital visitors) and 800 hospitalized mental patients to indicate whether or not each of hundreds of self-statements was true for them. Only statements that differentiated the hospitalized subjects from the normal subjects were incorporated into the inventory.

The items in the MMPI make up ten clinical scales:

Hypochondriasis (HS) Items showing abnormal concern with bodily functions ("I have chest pains several times a week").

Depression (D) Items showing extreme pessimism and hopelessness ("I often feel hopeless about the future").

Conversion hysteria (Hy) Items suggesting that the person may use physical or mental symptoms as a way of unconsciously avoiding conflicts and responsibilities ("My heart frequently pounds so hard I can feel it").

Psychopathic deviate (PD) Items showing a repeated and flagrant disregard for social customs and an emotional shallowness ("My activities and interests are often criticized by others").

Masculinity-femininity (Mf) Items that are thought to distinguish male and female respondents ("I like to arrange flowers").

Paranoia (Pa) Items that show abnormal suspiciousness and delusions of grandeur or persecution ("There are evil people trying to influence my mind").

NOW TAKING THE LEAD

According to surveys, 80 percent of professionals administering an MMPI in their work use the MMPI-2, 37 percent the MMPI, and 40 percent the MMPI-A (Downey, Sinnett, & Seeberger, 1998). Obviously, many testers use more than one version.

PERSONALITY INVENTORY A test designed to measure broad personality characteristics, consisting of statements about behaviors, beliefs, and feelings that people evaluate as either characteristic or uncharacteristic of them.

Psychasthenia (Pt) Items that show obsessions, compulsions, abnormal fears, and guilt and indecisiveness ("I save nearly everything I buy, even after I have no use for it").

Schizophrenia (Sc) Items that show bizarre or unusual thoughts or behavior, including extreme withdrawal, delusions, or hallucinations ("Things around me do not seem real").

Hypomania (Ma) Items that show emotional excitement, overactivity, and flight of ideas ("At times I feel very 'high' or very 'low' for no apparent reason").

Social introversion (Si) Items that show shyness, little interest in people, and insecurity ("I am easily embarrassed").

Scores for each scale can range from 0 to 120. When people score above 70, their functioning on that scale is considered deviant. When the scores are connected on a graph, a pattern called the *profile* takes shape, indicating the person's general personality and underlying emotional needs. Figure 4-3 shows the MMPI profile of John, a depressed 27-year-old man. It indicates that he is very depressed, feels anxious and threatened, is socially withdrawn, and is prone to physical complaints.

Each person is thought to approach a personality inventory such as the MMPI with a particular *response set*, a tendency to respond in set ways. Some individuals tend to respond affirmatively to statements regardless of their content ("yea-sayers"). Others try to answer in ways they believe are socially desirable. Obviously, their MMPI scores will be misleading. For this reason items have been built into the MMPI to detect whether respondents are lying, defensive, or careless in their answers (Baer et al., 1999; Iverson & Barton, 1999). For example, people who keep answering "true" to such items as "I smile at everyone I meet" and "false" to items like "I gossip a little at times" are thought to be lying and so may also be lying on many other responses.

The MMPI-2, the new version of the MMPI, contains 567 items—many identical to those in the original, some rewritten to reflect current language ("upset stomach," for instance, replaces "acid stomach"), and others that are new. To the original scales the MMPI-2 adds several new scales that cover issues such as eating problems, a tendency to abuse drugs, and poor functioning at work. Before being adopted, the MMPI-2 was tested on a more diverse group of people than was the original test. Thus scores on the new test may be more accurate indicators of personality and abnormal functioning.

Most clinicians have welcomed the MMPI-2 as a needed improvement and update. Initially, many feared that the new test might be inferior to the original and that the large body of research conducted on the original MMPI would not be applicable to the MMPI-2 (Humphrey & Dahlstrom, 1995). However, they have been won over by a growing body of research showing that the MMPI-2 is indeed a useful instrument and that the two versions produce comparable results (Butcher, 1999; Hargrave et al., 1994).

The MMPI and other personality inventories have several advantages over projective tests. Because they are paper-and-pencil tests, they do not take much time to administer, and they are objectively scored. Most of them are standardized, so one person's scores can be compared with many others'. Moreover, they often display greater test–retest reliability than projective tests. For example, people who take the MMPI a second time after an interval of less than two weeks receive approximately the same scores; studies have found the reliability correlation to be as high as .85 (Graham, 1987, 1977).

Personality inventories also appear to have greater validity, or accuracy, than projective tests (Garb, Florio, & Grove, 1998). However, they can hardly be considered *highly* valid. When clinicians have used these tests alone, they have not typically been able to judge a respondent's personality accurately (Johnson et al., 1996; Shedler et al., 1993). One problem is that the personality traits that the

ConsiderThis

In 1999, after a number of dog attacks, Spain's Agriculture Ministry proposed a law requiring the owners of potentially dangerous pets to undergo and pass a psychological test. Is this a good idea? • Is the field of clinical assessment equal to such a task?

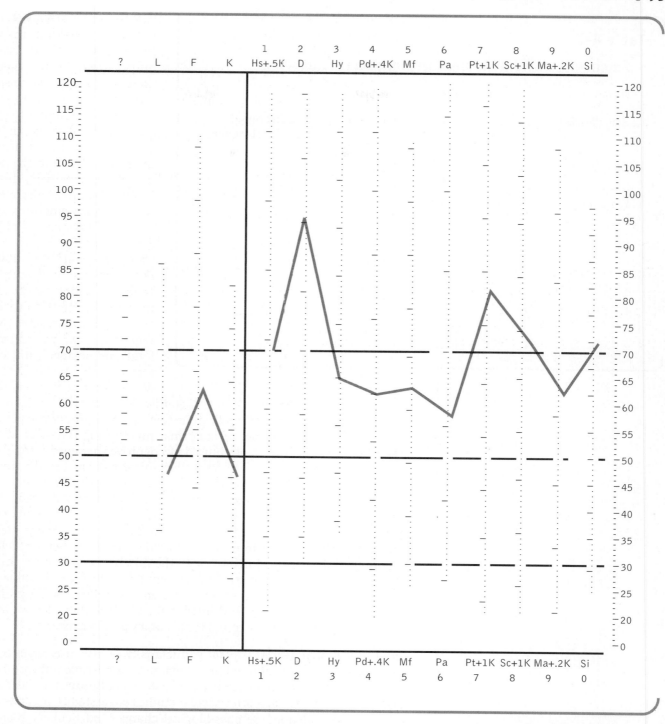

FIGURE 4-3 **An MMPI profile** *The profile of J. A. K., a 27-year-old man, suggests that he is depressed. He also appears to be anxious, prone to physical complaints, indecisive, introverted, and insecure. (From Graham, 1977, p. 164.)*

tests seek to measure cannot be examined directly. How can we fully know a person's character, emotions, and needs from self-reports alone?

Another problem is the tests' failure to allow for cultural differences in people's responses. Responses indicative of a psychological disorder in one culture may be normal responses in another (Butcher, Lim, & Nezami, 1998). In Puerto Rico, for example, where it is common to practice spiritualism, it would be normal to answer "true" to the MMPI item "Evil spirits possess me at times." In other populations, that response could indicate psychopathology (Rogler, Malgady, & Rodriguez, 1989).

Despite their limited validity, personality inventories continue to be popular (Archer, 1997). Research indicates that they can help clinicians learn about people's personal styles and disorders as long as they are used in combination with interviews or other assessment tools (Levitt, 1989).

> ### Table 4-1
>
> **Sample Items from the Beck Depression Inventory**
>
> | ITEMS | INVENTORY | |
> |---|---|---|
> | Suicidal ideas | 0 | I don't have any thoughts of killing myself. |
> | | 1 | I have thoughts of killing myself but I would not carry them out. |
> | | 2 | I would like to kill myself. |
> | | 3 | I would kill myself if I had the chance. |
> | Work inhibition | 0 | I can work about as well as before. |
> | | 1 | It takes extra effort to get started at doing something. |
> | | 2 | I have to push myself very hard to do anything. |
> | | 3 | I can't do any work at all. |
> | Loss of libido | 0 | I have not noticed any recent change in my interest in sex. |
> | | 1 | I am less interested in sex than I used to be. |
> | | 2 | I am much less interested in sex now. |
> | | 3 | I have lost interest in sex completely. |

RESPONSE INVENTORIES Like personality inventories, **response inventories** ask people to provide detailed information about themselves, but these tests focus on one specific area of functioning. For example, one such test may measure affect (emotion), another social skills, and still another cognitive processes. Clinicians can use them to determine the role such factors play in a person's disorder.

Affective inventories measure the severity of such emotions as anxiety, depression, and anger (Beidel, Turner, & Morris, 1995). In one of the most widely used affective inventories, the Beck Depression Inventory, shown in Table 4-1, people rate their level of sadness and its effect on their functioning across various spheres. *Social skill inventories*, used particularly by behavioral and sociocultural clinicians, ask respondents to indicate how they would react in a variety of social situations (Wiggins & Trobst, 1997). *Cognitive inventories* reveal a person's typical thoughts and assumptions, and can uncover counterproductive patterns of thinking that may be at the root of abnormal functioning (Glass & Merluzzi, 2000). They are, not surprisingly, often used by cognitive therapists and researchers.

Because response inventories collect information directly from the clients themselves, they have strong face validity. Thus both the number of these tests and the number of clinicians who use them have increased steadily in the past 25 years. At the same time, however, these inventories have major limitations (Schwarz, 1999; Shedler et al., 1993). Unlike the personality inventories, they rarely include questions to indicate whether people are being careless or inaccurate in their accounts. Moreover, with the notable exceptions of the Beck Depression Inventory and a few others (Richter et al., 1998), only some of them have been subjected to careful standardization, reliability, and validity procedures (Cox, Robb, & Russell, 1999; Winter et al., 1999). Often they are improvised as a need arises, without being tested for accuracy and consistency.

PSYCHOPHYSIOLOGICAL TESTS Clinicians may also use **psychophysiological tests**, which measure physiological responses as possible indicators of psychological problems (Cutmore & James, 1999; Stoyva & Budzynski, 1993). This practice began three decades ago after several studies suggested that states of anxiety are regularly accompanied by physiological changes, particularly increases in heart rate, body temperature, blood pressure, skin reactions (*galvanic skin response*), and muscle contraction. The measuring of physiological changes has since played a key role in the assessment of certain psychological disorders.

Psychophysiological tests have sometimes been used, for example, to help assess sexual functioning (Rowland, 1999). One such test, the *vaginal plethysmograph*, applied primarily in clinical research, can help measure sexual arousal in women. This instrument, a small tampon-shaped probe with a light at its end, is placed in a woman's vagina to measure the amount of light reflected by the vaginal wall. The reflected light increases when the wall arteries receive additional blood—that is, when the woman is sexually aroused. Studies have found that this instrument does detect a difference when female subjects are watching erotic films (Wincze & Lange, 1981; Heiman, 1977).

Another psychophysiological test is the *polygraph,* popularly known as a *lie detector.* Electrodes attached to various parts of a person's body detect changes in

FEAR WILL OUT

Some persons, so-called *repressive copers*, deny or ignore negative feelings in order to cope with unpleasant circumstances. While watching scary movies in one study, such individuals reported experiencing less fear than did nonrepressors. However, their bodily measures of fear (recorded by body sensors) were two to three times higher than those of the nonrepressing moviegoers (Sparks, Pellechia, & Irvine, 1999).

breathing, perspiration, and heart rate while the individual answers questions. The clinician observes these functions while the subject answers yes to *control questions*—questions whose answers are known to be yes, such as "Are your parents both alive?" Then the clinician observes the same physiological functions while the person answers *test questions*, such as "Did you commit this robbery?" If breathing, perspiration, and heart rate suddenly increase, the subject is suspected of lying (Raskin, 1982).

Like other kinds of clinical tests, psychophysiological tests have their drawbacks. One is logistical. Many require expensive equipment that must be carefully tuned and maintained (Cutmore & James, 1999; Nelson, 1981). In addition, psychophysiological measurements can be inaccurate and unreliable (see Box 4-2). The laboratory equipment itself—impressive, unusual, and sometimes

RESPONSE INVENTORIES Tests designed to measure a person's responses in one specific area of functioning, such as affect, social skills, or cognitive processes.

PSYCHOPHYSIOLOGICAL TEST A test that measures physical responses (such as heart rate and muscle tension) as possible indicators of psychological problems.

B O X **4-2**

Tests, Lies, and Videotape: The Public Misuse of Assessment

*I*n movies, criminals being grilled by the police reveal their guilt by sweating, shaking, cursing, or twitching. When they are hooked up to a *polygraph* (a lie detector), the needles bounce all over the paper. This image has been with us since World War I, when some clinicians developed the theory that people who are telling lies display systemic changes in their breathing, perspiration, and heart rate (Marston, 1917).

The danger of relying on polygraph tests is that there is no clear evidence that they work (Lykken, 1998; Steinbrook, 1992). The public did not pay much attention to this inconvenient fact until the mid-1980s, when the American Psychological Association officially reported that polygraphs were inaccurate and the United States Congress voted to restrict their use in criminal prosecution and employment screening.

With the polygraph's popularity in decline, businesses soon found themselves in need of a test to replace it. They were losing billions of dollars to theft, low productivity, and other dishonest behavior. *Integrity tests* seemed to be the answer. These personality tests seek to measure whether test takers are generally honest or dishonest—and whether it is safe to hire them for a particular job. More than forty of these written tests are now in use, supposedly revealing such characteristics as dependability, deviance, social conformity, wayward impulses,

and hostility to rules (Iacono & Patrick, 1997). Here again, however, research suggests that the tests have little validity, often yielding high rates of false accusations (Camara & Schneider, 1994; Guastello & Rieke, 1991).

Other psychological tests too have caused uproars. In Old Town, Maine, a police officer who had been accused of child sexual abuse lost his job after he refused to take a *penile plethysmograph* test, a test meant to evaluate his sexual impulses. To administer this psychophysiological test, a clinician places a rubber tube filled with mercury around a subject's penis and then shows him videotapes or slides of naked adults and children. When the subject becomes sexually aroused, the band stretches and the mercury registers the arousal. Clinicians can chart the results to determine whether a subject is more aroused by adults than by children, by males than by females, or by coerced sex than by consensual sex. Although this test does accurately report sexual arousal, it cannot predict whether a person will act on his feelings (Barker & Howell, 1992). That is, the test cannot determine whether someone has committed a sexual offense or predict whether he is likely to do so.

Although the charges against the police officer

in Maine were never confirmed, the police department required him to see a sex-abuse therapist and undergo testing to retain his job. The officer in turn charged the city of Old Town with violation of his civil rights. No government agency, he claimed, had the right to make such an intimate physical test a condition of employment. An arbitrator ordered the police department to reinstate the officer.

Lives can be changed dramatically when people are labeled, whether the label be "dishonest," "criminal," "depressive," or "sexually deviant." Questionable devices such as polygraph, integrity, and plethysmograph tests may violate more than the basic principles of science. They can also violate civil rights and hurt innocent people.

Polygraph, a test that lies?

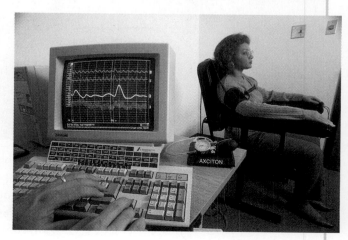

NEUROLOGICAL TEST A test that directly measures brain structure or activity.

NEUROPSYCHOLOGICAL TEST A test that detects brain impairment by measuring a person's cognitive, perceptual, and motor performances.

BATTERY A series of tests, each of which produces a different kind of data.

INTELLIGENCE TEST A test designed to measure a person's intellectual ability.

INTELLIGENCE QUOTIENT (IQ) A general score derived from intelligence tests that is considered to represent a person's overall level of intelligence.

PHOTO OPPORTUNITIES

Photography was invented in 1827. The first color photo was developed in 1892. The MRI was first used as a diagnostic tool in 1981.

The EEG *Electrodes pasted to a person's scalp detect electrical impulses from the brain. The electroencephalogram (EEG), used here to measure the brain waves of a 4-month-old being stimulated with toys, is only a gross indicator of the brain's activity.*

frightening—may arouse a subject's nervous system and thus alter his or her physical responses. Physiological responses may also change when they are elicited repeatedly in a single session. Galvanic skin responses, for example, often decrease upon repeated testing.

NEUROLOGICAL AND NEUROPSYCHOLOGICAL TESTS Some problems in personality or behavior are caused primarily by damage in the brain or changes in brain activity. Head injury, brain tumors, brain malfunctions, alcoholism, infections, and other disorders can all cause such impairment. If a psychological dysfunction is to be treated effectively, it is important to know whether its primary cause is a physical abnormality in the brain (Mattis & Wilson, 1997).

A number of techniques may help pinpoint brain abnormalities. Some procedures, such as brain surgery, biopsy, and X ray, have been used for years. More recently, scientists have developed a number of **neurological tests**, designed to evaluate brain structure and activity directly. One neurological test is the *electroencephalogram (EEG),* which records *brain waves,* the electrical activity taking place within the brain as a result of neurons firing. In this procedure, electrodes placed on the scalp send brain-wave impulses to a machine called an *oscillograph,* which amplifies and records them. When the encephalogram reveals an abnormal brain-wave pattern, or *dysrhythmia,* clinicians suspect the existence of brain injuries, tumors, seizures, or other brain abnormalities, and they turn to more precise and sophisticated techniques to ascertain the nature and scope of the problem.

Other neurological tests actually take "pictures" of brain structure or brain activity. These tests, called *neuroimaging* techniques, include *computerized axial tomography (CAT scan or CT scan),* in which X rays of the brain's structure are taken at different angles; *positron emission tomography (PET scan),* a computer-produced motion picture of chemical activity throughout the brain; and *magnetic resonance imaging (MRI),* a procedure that uses the magnetic property of certain atoms in the brain to create a detailed picture of the brain's structure and activity (see Box 4-3 on page 98).

Though elegant, these various techniques are sometimes unable to detect subtle brain abnormalities. Clinicians have therefore developed less direct but sometimes more revealing **neuropsychological tests** that measure cognitive, perceptual, and motor performances on certain tasks and interpret abnormal performances as an indicator of underlying neurological problems (Rao, 2000; Butters et al., 1995). Brain damage is especially likely to affect visual perception, recent memory, and visual-motor coordination, and so neuropsychological tests focus particularly on these areas.

The *Bender Visual-Motor Gestalt Test* (Bender, 1938), one of the most widely used neuropsychological tests, consists of nine cards, each displaying a simple design (see Figure 4-4). Test subjects look at the designs one at a time and copy each one on a piece of paper. Later they try to redraw the designs from memory. By the age of 12, most people can remember and redraw the designs accurately. Notable errors in accuracy are thought to reflect organic brain impairment.

The Bender-Gestalt test can detect general organic impairment in approximately 75 percent of cases, suggesting high validity (Heaton, Baade, & Johnson, 1978). However, no single neuropsychological test can consistently distinguish one *specific* kind of brain impairment from another (Lacks, 1999; Goldstein, 1990). This is the major limitation of all the neuropsychological tests: at best they are rough and general screening devices for neurological problems.

To achieve greater precision and accuracy, clinicians often use a comprehensive series, or **battery**, of neuropsychological tests, each targeting a specific skill

Original

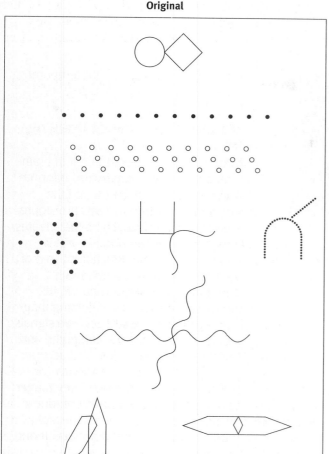

Copy

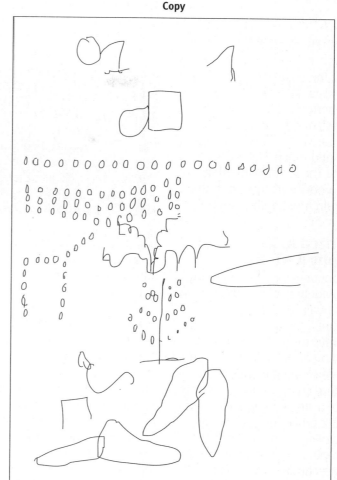

FIGURE 4-4 The Bender Visual-Motor Gestalt test *In this test subjects copy each of nine designs on a piece of paper, then produce them again from memory. Sizable errors in a drawing (as in the one on the right, which was done by a person with brain damage) may reflect organic brain dysfunction of some kind. (Adapted from Lacks, 1984, p. 33.)*

area (Baver, 2000). The *Halstead-Reitan Neuropsychology Battery* and the *Luria-Nebraska Battery* are two of the most widely used batteries (Reitan & Wolfson, 1985; Halstead, 1947).

INTELLIGENCE TESTS An early definition of intelligence described it as "the capacity to judge well, to reason well, and to comprehend well" (Binet & Simon, 1916, p. 192). Although most educators and clinicians would agree with this general statement, few of them would be in agreement about how to recognize and measure those capacities. Because intelligence is an *inferred* quality rather than a specific physical process, it can be measured only indirectly. In 1905 the French psychologist Alfred Binet and his associate Theodore Simon produced an **intelligence test** consisting of a series of tasks requiring people to use various verbal and nonverbal skills. The general score derived from this and subsequent intelligence tests is termed an **intelligence quotient**, or **IQ**, so called because initially it represented the ratio of a person's "mental" age to his or her "chronological" age, multiplied by 100.

There are now more than 100 intelligence tests available, including the widely used *Wechsler Adult Intelligence Scale*, *Wechsler Intelligence Scale for Children*, and *Stanford-Binet Intelligence Scale*. As we shall discuss in Chapter 18, intelligence tests play a key role in the diagnosis of mental retardation, but they can also help clinicians identify other problems, such as neurological disorders (Handler, 1998; Hackerman et al., 1996).

Intelligence tests are among the most carefully constructed of all clinical tests. They have been standardized on large groups of subjects, so clinicians have a good idea how each individual's score compares with the performance of the

ConsiderThis

How might IQ scores be misused by school officials, parents, or other individuals? • Why do you think our society is so preoccupied with the concept of intelligence and with IQ scores?

BOX 4-3

Taking Pictures of the Brain

During the past several decades scientists have developed techniques that permit clinicians to take actual pictures of the living brain—pictures that are much more detailed than X rays and much less invasive than surgery. These neuroimaging techniques produce pictures of brain structure, brain functioning, or both.

Computerized Axial Tomography (CAT)

The CAT scan, developed in the early 1970s, is a widely used procedure that has proved invaluable for locating brain structures. A machine passes a beam of X rays through the brain, to be recorded by an X-ray detector on the other side of the patient's head. This procedure creates a thin, horizontal picture of a single cross section of the brain. The procedure is repeated many times over the patient's entire head. A computer then combines the many cross-sectional views to construct a complete three-dimensional picture of the brain. Though the CAT scan does not provide information about the activity of the brain, it is extremely useful for identifying the precise locations, sizes, and shapes of various structures. It reveals tumors, injuries, and anatomical abnormalities much more clearly than a conventional X ray. Diagnosticians have found that the CAT scans of people who suffer from psychological disorders often deviate noticeably from the scans of people who display no behavioral abnormality.

Positron Emission Tomography (PET)

The development of PET has made it possible to measure and watch the activity of the brain, as opposed to its structure. A harmless radioactive isotope is injected into the patient's bloodstream and travels to the brain. The isotope emits subatomic particles—positrons—that collide with electrons to produce photons, which are

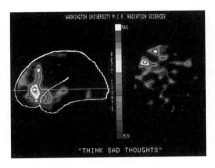

Sadness and the brain *A PET scan of a person thinking sad thoughts shows which areas of brain activity (shown in red, orange, and yellow) are related to such mood changes.*

then detected by a sensitive electronic device and recorded in a computer. The more physically active parts of the brain receive more of the isotope than the less active regions and produce a greater number of photons. The computer translates these data into a moving picture of the brain in which levels of blood flow and brain activity are represented by various colors. Very active areas, or "hot spots," on the PET scan are typically colored red or orange. Studies have demonstrated some fascinating correlations between specific kinds of brain activity and specific psychological disorders. PET scans of patients with obsessive-compulsive disorder, for example, show increased activity in the caudate nucleus, and those of patients with a bipolar disorder tend to show in-

creased activity in the right temporal region during manic episodes.

Magnetic Resonance Imaging (MRI)

MRI, the newest development in brain-imaging techniques, provides information on both the structure and the function of the brain. In this procedure, a person lies on a machine that creates a magnetic field around his or her head, affecting the direction of spin of the hydrogen atoms in the brain. When the magnet is turned off, the atoms return to normal, emitting magnetic signals in the process. The signals are recorded, read by a computer, and translated into a detailed and accurate picture of the brain. The MRI is now preferred to the CAT scan as an imager of brain structure because it produces pictures of extraordinary, almost photographic, quality and does so without emitting any radiation.

In recent years scientists have also developed the *functional MRI,* or *fMRI,* a special MRI procedure that takes numerous pictures of the brain in such rapid succession that it can detect brain changes as they are occurring from moment to moment. As such, the fMRI provides a new dimension in the study of the functioning brain. The fMRI is now considered superior to the PET scan as an imager of brain functioning because it can provide pictures of the brain's responses to extremely brief events such as hearing a particular sound.

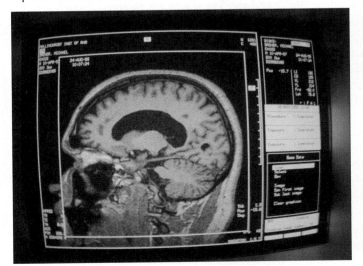

Crystal clear *This MRI of a person's brain, viewed from the side, is so detailed that it looks more like a photograph than a computer-based image.*

population at large. These tests have also shown very high reliability: people who repeat the same IQ test years later receive approximately the same score (Kline, 1993). Finally, the major IQ tests appear to have fairly high validity: children's IQ scores often correlate with their performance in school, for example (Ceci & Williams, 1997).

Nevertheless, intelligence tests have some important shortcomings. Factors that have nothing to do with intelligence, such as low motivation and high anxiety, can greatly influence a performance (Van der Molen et al., 1995). In addition, IQ tests may contain cultural biases in their language or tasks that place people of one background at an advantage over those of another (Lee, 1999; Jencks, 1998; Suzuki & Valencia, 1997). Similarly, members of some minority groups may have little experience with this kind of test, or they may be uncomfortable with test examiners of a majority ethnic background. Either way, their performances may suffer.

The Wechsler Adult Intelligence Scale-Revised (WAIS-R) *This widely used intelligence test has 11 subtests, which cover such areas as factual information, memory, vocabulary, arithmetic, design, and eye-hand coordination.*

Clinical Observations

In addition to interviewing and testing people, clinicians may systematically observe their behavior (Stricker & Trierweiler, 1995). In one technique, called **naturalistic observation**, clinicians observe clients in their everyday environments. In another, **structured observation**, they observe them in an artificial setting, such as a clinical office or laboratory. Finally, in **self-monitoring**, clients are instructed to observe themselves.

NATURALISTIC AND STRUCTURED OBSERVATIONS Naturalistic clinical observations usually take place in homes, schools, institutions such as hospitals and prisons, or community settings. Most of them focus on parent-child, sibling-child, or teacher-child interactions and on fearful, aggressive, or disruptive behavior (Kaplan, 1999). Generally, such observations are made by *participant observers,* key persons in the client's environment, and reported to the clinician (Auge & Auge, 1999).

When naturalistic observations are not practical, clinicians may observe people in a structured setting (Hackenberg, 1999). Observation rooms in offices or laboratories, equipped with videotape or a one-way mirror, have been used to observe children interacting with their parents, married couples attempting to settle a disagreement, speech-anxious people giving a speech, and fearful people approaching an object they find frightening (Floyd, O'Farrell, & Goldberg, 1987; Field, 1977).

Although much can be learned from actually witnessing behavior, clinical observations have certain disadvantages. For one thing, they are not always reliable (Banister et al., 1994; Foster & Cone, 1986). It is possible for various clinicians who observe the same person to focus on different aspects of behavior, assess the person differently, and arrive at different conclusions. Careful training of observers and the use of observer checklists can help reduce this problem (Blasko et al., 1998; Goodwin, 1995).

Similarly, observers may make errors that affect the validity, or accuracy, of their observations (Banister et al., 1994; Foster & Cone, 1986). The observer may suffer from *overload* and be unable to see or record all the important behaviors and events. Or the observer may experience *observer drift,* a steady decline in accuracy as a result of fatigue or of a gradual unintentional change in the standards of evaluation when an observation continues for a long period of time (O'Leary & Kent, 1973). Another possible problem is *observer bias*—the observer's judgments may be influenced by information and expectations he or she already has about the person (Goodwin, 1995; Shuller & McNamara, 1980).

A client's *reactivity* may also limit the validity of clinical observations; that is, his or her behavior may be affected by the very presence of the observer (Plante, 1999; Goodwin, 1995; Barker et al., 1994). If schoolchildren are aware that

THE POWER OF OBSERVATION

Everyday observations are more prone to error than clinical observations, and often more damaging. Mistaken eyewitness testimony is the primary cause of the conviction of innocent people (Wells et al., 1998). Confident eyewitnesses are as likely to be wrong as less confident eyewitnesses (Gruneber & Sykes, 1993).

NATURALISTIC OBSERVATION A method for observing behavior in which clinicians or researchers observe people in their everyday environments.

STRUCTURED OBSERVATION A method for observing behavior in which people are observed in artificial settings such as clinicians' offices or laboratories.

SELF-MONITORING A technique for observing behavior in which clients observe themselves.

An ideal observation *Using a one-way mirror, a clinical observer is able to view the classroom behaviors of young children without distracting the children or influencing their behaviors in any way.*

someone special is watching them, for example, they may change their usual classroom behavior, perhaps in the hope of creating a good impression.

Finally, clinical observations may lack *cross-situational,* or *external, validity.* A child who behaves aggressively in school is not necessarily aggressive at home or with friends after school. Because behavior is often specific to particular situations, observations in one setting cannot always be applied to other settings (Simpson & Halpin, 1986).

SELF-MONITORING As we saw earlier, personality and response inventories are tests in which persons report their own behaviors, feelings, or cognitions. In a related assessment procedure, *self-monitoring,* people observe themselves and carefully record the frequency of certain behaviors, feelings, or cognitions as they occur over time (Plante, 1999; Perrez, Horner, & Morval, 1998). How frequently, for instance, does a drug user have an urge for drugs or a headache sufferer have a headache? What kinds of circumstances bring those feelings about?

Self-monitoring is especially useful in assessing behavior that occurs so infrequently it is unlikely to be seen during other kinds of observations. It is also useful for behaviors that occur so frequently that any other method of observing them in detail would be impossible—for example, smoking, drinking, or other drug use. Third, self-monitoring may be the only way to observe and measure private thoughts or perceptions. In one study a woman was having auditory hallucinations, hearing voices and sounds that were not really occurring around her. She monitored the hallucinations for her clinician by raising a finger and keeping it raised throughout each such experience (Turner, Hersen, & Bellack, 1977).

Like all other clinical assessment procedures, however, self-monitoring has drawbacks. Here too validity is often a problem (Barker et al., 1994). People do not always receive proper instruction in this form of observation, nor do they always try to record their observations accurately. Furthermore, when people monitor themselves, they may change their behaviors unintentionally (Plante, 1999). Smokers, for example, often smoke fewer cigarettes than usual when they are monitoring themselves (Kilmann, Wagner, & Sotile, 1977), drug users take drugs less frequently (Hay, Hay, & Angle, 1977), and teachers give more positive and fewer negative comments to their students (Nelson, 1977).

BELIEVING IS SEEING

Persons' beliefs often wrongly influence their observations and recollections. Most moviegoers recall seeing Bambi's mother die in the snow and a knife slash Janet Leigh in the shower in *Psycho,* and hearing Tarzan say, "Me Tarzan, you Jane," and Humphrey Bogart say, "Play it again, Sam," in *Casablanca.* Yet none of these events took place in their respective movies.

Diagnosis: Does the Client's Syndrome Match a Known Disorder?

Clinicians use the data from interviews, tests, and observations to construct an integrated picture of the factors that are causing and sustaining a client's disturbance, a construction sometimes known as a *clinical picture* (Tucker, 1998; Stricker & Trierweiler, 1995). Clinicians typically follow their own implicit rules to form clinical pictures (Plante, 1999; Ganzach, 1995). Some, for example, use an *additive* or *linear* model, basing their conclusions on how many assessment responses point in the same direction (Hammond & Summers, 1965). As the number of concurring responses increases, the likelihood of a given conclusion increases as well. The clinician who worked with Angela Savanti, the troubled young woman whom we met at the beginning of the chapter, believed that Angela's assessment behaviors collectively pointed to a picture of depression, low self-concept, self-criticism, and an emotionally deprived family background.

> The long reaction times to verbal stimuli and the slowness of her motor responses [on the intelligence test] is [sic] consistent with the performance observed in persons who are depressed. The client's affect [feeling or emotion], as interpreted from the test material, was constricted and controlled. . . .
>
> A theme that emerged on several of the tests referred to a person who had an unrealistically high level of aspiration, who was extremely self-critical. As a result, this person labeled her accomplishments as poor or mediocre, no matter how hard she tried. She was constantly plagued with feelings of inadequacy, self-blame, and anger, because she could not live up to her high standards of performance.
>
> Maternal figures were depicted as controlling and lacking in empathy and warmth. The client described a scene [in the TAT] in which a woman was forcing her daughter to perform a chore that the mother did not want to do herself. The mother did not understand or care that the daughter was not willing to do the task, and the daughter eventually complied with the mother's wishes. . . . Male figures were described as nice, but not to be counted on.
>
> *(Leon, 1984, pp. 115–116)*

The clinical pictures drawn by clinicians are also influenced by their theoretical orientation (see Box 4-4 on the next page). The clinician who worked with Angela Savanti held a cognitive-behavioral view of abnormality, and so produced a picture that emphasized modeling and reinforcement principles and Angela's expectations, assumptions, and interpretations:

> Angela was rarely reinforced for any of her accomplishments at school, but she gained her mother's negative attention for what Mrs. Savanti judged to be poor performance at school or at home. Mrs. Savanti repeatedly told her daughter that she was incompetent, and any mishaps that happened to her were her own fault. . . . When Mr. Savanti deserted the family, Angela's first response was that somehow she was responsible. From her mother's past behavior, Angela had learned to expect that in some way she would be blamed. At the time that Angela broke up with her boyfriend, she did not blame Jerry for his behavior, but interpreted this event as a failing solely on her part. As a result, her level of self-esteem was lowered still more.
>
> The type of marital relationship that Angela saw her mother and father model remained her concept of what married life is like. She generalized from her observations of her parents' discordant interactions to an expectation of the type of behavior that she and Jerry would ultimately engage in. . . .
>
> Angela's uncertainties intensified when she was deprived of the major source of gratification she had, her relationship with Jerry. Despite the fact that she was overwhelmed with doubts about whether to marry him or not, she had gained a great deal of pleasure through being with Jerry. Whatever feelings she had been able to express, she had shared with him and no one else. Angela labeled Jerry's termination of their relationship as proof that she was not worthy of another person's interest. She viewed her present unhappiness as likely to continue, and she attributed it to some failing on her part. As a result, she became quite depressed.
>
> *(Leon, 1984, pp. 123–125)*

SPOTTING DEPRESSION

Family physicians recognize fewer than one-third of all cases of clinical depression that they encounter among their patients. Most undetected cases are mild, however. The physicians tend to identify correctly patients suffering from a major depressive disorder (Coyne, Schwenk, & Fechner-Bates, 1995).

"The mind . . . can make a heaven of hell, a hell of heaven."

Milton, *Paradise Lost*

BOX 4-4

Oppression and Mental Health: The Politics of Labeling

Throughout history, governments have applied the label of mental illness as a way of controlling or changing people whose views threaten the social order. This was a common practice in the former Soviet Union. There, political dissent was considered a symptom of abnormal mental functioning, and many dissidents were committed to mental hospitals.

In a more subtle process, a country's cultural values often influence the clinical assessments made by its practitioners. The historians Lynn Gamwell and Nancy Tomes (1995) have noted,

for example, the widespread clinical belief in the nineteenth-century United States that freedom would drive such "primitive" people as Native Americans insane. Medical experts of that time went so far as to claim that the forcible movement of tribal groups onto reservations was in their best interest because it would save them from the madness that awaited them in free society. The medical officer who supervised the "removal" of the Cherokees from their homeland to Oklahoma was later pleased to report that during the whole time he oversaw the migration

of 20,000 Cherokees (over 4,000 of whom died), he had not observed a single case of insanity.

Slave owners, too, liked to believe that slaves were psychologically comfortable with their subservience, and that those who tried to escape either were or would soon become insane. Secretary of State John Calhoun of South Carolina pointed to the 1840 census, conducted by his office, as evidence: it identified almost no insanity among slaves in the South, but many cases among former slaves living in the North. Calhoun asserted: "The data on insanity revealed in this census is unimpeachable. From it our nation must conclude that the abolition of slavery would be to the African a curse instead of a blessing."

The work of clinicians at that time lent support to this belief. One specialist claimed that several kinds of mental disorders were unique to African Americans, including *drapetomania* (from the Latin *drapeta*, fugitive)—an obsessive desire for freedom that drove some slaves to try to flee. Any slave who tried to run away more than twice was considered insane.

Drapetomania is long forgotten, but cultural views continue to influence psychological assessments and categories. Many clinicians have argued that categories such as "homosexuality," "sexual frigidity," and "masochistic personality"—each an established clinical category during much of the twentieth century—show all too well the impact of cultural beliefs on clinical categorizations and diagnoses.

A ride for liberty *Eastman Johnson's 1862 painting,* A Ride for Liberty—The Fugitive Slaves, *demonstrates the courage and clear-mindedness slaves needed to escape, in stark contrast to the mental instability of which they were accused.*

With the assessment data and clinical picture in hand, clinicians are ready to make a **diagnosis** (from Greek for "a discrimination")—that is, a determination that a person's psychological problems constitute a particular disorder. When clinicians decide, through diagnosis, that a client's pattern of dysfunction reflects a particular disorder, they are saying that the pattern is basically the same as one that has been displayed by many other people, has been observed and investigated in a variety of studies, and perhaps has responded to particular forms of treatment (Bourgeois, 1995). They can then apply what is generally known about the disorder to the particular individual they are trying to help. They can, for example, better predict the future course of the person's problem and the treatments that are likely to be helpful.

Classification Systems

The principle behind diagnosis is straightforward. When certain symptoms regularly occur together (a cluster of symptoms is called a **syndrome**) and follow a particular course, clinicians agree that those symptoms constitute a particular mental disorder. When people display this particular pattern of symptoms, diagnosticians assign them to that diagnostic category. A list of such categories, or disorders, with descriptions of the symptoms and guidelines for assigning individuals to the categories, is known as a **classification system**.

In 1883 Emil Kraepelin developed the first modern classification system for abnormal behavior (see Chapter 1). His categories have formed the foundation for the psychological part of the *International Classification of Diseases (ICD)*, the classification system now used by the World Health Organization (Jablensky, 1995). They have also influenced the *Diagnostic and Statistical Manual of Mental Disorders (DSM)*, a classification system developed by the American Psychiatric Association.

The DSM, like the ICD, has been changed over time as new findings keep emerging and clinical perspectives keep changing. First published in 1952, the DSM underwent major revisions in 1968, 1980, 1987, and 1994. The current edition, **DSM-IV**, published in 1994 and revised slightly in 2000, is by far the most widely used classification system in the United States. The descriptions of mental disorders presented throughout this book follow its categories. At the same time, not all of today's clinicians agree with the categories listed in DSM-IV (see Box 4-5). In fact, many actively debate the merits of this edition, just as clinicians continually argued over past versions of the DSM.

DIAGNOSIS A determination that a person's problems reflect a particular disorder.

SYNDROME A cluster of symptoms that usually occur together.

CLASSIFICATION SYSTEM A list of disorders, along with descriptions of symptoms and guidelines for making appropriate diagnoses.

DSM-IV The fourth, and current, edition of the *Diagnostic and Statistical Manual of Mental Disorders.*

BOX 4-5

The Battle over Premenstrual Dysphoric Disorder

Some categories of mental dysfunctioning are much more controversial than others, causing clinicians and public alike to battle over their appropriateness. After long and heated discussions two decades ago, for example, DSM-III dropped *homosexuality* as a category of mental dysfunctioning, citing a lack of evidence for including it and a concern about the social implications of calling a sexual orientation abnormal.

Battles were equally fierce in 1987 when many practitioners wanted to include *self-defeating* (or *masochistic*) *personality disorder* in DSM III-R to describe persons who are drawn repeatedly to relationships or situations in which they are made to suffer. Critics saw this as a female-targeted category that perpetuated the stereotype of abused women as the instigators of damaging relationships rather than

the victims of them. It was dropped after DSM III-R.

One of the biggest controversies in the development of DSM-IV centered on the category *premenstrual dysphoric disorder (PMDD)*. A DSM work group recommended in 1993 that PMDD be formally listed as a new and distinct kind of depressive disorder. The category was to be applied when a woman was regularly impaired by at least five of eleven symptoms during the week before her menses: sad or hopeless feelings; tense or anxious feelings; marked mood changes; frequent irritability or anger and increased interpersonal conflicts; decreased interest in her usual activities; lack of concentration; lack of energy; changes in appetite; insomnia or sleepiness; a subjective feeling of being overwhelmed or out of control; and physical symptoms such as swollen breasts, headaches, muscle

pain, a "bloated" sensation, or weight gain.

This recommendation set off an uproar. Many clinicians (including some dissenting members of the work group), several national organizations, interest groups, and the media warned that this diagnostic category would "pathologize" severe cases of *premenstrual syndrome*, or *PMS*, the premenstrual discomforts that are common and normal, and might cause women's behavior in general to be attributed largely to "raging hormones" (a stereotype that society is finally rejecting). They also argued that there were insufficient data to include the new category (Chase, 1993; DeAngelis, 1993).

The DSM solution? A compromise. PMDD is not currently listed as a formal category in DSM-IV, but the pattern is listed in the DSM appendix, with the suggestion that it be studied more thoroughly in the coming years.

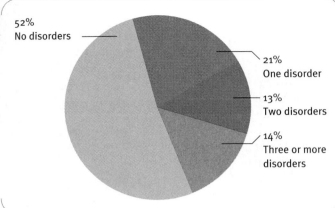

52%
No disorders

21%
One disorder

13%
Two disorders

14%
Three or more disorders

FIGURE 4-5 **How many people in the United States qualify for a DSM diagnosis during their lives?** *Almost half, according to one survey. Some of them even experience two or more different disorders, an occurrence known as co-morbidity. (Adapted from Kessler & Zhao, 1999; Kessler et al., 1994.)*

DSM-IV

DSM-IV lists approximately 400 mental disorders (see Figure 4-5). Each entry describes the criteria for diagnosing the disorder and key clinical features that are invariably present. It also describes related features, which are often but not always present, and age, culture, or gender trends. Finally, it includes a disorder's prevalence and risk, course, complications, predisposing factors, and family patterns. In a recent update, DSM-IV retained almost all of the criteria for diagnoses that it had established in 1994, while markedly revising its presentation of prevalence rates, family patterns, and other background information (APA, 2000).

DSM-IV requires clinicians to evaluate a client's condition on five separate *axes,* or branches of information, when making a diagnosis. First, they must decide whether the person is displaying one or more of the disorders found on *Axis I,* an extensive list of florid clinical syndromes that typically cause significant impairment (see Table 4-2). Some of the most frequently diagnosed disorders listed on this axis are the anxiety disorders and mood disorders—problems we shall discuss in later chapters:

Anxiety disorders People with anxiety disorders may experience general feelings of anxiety and worry (*generalized anxiety disorder*), anxiety centered on a specific situation or object (*phobias*), periods of panic (*panic disorder*), persistent thoughts or repetitive behaviors or both (*obsessive-compulsive disorder*), or lingering anxiety reactions to extraordinarily traumatic events (*acute stress disorder* and *posttraumatic stress disorder*).

Mood disorders People with mood disorders feel extremely sad or elated for long periods of time. These disorders include *major depressive disorder* and *bipolar disorder* (in which episodes of mania alternate with episodes of depression).

Next, diagnosticians must decide whether the person is displaying one of the disorders listed on *Axis II,* which includes long-standing problems that are frequently overlooked in the presence of the disorders on Axis I. There are only two groups of Axis II disorders: mental retardation and personality disorders. We will also examine these patterns in later chapters:

Mental retardation People with this disorder display significantly subaverage intellectual functioning and poor adaptive functioning by 18 years of age.

Personality disorders People with these disorders display a very rigid maladaptive pattern of inner experience and outward behavior that has endured for many years. People with *antisocial personality disorder,* for example, persistently disregard and violate the rights of others. People with *dependent personality disorder* are persistently dependent on others, clinging, obedient, and very afraid of separation.

Although people usually receive a diagnosis from *either* Axis I or Axis II, they may receive diagnoses from both axes. Angela Savanti would first receive a diagnosis of *major depressive disorder* from Axis I (a mood disorder) because her symptoms closely fit the DSM-IV criteria for this disorder. Let us suppose that the clinician judged that Angela also displayed a life history of dependent behavior. She might then also receive an Axis II diagnosis of *dependent personality disorder.*

The remaining axes of DSM-IV guide diagnosticians in reporting other relevant factors. *Axis III* asks for information concerning relevant general medical conditions from which the person is currently suffering. *Axis IV* asks about special psychosocial or environmental problems the person is facing, such as school or housing problems. And *Axis V* requires the diagnostician to make a *global assessment of functioning (GAF),* that is, to rate the person's psychological, social, and occupational functioning overall.

Table 4-2

Axis I Disorders in DSM-IV

Disorders usually first diagnosed in infancy, childhood, and adolescence	Disorders in this group tend to emerge and sometimes dissipate before adult life. They include *pervasive developmental disorders* (such as *autism*), *learning disorders, attention-deficit hyperactivity disorder, conduct disorder,* and *separation anxiety disorder.*
Delirium, dementia, amnestic, and other cognitive disorders	These disorders are dominated by impairment in cognitive functioning. They include *Alzheimer's disease* and *Huntington's disease.*
Mental disorders due to a general medical condition	These mental disorders are caused primarily by a general medical disorder. They include *mood disorder due to a general medical condition.*
Substance-related disorders	These disorders are brought about by the use of substances that affect the central nervous system. They include *alcohol use disorders, opioid use disorders, amphetamine use disorders, cocaine use disorders,* and *hallucinogen use disorders.*
Schizophrenia and other psychotic disorders	In this group of disorders, functioning deteriorates until the patient reaches a state of *psychosis,* or loss of contact with reality.
Mood disorders	Disorders in this group are marked by severe disturbances of mood that cause people to feel extremely and inappropriately sad or elated for extended periods of time. They include *major depressive disorder* and *bipolar disorders.*
Anxiety disorders	Anxiety is the predominant disturbance in this group of disorders. They include *generalized anxiety disorder, phobias, panic disorder, obsessive-compulsive disorder, acute stress disorder,* and *posttraumatic stress disorder.*
Somatoform disorders	These disorders, marked by physical symptoms that apparently are caused primarily by psychological rather than physiological factors, include *conversion disorder, somatization disorder,* and *hypochondriasis.*
Factitious disorders	People with these disorders intentionally produce or feign physical or psychological symptoms.
Dissociative disorders	These disorders are characterized by significant changes in consciousness, memory, identity, or perception, without a clear physical cause. They include *dissociative amnesia, dissociative fugue,* and *dissociative identity disorder (multiple personality disorder).*
Eating disorders	People with these disorders display abnormal patterns of eating that significantly impair their functioning. The disorders include *anorexia nervosa* and *bulimia nervosa.*
Sexual disorders and gender identity disorder	These disorders in sexual functioning, behavior, or preferences include *sexual dysfunctions, paraphilias,* and *gender identity disorder.*
Sleep disorders	People with these disorders display chronic sleep problems. The disorders include *primary insomnia, primary hypersomnia, sleep terror disorder,* and *sleepwalking disorder.*
Impulse-control disorders	People with these disorders are chronically unable to resist impulses, drives, or temptations to perform certain acts that are harmful to themselves or to others. The disorders include *pathological gambling, kleptomania, pyromania,* and *intermittent explosive disorder.*
Adjustment disorders	The primary feature of these disorders is a maladaptive reaction to a clear stressor, such as divorce or business difficulties, that first occurs within three months after the onset of the stessor.
Other conditions that may be a focus of clinical attention	This category consists of conditions or problems that are worth noting because they cause significant impairment, such as *relational problems, problems related to abuse or neglect, medication-induced movement disorders,* and *psychophysiological disorders.*

If Angela Savanti had diabetes, for example, the clinician might include that under Axis III information. Angela's recent breakup with her boyfriend would be noted on Axis IV. And because she seemed fairly dysfunctional at the time of diagnosis, Angela's GAF would probably be around 55 on Axis V, indicating a moderate level of dysfunction. The complete diagnosis for Angela Savanti would then be:

Axis I: Major depressive disorder

Axis II: Dependent personality disorder

Axis III: Diabetes

Axis IV: Problem related to the social environment (termination of engagement)

Axis V: GAF = 55 (current)

Because DSM-IV uses several kinds of diagnostic information, each defined by a different "axis," it is known as a *multiaxial system*. The diagnoses arrived at under this classification system are expected to be more informative and more carefully considered than those derived from the early DSMs.

Are Classifications Reliable and Valid?

A classification system, like an assessment method, is judged by its reliability and validity. Here *reliability* means that different diagnosticians are likely to agree on the diagnosis when using the system to diagnose the same client. Early versions of the DSM were at best moderately reliable (Nietzel et al., 1994; Kirk & Kutchins, 1992). In the early 1960s, for example, four clinicians, each relying on DSM-I, independently interviewed 153 patients (Beck et al., 1962). Only 54 percent of their diagnoses were in agreement. Because all four clinicians were experienced diagnosticians, their failure to agree suggested deficiencies in the classification system.

DSM-IV appears to have greater reliability than any of its predecessors (Nathan & Lagenbucher, 1999). Its framers conducted comprehensive reviews of

MUSICAL MALADIES

Psychological labels have inspired the names of a number of rock bands in recent years: 10,000 Maniacs, Moody Blues, Suicidal Tendencies, Xanax 25, Mental as Anything, The Insane Clown Posse, Unsane, Jane's Addiction, Therapy?, Psychotica, Multiple Personalities, The Self-Haters Orchestra.

The power of labeling *When looking at this late-nineteenth-century photograph of a baseball team at the State Homeopathic Asylum for the Insane in Middletown, New York, most observers assume that the players are patients. As a result, they tend to "see" depression or confusion in the players' faces and posture. In fact, the players are members of the asylum staff, some of whom even sought their jobs for the express purpose of playing for the hospital team.*

research to pinpoint which categories in past DSMs had been too vague and unreliable (Frances & Egger, 1999; Livesley, 1995). In turn, they developed a number of new diagnostic criteria and categories, and then ran extensive *field trials* to make sure that the new criteria and categories were in fact reliable. Still, many clinicians caution that firm conclusions cannot be drawn about DSM-IV's reliability until it has been more widely used and tested (Campbell, 1999; Kirk & Kutchins, 1992) (see Box 4-6).

The *validity* of a classification system is the accuracy of the information that its diagnostic categories provide. Categories are of most use to clinicians when they demonstrate *predictive validity*—that is, when they help predict future symptoms or events. A common symptom of major depressive disorder, for example, is either insomnia or hypersomnia (excessive sleep). When clinicians give Angela Savanti a diagnosis of major depressive disorder, they expect that she may eventually develop sleep problems even if none are present now. In addition, they expect her to respond to treatments that are effective for other depressed persons. The more often such predictions are accurate, the greater a category's predictive validity.

DSM-IV's framers tried to ensure the validity of this version of the DSM by again conducting comprehensive reviews of research and running extensive field studies before its publication. As a result, its criteria and categories appear to have stronger validity than those of earlier versions of the DSM (Nathan & Langenbucher, 1999). Yet, again, more research is needed to determine the precise strength of DSM-IV's validity (Wakefield, 1999; Hartung & Widiger, 1998).

LOVESICK

The distinguished psychologist Stuart Sutherland managed to slip the following definition into the 1989 *Macmillan Dictionary of Psychology:* "Love: a form of mental illness not yet recognized in any of the standard diagnostic manuals" (Sutherland, 1999).

BOX 4-6

David Helfgott: When Labels Fail

The Australian pianist David Helfgott burst onto the world stage during the winter of 1997. The story of his journey from a boy piano prodigy to a deeply troubled and dysfunctional young man and finally to an inspirational concert performer was told in the popular movie *Shine*. People around the world were moved and fascinated by his plight, and many attended his sold-out concerts in cities throughout the world.

Everyone who has seen *Shine* is familiar with Helfgott's symptoms, including his repeated hugs, hyperspeed commentaries, and self-addressed pep talks: "It's awesome it's awesome it's awesome"; "Keep smiling keep smiling you gotta keep smiling" (Chang & Gates, 1997, p. 62). Less clear to everyone is what these symptoms add up to. Stories about Helfgott speak vaguely of a "mental, or nervous, breakdown." His wife, Gillian, says that she prefers to think of him as "delightfully eccentric." His psychiatrist notes, "He's not autistic, not schizophrenic, and may be manic only in the colloquial rather than the clinical sense" (Chang & Gates, 1997, p. 63). The absence of a clear diagnostic label does not seem to trouble anyone, however. If anything, it adds to Helfgott's charm and to the public's fascination with him.

ConsiderThis
◉ Why is a clear diagnostic label of Helfgott's problem so elusive? • How may the lack of a label be helping people to see Helfgott as a person rather than as a disorder?

Can Diagnosis and Labeling Cause Harm?

Even with trustworthy assessment data and reliable and valid classification categories, clinicians will sometimes arrive at a wrong conclusion (Siegert, 1999; Stricker & Trierweiler, 1995). Like all human beings, they are flawed information processors. Studies show that they are influenced disproportionately by information gathered early in the assessment process (Meehl, 1996, 1960). They sometimes pay too much attention to certain sources of information, such as a parent's report about a child, and too little to others, such as the child's point of view (McCoy, 1976). And they can be unduly influenced by their expectations about the client (Shemberg & Doherty, 1999; Ben-Shakhar et al., 1998). They may assume, for example, that any person who consults them professionally must have some disorder. Because they are looking for abnormal functioning, clinicians may overreact to assessment data that suggest abnormality, a phenomenon that has been called the "reading-in syndrome" (Phares, 1979).

In a related problem, clinicians' judgments can be distorted by any number of personal biases—gender, age, race, and socioeconomic status, to name just a few (Baker & Bell, 1999; Rosenthal & Berven, 1999; Jenkins-Hall & Sacco, 1991). In one study, for example, white American therapists were asked to watch a videotaped clinical interview and then to evaluate either an African American or a white American woman who either was or was not depressed. Although the therapists rated the nondepressed African American woman much the same as the nondepressed white American woman, they rated the depressed African American woman with more negative adjectives and judged her to be less socially competent than the depressed white American woman.

Given the limitations of both assessment tools and assessors, it is small wonder that studies sometimes uncover shocking errors in diagnosis, especially in hospitals (Chen, Swann, & Burt, 1996). In one study a clinical team was asked to reevaluate at random the records of 131 patients at a mental hospital in New York, conduct interviews with many of these persons, and arrive at a diagnosis for each one (Lipton & Simon, 1985). The researchers then compared the team's diagnoses with the original diagnoses for which the patients were hospitalized. Although 89 of the patients had originally received a diagnosis of schizophrenia, only 16 received it upon reevaluation. And whereas 15 patients originally had been given a diagnosis of mood disorder, 50 received it now. Because treatment decisions rely heavily on proper diagnoses, it is obviously important for clinicians to be aware that such huge disagreements can occur.

Beyond the potential for misdiagnosis, the very act of classifying people can lead to unintended results. As we observed in Chapter 3, for example, many sociocultural theorists believe that diagnostic labels can become self-fulfilling prophecies (Lee, Uhlemann, & Barak, 1999; Scheff, 1999, 1975). When people are diagnosed as mentally disturbed, they may be viewed and reacted to correspondingly. If others see them as deficient and expect them to take on a sick role, they may begin to consider themselves sick as well and act that way. As the prophecy fulfills itself, the label "patient" seems justified. Furthermore, our society attaches a stigma to abnormality (Corrigan & Penn, 1999; Gabbard, 1998). People labeled mentally ill may find it difficult to get a job, especially a position of responsibility, or to be welcomed into social relationships. Once a label has been applied, it may stick for a long time.

> "*Health* is a state of complete physical, mental, and social well-being and not merely the absence of disease or infirmity."
>
> World Health Organization, 1948

(© The New Yorker Collection 1992, Shanahan, from cartoonbank.com)

Because of these problems, some clinicians would like to do away with diagnoses. Others disagree. They believe we must simply work to increase what is known about psychological disorders and improve diagnostic techniques (Barron, 1998; Reid, 1997; Chen et al., 1996). They hold that classification and diagnosis are critical to understanding and treating people in distress.

Treatment: How Might the Client Be Helped?

Over the course of ten months, Angela Savanti was treated for depression and related symptoms. She improved considerably during that time, as the following report describes.

> Angela's depression eased as she began to make progress in therapy. A few months before the termination of treatment, she and Jerry resumed dating. Angela discussed with Jerry her greater comfort in expressing her feelings and her hope that Jerry would also become more expressive with her. They discussed the reasons why Angela was ambivalent about getting married, and they began to talk again about the possibility of marriage. Jerry, however, was not making demands for a decision by a certain date, and Angela felt that she was not as frightened about marriage as she previously had been. . . .
>
> Psychotherapy provided Angela with the opportunity to learn to express her feelings to the persons she was interacting with, and this was quite helpful to her. Most important, she was able to generalize from some of the learning experiences in therapy and modify her behavior in her renewed relationship with Jerry. Angela still had much progress to make in terms of changing the characteristic ways she interacted with others, but she had already made a number of important steps in a potentially happier direction.
>
> *(Leon, 1984, pp. 118, 125)*

Clearly, treatment helped Angela, and by its conclusion she was a happier, more functional person than the woman who had first sought help ten months earlier. But how did her therapist decide on the treatment program that proved to be so helpful? And was the effectiveness of Angela's therapy typical of that offered by other therapists, to other clients, with other problems? Once again, the answers to these questions are far from clear.

Treatment Decisions

Angela's therapist began, like all therapists, with assessment information. Knowing the specific details and background of Angela's problem (idiographic data), and combining this information with established information about the nature and treatment of depression (nomothetic data), the clinician could arrive at a treatment plan for her.

Yet therapists may also be influenced by other factors when they make treatment decisions. Their treatment plans typically reflect their theoretical orientations and how they have learned to conduct therapy. As therapists apply a favored model in case after case, they become increasingly familiar with its principles and treatment techniques and tend to rely on them in work with still other clients (Witteman & Koele, 1999; Goldfried & Wolfe, 1996).

Current research may also play a role. Most clinicians say that they value research as a guide to practice (Beutler et al., 1995). However, not all of them actually read research articles, and so they cannot be directly influenced by them. Research articles tend to be written for other *researchers,* in technical language that is not typically accessible to clinicians or other kinds of readers. Thus, according to surveys, today's therapists actually gather most of their information about the latest developments in the field from secondary sources: colleagues, professional

"Newspapers usually take great care not to mention the race of those accused of violent crimes. But how many times have you seen the sentence, 'He had a history of mental illness'?"

Rob Morse, columnist, 1999

ConsiderThis

◉ How can persons make wise decisions about therapists and treatment approaches when they are seeking treatment? • What kinds of information about their approach and background should clinicians share with clients at the beginning of treatment?

newsletters, workshops, conferences, books, and the like (Goldfried & Wolfe, 1996; Beutler et al., 1995). Unfortunately, the accuracy and usefulness of these sources varies widely.

Finally, clinicians are influenced by the general state of knowledge in the clinical field when they make therapy decisions. What, in fact, does the field currently know about treatment and treatment effectiveness? And what implications does this have for the treatment of particular problems? We turn to this set of questions next.

The Effectiveness of Treatment

Altogether, as many as 400 forms of therapy are practiced in the clinical field today (Garfield & Bergin, 1994; Karasu, 1992). Naturally, the most important question to ask about each of them is whether it does what it is supposed to do (Lichtenberg & Kalodner, 1997). Does a particular treatment really help people overcome their psychological problems? On the surface, the question may seem simple. In fact, it is one of the most difficult questions for clinical researchers to answer (March & Curry, 1998).

The first problem is how to *define* "success" (Strupp, 1996, 1989). If, as Angela's therapist suggests, she still has much progress to make at the conclusion of therapy, should her recovery be considered successful? The second problem is how to *measure* improvement (Luborsky et al., 1999; Sechrest, McKnight, & McKnight, 1996). Should researchers give equal weight to the reports of clients, friends, relatives, therapists, and teachers? Should they use rating scales, inventories, therapy insights, observations, or some other measure? The various measures of improvement correlate only moderately with one another (Lambert & Hill, 1994).

Perhaps the biggest problem in determining the effectiveness of treatment is the *variety* and *complexity* of the treatments currently in use. People differ in their problems, personal styles, and motivations for therapy. Therapists differ in skill, experience, orientation, and personality (Garfield, 1998). And therapies differ in theory, format, and setting. Because an individual's progress is influenced by all

SUPPLEMENTARY TREATMENTS

In addition to traditional treatments for their psychological and physical problems, more than 4 of every 10 Americans try *alternative treatments* such as massage therapy, herbal medicines, or vitamins (Karel, 1998). Most such individuals fail to inform their practitioners of the additional interventions.

BOX **4-7**

Minority Groups and the Mental Health System

Researchers and clinicians around the world have become interested in the mental health experiences of members of ethnic and racial minority groups (Flaskerud, 2000; Burnett et al.,1999). In country after country, members of minority groups have been found to use mental health services less often than members of majority groups (Flaherty & Adams, 1998; Flaskerud & Hu, 1992). Nowhere is this trend more evident than in the United States.

Several factors may contribute to this underuse of mental health services. In some cases, cultural beliefs, a language barrier, and lack of informa-

tion about available services prevent minority individuals from seeking help. In other cases, members of minority groups do not trust the establishment, and rely instead on the traditional remedies prevalent in their immediate social environment (Cunningham, 1999; Lee, 1999). Some Hispanic persons in the United States, for example, continue to practice spiritualism, believing that bad spirits can enter the body and cause mental disorders, and that good spirits can cure those disorders (Rogler, Malgady, & Rodriguez, 1989). These individuals may seek help not from therapists but from folk healers, family members, and friends.

Research also finds that members of minority groups cease therapy sooner than persons from majority groups. In the United States, for example, African Americans, Native Americans, Asian Americans, and Hispanic Americans all have higher therapy dropout rates than white Americans (Flaherty & Adams, 1998; Wierzbicki & Pekarik, 1993). This finding may be a matter of economics. Dropping out of therapy is more common among clients who have less money, and members of minority groups have, on average, lower incomes. In addition, members of such groups may stop treatment because they do not feel they are benefiting from it or because

these factors and more, the findings of a particular study will not always apply to other clients and therapists.

Proper research procedures address some of these problems. By using control groups, random assignment, matched subjects, and the like, clinicians can draw certain conclusions about various therapies (see Box 4-7). Even in studies that are well designed, however, the variety and complexity of treatment limit the conclusions that can be reached (Kazdin, 1994).

Despite these difficulties, the job of evaluating therapies must be done, and clinical researchers have struggled on with it (Beutler, 1998; Kendall, 1998; Lambert & Bergin, 1994). Investigators have, in fact, conducted thousands of *therapy outcome studies,* studies that measure the effects of various treatments, and have tried to draw conclusions about the impact of treatment. The studies typically ask one of three questions:

1. Is therapy *in general* effective?
2. Are *particular* therapies generally effective?
3. Are *particular* therapies effective for *particular* problems?

IS THERAPY GENERALLY EFFECTIVE? Studies suggest that therapy is often more helpful than no treatment or than placebos (Cameron et al., 1999; Lambert & Bergin, 1994). A pioneering review examined 375 controlled studies, covering a total of almost 25,000 people seen in a wide assortment of therapies (Smith, Glass, & Miller, 1980; Smith & Glass, 1977). The reviewers combined the findings of these studies by standardizing their results, a special statistical technique called *meta-analysis.* They rated the level of improvement in each person treated and in each untreated control subject and computed the average difference between the two groups. According to this statistical analysis, the average person who received treatment was better off than 75 percent of the untreated control subjects (see Figure 4-6). Other meta-analyses have found similar relationships between treatment and improvement (Lambert, Weber, & Sykes, 1993; Crits-Christoph et al., 1991).

FIGURE 4-6 **Does therapy help?** *Combining subjects and results from hundreds of studies, investigators have determined that the average person who receives psychotherapy experiences greater improvement than do 75 percent of all untreated people with similar problems. (Adapted from Lambert, Weber, and Sykes, 1993; Smith, Glass, & Miller, 1980; Smith & Glass, 1977.)*

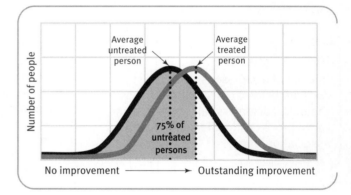

ethnic and racial differences prevent a strong rapport with their therapist (Whaley, 1998; Sue, 1991).

A number of studies in recent years have attempted to learn more about these patterns of therapy usage (Lee, 1999; Flaherty & Adams, 1998; Whaley, 1998; Sue, Zane, & Young, 1994). Some preliminary trends have emerged:

❖ In some comparative studies clients from minority groups improve as much as those from the majority group; in others they improve less. In no study, however, do they improve *more* than majority clients.

❖ Clients from minority groups tend to prefer therapists who are ethnically

and racially similar to themselves. Having an ethnically and racially similar therapist often improves the outcome of treatment among minority clients.

❖ Features that may increase the effectiveness of treatment are greater therapist sensitivity to cultural issues and inclusion of cultural morals and models in treatment (especially in therapies for children and adolescents).

❖ There is a shortage of therapists from ethnic and racial minority groups.

In light of such findings, clinicians have developed *culture-sensitive therapies,* which are designed to address the

unique issues faced by members of minority groups (Tan & Dong, 2000; Trugillo, 2000; Baker & Bell, 1999; Takeuchi et al., 1999). These approaches often include features such as (1) raising the consciousness of minority-group clients about the impact of the dominant culture and of their own culture on their self-views and behaviors, (2) helping clients express suppressed anger and pain, and (3) helping clients to make choices that work for them and to achieve a bicultural identity and balance that feel right for them.

HIRAM S. DUDSON
1930 – 1993

Member,
Placebo Group

(© The New Yorker Collection 1993, Donald Reilly, from cartoonbank.com)

HARDENED BELIEFS

One out of five persons surveyed still does *not* believe that people with psychological disorders can be treated and can improve (National Mental Health Association, 1999).

"Fortunately, [psycho]analysis is not the only way to resolve inner conflicts. Life itself still remains a very effective therapist."

Karen Horney,
Our Inner Conflicts, 1945

The widely read magazine *Consumer Reports* also conducted a survey a few years back, asking its readers about their experiences and satisfaction in therapy (Seligman, 1995). The 4,000 readers who responded indicated that therapy had often been helpful for them, or at least satisfying. Around 54 percent of the respondents who had felt "very poor" when they first began therapy reported that therapy "made things a lot better."

Some clinicians have debated an important related question: Can therapy be harmful? In his book *My Analysis with Freud,* the psychoanalyst Abraham Kardiner (1977) wrote, "Freud was always infuriated whenever I would say to him that you could not do harm with psychoanalysis. He said: 'When you say that, you also say it cannot do any good. Because if you cannot do any harm, how can you do good?'" In agreement with Freud, a number of studies have found that more than 5 percent of patients actually seem to get worse because of therapy (Plante, 1999; Lambert & Bergin, 1994). Their symptoms may become more intense, or the individuals may develop new ones, such as a sense of failure, guilt, reduced self-concept, or hopelessness, because of their inability to profit from therapy (Lambert, Shapiro, & Bergin, 1986; Hadley & Strupp, 1976).

ARE PARTICULAR THERAPIES GENERALLY EFFECTIVE? The studies we have looked at so far have lumped all therapies together to consider their general effectiveness. Many researchers, however, object to studies that treat all therapies alike. One critic describes them as operating under a *uniformity myth*—a false belief that all therapies are equivalent despite differences in the therapists' training, experience, theoretical orientations, and personalities (Kiesler, 1995, 1966).

Thus, an alternative approach examines the effectiveness of *particular* therapies. Most research of this kind shows each of the major forms of therapy to be superior to no treatment or to placebo treatment (Prochaska & Norcross, 1994). A number of other studies have compared particular therapies with one another and found that no one form of therapy generally stands out over all others (Cameron et al., 1999; Luborsky et al., 1999, 1975).

If different kinds of therapy have similar successes, might they have something in common? A **rapprochement movement** has tried to identify a set of common strategies that may run through the work of all effective therapists, regardless of the clinicians' particular orientation (Luborsky et al., 1999; Beutler, Machado, & Neufeldt, 1994). A survey of highly successful therapists suggests, for example, that most give feedback to patients, help patients focus on their own thoughts and behavior, pay attention to the way they and their patients are interacting, and try to promote self-mastery in their patients. In short, effective therapists of any type may practice more similarly than they preach (Korchin & Sands, 1983).

ARE PARTICULAR THERAPIES EFFECTIVE FOR PARTICULAR PROBLEMS? People with different disorders may respond differently to the various forms of therapy. Gordon Paul, an influential clinical theorist, said some years back that the most appropriate question regarding the effectiveness of therapy may be "*What* specific treatment, by *whom,* is most effective for *this* individual with *that* specific problem, and under *which* set of circumstances?" (Paul, 1967, p. 111). Researchers have investigated how effective particular therapies are at treating particular disorders, and they have often found sizable differences among the various therapies (DeRubeis & Crits-Christoph, 1998). Behavioral therapies, for example, appear to be the most effective of all in treating phobias (Wolpe, 1997; Emmelkamp, 1994), whereas drug therapy is the single most effective treatment for schizophrenia (Lieberman et al., 1996; Meltzer, 1992).

As we observed previously, studies also show that some clinical problems may respond better to *combined* approaches (Beitman, 1996, 1993). Drug therapy is sometimes combined with certain forms of psychotherapy, for example, to treat depression (Keller, 1999). In fact, it is now common for clients to be seen by two therapists—one of them a **psychopharmacologist** (or **pharmacotherapist**)—a psychiatrist who primarily prescribes medications—and the other a psychologist, social worker, or other therapist who conducts psychotherapy (Woodward, Duckworth, & Gutheil, 1993). Combination therapies are particularly useful in cases of **comorbidity**—the occurrence of two or more psychological disorders simultaneously (Newman et al., 1998).

Knowledge of how particular therapies fare with particular disorders can help therapists and clients alike make better decisions about treatment (Beutler, 1991, 1979). It can also lead researchers to a better understanding of why therapy works and ultimately of abnormal functioning. Thus this is a question to which we shall keep returning as we examine the disorders the therapies have been devised to combat.

> **RAPPROCHEMENT MOVEMENT** An effort to identify a set of common strategies that run through the work of all effective therapists.
>
> **PSYCHOPHARMACOLOGIST** A psychiatrist who primarily prescribes medications. Also known as a *pharmacotherapist.*
>
> **COMORBIDITY** The occurrence of two or more psychological problems in the same individual.

> **TREATMENT DELAY**
>
> People often wait a long time before seeking treatment for psychological disorders. Most individuals with mood, anxiety, or addictive disorders fail to contact a therapist until at least six years after the initial onset of their symptoms (Kessler, Olfson, & Berglund, 1998).

CROSSROADS:
Renewed Respect for Assessment and Diagnosis

Attitudes toward clinical assessment have changed over the past several decades (Nietzel et al., 1994). For many years, assessment was a highly regarded aspect of clinical practice. However, as the clinical models grew in number during the 1960s and 1970s, followers of each model favored certain tools over others, and the practice of assessment became fragmented. Meanwhile, research began to reveal that a number of tools were inaccurate or inconsistent. In this atmosphere, many clinicians lost confidence in systematic assessment and diagnosis, and some even came to approach these tasks casually.

Today therapists' respect for the role of assessment and diagnosis is on the rise once again. One reason for the renewed interest is the development of more precise diagnostic criteria, as presented in DSM-IV. Another is the drive by researchers for more rigorous tests to identify appropriate subjects for clinical studies. Still another factor is the clinical field's growing awareness that certain disorders can be properly identified only after careful and elaborate assessment procedures.

In Chapter 3 we observed that today's leading models of abnormal behavior often differ widely in their assumptions, conclusions, and treatments. It should not surprise us, then, that clinicians also differ considerably in their approaches to assessment and diagnosis or that those who prefer certain assessment techniques sometimes scoff at those who use other approaches. Yet when all is said and done, no technique stands out as superior to the rest. Each of the hundreds of available tools has major limitations, and each produces at best an incomplete picture of how a person is functioning and why.

In short, even though some assessment procedures have received more research support than others (and clinicians should pay close attention to such findings when deciding which ones to use), the present state of assessment and diagnosis argues against relying exclusively on any one approach (Bornstein, 1999). As a result, more and more clinicians now use batteries of assessment tools in their work. As we shall see later, such batteries are already providing invaluable guidance in the assessment of Alzheimer's disease, somatoform disorders, and certain other disorders that are particularly difficult to diagnose. Just as theorists and therapists are increasingly discovering the virtues of integrated perspectives and treatments, diagnosticians are appreciating the advantages of combining assessment tools.

Along with heightened respect for the importance of assessment and diagnosis has come increased research into the merits of the various assessment techniques (Chorpita & Lilienfeld, 1998; Exner, 1997; Cramer, 1996). This work is helping clinicians perform their work with more accuracy and consistency. Every major kind of assessment tool—from projective tests to personality inventories—is now undergoing careful scrutiny. This research, and more generally the renewed interest in systematic clinical assessment, is good news for people with psychological problems and welcome news for those who wish to help them.

SUMMARY AND REVIEW

■ **The practitioner's task** Clinical practitioners are interested primarily in gathering idiographic information about their clients. They seek an understanding of the specific nature and origins of a client's problems through clinical assessment and diagnosis. *p. 83*

■ **Clinical assessment** To be useful, assessment tools must be standardized, reliable, and valid. Most clinical assessment methods fall into three general categories: clinical interviews, tests, and observations. A clinical interview permits the practitioner to interact with a client and generally get a sense of who he or she is. It may be either unstructured or structured. Types of clinical tests include projective, personality, response, psychophysiological, neurological, neuropsychological, and intelligence tests. Types of observation include naturalistic observation and structured observation. Practitioners also employ self-monitoring: subjects observe themselves and record designated behaviors, feelings, or cognitions as they occur. *pp. 83–100*

■ **Diagnosis** After collecting assessment information, clinicians form a clinical picture and decide upon a diagnosis. The diagnosis is chosen from a classification system. The system used most widely in the United States is the Diagnostic and Statistical Manual of Mental Disorders (DSM). *pp. 100–103*

■ **DSM-IV** The most recent version of the DSM, known as DSM-IV, lists approximately 400 disorders. Clinicians must evaluate a client's condition on five axes, or categories of information. Because DSM-IV is relatively new, its reliability and validity continue to receive broad clinical review. *pp. 104–107*

■ **Dangers of diagnosis and labeling** Even with trustworthy assessment data and reliable and valid classification categories, clinicians will not always arrive at the correct conclusion. They are human and so fall prey to various biases, misconceptions, and expectations. Another problem related to diagnosis is the prejudice that labels arouse, which may be damaging to the person who is diagnosed. *pp. 108–109*

THE MADNESS OF KING GEORGE

Severe psychological problems can sometimes be traced to purely medical disorders. The legendary mental and physical dysfunctioning of England's King George III (1760–1820) has been documented and often exaggerated in movies, books, and numerous tales. The cause of his problems? *Porphyria,* a rare enzyme disease passed down from Mary, Queen of Scots, to George III, his son George IV, and Queen Victoria.

■ **Treatment** The treatment decisions of therapists may be influenced by assessment information, the diagnosis, the clinician's theoretical orientation and familiarity with research, and the field's state of knowledge. Determining the effectiveness of treatment is difficult because therapists differ in their ways of defining and measuring success. The variety and complexity of today's treatments also present a problem. Therapy outcome studies have led to three general conclusions: (*a*) People in therapy are usually better off than people with similar problems who receive no treatment; (*b*) the various therapies do not appear to differ dramatically in their general effectiveness; (*c*) certain therapies or combinations of therapies do appear to be more effective than others for certain disorders. *pp. 109–113*

▲ *See neuroimaging in action.* ▲ *How are unstructured and structured interviews conducted?* ▲ *Can violence be predicted?* ▲ *How does an EEG work?*

SEARCH THE *ABNORMAL PSYCHOLOGY* CD-ROM FOR

▲ Chapter 4 video cases and discussions
   "Mark"—Aggression, Violence, and the Brain
   The Mind of the Psychopath

▲ Chapter 4 practice test and feedback

▲ Additional video cases and discussions
   "Al"—Alcohol Disorders: Hereditary Factors
   "Derrick"—Hamilton Depression Scale

LOG ON TO THE COMER WEB PAGE

[www.worthpublishers.com/comerabnormalpsychology4e] **FOR**

▲ Suggested Web links, research exercises, FAQ page, additional Chapter 4 practice test questions

Generalized Anxiety Disorder and Phobias

Bob Donaldson was a 22-year-old carpenter referred to the psychiatric outpatient department of a community hospital. . . . During the initial interview Bob was visibly distressed. He appeared tense, worried, and frightened. He sat on the edge of his chair, tapping his foot and fidgeting with a pencil on the psychiatrist's desk. He sighed frequently, took deep breaths between sentences, and periodically exhaled audibly and changed his position as he attempted to relate his story:

> *Bob:* It's been an awful month. I can't seem to do anything. I don't know whether I'm coming or going. I'm afraid I'm going crazy or something.
>
> *Doctor:* What makes you think that?
>
> *Bob:* I can't concentrate. My boss tells me to do something and I start to do it, but before I've taken five steps I don't know what I started out to do. I get dizzy and I can feel my heart beating and everything looks like it's shimmering or far away from me or something—it's unbelievable.
>
> *Doctor:* What thoughts come to mind when you're feeling like this?
>
> *Bob:* I just think, "Oh, Christ, my heart is really beating, my head is swimming, my ears are ringing—I'm either going to die or go crazy."
>
> *Doctor:* What happens then?
>
> *Bob:* Well, it doesn't last more than a few seconds, I mean that intense feeling. I come back down to earth, but then I'm worrying what's the matter with me all the time, or checking my pulse to see how fast it's going, or feeling my palms to see if they're sweating.
>
> *Doctor:* Can others see what you're going through?
>
> *Bob:* You know, I doubt it. I hide it. I haven't been seeing my friends. You know, they say "Let's stop for a beer" or something after work and I give them some excuse—you know, like I have to do something around the house or with my car. I'm not with them when I'm with them anyway—I'm just sitting there worrying. My friend Pat said I was frowning all the time. So, anyway, I just go home and turn on the TV or pick up the sports page, but I can't really get into that either.

Bob went on to say that he had stopped playing softball because of fatigability and trouble concentrating. On several occasions during the past two weeks he was unable to go to work because he was "too nervous."

(Spitzer et al., 1983, pp. 11–12)

One does not need to be as troubled as Bob Donaldson to experience fear and anxiety. Think about a time when your breathing quickened, your muscles tensed, and your heart pounded with a sudden sense of dread. Was it when your car almost skidded off the road in the rain? When your professor announced a pop quiz? What about when the person you were in love with went out with someone else, or your boss suggested that your job performance ought to improve? Any time that you face what seems to be a

FEAR The central nervous system's physiological and emotional response to a serious threat to one's well-being.

ANXIETY The central nervous system's physiological and emotional response to a vague sense of threat or danger.

STRESSOR An event that creates a sense of threat by confronting a person with a demand or opportunity for change.

STRESS RESPONSE A person's particular reactions to stress.

serious threat to your well-being, you may react with the state of immediate alarm known as **fear**. Sometimes you cannot pinpoint a specific cause for your alarm, but still you feel tense and edgy, as if you expected something unpleasant to happen. The vague sense of being in danger is usually termed **anxiety**, and it has the same features—the same increase in breathing, muscular tension, perspiration, and so forth—as fear.

Although everyday experiences of fear and anxiety are not pleasant, they often have an adaptive function: they prepare us for action—for "fight or flight"—when danger threatens. They may lead us to drive more cautiously in a storm, keep up with our reading assignments, treat our dates more sensitively, and work harder at our jobs (Millar & Millar, 1996). Unfortunately, some people suffer such disabling fear and anxiety that they cannot lead a normal life. Their discomfort is too severe or too frequent; it lasts too long; or it is triggered too easily. These people are said to have an *anxiety disorder* or a related kind of disorder (see Box 5-1).

Anxiety disorders are the most common mental disorders in the United States (Zajecka, 1997). In any given year as many as 19 percent of the adult population suffer from one or another of the six anxiety disorders identified by DSM-IV

BOX 5-1

Adjustment Disorders: A Category of Compromise?

Some people react to a major stressor in their lives with extended and excessive feelings of anxiety, depressed mood, or antisocial behaviors. The symptoms do not quite add up to an anxiety or mood disorder, but they do cause considerable distress or interfere with the person's job, schoolwork, or social life. Should we consider such reactions normal? No, says DSM-IV. Somewhere between effective coping strategies and anxiety disorders lie the *adjustment disorders* (APA, 2000, 1994).

DSM-IV lists several types of adjustment disorders, including *adjustment disorder with anxiety* and *adjustment disorder with depressed mood.* People receive such diagnoses if they develop their symptoms within three months of the onset of a stressor. The symptoms may continue for as long as six months after the stressor subsides. If the stressor is long-term, such as a medical condition, the adjustment disorder may last indefinitely.

Up to 30 percent of all people in outpatient therapy receive this diagnosis—by far the one most frequently submitted to insurance companies for treatment-fee reimbursement (APA, 2000). However, some experts doubt that adjustment disorders are as common as this figure suggests. Rather, the

diagnosis seems to be a favorite among clinicians—it can easily be applied to a range of problems, yet is less stigmatizing than many other categories.

Almost any kind of stressor may trigger an adjustment disorder. Common ones are the breakup of a relationship, marital problems, business difficulties, and living in a crime-ridden neighborhood. The disorder may also be triggered by developmental events

such as going away to school, getting married, becoming a parent, or retiring from a job.

ConsiderThis

Have you, a friend, or a relative ever reacted to stress in ways that might suggest this diagnosis? • Is the category "adjustment disorder" too vague or too easily applied?

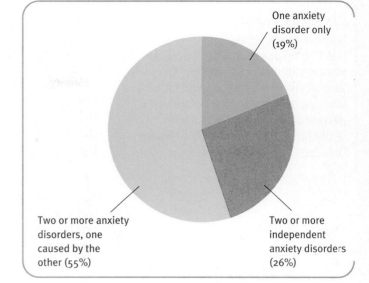

FIGURE 5-1   **Does anxiety beget anxiety?**
People with one anxiety disorder usually experience another as well, either simultaneously or at another point in their lives. One study of persons with anxiety disorders found that 81 percent actually suffered from multiple disorders. (Adapted from Hunt & Andrews, 1995.)

One anxiety disorder only (19%)

Two or more anxiety disorders, one caused by the other (55%)

Two or more independent anxiety disorders (26%)

(Kessler & Zhao, 1999). These disorders cost society at least $42 billion each year in health-care expenses, lost wages, and lost productivity (Greenberg et al., 1999; Kessler et al., 1999, 1994).

People with *generalized anxiety disorder* experience general and persistent feelings of anxiety. People with *phobias* experience a persistent and irrational fear of a specific object, activity, or situation. Individuals with *panic disorder* have recurrent attacks of terror. Those with *obsessive-compulsive disorder* feel overrun by recurrent thoughts that cause anxiety or by the need to perform repetitive actions to reduce anxiety. And those with *acute stress disorder* and *posttraumatic stress disorder* are tormented by fear and related symptoms well after a traumatic event (military combat, rape, torture) has ended. Most individuals with one anxiety disorder suffer from a second one as well (Fong & Silien, 1999; Goisman et al., 1995) (see Figure 5-1). Bob Donaldson, for example, experiences the excessive worry found in generalized anxiety disorder *and* the repeated attacks of terror that mark panic disorder.

In this chapter we shall look at generalized anxiety disorder and phobias, the most common anxiety disorders and the ones with the longest history of study. The other anxiety disorders—panic disorder, obsessive-compulsive disorder, and the stress disorders—have come to be understood and successfully treated only in recent years. They are the subject of Chapter 6.

Stress, Coping, and the Anxiety Response

Before we examine the various anxiety disorders, we need to take a closer look at the kinds of situations that normally cause us to feel threatened and the kinds of changes we experience in response to them. Actually, we feel some degree of threat—a state of *stress*—whenever we are faced with demands or opportunities that require us to change in some manner. A state of stress has two components: a **stressor**, the event that creates the demands, and a **stress response**, the person's reactions to the demands.

The stressors of life may include annoying everyday hassles, such as rush-hour traffic or the appearance of unexpected company; turning-point events, such as college graduation or marriage; long-term problems, such as poverty, poor health, or overcrowded living conditions; or traumatic events, such as major accidents, assaults, tornadoes, or military combat. Our response to such stressors is influenced by the way we appraise both the events and our capacity to react to them in an effective way (Pearlin, 1999; Lazarus & Folkman, 1984). People who sense that they have the ability and the resources to cope are more likely to take stressors in stride and to respond constructively (Aldwin et al., 1996). In short, one's response does not depend just on the nature of the stressor. It reflects one's own past experience, behavioral skills, self-concept, social support, and biological makeup.

When we appraise a stressor as threatening, a natural reaction is fear. Fear is actually a package of responses—physical, emotional, and cognitive. Physically, we perspire, our breathing quickens, our muscles tense, and our hearts beat faster. Turning pale, developing goose bumps, and feeling nauseated are other

THE PRESSURES OF EVERYDAY LIFE
Almost one-third of surveyed adults report always feeling rushed, nearly half say they would give up a day's pay for a day off, and more than half say they have felt considerable stress in the past two weeks (Americans' Use of Time Project for 1995).

physical reactions. Emotional responses to extreme threats include horror, dread, and even panic, while in the cognitive realm fear can disturb our ability to concentrate and distort our view of the world. We may exaggerate the harm that actually threatens us or remember things incorrectly after the threat has passed.

These features of the fear and anxiety response are produced by the action of the body's **autonomic nervous system (ANS)**, the extensive network of nerve fibers that connects the *central nervous system* (the brain and spinal cord) to all the other organs of the body. The ANS helps regulate the *involuntary* activities of these organs—breathing, heartbeat, blood pressure, perspiration, and the like (see Figure 5-2).

When our brain interprets a situation as dangerous, it excites a special group of ANS fibers that quicken our heartbeat and produce the other changes that we experience as fear or anxiety. These fibers are referred to collectively as the *sympathetic nervous system* (in a sense, they are "sympathetic" to our emergency needs). The sympathetic nervous system is also called the *fight-or-flight* system, precisely because it prepares us for some kind of action in response to danger.

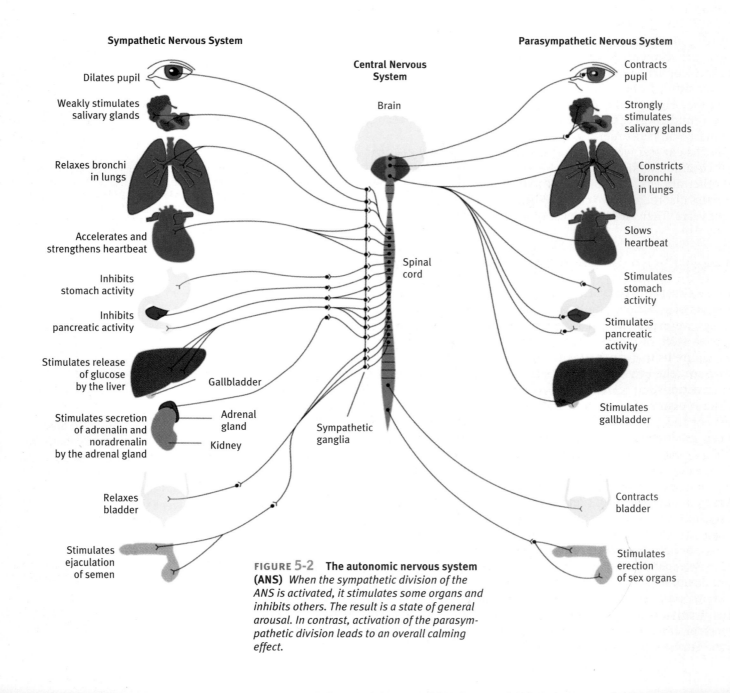

Sympathetic Nervous System

- Dilates pupil
- Weakly stimulates salivary glands
- Relaxes bronchi in lungs
- Accelerates and strengthens heartbeat
- Inhibits stomach activity
- Inhibits pancreatic activity
- Stimulates release of glucose by the liver
- Stimulates secretion of adrenalin and noradrenalin by the adrenal gland
- Relaxes bladder
- Stimulates ejaculation of semen

Gallbladder

Adrenal gland

Kidney

Central Nervous System

Brain

Spinal cord

Sympathetic ganglia

Parasympathetic Nervous System

- Contracts pupil
- Strongly stimulates salivary glands
- Constricts bronchi in lungs
- Slows heartbeat
- Stimulates stomach activity
- Stimulates pancreatic activity
- Stimulates gallbladder
- Contracts bladder
- Stimulates erection of sex organs

FIGURE 5-2 The autonomic nervous system (ANS) *When the sympathetic division of the ANS is activated, it stimulates some organs and inhibits others. The result is a state of general arousal. In contrast, activation of the parasympathetic division leads to an overall calming effect.*

Computer challenged *The modern world offers all kinds of opportunities for stress, both invited and uninvited. An audience watches as the human chess champion Gary Kasparov struggles against the computer champion Deep Blue.*

Individual experiences of anxiety *Although most people are terrified by the very thought of climbing a mountain, some are stimulated by the experience and others are even calmed by it. Such individual reactions represent differences in situation, or state, anxiety.*

When the perceived danger passes, a second group of ANS nerve fibers, the *parasympathetic nervous system,* returns our heartbeat and other body processes to normal. Together, these two parts of the ANS help control our fear and anxiety reactions. They enable our body to function reliably across all kinds of situations.

The ANS may stimulate organs directly. It may also affect them indirectly by stimulating *endocrine glands* throughout the body. As we observed in Chapter 3, these glands release *hormones* into the bloodstream, which propel various body organs into action. For example, when we are confronted by stressors, the ANS triggers the *adrenal glands,* located on top of the kidneys, to secrete a group of hormones called **corticosteroids**, including the hormone *cortisol.* These corticosteroids, in turn, stimulate various body organs and certain regions of the brain, setting in motion anxiety reactions. Eventually the corticosteroids stimulate the hippocampus, the brain part that seems to regulate emotional memories, and the hippocampus helps to turn off the body's anxiety reaction.

We all have our own patterns of ANS and endocrine functioning and our own ways of experiencing fear and anxiety. One person may respond to a threat by perspiring and being gripped by a sense of dread; another may breathe faster and have difficulty concentrating, yet perspire very little. Similarly, we all have our own level of ongoing anxiety. Some people are always relaxed, while others almost always feel some tension, even when no threat is apparent. A person's general level of anxiety is sometimes called **trait anxiety**, because it seems to be a trait or characteristic that each of us brings to the events in our lives (Soric, 1999; Spielberger, 1985, 1972, 1966). Psychologists have found that differences in trait anxiety appear soon after birth (Kagan & Snidman, 1999; Kalin, 1993; Pekrun, 1992).

People also differ in their sense of which situations are threatening (Pearlin, 1999; Soric, 1999; Walton et al., 1999). Walking through a forest may be fearsome for one person but relaxing for another. Flying in an airplane may arouse terror in some people and boredom in others. Such variations are called differences in **situation**, or **state**, **anxiety**. In most cases, however, these individual expressions of anxiety are quite different from the waves of tension and dread felt by those who suffer from an anxiety disorder.

AUTONOMIC NERVOUS SYSTEM (ANS) The network of nerve fibers that connects the central nervous system to all the other organs of the body.

CORTICOSTEROIDS A group of hormones, including cortisol, released by the adrenal glands at times of stress.

TRAIT ANXIETY The general level of anxiety that a person brings to the various events in his or her life.

SITUATION ANXIETY The various levels of anxiety produced in a person by different situations.

Generalized Anxiety Disorder

People with **generalized anxiety disorder** experience excessive anxiety under most circumstances and worry about practically anything. In fact, their problem is sometimes described as *free-floating anxiety*. Like the young carpenter Bob Donaldson, they typically feel restless, keyed up, or on edge, tire easily, have difficulty concentrating, suffer from muscle tension, and have sleep problems (see Table 5-1). The symptoms last at least six months. Many individuals with this disorder experience depression as well (Bakish, 1999; Kessler et al., 1999). Nevertheless, most people with generalized anxiety disorder are able, with some difficulty, to carry on social relationships and occupational activities (Maier et al., 2000).

Relatives and friends of people with this disorder sometimes accuse them of "wanting" to worry, "looking" for things to worry about, and being "happy" only when worrying. Most such accusations are unfair: people with the disorder hardly feel happy. They feel that they are in a constant struggle, always threatened and defending themselves, and always trying to escape their pain (Becker et al., 1998; Roemer et al., 1995).

Generalized anxiety disorder is common in Western society. Surveys suggest that as many as 4 percent of the United States population and 3 percent of Britain's population have the symptoms of this disorder in any given year (Kessler et al., 1999, 1994; Jenkins et al., 1997; Blazer et al., 1991). It may emerge at any age, but usually it first appears in childhood or adolescence. Women diagnosed with the disorder outnumber men 2 to 1 (see Table 5-2).

Table 5-1 DSM-IV Checklist

GENERALIZED ANXIETY DISORDER

1. Excessive or ongoing anxiety and worry, for at least six months, about numerous events or activities.
2. Difficulty controlling the worry.
3. At least three of the following symptoms: restlessness • easy fatigue • irritability • muscle tension • sleep disturbance.
4. Significant distress or impairment.

Based on APA, 2000, 1994.

Table 5-2

Anxiety Disorders Profile

	ONE-YEAR PREVALENCE (%)	FEMALE:MALE RATIO	TYPICAL AGE AT ONSET	PREVALENCE AMONG CLOSE RELATIVES	PERCENTAGE RECEIVING TREATMENT
Generalized anxiety disorder	4.0%	2:1	0–20 years	Elevated	27%
Specific phobias	9.0	2:1	Variable	Elevated	12%
Social phobias	8.0	3:2	10–20 years	Elevated	21%

Source: APA, 2000, 1994; Kessler et al., 1999, 1994; Regier et al., 1993; Blazer et al., 1991; Davidson et al., 1991; Eaton et al., 1991.

A variety of factors have been cited to explain the development of generalized anxiety disorder. We shall observe here the views and treatments offered by the sociocultural, psychodynamic, humanistic-existential, cognitive, and biological models. The behavioral perspective will be examined when we turn to phobias later in the chapter, because that model's approach to generalized anxiety disorder and phobias is basically the same.

The Sociocultural Perspective

According to sociocultural theorists, generalized anxiety disorder is most likely to develop in people who are faced with societal conditions that are truly dangerous. Studies have found that people in highly threatening environments are indeed more likely to develop the general feelings of tension, anxiety, and fatigue, the exaggerated startle reactions, and the sleep disturbances found in this disorder (Kendler, Karkowski, & Prescott, 1998; Staples, 1996).

GENERALIZED ANXIETY DISORDER A disorder marked by persistent and excessive feelings of anxiety and worry about numerous events and activities.

Take, for example, the psychological impact of living near the Three Mile Island nuclear power plant after the nuclear reactor accident of March 1979 (Baum, 1990; Bromet et al., 1984, 1982). In the months following the accident, local mothers of preschool children were found to display five times as many anxiety or depression disorders as mothers living elsewhere. Although the number of disorders decreased during the next year, the Three Mile Island mothers still displayed rather high levels of anxiety or depression a year later.

Do Societal Changes Contribute to Generalized Anxiety Disorder?

Stressful changes have occurred in our society over the past several decades (see Box 5-2 on page 125). Older workers have felt increasingly threatened by the introduction of computer technology, parents by the increased media attention to child abuse and abduction, and the general public by the dangers of nuclear energy. As sociocultural theorists might predict, these societal stresses have been accompanied by steady increases in the prevalence of generalized anxiety disorder throughout the United States. According to surveys, the proportion of the United States population suffering from generalized anxiety disorder has increased from 2.5 percent in 1975 to almost 4 percent today (Regier et al., 1993; Weissman et al., 1978). Elsewhere, the prevalence of generalized anxiety disorder is typically higher in urbanized countries that have greater numbers of stressful changes than in less urbanized countries (Compton et al., 1991). Similarly, studies around the world (Japan, Britain, Canada, Taiwan, Israel, and other countries) suggest that the prevalence of anxiety symptoms often increases along with societal changes caused by war, political oppression, modernization, and related national events (Compton et al., 1991; Hwu, Yeh, & Chang, 1989).

The role of society *Upon learning that her son was a victim of a drive-by shooting, a woman collapses in the arms of relatives at the scene. People who live in dangerous environments experience greater anxiety and have a higher rate of generalized anxiety disorder than those residing in other settings.*

Do Poverty and Race Contribute to Generalized Anxiety Disorder?

One of the most powerful forms of societal stress is poverty. People without secure financial means are likely to live in run-down communities with high crime rates, encounter fewer educational and job opportunities, experience less job security, and run a greater risk for health problems. As sociocultural theorists would predict, such people also have a higher rate of generalized anxiety disorder. In the United States, the rate is twice as high among people with incomes under $10,000 a year as among those with higher incomes (Blazer et al., 1991). As salaries and wages decrease in this country, the rate of generalized anxiety disorder steadily increases.

Since race is closely tied to income and job opportunity in the United States (Belle, 1990), it is also tied to the prevalence of generalized anxiety disorder. In any given year, approximately 6 percent of all African Americans suffer from this disorder, compared to 3.5 percent of white Americans. African American women, perhaps the country's most socially stressed group (Bennett, 1987), have the highest rate of all—6.6 percent (see Figure 5-3 on the next page).

Although poverty and other societal pressures may create a climate in which generalized anxiety disorder is more likely to develop, sociocultural variables are not the only factors at work. After all, most people in poor, war-torn, politically oppressed, or dangerous environments do not develop this anxiety disorder. Even if sociocultural factors play a broad role, theorists still must explain why some people develop the disorder and others do not. The psychodynamic, humanistic-existential, cognitive, and biological schools of thought have all tried to explain why and, on the basis of these explanations, to develop an effective form of treatment.

ConsiderThis

⦿ What kinds of factors might serve to relieve the stresses of modern society, and thus reduce the likelihood of people's developing generalized anxiety disorder?

FIGURE **5-3** **Poverty, race, and anxiety**
According to a survey of 1,738 parents in the United States, African Americans and Hispanic Americans are much more likely than white Americans to worry "a lot" about their children's safety, future, and survival. Similarly, poorer parents are much more likely than wealthier parents to worry about their children's welfare, regardless of race. The higher anxiety levels found in racial minority groups, then, may be largely a matter of living in poorer or more dangerous environments. (Adapted from National Commission on Children, 1991.)

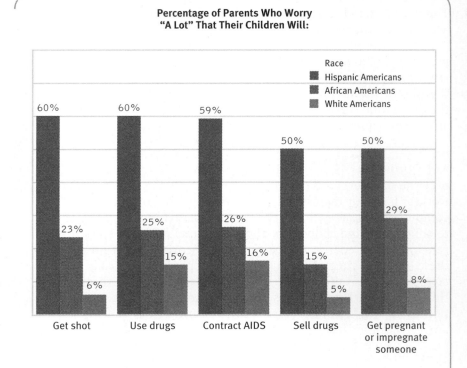

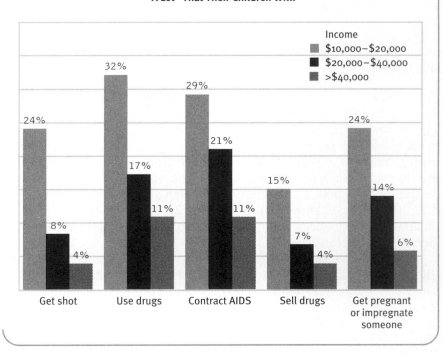

CROWDED CONDITIONS

Crowded living conditions are one form of societal stress that may raise anxiety. The most crowded cities in the world are Manila (108,699 people per square mile), Shanghai, Cairo, Paris, and Bombay. The most crowded states in the United States are New Jersey (1,042 people per square mile), Rhode Island, Massachusetts, Connecticut, and Maryland (Cohl, 1997).

The Psychodynamic Perspective

Sigmund Freud (1933, 1917) believed that all children experience some degree of anxiety as part of growing up. They feel *realistic anxiety* when they face actual danger. They experience *neurotic anxiety* when they are repeatedly prevented, by parents or by circumstances, from expressing their id impulses. And they experience *moral anxiety* when they are punished or threatened for expressing their id impulses. According to Freud, we all use ego defense mechanisms to help con-

BOX 5-2

Apocalypse Not: The Y2K Scare

As January 1, 2000, approached, more and more people became concerned—even anxious—about what this date would bring. Much of the concern centered on the so-called Y2K problem. Computers around the world, particularly older ones, had not been programmed to recognize the start of the new century, raising questions about their capacity to continue providing governmental, industrial, health, and personal services. As warnings vied with reassurances, the public's concern increased.

At first the concerns seemed realistic. There was, after all, a possibility that many services could be disrupted as the year 2000 began. As the countdown to the new millennium continued, however, the growing anxiety displayed by many people seemed disproportionate to and disconnected from any real societal dangers. In one survey, for example, 25 percent of Americans said they were worried because they didn't know what was going to happen in the new century, and 28 percent even agreed with the statement "We're approaching the end of the world" (Roper Starch Worldwide, 1999). Many people talked generally of doom and a number began to hoard food, cash, medicine, and gasoline.

Given such reactions, clinical theorists also suspected psychological reasons for the premillennial anxiety. Some, for example, described the Y2K computer problem as a magnet for the emotions of people who were already highly anxious (Rabasca, 1999). One theorist observed, "People may project some of their anxiety and fears and blame Y2K as a scapegoat" (Goldberg, 1999), and another noted that a person who "fears accidents and disasters is likely to fear the millennial change" (Kupfer, 1999). Theorists also pointed out that the anxiety surrounding the Y2K computer problem was similar to that which swept the world in A.D. 999 as people prepared for that millennial change (Landes, 1999; Rhodes, 1999).

Doomsaying is as old as humankind. Over the years, numerous religions have taught that the world would end by a particular date, bringing punishment to some people and rewards to others. Secular organizations have also predicted an apocalypse, though for other reasons—a squandering of natural resources, shortages of food, unchecked population growth, or a natural catastrophe (Moshinsky, 1995). When a new millennium approaches,

such beliefs and the people who embrace them increase precipitously.

Such theories suggest that the anxiety of the late 1990s was much more than a straightforward reaction to computer dangers, real as some of them were. Like other forms of anxiety, it represented a complex phenomenon in which sociocultural and psychological forces combined in just the right, or wrong, way.

trol these forms of anxiety; in some people, however, the anxiety is so strong and the defense mechanisms are so inadequate that generalized anxiety disorder develops.

PSYCHODYNAMIC EXPLANATIONS: WHEN CHILDHOOD ANXIETY GOES UNRESOLVED Freud proposed that generalized anxiety disorder arises when a person's defense mechanisms break down under stress and are overrun by neurotic or moral anxiety. It may be that the person's level of anxiety is just too high. Say that a boy is spanked every time he cries for milk as an infant, messes his pants as a 2-year-old, and explores his genitals as a toddler. He may eventually come to believe that his various id impulses are very dangerous, and he may experience overwhelming anxiety whenever he has such impulses. Or perhaps the ego defense mechanisms are too weak to cope with the resulting anxiety. Overprotected children, shielded by their parents from all frustrations and threats, have little opportunity to develop effective defense mechanisms. When they encounter the pressures of adult life, their defense mechanisms may be too weak to cope with the resulting anxieties.

"Why do you think you cross the road?"

Although today's psychodynamic theorists often disagree with many of Freud's specific notions, they believe, as Freud did, that generalized anxiety disorder can be traced to inadequacies in the early relationships between children and their parents. Object relations theorists, for example, believe that the children of overly strict or overly protective parents develop a fear of being attacked by "bad objects" (particularly their parents) or of losing "good objects." If they carry this internalized anxiety state into adulthood, they may develop a generalized anxiety disorder (Cirese, 1993; Zerbe, 1990).

Researchers have used various strategies to test these psychodynamic explanations. First, they have tried to show that people in general tend to use defense mechanisms in frightening situations. In some studies, experimenters have exposed subjects to threats of various kinds and have then measured how well they remember the fear-arousing events. As psychodynamic theorists would predict, the subjects tend to forget—that is, repress—many aspects of the events. In a famous study of this kind, subjects were manipulated into failing half of the problems on an important test. They later remembered less about the problems they had answered incorrectly than about those they had answered successfully (Rosenzweig, 1943, 1933).

Second, psychodynamic researchers have tried to show that people with generalized anxiety disorder are particularly likely to use defense mechanisms. In one study, investigators examined the early therapy transcripts of patients with this diagnosis. The transcripts provided evidence that the patients often reacted defensively. When asked by therapists to discuss upsetting experiences, they would quickly forget (repress) what they had just been talking about, change the direction of the discussion, or deny having negative feelings (Luborsky, 1973).

Third, researchers have studied people who as children suffered extreme punishment for id impulses. In accordance with psychodynamic theory, these people exhibit higher levels of anxiety later in life (Chiu, 1971). In cultures where children are regularly punished and threatened, for example, adults seem to have more fears and anxieties (Whiting et al., 1966). In addition, several studies have supported the psychodynamic position that extreme protectiveness by parents may also lead to high levels of anxiety in their children (Jenkins, 1968; Eisenberg, 1958).

Although these studies are consistent with psychodynamic explanations, some scientists question whether they show what they claim to show. When people have difficulty talking about upsetting events early in therapy, for example, they are not necessarily repressing those events. They may be purposely focusing on the positive aspects of their lives, or they may be too embarrassed to share personal negative events until they develop trust in the therapist.

Another problem is that some research studies and clinical reports have actually contradicted the psychodynamic explanations. In one, 16 people with generalized anxiety disorder were interviewed about their upbringing (Raskin et al., 1982). They reported relatively little of the excessive discipline or disturbed childhood environments that psychodynamic therapists might expect to find in the histories of people with this disorder.

WHAT HAPPENED TO NEUROSIS?

One of Freud's most famous concepts was *neurosis,* his term for any disorder in which a person's ego defense mechanisms repeatedly failed to reduce the intense anxiety aroused by unconscious conflicts. In some neurotic disorders (*phobic, anxiety,* and *obsessive-compulsive neuroses*) the uncontrolled anxiety was apparent, while in others (*hysterical, neurasthenic, depersonalization, depressive,* and *hypochondriacal neuroses*) the anxiety was thought to be hidden. Because the DSM now defines disorders by symptoms and without reference to possible causes, the notion of neurosis has been dropped from the diagnostic system. Disorders in which anxiety is apparent are now categorized as *anxiety disorders.* The other former neurotic disorders are now labeled *mood disorders, somatoform disorders,* and *dissociative disorders,* and are described in later chapters.

PSYCHODYNAMIC THERAPIES Psychodynamic therapists use the same general techniques to treat all psychological problems: free association and the therapist's interpretations of transference, resistance, and dreams. *Freudian psychodynamic therapists* use these methods to help clients with generalized anxiety disorder become less afraid of their id impulses and more able to control them successfully. Other psychodynamic therapists, particularly *object relations therapists,* use them to help anxious patients identify and work through the childhood relationship problems that continue to produce anxiety in adulthood (Zerbe, 1990; Diamond, 1987).

Here a therapist uses classic psychodynamic techniques and interpretations to help a young man overcome his generalized anxiety disorder. The client was financially successful but before therapy had felt inferior to others; he was not able to enjoy his success and experienced a very limited social life:

> In the course of analysis many facts were revealed that explained his inability to enjoy his financial success, and his despair of having an intimate relationship with a respectable girl. Briefly stated these difficulties were all rooted in guilt arising from unresolved . . . conflicts. . . . Material success and becoming the sole support of the family symbolized for him the childhood wish to replace and surpass his father. Hence when he accomplished his wholehearted desire to give his mother every comfort to compensate for her many years of hardship, he was faced with an acute conflict.
>
> He had always retained his strong attachment to his mother, since she was the only understanding and mild person in his whole miserable environment. He also had very tender feelings for his two young sisters. Toward the male members of his family who had always abused him he felt hatred, rebellion, and a desire to excel them. . . .
>
> [Over the course of treatment] he saw clearly how much his business was responsible for creating actual conflicts and neurotic difficulties because it was a stepping stone to realizing his competitive drives. Apart from the conscious reasons he also recognized the unconscious motivations for his ambitions to be an independent, successful businessman, the center of this being more powerful materially than his brothers and father and to have power over them, make them dependent, if he could, on him. He became also more aware as analysis progressed why he gradually became tired of the business, lost his ambition, began to have anxieties that grew worse. . . . The adult success revived the early striving and brought forth the early repressed guilt feeling that accompanied these strivings, and this chaos created his desire to run away from it all, in the neurosis and illness. . . .
>
> With this [insight] and working through of aggressiveness the patient began to achieve self-confidence in his business, social, and family relations. He became less afraid of his business associates and began to develop genuine feelings of affection for, or at least understanding of, various members of his family. He started meeting young people. . . . At this period he bought a better car, which he had hitherto avoided doing, and he also began to interest himself in sports.
>
> *(Lorand, 1950, pp. 37–43)*

Controlled research has not consistently shown psychodynamic approaches to be helpful in cases of generalized anxiety disorder (Goisman et al., 1999; Svartberg & Stiles, 1991). In most studies, such interventions have proved at best modestly helpful. An exception to this overall trend is *short-term psychodynamic therapy* (see Chapter 3), which has in some cases significantly reduced the levels of anxiety, worry, and interpersonal difficulty of patients with this disorder (Crits-Christoph et al., 1996, 1995).

The Humanistic and Existential Perspectives

Humanistic and existential theorists propose that generalized anxiety disorder, like other psychological disorders, arises when people stop looking at themselves honestly and acceptingly. Persistent denial and distortion of their true thoughts, emotions, and behavior make these people extremely anxious and unable to fulfill their potential as human beings.

PROPER CREDIT

The oft-cited psychodynamic concept known as the *inferiority complex* was developed by Alfred Adler, not Freud.

LAY TREATMENT

Besides seeking professional treatment, people are known to try informal techniques in an effort to feel better. "Worry beads," strings of beads that people rub between their fingers to help relieve anxiety, became very popular in the 1960s and are still used today. The practice began as a custom among peasants in Greece, who fingered sets of beads called *komboloi* in order to keep their hands occupied (Kahn & Fawcett, 1993).

HUMANISTIC EXPLANATIONS AND TREATMENTS: LACK OF SELF-ACCEPTANCE

The humanistic view of why people develop generalized anxiety disorder is best illustrated by Carl Rogers's explanation. As we saw in Chapter 3, Rogers believed children who fail to receive *unconditional positive regard* from others may become overly critical of themselves and develop harsh self-standards, what Rogers called *conditions of worth*. They try to meet these standards by repeatedly distorting and denying their true thoughts and experiences. Despite such efforts, however, threatening self-judgments keep breaking through and causing them intense anxiety. This onslaught of anxiety sets the stage for generalized anxiety disorder or some other form of psychological dysfunctioning.

Practitioners of Rogers's treatment approach, **client-centered therapy**, try to show unconditional positive regard for their clients and to empathize with them. The therapists hope that an atmosphere of genuine acceptance and caring will help clients feel secure enough to recognize their true needs, thoughts, and emotions (Raskin & Rogers, 1995). When clients eventually "experience" themselves—that is, trust their instincts and are honest and comfortable with themselves—their anxiety or other symptoms of psychological dysfunctioning will subside. In the following excerpt, Rogers describes the progress made by a client with anxiety and related symptoms:

> She was unusually sensitive to the process she was experiencing in herself. To use some of her expressions, she was feeling pieces of a jigsaw puzzle, she was singing a song without words, she was creating a poem, she was learning a new way of experiencing herself which was like learning to read Braille. Therapy was an experiencing of herself, in all its aspects, in a safe relationship. At first it was her guilt and her concern over being responsible for the maladjustments of others. Then it was her hatred and bitterness toward life for having cheated and frustrated her in so many different areas, particularly the sexual, and then it was the experiencing of her own hurt, of the sorrow she felt for herself for having been so wounded. But along with these went the experiencing of self as having a capacity for wholeness, a self which was not possessively loving toward others but was "without hate," a self that cared about others. This last followed what was, for her, one of the deepest experiences in therapy . . . the realization that the therapist cared, that it really mattered to him how therapy turned out for her, that he really valued her. She experienced the soundness of her basic directions. She gradually became aware of the fact that, though she had searched in every corner of herself, there was nothing fundamentally bad, but rather, at heart she was positive and sound. She realized that the values she deeply held were such as would set her at variance with her culture, but she accepted this calmly. . . .
>
> *(Rogers, 1954, pp. 261–264)*

In spite of such optimistic case reports, controlled studies have only sometimes found client-centered therapy more effective than placebo therapy or no therapy at all (Greenberg et al., 1994; Prochaska & Norcross, 1994). In addition, researchers have found, at best, only limited support for Rogers's explanation of generalized anxiety disorder and other forms of abnormal behavior. Nor have other humanistic theories and treatment received much research support. Remember, though, that most humanistic theorists do not consider traditional research methods to be a fair test for their explanations and treatments, and so they have not even tried to test their work by such means.

EXISTENTIAL EXPLANATIONS AND TREATMENTS: AVOIDING CHOICE AND RESPONSIBILITY

Existentialists believe that generalized anxiety disorder grows out of **existential anxiety**, a universal human fear of the limits and responsibilities of one's existence (May & Yalom, 1995; Tillich, 1952). We all experience existential anxiety, they say, because we know that life is limited and we fear the death that awaits us. We also know that our actions and choices may hurt others. Finally, we suspect that our own personal existence may ultimately lack meaning.

PET-CENTERED TREATMENT

To prevent or reduce anxiety in their pets, 33 percent of owners leave a radio or television playing when the pet is to be left alone, 50 percent leave toys out, and 41 percent leave lights on (Klein, 1998). Such efforts may comfort most pets, but for the 5 million dogs with extreme cases of separation anxiety, the Food and Drug Administration has also approved the drug *clomipramine hydrochloride*, brand name Clomicalm.

CLIENT-CENTERED THERAPY The humanistic therapy developed by Carl Rogers in which clinicians try to help clients by being accepting, empathizing accurately, and conveying genuineness.

EXISTENTIAL ANXIETY A universal fear of the limits and responsibilities of one's existence.

BASIC IRRATIONAL ASSUMPTIONS The inaccurate and inappropriate beliefs held by people with various psychological problems, according to Albert Ellis.

According to existentialists, people can confront their existential anxiety by taking responsibility for their actions, making deliberate decisions, finding ways to make their lives meaningful, and appreciating their own uniqueness. Or they can shrink from this confrontation and lead "inauthentic lives": deny their fears, overlook their freedom of choice, avoid taking responsibility, and conform excessively to society's guidelines (Bugental, 1992, 1965; May, 1967). According to existentialists, such a lifestyle fails to reduce a person's existential anxiety, which continues to erupt in the form of generalized and other anxiety disorders.

Existential therapists use a variety of techniques to help anxious people take more responsibility and live more meaningfully. Sometimes they support and encourage their clients; at other times they confront them. Like most humanists, however, existentialists believe that traditional research methods miss subtle, human experiences by looking only at what can be observed and defined objectively (Bugenthal, 1997, 1992). These theorists rely instead on reason, introspection, and case studies as evidence for their views and approaches.

"Just because you're Atilla the Hun, Dad, doesn't mean I have to be Atilla the Hun"

Finding one's own path *Humanists and existentialists believe that people must recognize and follow their own thoughts, emotions, and behaviors, not those set forth by others.* (© The New Yorker Collection 1993, P. Steiner, from cartoonbank.com. All rights reserved.)

The Cognitive Perspective

Proponents of the cognitive model suggest that psychological problems are often caused by dysfunctional ways of thinking. Given that excessive worry—a cognitive symptom—is a key characteristic of generalized anxiety disorder, it is not surprising that cognitive theorists have had much to say about the causes of and treatments for this particular disorder.

COGNITIVE EXPLANATIONS: MALADAPTIVE ASSUMPTIONS Several influential cognitive theories suggest that generalized anxiety disorder is caused by *maladaptive assumptions*. Albert Ellis, for example, believes that many people are guided by irrational beliefs that lead them to act and react in inappropriate ways (Ellis, 1999, 1977, 1962). Ellis calls these **basic irrational assumptions**, and he claims that people with generalized anxiety disorder often hold the following ones:

> "It is a dire necessity for an adult human being to be loved or approved of by virtually every significant other person in his community."

> "It is awful and catastrophic when things are not the way one would very much like them to be."

> "If something is or may be dangerous or fearsome, one should be terribly concerned about it and should keep dwelling on the possibility of its occurring."

> "One should be thoroughly competent, adequate, and achieving in all possible respects if one is to consider oneself worthwhile."

> *(Ellis, 1962)*

When people who make these basic assumptions are faced with a stressful event, such as an exam or a blind date, they are likely to interpret it as highly dangerous and threatening, to overreact, and to experience fear (see Box 5-3 on page 131). As they apply the assumptions to more and more life events, they may begin to develop a generalized anxiety disorder (Warren, 1997).

Similarly, the cognitive theorist Aaron Beck holds that people with generalized anxiety disorder constantly hold unrealistic silent assumptions that imply they are in imminent danger (Beck, 1997, 1991, 1976; Beck & Emery, 1985):

> "Any strange situation should be regarded as dangerous."

> "A situation or a person is unsafe until proven to be safe."

ConsiderThis

The word "worry" initially meant "to choke." Dogs who attack sheep are still said to "worry" them; otherwise, the term no longer connotes outward aggression (Ash, 1999). What connections do you see between the word's original meaning and its present one?

FACING FEAR

Studies find that subjects with generally high levels of anxiety are more likely than calmer subjects to notice and remember pictures of threatening faces. Attention to happy or neutral faces is about the same in both groups (Bradley et al., 1998).

"It is always best to assume the worst."

"My security and safety depend on anticipating and preparing myself at all times for any possible danger."

(Beck & Emery, 1985, p. 63)

Research has provided support for Ellis's and Beck's idea that maladaptive assumptions can induce anxiety. In several studies, nonanxious subjects who were manipulated into adopting negative views of themselves quickly developed signs of anxiety. For example, when normal college students were instructed to read to themselves such sentences as "My grades may not be good enough" and "I might flunk out of school," they temporarily showed greater respiratory changes and emotional arousal than did control subjects who read neutral sentences (Rimm & Litvak, 1969).

Other investigations have found that people with generalized anxiety disorder are particularly likely to hold maladaptive notions about dangerousness (Clark, 1999; Hollon & Beck, 1994). One study found that 32 participants with this disorder held many overblown beliefs that they would come to harm (Beck et al., 1974). Each person reported upsetting assumptions and images regarding such issues as physical injury, illness, or death; psychological dysfunctioning; failure and inability to cope; and rejection. Related studies have also found that people with generalized anxiety symptoms pay unusually close attention to threatening cues (Matthews & Mackintosh, 1998; Moo & Bradley, 1998).

What kinds of people are likely to have exaggerated expectations of danger? Some cognitive theorists point to those whose lives have been filled with *unpredictable negative events*. These individuals become generally fearful of the unknown and always wait for the boom to drop (Ladouceur, 1998; Pekrun, 1992). To avoid being blindsided, they keep trying to predict new and unforeseeable negative events. They look everywhere for signs of danger, and they wind up seeing danger everywhere, thus setting up a life of anxiety. In support of this idea, studies have demonstrated that both animal and human subjects respond more fearfully to unpredictable negative events than to predictable ones (Mineka, 1985) and that people with generalized anxiety disorder worry much more about the future than others do (Dugas et al., 1998). However, researchers have yet to determine whether people with this disorder have, in fact, experienced an unusual number of unpredictable negative events in life.

COGNITIVE THERAPIES Two kinds of cognitive approaches are commonly used in cases of generalized anxiety disorder. In one, based on the theories of Ellis and Beck, therapists help clients change the maladaptive assumptions that are supposedly at the root of their disorders. In the other, therapists teach clients how to cope during stressful situations (see Figure 5-4).

Fearful delights *Many people enjoy the feeling of fear as long as it occurs under controlled circumstances, as when they are safely watching the tension grow in the enormously popular* The Blair Witch Project.

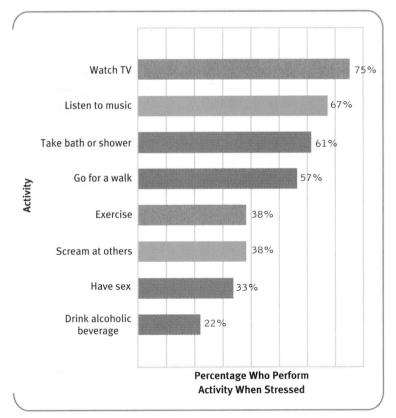

FIGURE 5-4 **What do people do to relieve stress?** *According to one large survey, most of us watch television or listen to music (Kanner, 1995).*

B O X **5-3**

Fears, Shmears: The Odds Are Usually on Our Side

People with anxiety disorders have many unreasonable fears, but millions of other people, too, worry about disaster every day. Most of the catastrophes they fear are not probable. Perhaps the ability to live by laws of *probability* rather than *possibility* is what separates the fearless from the fearful. What are the odds, then, that commonly feared events will happen? The range of probability is wide, but the odds are usually heavily in our favor.

A city resident will be a victim of a violent crime . . . 1 in 60

A suburbanite will be a victim of a violent crime . . . 1 in 1,000

A small-town resident will be a victim of a violent crime . . . 1 in 2,000

A child will suffer a high-chair injury this year . . . 1 in 6,000

The IRS will audit you this year . . . 1 in 100

You will be bumped off any given airline flight . . . 1 in 4,000

You will be murdered this year . . . 1 in 12,000

You will be killed on your next bus ride . . . 1 in 500 million

You will be hit by a baseball at a major-league game . . . 1 in 300,000

You will drown in the tub this year . . . 1 in 685,000

Your plane will arrive late . . . 1 in 6

Your house will have a fire this year . . . 1 in 200

You will die in a fire this year . . . 1 in 40,200

You will be killed by space debris . . . 1 in 5 billion

Build with care *The chance of a construction worker being injured at work during the year is 1 in 27.*

You will be struck by a meteorite . . . 1 in 10 trillion

Your carton will contain a broken egg . . . 1 in 10

You will develop a tooth cavity . . . 1 in 6

A young child will develop a tooth cavity . . . 1 in 10

You will contract AIDS from a blood transfusion . . . 1 in 100,000

Any given miner will be injured while working this year . . . 1 in 23

Any given factory worker will be injured at work this year . . . 1 in 37

Any given farmer will be injured while working this year . . . 1 in 19

You will die in a fall . . . 1 in 200,000

You will be attacked by a shark . . . 1 in 4 million

You will receive a diagnosis of cancer this year . . . 1 in 8,000

A woman will develop breast cancer during her lifetime . . . 1 in 9

You will develop a brain tumor this year . . . 1 in 25,000

A business owner will become insolvent or declare bankruptcy this year . . . 1 in 55

A piano player will eventually develop lower back pain . . . 1 in 3

You will be killed on your next automobile outing . . . 1 in 4 million

You will die in an automobile accident . . . 1 in 5,000

Condom use will eventually fail to prevent pregnancy . . . 1 in 10

An IUD will eventually fail to prevent pregnancy . . . 1 in 10

Coitus interruptus will eventually fail to prevent pregnancy . . . 1 in 5

(ADAPTED FROM KRANTZ, 1992)

CHANGING MALADAPTIVE ASSUMPTIONS In Ellis's technique of **rational-emotive therapy**, practitioners point out the irrational assumptions held by clients, suggest more appropriate assumptions, and assign homework that gives the individuals practice at challenging old assumptions and applying new ones (Ellis, 1999, 1995, 1962). Research has been limited, but studies do suggest that this approach brings at least modest relief to persons suffering from anxiety (Cowan &

RATIONAL-EMOTIVE THERAPY A cognitive therapy developed by Albert Ellis which helps clients to identify and change the irrational assumptions and thinking that help cause their psychological disorder.

Brunero, 1997; Lipsky et al., 1980). The approach is illustrated in the following discussion between Ellis and an anxious client who fears failure and disapproval at work, especially over a testing procedure that she has developed for her company:

> **Client:** I'm so distraught these days that I can hardly concentrate on anything for more than a minute or two at a time. My mind just keeps wandering to that damn testing procedure I devised, and that they've put so much money into; and whether it's going to work well or be just a waste of all that time and money. . . .
>
> **Ellis:** Point one is that you must admit that you are telling yourself something to start your worrying going, and you must begin to look, and I mean really look, for the specific nonsense with which you keep reindoctrinating yourself. . . . The false statement is: "If, because my testing procedure doesn't work and I am functioning inefficiently on my job, my co-workers do not want me or approve of me, then I shall be a worthless person." . . .
>
> **Client:** But if I want to do what my firm also wants me to do, and I am useless to them, aren't I also useless to me?
>
> **Ellis:** No—not unless you think you are. You are frustrated, of course, if you want to set up a good testing procedure and you can't. But need you be desperately unhappy because you are frustrated? And need you deem yourself completely unworthwhile because you can't do one of the main things you want to do in life?
>
> *(Ellis, 1962, pp. 160–165)*

"People are not disturbed by events themselves, but rather by the views they take of them."

Epictetus (A.D. c. 55–c. 135)

Beck's similar but more systematic approach, called, simply, *cognitive therapy,* is an adaptation of his influential and very effective treatment for depression (which is discussed in Chapter 8). Researchers are already finding that it and similar cognitive approaches often reduce generalized anxiety to more tolerable levels (Cameron et al., 1999; DeRubeis & Crits-Christoph, 1998).

TEACHING CLIENTS TO COPE The clinical innovator Donald Meichenbaum (1997, 1993, 1992, 1977) has developed a cognitive technique for coping with stress called **self-instruction training**, or **stress inoculation training**. It teaches clients to rid themselves of the unpleasant thoughts that keep raising their anxiety during difficult situations (so-called *negative self-statements*) and replace them with *coping self-statements* instead (see Box 5-4).

BOX 5-4

The Imaginary Spotlight

Many people with anxiety disorders worry about how they appear in the eyes of others. They may worry about sounding foolish, looking unattractive, or seeming insensitive. It turns out that they are wrong—not about how they are being viewed but that they are being viewed at all. People who are not excessively anxious often make this same mistake.

The psychologist Thomas Gilovich and his colleagues at Cornell University (1996) found that other people rarely notice our behaviors or appearance as much as we think they do. When these researchers asked a group of Cornell students to wear a Barry Manilow T-shirt, their embarrassed subjects predicted that at least half of all observers would notice the shirt the minute they walked into a room. Only a quarter of the observers actually did. Similarly, skiers overestimated the percentage of chair-lift riders who would be watching and judging their skiing ability as they skied by the lift.

ConsiderThis

● Why might people, including those with anxiety disorders, be so inclined to think that others are intensely interested in watching them? • Why are people so unaware of the actions and appearance of others?

In Meichenbaum's approach, people are taught coping self-statements that they can apply during four stages of a stressful situation—say, talking to their boss about a raise. First, they learn to say things to themselves that prepare them for the situation. Second, they learn self-statements that enable them to cope with the stressful situation as it is occurring—for instance, when they are actually in the boss's office. Third, they learn self-statements that will help them through the difficult moments when the situation seems to be going badly, as when the boss glares at them as they ask for more money. Finally, they learn to make self-congratulatory self-statements after they have coped effectively. Here are a few examples of the four kinds of self-statements:

Preparing for a Stressor
What is it you have to do?
You can develop a plan to deal with it.
Just think about what you can do about it. That's better than getting anxious.

Confronting and Handling a Stressor
Just psych yourself up—you can meet this challenge.
This tenseness can be an ally—a cue to cope.
Relax: you're in control. Take a slow, deep breath.

Coping with the Feeling of Being Overwhelmed
When fear comes, just pause.
Keep the focus on the present. What is it you have to do?
You should expect your fear to rise.
Don't try to eliminate fear totally. Just keep it manageable.

Reinforcing Self-Statements
It worked! You did it.
It wasn't as bad as you expected.
You made more out of your fear than it was worth.
Your damn ideas—that's the problem. When you control them, you control your fear.

Self-instruction training has proved to be of modest help in cases of generalized anxiety disorder (Sanchez-Canovas et al., 1991; Ramm et al., 1981) and moderately helpful to people who suffer from test-taking and performance anxiety, stress associated with life change, and mild forms of anxiety (Fausel, 1995; Meichenbaum, 1993, 1992, 1972). It has also been used with some success to help athletes compete better and to encourage people to behave less impulsively, control anger, and control pain (Meichenbaum, 1997, 1993; Crocker, 1989; Novaco, 1977).

In view of the limited effectiveness of self-instruction training in treating generalized and other anxiety disorders, Meichenbaum (1972) himself has suggested that it should be combined with other treatments. In fact, anxious people treated with a combination of self-instruction training and Ellis's rational-emotive therapy improve more than people treated by either approach alone (Glogower, Fremouw, & McCroskey, 1978).

The Biological Perspective

Biological theorists believe that generalized anxiety disorder is caused chiefly by biological factors. For years this claim was supported primarily by **family pedigree studies**, in which researchers determine how many and which relatives of a person with a disorder have the same disorder. If biological tendencies toward generalized anxiety disorder are inherited, people who are biologically related should have similar probabilities of developing this disorder. Studies have in fact

SELF-INSTRUCTION TRAINING A cognitive treatment developed by Donald Meichenbaum which teaches clients to use coping self-statements at times of stress. Also known as *stress inoculation training*.

FAMILY PEDIGREE STUDY A research design in which investigators determine how many and which relatives of a person with a disorder have the same disorder.

SPEAKING UP

Apparently most of us talk out loud to ourselves at least occasionally. In one study, researchers bugged the room in which subjects were trying to solve various mental tasks. Fully 132 of the 133 subjects were discovered to be talking to themselves during the tasks! Nevertheless, half of the participants later denied doing so (Duncan et al., 1999).

BENZODIAZEPINES The most common group of antianxiety drugs, which includes Valium and Xanax.

GABA The neurotransmitter gamma-aminobutyric acid, whose low activity has been linked to generalized anxiety disorder.

SEDATIVE-HYPNOTIC DRUGS Drugs that calm people at lower doses and help them to fall asleep at higher doses.

How Fast Is Fear?

Researchers in Germany momentarily flashed pictures of snakes and spiders for subjects who were afraid of the creatures. The subjects began to experience physical fear reactions (autonomic arousal) just 300 microseconds after each picture's brief appearance (Globisch et al., 1999).

A computer-drawn molecule of gamma-aminobutyric acid (GABA) *This neurotransmitter helps reduce anxiety by carrying an inhibitory message to neuron receptors.*

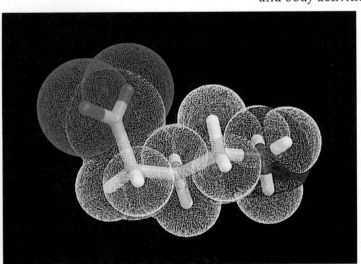

found that blood relatives of persons with generalized anxiety disorder are more likely than nonrelatives to have the disorder, too (Kendler et al., 1992; Carey & Gottesman, 1981). Approximately 15 percent of the relatives of people with the disorder display it themselves—much more than the 4 percent found in the general population. And the closer the relative (an identical twin, for example, as opposed to a fraternal twin or other sibling), the greater the likelihood that he or she will also have the disorder (APA, 2000; Marks, 1986; Slater & Shields, 1969).

Of course, investigators cannot have full confidence in biological interpretations of such studies. The findings could also be suggesting that generalized anxiety disorder is caused by environmental experiences. Because relatives are likely to share aspects of the same environment, their shared disorders may reflect similarities in environment and upbringing rather than similarities in biological makeup. The closer the relatives, the more similar their environmental experiences are likely to be (Kendler & Gardner, 1998). Because identical twins are more physically alike than fraternal twins, they may even experience more similarities in their upbringing (Tambs, Harris, & Magnus, 1995).

BIOLOGICAL EXPLANATIONS: GABA INACTIVITY In recent decades important discoveries by brain researchers have offered clearer evidence that generalized anxiety disorder is related to biological factors, in particular to biochemical dysfunction in the brain (Brawman-Mintzer & Lydiard, 1997). One of the first such discoveries occurred in the 1950s, when researchers determined that **benzodiazepines**, the family of drugs that includes diazepam (Valium) and alprazolam (Xanax), provide relief from anxiety. At first, no one understood why benzodiazepines reduce anxiety. Eventually, however, radioactive techniques were developed which enabled researchers to pinpoint the exact sites in the brain that are affected by benzodiazepines (Mohler & Okada, 1977; Squires & Braestrup, 1977). Apparently certain neurons have receptors that receive the benzodiazepines, just as a lock receives a key.

Investigators soon discovered that these benzodiazepine receptors ordinarily receive **gamma-aminobutyric acid (GABA)**, a common and important neurotransmitter in the brain (Leonard, 1999; Costa et al., 1978, 1975). As we observed in Chapter 3, neurotransmitters are chemicals that carry messages from one neuron to another. GABA carries *inhibitory* messages: when GABA is received at a receptor, it causes the neuron to stop firing.

On the basis of their findings, researchers have pieced together a scenario of how fear reactions occur. In normal fear reactions, key neurons throughout the brain fire more rapidly, triggering the firing of still more neurons and creating a general state of excitability throughout the brain and body. Perspiration, breathing, and muscle tension increase. This state is experienced as fear or anxiety. After neuron firing continues for a while, it triggers a *feedback system*—that is, brain and body activities that reduce the level of excitability. Some neurons throughout the brain release the neurotransmitter GABA, which then binds to GABA receptors on certain neurons and instructs those neurons to stop firing. The state of excitability is thereby curtailed, and the experience of fear or anxiety subsides (Costa, 1995, 1983; Sanders & Shekhar, 1995).

Researchers believe that a malfunction in this feedback system can cause fear or anxiety to go unchecked (Lloyd, Fletcher, & Minchin, 1992). In fact, when some investigators reduced GABA's ability to bind to GABA receptors, they found that animal subjects reacted with heightened anxiety (Costa, 1985; Mohler, Richards, & Wu, 1981). This finding suggests that people with generalized anxiety disorder may have ongoing problems in their anxiety feedback system. Perhaps their brain supplies of GABA are too low. Perhaps they have too few GABA receptors, or their GABA receptors do not readily capture the neurotransmitter.

This explanation is promising, but imperfect. One problem is that recent biological discoveries have complicated the picture. It has been found, for example, that GABA is only one of several body chemicals that can bind to the important GABA receptors (Leonard, 1999; Guidotti & Costa, 1998). Could these other chemicals also be critical factors in the brain's control of anxiety? Similarly, there is research suggesting that neurotransmitters that bind to yet other neuron receptors may also play key roles in anxiety and anxiety disorders—acting alone or in conjunction with GABA (Fernandez & Lopez, 1998; Maier, 1997). A second problem is that much of the research on the biology of anxiety has been done on laboratory animals. When researchers generate fear responses in animals, they assume that the animals are experiencing something similar to human anxiety, but it is impossible to be certain (Newman & Farley, 1995; Kalin, 1993). The animals may be experiencing a high level of arousal that is quite different from human anxiety.

Finally, biological theorists are faced with the problem of establishing a causal relationship. Although studies do tie physiological functioning to generalized anxiety disorder, they do not establish that the physiological events *cause* the disorder. The biological responses of anxious persons may be the result, rather than the cause, of their anxiety disorders. Perhaps long-term anxiety eventually leads to poorer GABA reception, for example.

BIOLOGICAL TREATMENTS The leading biological approach to treating generalized anxiety disorder is to prescribe *antianxiety drugs* (see Table 5-3). Indeed, it would be hard to find someone in our society who is not familiar with the words "tranquilizer," "Valium," and "Xanax." Other biological interventions are *relaxation training*, in which people learn to relax the muscles throughout their bodies, and *biofeedback*, in which clients learn to voluntarily control underlying biological processes that may be contributing to their problems.

ANTIANXIETY DRUGS Before the 1950s, a family of drugs labeled *barbiturates* were the major biological treatment for anxiety disorders (Miller, Klamen, & Costa, 1998; Ballenger, 1995). These drugs were used in low doses to calm people and in higher doses to help them fall asleep, and so they were generally known as **sedative-hypnotic drugs**. However, barbiturates created serious problems. They made people very drowsy, too high a dose could lead to death, and those who took them over a long period could become physically dependent on them.

In the late 1940s, Frank Berger, a pharmacologist who was trying to produce a more effective antibiotic drug, developed a compound called *meprobamate* that relaxed the muscles and reduced anxiety (Cole & Yonkers, 1995; Berger, 1970). It was released in the 1950s as a new kind of sedative-hypnotic medication under the brand name Miltown. This drug was less dangerous and less addictive than barbiturates, but it still caused great drowsiness.

Then in the late 1950s the researcher Lowell Randall found that a drug named *chlordiazepoxide,* a member of the family of drugs called *benzodiazepines,* was able to tranquilize animals without making them extremely tired (Randall, 1982; Sternbach, 1982). This drug had actually been developed in the 1930s and put aside as seemingly useless. After Randall's discovery, however, it was marketed as a sedative-hypnotic drug under the brand name Librium. Several years later another benzodiazepine drug, *diazepam,* was developed and marketed as Valium. Both doctors and patients considered these and other benzodiazepines to be totally safe for use as sedative-hypnotics, and the drugs soon became the most widely prescribed medications in the United States (Strange, 1992).

Do monkeys experience anxiety? *Clinical researchers must be careful in interpreting the reactions of animal subjects. This infant monkey was considered "fearful" after being separated from its mother. But perhaps it was feeling depression or another emotion, or experiencing a level of arousal that does not correspond to either human emotion.*

Table 5-3

Drugs That Reduce Anxiety

CLASS/GENERIC NAME	TRADE NAME
Benzodiazepines	
Alprazolam	Xanax
Chlordiazepoxide	Librium
Clonazepam	Klonopin
Clorazepate dipotassium	Tranxene
Diazepam	Valium
Lorazepam	Ativan
Oxazepam	Serax
Prazepam	Centrax
Azaspirones	
Buspirone	BuSpar
Beta blockers	
Propranolol	Inderal
Atenolol	Tenormin

Sprinkle lightly *In the early twentieth century, drug companies did not have to prove the safety or value of their products. Brain Salt, a patent medicine for anxiety and related difficulties, promised to cure nervous disability, headaches, indigestion, heart palpitations, and sleep problems.*

ConsiderThis

⦿ How might antianxiety drugs be administered so as to take advantage of their helpful effects yet minimize their undesired effects?

Only years later did investigators come to understand the reasons for their effectiveness. As we have noted, researchers eventually learned that there are specific neuron sites in the brain that receive benzodiazepines (Mohler & Okada, 1977; Squires & Braestrup, 1977), and that these same receptor sites ordinarily receive the neurotransmitter GABA (Leonard, 1999; Sanders & Shekhar, 1995). Apparently, when benzodiazepines bind to these neuron receptor sites, particularly those receptors known as *GABA-A* receptors, they increase the ability of GABA to bind to them as well, and so improve GABA's ability to stop neuron firing, slow bodily arousal, and reduce anxiety.

Benzodiazepines are prescribed for generalized anxiety disorder more than for most other kinds of anxiety disorders (Uhlenhuth et al., 1999, 1995). Controlled studies show that they do sometimes provide temporary and modest relief (Rickels et al., 2000). In recent years, however, clinicians have begun to realize the potential dangers of these drugs. First, when the medications are stopped, many persons' anxieties return as strong as ever. Second, we now know that people who take benzodiazepines in large doses for an extended time can become physically dependent on them. Third, the drugs can produce undesirable effects such as drowsiness, lack of coordination, memory loss, depression, and aggressive behavior. Fourth, long-term use of these drugs may impair a person's cognitive and psychomotor functioning, and these effects may persist even after the drugs are stopped. And finally, although benzodiazepines are not directly harmful to the body, clinicians have learned that they do *potentiate,* or multiply, the effects of other substances, such as alcohol. Breathing can slow dangerously, sometimes fatally, if people on these antianxiety drugs drink even small amounts of alcohol (Miller, 1999; Elsesser et al., 1996).

Since the 1980s several other kinds of antianxiety drugs have been developed which are now also available for people with generalized anxiety disorder (Hoehn Saric, 1998). One group, called *beta blockers*, binds to receptors in the brain called *beta-adrenergic receptors* and reduce specific physical symptoms of anxiety, such as palpitations and tremors (Tyrer, 1992). Unfortunately, beta blockers bring only minor improvement to people with generalized anxiety disorder (Meibach, Mullane, & Binstok, 1987), but they do seem to be helpful as a treatment for performance anxiety (Bruce & Saeed, 1999). For example, they have sometimes helped the performances of anxious bowlers, musicians, and public speakers (Taylor, 1995). Another kind of drug, *buspirone,* shows greater promise as a treatment for generalized anxiety disorder. Binding to a different set of receptors in the brain, this drug is often just as effective as benzodiazepines and may be less likely to lead to physical dependence (Lader & Scotto, 1998; Schweizer & Rickels, 1997).

RELAXATION TRAINING A nonchemical biological technique commonly used to treat generalized anxiety disorder is **relaxation training**. The premise behind

Modern relaxation *At the Brain Mind Gym, business executives receive pulsations of light and sound from goggles and headphones, which are meant to lull their brains into deep relaxation.*

this approach is that physical relaxation will lead to a state of psychological relaxation. In one version, therapists teach clients to identify individual muscle groups, tense them, release the tension, and ultimately relax the whole body. With continued practice, they can bring on a state of deep muscle relaxation at will, reducing their anxiety during stressful situations.

Research indicates that relaxation training is more effective than no treatment or placebo treatment in cases of generalized anxiety disorder (Fisher & Durham, 1999; DeRubeis & Crits-Christoph, 1998). The improvement it produces, however, tends to be modest (Butler et al., 1991), and other techniques that are known to induce relaxation, such as *meditation*, often seem to be equally effective (Kabat-Zinn et al., 1992; Mathews, 1984). Relaxation training is of greatest help to people with generalized anxiety disorder when it is combined with cognitive therapy or with biofeedback (Cameron et al., 1999; Taylor, 1995).

BIOFEEDBACK In **biofeedback**, therapists use electrical signals from the body to train people to control physiological processes such as heart rate, muscle tension, and blood pressure. Clients are connected to a monitor that gives them continuous information about their bodily activities. By attending to the therapist's instructions and the signals from the monitor, they may gradually learn to control even seemingly involuntary physiological processes.

The most widely applied method of biofeedback for the treatment of anxiety uses a device called an **electromyograph (EMG)**, which provides feedback about the level of muscular tension in the body (Brauer, 1999; Somer, 1995). Electrodes are attached to the client's muscles—usually the forehead muscles—where they detect the minute electrical activity that accompanies muscle tension (see Figure 5-5). The device then converts electric potentials coming from the muscles into an image, such as lines on a screen, or into a tone whose pitch changes along with changes in muscle tension. Thus clients "see" or "hear" when their muscles are becoming more or less tense. Through repeated trial and error, the individuals become skilled at voluntarily reducing muscle tension and, theoretically, at reducing tension and anxiety in everyday stressful situations. Research indicates that EMG biofeedback training helps both normal and anxious subjects reduce their anxiety somewhat (Rice, Blanchard, & Purcell, 1993; Hurley & Meminger, 1992). According to direct comparisons, this approach and relaxation training have similar effects on anxiety levels (Brown, Hertz, & Barlow, 1992).

In the 1960s and 1970s, many hailed biofeedback training as an approach that would revolutionize clinical treatment. So far, however, the techniques have proved more cumbersome, less efficient, and less productive than clinicians had envisioned (Brauer, 1999; Wittrock & Blanchard, 1992). Biofeedback appears to be most helpful when it plays an *adjunct* role in the treatment of certain medical

RELAXATION TRAINING A treatment procedure that teaches clients to relax at will so they can calm themselves in stressful situations.

BIOFEEDBACK A treatment technique in which a client is given information about physiological reactions as they occur and learns to control the reactions voluntarily.

ELECTROMYOGRAPH (EMG) A device that provides feedback about the level of muscular tension in the body.

IN SEARCH OF THE PERFECT WAVE

Brain-wave patterns are rhythmic electrical discharges in our brains. *Alpha waves* are desirable waves, produced when we are in a relaxed, wakeful state. Biofeedback therapists often use an *electroencephalograph (EEG)*, which records electrical activity in the brain, to teach clients to produce alpha waves voluntarily. Some people who can induce their own alpha-wave activity do in fact feel more relaxed and less anxious (Moore, 2000; Vanathy et al., 1998), but others do not, thus limiting this technique's appeal as a treatment for anxiety (Blanchard et al., 1992; Andrasik & Blanchard, 1983).

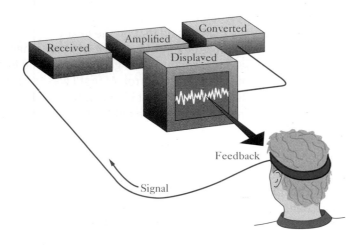

FIGURE 5-5 **Biofeedback at work** *This biofeedback system is recording tension in the forehead muscle of an anxious person. The system receives, amplifies, converts, and displays information about the tension, allowing the client to "observe" it and to try to reduce his tension responses.*

and houses. Behaviorists often account for these differences by proposing that human beings, as a species, have a *predisposition* to develop certain fears (Ohman & Soares, 1993; Seligman, 1971). This idea is referred to as **preparedness**, because human beings, theoretically, are "prepared" to acquire some phobias and not others. The following case description by I. M. Marks (1977) makes the point:

> A four-year-old girl was playing in the park. Thinking that she saw a snake, she ran to her parents' car and jumped inside, slamming the door behind her. Unfortunately, the girl's hand was caught by the closing car door, the results of which were severe pain and several visits to the doctor. Before this, she may have been afraid of snakes, but not phobic. After this experience, a phobia developed, not of cars or car doors, but of snakes. The snake phobia persisted into adulthood, at which time she sought treatment from me. (p. 192)

Marks concludes, "Certain stimuli seem to act as magnets for phobia . . . as if human brains were preprogrammed to make these preferential connections easily" (p. 194).

In a series of impressive tests of preparedness, the psychologist Arne Ohman and his colleagues have conditioned different kinds of fears in two groups of human subjects (Ohman & Soares, 1993; Ohman, Erixon, & Lofberg, 1975). In one study they showed all subjects slides of faces, houses, snakes, and spiders. One group received electric shocks whenever they observed the slides of faces and houses, while the other group received shocks in association with snakes and spiders. Were subjects more prepared to fear snakes and spiders? Using skin reactions, or *galvanic skin responses (GSRs)*, as a measure of fear, the experimenters found that both groups learned to fear the intended objects after repeated shock pairings. But then they noted an interesting distinction: after a short shock-free period, the persons who had learned to fear faces and houses stopped registering high GSRs in the presence of those objects, but the persons who had learned to fear snakes and spiders continued to show high GSRs in response to them for a long while. One interpretation is that animals and insects are stronger inducers of human phobias than faces or houses.

Researchers do not know whether human predispositions to fear are the result of biological or environmental factors. Proponents of a biological predisposition argue that a tendency to fear has been transmitted genetically through the evolutionary process. Among our ancestors, the ones who more readily acquired a fear of animals, darkness, heights, and the like were more likely to survive long enough to reproduce. Proponents of an environmental predisposition argue instead that experiences teach us early in life that certain objects are legitimate sources of fear, and this training predisposes many people to acquire corresponding phobias (Graham & Gaffan, 1997; Harris & Menzies, 1996).

How Are Phobias Treated?

Every theoretical model has its own approach to treating phobias, but behavioral techniques are more widely used than the rest, particularly for specific phobias. Research has shown them to be highly effective and to fare better than other approaches in most head-to-head comparisons (Ollendick & King, 1998; Wolpe, 1997). Thus we shall focus primarily on the behavioral interventions.

TREATMENTS FOR SPECIFIC PHOBIAS Specific phobias were among the first anxiety disorders to be treated successfully in clinical practice. The major behavioral approaches to treating them are *desensitization, flooding,* and *modeling.* Together, these approaches are called **exposure treatments**, because in all of them individuals are exposed to the objects or situations they dread.

People treated by **systematic desensitization**, a technique developed by Joseph Wolpe (1997, 1987, 1969), learn to relax while gradually confronting the

---

SPIDERS UNDER STRESS
Many people feel threatened by spiders, but what about when the tables are turned? Some species of tarantulas pluck hairs from their stomach and propel them like darts toward any creature that frightens them, causing the creature to itch.

PREPAREDNESS A predisposition to develop certain fears.

EXPOSURE TREATMENTS Behavioral treatments in which persons are exposed to the objects or situations they dread.

SYSTEMATIC DESENSITIZATION A behavioral treatment that uses relaxation training and a fear hierarchy to help clients with phobias react calmly to the objects or situations they dread.

FEAR HIERARCHY A list of objects or situations that frighten a person, starting with those that are slightly feared and ending with those that are feared greatly.

FLOODING A treatment for phobias in which clients are exposed repeatedly and intensively to a feared object and made to see that it is actually harmless.

objects or situations they fear. Since relaxation and fear are incompatible, the new relaxation response is thought to substitute for the fear response. Desensitization therapists first offer *relaxation training* to clients, teaching them to release all tension from their bodies. With continued practice, the clients are able to bring on a state of deep muscle relaxation at will. In addition, the therapists help clients create a **fear hierarchy**, a list of objects or situations in which the phobia is aroused. The items on the list are ranked from ones that evoke only a trace of fear to those that the person finds extremely frightening.

Then clients learn how to pair relaxation with the objects or situations they fear. While the client is in a state of relaxation, the therapist has the client face the event at the bottom of his or her hierarchy. This may be an actual confrontation, a process called *in vivo desensitization*. A person who fears heights, for example, may stand on a chair or climb a stepladder. Or the confrontation may be imagined, a process called *covert desensitization*. In this case, the person imagines the frightening event while the therapist describes it. The client moves through the entire list, pairing his or her relaxation responses with each feared item. Because the first item is only mildly frightening, it is usually only a short while before the person is able to relax totally in its presence. Over the course of several sessions, clients move up the ladder of their fears until they reach and overcome the one that frightens them most of all.

Another behavioral treatment for specific phobias is **flooding**. Flooding therapists believe that people will stop fearing things when they are exposed to them repeatedly and made to see that they are actually quite harmless. In flooding, people with phobias are forced to face their feared objects or situations without relaxation training and without a gradual buildup of tolerance. The flooding procedure, like desensitization, can be either in vivo or covert.

When flooding therapists guide clients in imagining feared objects or situations, they often exaggerate the description so that the clients experience intense emotional arousal. In the case of a woman with a snake phobia, the therapist had her imagine the following scene, among others:

> Close your eyes again. Picture the snake out in front of you, now make yourself pick it up. Reach down, pick it up, put it in your lap, feel it wiggling around in your lap, leave your hand on it, put your hand out and feel it wiggling around. Kind of explore its body with your fingers and hand. You don't like to do it, make yourself do it. Make yourself do it. Really grab onto the snake. Squeeze it a little bit, feel it. Feel it kind of start to wind around your hand. Let it. Leave your hand there, feel it touching your hand and winding around it, curling around your wrist.
>
> Okay, now put your finger out towards the snake and feel his head coming up. Its head is towards your finger and it is starting to bite at your finger. Let it, let it bite at your finger. Put your finger out, let it bite, let it bite at your finger, feel its fangs go right down into your finger. Oooh, feel the pain going right up your arm and into your shoulder.

(Hogan, 1968, p. 423)

In *modeling,* or *vicarious conditioning,* it is the therapist who confronts the feared object or situation while the client observes (Bandura, 1977, 1971; Bandura, Adams, & Beyer, 1977). The behavioral therapist acts as a model, to demonstrate that the person's fear is groundless. After several sessions many clients

Conquering coasterphobia *Missing out on thousands of dollars each year because many persons are afraid of riding on roller coasters, some amusement parks offer behavioral programs to help customers overcome their fears. After "treatment," some clients are able to ride the rails with the best of them. For others, it's back to the relative calm of the Ferris wheel.*

SNAKE DATA

The most dangerous snake in the world is the *black mamba,* whose bite kills in 95 of 100 cases. The *cobra* death rate is 18 to 35 percent, depending on the particular type, and the *tropical rattlesnake* death rate is 18 percent (Ash, 1999).

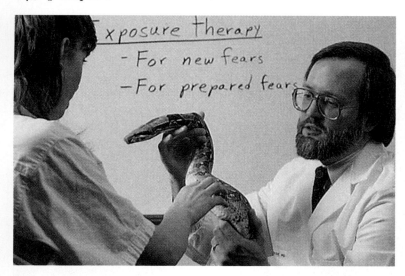

Participant modeling *In the exposure technique of participant modeling, a therapist treats a client with a snake phobia by first handling a snake himself, then encouraging the client to touch and handle it.*

are able to approach the objects or situations with composure. In one version of modeling, *participant modeling,* or *guided participation*, the client is actively encouraged to join in with the therapist.

Clinical researchers have repeatedly found that exposure treatments help with specific phobias (McGlynn et al., 1999; Ollendick & King, 1998; Emmelkamp, 1994). The key to success in all these therapies appears to be *actual* contact with the feared object or situation (Hellstrom & Ost, 1996; Emmelkamp, 1994). In vivo desensitization is more effective than covert desensitization, in vivo flooding more effective than covert flooding, and participant modeling more helpful than strictly observational modeling (Menzies & Clarke, 1993). Many behavioral therapists now combine features of each of the exposure approaches.

TREATMENTS FOR SOCIAL PHOBIAS Clinicians have only recently begun to have much success in treating social phobias (Heimberg et al., 1999, 1995). This progress is due in part to the growing recognition that social phobias have two distinct features that may feed upon each other: (1) people with the phobias may have overwhelming social fears, and (2) they may lack skill at initiating conversations, communicating their needs, or meeting the needs of others. Armed with this insight, clinicians now treat social phobias by trying to reduce social fears or by providing training in social skills, or both (Juster, Heimberg, & Holt, 1996).

HOW CAN SOCIAL FEARS BE REDUCED? Unlike specific phobias, which are typically unresponsive to psychotropic drugs, social fears are often reduced through medication (Montgomery, 1999; Pollack, 1999; Heimberg et al., 1998). Somewhat surprisingly, it is antidepressant medications that seem to be most helpful for this disorder, often more helpful than benzodiazepines or beta blockers—the drugs that specifically address performance anxiety.

Several types of psychotherapy have proved at least as effective as medication at reducing social fears. Moreover, people helped by these psychological treatments are apparently less likely to relapse than people treated with drugs alone (Liebowitz et al., 1999, 1997; Davidson, 1998). This suggests to some clinicians that the psychological approaches should always be included in the treatment of social fears.

One psychological approach is exposure therapy (DeRubeis & Crits-Christoph, 1998), the behavioral intervention so effective with specific phobias. Exposure therapists guide, encourage, and persuade clients with social fears to expose themselves to the dreaded social situations and to remain until their fears subside. Usually the exposure is gradual and often coupled with homework assignments in which the clients begin facing social situations on their own (Edelman & Chambless, 1995; Heimberg et al., 1990). Group therapy provides a particularly useful setting for exposure treatments by allowing people to confront the social situations they fear in an atmosphere of support and concern (Scholing & Emmelkamp, 1999, 1996; Shear & Beidel, 1998). In one group, a man who was afraid that his hands would tremble in the presence of others had to write on a blackboard in front of the group and serve tea to the other members (Emmelkamp, 1982).

Cognitive therapies have also been widely used to treat social fears, often in combination with behavioral techniques (Turk et al., 1999; Wells, 1998; Woody et al., 1997). In the following discussion, Albert Ellis uses rational-emotive therapy to help a man who fears he will be rejected if he speaks up at gatherings (see Box 5-7 on page 150). The discussion took place after the man had done a homework assignment in which he was to observe his self-defeating thoughts and beliefs and force himself to say anything he had on his mind in social situations, no matter how stupid it might seem to him:

FAMOUS VICTIM OF SOCIAL ANXIETY

Although the poet Emily Dickinson wrote movingly about love, she was not able to interact comfortably with people. She became so reclusive that she sometimes spoke to her visitors from an adjoining room rather than talking to them face to face (Asimov, 1997).

After two weeks of this assignment, the patient came into his next session of therapy and reported: "I did what you told me to do. . . . [Every] time, just as you said, I found myself retreating from people, I said to myself: 'Now, even though you can't see it, there must be some sentences. What are they?' And I finally found them. And there were many of them! And they all seemed to say the same thing."

"What thing?"

"That I, uh, was going to be rejected. . . . [If] I related to them I was going to be rejected. And wouldn't that be perfectly awful if I was to be rejected. And there was no reason for me, uh, to take that, uh, sort of thing, and be rejected in that awful manner." . . .

"And did you do the second part of the homework assignment?"

"The forcing myself to speak up and express myself?"

"Yes, that part."

"That was worse. That was really hard. Much harder than I thought it would be. But I did it."

"And?"

"Oh, not bad at all. I spoke up several times; more than I've ever done before. Some people were very surprised. Phyllis was very surprised, too. But I spoke up." . . .

"And how did you feel after expressing yourself like that?"

"Remarkable! I don't remember when I last felt this way. I felt, uh, just remarkable—good, that is. It was really something to feel! But it was so hard. I almost didn't make it. And a couple of other times during the week I had to force myself again. But I did. And I was glad!"

(Ellis, 1962, pp. 202–203)

As the case shows, Ellis also uses in vivo exposure techniques to help clients change their assumptions. He asks, "Unless phobic individuals act against their irrational beliefs that they must not approach fearsome objects or situations . . . , can they ever really be said to have overcome such beliefs?" (Ellis, 1979, p. 162). Behaviorists might argue that exposure is playing a more direct role in this cognitive treatment than Ellis acknowledges (Shear & Beidel, 1998).

Studies indicate that rational-emotive therapy and similar cognitive approaches do indeed help reduce social fears (Cameron et al., 1999). And these reductions persist for years (Heimberg et al., 1993, 1991). In fact, Ellis's therapy is more effective as a treatment for social anxiety than for most other problems. At the same time, research also suggests that cognitive therapy, like drug therapy and exposure therapy, does not typically overcome social phobias *fully* (Poulton & Andrews, 1996). It reduces social fear, but it does not consistently help people perform effectively in the social realm (Gardner et al., 1980). This is where social skills training has come to the forefront.

HOW CAN SOCIAL SKILLS BE IMPROVED? In **social skills training**, therapists combine several behavioral techniques to help people improve their social skills. They usually *model* appropriate social behaviors and encourage the clients to try them out. Clients then *role-play* with the therapists, rehearsing their new behaviors until they become proficient. Throughout the process, therapists provide frank *feedback* and *reinforce* (praise) the clients for effective performances.

Social reinforcement from others with similar social difficulties is often more powerful than reinforcement from a therapist alone. In *social skills training groups* and *assertiveness training groups,* members try out and rehearse new social behavior with or in front of other group members. The group can also provide guidance on what is socially appropriate.

Some practitioners have devised special exercises to help group members develop social skills (Mersch et al., 1991; Wlazlo et al., 1990; Rimm & Masters, 1979). One beginning exercise focuses on greetings. Each member turns to a

"It ain't so much the things we don't know that get us into trouble. It's the things we know that just ain't so."

Artemus Ward (1834–1867)

SOCIAL SKILLS TRAINING A therapy approach that helps people learn or improve social skills and assertiveness through role playing and rehearsing of desirable behaviors.

BOX 5-7

Clinician, Heal Thyself

Rational-emotive therapy teaches clients to challenge and change their irrational assumptions. And who was the first client treated by Albert Ellis, the founder of the approach? Why, none other than Albert Ellis!

| At 19 Ellis became active in a political group but was hampered by his terror of public speaking. Confronting his worst demons in the first of many "shame-attacking" exercises he would devise, Ellis repeatedly forced himself to speak up in any political context that would permit. . . . "Instead of just getting good at this, I found I was very good at it. And now you can't keep me away from a public platform."

[Next] Ellis decided to work on the terrors of more private communication. "I was always violently interested in women, . . . but I always made excuses not to talk to them and was terrified of being rejected.

"Since I lived near The New York Botanical Garden in the Bronx, I decided to attack my fear and shame with an exercise in the park. I vowed that when-

ever I saw a reasonably attractive woman up to the age of 35, . . . I would sit next to her with the specific goal of opening a conversation within one minute. I sat next to 130 consecutive women who fit my criteria. Thirty of the women got up and walked away, but about 100 spoke to me—about their knitting, the birds, a book, whatever. I made only one date out of all these contacts—and she stood me up. . . . But I realized that throughout this exercise no one vomited, no one called a cop and I didn't die. The process of trying new behaviors and understanding what happened in the real world instead of in my imagination led me to overcome my fear of speaking to women." |

(WARGO, 1988, P. 56)

neighbor and says, "Hello, how are you?" The neighbor replies, "Fine, how are you?" This exchange is to be made with warmth, good eye contact, and a strong, assertive tone of voice. Exchanging compliments is another exercise designed to help group members who have difficulty giving and receiving compliments.

Social skills training helps many people perform better in social situations (Cameron et al., 1999; Turk et al., 1999). Some people, however, continue to experience uncomfortable levels of fear despite such treatments (Juster et al., 1996; Marks, 1987).

No single approach—drug therapy, exposure treatment, cognitive therapy, or social skills training—consistently causes social phobias to disappear, and none is clearly superior to the others (Wlazlo et al., 1990). Yet each is helpful, and when the approaches are combined, the results have been especially encouraging (Franklin et al., 1999; Hope & Heimberg, 1993). One study compared the prog-

Contrary to popular belief . . . *The goal of assertiveness training groups is to teach people to express their needs in socially acceptable ways, not to encourage them to lash out at others without restraint.* (© 1993 Tribune Media Services, Inc. All rights reserved.)

ress of four treatment groups: people who received social skills training, people who received social skills training combined with rational-emotive therapy, people in a consciousness-raising group, and control subjects on a waiting list (Wolfe & Fodor, 1977). The group that received the combined treatment showed significantly more improvement in both fear reduction and social performance than the other three groups.

CROSSROADS:
Diathesis-Stress in Action

Clinicians and researchers have developed many ideas about generalized anxiety disorder and phobias. At times, however, the sheer quantity of concepts and findings makes it difficult to grasp what is and what is not really known about the disorders.

Overall, it is fair to say that clinicians do not yet have a clear understanding of generalized anxiety disorder. The explanations offered by each of the models have key limitations. Similarly, most treatments have had only modest success. Partly because progress has been so limited, growing numbers of clinical theorists are coming to believe that they can best understand the disorder by considering the various perspectives together. It may well be that people develop generalized anxiety disorder only when biological, psychological, and sociocultural factors are *all* operating.

Adopting a diathesis-stress perspective, for example, some theorists suggest that individuals with this disorder must have a biological vulnerability toward experiencing anxiety that is brought to fruition by psychological and sociocultural forces (Kazdin & Weisz, 1998). In fact, genetic investigators have discovered that certain genes may combine to help determine whether a person reacts to life's stressors calmly or in an uptight, anxious way (Plomin et al., 1997; Lesch et al., 1996; Flint et al., 1995), and developmental researchers have found that even during the earliest stages of life some infants consistently become very aroused when stimulated while other infants remain quiet (Kalin, 1993; Pekrun, 1992). It may be that the easily aroused infants have inherited defects in GABA functioning or other biological limitations that predispose them to generalized anxiety disorder. If, over the course of their lives, such individuals also confront intense societal pressures and learn to interpret the world as a dangerous place, they may indeed be candidates for developing the disorder.

A diathesis-stress perspective may also shed more light on phobias. Although today's leading phobia theories—especially the behavioral ones—are better supported than those for generalized anxiety disorder, combining them with genetic explanations may help us better predict who will and who will not develop phobias. We have already seen that humans as a species are more likely to fear some objects or situations (for example, snakes) than others (houses). It also appears that some individuals may be genetically predisposed to develop phobias, even phobias with particular themes. In one study, almost a third of subjects with a specific phobia had close relatives with a similar phobia (Fyer et al., 1990). In another, almost two-thirds of subjects with a blood-injection-injury phobia had close relatives with the same problem (Ost, 1989). And, in a related vein, several studies suggest that certain infants are born with a style of social inhibition or shyness that may increase their risk of developing a social phobia (Kagan & Snidman, 1999, 1991; Biederman et al., 1990). If such family patterns and infant traits do, in fact, reflect genetic tendencies, it could be that people must have both a genetic predisposition *and* unfortunate conditioning experiences in order to develop particular phobias.

Efforts at integration can also be seen in the treatment of generalized anxiety disorder and phobias. Many clinicians who treat people with these disorders are now combining principles and interventions from various models. As we noted earlier, treatment programs for social phobias may include a combination of

ConsiderThis

Almost half of all people with a major depressive disorder also experience an anxiety disorder (Regier et al., 1998). In such cases, the anxiety disorder usually begins during adolescence and the depressive disorder during young adulthood. How might problems with anxiety help cause a mood disorder? • How else might the relationship between these disorders be explained?

FAINTING AT THE SIGHT OF BLOOD

One of the most common specific phobias is the fear of blood, injections, and injury. Unlike people with other specific phobias, sufferers of this so-called *blood-injection-injury* phobia often faint when confronted by one of their dreaded objects or situations (Curtis et al., 1999; Bienvenu & Eaton, 1998; Antony, Brown, & Barlow, 1997).

STRESS MANAGEMENT PROGRAM An approach to treating generalized and other anxiety disorders that teaches clients techniques for reducing and controlling stress.

medications, exposure therapy, cognitive therapy, and social skills training. Similarly, cognitive techniques such as self-instruction training are now often combined with relaxation training or biofeedback in the treatment of generalized anxiety disorder—a package known as a **stress management program**.

The tendency to integrate concepts and techniques from various models has been even more apparent with regard to the remaining anxiety disorders—panic disorder, obsessive-compulsive disorder, and the stress disorders. Over the past 15 years great progress has been made in understanding and treating them. We shall turn to this very promising work in Chapter 6.

INSECURITY, ADULT STYLE

Children may cling to blankets or cuddly toys to feel more secure. Adults, too, may hug a beloved object in order to relax. One in five adult women and one in twenty men admit to sleeping with a stuffed animal on a regular basis (Kanner, 1995).

GENETICS OR MODELING?

Mothers of very shy preschoolers have a higher rate of anxiety disorders, particularly social phobia, than mothers of children who are not shy. In one study, 78 percent of the mothers of shy young children had a current or past anxiety disorder, a social phobia in half of the cases (Cooper & Eke, 1999).

SUMMARY AND REVIEW

■ **Coping, stress, and anxiety** Fear is a state of alarm that occurs in response to a specific, serious threat. Anxiety is the state of alarm that occurs when our sense of threat is vague. The features of fear and anxiety are produced by the activities of the autonomic nervous system and the endocrine glands, including the adrenal glands. *pp. 117–121*

■ **Generalized anxiety disorder** People with generalized anxiety disorder experience excessive anxiety and worry about a wide range of events and activities. The various explanations and treatments for this disorder have received only limited research support, although recent cognitive and biological approaches seem to be promising.

According to the sociocultural view, increases in societal dangers and pressures create a climate in which cases of generalized anxiety disorder are more likely to develop. *pp. 122–124*

In the original psychodynamic explanation, Freud said that generalized anxiety disorder may develop when anxiety is excessive and defense mechanisms break down and function poorly. Psychodynamic therapists use free association, interpretation, and related psychodynamic techniques to help people overcome this problem. *pp. 124–127*

Carl Rogers, the leading humanistic theorist, believed that people with generalized anxiety disorder fail to receive unconditional positive regard from significant others during their childhood and so become overly critical of themselves. He treated such individuals with client-centered therapy. Existentialists believe that generalized anxiety disorder results from existential anxiety—anxiety rooted in people's knowledge that life is finite and their suspicion that it may have no ultimate meaning. Existential therapists help anxious people take more responsibility for their choices and live more meaningfully. *pp. 127–129*

Cognitive theorists believe that generalized anxiety disorder is caused by maladaptive assumptions and beliefs that lead people to view most life situations as dangerous. Cognitive therapists help their clients change such thinking, and they teach them how to cope during stressful situations. *pp. 129–133*

Biological theorists hold that generalized anxiety disorder results from low activity of the neurotransmitter GABA. The most common biological treatment is antianxiety drugs, particularly benzodiazepines. Relaxation training and biofeedback are also applied in many cases. *pp. 133–138*

■ **Phobias** A phobia is a severe, persistent, and unreasonable fear of a particular object, activity, or situation. There are three main categories of phobias: specific phobias, social phobias, and agoraphobia. Behavioral explanations of phobias, particularly specific phobias, are the most influential today. Behaviorists believe that phobias are learned from the environment through classical conditioning or through modeling, and then are maintained because of avoidance behaviors. *pp. 138–146*

Specific phobias have been treated most successfully by behavioral exposure techniques in which people are led to confront the objects they fear. The exposure may be gradual and relaxed (desensitization), intense (flooding), or vicarious (modeling). *pp. 146–148*

Therapists who treat social phobias typically distinguish two components of this disorder: social fears and poor social skills. They try to reduce social fears by drug therapy, exposure techniques, group therapy, various cognitive approaches, or a combination of these interventions. They may try to improve social skills by social skills training. *pp. 148–151*

CYBER
STUDY

▲ *How might occupational stress affect mental health?* ▲ *How might stress and anxiety affect job performance?* ▲ *Observe the psychoanalytic treatment of an anxious person.* ▲ *See "fight-or-flight" reactions in action.* ▲ *What role does anxiety play in depression?*

SEARCH THE *ABNORMAL PSYCHOLOGY* CD-ROM FOR

▲ Chapter 5 video case and discussion
  "Claude & Claude"—Emotion, Stress, and Health

▲ Chapter 5 practice test and feedback

▲ Additional video cases and discussions
  "Larry"—Psychoanalytic Therapy Session
  "Derrick"—Hamilton Depression Scale

LOG ON TO THE COMER WEB PAGE

[www.worthpublishers.com/comerabnormalpsychology4e] **FOR**

▲ Suggested Web links, research exercises, FAQ page, additional
Chapter 5 practice test questions

Panic, Obsessive-Compulsive, and Stress Disorders

I was inside a very busy shopping precinct and all of a sudden it happened: in a matter of seconds I was like a mad woman. It was like a nightmare, only I was awake; everything went black and sweat poured out of me—my body, my hands and even my hair got wet through. All the blood seemed to drain out of me; I went as white as a ghost. I felt as if I were going to collapse; it was as if I had no control over my limbs; my back and legs were very weak and I felt as though it were impossible to move. It was as if I had been taken over by some stronger force. I saw all the people looking at me—just faces, no bodies, all merged into one. My heart started pounding in my head and in my ears; I thought my heart was going to stop. I could see black and yellow lights. I could hear the voices of the people but from a long way off. I could not think of anything except the way I was feeling and that now I had to get out and run quickly or I would die. I must escape and get into the fresh air.

(Hawkrigg, 1975)

Anxiety may take a form that is even more intense than the symptoms discussed in Chapter 5. In the excerpt above, for example, a woman describes a *panic attack,* an outbreak of terror that is the central feature of *panic disorder.* Anxiety may also pose problems that are different from the difficulties described in Chapter 5. People with *obsessive-compulsive disorder* are beset by recurrent unwanted thoughts that cause them anxiety or by the need to perform repetitive actions to reduce their anxiety. And people with *acute stress disorder* and *posttraumatic stress disorder* are tormented by fear and related symptoms well after a traumatic situation has ended and the threat has passed. During most of the twentieth century, clinicians and researchers paid much more attention to generalized anxiety disorder and phobias than to these other anxiety disorders in the belief that panic, obsessive-compulsive, and stress disorders were less common. Certainly they were less understood and treatments for them were less effective.

This situation has changed drastically in the past 15 years. Researchers are discovering that panic, obsessive-compulsive, and stress disorders are more common than anyone had realized. Moreover, they have uncovered very promising clues to the causes of these disorders, and therapists have developed treatments for them that are often quite helpful. In fact, this is where investigators of anxiety disorders are now focusing most of their attention (Norton et al., 1995).

Panic Disorder

Sometimes an anxiety reaction takes the form of a smothering, nightmarish panic in which people lose control of their behavior and, in fact, are practically unaware of what they are doing. Anyone can react with panic when a real threat looms up suddenly. Some people, however, experience *panic attacks*—periodic, discrete bouts of panic that occur suddenly, reach a peak within 10 minutes, and gradually pass. The attacks feature at least four of the following symptoms of panic: palpitations of the heart, tingling

"They just kept pushin' forward and they would just walk right on top of you, just trample over ya like you were a piece of the ground. They wouldn't even help ya; people were just screamin' 'help me' and nobody cared."

Patron at The Who concert, Cincinnati, 1979, where 11 people were trampled to death (Johnson, 1987)

Table 6-1 | DSM-IV Checklist

PANIC ATTACK

A discrete period of intense fear in which at least four of the following symptoms develop suddenly and reach a peak within 10 minutes:

✛ Palpitations, pounding heart, or accelerated heart rate
✛ Sweating
✛ Trembling or shaking
✛ Sensations of shortness of breath or smothering
✛ A feeling of choking
✛ Chest pain or discomfort
✛ Nausea or abdominal distress
✛ Feeling dizzy, unsteady, lightheaded, or faint
✛ Derealization or depersonalization
✛ Fear of losing control or going crazy
✛ Fear of dying
✛ Numbness or tingling sensations
✛ Chills or hot flashes

Based on APA, 2000, 1994.

in the hands or feet, shortness of breath, sweating, hot and cold flashes, trembling, chest pains, choking sensations, faintness, dizziness, and a feeling of unreality (see Table 6-1). Small wonder that during a panic attack many people fear they will die, go crazy, or lose control.

People with any of the anxiety disorders (or, for that matter, people without an anxiety disorder) may experience a panic attack when they are faced with something they dread. Some people, however, have panic attacks repeatedly and unexpectedly without apparent reason. They may be suffering from **panic disorder**. In addition to the panic attacks, people who are diagnosed with panic disorder also must experience dysfunctional changes in their thinking or behavior as a result of the attacks for a period of a month or more. For example, they may worry persistently about having another attack, have concerns about what such an attack means ("Am I losing my mind?" "Am I having a heart attack?"), or plan their behavior around the possibility of a future attack.

Many people (and their physicians) mistake their first panic attack for a general medical problem (Ballenger, 1997; Stahl & Soefje, 1995). Conversely, certain medical problems—thyroid disease or mitral valve prolapse, a cardiac malfunction marked by periodic episodes of heart palpitations—may initially be misdiagnosed as panic disorder (Carter et al., 1997; Pollock et al., 1996).

Panic disorder is often accompanied by **agoraphobia,** one of the three categories of phobia mentioned in Chapter 5. People with agoraphobia (from the Greek for "fear of the marketplace") are afraid to leave the house and travel to public places or other locations where escape might be difficult or help unavailable should panic symptoms develop. The intensity of agoraphobia may fluctuate. In severe cases, people become virtual prisoners in their own homes. Their social life dwindles, and they cannot hold a job.

The experience of agoraphobia *George Tooker's painting* Subway *expresses the sense of threat and entrapment that many people with agoraphobia experience when they enter public places.*

Until recently, clinicians failed to recognize the close link between agoraphobia and panic attacks. They believed that this intense fear of public places was acquired much as other phobias are, by classical conditioning or modeling. They now realize that panic attacks, or at least some paniclike symptoms, typically set the stage for agoraphobia (Goisman et al., 1995): after experiencing one or more unpredictable attacks, certain individuals become fearful of having new attacks in public places where help or escape might be elusive (Cox, Endler, & Swinson, 1995). Anne Watson's plight illustrates a typical onset of agoraphobia:

> Ms. Watson reported that until the onset of her current problems two years ago, she had led a normal and happy life. At that time an uncle to whom she had been extremely close in her childhood died following a sudden unexpected heart attack.... Six months after his death she was returning home from work one evening when suddenly she felt that she couldn't catch her breath. Her heart began to pound, and she broke out into a cold sweat. Things began to seem unreal, her legs felt leaden, and she became sure she would die or faint before she reached home. She asked a passerby to help her get a taxi and went to a nearby hospital emergency room. The doctors there found her physical examination, blood count and chemistries, and electrocardiogram all completely normal....
>
> Four weeks later Ms. Watson had a second similar attack while preparing dinner at home. She made an appointment to see her family doctor, but again, all examinations were normal. She decided to put the episodes out of her mind and continue with her normal activities. Within the next several weeks, however, she had four attacks and noticed that she began to worry about when the next one would occur....
>
> She then found herself constantly thinking about her anxieties as attacks continued; she began to dread leaving the house alone for fear she would be stranded, helpless and alone, by an attack. She began to avoid going to movies, parties, and dinners with friends for fear she would have an attack and be embarrassed by her need to leave. When household chores necessitated driving she waited until it was possible to take her children or a friend along for the ride. She also began walking the twenty blocks to her office to avoid the possibility of being trapped in a subway car between stops when an attack occurred.
>
> *(Spitzer et al., 1983, pp. 7–8)*

PANIC DISORDER An anxiety disorder marked by recurrent and unpredictable panic attacks.

AGORAPHOBIA An anxiety disorder in which a person is afraid to be in places or situations from which escape might be difficult (or embarrassing) or help unavailable if paniclike symptoms were to occur.

FEARING FEAR

Researchers had persons with agoraphobia record their thoughts while engaging in fear-arousing situations such as driving alone. The subjects' most common thoughts (29 percent) were about how frightened they were feeling (Williams et al., 1997).

Not everyone with panic disorder develops agoraphobia, but many such persons do. Thus DSM-IV distinguishes *panic disorder without agoraphobia* from *panic disorder with agoraphobia* (see Table 6-2). Around 2.3 percent of all people in the United States suffer from one or the other of these patterns in a given year; 3.5 percent develop one of the patterns at some point in their lives (Kessler & Zhao, 1999; Kessler et al., 1994). Both kinds of panic disorder are likely to develop between late adolescence and the mid-30s, and are at least twice as common among women as among men (APA, 2000). Similar prevalence rates and patterns of development are found in most other countries across the world (Weissman et al., 1997) and in all racial and ethnic groups. Around half of the individuals with either form of panic disorder receive treatment, often very successfully (Beamish et al., 1996; Narrow et al., 1993). In some cases of agoraphobia, the panic symptoms that initiate the phobic pattern never reach the full status of panic disorder. These cases receive a diagnosis of *agoraphobia without history of panic disorder*.

Table 6-2   DSM-IV Checklist

PANIC DISORDER WITHOUT AGORAPHOBIA

1. Recurrent unexpected panic attacks.
2. A month or more of one of the following after at least one of the attacks.
   (a) Persistent concern about having additional attacks.
   (b) Worry about the implications or consequences of the attack.
   (c) Significant change in behavior related to the attacks.

PANIC DISORDER WITH AGORAPHOBIA

1. Symptoms of panic disorder.
2. Anxiety about being in places or situations from which escape might be difficult (or embarrassing) or in which help might not be available if paniclike symptoms were to occur.
3. Situations either avoided, endured with marked distress, or manageable only with the presence of a companion.

Based on APA, 2000, 1994.

DOCTOR VISITS

People with panic disorder report making seven times more visits to physicians than other people do (Carr, 1998).

AGE LIMITS

Typically a person must reach a certain level of physical or cognitive maturity before experiencing a full-blown panic attack. One study found that over 5 percent of sixth- and seventh-grade girls had experienced a panic attack (Hayward, 1992). In the subgroup of girls rated most physically immature, none reported panic attacks, but 8 percent of those who had completed puberty did report having them.

NOREPINEPHRINE A neurotransmitter whose abnormal activity is linked to panic disorder and depression.

LOCUS CERULEUS A small area of the brain that seems to be active in the regulation of emotions. Many of its neurons use norepinephrine.

The Biological Perspective

In the 1960s, clinicians made the surprising discovery that panic disorder responded less to benzodiazepine drugs, the drugs useful in treating generalized anxiety disorder, than to certain antidepressant drugs, drugs that are usually used to reduce the symptoms of depression (Klein, 1964; Klein & Fink, 1962). This observation led to the first biological explanations and treatments for panic disorder.

To understand the biology of panic disorder, researchers worked backward from their understanding of the antidepressant drugs that seemed to control it. They knew that many of the antidepressant drugs in question change the activity of **norepinephrine**, one of the neurotransmitters that carry messages from neuron to neuron in the brain. If the drugs also eliminated panic attacks, researchers wondered, might panic disorder be caused in the first place by abnormal norepinephrine activity?

Several studies have produced evidence that norepinephrine activity is indeed irregular in people who suffer from panic attacks (Levy et al., 1996; Gorman, Papp, & Coplan, 1995). For example, the **locus ceruleus** is a brain area rich in neurons that use norepinephrine. When this area is electrically stimulated in monkeys, the monkeys display a paniclike reaction. Conversely, when this norepinephrine-rich brain area is surgically damaged, monkeys show no reaction at all, even in the face of unmistakable danger. Perhaps panic reactions are related to changes in norepinephrine activity in the locus ceruleus (Redmond, 1981, 1979, 1977) (see Figure 6-1).

In another line of research, scientists have induced panic attacks in human beings by injecting them with chemicals known to affect the activity of norepinephrine (Bourin et al., 1995). When low doses of one such chemical, *yohimbine,* are given to subjects who suffer from panic disorder, many of them immediately experience a panic attack (Charney et al., 1990, 1987). Some studies have successfully used yohimbine to induce panic symptoms even in people with no history of panic (Charney et al., 1992, 1984, 1983). These findings strongly implicate norepinephrine in panic attacks, because yohimbine alters norepinephrine functioning, particularly in the locus ceruleus, without affecting other neurotransmitters.

Just what goes wrong in panic attacks, however, is still not fully understood. It is not clear, for example, whether the problem is excessive activity, deficient activity, or some other form of dysfunctioning involving norepinephrine. To complicate matters, there is growing evidence that other neurotransmitters also may have roles to play in panic disorder (Emmanuel et al., 1999; Gorman et al., 1995).

Furthermore, investigators do not know why some people have such biological abnormalities. One possibility is that a predisposition to develop panic disorder is inherited (Stein, Jang, & Livesley, 1999; Kendler et al., 1995; Torgersen, 1990, 1983). If a genetic factor is indeed at work, close relatives should have higher rates of panic disorder than more distant relatives (see Table 6-3). One study did find that among identical twins (twins who share all of their genes), if one twin had panic disorder, the other twin had the same disorder in 24 percent of cases. Among fraternal twins (who share only some of their genes), if one twin had panic disorder, the other twin had the same disorder in only 11 percent of cases (Kendler et al., 1993). Other twin studies, however, have not always yielded such clear trends (Stein & Uhde, 1995). Thus the issue of genetic predisposition is still open to debate.

In 1962 Donald Klein and Max Fink discovered that certain antidepressant drugs could prevent panic attacks or reduce their frequency. As we have seen, this finding was a surprise at first. Since then, however, studies across the world have repeatedly confirmed this observation. In fact, the drugs seem to be helpful whether or not the panic disorder is accompanied by depressive symptoms (Silberman, 1999; Hirschfeld, 1996, 1992).

Table 6-3

Anxiety Disorders Profile

	ONE-YEAR PREVALENCE (%)	FEMALE:MALE RATIO	TYPICAL AGE AT ONSET	PREVALENCE AMONG CLOSE RELATIVES	PERCENTAGE RECEIVING TREATMENT
Panic disorder	2.3%	5:2	15–35 years	Elevated	54.4%
Obsessive-compulsive disorder	2.0	1:1	4–25 years	Elevated	41.3
Acute and posttraumatic stress disorders	3.9	2:1	Variable	Unknown	Unknown

Source: APA, 2000, 1994; Kessler et al., 1994; Regier et al., 1993; Davidson et al., 1991; Eaton et al., 1991; Boyd et al., 1990.

Many of these antidepressant drugs seem to act to restore appropriate activity of the neurotransmitter norepinephrine, particularly at neurons in the locus ceruleus (Gorman et al., 1996; Redmond, 1985). They bring at least some improvement to 80 percent of patients who have panic disorder (Ballenger, 1998; Hirschfeld, 1992). Approximately 40 to 60 percent recover markedly or fully, and the improvements can last indefinitely, as long as the drugs are not stopped (Tiller et al., 1999; Lecrubier et al., 1997). Otherwise, relapse rates are high. Recently alprazolam (Xanax) and a few other powerful benzodiazepine drugs have also proved very effective, yielding similar success rates (Holland, Musch, & Hindmarch, 1999; Davidson, 1997).

Clinicians have also found the antidepressant drugs or powerful benzodiazepines to be helpful in most cases of panic disorder with agoraphobia (Uhlenhuth et al., 1995; Rickels et al., 1993). The drugs apparently help break the cycle of attack, anticipation, and fear. As the drugs eliminate or reduce their panic attacks, people become confident enough to journey out into public places once again.

At the same time, psychotropic drugs alone are not always enough to overcome panic disorder with agoraphobia. Perhaps the client's anticipatory anxiety has become so severe that fears continue even after the panic attacks are gone (Marks & Swinson, 1992). For these people, a combination of medication and behavioral exposure treatment may be more effective than either treatment alone (de-Beurs et al., 1995; Nagy et al., 1993). In such instances, the exposure approach is similar to that used with other kinds of phobias. Therapy, often conducted in conjunction with a support group, helps the clients venture farther and farther from their homes and gradually to function in outside places. Therapists may use rewards, encouragement, praise, reasoning, and coaxing to get these individuals to face the outside world (Emmelkamp, 1994).

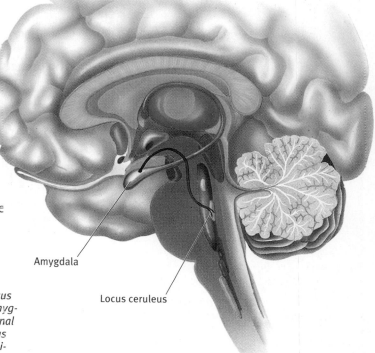

Amygdala

Locus ceruleus

FIGURE 6-1 **The biology of panic** *The locus ceruleus sends its major messages to the amygdala, a brain region known to trigger emotional reactions. Many neurons in the locus ceruleus use norepinephrine, a neurotransmitter implicated in panic disorder and in depression.*

NOCTURNAL PANIC

Around 60 percent of people with panic disorder experience panic attacks at night in addition to their daytime attacks (Sloan et al., 1999; Craske & Rowe, 1997). Usually they are awakened from a deep sleep by their symptoms and fear that they are dying.

ConsiderThis

⦿ Why might people whose childhoods were marked by unpredictable or uncontrollable events or by chronic family illnesses be inaccurate interpreters of their bodily sensations?

The Cognitive Perspective

Cognitive theorists and practitioners have come to recognize that biological factors are only part of the cause of panic attacks. In their view, full panic reactions are experienced only by people who misinterpret certain physiological events that are occurring within their bodies. Cognitive treatments are aimed at correcting such misinterpretations.

THE COGNITIVE EXPLANATION: MISINTERPRETING BODILY SENSATIONS Cognitive theorists believe that panic-prone people may be very sensitive to certain bodily sensations, and when such sensations occur unexpectedly, may misinterpret them as signs of a medical catastrophe (McNally, 1999; Cox, 1996). Rather than understanding the probable cause of such sensations as "something I ate" or "a fight with the boss," the panic-prone grow increasingly worried about losing control, fear the worst, lose all perspective, and rapidly plunge into panic. Constant concern over the possibility that the "dangerous" sensations may return at any time only increases the likelihood of future panic attacks.

Why might some people be prone to such misinterpretations? Clinicians have identified several possible factors (McGlynn & Bates, 1999; Barlow, 1989, 1988). Perhaps the individuals have poor coping skills or lack social support. Perhaps their childhoods were filled with unpredictable events, lack of control, chronic illnesses in the family, or parental overreactions to their children's bodily symptoms. It may also be that the misinterpretations are caused by some dysfunction in the locus ceruleus, the brain area that we just discussed. The British psychologist Jeffrey Gray has proposed that this area of the brain is part of a brain circuit known as the *behavioral inhibition system (BIS)*, which alerts people to possible danger (Gray & McNaughton, 1996; Gray, 1995, 1985, 1982). When signs of danger are present—including signs such as changes in our body's functioning—this brain circuit ordinarily increases its production of neurotransmitters, which carry messages of the impending danger to yet other brain areas. The people then stop what they are doing, experience fear, and try to assess how much danger they are in. Clearly, abnormal functioning in the locus ceruleus, such as that found in panic-prone people, could lead to dysfunctions in the BIS, resulting in overattentiveness to one's bodily changes, overassessments of actual danger, or both.

Whatever the precise causes, research suggests that panic-prone individuals have a high degree of what cognitive theorists have come to call **anxiety sensitivity**: they are generally preoccupied with their bodily sensations, are unable to assess them logically, and interpret them as potentially harmful (Stein & Rapee, 1999; Taylor, 1995; Reiss et al., 1986). One study found that people who scored high on an anxiety sensitivity survey were five times more likely than other subjects to develop panic disorder (Maller & Reiss, 1992). Other studies have found

Joy turns to panic *Anyone is capable of experiencing panic in the face of a clear and overwhelming threat that unfolds at breakneck speed. Uncontrollable crowds led to panic when a wall collapsed at the European Cup soccer finals in Brussels in 1985. Thousands of persons were injured and 38 were killed.*

that individuals with panic disorder are indeed more aware of and frightened by bodily sensations than other people (McNally, 1999; Taylor, Koch, & McNally, 1992).

According to cognitive theorists, people with high anxiety sensitivity are likely to experience and misinterpret certain kinds of sensations more than others. Many seem to "overbreathe," or hyperventilate, in stressful situations. Apparently the abnormal breathing makes them think they are in danger or even dying of suffocation, so they panic (McGlynn & Bates, 1999). Other physical sensations that can be misinterpreted include excitement, breathing discomfort, fullness in the abdomen, and acute anger (McNally, Hornic, & Donnell, 1995; Verburg et al., 1995). One person, on learning that her artwork had been accepted for exhibit at a gallery, became so excited that she experienced "palpitations of the heart." Misinterpreting them as a sign of a heart attack, she panicked.

In **biological challenge tests**, researchers produce hyperventilation or other biological sensations by administering drugs or by instructing subjects to breathe, exercise, or simply think in certain ways (Stein & Rapee, 1999; Bertani et al., 1997). As one might expect, people with panic disorder experience greater anxiety during these tests than people without the disorder, particularly when they believe that their bodily sensations are dangerous or out of control.

Although the cognitive explanation of panic disorder is relatively new, researchers have already collected considerable evidence in its favor. In particular, they have found that people who are prone to panic often interpret bodily sensations in ways that are not at all common. Precisely how different their misinterpretations are and how the misinterpretations interact with biological factors are questions that remain to be answered more fully.

COGNITIVE THERAPY Cognitive therapists try to correct people's misinterpretations of their body sensations (McGlynn & Bates, 1999; Beck & Weishaar, 1995). The first step is to educate clients about the general nature of panic attacks, the actual causes of bodily sensations, and the tendency of clients to misinterpret their sensations. The next step is to teach clients to apply more accurate interpretations during stressful situations, thus short-circuiting the panic sequence at an early point. Therapists may also teach clients to cope better with anxiety—by applying relaxation and breathing techniques, for example—and to distract themselves from their sensations, perhaps by striking up a conversation with someone.

Cognitive therapists may also use biological challenge procedures to induce panic sensations in therapy, so that clients can apply their new skills under watchful supervision. Individuals whose attacks are typically triggered by a rapid heart rate, for example, may be told to jump up and down for several minutes or to run up a flight of stairs (Clark, 1993; Rapee, 1993). They can then practice interpreting the resulting sensations appropriately and not dwelling on them.

According to research, cognitive treatments often help people with panic disorder (Penava et al., 1998; Craske et al., 1997). In international studies, 85 percent of subjects given these treatments were free of panic for as long as two years or more, compared to only 13 percent of control subjects (Clark & Wells, 1997; Ost & Westling, 1995). As with drug therapy, cognitive treatments are only sometimes sufficient for persons whose panic disorders are accompanied by agoraphobia (Oei, Llamas, & Devilly, 1999). For many such persons, therapists add exposure techniques to the cognitive treatment program—an addition that has produced high success rates.

Cognitive therapy has proved to be at least as helpful as antidepressant drugs or alprazolam in the treatment of panic disorder, sometimes more so (Zauber &

"I'm sorry, I didn't hear what you said. I was listening to my body."

THE ROOTS OF PANIC

According to a Greek myth, Pan, the cloven-hoofed god of pastures, flocks, and shepherds, used to take naps in caves or thickets along country roads. When travelers disturbed the foul-looking god, he would let out a horrifying scream. The god's appearance and scream terrified the travelers—a reaction henceforth known as *panic*.

ANXIETY SENSITIVITY A tendency to focus on one's bodily sensations, assess them illogically, and interpret them as harmful.

BIOLOGICAL CHALLENGE TEST A procedure used to produce panic in subjects or clients by having them exercise vigorously or perform some other potentially panic-inducing task in the presence of a researcher or therapist.

OBSESSION A persistent thought, idea, impulse, or image that is experienced repeatedly, feels intrusive, and causes anxiety.

COMPULSION A repetitive and rigid behavior or mental act that a person feels driven to perform in order to prevent or reduce anxiety.

OBSESSIVE-COMPULSIVE DISORDER A disorder in which a person has recurrent and unwanted thoughts, a need to perform repetitive and rigid actions, or both.

Katon, 1998; Margraf et al., 1993). In view of the effectiveness of both cognitive and drug treatments, many clinicians have tried combining them. It is not yet clear, however, whether or not this strategy is more effective than cognitive therapy alone (Loerch et al., 1999; Schmidt, 1999).

Obsessive-Compulsive Disorder

Obsessions are persistent thoughts, ideas, impulses, or images that seem to invade a person's consciousness. **Compulsions** are repetitive and rigid behaviors or mental acts that people feel compelled to perform in order to prevent or reduce anxiety. As Figure 6-2 indicates, minor obsessions and compulsions are familiar to almost everyone (Muris, Murckelbach, & Clavan, 1997). We may find ourselves filled with thoughts about an upcoming performance, date, examination, or vacation; worry that we forgot to turn off the stove or lock the door; or be

FIGURE 6-2 **Normal routines** *Most people find it comforting to follow set routines when they carry out everyday activities, and in fact, 40 percent become irritated if they are forced to depart from their routines. (Adapted from Kanner, 1998, 1995.)*

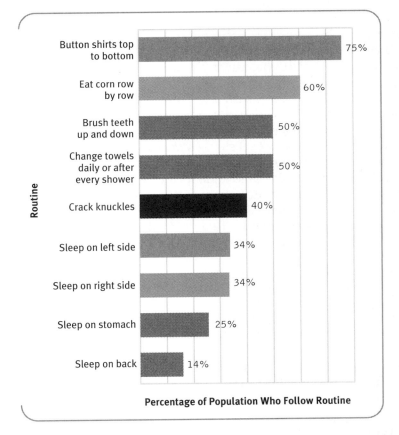

haunted for days by the same song, melody, or poem. We may feel better when we avoid stepping on cracks, turn away from black cats, follow a strict routine every morning, or arrange our closets in a particular manner.

Minor obsessions and compulsions can play a helpful role in life. Distracting tunes or little rituals often calm us during times of stress. A man who repeatedly hums a tune or taps his fingers during a test may be releasing tension and thus improving his performance. Many people find it comforting to repeat religious or cultural rituals, such as touching a mezuzah, sprinkling holy water, or fingering rosary beads.

According to DSM-IV, a diagnosis of **obsessive-compulsive disorder** may be called for when obsessions or compulsions are severe, perceived by the person as excessive or unreasonable, cause great distress, consume considerable time, or interfere with daily functions (see Table 6-4). Obsessive-compulsive disorder is classified as an anxiety disorder because the victims' obsessions cause in-

Table 6-4 **DSM-IV Checklist**

OBSESSIVE-COMPULSIVE DISORDER

1. Recurrent obsessions or compulsions.
2. Past or present recognition that the obsessions or compulsions are excessive or unreasonable.
3. Significant distress or impairment, or disruption by symptoms for more than one hour a day.

Based on APA, 2000, 1994.

tense anxiety, while their compulsions are aimed at preventing or reducing anxiety. In addition, their anxiety rises if they try to resist their obsessions or compulsions. The pattern displayed by Georgia is described by her husband:

> "You remember that old joke about getting up in the middle of the night to go to the john and coming back to the bedroom to find your wife has made the bed? It's no joke. Sometimes I think she never sleeps. I got up one night at 4 A.M. and there she was doing the laundry downstairs. Look at your ash tray! I haven't seen one that dirty in years! I'll tell you what it makes me feel like. If I forget to leave my dirty shoes outside the back door she gives me a look like I had just crapped in the middle of an operating room. I stay out of the house a lot and I'm about half-stoned when I do have to be home. She even made us get rid of the dog because she said he was always filthy. When we used to have people over for supper she would jitterbug around everybody till they couldn't digest their food. I hated to call them up and ask them over because I could always hear them hem and haw and make up excuses not to come over. Even the kids are walking down the street nervous about getting dirt on them. I'm going out of my mind but you can't talk to her. She just blows up and spends twice as much time cleaning things. We have guys in to wash the walls so often I think the house is going to fall down from being scrubbed all the time. About a week ago I had it up to here and told her I couldn't take it any more. I think the only reason she came to see you was because I told her I was going to take off. . . ."
>
> Georgia's obsessive concern with cleanliness forced her to take as many as three showers a day, one in the morning, one before supper, and one before going to bed, and on hot days the number of showers would rise in direct proportion to the temperature. . . . Georgia was aware, in part, of the effect she was having on her family and friends, but she also knew that when she tried to alter her behavior she got so nervous that she felt she was losing her mind. She was frightened by the possibility that "I'm headed for the funny-farm." As she said, "I can't get to sleep unless I am sure everything in the house is in its proper place so that when I get up in the morning, the house is organized. I work like mad to set everything straight before I go to bed, but, when I get up in the morning, I can think of a thousand things that I ought to do. I know some of the things are ridiculous, but I feel better if I get them done, and I can't stand to know something needs doing and I haven't done it."
>
> (McNeil, 1967, pp. 26–28)

As many as 2 percent of the people in the United States and Great Britain suffer from obsessive-compulsive disorder in any given year (APA, 2000; Bebbington, 1998; Regier et al., 1993). It is equally common in men and women; however, among children, it is more common in boys (APA, 2000). The disorder usually begins by young adulthood. As with Georgia, obsessive-compulsive disorder typically persists for many years, but the symptoms and their severity fluctuate over time. Many sufferers are also depressed, and some develop an eating disorder as well (Crino & Andrews, 1996).

What Are the Features of Obsessions and Compulsions?

Obsessions are not the same as pervasive worries about real problems, and compulsions are not repetitive actions that feel voluntary and seem harmless to the people who perform them (Langlois et al., 2000).

THE FEATURES OF OBSESSIONS Obsessions are thoughts that feel both intrusive ("ego dystonic") and foreign ("ego alien") to the people who experience them. Attempts to ignore or resist these thoughts may arouse even more anxiety, and before long they come back more strongly than ever. Like Georgia, people with obsessions are quite aware that their thoughts are excessive and inappropriate. Many experience them as repugnant and painful.

AND THE WINNER IS . . .

Jack Nicholson won an Academy Award in 1998 for his portrayal of a man with obsessive-compulsive disorder in the film *As Good as It Gets*. The long list of actors and actresses who have received Oscars for their portrayals of people with psychological disorders includes Ray Milland (*The Lost Weekend*), Joanne Woodward (*The Three Faces of Eve*), Cliff Robertson (*Charly*), Jack Nicholson again (*One Flew Over the Cuckoo's Nest*), Timothy Hutton (*Ordinary People*), Peter Finch (*Network*), Dustin Hoffman (*Rain Man*), Anthony Hopkins (*The Silence of the Lambs*), Jessica Lange (*Blue Skies*), Geoffrey Rush (*Shine*), and Angelina Jolie (*Girl, Interrupted*).

AN OBSESSION THAT CHANGED THE WORLD

The experiments that led Louis Pasteur to the pasteurization process may have been driven in part by his obsession with contamination and infection. Apparently he would not shake hands, and regularly wiped his glass and plate before dining (Asimov, 1997).

The great pursuit *Captain Ahab's preoccupation with the great white whale in Herman Melville's* Moby Dick *(1851) is one of literature's most famous presentations of obsessive thinking.*

COMMON CLEANING
According to surveys, most people take a ten-minute shower, although research suggests that only four minutes are actually spent washing (Kanner, 1995).

Obsessions often take the form of obsessive *wishes* (for example, repeated wishes that one's spouse would die), *impulses* (repeated urges to yell out obscenities at work or in church), *images* (fleeting visions of forbidden sexual scenes), *ideas* (notions that germs are lurking everywhere), or *doubts* (concerns that one has made or will make a wrong decision). In the following excerpt, a clinician describes a 20-year-old college junior who was plagued by obsessive doubts.

> He now spent hours each night "rehashing" the day's events, especially interactions with friends and teachers, endlessly making "right" in his mind any and all regrets. He likened the process to playing a videotape of each event over and over again in his mind, asking himself if he had behaved properly and telling himself that he had done his best, or had said the right thing every step of the way. He would do this while sitting at his desk, supposedly studying; and it was not unusual for him to look at the clock after such a period of rumination and note that, to his surprise, two or three hours had elapsed.
>
> *(Spitzer et al., 1981, pp. 20–21)*

Certain basic themes run through the thoughts of most people troubled by obsessive thinking (APA, 2000, 1994). The most common theme appears to be *dirt* or *contamination* (see Box 6-1). Other common themes are *violence* and *aggression, orderliness, religion,* and *sexuality.*

THE FEATURES OF COMPULSIONS Although compulsive behaviors are technically under voluntary control, the people who feel they must do them have little sense of choice in the matter. Most of these individuals recognize that their behavior is unreasonable, but they believe at the same time something terrible will happen if they don't perform the compulsions (Foa & Kozak, 1995). After performing a compulsive act, they usually feel less anxious for a short while. Some people develop the act into a detailed and often elaborate *compulsive ritual.* They must go through the ritual in exactly the same way every time, according to certain rules.

Like obsessions, compulsions take various forms (Ball, Baer, & Otto, 1996; Tallis, 1996). *Cleaning compulsions* are very common. Like Georgia, people with these compulsions feel compelled to keep cleaning themselves, their clothing, or their homes. The cleaning may follow ritualistic rules and be repeated dozens or hundreds of times a day, making it almost impossible to have a normal life:

> Ruth complained that . . . she was spending most of her time engaged in some type of behavior she felt driven to carry out. In addition, each ritual activity was becoming more involved and time consuming. At the time of the interview, she was washing her hands at least three or four times an hour, showering six or seven times a day, and thoroughly cleaning her apartment at least twice a day. . . .
>
> Ruth stated that she felt frustrated and tired most of the time, due to the amount of effort involved in these rituals. She experienced a great deal of pain in her hands because the outer layer of skin was virtually rubbed off. Nonetheless, she felt compelled to thoroughly wash her hands and repeatedly clean her apartment each time she felt that she or her environment was contaminated in some way.
>
> *(Leon, 1977, pp. 127–132)*

People with *checking compulsions* check the same items over and over—door locks, gas taps, ashtrays, important papers—to make sure that all is as it should be. Another common compulsion is the constant striving for *symmetry, order,* or *balance* in one's actions and surroundings. People with this compulsion must place certain items (clothing, books, foods) in perfect order in accordance with strict rules.

> Ted is a 13-year-old referred to a Midwestern inpatient psychiatric research ward because of "senseless rituals and attention to minutiae." He can spend 3 hours centering the toilet paper roll on its holder or rearranging his bed and other objects in his room. When placing objects down, such as books or shoelaces after tying them, he picks them up and replaces them several times until they seem "straight." Although usually placid, he becomes abusive with family members who try to enter his room for fear they will move or break his objects. When he is at school, he worries that people may disturb his room. He sometimes has to be forced to interrupt his routine to attend meals. Last year he hid pieces of his clothing around the house because they wouldn't lie straight in his drawers. Moreover, he often repeats to himself, "This is perfect; you are perfect."
>
> *(Spitzer et al., 1983, p. 15)*

Touching, verbal, and counting compulsions are also common. People with *touching compulsions* repeatedly touch or avoid touching certain items whenever they see them. Individuals with *verbal rituals* feel compelled to repeat expressions, phrases, or chants. And those with *counting compulsions* feel driven to count the things they see around them throughout the day.

COMMON CHECKING

According to one survey, almost half of adults double back after leaving home to make sure they have turned off an appliance. More than half of all people who use an alarm clock check it repeatedly to be sure they've set it (Kanner, 1995).

BOX 6-1

Terror behind the Smile

Many of today's college students grew up watching *Double Dare* and *Family Double Dare,* two of the messiest game shows in television history. Young contestants were regularly splattered with goo and dunked in slime and muck (Summers, 1996). All the while, the host, Marc Summers, seemed to be having a great time, especially when the kids would pick him up and throw him into the mess as well. In 1996, however, Summers revealed that his years on the show had been a personal nightmare. He had an obsessive-compulsive disorder.

Summers says that his disorder dates back to the age of 8. He remembers cleaning his room for hours, removing and dusting every book in his bookcase. When he got the opportunity to host *Double Dare,* he couldn't turn down the career opportunity. But the price was high. After the shows, he would spend hours in the shower. "It was the most uncomfortable feeling in the world—a feeling of physical revulsion." Only recently did Summers recognize his disorder. He now takes medications for it, and his symptoms are diminishing.

ConsiderThis

⦿ Might Summers have agreed to host the show to somehow help him face his fears and compulsions? • If it was a form of self-treatment, why did it not help? • What other examples of so-called counterphobic behavior pervade our culture?

HARD TO AVOID

People who try to avoid all contamination and rid themselves and their world of all germs are fighting a losing battle. While talking, the average person sprays 300 microscopic saliva droplets per minute, or 2.5 per word.

ARE OBSESSIONS AND COMPULSIONS RELATED? Although some people with obsessive-compulsive disorder experience obsessions only or compulsions only, most of them experience both. In fact, compulsive acts are often a response to obsessive thoughts (Pato & Pato, 1997). One investigation found that in most cases, compulsions seemed to represent a *yielding* to obsessive doubts, ideas, or urges (Akhtar et al., 1975). A woman who keeps doubting that her house is secure may yield to that obsessive doubt by repeatedly checking locks and gas jets. Or a man who obsessively fears contamination may yield to that fear by performing cleaning rituals. The investigation also found that compulsions sometimes serve to *control* obsessions. Below, a teenager describes how she tried to control her obsessive fears of contamination by performing counting and verbal rituals:

> *Patient:* If I heard the word, like, something that had to do with germs or disease, it would be considered something bad, and so I had things that would go through my mind that were sort of like "cross that out and it'll make it okay" to hear that word.
>
> *Interviewer:* What sort of things?
>
> *Patient:* Like numbers or words that seemed to be sort of like a protector.
>
> *Interviewer:* What numbers and what words were they?
>
> *Patient:* It started out to be the number 3 and multiples of 3 and then words like "soap and water," something like that; and then the multiples of 3 got really high, and they'd end up to be 124 or something like that. It got real bad then.
>
> *(Spitzer et al., 1981, p. 137)*

Many people with obsessive-compulsive disorder worry that they will act out their obsessions. A man with obsessive images of wounded loved ones may worry that he is but a step away from committing murder; or a woman with obsessive urges to yell out in church may worry that she will one day give in to them and embarrass herself. Most such concerns are unfounded. Although many obsessions lead to compulsive acts—particularly to cleaning and checking compulsions—they do not usually lead to violence or immoral conduct.

Obsessive-compulsive disorder, like panic disorder, was once among the least understood of the psychological disorders. In recent years, however, researchers have begun to learn more about it. The most influential explanations and treatments come from the psychodynamic, behavioral, cognitive, and biological models.

The Psychodynamic Perspective

As we have observed, psychodynamic theorists believe that an anxiety disorder develops when children come to fear their own id impulses and use ego defense mechanisms to lessen the resulting anxiety. What distinguishes obsessive-compulsive disorder from other anxiety disorders, in their view, is that here the battle between anxiety-provoking id impulses and anxiety-reducing defense mechanisms is not buried in the unconscious but is played out in explicit and dramatic thoughts and actions. The id impulses usually take the form of obsessive thoughts, and the ego defenses appear as counterthoughts or compulsive actions. A woman who keeps imagining her mother lying broken and bleeding, for example, may counter those thoughts with repeated safety checks throughout the house.

PSYCHODYNAMIC EXPLANATIONS: THE BATTLE BETWEEN THE ID AND THE EGO

According to psychodynamic theorists, three ego defense mechanisms are particularly common in obsessive-compulsive disorder: *isolation, undoing,* and *reaction formation* (Hollander et al., 1994). People who resort to **isolation** simply disown their undesirable and unwanted thoughts and experience them as foreign intru-

ISOLATION An ego defense mechanism in which people unconsciously isolate and disown undesirable and unwanted thoughts, experiencing them as foreign intrusions.

UNDOING An ego defense mechanism whereby a person unconsciously cancels out an unacceptable desire or act by performing another act.

REACTION FORMATION An ego defense mechanism whereby a person suppresses an unacceptable desire by taking on a lifestyle that expresses the opposite desire.

sions. People who engage in **undoing** perform acts that are meant to cancel out their undesirable impulses. Those who wash their hands repeatedly, for example, may be symbolically undoing their unacceptable id impulses. People who develop a **reaction formation** take on a lifestyle that directly opposes their unacceptable impulses. A person may live a life of compulsive kindness and devotion to others in order to counter unacceptably aggressive impulses. Another may lead a life of chastity to counteract obsessive sexual impulses.

Sigmund Freud believed that during the *anal stage* of development (occurring at about 2 years of age) some children experience intense rage and shame that fuel the battle between id and ego. He theorized that children at this stage get pleasure from their bowel movements. When their parents try to toilet train them, the children must learn to delay their anal gratification. If parents are premature or too harsh in their toilet training, the children may feel such rage that they develop *aggressive id impulses*—antisocial impulses that repeatedly seek expression. They may soil their clothes all the more frequently and become generally destructive, messy, or stubborn.

If parents handle the child's aggressiveness by further pressure and embarrassment, the child may also feel ashamed, guilty, and dirty. The aggressive impulses will now compete with a strong desire to control them; the child who wants to soil will also have a desire to retain. If this intense conflict between the id and the ego continues, it may eventually blossom into obsessive-compulsive disorder.

Not all psychodynamic theorists agree with Freud's explanation. Some object relations theorists, for example, propose that disturbed relationships early in life leave certain people with an all-or-nothing view of the world. Believing that people are either all good or all bad, they must experience their negative thoughts as "foreign" obsessions in order to tolerate them (Oppenheim & Rosenberger, 1991). In another departure from Freud, some ego psychologists believe that the aggressive impulses of people with this disorder are rooted in feelings of insecurity rather than poor toilet-training experiences (Erikson, 1963; Sullivan, 1953; Horney, 1937). Even these theorists, however, agree with Freud that people with the disorder have intense aggressive impulses and a competing need to control them. Overall, research has not clearly supported the various psychodynamic theories (Fitz, 1990).

PSYCHODYNAMIC THERAPIES Psychodynamic therapists try to help people with obsessive-compulsive disorder uncover and overcome their underlying conflicts and defenses, using the customary techniques of free association and therapist interpretation. Research has offered little evidence, however, that a traditional psychodynamic approach is of much help (Salzman, 1980).

In fact, there is some suspicion that psychodynamic therapy may actually add to the difficulties of patients with obsessive-compulsive disorder (Salzman, 1980). Free association and interpretation may play into their tendency to "think too much" (Noonan, 1971). Thus some psychodynamic therapists now prefer to treat these patients with *short-term psychodynamic therapies,* which, as we observed in Chapter 3, are more direct and action-oriented than the classical techniques. In one approach, the therapist directly advises clients that their compulsions are defense mechanisms and urges them to stop acting compulsively (Salzman, 1985, 1980).

At the hospital for mothers whose children stepped on sidewalk cracks

ConsiderThis

○ What might psychodynamic theorists say in response to the following statement by the parks commissioner of New York City? "You cannot believe the savagery with which people attack toilets. They break the plumbing, they smash them. They go wild. I can see how people might injure schools or places where they've had difficulties, but I do not see how anyone can bear a grudge against a toilet."

The Behavioral Perspective

Behaviorists have concentrated on explaining and treating compulsions rather than obsessions. Although the behavioral explanation itself has received little support, behavioral treatments for compulsive behaviors have been very successful and have helped change the once gloomy treatment picture for this disorder.

Touch for luck *An LSU football player touches a statue of the school mascot, a bulldog, before the homecoming game. Athletes often follow rituals that they believe will help them perform better on the field. Like compulsions, their superstitious behaviors may be reinforced by reductions in anxiety.*

THE BEHAVIORAL EXPLANATION: LEARNING BY CHANCE

Behaviorists propose that people happen upon their compulsions quite randomly. In a fearful situation, they happen just coincidentally to wash their hands, say, or dress a certain way. When the threat lifts, they link the improvement to that particular action. After repeated accidental associations, they believe that the action is bringing them good luck or actually changing the situation, and so they perform the same actions again and again in similar situations. The act becomes a key method of avoiding or reducing anxiety (Steketee et al., 1996). This explanation, however, has nothing to say about why some people develop compulsions and others do not. Certainly everyone experiences some accidental associations, yet relatively few become compulsive.

The influential clinical investigator Stanley Rachman and his associates have shown that compulsions do appear to be rewarded by a reduction in anxiety. In one of their experiments, for example, 12 people with compulsive hand-washing rituals were placed in contact with objects that they considered contaminated (Hodgson & Rachman, 1972). As behaviorists would predict, the hand-washing rituals of these subjects seemed to lower their anxiety. Of course, although such investigations suggest that compulsions may eventually be rewarded by a reduction in anxiety, they do not show that compulsions are acquired in the first place as a result of such reductions.

BEHAVIORAL THERAPY

In the mid-1960s, when V. Meyer (1966) was treating two patients with chronic obsessive-compulsive disorder, he instructed the hospital staff to keep a watchful eye on them and prevent them from performing their compulsive acts. The patients' compulsive behavior improved significantly and continued to show the same improvement after 14 months. In the 1970s Stanley Rachman eliminated the staff supervision: he simply instructed clients to try to stop themselves from performing their compulsive acts (Rachman, 1985; Rachman & Hodgson, 1980).

In Rachman's procedure, **exposure and response prevention**, people are repeatedly exposed to objects or situations that produce anxiety, obsessive fears, and compulsive behaviors, but they are told to resist performing the behaviors they feel bound to perform. Because people find it very difficult to stop, therapists often set an example. As the clients watch, the therapists put themselves in the anxiety-producing situation without performing any compulsive actions, and then they encourage the clients to do the same (see Figure 6-3).

Many behavioral therapists now use Rachman's procedure. Some of them have people also carry out *self-help* procedures at home (Knox, Albano, & Barlow, 1996; Emmelkamp, 1994). That is, they assign homework in exposure and response prevention, such as these assignments given to a woman with a cleaning compulsion:

- Do not mop the floor of your bathroom for a week. After this, clean it within three minutes, using an ordinary mop. Use this mop for other chores as well without cleaning it.

- Buy a fluffy mohair sweater and wear it for a week. When taking it off at night do not remove the bits of fluff. Do not clean your house for a week.

ConsiderThis

⦿ Can you think of instances in your own life when you instinctively tried a simple version of exposure and response prevention in order to stop behaving in certain ways? • Were your efforts successful? • What does this suggest about the need for systematic and perhaps supervised applications of the technique?

■ You, your husband, and children all have to keep shoes on. Do not clean the house for a week.

■ Drop a cookie on the contaminated floor, pick the cookie up and eat it.

■ Leave the sheets and blankets on the floor and then put them on the beds. Do not change these for a week.

(Emmelkamp, 1982, pp. 299–300)

Eventually this woman was able to set up a reasonable routine for cleaning herself and her home.

Exposure and response prevention has been offered in both individual and group therapy. Between 60 and 90 percent of clients with obsessive-compulsive disorder have been found to improve considerably with this approach (Albucher, Abelson, & Nesse, 1998; Riggs & Foa, 1993). They also function better at home, socially, and at work. These changes continue to be observed for years (Bolton, Luckie, & Steinberg, 1995).

The effectiveness of this approach suggests that people with obsessive-compulsive disorder are like the superstitious man in the old joke who keeps snapping his fingers to keep elephants away. When someone points out, "But there aren't any elephants around here," the man replies, "See? It works!" One review concludes, "With hindsight, it is possible to see that the obsessional individual has been snapping his fingers, and unless he stops (response prevention) and takes a look around at the same time (exposure), he isn't going to learn much of value about elephants" (Berk & Efran, 1983, p. 546).

The same studies and statistics indicate the limitations of exposure and response prevention. Few clients who receive the treatment overcome all their symptoms, and as many as one-quarter fail to improve at all (Marks & Swinson, 1992; Greist, 1990). Also, the approach is of limited help to those who have obsessions but no compulsions (Hohagen et al., 1998; Jenike, 1992). After all, the treatment makes its impact on obsessions by blocking closely linked compulsive acts. Moreover, the favorable findings come mainly from studies of cleaning and checking compulsions. The effectiveness of this approach with other kinds of compulsions or with multiple compulsions is unclear (Ball, Baer, & Otto, 1996).

The Cognitive Perspective

Cognitive theorists have developed a promising explanation and treatment for obsessive-compulsive disorder. Their theory and treatment techniques also include a number of behavioral principles, leading some observers to describe the approach as cognitive-behavioral.

THE COGNITIVE EXPLANATION: INTERPRETING UNWANTED THOUGHTS The cognitive explanation of obsessive-compulsive disorder begins with the observation that everyone has repetitive, unwanted, and intrusive thoughts. Anyone might have thoughts of harming others, engaging in unacceptable sexual acts, or being contaminated by germs, but most people dismiss or ignore them with ease. Those who develop obsessive-compulsive disorder, however, typically blame themselves for such thoughts and expect that somehow terrible consequences will ensue (Salkovskis, 1999, 1989, 1985). To avoid the consequences, they try to **neutralize** the thoughts—thinking or behaving in ways meant to eliminate them, to put matters right internally, or to make amends.

Neutralizing acts might include requesting special reassurance from others, deliberately thinking "good" thoughts, washing one's hands, or checking for

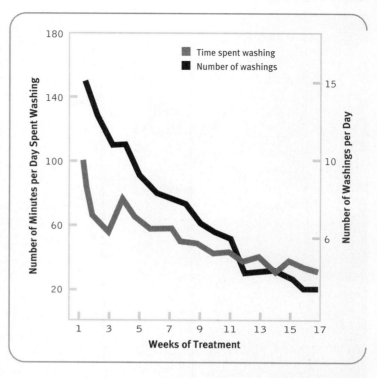

FIGURE 6-3 **Successful treatment for cleaning compulsions** *When a client was treated by exposure and response prevention, he showed a steady decline in the frequency of his daily washings and in the total amount of time he spent at them. (Adapted from Rachman, Hodgson, & Marzillier, 1970, p. 390.)*

EXPOSURE AND RESPONSE PREVENTION A behavioral treatment for obsessive-compulsive disorder that exposes clients to anxiety-arousing thoughts or situations and then prevents them from performing their compulsive acts.

NEUTRALIZING A person's attempt to eliminate unwanted thoughts by thinking or behaving in ways that put matters right internally, that make up for the unacceptable thoughts.

Painful thoughts *Like the man in George Cruik-shank's painting* The Blue Devils, *some people may find unwanted thoughts particularly threatening and debilitating. According to cognitive theorists, their reactions to intrusive thoughts may set the stage for obsessive-compulsive disorder.*

HABITUATION TRAINING A therapeutic technique in which a therapist tries to call forth a client's obsessive thoughts again and again, with the expectation that the thoughts will eventually lose their power to frighten and thus to cause anxiety.

SEROTONIN A neurotransmitter whose abnormal activity is linked to depression, obsessive-compulsive disorder, and eating disorders.

ORBITAL FRONTAL CORTEX A region of the brain in which impulses involving excretion, sexuality, violence, and other primitive activities normally arise.

CAUDATE NUCLEI Structures in the brain, within the region known as the basal ganglia, that help convert sensory information into thoughts and actions.

possible sources of danger (Freeston & Ladouceur, 1997). When a neutralizing effort of some kind brings about a temporary reduction in discomfort, it is reinforced and will likely be repeated. Eventually the neutralizing thought or act is used so often that it becomes, by definition, an obsession or compulsion. At the same time, the individual becomes more and more convinced that his or her unpleasant intrusive thoughts are dangerous and are in need of elimination. As the person's fear of such thoughts increases, the thoughts begin to occur more frequently and they, too, become obsessions.

While everyone sometimes has undesired thoughts, only some people develop obsessive-compulsive disorder. Why do these individuals find such normal thoughts so disturbing to begin with? Researchers have found that this population tends (1) to have a higher rate of depression (Sobin et al., 1999; Clark & Purdon, 1993); (2) to have exceptionally high standards of conduct and morality (Rachman, 1993; Rachman & Hodgson, 1980); (3) to believe that their intrusive negative thoughts are equivalent to actions and capable of causing harm to themselves or others, and to feel responsible for eliminating the imagined danger (Wilson & Chambless, 1999); and (4) generally to believe that they can and should have perfect control over all thoughts and behaviors (Bouchard, Rhéaume, & Ladouceur, 1999).

Other aspects of this cognitive theory have also received clarification and support from research. Several investigators have found, for example, that people with obsessive-compulsive disorder more frequently experience intrusive thoughts than other people (Clark, 1992). In addition, studies have confirmed that people who develop this disorder resort at least sometimes to more elaborate neutralizing strategies than other people when trying to stop unwanted thoughts (Freeston et al., 1992). The neutralizing techniques do seem to reduce their discomfort temporarily (Roper, Rachman, & Hodgson, 1973).

COGNITIVE THERAPIES Cognitive practitioners have developed approaches to obsessive-compulsive disorder that combine cognitive and behavioral techniques (Freeston et al., 1996). In **habituation training**, for example, the client's obsessive thoughts are intentionally elicited again and again. The rationale is that intense exposure to the thoughts will diminish their power to frighten, so that the thoughts produce less anxiety and trigger fewer new obsessive thoughts or compulsive acts (Salkovskis & Westbrook, 1989; Rachman & Hodgson, 1980). In one version of habituation training, clients are simply instructed to summon obsessive thoughts or images to mind and hold them for a while. In another version, clients spend up to an hour once or twice a day listening to their own voices on tape stating their obsessive thoughts again and again.

For people who experience obsessions only, habituation training is often the entire plan of treatment (Rachman & Hodgson, 1980). For others, however, therapists may add *covert-response prevention,* which teaches clients to distract or otherwise prevent themselves from carrying out the compulsive actions they wish to perform in response to the obsessive thoughts that arise in habituation training. So far, support for these approaches has come mostly from case studies rather than empirical investigations (Ladouceur et al., 1995).

The Biological Perspective

Partly because obsessive-compulsive disorder was so difficult to explain in the past, researchers tried repeatedly to identify hidden biological factors that might contribute to it. Their efforts have been rewarded in recent years, and promising biological treatments have been developed as well.

BIOLOGICAL EXPLANATIONS   Two lines of research now offer great promise for explaining the biology of obsessive-compulsive disorder. One points to abnormally low activity of the neurotransmitter *serotonin*, the other to abnormal functioning in key areas of the brain.

Serotonin, like GABA and norepinephrine, is a brain chemical that carries messages from neuron to neuron. The first clue to its role in obsessive-compulsive disorder was the surprising finding by clinical researchers that two antidepressant drugs, *clomipramine* and *fluoxetine* (Anafranil and Prozac), reduce obsessive and compulsive symptoms (Klerman et al., 1994; Rapoport, 1991, 1989). Since these particular drugs also increase serotonin activity, some researchers concluded that the disorder is caused by low serotonin activity. In fact, only those antidepressant drugs that increase serotonin activity help in cases of obsessive-compulsive disorder; antidepressants that mainly affect other neurotransmitters have no effect on it (Jenike, 1992).

Another line of research has linked obsessive-compulsive disorder to abnormal brain functioning in specific regions of the brain: the **orbital region of the frontal cortex** (just above each eye) and the **caudate nuclei** (structures located within the brain region known as the *basal ganglia,* which lies under the cerebral cortex). Together, these parts set up a brain circuit that converts sensory information into thoughts and actions. The circuit begins in the orbital region, where sexual, violent, and other primitive impulses normally arise. These impulses next move on to the caudate nuclei, which act as filters that send only the most powerful impulses on to the *thalamus,* the next stop on the circuit (see Figure 6-4). If impulses reach the thalamus, the person is driven to think further about them and perhaps to act. Many biological theorists now believe that either the orbital region or the caudate nuclei of some people are too active, leading to a constant eruption of troublesome thoughts and actions (Peterson et al., 1999).

In support of this theory, medical scientists have observed for years that obsessive-compulsive symptoms do sometimes arise or subside after the orbital region, caudate nuclei, or related brain areas are damaged by accident or illness (Max et al., 1995; Paradis et al., 1992). In one highly publicized case, a patient with obsessive-compulsive disorder tried to commit suicide by shooting himself in the head. Although he survived the shot, he did considerable damage to the brain areas in question. Perhaps as a result of the injury, his obsessive and compulsive symptoms declined dramatically. Similarly, PET scans, which offer pictures of brain functioning, have shown that the caudate nuclei and the orbital region of patients with obsessive-compulsive disorder are more active than those of control subjects (Saxena et al., 1999; Baxter et al., 1990).

The serotonin and anatomical hypotheses may themselves be linked. It turns out that the neurotransmitter serotonin plays a very active role in the operation of the orbital region and the caudate nuclei, so low serotonin activity might well disrupt the proper functioning of those brain parts.

BIOLOGICAL THERAPIES   As we have seen, researchers have learned that certain antidepressant drugs are very useful in the treatment of obsessive-compulsive disorder (German & Kent, 1999). Not only do they increase brain serotonin activity; they also produce more normal activity in the orbital region and caudate nuclei, the brain areas that have been implicated in the disorder (Baxter et al.,

IS LOVE AN OBSESSION?

One team of researchers found that the serotonin activity of subjects who claimed to be newly in love was about as low as that of subjects with obsessive-compulsive disorder (Marazziti et al., 1999).

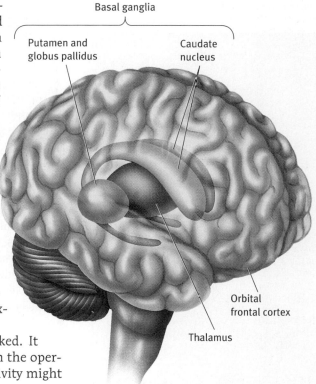

Basal ganglia

Putamen and globus pallidus

Caudate nucleus

Orbital frontal cortex

Thalamus

FIGURE 6-4   **The biology of obsessive-compulsive disorder**   *A three-dimensional view of the brain shows the regions that have been linked to obsessive-compulsive disorder. These areas may be too active in people with the disorder. (Adapted from Rapoport, 1989, p. 85.)*

1992; Swedo et al., 1992). Studies have found that clomipramine, fluoxetine, and fluvoxamine (Anafranil, Prozac, and Luvox) bring improvement to between 50 and 80 percent of those with obsessive-compulsive disorder (Black et al., 1997; Taylor, 1995). The obsessions and compulsions do not usually disappear totally, but on average they are cut almost in half within eight weeks of treatment (DeVeaugh-Geiss et al., 1992). People whose improvement is based on the drugs alone, however, tend to relapse if the medication is stopped (Eisen et al., 1999; Ravizza et al., 1998). Drug therapy is increasingly being combined with psychotherapy, particularly with exposure and response prevention, but it is not yet clear that such integrated treatments are consistently superior to one of the approaches alone (Hohagen et al., 1998).

Thus the treatment of obsessive-compulsive disorder, like that of panic disorder, has improved greatly over the past decade. Once a very stubborn problem, obsessive-compulsive disorder is now responding to several forms of treatment, particularly exposure and response prevention and antidepressant drugs, often used in combination (Riggs & Foa, 1993). Interestingly, at least two important studies suggest that the behavioral and biological approaches may ultimately have the same effect on the brain. In these investigations, subjects who responded to exposure and response prevention and subjects who responded to antidepressant drugs all showed marked reductions in activity in the caudate nuclei (Schwartz et al., 1996; Baxter et al., 1992). These studies were the first to provide evidence tying psychotherapy for a mental disorder directly to changes in brain function.

Stress Disorders

Mark remembers his first "firefight" and encountering the VC [Viet Cong] for the first time. He lost all bladder and bowel control—in a matter of a few minutes. In his own words, "I was scared and literally shitless; I pissed all over myself, and shit all over myself too. Man, all hell broke loose. I tell you, I was so scared, I thought I would never make it out alive. I was convinced of that. Charlie had us pinned down and [was] hitting the shit out of us for hours. We had to call in the napalm and the bombing." During the first fight, Mark, an infantryman, experienced gruesome sights and strange sounds in battle. He witnessed headless bodies. "One guy said to me, 'Hey, Mark, new greenhorn boy, you saw that head go flying off that gook's shoulder. Isn't that something?'" Within 2 weeks Mark saw the head of a running comrade blown off his shoulders, the headless body moving for a few feet before falling to the ground. Mark, nauseous and vomiting for a long time, couldn't see himself surviving much longer: "I couldn't get that sight out of my head; it just kept on coming back to me in my dreams, nightmares. Like clockwork, I'd see R's head flying, and his headless body falling to the ground. I knew the guy. He was very good to me when I first got to the unit. Nobody else seemed to give a damn about me; he broke me in. It's like I would see his head and body, you know, man, wow!" Mark often found himself crying during his first weeks of combat. "I wanted to go home. I was so lonely, helpless, and really scared. But I knew I could not go home until my year was up."

(Brende & Parson, 1985, pp. 23-24)

The horror of combat *Soldiers often react to combat with severe anxiety or depression or both. These immediate responses to battle have at various times been called "shell shock," "combat fatigue," or most recently, "acute stress disorder."*

Mark's reaction to combat experience is normal and understandable. During or immediately after a traumatic situation, many people become highly anxious and depressed. For some, however, anxiety and depression persist well after the situation is over. These people may be suffering from **acute stress disorder** or **post-traumatic stress disorder**, patterns that arise in reaction to a psychologically traumatic event. The event usually involves actual or threatened serious injury or threatened death to the person or to a family member or friend. Unlike other anxiety disorders, which typically are triggered by objects or situations that most

Working with Death

One of the least pleasant jobs in our society is to tie up loose ends after a horrifying disaster or murder. Yet the work must be done, regardless of the toll it may take on the workers. It turns out that reactions to such responsibilities vary widely.

In 1993, 83 persons died in the fire at the Branch Davidian compound in Waco, Texas. Thirty-one dentists had to examine the dental remains of the dead. A study later revealed that these dentists had more symptoms of posttraumatic stress disorder than were observed in a control group of other dentists (McCarroll et al., 1996).

Then there are Ray and Louise Barnes (see photo), who run a business called Crime Scene Clean-Up. They and their staffers are hired by police departments, funeral homes, and grieving families to clean up after homicides, suicides, and accidents. They use latex gloves, mops, respirators, and other tools of the trade

to "scrub away the detritus of human disaster" (Howe & Nugent, 1996). Ray Barnes says that his former jobs with a funeral home and a medical examiner's office helped prepare him for this work. While hardly indifferent to the grisly scenes, he has grown somewhat used to them, and he and his wife now have a thriving business.

Consider This

● Why might the dentists and the Barneses react so differently to the situations they have faced? • Is it possible to "adjust" to situations of horror over time, or might repeated exposure take a toll in other ways? • What other jobs in our society might be traumatizing?

---

people would not find threatening, the situations that cause acute stress disorder or posttraumatic stress disorder—combat, rape, an earthquake, an airplane crash—would be traumatic for anyone (see Box 6-2).

If the symptoms begin within four weeks of the traumatic event and last for less than a month, DSM-IV assigns a diagnosis of *acute stress disorder* (APA, 2000, 1994). If the symptoms continue longer than a month, a diagnosis of *posttraumatic stress disorder* is assigned. The symptoms of posttraumatic stress disorder may begin either shortly after the traumatic event or months or years afterward (see Table 6-5 on the next page). Many cases of acute stress disorder develop into posttraumatic stress disorder (Brewin et al., 1999; Koopman et al., 1995). Apart from the differences in onset and duration, the symptoms of these two anxiety disorders are almost identical (Taylor et al., 1998; Wilmer, 1996):

Reexperiencing the traumatic event People may be battered by recurring memories, dreams, or nightmares connected to the event. A few relive the event so vividly in their minds (*flashbacks*) that they think it is actually happening again.

Avoidance People will usually avoid activities that remind them of the traumatic event and will try to avoid related thoughts, feelings, or conversations.

Reduced responsiveness Reduced responsiveness to events in the external world, often called "psychic numbing" or "emotional anesthesia," may begin during or soon after the traumatic event. The person feels detached or estranged from other people or loses interest in activities that once brought enjoyment. The ability to experience such intimate emotions as tenderness and sexuality is often impaired. Reduced responsiveness is particularly prominent in acute stress disorder, where it may include signs of *dissociation*, or psychological separation: dazedness, loss of memory, derealization (feeling that the environment is unreal or strange), or depersonalization (feeling that one's thinking or body is unreal or foreign).

Increased arousal, anxiety, and guilt People with these disorders may experience hyperalertness, an exaggerated startle response, sleep disturbances, or

ACUTE STRESS DISORDER An anxiety disorder in which fear and related symptoms are experienced soon after a traumatic event and last less than a month.

POSTTRAUMATIC STRESS DISORDER An anxiety disorder in which fear and related symptoms continue to be experienced long after a traumatic event.

Table 6-5 **DSM-IV Checklist**

POSTTRAUMATIC STRESS DISORDER

1. A history of having experienced, witnessed, or confronted event(s) involving death, serious injury, or threat to the physical integrity of self or others. Reaction of intense fear, helplessness, or horror produced by event.
2. Event persistently reexperienced in at least one of the following ways:
   (a) Recurrent distressing recollections.
   (b) Recurrent distressing dreams, illusions, flashbacks, or a sense of reliving the experience.
   (c) Distress caused by reminders of event.
   (d) Physical arousal produced by reminders of event.
3. Persistent avoidance of reminders of the event and a subjective sense of numbing, detachment, or emotional unresponsiveness.
4. At least two marked symptoms of increased arousal:
   (a) Difficulty sleeping.
   (b) Irritability.
   (c) Poor concentration.
   (d) Hypervigilance.
   (e) Exaggerated startle response.
5. Significant distress or impairment, with symptoms lasting at least one month.

Based on APA, 2000, 1994.

---

other signs of increased arousal, and may also have trouble concentrating or remembering things. They may feel extreme guilt because they survived the traumatic event while others did not. Some also feel guilty about what they may have had to do to survive.

We can see these symptoms in the recollections of Vietnam combat veterans years after they returned home:

> **Alan:** I can't get the memories out of my mind! The images come flooding back in vivid detail, triggered by the most inconsequential things, like a door slamming or the smell of stir-fried pork. Last night I went to bed, was having a good sleep for a change. Then in the early morning a storm-front passed through and there was a bolt of crackling thunder. I awoke instantly, frozen in fear. I am right back in Vietnam, in the middle of the monsoon season at my guard post. I am sure I'll get hit in the next volley and convinced I will die. My hands are freezing, yet sweat pours from my entire body. I feel each hair on the back of my neck standing on end. I can't catch my breath and my heart is pounding. I smell a damp sulfur smell.
>
> *(Davis, 1992)*

> **Lucas:** [My wife] said that I wasn't the loving guy she used to know and love, that something horrible must have happened to me over there to change me so completely. . . . She said that the look in my eyes was the look of a deeply terrorized person, with a long-distance stare, looking off into the beyond—not into the present with her at this time. She also mentioned that my frightened look and pallid complexion, my uptight way of sitting, talking, walking, you name it, my aloofness, and all that, made her too uncomfortable for us to continue our relationship. . . . Finally, as time went on, I realized that so many people couldn't be wrong about me. The change in me began to seem deep to me—deeper than I would ever have imagined to be the case.
>
> *(Brende & Parson, 1985, pp. 46–47)*

RETURNING HOME

One-quarter of the 1.5 million combat soldiers who returned from Vietnam were arrested within two years of their return. The divorce rate among the veterans was nearly double that of the general population, and their suicide rate was nearly 25 percent higher (Williams, 1983).

What Triggers Stress Disorders?

An acute or posttraumatic stress disorder can occur at any age, even in childhood, and can impair personal, family, social, or occupational life (Putnam, 1996). People with a stress disorder may also experience depression or substance abuse. A number become suicidal (Amir et al., 1999). Around 3.9 percent of people in the United States experience one of the stress disorders in any given year; 7.6 percent suffer from one of them within their lifetimes (Kessler & Zhao, 1999; Kessler et al., 1994). Women are at least twice as likely as men to develop the disorders: around 20 percent of women who are exposed to a serious trauma may develop one, compared to 8 percent of men (Ursano et al., 1999; Kessler et al., 1995). While any traumatic event can trigger a stress disorder, some are particularly likely to do so. Among the most common are combat, disasters, and abuse and victimization.

COMBAT AND STRESS DISORDERS For years clinicians have recognized that many soldiers develop symptoms of severe anxiety and depression *during* combat (Oei, Lim, & Hennessy, 1990). The pattern of symptoms was called "nostalgia" during the American Civil War because it was considered to be the result of extended absence from home (Bourne, 1970). It was called "shell shock" during World War I because it was thought to result from small brain hemorrhages or concussions caused by constant artillery explosions. During World War II and the Korean War, it was referred to as "combat fatigue" (Figley, 1978). Not until after the Vietnam War, however, did clinicians learn that a great many soldiers also experience serious psychological symptoms *after* combat (Schlenger et al., 1999).

In the first years after the Vietnam War, the psychological problems of combat veterans were generally overlooked, perhaps in part because of the nation's desire to leave this unpopular war behind. By the late 1970s, however, it had become apparent that many Vietnam combat veterans were still experiencing war-related psychological difficulties (Williams, 1983). We now know that as many as 29 percent of all veterans, male and female, who served in Vietnam suffered an acute or posttraumatic stress disorder, while another 22 percent suffered from at least some stress symptoms (Weiss et al., 1992). In fact, 10 percent of the veterans of this war still experience significant posttraumatic stress symptoms, including flashbacks, night terrors, nightmares, and persistent images and thoughts. Similarly, in a study of combat veterans of the Persian Gulf War, over one-third reported six months later that they were experiencing nightmares and were drinking more than before (Labbate & Snow, 1992).

DISASTERS AND STRESS DISORDERS Acute and posttraumatic stress disorders may also follow natural and accidental disasters such as earthquakes, floods, tornadoes, fires, airplane crashes, and serious car accidents (see Table 6-6 on the next page). Studies have found, for example, that around one-third of victims—adult or child—of serious traffic accidents may develop posttraumatic stress disorder within a year of the accident (Ursano et al., 1999; Stallard, Velleman, & Baldwin, 1998). Similarly, several studies found stress reactions among the survivors of Hurricane Andrew, the storm that ravaged Florida and other parts of the southeastern United

ConsiderThis

⦿ What types of events in modern society might be likely to trigger acute and posttraumatic stress disorders? • Do you think the vivid images seen daily on television, in movies, in rock videos, and the like would make people more vulnerable to developing such disorders or less vulnerable?

Human aftershocks *These Armenian citizens seek solace in church after a devastating earthquake. Strong institutional and social ties can sometimes, but not always, reduce individual stress reactions after disasters and other traumatic events.*

Table 6-6			
Worst Natural Disasters of the Twentieth Century			
DISASTER	YEAR	LOCATION	NUMBER KILLED
Flood	1931	Huang He River, China	3,700,000
Earthquake	1926	Tangshan, China	242,419
Volcanic eruption	1902	Mont-Pélée, Martinique	40,000
Landslide	1970	Yungay, Peru	17,500
Tidal wave	1960	Agadir, Morocco	12,000
Avalanche	1916	Italian Alps	10,000
Tornado	1989	Shaturia, Bangladesh	1,300

Adapted from Ash, 1999, 1998.

States in 1992 (Vernberg et al., 1996; Gelman & Katel, 1993). By a month after the storm the number of calls received by the domestic violence hot line in Miami and the number of women applying for police protection had doubled (Treaster, 1992). By six months after the storm it was apparent that many elementary-school-age children were also victims of posttraumatic stress disorder; their symptoms ranged from misbehavior in school to failing grades and problems with sleep (Vernberg et al., 1996; Gelman & Katel, 1993). One child said months afterward, "When I go to sleep, I think the storm is going to come, so I can't go to sleep." Another recalled, "I was sleeping, and I thought it was coming again" (Gelman & Katel, 1993, p. 65).

VICTIMIZATION AND STRESS DISORDERS People who have been abused or victimized often experience lingering stress symptoms. For example, interviews with survivors of Nazi concentration camps years after their liberation have indicated that as many as 46 percent of them eventually qualified for a diagnosis of posttraumatic stress disorder (Kuch & Cox, 1992; Eitinger, 1973, 1969, 1964).

A common form of victimization in our society today is sexual assault. **Rape** is forced sexual intercourse or another sexual act upon a nonconsenting person or intercourse with an underage person. Surveys suggest that in the United States more than 876,000 persons are victims of rape each year (NCVS, 1998). Most rapists are men, and most victims are women. Around one in seven women are raped at some time during their lives. Surveys also suggest that most rape victims are young: 29 percent are under 11 years old, 32 percent are between the ages of 11 and 17, and 29 percent are between 18 and 29. More than 80 percent of the victims are raped by acquaintances or relatives (NCVS, 1998; Koss, 1992; Youngstrom, 1992).

The psychological impact of rape on a victim is immediate and may last a long time. Rape victims typically experience enormous distress during the week after the assault. Stress continues to rise

Victimization and posttraumatic stress disorder *Many survivors of Nazi concentration camps faced a long road back to psychological health. Because knowledge of posttraumatic stress disorder was nonexistent until recent years, most survivors had to find their way back without professional help.*

for the next three weeks, maintains a peak level for another month or so, and then starts to improve (Koss, 1993). In one study, 94 percent of rape victims fully qualified for a clinical diagnosis of acute stress disorder when they were observed an average of twelve days after the assault (Rothbaum et al., 1992). Although most rape victims improve psychologically within three or four months, the effects may persist for up to eighteen months or longer. Victims typically continue to have higher than average levels of anxiety, suspiciousness, depression, self-esteem problems, self-blame, flashbacks, sleep problems, and sexual dysfunction (Arata, 1999; Moncrieff et al., 1996; Koss, 1993). The lingering psychological impact of rape is apparent in the following case description:

> Mary Billings is a 33-year-old divorced nurse, referred to the Victim Clinic at Bedford Psychiatric Hospital for counseling by her supervisory head nurse. Mary had been raped two months ago. The assailant gained entry to her apartment while she was sleeping, and she awoke to find him on top of her. He was armed with a knife and threatened to kill her and her child (who was asleep in the next room) if she did not submit to his demands. He forced her to undress and repeatedly raped her vaginally over a period of 1 hour. He then admonished her that if she told anyone or reported the incident to the police he would return and assault her child.
>
> After he left, she called her boyfriend, who came to her apartment right away. He helped her contact the Sex Crimes Unit of the Police Department, which is currently investigating the case. He then took her to a local hospital for a physical examination and collection of evidence for the police (traces of sperm, pubic hair samples, fingernail scrapings). She was given antibiotics as prophylaxis against venereal disease. Mary then returned home with a girlfriend who spent the remainder of the night with her.
>
> Over the next few weeks Mary continued to be afraid of being alone and had her girlfriend move in with her. She became preoccupied with thoughts of what had happened to her and the possibility that it could happen again. Mary was frightened that the rapist might return to her apartment and therefore had additional locks installed on both the door and the windows. She was so upset and had such difficulty concentrating that she decided she could not yet return to work. When she did return to work several weeks later, she was still clearly upset, and her supervisor suggested that she might be helped by counseling.
>
> During the clinic interview, Mary was coherent and spoke quite rationally in a hushed voice. She reported recurrent and intrusive thoughts about the sexual assault, to the extent that her concentration was impaired and she had difficulty doing chores such as making meals for herself and her daughter. She felt she was not able to be effective at work, still felt afraid to leave her home, to answer her phone, and had little interest in contacting friends or relatives.
>
> . . . [Mary] talked in the same tone of voice whether discussing the assault or less emotionally charged topics, such as her work history. She was easily startled by an unexpected noise. She also was unable to fall asleep because she kept thinking about the assault. She had no desire to eat, and when she did attempt it, she felt nauseated. Mary was repelled by the thought of sex and stated that she did not want to have sex for a long time, although she was willing to be held and comforted by her boyfriend.
>
> *(Spitzer et al., 1983, pp. 20–21)*

Although many rape victims are injured by their attacker or experience other physical problems as a result of their assault, only half receive the kind of formal medical care afforded Mary (Beebe, 1991; Koss, Woodruff, & Koss, 1991). Between 4 and 30 percent of victims develop a sexually transmitted disease (Koss, 1993; Murphy, 1990) and 5 percent become pregnant (Beebe, 1991; Koss et al., 1991), yet a national survey revealed that 60 percent of rape victims received no

GENDER DIFFERENCES

Rates of reported rape and other sexual assaults against women are 10 times higher than those against men (U.S. Dept. of Justice, 1995). Over 80 percent of male rapes are committed by other men (NCVS, 1998).

VIOLENCE TIMETABLE

In the United States, a violent crime is committed every 16 seconds, a rape every 5 minutes, a murder every 21 minutes (FBI Uniform Crime Report).

RAPE Forced sexual intercourse or another sexual act upon a nonconsenting person or intercourse with an underage person.

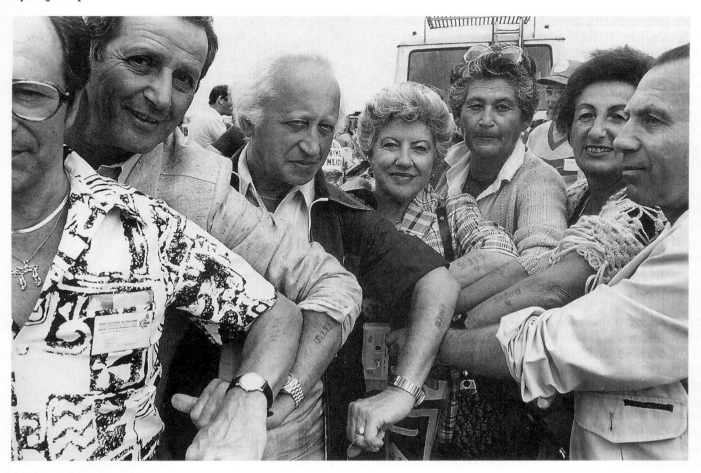

Recovery from trauma *Many people eventually overcome the effects of traumatic stress. During a reunion, these concentration camp survivors proudly display their tattooed camp identification numbers as symbols of their triumph over their psychological wounds.*

BOSNIAN VICTIMS

Studies indicate that between 18 and 50 percent of refugees from the wars in Bosnia and Kosovo developed a post-traumatic stress disorder (Favaro et al., 1999; Thulesius & Hakansson, 1999).

pregnancy testing or preventive measures and 73 percent received no information or testing for exposure to HIV (National Victims Center, 1992). Female victims of rape and other crimes are also much more likely than nonvictimized women to suffer serious long-term health problems (Leserman et al., 1996; Koss & Heslet, 1992). Interviews with 390 women revealed that such victims experienced a decline in physical well-being for at least five years after the crime and made twice as many visits to physicians. It is not yet clear why rape and other assaults lead to these long-term health problems.

As we see in Box 6-3 on page 180, ongoing victimization and abuse in the family—specifically spouse and child abuse—may also lead to stress disorders (Thompson et al., 1999; McLeer et al., 1998). Because these forms of abuse may occur over a long span of time and violate family roles and trust, many victims develop other symptoms and disorders as well (Kemp et al., 1995; Mathias, Mertin, & Murray, 1995).

Finally, living in a violent neighborhood or attending schools plagued by violence can be a source of ongoing trauma (Purnell, 1999; Kliewer et al., 1998). A study of one neighborhood found that fully 14 percent of fifth- and sixth-graders had witnessed a shooting and 43 percent had observed a mugging. These children showed more symptoms of stress than other children (Martinez & Richters, 1993; Richters & Martinez, 1993).

Explanations of Stress Disorders

Clearly, extraordinary trauma can cause a stress disorder. The stressful event alone, however, may not be the entire explanation. Certainly, anyone who experiences an unusual trauma will be affected by it, but only some people develop a disorder. To understand the development of stress disorders more fully, researchers have looked to the survivors' biological processes, personalities, childhood experiences, and social support systems and to the severity of the traumas; a growing number suspect that these variables may interrelate in the development of the disorders.

BIOLOGICAL AND GENETIC FACTORS Investigators have gathered evidence that traumatic events trigger physical changes in the brain and body that may lead to severe stress reactions and, in some cases, to stress disorders. They have, for example, found abnormal activity of the neurotransmitter *norepinephrine* and the hormone *cortisol* in the urine and blood of combat soldiers, rape victims, concentration camp survivors, and survivors of other severe stresses (Baker et al., 1999; Yehuda et al., 1998, 1995, 1994).

Perhaps people whose biochemical reactions to stress are particularly strong are more likely than others to develop acute and posttraumatic stress disorders (Kellner & Yehuda, 1999; Shalev, 1999). But why would certain people be prone to such strong biological reactions? It may be that the propensity is inherited. One study of approximately 4,000 pairs of twins who had served in the Vietnam War found that if one twin developed stress symptoms after combat, an identical twin was more likely than a fraternal twin to develop the same problems (True & Lyons, 1999; True et al., 1993). We must remember, though, that the similarities seen in identical twins do not always reflect genetic influences: childhood experiences, personalities, and support systems may also be more similar in identical twins than in fraternal twins and explain the greater similarity in their reactions to stress.

There is also evidence that once a stress disorder unfolds, other biological changes follow. Research suggests, for example, that people with posttraumatic stress disorder experience more health problems after the trauma than before it (Schnurr & Spiro, 1999; Taft et al., 1999). Apart from these changes, the heightened biochemical arousal that these victims continue to experience may eventually damage their *hippocampus*, the brain area that regulates the body's stress hormones (Bremner, 1999; Bremner, Southwick, & Charney, 1999). Such damage and the abnormal biochemical activity it produces may exacerbate the stress disorder.

PERSONALITY Some studies suggest that people with certain personality profiles, attitudes, and coping styles are more likely to develop stress disorders (McFarlane, 1999; Schnurr & Vielhauer, 1999; Williams, 1999). In the aftermath of Hurricane Hugo, for example, children who had been highly anxious before the storm were more likely than other children to develop severe stress reactions (Lonigan et al., 1994). Similarly, the victims who are most likely to develop stress disorders after being raped are the ones who had psychological problems before they were raped, or who were struggling with stressful life situations (Darvres-Bornoz et al., 1995). The same is true of war veterans who had psychological problems before they went into combat (Orsillo et al., 1996). Finally, people who generally view life's negative events as beyond their control tend to develop more severe stress symptoms after sexual or other kinds of criminal assaults than people who feel greater control over their lives (Regehr, Cadell, & Jansen, 1999; Kushner et al., 1992). These findings coincide with another discovery: that many people respond to stress with a set of positive attitudes, collectively called *hardiness*, that enables them to carry on their lives with a sense of fortitude, control, and commitment (Kobasa, 1990, 1987, 1979).

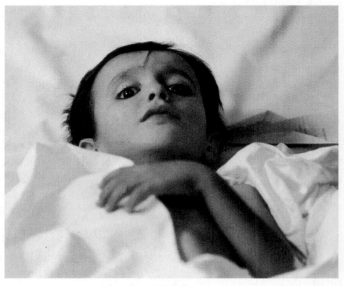

No age minimum *Confusion and fear fill the eyes of this child, rescued after being trapped under rubble for 146 hours following a Turkish earthquake. His risk of developing a stress disorder will depend on various factors, including genetic influences and his family and social supports.*

Protection by personality *Millions reacted to the San Francisco earthquake of 1989 with dread and panic, but some laid-back individuals thrived on all the excitement. Their "hardy" personality styles may have helped to protect them from the development of stress disorders.*

BOX 6-3

Spouse Abuse: Victimization in the Family

❙ He told me that he was never going to let me go. He said that he married me, and whether he loved me or not, and whether I loved him or not, I was going to stay with him, and if I tried to leave him, he was going to kill me—one day at a time, like dripping water on a rock, until I broke apart. Although I never knew exactly what he would do, I knew that he was capable of torture. He broke my arm once and dangled it in front of me, playing with it, telling me it wasn't broken. ❙

(JONES & SCHECHTER, 1992)

Spouse abuse, the physical mistreatment or misuse of one spouse by the other, takes numerous forms, from shoving to battering. Ninety-three percent of abused spouses are women, married or cohabiting (Walker, 1999; National Crime Victimization Survey, 1993). It is estimated that spouse abuse occurs in 2 to 4 million homes in the United States each year and that as many as a third of all U.S. women have been abused at least once by their husbands (Brannen et al., 1999; Dearwater et al., 1999; AMA, 1992). Spouse abuse is seen in all races, religions, educational levels, and socioeconomic groups (U.S. Dept. of Justice, 1995). The U.S. surgeon general has ranked it as the leading cause of injuries to women between the ages of 15 and 44.

For years this behavior was viewed as a private matter; until 1874 a husband actually had a legal right to beat his wife in the United States. Even after that time, abusers were rarely punished. Police were reluctant to do anything other than attempt to quell an episode of domestic violence, and the courts rarely prosecuted an abuser. Thanks to the civil rights movement in the 1970s and the efforts of women's groups, state legislatures have increasingly passed laws that empower the courts to prosecute abusers and protect victims. As a result, the police are now able to intervene more actively, and nearly half of all U.S. police departments have established special units to deal with spouse abuse (LEMAS, 1990). In fact, 25 states have laws requiring the police to make an arrest when they are called to a scene. Arrests do not necessarily lead to convictions, however, nor do convictions always produce sentences that prevent future abuse.

Abusers

There is no uniform personality profile for abusers. Many of them, though, have a need to control their wives, but are emotionally dependent on them at the same time and fear losing them (Murphy et al., 1994). Often these men consider their wives to be their personal property, and they become most assaultive when the wife shows independence. In some cases the abuse increases when the wives pursue outside friendships, attempt to work outside the home, or even attend to the children's needs first. These husbands may also belittle and isolate their wives and make them feel inept, worthless, and dependent.

"Honeymoon phases" seem to be common in abusive relationships (Walker, 1984, 1979). Periodically the husband, concerned that the latest violent incident will cause his wife to leave him, performs acts of kindness and contrition, and promises that the abuse will never happen again (Jones & Schechter, 1992). Unfortunately, in most cases the abuse does happen again, and over time, battering may even increase.

Many persons who abuse their spouses have alcohol-related or other substance-related problems (Mollerstrom et al., 1992; Saunders, 1992), but these problems are not usually the key cause of battering, and treating only an abuser's substance problem seldom stops the violence (ADVTP, 1996; Jones & Schechter, 1992). Many abusers were themselves beaten as children or saw their mothers beaten (Walker, 1999; Saunders, 1992). Often they suffer from low self-esteem and feel generally stressed and frustrated with their lives (Russell & Hulson, 1992).

Victims

As a result of physical abuse, threats, and intimidation, a victim of abuse typically feels very dependent on her husband and unable to function on her own. These feelings tend to keep her in the relationship despite the obvious physical dangers. Abused women are not masochistic, as many clinical theorists once believed (Walker, 1984; Finkelhor et al., 1983). In fact, 80 percent of them try to defend themselves either physically or verbally. This is the same as the percentage of women in general who defend themselves when assaulted by a stranger (U.S. Dept. of Justice, 1994).

Many victims stay with their husbands out of economic need. Research shows

CHILDHOOD EXPERIENCES A recent wave of studies has identified childhood experiences that seem to leave some people at risk for later acute and posttraumatic stress disorders. People whose childhoods have been marked by poverty appear more likely to develop these disorders in the face of later trauma. So do people whose family members suffered from psychological disorders; who experienced assault, abuse, or catastrophe at an early age; or who were younger than 10 when their parents separated or divorced (Breslau et al., 1999; Bremner et al., 1993).

Such childhood experiences may help produce the personality styles or attitudes that have been linked to stress disorders. Perhaps their early situations

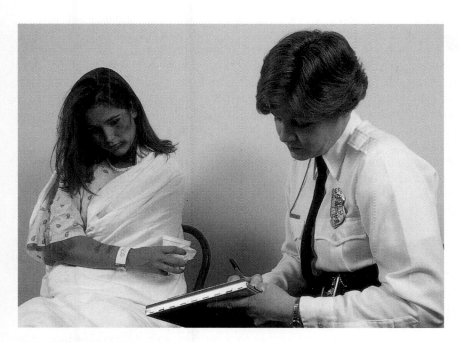

Police intervention *A victim of spouse abuse is interviewed by a police officer after being hospitalized. Many police departments now have special units to ensure that victims receive medical help, counseling, and legal guidance.*

Treatments for Spouse Abuse

Clinicians used to propose couple therapy as the treatment of choice for spouse abuse, but too often, as they have learned, the woman continues to be abused at home, and the intervention is only a charade. In fact, couple therapy alone sometimes increases the risk of serious injury or death (ADVTP, 1996; Jones & Schechter, 1992). The treatment that is now preferred has three steps: (1) providing a woman with a safe place to live, away from her abusive husband; (2) counseling for the victim to help her understand her situation, recognize her choices, and develop a more positive self-image; and (3) counseling for the abuser to help him cope better with stress, develop appropriate attitudes toward his wife, and learn proper ways of expressing anger (Austin & Dankwort, 1999; Wexler, 1999; Ganley, 1981).

Many community programs have been established to provide these services—hot lines; emergency shelters, or "safe houses," for women; and public organizations and self-help groups to provide education and aid (Page, 1996; Sullivan et al., 1992). In some areas, the legal system also plays a role by requiring that arrested abusers attend a batterers' program as an alternative to jail (Walker, 1999). In spite of much progress, spouse abuse remains a difficult and poorly understood problem. Nevertheless, the fact that treatment programs now exist is an important development for both victims and our society, and most clinicians believe that many of these programs are on the right track.

that most women's standard of living falls drastically after a divorce (Glazer, 1993; Heise & Chapman, 1990). Others stay for fear of what their husbands may do if they go. This fear is often justified: violence against the victim increases by as much as 75 percent when she tries to leave the relationship (Hart, 1992; U.S. Dept. of Justice, 1992). In one study of spouse abuse, 70 percent of the reported injuries were inflicted after the couple separated (Liss & Stahly, 1993). Another study found that half of all women murdered by their husbands were killed after they had left home (Hart, 1993). Victims of spouse abuse may also be justifiably afraid to report the abuse and ask for help (U.S. Dept. of Justice, 1994).

About 50 percent of victims of spouse abuse grew up in homes where they or their mothers were abused, and most come from families in which male and female roles follow old stereotypes. Many victims have very low self-esteem, partly as a result of the ongoing abuse (Cornell & Gelles, 1983). They often blame themselves for the abuse and agree when their husbands accuse them of triggering it. Usually the pattern of abuse did not begin until after the couple married.

teach children that the world is an unpredictable and dangerous place. In Chapter 5 we observed that such a worldview may set the stage for generalized anxiety disorder. Similarly, it may lead people to react more hopelessly and fearfully to extraordinary trauma, and so increase their risk of developing a stress disorder.

SOCIAL SUPPORT It has been found that people whose social support systems are weak are also more likely to develop a stress disorder after a traumatic event (Pickens et al., 1995; Perry et al., 1992). Rape victims who feel loved, cared for, valued, and accepted by their friends and relatives recover more successfully. So

ConsiderThis

● Rape victims need support from the medical and legal systems in order to deal effectively with their trauma and its aftermath. How might physicians, police, the courts, and other agents better meet the needs of these victims?

REBOUND EFFECT

In one study, rape victims suffering from posttraumatic stress disorder were instructed to deliberately suppress all thoughts about their sexual assault. This strategy not only failed to help them but led to a rise in rape-related thoughts (Shipherd & Beck, 1999).

do those treated with dignity and respect by the criminal justice system (Davis, Brickman, & Baker, 1991; Sales, Baum, & Shore, 1984). In contrast, clinical reports have suggested that poor social support has contributed to the development of posttraumatic stress disorder in some combat veterans (Taft et al., 1999; Figley & Leventman, 1990).

SEVERITY OF TRAUMA As one might expect, the severity and nature of traumatic events also play a role in determining whether an individual will develop a stress disorder. Some events can override even a nurturing childhood, positive attitudes, and social support. One study examined 253 Vietnam War prisoners five years after their release. Some 23 percent qualified for a clinical diagnosis, though all had been evaluated as well adjusted before their imprisonment (Ursano, Boydstun, & Wheatley, 1981).

Generally, the more severe the trauma and the more direct one's exposure to it, the greater the likelihood of developing a stress disorder (King et al., 1996; Putnam, 1996). Among the Vietnam prisoners of war, for example, it was the men who had been imprisoned longest and treated most harshly that had the highest percentage of disorders. Mutilation and severe physical injury in particular seem to increase the risk of stress reactions, as does witnessing the injury or death of other people (Putnam, 1996; Kessler et al., 1995). It is, as a survivor of trauma once said, "hard to be a survivor" (Kolff & Doan, 1985, p. 45).

How Do Clinicians Treat Stress Disorders?

Treatment can make a major difference to a person with a stress disorder. One survey found that posttraumatic stress symptoms lasted an average of three years with treatment but five and a half years without (Kessler & Zhao, 1999; Kessler et al., 1995). Today's treatment procedures for troubled survivors typically vary from trauma to trauma. Was it combat, sexual molestation, or a major accident? Yet all the programs share basic goals: they try to help survivors put an end to the lingering stress reactions, gain perspective on their traumatic experiences, and return to constructive living. Programs for combat veterans who suffer from posttraumatic stress disorder illustrate how these issues may be addressed.

TREATMENT FOR COMBAT VETERANS Therapists have used a variety of techniques to reduce veterans' posttraumatic symptoms (van der Kolk et al., 1999; Shalev, Bonne, & Eth, 1996). Among the most common are *drug therapy*, *exposure techniques*, *insight therapy*, *family therapy*, and *group therapy*. Typically the approaches are combined, as no one of them successfully reduces all the symptoms (Boudewins, 1996).

Antianxiety drugs help control the tension and exaggerated startle responses that many veterans experience. In addition, antidepressant medications may reduce the occurrence of nightmares, panic attacks, flashbacks, unwanted recollections, and feelings of depression (Friedman, 1999; Mirabella, Frueh, & Fossey, 1995).

Behavioral exposure techniques, too, have helped reduce specific symptoms, and they have often led to improvements in overall adjustment (DeRubeis & Crits-Christoph, 1998; Woodward et al., 1997). Flooding, along with relaxation training, helped rid a 31-year-old veteran of frightening flashbacks and nightmares (Fairbank & Keane, 1982). The therapist and the veteran first singled out combat scenes that the man had been reexperiencing frequently. The therapist then helped the veteran to imagine one of these scenes in great detail and urged him to hold on to the image until his anxiety stopped. After each of these flooding exercises, the therapist had the veteran switch to a positive image and led him through relaxation exercises.

Recently a relatively new form of exposure therapy has been gaining attention. In **eye movement desensitization and reprocessing**, clients move their eyes in a *saccadic,* or rhythmic, manner from side to side while flooding their minds with images of their phobic objects and situations. According to some case studies, a variety of psychological problems have improved dramatically when treated with this approach, including posttraumatic fears and memories. In fact, a few clients are said to have improved after only one session (Lipke & Botkin, 1992; Puk, 1991). Controlled studies of the approach have reported more modest successes, but at least some of them suggest that this treatment can be helpful (Cahill, Carrigan, & Frueh, 1999; Boudewins et al., 1991).

Although drug therapy and exposure techniques bring some relief, most clinicians believe that veterans with posttraumatic stress disorder cannot fully recover with these approaches alone: they must also come to grips in some way with their combat experiences and the impact those experiences continue to have (Marmar et al., 1993). Thus clinicians often try to help veterans bring out deep-seated feelings, accept what they have done and experienced, become less judgmental of themselves, and learn to trust other people once again (Shay & Munroe, 1999). In research along these lines, the psychologist James Pennebaker (1997) has found that talking (or even writing) about traumatic experiences can reduce lingering anxiety and tension.

People who have a stress disorder are sometimes helped to express their feelings and develop insight in couple or family therapy formats (Glynn et al., 1995; Johnson, Feldman, & Lubin, 1995). The symptoms of posttraumatic stress disorder tend to be particularly apparent to family members, who may be directly affected by the client's anxieties, depressive mood, or angry outbursts (Catherall, 1999). With the help and support of their family members, trauma victims may come to recognize the feelings they are grappling with, examine their impact on others, learn to communicate better, and improve their problem-solving skills.

Veterans may also benefit from **rap groups**, where they meet with others like themselves to share experiences and feelings, develop insights, and give mutual support. This form of group therapy was originated in 1971 by an organization called Vietnam Veterans Against the War. Many veterans find it easier to recall events in a rap group and to confront feelings they have been trying to avoid for

EYE MOVEMENT DESENSITIZATION AND REPROCESSING A behavioral exposure treatment in which clients move their eyes in a saccadic (rhythmic) manner from side to side while flooding their minds with images of phobic objects and situations.

RAP GROUP A group that meets to talk about and explore members' problems in an atmosphere of mutual support.

Sharing painful memories and feelings *Rap groups have helped many Vietnam veterans overcome the anxiety, depression, sleep problems, and flashbacks that still linger years after the war.*

years (Ford & Stewart, 1999). One of the major issues rap groups deal with is guilt—guilt about things the members may have done to survive or about the very fact that they did survive while close friends died. Once the veterans are finally able to talk openly about their combat experiences and guilt feelings, they may finally start to recover from them and weigh their responsibility for past actions more accurately (Lifton, 1973). Rap groups may also focus on the rage many combat veterans feel. Well after the Vietnam War, for example, many veterans remained deeply angry that they had to fight for a questionable cause, face unbearable conditions and tensions in Vietnam, and then deal with an accusing society after they returned home.

Today hundreds of small *Veteran Outreach Centers* across the country, as well as numerous treatment programs in Veterans Administration hospitals and mental health clinics, specialize in rap groups (Ford & Stewart, 1999). These agencies also offer individual therapy, counseling for the spouses and children of troubled veterans, family therapy, and aid in seeking jobs, education, and benefits (Brende & Parson, 1985; Blank, 1982).

Research into the effectiveness of Veteran Outreach Centers has been limited (Funari, Piekarski, & Sherwood, 1991). However, the clinical reports and empirical studies that have been done suggest that they offer a necessary, sometimes life-saving treatment opportunity. Julius's search for help upon his return from Vietnam was, unfortunately, an ordeal that many veterans have shared:

> When I got back from the 'Nam, I knew I needed psychotherapy or something like that. I just knew that if I didn't get help I was going to kill myself or somebody else. . . . I went to see this doctor; he barely looked at me. I felt he "saw me coming" and knew all about my sickness. I was the "sicky" to him. He just kept on asking me all that bullshit about how many children I had killed and was I guilty and depressed about it. He asked how it felt to kill people. He also kept on asking me about my brothers and sisters. But he never asked me about what my experiences were like in Vietnam. He never did. I saw him for treatment for about a month—about three visits, but I quit because we weren't getting anywhere. . . . He just kept on giving me more and more medications. I could've set up my own pharmacy. I needed someone to talk to about my problems, my real problems, not some bullshit about my childhood. I needed someone who wanted to help. The clinic later referred me to another shrink. . . . I guess she thought she was being honest with me, by telling me that she was not a veteran, was not in Vietnam, and did not know what was wrong with me. She also told me that she had no experience working with Vietnam veterans, and that I should go to the Veterans Administration for help. . . .
>
> It was only in the last 3 years when my wife made an important phone call to a local Veterans Outreach Center that I started feeling I had hope, that something could be done for me. I received the help that I have always needed. Finally, I found it easier to hold a job and take care of my family. My nightmares are not as frightening or as frequent as they used to be. Things are better now; I am learning to trust people and give more to my wife and children.
>
> *(Brende & Parson, 1985, pp. 206–208)*

COMMUNITY THERAPY: THE SOCIOCULTURAL MODEL IN ACTION People who are traumatized by disasters, victimization, or accidents may profit from many of the same treatments that are used to help survivors of combat. In addition, because their traumas occur in their own community, where mental health resources are close at hand, these individuals may profit from immediate community interventions. A case in point is the rapidly mobilized community care now offered by mental health professionals across the world to victims of large-scale disasters.

Everyone is affected *A fire captain cradles one-year-old Baylee Almon, a child killed in the bombing of the Oklahoma City federal building. This famous photograph reminds us that rescue workers are themselves subjected to enormous stress and trauma during disasters (Bryant & Harvey, 1995).*

Psychological interventions by community workers were first offered in the early 1980s when fire and emergency rescue workers began receiving **critical incident stress debriefing**—training in how to help victims talk about their feelings and reactions to traumatic incidents (McClelland, 1998). Since then, thousands of professionals have received training and certification in the delivery of emergency mental health services, and they stand ready to act wherever a disaster strikes (Clay, 1999).

One of the largest such programs is the *Disaster Response Network (DRN)*, developed in 1991 by the American Psychological Association and the American Red Cross. The network is made up of more than 2,500 volunteer psychologists who offer free emergency mental health services at disaster sites throughout North America (Peterson, 1996). They have been mobilized for such disasters as Hurricane Andrew in 1992, earthquakes in Southern California, the Oklahoma City bombing, the World Trade Center bombing, and the explosion of TWA Flight 800.

Traditional long-term mental health services may not always be appropriate, available, or sought after a disaster. In fact, many survivors do not even recognize their own degree of upset in the aftermath of disaster (Michaelson, 1993). Thus the short-term community intervention provided by the Disaster Response Network and similar programs seems to fill a real need (Joyner & Swenson, 1993). People who live in poverty are in particular need of community-level interventions. These survivors apparently experience more psychological distress after disasters than survivors with higher incomes (Gibbs, 1989), they cannot afford private counseling, and they are less likely to know where to seek counseling.

The first aim of mental health professionals in disaster settings is to help survivors meet their basic needs as quickly as possible. During the Midwest flood of 1993, for example, professionals worked in shelters and service centers and rode in Red Cross emergency vehicles to deliver food and water along with counseling services. Some counselors joined flood victims in piling sandbags to protect their homes from further damage. The counselors also used these early contacts to determine which victims were most in need of psychological help.

Once mental health volunteers become involved in the community, they may act more directly to help meet the psychological needs of the disaster victims. They often use a four-stage approach (Michaelson, 1993):

1. **Normalize people's responses to the disaster.** The counselors educate survivors about the symptoms they may be experiencing, such as sleep disturbances, difficulty concentrating, or feelings of grief. Essentially, survivors are given permission to have these reactions and told that they are normal responses to a disaster.

2. **Encourage expressions of anxiety, anger, and frustration.** To reduce the anxiety, anger, and frustration that survivors often feel after a disaster, counselors help them talk about their experiences and their feelings.

3. **Teach self-helping skills.** Counselors train survivors to develop stress management and other self-help skills.

CRITICAL INCIDENT STRESS DEBRIEFING Training in how to help victims talk about their feelings and reactions to traumatic incidents.

4. **Provide referrals.** The workers eventually may refer survivors to other professionals who can provide long-term counseling (Sleek, 1997). It is estimated that between 15 and 25 percent of survivors need this specialized assistance.

Relief workers, too, can become overwhelmed by the traumas they witness (Ursano et al., 1999). During the Los Angeles riots, for example, a key responsibility of many community mental health counselors was to help Red Cross workers vent and accept their own feelings as well as teach them about stress disorders and how to identify victims who need further treatment. Many mental health professionals who live in a disaster area need counseling themselves, since they, too, are survivors. The dual role they are thrown into may make it difficult for them to deal with their own experiences.

Although this approach has detractors (see Box 6-4), most professionals believe that intervention at the community level is highly useful after a disaster. And sadly, our world seems to offer ever-increasing opportunities to test that be-

"IT COULD HAVE BEEN SAMMY"
Disaster workers who deal with the remains of deceased victims are more likely to develop a stress disorder if they identify with the victims—"It could have been my family." (Ursano et al., 1999).

BOX 6-4

Disaster Counseling: The Other Side

Rapid-mobilization mental health programs for disaster victims are growing in number and popularity. A number of investigations of these programs seem to yield favorable results, and personal testimonials are supportive as well. At the same time, the programs have a number of detractors, who question the effectiveness of the interventions (Gist & Woodall, 1999).

A study conducted several years back was among the first to raise concerns about the disaster mental health programs (Bisson & Deahl, 1994). Crisis counselors worked with 62 British soldiers whose job during the Gulf War was to handle and identify the bodies of individuals who had been killed. After receiving nine months of crisis counseling, half of the soldiers nevertheless displayed posttraumatic stress symptoms, leading some theorists to conclude that disaster intervention programs do not really make much difference. Still worse, some clinicians now worry that the programs may encourage victims to dwell too long on the traumatic events that they have experienced. Moreover, certain clinicians are concerned that early disaster counseling may inadvertently

"suggest" problems to victims, thus helping to produce stress disorders in the first place (McClelland, 1998).

The current clinical climate continues to favor disaster counseling, and such programs may indeed prove to be as helpful as many clinicians believe. However, the concerns of detractors merit se-

rious consideration. We are reminded here, as elsewhere, of the constant need for careful research in the field of abnormal psychology.

Essential or excessive? *A relief worker comforts the family member of a victim of Egypt Air Flight 990, the plane which crashed off Nantucket Island in 1999 under mysterious circumstances, killing all 217 aboard.*

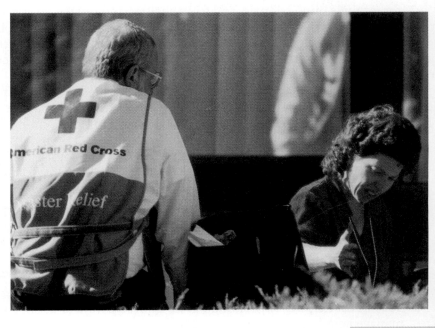

lief. In the immediate aftermath of the explosion of TWA Flight 800 in July 1996, close to 500 mental health professionals were mobilized to counsel family members, flight crews, rescue personnel, and others affected by the disaster (Seppa, 1996). Similarly, hundreds of counselors were called to action after the 1998 crash of Swissair Flight 111 in Peggy's Cove, Nova Scotia, and after the 1999 shooting of 23 persons at Columbine High School in Littleton, Colorado.

CROSSROADS:
Lessons to Be Learned

Panic, obsessive-compulsive, and stress disorders—once known in clinical circles simply as the "other" anxiety disorders—have received intense study over the past decade. Lessons can be learned from the history of these disorders, not just about the disorders themselves, but about the general study and treatment of psychological abnormality.

First, we learn that effort pays off. For many years, the study and treatment of panic disorder and obsessive-compulsive disorder seemed to be going nowhere. Early theoretical explanations provided few insights, and clinical interventions brought little change. Recent work in the biological, cognitive, and behavioral spheres has changed all that. Today research into these problems is flourishing, the new explanations are enlightening, and treatment is highly effective.

A second lesson is that we can always improve upon the identification and classification of psychological disorders. Panic disorder was not distinguished from generalized anxiety disorder until the 1960s, and the stress disorders did not even enter the diagnostic system until the 1980s. These newer classifications have been much more than clinical window dressing. Clinical theorists, researchers, and practitioners were able to make significant progress in understanding and treating these problems only after they were properly identified.

A third lesson is that insights and techniques from the various models not only *can* be combined but often *should* be combined for greater clarity and effectiveness. Not until clinical theorists took a cross-model look at the disorders discussed in this chapter were they able to develop explanations and treatments that were informative and helpful. The cognitive explanation of panic disorder, for example, builds squarely on the biological idea that the disorder begins with unusual physical sensations. Similarly, the stress disorders seem best explained by the interrelationships of the genetic, childhood, and personality factors that set the stage for them; the overpowering events and biological reactions that trigger them; *and* the sociocultural climate the victims must live in.

In a similar vein, therapists have found that treatment is at least sometimes more effective when medications are combined with cognitive techniques to treat panic disorder, with behavioral techniques to treat obsessive-compulsive disorder, and with various psychotherapeutic techniques to treat stress disorders. For the millions of people who suffer from these anxiety disorders, such integrated insights and interventions are most positive and momentous developments.

Finally, we can learn a lesson of caution from the recent work on these disorders. When problems are heavily studied, it is common for researchers and clinicians to make claims and draw conclusions that may be too bold. Take post-traumatic stress disorder. Because its symptoms are many, because a variety of life events can be considered traumatic, and because the disorder has received so much attention, many people—perhaps too many—are now receiving this diagnosis. We shall see this potential problem again when we look at attention-deficit hyperactivity disorder, repressed memories of childhood abuse, and multiple personality disorder. The line between enlightenment and overenthusiasm is often thin.

UNNATURAL DISASTER

Around one-third of the adults who were inside or just outside the Oklahoma City federal building at the time of the 1995 bombing developed post-traumatic stress disorder (North et al., 1999).

SUMMARY AND REVIEW

■ **Recent developments** Discoveries in recent years have shed light on the causes of panic disorder, obsessive-compulsive disorder, and stress disorders, and promising treatments have been developed. *p. 155*

■ **Panic disorder** Panic attacks are periodic, discrete bouts of panic that occur suddenly. Sufferers of panic disorder experience panic attacks repeatedly and unexpectedly, and without apparent reason. When panic disorder leads to agoraphobia, it is termed panic disorder with agoraphobia.

Biological theorists believe that abnormal norepinephrine activity in the brain's locus ceruleus is the key to panic disorder. Biological therapists use certain antidepressant drugs or powerful benzodiazepines to treat people with this disorder. Patients whose panic disorder is accompanied by agoraphobia may need a combination of drug therapy and behavioral exposure treatment.

Cognitive theorists suggest that panic-prone people become preoccupied with some of their bodily sensations, misinterpret them as signs of medical catastrophe, panic, and in some cases develop panic disorder. Such persons have a high degree of anxiety sensitivity and also experience greater anxiety during biological challenge tests. Cognitive therapists teach patients to interpret their physical sensations more accurately and to cope better with anxiety. In cases of panic disorder with agoraphobia, practitioners might combine a cognitive approach with behavioral exposure techniques. *pp. 155-162*

■ **Obsessive-compulsive disorder** People with obsessive-compulsive disorder are beset by obsessions, perform compulsions, or display both. Common themes in obsessions are contamination and violence. Compulsions commonly center on cleaning or checking. Other common compulsions involve touching, verbal rituals, or counting. Compulsions are often a response to a person's obsessive thoughts.

According to the psychodynamic view, obsessive-compulsive disorder arises out of a battle between id impulses, which appear as obsessive thoughts, and ego defense mechanisms, which take the form of counterthoughts or compulsive actions. Behaviorists believe that compulsive behaviors develop through chance associations. The leading behavioral treatment combines prolonged exposure with response prevention.

Cognitive theorists believe that obsessive-compulsive disorder grows from a normal human tendency to have unwanted and unpleasant thoughts. The efforts of some people to understand, eliminate, or avoid such thoughts actually lead to obsessions and compulsions. A promising cognitive-behavioral treatment is habituation training, during which therapists encourage clients to summon their obsessive thoughts to mind for a prolonged period, expecting that such prolonged exposure will cause the thoughts to feel less threatening and to generate less anxiety. Biological researchers have tied obsessive-compulsive disorder to low serotonin activity and abnormal functioning in the orbital region of the frontal cortex and in the caudate nuclei. Antidepressant drugs that raise serotonin activity are a useful form of treatment. *pp. 162-172*

■ **Stress disorders** People with acute stress disorder or posttraumatic stress disorder react with anxiety and related symptoms after a traumatic event, including reexperiencing the traumatic event, avoiding related events, being markedly less responsive than normal, and experiencing increased arousal, anxiety, and guilt. The traumatic event may be combat experience, a disaster, or victimization. The symptoms of acute stress disorder begin soon after the trauma and last less than a month. Those of posttraumatic stress disorder may begin at any time (even years) after the trauma, and may last for months or years.

In attempting to explain why some people develop a stress disorder and others do not, researchers have focused on biological factors, personality,

---

COMPULSION FOR COMPOSING
Beethoven is said to have habitually dipped his head in cold water before trying to compose music.

NUCLEAR TRAUMA
Major Claude Robert Eatherly was one of the pilots who dropped atom bombs on Hiroshima and Nagasaki in 1945. In subsequent years, feeling personally responsible for the nuclear devastation of the two cities, he made two suicide attempts and was hospitalized for psychological problems on several occasions (Hirsch et al., 1974).

childhood experiences, social support, and the severity of the traumatic event. Techniques used to treat the stress disorders include drug therapy and behavioral exposure techniques. Clinicians may also use insight therapy, family therapy, and group therapy (including rap groups for combat veterans) to help sufferers develop insight and perspective. Rapidly mobilized community therapy, such as that offered by the Disaster Response Network, follows the principles of critical incident stress debriefing. It can be helpful after large-scale disasters. *pp. 172–187*

CYBER STUDY

▲ *How do persons with obsessive-compulsive disorder explain their behaviors?*
▲ *How disruptive are obsessions and compulsions?* ▲ *How do obsessions and compulsions interrelate?* ▲ *How do persons react to the trauma of losing a loved one to suicide?*

SEARCH THE *ABNORMAL PSYCHOLOGY* CD-ROM FOR

▲ Chapter 6 video cases and discussions
   "Jennifer"—Obsessive-Compulsive Disorder
   "Bill"—Obsessive-Compulsive Disorder

▲ Chapter 6 practice test and feedback

▲ Additional video cases and discussions
   "Bonnie"—Suicide
   "Jed"—Suicide

LOG ON TO THE COMER WEB PAGE

[www.worthpublishers.com/comerabnormalpsychology4e] **FOR**

▲ Suggested Web links, research exercises, FAQ page, additional Chapter 6 practice test questions

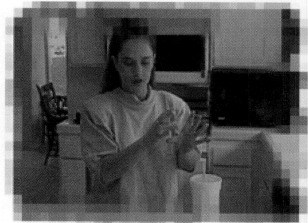

Mood Disorders

. . . a six-month period, her irritability bordered on the irrational. She screamed in anger or sobbed in despair at every dirty dish left on the coffee table or on the bedroom floor. Each day the need to plan the dinner menu provoked agonizing indecision. How could all the virtues or, more likely, vices of hamburgers be accurately compared to those of spaghetti? . . . She had her whole family walking on eggs. She thought they would be better off if she were dead.

Beatrice could not cope with her job. As a branch manager of a large chain store, she had many decisions to make. Unable to make them herself, she would ask employees who were much less competent for advice, but then she could not decide whose advice to take. Each morning before going to work, she complained of nausea. . . .

Beatrice's husband loved her, but he did not understand what was wrong. He thought that she would improve if he made her life easier by taking over more housework, cooking, and child care. His attempt to help only made Beatrice feel more guilty and worthless. She wanted to make a contribution to her family. She wanted to do the chores "like normal people" did but broke down crying at the smallest impediment to a perfect job. . . . Months passed, and Beatrice's problem became more serious. Some days she was too upset to go to work. She stopped seeing her friends. She spent most of her time at home either yelling or crying. Finally, Beatrice's husband called the psychiatrist and insisted that something was seriously wrong.

(Lickey & Gordon, 1991, p. 181)

Most people's moods come and go. Their feelings of elation or sadness are understandable reactions to daily events and do not affect their lives greatly. The moods of people with mood disorders, in contrast, tend to last a long time. As in Beatrice's case, the mood colors all of their interactions with the world and interferes with normal functioning.

Depression and mania are the key emotions in mood disorders. **Depression** is a low, sad state in which life seems dark and its challenges overwhelming. **Mania**, the opposite of depression, is a state of breathless euphoria, or at least frenzied energy, in which people may have an exaggerated belief that the world is theirs for the taking. Most people with a mood disorder suffer only from depression, a pattern called **unipolar depression**. They have no history of mania and return to a normal or nearly normal mood when their depression lifts. Others experience periods of mania that alternate with periods of depression, a pattern called **bipolar disorder**. One might logically expect a third pattern of mood disorder, *unipolar mania,* in which people suffer from mania only, but this pattern is so rare that many experts doubt its existence, except when it is brought on by a medical condition (APA, 2000, 1994).

Mood disorders have always captured people's interest, in part because so many famous people have suffered from them (see Box 7-1 on the next page). The Bible speaks of the severe depressions of Nebuchadnezzar, Saul, and Moses. Queen Victoria of England and Abraham Lincoln seem to have

DEPRESSION A low, sad state marked by significant levels of sadness, lack of energy, low self-worth, guilt, or related symptoms.

MANIA A state or episode of euphoria or frenzied activity in which people may have an exaggerated belief that the world is theirs for the taking.

UNIPOLAR DEPRESSION Depression without a history of mania.

BIPOLAR DISORDER A disorder marked by alternating or intermixed periods of mania and depression.

BOX 7-1

Depression, Politics, and Public Perceptions

When George McGovern ran for president of the United States in 1972, word leaked out that his running mate, Senator Thomas Eagleton, had once suffered from depression and had received electroconvulsive therapy. The news, as well as the perception that Eagleton may have tried to hide his past problems, led to Eagleton's withdrawal from the race and no doubt contributed to McGovern's overwhelming defeat.

When General Colin Powell was being touted as a possible presidential candidate in 1996, rumors emerged that his wife, Alma, had suffered from depression. During a news conference announcing his decision not to run, Powell straightforwardly acknowledged his wife's past episode of depression, discussed her successful response to antidepressant drug treatment, and encouraged everyone with this problem to seek treatment. In this instance, the public responded with admiration and respect. Indeed, support for Powell seemed to rise.

Similarly, in 1999 Tipper Gore, wife of then-Vice President Al Gore, disclosed at a White House conference that she had experienced a major depressive episode ten years earlier after her son had been hit by a car. Again the public reacted with empathy and admiration.

ConsiderThis

● Recently McGovern said he regrets having dropped Eagleton from the 1972 ticket, noting, "I think today we probably would have gotten different advice." Why might he receive different advice today? ● Do the different public reactions to Eagleton, Powell, and Gore suggest that the perception of depression is less negative in our society today than it was a generation ago? ● If Colin Powell or Al Gore themselves, rather than their wives, had experienced bouts of depression, would the public reaction have been more similar to that accorded Senator Eagleton?

experienced recurring depressions. Mood disorders also have plagued such writers as Ernest Hemingway, Eugene O'Neill, Virginia Woolf, and Sylvia Plath (Andreasen, 1980). Their mood problems have been shared by millions, and today the economic costs (work loss, treatment, hospitalization) amount to more than $40 billion each year (Nordenberg, 1998; Simon & Katzelnick, 1997). Of course, the human suffering that the disorders cause is beyond calculation.

ConsiderThis

● Almost every day we experience ups and downs in mood. How can we separate the everyday blues from clinical depression?

Unipolar Depression

Whenever we feel particularly unhappy, we are likely to describe ourselves as "depressed." In all likelihood, we are merely responding to sad events, fatigue, or unhappy thoughts (see Figure 7-1). This loose use of the term confuses a perfectly normal mood swing with a clinical syndrome. All of us experience dejection from time to time; but only some experience unipolar depression.

Normal dejection is seldom so severe as to influence daily functioning significantly or to persist very long. Such downturns in mood can even be beneficial (Nesse, 2000). Periods spent in contemplation can lead us to explore our inner selves, our values, and our way of life, and we often emerge with a sense of greater strength, clarity, and resolve.

Clinical depression, on the other hand, has no redeeming characteristics. It brings severe and long-lasting psychological pain that may intensify as time goes by. Those who suffer from it may lose their will to carry out the simplest of life's activities; some even lose their will to live.

How Common Is Unipolar Depression?

Between 5 and 10 percent of adults in the United States suffer from a severe unipolar pattern of depression in any given year, while another 3 to 5 percent suffer from mild forms (Kessler & Zhao, 1999; Kessler et al., 1994; Regier et al., 1993). The prevalence is similar in Canada, England, and many other countries (Smith & Weissman, 1992). Around 17 percent of all adults in the world may experience an episode of severe unipolar depression at some point in their lives (Angst, 1999, 1995). A worldwide research project suggests that the risk of experiencing this problem has steadily increased since 1915. Although unipolar depression may begin at any age, the average age for its onset, now 27 in the United States, has dropped with each generation (Weissman et al., 1992, 1991).

In almost all countries, women are at least twice as likely as men to experience episodes of severe unipolar depression (Weissman et al., 1995). As many as 26 percent of women may have an episode at some time in their lives, compared with 12 percent of men (APA, 1993). Among children, the prevalence of unipolar depression is similar for girls and boys (Hankin et al., 1998).

All of these rates hold steady across the various socioeconomic classes. Similarly, few differences in prevalence of unipolar depression have been found

ConsiderThis

In one study, students who listened to a sad song became more depressed than those who listened to a happy song (Stratton & Zalanow, 1999, 1994). Yet the sad-song students reported "enjoying" their musical experience more than the happy-song students. What might be going on here?

WORLD COUNT

Around 122,865,000 new cases of mood disorder emerge each year worldwide (World Health Organization).

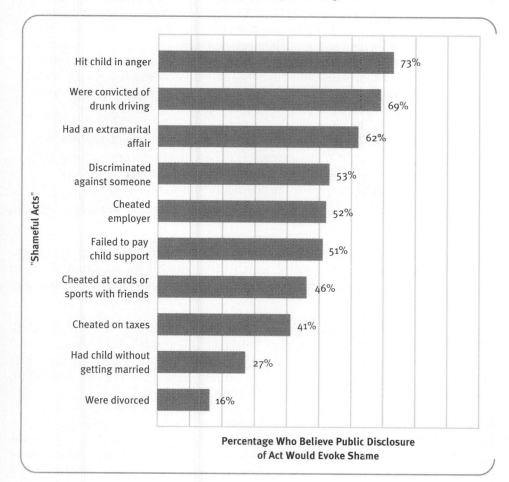

Percentage Who Believe Public Disclosure of Act Would Evoke Shame

FIGURE 7-1 **What makes people feel ashamed?** *Even people who are not depressed feel shame from time to time. In one survey, most respondents believed that people would feel shame if they were discovered to have hit a child in anger or been convicted of drunk driving. (From Newsweek Poll, 1995.)*

DUBIOUS DISTINCTION
The World Health Organization cites depression as the leading cause of disability in the world (Kaufman, 1999).

among ethnic groups. In the United States, middle-aged white Americans have a somewhat higher rate than middle-aged African Americans, but the rates for younger and older adults are the same in both populations (Weissman et al., 1991). Approximately two-thirds of people with unipolar depression recover within four to six months, some without treatment (APA, 2000, 1994; Keller, 1988). However, most of them have at least one other episode of depression later in their lives (Angst, 1999; Kessing et al., 1998).

What Are the Symptoms of Depression?

The picture of depression may differ from person to person. Earlier, we saw how Beatrice's indecisiveness, uncontrollable sobbing, and feelings of despair, anger, and worthlessness brought her job and social life to a standstill. Other depressed people have symptoms that are less severe. They manage to function, although their depression typically robs them of much effectiveness or pleasure, as we see in the case of Derek:

Derek has probably suffered from depression all of his adult life but was unaware of it for many years. Derek called himself a night person, claiming that he could not think clearly until after noon even though he was often awake by 4:00 A.M. He tried to schedule his work as editorial writer for a small town newspaper so that it was compatible with his depressed mood at the beginning of the day. Therefore, he scheduled meetings for the mornings; talking with people got him moving. He saved writing and decision making for later in the day.

. . . Derek's private thoughts were rarely cheerful and self-confident. He felt that his marriage was a mere business partnership. He provided the money, and she provided a home and children. Derek and his wife rarely expressed affection for each other. Occasionally, he had images of his own violent death in a bicycle crash, in a plane crash, or in a murder by an unidentified assailant.

Derek felt that he was constantly on the edge of job failure. He was disappointed that his editorials had not attracted the attention of larger papers. He was certain that several of the younger people on the paper had better ideas and wrote more skillfully than he did. He scolded himself for a bad editorial that he had written ten years earlier. Although that particular piece had not been up to his usual standards, everyone else on the paper had forgotten it a week after it appeared. But ten years later, Derek was still ruminating over that one editorial. . . .

Derek brushed off his morning confusion as a lack of quick intelligence. He had no way to know that it was a symptom of depression. He never realized that his death images might be suicidal thinking. People do not talk about such things. For all Derek knew, everyone had similar thoughts.

(Lickey & Gordon, 1991, pp. 183–185)

As the cases of Beatrice and Derek indicate, depression has many symptoms other than sadness. The symptoms, which often exacerbate one another, span five areas of functioning: emotional, motivational, behavioral, cognitive, and physical.

EMOTIONAL SYMPTOMS Most people who are depressed feel sad and dejected. They describe themselves as feeling "miserable," "empty," and "humiliated." They report getting little pleasure from anything, and they tend to lose their sense of humor. Some also experience anxiety, anger, or agitation (see Box 7-2 on page 197). This sea of misery may lead to crying spells.

MOTIVATIONAL SYMPTOMS Depressed people typically lose the desire to pursue their usual activities. Almost all report a lack of drive, initiative, and spontaneity. They may have to force themselves to go to work, talk with friends, eat meals, or have sex (Buchwald & Rudick-Davis, 1993). This state has been described as a

THE DARKNESS OF DEPRESSION
In Western society, black is often the color of choice in describing depression. The British prime minister Winston Churchill called his recurrent episodes a "black dog always waiting to bare its teeth." The American novelist Ernest Hemingway referred to his bouts as "black-assed" days. And the Rolling Stones sing about depressive thinking: "I see a red door and I want to paint it black."

Lincoln's private war *In 1841, Abraham Lincoln wrote to a friend, "I am now the most miserable man living. If what I feel were equally distributed to the whole human family, there would be not one cheerful face on earth."*

Behind the mask *Like the movie star Marilyn Monroe, some people hide their depression by smiling and looking happy most of the time. Many children, in particular, are thought to have "masked" depressions.*

"paralysis of will" (Beck, 1967). One individual recalls, "I didn't want to do anything—just wanted to stay put and be let alone" (Kraines & Thetford, 1972, p. 20).

Suicide represents the ultimate escape from life's challenges. As we shall see in Chapter 9, many depressed people become uninterested in life or wish to die; others wish they could kill themselves, and some actually try. It has been estimated that between 6 and 15 percent of people who suffer from severe depression commit suicide (Inskip, Harris, & Barraclough, 1998; Rossow & Amundsen, 1995).

BEHAVIORAL SYMPTOMS Depressed people are usually less active and less productive. They spend more time alone and may stay in bed for long periods. One man recalls, "I'd awaken early, but I'd just lie there—what was the use of getting up to a miserable day?" (Kraines & Thetford, 1972, p. 21). Depressed people may also move and even speak more slowly, with seeming reluctance and lack of energy (Sobin & Sackeim, 1997; Parker et al., 1993).

COGNITIVE SYMPTOMS Depressed people hold extremely negative views of themselves (Gable & Shean, 2000; Joiner et al., 1995). They consider themselves inadequate, undesirable, inferior, perhaps evil. They also blame themselves for nearly every unfortunate event, even things that have nothing to do with them, and they rarely credit themselves for positive achievements.

Another cognitive symptom of depression is pessimism. Sufferers are usually convinced that nothing will ever improve, and they feel helpless to change any aspect of their lives (Dixon et al., 1993; Metalsky et al., 1993). Because they expect the worst, they are likely to procrastinate. Their sense of hopelessness and helplessness makes them especially vulnerable to suicidal thinking. A successful businessman recalls, "Everything seemed black. The whole world was going to the devil, the country was going bankrupt, and my business was doomed to fail" (Kraines & Thetford, 1972, p. 20).

PHILOSOPHICAL MOODS

Heraclitus (c. 535–c. 475 B.C.) was called "the weeping philosopher" because his views were so pessimistic. Democritus (c. 460 –c. 370 B.C.) was called "the laughing philosopher" because of his optimistic teachings and his cheerful disposition (Asimov, 1997).

MAJOR DEPRESSIVE DISORDER A severe pattern of depression that is disabling and is not caused by such factors as drugs or a general medical condition.

DYSTHYMIC DISORDER A mood disorder that is similar to but longer-lasting and less disabling than a major depressive disorder.

TOO TIRED

According to one survey, 12 percent of adults suffer from substantial fatigue that has lasted six months or longer (Loge, Ekeberg, & Kaasa, 1998).

People with depression frequently complain that their intellectual ability is poor. They feel confused, unable to remember things, easily distracted, and unable to solve even small problems. In laboratory studies, depressed subjects do perform more poorly than nondepressed subjects on some tasks of memory, attention, and reasoning (Kalska et al., 1999; Hertel, 1998). It may be, however, that these difficulties reflect motivational problems rather than cognitive ones (Lachner & Engel, 1994).

PHYSICAL SYMPTOMS People who are depressed frequently have such physical ailments as headaches, indigestion, constipation, dizzy spells, and general pain (Fishbain, 2000). In fact, many depressions are misdiagnosed as medical problems at first (Simon & Katzelnick, 1997). Disturbances in appetite and sleep are particularly common. Most depressed people eat less, sleep less, and feel more fatigued than they did prior to the disorder. Some, however, eat and sleep excessively. Even if they get rest and sleep, they feel tired most of the time (Kazes et al., 1994; Spoov et al., 1993).

Diagnosing Unipolar Depression

According to DSM-IV, a *major depressive episode* is a period marked by at least five symptoms of depression and lasting for two weeks or more (see Table 7-1). In extreme cases, the episode may include psychotic symptoms, ones marked by a loss of contact with reality, such as *delusions*—bizarre ideas without foundation—or *hallucinations*—perceptions of things that are not actually present (Parker et al., 1997; Coryell et al., 1996). A depressed man with psychotic symptoms may imagine that he can't eat "because my intestines are deteriorating and will soon stop working," or he may believe that he sees his dead wife.

Table 7-1 DSM-IV Checklist

MAJOR DEPRESSIVE EPISODE

1. The presence of at least five of the following symptoms during the same two-week period: • depressed mood most of the day, nearly every day • markedly diminished interest or pleasure in almost all activities most of the day, nearly every day • significant weight loss or weight gain, or decrease or increase in appetite nearly every day • insomnia or hypersomnia nearly every day • psychomotor agitation or retardation nearly every day • fatigue or loss of energy nearly every day • feelings of worthlessness or excessive guilt nearly every day • reduced ability to think or concentrate, or indecisiveness, nearly every day • recurrent thoughts of death or suicide, a suicide attempt, or a specific plan for committing suicide.
2. Significant distress or impairment.

MAJOR DEPRESSIVE DISORDER

1. The presence of a major depressive episode.
2. No history of a manic or hypomanic episode.

DYSTHYMIC DISORDER

1. Depressed mood for most of the day, for more days than not, for at least two years.
2. Presence, while depressed, of at least two of the following: • poor appetite or overeating • insomnia or hypersomnia • low energy or fatigue • low self-esteem • poor concentration or difficulty making decisions • feelings of hopelessness.
3. During the two-year period, symptoms not absent for more than two months at a time.
4. No history of a manic or hypomanic episode.
5. Significant distress or impairment.

Based on APA, 2000, 1994.

BOX 7-2

Anxiety Plus Depression: Two Sides of the Same Coin?

Traditionally diagnosticians have viewed anxiety and depression as separate problems, but more and more clinicians are coming to believe that the two reflect a single underlying problem, or at the very least are closely related reactions that feed off each other.

Indications abound that anxiety and depression are often linked: (1) People with each of the anxiety disorders have much higher rates of depression than do the rest of the population (Bakish, 1999; APA, 1994). Similarly, around half of all people with major depressive disorder also have an anxiety disorder (Fava et al., 2000; Regier et al., 1998). (2) Treatments for one of these disorders are sometimes helpful for the other as well. In 1999, for example, the antidepressant drug *venlafaxine* (Effexor) received approval as a treatment for generalized

anxiety disorder. (3) Sometimes anxiety and depression have common features, such as worry, demoralization, and social withdrawal. Even when symptoms are distinct (fear versus loss of pleasure, for example), they may become intermingled, leaving clinicians incapable of determining whether the person is suffering primarily from an anxiety disorder or a mood disorder.

How can we explain this overlap between anxiety and depression? Perhaps they have a common basis. Each, for example, has been linked to such biological variables as heightened secretions of the stress hormone *cortisol* and low activity of the neurotransmitter *serotonin*. Or perhaps intense anxiety leads to depression. That is, anxiety may be so disabling and upsetting for some people that they become worn down and de-

pressed (Parker et al., 1999). Adults who suffer from both severe anxiety and severe depression develop their anxiety symptoms, on average, at 16 years of age and their depression at 23 years (Regier et al., 1998).

While the relationship between anxiety and depression is being sorted out, two things have already become clear. First, it is more complex and disabling to experience both of these problems than one of them alone (Lydiard & Brawman-Mintzer, 1998). Symptoms of depression, for example, last longer in persons whose mood disorder is accompanied by an anxiety disorder (Gaynes et al., 1999). Second, distinguishing between anxiety and depression is a much more difficult task for diagnosticians than it may seem to be.

People who experience a major depressive episode, without having any history of mania, receive a diagnosis of **major depressive disorder**. The disorder may be additionally categorized as *recurrent* if it has been preceded by previous episodes; *seasonal* if it changes with the seasons (for example, if the depression recurs each winter); *catatonic* if it is marked by either immobility or excessive activity; *postpartum* if it occurs within four weeks of giving birth; or *melancholic* if the person is almost totally unaffected by pleasurable events (APA, 2000, 1994; Kendler, 1997).

People who display a longer-lasting (at least two years) but less disabling pattern of unipolar depression may receive a diagnosis of **dysthymic disorder**. When dysthymic disorder leads to major depressive disorder, the sequence is called double depression (Miller, Norman, & Keitner, 1999; Donaldson et al., 1997).

GREEK ROOTS

The term "dysthymia" comes from the Greek for "despondent."

Triggers of depression *At a 1999 White House conference, Mike Wallace (CBS newsman) and Tipper Gore (wife of then-Vice President Al Gore) discuss their bouts of depression. Wallace's episode was triggered by a lengthy civil trial, Gore's by her son's near-fatal accident.*

What Causes Unipolar Depression?

Episodes of unipolar depression often seem to be triggered by stressful events. In fact, researchers have found that depressed people experience a greater number of stressful life events during the month just before the onset of their disorder than do other people during the same period of time ((Kendler, Karkowski, & Prescott, 1999; Paykel & Cooper, 1992). Stressful life events also precede other psychological disorders, but depressed people report more such events than anybody else.

Some clinicians consider it important to distinguish a *reactive (exogenous) depression,* which follows clear-cut stressful events, from an *endogenous depression,* which seems to be a response to internal factors. But can one ever know for certain whether a depression is reactive or not? Even if stressful events occurred before the onset of depression, that depression may not be reactive. The events could actually be a coincidence (Paykel, 1982). Conversely, even when depression emerges in the seeming absence of stressful events and appears to be endogenous, it could be that a subtle stressor has escaped notice (Paykel, Rao, & Taylor, 1984). Thus, today's clinicians usually concentrate on recognizing both the situational and the internal aspects of any given case of unipolar depression.

The current explanations of unipolar depression point to biological, psychological, and sociocultural factors. Just as clinicians now recognize both internal and situational features in each case of depression, many believe that the various explanations should be viewed collectively in order for unipolar depression to be fully understood.

The Biological View

Medical researchers have been aware for years that certain diseases and drugs produce mood changes. Could unipolar depression itself have a biological foundation? Evidence from genetic and biochemical studies suggest that often it does (Judd, 1995).

GENETIC FACTORS Three kinds of research—family pedigree, twin, and adoption studies—suggest that some people inherit a predisposition to unipolar depression; as we have observed, however, findings from such studies can also be interpreted in other ways. *Family pedigree studies* select people with unipolar depression as *probands* (the proband is the person who is the focus of a genetic study), examine their relatives, and see whether depression also afflicts other members of the family. If a predisposition to unipolar depression is inherited, a proband's relatives should have a higher rate of depression than the population at large. Researchers have in fact found that as many as 20 percent of those relatives are depressed (see Table 7-2), compared with fewer than 10 percent of the general population (Harrington et al., 1993).

If a predisposition to unipolar depression is inherited, we would also expect to find more cases among the probands' close relatives than among their distant relatives. *Twin studies* have supported this expectation (Gershon & Nurnberger, 1995; Nurnberger & Gershon, 1992, 1984). One recent study looked at nearly 200 pairs of twins. When a *monozygotic (identical) twin* had unipolar depression, there was a 46 percent chance that the other twin would have the same disorder. In contrast, when a *dizygotic (fraternal) twin* had unipolar depression, the other twin had only a 20 percent chance of developing the disorder (McGuffin et al., 1996).

Finally, *adoption studies* have also implicated a genetic factor, at least in cases of severe unipolar depression. One study looked at the families of adopted persons who had been hospitalized for this disorder in Denmark. The biological parents of these adoptees turned out to have a higher incidence of severe depression (but not mild depression) than did the biological parents of a control group of nondepressed adoptees (Wender et al., 1986). Some theorists interpret these findings to mean that severe depression is more likely than mild depression to be caused by genetic factors.

MUTUAL DAMAGE

Investigators have long known that physical decline in the elderly can lead to depression. Recent studies also reveal that depression itself often causes physical decline and physical impairment in the elderly (Callahan et al., 1998; Penninx et al., 1998).

NOREPINEPHRINE A neurotransmitter whose abnormal activity is linked to depression and panic disorder.

SEROTONIN A neurotransmitter whose abnormal activity is linked to depression, obsessive-compulsive disorder, and eating disorders.

CATECHOLAMINE THEORY The view that unipolar depression is related to low activity of norepinephrine (a catecholamine).

INDOLEAMINE THEORY The view that unipolar depression is caused by deficiencies in the activity of serotonin (an indoleamine).

Table 7-2

Mood Disorders Profile

	ONE-YEAR PREVALENCE (%)	FEMALE: MALE RATIO	TYPICAL AGE AT ONSET (YEARS)	PREVALENCE AMONG FIRST-DEGREE RELATIVES	PERCENTAGE RECEIVING TREATMENT
Major depressive disorder	5–10%	2:1	24–29	Elevated	49%
Dysthymic disorder	2.5–5.4	Between 3:2 and 2:1	10–25	Elevated	37.8
Bipolar I disorder	0.7	1:1	15–44	Elevated	58.9
Bipolar II disorder	0.5	1:1	15–44	Elevated	58.9
Cyclothymic disorder	0.4	1:1	15–25	Elevated	Unknown

Source: APA, 2000, 1994; Kessler et al., 1994; Regier et al., 1993; Weissman et al., 1991.

BIOCHEMICAL FACTORS As we have seen, neurotransmitters are the brain chemicals that carry messages from one nerve cell, or neuron, to another. Low activity of two such chemicals, **norepinephrine** and **serotonin**, has been strongly linked to unipolar depression (Delgado & Moreno, 2000). In the 1950s, several pieces of evidence began to point to this relationship. First, medical researchers discovered that *reserpine* and other medications for high blood pressure often caused depression (Ayd, 1956). As it turned out, some of these medications lowered norepinephrine activity and others lowered serotonin. A second piece of evidence was the discovery of the first truly effective antidepressant drugs. Although these drugs were discovered by accident, researchers soon learned that they relieve depression by increasing either norepinephrine or serotonin activity.

Such findings led some theorists to conclude that unipolar depression is a product of low norepinephrine activity (Bunney & Davis, 1965; Schildkraut, 1965), and others reasoned that depression is caused by low serotonin activity (Golden & Gilmore, 1990; Glassman & Platman, 1969). Because norepinephrine belongs to the class of chemicals called catecholamines, the theory tying it to depression became known as the **catecholamine theory**. Correspondingly, the theory linking serotonin to depression was called the **indoleamine theory**, because serotonin belongs to the class of chemicals known as indoleamines.

POPULAR PERCEPTION

Ninety percent of persons surveyed believe that a brain chemistry imbalance is the cause of chronic clinical depression and schizophrenia (NAMI, 1996).

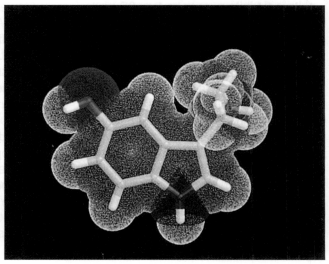
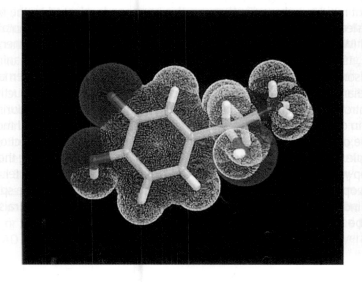

The biochemical culprits *Computer-drawn molecules of the neurotransmitters norepinephrine (left) and serotonin (right), each linked to unipolar depression.*

Psychological Views

The psychological models that have been most widely applied to unipolar depression are the psychodynamic, behavioral, and cognitive models. The psychodynamic explanation has not been strongly supported by research, and the behavioral view has received only modest support. In contrast, cognitive explanations have received considerable research support and have gained a large following.

THE PSYCHODYNAMIC VIEW Sigmund Freud and his student Karl Abraham developed the first psychodynamic explanation of depression (Freud, 1917; Abraham, 1916, 1911). They began by noting the similarity between clinical depression and grief in people who lose loved ones: constant weeping, loss of appetite, difficulty sleeping, loss of pleasure in life, and general withdrawal (Beutel et al., 1995).

According to Freud and Abraham, a series of unconscious processes is set in motion when a loved one dies. Unable to accept the loss, mourners at first regress to the oral stage of development, the period of total dependency when infants cannot distinguish themselves from their parents. By regressing to this stage, the mourners merge their own identity with that of the person they have lost, and so symbolically regain the lost person. In this process, called *introjection*, they direct all their feelings for the loved one, including sadness and anger, toward themselves.

For most mourners, introjection is temporary. For some, however, grief worsens. They feel empty, they continue to avoid social relationships, and their sense of loss increases. They may introject feelings of intense anger toward the loved one for departing, or perhaps because of unresolved conflicts from the past. They therefore experience self-hatred, and become more and more depressed.

Freud and Abraham believed that two kinds of people are particularly likely to become depressed in the face of loss: those whose parents failed to nurture them and meet their needs during the oral stage and those whose parents gratified those needs excessively. Infants whose needs are inadequately met remain overly dependent on others throughout their lives, feel unworthy of love, and have low self-esteem. Those whose needs are excessively gratified find the oral stage so pleasant that they resist moving on to subsequent stages. Either way, the individuals may devote their lives to others, desperately in search of love and approval (Bemporad, 1992). They are likely to feel a greater sense of loss when a loved one dies.

Of course, many people become depressed without losing a loved one. To explain why, Freud proposed the concept of **symbolic**, or **imagined**, **loss**, in which other kinds of events are equated with loss of a loved one. A college student may, for example, experience failure in a calculus course as the loss of her parents, believing that they love her only when she excels academically.

Although many psychodynamic theorists have departed from Freud and Abraham's original theory of depression (Bemporad & Vasile, 1999), it continues to influence current psychodynamic thinking. For example, *object relations theorists,* the psychodynamic theorists who emphasize relationships, propose that depression results when people's relationships leave them feeling unsafe and insecure (Kernberg, 1997, 1976; Horner, 1991). People whose parents pushed them toward either excessive dependence or excessive self-reliance are more likely to become depressed when they later lose important relationships.

The following therapist description of a depressed middle-aged woman illustrates the psychodynamic concepts of dependence, loss of a loved one, symbolic loss, and introjection:

> Mrs. Marie Carls . . . had always felt very attached to her mother. As a matter of fact, they used to call her "Stamp" because she stuck to her mother as a stamp to a letter. She always tried to placate her volcanic mother, to please her in every possible way. . . .

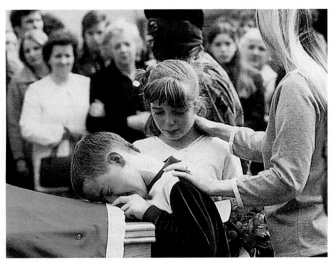

Early loss *Research has found that people who lose their parents as children have an increased likelihood of experiencing depression as adults.*

After marriage [to Julius], she continued her pattern of submission and compliance. Before her marriage she had difficulty in complying with a volcanic mother, and after her marriage she almost automatically assumed a submissive role. . . .

Several months after beginning treatment, the patient reported a dream. Ignatius and she had decided not to see each other again. She would have to leave him forever. I asked who Ignatius was, because I had not heard the name until then. The patient replied almost with surprise, "But the first time I came to see you, I told you that in the past I had had an infatuation." She then told me that when she was thirty years old . . . [she] and her husband invited Ignatius, who was single, to come and live with them. Ignatius and the patient soon discovered that they had an attraction for each other. They both tried to fight that feeling; but when Julius had to go to another city for a few days, the so-called infatuation became much more than that. There were a few physical contacts. . . . There was an intense spiritual affinity. . . . A few months later everybody had to leave the city. Ignatius and Marie promised to keep in touch, but both of them were full of hesitation because of Julius, a devoted husband to Marie and a devoted friend to Ignatius. Nothing was done to maintain contact. Two years later, approximately a year after the end of the war, Marie heard that Ignatius had married. She felt terribly alone and despondent. . . .

Her suffering had become more acute as she realized that old age was approaching and she had lost all her chances. Ignatius remained as the memory of lost opportunities. . . . Her life of compliance and obedience had not permitted her to reach her goal. . . . When she became aware of these ideas, she felt even more depressed. . . . She felt that everything she had built in her life was false or based on a false premise.

(Arieti & Bemporad, 1978, pp. 275–284)

SYMBOLIC LOSS According to Freudian theory, the loss of a valued object (for example, a loss of employment) which is unconsciously interpreted as the loss of a loved one. Also called *imagined loss.*

ANACLITIC DEPRESSION A pattern of depressed behavior found among very young children that is caused by separation from one's mother.

Studies have offered general support for the psychodynamic idea that depression may be triggered by a major loss (APA, 1993). In a famous study of 123 infants who were placed in a nursery after being separated from their mothers, René Spitz (1946, 1945) found that 19 of the infants became very weepy and sad upon separation, and withdrew from their surroundings—a pattern called **anaclitic depression**. Studies of infant monkeys who are separated from their mothers have noted a similar pattern of apparent depression (Harlow & Harlow, 1965).

Other research suggests that losses suffered early in life may set the stage for later depression (Agid et al., 1999; Lara & Klein, 1999). When, for example, a depression scale was administered to 1,250 medical patients during visits to their family physicians, the patients whose fathers had died during their childhood scored higher on depression (Barnes & Prosen, 1985).

Related research supports the psychodynamic idea that people whose childhood needs were improperly met are particularly likely to become depressed after experiencing loss (Young et al., 1997; Parker, 1992, 1983). In some studies, depressed subjects have filled out a scale called the *Parental Bonding Instrument,* which indicates how much care and protection people feel they received as children. Many have identified their parents' child-rearing style as "affectionless control," consisting of a mixture of low care and high protection (Sato et al., 1997; Shah & Waller, 2000; Parker et al., 1995). In addition, depressed persons who describe their parents' style in this way tend to respond less well to treatment (Sakado et al., 1999).

Attachment and separation *Holding that people are more prone to develop depression if their childhood relationships were disrupted, object relations theorists worry about children who are returned to their biological parents after living for an extended time with adoptive parents. In 1995 "Baby Richard," as the courts referred to him, was taken from his adoptive parents and placed with his biological parents after a legal battle that spanned his entire four years.*

Across the species *Harry Harlow and his colleagues found that infant monkeys reacted with apparent despair to separation from their mothers. Even monkeys raised with surrogate mothers—wire cylinders wrapped with foam rubber and covered with terry cloth—formed an attachment to them and mourned their absence.*

These studies offer some support for the psychodynamic view of unipolar depression, but this support has key limitations. First, although the findings indicate that losses and inadequate parenting sometimes trigger depression, they do not establish that such factors are *typically* responsible for the disorder. In the studies of young children and young monkeys, for example, only some of the subjects who were separated from their mothers showed depressive reactions. In fact, it is estimated that less than 10 percent of all people who experience major losses in life actually become depressed (Paykel & Cooper, 1992; Paykel, 1982).

A second problem with the psychodynamic evidence is that many findings are inconsistent. Though some studies find evidence of a relationship between childhood loss and later depression, others do not (Parker, 1992; Owen, Lancee, & Freeman, 1986).

A third problem is that certain features of the psychodynamic explanation are nearly impossible to test. Because symbolic loss, fixation at the oral stage, and introjection are said to operate at an unconscious level, it is difficult for researchers to determine if and when they are occurring. Similarly, other psychodynamic ideas can be measured only by retrospective self-reports of people who are or have been depressed. When subjects fill out the Parental Bonding Instrument, for example, how can we be sure that they are indicating their parents' actual behaviors?

THE BEHAVIORAL VIEW Behaviorists believe that unipolar depression results from major shifts in the rewards and punishments people receive in their lives. During the 1970s and 1980s, the clinical researcher Peter Lewinsohn developed one of the leading behavioral explanations (Lewinsohn et al., 1990, 1984). He suggested that the positive rewards in life dwindle for some persons, leading them to perform fewer and fewer constructive behaviors. The rewards of campus life, for example, may disappear when a young woman graduates from college and takes a job; or an aging baseball player may lose the rewards of high salary and adulation when his skills deteriorate. Although many people manage to put such changes in perspective and fill their lives with other forms of gratification, some become disheartened. The positive features of their lives decrease even more, and the decline in rewards leads them to perform still fewer constructive behaviors. In this manner, a person may spiral toward depression.

In a series of studies, Lewinsohn and his colleagues found that the number of rewards people receive in life is indeed related to the presence or absence of depression. Not only did depressed subjects in his studies report fewer positive rewards than nondepressed subjects, but when their rewards began to increase, their mood improved as well (Lewinsohn, Youngren, & Grosscup, 1979). Similarly, recent investigations have found a strong relationship between positive life events and feelings of life satisfaction and happiness (Lui, 1999).

Lewinsohn and other behaviorists further contended that social rewards are particularly important in the downward spiral of depression (Peterson, 1993; Lewinsohn et al., 1984). Their idea is supported by research showing that depressed persons experience fewer social rewards than nondepressed persons, and that as their mood improves, their social rewards increase. Although depressed people are sometimes the victims of social circumstances, it may be that depressive characteristics such as flat behaviors, dark mood, or excessive need for reassurance help produce a decline in social rewards (Joiner & Coyle, 1999; Lara & Klein, 1999). Nondepressed subjects in one study reported feeling worse after a short phone conversation with a depressed person (Coyne, 1976), and subjects in another study became less verbal, less supportive, and less cheerful when interacting with someone who was mildly depressed (Gotlib & Robinson, 1982).

Behaviorists have done an admirable job of compiling data to support this theory, but this research, too, has limitations. It has relied heavily on the self-reports of depressed subjects, and as we saw in Chapter 4, measures of this kind can be biased and inaccurate; depressed people's reports may be influenced heavily by a gloomy mood and negative outlook (Youngren & Lewinsohn, 1980).

Saying goodbye *As highlights of his glorious career appear on a screen, Wayne Gretsky announces his retirement from ice hockey. According to behaviorists, the reduction in rewards brought about by retirement places sports stars and other high achievers at risk for depression unless they can develop a healthy perspective about the change and add new sources of gratification to their lives.*

Moreover, the behavioral studies have been largely correlational and do not establish that decreases in rewarding events are the initial cause of depression. A depressed mood in itself may lead to a decrease in activities and hence to fewer rewards.

COGNITIVE VIEWS Cognitive theorists believe that people with unipolar depression persistently interpret events in negative ways and that such perspectives lead to their disorder (Lara & Klein, 1999). The two most influential cognitive explanations are the theory of *negative thinking* and the theory of *learned helplessness.*

NEGATIVE THINKING Aaron Beck believes that negative thinking, rather than underlying conflicts or a reduction in positive rewards, lies at the heart of depression (Clark, Beck, & Alford, 1999; Beck, 1997, 1991, 1967). Other cognitive theorists—Albert Ellis, for one—also point to maladaptive thinking as a key to depression, but Beck's theory is the one most often associated with the disorder. According to Beck, *maladaptive attitudes,* a *cognitive triad, errors in thinking,* and *automatic thoughts* combine to produce unipolar depression.

Beck believes that some people develop maladaptive attitudes as children, such as "My general worth is tied to every task I perform" or "If I fail, others will feel repelled by me." The attitudes result from their own experiences, their family relationships, and the judgments of the people around them (see Figure 7-2). Many failures are inevitable in a full, active life, so such attitudes are inaccurate and self-defeating. The attitudes become *schemas,* or abstract principles, against which the child evaluates every experience (Young et al., 1993; Beck et al., 1990).

The negative schemas of these persons may lie dormant for years. But later in life, upsetting situations can trigger an extended round of negative thinking. According to Beck, the thinking typically takes three forms, which he calls the

"There is nothing either good or bad, but thinking makes it so."

William Shakespeare, *Hamlet*

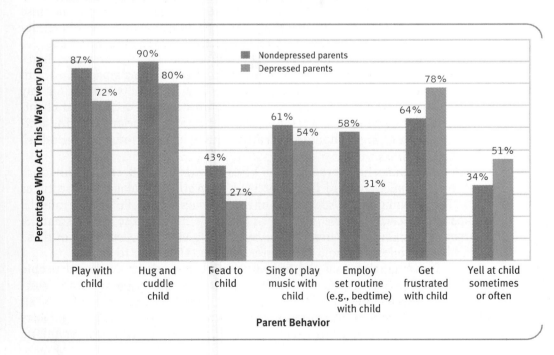

FIGURE 7-2 How depressed parents and their children interact *Depressed parents are less likely than nondepressed parents to play with, hug, read to, or sing to their young children each day or to employ the same routine each day. They are also more likely to get frustrated with their children on a daily basis. (Adapted from Princeton Survey Research Associates, 1996).*

cognitive triad: the individuals repeatedly interpret (1) their *experiences,* (2) *themselves,* and (3) their *futures* in negative ways that lead them to feel depressed. That is, depressed people interpret their experiences as burdens that repeatedly defeat or deprive them. They view themselves as undesirable, worthless, and inadequate. And they regularly see the future as bleak. The cognitive triad is at work in the thinking of this depressed person:

> I can't bear it. I can't stand the humiliating fact that I'm the only woman in the world who can't take care of her family, take her place as a real wife and mother, and be respected in her community. When I speak to my young son Billy, I know I can't let him down, but I feel so ill-equipped to take care of him; that's what frightens me. I don't know what to do or where to turn; the whole thing is too overwhelming. . . . I must be a laughing stock. It's more than I can do to go out and meet people and have the fact pointed up to me so clearly.
>
> *(Fieve, 1975)*

According to Beck, depressed people also make *errors in their thinking.* Repeated errors in logic help build and maintain the cognitive triad. In one common error of logic, they draw *arbitrary inferences*—negative conclusions based on little evidence. A man walking through the park, for example, passes a woman who is looking at nearby flowers, and he concludes, "She's avoiding looking at me." Similarly, depressed people often *minimize* the significance of positive experiences or *magnify* that of negative ones. A college student receives an A on a difficult English exam, for example, but concludes that the grade reflects the professor's generosity rather than her own ability (minimization). Later in the week the same student must miss an English class and is convinced that she will be unable to keep up the rest of the semester (magnification). Other errors of logic commonly displayed by depressed people are *selective abstraction,* in which persons focus on one negative detail of a situation while ignoring the larger context; *overgeneralization,* in which they draw a broad conclusion from a single, often insignificant event; and *personalization,* in which they incorrectly point to themselves as the cause of negative events. A father is displaying personalization, for example, when he responds to a sudden rainstorm in the middle of a picnic by blaming himself for picking the wrong day for a family outing.

Finally, depressed people experience **automatic thoughts**, a steady train of unpleasant thoughts that keep suggesting to them that they are inadequate and that their situation is hopeless. Beck labels these thoughts "automatic" because they seem to just happen, as if by reflex. In the course of only a few hours, depressed people may be visited by hundreds of such thoughts: "I'm worthless. . . . I'll never amount to anything. . . . I let everyone down. . . . Everyone hates me. . . . My responsibilities are overwhelming. . . . I've failed as a parent. . . . I'm stupid. . . . Everything is difficult for me. . . . I've caused problems for my friends. . . . Things will never change." One therapist said of a depressed client, "By the end of the day, she is worn out, she has lived a thousand painful accidents, participated in a thousand deaths, mourned a thousand mistakes" (Mendels, 1970).

Numerous studies have produced evidence in support of Beck's explanation. Several, for example, confirm that depressed people hold maladaptive attitudes such as "People will probably think less of me if I make a mistake" and "I must be a useful, productive, creative person, or life has no purpose" (Whisman & McGarvey, 1995; Garber, Weiss, & Shanley, 1993). Moreover, the more of these maladaptive attitudes they hold, the more depressed they tend to be.

Other research has found the cognitive triad at work in depressed people (Cole & Turner, 1993). In various studies, depressed subjects have recalled unpleasant experiences more readily than positive ones (Lloyd & Lishman, 1975); rated their performances on laboratory tasks lower than nondepressed subjects do (Slife & Weaver, 1992); and selected pessimistic statements in storytelling

"Depression is an insidious vacuum that crawls into your brain and pushes your mind out of the way."

Depressed woman (Karp, 1996)

tests (Weintraub, Segal, & Beck, 1974). In such tests, they tend to choose options such as "I expect my plans will fail" and "I feel like I'll never meet anyone who's interested in me."

Beck's claims about errors in logic have also received research support (Cole & Turner, 1993; Yost, Cook, & Peterson, 1986). In one study, female subjects—some depressed, some not—were asked to read and interpret paragraphs about women in difficult situations. Depressed subjects made more errors in logic (such as arbitrary inference or magnification) in their interpretations than nondepressed women did (Hammen & Krantz, 1976). In another study elementary school children who were depressed scored significantly higher on the *Children's Negative Cognitive Error Questionnaire* than those who were not depressed (Leitenberg et al., 1986).

Finally, research has supported Beck's claim that automatic thoughts are tied to depression (Philpot, Holliman, & Madona, 1995; Garber et al., 1993). In several studies, nondepressed subjects who are manipulated into reading negative automatic thoughtlike statements about themselves become increasingly depressed (Bates, Thompson, & Flanagan, 1999; Strickland, Hale, & Anderson, 1975). Related investigations have revealed that people who consistently make *ruminative* responses during their depressed moods—that is, repeatedly dwell mentally upon their mood without acting to change it—experience depressed moods for longer periods and are more likely to develop a clinical depression than people who are able to avoid such thoughts (Nolen-Hoeksema, 1998, 1995; Just & Alloy, 1997).

This body of research shows that negative thinking is indeed linked to depression, but it fails to show that such patterns of thought are the cause and core of unipolar depression. It could be that a central mood problem leads to thinking difficulties, which then take a further toll on mood, behavior, and physiology (Scott, Winters, & Beevers, 2000; Miranda & Persons, 1988). Some studies have tried to establish that negative thinking does indeed precede the negative mood of depressed people. In one, investigators followed the progress of 15 severely depressed women and interviewed them after their depressive symptoms had improved to determine whether they still held maladaptive attitudes (Rush et al., 1986). The researchers found that the women who continued to hold such attitudes were more likely to develop depressive symptoms again six months later. That is, their negative schemas remained in place even during periods of improved mood, possibly setting the stage for renewed depression at a later point.

LEARNED HELPLESSNESS Feelings of helplessness fill this account of a young woman's depression:

Family impact *Children of depressed parents are at greater risk of later experiencing depression than are children of nondepressed parents. Various factors may account for this relationship, including modeling effects, negative thinking and judgments by parents, social deprivation, and genetic influence.*

> Mary was 25 years old and had just begun her senior year in college. . . . Asked to recount how her life had been going recently, Mary began to weep. Sobbing, she said that for the last year or so she felt she was losing control of her life and that recent stresses (starting school again, friction with her boyfriend) had left her feeling worthless and frightened. Because of a gradual deterioration in her vision, she was now forced to wear glasses all day. "The glasses make me look terrible," she said, and "I don't look people in the eye much any more." Also, to her dismay, Mary had gained 20 pounds in the past year. She viewed herself as overweight and unattractive. At times she was convinced that with enough money to buy contact lenses and enough time to exercise she could cast off her depression; at other times she believed nothing would help. . . .
>
> Mary saw her life deteriorating in other spheres, as well. She felt overwhelmed by schoolwork and, for the first time in her life, was on academic probation. Twice before in the past seven years feelings of inadequacy and pressure from part-time jobs (as a waitress, bartender, and salesclerk) had caused her to leave school. She felt certain that unless she could stop her current downward

spiral she would do so again—this time permanently. She despaired of ever getting her degree.

In addition to her dissatisfaction with her appearance and her fears about her academic future, Mary complained of a lack of friends. Her social network consisted solely of her boyfriend, with whom she was living. Although there were times she experienced this relationship as almost unbearably frustrating, she felt helpless to change it and was pessimistic about its permanence. . . .

(Spitzer et al., 1983, pp. 122–123)

Mary feels that she is "losing control of her life." According to the psychologist Martin Seligman, such feelings of helplessness are at the center of her depression. Since the mid-1960s Seligman has developed the **learned helplessness** theory of depression (Seligman 1992, 1975). It holds that people become depressed when they think (1) that they no longer have control over the reinforcements in their lives and (2) that they themselves are responsible for this helpless state.

Seligman's theory first began to take shape when he was working with laboratory dogs. In one procedure, he strapped dogs into an apparatus called a *hammock,* in which they received shocks periodically no matter what they would do. The next day each dog was placed in a **shuttle box**, a box partitioned in half by a barrier over which the animal could jump to reach the other side (see Figure 7-3). Seligman applied shocks to the dogs in the box, expecting that they, like other dogs in this situation, would soon learn to escape by jumping over the barrier. However, most of these dogs failed to learn anything in the shuttle box. After a flurry of activity, they simply "lay down and quietly whined" and accepted the shock.

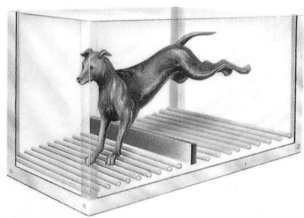

FIGURE 7-3 **Jumping to safety** *Experimental animals learn to escape or avoid shocks that are administered on one side of a shuttle box by jumping to the other (safe) side.*

Seligman decided that while receiving inescapable shocks in the hammock the day before, the dogs had learned that they had no control over unpleasant reinforcements (shocks) in their lives. That is, they had learned that they were helpless to do anything to change negative situations. Thus, when later they were placed in a new situation (the shuttle box) where they could in fact control their fate, they continued to believe that they were generally helpless. Seligman noted that the effects of learned helplessness greatly resemble the symptoms of human depression, and he proposed that people in fact become depressed after developing a general belief that they have no control over reinforcements in their lives.

In numerous human and animal studies, subjects who undergo helplessness training have displayed reactions similar to depressive symptoms. They display passivity, for example. In one study, nondepressed human subjects were pretreated in one of three ways: one group of subjects was exposed to a very loud noise that they could stop by pushing a button; a second group was also exposed to the loud noise but could do nothing to stop it; and a third group (naive subjects) heard no loud noise at all (Hiroto, 1974). All subjects were then placed in front of a finger shuttle box (a rectangular box with a handle on top) and subjected to a loud noise. Without the subjects' knowledge, the box was rigged so that the noise would stop when the handle was moved from one side to the other. Both the naive subjects and those who had previously had control over the loud noise quickly learned to move the handle to turn off the new noise. Most of the subjects who had been pretreated with unavoidable loud noise, however, failed to learn the simple task of moving the handle across the box. They simply sat passively and accepted the abrasive sound.

Human and animal subjects who undergo helplessness training also display other reactions that are similar to depressive symptoms. When human subjects are given uncontrollable negative reinforcements, they later score higher on a depressive mood survey than other subjects (Miller & Seligman, 1975). Similarly, helplessness-trained animal subjects lose interest in sexual and social activities—a common symptom of human depression (Lindner, 1968). Finally, uncontrollable negative events result in lower norepinephrine and serotonin activity in rats

ConsiderThis

One-third of people who feel unhappy as children continue to feel unhappy as adults. In contrast, fewer than one-tenth of those who are happy as children become unhappy adults (Freeman, Templer, & Hill, 1999). How might different theorists explain this correlation between childhood and adult happiness?

(Wu et al., 1999; Neumaier et al., 1997). This, of course, is similar to the neurotransmitter activity found in the brains of people with unipolar depression.

Why do some people react helplessly and become depressed when they experience loss of control while others do not? The learned helplessness explanation of depression has been revised somewhat over the past two decades to help explain such differences. According to a new version of the theory, when people view events as beyond their control, they ask themselves why this is so (Abramson, Metalsky, & Alloy, 1989; Abramson, Seligman, & Teasdale, 1978). If they attribute their present lack of control to some *internal* cause that is both *global* and *stable* ("I am inadequate at everything and I always will be"), they may well feel helpless to prevent future negative outcomes and they may experience depression. If they make other kinds of **attributions**, this reaction is unlikely (see Table 7-3).

Consider a college student whose girlfriend breaks up with him. If he attributes this loss of control to an internal cause that is both global and stable— "It's my fault [internal], I ruin everything I touch [global], and I always will [stable]"—he then has reason to expect similar losses of control in the future and may generally experience a sense of helplessness. According to the learned helplessness view, he is a prime candidate for depression. If the student had instead attributed the breakup to causes that were more *specific* ("The way I've behaved the past couple of weeks blew this relationship"), *unstable* ("I don't know what got into me—I don't usually act like that"), or *external* ("She never did know what she wanted"), he might not expect to lose control again and would probably not experience helplessness and depression.

Hundreds of studies have supported the relationship between styles of attribution, helplessness, and depression (Kinderman & Bentall, 1997). In one study, depressed persons were asked to fill out an *Attributional Style Questionnaire* both before and after successful therapy. Before therapy, their depression was accompanied by the internal / global / stable pattern of attribution. At the end of therapy and again one year later, their depression was improved and their attribution styles were less likely to be limited to internal, global, and stable explanations for their problems (Seligman et al., 1988).

It is worth noting that some theorists have refined the helplessness model yet again in recent years. They suggest that attributions are likely to cause depression only when they further produce a sense of *hopelessness* in an individual (Abramson et al., 1999,

LEARNED HELPLESSNESS The perception, based on past experiences, that one has no control over one's reinforcements.

SHUTTLE BOX A box partitioned by a barrier that an animal can jump over in order to escape or avoid shock.

ATTRIBUTION An explanation of events as resulting from particular causes.

"I FEEL BETTER TODAY TOO, BUT AROUND HERE I'VE LEARNED NOT TO BE TOO OPTIMISTIC."

(© 1998 Sidney Harris)

Table 7-3

Internal and External Attributions

Event: "I failed my psych test today"

	INTERNAL		EXTERNAL	
	STABLE	UNSTABLE	STABLE	UNSTABLE
Global	"I have a problem with test anxiety."	"Getting into an argument with my roommate threw my whole day off."	"Written tests are an unfair way to assess knowledge."	"No one does well on tests that are given the day after vacation."
Specific	"I just have no grasp of psychology."	"I got upset and froze when I couldn't answer the first two questions."	"Everyone knows that this professor enjoys giving unfair tests."	"This professor didn't put much thought into the test because of the pressure of her book deadline."

ConsiderThis

⦿ Why might depression feature more physical symptoms in non-Western cultures and more psychological symptoms in Western cultures?

Non-Western depression *Depressed people in non-Western countries tend to have fewer cognitive symptoms, such as self-blame, and more physical symptoms, such as fatigue, weakness, and sleep disturbances.*

1989; Alloy et al., 1990). By taking this factor into consideration, clinicians are often able to predict depression with still greater precision (Waikar & Craske, 1997).

Although the learned helplessness model of unipolar depression has been widely applied, it too has imperfections. First, laboratory helplessness does not parallel depression in every respect. Uncontrollable shocks in the laboratory, for example, almost always produce anxiety along with the helplessness effects (Seligman, 1975), but human depression is not always accompanied by anxiety. Second, much of the learned helplessness research relies on animal subjects. While the animals' passivity and social withdrawal in learned helplessness studies seem to correspond to symptoms of human depression, it is impossible to know whether they do in fact reflect the same psychological phenomena. In particular, the attributional feature of the theory raises difficult questions. What about the dogs and rats who learn helplessness? Are they too attributing their lack of control to internal, global, and stable causes? Can animals make attributions, even implicitly?

The Sociocultural View

Sociocultural theorists propose that unipolar depression is greatly influenced by the social structure in which people live. Their belief is consistent with the finding, discussed earlier, that this disorder is often triggered by outside stressors. In addition, researchers have found ties between depression and factors such as culture, gender and race, and social support.

HOW ARE CULTURE AND DEPRESSION RELATED? On the one hand, depression is a worldwide phenomenon: persons in all countries and cultures are at risk for it (Chen, Rubin, & Li, 1995). On the other hand, the precise picture of depression varies from culture to culture. Depressed people in non-Western countries, for example, are more likely to be troubled by physical symptoms such as fatigue, weakness, sleep disturbances, and weight loss (Manson & Good, 1993; Marsella, 1980). Depression in these countries is less often marked by such psychological symptoms as self-blame and guilt. Interestingly, as these countries have become more Westernized, depression there has taken on the more psychological character it has in the West.

HOW DO GENDER AND RACE RELATE TO DEPRESSION? The rates of unipolar depression also vary from subgroup to subgroup within a society. As we have already noted, the rate of depression is much higher among women than among men. One sociocultural theory holds that the quality of women's roles in society leaves them particularly vulnerable to this disorder (see Box 7-4).

Similarly, although few differences in the overall rate of unipolar depression have been found among white Americans, African Americans, and Hispanic Americans (Weissman et al., 1991), researchers sometimes find striking differences when they look at specific ethnic populations living under special circumstances. A study of one Native American village in the United States, for example, showed that the lifetime risk of developing depression was 37 percent among women, 19 percent among men, and 28 percent overall, much higher than the risk in the general United States population (Kinzie et al., 1992). Many sociocultural theorists explain

BOX 7-4

Depressing News for Women

Women in places as far apart as Paris, Sweden, Beirut, New Zealand, and the United States are at least twice as likely as men to receive a diagnosis of unipolar depression (Maier et al., 1999; Olsson & von Knorring, 1999; Weissman & Olfson, 1995). Women also appear to be younger when depression strikes, to have more frequent and longer-lasting bouts, and to respond less successfully to treatment (Pajer, 1995; Weissman & Olfson, 1995). Why the huge difference between the sexes? Several theories have been offered (Blehar & Oren, 1995; Nolen-Hoeksema, 1995, 1990, 1987).

The artifact theory One theory holds that women and men are equally prone to depression, but that clinicians fail to detect depression in men. Perhaps men find it less socially acceptable to admit feeling depressed or to seek treatment. Perhaps depressed women display more emotional symptoms, such as sadness and crying, which are easily diagnosed, while depressed men mask their depression behind traditionally "masculine" symptoms such as anger (Mirowsky & Ross, 1995). This explanation lacks consistent research support (Fennig, Schwartz, & Bromet, 1994). It turns out that women are actually no more willing or able than men to identify their depressive symptoms and seek treatment (Nolen-Hoeksema, 1990; Amenson & Lewinsohn, 1981).

The hormone theory Another theory holds that hormone changes trigger depression in many women (Young & Korszun, 1999; Pajer, 1995). A woman's biological life from her early teens to middle age is characterized by frequent and significant changes in hormone levels. Gender differences in rates of depression also span these same years (Weissman & Olfson, 1995). It is unlikely, however, that hormone changes alone are responsible for the high levels of depression in women. Important social and life events that occur at puberty, pregnancy, and menopause could likewise have an effect. Hormone explanations have also been criticized as sexist, since they imply that a woman's normal biology is flawed (Nolen-Hoeksema, 1990).

The quality-of-life theory Perhaps women in our society experience more stress than men (Stoppard, 2000: Gold, 1998). On average they face more poverty, more menial jobs, less adequate housing, and more discrimination than men—all factors that have been linked to depression (Wu & DeMaris, 1996; Brems, 1995). And in many homes, women bear a disproportionate share of responsibility for child care and housework.

The societal pressure theory Almost from birth, females in Western society are taught to aspire to a low body weight and slender body shape—goals that are unreasonable, unhealthy, and often unattainable. The cultural standard for males is much more lenient. As girls approach adolescence, peer pressure and self-focus intensify, leading to greater and greater dissatisfaction with their weight and body. In turn, such dissatisfaction may increase the likelihood of depression. Consistent with this theory, gender differences in depression do indeed first appear during adolescence (Wichstrom, 1999; Nolen-Hoeksema & Girgus, 1995) and persons with eating disorders often experience high levels of depression (Paxton & Diggens, 1997). However, it is not clear that eating and weight concerns actually cause depression; they may be the result of depression instead.

The lack-of-control theory According to this theory, women are more prone to depression because they feel less control over their lives. Studies have, in fact, confirmed that women are more prone to develop learned helplessness in the laboratory than men (Le Unes, Nation, & Turley, 1980). In addition, it has been found that victimization of any kind, from burglary to rape, often produces a general sense of helplessness and increases the symp-

Female melancholy *Edvard Munch's painting* Melancholy (Laura) *was inspired by his sister's bouts of severe depression.*

toms of depression; and women in our society are more likely than men to be victims, particularly of sexual assault and child abuse (Zuravin & Fontanella, 1999). Despite these correlations, researchers have yet to subject this idea to strict testing (Nolen-Hoeksema, 1990, 1987).

The self-blame theory Research indicates that women are more likely than men to blame their failures on lack of ability and to attribute their successes to luck—an attribution style that has also been linked to depression (Wolfe & Russianoff, 1997). Perhaps not so coincidentally, these gender differences in attribution begin during adolescence, about the same time that the gender differences in depression first appear (Cyranowski et al., 2000; Nolen-Hoeksema & Girgus, 1995). On the other hand, recent research suggests that today's women and men may not differ as much as they used to in their levels of self-esteem and self-blame (Kling et al., 1999).

Each of these explanations for the gender difference in unipolar depression offers food for thought. Each has gathered just enough supporting evidence to elicit interest and, at the same time, just enough nonsupporting evidence to raise questions about its usefulness. Thus, at present, the gender difference in depression remains one of the most talked-about but least understood phenomena in the clinical field.

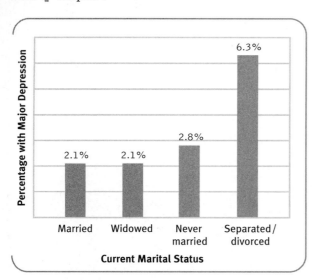

FIGURE 7-4 **Marital status and major depressive disorder** *Currently separated or divorced people are three times more likely to be depressed than people who currently are married. (Adapted from Weissman et al., 1991.)*

high prevalence rates of this kind by pointing to the terrible social and economic pressures faced by the people who live on Native American reservations.

HOW DOES SOCIAL SUPPORT RELATE TO DEPRESSION? The availability of social support seems to influence the likelihood of depression (Hammen, 1999; Champion & Power, 1995). As we see in Figure 7-4, across the United States, people who are separated or divorced display three times the depression rate of married or widowed persons and double the rate of people who have never been married (Weissman et al., 1991). In some cases, the spouse's depression may contribute to a separation or divorce (Spangenberg & Theron, 1999; Beach, Sandeen, & O'Leary, 1990), but more often, the interpersonal conflicts and lack of mutual support found in troubled relationships seem to lead to depression (Bruce & Kim, 1992; Barnett & Gotlib, 1990).

People whose lives are isolated and bereft of intimacy seem particularly likely to become depressed at times of stress (Nezlek et al., 2000; Paykel & Cooper, 1992). Some highly publicized studies conducted in England a few decades ago showed that women who had three or more young children, lacked a close confidante, and had no outside employment were more likely than other women to become depressed after experiencing stressful life events (Brown, 1988; Brown & Harris, 1978). Studies have also found that depressed people who lack social support remain depressed longer than those who have a supportive spouse or warm friendships (Moos & Cronkite, 1999; Goodyer et al., 1997). Similarly, persons who live with families that are very nagging, critical, and prone to emotional outbursts (that is, families with so-called *high expressed emotion*) are particularly likely to relapse after recovering from depression (Hooley & Teasdale, 1989; Hooley, Orley, & Teasdale, 1986).

ANIMAL SUPPORT

There are 66 million pet cats and 58 million pet dogs in the United States (Ash, 1998). Studies find that animal companionship often helps prevent or reduce depression, improve cardiovascular functioning, lower stress, and enhance self-esteem (Barker, 1999).

Bipolar Disorders

People with a *bipolar disorder* experience both the lows of depression and the highs of mania. Many describe their life as an emotional roller coaster. They shift back and forth between extreme moods. This roller-coaster ride and its impact on relatives and friends is dramatically depicted in the following case study:

In his early school years he had been a remarkable student and had shown a gift for watercolor and oils. Later he had studied art in Paris and married an English girl he had met there. Eventually they had settled in London.

Ten years later, when he was thirty-four years old, he had persuaded his wife and only son to accompany him to Honolulu, where, he assured them, he would be considered famous. He felt he would be able to sell his paintings at many times the prices he could get in London. According to his wife, he had been in an accelerated state, but at that time the family had left, unsuspecting, believing with the patient in their imminent good fortune. When they arrived they found almost no one in the art world that he was supposed to know. There were no connections for sales and deals in Hawaii that he had anticipated. Settling down, the patient began to behave more peculiarly than ever. After enduring several months of the patient's exhilaration, overactivity, weight loss, constant talking, and unbelievably little sleep, the young wife and child began to fear for his sanity. None of his plans materialized. After five months in the Pacific, with finances growing thin, the patient's overactivity subsided and he fell into a depression.

During that period he refused to move, paint, or leave the house. He lost twenty pounds, became utterly dependent on his wife, and insisted on seeing none of the friends he had accumulated in his manic state. His despondency became so severe that several doctors came to the house and advised psychiatric hospitalization. He quickly agreed and received twelve electroshock treatments, which relieved his depressed state. Soon afterward he began to paint again and to sell his work modestly. Recognition began to come from galleries and critics in the Far East. Several reviews acclaimed his work as exceptionally brilliant.

This was the beginning of the lifelong career of his moodswing. In 1952, while still in Honolulu, he once again became severely depressed. . . . Four years later he returned to London in a high. . . . When this manic period subsided and he surveyed the wreckage of his life, an eight-month interval of normal mood followed, after which he again switched into a profound depression.

(Fieve, 1975, pp. 64–65)

What Are the Symptoms of Mania?

Unlike people sunk in the gloom of depression, those in a state of mania typically experience dramatic and inappropriate rises in mood. The symptoms of mania span the same areas of functioning—*emotional, motivational, behavioral, cognitive,* and *physical*—as those of depression, but mania affects those areas in an opposite way.

In mania a person has active, powerful emotions in search of an outlet. The mood of euphoric joy and well-being is out of all proportion to the actual happenings in the person's life. One person with mania explained, "I feel no sense of restriction or censorship whatsoever. I am afraid of nothing and no one" (Fieve, 1975, p. 68). Not every person with mania is a picture of happiness, however (see Box 7-5 on the next page). Some instead become irritable and angry—especially when others get in the way of their exaggerated ambitions—like this man:

All by himself, he had been building a magnificent swimming pool for his country home in Virginia, working eighteen hours a day at it. He decided to make the pool public and open a concession stand at one end to help defray the mounting costs of the project. When his wife suggested that he might be going overboard, he became furious and threatened to leave her for another woman. Soon afterward, when his wife was out, he took many valuables from the house—his share, he claimed—and sold or pawned them. Complaining that his wife was a stick in the mud, he decided to throw a round-the-clock party, and he invited to the house almost everyone he passed on the street.

(Fieve, 1975, p. 148)

In the motivational realm, people with mania seem to want constant excitement, involvement, and companionship. They enthusiastically seek out new friends and old, new interests and old, and have little awareness that their social style is overwhelming, domineering, and excessive:

He was interested in everything and everyone around him. He talked familiarly to patients, attendants, nurses, and physicians. He took a fancy to the woman physician on duty in the admission building, calling her by her first name and annoying her with letters and with his familiar, ill mannered, and obtrusive attentions. . . . He made many comments and asked many questions about other patients and promised that he would secure their discharge. He interfered with their affairs and soon received a blow on the jaw from one patient and a black eye from another.

(Kolb, 1973, p. 372)

Famous victim *The English novelist and essayist Virginia Woolf (1882–1941) had an enormous influence on the development of the twentieth-century novel. Yet she suffered from severe mood disturbances, possibly a bipolar disorder, that eventually led her to take her own life by drowning.*

BOX 7-5

Happiness: More Common Than We Think

Judging from the evening news and the spread of self-help books, one would think that happiness was rare. Even psychologists seem far more interested in studying heartache than happiness (Myers, 2000).

But there's good news. A growing body of research indicates that most people's lives are more upbeat than we think. In fact, most people around the world say they're happy—including most of those who are poor, unemployed, elderly, and disabled (Myers & Diener, 1996). Over 90 percent of people with quadriplegia say they're glad to be alive, and overall, people with spinal cord injuries report feeling only slightly less happy than other people (Diener & Diener, 1996). Men and women are equally likely to declare themselves satisfied or very happy. There is truth too to the old adage "Money can't buy happiness." Wealthy people appear only slightly happier than those of modest means (Diener et al., 1993). Overall, only one person in ten reports being "not too happy" (Myers, 2000; Myers & Diener, 1996).

Although people aren't happy every day, most seem able to bounce back well from disappointments. Happy people also seem to remain happy from decade to decade, regardless of job changes, moves, and family changes (Myers & Diener, 1996). Some research indicates that happiness is only briefly affected by events in life (Suh, Diener, & Fujita, 1996). Happy people adjust to negative events and return to their usual cheerful state within a few months (Diener et al., 1992). Conversely, unhappy people are not cheered in the long term even by positive events.

If gender, race, income, and life events have but limited effects on long-term happiness, what makes so many people upbeat? Some research indicates that happiness is dependent on personality characteristics and interpretive styles (Diener, 2000). Happy people are generally optimistic and extroverted, and they tend to have several close friends (Francis, 1999; Lu, 1999; Diener et al., 1992). Happy people also have high self-esteem and believe that they have control over their lives.

Some researchers believe that people have a "happiness set point" to which they consistently return, despite life's ups and downs. An investigation of 2,300 twins suggested to the researchers who conducted the study that as much as half of one's sense of happiness is related to genetic factors (Lykken & Tellegen, 1996).

A better understanding of the roots of happiness may come from the present flurry of research, perhaps providing useful solutions to people who are not so happy and even those who are clinically depressed. In the meantime, we have the comfort of knowing that the human condition isn't quite as unhappy as news stories (and textbooks on abnormal psychology) may make it seem.

FRENZIED MASTERPIECE
George Frideric Handel wrote his *Messiah* in less than a month during a manic episode (Roesch, 1991).

The behavior of people with mania is usually very active. They move quickly, as though there were not enough time to do everything they want to do. They may talk rapidly and loudly, their conversations filled with jokes and efforts to be clever or, conversely, with complaints and verbal outbursts. Flamboyance is not uncommon: dressing in flashy clothes, giving large sums of money to strangers, or even getting involved in dangerous activities. Several of these qualities are evident in the monologue delivered by Joe to the two policemen who escorted him to a mental hospital:

> You look like a couple of bright, alert, hardworking, clean-cut, energetic go-getters and I could use you in my organization! I need guys that are loyal and enthusiastic about the great opportunities life offers on this planet! It's yours for the taking! Too many people pass opportunity by without hearing it knock because they don't know how to grasp the moment and strike while the iron is hot! You've got to grab it when it comes up for air, pick up the ball and run! You've got to be decisive! decisive! decisive! No shilly-shallying! Sweat! Yeah, sweat with a goal! Push, push, push, and you can push over a mountain! Two mountains, maybe. It's not luck! Hell, if it wasn't for bad luck I wouldn't have any luck at all! Be there firstest with the mostest! My guts and your blood! That's the system! I know, you

know, he, she or it knows it's the only way to travel! Get 'em off balance, baby, and the rest is leverage! Use your head and save your heels! What's this deal? Who are these guys? Have you got a telephone and a secretary I can have instanter if not sooner? What I need is office space and the old LDO [long-distance operator].

(McNeil, 1967, p. 147)

In the cognitive realm, people with mania usually show poor judgment and planning, as if they feel too good or move too fast to consider possible pitfalls. Filled with optimism, they rarely listen when others try to slow them down, interrupt their buying sprees, or prevent them from investing money unwisely. They may also hold an inflated opinion of themselves, and sometimes their self-esteem approaches grandiosity (Silverstone & Hunt, 1992). During severe episodes of mania, some have trouble remaining coherent or in touch with reality.

Finally, in the physical realm, people with mania feel remarkably energetic. They typically get little sleep, yet feel and act wide awake (Silverstone & Hunt, 1992). Even if they miss a night or two of sleep, their energy level may remain high.

MANIC ATTENTION

People with mania may be easily distracted by random stimuli from the environment (Double, 1991; Harrow et al., 1988). A number also report that their sensory impressions seem sharper, brighter, more colorful, and more pleasurable than when they are not in a state of mania.

Diagnosing Bipolar Disorders

People are considered to be in a full *manic episode* when for at least one week they display an abnormally high or irritable mood, along with at least three other symptoms of mania (see Table 7-4). The episode may include psychotic features such as delusions or hallucinations. When the symptoms of mania are less severe (causing little impairment), the person is said to be experiencing a *hypomanic episode* (APA, 2000, 1994).

DSM-IV distinguishes two kinds of bipolar disorders—bipolar I and bipolar II. People with **bipolar I disorder** have full manic and major depressive episodes.

Table 7-4 DSM-IV Checklist

MANIC EPISODE

1. A period of abnormally and persistently elevated, expansive, or irritable mood, lasting at least one week.
2. Persistence of at least three of the following: • inflated self-esteem or grandiosity • decreased need for sleep • more talkativeness than usual, or pressure to keep talking • flight of ideas or the experience that thoughts are racing • distractibility • increase in activity or psychomotor agitation • excessive involvement in pleasurable activities that have a high potential for painful consequences.
3. Significant distress or impairment.

BIPOLAR I DISORDER

1. The presence of a manic, hypomanic, or major depressive episode.
2. If currently in a hypomanic or major depressive episode, history of a manic episode.
3. Significant distress or impairment.

BIPOLAR II DISORDER

1. The presence of a hypomanic or major depressive episode.
2. If currently in a major depressive episode, history of a hypomanic episode. If currently in a hypomanic episode, history of a major depressive episode. No history of a manic episode.
3. Significant distress or impairment.

Based on APA, 2000, 1994.

produce shifting misalignments along neural membranes and consequent fluctuations from one mood extreme to the other. In support of this theory, investigators have found membrane defects in the neurons of persons with bipolar disorders and have observed abnormal functioning in the proteins that help transport ions across a neuron's membrane (Wang et al., 1999; Kato et al., 1993; Meltzer, 1991).

GENETIC FACTORS Many experts believe that people inherit a biological predisposition to develop bipolar disorders. Findings from *family pedigree studies* support this idea. Identical twins of persons with a bipolar disorder have a 40 percent likelihood of developing the same disorder, and fraternal twins, siblings, and other close relatives of such persons have a 5 to 10 percent likelihood, compared to the 1 percent prevalence rate in the general population (Craddock & Jones, 1999; Gershon & Nurnberger, 1995).

Researchers have also conducted *genetic linkage studies* to identify possible patterns in the inheritance of bipolar disorders. These studies select large families that have had high rates of a disorder over several generations, observe the pattern of distribution of the disorder among family members, and determine whether it closely follows the distribution pattern of a known genetically transmitted family trait (called a *genetic marker*), such as color blindness, red hair, or a particular medical syndrome.

After studying the records of Israeli, Belgian, and Italian families that had shown high rates of bipolar disorders across several generations, one team of researchers seemed for a while to have linked bipolar disorders to genes on the X chromosome (Baron et al., 1987; Mendlewicz et al., 1987, 1980). Other research teams, however, later used techniques from *molecular biology* to examine genetic patterns in large families, and they linked bipolar disorders to genes on chromosomes 4, 6, 11, 12, 13, 15, 18, and 22 (Berrettini, 2000). Such wide-ranging findings may mean that the logic behind the various gene studies is flawed (Gershon, 2000; Bellivier et al., 1999). Alternatively, a variety of genetic abnormalities may combine to bring about bipolar disorders (Meltzer, 2000; Craddock & Jones, 1999).

Extended families and genetic research
Closely knit families in which there is little intermarriage across the generations are attractive candidates for genetic linkage studies, which seek to identify possible patterns in the inheritance of disorders. The possible genetic patterns of bipolar disorders have, for example, been studied in some Amish families in Pennsylvania.

CROSSROADS:
Making Sense of All That Is Known

With mood disorders so prevalent in all societies, it is no wonder that they have been the focus of so much research. Great quantities of data about these disorders have been gathered. Still clinicians have yet to understand fully all that they know.

Several factors have been closely tied to unipolar depression, including biological abnormalities, a reduction in positive reinforcements, negative ways of thinking, a perception of helplessness, and sociocultural influences. Moreover, in a number of cases life stress, such as the loss of a loved one, seems to help trigger the disorder. Indeed, more contributing factors have been associated with unipolar depression than with most other psychological disorders. Precisely how all of these factors relate to unipolar depression is, however, unclear (Flett, Vredenburg, & Krames, 1997). Several relationships are possible:

1. *One* of the factors may be the key cause of unipolar depression. That is, one theory may be more useful than any of the others for predicting and explaining how unipolar depression occurs. If so, theories pointing to cognitive or biological factors are leading candidates, for these kinds of factors have each been found, at times, to precede and predict depression.

2. *Different* factors may be capable of initiating unipolar depression in different persons. Some people may, for example, begin with low serotonin activity, which predisposes them to react helplessly in stressful situations, interpret events negatively, and enjoy fewer pleasures in life. Others may first suffer a severe loss, which triggers helplessness reactions, low serotonin activity, and reductions in positive rewards. Regardless of the initial cause, these factors may merge into a "final common pathway" of unipolar depression.

3. An *interaction* between two or more specific factors may be necessary to produce unipolar depression (Klocek, Oliver, & Ross, 1997). Perhaps people will become depressed only if they have low levels of serotonin activity, feel helpless, and repeatedly blame themselves for negative events. This would help explain why only some helplessness-trained persons actually come to exhibit helplessness in laboratory studies, and why only some people with low serotonin activity become depressed.

4. The various factors may play *different roles* in unipolar depression. Some may *cause* the disorder, some may *result* from it, and some may *keep it going*. Peter Lewinsohn and his colleagues (1988) assessed more than 500 nondepressed persons on the various factors linked to depression. They then assessed the subjects again eight months later to see who had in fact become depressed and which of the factors had predicted depression. Negative thinking, self-dissatisfaction, and life stress were found to precede and predict depression; poor social relationships and reductions in positive rewards did not. The research team concluded that the former factors help cause unipolar depression, while the latter simply accompany or result from depression, and perhaps help maintain it.

As with unipolar depression, clinicians and researchers have learned much about bipolar disorders in recent years. But, unlike unipolar depression, bipolar disorders appear to be best explained by focusing largely on one kind of variable—biological factors. The evidence suggests that biological abnormalities, perhaps inherited and perhaps triggered by life stress, cause bipolar disorders. Whatever roles other factors may play, the primary one appears to lie in this realm.

PERVASIVE PROBLEM

It is estimated that clinical depression is experienced by half of all people who have suffered a stroke, 17 percent of those who have had a heart attack, 30 percent of cancer patients, and between 9 and 27 percent of people with diabetes (Simpson, 1996).

Treatments for Mood Disorders

"I think depression has made me a stronger person somehow. I mean in learning to handle this kind of thing. I think that I've had to develop skills and abilities that I wouldn't otherwise. And sensitivities too. I think it's made me more compassionate. I think, because of it, I know what it's like to go through something like that and I'm more curious about other people and what they're going through. [I'm also] more intent in trying to make some meaning out of the whole thing [life]. . . ."

Anonymous (in Karp, 1995, p. 130)

"I will take Zoloft for the rest of my life. I'm quite content to do it."

Mike Wallace, television news journalist (in Biddle et al., 1996)

"In my case, ECT [electroconvulsive therapy] was miraculous. My wife was dubious, but when she came into my room afterward, I sat up and said, 'Look who's back among the living.' It was like a magic wand."

Dick Cavett, talk show host (in People, 1992)

". . . the hospital was my salvation, and it is something of a paradox that in this austere place with its locked and wired doors and desolate green hallways . . . I found the repose, the assuagement of the tempest in my brain, that I was unable to find in my quiet farmhouse. . . . For me the real healers were seclusion and time."

William Styron, novelist (in Styron, 1990, pp. 68–69)

"Because I thought I ought to be able to handle my increasingly violent mood swings by myself, for the first ten years I did not seek any kind of treatment. Even after my condition became a medical emergency, I still intermittently resisted the medications. . . . Having finally cottoned onto the disastrous consequences of starting and stopping lithium, I took it faithfully and found that life was a much stabler and more predictable place than I had ever reckoned. My moods were still intense and my temperament rather quick to the boil, but I could make plans with far more certainty and the periods of absolute blackness were fewer and less extreme. . . . I am [now] too frightened that I will again become morbidly depressed or virulently manic—either of which would, in turn, rip apart every aspect of my life, relationships, and work that I find most meaningful—to seriously consider any change in my medical treatment."

Kay Redfield Jamison, clinical researcher (in Jamison, 1995, pp. 5, 153, 212)

Each of these persons suffered from and overcame a severe mood disorder. And, clearly, all believe that the treatment they received was the key to their improvement—the key that opened the door to a normal, stable, and productive life. Yet the treatments that seemed to help them differed greatly. Psychotherapy helped bring control, compassion, and meaning back to the life of the first individual. Electroconvulsive therapy, popularly known as

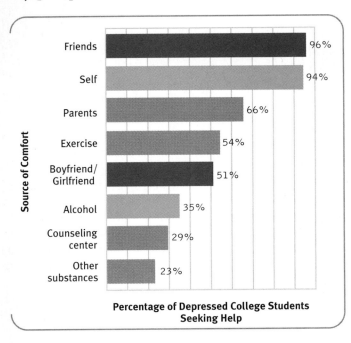

Friends 96%
Self 94%
Parents 66%
Exercise 54%
Boyfriend/ Girlfriend 51%
Alcohol 35%
Counseling center 29%
Other substances 23%

Percentage of Depressed College Students Seeking Help

Source of Comfort (y-axis label)

FIGURE 8-1 **Where do college students turn when they feel depressed?** *Typically they turn to friends and to themselves. Fewer than one-third go to a counseling center. (Adapted from Oswalt & Finkelberg, 1995.)*

EARLY CONTACT

Therapists are not necessarily the first health professionals to be contacted when depression strikes. Initially, 41 percent of persons with this disorder go to a physician with complaints of feeling generally ill, 37 percent complain of pain, and 12 percent report general tiredness and fatigue (Katon & Walker, 1998).

ConsiderThis

● What kinds of transference issues might psychodynamic therapists expect to arise in treatment with depressed persons?

shock treatment, lifted Dick Cavett from the black hole of severe unipolar depression. Hospitalization and its temporary retreat was the answer for William Styron, and antidepressant drugs the key for Mike Wallace. Kay Jamison escaped the roller-coaster ride of bipolar disorders with the help of lithium, a common, inexpensive element found in mineral salts.

How could such diverse therapies be so helpful to people suffering from the same or similar disorders? As this chapter will show, mood disorders—as extraordinarily painful and disabling disorders as they tend to be—respond more successfully to more kinds of treatment than do most other forms of psychological dysfunction (see Figure 8-1). This diversity of successful treatments is in some ways puzzling to today's clinical theorists and researchers, but it is also a source of reassurance and hope for the millions of people who desire desperately to regain some measure of control over their moods. More than 41 percent of people with mood disorders enter treatment in any given year; most find that they improve as a result (Shelton et al., 1997; Regier et al., 1993).

Treatments for Unipolar Depression

Ten percent of the clients of psychologists, psychiatrists, and social workers suffer primarily from unipolar depression (Knesper et al., 1985). In addition, many other people in therapy experience depressed feelings as part of another disorder, such as an eating disorder, or in association with general problems that they are encountering in life. Thus much of the therapy being administered today is for unipolar depression.

A variety of treatment approaches are currently in widespread use for unipolar disorder. We shall look first at the psychological approaches, focusing on the psychodynamic, behavioral, and cognitive therapies. We will then turn to the sociocultural approaches, including a highly regarded intervention called interpersonal psychotherapy. Lastly, we will consider two effective biological approaches—electroconvulsive therapy and antidepressant drugs. In the process, it will become evident that unipolar patterns of depression are indeed among the most successfully treated of all psychological disorders.

Psychological Approaches

The psychological treatments used most often to combat unipolar depression come from the psychodynamic, behavioral, and cognitive schools of thought. Psychodynamic therapy, the oldest of all modern psychotherapies, continues to be used widely for depression even though research has not offered strong evidence of its effectiveness. Behavioral therapy, effective primarily for mild or moderate depression, is practiced less often today than in past decades. Cognitive therapy has performed so well in research that it has a large and growing following among clinicians.

PSYCHODYNAMIC THERAPY Believing that unipolar depression results from unconscious grief over real or imagined losses, compounded by excessive dependence on other people, psychodynamic therapists seek to help clients bring these underlying issues to consciousness and work them through (see Box 8-1 on page 226). Using the arsenal of basic psychodynamic procedures, they encourage the depressed client to associate freely during therapy; suggest interpretations of the client's associations, dreams, and displays of resistance and transference; and help the person reexperience and review past events and feelings. Free association, for example, helped one man recall the early experiences of loss that, according to his therapist, had set the stage for his depression:

> Among his earliest memories, possibly the earliest of all, was the recollection of being wheeled in his baby cart under the elevated train structure and left there alone. Another memory that recurred vividly during the analysis was of an operation around the age of five. He was anesthetized and his mother left him with the doctor. He recalled how he had kicked and screamed, raging at her for leaving him.
>
> (Lorand, 1968, pp. 325–326)

In the following excerpt, the therapist interpreted a depressed client's dream and traced his mood problem to early dependence and to real and symbolic losses:

> The patient reported a dream in which he was at his father's gravesite, in which his dead father was lying. In the dream the patient was crying and others were trying to comfort him. He had the feeling that everyone close to him was sick. He woke from the dream crying. In his associations this patient remembered the actual death of his father, stating that at the time, "I felt as if my purpose in life had been extinguished." The patient had had a quasi-symbiotic relationship with his father, who had preferred him over the other children. He followed his father's orders to the letter, in return for which his father lavished praise on him and gave him substantial sums of money. He never dared to cross his father since he had the experience of witnessing what had occurred to his brothers when they disagreed even slightly with the father. This patient had grown up in a rural area where the father, a wealthy and influential businessman, had ruled over a large estate like a small monarch. Although he had slavishly followed his father's instructions, the patient often had been irresponsible in his own affairs, and had lost moderate sums of money because of his naiveté. He had the dream after losing a considerable sum of money at cards. The dream may have represented an awareness that he was now on his own, yet there remained within him a desperate desire to be taken care of once again by a powerful other. The dream showed his characteristic turning to others to make things right, as his father had done in the past whenever he was in trouble.
>
> (Arieti & Bemporad, 1978, p. 300)

Psychodynamic therapists expect that in the course of treatment depressed clients will eventually become less dependent on others, cope with losses more effectively, make corresponding changes in their daily lives, and join the majority of people who describe themselves as happy. The transition of a therapeutic insight into a real-life change is seen in the case of a middle-aged executive:

> The patient's father was still living and in a nursing home, where the patient visited him regularly. On one occasion, he went to see his father full of high expectations, as he had concluded a very successful business transaction. As he began to describe his accomplishments to his father, however, the latter completely ignored his son's remarks and viciously berated him for wearing a pink shirt, which he considered unprofessional. Such a response from the father was not unusual, but this time, as a result of the work that had been accomplished in therapy, the patient could objectively analyze his initial sense of disappointment and deep feeling of failure for not pleasing the older man. Although this experience led to a transient state of depression, it also revealed to the patient his whole dependent lifestyle—his use of others to supply him with a feeling of worth. This experience added a dimension of immediate reality to the insights that had been achieved in therapy and gave the patient the motivation to change radically his childhood system of perceiving himself in relation to paternal transference figures.
>
> (Bemporad, 1992, p. 291)

LOSS OF A FATHER

Before the 1960s, the most common cause of fatherlessness was death. Since then, the leading cause has been separation or divorce (Coney & Mackey, 1998).

BOX 8-1

The Grieving Process

Each year tens of millions of people experience the death of a close relative or friend. Reactions to such painful losses can be so similar to clinical depression that Freud and Abraham based the psychoanalytic explanation of depression on them. But mourning is a natural process that allows us eventually to come to grips with our loss and resume our lives.

Unfortunately, there are many common misconceptions about grieving. The most common is the belief that there is a set timetable for mourning (Doka, 1999). Friends and acquaintances often allow the mourner only a few weeks to return to normal life. In fact, it is sometimes many months before a person is ready to do so (Jacobs, 1999). The amount of time needed depends on such factors as the relationship of the mourner to the deceased, the age of the mourner, and, clearly, the mourner's personality (Stroebe et al., 2000).

The bereavement process is also experienced differently in different cultural groups (Stroebe et al., 1992). Japanese Buddhists believe in maintaining contact with dead ancestors, and almost all homes have an altar dedicated to them. Offering food and speaking to the dead are common practices. The Hopi Indians, though, believe that contact with death brings pollution, so they quickly rid the home of all reminders of their deceased relatives. Muslims in Egypt believe that the bereaved should dwell on their loss and surround themselves with others who share their sorrow, but Muslims in Bali are taught to contain their grief, to laugh and be joyful (Wikan, 1991).

Western society tends to view bereavement as an interference in the daily routine of life, a troublesome, debilitating emotional response that one must overcome as quickly and efficiently as possible. This view was not always the norm in the West. In the mid-nineteenth century, for example, communication with the dead through séances and mediums was popular. The amount of grief one felt after the death of a loved one was held to indicate the relationship's strength and significance, and the bereaved were expected to focus on a reunion with the deceased in heaven.

Despite individual variations, many mourners in Western society today go through a predictable sequence of emotions (Osterweis & Townsend, 1988). The bereavement process may begin with *shock:* the survivor has difficulty believing that the person has died. This is frequently followed by a sense of *loss and separation,* a feeling that sometimes leads to misperceptions and illusions—glimpses of the dead person in the street or dreams that the person is alive. Once the mourner fully accepts the fact that the deceased is not coming back, *despair* may set in. Depression, irritability, guilt, and anger are natural responses at this stage. Social relationships may deteriorate at this time, and some mourners may suffer from medical problems (Arnette, 1996).

Once the mourning process is complete, it becomes possible to think of the deceased person without being overwhelmed by despair and a sense of loss.

Depression among the elderly *Old age may be accompanied by the loss of good health, of close relatives and friends, and of control over one's life. Both psychodynamic and behavioral therapists link such losses to the high rate of depression found among the elderly. Yet depression is not inevitable as people age.*

Despite successful case reports such as this, researchers have found that long-term psychodynamic therapy is only occasionally helpful in cases of unipolar depression (APA, 1993; Prochaska, 1984). Two features of the approach may help limit its effectiveness. First, depressed clients may be too passive and feel too fatigued to join fully in the subtle therapy discussions required in psychodynamic therapy (Bose, 1995). Second, they may become discouraged and end treatment too early when this long-term approach is unable to provide the quick relief that they desperately seek. Generally, psychodynamic therapy seems to be of greatest help in cases of depression that clearly involve a history of childhood loss or trauma, a chronic sense of emptiness, perfectionism, extreme self-criticism, or rigid expectations for oneself (Blatt, 1999, 1995; APA, 1993). Short-term psychodynamic therapies have performed better than the traditional approaches (Jefferson & Greist, 1994; Svartberg & Stiles, 1991).

BEHAVIORAL THERAPY Peter Lewinsohn, whose theory of depression tied mood to the rewards in a person's life, also developed a behavioral treatment for unipolar depression in the 1970s. In this approach, therapists (1) reintroduce clients to pleasurable events and activities, (2) appropriately reinforce their depressive and nondepressive behaviors, and (3) help them improve their social skills (Lewinsohn et al., 1990, 1982; Teri & Lewinsohn, 1986).

First, guided by a client's responses on a *Pleasant Events Schedule* and an *Activity Schedule,* the therapist selects activities that the client

At this point, one is prepared to get on with one's life, although anniversaries and other special dates may cause flare-ups of mourning for many years to come.

Social support can often be very helpful during the bereavement process (Doka, 1999). In fact, numerous self-help bereavement groups allow mourners opportunities to gather with others who have lost loved ones and discuss the emotional and practical problems they all face. Group members do not avoid the topic of death, and no one promises or demands a speedy return to normal. Such groups are helpful for many mourners (Allumbaugh & Hoyt, 1999), allowing a necessary process to proceed as it should—without pressure, misinterpretation, or judgment.

Mass grief *The recent deaths of Princess Diana, John Kennedy, Jr., and the Columbine High School students have each triggered mass grief reactions. Tens of thousands of people spontaneously came together to mourn these losses and built extemporaneous memorial sites with endless offerings of flowers, candles, notes, drawings, balloons, and other personal items, as at this site honoring Diana outside of Kensington Palace in London.*

considers pleasurable, such as going shopping or taking photographs, and encourages the person to set up a weekly schedule for engaging in them. Studies have shown that adding positive activities to a person's life can indeed lead to a better mood (Leenstra, Ormel, & Giel, 1995; Teri & Lewinsohn, 1986). The following case description exemplifies this process:

> This patient was a forty-nine-year-old housewife whose children were grown and no longer living at home. Her major interest in life was painting, and indeed she was an accomplished artist. She developed a depression characterized by apathy, self-derogation, and anxiety while she was incapacitated with a severe respiratory infection. She was unable to paint during her illness and lost interest and confidence in her art work when she became depressed. Her therapist thought that she could reinstitute her sources of "reinforcement" if she could be motivated to return to the easel. After providing a supportive relationship for a month, the therapist scheduled a home visit to look at her paintings and to watch and talk with her while she picked up her brush and put paint to canvas. By the time he arrived, she had already begun to paint and within a few weeks experienced a gradual lessening of her depression.
>
> *(Liberman & Raskin, 1971, p. 521)*

While reintroducing pleasurable events into a client's life, the therapist also makes sure that the person's various behaviors are rewarded correctly. Behaviorists have argued that when people become depressed, their negative behaviors—

LAST-MINUTE EDIT

Early drafts of the Declaration of Independence called for the right to "life, liberty and the protection of property." The founding fathers are believed to have changed this phrase to "life, liberty and the pursuit of happiness" in order to divert attention from the large real estate holdings that many of them had (Johnsen, 1994).

Preventing depression among the elderly
Behaviorists propose that people need pleasurable events in their lives in order to thrive and to avoid depression. With this in mind, more and more activities, such as the Senior Olympics, are being made available to elderly persons, providing important rewards, stimulation, and satisfaction.

crying, complaining, or self-depreciation—keep others at a distance, reducing chances for positive reinforcement. To reverse this pattern, the therapist may use a *contingency management approach,* systematically ignoring a client's depressive behaviors while praising or otherwise rewarding constructive statements and behavior, such as going to work. Sometimes family members and friends are recruited to help with this feature of treatment (Liberman & Raskin, 1971).

Finally, behavioral therapists may train clients in effective social skills (Segrin, 2000; Hersen et al., 1984). In group therapy programs, members, for example, may work together to improve eye contact, facial expression, tone of voice, posture, and other behaviors that convey social messages.

These behavioral techniques seem to be of only limited help when just one of them is applied. A group of depressed people who were instructed to increase their pleasant activities, for example, showed no more improvement than a control group who were told simply to keep track of their activities (Hammen & Glass, 1975). However, when the treatment program combines two or three of these behavioral techniques, much as Lewinsohn had envisioned, it does appear to reduce depressive symptoms, particularly if the depression is mild (Jacobson et al., 1996; Teri & Lewinsohn, 1986). The behavioral techniques have sometimes been offered as part of a package, with lectures, classroom activities, homework assignments, and an explanatory guidebook. It is worth noting that Lewinsohn himself has combined behavioral techniques with cognitive strategies in recent years, in an approach similar to the cognitive treatment that we shall turn to next (Clarke et al., 1999; Lewinsohn & Clarke, 1999).

COGNITIVE THERAPY In Chapter 7 we saw that Aaron Beck views unipolar depression as resulting from a chain of cognitive problems. *Maladaptive attitudes* lead people to repeatedly view themselves, their world, and their future in negative ways—the so-called *cognitive triad*. Such biased views combine with *illogical thinking* to produce *automatic thoughts,* unrelentingly negative thoughts that flood the mind and produce the symptoms of depression.

Beck's **cognitive therapy**, the leading cognitive treatment for unipolar depression, is designed to help clients recognize and change their negative cognitive processes and thus to improve both their mood and their behavior (Beck, 1997, 1985, 1967). The approach is similar to Albert Ellis's *rational-emotive therapy* (discussed in Chapters 3 and 5), but it is tailored to the specific cognitive errors found in depression. Beck's approach follows four successive phases and usually requires fewer than 20 sessions (see Table 8-1).

Phase 1: Increasing activities and elevating mood Using behavioral techniques to set the stage for cognitive treatment, therapists first encourage individuals to become more active and confident. Clients spend time during each session preparing a detailed schedule of hourly activities for the coming week (see Figure 8-2). As they become more active from week to week, their mood is expected to improve. Inasmuch as this early stage of treatment incorporates behavioral techniques, Beck's approach should probably be considered a cognitive-behavioral approach rather than a purely cognitive intervention (Jacobson and Gortner, 2000).

Phase 2: Challenging automatic thoughts Once people are more active and feeling some emotional relief, cognitive therapists begin to educate them about their negative automatic thoughts. The individuals are instructed to recognize and record automatic thoughts as they occur and bring their lists to each session. Therapist and client then test the reality behind the

	Monday	Tuesday	Wednesday	Thursday	Fr
9-10		Go to grocery store	Go to museum	Get ready to go out	
10-11		Go to grocery store	Go to museum	Drive to Doctor's appointment	
11-12	Doctor's appointment	Call friend	Go to museum	Doctor's appointment	
12-1	Lunch	Lunch	Lunch at museaum		
1-2	Drive home	Clean front room	Drive home		
2-3	Read novel	Clean front room	Washing		
3-4	Clean bedroom	Read novel	Washing		
4-5	Watch TV	Watch TV	Watch TV		
5-6	Fix dinner	Fix dinner	Fix dinner		
6-7	Eat with family	Eat with family	Eat with family		
7-8	Clean kitchen	Clean kitchen	Clean kitchen		
8-12	Watch TV, read novel, sleep	Call sister, watch TV, read novel, sleep	Work on rug, read novel, sleep		

FIGURE 8-2 Increasing activity *In the early stages of cognitive therapy for depression, the client and therapist prepare an activity schedule such as this. Activities as simple as watching television and calling a friend are specified. (Adapted from Beck et al., 1979, p. 122.)*

Table 8-1

Mood Disorders and Treatment

DISORDER	MOST EFFECTIVE TREATMENT	AVERAGE LENGTH OF INITIAL TREATMENT (WEEKS)	PERCENT IMPROVED BY TREATMENT
Major depressive disorder	Cognitive or interpersonal psychotherapy	20	60%
	Antidepressant drugs	20	60
	ECT	2	60
Dysthymic disorder	Cognitive or interpersonal psychotherapy	20	60
	Antidepressant drugs	20	60
Bipolar I disorder	Antibipolar drugs	Indefinite	60
Bipolar II disorder	Antibipolar drugs	Indefinite	60
Cyclothymic disorder	Psychotherapy or antibipolar drugs	20 to indefinite	Unknown

thoughts, often concluding that they are groundless. Beck offers the following exchange as an example of this sort of review:

Therapist: Why do you think you won't be able to get into the university of your choice?

Patient: Because my grades were really not so hot.

Therapist: Well, what was your grade average?

Patient: Well, pretty good up until the last semester in high school.

Therapist: What was your grade average in general?

...ly grades were A's but I got terrible

...?

...ould seem to me to come out to almost all
...on't be able to get into the university?
...ng so tough.
...e average grades are for admissions to

...t a B+ average would suffice.
...an that?

(Beck et al., 1979, p. 153)

...g and biases As people begin to recognize
...ghts, cognitive therapists show them
...contributing to these thoughts. The de-
...ing dichotomous (all-or-nothing) think-
...ade lower than A was "terrible." The ther-
...that almost all their interpretations of
...hange that style of interpretation.

...Therapists help clients change the mal-
...for their depression in the first place. As

COGNITIVE THERAPY A therapy developed by Aaron Beck that helps people identify and change the maladaptive assumptions and ways of thinking that help cause their psychological disorders.

INTERPERSONAL PSYCHOTHERAPY (IPT)
A treatment for unipolar depression that is based on the belief that clarifying and changing one's interpersonal problems will help lead to recovery.

part of the process, therapists often encourage clients to test their attitudes, as in the following therapy discussion:

Therapist: On what do you base this belief that you can't be happy without a man?

Patient: I was really depressed for a year and a half when I didn't have a man.

Therapist: Is there another reason why you were depressed?

Patient: As we discussed, I was looking at everything in a distorted way. But I still don't know if I could be happy if no one was interested in me.

Therapist: I don't know either. Is there a way we could find out?

Patient: Well, as an experiment, I could not go out on dates for a while and see how I feel.

Therapist: I think that's a good idea. Although it has its flaws, the experimental method is still the best way currently available to discover the facts. You're fortunate in being able to run this type of experiment. Now, for the first time in your adult life you aren't attached to a man. If you find you can be happy without a man, this will greatly strengthen you and also make your future relationships all the better.

(Beck et al., 1979, pp. 253–254)

ConsiderThis

◉ Friends and family members try, with limited success, to convince depressed people that their gloom-and-doom view of things is wrong. How does the successful cognitive approach to unipolar depression differ from such efforts at friendly persuasion?

Over the past three decades, literally hundreds of studies have shown that cognitive therapy helps with unipolar depression (DeRubeis et al., 2000). Depressed people who receive this therapy improve much more than those who receive placebos or no treatment at all (Shaw & Segal, 1999; Hollon & Beck, 1994). Around 50 to 60 percent show a near total elimination of their symptoms. The individuals improve steadily in their cognitive functioning over the course of therapy, becoming less pessimistic and more positive in their self-concepts, and their improvements correspond closely to improvements in their depression (Segal, Gemar, & Williams, 1999; Pace & Dixon, 1993). In view of this strong research support, many therapists have adopted the cognitive approach, some offering it in a group therapy format (Bristow & Bright, 1995).

"I see no problem with a limited period of grief, as long as you keep in mind that agent Fox Mulder was a fictional character."

Sociocultural Approaches

As we observed in Chapter 7, sociocultural theorists trace the causes of unipolar depression to the broader social structure in which people live and the roles they are required to play. The most effective sociocultural approaches to depression are *interpersonal psychotherapy* and *couple therapy*. The techniques used in these approaches often borrow from the other models, but they are used in this instance primarily to help persons overcome the social difficulties that may underlie their depression.

INTERPERSONAL PSYCHOTHERAPY Developed during the 1980s by the clinical researchers Gerald Klerman and Myrna Weissman, **interpersonal psychotherapy (IPT)** holds that any of four interpersonal problem areas may lead to depression and must be addressed: interpersonal loss, interpersonal role dispute, interpersonal role transition, and interpersonal deficits (Klerman & Weissman, 1992; Klerman et al., 1984). Over the course of around 16 sessions, IPT therapists address these areas.

First, depressed persons may, as psychodynamic theorists suggest, be experiencing a grief reaction over an *interpersonal loss,* the loss of an important loved one. In such cases, IPT therapists encourage clients to explore their relationship with the departed person and express any feelings of anger they may discover. Eventually clients develop new ways of remembering the lost person and also seek new relationships.

Second, depressed people may find themselves in the midst of an *interpersonal role dispute.* Role disputes occur when two people have different expectations of their relationship and of the role each should play. IPT therapists help clients examine whatever role disputes they may be involved in and to develop ways of solving them.

Depressed people may also be experiencing an *interpersonal role transition*, brought about by major life changes such as divorce or the birth of a child. They may feel overwhelmed by the role changes that accompany the life change (see Box 8-2 on page 233). In such cases IPT therapists help them develop the social supports and skills the new roles require.

Finally, some depressed people display *interpersonal deficits,* such as extreme shyness, insensitivity to others' needs, or social awkwardness. According to Klerman and Weissman, many depressed people experienced disrupted relationships as children and have failed to establish intimate relationships as adults. IPT therapists may help them recognize the nature and sources of their deficits and may teach them social skills and assertiveness in order to improve their social effectiveness.

In the following discussion, the therapist encourages a depressed man to recognize the effect his behavior has on others:

> ***Client:*** *(After a long pause with eyes downcast, a sad facial expression, and slumped posture)* People always make fun of me. I guess I'm just the type of guy who really was meant to be a loner, damn it. *(Deep sigh)*
> ***Therapist:*** Could you do that again for me?
> ***Client:*** What?
> ***Therapist:*** The sigh, only a bit deeper.
> ***Client:*** Why? *(Pause)* Okay, but I don't see what . . . okay. *(Client sighs again and smiles)*
> ***Therapist:*** Well, that time you smiled, but mostly when you sigh and look so sad I get the feeling that I better leave you alone in your misery, that I should walk on eggshells and not get too chummy or I might hurt you even more.

DIFFERING OPINIONS

According to a survey in Australia, clinicians believe that psychotherapy and antidepressant drugs are of more help to depressed persons than other kinds of intervention. The majority of Australians, however, place greater faith in family members, close friends, and vitamins (Jorm et al., 1997).

Role transition *Major life changes such as marriage, the birth of a child, or divorce can present difficulties in role transition, one of the interpersonal problem areas addressed by IPT therapists in their work with depressed clients.*

> *Client:* (A bit of anger in his voice) Well, excuse me! I was only trying to tell you how I felt.
>
> *Therapist:* I know you felt miserable, but I also got the message that you wanted to keep me at a distance, that I had no way to reach you.
>
> *Client:* (Slowly) I feel like a loner, I feel that even you don't care about me— making fun of me.
>
> *Therapist:* I wonder if other folks need to pass this test, too?
>
> (Young & Beier, 1984, p. 270)

Research suggests that IPT and related interpersonal interventions for depression have a success rate similar to that of cognitive therapy (Mufson et al., 1999; Swartz, 1999; Stuart & O'Hara, 1995). That is, symptoms almost totally disappear in 50 to 60 percent of clients who receive treatment. After IPT, clients not only experience a reduction of depressive symptoms, but also function more effectively in their social and family interactions (Klerman & Weissman, 1992). Not surprisingly, IPT is considered particularly useful for depressed people who are struggling with social conflicts or undergoing changes in their careers or social roles (APA, 1993).

COUPLE THERAPY As we have seen, depression can result from marital discord, and recovery from depression is often slower for people who do not receive support from their spouse (Bruce & Kim, 1992). In fact, as many as half of all depressed clients may be in a dysfunctional relationship. Thus it is not surprising that many cases of depression have been treated by *couple therapy*, the approach in which a therapist works with two people who share a long-term relationship.

Therapists who offer *behavioral marital therapy* help spouses change harmful marital behavior by teaching them specific communication and problem-solving skills (see Chapter 3) (Lebow & Gurman, 1995). When the depressed person's marriage is laden with conflict, this and similar approaches may be as effective as individual cognitive therapy or interpersonal psychotherapy in helping to reduce depression (Baucom et al., 1998; Teichman et al., 1995). In addition, such clients who receive couple therapy are more likely than those in individual therapy to be more satisfied with their marriage after treatment.

Biological Approaches

Like several of the psychological and sociocultural therapies, biological treatments can bring great relief to people with unipolar depression. Usually biological treatment means antidepressant drugs, but for severely depressed persons who do not respond to other forms of treatment, it sometimes means electroconvulsive therapy. Many people are surprised to learn that electroconvulsive therapy is, in fact, a highly effective approach for unipolar depression.

ELECTROCONVULSIVE THERAPY One of the most controversial forms of treatment for depression is **electroconvulsive therapy**, or **ECT**. One patient describes his experience:

> Strapped to a stretcher, you are wheeled into the ECT room. The electroshock machine is in clear view. It is a solemn occasion; there is little talk. The nurse, the attendant, and the anesthetist go about their preparation methodically. Your psychiatrist enters. He seems quite matter-of-fact, businesslike—perhaps a bit rushed. "Everything is going to be just fine. I have given hundreds of these treatments. No one has ever died." You flinch inside. Why did he say that? But there is no time to dwell on it. They are ready. The electrodes are in place. The long clear plastic tube running from the bottle above ends with a needle in your vein. An injection is given. Suddenly—terrifyingly—you can no longer breathe; and then . . . You awaken in your hospital bed. There is a soreness in your legs and a

SPECIAL TRAINING NOT REQUIRED Any psychotherapist, trained in couple therapy or not, may practice this complex form of treatment. The majority of clinicians now doing couple therapy have had no formal training in it (Doherty, 1999).

ELECTROCONVULSIVE THERAPY (ECT) A treatment for depression in which electrodes attached to a patient's head send an electric current through the brain, causing a convulsion.

BOX 8-2

Sadness at the Happiest of Times

Women usually expect the birth of a child to be a happy experience. But for 10 to 30 percent of new mothers, the weeks and months after childbirth bring clinical depression (Nonacs & Cohen, 1998; Terry, Mayocchi, & Hynes, 1996; Horowitz et al., 1995). *Postpartum depression* typically begins within four weeks after the birth of a child (APA, 2000, 1994), and it is far more severe than simple "baby blues." It is also different from other postpartum syndromes such as postpartum psychosis (Terp et al., 1999) and postpartum panic disorder.

The "baby blues" are so common—as many as 80 percent of women experience them—that most researchers consider them normal. As new mothers try to cope with the wakeful nights, rattled emotions, and other stresses that accompany the arrival of a new baby, they may experience crying spells, fatigue, anxiety, insomnia, and sadness. These symptoms usually disappear within days or weeks (Najman et al., 2000; Horowitz et al., 1995).

In postpartum depression, however, depressive symptoms continue, and may last up to a year (Terry et al., 1996). The symptoms include extreme sadness, despair, tearfulness, insomnia, anxiety, intrusive thoughts, compulsions, panic attacks, feelings of inability to cope, and suicidal thoughts. The mother-infant relationship and the health of the child may suffer as a result.

Many clinicians believe that the hormonal changes accompanying childbirth trigger postpartum depression (Parry, 1999). All women experience a kind of hormone "withdrawal" after delivery, as estrogen and progesterone levels, which rise as much as 50 times above normal during pregnancy, now drop sharply to levels far below normal (Horowitz et al., 1995). The levels of thyroid hormones, prolactin, and cortisol also change (Abou et al., 1999). Perhaps some women are particularly influenced by these dramatic hormone changes (Horowitz et al., 1995). Still other theorists suggest a genetic predisposition to postpartum depression. A woman with a family history of mood disorders appears to be at high risk, even if she herself has not previously had a mood disorder (APA, 2000, 1994; Steiner & Tam, 1999).

At the same time, psychological and sociocultural factors may play important roles in the disorder. The birth of a baby brings enormous psychological and social change (Nicolson, 1999; Hopkins et al., 1984). A woman typically faces changes in her marital relationship, daily routines, and social roles. Sleep and relaxation are likely to decrease and financial pressures may increase. Perhaps she feels the added stress of giving up a career—or of trying to maintain one. This pileup of stress may heighten the risk of depression (Swendsen & Mazure, 2000; Terry et al., 1996). Mothers whose infants are sick or temperamentally "difficult" seem to be particularly at risk (Terry et al., 1996).

Fortunately, treatment can make a big difference for most women with post-

Behind the smile *Singer Marie Osmond, performing here with her brother Donny, recently revealed that she suffered from postpartum depression after giving birth in 1999.*

partum depression. Self-help support groups have proved enormously helpful for many women with the disorder (Honikman, 1999; Taylor, 1999). In addition, many respond well to the same approaches that are applied to other forms of unipolar depression—antidepressant medications, cognitive therapy, interpersonal psychotherapy, or a combination of these approaches (Stuart, 1999; Stowe et al., 1995). Some clinicians in Great Britain have even added an *estrogen patch* to the usual arsenal of treatment weapons: a skin patch that delivers estrogen into the bloodstream (Gilbert, 1996; Gregoire et al., 1996).

However, many women who would benefit from treatment do not seek help because they feel ashamed about being sad at a time that is supposed to be joyous or they are concerned about being judged harshly (APA, 1994). For them, and for the spouses and family members close to them, a large dose of education is in order. Even positive events can be stressful and upsetting if they also bring major change to one's life. Recognizing and addressing such upsets is in everyone's best interest.

bruise on your arm you can't explain. You are confused to find it so difficult to recover memories. Finally, you stop struggling in the realization that you have no memory for what has transpired. You were scheduled to have ECT, but something must have happened. Perhaps it was postponed. But the nurse keeps coming over to you and asking, "How are you feeling?" You think to yourself: "It must have been given"; but you can't remember. Confused and uncomfortable, you begin the dread return to the ECT room. You have forgotten, but something about it remains. You are frightened.

(Taylor, 1975)

Clinicians and patients alike vary greatly in their opinions of ECT. Some consider it a safe biological procedure with minimal risks; others believe it to be an extreme measure that can cause troublesome memory loss and even neurological damage. Despite the heat of this controversy, ECT is used frequently, largely because it is an effective and fast-acting intervention for unipolar depression (APA, 1993).

THE TREATMENT PROCEDURE In an ECT procedure, two electrodes are attached to the patient's head, and an electric current of 65 to 140 volts is sent through the brain for half a second or less. The current causes a brain seizure that lasts from 25 seconds to a few minutes. After six to twelve such treatments, spaced over two to four weeks, most patients feel less depressed (Bailine et al., 2000; Fink, 1992). In *bilateral ECT* one electrode is applied to each side of the forehead and a current passes through both sides of the brain. In *unilateral ECT*, a method used increasingly in recent years, the electrodes are placed so that the current passes through only one side.

THE ORIGINS OF ECT The discovery that electric shock can be therapeutic was made by accident. In the 1930s, clinical researchers mistakenly came to believe that brain seizures, or the *convulsions* (severe body spasms) that accompany them, could cure schizophrenia and other psychotic disorders. They observed that people with psychosis rarely suffered from *epilepsy* (*brain seizure disorder*) and that people with epilepsy rarely were psychotic, and so concluded that brain seizures or convulsions somehow prevented psychosis. We now know that the observed correlation between seizures and lack of psychotic symptoms does not necessarily imply that one event caused the other. Nevertheless, swayed by faulty logic, clinicians in the 1930s searched for ways to induce seizures as a treatment for patients with psychosis.

A Hungarian physician named Joseph von Meduna gave the drug *metrazol* to patients suffering from psychosis, and a Viennese physician named Manfred Sakel gave them large doses of *insulin* (*insulin coma therapy*). These procedures produced the desired brain seizures, but each was quite dangerous and sometimes even caused death. Finally, an Italian psychiatrist named Ugo Cerletti discovered that he could induce seizures more safely by applying electric currents to patients' heads, and he and his colleague Lucio Bini soon developed electroconvulsive therapy as a treatment for psychosis (Cerletti & Bini, 1938). As one might expect, much uncertainty and confusion accompanied their first clinical application of ECT. Did experimenters have the right to impose such an untested treatment against a patient's will?

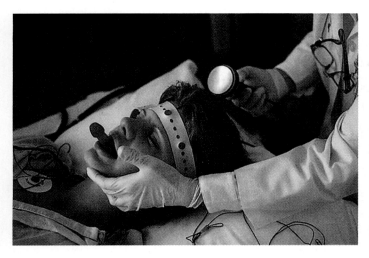

ECT today *During ECT, patients are now given drugs to help them sleep, muscle relaxants to prevent severe jerks of the body and broken bones, and oxygen to guard against brain damage.*

WHY INSULIN?

When patients were given large doses of insulin, their blood sugar dropped so dramatically that they sank into a coma.

The schizophrenic arrived by train from Milan without a ticket or any means of identification. Physically healthy, he was bedraggled and alternately was mute or expressed himself in incomprehensible gibberish made up of odd neologisms. The patient was brought in but despite their vast animal experience there was great apprehension and fear that the patient might be damaged, and so the shock was cautiously set at 70 volts for one-tenth of a second. The low dosage predictably produced only a minor spasm, after which the patient burst into song. Cerletti suggested another shock at a higher voltage, and an excited and voluble discussion broke out among the spectators. . . . All of the staff objected to a further shock, protesting that the patient would probably die. Cerletti was familiar with committees and knew that postponement would inevitably mean prolonged and possibly permanent procrastination, and so he decided to proceed at 110 volts for one-half second. However, before he could do so, the patient who had heard but so far not participated in the discussion sat up and pontifically proclaimed in clear Italian without hint of jargon, "Non una seconda! Mortifera!" (Not again! It will kill me!). Professor Bini hesitated but gave the order to proceed. After recovery, Bini asked the patient "What has been happening to you?" and the man replied "I don't know; perhaps I've been asleep." He remained jargon-free and gave a complete account of himself, and was discharged completely recovered after 11 complete and 3 incomplete treatments over a course of 2 months.

(Brandon, 1981, pp. 8–9)

ECT soon became popular and was tried out on a wide range of psychological problems, as new techniques so often are. Its effectiveness with severe depression in particular became quite apparent. Ironically, however, doubts were soon raised concerning its usefulness for psychosis, and many researchers have since judged it ineffective for most psychotic disorders (Taylor & Carroll, 1987).

CHANGES IN ECT PROCEDURES Although Cerletti gained international fame for his procedure, eventually he abandoned ECT and spent his later years seeking other treatments for mental disorders (Karon, 1985). The reason: he abhorred the broken bones and dislocations of the jaw or shoulders that sometimes resulted from ECT's severe convulsions, as well as the memory loss, confusion, and brain damage that the seizures could cause. Other clinicians have stayed with the procedure, however, and have changed it over the years to reduce its undesirable consequences. Today's practitioners give patients strong *muscle relaxants* to minimize convulsions, thus eliminating the danger of fractures or dislocations. They also use *anesthetics* (*barbiturates*) to put patients to sleep during the procedure, reducing their terror (Fink, 1992). With these precautions, ECT is medically more complex than it used to be, but also less dangerous and somewhat less disturbing (Mehta & Bedient, 1999; Salzman, 1998).

Patients who receive ECT, particularly bilateral ECT, typically have difficulty remembering the events before and immediately after their treatments. In most cases, this memory loss clears up within a few months (Calev et al., 1995, 1991; Squire & Slater, 1983). Some patients, however, experience gaps in more distant memory, and this form of amnesia can be permanent (Squire, 1977). Understandably, these individuals may be left embittered by the procedure.

EFFECTIVENESS OF ECT ECT is clearly effective in treating unipolar depression. Studies find that between 60 and 70 percent of ECT patients improve (Rey & Walter, 1997). The procedure seems to be particularly effective in severe cases of depression that include delusions (O'Leary et al., 1995; Buchan et al., 1992). It has been difficult, however, to determine why ECT works so well. After all, this procedure delivers a broad insult to the brain that causes neurons all over the brain to fire and all kinds of neurotransmitters to be released, and it affects many other systems throughout the body as well (Kellner, 1999; Fink, 1992).

Although ECT is effective and ECT techniques have improved, its use has generally declined since the 1950s. Apparently more than 100,000 patients a year underwent ECT during the 1940s and 1950s. Today as few as 50,000 per year are believed to receive it (Cauchon, 1999; Foderaero, 1993). Two of the reasons for this decline are the memory loss caused by ECT and the frightening nature of this procedure. Another is the emergence of effective *antidepressant drugs*.

SOURCE OF INSPIRATION

Like everyone else, Ugo Cerletti initially believed that the application of electric currents to people's heads would kill them. One day, however, he visited a slaughterhouse where he observed that before slaughtering hogs with a knife, butchers clamped the animals' heads with metallic tongs and applied an electric current. The hogs fell unconscious and had convulsions, but they did not die from the current itself. Their comas merely made it easier for the butchers to kill them by other means. Said Cerletti: "At this point I felt we could venture to experiment on man."

ON THE HORIZON?

Some clinicians predict that a new procedure called *transcranial magnetic stimulation (TMS)* will eventually replace electroconvulsive therapy (ECT). In TMS, a coil that transmits a magnetic field is held close to a patient's scalp, sending a small electric current into just one area of the brain (the prefrontal cortex), in contrast to ECT's stimulation of the entire brain. The new procedure is painless and has less serious undesired effects. In recent studies, TMS brought significant improvement to half of the severely depressed patients who received it (Klein et al., 1999).

MAO INHIBITOR An antidepressant drug that prevents the action of the enzyme monoamine oxidase.

TRICYCLIC An antidepressant drug such as imipramine that has three rings in its molecular structure.

ON THE RISE

Antidepressant medications are now the second most prescribed class of drugs, just behind drugs for high blood pressure (Express Scripts, 1999).

ANTIDEPRESSANT DRUGS Two kinds of drugs discovered in the 1950s reduce the symptoms of depression: *monoamine oxidase (MAO) inhibitors* and *tricyclics*. These drugs have recently been joined by a third group, the so-called *second-generation antidepressants* (see Table 8-2). Before these discoveries the only drugs that provided any relief for depression were amphetamines, stimulant drugs that we shall be observing in Chapter 12. Amphetamines stimulated some depressed people to greater activity, but they did not result in greater joy.

MAO INHIBITORS The effectiveness of **MAO inhibitors** as a treatment for unipolar depression was discovered accidentally. Physicians noted that *iproniazid,* a drug being tested on patients with tuberculosis, had an interesting effect: it seemed to make the patients happier (Sandler, 1990). It was found to have the same effect on depressed patients (Kline, 1958; Loomer, Saunders, & Kline, 1957). What this and several related drugs had in common biochemically was that they slowed the body's production of the enzyme *monoamine oxidase (MAO).* Thus they were called MAO inhibitors.

Normally, brain supplies of the enzyme MAO break down, or degrade, the neurotransmitter norepinephrine. MAO inhibitors block MAO from carrying out this degradation and thereby stop the destruction of norepinephrine. The result is a rise in norepinephrine activity and, in turn, a reduction of depressive symptoms. Approximately half of depressed patients who take MAO inhibitors are helped by them (Thase, Trivedi, & Rush, 1995).

As clinicians have gained experience with MAO inhibitors, they have learned that the drugs can also create serious medical problems. Apparently many of the foods we eat—including cheeses, certain fish, bananas, and certain wines—contain *tyramine,* a chemical that can raise blood pressure dangerously if too much of it accumulates (Stahl, 1998). Normally, MAO in the liver serves the beneficial role of quickly breaking tyramine down into another chemical, hence keeping blood pressure under control. Unfortunately, when MAO inhibitors are taken to combat depression, they also block the production of MAO in the liver and intestines. This action allows tyramine to accumulate and puts the person in great danger of high blood pressure and perhaps sudden death.

Thus people who take MAO inhibitors must typically avoid any of the long list of foods that contain tyramine. In recent years, new MAO inhibitors have been discovered that affect norepinephrine levels without disturbing the breakdown of tyramine, thus posing fewer of the dietary dangers of traditional MAO inhibitors (Lotufo-Neto, Tivedi, & Thase, 1999; Lecrubier, 1995; Paykel, 1995). Some of these so-called *reversible selective MAO inhibitors* are now available in Canada and Europe but have yet to be approved for use in the United States.

TRICYCLICS The discovery of **tricyclics** in the 1950s was also accidental. Researchers who were looking for a new drug to combat schizophrenia ran some tests on a drug called *imipramine* (Kuhn, 1958). They discovered that imipramine was of no help in cases of schizophrenia, but it did relieve unipolar depression in many people. The new drug (trade name Tofranil) and related compounds became known as tricyclic antidepressants because they all share a three-ring molecular structure.

In hundreds of studies, depressed patients taking tricyclics have improved much more than similar patients taking placebos, although the drugs must be taken for at least ten days before such improvements take hold (APA, 1993). About 60 to 65 percent of patients who

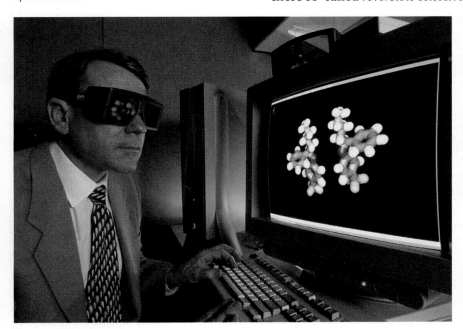

The antidepressant revolution *A clinical scientist studies the molecular structure of Prozac. Sales of antidepressant drugs total $10 billion each year, with Prozac accounting for one-third of this amount.*

take tricyclics are helped by them (Einarson et al., 1999; Hirschfeld, 1999). The case of Derek, whom we met in Chapter 7, is typical:

> One winter Derek signed up for an evening course called "The Use and Abuse of Psychoactive Drugs" because he wanted to be able to provide accurate background information in future newspaper articles on drug use among high school and college students. The course covered psychiatric as well as recreational drugs. When the professor listed the symptoms of affective mood disorders on the blackboard, Derek had a flash of recognition. Perhaps he suffered from depression with melancholia.
>
> Derek then consulted with a psychiatrist, who confirmed his suspicion and prescribed imipramine. A week later, Derek was sleeping until his alarm went off. Two weeks later, at 9:00 A.M. he was writing his column and making difficult decisions about editorials on sensitive topics. He started writing some feature stories on drugs just because he was interested in the subject. Writing was more fun than it had been in years. His images of his own violent death disappeared. His wife found him more responsive. He conversed with her enthusiastically and answered her questions without . . . long delays.
>
> *(Lickey & Gordon, 1991, p. 185)*

If depressed people stop taking tricyclics immediately after obtaining relief, they run as much as a 50 percent risk of relapsing within a year (Montgomery et al., 1993); if, however, they continue taking the drugs at full dose for five months or so after being free of depressive symptoms—a practice called "continuation therapy"—their chances of relapse decrease considerably (Kocsis et al., 1995; Montgomery et al., 1993, 1988). Some studies further suggest that patients who take these antidepressant drugs at full dosage for three or more years after initial improvement—a practice called "maintenance therapy"—may reduce the risk of relapse even more. As a result, many clinicians keep certain patients on antidepressant drugs indefinitely (Franchini et al., 1997; Kupfer, 1995).

Most researchers have concluded that tricyclics reduce depression by acting on neurotransmitter "reuptake" mechanisms (Stahl, 1998; Blier & de Montigny, 1994). We have seen that messages are carried from one neuron across the synaptic space to a receiving neuron by a neurotransmitter, a chemical released from the nerve ending of the sending neuron. However, there is a complication in this process. While the nerve ending is releasing the neurotransmitter, a pumplike mechanism in the same ending is trying to recapture it. The purpose of this mechanism is to prevent the neurotransmitter from remaining in the synapse too long and repeatedly stimulating the receiving neuron. Perhaps this pumplike reuptake mechanism is too successful in some people, reducing norepinephrine or serotonin activity too much. The reduced activity of these neurotransmitters may, in turn, result in clinical depression. Apparently tricyclics block this reuptake process, thus increasing neurotransmitter activity (see Figure 8-3 on the next page).

If tricyclics act immediately to increase norepinephrine and serotonin activity and efficiency, why do the symptoms of depression continue for ten or more days after drug therapy begins? There is now growing evidence that when tricyclics are ingested, they initially *slow down* the activity of the neurons that use norepinephrine and serotonin (Gardner, 1996; Blier & de Montigny, 1994). Granted, the reuptake mechanisms of these

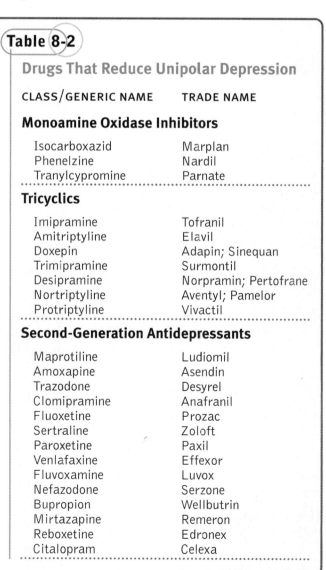

Table 8-2

Drugs That Reduce Unipolar Depression

CLASS/GENERIC NAME	TRADE NAME
Monoamine Oxidase Inhibitors	
Isocarboxazid	Marplan
Phenelzine	Nardil
Tranylcypromine	Parnate
Tricyclics	
Imipramine	Tofranil
Amitriptyline	Elavil
Doxepin	Adapin; Sinequan
Trimipramine	Surmontil
Desipramine	Norpramin; Pertofrane
Nortriptyline	Aventyl; Pamelor
Protriptyline	Vivactil
Second-Generation Antidepressants	
Maprotiline	Ludiomil
Amoxapine	Asendin
Trazodone	Desyrel
Clomipramine	Anafranil
Fluoxetine	Prozac
Sertraline	Zoloft
Paroxetine	Paxil
Venlafaxine	Effexor
Fluvoxamine	Luvox
Nefazodone	Serzone
Bupropion	Wellbutrin
Mirtazapine	Remeron
Reboxetine	Edronex
Citalopram	Celexa

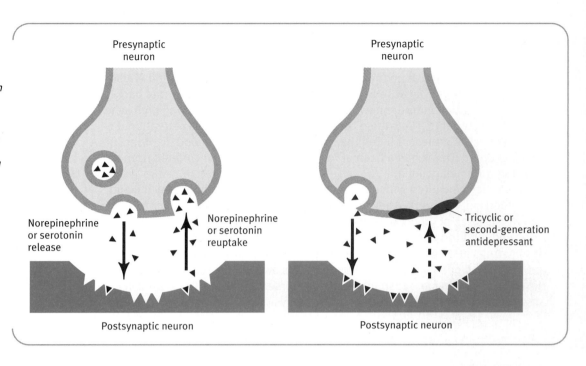

FIGURE 8-3 **Reuptake and antidepressants** (Left) *When a neuron releases norepinephrine or serotonin from its endings, a pumplike reuptake mechanism immediately starts to recapture the neurotransmitters before they are received by the postsynaptic (receptor) neuron. (Right) Tricyclic and most second-generation antidepressant drugs block this reuptake process, enabling more norepinephrine or serotonin to reach the postsynaptic neuron. (Adapted from Snyder, 1986, p. 106.)*

Presynaptic neuron

Presynaptic neuron

Norepinephrine or serotonin release

Norepinephrine or serotonin reuptake

Tricyclic or second-generation antidepressant

Postsynaptic neuron

Postsynaptic neuron

ConsiderThis

Some clinicians argue that antidepressant drugs serve to curb useful behaviors, destroy individuality, and blunt people's concerns about societal ills. Are such concerns justified?

cells are immediately corrected, thus allowing more efficient transmission of the neurotransmitters, but the neurons themselves respond to the change by releasing smaller amounts of the neurotransmitters. After a week or two, the neurons finally adapt to the tricyclic drugs and go back to releasing normal amounts of the neurotransmitters. Now the corrections in the reuptake mechanisms begin to have the desired effect: the neurotransmitters reach the receptor neurons in greater numbers, hence triggering more neural firing and producing a decrease in depression.

Today tricyclics are prescribed more often than MAO inhibitors. They are less dangerous than most MAO inhibitors, and they do not require restrictions of the person's diet (Montgomery et al., 1993). Also, persons taking tricyclics typically show higher rates of improvement than those taking MAO inhibitors (Swonger & Constantine, 1983). On the other hand, some individuals respond better to MAO inhibitors than to either tricyclics or the new antidepressants described next, and they continue to be given these drugs (Paykel, 1995; Thase et al., 1995).

SECOND-GENERATION ANTIDEPRESSANTS A third major group of effective antidepressant drugs, structurally different from the MAO inhibitors and tricyclics, has been developed during the past several years. Most of these *second-generation antidepressants* are labeled **selective serotonin reuptake inhibitors (SSRIs)**, because they increase serotonin activity specifically, without affecting norepinephrine or other neurotransmitters. The SSRIs include *fluoxetine* (trade name Prozac) and *sertraline* (Zoloft) (see Box 8-3). Newly developed *selective norepinephrine reuptake inhibitors* (which increase norepinephrine activity only) and *serotonin-norepinephrine reuptake inhibitors* (which increase both serotonin and norepinephrine activity) are also now available (Ferrier, 1999; Montgomery, 1999).

In effectiveness the second-generation antidepressant drugs are about on a par with the tricyclics (Hirschfeld, 1999; Einarson et al., 1999), yet their sales have skyrocketed. Prozac alone produces nearly $3 billion in sales each year. Clinicians often prefer the new antidepressants because it is harder to overdose on them than on tricyclics. In addition, they do not typically produce some of the unpleasant effects of the tricyclics, such as dry mouth and constipation (Leonard, 1997). At the same time, the new antidepressants can result in undesired effects of their own. Some people, for example, experience a reduction in their sex drive (Segraves, 1998).

SELECTIVE SEROTONIN REUPTAKE INHIBITORS (SSRIs) A group of second-generation antidepressant drugs that increase serotonin activity specifically, without affecting other neurotransmitters.

Prozac, Dog's Best Friend?

The popularity of Prozac and related antidepressant drugs skyrocketed in the 1990s. Many clinicians believe that Prozac is being prescribed much too often. They worry in particular about its use with children, elderly people, and people whose psychological problems are relatively minor. Now they have been given something else to worry about: Prozac is also being prescribed for *dogs* with mood or behavioral problems (Millward, 1996).

In a 1996 article for *Dogs Today* magazine, Dr. Peter Neville, an expert on animal behavior, described dogs given Prozac. Jannie, a pointer with a shadow-chasing problem, was prescribed the drug for an obsessive-compulsive disorder. George, a Staffordshire bull terrier, was given it to combat "sustained rage assaults" on other dogs. And Henry, an English bull terrier, kept pinning his owner every time she tried to leave home (Millward, 1996).

ConsiderThis

⦿ Is there something odd or wrong about human beings serving as a testing ground for a medication that is later given to animals? • What other human treatments (psychological or medical) are applied to pets? • Is the prescription of Prozac for troubled pets inappropriate?

How Do the Treatments for Unipolar Depression Compare?

For most kinds of psychological disorders, no more than one or two treatments or combinations of treatments, if any, emerge as highly successful. Unipolar depression seems to be an exception. One of the most treatable of all abnormal patterns, it may respond to any of several approaches. During the past decade researchers have conducted a number of treatment outcome studies, revealing some important trends:

1. Cognitive, interpersonal, and biological therapies are each highly effective treatments for unipolar depression, from mild to severe (Cameron et al., 1999; DeRubeis & Crits-Christoph, 1998). In most head-to-head comparisons, they seem to be equally effective at reducing depressive symptoms; however, there are indications that some populations of depressed patients respond better to one therapy than to another (Jarrett et al., 1999; Stewart et al., 1993).

   One of the most ambitious studies of depression therapy was a six-year, $10 million investigation sponsored by the National Institute of Mental Health (Elkin, 1994; Elkin et al., 1989, 1985). Experimenters separated 239 moderately and severely depressed people into four treatment groups. One group was treated with 16 weeks of Beck's cognitive therapy, another with 16 weeks of interpersonal psychotherapy, and a third group with the antidepressant drug imipramine. The fourth group received a placebo. A total of 28 therapists conducted these treatments.

   Using a depression assessment instrument called the Hamilton Rating Scale for Depression, the investigators found that each of the three therapies almost completely eliminated depressive symptoms in 50 to

SAME INGREDIENTS, DIFFERENT NAME

While developing and gaining approval for a drug, a pharmaceutical company files for an exclusive patent on the drug. The patent runs for 20 years, with certain extensions possible. Then other companies may also manufacture the drug, as a "generic." More than 8,000 generic drugs are currently approved for sale in the United States, costing 30 to 80 percent less than the name brands (Johnsen, 1994). The patent on fluoxetine (Prozac) expires in 2003.

"*It's amazing. Since I've been taking Prozac the whole damn kingdom is happier.*"

THE INSURANCE FACTOR

Insurance coverage helps dictate the type of treatment people receive for depression. Privately insured patients are more likely than Medicaid patients to receive psychotherapy. Moreover, among those receiving medications, the privately insured are more likely to receive selective serotonin reuptake inhibitors than the cheaper tricyclics (Melf, Croghan, & Hanna, 1999).

60 percent of the subjects who completed treatment, whereas only 29 percent of those who received the placebo showed such improvement—a trend that also held, although somewhat less powerfully, when other assessment measures were used. These findings are consistent with those of most other comparative outcome studies (Stravynski & Greenberg, 1992; Frank et al., 1991, 1990).

The study found that drug therapy reduced depressive symptoms more quickly than the cognitive and interpersonal therapies did, but these psychotherapies had matched the drugs in effectiveness by the final four weeks of treatment. In addition, some recent studies suggest that cognitive therapy may be more effective than drug therapy at preventing recurrences of depression except when drug therapy is continued for an extended period of time (Segal et al., 1999; Beck, 1997; Haaga & Beck, 1992). Despite the comparable or even superior showing of cognitive therapy, the 1980s and 1990s witnessed a significant increase in the number of physicians prescribing antidepressants. The number of office visits in which an antidepressant was prescribed grew from 2.5 million in 1980 to 4.7 million in 1987 (Olfson & Klerman, 1993). That trend continued throughout the 1990s with the emergence of second-generation antidepressants.

2. Although the cognitive and interpersonal therapies may lower the likelihood of relapse, they are hardly relapse-proof. Some studies suggest that as many as 30 percent of the depressed patients who respond to these approaches may, in fact, relapse within a few years after the completion of treatment (Cameron et al., 1999; Shea et al., 1992). In an effort to head off relapse, some of today's cognitive and interpersonal therapists continue to offer treatment, perhaps on a less frequent basis, after the depression lifts—an approach similar to the "continuation" or "maintenance" approaches used with antidepressant drugs (Clarke et al., 1999; Spanier et al., 1999). Early indications are that treatment extensions of this kind do in fact reduce the rate of relapse among successfully treated patients. In fact, some research now suggests that persons who have recovered from depression are less likely to relapse if they receive continuation or maintenance therapy in either drug or psychotherapy form, irrespective of which kind of therapy they originally received (Reynolds et al., 1999).

Is laughter the best medicine? *Members of this laughter club in Bombay, India, practice therapeutic laughing, or Hasyayog. The club represents a new kind of group therapy, founded on the belief that laughing at least 15 minutes each day will drive away depression, stress, and other ills. Laughter clubs, currently 400 in number, have recently spread to the United States.*

3. When persons with depression experience significant discord in their marriages, couple therapy tends to be as helpful as cognitive, interpersonal, or drug therapy.

4. In head-to-head comparisons, depressed people who receive strictly behavioral therapy have shown less improvement than those who receive cognitive, interpersonal, or biological therapy. Behavioral therapy has, however, proved more effective than placebo treatments or no attention at all (Emmelkamp, 1994; Shaw, 1977, 1976). Also, as we have seen, behavioral therapy is of less help to people who are severely depressed than to those with mild or moderate depression.

5. Most studies suggest that psychodynamic therapies are less effective than these other therapies in treating all levels of unipolar depression (Svartberg & Stiles, 1991; McLean & Hakstian, 1979). Many psychodynamic clinicians argue, however, that this system of therapy simply does not lend itself to empirical research, and its effectiveness should be judged by therapists' reports of individual recovery and progress (Bemporad, 1992).

6. Studies have found that a combination of psychotherapy (usually cognitive or interpersonal) and drug therapy are modestly more helpful to depressed people than either treatment alone (Frank et al., 2000; Miller et al., 1999).

7. Among the biological treatments, antidepressant drugs and ECT appear to be equally effective for reducing depression, although ECT seems to act more quickly (Fogel, 1986). Half of all patients treated by either intervention, however, relapse within a year unless the initial treatment is followed up by continuing drug treatment or by psychotherapy (Feinberg, 1999; Fink, 1992; Prien, 1992).

When clinicians today choose a biological treatment for mild to severe unipolar depression, they generally prescribe one of the antidepressant medications. Alternatively, some may suggest one of the popular herbal supplements now in the marketplace (see Box 8-4 on the next page). They are not likely to refer patients for ECT unless the depression is severe and has been unresponsive to all other forms of treatment (Fink, 1992, 1988). ECT appears to be helpful for 50 to 80 percent of the severely depressed patients who do not respond to antidepressant drugs (APA, 1993; Avery & Lubrano, 1979). If depressed persons seem to be a high suicide risk, clinicians sometimes refer them for ECT treatment more readily (Prudic & Sackeim, 1999; Fink, 1992). Although ECT clearly has a beneficial effect on suicidal behavior in the short run, studies have not clearly indicated that it has a long-term effect on suicide rates (Prudic & Sackeim, 1999).

Stretching one's emotions *Exercise apparently contributes to both physical and emotional health. Research shows that regular exercise can help prevent or reduce feelings of depression and other psychological symptoms.*

NEW KID ON THE BLOCK

In 1999, *s-adenosylmethionine*, or *SAMe* (pronounced "Sammy"), joined conventional antidepressant drugs and St. John's wort in the United States marketplace as a hugely popular biological treatment for unipolar depression. Sold as an over-the-counter dietary supplement, SAMe is a common molecule produced by all living cells. Although sold in Italy and 13 other countries for more than 20 years, SAMe is just now beginning to receive broad and systematic study.

Treatments for Bipolar Disorders

Until the past few decades, people with bipolar disorders were destined to spend their lives on an emotional roller coaster. Psychotherapists reported almost no success (Lickey & Gordon, 1991), and antidepressant drugs were of limited help (Prien et al., 1974). In fact, the drugs sometimes triggered a manic episode (Barak, Kimhi, & Weizman, 2000; Altshuler et al., 1995; Dilsaver & Swann, 1995). ECT, too, only occasionally relieved either the depressive or the manic episodes of bipolar disorders (Jefferson & Greist, 1994).

BOX 8-4

St. John's Wort: A Natural Answer to Depression?

It's natural. It's inexpensive. It's available without prescription. Many people say it rescued them from clinical depression. And it has been endorsed in television shows, magazines, and newspapers around the world. *Hypericum perforatum,* popularly known as *St. John's wort* ("wort" is an archaic word for "plant"), is one of today's hottest-selling products.

St. John's wort is a low, wild-growing shrub with yellow flowers that has been used for 2,400 years in folk and herbal remedies (Bloomfield & McWilliams, 1996). Research into the use of its extracts as a treatment for depression took off a decade ago, particularly in Germany. Since then, a growing number of studies have suggested that these extracts may be of help to 60 percent of people with mild to moderate depression, while producing few of the undesired effects of conventional antidepressant drugs (Schrader, 2000; Volz & Laux, 2000). The publicity generated by this research has led to a dramatic increase in sales. In Germany the herb already outsells Prozac by as much as 24 to 1

(Bloomfield & McWilliams, 1996). In the United States, where plants cannot be patented, pharmaceutical companies have little incentive to carry out expensive research on the herb, but health food stores offer it as a dietary supplement, and it has become a best-seller for them. More than one million Americans spent an estimated $400 million on the herb last year alone (Mazo, 1999).

Many researchers caution, however, that too little is known about St. John's wort to regard it as safe and effective. What are the effects and possible dangers of long-term use? What is the herb's impact on severe depression? What is its proper dosage? How might it mix with antidepressant drugs? And how can consumers know the strength and possible effects of the particular extract that they buy? These and other important questions are currently being addressed in research. A very interested public awaits the answers.

ConsiderThis

● If antidepressant drugs are already highly effective, why are people so intent on finding alternative biological treatments for depression? ● How can consumers know whether a popular new approach has genuine merit or is a passing fad?

Lithium Therapy

The use of **lithium** has so dramatically changed this gloomy picture that many people view the silvery-white element—found in various simple mineral salts throughout the natural world—as a true miracle drug. Anna started taking lithium in the 1960s, when lithium was still considered an experimental drug. Her experience shows the extraordinary impact it can have.

> Anna was a 21-year-old college student. Before she became ill, Anna was sedate and polite, perhaps even a bit prim. During the fall of her sophomore year at college, she had an episode of mild depression that began when she received a C on a history paper she had worked quite hard on. The same day she received a sanctimonious letter from her father reminding her of the financial hardships he was undergoing to send her to college. He warned her to stick to her books and not to play around with men. Anna became discouraged. She doubted that she deserved her parents' sacrifice. Anna's depression did not seem unusual to her roommate, to her other friends, or even to Anna herself. It seemed a natural reaction to her father's unreasonable letter and her fear that she could not live up to the standards he set. In retrospect, this mild depression was the first episode of her bipolar illness.
>
> Several months later, Anna became restless, angry, and obnoxious. She talked continuously and rapidly, jumping from one idea to another. Her speech was

LITHIUM A metallic element that occurs in nature as a mineral salt and is an effective treatment for bipolar disorders.

filled with rhymes, puns, and sexual innuendoes. During Christmas vacation, she made frequent and unwelcome sexual overtures to her brother's friend in the presence of her entire family. When Anna's mother asked her to behave more politely, Anna began to cry and then slapped her mother across the mouth. Anna did not sleep that night. She sobbed. Between sobs she screamed that no one understood her problems, and no one would even try. The next day, Anna's family took her to the hospital. . . . When she was discharged two weeks later, she was less angry and no longer assaultive. But she was not well and did not go back to school. Her thought and speech were still hypomanic. She had an exaggerated idea of her attractiveness and expected men to fall for her at the first smile. She was irritated when they ignored her attentions. Depressive symptoms were still mixed with the manic ones. She often cried when her bids for attention were not successful or when her parents criticized her dress or behavior.

Anna returned to school the following fall but suffered another depressive episode, followed by another attack of mania within seven months. She had to withdraw from school and enter the hospital. This time . . . the psychiatrists diagnosed her illness as bipolar disorder [and] began treatment with . . . lithium. . . . After seventeen days on lithium, Anna's behavior was quite normal. She was attractively and modestly dressed for her psychiatric interviews. Earlier, she had been sloppily seductive; hair in disarray, half-open blouse, smeared lipstick, bright pink rouge on her cheeks, and bright green make-up on her eyelids. With the help of lithium, she gained some ability to tolerate frustration. During the first week of her hospital stay, she had screamed at a nurse who would not permit her to read late into the night in violation of the ward's 11:00 P.M. "lights out" policy. On lithium, Anna was still annoyed by this "juvenile" rule, but she controlled her anger. She gained some insight into her illness, recognizing that her manic behavior was destructive to herself and others. She also recognized the depression that was often mixed with the mania. . . . She admitted, "Actually, when I'm high, I'm really feeling low. I need to exaggerate in order to feel more important."

Because Anna was on a research ward, the effectiveness of lithium had to be verified by removal of the drug. When she had been off lithium for four to five days, Anna began to show symptoms of both mania and depression. She threatened her psychiatrist, and as before, the threats were grandiose with sexual overtones. In a slinky voice, she warned, "I have ways to put the director of this hospital in my debt. He crawled for me before and he'll do it again. When I snap my fingers, he'll come down to this ward and squash you under his foot." Soon afterward, she threatened suicide. She later explained, "I felt so low last night that if someone had given me a knife or gun, POW." By the ninth day off lithium, Anna's speech was almost incomprehensible: "It's sad to be so putty, pretty, so much like water dripping from a faucet. . . ." Lithium therapy was reinstituted, and within about sixteen days, Anna again recovered and was discharged on lithium.

(Lickey & Gordon, 1991, pp. 236–239)

Determining the correct lithium dosage for a given patient is a delicate process, requiring regular analyses of blood and urine samples and other laboratory tests (Schou, 1997). Too low a dose will have little or no effect on the bipolar mood swings, but too high a dose can result in lithium *intoxication* (literally, poisoning), which can cause nausea, vomiting, sluggishness, tremors, dizziness, slurred speech, sodium imbalance, seizures, kidney dysfunction, and even death (Moncrieff, 1997). With the correct dose, however, lithium often produces a noticeable change in mood within five to fourteen days, as it did for Anna. Some patients respond better to other drugs, such as the antiseizure drugs *carbamazepine* (Tegretol) or *valproate* (Depakote), or to a combination of such drugs (Lennkh & Simhandl, 2000; Nolen, 1999; Freeman & Stoll, 1998).

"Depression is terrifying, and elation, its nonidentical twin sister, is even more terrifying—attractive as she may be for a moment."

Film director Joshua Logan, describing his bipolar disorder, 1973

TAKING THE LEAD

In 1998 valproate (Depakote) actually surpassed lithium to become the drug most prescribed for treating mania in bipolar disorders (UTMB, 1999).

"More lithium."

ORIGINS OF LITHIUM TREATMENT The discovery that lithium effectively reduces bipolar symptoms was, like so many other medical discoveries, quite accidental. In 1949 an Australian psychiatrist, John Cade, hypothesized that manic behavior is caused by a toxic level of *uric acid* in the body. He set out to test this theory by injecting guinea pigs with uric acid, but first he combined it with lithium to increase its solubility.

To Cade's surprise, the guinea pigs became not manic but quite lethargic after their injections. Cade suspected that the lithium had produced this effect. When he later administered lithium to ten human beings who had mania, he discovered that it calmed and normalized their mood. Although many countries began using lithium for bipolar disorders soon after, it was not until 1970 that the U.S. Food and Drug Administration approved it.

EFFECTIVENESS OF LITHIUM All manner of research has attested to lithium's effectiveness in treating manic episodes. More than 60 percent of patients with mania improve on this medication. In addition, most of them experience fewer new episodes as long as they continue taking lithium (Viguera et al., 2000; Maj et al., 1998). One study found that the risk of relapse is twenty-eight times greater if patients stop taking lithium (Suppes et al., 1991). These findings suggest that lithium may also be a *prophylactic drug,* one that actually helps prevent symptoms from developing (Lenox et al., 1998; Schou, 1997). Accordingly, today's clinicians usually continue patients on some level of lithium even after their manic episodes subside (Nolen, 1999; Jefferson & Greist, 1994).

Lithium also helps those with bipolar disorder overcome their depressive episodes, though to a lesser degree than it helps with their manic episodes (Hlastala et al., 1997). In addition, continued doses of lithium apparently reduce

GOING IT ALONE

Within one year after lithium is stopped, two-thirds of successfully treated bipolar patients develop a new depressive or manic episode. The suicide rate of these individuals also increases twentyfold (Baldessarini et al., 1999).

the risk of future depressive episodes, just as they seem to prevent the return of manic episodes (Baldessarini, Tondo, & Hennen, 1999; Simpson & Jamison, 1999).

These findings have led researchers to wonder whether lithium might also be helpful in cases of unipolar depression. Here the results have been mixed. A few studies suggest that lithium does help some patients with unipolar depression (Lenox et al., 1998; Jefferson & Greist, 1994) and occasionally prevents recurrences of that pattern (Coppen, 1994; Abou-Saleh, 1992). Of course, it is possible that the "unipolar" patients helped by lithium actually have a bipolar disorder whose manic aspect has yet to appear.

In the same vein, lithium often seems to enhance the effectiveness of antidepressant drugs prescribed for unipolar depression (Fava, 2000; Shelton, 1999; Katona, 1995). In one study, up to two-thirds of "tricyclic nonrespondent" patients were converted to "responders" when lithium was added to their antidepressant drug therapy (Joffe et al., 1993).

LITHIUM'S MODE OF OPERATION Researchers do not fully understand how lithium operates. They suspect that it changes synaptic activity in neurons, but in a different way than antidepressant drugs (Ghaemi, Boiman, & Goodwin, 1999). The firing of a neuron actually consists of several phases that ensue at lightning speed. When the neurotransmitter binds to a receptor on the receiving neuron, a series of changes occur within the receiving neuron to set the stage for firing. The substances in the neuron that carry out those changes are often called **second messengers** because they relay the original message from the receptor site to the firing mechanism of the neuron. Whereas antidepressant drugs affect a neuron's initial reception of neurotransmitters, lithium appears to affect a neuron's second messengers.

Different second-messenger systems are at work in different neurons. In one of the most important systems, chemicals called *phosphoinositides* (consisting of sugars and lipids) are produced once neurotransmitters are received. Lithium apparently affects this particular messenger system (Manji et al., 1999; Belmaker et al., 1995). Lithium may in fact affect the activity of any neuron that uses this second-messenger system, and in so doing may correct the neural abnormalities that lead to bipolar disorders.

Alternatively, it may be that lithium corrects bipolar functioning by directly changing sodium and potassium ion activity in neurons (Swonger & Constantine, 1983). In Chapter 7 we noted the theory that bipolar disorders are triggered by unstable alignments of ions along the membranes of certain neurons in the brain. If this instability is the key to bipolar problems, lithium would be expected

SECOND MESSENGERS Chemical changes within a neuron just after the neuron receives a neurotransmitter message and just before it responds.

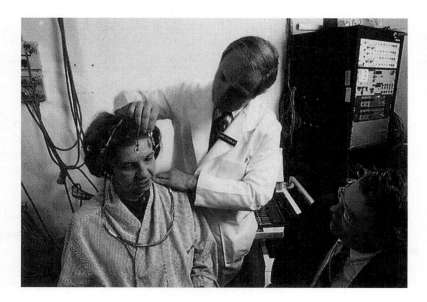

Sleep and mood *The sleep cycle is often disturbed in people with depression, either unipolar or bipolar (Thase et al., 1997, 1995). Electroencephalogram recordings taken of patients while they sleep can help clinicians assess and treat mood disorders more effectively.*

BOX 8-5

Abnormality and Creativity: A Delicate Balance

Up to a point, states of depression, mania, anxiety, and even confusion can be valuable and functional. This may be particularly true in the arts. The ancient Greeks believed that various forms of "divine madness" inspired creative acts, from poetry to performance (Ludwig, 1995). In the eighteenth century, romantic notions of the "mad genius" led asylum superintendents to encourage their patients to write; the patients' creations were published in asylum literary journals (Gamwell & Tomes, 1995).

Even today many people expect "creative geniuses" to be psychologically disturbed. A popular image of the artist includes a glass of liquor, a cigarette, and a tormented expression. Classic examples include the writer William Faulkner, who suffered from alcoholism and re-

ceived electroconvulsive therapy for depression; the poet Sylvia Plath, who experienced depression most of her life and eventually committed suicide; and the dancer Vaslav Nijinsky, who suffered from schizophrenia and spent many years in institutions. In fact, a number of studies indicate that artists and writers are somewhat more likely than others to suffer from mental disorders, particularly mood disorders; on average, such individuals also experience psychological difficulties for longer periods of time (Jamison, 1995; Ludwig, 1995, 1994).

Why might creative people be prone to psychological disorders? Some may be predisposed to such disorders long before they begin their artistic careers; the careers may simply bring attention to their emotional struggles (Ludwig, 1995). Indeed, creative people often have a

Personal expertise *Kay Redfield Jamison, one of the world's most productive researchers on bipolar disorders and their relationship to creativity, recently revealed in an autobiography,* An Unquiet Mind, *that she herself has suffered from the disorder throughout her adult life.*

family history of psychological problems. A number also have experienced intense psychological trauma during childhood, including physical and sexual abuse. Vir-

to have some kind of effect on the ion activity. Several studies in fact suggest that lithium ions often substitute, although imperfectly, for sodium ions (Baer et al., 1971), and other research suggests that lithium changes the transport mechanisms that move ions back and forth across the neural membrane (Soares et al., 1999; Lenox et al., 1998).

Adjunctive Psychotherapy

Psychotherapy alone is rarely helpful for persons with bipolar disorders (Klerman et al., 1994). At the same time, clinicians have learned that lithium therapy alone is not always sufficient either. Thirty percent or more of patients with these disorders may not respond to lithium or a related drug, may not receive the proper dose, or may relapse while taking it (Kulhara et al., 1999; Solomon et al., 1995). In addition, a number of patients stop taking lithium because they are bothered by the drug's unwanted effects, feel too well to recognize the need for it, miss the euphoria felt during manic episodes, or worry about becoming less productive or creative when they take the drug (Goodwin & Jamison, 1990; Wulsin et al., 1988) (see Box 8-5).

In view of these problems, many clinicians now use individual, group, or family therapy as an *adjunct* to lithium treatment (George, Friedman, & Miklowitz, 2000; Scott, 1995). Most often, therapists use these formats to stress the need for proper management of medications (Goodwin & Jamison, 1990), to improve social skills and relationships that may be affected by bipolar episodes (Frank et al., 1999; Klerman & Weissman, 1992), to educate patients and families about bipolar disorders (Bland & Harrison, 2000; Tohen & Grundy, 1999), and to help patients solve the special family, school, and occupational problems caused by their disorder (Hammen et al., 2000; Honig et al., 1995).

Few controlled studies have tested the effectiveness of psychotherapy as an adjunct to drug therapy for severe bipolar disorders, but a growing number of clinical reports suggest that it helps reduce hospitalization, improves social func-

ConsiderThis

● What issues of lifestyle, family and social relationships, and other areas of functioning might need to be addressed in adjunctive psychotherapy for persons with a bipolar disorder?

ginia Woolf, for example, endured sexual abuse as a child.

Another reason for the creativity link may be that creative endeavors create emotional turmoil that is overwhelming, even for those who would not otherwise be prone to psychological problems. Truman Capote said that writing his famous book *In Cold Blood* "killed" him psychologically. Before writing this account of a brutal murder, he considered himself "a stable person. . . . Afterward something happened to me" (Ludwig, 1995).

Yet a third explanation for the link between creativity and psychological disorders is that the creative professions offer a welcome climate for those with psychological disturbances. In the worlds of poetry, painting, and acting, for example, emotional expression and personal turmoil are valued as sources of inspiration and success (Ludwig, 1995). Additionally, in artistic milieus less stigma is attached to extreme feelings and unconventional behavior (Ludwig, 1995).

Much remains to be learned about the relationship between emotional turmoil and creativity, but work in this area has already clarified two important points. First, psychological disturbance is hardly a requirement for creativity. Many "creative geniuses" are, in fact, psychologically stable and happy throughout their entire lives. Second, *mild* psychological disturbances correlate with creative achievement much more strongly than severe disturbances do. For example, mild patterns of mania, or *hypomania,* often produce sharpened and creative thinking and greater productivity (Jamison, 1995). Extreme disturbance, however, such as severe mania, depression, or anxiety, or patterns of alcoholism, tends to reduce the quality and quantity of creative work and often ruins careers (Ludwig, 1995). The nineteenth-century composer Robert Schumann produced twenty-seven works during one hypomanic year but next to nothing during years when he was severely depressed and suicidal (Jamison, 1995).

Some artists worry that if their psychological suffering stops, their creativity will disappear as well. In fact, however, research suggests that successful treatment for severe psychological disorders can actually improve the creative process (Jamison, 1995; Ludwig, 1995; Whybrow, 1994). Romantic notions aside, severe mental dysfunctioning has little redeeming value, in the arts or anywhere else.

tioning, and increases clients' ability to obtain and hold a job (Frank et al., 1999; Scott, 1995; Solomon et al., 1995; Werder, 1995). Psychotherapy plays a more central role in the treatment of *cyclothymic disorder,* the mild bipolar pattern that was described in Chapter 7. In fact, patients with this problem typically receive psychotherapy, alone or in combination with lithium. As yet, however, few studies have investigated whether such approaches help people with this milder pattern (Klerman et al., 1994).

CROSSROADS:
With Success Come New Questions

Mood disorders are among the most treatable of all psychological disorders. The choice of treatment for bipolar disorders is narrow and simple: drug therapy, perhaps accompanied by psychotherapy, is the single most successful approach. The picture for unipolar depression is more varied and complex, although no less promising. Cognitive therapy, interpersonal psychotherapy, and antidepressant drugs are all helpful in cases of any severity; couple therapy is helpful in select cases; behavioral therapy helps in mild to moderate cases; and ECT is useful and effective in severe cases.

Why should several very different approaches be highly effective in the treatment of unipolar depression? Two explanations have been proposed. First, if many factors contribute to unipolar depression, it is plausible that the removal of any one of them could improve all areas of functioning. In fact, studies have sometimes found that when one kind of therapy is effective, clients tend to function better in all spheres. When certain antidepressant drugs are effective, for instance, clients make the same improvements in their thinking and social functioning that cognitive and interpersonal therapy would bring about (Bosc, 2000; Weissman, 2000).

DRUGS FOR EVERYONE?

Can antidepressants also improve the spirits of nondepressed persons? Yes and no, it appears. When given to volunteers who had no clinical symptoms, antidepressants seemed to help reduce negative emotions such as hostility and fear, but failed to increase positive feelings such as happiness and excitement (Knutson et al., 1998).

A second explanation suggests that there are various kinds of unipolar depression, each of which responds to a different kind of therapy. There is evidence that interpersonal psychotherapy is more helpful in depressions brought on by social problems than in depressions that seem to occur spontaneously (Thase et al., 1997; Prusoff et al., 1980). Similarly, antidepressant medications seem more helpful than other treatments in cases marked by appetite and sleep problems, sudden onset, and a family history of depression (McNeal & Cimbolic, 1986; Schatzberg et al., 1982).

Whatever the ultimate explanation, the treatment picture is very promising both for people with unipolar depression and for those with bipolar disorders. The odds are that one or a combination of the therapies now in use will relieve their symptoms. Yet the sobering fact remains that as many as 40 percent of people with a mood disorder do not improve under treatment, and must suffer their mania or depression until it has run its course.

SUMMARY AND REVIEW

- **Treatments for mood disorders** More than 60 percent of people with mood disorders can be helped by treatment. *p. 224*

- **Treatments for unipolar depression** Various treatments have been used with unipolar depression. Psychodynamic therapists try to help depressed persons become aware of and work through their real or imagined losses and their excessive dependence on others. Behavioral therapists reintroduce clients to events and activities that they once found pleasurable, reinforce nondepressive behaviors, and teach interpersonal skills. Cognitive therapists help depressed persons identify and change their dysfunctional cognitions. *pp. 224–230*

  Sociocultural theorists trace unipolar depression to such factors as social structure and social roles. One sociocultural approach, interpersonal psychotherapy, is based on the premise that depression stems from social problems, and so therapists try to help clients develop insight into their interpersonal problems, change them and the conditions that are causing them, and learn skills to protect themselves in the future. Another sociocultural approach, couple therapy, may be used when depressed people are in a dysfunctional relationship. *pp. 231–232*

  Most biological treatments consist of antidepressant drugs, but electroconvulsive therapy is still used to treat some severe cases of depression. Electroconvulsive therapy (ECT) remains a controversial procedure, although it is a fast-acting intervention that is particularly effective when depression is severe, unresponsive to other kinds of treatment, or characterized by delusions. Antidepressant drugs include three classes: MAO inhibitors, tricyclics, and second-generation antidepressants. MAO inhibitors block the degradation of norepinephrine, allowing the levels of this neurotransmitter to build up and relieve depressive symptoms. People taking MAO inhibitors must be careful to avoid eating foods with tyramine. Tricyclics improve depression by blocking neurotransmitter reuptake mechanisms, thereby increasing the activity of norepinephrine and serotonin. The second-generation antidepressants include selective serotonin reuptake inhibitors, or SSRIs, drugs that selectively increase the activity of serotonin. These drugs are as effective as tricyclics and have fewer undesired effects. *pp. 232–239*

- **Comparing treatments for unipolar depression** The cognitive, interpersonal, and biological therapies appear to be the most successful for mild to severe depression. Couple therapy is helpful when the individual's depression is accompanied by significant marital discord. Behavioral therapy is helpful in mild to moderate cases. And ECT is effective in severe cases. Combinations of psychotherapy and drug therapy tend to be modestly more helpful than any one approach on its own. *pp. 239–241*

EXERCISE REALLY HELPS

Research is now catching up to a piece of common wisdom: exercise helps relieve depression. Numerous studies clarify that various kinds of regular exercise often alleviate mild to moderate depression and sometimes play a useful role in more severe episodes (Tkachuk & Martin, 1999).

■ **Treatments for bipolar disorders** Lithium (or, alternatively, carbamazepine or valproate) has proved to be very effective in alleviating and preventing both the manic and the depressive episodes of bipolar disorders. It is helpful in 60 percent or more of cases. This drug may reduce bipolar symptoms by affecting the activity of second-messenger systems in certain neurons throughout the brain. Alternatively, lithium may directly change the activity of sodium and other ions in neurons, for example, by altering the transportation of the ions across neural membranes.

   In recent years clinicians have learned that patients may fare better when lithium is supplemented by adjunctive psychotherapy. The issues most often addressed by psychotherapists are medication management, social skills and relationships, patient education, and solving the family, school, and occupational problems caused by bipolar episodes. *pp. 241–247*

CYBER STUDY

▲ *How do medications alleviate mood disorders?* ▲ *Observe psychological and biological treatments working together.* ▲ *How do clinicians determine the optimal medication (and dosage) for unipolar depression?* ▲ *How has ECT changed over the years?*

SEARCH THE *ABNORMAL PSYCHOLOGY* CD-ROM FOR

▲ Chapter 8 video cases and discussions
   "Doug"—Mood Disorders: Medication and Talk Therapy
   Early Electroconvulsive Therapy
   "Meredith"—Mood Disorders: Medication and Talk Therapy

▲ Chapter 8 practice test and feedback

▲ Additional video cases and discussions
   Mood Disorders: Hereditary Factors
   "Derrick"—Hamilton Depression Scale

LOG ON TO THE COMER WEB PAGE

[www.worthpublishers.com/comerabnormalpsychology4e] **FOR**

▲ Suggested Web links, research exercises, FAQ page, additional Chapter 8 practice test questions

Suicide

I had done all I could and I was still sinking. I sat many hours seeking answers, and all there was was a silent wind. The answer was in my head. It was all clear now: Die. . . .

The next day a friend offered to sell me a gun, a .357 magnum pistol. I bought it. My first thought was: What a mess this is going to make. That day I began to say goodbye to people: not actually saying it but expressing it silently.

Friends were around, but I didn't let them see what was wrong with me. I could not let them know lest they prevent it. My mind became locked on my target. My thoughts were: Soon it will all be over. I would obtain the peace I had so long sought. The will to survive and succeed had been crushed and defeated. I was like a general on a battlefield being encroached on by my enemy and its hordes: fear, hate, self-depreciation, desolation. I felt I had to have the upper hand, to control my environment, so I sought to die rather than surrender. . . .

I was only aware of myself and my plight. Death swallowed me long before I pulled the trigger. The world through my eyes seemed to die with me. It was like I was to push the final button to end this world. I committed myself to the arms of death. There comes a time when all things cease to shine, when the rays of hope are lost.

I placed the gun to my head. Then, I remember a tremendous explosion of lights like fireworks. Thus did the pain become glorious, an army rallied to the side of death to help destroy my life, which I could feel leaving my body with each rushing surge of blood. I was engulfed in total darkness.

(Shneidman, 1987, p. 56)

Salmon spawn and then die, after an exhausting upstream journey to their breeding ground. But only humans knowingly take their own lives. The actions of salmon and lemmings are instinctual responses that may even help their species survive in the long run. Only in the human act of suicide do beings act for the specific purpose of putting an end to their lives.

Suicide has been recorded throughout history. The Old Testament described King Saul's suicide: "There Saul took a sword and fell on it." The ancient Chinese, Greeks, and Romans also provided examples. In more recent times, suicides by such celebrated individuals as the writer Ernest Hemingway, the actress Marilyn Monroe, and the rock star Kurt Cobain have both shocked and fascinated the public (see Box 9-1 on page 253). Even more disturbing are mass suicides such as those of the Heaven's Gate cult in 1997.

Before you finish reading this page, someone in the United States will try to kill himself. At least 60 Americans will have taken their own lives by this time tomorrow. . . . Many of those who attempted will try again, a number with lethal success.

(Shneidman & Mandelkorn, 1983)

Table 9-1

Most Common Causes of Death in the United States

RANK	CAUSE	DEATHS PER YEAR	PERCENTAGE OF TOTAL DEATHS
1	Heart disease	733,834	31.6%
2	Cancer	544,278	23.4
3	Stroke	160,431	6.9
4	Lung diseases	106,146	4.6
5	Accidents	93,874	4.0
6	Pneumonia and influenza	82,579	3.6
7	Diabetes	61,559	2.7
8	AIDS	32,655	1.4
9	Suicide	30,862	1.3
10	Liver disease	25,135	1.1

Source: Ash, 1999; U.S. National Center for Health Statistics.

Fatal attraction *A tiny male redback spider prepares to be eaten by his large female partner during copulation, and even aids in his own death. While placing his intromittent organ into his partner, he also spins around and dangles his enticing abdomen in front of her mouth. The male may be shortsighted, but he is not intending to die. In fact, by keeping his partner busy eating him, he can deposit a maximum amount of sperm, thus increasing the chances of reproduction and the birth of an offspring with similar tendencies (Andrade, 1996).*

Today suicide ranks among the top ten causes of death in the world. It has been estimated that as many as 700,000 people may die by it each year, 31,000 in the United States alone (Kaplan, 1999; Phillips, Liu, & Zhang, 1999; NCIPC, 1999) (see Table 9-1). Millions of other people throughout the world—600,000 in the United States—make unsuccessful attempts to kill themselves; such attempts are called **parasuicides** (Crosby, Cheltenham, & Sacks, 1999; McIntosh, 1991). Actually, it is difficult to obtain accurate figures on suicide, and many investigators believe that estimates are often low. For one thing, suicide can be difficult to distinguish from unintentional drug overdoses, automobile crashes, drownings, and other accidents (Ohberg, Penttila, & Lonnqvist, 1997). Many apparent "accidents" were probably intentional. For another, suicide is frowned on in our society, causing relatives and friends to refuse to acknowledge that loved ones have taken their own lives.

Suicide is not classified as a mental disorder by DSM-IV, but clinicians are aware of the high frequency with which psychological dysfunctioning—a breakdown of coping skills, emotional turmoil, a distorted view of life—plays a role in this act. Although suicide is frequently linked to depression, at least half of all suicides result from other mental disorders, such as schizophrenia or alcohol dependence, or involve no clear psychological disorder at all (Murphy, 1998).

Many people are misinformed about the symptoms and causes of suicide. A generation ago, when researchers gave a suicide "fact test" to several hundred undergraduates, the average score was only 59 percent correct (McIntosh, Hubbard, & Santos, 1985). As suicide has become a major focus of the clinical field, however, people's insights are improving, and more recent scores on a similar test by students in both Canada and the United States have been higher (Leenaars & Lester, 1992).

BOX 9-1

Suicide in the Family

On July 1, 1996, the model and actress Margaux Hemingway killed herself by taking an overdose of barbiturates. She was the fifth person in four generations of her family to commit suicide. Her death came almost 35 years to the day after the suicide of her famous grandfather, novelist Ernest Hemingway, by shotgun. Severely depressed about his progressive physical illness, he had failed to respond to two series of electroconvulsive treatments.

Margaux Hemingway had suffered from severe depression, alcoholism, and bulimia nervosa. She had had a successful modeling and acting career in the 1970s, but in later years her work consisted primarily of infomercials and low-budget movies. According to friends, she had tried for years to handle her anguish and setbacks with grace. "I was taught it was Hemingwayesque to take your blows and walk stoically through them."

ConsiderThis

⦿ Suicide sometimes runs in families. Why might this be the case? • Some family names bring instant recognition, as "Hemingway" does. What special challenges and pressures might such recognition bring to a person's life?

What Is Suicide?

Not every self-inflicted death is a suicide. A man who crashes his car into a tree after falling asleep at the steering wheel is not trying to kill himself. Thus Edwin Shneidman (1999, 1993, 1981, 1963), one of the most influential writers on this topic, defines **suicide** as an intentioned death—a self-inflicted death in which one makes an intentional, direct, and conscious effort to end one's life.

Intentioned deaths may take various forms. Consider the following examples. All three of these people intended to die, but their motives, concerns, and actions differed greatly.

> **Dave** was a successful man. By the age of 50 he had risen to the vice presidency of a small but profitable office machine firm. He had a devoted wife and two teenage sons who respected him. They lived in an upper-middle-class neighborhood, had a spacious house, and enjoyed a life of comfort and contentment.
>
> In August of his fiftieth year, everything changed. Dave was fired. Just like that, after many years of loyal and effective service. The firm's profits were down and the president wanted to try new, fresher marketing approaches. He wanted to try a younger person in Dave's position.
>
> Dave was shocked. The experience of rejection, loss, and emptiness was overwhelming. He looked for another position, but found only low-paying jobs for which he was overqualified. Each day as he looked for work Dave became more depressed, anxious, and desperate. He was convinced that his wife and sons would not love him if he could not maintain their lifestyle. Even if they did, he could not love himself under such circumstances. He kept sinking, withdrew from others, and became increasingly hopeless.

WHALE DEATHS

Whales that beach themselves are not committing suicide. The sand disturbs their sonar and throws them off course (Jordan, 1997).

PARASUICIDE A suicide attempt that does not result in death.

SUICIDE A self-inflicted death in which the person acts intentionally, directly, and consciously.

SOCIETAL PUNISHMENT

In times past, the bodies of people who committed suicide were treated disrespectfully. As late as 1811 it was a common practice in England to bury the victim at a crossroad by night with a stake driven through the heart. In eighteenth-century France and England, the body was dragged through the streets on a frame, head downward, the way criminals were dragged to their executions (Roesch, 1991; Evans & Farberow, 1988).

SUICIDE AND HOSPITALIZATION

Suicidal behavior or thinking is the most common precipitant for admission to a mental hospital. Between 60 and 75 percent of patients who are admitted have aroused concern that they will harm themselves (Jacobson, 1999).

Six months after losing his job, Dave began to consider ending his life. The pain was too great, the humiliation unending. He hated the present and dreaded the future. Throughout February he went back and forth. On some days he was sure he wanted to die. On other days, an enjoyable evening or uplifting conversation might change his mind temporarily. On a Monday late in February he heard about a job possibility, and the anticipation of the next day's interview seemed to lift his spirits. But Tuesday's interview did not go well. It was clear to him that he would not be offered the job. He went home, took a recently purchased gun from his locked desk drawer, and shot himself.

Billy never truly recovered from his mother's death. He was only 7 years old and unprepared for such a loss. His father sent him to live with his grandparents for a time, to a new school with new kids and a new way of life. In Billy's mind, all these changes were for the worse. He missed the joy and laughter of the past. He missed his home, his father, and his friends. Most of all he missed his mother.

He did not really understand her death. His father said that she was in heaven now, at peace, happy; that she had not wanted to die or leave Billy; that an accident had taken her life. Billy's unhappiness and loneliness continued day after day and he began to put things together in his own way. He believed he would be happy again if he could join his mother. He felt she was waiting for him, waiting for him to come to her. These thoughts seemed so right to him; they brought him comfort and hope. One evening, shortly after saying good night to his grandparents, Billy climbed out of bed, went up the stairs to the roof of their apartment house, and jumped to his death. In his mind he was joining his mother in heaven.

Margaret and Bob had been going together for a year. It was Margaret's first serious relationship; it was her whole life. Thus when Bob told her that he no longer loved her and was leaving her for someone else, Margaret was shocked and shaken.

As the weeks went by, Margaret was filled with two competing feelings— depression and anger. Several times she called Bob, begged him to reconsider, and pleaded for a chance to win him back. At the same time, she hated him for putting her through such misery. She didn't deserve this treatment. Sometimes when she was talking to him, her pleas would change to demands, her cries to yells.

Margaret's friends became more and more worried about her. At first they sympathized with her pain, assuming it would soon lift. But as time went on, her depression and anger worsened, and Margaret began to act strangely. She started to drink heavily and to mix her drinks with all kinds of pills. She seemed to be flirting with danger.

One night Margaret went into her bathroom, reached for a bottle of sleeping pills, and swallowed a handful of them. She wanted to make her pain go away, and she wanted Bob to know just how much pain he had caused her. She continued swallowing pill after pill, crying and swearing as she gulped them down. When she began to feel drowsy, she decided to call her close friend Cindy. She was not sure why she was calling, perhaps to say good-bye, to explain her actions, or to make sure that Bob was told; or perhaps to be talked out of it. Cindy pleaded and reasoned with Margaret and tried to motivate her to live. Margaret was trying to listen, but she became less and less coherent. Cindy hung up the phone and quickly called Margaret's neighbor and the police. When reached by her neighbor, Margaret was already in a coma. Seven hours later, while her friends and family waited for news in the hospital lounge, Margaret died.

While Margaret seemed to have mixed feelings about her death, Dave was clear in his wish to die. Whereas Billy viewed death as a trip to heaven, Dave saw it as an end to his existence. Such differences can be important in efforts to understand and treat suicidal persons. Accordingly, Shneidman has distinguished four kinds of people who intentionally end their lives: the *death seeker, death initiator, death ignorer,* and *death darer.*

Death seekers clearly intend to end their lives at the time they attempt suicide. This singleness of purpose may last only a short time. It can change to confusion the very next hour or day, and then return again in short order. Dave, the middle-aged executive, was a death seeker. He had many misgivings about suicide and was ambivalent about it for weeks, but on Tuesday night he was a death seeker—clear in his desire to die and acting in a manner that virtually guaranteed a fatal outcome.

Death initiators also clearly intend to end their lives, but they act out of a belief that the process of death is already under way and that they are simply hastening the process. Some expect that they will die in a matter of days or weeks. Many suicides among the elderly and very sick fall into this category (Clark, 1999; Valente & Saunders, 1995). The robust novelist Ernest Hemingway was profoundly concerned about his failing body—a concern that some observers believe was at the center of his suicide.

Death ignorers do not believe that their self-inflicted death will mean the end of their existence. They believe they are trading their present lives for a better or happier existence. Many child suicides, like Billy's, fall into this category, as do those of adult believers in a hereafter who commit suicide to reach another form of life. The thirty-nine members of the Heaven's Gate cult acted out of the belief that their deaths would free their spirits and enable them to ascend to a "Higher Kingdom."

Death darers experience mixed feelings, or ambivalence, in their intent to die even at the moment of their attempt, and they show this ambivalence in the act itself. Although to some degree they wish to die, and they often do die, their risk-taking behavior does not guarantee death. The person who plays Russian roulette—that is, pulls the trigger of a revolver randomly loaded with one bullet—is a death darer. Many death darers are as interested in gaining attention, making someone feel guilty, or expressing anger as in dying per se (Brent et al., 1988). Margaret might be considered a death darer. Although her unhappiness and anger were great, she was not sure that she wanted to die. Even while taking pills, she called her friend, reported her actions, and listened to her friend's pleas.

When individuals play *indirect, covert, partial,* or *unconscious* roles in their own deaths, Shneidman classifies them in a suicide-like category called **subintentional death** (Shneidman, 1993, 1981). Seriously ill people who consistently mismanage their medicines may belong in this category. In related work, the influential clinical theorist Karl Menninger (1938) distinguished a category called *chronic suicide.* These people behave in life-endangering ways over an extended period of time, perhaps consuming excessive alcohol, abusing drugs, or indulging in risky activities or occupations. Although their deaths may represent a form of suicide, their true intent is unclear, and so these individuals are not included in the discussions of this chapter.

How Is Suicide Studied?

Suicide researchers face a major obstacle: their subjects are no longer alive. How can investigators draw accurate conclusions about the intentions, feelings, and circumstances of people who can no longer explain their actions? Two research methods attempt to deal with this problem, each with only partial success.

One strategy is **retrospective analysis**, a kind of psychological autopsy in which clinicians and researchers piece together data from the suicide victim's past (Moscicki, 1999; Hawton et al., 1998). Relatives, friends, therapists, or physicians may remember past statements, conversations, and behavior that shed light on a self-inflicted death. Retrospective information may also be provided by the suicide notes that some victims leave behind (see Box 9-2 on the next page).

Death darers? *A sky surfer tries to ride the perfect cloud over Sweden. Are thrill-seekers daredevils searching for new highs, as many of them claim, or are some actually death darers?*

DEATH SEEKER A person who clearly intends to end his or her life at the time of a suicide attempt.

DEATH INITIATOR A person who attempts suicide believing that the process of death is already under way and that he or she is simply hastening the process.

DEATH IGNORER A person who attempts suicide without recognizing the finality of death.

DEATH DARER A person who is ambivalent about the wish to die even as he or she attempts suicide.

SUBINTENTIONAL DEATH A death in which the victim plays an indirect, hidden, partial, or unconscious role.

RETROSPECTIVE ANALYSIS A psychological autopsy in which clinicians and researchers piece together information about a person's suicide from the person's past.

However, such sources of information are not always available. Less than one-quarter of all suicide victims have been in psychotherapy (Fleer & Pasewark, 1982), and less than one-third leave notes (Black, 1993; Leenaars, 1992, 1989). Nor is retrospective information necessarily valid. A grieving, perhaps guilt-ridden, relative may be incapable of objective recollection (Hawton et al., 1998).

BOX 9-2

Suicide Notes

Dear Bill: I am sorry for causing you so much trouble. I really didn't want to and if you would have told me at the first time the truth probably both of us would be very happy now. Bill I am sorry but I can't take the life any more, I don't think there is any goodness in the world. I love you very very much and I want you to be as happy in your life as I wanted to make you. Tell your parents I am very sorry and please if you can do it don't ever let my parents know what happened.

Please, don't hate me Bill, I love you.

Mary

(LEENAARS, 1991)

Many suicides go undetected or unconfirmed because the only people who could tell us the truth are gone from the world. Many other people who commit suicide, however—an estimated 12 to 33 percent—leave notes that reveal their intentions and psychological state only hours or minutes before they died (Black, 1993; Leenaars, 1992, 1989).

Each suicide note is a personal document, unique to the writer and the circumstances (Leenaars, 1989). Some are barely a single sentence; others run several pages. People who leave notes clearly wish to send a powerful message to those they leave behind (Leenaars, 1989), whether it be "a cry for help, an epitaph, or a last will and testament" (Frederick, 1969, p. 17). Most suicide notes are addressed to specific individuals.

Survivors' reactions to suicide notes vary (Leenaars, 1989). A note can clarify the cause of death, thus saving relatives the ordeal of a legal investigation. Friends and relatives may find that it

Suicide note left by Paul Bern to his wife, famed actress Jean Harlow, in 1932.

eases their grief to know the person's reasons for committing suicide (Chynoweth, 1977). Yet some suicide notes add to the guilt and horror that survivors experience, as in the following case:

Rather than permit his wife to leave him, twenty-year-old Mr. Jefferson hanged himself in the bathroom, leaving a note on the front door for his wife, saying, "Cathy I love you. You're right, I am crazy . . . and thank you for trying to love me. Phil." Mrs. Jefferson felt and frequently insisted that she "killed Phil." She attempted suicide herself a week after.

(WALLACE, 1981, P. 79)

Clinical researchers have tried to improve their understanding of suicide by studying differences between genuine and fake suicide notes, the age and sex of note writers, the grammar of notes, the type and frequency of words used, conscious and unconscious contents, handwriting, and emotional, cognitive, and motivational themes (Lester & Linn, 1998; Leenaars, 1989). One important finding is that suicide notes vary significantly with age (Lester, 1998). Younger persons express more hostility toward themselves and cite more interpersonal problems in their notes; those between 40 and 49 report being unable to cope with life; those between 50 and 59 tend not to cite a reason for their suicide; and those over 60 are motivated by such problems as illness, pain, disability, and loneliness (Lester, 1998).

Studies of notes have also revealed that the nature of suicide has changed little since the 1940s. Suicide notes written in the 1940s and 1950s are similar in content to modern notes, with one exception: modern notes show less confusion and more limited thinking.

A note provides only a partial picture of the writer's experiences, perceptions, thoughts, and emotions. Moreover, as Edwin Shneidman remarks, the writers themselves may not be fully aware of their motives; their desperate thinking prevents them from being truly insightful. Suicide notes are "not the royal road to an easy understanding of suicidal phenomena" (Shneidman, 1973, p. 380), but in combination with other sources they can point clinicians and researchers in the right direction (Black, 1995).

Because of these limitations, many researchers also use a second strategy—*studying people who survive their suicide attempts*. Of course, people who survive suicide may differ in important ways from those who do not (Krupinski et al., 1998; Diekstra et al., 1995). Many of them may not really have wanted to die, for example. Nevertheless, suicide researchers have found it useful to study survivors of suicide; and we shall consider those who attempt suicide and those who commit suicide as more or less alike.

Patterns and Statistics

Suicide happens within a larger social setting, and researchers have gathered many statistics regarding the social contexts in which such deaths take place. They have found, for example, that suicide rates vary from country to country (Schmidtke et al., 1999). Russia, Hungary, Germany, Austria, Finland, Denmark, China, and Japan have very high rates, more than 20 suicides annually per 100,000 persons; conversely, Egypt, Mexico, Greece, and Spain have relatively low rates, fewer than 5 per 100,000. The United States and Canada fall in between, each with a suicide rate of around 12 per 100,000 persons, and England has a rate of 9 per 100,000 (NCHS, 1994; WHO, 1992).

Religious affiliation and beliefs may help account for these national differences (Kelleher et al., 1998; Shneidman, 1987). For example, countries that are largely Catholic, Jewish, or Muslim tend to have low suicide rates. Perhaps in these countries, strict prohibitions against suicide or a strong religious tradition deter many people from committing suicide. Yet there are exceptions to this tentative rule. Austria, a predominantly Roman Catholic country, has one of the highest suicide rates in the world (Kelleher et al., 1998).

Research is beginning to suggest that religious doctrine may not help prevent suicide as much as the degree of an individual's *devoutness*. Regardless of their particular persuasion, very religious people seem less likely to commit suicide (Jahangir, urRehman, & Jan, 1998; Martin, 1984). Similarly, it seems that people who hold a greater reverence for life are less prone to consider or attempt self-destruction (Lee, 1985).

The suicide rates of men and women also differ. Three times as many women attempt suicide as men, yet men succeed at more than three times the rate of women (Moscicki, 1999; Weissman et al., 1999; Stillion & McDowell, 1996). Around the world 19 of every 100,000 men kill themselves each year; the suicide rate for women, which has been increasing in recent years, is 5 per 100,000 (Schmidtke et al., 1999).

One reason for these differing rates appears to be the different methods used by men and women (Ayd & Palma, 1999; Kushner, 1995). Men tend to use more violent methods, such as shooting, stabbing, or hanging themselves, whereas women use less violent methods, such as drug overdose. Guns are used in nearly two-thirds of the male suicides in the United States, compared to 40 percent of the female suicides (Canetto & Lester, 1995; NCHS, 1990).

Suicide is also related to marital status (see Figure 9-1 on the next page). Married people, especially those with children, have a fairly low suicide rate; single and widowed people have higher rates; and divorced people have the highest rate of all (Weissman et al., 1999; Canetto & Lester, 1995). One study compared 90 persons who committed suicide with 90 psychologically troubled patients who had never attempted suicide (Roy, 1982). Only 16 percent of the suicides were married or living with someone else at the time of the suicide, compared to 30 percent of the control group. Similarly, an analysis conducted in Canada over four decades revealed a strong positive correlation between national divorce rates and suicide rates (Leenaars & Lester, 1999).

Suicide's broad impact *The suicide of Nirvana's Kurt Cobain in April 1994 shocked young rock fans throughout the world and led to widespread grief and confusion. In Seattle, Cobain's hometown, a candlelight vigil was attended by about 5,000 people, including these two fans.*

ConsiderThis

⦿ Suicide rates vary widely from country to country. What factors besides religion might help account for the differences?

STATE BY STATE

Suicide rates vary by state in the United States. Western states have the highest rate of suicide (15 per 100,000 persons), followed by the South (13 per 100,000), the Midwest (10 per 100,000), and the Northeast (8 per 100,000). Guns are used in 70 percent of southern suicides, 58 percent in the West and Midwest, and 45 percent in the Northeast (Klein, 1998).

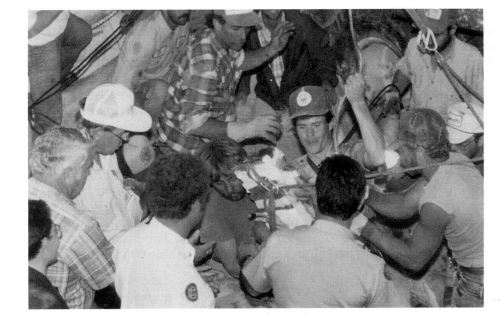

Lingering impact *While the world watched in 1987, paramedic Robert O' Donnell squirmed down a narrow rescue shaft in Midland, Texas, reached 2-year-old Jessica McClure (who had fallen down an unused well), and handed her to the rescue workers seen in this famous photograph. Some friends say that O' Donnell never recovered from his "quicksilver" fame nor the subsequent loss of celebrity. A decade after his heroic act, he shot himself to death.*

THE IMPACT OF INTERNMENT

The suicide rate among the 110,000 Japanese Americans who were interned in "relocation centers" during World War II rose to double that of the national population (Jensen, 1998).

keep seriously ill people alive much longer, they often fail to extend the quality and comfort of the patients' lives (Werth, 1995).

ABUSIVE ENVIRONMENT Victims of an abusive or repressive environment from which they have little or no hope of escape sometimes commit suicide. For example, prisoners of war, inmates of concentration camps, abused spouses, abused children, and prison inmates have tried to end their lives (Gore, 1999; McKee, 1998; Fondacaro & Butler, 1995; Rodgers, 1995) (see Figure 9-3). Like those who have serious illnesses, these people may have felt that they could endure no more suffering and believed that there was no hope for improvement in their condition.

OCCUPATIONAL STRESS Some jobs create feelings of tension or dissatisfaction that may precipitate suicide attempts. Research has found particularly high suicide rates among psychiatrists and psychologists, physicians, dentists, lawyers, and unskilled laborers (Holmes & Rich, 1990; Stillion, 1985). Such correlations do not necessarily mean that occupational pressures directly cause suicidal ac-

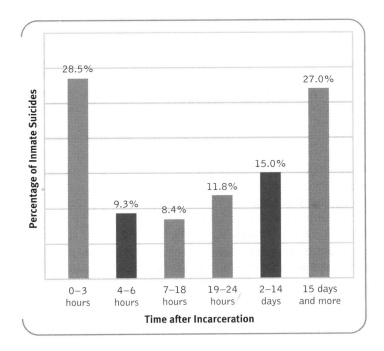

FIGURE 9-3 Suicide in prisons *Approximately 107 of every 100,000 inmates in U.S. jails commit suicide each year, many times the national prevalence. Most such suicides occur during the first day of incarceration. (Adapted from Bonner, 1990; Hayes & Rowan, 1988.)*

tions. Perhaps unskilled workers are responding to financial insecurity rather than job stress when they attempt suicide (Wasserman & Stack, 2000; Chastang et al., 1998). Similarly, rather than reacting to the emotional strain of their work, suicidal psychiatrists and psychologists may have long-standing emotional problems that stimulated their career interest in the first place (Johnson, 1991).

Clinicians once believed that married women who held jobs outside the home had higher suicide rates than other women, perhaps because of conflicts between the demands of their families and their jobs (Stack, 1987; Stillion, 1985). However, recent studies call these notions into question and some even suggest that work outside the home may be linked to lower suicide rates among women, just as it is among men (Stack, 1998; Yang & Lester, 1995).

Mood and Thought Changes

Many suicide attempts are preceded by a change in mood. The change may not be severe enough to warrant a diagnosis of a mental disorder, but it does represent a significant shift from the person's past mood. The most common change is an increase in sadness (Kienhorst et al., 1995; Tishler, McKenry, & Morgan, 1981). Also common are increases in feelings of anxiety, tension, frustration, anger, or shame (Fawcett, 1999; Kienhorst et al., 1995). In fact, Shneidman (1999, 1991) suggests that the key to suicide is "psychache," a feeling of psychological pain that seems intolerable to the person.

Suicide attempts may also be preceded by shifts in patterns of thinking. Individuals may become preoccupied with their problems, lose perspective, and see suicide as the only effective solution to their difficulties (Shneidman, 1999, 1993, 1987). They often develop a sense of **hopelessness**—a pessimistic belief that their present circumstances, problems, or mood will not change (Weishaar, 2000; Jacobs et al., 1999). Some clinicians believe that a feeling of hopelessness is the single most likely indicator of suicidal intent, and they take special care to look for signs of hopelessness when they assess the risk of suicide (Hewitt et al., 1997; Levy, Jurkovic, & Spirito, 1995).

Many people who attempt suicide fall victim to **dichotomous thinking**, viewing problems and solutions in rigid either/or terms (Weishaar, 2000; Shneidman, 1993, 1987). In the following statement a woman who survived her leap from a building describes her dichotomous thinking at the time. She saw death as the only alternative to her pain:

> I was so desperate. I felt, my God, I couldn't face this thing. Everything was like a terrible whirlpool of confusion. And I thought to myself: There's only one thing to do. I just have to lose consciousness. That's the only way to get away from it. The only way to lose consciousness, I thought, was to jump off something good and high....
>
> *(Shneidman, 1987, p. 56)*

Alcohol and Other Drug Use

Studies indicate that as many as 60 percent of the people who attempt suicide drink alcohol just before the act (Suokas & Lonnqvist, 1995; Hirschfeld & Davidson, 1988). Autopsies reveal that about one-fourth of these people are legally intoxicated (Flavin et al., 1990; Abel & Zeidenberg, 1985). In fact, considering that coroners are more likely to classify deaths as accidental when they detect high alcohol levels (Crompton, 1985), the excessive use of alcohol just before suicide is probably much higher. Such statistics suggest to many clinical researchers that alcohol often contributes to suicidal behavior (Lester, 1999; Wasserman, 1992).

A number of factors may account for this relationship between alcohol use and suicide (Weiss & Hufford, 1999). Alcohol's disinhibiting effects may allow

ConsiderThis

Countries with a large number of women in the labor force do not typically experience a rise in the rate of female suicides; some, however, do experience an increase in the rate of male suicides (Stack, 1998). How might this trend be explained?

"To be, or not to be: that is the question . . ."

William Shakespeare, *Hamlet*

HOPELESSNESS A pessimistic belief that one's present circumstances, problems, or mood will not change.

DICHOTOMOUS THINKING Viewing problems and solutions in rigid "either/or" terms.

people who are considering suicide to overcome the fears that would otherwise restrain them. Alternatively, alcohol may contribute to suicide by lowering an individual's inhibitions against violence and helping to release underlying aggressive feelings. Yet another possibility is that alcohol further impairs a suicidal person's judgment and problem-solving abilities.

Research suggests that the use of other kinds of drugs may have a similar tie to suicide, particularly in teenagers and young adults (Rich et al., 1998; Garrison et al., 1993; Marzuk et al., 1992). A high level of heroin, for example, was found in the blood of Kurt Cobain at the time of his suicide in 1994 (Colburn, 1996).

Mental Disorders

Although people who attempt suicide may be troubled or anxious, they do not necessarily have a psychological disorder as defined in DSM-IV. Nevertheless, more than half of all suicide attempters do display a diagnosable mental disorder (Jacobs et al., 1999; Murphy, 1998; Harris & Barraclough, 1997). The ones linked most strongly to suicide are *mood disorders* (unipolar and bipolar depression), *substance-related disorders* (particularly alcoholism), and *schizophrenia* (see Table 9-2). Research suggests that as many as 15 percent of people with each of these disorders try to kill themselves (Kelleher et al., 1998; Meltzer, 1998; Rossow & Amundsen, 1995). People who are both depressed and dependent on alcohol seem particularly prone to suicidal impulses (Weiss & Hufford, 1999; Cornelius et al., 1995). Panic and other anxiety disorders have also been linked to suicide, but in most cases these disorders occur in conjunction with depression, a substance-related disorder, or schizophrenia (Fawcett, 1999; Overbeek et al., 1998; King et al., 1995).

As we observed in Chapter 7, people with major depressive disorder often experience suicidal thoughts. Those whose disorder includes a particularly strong sense of hopelessness seem most likely to attempt suicide (Fawcett et al., 1987).

Multiple risks *People who experience multiple suicide factors are at particular risk for self-destruction. The actor Herve Villechaize (right) killed himself after losing his lucrative role in the television series* Fantasy Island *and also developing a chronic, painful medical condition.*

"The man, who in a fit of melancholy, kills himself today, would have wished to live had he waited a week."

Voltaire, "Cato,"
Philosophical Dictionary, 1764

Table 9-2

Common Predictors of Suicide

1. Depressive disorder and certain other mental disorders
2. Alcoholism and other forms of substance abuse
3. Suicide ideation, talk, preparation; certain religious ideas
4. Prior suicide attempts
5. Lethal methods
6. Isolation, living alone, loss of support
7. Hopelessness, cognitive rigidity
8. Being an older white male
9. Modeling, suicide in the family, genetics
10. Economic or work problems; certain occupations
11. Marital problems, family pathology
12. Stress and stressful events
13. Anger, aggression, irritability
14. Physical illness
15. Repetition and combination of factors 1 to 14

Source: Adapted from Maris, 1992.

One program in Sweden was able to reduce the community suicide rate by teaching physicians how to recognize and treat depression at an early stage (Rihmer, Rutz, & Pihlgren, 1995). Even when depressed people are showing improvements in mood, however, they may remain high suicide risks. In fact, among those who are severely depressed, the risk of suicide may actually increase as their mood improves and they have more energy to act on their suicidal wishes.

Severe depression also may play a key role in suicide attempts by persons with serious physical illnesses (Hendin, 1999; Henriksson et al., 1995). A study of 44 patients with terminal illnesses revealed that fewer than one-quarter of them had thoughts of suicide or wished for an early death, and that those who did were all suffering from major depressive disorder (Brown et al., 1986).

A number of the people who drink alcohol or use drugs just before a suicide attempt actually have a long history of abusing such substances (Pirkola et al., 2000; Jones, 1997; Neeleman & Farrell, 1997). The basis for the link between substance-related disorders and suicide is not clear (Weiss & Hufford, 1999). Perhaps the tragic lifestyle of many persons with these disorders or their sense of being hopelessly trapped by a substance leads to suicidal thinking. Alternatively, a third factor—psychological pain, for instance, or desperation—may cause both substance abuse and suicidal thinking (Frances & Franklin, 1988). Such people may be caught in a downward spiral: they are driven toward substance use by psychological pain or loss, only to find themselves caught in a pattern of substance abuse that aggravates rather than solves their problems (Downey, 1991; Miller et al., 1991). Nor should the medical complications of chronic substance abuse be overlooked. Many suicides by people with alcoholism, for example, occur in the late stages of the disorder, when cirrhosis of the liver and other medical complications arise. At least some of these people may be acting as "death initiators" in the belief that a journey toward death has already begun (Miles, 1977; Barraclough et al., 1974).

People with schizophrenia, as we shall see in Chapter 14, may hear voices that are not actually present (hallucinations) or hold beliefs that are clearly false and perhaps bizarre (delusions). There is a popular notion that when such persons kill themselves, they must be responding to an imagined voice commanding them to do so or to a delusion that suicide is a grand and noble gesture. Research indicates, however, that suicides by people with schizophrenia more often reflect feelings of *demoralization* (Reid, 1998; Krausz et al., 1995; Peuskens et al., 1997). For example, many young and unemployed sufferers who have had relapses over several years come to believe that the disorder will forever disrupt their lives (see Box 9-3 on the next page). Still others seem to be disheartened by their unfortunate, sometimes dreadful, living conditions. Suicide is the leading cause of premature death in this population (Tsuang et al., 1999; Meltzer, 1998).

Modeling: The Contagion of Suicide

It is not unusual for people, particularly teenagers, to try to commit suicide after observing or reading about someone else who has done so (Grossman & Kruesi, 2000; Joiner, 1999; Phillips et al., 1992). Perhaps these people have been struggling with major problems, and the other person's suicide seems to reveal a possible solution; or they have been thinking about suicide and the other person's suicide seems to give them permission or finally persuades them to act. Either way, one suicidal act apparently serves as a *model* for another. Suicides by celebrities, other highly publicized suicides, and suicides by co-workers or colleagues are particularly common triggers.

CELEBRITIES When the researcher Steven Stack (1987) analyzed U.S. suicide data spanning 1948 to 1983, he found that suicides by entertainers and political figures are regularly followed by unusual increases in the number of suicides across the nation. During the week after the suicide of Marilyn Monroe in 1963, for example, the national suicide rate rose 12 percent (Phillips, 1974).

THE DANGER OF COMORBIDITY
A European study found that people with three or more mental disorders (for example, depression, panic disorder, *and* a substance-related disorder) are 18 times more likely to attempt suicide than people without a disorder (Wunderlich et al., 1998).

Murder-suicide *The lives of comedic actor Phil Hartman and his wife Brynne ended in 1998 when she shot him and then herself. Around 1.5 percent of all suicides occur in the context of murder-suicide, usually involving spouses or lovers who have been in conflict (Nock & Marzuk, 1999).*

BOX 9-3

"I'm All Traveled Out"

On October 5, 1998, Margaret Mary Ray knelt down in front of an oncoming 105-car coal train in Hotchkiss, Colorado, and brought her life to an immediate end. Ms. Ray, 46, had suffered from schizophrenia for years, holding delusions that she was in intimate relationships with famous people and even stalking them in their residences. Like a number of other people with schizophrenia, she eventually grew weary and hopeless about the chances that her disorder would ever improve. In a suicide note sent to her mother, she said, "I'm all traveled out. . . . I choose a painless and instantaneous way to end my life. . . ."

One difference between Ms. Ray and most other people with schizophrenia is that millions of people knew something about her dysfunction. She gained notoriety during her last decade as the woman who believed that she was romantically involved with the television comedian David Letterman, repeatedly breaking into his home, sleeping on his tennis court, and on one occasion stealing his car. Her delusion first came to light in 1988 when she was arrested while driving Letterman's car at the entrance to the Lincoln Tunnel in New York City. When she was unable to pay the toll, she identified herself as Letterman's wife and her son as his son. Over the next decade, she was arrested repeatedly for trespassing and was forced to spend a total of ten months in prison and fourteen months in a state hospital. Newspaper accounts, particularly the supermarket tabloids, usually described her exploits in a lighthearted way, and readers generally considered her to be a strange and comical character.

Not until Ms. Ray killed herself did most people become aware of just how

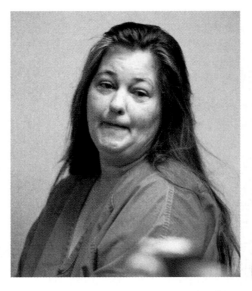

A weary Margaret Ray faces charges of stalking in 1997.

disturbed she was. In fact, two of her three brothers had also suffered from schizophrenia and killed themselves years earlier. Her adult life consisted of sudden jaunts across the country, strange ideas, and impulsive and erratic behavior that extended well beyond her focus on Letterman. Her surviving brother remembers times when she spoke in sentences and syntax that made no sense and warm days when she wore three layers of clothing (Bruni, 1998). Her daughter observes, "She had a running commentary on the world that was very inappropriate and a few decibels too loud." Medications often seemed to help her, but she usually stopped taking them outside of prison or the state hospital.

Letterman himself recognized the seriousness of Ms. Ray's problem and grappled with how best to handle things. He rarely talked about

her, never mentioned her name on the air, and often declined to press charges against her. Expressing compassion for her, he recalls that she sent him many letters between her uninvited house visits, and it was apparent in each letter whether she was taking her medications (Bruni, 1998). "When she was on them, it was like hearing from your aunt. When she was off them, it was like hearing from your aunt on Neptune." On the day after her death, he observed, "This is a sad end to a confused life."

Consider This

○ Why do people tend to overlook or dismiss the psychological pain of people with bizarre ideas or erratic behaviors? • How might such oversights add to the suffering or symptoms of such people?

OTHER HIGHLY PUBLICIZED CASES Suicides with bizarre or unusual aspects often receive intense coverage by the news media. Such highly publicized accounts may lead to similar suicides (Etzersdorfer & Sonneck, 1998; Martin, 1998). During the year after a widely publicized, politically motivated suicide by self-burning in England, for example, 82 other people set themselves on fire, with equally fatal results (Ashton & Donnan, 1981). Inquest reports revealed that most of those people had histories of emotional problems and that none of the suicides had the political motivation of the publicized suicide. The imitators seemed to be responding to their own problems in a manner triggered by the suicide they had observed or read about.

Even a media program that is clearly intended to educate and help viewers may have the paradoxical effect of spurring imitators. One study found a dramatic increase in the rate of suicide among West German teenagers after the airing of a television documentary showing the suicide of a teenager who jumped under a train (Schmidtke & Häfner, 1988). The number of railway suicides by male teenagers increased by 175 percent after the program was aired.

Some clinicians argue that more responsible reporting could reduce this undesirable aftereffect of highly publicized suicides (Etzersdorfer & Sonneck, 1998; Mulder, 1996; Motto, 1967). One innovative approach to reporting was seen in the media's coverage of the suicide of Kurt Cobain. MTV's repeated theme on the evening of the suicide was "Don't do it!" In fact, thousands of young people called MTV and other radio and television stations in the hours after Cobain's death, distraught, frightened, and in some cases suicidal. Some of the stations responded by posting the phone numbers of suicide prevention centers, presenting interviews with suicide experts, and offering counseling services and advice directly to callers. Perhaps because of such efforts, the usual rate of suicide both in Seattle, Cobain's hometown, and elsewhere held steady during the weeks that followed.

CO-WORKERS AND COLLEAGUES The word-of-mouth publicity that attends suicides in a school, workplace, or small community may trigger suicide attempts. The suicide of a recruit at a U.S. Navy training school, for example, was followed within two weeks by another and also by an attempted suicide at the school. To head off what threatened to become a suicide epidemic, the school began a program of staff education on suicide and group therapy sessions for recruits who had been close to the suicide victims (Grigg, 1988).

Explanations of Suicide

Most people faced with difficult situations never try to kill themselves. In an effort to understand why some people are more prone to suicide than others, theorists have proposed more fundamental explanations for self-destructive action than the immediate triggers considered in the previous section. The leading theories come from the psychodynamic, sociocultural, and biological perspectives. As a group, however, these hypotheses have received limited research support and fail to address the full range of suicidal acts. Thus the clinical field currently lacks a satisfactory understanding of suicide.

The Psychodynamic View

Many psychodynamic theorists believe that suicide results from depression and from anger at others that is redirected toward oneself. This theory was first stated by Wilhelm Stekel at a meeting in Vienna in 1910, when he proclaimed that "no one kills himself who has not wanted to kill another or at least wished the death of another" (Shneidman, 1979). Some years later Sigmund Freud (1920) wrote, "No neurotic harbors thoughts of suicide which he has not turned back upon himself from murderous impulses against others."

As we saw in Chapter 7, Freud (1917) and Abraham (1916, 1911) proposed that when people experience the real or symbolic loss of a loved one, they come to "introject" the lost person; that is, they unconsciously incorporate the person into their own identity and feel toward themselves as they had felt toward the other. For a short while, negative feelings toward the lost loved one are experienced as self-hatred. Anger toward the loved one may turn into intense anger against oneself and finally into a pervasive depression. Suicide is thought to be an

COPYCAT SUICIDES

In 1999 a character in the popular British medical television show *Casualty* intentionally killed himself by overdosing on a drug. During the two weeks after the episode was aired, the number of attempted suicides in England rose 17 percent, most of them involving the same method (O'Connor et al., 1999).

ConsiderThis

● What precautions or actions should the media and the arts take in their presentations of famous cases of suicide?

HOLIDAY EFFECTS

Studies in countries throughout Europe indicate that suicide rates tend to drop before Christmas and Easter, but then increase after those holidays (Jessen et al., 1999). How might we explain these trends?

extreme expression of this self-hatred. The following description of a suicidal patient demonstrates how such forces may operate:

> A 27-year-old conscientious and responsible woman took a knife to her wrists to punish herself for being tyrannical, unreliable, self-centered, and abusive. She was perplexed and frightened by this uncharacteristic self-destructive episode and was enormously relieved when her therapist pointed out that her invective described her recently deceased father much better than it did herself.
>
> *(Gill, 1982, p. 15)*

In support of Freud's view, researchers have often found a relationship between childhood losses and later suicidal behaviors (Kaslow et al., 1998; Lester, 1998; Paykel, 1991). One study of 200 family histories found that early parental loss was much more common among suicide attempters (48 percent) than among nonsuicidal control subjects (24 percent) (Adam, Bouckoms, & Streiner, 1982). Common forms of loss were death of the father and divorce or separation of the parents, especially during either the early years of life or late adolescence.

Late in his career, Freud proposed that human beings have a basic "death instinct." He called this instinct *Thanatos*, and described it as opposing the "life instinct." According to Freud, while most people learn to redirect their death instinct, by aiming it toward others, suicidal people, caught in a web of self-anger, direct it squarely upon themselves.

Sociological findings are consistent with this explanation of suicide. National suicide rates have been found to drop in times of war, when, one could argue, people are encouraged to direct their self-destructive energy against "the enemy." In addition, societies with high rates of homicide tend to have low rates of suicide, and vice versa (Somasundaram & Rajadurai, 1995). However, research has failed to establish that suicidal people are in fact dominated by intense feelings of anger. Although hostility is an important element in some suicides, several studies find that other emotional states are even more prevalent (Castrogiovanni, Pieraccini, & DiMuto, 1998; Linehan & Nielsen, 1981).

By the end of his career, Freud himself expressed dissatisfaction with his theory of suicide. Other psychodynamic theorists have also challenged his ideas over the years, yet themes of loss and self-directed aggression generally remain at the center of most psychodynamic explanations (Maltsberger, 1999; Bose, 1995).

The picture of suicide *For most people, the subject of suicide calls forth the image of a determined man sitting with a gun, much like the subject of Alex Colville's striking painting* Target Pistol and Man, *1988. This image is often accurate—men commit suicide more than women and they usually use a firearm.*

The Sociocultural View

Toward the end of the nineteenth century, Emile Durkheim (1897), a sociologist, developed a comprehensive theory of suicidal behavior. Today this theory continues to be influential. According to Durkheim, the probability of suicide is determined by how attached a person is to such social groups as the family, religious institutions, and community. The more thoroughly a person belongs, the lower the risk of suicide. Conversely, people who have poor relationships with their society are at greater risk of killing themselves. He defined several categories of suicide, including *egoistic, altruistic,* and *anomic* suicide.

Egoistic suicides are committed by people over whom society has little or no control. These people are not concerned with the norms or rules of society, nor are they integrated into the social fabric. According to Durkheim, this kind of suicide is more likely in people who are isolated, alienated, and nonreligious. The larger the number of such people living in a society, the higher that society's suicide rate.

EGOISTIC SUICIDE Suicide committed by people over whom society has little or no control, people who are not inhibited by the norms or rules of society.

ALTRUISTIC SUICIDE Suicide committed by people who intentionally sacrifice their lives for the well-being of society.

ANOMIC SUICIDE Suicide committed by individuals whose social environment fails to provide stability, thus leaving them without a sense of belonging.

Altruistic suicides, in contrast, are committed by people who are so well integrated into the social structure that they intentionally sacrifice their lives for its well-being. Soldiers who threw themselves on top of a live grenade to save others, Japanese kamikaze pilots who gave their lives in air attacks, and Buddhist monks and nuns who protested the Vietnam War by setting themselves on fire—all were committing altruistic suicide. According to Durkheim, societies that encourage altruistic deaths and deaths to preserve one's honor (as Far Eastern societies do) are likely to have higher suicide rates.

Anomic suicides, another category proposed by Durkheim, are those committed by people whose social environment fails to provide stable structures, such as family and religion, to support and give meaning to life. Such a societal condition, called *anomie* (literally, "without law"), leaves individuals without a sense of belonging. Unlike egoistic suicide, which is the act of a person who rejects the structures of a society, anomic suicide is the act of a person who has been let down by a disorganized, inadequate, often decaying society.

Durkheim argued that when societies go through periods of anomie, their suicide rates increase. Historical trends support this claim. Periods of economic depression may bring about some degree of anomie in a country, and national suicide rates tend to rise during such times (Yang et al., 1992; Lester, 1991). Periods of population change and increased immigration, too, tend to bring about a state of anomie, and again suicide rates rise (Burvill, 1998; Ferrada et al., 1995). Steven Stack (1981) examined suicide rates and immigration increases in 34 countries and he found that each 1 percent increase in immigration was associated with an increase of 0.13 percent in the suicide rate.

A major change in an individual's immediate surroundings, rather than general societal problems, can also lead to anomic suicide. People who suddenly inherit a great deal of money, for example, may go through a period of anomie as their relationships with social, economic, and occupational structures are changed. Thus Durkheim predicted that societies with greater opportunities for change in individual wealth or status would have higher suicide rates, and this prediction, too, is supported by research (Lester, 1985).

Durkheim's theory of suicide highlights the importance of social and societal factors. Although today's sociocultural theorists do not always embrace Durkheim's particular ideas, most agree that social structure and cultural stress often

In the service of others *According to Emile Durkheim, people who intentionally sacrifice their lives for others are committing altruistic suicide. Betsy Smith, a heart transplant recipient who was warned that she would probably die if she did not terminate her pregnancy, elected to have the baby and died giving birth.*

Clash of cultures *The sudden introduction of modern technology into a relatively undeveloped society, illustrated by this satellite television disk alongside a nomad's ger in Mongolia, can produce a climate of disorganization and anomie, leaving some members confused and troubled.*

BOX 9-4

Suicide among the Japanese

According to a comparison of American and Japanese medical students, Americans tend to regard suicide as an expression of anger or aggression, whereas the Japanese view it as normal, reasonable behavior (Domino & Takahashi, 1991). The sociologist Mamoru Iga (1993) holds that this difference reflects the cultures' religious and philosophical understandings of life and death.

The Shinto and Buddhist traditions stress eternal change and the transience of life. In the Buddhist view, life is sorrowful, and death is a way of freeing oneself from illusion and suffering. Furthermore, the highest aim of many Japanese is complete detachment from earthly concerns, total self-negation. Within this framework, death can be seen as beautiful, as an expression of sincerity (*makoto*), or an appropriate reaction to shame. Thus, according to Iga, "In Japan, suicide has traditionally been an accepted, if not a welcomed, way of solving a serious problem. . . . Suicide is not a sin in Japan; it is not punishable by God. Suicide is not viewed as a social or national issue but a personal problem."

Many of the factors that trigger suicide in the West—physical illness, alcohol abuse, mental disorders—are also at work in Japanese suicides (Lester & Saito, 1999). However, the different attitudes of the two cultures toward death and suicide may help explain the sizable difference between the rates of suicide in Japan (26 per 100,000 persons) and the United States (12 per 100,000).

Iga also points to the absence of a humanistic tradition in Japan. Self-expression, self-love, and self-enhancement are prominent values in the West, and out of such a tradition comes the impulse to prevent suicide. Japanese society, however, values the subjugation of the individual to the social order and stresses harmony between humanity and nature: humans must bow to nature. Thus no deep-rooted principle in Japan requires that people be stopped from taking their own lives.

Finally, Iga points to several sociocultural factors that may further contribute to the high rate of suicide in Japan. One is the long-standing, pervasive sexism in Japanese culture. Others are increasing academic pressure on young people and increasing work pressure on middle-aged men. Nor should economic pressure in Japan be overlooked. During the country's severe recession of 1998, the number of suicides increased by more than one-third.

Of course, in today's world East and West meet regularly, and in fact interactions between the cultures have had an impact on Japanese attitudes in respect to one facet of suicide—suicide prevention. After visiting the Los Angeles Suicide Prevention Center, some Japanese psychologists and psychiatrists opened the first suicide prevention center in Japan in 1971. They worried at first that shame would deter the Japanese from seeking help, but the center was so successful that by 1990 it was operating branches in 33 Japanese cities. Still other efforts at suicide prevention have followed (Takahashi, 1998).

Academic stress *The students in this classroom are participating in summer* juku, *a Japanese camp where they receive remedial help, extra lessons, and exam practice eleven hours a day.*

play major roles in suicide (Hassan, 1998) (see Box 9-4). In fact, the sociocultural view pervades the study of suicide. We saw its impact earlier when we observed the many studies linking suicide to broad factors such as religious affiliation, marital status, gender, race, and societal stress. We will also see it when we consider the ties between suicide and age.

Despite the influence of sociocultural theories, they cannot by themselves explain why some people who experience particular societal pressures commit suicide whereas the majority do not. Durkheim himself concluded that the final explanation probably lies in the interaction between societal and individual factors.

The Biological View

For years biological researchers relied largely on family pedigree studies to support their position that biological factors contribute to suicidal behavior. They have repeatedly found higher rates of suicide among the parents and close relatives of suicidal people than among those of nonsuicidal people (Brent et al., 1998, 1996). Indeed, one study found that over one-third of teenage subjects who committed suicide had a close relative who had attempted suicide (Gould, Shaffer, & Davies, 1990). Such findings may suggest that genetic, and so biological, factors are at work (Roy et al., 1999; Statham et al., 1998).

Studies of twins also have supported this view of suicide. Researchers who studied twins born in Denmark between 1870 and 1920, for example, located nineteen identical pairs and fifty-eight fraternal pairs in which at least one twin had committed suicide (Juel-Nielsen & Videbech, 1970). In four of the identical pairs the other twin also committed suicide (21 percent), while none of the other twins among the fraternal pairs had done so.

As with all family pedigree and twin research, there are nonbiological interpretations for these findings as well (Brent et al., 1998). Psychodynamic clinicians might argue that children whose close relatives commit suicide are prone to depression and suicide because they have lost a loved one at a critical stage of development (Stimming & Stimming, 1999). Behavioral theorists might emphasize the modeling role played by parents or close relatives who attempt suicide.

In the past two decades, laboratory research has offered more direct support for a biological view of suicide. The activity level of the neurotransmitter *serotonin* has often been found to be low in people who commit suicide (Mann & Arango, 1999; Mann et al., 1999). An early hint of this relationship came from a study by the psychiatric researcher Marie Asberg and her colleagues (1976). They studied 68 depressed patients and found that 20 of the patients had particularly low levels of serotonin activity. It turned out that 40 percent of the low-serotonin people attempted suicide, compared with 15 percent of the higher-serotonin subjects. The researchers interpreted this to mean that low serotonin activity may be "a predictor of suicidal acts." Later studies found that suicide attempters with low serotonin activity are ten times more likely to make a repeat attempt and succeed than are suicide attempters with higher serotonin activity (Roy, 1992; Asberg et al., 1976).

Studies that examine the autopsied brains of suicide victims point in the same direction (Mann & Arango, 1999; Stanley et al., 1986, 1982). Some of these studies measure serotonin activity by determining the number of *imipramine receptor* sites in the brain. Recall that imipramine is an antidepressant drug that binds to certain neuron receptors throughout the brain (see Chapter 8). It is believed that the degree of imipramine binding reflects the usual activity level of serotonin; the less imipramine binding, the less serotonin activity (Langer & Raisman, 1983). Fewer imipramine binding sites have been found in the brains of persons who died by suicide than in the autopsied brains of nonsuicides—in fact, approximately half as many binding sites has been the usual finding.

At first glance, these and related studies may appear to tell us only that depressed people often attempt suicide. After all, depression is itself related to low serotonin activity. On the other hand, there is evidence of low serotonin activity even among suicidal subjects who have no history of depression (Van Praag, 1983; Brown et al., 1982). That is, low serotonin activity seems also to have a role in suicide separate from depression.

How, then, might low serotonin activity increase the likelihood of suicidal behavior? One possibility is that it contributes to aggressive behavior. It has been found, for example, that serotonin activity is lower in aggressive men than in nonaggressive men and that serotonin activity is often low in those who commit such aggressive acts as arson and murder (Stanley et al., 2000; Moffitt et al., 1998; Bourgeois, 1991). Moreover, other studies have found that depressed patients with lower serotonin activity try to commit suicide more often, use more lethal methods, and score higher in hostility on various personality inventories than do depressed patients with higher serotonin activity (Malone et al., 1996; Van Praag, 1986). Such findings suggest that low serotonin activity helps produce aggressive feelings and perhaps impulsive behavior (Mann & Arango, 1999; Volavka, 1995; Bourgeois, 1991). In people who are clinically depressed, low

ConsiderThis

◉ Although findings are sometimes mixed, many studies suggest that suicides committed by violent methods are highest during the spring and lowest in late fall (Pretti & Miotto, 2000). How might this trend be explained?

MOST COMMON KILLINGS

More suicides (31,000) than homicides (23,000) are committed in the United States each year.

serotonin activity may produce aggressive tendencies that cause them to be particularly vulnerable to suicidal thinking and action. Even in the absence of a depressive disorder, however, people with low serotonin activity may develop such aggressive feelings that they too are dangerous to themselves or to others.

Is Suicide Linked to Age?

The likelihood of committing suicide generally increases with age, although people of all ages may try to kill themselves. Recently clinicians have paid particular attention to self-destructive behavior in three age groups: *children,* partly because suicide at their young age contradicts society's perception that childhood is an enjoyable period; *adolescents,* because of the steady and highly publicized rise in their suicide rate; and the *elderly,* because suicide is more prevalent in this age group than in any other (see Figure 9-4). Although the features and theories of suicide discussed throughout this chapter apply to all age groups, each of these groups faces unique problems that may play key roles in the suicidal acts of its members (Richman, 1999).

Children

> Tommy [age 7] and his younger brother were playing together, and an altercation arose that was settled by the mother, who then left the room. The mother recalled nothing to distinguish this incident from innumerable similar ones. Several minutes after she left, she considered Tommy strangely quiet and returned to find him crimson-faced and struggling for air, having knotted a jumping rope around his neck and jerked it tight.
>
> *(French & Berlin, 1979, p. 144)*

> Dear Mom and Dad,
>   I love you. Please tell my teacher that I cannot take it anymore. I quit. Please don't take me to school anymore. Please help me. I will run away so don't stop me. I will kill myself. So don't look for me because I will be dead. I love you. I will always love you. Remember me.
>   Help me.
>   Love Justin [age 10]
>
> *(Pfeffer, 1986, p. 273)*

Although suicide is infrequent among children, it has been increasing over the past several decades (Pfeffer, 2000). Approximately 500 children under 14 years of age in the United States now commit suicide each year—around 0.9 per 100,000 in this age group, a rate nearly 800 percent higher than that of 1950 (Goldman & Beardslee, 1999; Stillion & McDowell, 1996). Boys outnumber girls by as much as five to one. In addition, it has been estimated that one of every 100 children try to harm themselves, and many thousands of children are hospitalized each year for deliberately self-destructive acts, such as stabbing, cutting, burning, overdosing, or jumping from high places.

One study of suicide attempts by children revealed that the majority had taken an overdose of drugs at home, half were living with only one parent, and a quarter had attempted suicide before (Kienhorst et al., 1987). Recent studies further suggest that the use of guns is increasing among children who attempt suicide (Cytryn & McKnew, 1996).

Researchers have found that suicide attempts by the very young are commonly preceded by such behavioral patterns as running away from home, accident-proneness, acting out, temper tantrums, self-depreciation, social withdrawal and

---

ConsiderThis

⊙ Often people view the suicide of an elderly or chronically sick person as less tragic than that of a young or healthy person. Why might they think this way, and is their reasoning valid?

SOURCES OF INFORMATION

Interviews indicate that elementary school children learn about suicide most often from television and discussions with other children, and rarely discuss suicide with adults (Mishara, 1999).

loneliness, extreme sensitivity to criticism, low tolerance of frustration, dark fantasies and daydreams, marked personality change, and overwhelming interest in death and suicide (Cytryn & McKnew, 1996; McGuire, 1982). Studies have further linked child suicides to the recent or anticipated loss of a loved one, family stress and parent unemployment, abuse by parents, and a clinical level of depression (Pfeffer, 2000; Goldman & Beardsley, 1999; Cytryn & McKnew, 1996; Pfeffer et al., 1993).

Most people find it hard to believe that children fully comprehend the meaning of a suicidal act. They argue that because a child's thinking is so limited, children who attempt suicide fall into Shneidman's category of "death ignorers," like Billy, who sought to join his mother in heaven (Fasko & Fasko, 1991). Many child suicides, however, appear to be based on a clear understanding of death and on a clear wish to die (Carlson et al., 1994; Pfeffer, 1993, 1986). In addition, suicidal thinking among even normal children is apparently more common than most people once believed (Kovacs et al., 1993; Pfeffer et al., 1984). Clinical interviews with schoolchildren have revealed that between 6 and 33 percent have thought about suicide (Culp, Clyman, & Culp, 1995; Jacobsen et al., 1994).

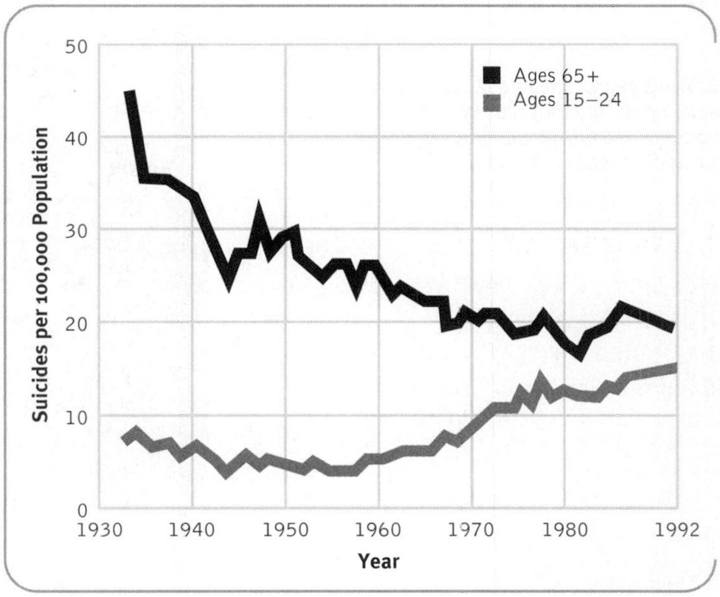

Adolescents

> Dear Mom, Dad, and everyone else,
>   I'm sorry for what I've done, but I loved you all and I always will, for eternity. Please, please, please don't blame it on yourselves. It was all my fault and not yours or anyone else's. If I didn't do this now, I would have done it later anyway. We all die some day, I just died sooner.
>
>   Love,
>
>   John
>
> *(Berman, 1986)*

The suicide of John, age 17, was not an unusual occurrence. Suicidal actions become much more common after the age of 14 than at any earlier age. According to official records, over 2,000 teenagers, or 11 of every 100,000, commit suicide in the United States each year, although some clinicians believe the actual rate to be up to three times higher than this (Madge & Harvey, 1999). In addition, as many as 500,000 teenagers may make attempts (Popenhagen & Qualkley, 1998). Because fatal illnesses are uncommon among the young, suicide has become the third leading cause of death in this age group, after accidents and homicides. Furthermore, as many as half of all teenagers have thought about killing themselves (Goldman & Beardsley, 1999; Diekstra et al., 1993).

Although young white Americans are more prone to suicide than young African Americans, the rates of the two groups are becoming closer (Center for Disease Control, 1998). The white American rate was 157 percent greater than the African American rate in 1980; today it is only 42 percent greater. This trend may reflect increasingly similar pressures on young African Americans and young white Americans—competition for grades and college opportunities, for example, is now intense for both groups. The growing suicide rate for young African Americans may also be linked to rising unemployment among them, the many anxieties of inner-city life, and the rage felt by many young African Americans over racial inequities in our society (Burr, Hartman, & Matteson, 1999; Lipschitz, 1995).

FIGURE 9-4 **Changing suicide rates** *The suicide rate of elderly people has been generally declining for at least a half-century, while that of young adults is increasing. Still, older people continue to be at higher risk for suicide. (Adapted from McIntosh, 1996, 1991, 1987.)*

WHERE TO TURN

One survey of 396 high school students indicated that teenagers are unlikely to initiate contact with a counselor during a suicidal crisis, but over half would probably tell a friend (Hennig, Crabtree, & Baum, 1998).

Difficult years *The angst, confusion, conflict, and impulsivity that typically characterize adolescence provide fertile ground for the growth of suicidal thoughts and attempts.*

SEXUAL STRESS

Sexual orientation is one of the most stressful issues for adolescents, particularly in a society biased against homosexuality. Although most studies have been unclear about links between sexual orientation and suicide, one survey of 736 public high school students found that suicide had been considered or attempted by 28 percent of the bisexual or homosexual males, 21 percent of bisexual or homosexual females, 15 percent of heterosexual females, and 4 percent of heterosexual males (Remafedi et al., 1998).

TEENAGE ANOMIE

In a study across several midwestern states, half of 300 homeless and runaway teenagers said that they had thoughts of suicide, and over one-quarter had attempted suicide in the previous year (Yoder et al., 1998).

About half of teenage suicides, like those of people in other age groups, have been tied to clinical depression, low self-esteem, and feelings of hopelessness, but many teenagers who try to kill themselves also appear to struggle with anger and impulsiveness (Goldman & Beardsley, 1999; Boergers et al., 1998; Stein et al., 1998). In addition, a number of adolescents who consider or attempt suicide may have deficiencies in their ability to sort out and solve problems (Carris, Sheeber, & Howe, 1998). Furthermore, such teenagers are often under great stress (Haliburn, 2000; Huff, 1999; de Wilde et al., 1998, 1992). Many of them experience long-term pressures such as poor (or missing) relationships with parents, family conflict, inadequate peer relationships, and social isolation (Pfeffer, Normandin, & Rakuma, 1998; Garnefski & Diekstra, 1997). Their actions also may be triggered by more immediate stress, such as a parent's unemployment or medical illness, financial setbacks for the family, or problems with a boyfriend or girlfriend (Fergusson, Woodward, & Horwood, 2000; Brent et al., 1998). Stress at school seems to be a particularly common problem for teenagers who attempt suicide (Ho et al., 1995; Brent et al., 1988). Some have trouble keeping up at school, while others may be high achievers who feel pressured to be perfect and to stay at the top of the class (Delisle, 1986; Leroux, 1986).

Some theorists believe that the period of adolescence itself produces a stressful climate in which suicidal actions are more likely (Goldman & Beardsley, 1999; Harter & Marold, 1994). Adolescence is a period of rapid growth, and it is often marked by conflicts, depressed feelings, tensions, and difficulties at home and school. Adolescents tend to react to events more sensitively, angrily, dramatically, and impulsively than individuals in other age groups; thus the likelihood of suicidal acts during times of stress is increased (Kaplan, 1984; Taylor & Stansfeld, 1984). Finally, the suggestibility of adolescents and their eagerness to imitate others, including others who attempt suicide, may set the stage for suicidal action (Hazell & Lewin, 1993; Berman, 1986). One study found that 93 percent of adolescent suicide attempters had known someone who had attempted suicide (Conrad, 1992).

Far more teenagers attempt suicide than actually kill themselves—the ratio may be as high as 200 to 1. The unusually large number of unsuccessful suicides may mean that teenagers are less certain than older persons who make such attempts. While some do indeed wish to die, many may simply want to make others understand how desperate they are, get help, or teach others a lesson (Boergers et al., 1998; Hawton, 1986). Up to half of teenage attempters make new suicide attempts in the future, and as many as 14 percent eventually die by suicide (Diekstra et al., 1995; Diekstra, 1989).

In countries around the world, the suicide rate for adolescents is not only high but increasing (Hawton et al., 2000). Overall, it has more than doubled in recent decades, as has the rate for young adults (Mehlum et al., 1999; McIntosh, 1996, 1991). Several theories, most pointing to societal changes, have been proposed to explain the dramatic rises in these two age groups. First, as the number and proportion of teenagers and young adults in the general population keep rising, the competition for jobs, college positions, and academic and athletic honors intensifies for them, leading increasingly to shattered dreams and ambitions (Holinger & Offer, 1993, 1991, 1982). Other explanations point to weakening ties in the family (which may produce feelings of alienation and rejection in many of today's young people) and to the increased availability of alcohol and other drugs and the pressure to use them among teenagers and young adults (Goldman & Beardsley, 1999; Jones, 1997). Two studies found that 70 percent of teenage suicide attempters abused drugs or alcohol to some degree (Miller et al., 1991; Shafii et al., 1985).

The mass media coverage of suicide attempts by teenagers and young adults may also contribute to the rise in the suicide rate among the young (Grossman & Kruesi, 2000; Moscicki, 1999). The detailed descriptions of teenage suicide that the media and the arts have offered in recent years may serve as models for young people who are contemplating suicide. Within days of the highly publicized suicides of four adolescents in one New Jersey town in 1987, dozens of teenagers across the United States took similar actions (at least twelve of them fatal)—two in the same garage just one week later.

The Elderly

Rose Ashby walks to the dry cleaner's to pick up her old but finest dinner dress. Although shaken at the cost of having it cleaned, Rose tells the sympathetic girl behind the counter, "Don't worry. It doesn't matter. I won't be needing the money any more."

Walking through the streets of St. Petersburg, Florida, she still wishes it had been Miami. The west coast of the fountain-of-youth peninsula is not as warm as the east. If only Chet had left more insurance money, Rose could have afforded Miami. In St. Petersburg, Rose failed to unearth de León's promised fount.

Last week, she told the doctor she felt lonely and depressed. He said she should perk up. She had everything to live for. What does he know? Has he lost a husband like Chet and his left breast to cancer all in one year? Has he suffered arthritis all his life? Were his ovaries so bad he had to undergo a hysterectomy? Did he have to suffer through menopause just to end up alone without family or friends? Does he have to live in a dungeon? Is his furniture worn, his carpet threadbare? What does he know? Might his every day be the last one for him?

As Rose turns into the walk to her white cinderblock apartment building, fat Mrs. Green asks if she is coming to the community center that evening. Who needs it? The social worker did say Rose should come. Since Rose was in such good health, she could help those not so well as she.

Help them do what? Finger-paint like little children? Make baskets like insane people? Sew? Who can see to sew? Besides, who would appreciate it? Who would thank her? Who could she tell about her troubles? Who cares?

When she told the doctor she couldn't sleep, he gave her the prescription but said that all elderly people have trouble sleeping. What does he know? Does he have a middle-aged daughter who can only think about her latest divorce, or grandchildren who only acknowledge her birthday check by the endorsement on the back? Are all his friends dead and gone? Is all the money from her dead husband's insurance used up? What does he know? Who could sleep in this dungeon?

THE HEAVY METAL LINK

Research finds that fans of heavy metal rock consider suicide more acceptable than do people who are not fans (Stack, 1998). But this attitude does not seem to result from the music or the lifestyle it espouses. Rather, heavy metal fans tend to be low in religiosity, and low religiosity relates to greater acceptability of suicide. Fans who are religious rate suicide just as unacceptable as non-fans do.

CRITICAL DOCTOR CALLS

Around 83 percent of persons who commit suicide have seen a family doctor in the previous year, 66 percent in the previous month, 40 percent in the previous week, and 20 percent within the past day (Pirkis & Burgess, 1998; Hirschfeld & Russell, 1997).

Back in her apartment, Rose washes and sets her hair. It's good she has to do it herself. Look at this hair. So thin, so sparse, so frowsy. What would a hairdresser think?

Then make-up. Base. Rouge. Lipstick. Bright red. Perfume? No! No cheap perfume for Rose today. Remember the bottles of Joy Chet would buy for her? He always wanted her to have the best. He would boast that she had everything, and that she never had to work a day in her life for it.

"She doesn't have to lift her little finger," Chet would say, puffing on his cigar. Where is the Joy now? Dead and gone. With Chet. Rose manages a wry laugh at the play on words.

Slipping into her dinner dress, she looks into the dresser mirror. "It's good you can't see this face now, Chet. How old and ugly it looks."

Taking some lavender notepaper from the drawer, she stands at the dresser to write. Why didn't anyone warn her that growing old was like this? It is so unfair. But they don't care. People don't care about anyone except themselves.

Leaving the note on the dresser, she suddenly feels excited. Breathing hard now, she rushes to the sink—who could call a sink in the counter in the living room a kitchen?—and gets a glass of water.

Trying to relax, Rose arranges the folds in her skirt as she settles down on the chaise. Carefully sipping the water as she takes all the capsules so as to not smear her lipstick, Rose quietly begins to sob. After a lifetime of tears, these will be her last. Her note on the dresser is short, written to no one and to everyone.

> You don't know what it is like
> to have to grow old and die.

(Gernsbacher, 1985, pp. 227–228)

HOMICIDE-SUICIDE IN THE ELDERLY

The rate of homicide-suicides among elderly couples (typically a husband shoots an ailing wife, then himself) increased nearly four times, from 0.12 per 100,000 population to 0.47, in Florida between 1988 and 1994. Most of the perpetrators had mental health problems, such as depression or alcohol abuse, but were not receiving treatment (Cohen et al., 1998).

In Western society the elderly are more likely to commit suicide than people in any other age group. About 19 of every 100,000 persons over the age of 65 in the United States commit suicide (McIntosh, 1995, 1992). Elderly persons committed over 19 percent of all suicides in the United States during the 1980s, yet they accounted for only 12 percent of the total population (McIntosh, 1992).

Many factors contribute to this high suicide rate (Pearson, 2000; Steffens & Blazer, 1999). As people grow older, all too often they become ill, lose close friends and relatives, lose control over their lives, and lose status in our society. Such experiences may result in feelings of hopelessness, loneliness, depression, or inevitability among aged persons and so increase the likelihood that they will attempt suicide. In one study, 44 percent of elderly people who committed suicide gave some indication that their act was prompted by the fear of being placed

The power of respect *Elderly persons are held in high esteem in many traditional societies because of the store of knowledge they have accumulated. Perhaps not so coincidentally, suicides among the elderly seem to be less common in these cultures than in those of many modern industrialized nations.*

in a nursing home (Loebel et al., 1991). Also, the suicide rate of elderly people who have recently lost a spouse is quite high (Duberstein, Conwell, & Cox, 1998; McIntosh, 1995, 1992). The risk is greatest during the first year of bereavement, but it remains high in later years as well.

Elderly persons are typically more determined than younger persons in their decision to die and they give fewer warnings of their intent, so their success rate is much higher (Clark, 1999; Conwell et al., 1998). Apparently one of every four elderly persons who attempts suicide succeeds. Given the resolve of aged persons and their physical decline, some people argue that older persons who want to die are clear in their thinking and should be allowed to carry out their wishes (see Box 9-5 on the next page). However, clinical depression appears to play an important role in as many as 60 percent of suicides by the elderly, suggesting that more elderly persons who are suicidal should be receiving treatment for their depressive disorders (Pearson, 2000; Haight et al., 1998).

The suicide rate among the elderly in the United States is lower in some minority groups (Kettl, 1998). Although Native Americans have the highest overall suicide rate, for example, the rate among elderly Native Americans is relatively low (NIH, 1999; McIntosh & Santos, 1982). The aged are held in high esteem by Native Americans and looked to for the wisdom and experience they have acquired over the years, and this may help account for their low suicide rate. Such high regard is in sharp contrast to the loss of status often experienced by elderly white Americans (Butler, 1975).

Similarly, the suicide rate is only one-third as high among elderly African Americans as among elderly white Americans (McIntosh, 1992). One reason for this low suicide rate may be the pressures assailing African Americans: "only the strongest survive" (Seiden, 1981). Those who reach an advanced age have overcome great adversity and often feel proud of what they have accomplished. Because reaching old age is not in itself a form of success for white Americans, their attitude toward aging is more negative. Another possible explanation is that aged African Americans have successfully overcome the rage that prompts many suicides in younger African Americans.

"Old age, more to be feared than death."

Juvenal, *Satires* XI

Treatment and Suicide

Treatment of suicidal people falls into two major categories: *treatment after suicide has been attempted* and *suicide prevention*. While treatment may also be beneficial to relatives and friends, whose feelings of loss, guilt, and anger after a suicide fatality or attempt can be intense, the discussion here is limited to the treatment afforded suicidal people themselves (Provini et al., 2000; McIntosh, 1999).

What Treatments Are Used after Suicide Attempts?

After a suicide attempt, most victims need medical care. Some are left with severe injuries, brain damage, or other medical problems. Once the physical damage is treated, psychotherapy or drug therapy may begin, on either an inpatient or outpatient basis.

Unfortunately, even after trying to kill themselves, many suicidal people fail to receive systematic psychotherapy (Beautrais, Joyce, & Mulder, 2000; Rhodes & Links, 1998). In a random survey of several hundred teenagers, 9 percent were found to have made at least one suicide attempt, and of those only half had received later psychological treatment (Harkavy & Asnis, 1985). Similarly, in another study, one-third of adolescent attempters reported that they had not received any help after trying to end their lives (Larsson & Ivarsson,

Words of despair *The poet and author Sylvia Plath committed suicide in 1963 at age 31. One of her poems reads "I saw the years of my life spaced along a road in the form of telephone poles, threaded together by wires. I counted one, two, three . . . nineteen poles, and then the wires dangled into space . . . I couldn't see a single pole beyond the nineteenth."*

BOX **9-5**

The Right to Commit Suicide

▌ In the fall of 1989, a Michigan doctor, Jack Kevorkian, built a "suicide device." A person using it could, at the touch of a button, change a saline solution being fed intravenously into the arm to one containing chemicals that would bring

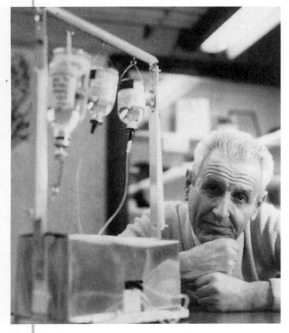

Dr. Jack Kevorkian and his suicide device.

unconsciousness and a swift death. The following June, under the doctor's supervision, Mrs. J. Adkins took her life. She left a note explaining: "This is a decision taken in a normal state of mind and is fully considered. I have Alzheimer's disease and I do not want to let it progress any further. I do not want to put my family or myself through the agony of this terrible disease." Mrs. Adkins believed that she had a right to choose death. Michigan authorities promptly prohibited further use of Kevorkian's device, but the physician continued to assist in the suicides of medically ill persons throughout the 1990s until his conviction in 1999 for second-degree murder in one case. ▌

(ADAPTED FROM BELKIN, 1990; MALCOLM, 1990)

*D*o individuals have a right to commit suicide, or does society have the right to stop them? Dr. Kevorkian's series of court battles have made many people ask just that.

The ancient Greeks valued physical and mental well-being in life and dignity in death. Therefore, individuals with a grave illness or mental anguish were permitted to commit suicide. Athenians could obtain official permission from the Senate to take their own lives, and judges were allowed to give them hemlock (Humphry & Wickett, 1986).

American traditions, in contrast, discourage suicide, on the basis of belief in the "sanctity of life" (Eser, 1981). We speak of "committing" suicide, as though it were a criminal act (Barrington, 1980), and we allow the state to use force, including involuntary commitment to a mental hospital, to prevent it. But times and attitudes are changing. Today the ideas of a "right to suicide" and "rational suicide" are receiving more support from the public, psychotherapists, and physicians. In fact, surveys suggest that half of today's physicians believe that suicide can be rational in some circumstances (Ganzini et al., 2000; Duberstein et al., 1995).

Public support for a right to suicide seems strongest in connection with great pain and terminal illness (Palmore, 1999; Werth, 2000, 1999, 1996). Studies show that about half or more of all Americans believe that terminally ill persons should be free to take their lives or

---

FATAL REPETITION

In Finland 19 percent of all males and 39 percent of all females who committed suicide in the late 1980s had made an earlier attempt the previous year (Isometsae & Loennqvist, 1998).

1998). In some cases, health-care professionals are at fault. In others, the person who has attempted suicide refuses follow-up therapy. One study of adolescents who had attempted to kill themselves found that 40 percent failed to attend available follow-up outpatient treatment sessions (Piacentini et al., 1995).

The goals of therapy are to keep people alive, help them achieve a nonsuicidal state of mind, and guide them to develop better ways of handling stress (Jacobson, 1999; Shneidman, 1999, 1993). Various therapies have been employed, including drug, psychodynamic, cognitive, group, and family therapies (Salzman, 1999; Rudd, 1998; Canetto, 1995). Treatment appears to help. Studies have found that 30 percent of suicide attempters who do not receive treatment try again, compared with 16 percent of patients in treatment (Nordstrom, Samuelsson, & Asberg, 1995; Allard et al., 1991). It is not clear, however, whether any one approach is more effective than the others (Canetto, 1995).

What Is Suicide Prevention?

During the past 30 years, emphasis around the world has shifted from suicide treatment to suicide prevention (Goldney, 1998; Kosky et al., 1998). In some respects this change is most appropriate: the last opportunity to keep many potential suicide victims alive comes before the first attempt.

to seek a physician's assistance to do so (Drane, 1995; Duberstein et al., 1995). There is also evidence that doctors and patients are acting on these beliefs. One survey of 118 doctors specializing in AIDS in San Francisco found that half of the respondents had helped patients commit suicide by giving them prescriptions for lethal amounts of narcotics (Slome et al., 1997).

Many people consider suicide a "natural right," comparable to the rights to life, ownership of property, and freedom of speech (Battin, 1999, 1982). Most, however, would limit this right to situations in which the act of suicide is indeed "rational," a choice made only when life stops being enriching and fulfilling (Ganzini et al., 2000; Weir, 1992). Most do not believe suicide appropriate in "irrational" cases, those motivated by psychological disorders such as depression (Werth, 2000; Battin, 1999, 1982; Clay, 1997; Weir, 1992). In line with such reasoning, the state of Oregon in 1997 passed the "Death with Dignity" Act, allowing a doctor to assist a suicide (by administering a lethal dose of drugs) if two physicians determine that the patient has less than six months to live and is not basing his or her decision to die on depression or another mental disorder.

It turns out, however, that even in cases of severe illness it is difficult to know whether a person's wish to commit suicide is rational (Kelly et al., 1999). Is the hopelessness of an AIDS patient realistic or a symptom of depression? Some research suggests that the suicidal acts of cancer and AIDS patients often spring largely from psychological and social distress (Breitbart, Rosenfeld, & Passik, 1996). Half or more of those patients who are suicidal may be clinically depressed (Chochinov et al., 1995; Brown et al., 1986). In some cases, then, it may be more beneficial to help individuals come to terms with a fatal illness than to offer them a license to end their lives (Hendin, 1999).

Some clinicians also worry that the right to suicide could be experienced more as a "duty to die" than as the ultimate freedom (McIntosh, 1999; Seale & Addington-Hall, 1995). Elderly people might feel selfish in expecting relatives to support and care for them when suicide is a socially approved alternative (Sherlock, 1983). Indeed, many already feel that they are "too old" and a burden to their families (Breitbart et al., 1996).

Finally, if suicide is accepted as rational, some people argue, it might be all too easy to accept forced euthanasia and infanticide as well (Annas, 1993; Battin, 1982). As care for the terminally ill grows ever more costly, would suicide be subtly encouraged among the poor and disadvantaged? Could assisted suicide become a form of medical cost control (Hendin, 1999; SHHV Task Force, 1995)? In the Netherlands, where assisted suicide and euthanasia are legal, "termination of the patient without explicit request" (involuntary euthanasia) occurs about 1,000 times each year (Hendin, 1999, 1995; Seale & Addington-Hall, 1995).

How are these issues to be resolved? Understanding and preventing suicide remain challenges for the future, and so do questions about whether and when we should stand back and do nothing. Whatever one's position on this issue, it is a matter of life and death.

The first **suicide prevention program** in the United States was founded in Los Angeles in 1955; the first in England, called the *Samaritans,* was started in 1953. There are now more than 200 suicide prevention centers in the United States and over 100 in England (Lester, 1989; Roberts, 1979). In addition, many mental health centers, hospital emergency rooms, pastoral counseling centers, and poison control centers now include suicide prevention programs among their services (Dorwart & Ostacher, 1999).

There are also more than 1,000 *suicide hot lines* in the United States, 24-hour-a-day telephone services (Garland, Shaffer, & Whittle, 1989). Callers reach a counselor, typically a *paraprofessional,* a person trained in counseling but without a formal degree, who provides services under the supervision of a mental health professional (Neimeyer & Bonnelle, 1997).

Suicide prevention programs and hot lines respond to suicidal people as individuals *in crisis*—that is, under great stress, unable to cope, feeling threatened or hurt, and interpreting their situations as unchangeable. Thus the programs offer *crisis intervention:* they try to help suicidal people see their situations more accurately, make better decisions, act more constructively, and overcome their crises (Frankish, 1994). Because crises can occur at any time, the centers advertise their hot lines and also welcome people who walk in without appointments.

Although specific features vary from center to center, the general approach used by the *Los Angeles Suicide Prevention Center* reflects the goals and techniques

"Passions unguided are for the most part mere madness."

Thomas Hobbes, *Leviathan,* 1651

SUICIDE PREVENTION PROGRAM A program that tries to identify people who are at risk of killing themselves and to offer them crisis intervention.

of many such organizations (Jacobs, 1999; Litman, 1995; Maris & Silverman, 1995). During the initial contact, the counselor has several tasks (Shneidman & Farberow, 1968):

Establishing a positive relationship As callers must trust counselors in order to confide in them and follow their suggestions, counselors try to set a positive and comfortable tone for the discussion. They convey that they are listening, understanding, interested, nonjudgmental, and available (see Box 9-6).

Understanding and clarifying the problem Counselors first try to understand the full scope of the caller's crisis and then help the person see the crisis in clear and constructive terms. In particular, they try to help callers see the central issues and the transient nature of their crises and recognize the alternatives to suicide.

Assessing suicide potential Crisis workers at the Los Angeles Suicide Prevention Center fill out a questionnaire, often called a *lethality scale,* to estimate the caller's potential for suicide. It helps them determine the degree of stress the caller is under, relevant personality characteristics, how detailed the suicide plan is, the severity of symptoms, and the coping resources available to the caller.

Assessing and mobilizing the caller's resources Although they may view themselves as ineffectual and helpless, people who are suicidal usually have many strengths and resources, including relatives and friends. It is the counselor's job to recognize, point out, and activate those resources.

Formulating a plan Together the crisis worker and caller develop a plan of action. In essence, they are agreeing on a way out of the crisis, an alternative to suicidal action. Most plans include a series of follow-up counseling sessions over the next few days or weeks, either in person at the center or by phone. Each plan also requires the caller to take certain actions and make certain changes in his or her personal life. Counselors usually negotiate a *no-suicide contract* with the caller—a promise not to attempt suicide, or at least a promise to reestablish contact if the caller again considers suicide. Although popular, the usefulness of such contracts has been called into question in recent years (Miller et al., 1998). In addition, if callers are in the midst of a suicide attempt, counselors will try to find out their whereabouts and get medical help to them immediately.

Although crisis intervention appears to be sufficient treatment for some suicidal people (Hawton, 1986), longer-term therapy is needed for most (Rudd, 2000;

ConsiderThis

◉ A person's wish to die is often ambivalent. In addition, most people who think about suicide do not act. How, then, should clinicians decide whether to hospitalize a person who is considering suicide or even one who has made an attempt?

BOX **9-6**

Attitudes toward Suicide: The Gender Factor

We already know that men and women have very different rates of suicide and, on average, use different methods when they attempt suicide. It turns out that men and women also have a different level of understanding of suicide and hold different attitudes toward people who try to kill themselves.

Judith Stillion (1995) has reported, for example, that women tend to know more of the facts about suicidal behavior than men do. They are also more willing to discuss the subject with suicidal people, and they report feeling more sympathy for those who are considering suicide. Yet women are more disapproving of suicide as a "solution" to problems.

ConsiderThis

◉ Why might women and men hold different attitudes toward suicide? • How might these attitudes relate to patterns of suicidal behavior for women and men? • Are there implications here for suicide peer counseling and crisis intervention?

Working with suicide *An individual breaks free from police and falls from a bridge in New York City. The scene reminds us that many kinds of professionals face suicidal behavior. Police departments typically provide special crisis intervention training so that officers can develop the skills to address suicidal individuals.*

Berman & Jobes, 1995; Litman, 1995). If the crisis intervention center does not offer this kind of therapy, the counselors will refer the clients elsewhere.

As the suicide prevention movement spread during the 1960s, many clinicians reasoned that **crisis intervention** techniques should also be applied to problems other than suicide. Crisis intervention has emerged during the past three decades as a respected form of treatment for such wide-ranging problems as teenage confusion, drug and alcohol abuse, rape victimization, and spouse abuse (Lester, 1989; Bloom, 1984).

Yet another way to help prevent suicide may be to reduce the public's access to common means of suicide (Leenaars & Lester, 1998; Lester, 1998). In 1960, for example, around 12 of every 100,000 persons in Britain killed themselves by inhaling coal gas (which contains carbon monoxide). In the 1960s Britain replaced coal gas with natural gas (which contains no carbon monoxide) as an energy source, and by the mid-1970s the rate of coal gas suicide fell to zero (Diekstra et al., 1995). In fact, England's overall rate of suicide, at least for older people, dropped as well. On the other hand, the Netherlands' drop in gas-induced suicides was compensated for by an increase in other methods, particularly drug overdoses. Thus, while it is hoped that such measures as gun control, safer medications, and car emission controls may lower suicide rates (Cantor & Baume, 1998; Lambert & Silva, 1998), there is no guarantee that they will (Stack, 1998; Lester, 1992).

Do Suicide Prevention Programs Work?

It is difficult for researchers to measure the effectiveness of suicide prevention programs (Reisch, Schlatter, & Tschacher, 1999; Goldney, 1998; Maris & Silverman, 1995). There are many kinds of programs, each with its own procedures

CRISIS INTERVENTION A treatment approach that tries to help people in a psychological crisis to view their situation more accurately, make better decisions, act more constructively, and overcome the crisis.

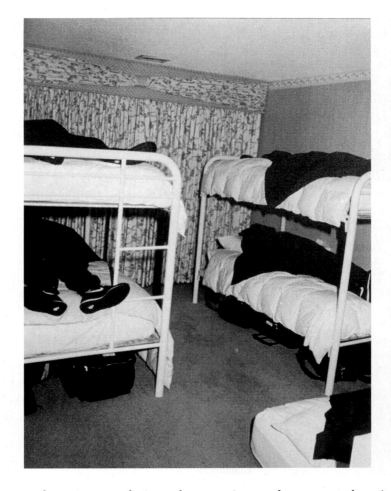

Mass suicide *Group suicides are not well understood nor effectively prevented by the clinical field. The nation will not soon forget the suicide by 39 members of the Heaven's Gate cult near San Diego, California, nor the eerie death scene. Each member lay neatly in new black sneakers, under a diamond-shaped purple shroud. Nearby was an overnight bag, packed with clothes, a notebook, and lip balm.*

AIDS AND SUICIDE

The suicide risk of men who have AIDS or who test positive for HIV is 36 times that of men without these diagnoses (Mishara, 1998).

and serving populations that vary in number, age, and environmental pressures. Communities with high suicide risk factors, such as a high elderly population or economic problems, may continue to have higher suicide rates than other communities regardless of the effectiveness of their local prevention centers.

Do suicide prevention centers reduce the number of suicides in a community? Clinical researchers do not know (Dorwart & Ostacher, 1999; Canetto, 1995). Studies comparing local suicide rates before and after the establishment of community prevention centers have yielded different findings. Some find a decline in a community's suicide rates, others no change, and still others an increase (Lester, 1997; Dew et al., 1987; Weiner, 1969). Then again, even an increase may represent a positive impact, if it is lower than the larger society's overall increase in suicidal behavior. One investigator found that although suicide rates did increase in certain cities with prevention programs, they increased even more in cities without such programs (Lester, 1991, 1974).

Do suicidal people contact prevention centers? Apparently only a small percentage do. Moreover, the typical caller to an urban prevention center appears to be young, African American, and female, whereas the greatest number of suicides are committed by elderly white men (Canetto, 1995; Lester, 1989, 1972).

Prevention programs do seem to reduce the number of suicides among those high-risk people who do call. One study identified 8,000 high-risk individuals who contacted the Los Angeles Suicide Prevention Center. Approximately 2 percent of these callers later committed suicide, compared to the 6 percent suicide rate usually found in similar high-risk groups. Clearly, centers need to be more visible and available to people who are thinking of suicide. The growing number of advertisements and announcements in newspapers and on television, radio, and billboards indicate a movement in this direction.

Partly because of the many suicide prevention programs and the data they have generated, today's clinicians have a better understanding of suicide and greater ability to assess its risk than those of the past (Clum & Yang, 1995; McIntosh et al., 1985). Studies reveal that the professionals who are most knowledgeable about suicide are psychologists, psychiatrists, and personnel who actually work in prevention programs (Domino & Swain, 1986). Other professionals whom suicidal persons might contact, such as members of the clergy, are sometimes less well informed (Leane & Shute, 1998; Domino & Swain, 1986).

Shneidman (1987) has called for broader and more effective public education about suicide as the ultimate form of prevention. And at least some *suicide education* programs—most of them concentrating on teachers and students—have begun to emerge (Kalafat & Ryerson, 1999; Mauk & Sharpnack, 1998; Metha, Weber, & Webb, 1998). The curriculum for such programs has been the subject of much debate and their merits have yet to be widely investigated (Dorwart & Ostacher, 1999; Kalafat & Elias, 1995). Nevertheless, clinicians typically agree with the goals behind these programs and, more generally, with Shneidman when he states:

> The primary prevention of suicide lies in education. The route is through teaching one another and . . . the public that suicide can happen to anyone, that there are verbal and behavioral clues that can be looked for . . . , and that help is available. . . .
>
> In the last analysis, the prevention of suicide is everybody's business.
>
> *(Shneidman, 1985, p. 238)*

ConsiderThis

Some schools are reluctant to offer suicide education programs, especially if they have never experienced a suicide attempt by one of their students. What might be their concerns? • How valid is their position?

CROSSROADS:
Psychological and Biological Insights Lag Behind

Once a mysterious and hidden problem, hardly acknowledged by the public and barely investigated by professionals, suicide today is the focus of much attention. During the past 25 years in particular, investigators have learned a great deal about this life-or-death problem.

In contrast to most other problems covered in this textbook, suicide has received more productive examination from proponents of the sociocultural model than from those of any other (Aldridge, 1998). Sociocultural theorists have, for example, highlighted the importance of societal change and stress, national and religious affiliation, marital status, gender, race, and the mass media. The insights and information gathered by psychological and biological researchers have been more limited.

Although sociocultural factors certainly shed light on the general background and triggers of suicide, they typically leave us unable to predict that a given person will attempt suicide. When all is said and done, clinicians do not yet fully understand why some people kill themselves while others in similar circumstances manage to find better ways of addressing their problems. Psychological and biological insights must catch up to the sociocultural insights if clinicians are truly to explain and understand suicide.

Treatments for suicide also pose some difficult problems. Clinicians have yet to develop clearly successful therapies for suicidal persons. Suicide prevention programs have been designed by the clinical community and certainly reflect its commitment to helping people who are suicidal, but it is not yet clear how much such programs actually reduce the overall risk or rate of suicide.

At the same time, the growth in the amount of research on suicide offers great promise. And perhaps most promising of all, clinicians are now enlisting the public in the fight against this problem. They are calling for broader public education about suicide—programs aimed at both young and old. It is reasonable to expect that the current commitment will lead to a better understanding of suicide and to more successful interventions. Such goals are of importance to

POLITICAL INTEGRATION AND DISINTEGRATION

After the reunification of Germany, East Germany's suicide rate dropped by one-third and West Germany's declined by one-quarter (Schmidtke et al., 1999). In contrast, suicide rates increased in the nations formed after the formal breakup of the Soviet Union in 1991 (Lester, 1998).

everyone. Although suicide itself is typically a lonely and desperate act, the impact of such acts is very broad indeed.

SUMMARY AND REVIEW

■ **What is suicide?** Suicide is a self-inflicted death in which one makes an intentional, direct, and conscious effort to end one's life. Four kinds of people who intentionally end their lives have been distinguished: the death seeker, the death initiator, the death ignorer, and the death darer. *pp. 253–255*

■ **Research strategies** Two major strategies are used in the study of suicide: retrospective analysis (a psychological autopsy) and the study of people who survive suicide attempts, on the assumption that they are similar to those who commit fatal suicides. Each strategy has limitations. *pp. 255–257*

■ **Patterns and statistics** Suicide ranks among the top ten causes of death in Western society. Rates vary from country to country. One reason seems to be cultural differences in religious affiliation, beliefs, or degree of devoutness. Suicide rates also vary according to race, gender, and marital status. *pp. 257–258*

■ **Factors that trigger suicide** Many suicidal acts are triggered by the current events or conditions in a person's life. The acts may be triggered by recent stressors, such as loss of a loved one and job loss, or long-term stressors like serious illness, an abusive environment, and job stress. They may also be preceded by changes in mood or thought, particularly increases in one's sense of hopelessness. In addition, the use of alcohol or other kinds of substances, mental disorders, or news of another's suicide may precede suicide attempts. *pp. 258–265*

■ **Explanations** The leading explanations for suicide come from the psychodynamic, sociocultural, and biological models. Each has received only limited support. Psychodynamic theorists believe that suicide usually results from depression and self-directed anger. Emile Durkheim's sociocultural theory defines three categories of suicide based on the person's relationship with society: egoistic, altruistic, and anomic suicides. And biological theorists suggest that the activity of the neurotransmitter serotonin is particularly low in individuals who commit suicide. *pp. 265–270*

■ **Suicide in different age groups** The likelihood of suicide varies with age. It is uncommon among children, although it has been increasing in that group during the past several decades. Suicide by adolescents, a more common occurrence, is also on the increase. In particular, suicide attempts by this age group are numerous. Adolescent suicide has been linked to clinical depression, anger, impulsiveness, major stress, and adolescent life itself. The rising suicide rate among adolescents and young adults may be related to the growing number and proportion of young people in the general population, the weakening of family ties, the increased availability and use of drugs among the young, and the broad media coverage of suicide attempts by the young.

In Western society the elderly are more likely to commit suicide than people in any other age group. The loss of health, friends, control, and status may produce feelings of hopelessness, loneliness, depression, or inevitability in this age group. *pp. 270–275*

■ **Treatment and suicide** Treatment may follow a suicide attempt. In such cases, therapists seek to help the person achieve a nonsuicidal state of mind and develop better ways of handling stress and solving problems.

Over the past 30 years, emphasis has shifted to suicide prevention. Suicide prevention programs include 24-hour-a-day hot lines and walk-in centers staffed largely by paraprofessionals. During their initial contact with a suicidal person, counselors seek to establish a positive relationship, to understand and clarify the problem, to assess the potential for suicide, to assess and mobilize the caller's resources, and to formulate a plan for overcoming the crisis. Beyond such crisis intervention, most suicidal people also need longer-term therapy. In a still broader attempt at prevention, suicide education programs for the public are beginning to appear. *pp. 275–281*

PSYCHOLOGICAL DAMAGE CONTROL
The term "postvention" describes services offered after a trauma (for example, after a schoolmate's suicide) to head off psychological aftereffects.

CYBER STUDY

▲ *Observe the behaviors, thought processes, and feelings of suicidal persons.*
▲ *What role might alcohol or weapon availability play in suicide?* ▲ *How might unemployment relate to suicidal thinking?* ▲ *Does treatment eliminate (or reduce) suicidal thinking?* ▲ *What are the reactions of relatives and friends after a suicide?*

SEARCH THE *ABNORMAL PSYCHOLOGY* CD-ROM FOR

▲ Chapter 9 video cases and discussions
 "Andy"—Suicide
 "Sue"—Suicide
 "Bonnie"—Suicide
 "Jed"—Suicide

▲ Chapter 9 practice test and feedback

▲ Additional video cases and discussions
 "Meredith"—Mood Disorders: Medication and Talk Therapy
 "Derrick"—Hamilton Depression Scale

LOG ON TO THE COMER WEB PAGE

[www.worthpublishers.com/comerabnormalpsychology4e] **FOR**

▲ Suggested Web links, research exercises, FAQ page, additional Chapter 9 practice test questions

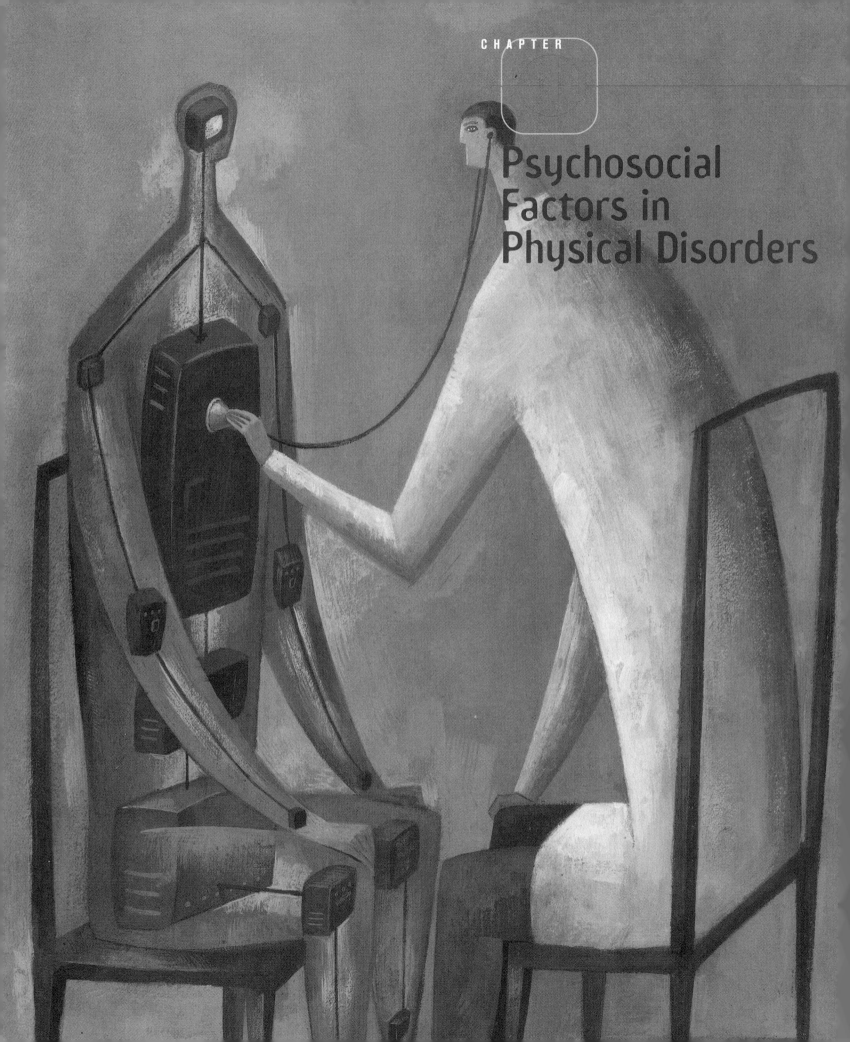

Psychosocial Factors in Physical Disorders

It was Wednesday. The big day. Midterms in History and Physics back to back, beginning at 11:30, and an oral presentation in Psych at 3:30. Jerry had been preparing for, and dreading, this day for weeks, calling it "D-day" to his friends. He had been up until 3:30 A.M. the night before, studying, trying to nail everything down. It seemed like he had fallen asleep only minutes ago, yet here it was 9:30 A.M. and the killer day was under way.

As soon as he woke, Jerry felt a tight pain grip his stomach. He also noticed buzzing in his ears, a lightheadedness, and even aches throughout his body. He wasn't surprised, given the day he was about to face. One test might bring a few butterflies of anxiety; two and a presentation were probably good for a platoon of dragonflies.

As he tried to get going, however, Jerry began to suspect that this was more than butterflies. His stomach pain soon turned to spasms, and his lightheadedness became outright dizziness. He could barely make it to the bathroom without falling. Thoughts of breakfast made him nauseous. He knew he couldn't keep anything down.

Jerry began to worry, even panic. This was hardly the best way to face what was in store for him today. He tried to shake it off, but the symptoms stayed. Finally, his roommate convinced him that he had better go to a doctor. At 10:30, just an hour before the first exam, he entered the big brick building called "Student Health." He felt embarrassed, like a wimp, but what could he do? Persevering and taking two tests under these conditions wouldn't prove anything—except maybe that he was foolish.

Psychosocial factors—factors that are either psychological or sociocultural—may contribute to somatic, or bodily, illnesses in a variety of ways. The physician who sees Jerry has some possibilities to sort out. Jerry could be *faking* his pain and dizziness to avoid taking a tough test. Alternatively, he may be *imagining* his illness, that is, faking to himself. Then again, his physical symptoms could be very real, yet triggered by *stress:* whenever he feels extreme pressure, such as a person can feel before an important test, Jerry's gastric juices may become more active and irritate his intestines, and his blood pressure may rise and cause him to become dizzy. Or he may be coming down with the flu. Even this *purely medical* problem, however, could be linked to psychosocial factors. Perhaps weeks of constant worry about the exams and presentation have weakened Jerry's body so that he was not able to fight off the flu virus. Whatever the diagnosis, Jerry's state of mind and his social environment are affecting his body. The physician's view of the role played by these psychosocial factors will in turn affect the treatment Jerry receives.

We have observed that psychological disorders frequently have physical causes. Abnormal neurotransmitter activity, for example, contributes to generalized anxiety disorder, panic disorder, and depression. Is it surprising, then, that bodily illnesses may have psychosocial causes? Today's clinicians recognize the wisdom of Socrates's fourth century B.C. assertion: "You should not treat body without soul."

The idea that psychological and sociocultural factors may contribute to somatic illnesses has ancient roots, yet it had few proponents before the twentieth century. It was particularly unpopular during the Renaissance, when medicine began to be a physical science and scientists became committed to the pursuit of objective "fact" (Gatchel & Baum, 1983). At that time the mind was considered the province of priests and philosophers, not of physicians and scientists. By the seventeenth century, the French philosopher René Descartes went so far as to claim that the mind, or soul, is separate from the body—a position called **mind-body dualism**.

Not until the twentieth century were medical scientists persuaded that psychosocial factors such as stress, worry, and unconscious needs can contribute in major ways to physical illness. Today, in fact, certain kinds of physical illnesses, known as *factitious disorder* and the *somatoform disorders,* are thought to be caused almost entirely by psychosocial factors. Other kinds, called *psychophysiological disorders*, are believed to result from an interaction of biological, psychological, and sociocultural factors.

Factitious Disorder

Like Jerry, people who become physically sick usually go to a physician. Sometimes, however, the physician cannot find a medical cause for the problem and may suspect that other factors are involved. Perhaps the patient is *malingering*—intentionally feigning illness to achieve some external gain, such as financial compensation or deferment from military service (LoPiccolo, Goodkin, & Baldewicz, 1999).

Alternatively, a patient may intentionally produce or feign physical symptoms simply from a wish to be a patient; that is, the motivation for assuming the sick role may be the role itself. Physicians would then decide that the patient is manifesting **factitious disorder** (see Table 10-1).

> A 29-year-old female laboratory technician was admitted to the medical service via the emergency room because of bloody urine. The patient said that she was being treated for lupus erythematosus by a physician in a different city. She also mentioned that she had had Von Willebrand's disease (a rare hereditary blood disorder) as a child. On the third day of her hospitalization, a medical student mentioned to the resident that she had seen this patient several weeks before at a different hospital in the area, where the patient had been admitted for the same problem. A search of the patient's belongings revealed a cache of anticoagulant medication. When confronted with this information she refused to discuss the matter and hurriedly signed out of the hospital against medical advice.
>
> *(Spitzer et al., 1981, p. 33)*

Table 10-1 DSM-IV Checklist

FACTITIOUS DISORDER

1. Intentional production or feigning of physical signs or symptoms.
2. Physical symptoms motivated by a desire to assume the sick role.
3. Absence of economic or other external incentives for the behavior.

Based on APA, 2000, 1994.

People with factitious disorder often go to extremes to create the appearance of illness. Many give themselves medications secretly. Some, like the woman just described, inject drugs to cause bleeding. Still others use laxatives to produce chronic diarrhea. High fevers are especially easy to create. In one study of patients with prolonged mysterious fever, more than 9 percent were eventually diagnosed with factitious disorder (Feldman, Ford, & Reinhold, 1994).

People with factitious disorder often research their supposed ailments and are impressively knowledgeable about medicine (Miner & Feldman, 1998). Many eagerly undergo painful testing or treatment, even surgery (Stern & Cremens, 1998). When confronted with evidence that their symptoms are factitious, they typically deny the charges and leave the hospital; they may enter another hospital the same day.

"I hope you're not going to be like the twenty incompetent doctors who couldn't find anything wrong with me."

MIND-BODY DUALISM René Descartes's position that the mind is separate from the body.

FACTITIOUS DISORDER An illness with no identifiable physical cause, in which the patient is believed to be intentionally producing or faking symptoms in order to assume a sick role.

MUNCHAUSEN SYNDROME The extreme and chronic form of factitious disorder.

MUNCHAUSEN SYNDROME BY PROXY A disorder in which parents make up or induce physical illnesses in their children.

Munchausen syndrome is the extreme and chronic form of factitious disorder. It is named after Baron Munchausen, an eighteenth-century cavalry officer who journeyed from tavern to tavern in Europe telling fantastical tales about his supposed military adventures (Feldman et al., 1994; Zuger, 1993). In a related disorder, **Munchausen syndrome by proxy**, parents make up or produce physical illnesses in their children, leading in some cases to repeated painful diagnostic tests, medication, and surgery (Libow & Schreier, 1998; Parnell, 1998). If the children are removed from their parents and placed in the care of others, their symptoms disappear (see Box 10-1 on the next page).

Clinical researchers have had a hard time determining the prevalence of factitious disorder, since patients hide the true nature of their problem (Bauer & Boegner, 1996). Overall, the pattern is more common in women than men (APA, 2000). Severe cases, however, seem to be more frequent among men. The disorder usually begins during early adulthood.

Factitious disorder seems to be most common among people who (1) as children received extensive medical treatment for a true physical disorder, (2) experienced family disruptions or physical or emotional abuse in childhood, (3) carry a grudge against the medical profession, (4) have worked as a nurse, laboratory technician, or medical aide, or (5) have an underlying personality problem such as extreme dependence (APA, 2000; Feldman et al., 1994). They often have poor social support, few enduring social relationships, and little family life (Feldman et al., 1994).

The precise causes of factitious disorder are not understood, although clinical reports have suggested depression, unsupportive parental relationships during childhood, and an extreme need for social support that is not otherwise forthcoming (Ozden & Canat, 1999; Feldman et al., 1994). Nor have clinicians been able to develop dependably effective treatments for it (Simon, 1998; Feldman & Feldman, 1995). Some cases, however, have responded to joint treatment by psychotherapists and medical practitioners (Parker, 1993; Schwarz et al., 1993).

Psychotherapists and medical practitioners often report feelings of annoyance or anger toward people with factitious disorder, feeling that these people are, at the very least, wasting their time. Yet people with this disorder, like most people with psychological disorders, feel they have no control over their problem, and they often experience great distress. They need effective therapy rather than scorn, but such help is often not available to them.

PSEUDOLOGIA FANTASTICA

Some people with factitious disorder are able to provide an elaborate (and false) medical history, a fabrication called *pseudologia fantastica*.

"Mental disorders arise from physical ones, and likewise physical disorders arise from mental ones."

The Mahabharata, c. A.D. 200

BOX 10-1

Munchausen Syndrome by Proxy

I [Jennifer] had been hospitalized 200 times and undergone 40 operations. Physicians removed her gallbladder, her appendix and part of her intestines, and inserted tubes into her chest, stomach and intestines. [The 9-year-old from Florida] was befriended by the Florida Marlins and served as a poster child for health care reform, posing with Hillary Rodham Clinton at a White House rally. Then police notified her mother that she was under investigation for child abuse. Suddenly, Jennifer's condition improved dramatically. In the next nine months, she was hospitalized only once, for a viral infection. . . . Experts said Jennifer's numerous baffling infections were "consistent with someone smearing fecal matter" into her feeding line and urinary catheter. I

(KATEL & BECK, 1996)

Recent cases like Jennifer's have horrified the public and called attention to *Munchausen syndrome by proxy*. This disorder is caused by a caregiver who uses various techniques to induce symptoms in a child—giving the child drugs, tampering with medications, contaminating a feeding tube, or even smothering the child, for example. The illness can take almost any form, but the most common symptoms are bleeding, seizures, asthma, comas, diarrhea, vomiting, "accidental" poisonings, infections, fevers, and sudden infant death syndrome (Libow & Schreier, 1998; Boros et al., 1995).

Between 10 and 30 percent of the victims of Munchausen syndrome by proxy die as a result of their symptoms, and 8 percent of those who survive are permanently disfigured or physically impaired (Boros et al., 1995; Von Burg & Hibbard, 1995). Psychological, educational, and physical development are also affected (Libow & Schreier, 1998; Libow, 1995; Skau & Mouridsen, 1995). Jennifer missed so much school that at age 9 she could barely read or write.

The syndrome is very hard to diagnose (Pankratz, 1999) and may be more common than clinicians once thought. The parent (usually the mother) seems to be so devoted and caring that others sympathize with and admire her. Yet the physical problems disappear when child and parent are separated. In many cases siblings of the sick child have also been victimized (Skau & Mouridsen, 1995; Smith & Killam, 1994).

What kind of parent carefully inflicts pain and illness on her own child? The typical Munchausen mother is emotionally needy: she craves the attention and praise she receives for the devoted care of her sick child. She may have little social support outside the medical system, and her husband tends to be absent, physically or emotionally. Many of these mothers are intelligent; often they have a medical background of some kind—perhaps having worked formerly in a doctor's office. Typically they deny their actions, even in the face of clear evidence, and refuse to undergo therapy. In fact, successful treatment has rarely been documented.

Law enforcement authorities are reluctant to consider Munchausen syndrome by proxy a psychological disorder and instead approach it as a crime—a meticulously planned form of child abuse (Libow & Schreier, 1998). They almost always require that the child be permanently separated from the mother (Skau & Mouridsen, 1995). At the same time, a parent who resorts to such actions is obviously experiencing serious psychological disturbance and greatly needs clinical help. Thus clinical researchers and practitioners must now work to develop clearer insights and more effective treatments for such parents and for their small victims.

Convalescent, 1994, by Frank Holl

Somatoform Disorders

When a physical illness has no apparent medical cause, physicians may alternatively suspect a **somatoform disorder**, another pattern of physical complaints with largely psychosocial causes (Taylor & Mann, 1999). In contrast to people with factitious disorder, those with somatoform disorders do not consciously want or purposely induce their symptoms; they almost always believe that their problems are genuinely medical. In some somatoform disorders, known as *hys-*

terical somatoform disorders, there is an actual change in physical functioning. In others, the *preoccupation somatoform disorders,* people who are healthy become preoccupied with the mistaken belief that there is something physically wrong with them.

What Are Hysterical Somatoform Disorders?

People with **hysterical somatoform disorders** exhibit actual changes in their physical functioning. These somatoform disorders are often hard to distinguish from genuine medical problems (Hickie et al., 2000; Fink et al., 1999). In fact, it is always possible that a diagnosis of hysterical disorder is a mistake and that the patient's problem actually has an undetected organic cause (Kulisevsky et al., 1998; Johnson et al., 1996). The tools of medical science are too imprecise to eliminate physical factors completely. DSM-IV lists three hysterical somatoform disorders: *conversion disorder, somatization disorder,* and *pain disorder associated with psychological factors.*

CONVERSION DISORDER In **conversion disorder**, a psychosocial conflict or need is converted into dramatic physical symptoms that affect voluntary motor or sensory functioning (see Table 10-2). The symptoms often seem neurological,

MISTAKEN IDENTITY

Many medical problems with vague and confusing symptoms—hyperparathyroidism, multiple sclerosis, and lupus are examples—are frequently misdiagnosed as hysterical disorders. In the past, whiplash was regularly diagnosed as hysteria (Merskey, 1986).

Table 10-2 DSM-IV Checklist

CONVERSION DISORDER

1. One or more physical symptoms or deficits affecting voluntary motor or sensory function that suggest a neurological or other general medical condition.
2. Psychological factors judged to be associated with the symptom or deficit.
3. Symptom or deficit not intentionally produced or feigned.
4. Symptom or deficit not fully explained by a general medical condition or a substance.
5. Significant distress or impairment.

SOMATIZATION DISORDER

1. A history of many physical complaints, beginning before the age of 30, that occur over a period of several years and result in treatment being sought or in significant impairment.
2. Physical complaints over the period include all of the following:
   (a) Four different kinds of pain symptoms.
   (b) Two gastrointestinal symptoms.
   (c) One sexual symptom.
   (d) One neurological-type symptom.
3. Physical complaints not fully explained by a known general medical condition or a drug, or extending beyond the usual impact of such a condition.
4. Symptoms not intentionally produced or feigned.

PAIN DISORDER ASSOCIATED WITH PSYCHOLOGICAL FACTORS

1. Significant pain as the primary problem.
2. Psychological factors judged to have the major role in the onset, severity, exacerbation, or maintenance of the pain.
3. Symptom or deficit not intentionally produced or feigned.
4. Significant distress or impairment.

Based on APA, 2000, 1994.

SOMATOFORM DISORDER A physical illness or ailment that is explained largely by psychosocial causes, in which the patient experiences no sense of wanting or guiding the symptoms.

HYSTERICAL SOMATOFORM DISORDERS Somatoform disorders in which people suffer actual changes in their physical functioning.

CONVERSION DISORDER A somatoform disorder in which a psychosocial need or conflict is converted into dramatic physical symptoms that affect voluntary motor or sensory function.

Mind over matter *The opposite of hysterical disorders—though again demonstrating the power of psychological processes—are instances in which people "ignore" pain or other physical symptoms. Despite a badly injured leg, Kerri Strug completes a near perfect vault routine and landing, leading the United States gymnastics team to an Olympic gold medal in 1996.*

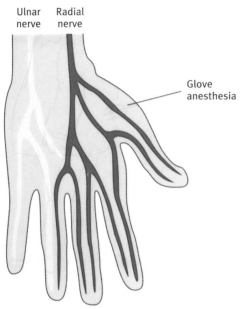

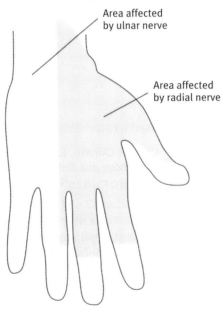

FIGURE 10-1 **Glove anesthesia** *In this conversion symptom the entire hand, extending from the fingertips to the wrist, becomes numb. Actual physical damage to the ulnar nerve, in contrast, causes anesthesia in the ring finger and little finger and beyond the wrist partway up the arm; and damage to the radial nerve causes loss of feeling only in parts of the ring, middle, and index fingers and the thumb and partway up the arm. (Adapted from Gray, 1959.)*

the way the nervous system is known to work (APA, 2000, 1994; Tiihonen et al., 1995). In a conversion symptom called *glove anesthesia*, numbness begins sharply at the wrist and extends evenly right to the fingertips. As Figure 10-1 shows, real neurological damage is rarely as abrupt or equally distributed. Even the numbness, tingling, and pain of the neurological disease *carpal tunnel syndrome* rarely spread uniformly throughout the hand.

The physical effects of a hysterical disorder may also differ from those of the corresponding medical problem (Levy, 1985). For example, when paralysis from the waist down, or *paraplegia*, is caused by damage to the spinal cord, a person's leg muscles may *atrophy*, or waste away, unless physical therapy is applied. People whose paralysis is the result of a conversion disorder, in contrast, do not usually experience atrophy. Perhaps they exercise their muscles without being aware that they are doing so. Similarly, people with conversion blindness have fewer accidents than people who are organically blind, an indication that they have at least some vision even if they are unaware of it.

What Are Preoccupation Somatoform Disorders?

Hypochondriasis and *body dysmorphic disorder* are **preoccupation somatoform disorders**. People with these problems misinterpret and overreact to bodily symptoms or features no matter what friends, relatives, and physicians may say. Although preoccupation disorders also cause great distress, their impact upon an individual's personal, social, and occupational life differs from that of hysterical disorders.

HYPOCHONDRIASIS People who suffer from **hypochondriasis** unrealistically interpret bodily symptoms as signs of a serious illness (see Table 10-3). Often their symptoms are merely normal bodily changes, such as occasional coughing,

Table 10-3 DSM-IV Checklist

HYPOCHONDRIASIS

1. Preoccupation with fears or beliefs that one has a serious disease, based on misinterpretation of bodily symptoms, lasting at least six months.
2. Persistence of preoccupation despite appropriate medical evaluation and reassurance.
3. Absence of delusions.
4. Significant distress or impairment.

BODY DYSMORPHIC DISORDER

1. Preoccupation with an imagined or exaggerated defect in appearance.
2. Significant distress or impairment.

Based on APA, 2000, 1994.

sores, or sweating. Although some patients recognize that their concerns are excessive, many do not.

Hypochondriasis can present a picture very similar to that of somatization disorder (Leibbrand et al., 2000). Each typically involves numerous physical symptoms and frequent visits to doctors, and each arouses great concern. If the anxiety is great and the bodily symptoms are relatively minor, a diagnosis of hypochondriasis is probably in order; if the symptoms overshadow the patient's anxiety, they may indicate somatization disorder (Hollifield et al., 1999; Noyes, 1999).

Although hypochondriasis can begin at any age, it starts most often in early adulthood, among men and women in equal numbers (APA, 2000, 1994). Between 1 and 5 percent of all people experience the disorder (APA, 2000). As with pain disorder associated with psychological factors, physicians report seeing many cases (Fink et al., 1999; Escobar et al., 1998). For most patients, the symptoms wax and wane over the years.

BODY DYSMORPHIC DISORDER People who experience **body dysmorphic disorder**, also known as **dysmorphophobia**, become deeply concerned about some imagined or minor defect in their appearance (see again Table 10–3). Most often, they focus on wrinkles, spots on the skin, excessive facial hair, swelling of the face, or a misshapen nose, mouth, jaw, or eyebrow. Some worry about the appearance of their feet, hands, breasts, penis, or other body parts. Still others are concerned about bad odors coming from sweat, breath, genitals, or the rectum (Neziroglu, 1998; Marks, 1987). Here we see such a case:

> A woman of 35 had for 16 years been worried that her sweat smelled terrible. The fear began just before her marriage when she was sharing a bed with a close friend who said that someone at work smelled badly, and the patient felt that the remark was directed at her. For fear that she smelled, for 5 years she had not gone out anywhere except when accompanied by her husband or mother. She had not spoken to her neighbors for 3 years because she thought she had overheard them speak about her to some friends. She avoided cinemas, dances, shops, cafes, and private homes. Occasionally she visited her in-laws, but she always sat at a distance from them. Her husband was not allowed to invite any friends home; she constantly sought reassurance from him about her smell; and strangers who rang the doorbell were not answered. Television commercials about deodorants made her very anxious. She refused to attend the local church

STRICTLY A COINCIDENCE?

On February 17, 1673, the French actor-playwright Molière collapsed on stage and died while performing in *Le Malade imaginaire (The Hypochondriac)* (Ash, 1999).

PREOCCUPATION SOMATOFORM DISORDERS Somatoform disorders in which people misinterpret and overreact to minor, even normal, bodily symptoms or features.

HYPOCHONDRIASIS A somatoform disorder in which people mistakenly fear that minor changes in their physical functioning indicate a serious disease.

BODY DYSMORPHIC DISORDER A somatoform disorder marked by excessive worry that some aspect of one's physical appearance is defective. Also known as *dysmorphophobia*.

because it was small and the local congregants might comment on her. The family had to travel to a church 8 miles away in which the congregants were strangers; there they sat or stood apart from the others. Her husband bought all her new clothes as she was afraid to try on clothes in front of shop assistants. She used vast quantities of deodorant and always bathed and changed her clothes before going out, up to 4 times daily.

(Marks, 1987, p. 371)

SEEKING FRESHNESS
Around 45 percent of American adults use mouthwash every day (Kanner, 1995).

It is common in our society to be concerned about appearance (see Box 10-2 on page 297). Many teenagers and young adults worry about acne, for instance. The concerns of people with body dysmorphic disorder, however, are extreme. Sufferers may be unable to look others in the eye, or they may go to great lengths to conceal their "defects"—say, always wearing sunglasses to hide their supposedly misshapen eyes. Some seek plastic surgery (Hollander & Aronowitz, 1999). One study found that 30 percent of subjects with the disorder were housebound, and 17 percent had attempted suicide (Phillips et al., 1993).

Most cases of the disorder begin during adolescence. Often, however, people don't reveal their concerns for many years. Up to 2 percent of people in the United States suffer from body dysmorphic disorder (Hollander & Aronowitz, 1999). Clinical reports suggest that it may be equally common among men and women (APA, 2000; Bower, 1995).

What Causes Somatoform Disorders?

Theorists typically explain the preoccupation somatoform disorders much as they do anxiety disorders (Phillips, 2000; Noyes, 1999; Phillips et al., 1995). Behaviorists, for example, believe that the fears found in hypochondriasis and body dysmorphic disorder have been acquired earlier in life through classical conditioning or modeling (Whitehead et al., 1994) (see Figure 10-2). Cognitive theorists suggest that people with the disorders are so sensitive to and threatened by bodily cues that they come to overinterpret them (Cox, Borger, & Enns, 1999; Marcus, 1999).

In contrast, the hysterical somatoform disorders—conversion, somatization, and pain disorders—are widely considered unique and in need of special explanations. The ancient Greeks believed that only women had hysterical disorders. The uterus of a sexually ungratified woman was supposed to wander throughout her body in search of fulfillment, producing a physical symptom wherever it lodged. Thus Hippocrates suggested marriage as the most effective treatment for such disorders.

LINGUISTIC ROOTS
The term "hysteria" comes from *hustera,* the Greek word for "uterus."

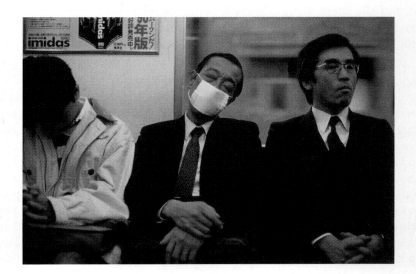

An extreme case of hypochondriasis? *Not necessarily. After a 1918 flu epidemic killed 20 million people, people in Japan started wearing a* masuku *to protect them from stray germs. Some, like this commuter, continue the tradition during cold and flu season.*

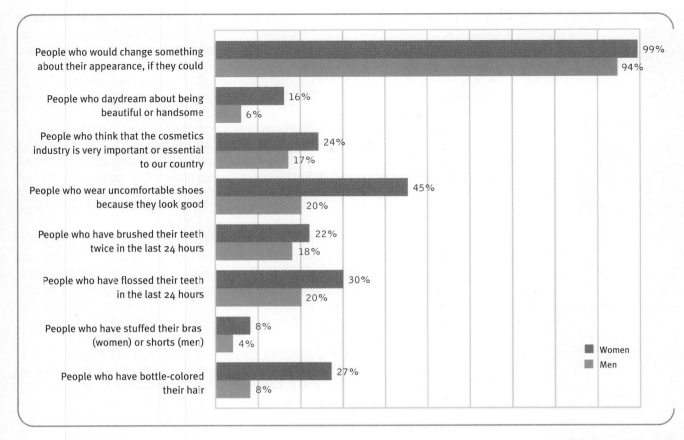

People who would change something about their appearance, if they could — 99% Women, 94% Men

People who daydream about being beautiful or handsome — 16% Women, 6% Men

People who think that the cosmetics industry is very important or essential to our country — 24% Women, 17% Men

People who wear uncomfortable shoes because they look good — 45% Women, 20% Men

People who have brushed their teeth twice in the last 24 hours — 22% Women, 18% Men

People who have flossed their teeth in the last 24 hours — 30% Women, 20% Men

People who have stuffed their bras (women) or shorts (men) — 8% Women, 4% Men

People who have bottle-colored their hair — 27% Women, 8% Men

■ Women ■ Men

FIGURE 10-2 **"Mirror, mirror, on the wall . . ."** *People with body dysmorphic disorder are not the only ones who have concerns about their appearance. Surveys find that in our appearance-conscious society, large percentages of people regularly think about and try to change the way they look (Kimball, 1993; Poretz & Sinrod, 1991; Weiss, 1991; Simmon, 1990).*

Work by Ambroise-Auguste Liébault and Hippolyte Bernheim in the late nineteenth century set the stage for today's prevailing opinion that psychosocial factors cause hysterical disorders. These researchers founded the Nancy School in Paris for the study and treatment of mental disorders. There they were able to produce hysterical symptoms in normal people—deafness, paralysis, blindness, and numbness—by hypnotic suggestion, and they could remove the symptoms by the same means (see Chapter 1). If hypnotic suggestion could both produce and reverse physical dysfunctioning, they concluded, hysterical disorders might themselves be caused by psychological processes.

Today's leading explanations for hysterical somatoform disorders come from the psychodynamic, behavioral, and cognitive models. None has received compelling research support, however, and the disorders are still poorly understood (Lautenbacher & Rollman, 1999; Kirmayer, Robbins, & Paris, 1994).

THE PSYCHODYNAMIC VIEW As we noted in Chapter 1, Freud's theory of psychoanalysis began with his efforts to explain hysterical symptoms. Indeed, he was one of the few clinicians of his day to treat patients with these symptoms seriously, as people with a genuine problem. After studying hypnosis in Paris and becoming acquainted with the work of Liébault and Bernheim, Freud became interested in the work of an older physician, Josef Breuer (1842–1925). Breuer had successfully used hypnosis to treat a woman he called Anna O., who suffered from hysterical deafness, disorganized speech, and paralysis. Critics have since questioned whether Anna's ailments were entirely hysterical and whether Breuer's treatment helped her as much as he claimed (Ellenberger, 1972). But on the basis of this and similar cases, Freud (1894) came to believe that hysterical disorders represented a *conversion* of underlying emotional conflicts into physical symptoms.

Observing that most of his patients with hysterical disorders were women, Freud centered his explanation of hysterical disorders on the needs and conflicts

"A cheerful heart is a good medicine, but a downcast spirit dries up the bones."

Proverbs 17:22

The real Anna O *Historians have identified Bertha Pappenheim, a wealthy Viennese woman, as the subject of Joseph Breuer's famous case of "Anna O," in which a patient with hysterical symptoms was said to be cured by hypnosis (Ellenberger, 1972).*

experienced by girls during their phallic stage (ages 3 through 5). At that time in life, he believed, all girls develop a pattern of desires called the *Electra complex:* each girl experiences sexual feelings for her father and, at the same time, recognizes that she must compete with her mother for his affection. However, in deference to her mother's more powerful position and to cultural taboos, the child typically represses her sexual feelings and rejects these early desires for her father.

Freud believed that if a child's parents overreact to her sexual feelings—with strong condemnations or punishments, for example—the Electra conflict will be unresolved and the child may reexperience sexual anxiety throughout her life. Whenever events trigger sexual feelings, she may experience an unconscious need to hide them from both herself and others. Freud concluded that some women hide their sexual feelings by unconsciously converting them into physical symptoms.

Most of today's psychodynamic theorists have modified Freud's explanation of hysterical disorders, particularly his notion that the disorders can always be traced to an unresolved Electra conflict (Hess, 1995; Scott, 1995). They continue to believe, however, that sufferers of these disorders have unconscious conflicts carried forth from childhood which arouse anxiety and that the individuals convert this anxiety into "more tolerable" physical symptoms (Stuart & Noyes, 1999).

Psychodynamic theorists propose that two mechanisms are at work in hysterical somatoform disorders—primary gain and secondary gain (Colbach, 1987). People achieve **primary gain** when their hysterical symptoms keep their internal conflicts out of awareness. During an argument, for example, a man who has underlying fears about expressing anger may develop a conversion paralysis of the arm, thus preventing his feelings of rage from reaching consciousness. People achieve **secondary gain** when their hysterical symptoms further enable them to avoid unpleasant activities or to receive kindness or sympathy from others. When, for example, a conversion paralysis allows a soldier to avoid combat duty or conversion blindness prevents the breakup of a relationship, secondary gain may be operating. In short, primary gains initiate hysterical symptoms; secondary gains are by-products of the symptoms. Both forms of gain help to lock in the conversion symptoms, according to psychodynamic theorists.

Electra complex goes awry *Freud argued that a hysterical disorder may result when parents overreact to their daughter's early displays of affection for her father. The child may go on to exhibit sexual repression in adulthood and convert sexual feelings into physical ailments.*

BOX **10-2**

Cultural Dysmorphophobia?

*P*eople almost everywhere want to be attractive, and they tend to worry about how they appear in the eyes of others. At the same time, these concerns take different forms in different cultures.

Whereas people in Western society worry in particular about their body size and facial features, women of the Padaung tribe in Burma focus on the length of their neck and wear heavy stacks of brass rings to try to extend it. Although many such women are trying to make money as a tourist attraction, others are striving desperately to achieve what their culture has taught them is the perfect neck size. Said one, "It is most beautiful when the neck is really long. The longer it is, the more beautiful it is. I will never take off my rings . . . I'll be buried in them" (Mydans, 1996).

ConsiderThis

◉ How might a culture help create individual cases of body dysmorphic disorder (dysmorphophobia)? • Why do some people in a society carry cultural ideals to an extreme, while others stay within normal bounds?

THE BEHAVIORAL VIEW Behavioral theorists propose that the physical symptoms of hysterical disorders bring *rewards* to sufferers (see Table 10-4 on the next page). Perhaps the symptoms remove the individuals from an unpleasant work situation or relationship or bring attention to the individuals (Whitehead et al., 1994; Ullmann & Krasner, 1975). In response to such rewards, the sufferers learn to display the symptoms more and more. Behaviorists also hold that people who are familiar with an illness will more readily adopt its physical symptoms (Garralda, 1996). In fact, studies find that many sufferers develop their hysterical symptoms after they or their close relatives or friends have had similar medical problems (Stuart & Noyes, 1999; Livingston, Witt, & Smith, 1995).

The behavioral focus on rewards is similar to the psychodynamic idea of secondary gains. The key difference is that psychodynamic theorists view the gains as indeed secondary—that is, as rewards that come only after underlying conflicts produce the disorder. Behaviorists view them as the primary cause of the development of the disorder.

Like the psychodynamic explanation, the behavioral view of hysterical disorders has received little support from empirical research. Even clinical case reports

PRIMARY GAIN In psychodynamic theory, the gain achieved when hysterical symptoms keep internal conflicts out of awareness.

SECONDARY GAIN In psychodynamic theory, the gain achieved when hysterical symptoms elicit kindness from others or provide an excuse to avoid unpleasant activities.

PSYCHOPHYSIOLOGICAL DISORDERS Illnesses that result from an interaction of psychosocial and organic factors. Also known as *psychosomatic disorders.*

ULCER A lesion that forms in the wall of the stomach or of the duodenum.

ASTHMA A medical problem marked by narrowing of the trachea and bronchi, which results in shortness of breath, wheezing, coughing, and a choking sensation.

INSOMNIA Difficulty falling or staying asleep.

MUSCLE CONTRACTION HEADACHE A headache caused by the narrowing of muscles surrounding the skull. Also known as *tension headache.*

MIGRAINE HEADACHE An extremely severe headache that occurs on one side of the head, often preceded by a warning sensation and sometimes accompanied by dizziness, nausea, or vomiting.

HYPERTENSION Chronic high blood pressure.

CORONARY HEART DISEASE Illness of the heart caused by a blocking of the coronary arteries.

antidepressant medications to treat people with hysterical disorders. Research has, in fact, suggested that this treatment does bring improvement—particularly a reduction in pain symptoms (Fishbain et al., 1998).

Psychophysiological Disorders

About 75 years ago clinicians identified a group of physical illnesses that seemed to result from an *interaction* of psychosocial and physical factors (Dunbar, 1948; Bott, 1928). These illnesses differed from somatoform disorders in that both psychosocial *and* physical factors helped cause them and the illnesses further brought about actual physical damage. Whereas early versions of the DSM labeled these illnesses **psychophysiological**, or **psychosomatic, disorders**, DSM-IV labels them *psychological factors affecting medical condition* (see Table 10-5). We shall use the more familiar term "psychophysiological" in discussing them.

Table 10-5 DSM-IV Checklist

PSYCHOLOGICAL FACTORS AFFECTING GENERAL MEDICAL CONDITION

1. The presence of a general medical condition.
2. Psychological factors adversely affecting the general medical condition in one of the following ways:
   (a) Influencing the course of the general medical condition.
   (b) Interfering with the treatment of the general medical condition.
   (c) Posing additional health risks.
   (d) Stress-related physiological responses precipitating or exacerbating the general medical condition.

Based on APA, 2000, 1994.

Traditional Psychophysiological Disorders

Before the 1970s, clinicians believed that only a limited number of illnesses were psychophysiological. The best known and most common of these were ulcers, asthma, insomnia, chronic headaches, high blood pressure, and coronary heart disease. Recent research, however, has shown that many other physical illnesses—including bacterial and viral infections—may be caused by an interaction of psychosocial and physical factors. We will focus first on the traditional psychophysiological disorders and then the newer illnesses in this category.

Ulcers are lesions (holes) that form in the wall of the stomach or of the duodenum, resulting in burning sensations or pain in the stomach, occasional vomiting, and stomach bleeding. This disorder is experienced by up to 10 percent of all people in the United States and is responsible for more than 6,000 deaths each year. Ulcers are often caused by an interaction of psychosocial factors, such as environmental stress, intense feelings of anger or anxiety, or a dependent personality style (Tennant, 1988; Weiner et al., 1957), and physiological factors, such as bacterial infections (Blaser, 1996; McDaniel et al., 1994).

Asthma causes the body's airways (the trachea and bronchi) to narrow periodically, making it hard for air to pass to and from the lungs (Simeonsson et al., 1995). The resulting symptoms are shortness of breath, wheezing, coughing, and a terrifying choking sensation. Some 15 million people in the United States suffer from asthma, twice as many as 15 years ago (NCHS, 1999). Most victims are children or young teenagers at the time of the first attack

Treating asthma *Children who suffer from asthma may use an aerochamber, or inhaler, to help them inhale helpful medications. The child pumps the medication into the device's plastic tube and then inhales it.*

(DeAngelis, 1994). Seventy percent of all cases appear to be caused by an interaction of psychosocial factors, such as environmental pressures, troubled family relationships, anxiety, or high dependency needs, and physiological factors, such as allergies to specific substances, a slow-acting sympathetic nervous system, or a weakened respiratory system traceable to respiratory infections or genetic inheritance (Lehrer, 1998; Carr, 1998; Godding, Kruth, & Jamart, 1997).

Insomnia, difficulty initiating or maintaining sleep, plagues approximately 20 to 45 percent of the population each year (APA, 2000; Mendelson et al., 1999). Although many of us have transient bouts of insomnia that last a few nights or so, a large number of people experience ongoing *chronic* insomnia that lasts months or years (see Box 10-3 on the next page). They feel as though they are almost constantly awake. Chronic insomniacs are often very sleepy during the day and may have difficulty functioning effectively. Insomnia may be caused by a combination of psychosocial factors, such as high levels of anxiety or depression, and physiological problems, such as an overactive arousal system or certain medical ailments (Mendelson et al., 1999; Ohayon, Caulet, & Lemoine, 1998).

Chronic headaches are frequent intense aches of the head or neck that are not caused by another physical disorder. There are two types. **Muscle contraction**, or **tension**, **headaches** are identified by pain at the back or front of the head or the back of the neck (Peterson et al., 1995). These occur when the muscles surrounding the skull tighten, narrowing the blood vessels. Approximately 40 million Americans suffer from such headaches. **Migraine headaches** are extremely severe, often near-paralyzing aches located on one side of the head. They are often preceded by a warning sensation called an *aura* and are sometimes accompanied by dizziness, nausea, or vomiting. Migraine headaches are thought by some medical theorists to develop in two phases: (1) blood vessels in the brain narrow, so that the flow of blood to parts of the brain is reduced, and (2) the same blood vessels later expand, so that blood flows through them rapidly, stimulating many neuron endings and causing pain. Migraines are suffered by about 23 million people in the United States.

Research suggests that chronic headaches are caused by an interaction of psychosocial factors, such as environmental pressures, a passive personality style, or general feelings of helplessness, anger, anxiety, or depression (Berliner et al., 1999; Stronks et al., 1999; Merikangas, Stevens, & Angst, 1994), and physiological factors, such as abnormal activity of the neurotransmitter serotonin, vascular problems, or muscle weakness (Hargreaves & Shepheard, 1999; Park, 1996).

Hypertension is a state of chronic high blood pressure. That is, the blood pumped through the body's arteries by the heart produces too much pressure against the artery walls. Hypertension has few outward symptoms (Fahrenberg et al., 1995), but it interferes with the proper functioning of the entire cardiovascular system, greatly increasing the likelihood of stroke, coronary heart disease, and kidney problems. It is estimated that 40 million people in the United States have hypertension, 14,000 die directly from it annually, and millions more perish because of illnesses caused by it (NCHS, 1999; Johnson, Gentry, & Julius, 1992). Fewer than 15 percent of all cases are caused by physiological abnormalities alone; the rest result from a combination of psychosocial and physiological factors and are called *essential hypertension* (McDaniel et al., 1994). Some of the leading psychosocial causes of essential hypertension are constant environmental danger, general feelings of anger or depression, and an unexpressed need for power (Gidron, Davidson, & Bata, 1999; Dubbert, 1995). Physiological causes include faulty *baroreceptors*—sensitive nerves in the blood vessels responsible for signaling the brain that blood pressure is becoming too high (Julius, 1992; Schwartz, 1977).

Coronary heart disease is caused by a blocking of the *coronary arteries*—the blood vessels that surround the heart and are responsible for carrying oxygen to the heart muscle. The term actually refers to several problems, including *angina pectoris*, extreme chest pain caused by a partial blockage of the coronary arteries; *coronary occlusion*, a complete blockage of a coronary artery that halts the flow of

SOURCE OF INSPIRATION

The surreal world of *Alice's Adventures in Wonderland* may have been inspired by the migraine aura perceptions of its author, Lewis Carroll. Diary entries and sketches by Carroll indicate that he experienced migraine hallucinations in the years leading to the book's writing (Podoll & Robinson, 1999).

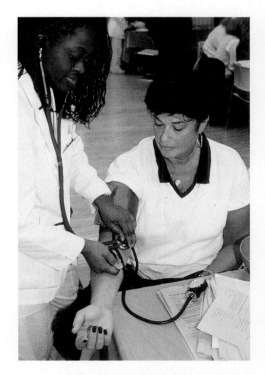

The silent killer *High blood pressure, a psychophysiological disorder with few outward signs, kills tens of thousands of people each year, prompting health care professionals to regularly provide free blood pressure checks in the workplace or other community settings.*

DISREGULATION MODEL A theory that explains psychophysiological disorders as breakdowns in the body's negative feedback loops, which lead to interruption of the body's smooth, self-regulating operation.

blood to various parts of the heart muscle; and *myocardial infarction* (a "heart attack"). Together such problems are the leading cause of death in men over the age of 35 and of women over 40 in the United States, accounting for over 700,000 deaths each year, almost one-third of all deaths in the nation (Blanchard, 1994; Matarazzo, 1984). The majority of all cases of coronary heart disease are related to an interaction of psychosocial factors, such as job stress or high levels of anger or depression, and physiological factors, such as a high level of cholesterol, obesity, hypertension, the effects of smoking, or lack of exercise (Wulsin, Vaillant, & Wells, 1999; Glassman & Shapiro, 1998; Mancini, 1998).

DISREGULATION AND PSYCHOPHYSIOLOGICAL DISORDERS By definition, psychophysiological disorders are caused by an interaction of psychosocial and physical factors. How do these factors combine to produce a given illness? Gary Schwartz, a leading researcher, has proposed the **disregulation model** to answer this question (see Figure 10-3). Schwartz suggests that the brain and body ordinarily set up *negative feedback loops* that sustain the smooth operation of the body (Schwartz, 1982, 1977). The brain receives information about events from the environment, processes this information, and then stimulates body organs to act. Mechanisms in the organs then provide critical negative feedback, telling the brain that its stimulation has been sufficient and should now stop.

A typical feedback loop is the one that governs blood pressure (Egan, 1992; Julius, 1992). In one part of the loop the brain receives a stimulus that signals

B O X **10-3**

Sleep and Sleep Disorders: Another Mind-Body Connection

Sleep, a physical activity crucial to health and well-being, is affected by both physical and psychosocial factors. Sleep deprivation for 100 hours or more leads to hallucinations, paranoia, and bizarre behavior. When people remain awake for over 200 hours, they frequently experience periods of "microsleep," naps lasting two to three seconds. The body simply refuses to be entirely deprived of sleep for long.

To learn more about sleep, researchers bring people into the laboratory and record their activities as they sleep. They use three types of recording devices, usually simultaneously: the *electroencephalograph* (*EEG*), which records electrical activity in the brain; the *electrooculograph,* which records the movement of the eyes; and the *electromyograph* (*EMG*), which measures muscle tension and activity.

One important discovery has been that eyes move rapidly about 25 percent of the time a person is asleep (Aserinsky & Kleitman, 1953), a phenomenon known as *rapid eye movement,* or *REM.* REM sleep is often called "paradoxical

sleep" because it resembles both deep sleep and wakefulness. Despite small movements and muscle twitches, the body is immobilized—essentially paralyzed. At the same time, the eyes are darting back and forth. Blood flow to the brain increases, and the EEG shows brain wave activity that is almost identical to that of an awake and alert person. Eighty percent of the subjects who are awakened from REM sleep report that they were dreaming.

DSM-IV identifies a number of sleep disorders. Like psychophysiological disorders, most of them result from an interaction of physical and psychosocial causes. The *dyssomnias* are sleep disorders that involve disturbances in the amount, quality, or timing of sleep. The *parasomnias* involve abnormal events that occur during sleep (APA, 2000, 1994; Stores, 1996).

Dyssomnias

Insomnia, difficulty falling or staying asleep, is the most common dyssomnia. For a diagnosis of *primary insomnia,* this problem must be the *main* complaint, last at least one month, and cause significant dysfunctioning (APA, 2000, 1994; Ohayon, 1997). Between 1 and 10 percent of all adults qualify for a diagnosis

***Sleep*, by George Tooker**

dangers in the environment, such as nearby lightning or cars speeding by. In the next part of the loop, the brain processes this information and alerts the nervous system, which causes bodily organs to raise blood pressure. In a subsequent part of the loop, *baroreceptors,* the pressure-sensitive cells in the body's blood vessels, alert the nervous system when the blood pressure rises too high, and the nervous system then lowers the blood pressure. In short, the various parts of the feedback loop work together to help keep blood pressure at an appropriate level.

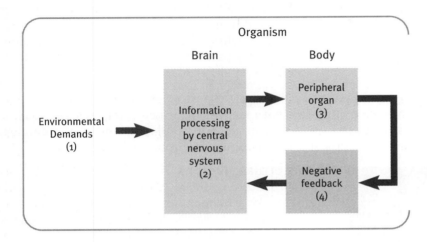

FIGURE 10-3 **Negative feedback loop**
According to Schwartz's disregulation model, in the normal process of regulation the organism receives environmental pressure (1); the brain processes information about this pressure (2); the brain stimulates body organs into action (3); and the organs provide negative feedback to the brain, sending the message that the stimulation has been sufficient and should stop (4). (Adapted from Schwartz, 1977.)

of primary insomnia each year (APA, 2000). Contrasting with insomnia, *primary hypersomnia* is a dyssomnia characterized by excessive sleepiness that lasts for at least a month. The person with hypersomnia may need extra hours of sleep each night and may need to sleep during the daytime as well (APA, 2000, 1994).

Narcolepsy, a disorder marked by more than three months of sudden bouts of REM sleep during waking hours, afflicts more than 135,000 people in the United States. Although narcolepsy is a biological disorder, the bouts of REM sleep are often triggered by strong emotion. Sufferers may suddenly fall into REM sleep in the midst of an argument or during an exciting part of a football game.

Breathing-related sleep disorder disrupts sleep by depriving the brain of oxygen. *Sleep apnea,* the most common form of this disorder, is found in up to 10 percent of the adult population (APA, 2000). Its victims, typically overweight men who are heavy snorers, actually stop breathing for up to 30 seconds or more as they sleep. Hundreds of

episodes may occur nightly without the victim's awareness.

People with *circadian rhythm sleep disorder* experience excessive sleepiness or insomnia as a result of a mismatch between their own sleep-wake pattern and the sleep-wake schedule of most other people in their environment. Often the disorder takes the form of falling asleep late and awakening late. This dyssomnia can be induced by night-shift work, frequent changes in work shifts, or repeated episodes of jet lag.

Parasomnias

Nightmare disorder is the most common of the parasomnias. Most people experience nightmares from time to time, but in some cases nightmares become frequent and cause such great distress that the individual must receive treatment. Such nightmares often increase under stress.

Persons with *sleep terror disorder* awaken suddenly during the first third of their evening sleep, screaming in extreme fear and agitation. They are in a state of panic, are often incoherent, and

have a heart rate to match. Generally the sufferer does not remember the episode the next morning. Sleep terrors most often appear in children and disappear during adolescence. Up to 6 percent of children experience them at some time (APA, 2000).

People with a *sleepwalking disorder*— usually children—repeatedly leave their beds and walk around, without being conscious of the episode or remembering it later. The episodes occur in the first third of the night. People who are awakened while sleepwalking are confused for several moments. If allowed to continue sleepwalking, they eventually return to bed. Sleepwalkers usually manage to avoid obstacles, climb stairs, and perform complex activities, in a seemingly emotionless state. Accidents do happen, however: tripping, bumping into furniture, and even falling out of windows have all been reported. Up to 5 percent of children experience this disorder for a period of time, and as many as 30 percent have occasional episodes. Sleepwalking usually disappears by age 15 (APA, 2000, 1994).

WHITE COAT HYPERTENSION

A British study found that one-third of patients who had high blood pressure during a doctor's visit were merely experiencing a temporary rise, caused largely by nervousness about the visit or test (Lahiri et al., 1998). Their blood pressure dropped to near normal levels once they left the doctor's office.

According to Schwartz, if one part of a feedback loop fails to operate properly, the body will enter a state of *disregulation* rather than effective self-regulation; problems will occur throughout the loop; and a psychophysiological disorder may ultimately develop. Hypertension, for example, may result from a problem in any part of the blood-pressure feedback loop. Should information from the environment be excessive (as when one is faced with unrelenting job stress or long-term unemployment), should the processing of information be generally faulty (as when one keeps misinterpreting everyday events), should an organ malfunction (as when the aorta narrows abnormally), or should a feedback mechanism fail (as when baroreceptors fail to inform the brain that blood pressure is rising too high), inaccurate messages will be fed to the next part of the loop and then relayed to the next, until every part in the loop has been alerted to keep the blood pressure high (Landsbergis et al., 1994).

WHAT FACTORS CONTRIBUTE TO PSYCHOPHYSIOLOGICAL DISORDERS? Over the years, clinicians have identified sociocultural, psychological, and biological variables that may contribute to disregulation and to the development of psychophysiological disorders. Some are particularly common.

SOCIOCULTURAL FACTORS The stressful demands placed on people by their culture or social group may lead to disregulation and set the stage for psychophysiological disorders. The stress may come from *cataclysmic, background,* or *personal stressors* (Lazarus & Cohen, 1977). *Cataclysmic stressors* are events that have a powerful and lingering effect on a whole population, such as wars or natural disasters. After a 1979 nuclear accident at Three Mile Island in Pennsylvania, for example, people who lived near the nuclear plant experienced a high number of psychophysiological disorders, and they continued to do so for years (Schneiderman & Baum, 1992; Baum et al., 1983). *Background stressors* are ongoing, local social conditions that produce persistent feelings of tension, such as life in a crime-ridden neighborhood or working in an unsatisfying job (Landsbergis et al., 1994). For example, hypertension is twice as common among African Americans as among white Americans (Johnson et al., 1992). Although physiological factors may largely explain this difference, some theorists believe that it is also linked to the dangerous environments in which so many African Americans live, the unsatisfying jobs at which so many must work, and the racial discrimination most face (Clark et al., 1999; Dorr, 1998). Finally, *personal stressors* are temporary negative events that occur in one's immediate environment, such as a death in the family, divorce, or loss of a job (Luecken, 1998; Levy et al., 1997; Johnson et al., 1992).

Risky business *A currency dealer shouts orders during trading at the Paris Stock Exchange. The stresses of working in high-pressure environments apparently increase one's risk of developing a medical illness, including coronary heart disease.*

PSYCHOLOGICAL FACTORS According to many theorists, certain needs, attitudes, emotions, or coping styles may cause people to overreact repeatedly to stressors, and so increase their chances of developing psychophysiological disorders (Watten et al., 1997). Researchers have found, for example, that men with a *repressive coping style* (a reluctance to express discomfort, anger, or hostility) tend to experience a particularly sharp rise in blood pressure, heart rate, and autonomic activity during experimentally induced stress (Coy, 1998; NAMHC, 1996; Vogele & Steptoe, 1993). Increased rates of asthma have also been found among some people with this coping style (Lehrer, 1998; DeAngelis, 1992).

Another personality style that may contribute to psychophysiological disorders is the **Type A personality style**, an idea introduced by two cardiologists, Meyer Friedman and Raymond Rosenman (1959). People with this personality style are said to be consistently angry, cynical, driven, impatient, competitive, and ambitious. They interact with the world in a way that, according to Friedman and Rosenman, produces continual stress and often leads to coronary heart disease. People with a **Type B personality style**, by contrast, are thought to be more relaxed, less aggressive, and less concerned about time. They are less likely

JOB DISSATISFACTION

In surveys, 35 percent of white Americans report being dissatisfied with their jobs, as compared with 44 percent of African Americans (Watson Wyatt Worldwide, 1995).

to experience cardiovascular deterioration. In reality, of course, most people fall between these two extremes, tending toward one or the other but showing features of both.

The link between the Type A personality style and coronary heart disease has been supported by many studies (Rosenman, 1990; Williams, 1989). In one well-known investigation of more than 3,000 people, Friedman and Rosenman (1974) separated healthy men in their 40s and 50s into Type A and Type B categories and then followed their health over the next eight years. More than twice as many Type A men developed coronary heart disease. Later studies found that Type A functioning correlates similarly with heart disease in women (Haynes, Feinleib, & Kannel, 1980).

In recent studies the link found between the Type A personality style and heart disease has not been as strong as the earlier studies suggest. They do show, nevertheless, that some of the characteristics that supposedly make up the Type A style, particularly hostility, are very likely to be related to heart disease (Gallacher et al., 1999; Morren, 1998). In fact, some studies have found that feelings of anger may directly impair the heart's pumping action and efficiency (Ironson et al., 1992).

BIOLOGICAL FACTORS We saw in Chapter 3 that the brain activates body organs through the operation of the *autonomic nervous system (ANS)*, the network of nerve fibers that connect the central nervous system to the body's organs. If we see a frightening animal, for example, a group of ANS fibers known as the *sympathetic nervous system* increases its activity. As the danger passes, another group of ANS fibers, the *parasympathetic nervous system*, takes over to counter the activity of the ANS, causing our heartbeat, respiration, and other bodily functions to return to normal. These two complementary parts of the ANS are constantly working in opposition to help our bodies operate in a smooth and stable manner—a condition called *homeostasis* (Cannon, 1927).

Hans Selye (1976, 1974) was one of the first researchers to describe the relationship between stress and the ANS. He proposed that people typically respond to stress in three stages, which he called, collectively, the *general adaptation syndrome*. In the presence of threat, the sympathetic nervous system increases its activity and arouses responses throughout the body (*alarm stage*). The parasympathetic nervous system next attempts to counteract these responses (*resistance stage*). Finally, if exposure to stress continues, the resistance may fail and organs controlled by the ANS may become overworked and break down (*exhaustion stage*).

Because the ANS is the body system responsible for "normal" stress reactions, defects in this system are believed to contribute to the development of psychophysiological disorders (Boyce et al., 1995; Hugdahl, 1995). If one's ANS is stimulated too easily, for example, it may overreact to situations that most people find only mildly stressful, eventually damaging certain organs and causing a psychophysiological disorder (Boyce et al., 1995).

Other more specific biological problems may also contribute to psychophysiological disorders. People may, for example, have *local biological weaknesses*: certain organs may be defective or abnormally prone to break down under stress (Rees, 1964). Thus a person with a weak gastrointestinal system may be a prime candidate for an ulcer, whereas someone with a weak respiratory system may develop asthma readily. Alternatively, people may display *individual biological reactions* that heighten their chances of developing psychophysiological disorders. Some individuals perspire in response to stress, others develop stomachaches, and still others experience a rise in blood pressure (Fahrenberg, Foerster, & Wilmers, 1995). Although such variations are perfectly normal, the repeated overuse of a single system may wear it down and eventually help cause a psychophysiological disorder. Research has indicated, for example, that some individuals are particularly likely to experience temporary rises in blood pressure when stressed (McDaniel et al., 1994). It may be that they are prone to develop hypertension. Similarly, some infants secrete much more gastric acid under stress than other

ConsiderThis

⊙ One study found that the heart rate responses of angry subjects were higher when their anger was triggered by imagined or recalled events than by current events (Foster, Smith, & Webster, 1999). Why might imagined or recollected anger be particularly powerful?

"SO SCARED, MY HEART STOPPED"

Monitoring high school students as they were watching a scary movie, researchers found that a half hour into the movie the students' heart rate slowed down by five beats per minute, skin temperature dropped 10 degrees, and palms became more moist (Sparks & Cantor, 1998).

TYPE A PERSONALITY STYLE A personality pattern characterized by hostility, cynicism, drivenness, impatience, competitiveness, and ambition.

TYPE B PERSONALITY STYLE A personality pattern in which persons are more relaxed, less aggressive, and less concerned about time.

ACID STOMACH

Each day the stomach produces as much as 3.5 pints (2 liters) of hydrochloric acid. Around 500,000 cells are replaced every minute so the acid will not damage the stomach walls (Ash, 1999).

infants (Weiner, 1977; Mirsky, 1958). Perhaps, over the years, this physical reaction wears down the lining of the stomach or duodenum, leaving the individuals more vulnerable to ulcers.

Clearly, sociocultural, psychological, and biological variables combine to produce psychophysiological disorders. The interaction of such variables to produce medical problems was once considered an unusual occurrence. According to the disregulation model, however, the interaction of psychosocial and physical factors is the rule of bodily functioning, not the exception, and as the years have passed, more and more illnesses have been added to the list of traditional psychophysiological disorders. Let us turn next to the "new" psychophysiological disorders.

New Psychophysiological Disorders

Since the 1960s, researchers have found many links between psychosocial stress and a wide range of physical illnesses. Let us look first at how these links were established and then at *psychoneuroimmunology*, a new area of study that further ties stress and illness to the body's immune system.

ARE PHYSICAL ILLNESSES RELATED TO STRESS? In 1967 two researchers, Thomas Holmes and Richard Rahe, developed the *Social Adjustment Rating Scale*, which assigns numerical values to the stresses that most people experience at some time in their lives (see Table 10-6). Answers given by a large sample of subjects indicated that the most stressful event on the scale should be the death of a spouse, which receives a score of 100 *life change units* (*LCUs*). Lower on the scale

Table 10-6

Most Stressful Life Events

ADULTS: "SOCIAL ADJUSTMENT RATING SCALE"*

1. Death of spouse	12. Pregnancy
2. Divorce	13. Sex difficulties
3. Marital separation	14. Gain of new family member
4. Jail term	15. Business readjustment
5. Death of close family member	16. Change in financial state
6. Personal injury or illness	17. Death of close friend
7. Marriage	18. Change to different line of work
8. Fired at work	19. Change in number of arguments with spouse
9. Marital reconciliation	20. Mortgage over $10,000
10. Retirement	21. Foreclosure of mortgage or loan
11. Change in health of family member	22. Change in responsibilities at work

STUDENTS: "UNDERGRADUATE STRESS QUESTIONNAIRE"†

1. Death (family member or friend)	12. Went into a test unprepared
2. Had a lot of tests	13. Lost something (especially wallet)
3. It's finals week	14. Death of a pet
4. Applying to graduate school	15. Did worse than expected on test
5. Victim of a crime	16. Had an interview
6. Assignments in all classes due the same day	17. Had projects, research papers due
7. Breaking up with boy-/girlfriend	18. Did badly on a test
8. Found out boy-/girlfriend cheated on you	19. Parents getting divorce
9. Lots of deadlines to meet	20. Dependent on other people
10. Property stolen	21. Having roommate conflicts
11. You have a hard upcoming week	22. Car/bike broke down, flat tire, etc.

*Full scale has 43 items.
†Full scale has 83 items.

Source: Holmes & Rahe, 1967; Crandall et al., 1992.

is retirement (45 LCUs), and still lower is a minor violation of the law (11 LCUs). Even positive events, such as an outstanding personal achievement (28 LCUs), are somewhat stressful. This scale gave researchers a yardstick for measuring the total amount of stress a person faces over a period of time. If, for example, in the course of a year a businesswoman started a new business (39 LCUs), sent her son off to college (29 LCUs), moved to a new house (20 LCUs), and witnessed the death of a close friend (37 LCUs), her stress score for the year would be 125 LCUs, a considerable amount of stress for such a period of time.

With the Social Adjustment Rating Scale in hand, the researchers were able to examine the relationship between life stress and the onset of illness. They found that the LCU scores of sick people during the year before they fell ill were much higher than those of healthy people (Holmes & Rahe, 1989, 1967). If a person's life changes totaled more than 300 LCUs over the course of a year, that person was particularly likely to develop a serious health problem.

In one study Rahe (1968) divided 2,500 healthy naval personnel into a high-risk group (highest LCU scores over the previous six months) and a low-risk group (lowest LCU scores); he then kept track of the health changes of the two groups when they went to sea. Twice as many high-risk as low-risk sailors developed illnesses during their first month at sea; the high-risk sailors also continued to develop more illnesses each month for the next five months.

The Social Adjustment Rating Scale has been updated and revised by various researchers over the years (Hobson et al., 1998; Miller & Rabe, 1997). Using either the original or the revised scales, studies have linked stresses of various kinds to a wide range of physical conditions, from trench mouth and upper respiratory infection to cancer (Cobb & Steptoe, 1998; Kiecolt-Glaser et al., 1991). Overall, the greater the amount of life stress, the greater the likelihood of illness (see Figure 10-4 on the next page). Researchers even have found a relationship between traumatic stress and death. When, for example, investigators examined the medical records of 4,486 British widowers 55 years of age or older, they discovered that 213 of these men had died during the stressful first six months of their bereavement—a fatality rate significantly higher than usual for married men in this age range (Young, Benjamin, & Wallis, 1963). After six months the mortality rate of the widowers returned to a normal level. Another study of 903 close relatives of persons who had died in a community in Wales found that almost 5 percent of the relatives died during the stressful first year of their bereavement (Rees & Lutkin, 1967). In fact, the widows and widowers in this group had a mortality rate of 12 percent, compared to a rate of less than 1 percent for age-matched control subjects.

A particularly striking instance of death after the loss of a loved one is seen in the following case:

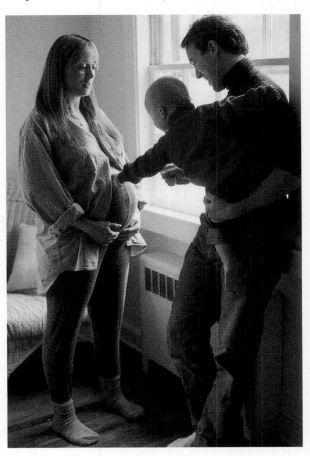

Joyful stress *According to the Social Adjustment Rating Scale, even positive events such as pregnancy are stressful for everyone involved.*

ConsiderThis

◉ The Social Adjustment Rating Scale has been criticized for assigning a specific number to each major life event. Why might this number fail to be a good indicator of the amount of stress the event actually causes for a particular individual?

> Charlie and Josephine had been inseparable companions for 13 years. In a senseless act of violence Charlie, in full view of Josephine, was shot and killed in a melee with police. Josephine first stood motionless, then slowly approached his prostrate form, sunk to her knees, and silently rested her head on the dead and bloody body. Concerned persons attempted to help her away, but she refused to move. Hoping she would soon surmount her overwhelming grief, they let her be. But she never rose again; in 15 minutes she was dead. Now the remarkable part of the story is that Charlie and Josephine were llamas in the zoo! They had escaped from their pen during a snow storm and Charlie, a mean animal to begin with, was shot when he proved unmanageable. I was able to establish from the zoo keeper that to all intents and purposes Josephine had been normally frisky and healthy right up to the moment of the tragic event.
>
> *(Engel, 1968)*

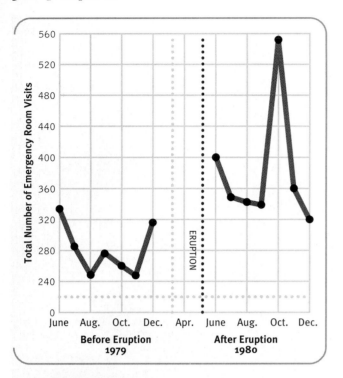

FIGURE 10-4 **Catastrophic stress** *Paul and Gerald Adams (1984) found that during the months immediately after the eruption of Mount St. Helens on May 18, 1980, there was a 34 percent increase in emergency room visits and a 19 percent rise in deaths in nearby Othello, Washington.*

PSYCHONEUROIMMUNOLOGY The study of the connections between stress, the body's immune system, and illness.

IMMUNE SYSTEM The body's network of activities and cells that identify and destroy antigens and cancer cells.

ANTIGEN A foreign invader of the body, such as a bacterium or virus.

LYMPHOCYTES White blood cells that circulate through the lymph system and bloodstream, helping the body identify and destroy antigens and cancer cells.

One shortcoming of Holmes and Rahe's Social Adjustment Rating Scale is that it does not take into consideration the particular life stress factors of specific populations. For example, in their development of the scale, the researchers sampled white Americans predominantly. Less than 5 percent of the subjects were African Americans. But since their ongoing life experiences often differ in significant ways, might not African Americans and white Americans differ in their stress reactions to various kinds of life events? One study indicates that indeed they do (Komaroff, Masuda, & Holmes, 1989, 1986). Both white and African Americans rank death of a spouse as the single most stressful life event, but African Americans experience greater stress than white Americans from such events as a major personal injury or illness, a major change in work responsibilities, or a major change in living conditions. Similarly, recent studies have shown that women and men differ in their reactions to certain life changes on the scale (Miller & Rahe, 1997). Women, for example, tend to experience more stress than men when confronted with the death of a close family member, loss of a job, a major injury or illness, a decrease in income, credit problems, or a change in residence.

Finally, college students may face stressors that are different from those listed in the Social Adjustment Rating Scale (Crandall et al., 1992). Instead of having marital difficulties, being fired, or applying for a job, a college student may have trouble with a roommate, fail a course, or apply to graduate school. When researchers developed special scales to measure life events more accurately in this population (see bottom half of Table 10-6), they again found relationships between stressful events and illness (Crandall et al., 1992).

PSYCHONEUROIMMUNOLOGY How do stressful events result in a viral or bacterial infection? Researchers have increasingly focused on the body's immune system as the key to this relationship and have developed a new area of study called **psychoneuroimmunology** to examine the links between psychosocial stress, the immune system, and health (Coe, 1999).

The **immune system** is the body's network of activities and cells that identify and destroy **antigens**—foreign invaders, such as bacteria, viruses, fungi, and parasites—and cancer cells. Immune cells are located in the bone marrow, thymus, lymph nodes, spleen, tonsils, appendix, and small intestine (Cohen & Herbert, 1996). Among the most important cells in this system are billions of **lymphocytes**, white blood cells that circulate through the lymph system and the bloodstream. When stimulated by antigens, lymphocytes spring into action to help the body overcome the invaders.

One group of lymphocytes, called *helper T-cells,* identify antigens and then multiply and trigger the production of other kinds of immune cells (see Box 10-4 on page 310). Another group, *natural killer T-cells,* seek out and destroy body cells that have already been infected by viruses, thus helping to stop the spread of a viral infection. A third group of lymphocytes, *B-cells,* produce *antibodies,* protein molecules that recognize and bind to antigens, mark them for destruction, and prevent them from causing infection.

Researchers now believe that stress can interfere with the activity of lymphocytes, slowing them down and thus increasing a person's susceptibility to viral and bacterial infections (Sternberg & Gold, 1997; Ader, Felten, & Cohen, 1991). When laboratory animals have been subjected to stressors of various kinds, their lymphocytes and antibodies reproduce more slowly than usual and destroy antigens less effectively (Hibma & Griffin, 1994; Maier et al., 1994). Studies of humans tell a similar story. For example, scientists who monitored Skylab astronauts during various phases of their extended space mission discovered that their T-cell reactions to antigens decreased within a few hours after the stress of splashdown and returned to normal three days later (Kimzey et al., 1976; Kimzey, 1975).

In a landmark study, R. W. Bartrop and his colleagues (1977) in New South Wales, Australia, compared the immune systems of 26 people whose spouses had died eight weeks earlier with those of 26 matched control subjects whose spouses had not died. Blood samples revealed that lymphocyte functioning was much lower in the bereaved people than in the controls. Still other studies have shown slow immune functioning in persons who are exposed to long-term stress. For example, researchers have found poorer immune functioning among people who face the challenge of providing ongoing care for a relative with Alzheimer's disease (Kiecolt-Glaser et al., 1996, 1991, 1987).

These studies seem to be telling a remarkable story. During periods when healthy individuals happened to experience unusual levels of stress, they remained healthy on the surface, but their experiences apparently slowed their immune systems so that they became susceptible to illness. If stress affects our capacity to fight off illness, it is no wonder that researchers have repeatedly found a relationship between life stress and illnesses of various kinds. But why and when does stress interfere with the immune system? Several factors influence whether stress will result in a slowdown of the system, including *biochemical activity, behavioral changes, personality style,* and *degree of social support.*

Killer T-cells at work *These killer T-cells surround a larger cancer cell and destroy it, thus helping to prevent the spread of cancer.*

BIOCHEMICAL ACTIVITY As we have seen, stress leads to increased activity by the sympathetic nervous system, including an increase in the release of the neurotransmitter *norepinephrine* throughout the brain and body. It appears that, beyond supporting the activity of the sympathetic nervous system, this chemical eventually helps slow the functioning of the immune system (Schorr & Arnason, 1999; Whitacre et al., 1994). During low stress or early stages of stress, norepinephrine travels to certain lymphocyte receptors and gives a message for the lymphocytes to increase their activity. As the stress continues or heightens, however, the neurotransmitter travels to yet other receptors on the lymphocytes and gives them an *inhibitory message* to stop their activity. Thus, while the release of norepinephrine improves immune functioning at low levels of stress, it actually slows down immune functioning at higher levels.

Similarly, the body's endocrine glands help reduce immune system functioning during periods of prolonged stress. Remember that under various circumstances, glands throughout the body release *hormones,* chemical messengers that propel body organs into action. When a person is under stress, the *adrenal glands,* which are located on top of the kidneys, release *corticosteroids*—cortisone and other so-called stress hormones. At first, the body's release of the corticosteroids stimulates body organs to greater activity. However, after stress continues for

MARITAL STRESS

During and after marital spats, women typically experience a greater release of stress hormones than men, and so a greater decrease in immune functioning (Kiecolt-Glaser et al., 1996).

Laboratory insights *Laboratory animals are widely used in research on the immune system. The destruction of the immune systems of these mice, which has caused their hair to fall out, enables researchers to produce and investigate invasions by various cells and viruses.*

BOX 10-4

The Psychological Effects of HIV and AIDS

The *human immunodeficiency virus* (HIV) is a virus that invades certain cells and causes their death. The virus particularly infects *T-4 helper lymphocytes,* the immune cells that normally protect the body from disease by telling the rest of the immune system which invaders to kill (Richardson, 1997; Batchelor, 1988). The infected lymphocytes in turn carry the killer deep into the immune system, where it produces further destruction. In many cases, HIV develops into *acquired immune deficiency syndrome* (*AIDS*), a full-scale attack on the immune system.

Without treatment, the progression from HIV infection to AIDS may take weeks, months, or years (Barroso, 1999; Richardson, 1997; Travis, 1996). In recent years, scientists have developed powerful combinations of drugs that can suppress the virus and greatly delay the onset of AIDS (Ostrow et al., 1999). Generally, however, much remains to be learned about how and why persons who are infected with HIV develop AIDS, whether slowly or rapidly. Most sufferers do not die of AIDS per se but instead fall victim to infections that would not survive in a healthy immune system. The psychological suffering of both people who are HIV-positive and people with AIDS is increasingly receiving attention from researchers and health-care workers (Crystal & Schlosser, 1999).

Psychological disorders associated with HIV may be caused by factors that are primarily organic. The HIV may invade the brain, for example, causing *AIDS dementia complex* (*ADC*), a disease that can result in lack of energy, manic-depressive symptoms, and psychosis. More commonly, there is a general decline in cognitive functioning—it takes longer to think or remember (Brew, 1999; Grant et al., 1999). In a vicious cycle, the patient's psychological well-being declines, causing the immune system to weaken further. Not a great deal is known about ADC, but some researchers believe that it may affect many AIDS sufferers and that it may be one of the earliest symptoms to develop (Ungvarski & Trzcianowska, 2000; Grassi et al., 1999).

Psychological problems of HIV sufferers may also result from sociocultural factors (Crystal & Schlosser, 1999; Kaplan, Marks, & Mertends, 1997). Although not all HIV sufferers develop AIDS dementia complex, almost all are subjected to severe environmental stress, which can reduce the ability of the immune system to ward off illness (Nott & Vedhara, 1999). A weakened immune system leaves HIV sufferers even less able to fight off the AIDS virus or, indeed, any other infection.

Society does not provide AIDS sufferers with a supportive environment in which to wage their war. Indeed, it attaches considerable stigma to the disease and to those who contract it. Surveys show that some people view AIDS as a proper punishment for gay men, intravenous drug users, and people who associate with them (Herek & Glunt, 1988). When Magic Johnson revealed a number of years ago that he had contracted HIV through means other than homosexual contact or intravenous drug use, AIDS activists hoped that such views would change. But even Magic Johnson was not safe from the repercussions of the public's attitudes about AIDS. This celebrated athlete lost lucrative endorsement contracts and found other professional players unwilling to face him on the basketball court for fear of contracting his disease.

Experts agree that casual contact with AIDS sufferers does not lead to infection (Herek et al., 1993). Yet prejudice and misunderstanding continue. Patients with HIV may face discrimination and harassment, along with loss of their jobs, health insurance, and police protection (Tross & Hirsch, 1988). Many victims must also deal with the loss of friends who die of AIDS and with others who reject them, along with the prospect of their own death. The stress can lead to apathy, depression, preoccupation with the illness, anxiety-related disorders, and other problems (Carels et al., 1998; Lyketsos et al., 1996; Taylor et al., 1996). Once again, in a vicious cycle, all of these stressors can themselves affect the ability of the immune system to fight off the disease (Nott & Vedhara, 1999; Fleishman & Fogel, 1994).

Some promising studies find that psychological treatments, particularly *cognitive-behavioral stress management techniques,* can help prevent or reduce the anxiety and depression in HIV sufferers and may even slow down progression of the disease (Schneiderman, 1999; Lutgendorf et al., 1997; Ironson et al., 1994). More generally, to reduce the psychologically based problems that accompany HIV and AIDS, we must give victims the support, compassion, and hope that is available to sufferers of other life-threatening illnesses. We can do so only by educating the public about the facts. Today millions of dollars are spent to educate both youngsters and adults about AIDS (Jacobs, 1993). Yet it is very difficult to overcome deeply felt prejudices—against people and against a mysterious and deadly disease. Only when sufferers are accepted as people deserving of help and understanding will their environment serve to help their recovery rather than hasten their deaths.

30 minutes or more, the stress hormones travel to certain receptor sites in the body and give inhibitory messages, which help calm down the overstressed body (Manuck et al., 1991). One such group of receptor sites is located on the lymphocytes. When the corticosteroids bind to these receptors, their inhibitory messages actually slow down the activity of the lymphocytes (Bellinger et al., 1994; Zwilling et al., 1993). Thus, again, the very chemicals that initially help people to deal with stress eventually act to slow the immune system.

BEHAVIORAL CHANGES Stress may set in motion a series of behavioral changes that indirectly affect the immune system. Some people under intense or chronic stress may, for example, become anxious or depressed, perhaps even develop an anxiety or mood disorder. As a result, they may sleep badly, eat poorly, exercise less, or smoke or drink more—behaviors known to slow down the immune system (Kiecolt-Glaser & Glaser, 1999, 1988; Jung & Irwin, 1999; Cohen & Herbert, 1996).

PERSONALITY STYLE An individual's personality style may also play a role in determining how much the immune system is slowed down by stress (Kemeny & Laudenslager, 1999). According to research, people who generally respond to life stress with optimism, constructive coping strategies, and resilience—that is, people who welcome challenge and are willing to take control in their daily encounters—experience better immune system functioning and are better prepared to fight off illness (Taylor et al., 2000; Lee et al., 1998). Some studies find, for example, that people with a so-called "hardy" personality remain healthy after stressful events, while those whose personalities are less hardy seem more susceptible to illness (Kobasa, 1990, 1987, 1984, 1982). One study even discovered that men with an enduring sense of hopelessness die at above-average rates from heart disease, cancer, and other causes (Everson et al., 1996) (see Figure 10-5).

In related work, the psychology researcher David McClelland and his associates have identified what they call the *inhibited power motive style* (McClelland, 1993, 1985). People who display this personality style are thought to have a strong need for power; they strive for prestige and influence over others. However, they have been taught to satisfy this need in indirect ways—by serving other people or worthy causes, for example, or by upholding high principles. Apparently, people with inhibited power motives are more likely than others to develop physical illnesses, particularly upper respiratory infections, in the face of

DIRECT IMPACT
Studies indicate that the abnormal biochemical activity that accompanies depression also directly disrupts lymphocyte activity (Azar, 1996). Correspondingly, the immune systems of depressed people—even merely dejected individuals—do not function as well as those of other people (Schleifer et al., 1999, 1996; Cohen & Herbert, 1996).

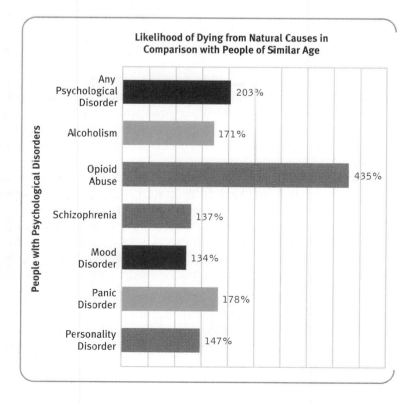

Likelihood of Dying from Natural Causes in Comparison with People of Similar Age

People with Psychological Disorders

- Any Psychological Disorder — 203%
- Alcoholism — 171%
- Opioid Abuse — 435%
- Schizophrenia — 137%
- Mood Disorder — 134%
- Panic Disorder — 178%
- Personality Disorder — 147%

FIGURE 10-5 **Warning: psychological disorders may be dangerous to your health** *Psychological disorders are themselves a source of stress that can lead to medical problems. People with such disorders are twice as likely to die of natural causes (medical illnesses) as people in the same age group without psychological difficulties. (Adapted from Harris & Barraclough, 1998.)*

Staying healthy amidst chaos *A rescue worker in Turkey carries a baby to safety. Although such workers are inevitably affected by their very stressful experiences, those with so-called hardy or resilient personalities are less likely to develop immune system problems or significant medical illnesses.*

academic and other power-related stresses (McClelland, 1993; Jemmott, 1987). According to McClelland, such stress arouses the power needs of these people, and so triggers their sympathetic nervous system into action. All of this arousal, in turn, increases the release of norepinephrine, which, as we observed earlier, eventually inhibits the functioning of the immune system (McClelland, 1993, 1979).

In one study designed to test this theory, 64 dental students were examined at five points in the school year: September, November, April, June, and July (Jemmott et al., 1983). Samples of saliva were collected from the subjects at each point and analyzed for *s-IgA,* an antibody that typically protects the body from upper respiratory infections: the lower a person's s-IgA reading, the poorer his or her immune functioning. As expected, the average s-IgA measures of the dental students were normal during the calm of September, dropped significantly during the academically stressful months of November, April, and June, and rebounded in July. In short, during periods of increased stress, the subjects' immune systems seemed less able to ward off upper respiratory infections. The investigators then looked separately at the s-IgA measures of those dental students who scored high in inhibited power motive style. Their s-IgA levels tended to be low even during the calm periods of September and July. That is, they remained highly susceptible to illness over a longer period of time than those with a low power motive.

Finally, some studies have noted a relationship between certain personality characteristics and recovery from cancer (Greer, 1999; Garssen & Goodkin, 1999). They have found that patients with certain forms of cancer who display a helpless coping style and who cannot easily express their feelings, particularly anger, tend to have less successful recoveries than patients who do express their emotions. Other studies, however, have found no relationship between personality and cancer outcome (Garssen & Goodkin, 1999; Holland, 1996).

SOCIAL SUPPORT Finally, people who have few social supports and feel lonely seem to display poorer immune functioning in the face of stress than people who do not feel lonely (Cohen & Herbert, 1996; Kiecolt-Glaser et al., 1988, 1987). In one study, medical students were given the *UCLA Loneliness Scale* and then divided into "high" and "low" loneliness groups (Kiecolt-Glaser et al., 1984). The high-loneliness group showed lower lymphocyte responses during a final exam period.

Other studies have found that social support and affiliation may actually help protect people from stress, poor immune system functioning, and subsequent illness, or help speed up recovery from illness or surgery (Kiecolt-Glaser et al., 1998, 1991; Uchino & Garvey, 1997; Cohen et al., 1992). In one study, hepatitis B vaccine inoculations were administered to 48 medical students on the last day of a three-day examination period (Glaser et al., 1992). The students who reported the greatest amount of social support had stronger immune responses to the hepatitis B vaccine. Similarly, some studies have suggested that patients with certain forms of cancer who receive social support in their personal lives or supportive therapy often have better immune system functioning and, in turn, more successful recoveries than patients without such supports (Spiegel & Classen, 2000; Garssen & Goodkin, 1999; Koopman et al., 1998) (see Box 10-5).

BOX 10-5

He Ain't Heavy

A few years ago, thirteen fifth-grade boys in San Marcos, California, went to a barbershop and proceeded to have their heads shaved. The purpose of this seemingly strange group action? To show support and compassion for their 11-year-old friend and classmate Ian O'Gorman. Ian was undergoing chemotherapy for cancer at the time and was beginning to lose his hair. His

friends didn't want him to feel left out or further traumatized, so they undertook this selfless display of support. Their teacher, who had his head shaved too, said that the idea came from the boys, who nicknamed themselves the Bald Eagles. All parents gave their blessings to the group action. Ian gratefully reported, "What my friends did really made me feel stronger. It helped me get through all this. . . . I was really amazed that they would do something like this for me."

ConsiderThis

⬤ No doubt the generous behavior of his friends had an enormous impact on Ian's state of mind. Might it also have affected his health and recovery? • Is our society more sensitive today than in the past to the psychosocial issues at work in illnesses such as Ian's?

Psychological Treatments for Physical Disorders

As clinicians have discovered that psychosocial factors may contribute to physical disorders, they have applied psychological treatments to more and more medical problems (Compas et al., 1998; Cassem & Hyman, 1995). The most common of these interventions are relaxation training, biofeedback training, meditation, hypnosis, cognitive interventions, insight therapy, and support groups. The field of treatment that combines psychological and physical interventions to treat or prevent medical problems is known as **behavioral medicine** (Feinstein & Brewer, 1999; Blanchard, 1994).

BEHAVIORAL MEDICINE A field of treatment that combines psychological and physical interventions to treat or prevent medical problems.

Relaxation, the hard way *Clinicians are always developing techniques to help people relax. A climber dangles from Alaska's Mount Barrile to demonstrate the use of "Tranquilite" sleep goggles, which are supposed to produce relaxation with blue light and a soothing "pink sound."*

IMPORTANT, BUT INSENSITIVE

The brain has no feelings. Even cutting into it will not cause pain. Headache pain, for example, comes from nerve endings in the muscles and blood vessels on the outside of the skull (Jordan, 1998; Johnsen, 1994).

RELAXATION TRAINING As we saw in Chapter 5, people can be taught to relax their muscles at will, a process that sometimes reduces feelings of anxiety. Given the positive effects of relaxation on anxiety and the nervous system, clinicians believe that **relaxation training** can be of help in preventing or treating medical illnesses that are related to stress.

Relaxation training, often in combination with medication, has been widely used in the treatment of high blood pressure (Dubbert, 1995; Canino et al., 1994). One study assigned hypertensive subjects to one of three forms of treatment: medication, medication plus relaxation training, or medication plus supportive psychotherapy (Taylor et al., 1977). Only those who received relaxation training in combination with medication showed a significant reduction in blood pressure. Relaxation training has also been of some help in treating headaches, insomnia, asthma, the undesirable effects of cancer treatments, pain after surgery, and Raynaud's disease, a disorder of the vascular system characterized by throbbing, aching, and pain (Good et al., 1999; McGrath 1999; Good, 1995).

BIOFEEDBACK TRAINING As we also have seen in Chapter 5, patients given **biofeedback training** are connected to machinery that gives them continuous readings about their involuntary body activities. This information enables them gradually to gain control over those activities. Moderately helpful in the treatment of anxiety disorders, the procedure has also been applied to a growing number of physical disorders.

In one study, *electromyograph* (*EMG*) feedback was used to treat sixteen patients who were experiencing facial pain caused in part by tension in their jaw muscles (Dohrmann & Laskin, 1978). In an EMG procedure, electrodes are attached to a person's muscles so that the muscle contractions are detected and converted into a tone for the individual to hear (see page 137). Changes in the pitch and volume of the tone indicate changes in muscle tension. After "listening" to EMG feedback repeatedly, the sixteen patients in this study learned how to relax their jaw muscles at will and later reported a reduction in facial pain. In contrast, eight control subjects, who were wired to similar equipment but not given biofeedback training, showed little improvement in muscle tension or pain.

EMG feedback has also been used successfully in the treatment of headaches and muscular disabilities caused by strokes or accidents (Brauer, 1999; Blanchard, 1994). Still other forms of biofeedback training have been of some help in the treatment of heartbeat irregularities (arrhythmia), asthma, migraine headaches, high blood pressure, stuttering, pain from burns, and Raynaud's disease (McGrath, 1999; Compas et al., 1998; Nakao et al., 2000; Labbe, 1995).

MEDITATION Although meditation has been practiced since ancient times, Western health-care professionals have only recently become aware of its effectiveness in relieving physical distress (Carrington, 1993). **Meditation** is a technique of turning one's concentration inward, achieving a slightly changed state of consciousness, and temporarily ignoring all stressors. In the most common approach, meditators go to a quiet place, assume a comfortable posture, utter or think a particular sound (called a *mantra*) to help focus their attention, and allow their minds to turn away from all outside thoughts and concerns (Del Monte, 1995).

Many people who meditate regularly report feeling more peaceful, engaged, and creative (Carrington, 1993, 1978; Schneider et al., 1992). Meditation has been used to help manage pain in cancer patients (Goleman & Gurin, 1993) and to help treat high blood pressure, heart problems, asthma, skin disorders, dia-

Blocking out worldly events *In the past, meditation served as a pathway to enlightenment and spiritual awakening. Though still often used for such ends, today the technique is commonly employed by people who seek a better state of physical or psychological health.*

betes, and even viral infections (Carrington, 1993, 1978; Shapiro, 1982). It has also been useful in relieving the stress-related problem of insomnia (Woolfolk et al., 1976).

HYPNOSIS As described in Chapter 1, individuals who undergo **hypnosis** are guided by a hypnotist into a sleeplike, suggestible state during which they can be directed to act in unusual ways, to experience unusual sensations, to remember seemingly forgotten events, or to forget remembered events. With training some people are even able to induce their own hypnotic state (*self-hypnosis*). Hypnosis is now used as an aid to psychotherapy; to help conduct research on pain, memory, and various other topics; and to help treat many physical conditions (Temes, 1999; Barber, 1993, 1984).

Hypnosis seems to be particularly helpful in the control of pain, whether caused by a medical condition or by medical procedures (Kiecolt-Glaser et al., 1998; Holroyd, 1996). One case study describes a patient who underwent dental surgery under hypnotic suggestion: after a hypnotic state was induced, the dentist suggested to the patient that he was in a pleasant and relaxed setting listening to a friend describe his own success at undergoing similar dental surgery under hypnosis. The dentist then proceeded to perform a successful 25-minute operation (Gheorghiu & Orleanu, 1982).

Although only some people are able to undergo surgery while anesthetized by hypnosis alone, hypnosis combined with chemical forms of anesthesia is apparently beneficial to many patients (Wadden & Anderton, 1982). Beyond its use in the control of pain, hypnosis has been used successfully to help treat such problems as skin diseases, asthma, insomnia, high blood pressure, warts, and other forms of infection (Hackman et al., 2000; Hornyak et al., 2000; Agras, 1984).

COGNITIVE INTERVENTIONS People with physical ailments have sometimes been taught new attitudes or cognitive responses toward their ailments as part of treatment (Kiecolt-Glaser et al., 1998; Compas et al., 1998). For example, **self-instruction training** has helped patients cope with severe pain, including pain from burns, arthritis, surgical procedures, headaches, back disorders, ulcers, multiple sclerosis, and cancer treatment (Meichenbaum, 1997, 1993, 1977, 1975; Vlaeyen et al., 1995). As we saw in Chapter 5, self-instruction therapists teach people to rid themselves of negative self-statements ("Oh, no, I can't take

"I forgot my mantra."

Unnamed character in the film
Annie Hall, 1977

RELAXATION TRAINING A treatment procedure that teaches clients to relax at will.

BIOFEEDBACK TRAINING A treatment technique in which a client is given information about physiological reactions as they occur and learns to control the reactions voluntarily.

MEDITATION A technique of turning one's concentration inward and achieving a slightly changed state of consciousness.

HYPNOSIS A sleeplike suggestible state during which a person can be directed to act in unusual ways, to experience unusual sensations, to remember seemingly forgotten events, or to forget remembered events.

SELF-INSTRUCTION TRAINING A cognitive treatment that teaches clients to use coping self-statements at times of stress or discomfort.

Fighting HIV on all fronts *As part of his treatment at the Wellness Center in San Francisco, this man meditates and writes letters to his HIV virus.*

ROOM WITH A VIEW

According to one hospital's records of individuals who underwent gall bladder surgery, those in rooms with a good view from their window had shorter hospitalizations and needed fewer pain medications than those in rooms without a good view (Ulrich, 1984).

"NO TIME" IS THE ENEMY

Are feelings of time pressure a safety hazard as well as a health hazard? In Sweden, car drivers with a greater sense of time pressure had more accidents or near-accidents than other drivers (Karlberg et al., 1998).

this pain") and to replace them with coping self-statements ("When pain comes, just pause; keep focusing on what you have to do").

INSIGHT THERAPY AND SUPPORT GROUPS If anxiety, depression, anger, and the like contribute to a person's physical ills, therapy to reduce these negative emotions should help reduce the ills. In such cases, physicians may recommend insight therapy, support groups, or both to help patients overcome their medical difficulties. Research suggests that the discussion of past and present upsets may indeed have beneficial effects on one's health (Smyth, 1998; Francis & Pennebaker, 1992). In one study, asthma and arthritis patients who simply wrote down their thoughts and feelings about stressful events for a handful of days showed lasting improvements in their conditions (Smyth et al., 1999). In addition, studies indicate that asthmatic children who receive individual or family therapy often adjust better to their life situations, experience less panic during asthma attacks, have fewer and milder attacks, and miss fewer days of school (Campbell & Patterson, 1995; Simeonsson et al., 1995; Alexander, 1981). Finally, as we have seen, recovery from cancer and certain other illnesses is sometimes improved by participation in support groups (Garssen & Goodkin, 1999; Fawzy et al., 1993; Spiegel et al., 1989).

COMBINATION APPROACHES Studies have found that the various psychological interventions for physical problems tend to be equal in effectiveness (Brauer, 1999; Newton et al., 1995; Wittrock et al., 1995). Relaxation and biofeedback training, for example, are equally helpful (and more helpful than placebos) in the treatment of high blood pressure, headaches, asthma, and Raynaud's disease. Psychological interventions are, in fact, often of greatest help when they are combined with other psychological interventions and with medical treatments (Canty, 1996; Hermann et al., 1995). In one study, ulcer patients who were given relaxation, self-instruction, and assertiveness training along with medication were found to be less anxious and more comfortable, to have fewer symptoms, and to have a better long-term outcome than patients who received medication only (Brooks & Richardson, 1980).

Combination interventions have also been helpful in changing Type A behavior patterns and in reducing the risk of coronary heart disease among Type A people (Cohen, Ardjoen, & Sewpersad, 1997; Johnston, 1992). In one study, 862 patients who had suffered a heart attack within the previous six months were assigned to one of two groups (Friedman et al., 1984). The control group was given three years of cardiological counseling (diet, exercise, and medical advice). The experimental group received the same counseling plus Type A behavioral counseling. They were taught about the Type A personality style and to recognize their excessive physiological, cognitive, and behavioral responses in stressful situations. They were also trained in relaxation and taught to change counterproductive attitudes.

The addition of the Type A behavioral counseling led to major differences in lifestyle and health. Type A behavior was reduced in almost 80 percent of the patients who received both Type A counseling and cardiological counseling for three years, compared to only 50 percent of those who received cardiological counseling alone. Moreover, fewer of those who received the combined counseling suffered another heart attack—only 7 percent, compared to 13 percent of the subjects in the control group.

Clearly, the treatment picture for physical illnesses has been changing markedly (see Box 10-6). While medical treatments continue to dominate, the use of psychological approaches is on the rise. Today's scientists and practitioners are traveling a course far removed from the mind-body dualism of centuries past.

BOX 10-6

One More for the Road

People in Toronto are flocking to a new kind of bar, the O_2 Spa Bar. There they pay their hard-earned money for a 20-minute drink of fresh air. Customers hook up to oxygen tanks and inhale nearly pure oxygen. Patrons swear that repeated "drinks" of oxygen help them feel more energetic and less stressed. Many claim to be cured of everything from hangovers to hot flashes. Similar oxygen bars have been around for a while in Asian cities; they are just now getting started in North America.

ConsiderThis

● Might a placebo effect be operating for at least some of the people who respond so positively to oxygen bars or other health-enhancement techniques?
• Why do people in our society keep searching for new ways to bring about more pleasant physical or psychological states?

CROSSROADS:
Expanding the Boundaries of Abnormal Psychology

Once considered outside the field of abnormal psychology, physical disorders are now seen as problems that fall squarely within its boundaries. Just as physical factors have long been recognized as playing a role in abnormal mental functioning, psychosocial events are now considered important contributors to abnormal physical functioning. In fact, many of today's clinicians believe that psychological and sociocultural factors contribute to the onset and course of virtually all physical ailments.

The number of studies devoted to this relationship has risen steadily during the past 30 years. What researchers once saw as a vague tie between stress and physical illness is now understood as a complex interaction of many variables. Such factors as life stress, individual psychological reactions, neurotransmitter activity, and depression of the immune system are all recognized as contributors to disorders once considered purely physical.

Insights into the treatment of physical illnesses have been accumulating just as rapidly. Psychological approaches such as relaxation training and cognitive therapy are being applied more and more to physical ills, usually in combination with traditional medical treatments. Although such approaches have yielded only modest results so far, many clinicians are convinced that psychological interventions will become increasingly important in the treatment of many physical ailments.

While the increasing focus on psychosocial aspects of physical illness seems promising, perhaps even more exciting is the growing emphasis on the *interrelationship* of the social environment, the brain, and the rest of the body. Researchers have observed repeatedly that mental disorders are often best understood and treated when sociocultural, psychological, and biological factors are all taken into consideration. They now know that this interaction also helps explain medical problems. We are reminded that the brain is part of the body and that both are part of a social context. For better and for worse, the three are inextricably linked.

"Under our holistic approach, Mr. Wyndot, we not only treat your symptoms, we also treat your dog."

In the past, physicians failed to recognize that psychosocial factors often contribute to physical illness. Some observers now fear that today there may be too much emphasis on such factors. What problems might result from an overemphasis on the role of psychosocial factors in physical illness or, conversely, from too rigid a distinction between the mind and body?

SUMMARY AND REVIEW

■ **Bodily illness and psychosocial factors** Before the twentieth century, medical theory was dominated by mind-body dualism, the belief that the mind and body were totally separate entities. Today's clinicians recognize that bodily illnesses can have psychosocial causes. *pp. 285–286*

■ **Factitious disorder** Persons with factitious disorder feign or induce physical disorders in order to assume the role of a sick person. Munchausen syndrome is the extreme and long-term form of factitious disorder. In a related disorder, Munchausen syndrome by proxy, a parent fabricates or induces a physical illness in his or her child. *pp. 286–288*

■ **Somatoform disorders** Patients with somatoform disorders have physical complaints whose causes are largely psychosocial. Unlike people with factitious disorder, these sufferers genuinely believe that their illnesses are organic.

Hysterical somatoform disorders involve an actual loss or change of physical functioning. They include conversion disorder, somatization disorder (or Briquet's syndrome), and pain disorder associated with psychological factors. Diagnosticians are sometimes able to distinguish hysterical somatoform disorders from "true" medical problems by observing oddities in the patient's medical picture.

Freud developed the initial psychodynamic view of hysterical somatoform disorders, proposing that the disorders represent a conversion of underlying emotional conflicts into physical symptoms. According to behaviorists, the physical symptoms of these disorders bring rewards to the sufferer, and such reinforcement helps maintain the symptoms. Some cognitive theorists propose that the disorders are forms of communication, and that people express their emotions through their physical symptoms. Treatments for hysterical disorders emphasize either insight, suggestion, reinforcement, or confrontation.

People with preoccupation somatoform disorders are preoccupied with the notion that something is wrong with them physically. In this category are hypochodriasis and body dysmorphic disorder. Theorists explain preoccupation somatoform disorders much as they do anxiety disorders. Treatment for the disorders includes medications, exposure and response prevention, and other treatments originally developed for anxiety disorders. *pp. 288–300*

■ **Psychophysiological disorders** Psychophysiological disorders are those in which psychosocial and physiological factors interact to cause a physical problem. These disorders have been explained by the disregulation model, which proposes that our brain and body ordinarily set up negative feedback loops that ensure the smooth operation of the body. When this system fails, psychophysiological problems may result. Factors linked to these disorders are sociocultural factors, such as society-wide stressors or persistent social conditions; psychological factors, such as particular needs, attitudes, or personality styles; and biological factors, such as defects in the ANS or particular organs.

For years clinical researchers singled out a limited number of physical illnesses as psychophysiological. These traditional psychophysiological disorders include ulcers, asthma, insomnia, chronic headaches, hypertension, and coronary heart disease. Recently many other psychophysiological disorders have been identified. Scientists have linked many physical illnesses to stress and have developed a new area of study called psychoneuroimmunology. *pp. 300–308*

■ **Psychoneuroimmunology** The body's immune system consists of lymphocytes and other cells that fight off antigens—bacteria, viruses, and other foreign invaders—and cancer cells. Stress can slow lymphocyte activity, thereby interfering with the immune system's ability to protect against illness during times of stress. Factors that seem to affect immune functioning include

VIRTUES OF LAUGHTER

After watching a humorous video, subjects who had laughed at and enjoyed the film showed decreases in stress and improvements in natural killer cell activity—reactions not found in control subjects observing a travel tour video (Bennett, 1998).

norepinephrine and hormone activity, behavioral changes, personality style, and social support. *pp. 308–313*

■ **Psychological treatments for physical disorders** Behavioral medicine combines psychological and physical interventions to treat or prevent medical problems. Psychological approaches such as relaxation training, biofeedback training, meditation, hypnosis, cognitive techniques, insight therapy, and support groups are increasingly being included in the treatment of various medical problems. *pp. 313–317*

MEDICAL EXPENSES

The medical expenses of people who feel under constant stress are 46 percent higher than those of stress-free persons (Goetzel, 1998).

CYBER STUDY

▲ *How do physical, psychological, and sociocultural factors combine to exacerbate pain?* ▲ *Observe pain interventions in action.* ▲ *See the impact of stress on judgment, emotions, job performance, and health.* ▲ *Compare body dysmorphic disorder with a compulsion to check oneself in the mirror and with eating disorders.*

SEARCH THE *ABNORMAL PSYCHOLOGY* CD-ROM FOR

▲ Chapter 10 video case and discussion
  "Fran"—Treating Chronic Pain

▲ Chapter 10 practice test and feedback

▲ Additional video cases and discussions
  "Claude & Claude"—Emotion, Stress, and Health
  "Jennifer"—Obsessive-Compulsive Disorder
  "Liz"—Bulimia Nervosa

LOG ON TO THE COMER WEB PAGE

[www.worthpublishers.com/comerabnormalpsychology4e] **FOR**

▲ Suggested Web links, research exercises, FAQ page, additional Chapter 10 practice test questions

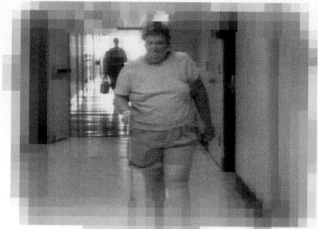

Eating Disorders

"Girls should be encouraged to take an interest in their appearance when they are very young."

Ladies' Home Journal, 1940

Janet Caldwell was . . . five feet, two inches tall and weighed 62 pounds. . . . Janet began dieting at the age of 12 when she weighed 115 pounds and was chided by her family and friends for being "pudgy." She continued to restrict her food intake over a two-year period, and as she grew thinner, her parents became increasingly more concerned about her eating behavior. . . .

Janet . . . felt that her weight problem began at the time of puberty. She said that her family and friends had supported her efforts to achieve a ten-pound weight loss when she first began dieting at age 12. Janet did not go on any special kind of diet. Instead, she restricted her food intake at meals, generally cut down on carbohydrates and protein intake, tended to eat a lot of salads, and completely stopped snacking between meals. At first, she was quite pleased with her progressive weight reduction, and she was able to ignore her feelings of hunger by remembering the weight loss goal she had set for herself. However, each time she lost the number of pounds she had set for her goal she decided to lose just a few more pounds. Therefore she continued to set new weight goals for herself. In this manner, her weight dropped from 115 pounds to 88 pounds during the first year of her weight loss regimen.

Janet felt that, in her second year of dieting, her weight loss had continued beyond her control. . . . She became convinced that there was something inside of her that would not let her gain weight. . . . Janet commented that although there had been occasions over the past few years when she had been fairly "down" or unhappy, she still felt driven to keep on dieting. As a result, she frequently went for walks, ran errands for her family, and spent a great deal of time cleaning her room and keeping it in a meticulously neat and unaltered arrangement.

When Janet's weight loss continued beyond the first year, her parents insisted that she see their family physician, and Mrs. Caldwell accompanied Janet to her appointment. Their family practitioner was quite alarmed at Janet's appearance and prescribed a high-calorie diet. Janet said that her mother spent a great deal of time pleading with her to eat, and Mrs. Caldwell planned various types of meals that she thought would be appealing to Janet. Mrs. Caldwell also talked a great deal to Janet about the importance of good nutrition. Mr. Caldwell, on the other hand, became quite impatient with these discussions and tended to order Janet to eat. Janet then would try to eat something, but often became tearful and ran out of the room because she could not swallow the food she had been ordered to eat. The youngster said that she often responded to her parents' entreaties that she eat by telling them that she indeed had eaten but they had not seen her do so. She often listed foods that she said she had consumed which in fact she had flushed down the toilet. She estimated that she only was eating about 300 calories a day.

(Leon, 1984, pp. 179–184)

It has not always done so, but Western society today equates thinness with health and beauty (see Figure 11-1 on the next page). In fact, in the United

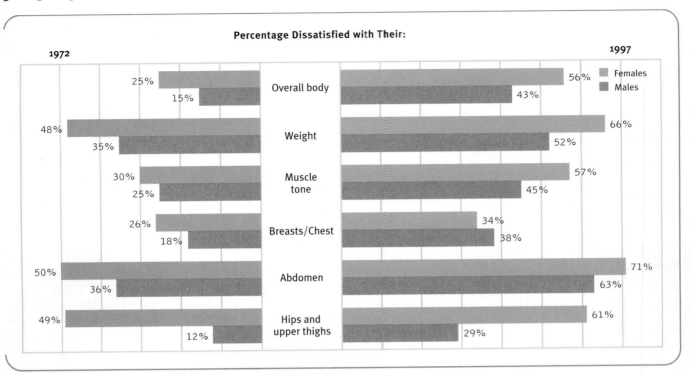

Percentage Dissatisfied with Their:

1972   1997

Females
Males

	1972 Females	1972 Males	1997 Females	1997 Males
Overall body	25%	15%	56%	43%
Weight	48%	35%	66%	52%
Muscle tone	30%	25%	57%	45%
Breasts/Chest	26%	18%	34%	38%
Abdomen	50%	36%	71%	63%
Hips and upper thighs	49%	12%	61%	29%

FIGURE 11-1 **Body dissatisfaction on the rise** *According to surveys on body image, people in our society are much more dissatisfied with their bodies now than they were a generation ago. Women are still more dissatisfied than men, but today's men are more dissatisfied with their bodies than the men of a generation past. (Adapted from Garner, Cooke, & Marano, 1997, p. 42; Rodin, 1992, p. 57.)*

MISLEADING LABEL

The term "anorexia," which means "lack of appetite," is actually a misnomer. Sufferers usually continue to have strong feelings of hunger.

States thinness has become a national obsession. Most of us are as preoccupied with how much we eat as with the taste and nutritional value of our food. It is not surprising, then, that during the past three decades we have also witnessed an increase in two eating disorders that have at their core a morbid fear of gaining weight (Gordon, 2000; Russell, 1995). Sufferers of *anorexia nervosa,* like Janet Caldwell, are convinced that they need to be extremely thin, and they lose so much weight that they may starve themselves to death. People with *bulimia nervosa* go on frequent eating binges, during which they uncontrollably consume large quantities of food, then force themselves to vomit or take other exteme steps to keep from gaining weight.

The news media have published many reports about anorexic or bulimic behavior. One reason for the surge in public interest is the frightening medical consequences that can result. The death in 1982 of Karen Carpenter, a popular singer and entertainer, from medical problems related to anorexia nervosa serves as a reminder. Another reason for concern is the disproportionate prevalence of these disorders among adolescent girls and young women (Russell, 1995).

Clinicians now understand that the similarities between anorexia nervosa and bulimia nervosa can be as important as the differences between them (van der Ham et al., 1997; Williams et al., 1996). For example, many people with anorexia nervosa binge as they persist in losing dangerous amounts of weight; some later develop bulimia nervosa (APA, 2000; Mizes, 1995). Conversely, people with bulimia nervosa sometimes develop anorexia nervosa as time goes on.

Anorexia Nervosa

Janet Caldwell, 14 years old and in the eighth grade, displays many symptoms of **anorexia nervosa:** she refuses to maintain more than 85 percent of her normal body weight, intensely fears becoming overweight, has a distorted view of her weight and shape, and has stopped menstruating (see Table 11-1).

Like Janet, at least half of the people with anorexia nervosa reduce their weight by restricting their intake of food, a pattern called *restricting-type anorexia nervosa.* At first they tend to cut out sweets and fattening snacks and then, increasingly, other foods (APA, 2000, 1994). Eventually people with this kind of anorexia nervosa show almost no variability in diet. Others, however, lose weight by forcing themselves to vomit after meals or by abusing laxatives or diuretics, and they may even engage in eating binges, a pattern called *binge-eating/purging-type anorexia nervosa,* which we shall discuss in more detail when we turn to bulimia nervosa (APA, 2000, 1994).

Approximately 90 to 95 percent of all cases of anorexia nervosa occur in females (see Box 11-1 on page 325). Although the disorder can appear at any age, the peak age of onset is between 14 and 18 years (APA, 2000). Around 0.5 percent of all females in Western countries develop the disorder in their lifetime, and many more display at least some of its symptoms. It seems to be on the increase in North America, Europe, and Japan (Battle & Brownell, 1996; Szmukler & Patton, 1995).

Typically the disorder begins after a person who is slightly overweight or of normal weight has been on a diet. The escalation toward anorexia nervosa may follow a stressful event such as separation of parents, a move away from home, or an experience of personal failure (Gowers et al., 1996; Horesh et al., 1995). Although most victims recover, between 2 and 6 percent of them become so seriously ill that they die, usually from medical problems brought about by starvation or from suicide (Nielsen et al., 1998; Neumarker, 1997; Slade, 1995).

The Clinical Picture

Becoming thin is the key goal for people with anorexia nervosa, but *fear* provides their motivation (Russell, 1995). People with this disorder are afraid of becoming obese, of giving in to their growing desire to eat, and more generally of losing control over the size and shape of their bodies. In addition, despite their focus on thinness and the severe restrictions they may place on their food intake, people with anorexia are *preoccupied with food.* They may spend considerable time thinking and even reading about food and planning their limited meals (King, Polivy, & Herman, 1991). Many report that their dreams are filled with images of food and eating (Frayn, 1991; Levitan, 1981).

This preoccupation with food may in fact be a result of food deprivation rather than its cause. In a famous "starvation study" conducted in the late 1940s, 36 normal-weight conscientious objectors were put on a semistarvation diet for six months (Keys et al., 1950). Like people with anorexia nervosa, the volunteers became preoccupied with food and eating. They spent hours each day planning their small meals, talked more about food than about any other topic, studied cookbooks and recipes, mixed food in odd combinations, and dawdled over their meals. Many also had vivid dreams about food.

Persons with anorexia nervosa also *think in distorted ways.* They usually have a low opinion of their body shape, for example, and consider themselves unattractive (Gupta & Johnson, 2000). In addition, they are likely to overestimate their actual proportions. While most women in Western society overestimate their body size, the estimates of those with anorexia nervosa are particularly high. A 23-year-old patient said:

> I look in a full-length mirror at least four or five times daily and I really cannot see myself as too thin. Sometimes after several days of strict dieting, I feel that my shape is tolerable, but most of the time, odd as it may seem, I look in the mirror and believe that I am too fat.
>
> *(Bruch, 1973)*

This tendency to overestimate body size has been tested in the laboratory (Rushford & Ostermeyer, 1997). In a popular assessment technique, subjects look at a photograph of themselves through an adjustable lens. They are asked to adjust the lens until the image that they see matches

ANOREXIA NERVOSA A disorder marked by the pursuit of extreme thinness and by an extreme loss of weight.

CULTURAL DIFFERENCES

In Hong Kong and India, anorexia nervosa is motivated not by a fear of weight gain but rather by a desire to fast for religious purposes or by eccentric nutritional ideas (Castillo, 1997).

Table 11-1 DSM-IV Checklist

ANOREXIA NERVOSA

1. Refusal to maintain body weight above a minimally normal weight for age and height.
2. Intense fear of gaining weight, even though underweight.
3. Disturbed body perception, undue influence of weight or shape on self-evaluation, or denial of the seriousness of the current low weight.
4. In postmenarcheal females, amenorrhea.

Based on APA, 2000, 1994.

Famous victim *Perhaps the most publicized sufferer of anorexia nervosa during recent decades was Karen Carpenter, the young singer who developed this disorder at the height of her career and died of related medical problems.*

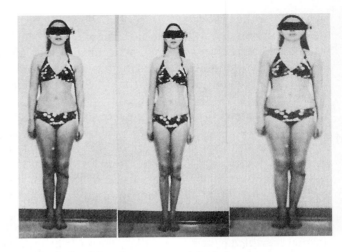

Seeing is deceiving *In one research technique, people look at photographs of themselves through a special lens and adjust the lens until they see what they believe is their actual image. A subject may change her actual image (left) from 20 percent thinner (middle) to 20 percent larger (right).*

their actual body size. The image can be made to vary from 20 percent thinner to 20 percent larger than actual appearance. In one study, more than half of the subjects with anorexia nervosa were found to overestimate their body size, stopping the lens when the image was larger than they actually were.

The distorted thinking of anorexia nervosa also takes the form of certain maladaptive attitudes and misperceptions (DeSilva, 1995; Garner & Bemis, 1985, 1982). Sufferers tend to hold such beliefs as "I must be perfect in every way"; "I will become a better person if I deprive myself"; and "I can avoid guilt by not eating." Gertrude, who recovered from anorexia nervosa, recalls that at age 15 "my thought processes became very unrealistic. I felt I had to do something I didn't want to do for a higher purpose. That took over my life. It all went haywire" (Bruch, 1978, p. 17).

People with anorexia nervosa also display certain *psychological problems,* such as at least mild depression and anxiety and low self-esteem (Weiderman & Pryor, 2000; Halmi, 1995). Some also experience insomnia or other sleep disturbances (APA, 2000). A number grapple with substance abuse (Wilson, 1993). And many display obsessive-compulsive patterns (APA, 2000). They may set rigid rules for food preparation or even cut food into specific shapes. Broader obsessive-compulsive patterns are common as well. In one study, people with anorexia nervosa and others with obsessive-compulsive disorder scored equally high for obsessiveness and compulsiveness (Bastiani et al., 1996). Similarly, persons with anorexia nervosa tend to be perfectionistic (Bastiani et al., 1995). Again, studies of normal subjects placed on semistarvation diets have reported similar psychological problems, suggesting that some of these features too may be the result of starvation (Fichter & Pirke, 1995; Keys et al., 1950).

ORDERLY EATING

Rules to eat by are not by themselves uncommon or abnormal. Almost a third of Americans eat meals in a distinct order, such as consuming all of one food on the plate before proceeding to the next (Kanner, 1995).

Medical Problems

The starvation habits of anorexia nervosa cause a range of medical problems (Baker et al., 2000; Ward et al., 1997; Casper, 1995). Women develop *amenorrhea,* the absence of menstrual cycles. Other problems include lowered body temperature, low blood pressure, body swelling, reduced bone mineral density, and slow heart rate. Metabolic and electrolyte imbalances also may occur and can

Not for Women Only

The number of young men with eating disorders appears to be on the rise, and more men are now seeking treatment for these disorders (Gilbert, 1996). Nevertheless, males account for only 5 to 10 percent of all cases of eating disorders (Frasciello & Willard, 1995). The reasons for this striking gender difference are not entirely clear.

One possible explanation is that men and women are subject to different sociocultural pressures. For example, a survey of college men found that the majority selected "muscular, strong and broad shoulders" to describe the ideal male body, and "thin, slim, slightly underweight" to describe the ideal female body (Kearney-Cooke & Steichen-Ash, 1990). Although the emphasis on a muscular, strong, and athletic body as the male ideal tends to lower the likelihood of eating disorders in men, it may nevertheless create other problems, such as steroid abuse or excessive weight lifting to increase muscle mass and strength (Mickalide, 1990).

A second reason for the different rates of eating disorders may be the different methods of weight loss favored by men and women. According to some clinical observations, men are more likely to use exercise to lose weight, whereas women more often diet (Braun, 1996; Mickalide, 1990). And dieting often causes the onset of eating disorders.

Perhaps a third reason for the difference in reported cases is that eating disorders in men may be underdiagnosed. Some men do not want to admit that they have what many consider a "female problem." In addition, it may be more difficult for clinicians to identify eating disorders in men because the clinical manifestations are different. For example, amenorrhea, an obvious symptom of anorexia nervosa among females, does not occur in men. While anorexia nervosa does cause some reproductive problems in males, such as low levels of testosterone, they are not problems that are easy to identify by diagnostic tests (Andersen, 1990).

Many of the men who develop eating disorders struggle with the same issues

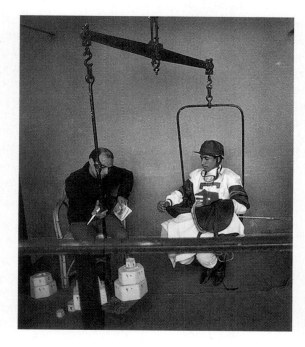

The weigh-in *Although this jockey does not have an eating disorder, his prerace weigh-in illustrates the weight standards and pressures to which such athletes are subjected.*

as women. Some, for example, report that they want a "lean, toned, thin" shape similar to the ideal female body, rather than the muscular, broad-shouldered shape of the typical male ideal (Kearney-Cooke & Steichen-Ash, 1990). In many cases, however, the triggers of male eating disorders are different from those of female eating problems (Joiner et al., 2000; Costanzo et al., 1999). For example, males are more likely than women to develop eating disturbances because of the requirements and pressures of a job or sport (Thompson & Sherman, 1993). According to one study, 37 percent of males with eating disorders had jobs or played sports for which weight control was important, compared to 13 percent of women (Braun, 1996). The highest rates have been found among jockeys, wrestlers, distance runners, bodybuilders, and swimmers. Jockeys commonly spend hours before a race in a sauna, shedding up to seven pounds of weight, and may restrict their food intake, abuse laxatives and diuretics, and force vomiting (King & Mezey, 1987). Similarly, male wrestlers in high school and college commonly restrict their food for up to three days before a match in order to "make weight," often losing between 2 and 12 percent of their body weight. Some lose up to five pounds of water weight by practicing or running in

several layers of warm or rubber clothing before weighing in for a match (Thompson & Sherman, 1993).

Whereas most women with eating disorders are obsessed with thinness at all times, wrestlers and jockeys are usually preoccupied with weight reduction only during their active season. After "making weight," many wrestlers go on eating and drinking binges in order to gain strength for the upcoming match, only to resume the weight-loss regimen after the match in preparation for the next weigh-in. Similarly, one study of male bodybuilders found that nearly half of the subjects binged after competitions and most gained significant weight in the off season, followed by dieting to lose weight in preparation for new competitions (Andersen et al., 1995). A cycle of losing and regaining weight each season alters metabolic activity and jeopardizes the person's health and future efforts at weight control (Mickalide, 1990; Steen et al., 1988).

As the number of males with eating disturbances increases, researchers are intensifying their efforts to understand both the similarities and the differences between males and females with these disorders (Andersen, 1992). Since eating disturbances cause problems for both men and women, investigators must unravel and deal with the important factors that operate across the gender divide.

lead to death by heart failure or circulatory collapse. The severe nutritional deficiencies of anorexia nervosa may also cause skin to become rough, dry, and cracked; nails to become brittle; and hands and feet to be cold and blue. Some people lose hair from the scalp and some grow *lanugo* (the fine, silky hair that covers some newborns) on their trunk, extremities, and face.

An overview of anorexia nervosa suggests that people with this disorder are caught in a vicious cycle. Their fear of obesity and distorted body image lead them to starve themselves. Starvation in turn leads to a preoccupation with food, increased anxiety and depression, and medical problems, causing them to feel even more afraid that they will lose control over their weight, their eating, and themselves. They then try still harder to achieve thinness by not eating.

Bulimia Nervosa

People with **bulimia nervosa**—a disorder also known as **binge-purge syndrome**—engage in repeated episodes of uncontrollable overeating, or **binges**. A binge occurs over a limited period of time, often an hour, during which the person eats much more food than most people would eat during a similar time span (APA, 2000, 1994). In addition, people with this disorder repeatedly perform inappropriate *compensatory behaviors,* such as forcing themselves to vomit; misusing laxatives, diuretics, or enemas; fasting; or exercising excessively (see Table 11-2). If the compensatory behaviors regularly include forced vomiting or misuse of laxatives, diuretics, or enemas, the specific diagnosis is *purging-type bulimia nervosa.* If individuals instead compensate by fasting or exercising frantically, the specific diagnosis is *nonpurging-type bulimia nervosa.* A married woman with the former pattern, since recovered, describes a morning during her disorder:

> Today I am going to be really good and that means eating certain predetermined portions of food and not taking one more bite than I think I am allowed. I am very careful to see that I don't take more than Doug does. I judge by his body. I can feel the tension building. I wish Doug would hurry up and leave so I can get going!
>
> As soon as he shuts the door, I try to get involved with one of the myriad of responsibilities on the list. I hate them all! I just want to crawl into a hole. I don't want to do anything. I'd rather eat. I am alone, I am nervous, I am no good, I always do everything wrong anyway, I am not in control, I can't make it through the day, I just know it. It has been the same for so long.
>
> I remember the starchy cereal I ate for breakfast. I am into the bathroom and onto the scale. It measures the same, BUT I DON'T WANT TO STAY THE SAME! I want to be thinner! I look in the mirror, I think my thighs are ugly and deformed looking. I see a lumpy, clumsy, pear-shaped wimp. There is always something wrong with what I see. I feel frustrated trapped in this body and I don't know what to do about it.
>
> I float to the refrigerator knowing exactly what is there. I begin with last night's brownies. I always begin with the sweets. At first I try to make it look like nothing is missing, but my appetite is huge and I resolve to make another batch of brownies. I know there is half of a bag of cookies in the bathroom, thrown out the night before, and I polish them off immediately. I take some milk so my vomiting will be smoother. I like the full feeling I get after downing a big glass. I get out six pieces of bread and toast one side in the broiler, turn them over and load them with patties of butter and put them under the broiler again till they are bubbling. I take all six pieces on a plate to the television and go back for a bowl of cereal and a banana to have along with them. Before the last toast is finished, I am already preparing the next batch of six more pieces. Maybe another brownie or five, and a couple of large bowlfuls of ice cream, yogurt or cottage cheese. My stomach is stretched into a huge ball below my ribcage. I know I'll have to go

into the bathroom soon, but I want to postpone it. I am in never-never land. I am waiting, feeling the pressure, pacing the floor in and out of the rooms. Time is passing. Time is passing. It is getting to be time.

I wander aimlessly through each of the rooms again tidying, making the whole house neat and put back together. I finally make the turn into the bathroom. I brace my feet, pull my hair back and stick my finger down my throat, stroking twice, and get up a huge pile of food. Three times, four and another pile of food. I can see everything come back. I am glad to see those brownies because they are SO fattening. The rhythm of the emptying is broken and my head is beginning to hurt. I stand up feeling dizzy, empty and weak. The whole episode has taken about an hour.

(Hall, 1980, pp. 5–6)

BULIMIA NERVOSA A disorder marked by frequent eating binges that are followed by forced vomiting or other extreme compensatory behaviors to avoid gaining weight. Also known as *binge-purge syndrome*.

BINGE An episode of uncontrollable eating during which a person ingests a very large quantity of food.

BINGE-EATING DISORDER A type of eating disorder in which a person displays a pattern of binge eating without any accompanying compensatory behaviors.

Like anorexia nervosa, bulimia nervosa usually occurs in females (again in 90 to 95 percent of the cases) and begins in adolescence or young adulthood (most often between 15 and 21 years of age). It often lasts for several years, with periodic letup. The weight of people with bulimia nervosa usually stays within a normal range, although it may fluctuate markedly within that range (APA, 2000, 1994). Some people with this disorder, however, become seriously underweight and may eventually qualify for a diagnosis of anorexia nervosa instead (see Figure 11-2). Clinicians have also observed that certain people, a number of them overweight (see Box 11-2 on the next page), display a pattern of binge eating without vomiting or other inappropriate compensatory behaviors. This pattern, often called **binge-eating disorder**, is being considered for inclusion as a category in the next edition of the DSM (Joiner, Vohs, & Heatherton, 2000; Mussell et al., 1996). It may be manifested by as many as 30 percent of people in weight-control programs (Ricca et al., 2000; Spitzer et al., 1992).

Many adolescents and young adults go on occasional eating binges or experiment with vomiting or laxatives after they hear about these behaviors from their friends or the media (Pyle, 1999; Johnson et al., 1995). In one study, 50 percent of the college students surveyed reported periodic binges, 6 percent had tried vomiting, and 8 percent had experimented with laxatives at least once (Mitchell et al., 1982). Only some of these individuals, however, qualify for a diagnosis of bulimia nervosa. Surveys in several countries suggest that as many as 3 percent of women develop the full syndrome (APA, 2000; Foreyt et al., 1996).

Table 11-2 DSM-IV Checklist

BULIMIA NERVOSA

1. Recurrent episodes of binge eating.
2. Recurrent inappropriate compensatory behavior in order to prevent weight gain.
3. Symptoms continuing, on average, at least twice a week for three months.
4. Undue influence of weight or shape on self-evaluation.

Based on APA, 2000, 1994.

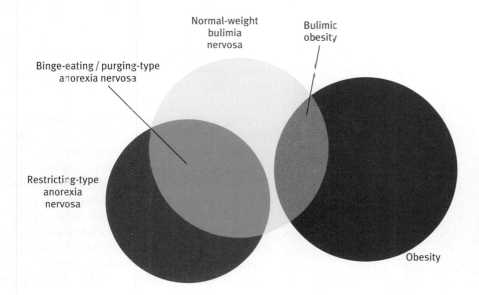

Normal-weight bulimia nervosa

Bulimic obesity

Binge-eating / purging-type anorexia nervosa

Restricting-type anorexia nervosa

Obesity

FIGURE 11-2 Overlapping patterns of anorexia nervosa, bulimia nervosa, and obesity *Some people with anorexia nervosa binge and purge their way to weight loss, and some obese persons binge-eat. However, most people with bulimia nervosa are not obese, and most overweight people are not bulimic. (Adapted from APA, 2000, 1994; Garner & Fairburn, 1988; Russell, 1979.)*

BOX 11-2

Obesity: To Lose or Not to Lose

By medical standards, one-third of adults in the United States weigh at least 20 percent more than people of their height typically do (Foreyt et al., 1996). In fact, despite the public's focus on thinness, low-fat foods, and healthful lifestyles, obesity has become increasingly common in the United States (NCHS, 1999; Kuczmarski et al., 1994). Being overweight is not a mental disorder, nor in most cases is it the result of abnormal psychological processes. Nevertheless, it causes great anguish, and not just because of its physical effects. The media, people on the streets, and even many health professionals treat obesity as shameful. Obese people are often the unrecognized victims of discrimination in efforts to gain admission to college, jobs, and promotions (Rothblum, 1992).

Mounting evidence indicates that overweight persons are not to be sneered at as weak and out of control and that obesity results from multiple factors. First, genetic and biological factors seem to play a large role. Researchers have found that children of obese biological parents are more likely

Laboratory obesity *By electrically stimulating parts of a rodent's hypothalamus, researchers can induce overeating and massive weight gain.*

to be obese than children whose biological parents are not obese, whether or not the people who raise those children are obese (Stunkard et al., 1986). Other researchers have identified several genes

that seem to be linked to obesity (Nagle et al., 1999; Halaas et al., 1995). And still others have identified chemicals in the body, including a hormone called *leptin* and a protein called *glucagon-like peptide-1 (GLP-1),* that apparently act as natural appetite suppressants (Turton et al., 1996; Tartaglia et al., 1995). Suspicion is growing that the brain receptors for these chemicals may be defective in overweight persons.

Environment also plays a causal role in obesity. Studies have shown that people eat more when they are in the company of others, particularly if the other people are eating (Logue, 1991). In addition, research finds that people from low socioeconomic environments are more likely to be obese than those from high socioeconomic backgrounds (Ernst & Harlan, 1991).

Health Risk?

Do mildly to moderately obese people have a greater risk of coronary disease or cancer or other disease? Investigations into this question have produced conflicting results (Bender et al., 1999;

Harmful advertising *When Calvin Klein posed young teenagers in sexually suggestive clothing ads in 1995, the public protested and the ads were halted. However, what some researchers consider even more damaging—the use of very thin young models who influence the body ideals and dietary habits of millions of teenage girls—continued uninterrupted.*

Binges

People with bulimia nervosa may have two to forty binge episodes per week, although the number is usually closer to ten (Mizes, 1993). In most cases, the binges are carried out in secret. The person eats massive amounts of food very rapidly, with minimal chewing—usually sweet, high-calorie foods with a soft texture, such as ice cream, cookies, doughnuts, and sandwiches. As suggested by the Greek term *bous limos,* or "cattle hunger," from which the word "bulimia" is derived, the food is hardly tasted or thought about. Binge-eaters commonly consume more than 1,500 calories (often more than 3,000) during an episode (Agras, 1995).

Binges are usually preceded by feelings of great tension (Johnson et al., 1995). The person feels irritable, "unreal," and powerless to control an overwhelming need to eat "forbidden" foods (Levine, 1987). During the binge, the person feels unable to stop eating. Although the binge itself may be experienced as pleasurable in the sense that it relieves the unbearable tension, it is followed by feelings of extreme self-blame, guilt, and depression, as well as fears of gaining weight and being discovered (APA, 2000; Porzelius et al., 1999).

Lean, Han, & Seidell, 1999). One long-term study found that while moderately overweight subjects had a 30 percent higher risk of early death, underweight subjects had a low likelihood of dying at an early age as long as their thinness could not be attributed to smoking or illness (Manson et al., 1995). However, another study found that the mortality rate of underweight subjects was as high as that of overweight subjects regardless of smoking behavior or illness (Troiano et al., 1996). These findings suggest that the jury is still out on this issue.

Does Dieting Work?

There are scores of diets and diet pills. There is almost no evidence, however, that any diet yet devised can ensure long-term weight loss (Wilson, 1994). In fact, long-term studies reveal a *rebound effect,* a net gain in weight in obese people who have lost weight on very low-calorie diets. Research also suggests that the feelings of failure that accompany diet rebounds may lead to dysfunctional eating patterns, including binge eating (Venditti et al., 1996).

Most low-calorie dieters shift from weight loss to weight gain, then to loss again, and so on. In the end this yo-yo pattern may itself be a health risk, increasing the likelihood of high blood pressure and cardiovascular disease (Brownell & O'Neill, 1995, 1993; Lissner et al., 1991). In cases of extreme obesity, where weight is indeed a clear health hazard and weight loss is advisable, establishing a realistic, attainable goal rather than an unrealistic ideal appears to be the most promising path to long-term weight loss (Brownell & O'Neil, 1993; Brownell & Wadden, 1992).

Efforts are now under way to develop new kinds of drugs that will operate directly on the genes, hormones, and proteins that have been linked to obesity (Carek & Dickerson, 1999; Greenberg, Chan, & Blackburn, 1999). Theoretically, these treatments will counteract the bodily reactions that undermine efforts at dieting. Whether such interventions can provide safe and permanent weight loss remains to be seen.

What Is the Proper Goal?

Some researchers argue that attempts to reduce obesity should focus less on weight loss and more on improving general health and attitudes (Rosen et al., 1995). If poor eating habits can be corrected, if a poor self-concept and distorted body image can be improved, and if overweight people can be educated about the myths and truths regarding obesity, perhaps everyone will be better off.

Thus a growing number of experts are suggesting that people who are mildly and perhaps even moderately obese should be left alone, at least so far as weight loss is concerned. At the very least, their weight-loss programs should set more modest and realistic goals. In addition, it is critical that the public overcome its prejudice against people who are overweight and come to appreciate that obesity is, at worst, a problem that requires treatment, and perhaps simply another version of the normal human condition.

Compensatory Behaviors

After a binge, people with bulimia nervosa try to compensate for and undo its effects. Many resort to vomiting. But vomiting actually fails to prevent the absorption of half of the calories consumed during a binge. Furthermore, repeated vomiting affects one's general ability to feel satiated; thus it leads to greater hunger and more frequent and intense binges (Wooley & Wooley, 1985). Similarly, the use of laxatives or diuretics fails almost completely to undo the caloric effects of bingeing (Garner et al., 1985).

Vomiting and other compensatory behaviors may temporarily relieve the uncomfortable physical feelings of fullness or reduce the feelings of anxiety, self-disgust, and lack of control attached to binge eating (DeSilva, 1995; Mizes, 1995). Over time, however, a cycle develops in which purging allows more bingeing and bingeing necessitates more purging (Porzelius et al., 1999). The cycle eventually causes people with this disorder to feel powerless, useless, and disgusted with themselves (Kanakis & Thelen, 1995). Most recognize fully that they have an eating disorder. The woman we met earlier recalls how the pattern of bingeing, purging, and self-disgust took hold while she was a teenager in boarding school:

> Every bite that went into my mouth was a naughty and selfish indulgence, and I became more and more disgusted with myself. . . .
> The first time I stuck my fingers down my throat was during the last week of school. I saw a girl come out of the bathroom with her face all red and her eyes

WEIGHING IN

Five percent of Americans weigh themselves more than once per day, 8 percent once per day, 10 percent twice per week, and 36 percent twice per month. Women are three times more likely than men to check the scale (Kanner, 1995).

puffy. She had always talked about her weight and how she should be dieting even though her body was really shapely. I knew instantly what she had just done and I had to try it. . . .

I began with breakfasts which were served buffet-style on the main floor of the dorm. I learned which foods I could eat that would come back up easily. When I woke in the morning, I had to make the decision whether to stuff myself for half an hour and throw up before class, or whether to try and make it through the whole day without overeating. . . . I always thought people noticed when I took huge portions at mealtimes, but I figured they assumed that because I was an athlete, I burned it off. . . . Once a binge was under way, I did not stop until my stomach looked pregnant and I felt like I could not swallow one more time.

That year was the first of my nine years of obsessive eating and throwing up. . . . I didn't want to tell anyone what I was doing, and I didn't want to stop. . . . [Though] being in love or other distractions occasionally lessened the cravings, I always returned to the food.

(Hall, 1980, pp. 9–12)

Models and mannequins *Mannequins were once made extra thin to show the lines of the clothing for sale to best advantage. Today the shape of the ideal woman is indistinguishable from that of a mannequin, and a growing number of young women try to achieve this ideal through a pattern of bingeing and purging.*

As with anorexia nervosa, a bulimic pattern typically begins during or after a period of intense dieting, often one that has been successful and earned praise from family members and friends (Lowe et al., 1996; Szmukler & Patton, 1995). Research has found that normal subjects placed on very strict diets also develop a tendency to binge. Some of the subjects in the conscientious objector "starvation study," for example, later binged when they were allowed to return to regular eating, and a number of them continued to be hungry even after large meals (Keys et al., 1950). A more recent study examined the binge-eating behavior of subjects at the end of a very low-calorie weight-loss program (Telch & Agras, 1993). Immediately after the program, 62 percent of the subjects, who had not previously been binge eaters, reported binge-eating episodes, although the episodes did decrease during the three months after treatment stopped.

Bulimia Nervosa vs. Anorexia Nervosa

Bulimia nervosa is similar to anorexia nervosa in many ways. Both disorders typically begin after a period of dieting by people who are fearful of becoming obese; driven to become thin; preoccupied with food, weight, and appearance; and struggling with feelings of depression, anxiety, and the need to be perfect (Lehoux, Steiger, & Jabalpurlawa, 2000; Joiner et al., 1997, 1995). Substance abuse may accompany either disorder, perhaps beginning with the excessive use of diet pills (APA, 2000; Wiederman & Pryor, 1996). People with either disorder believe that they weigh too much and look too heavy regardless of their actual weight or appearance (Mizes, 1995; Ledoux et al., 1993). And both disorders are marked by disturbed attitudes toward eating (Porzelius et al., 1999; DeSilva, 1995). One study found, for example, that women with bulimia nervosa generally perceived their body size to be larger than did control subjects of similar size and believed that their body size became larger still after they ate a small snack (McKenzie et al., 1993).

Yet the two disorders also differ in important ways (see Table 11-3). Although people with either disorder worry about the opinions of others, those with bulimia nervosa tend to be more concerned about pleasing others, being attractive to others, and having intimate relationships (Striegel-Moore, Silberstein, & Rodin, 1993; Muuss, 1986). They also tend to be more sexually experienced and active than people with anorexia nervosa. On the positive side, people with bulimia nervosa display fewer of the obsessive qualities that drive people with

DIETARY TRIGGERS
Although most dieters do not develop an eating disorder, female teenagers who follow a severely restrictive diet are 18 times more likely than nondieters to develop an eating disorder within one year of the diet (Patton et al., 1999).

Table 11-3

Anorexia Nervosa vs. Bulimia Nervosa

RESTRICTING-TYPE ANOREXIA NERVOSA	BULIMIA NERVOSA
Refusal to maintain a minimum body weight for healthy functioning	Underweight, normal weight, near-normal weight, or overweight
Hunger and disorder denied; often proud of weight management and more satisfied with body	Intense hunger experienced; binge–purge experienced as abnormal; greater body dissatisfaction
Less antisocial behavior	Greater tendency to antisocial behavior and alcohol abuse
Amenorrhea of at least 3 months' duration common	Irregular menstrual periods common; amenorrhea uncommon unless body weight is low
Mistrust of others, particularly professionals	More trusting of people who wish to help
Tend to be obsessional	Tend to be dramatic
Greater self-control, but emotionally over-controlled, with problems experiencing and expressing feelings	More impulsivity and emotional instability
More likely to be sexually immature and inexperienced	More sexually experienced and sexually active
Females more likely to reject traditional feminine role	Females more likely to embrace traditional feminine role
Age of onset often around 14–18	Age of onset around 15–21
Greater tendency for maximum pre-disorder weight to be near normal for age	Greater tendency for maximum pre-disorder weight to be slightly greater than normal
Lesser familial predisposition to obesity	Greater familial predisposition to obesity
Greater tendency toward pre-disorder compliance with parents	Greater tendency toward pre-disorder conflict with parents
Tendency to deny family conflict	Tendency to perceive intense family conflict

Source: APA, 2000, 1994; Levine, 1987; Andersen, 1985; Garner et al., 1985; Neuman & Halvorson, 1983.

restricting-type anorexia nervosa to control their caloric intake so rigidly (Halmi, 1995; Andersen, 1985). On the negative side, they are more likely to have long histories of mood swings, become easily frustrated or bored, and have trouble coping effectively or controlling their impulses (APA, 2000; Sanftner & Crowther, 1998). Individuals with bulimia nervosa also tend to be ruled by strong emotions and may change friends and relationships frequently. And more than one-third of them display the characteristics of a personality disorder, which we shall examine more closely in Chapter 17 (APA, 2000; Matsunaga et al., 2000; Braun et al., 1995).

Another difference is the nature of the medical complications that accompany each disorder (Keel & Mitchell, 1997). Only half of women with bulimia nervosa are amenorrheic or have very irregular menstrual periods, compared to almost all of those with

Laboratory starvation *Thirty-six conscientious objectors who were put on a semistarvation diet for six months developed many of the symptoms seen in anorexia nervosa and bulimia nervosa (Keys et al., 1950).*

MULTIDIMENSIONAL RISK PERSPECTIVE
A theory that identifies several kinds of risk factors that are thought to combine to help cause a disorder. The more factors present, the greater the risk of developing the disorder.

anorexia nervosa (Treasure & Szmukler, 1995). On the other hand, repeated vomiting bathes teeth and gums in hydrochloric acid, leading some women with bulimia nervosa to experience serious dental problems, such as breakdown of enamel and even loss of teeth (Casper, 1995; Treasure & Szmukler, 1995). Moreover, frequent vomiting or chronic diarrhea (from the use of laxatives) can cause dangerous potassium deficiencies, which may lead to weakness, intestinal disorders, kidney disease, or heart damage (Turner et al., 2000; Halmi et al., 1994; Sharp & Freeman, 1993).

What Causes Eating Disorders?

Currently, theorists and researchers are using a **multidimensional risk perspective** to explain eating disorders. That is, they cite several key factors as placing individuals at risk for these disorders (Lask, 2000). The more of these factors that are present, the greater the likelihood that a person will develop an eating disorder (Lyon et al., 1997). Among the leading factors identified to date are sociocultural conditions (societal and family pressures), psychological problems (ego, cognitive, and mood disturbances), and biological variables.

Societal Pressures

Many theorists believe that the current Western standards of female attractiveness have contributed to increases in eating disorders (Wertheim et al., 1997; Abramson & Valene, 1991). These standards have changed throughout history, with a noticeable shift toward preference for a thin female frame in recent decades. The shift to a thinner frame has been steady since the 1950s. One study that tracked the height, weight, and age of contestants in the Miss America Pageant from 1959 through 1978 found an average decline of 0.28 pound per year among the contestants and 0.37 pound per year among winners (Garner et al., 1980). The researchers also examined data on all *Playboy* magazine centerfold models over the same time period and found that the average weight, bust, and hip measurements of these women had decreased steadily. More recent studies of Miss America contestants and *Playboy* centerfolds indicate that these trends have continued (Rubinstein & Caballero, 2000; Wiseman et al., 1992).

Consider This

⦿ The prevalence of eating disorders is particularly low in cultures that restrict female social roles and reduce a woman's freedom to make decisions about her life (Miller & Pumariega, 1999; Bemporad, 1997). How might you explain this relationship?

Occupational hazard *The thin frames of these dance students are apparent as they warm up for a class outside a rehearsal hall. Certain professionals, such as dancers, models, and athletes, have high rates of eating concerns and disorders, largely because of their professions' emphasis on weight and size.*

Because thinness is especially valued in the subcultures of fashion models, actors, dancers, and certain athletes, members of these groups are likely to be particularly concerned about their weight (Powers, 1999; Williamson et al., 1995). As sociocultural theorists would predict, studies have found that people in these professions are more prone than others to eating disorders (Thompson & Sherman, 1999; Attie & Brooks-Gunn, 1992), and a number of famous young women from these fields have publicly acknowledged grossly disordered eating patterns in recent years. One survey of 1,443 athletes at ten colleges around the United States revealed that more than 9 percent of female college athletes suffer from an eating disorder and another 50 percent admit to eating behaviors that put them at risk for such disorders (Johnson, 1995). A full 20 percent of the gymnasts surveyed manifested an eating disorder (see Figure 11-3).

Attitudes toward thinness may also help explain economic and racial differences in the rates of eating disorders (see Box 11-3 on page 335). In the past, white American women in the upper socioeconomic classes expressed more concern about thinness and dieting than did African American women or white American women of the lower socioeconomic classes (Margo, 1985; Stunkard, 1975). Correspondingly, eating disorders were more common among white American women higher on the socioeconomic scale (Foreyt et al., 1996; Rosen et al., 1991). In more recent years, however, dieting and preoccupation with thinness have increased to some degree in all classes and minority groups, as has the prevalence of eating disorders (Striegel-Moore & Smolak, 2000; Miller & Pumariega, 1999).

Cultural differences may also help explain the striking gender gap for eating disorders. Our society's emphasis on a thin appearance is aimed at women much more than men (Nichter & Nichter, 1991; Rolls et al., 1991). Some theorists believe that this double standard has made women much more intent upon being thin, more inclined to diet, and more prone to eating disorders (Rand & Kuldau, 1991).

Western society not only glorifies thinness but creates a climate of prejudice against overweight people of all ages. Whereas slurs based on ethnicity, race, and gender are considered unacceptable, cruel jokes about obesity are standard fare on television shows and in movies, books, and magazines. Research indicates that the prejudice against obese people is deep-rooted (Tiggeman & Wilson-Barrett, 1998; Brownell & O'Neil, 1993). Prospective parents who were shown pictures of a chubby child and a medium-weight or thin child rated the former as less friendly, energetic, intelligent, and desirable than the latter. In another study, preschool children who were given a choice between a chubby and a thin rag doll chose the thin one, although they could not say why. It is small wonder that as many as half of elementary school girls have tried to lose weight (Shisslak et al., 1998) and 61 percent of middle school girls are currently dieting (Hunnicut & Newman, 1993).

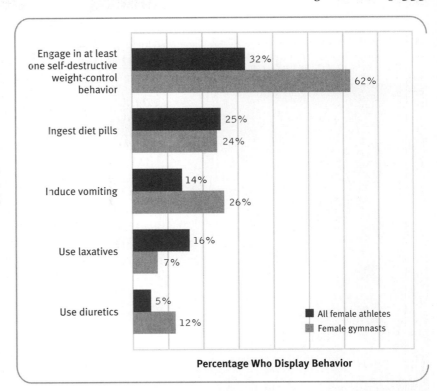

Percentage Who Display Behavior

FIGURE **11-3** **Dangerous shortcuts** *According to surveys, in sports ranging from field hockey to gymnastics, almost a third of all female athletes engage in one or more self-destructive behaviors to control their weight. Close to two-thirds of female college gymnasts engage in at least one such behavior. (Adapted from Rosen & Hough, 1988; Rosen et al., 1986.)*

Unfair game *In Western society, overweight people are typically treated with insensitivity. They are also the targets of humor in magazines, books, television shows, and movies, such as the highly successful film* The Nutty Professor.

Family Environment

Families may play a critical role in the development of eating disorders. Research suggests that as many as half of the families of people with eating disorders have a long history of emphasizing thinness, physical appearance, and dieting (Haworth-Hoeppner, 2000; Lieberman, 1995). In fact, the mothers in these families are more likely to diet themselves and to be generally perfectionistic than are the mothers in other families (Pike & Rodin, 1991). Abnormal interactions and forms of communication within a family may also set the stage for an eating disorder. Family systems theorists argue that the families of people who develop eating disorders are often dysfunctional to begin with and that the eating disorder of one member is simply a reflection of the larger problem (Dalzell, 2000; Vandereycken, 1994; Lundholm & Waters, 1991). The influential family theorist Salvador Minuchin, for example, believes that what he calls an **enmeshed family pattern** often leads to eating disorders (Minuchin, Rosman, & Baker, 1978).

In an enmeshed system, family members are overinvolved in each other's affairs and overconcerned with the details of each other's lives. On the positive side, enmeshed families can be affectionate and loyal. On the negative side, they can be clinging and foster dependency. Parents are too involved in the lives of their children, allowing little opportunity for individuality and independence. Minuchin argues that adolescence poses a special problem for these families. The teenager's normal push for independence threatens the family's apparent harmony and closeness. In response, the family may subtly force the child to take on a "sick" role—to develop an eating disorder or some other illness. The child's disorder enables the family to maintain its appearance of harmony. A sick child needs her family, and family members can rally to protect her.

Some case studies have supported such family systems explanations, but empirical studies fail to show that particular family patterns consistently set the stage for the development of eating disorders (Wilson et al., 1996; Colahan & Senior, 1995). In fact, the families of people with either anorexia nervosa or bulimia nervosa vary widely (Eisler, 1995).

Ego Deficiencies and Cognitive Disturbances

Hilde Bruch, a pioneer in the study and treatment of eating disorders, developed a theory built on both psychodynamic and cognitive notions. She argued that disturbed mother–child interactions lead to serious *ego deficiencies* in the child (including a poor sense of autonomy and control) and to severe *cognitive disturbances* that jointly help produce disordered eating patterns (Bruch, 1991, 1983, 1981, 1962).

According to Bruch, parents may respond to their children either effectively or ineffectively. *Effective parents* accurately attend to their children's biological and emotional needs, giving them food when they are crying from hunger and comfort when they are crying out of fear. *Ineffective parents,* by contrast, fail to attend to their children's internal needs, deciding that their children are hungry, cold, or tired without correctly interpreting the children's actual condition. They may feed the children at times of anxiety rather than hunger or comfort them at times of tiredness rather than anxiety. Children who receive such parenting may grow up confused and unaware of their own internal needs, not knowing for themselves when they are hungry or full, and unable to identify their own emotions.

Unable to rely on internal signals, these children turn instead to external guides, such as their parents. They seem to be "model children," but they fail to

Changing times Seated Bather, *by Pierre-Auguste Renoir (1841–1919), shows that the aesthetically ideal woman of the past was considerably larger than today's ideal.*

ENMESHED FAMILY PATTERN A family system in which members are overinvolved with each other's affairs and overconcerned about each other's welfare.

BOX **11-3**

Eating Disorders | 335

Body Image: A Matter of Race?

In the popular movie *Clueless,* Cher and Dionne, wealthy teenage friends of different races, have similar tastes, beliefs, and values about everything from boys to schoolwork. In particular, they have the same kinds of eating habits and beauty ideals, and they are even similar in weight and physical form. But does the story of these young women reflect the realities of white and African American females in our society? The answer, according to some recent investigations, appears to be no (Miller et al., 2000; Cash & Henry, 1995; Parker et al., 1995).

Although young African American women seem to be more worried about their weight and more prone to diet and to develop eating disorders today than in the past, their values, goals, and behaviors in these areas remain healthier than those of young white women. A widely publicized study done at the University of Arizona explored the body image ideals and dieting behaviors of 296 eighth- and ninth-grade girls over a three-year span (Parker et al., 1995). Its findings: nearly 90 percent of the white teens said they were dissatisfied with their weight and body shape, whereas nearly 70 percent of the African American teens were satisfied with their bodies. The African American teens expressed satisfaction regardless of their actual weight; even those who were overweight described themselves as happy.

Beauty Ideals

The study also suggests that white and African American adolescent girls have very different ideals of beauty. The white teens, asked to define the "perfect girl," described a girl of 5'7" weighing between 100 and 110 pounds—proportions that mirror those of today's so-called supermodels. Attaining a perfect weight, many said, was the key to being "totally happy," and they indicated that thinness was a requirement for popularity. Several explained that "being skinny makes you fit in more."

In contrast, the African American respondents tended to emphasize personality traits over physical characteristics when they described the ideal girl. They defined the "perfect" African American girl as smart, fun, easy to talk to, not conceited, and funny; she did not necessarily need to be "pretty," as long as she was well groomed. The body dimensions the African American teens described were more attainable for the typical girl; they favored fuller hips, for example. Perhaps the key difference was the African American subjects' greater emphasis on true beauty as an inner quality. Two-thirds of them defined beauty as "the right attitude," and approximately the same percentage indicated that women become more beautiful as they grow older.

Health and Diet

Given such definitions of beauty, it is not surprising that the African American subjects were far less likely than the white American respondents to diet for extended periods. Although a full 52 percent of the African American teens had dieted at some point in the previous year, they did not tend to stick to a strict diet, explaining that it is better to be a "little" overweight than underweight. Meanwhile, the white teens, 61 percent of whom had dieted in the previous year, stressed dieting as a way both to become thinner and to gain control over other aspects of their lives, such as their social life. Body dissatisfaction and talk about feeling fat seemed to be one way for the white teenagers to show that they were concerned about their appearance and were working toward their standard of beauty (Nichter & Vuckovic, 1994).

Although the African American teenagers in this study, and in other settings as well, expressed positive feelings about their bodies and about beauty in general, clinical theorists warn that problems may lie ahead for them (Williamson, 1998). The University of Arizona investigators observe, "It remains to be seen whether they will be able to maintain these self-perceptions as they become older and obtain jobs in mainstream American society. . . . [They] may be more likely to deemphasize their black identities in order to get ahead. . . . Will this translate into body discipline in the form of dieting to obtain a thin body by girls who aspire to make it?" (Parker et al., 1995, p. 111).

Racial differences *While women within each race differ, evidence is mounting that African American teens are, on average, more satisfied with their weight and body shape than white American teens and less inclined to diet for extended periods.*

ConsiderThis

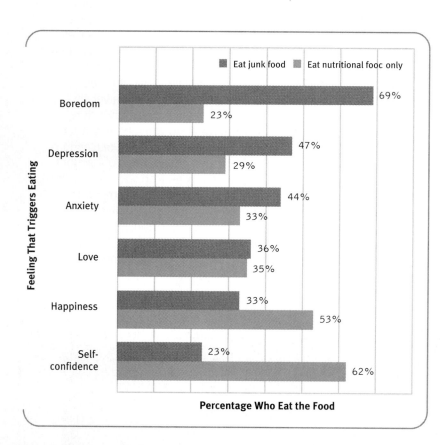

● The most successful of today's fashion models, often referred to as supermodels, have a celebrity status that was not conferred upon models in the past. Why do you think the fame and status of models has risen in this way?

develop genuine self-reliance, and "experience themselves as not being in control of their behavior, needs, and impulses, as not owning their own bodies" (Bruch, 1973, p. 55). Adolescence increases their innate desire to establish autonomy, yet they feel unable to do so (Strauss & Ryan, 1987). To overcome their sense of helplessness, they seek excessive control over their body size and shape and over their eating habits. Helen, an 18-year-old, describes her experience:

> There is a peculiar contradiction—everybody thinks you're doing so well and everybody thinks you're great, but your real problem is that you think that you are not good enough. You are afraid of not living up to what you think you are expected to do. You have one great fear, namely that of being ordinary, or average, or common—just not good enough. This peculiar dieting begins with such anxiety. You want to prove that you have control, that you can do it. The peculiar part of it is that it makes you feel good about yourself, makes you feel "I can accomplish something." It makes you feel "I can do something nobody else can do."
>
> *(Bruch, 1978, p. 128)*

Clinical reports and research have provided some support for Bruch's theory. Clinicians have observed that the parents of teenagers with eating disorders do tend to define their children's needs rather than allow the children to define their own needs (Hart & Kenny, 1995; Steiner et al., 1991). When Bruch interviewed the mothers of 51 children with anorexia nervosa, many proudly recalled that they had always "anticipated" their young child's needs, never permitting the child to "feel hungry" (Bruch, 1973).

Research has also supported Bruch's belief that people with eating disorders perceive internal cues inaccurately (Fukunishi, 1998; Halmi et al., 1989). When subjects with bulimia nervosa are anxious or upset, for example, many of them mistakenly think they are also hungry (see Figure 11-4), and they respond as they might respond to hunger—by eating (Rebert, Stanton, & Schwartz, 1991). Finally, studies support Bruch's argument that people with eating disorders rely excessively on the opinions, wishes, and views of others. They are more likely than other people to worry about how others view them, to seek approval, to be conforming, and to feel a lack of control over their lives (Walters & Kendler, 1995; Vitousek & Manke, 1994).

FIGURE 11-4 **When do people seek junk food?** *Apparently, when they feel bad. People who eat junk food when they are feeling bad outnumber those who eat nutritional food under similar circumstances. In contrast, more people seek nutritional food when they are feeling good. (Adapted from Lyman, 1982.)*

Mood Disorders

Many people with eating disorders, particularly those with bulimia nervosa, experience symptoms of depression, such as sadness, low self-esteem, shame, pessimism, and errors in logic (Burney & Irwin, 2000; Lehoux et al., 2000; Paxton & Diggens, 1997). This finding has led some theorists to suggest that mood disorders set the stage for eating disorders (Hsu et al., 1992).

Their claim is supported by four kinds of evidence. First, many more people with an eating disorder qualify for a clinical diagnosis of major depressive disorder than do people in the general population (Brewerton et al., 1995; Pope & Hudson, 1984). Second, the close relatives of people with eating disorders seem to have a higher rate of mood disorders than do close relatives of people without such disorders (APA, 2000). Third, as we shall see, many people with eating disorders, particularly bulimia nervosa, have low activity of the neurotransmitter serotonin, similar to the serotonin abnormalities found in depressed people. And finally, people with eating disorders are often helped by some of the same antidepressant drugs that reduce depression (Advokat & Kutlesic, 1995; Mitchell & de Zwaan, 1993).

Although such findings sugggest that depression may be linked to eating disorders, other explanations are possible (Wade et al., 2000). For example, the pressure and pain of having an eating disorder may *cause* a mood disorder (Silverstone, 1990). Whatever the correct interpretation, many people struggling with eating disorders also suffer from depression, among other psychological problems.

Biological Factors

Biological theorists suspect that some people inherit a genetic tendency to develop an eating disorder. Consistent with this notion, relatives of people with these disorders are up to six times more likely than other individuals to develop the disorders themselves (Strober et al., 2000; Gorwood et al., 1998). Moreover, if one identical twin has bulimia nervosa, the other twin also develops the disorder in 23 percent of cases; in contrast, the concordance rate for fraternal twins, who are genetically less similar, is 9 percent (Walters & Kendler, 1995; Kendler et al., 1991). Although such data do not rule out environmental explanations, they have encouraged biological researchers to look further still for specific biological causes.

One factor that has interested investigators is the possible role of *serotonin*. Several researcher teams have found a link between eating disorders and the genes responsible for the production of this neurotransmitter (Enoch et al., 1998), while others have measured low serotonin activity in many people with eating disorders (Carrasco et al., 2000; Smith, Fairburn, & Cowen, 1999). Given serotonin's role in depression and obsessive-compulsive disorder—problems that often accompany eating disorders—it is possible that low serotonin activity has more to do with those other disorders than with the eating disorders per se. On the other hand, perhaps low serotonin activity contributes directly to eating disorders—for example, by causing the body to crave and binge on higher-carbohydrate foods (Kaye et al., 2000; Wurtman, 1987). Some researchers even believe that persons with eating disorders are born with excessively high levels of serotonin activity, which they instinctively try to reduce by starving or purging themselves (Kaye et al., 1998). Eventually their disordered eating patterns may reduce the neurotransmitter activity to a level that is abnormally low.

Multiple influences *An individual's weight set point is influenced by a range of factors, from genetic to sociocultural. Although the Pima Native Americans in Arizona (left) and their relatives in Mexico (right, during a Holy Week festival) share common genetics, the former weigh more on average. High-fat foods dominate the diets of Arizonan Pimas, while Mexican Pimas subsist on grains and vegetables.*

Common goal *As we are reminded by these junior high school students in gym class, children approach puberty with a wide range of body sizes and metabolism rates. Yet, because of societal and psychological influences, the majority of them, particularly girls, aspire to a similar ultra-thin body size that is unattainable for most.*

FOOD PROCESSING

The adult human stomach can hold up to two liters. Ingested food remains in the stomach for three to five hours, exiting the body completely in fifteen hours or so.

HYPOTHALAMUS A part of the brain that helps regulate various bodily functions, including eating and hunger.

LATERAL HYPOTHALAMUS (LH) The region of the hypothalamus that, when activated, produces hunger.

VENTROMEDIAL HYPOTHALAMUS (VMH) The region of the hypothalamus that, when activated, depresses hunger.

WEIGHT SET POINT The weight level that a person is predisposed to maintain, controlled in part by the hypothalamus.

Other biological researchers explain eating disorders by pointing to the **hypothalamus**, a part of the brain that regulates many bodily functions through the activity of the endocrine system (Tataranni et al., 1999; Leibowitz & Hoebel, 1998). With its rich supply of blood vessels, the hypothalamus can detect changes in blood chemistry as well as respond to incoming neural information about what is happening throughout the body.

Researchers have located two separate areas in the hypothalamus that help control eating (Grossman, 1990; Bray et al., 1980). One, the **lateral hypothalamus (LH)**, consisting of the side areas of the hypothalamus, produces hunger when it is activated. When the LH of a laboratory animal is stimulated electrically, the animal eats, even if it has been fed recently. But if the LH is destroyed, the animal will refuse to eat, even if it has been starved. In contrast, another area, the **ventromedial hypothalamus (VMH)**, consisting of the bottom and middle of the hypothalamus, reduces hunger when it is activated. When the VMH is electrically stimulated, laboratory animals stop eating. When it is destroyed, the stomach and intestines of animals increase their rate of processing food, causing the animals to eat more often and eventually to become obese (Duggan & Booth, 1986; Hoebel & Teitelbaum, 1966).

These different centers of the hypothalamus are apparently activated by chemicals from the brain and body, depending on whether the person is eating or fasting. One such brain chemical is *glucagon-like peptide-1* (*GLP-1*), a natural appetite suppressant that operates in both animals and humans. When a team of researchers collected and injected GLP-1 into the brains of rats, the chemical traveled to receptors in the hypothalamus and caused the rats to reduce their food intake up to 95 percent even though they had not eaten for 24 hours (Turton et al., 1996). Conversely, when "full" rats were injected with a substance that blocked the reception of GLP-1 in the hypothalamus, they more than doubled their food intake.

Some researchers believe that the LH and VMH and chemicals such as GLP-1, working together, comprise a "weight thermostat" of sorts in the body, responsible for keeping an individual at a particular weight level called the **weight set point** (Garner et al., 1985; Keesey & Corbett, 1983). Genetic inheritance and early eating practices seem to determine each person's weight set point. When a person's weight falls below his or her particular set point, the LH is activated and seeks to restore the lost weight by producing hunger and lowering the body's *metabolic rate,* the rate at which the body expends energy. When a person's weight rises above his or her set point, the VMH is activated, and it seeks to remove the excess weight by reducing hunger and increasing the body's metabolic rate.

According to the weight set point theory, when people diet and fall to a weight below their weight set point, their brain begins to try to restore the lost weight (see Box 11-4). Hypothalamic activity produces a preoccupation with food and a desire to binge. It also triggers bodily changes designed to prevent further loss of weight and promote the gaining of weight, however little is eaten (Spalter et al., 1993; Hill & Robinson, 1991). Once the brain and body begin conspiring to raise weight in this way, dieters actually enter into a battle against themselves. Some people apparently manage to shut down the inner "thermostat" and control their eating almost completely. These people move toward restricting-type anorexia nervosa. For others, the battle spirals toward a binge–purge pattern. Perhaps the obsessive personality style of the former group helps them stick to a rigid regimen of dieting despite the brain's push for weight gain, while the impulsive style of the latter makes it particularly hard for them to resist the increasing urge to eat.

BOX **11-4**

And She Lived Happily Ever After?

In May 1996 Alicia Machado, a 19-year-old woman from Venezuela, was crowned Miss Universe. Then her problems began. During the first eight months of her reign, her weight rose from 118 to 160 pounds, angering pageant officials and sparking rumors that she was about to be relieved of her crown. The "problem" received broad newspaper and television coverage and much ridicule on talk radio programs around the world.

Ms. Machado explained, "I was a normal girl, but my life has had big changes. I travel to many countries, eat different foods." Nevertheless, in response to all the pressure, she undertook a special diet and an extensive exercise program to lose at least some of the weight she had gained. Her trainer claimed that a weight of 118 pounds was too low for her frame and explained that she had originally attained it by taking diet pills.

ConsiderThis

What does this episode suggest about the role of societal factors in the development of eating problems? • Why did so many people hold such strong, often critical opinions about Ms. Machado's weight? • What messages did this controversy and its resolution convey to women around the world?

Treatments for Eating Disorders

Today's treatments for eating disorders have two goals. The first is to correct as quickly as possible the abnormal eating pattern that is endangering the person's health. The second is to address the broader psychological and situational factors that have led to and now maintain the eating problem. Family and friends can also play an important role in helping to overcome the disorder (Sherman & Thompson, 1990).

Treatments for Anorexia Nervosa

The immediate aims of treatment for anorexia nervosa are to help individuals regain their lost weight, recover from malnourishment, and eat normally again. Therapists must then help them to make psychological and perhaps family changes to preserve those gains.

HOW ARE PROPER WEIGHT AND NORMAL EATING RESTORED? A variety of treatment methods are used to help patients with anorexia nervosa gain weight quickly and return to health within weeks. In the past, treatment was almost always provided in a hospital, but now it is often offered in outpatient settings (Pyle, 1999; Battle & Brownell, 1996).

In life-threatening cases, clinicians may need to *force tube and intravenous feedings* on a patient who refuses to eat. Unfortunately, this use of force may breed distrust in the patient and set up a power struggle between patient and therapist (Treasure, Todd, & Szmuckler, 1995; Zerbe, 1993). In contrast, *behavioral* weight-restoration approaches have clinicians reward patients whenever they eat properly or gain weight and offer no rewards when they eat improperly or fail to gain weight (Griffiths et al., 1998; Halmi, 1985).

Perhaps the most popular weight-restoration technique of recent years has been a combination of *supportive nursing care* and a high-calorie diet (Andersen, 1995; Treasure et al., 1995). Here nurses gradually increase a patient's diet over the course of several weeks to more than 2,500 calories a day. The nurses educate

IN SEARCH OF A NAME

In the past, names for anorexia nervosa and its victims have included *inedia prodigiosa* ("a great starvation"), *fasting girl, wasting disease, morbid appetite, sitophobia* (fear of grain), and *hysterical anorexia.*

patients about the program, track their progress, provide encouragement, and help them recognize that their weight gain is under control and will not be permitted to continue into obesity. Studies find that patients in nursing-care programs usually gain the necessary weight over eight to twelve weeks (Treasure et al., 1995; Garfinkel & Garner, 1982).

HOW ARE LASTING CHANGES ACHIEVED? Clinical researchers have found that individuals with anorexia nervosa must address their underlying psychological problems in order to achieve lasting improvement. Therapists typically offer a mixture of therapy and education in pursuit of this broader goal, using a combination of individual, group, and family approaches (Wright, 2000; Pyle, 1999).

BUILDING AUTONOMY AND SELF-AWARENESS One focus of treatment is to help patients with anorexia nervosa recognize their need for independence and teach them more appropriate ways to exercise control (Dare & Crowther, 1995; Robin et al., 1995). Therapists may also teach them to recognize and trust their internal sensations and feelings (Kaplan & Garfinkel, 1999; Bruch, 1973). In the following exchange, a therapist tries to help a 15-year-old client recognize and share her feelings:

> *Patient:* I don't talk about my feelings; I never did.
> *Therapist:* Do you think I'll respond like others?
> *Patient:* What do you mean?
> *Therapist:* I think you may be afraid that I won't pay close attention to what you feel inside, or that I'll tell you not to feel the way you do—that it's foolish to feel frightened, to feel fat, to doubt yourself, considering how well you do in school, how you're appreciated by teachers, how pretty you are.
> *Patient:* (*Looking somewhat tense and agitated*) Well, I was always told to be polite and respect other people, just like a stupid, faceless doll. (*Affecting a vacant, doll-like pose*)
> *Therapist:* Do I give you the impression that it would be disrespectful for you to share your feelings, whatever they may be?
> *Patient:* Not really; I don't know.
> *Therapist:* I can't, and won't, tell you that this is easy for you to do. . . . But I can promise you that you are free to speak your mind, and that I won't turn away.
>
> (*Strober & Yager, 1985, pp. 368–369*)

CORRECTING DISTURBED COGNITIONS Another focus of treatment is to help people with anorexia nervosa change their misconceptions and attitudes about eating and weight (Christie, 2000) (see Table 11-4). Using cognitive approaches, therapists may guide clients to recognize, challenge, and change maladaptive assumptions, such as "I must always be perfect" or "My weight and shape determine my value" (Lask & Bryant-Waugh, 2000; Freeman, 1995). Therapists may also educate clients about the perceptual distortions typical of anorexia nervosa and help them see that their own assessments of their size are incorrect (Mitchell & Peterson, 1997; Garner & Bemis, 1985, 1982). Even if a client never learns to judge her body shape accurately, she may at least reach a point where she says, "I know that a cardinal feature of anorexia nervosa is a misperception of my own size, so I can expect to feel fat no matter what size I really am."

CHANGING FAMILY INTERACTIONS Family therapy is often part of the treatment program for anorexia nervosa (Geist et al., 2000; Honig, 2000). As in other family therapy situations, the therapist meets with the family as a whole, points out troublesome family patterns (including inappropriate family communications and attitudes about food, eating, and body shape), and helps the members make appropriate changes. In particular, family therapists may try to help the person

Table 11-4

Sample Items from the Eating Disorder Inventory II

For each item, decide if the item is true about you ALWAYS (A), USUALLY (U), OFTEN (O), SOMETIMES (S), RARELY (R), or NEVER (N). Circle the letter that corresponds to your rating.

A	U	O	S	R	N	I think that my stomach is too big.
A	U	O	S	R	N	I eat when I am upset.
A	U	O	S	R	N	I stuff myself with food.
A	U	O	S	R	N	I think about dieting.
A	U	O	S	R	N	I think that my thighs are too large.
A	U	O	S	R	N	I feel ineffective as a person.
A	U	O	S	R	N	I feel extremely guilty after overeating.
A	U	O	S	R	N	I am terrified of gaining weight.
A	U	O	S	R	N	I get confused about what emotion I am feeling.
A	U	O	S	R	N	I feel inadequate.
A	U	O	S	R	N	I have gone on eating binges where I felt that I could not stop.
A	U	O	S	R	N	As a child, I tried very hard to avoid disappointing my parents and teachers.
A	U	O	S	R	N	I have trouble expressing my emotions to others.
A	U	O	S	R	N	I get confused as to whether or not I am hungry.
A	U	O	S	R	N	I have a low opinion of myself.
A	U	O	S	R	N	I think my hips are too big.
A	U	O	S	R	N	If I gain a pound, I worry that I will keep gaining.
A	U	O	S	R	N	I have the thought of trying to vomit in order to lose weight.
A	U	O	S	R	N	I think my buttocks are too large.
A	U	O	S	R	N	I eat or drink in secrecy.
A	U	O	S	R	N	I would like to be in total control of my bodily urges.

Source: Garner, Olmsted, & Polivy, 1991, 1984.

with anorexia nervosa separate her feelings and needs from those of other family members. Although the role of family in the development of anorexia nervosa has not been clarified fully, research strongly suggests that family therapy (or at least parent counseling) can be quite helpful in the treatment of this disorder (Dare & Eisler, 1997, 1995; Russell et al., 1992).

> *Mother:* I think I know what [Susan] is going through: all the doubt and insecurity of growing up and establishing her own identity. (*Turning to the patient, with tears*) If you just place trust in yourself, with the support of those around you who care, everything will turn out for the better.
>
> *Therapist:* Are you making yourself available to her? Should she turn to you, rely on you for guidance and emotional support?
>
> *Mother:* Well, that's what parents are for.
>
> *Therapist:* (*Turning to patient*) What do you think?
>
> *Susan:* (*To mother*) I can't keep depending on you, Mom, or everyone else. That's what I've been doing, and it gave me anorexia. . . .

"All philosophy in two words—sustain and abstain."

Epictetus, (A.D. c. 55–c. 135)

> *Therapist:* Do you think your mom would prefer that there be no secrets between her and the kids—an open door, so to speak?
> *Older sister:* Sometimes I do.
> *Therapist:* (*To patient and younger sister*) How about you two?
> *Susan:* Yeah. Sometimes it's like whatever I feel, she has to feel.
> *Younger sister:* Yeah.
>
> (*Strober & Yager, 1985, pp. 381–382*)

WHAT IS THE AFTERMATH OF ANOREXIA NERVOSA? The use of combined treatment approaches has greatly improved the outlook for people with anorexia nervosa, although the road to recovery can be difficult. The course and outcome of this disorder are highly variable (Miller, 1996), but researchers have noted certain trends.

Daily record *A teenager with anorexia nervosa writes in her journal as part of an inpatient treatment program. The writing helps her identify the fears, emotions, and needs that have contributed to her disorder.*

On the positive side, weight is often quickly restored once treatment begins, and treatment gains may continue for years. In one study, 83 percent of patients continued to show improvement when they were interviewed several years or more after their initial recovery: around 33 percent were fully recovered and 50 percent partially improved (Herzog et al., 1999; Treasure et al., 1995). Other studies have found that most individuals perform effectively at their jobs and express job satisfaction years after their recovery (Fombonne, 1995; Theander, 1970). Furthermore, those who recover are likely to marry or have intimate relationships at rates similar to those of other persons (Hsu, Crisp, & Harding, 1979; Theander, 1970).

Another positive note is that most females with anorexia nervosa menstruate again when they regain their weight (Fombonne, 1995; Crisp, 1981), and other medical improvements follow (Iketani et al., 1995). Also encouraging is that the death rate from anorexia nervosa seems to be declining (Neumarker, 1997; Treasure & Szmukler, 1995). Earlier diagnosis and safer and faster weight-restoration techniques may account for this trend. Deaths that do occur are usually caused by suicide, starvation, infection, gastrointestinal problems, or electrolyte imbalance (Nielsen et al., 1998; Treasure & Szmukler, 1995).

On the negative side, close to 20 percent of persons with anorexia nervosa remain impaired for years (APA, 2000; Halmi et al., 1991). Furthermore, recovery, when it does occur, is not always permanent (Herzog et al., 1999). Anorexic behavior recurs in one-third of recovered patients, usually triggered by new stresses, such as marriage, pregnancy, or a major relocation (Strober, Freeman, & Morrell, 1997; Sohlberg & Norring, 1992). Even years later, many recovered individuals continue to express concerns about their weight and appearance. Some continue to restrict their diets to some degree, experience anxiety when they eat with other people, or hold some distorted ideas about food, eating, and weight (Fichter & Pirke, 1995; Pirke et al., 1992).

About half of those who have suffered from anorexia nervosa continue to experience certain emotional problems—particularly depression, social anxiety, and obsessiveness—years after treatment. Such problems are particularly common in those who have not succeeded in reaching a fully normal weight (Halmi, 1995; Hsu et al., 1992). Similarly, family problems persist for approximately half of recovered individuals (Hsu, 1980).

The more weight a person has lost and the more time passed before the patient entered treatment, the poorer the prognosis for recovery (Pyle, 1999; Steinhausen, 1997). Individuals who had psychological or sexual problems before the

SOCIETAL DISAPPROVAL

In 1992 Canada canceled national beauty contests, claiming they were too degrading.

onset of the disorder tend to have a poorer recovery rate than those without such a history (Lewis & Chatoor, 1994; Burns & Crisp, 1985). Teenagers seem to have a better recovery rate than older patients (APA, 2000; Steinhausen et al., 2000). Females have a better recovery rate than males.

Treatments for Bulimia Nervosa

Treatment programs tailored to bulimia nervosa are relatively new, but they have risen rapidly in popularity. Many of these programs are offered in eating disorder clinics. All share the immediate goal of helping clients to eliminate their binge-purge patterns and establish good eating habits (see Box 11-5 on the next page) and the more general goal of eliminating the underlying causes of bulimic patterns. The programs emphasize education as much as therapy (Davis et al., 1997; Button, 1993). Like programs for anorexia nervosa, they often combine several treatment strategies, including individual insight therapy, group therapy, behavioral therapy, and antidepressant drug therapy (Tobin, 2000; Mizes, 1995; Wakeling, 1995).

INDIVIDUAL INSIGHT THERAPY Psychodynamic therapy has often been applied to cases of bulimia nervosa (Bloom et al., 1994; Fichter, 1990). The therapist uses free association and gentle interpretations to help patients uncover and work through their frustrations, lack of self-trust, need for control, and feelings of powerlessness (Dare & Crowther, 1995; Lerner, 1986). Only a few research studies have tested the effectiveness of psychodynamic therapy in bulimia nervosa, but those studies are generally supportive (Garner et al., 1993; Yager, 1985).

The insight approach that is now receiving the most attention in cases of bulimia nervosa is cognitive therapy, which tries to help clients recognize and change their maladaptive attitudes toward food, eating, weight, and shape (Porzelius et al., 1999; Freeman, 1995). Cognitive therapists typically teach the individuals to identify and challenge the negative thoughts that regularly precede their urge to binge—"I have no self-control," "I might as well give up," "I look fat" (Mitchell & Peterson, 1997; Fairburn, 1985). They may also guide clients to recognize, question, and eventually change their perfectionistic standards, sense of helplessness, and low self-concept (Freeman, 1995; Mizes, 1995).

Cognitive therapy seems to help as many as 65 percent of patients to stop bingeing and purging (Compas et al., 1998; Walsh et al., 1997). Approaches that mix cognitive and psychodynamic techniques also appear to be helpful (Brisman, 1992; Yager, 1985). Therapists have had considerable success with *interpersonal psychotherapy* as well, the treatment that seeks to improve interpersonal functioning (Wilfley & Cohen, 1997; Fairburn et al., 1995, 1993), and with *self-care manuals,* which describe numerous education and treatment strategies for sufferers (Treasure et al., 1996; Schmidt & Treasure, 1993).

GROUP THERAPY Most bulimia nervosa programs now include group therapy to give people an opportunity to share their thoughts, concerns, and experiences with one another (Leung et al., 2000; Pyle, 1999). Group members learn that their disorder is not unique or shameful, and they receive support and understanding from one another, along with candid feedback and insights (Manley & Needham, 1995). In the group they can also work directly on underlying fears of displeasing others or being criticized. Research suggests that group therapy is at least somewhat helpful in as many as 75 percent of bulimia nervosa cases, particularly when it is combined with individual insight therapy (McKisack & Waller, 1997; Wilfley et al., 1993).

IS PREVENTION POSSIBLE?

In a psychoeducation program, 11- to 13-year-old girls who were extremely worried about gaining weight were taught that female weight gain after puberty is normal and that excessive restriction of food can actually lead to weight gain. The concerns of the girls lessened markedly, in contrast to those of similar subjects who did not receive the instruction (Killen, 1996; Killen et al., 1994).

Early lessons *Many clinicians believe that beauty contests for children harshly underline society's emphasis on appearance and thinness. The contests teach participants at a very young age that their appearance is key to pleasing others and that they may be judged by demanding aesthetic standards throughout their lives.*

ConsiderThis

◉ Many, perhaps most, women in Western society feel as if they are dieting, or between diets, their entire adult lives. Is it possible to be a woman in this society and not struggle with at least some issues of eating and appearance? • Who is responsible for the standards and pressures that affect so many women?

BEHAVIORAL THERAPY Behavioral techniques are often incorporated into treatment programs for bulimia nervosa. Clients may, for example, be asked to keep diaries of their eating behavior, changes in sensations of hunger and fullness, and the ebb and flow of other feelings (Mitchell & Peterson, 1997; Goleman, 1995). This approach helps them to evaluate their eating patterns more objectively and recognize the emotions that trigger their desire to binge.

Some behaviorists use the technique of *exposure and response prevention* to help break the binge-purge cycle. As we saw in Chapter 6, this approach consists of exposing people to situations that would ordinarily raise anxiety and then preventing them from performing their usual compulsive responses until they learn that the situations are actually harmless and their compulsive acts unnecessary. For bulimia nervosa, the therapists require clients to eat particular kinds and amounts of food and then prevent them from vomiting, to show that eating can be a harmless and indeed constructive activity that needs no undoing (Rosen & Leitenberg, 1985, 1982). Typically the therapist sits with the client during the eating of forbidden foods and stays until the urge to purge has passed (Porzelius et al., 1999). Studies find that this treatment often helps reduce eating-related anxieties, bingeing, and vomiting (Bulik et al., 1998; Kennedy, Katz, & Neitzert, 1995).

ANTIDEPRESSANT MEDICATIONS During the past decade, antidepressant drugs such as fluoxetine, or Prozac, have been used in treatments for bulimia nervosa (Walsh et al., 1997). According to research, the drugs help 25 to 40 percent of patients, reducing their binges by an average of 67 percent and vomiting by 56 percent. Once again, drug therapy seems to work best in combination with other forms of therapy (Walsh et al., 1997; Agras, 1995, 1994).

BOX 11-5

A Big McProblem

*I*f the aesthetic ideal is a small frame, if people want to curb their eating, and if rates of eating disorders are increasing, why are fast-food servings getting bigger and more profitable? A Macho Meal sold by the Del Taco Mexican fast-food chain weighs almost four pounds—more than the Manhattan telephone book (Horovitz, 1996). A Double Gulp drink from 7-Eleven is larger than five cans of cola. Four slices of Pizza Hut's Triple Decker pizza contain more than the average allowance of calories, salt, and saturated fat for an entire day.

Meanwhile, McLean Deluxe lower-fat burgers and Taco Bell's Border Lights have struggled in the marketplace. Altogether, customers spend more than $2.5 billion on "big" fast-food products each year.

ConsiderThis

◉ How may these generously sized products be related to the increase in eating disturbances seen throughout society? • Does their availability create a climate for bingeing and purging? • Or are people actually driven to consume such products by the effects of excessive concern about dieting and eating?

Eating for sport *Few people go to the extremes of these participants at the World Pizza Eating Championships in New York City, but eating outrageous portions at fast-food restaurants and pizzerias is a growing trend around the United States.*

THE AFTERMATH OF BULIMIA NERVOSA Left untreated, bulimia nervosa can last for years, sometimes improving temporarily but then returning (APA, 2000). Treatment, however, produces immediate, significant improvement in approximately 40 percent of clients: they stop or greatly reduce their bingeing and purging, eat properly, and maintain a normal weight. Another 40 percent show a moderate response—at least some decrease in bingeing and purging. As many as 20 percent show little immediate improvement (Keel & Mitchell, 1997; Button, 1993). Follow-up studies suggest that by 10 years after treatment, 89 percent of persons with bulimia nervosa have recovered either fully (70 percent) or partially (19 percent) (Herzog et al., 1999; Keel et al., 1999). Those with partial recoveries continue to have recurrent binges or purges.

Relapse can be a problem even among people who respond successfully to treatment (Herzog et al., 1999; Keel & Mitchell, 1997). As with anorexia nervosa, relapses are usually triggered by a new life stress, such as an upcoming exam, job change, illness, marriage, or divorce (Abraham & Llowellyn-Jones, 1985). One study found that close to one-third of persons who had recovered from bulimia nervosa relapsed within two years of treatment, usually within six months (Olmsted, Kaplan, & Rockert, 1994). Relapse is more likely among persons who had longer histories of bulimia nervosa prior to treatment, had vomited more frequently during their disorder, had histories of substance abuse, and continue to distrust others after treatment (Keel et al., 2000, 1999; Olmsted et al., 1994).

Research also indicates that treatment helps many, but not all, people with bulimia nervosa attain lasting improvements in their overall psychological and social functioning (Keel et al., 2000; Yager et al., 1995). Follow-up studies find former patients to be less depressed than they had been at the time of diagnosis (Halmi, 1995). Approximately one-third of former patients interact in healthier ways at work, at home, and in social settings, while another third interact effectively in two of these areas (Hsu & Holder, 1986).

A new look for Barbie *Partly in response to clinical concerns, the manufacturer of "Barbie" recently changed the proportions of the doll with whom so many women grow up. A 5-foot-2, 125-pound woman who aspires to Barbie's old proportions would have to grow to be 7-foot-2, add 5 inches to her chest and 3.2 inches to her neck length, and lose 6 inches from her waist (Brownell & Napolitano, 1995).*

CROSSROADS:
A Standard for Integrating Perspectives

We have observed throughout this book that it is often useful to consider sociocultural, psychological, and biological factors jointly when one tries to explain or treat various forms of abnormal functioning. Nowhere is the argument for combining these perspectives more powerful than in the case of eating disorders. According to the multidimensional risk perspective, embraced by the many theorists and therapists, varied factors act together to encourage the development of eating disorders (Lyon et al., 1997; Gleaves, Williamson, & Barker, 1993). One person may succumb to societal pressures, autonomy problems, the changes of adolescence, and hypothalamic overactivity, while another person's dysfunction may result from family pressures, depression, and the effects of dieting. No wonder that the most helpful treatment programs for eating disorders combine sociocultural, psychological, and biological approaches. It makes sense that treatment programs need to be wide-ranging and flexible, tailored to the unique interacting problems of the patient. When the multidimensional risk perspective is applied to eating disorders, it demonstrates that scientists and practitioners from very different models can work together productively in an atmosphere of mutual respect.

Today's many investigations of eating disorders keep revealing new surprises that force clinicians to adjust their theories and treatment programs. For example, in recent years researchers have learned that people with bulimia nervosa sometimes feel strangely positive about their symptoms. A recovered patient said, "I still miss my bulimia as I would an old friend who has died" (Cauwels, 1983,

FORBIDDEN FRUIT (AND CRACKERS)

In one study, preschool children showed no special interest in fruit bars and Goldfish crackers until the foods were placed in a "no-no" jar. Once the foods had been given taboo status, the children made more positive comments about them, requested them more often, tried to gain access to them, and grabbed more of them when they were available (Fisher & Birch, 1999).

p. 173). Only when feelings like these are understood will treatment become fully effective—another reason why the cooperation and commitment of different kinds of theorists, clinicians, and researchers are so important.

While clinicians and researchers seek more answers about eating disorders, clients themselves have begun to take an active role. A number of patient-run organizations now provide information, education, and support through a national telephone hot line, professional referrals, newsletters, workshops, and conferences. The National Anorexic Aid Society, the American Anorexia and Bulimia Association, the National Association of Anorexia Nervosa and Associated Disorders, and Anorexia Nervosa and Related Eating Disorders, Inc., help combat the isolation and shame to which people with eating disorders are vulnerable. They show countless sufferers that they are hardly alone or powerless.

SUMMARY AND REVIEW

▪ **Eating disorders** Rates of eating disorders have increased dramatically as thinness has become a national obsession. The two leading disorders in this category, anorexia nervosa and bulimia nervosa, share many similarities, as well as key differences. *pp. 321–322*

▪ **Anorexia nervosa** People with anorexia nervosa pursue extreme thinness and lose dangerous amounts of weight. They may follow a pattern of restricting-type anorexia nervosa or binge-eating/purging-type anorexia nervosa. The central features of anorexia nervosa are a drive for thinness, fear of weight, preoccupation with food, cognitive disturbances, psychological problems such as depressed feelings or obsessive functioning, and consequent medical problems, including amenorrhea. *pp. 322–326*

▪ **Bulimia nervosa** Individuals with bulimia nervosa go on frequent eating binges and then force themselves to vomit or perform other inappropriate compensatory behaviors. They may follow a pattern of purging-type bulimia nervosa or nonpurging-type bulimia nervosa. The binges often occur in response to increasing tension and are followed by feelings of guilt and self-blame. Compensatory behavior is at first reinforced by the temporary relief from uncomfortable feelings of fullness or the reduction of feelings of anxiety, self-disgust, and loss of control attached to bingeing. Over time, however, people come to feel generally disgusted with themselves, depressed, and guilty.

People with bulimia nervosa may experience mood swings or have difficulty controlling their impulses. Some display a personality disorder. Around half are amenorrheic, a number develop dental problems, and some develop a potassium deficiency. *pp. 326–333*

▪ **Explanations** Most theorists now apply a multidimensional risk perspective to explain eating disorders, and identify several key contributing factors. Principal among these are society's emphasis on thinness and bias against obesity; family environment, including, perhaps, an enmeshed family pattern; ego and cognitive disturbances, including a poor sense of autonomy and control; a mood disorder; and biological factors, such as activity of the hypothalamus, biochemical activity, and the body's weight set point. *pp. 332–338*

▪ **Treatments** Therapists aim first to help people with eating disorders resume normal eating and regain their health; then they tackle the broader problems that led to the disorder. The first step in treating anorexia nervosa, for example, is to increase calorie intake and quickly restore the person's weight, using a strategy such as supportive nursing care. The second step is to deal with the underlying psychological and family problems, using a mixture of therapy and education. About 83 percent of people who receive successful treatment for anorexia nervosa continue to show full or partial improvements years later.

However, some of them relapse along the way, many continue to worry about their weight and appearance, and half continue to experience some emotional or family problems. Most menstruate again when they regain weight. Most of those who recover are later found to enjoy work and perform effectively at their jobs, and to marry or have intimate relationships at the usual rates. *pp. 339–343*

Treatments for bulimia nervosa focus first on stopping the binge–purge pattern and then on addressing the underlying causes of the disorder. Often several treatment strategies are combined, including individual insight therapy, group therapy, behavioral therapy, and antidepressant medications. Approximately 89 percent of those who receive treatment eventually improve either fully or partially. While relapse can be a problem and may be precipitated by a new stress, treatment leads to lasting improvements in psychological and social functioning for many individuals. *pp. 343–345*

ConsiderThis

⦿ Relapse is a problem for some people who recover from anorexia nervosa and bulimia nervosa. Why might people remain vulnerable even after recovery? • How might they and therapists reduce the chances of relapse?

CYBER STUDY

▲ *Witness the feelings behind bingeing and purging.* ▲ *How does bulimia nervosa begin?* ▲ *Why might relapse occur in cases of eating disorders?* ▲ *How do individuals feel toward their eating disorders?* ▲ *Do either obsessive-compulsive disorders or body dysmorphic disorders set the stage for eating disorders?*

SEARCH THE *ABNORMAL PSYCHOLOGY* CD-ROM FOR

▲ Chapter 11 video case and discussion
  "Liz"—Bulimia Nervosa

▲ Chapter 11 practice test and feedback

▲ Additional video case and discussion
  "Jennifer"—Obsessive-Compulsive Disorder

LOG ON TO THE COMER WEB PAGE

[www.worthpublishers.com/comerabnormalpsychology4e] **FOR**

▲ Suggested Web links, research exercises, FAQ page, additional Chapter 11 practice test questions

Substance
Related
Disorders

"I am Duncan. I am an alcoholic." The audience settled deeper into their chairs at these familiar words. Another chronicle of death and rebirth would shortly begin [at] Alcoholics Anonymous. . . .

. . . "I must have been just past my 15th birthday when I had that first drink that everybody talks about. And like so many of them . . . it was like a miracle. With a little beer in my gut, the world was transformed. I wasn't a weakling anymore, I could lick almost anybody on the block. And girls? Well, you can imagine how a couple of beers made me feel, like I could have any girl I wanted. . . .

"Though it's obvious to me now that my drinking even then, in high school, and after I got to college, was a problem, I didn't think so at the time. After all, everybody was drinking and getting drunk and acting stupid, and I didn't really think I was different. . . . I guess the fact that I hadn't really had any blackouts and that I could go for days without having to drink reassured me that things hadn't gotten out of control. And that's the way it went, until I found myself drinking even more—and more often—and suffering more from my drinking, along about my third year of college.

. . . "My roommate, a friend from high school, started bugging me about my drinking. It wasn't even that I'd have to sleep it off the whole next day and miss class, it was that he had begun to hear other friends talking about me, about the fool I'd made of myself at parties. He saw how shaky I was the morning after, and he saw how different I was when I'd been drinking a lot— almost out of my head was the way he put it. And he could count the bottles that I'd leave around the room, and he knew what the drinking and carousing was doing to my grades. . . . [P]artly because I really cared about my roommate and didn't want to lose him as a friend, I did cut down on my drinking by half or more. I only drank on weekends—and then only at night. . . . And that got me through the rest of college and, actually, through law school as well. . . .

"Shortly after getting my law degree, I married my first wife, and . . . for the first time since I started, my drinking was no problem at all. I would go for weeks at a time without touching a drop. . . .

"My marriage started to go bad after our second son, our third child, was born. I was very much career-and-success oriented, and I had little time to spend at home with my family. . . . My traveling had increased a lot, there were stimulating people on those trips, and, let's face it, there were some pretty exciting women available, too. So home got to be little else but a nagging, boring wife and children I wasn't very interested in. My drinking had gotten bad again, too, with being on the road so much, having to do a lot of entertaining at lunch when I wasn't away, and trying to soften the hassles at home. I guess I was putting down close to a gallon of very good scotch a week, with one thing or another.

"And as that went on, the drinking began to affect both my marriage and my career. With enough booze in me and under the pressures of guilt over my failure to carry out my responsibilities to my wife and children, I sometimes got kind of rough physically with them. I would break furniture, throw things

SUBSTANCE ABUSE A pattern of behavior in which people rely on a drug excessively and regularly, bringing damage to their relationships, functioning poorly at work, or putting themselves or others in danger.

SUBSTANCE DEPENDENCE A pattern of behavior in which people organize their lives around a drug, possibly building a tolerance to it or experiencing withdrawal symptoms when they stop taking it, or both. Also called *addiction*.

TOLERANCE The adjustment that the brain and the body make to the regular use of certain drugs so that ever larger doses are needed to achieve the earlier effects.

WITHDRAWAL Unpleasant, sometimes dangerous reactions that may occur when people who use a drug regularly stop taking or reduce their dosage of the drug.

ALCOHOL Any beverage containing ethyl alcohol, including beer, wine, and liquor.

around, then rush out and drive off in the car. I had a couple of wrecks, lost my license for two years because of one of them. Worst of all was when I tried to stop. By then I was totally hooked, so every time I tried to stop drinking, I'd experience withdrawal in all its horrors . . . with the vomiting and the "shakes" and being unable to sit still or to lie down. And that would go on for days at a time. . . .

"Then, about four years ago, with my life in ruins, my wife given up on me and the kids with her, out of a job, and way down on my luck, [Alcoholics Anonymous] and I found each other. . . . I've been dry now for a little over two years, and with luck and support, I may stay sober. . . ."

(*Spitzer et al., 1983, pp. 87–89*)

Human beings enjoy a remarkable variety of foods and drinks. Every substance on earth probably has been tried by someone, somewhere, at some time. We also have discovered substances that have interesting nonnutritive effects—both medical and pleasurable—on our brains and the rest of our bodies. We may swallow an aspirin to quiet a headache, an antibiotic to fight an infection, or a tranquilizer to calm us down. We may drink coffee to get going in the morning or wine to relax with friends. We may smoke cigarettes to soothe our nerves. However, many of the substances we consume can harm us or disrupt our behavior or mood. The misuse of such substances has become one of society's biggest problems; it has been estimated that the cost of drug misuse is at least $276 billion each year in the United States alone (NIDA, 1998).

A *drug* is defined as any substance other than food that affects our bodies or minds. It need not be a medicine or be illegal. The term *substance,* or *controlled substance,* is now frequently used in place of "drug," in part because many people fail to see that such substances as alcohol, tobacco, and caffeine are drugs, too. When a person ingests a substance—whether it be alcohol, cocaine, marijuana, or some form of medication—trillions of powerful molecules surge through the bloodstream and into the brain (Nash, 1997). Once there, the molecules set off a series of biochemical events that disturb the normal operation of the brain and body. Not surprisingly, then, substance misuse may lead to various kinds of abnormal functioning.

Drugs may cause *temporary* changes in behavior, emotion, or thought. As Duncan found out, for example, an excessive amount of alcohol may lead to *intoxication* (literally, "poisoning"), a temporary state of poor judgment, mood changes, irritability, slurred speech, and poor coordination. Drugs such as LSD may produce a particular form of intoxication, sometimes called *hallucinosis,* consisting of perceptual distortions and hallucinations.

Some substances can also lead to *long-term* problems. People who regularly ingest them may develop maladaptive patterns of behavior and changes in their body's physical responses (APA, 2000). In one such pattern, called **substance abuse**, they rely on the drug excessively and chronically, and in so doing damage their family and social relationships, function poorly at work, or put themselves and others in danger. A more advanced pattern, **substance dependence**, is also known as **addiction**. In this pattern, people not only abuse the drug but center their lives on it and perhaps acquire a physical dependence on it, marked by a *tolerance* for it, *withdrawal symptoms,* or both (see Table 12-1). When people develop **tolerance**, they need increasing doses of a drug in order to keep getting the desired effect. **Withdrawal** consists of unpleasant and even dangerous symptoms—cramps, anxiety attacks, sweating, nausea—that occur when individuals suddenly stop taking or cut back on the drug.

Duncan, who described his problems to fellow members at an Alcoholics Anonymous meeting, was caught in a pattern of alcohol dependence. When he was a college student and later a lawyer,

Heroin chic *Over the years, different substances may rise and fall and rise again in popularity. During the 1980s heroin was associated with crime, immorality, and street life, and its use declined. In the 1990s, however, its popularity rose greatly. For a time the drug even defined a new look in the fashion industry—"heroin chic"—and it was prominently featured in movies such as* Trainspotting.

alcohol damaged his family, social, academic, and work life. He also built up a tolerance for the substance over time and experienced withdrawal symptoms such as vomiting and shaking when he tried to stop using it. In any given year, 11.3 percent of all adults in the United States exhibit substance abuse or dependence. Only 20 percent of them receive treatment (Kessler & Zhao, 1999; Regier et al., 1993).

Many drugs are available in our society, and new ones are introduced almost every day. Some are harvested from nature, others derived from natural substances, and still others produced in the laboratory. Some, such as antianxiety drugs and barbiturates, require a physician's prescription for legal use. Others, such as alcohol and nicotine, are legally available to adults. Still others, such as heroin, are illegal under all circumstances. In 1962 only 4 million people in the United States had ever used marijuana, cocaine, heroin, or another illegal substance; today the number has climbed to more than 72 million (NHSDA, 1998; Kleber, 1995). In fact, over 23 million people have used illegal substances within the past year, and 14 million are using one currently. Ten percent of teenagers have used an illegal drug within the past month.

The substances people misuse fall into several categories: *depressants,* such as alcohol and opioids, which slow the central nervous system; *stimulants* of the central nervous system, such as cocaine and amphetamines; *hallucinogens,* such as LSD, which cause delusions, hallucinations, and other powerful changes in sensory perception; and *cannabis* substances, such as marijuana, which cause a mixture of hallucinogenic, depressant, and stimulant effects. Many people take more than one of these substances at a time, a practice known as *polydrug use.* In this chapter we shall look at some of the most problematic substances and the abnormal patterns they may produce. After first examining the substances separately, we shall consider the causes and treatments of substance-related disorders together as a group.

Table 12-1 DSM-IV Checklist

SUBSTANCE ABUSE

1. A maladaptive pattern of substance use leading to significant impairment or distress
2. At least one of the following features occurring within one year:
   (a) Recurrent substance use, resulting in failure to fulfill major role obligations at work, school, or home
   (b) Recurrent substance use in situations in which it is physically hazardous
   (c) Recurrent substance-related legal problems
   (d) Substance use that continues despite its causing or increasing persistent social or interpersonal problems

SUBSTANCE DEPENDENCE

1. A maladaptive pattern of substance use leading to significant impairment or distress
2. At least three of the following:
   (a) Tolerance
   (b) Withdrawal
   (c) Substance often taken in larger amounts over a longer period than was intended
   (d) Persistent desire for substance or unsuccessful efforts to control substance use
   (e) Considerable time spent trying to obtain, use, or recover from the substance
   (f) Substance use in place of important activities
   (g) Substance use that continues despite its causing or increasing persistent physical or psychological problems

Based on APA, 2000, 1994.

Depressants

Depressants slow the activity of the central nervous system. They reduce tension and inhibitions and may interfere with a person's judgment, motor activity, and concentration. The three most widely used groups of depressants are *alcohol, sedative-hypnotics,* and *opioids.*

Alcohol

Two-thirds of the people in the United States drink beverages that contain **alcohol**, at least occasionally. Purchases of beer, wine, and liquor amount to tens of billions of dollars each year in the United States alone. Around 6 percent of all adults are heavy drinkers, consuming at least five drinks on at least five occasions each month (NHSDA, 1998). Among heavy drinkers, men outnumber women by more than four to one, 9.7 percent to 2.4 percent (Wilsnack et al., 2000).

All alcoholic beverages contain *ethyl alcohol,* a chemical that is quickly absorbed into the blood through the lining of the stomach and the intestine. The ethyl alcohol immediately begins to take effect as it is carried in the bloodstream

BEER SALES

Each year Americans pay $60 billion for 196 million barrels of beer. Light beer accounts for more than one-third of beer sales. The state of Nevada has the highest beer consumption (on average 49 gallons per person) and Utah the lowest (21 gallons) (Weissman, 1999).

Rewriting history *An 1848 lithograph of George Washington saying farewell to his officers, at left, shows him drinking a toast to his compatriots. But the wine glasses and bottles are mysteriously absent in an edition released in 1876, when alcohol was out of favor.*

"Wine is the most healthful and most hygienic of beverages."

Louis Pasteur

COLLEGE EXPENSES

Each year college students spend $5.5 billion on alcohol (mostly beer)—more than they spend on books, soda, coffee, juice, and milk combined (Eigan, 1991).

to the central nervous system (the brain and spinal cord), where it acts to depress, or slow, functioning by binding to various neurons. One important group of neurons to which ethyl alcohol binds are those that normally receive the neurotransmitter GABA. As we observed in Chapter 5, GABA carries an *inhibitory* message—a message to stop firing—when it is received at certain neurons. When alcohol binds to receptors on those neurons, it apparently helps GABA to shut down the neurons, thus helping to relax the drinker (Gordis, 1991).

At first ethyl alcohol depresses the areas of the brain that control judgment and inhibition; people become looser, more talkative, and often more friendly. As their inner control breaks down, they may feel relaxed, confident, and happy. When more alcohol is absorbed, it slows down additional areas in the central nervous system, leaving the drinkers less able to make sound judgments, their speech less guarded and less coherent, and their memory impaired (Fromme, Katz, & D'Amico, 1997; Goldstein, 1994). Many people become highly emotional and perhaps loud and aggressive.

Motor difficulties increase as drinking continues, and reaction times slow. People may be unsteady when they stand or walk and clumsy in performing even simple activities. They may drop things, bump into doors and furniture, and misjudge distances. Their vision becomes blurred, particularly peripheral, or side, vision, and they have trouble hearing. As a result, people who have drunk too much alcohol may have great difficulty driving or solving simple problems.

The extent of the effect of ethyl alcohol is determined by its *concentration,* or proportion, in the blood. Thus a given amount of alcohol will have less effect on a large person than on a small one (see Table 12-2). Gender also affects the concentration of alcohol in the blood. Women have less of the stomach enzyme *alcohol dehydrogenase,* which breaks down alcohol in the stomach before it enters the blood. So women become more intoxicated than men on equal doses of alcohol.

Levels of impairment are closely related to the concentration of ethyl alcohol in the blood. When the alcohol concentration reaches 0.06 percent of the blood volume, a person usually feels relaxed and comfortable without being intoxicated. By the time it reaches 0.09 percent, however, the drinker crosses the line into intoxication. If the level goes as high as 0.55 percent, death will probably result. Most people, however, lose consciousness before they can drink enough to reach this level.

The effects of alcohol subside only when the alcohol concentration in the blood declines. Most of the alcohol is broken down, or *metabolized,* by the liver into carbon dioxide and water, which can be exhaled and excreted. The average rate of this metabolism is 10 to 15 percent of an ounce per hour, but different people's livers work at different speeds; thus rates of "sobering up" vary. Despite popular belief, only time and metabolism can make a person sober. Drinking black coffee, splashing cold water on one's face, or "pulling oneself together" cannot hurry the process.

Table 12-2

Relationships between Sex, Weight, Oral Alcohol Consumption, and Blood Alcohol Level

ABSOLUTE ALCOHOL (OUNCES)	BEVERAGE INTAKE*	BLOOD ALCOHOL LEVEL (PERCENT)					
		FEMALE (100 LB.)	MALE (100 LB.)	FEMALE (150 LB.)	MALE (150 LB.)	FEMALE (200 LB.)	MALE (200 LB.)
1/2	1 oz. spirits† 1 glass wine 1 can beer	0.045	0.037	0.03	0.025	0.022	0.019
1	2 oz. spirits 2 glasses wine 2 cans beer	0.090	0.075	0.06	0.050	0.045	0.037
2	4 oz. spirits 4 glasses wine 4 cans beer	0.180	0.150	0.12	0.100	0.090	0.070
3	6 oz. spirits 6 glasses wine 6 cans beer	0.270	0.220	0.18	0.150	0.130	0.110
4	8 oz. spirits 8 glasses wine 8 cans beer	0.360	0.300	0.24	0.200	0.180	0.150
5	10 oz. spirits 10 glasses wine 10 cans beer	0.450	0.370	0.30	0.250	0.220	0.180

*In 1 hour.
†100-proof spirits

Source: Ray & Ksir, 1993, p. 194.

ALCOHOL ABUSE AND DEPENDENCE Though legal, alcohol is actually one of the most dangerous of recreational drugs, whose reach extends across the life span (Scheier & Botvin, 1997). In fact, around 10 percent of elementary school students admit to some alcohol use, while 51 percent of high school seniors drink alcohol each month (most to the point of intoxication) and 3.5 percent report drinking every day (Johnston et al., 1999, 1993; NIDA, 1995) (see Figure 12-1 on the next page). Similarly, alcohol misuse is a major problem on college campuses (Babor et al., 1999; Clements, 1999) (see Box 12-1 on page 355).

Surveys indicate that over a one-year period, as many as 10 percent of all adults in the United States exhibit a long-term pattern of alcohol abuse or dependence, either of which is known in popular terms as *alcoholism* (Kessler & Zhao, 1999; Regier et al., 1993). Between 13 and 18 percent of the nation's adults display one of the patterns at some time in their lives, with men outnumbering women by as much as 5 to 1. Many teenagers also experience alcohol abuse and dependence (Scheier & Botvin, 1997).

The prevalence of alcoholism in a given year is around 7 percent for both white and African Americans and 9 percent for Hispanic Americans (APA, 2000; Anthony et al., 1995; Helzer et al., 1991). The men in these groups, however, show strikingly different age patterns. For white and Hispanic American men, the rate of alcoholism is highest—over 18 percent—during young adulthood, compared to 8 percent among African American men in that age group. For African American men, the rate is highest during late middle age, 15 percent compared to 8 percent among white and Hispanic American men in that age group. Generally,

FIGHTING BLACK DEATH

A popular theory in the mid-1300s was that strong drinks of alcohol offered protection from the Black Death, the bubonic plague that was sweeping Europe. This mistaken belief led to a plague of drunkenness as widespread as the plague of contagion (Asimov, 1997).

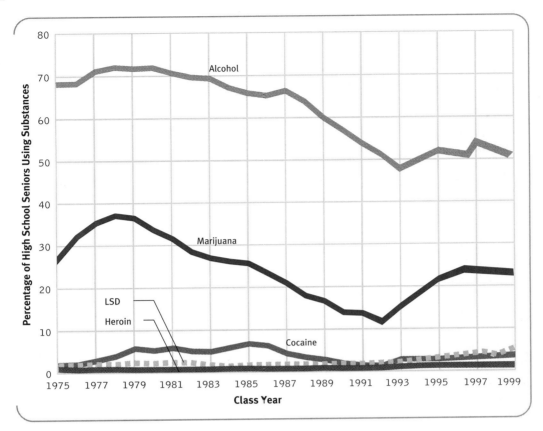

FIGURE 12-1 **Teenagers and substance use**
The overall percentage of high school seniors who admitted to using substances illicitly at least once within 30 days of being surveyed rose in the 1970s, declined in the 1980s, and rose again in the 1990s (Johnston et al., 1999; NIDA, 1996).

Asians in the United States and elsewhere have lower rates of alcoholism than do people from other cultures. As many as one-half of these individuals have a deficiency of alcohol dehydrogenase, the chemical responsible for breaking down alcohol, so they react quite negatively to even a modest intake of alcohol. Such reactions in turn prevent extended use (APA, 2000).

ALCOHOL ABUSE Generally speaking, people who abuse alcohol drink excessive amounts regularly and rely on it to enable them to do things that would otherwise make them anxious. Eventually the drinking interferes with their social behavior and ability to think and work. They may have frequent arguments with family members or friends, miss work repeatedly, and even lose their jobs (Bray et al., 2000; Schmidt et al., 2000).

Individually, however, people vary in their patterns of alcohol abuse (Walker et al., 1996). Some drink large amounts of alcohol every day and keep drinking until intoxicated. Others go on periodic binges of heavy drinking that can last weeks or months. They may remain intoxicated for days and later be unable to remember anything about the period. Still others may limit their excessive drinking to weekends or evenings, or both. The actor Dick Van Dyke commented:

> I didn't miss work ever because of drinking. And I never drank at work. Never drank during the day—only at home and only in the evenings. . . . I never craved a drink during the day. I was never a morning drinker—I didn't want one then. The idea made me as sick as it would make anyone else. But evening drinking is a form of alcoholism, just like periodic drinking is a form of alcoholism. . . .
>
> *(HEW, 1976, p. 76)*

AT RISK

Individuals who begin drinking before age 15 are twice as likely to develop alcohol abuse and four times as likely to develop alcohol dependence as those who begin drinking at age 21 (Grant & Dawson, 1998).

ALCOHOL DEPENDENCE For many people, the pattern of alcohol misuse includes dependence. Their bodies build up a tolerance for alcohol and they need to drink ever-greater amounts to feel its effects. They also experience withdrawal when they stop drinking. Within hours their hands, tongue, and eyelids begin to shake;

BOX 12-1

College Binge Drinking: An Extracurricular Crisis

*D*rinking large amounts of alcohol in a short time, or *binge drinking,* is a serious problem on college campuses. Studies show that more than one-third of college students binge-drink at times, around half of them at least six times per month (Bennett et al., 1999; Wechsler et al., 1997, 1994). These are higher rates than those displayed by people of the same age who are not in college. In fact, college students drink an estimated 430 million gallons of alcohol each year, and spend $5.5 billion to do so (Eigan, 1991).

In many circles, alcohol use is an accepted aspect of college life. Are we as a society taking the issue too lightly? Consider some of the following statistics:

- Alcohol is a factor in nearly 40 percent of academic problems and 28 percent of all college dropouts (Anderson, 1994).

- Although 84 percent of incoming freshmen consider heavy alcohol use to be a problem on campus, 68 percent drink during their first semester, at least half of them during their first week on campus (Harvard School of Public Health, 1995).

- The average student spends $466 a year on alcohol (Eigan, 1991).

- Binge drinking has been linked to severe health problems and serious injury, auto crashes, unplanned and unprotected sex, aggressive behaviors, and various psychological problems (Wechsler et al., 1995; Wechsler & Isaac, 1992).

These findings have led some educators to describe binge drinking as "the

No. 1 public health hazard" for full-time college students, and many researchers and clinicians have turned their attention it. Henry Wechsler and his colleagues (1995) at the Harvard School of Public Health mailed a questionnaire about drinking patterns to students at 140 college campuses around the United States and received close to 18,000 replies. According to the responses, people most likely to binge-drink were those who lived in a fraternity or sorority, pursued a party-centered lifestyle, and engaged in high-risk behaviors such as smoking marijuana, having multiple sex partners, and smoking cigarettes. Other variables—including being male, white, involved in athletics, and a business major—also raised the risk of binge drinking. These variables have been cited in other studies as well (Meilman et al., 1999). The researchers expressed

concern "that college binge drinking is tied to some of the most desired aspects of American college life—parties, social lives, dormitory living, athletics, and interaction with friends" (Wechsler et al., 1995, p. 925). The study also found that students who were binge drinkers in high school were more likely to binge-drink in college.

The results of such studies are based on self-administered questionnaires, and subjects' responses may have been biased. Perhaps binge drinkers are more likely than nondrinkers to respond to such questionnaires. Still, the implications are clear: college drinking, certainly binge drinking, may be more pervasive and more harmful than was previously believed. At the very least, it is a problem whose research time has come.

Testing the limits *Binge drinking, similar to this display at a college campus party, has led to a number of deaths in recent years.*

they feel weak and nauseated; they sweat and vomit; their heart beats rapidly; and their blood pressure rises. They may also become anxious, depressed, unable to sleep, or irritable (APA, 2000; Thompson et al., 1995).

A small percentage of people who are dependent on alcohol experience a particularly dramatic withdrawal reaction called **delirium tremens ("the DTs")**, or **alcohol withdrawal delirium**. It consists of terrifying visual hallucinations that begin within three days after the cessation or reduction of drinking. Some people see small, frightening animals chasing or crawling on them, or objects dancing about in front of their eyes. Mark Twain gave a classic picture of delirium tremens in Huckleberry Finn's description of his father:

DELIRIUM TREMENS (DTs) A dramatic withdrawal reaction experienced by some people who are alcohol-dependent. It consists of confusion, clouded consciousness, and terrifying visual hallucinations. Also called *alcohol withdrawal delirium.*

I don't know how long I was asleep, but . . . there was an awful scream and I was up. There was Pap looking wild, and skipping around every which way and yelling about snakes. He said they was crawling up on his legs; and then he would give a jump and scream, and say one had bit him on the cheek—but I couldn't see no snakes. He started and run round . . . hollering "Take him off! he's biting me on the neck!" I never see a man look so wild in the eyes. Pretty soon he was all fagged out, and fell down panting; then he rolled over . . . kicking things every which way, and striking and grabbing at the air with his hands, and screaming . . . there was devils a-hold of him. He wore out by and by. . . . He says . . .

"Tramp-tramp-tramp: that's the dead; tramp-tramp-tramp; they're coming after me; but I won't go. Oh, they're here; don't touch me . . . They're cold; let go . . ."

Then he went down on all fours and crawled off, begging them to let him alone. . . .

(Twain, 1885)

Like most other alcohol withdrawal symptoms, the DTs usually run their course in two to three days. However, people who experience them or a related severe withdrawal reaction may also have seizures, lose consciousness, suffer a stroke, or even die. Today certain medical procedures can help prevent or reduce such extreme reactions (D'Onofrio et al., 1999).

WHAT ARE THE PERSONAL AND SOCIAL CONSEQUENCES OF ALCOHOLISM? Alcoholism destroys millions of families, social relationships, and careers. Medical treatment, lost productivity, and losses due to deaths from alcoholism cost society as much as $148 billion annually (NIDA, 1998; Cornish et al., 1995). The disorder also plays a role in more than one-third of all suicides, homicides, assaults, rapes, and accidental deaths, including 41 percent of all fatal automobile accidents in the United States (CDC, 1998; Mustane & Tewksbury, 1998). Altogether, intoxicated drivers are responsible for 17,000 deaths each year (CDC, 1998; NCHS, 1997). At the same time, intoxicated pedestrians are four times more likely than sober pedestrians to be hit by a car (Painter, 1992).

Alcoholism has serious effects on the 30 million children of persons with this disorder. Home life for these children is likely to be marred by high levels of conflict and perhaps by sexual or other forms of abuse (Mathew et al., 1993; Velleman & Orford, 1993). In turn, the children themselves have higher rates of psychological problems such as anxiety, depression, phobias, conduct disorder, attention-deficit disorder, and substance-related disorders during their lifetimes (Kuperman et al., 1999; Hill & Muka, 1996). Many have low self-esteem, poor communication skills, poor sociability, and marital problems (Lewis-Harter, 2000; Kelly & Myers, 1996; Greenfield et al., 1993).

Long-term excessive drinking can also seriously damage one's physical health. It so overworks the liver that people may develop an irreversible condition called *cirrhosis,* in which the liver becomes scarred and dysfunctional. Cirrhosis is the tenth most frequent cause of death in the United States, accounting for some 25,000 deaths each year (NCHS, 1999). Alcohol abuse and dependence may also damage the heart and lower the immune system's ability to fight off

IMPAIRED DRIVING

Each year over 1.4 million arrests are made in the United States for driving under the influence of alcohol or opioids, involving one of every 123 drivers (Uniform Crime Reports, 1997). In 60 percent of the 500 child passenger deaths linked to alcohol in 1996, it was the driver of the child's own car who was alcohol-impaired (CDC, 1997).

Spreading the word *Educating the public with billboard, television, and radio ads about the dangers of alcohol has helped reduce the number of alcohol-related automobile deaths by over 25 percent in recent years (CDC, 1997).*

cancer and bacterial infections and to resist the onset of AIDS after infection (NIAAA, 1992).

Long-term excessive drinking also causes major nutritional problems. Alcohol makes people feel full and lowers their desire for food, yet it has no nutritional value. As a result, chronic drinkers become malnourished, weak, and prone to disease. Their vitamin and mineral deficiencies may also cause certain mental disorders. An alcohol-related deficiency of vitamin B (thiamine), for example, may lead to **Korsakoff's syndrome**, a disease marked by extreme confusion, memory loss, and other neurological symptoms (Krabbendam et al., 2000; Kopelman, 1995). People with Korsakoff's syndrome cannot remember the past or learn new information, and may make up for their memory losses by *confabulating*—reciting made-up events to fill in the gaps.

Finally, women who drink during pregnancy place their fetuses at risk. Excessive alcohol use during pregnancy may cause a baby to be born with **fetal alcohol syndrome**, a pattern of abnormalities that can include mental retardation, hyperactivity, head and face deformities, heart defects, and slow growth (Doweiko, 1999; CDC, 1998; Ray & Ksir, 1993). It has been estimated that in the overall population fewer than 3 of every 1,000 babies are born with this syndrome. The rate increases to as many as 29 of every 1,000 babies of women who are problem drinkers (Doweiko, 1999; Ray & Ksir, 1993). In addition, heavy drinking early in pregnancy often leads to a miscarriage.

Sedative-Hypnotic Drugs

Sedative-hypnotic drugs, also called *anxiolytic* (meaning "anxiety-reducing") *drugs*, produce feelings of relaxation and drowsiness. At low dosages, the drugs have a calming or sedative effect. At higher dosages, they are sleep inducers, or hypnotics. The sedative-hypnotic drugs include *barbiturates* and *benzodiazepines*.

BARBITURATES First discovered in Germany more than 100 years ago, **barbiturates** were widely prescribed in the first half of the twentieth century to fight anxiety and to help people sleep. Despite the recent development of the safer benzodiazepines, some physicians still prescribe barbiturates, especially for sleep problems. The drugs can cause many problems, however, not the least of which are abuse and dependence. Several thousand deaths a year are caused by accidental or suicidal overdoses.

Barbiturates are usually taken in pill or capsule form. In low doses they reduce a person's level of excitement in the same way that alcohol does, by binding to the neuron receptors that receive the inhibitory neurotransmitter GABA and by helping GABA operate at those receptors (Doweiko, 1999; Frey et al., 1995; Morgan & London, 1995). People can get intoxicated from large doses of barbiturates, just as they do from alcohol. And, like alcohol, barbiturates are broken down in the liver (Nishino et al., 1995).

At high doses, barbiturates also depress the *reticular formation*, the part of the brain that normally keeps people awake. This explains the drugs' sedative effect. At still higher doses, the drugs slow down spinal reflexes and muscles and are often used as surgical anesthetics. At too high a level, they can halt breathing, lower blood pressure, and lead to coma and death.

Repeated use of barbiturates can quickly result in a pattern of abuse. Users may spend much of the day intoxicated, irritable, and unable to do their work. Dependence can also result. The user organizes his or her life around the drug and needs increasing amounts of it to calm down or fall asleep. A great danger of barbiturate dependence is that the lethal dose of the drug remains the same even while the body is building up a tolerance for its sedating effects (Landry, 1994; Gold, 1986). Once the prescribed dose stops reducing anxiety or inducing sleep, the user is all too likely to increase it without medical supervision, and eventually may ingest a dose that proves fatal. Those caught in a pattern of barbiturate dependence may also experience withdrawal symptoms such as nausea, anxiety,

BENZODIAZEPINES The most common group of antianxiety drugs, which includes Valium and Xanax.

OPIOID Opium or any of the drugs derived from opium, including morphine, heroin, and codeine.

OPIUM A highly addictive substance made from the sap of the opium poppy.

MORPHINE A highly addictive substance derived from opium that is particularly effective in relieving pain.

HEROIN One of the most addictive substances derived from opium, illegal in the United States under all circumstances.

ENDORPHINS Neurotransmitters that help relieve pain and reduce emotional tension. They are sometimes referred to as the body's own opioids.

and sleep problems. Barbiturate withdrawal—which in extreme cases may resemble delirium tremens—is particularly dangerous, for it can cause convulsions.

BENZODIAZEPINES Chapter 5 described **benzodiazepines**, the antianxiety drugs developed in the 1950s, as the most popular sedative-hypnotic drugs available. Xanax and Valium are just two of the dozens of these compounds in clinical use (Frey et al., 1995). Like alcohol and barbiturates, they calm people by binding to neuron receptors that receive GABA and by increasing GABA's activity at those receptors. These drugs, however, relieve anxiety without making people as drowsy as other kinds of sedative-hypnotics. They are also less likely to slow a person's breathing, so they are less likely to cause death in the event of an overdose (Nishino et al., 1995).

When benzodiazepines were first discovered, they seemed so safe and effective that physicians prescribed them generously, and their use spread. Eventually it became apparent that in high enough doses the drugs can cause intoxication and lead to abuse or dependence (Ashton, 1995; Cornish et al., 1995). As many as 1 percent of the adults in the United States abuse or become physically dependent on antianxiety drugs at some point in their lives (APA, 2000; Anthony et al., 1995) and thus become subject to some of the same dangers that researchers have identified in barbiturate misuse.

Opioids

Opioids include opium—extracted from the sap of the opium poppy—and the drugs derived from it, such as heroin, morphine, and codeine. **Opium** itself has been in use for thousands of years. In the past it was used widely in the treatment of medical disorders because of its ability to reduce both physical and emotional pain. Physicians eventually discovered, however, that the drug was physically addictive.

In 1804 a new substance, **morphine**, was derived from opium. It was named after Morpheus, the Greek god of sleep. Morphine relieved pain even more effectively than opium and was originally touted as nonaddictive. However, wide use of this drug eventually revealed that it too could lead to addiction. So many wounded soldiers in the United States received morphine injections during the Civil War that morphine dependence became known as "soldiers' disease."

In 1898 morphine was converted into yet another new pain reliever, **heroin**. For several years heroin was viewed as a wonder drug and was used as a cough medicine and for other medical purposes. Eventually, however, physicians learned that heroin is even more addictive than the other opioids. By 1917 the U.S. Congress concluded that all drugs derived from opium were addictive (see Table 12-3), and it passed a law making opioids illegal except for medical purposes.

Purer blend *In the past, heroin was usually injected. However, today's heroin, derived from poppy fields such as this one in Mexico, is purer than it was in the 1980s (65 percent pure versus 5 percent), making it possible for users to snort or smoke the drug with considerable impact.*

Still other drugs have been derived from opium, and *synthetic* (laboratory-blended) opioids such as *methadone* have also been developed. All these opioid drugs—natural and synthetic—are known collectively as *narcotics*. Each drug has a different potency, speed of action, and tolerance level. Morphine and codeine are medical narcotics usually prescribed to relieve pain. Heroin is illegal in the United States under all circumstances.

Narcotics are smoked, inhaled, snorted, injected by needle just beneath the skin ("skin popped"), or injected directly into the bloodstream ("mainlined"). Injection seems to be the most common method of narcotic use, although the other techniques have been used increasingly in recent years (NHSDA, 1998). An injection quickly brings on a *rush*—a spasm of warmth and ecstasy that is sometimes compared with orgasm.

Table 12-3

Risks and Consequences of Drug Misuse

	INTOXICATION POTENTIAL	DEPENDENCY POTENTIAL	RISK OF ORGAN DAMAGE OR DEATH	RISK OF SEVERE SOCIAL OR ECONOMIC CONSEQUENCES	RISK OF SEVERE OR LONG-LASTING MENTAL AND BEHAVIORAL CHANGE
Opioids	High	High	Low	High	Low to moderate
Sedative-hypnotics Barbiturates	Moderate	Moderate to high	Moderate to high	Moderate to high	Low
Benzodiazepines	Moderate	Low	Low	Low	Low
Stimulants (cocaine, amphetamines)	High	High	Moderate	Low to moderate	Moderate to high
Alcohol	High	Moderate	High	High	High
Cannabis	High	Low to moderate	Low	Low to moderate	Low
Mixed drug classes	High	High	High	High	High

Source: APA, 2000, 1994; Gold, 1986, p. 28.

The brief spasm is followed by several hours of a pleasant feeling called a *high* or *nod*. During a high, the drug user feels relaxed, happy, and unconcerned about food, sex, or other bodily needs.

Opioids create these effects by depressing the central nervous system, particularly the centers that help control emotion. The drugs attach to brain receptor sites that ordinarily receive **endorphins**—neurotransmitters that help relieve pain and reduce emotional tension (Doweiko, 1999; Snyder, 1991, 1986). When neurons at these receptor sites receive opioids, they produce pleasurable and calming feelings just as they would do if they were receiving endorphins. In addition to reducing pain and tension, opioids cause nausea, narrowing of the pupils ("pinpoint pupils"), and constipation—bodily reactions that can also be brought about by releases of endorphins in the brain.

HEROIN ABUSE AND DEPENDENCE Heroin use exemplifies the kinds of problems posed by opioids. After taking heroin repeatedly for just a few weeks, users may become caught in a pattern of abuse: the drug interferes significantly with their social and occupational functioning. In most cases, heroin abuse leads to a pattern of dependence as well, and users soon center their lives on the substance, build a tolerance for it, and experience a withdrawal reaction when they stop taking it. At first the withdrawal symptoms are anxiety, restlessness, sweating, and rapid breathing; later they include severe twitching, aches, fever, vomiting, diarrhea, loss of appetite, high blood pressure, and weight loss of up to 15 pounds (due to loss of bodily fluids). These symptoms usually peak by the third day, gradually subside, and disappear by the eighth day. A person in withdrawal can either wait out the symptoms or end withdrawal by taking heroin again.

People who are dependent on heroin soon need the drug just to avoid going into withdrawal, and they must continually increase their doses in order to achieve even that. The temporary high becomes less intense and less important. Most such individuals organize their lives around efforts to get their next dose, in many cases

Injecting heroin *Opioids may be taken by mouth, inhaled, snorted, injected just beneath the surface of the skin, or, as here, injected intravenously. Those who share needles to inject themselves risk developing AIDS or hepatitis.*

turning to criminal activities, such as theft and prostitution, to support the expensive "habit."

Surveys suggest that close to 1 percent of adults in the United States become addicted to heroin or other opioids at some time in their lives (APA, 2000, 1994). The rate of addiction dropped considerably during the 1980s, rose in the early 1990s, and now seems to have fallen once again. The number of persons currently addicted to these drugs is estimated to be less than 150,000 (NHSDA, 1998; Elias, 1993). The actual number may be even higher, however, given the reluctance of many people to admit to participation in an illegal activity (Morral et al., 2000; NHSDA, 1998).

WHAT ARE THE DANGERS OF HEROIN ABUSE? The most immediate danger of heroin use is an overdose, which closes down the respiratory center in the brain, almost paralyzing breathing and in many cases causing death. Death is particularly likely during sleep, when a person is unable to fight this effect by consciously working to breathe. People who resume heroin use after having abstained for some time often make the fatal mistake of taking the same dose they had built up to before. Because their bodies have been without heroin for some time, however, they can no longer tolerate this high level. Each year approximately 2 percent of persons dependent on heroin and other opioids die under the drug's influence, usually from an overdose (APA, 2000; Sporer, 1999).

Users run other risks as well. Often pushers mix heroin with a cheaper drug, such as a barbiturate or LSD, or even a deadly substance such as cyanide or battery acid. In addition, dirty needles and other unsterile equipment spread infections such as AIDS, hepatitis, and skin abscesses. In some areas of the United States the HIV infection rate among persons dependent on heroin is reported to be as high as 60 percent (APA, 2000, 1994).

Stimulants

Stimulants are substances that increase the activity of the central nervous system, resulting in increased blood pressure and heart rate, greater alertness, and speeded-up behavior and thinking. Among the most troublesome stimulants are *cocaine* and *amphetamines*, which have effects on behavior and emotions that are very similar. When users report different effects, it is often because they have ingested different amounts of the drugs. Two other widely used and legal stimulants are *caffeine* and *nicotine* (see Box 12-2 on page 364).

Cocaine

Cocaine—the central active ingredient of the coca plant, found in South America—is the most powerful natural stimulant now known. The drug was first isolated from the plant in 1865. South American natives, however, have chewed the leaves of the plant since prehistoric times for the energy and alertness the drug offers.

Processed cocaine (*hydrochloride powder*) is an odorless, white, fluffy powder. For recreational use, it is most often snorted so that it is absorbed through the mucous membrane of the nose. Some users prefer the more powerful effects of injecting cocaine intravenously or smoking it in a pipe or cigarette.

Wonder drug *Legal in the United States until 1914, cocaine was an ingredient in over-the-counter medicines, such as Cocaine Toothache Drops. This 1885 ad shows that it was used to treat children as well as adults. Cocaine was also part of Coca-Cola's formula until 1903.*

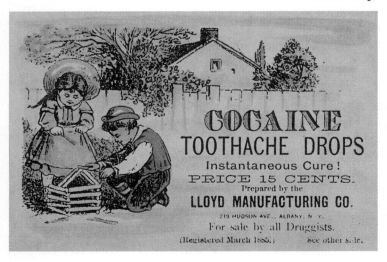

Sherlock Holmes took his bottle from the corner of the mantelpiece, and his hypodermic syringe from its neat morocco case. With his long white nervous fingers, he adjusted the delicate needle and rolled back his left shirt-cuff. For some little time his eyes rested thoughtfully upon the sinewy forearm and wrist, all dotted and scarred with innumerable puncture-marks. Finally, he thrust the sharp point home, pressed down the tiny piston, and sank back into the velvet-lined armchair with a long sigh of satisfaction.

Three times a day for many months I had witnessed this performance, but custom had not reconciled my mind to it. . . .

"Which is it today," I asked, "morphine or cocaine?"

He raised his eyes languidly from the old black-letter volume which he had opened.

"It is cocaine," he said, "a seven-per-cent solution. Would you care to try it?"

"No, indeed," I answered brusquely. "My constitution has not got over the Afghan campaign yet. I cannot afford to throw any extra strain upon it."

He smiled at my vehemence. "Perhaps you are right, Watson," he said. "I suppose that its influence is physically a bad one. I find it, however, so transcendently stimulating and clarifying to the mind that its secondary action is a matter of small moment."

"But consider!" I said earnestly. "Count the cost! Your brain may, as you say, be roused and excited, but it is a pathological and morbid process which involves increased tissue-change and . . . a permanent weakness. You know, too, what a black reaction comes upon you. Surely, the game is hardly worth the candle."

(Doyle, 1938, pp. 91–92)

COCAINE An addictive stimulant obtained from the coca plant. It is the most powerful natural stimulant known.

FREUD'S FOLLY

Early in his career, Sigmund Freud was a staunch advocate of cocaine use. He proclaimed, "Cocaine brings about an exhilaration and lasting euphoria . . . an increase in self-control and . . . more vitality and capacity for work. . . . In other words, you are simply normal" (Freud, 1885).

For years people believed that cocaine posed few problems aside from intoxication and, on occasion, temporary psychosis. Like Sherlock Holmes, many felt that the benefits outweighed the costs. Only later did researchers come to appreciate its many dangers. Their insights came only after society witnessed a dramatic increase in the drug's popularity and in problems related to its use. In the early 1960s an estimated 10,000 persons in the United States had tried cocaine. Today more than 21 million people have tried it, and 1.8 million—most of them teenagers or young adults—are using it currently (NHSDA, 1999; Kleber, 1995). Altogether, close to 3 percent of the population become dependent on cocaine at some point in their lives (Anthony et al., 1995).

Cocaine brings on a euphoric rush of well-being and confidence. Given a high enough dose, this rush can be almost orgasmic, like the one produced by heroin. At first cocaine stimulates the higher centers of the central nervous system, making users feel excited, energetic, talkative, and even euphoric. As more is taken, it stimulates other centers of the central nervous system, producing a faster pulse, higher blood pressure, faster and deeper breathing, and further arousal and wakefulness.

Cocaine apparently produces these effects largely by increasing supplies of the neurotransmitter *dopamine* at key neurons throughout the brain (see Figure 12-2). More precisely, cocaine prevents the neurons that release dopamine from reabsorbing it, as they normally would do. So excessive amounts of dopamine travel to receiving neurons throughout the central nervous system and overstimulate them. In addition, cocaine appears to increase the activity of the neurotransmitters *norepinephrine* and *serotonin* in some areas of the brain (Panikkar, 1999; Volkow et al., 1999, 1997).

High doses of the drug produce *cocaine intoxication,* whose symptoms are poor muscle coordination, grandiosity, bad judgment, anger, aggression, compulsive behavior, anxiety, and confusion. Some people experience hallucinations or delusions, or both, a condition known as *cocaine-induced psychotic disorder* (APA, 2000; Rosse et al., 1993; Yudofsky, Silver, & Hales, 1993).

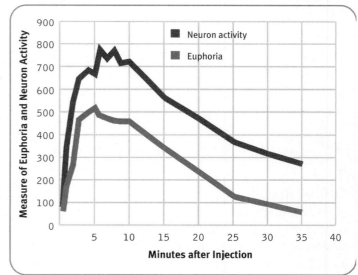

FIGURE 12-2 **Biochemical euphoria** *The subjective experiences of euphoria after a cocaine injection closely parallel cocaine's action at dopamine-using neurons. The peak experience of euphoria seems to occur around the same time as the peak of neuron activity (Fowler, Volkow, & Wolf, 1994, p. 110; Cook, Jeffcoat, & Perez-Reyes, 1985).*

> A young man described how, after free-basing, he went to his closet to get his clothes, but his suit asked him, "What do you want?" Afraid, he walked toward the door, which told him, "Get back!" Retreating, he then heard the sofa say, "If you sit on me, I'll kick your ass." With a sense of impending doom, intense anxiety, and momentary panic, the young man ran to the hospital where he received help.
>
> *(Allen, 1985, pp. 19–20)*

As the stimulant effects of cocaine subside, the user experiences a depression-like letdown, popularly called *crashing*, a pattern that may also include headaches, dizziness, and fainting (Cornish et al., 1995). For occasional users, the aftereffects usually disappear within twenty-four hours, but they may last longer for people who have taken a particularly high dose. These individuals may sink into a stupor, deep sleep, or, in some cases, coma (Coambs & McAndrews, 1994).

COCAINE ABUSE AND DEPENDENCE Regular use of cocaine may lead to a pattern of abuse in which the person remains under its effects much of each day to the detriment of social relationships and work. Regular drug use may also cause problems in short-term memory or attention (Rosselli & Ardila, 1996; Washton & Gold, 1984). Dependence may also develop, so that cocaine dominates the person's life, higher doses are needed to gain the desired effects, and abstinence results in depression, fatigue, sleep problems, irritability, and anxiety (APA, 2000). These withdrawal symptoms may last for weeks or even months after drug use has ceased.

In the past, cocaine use was restricted by the drug's high cost. Moreover, cocaine was usually snorted, and constriction of the blood vessels in the nose limited the amount of drug entering the bloodstream. Since 1984, however, newer, more powerful, and sometimes cheaper forms of cocaine have become popular and produced an enormous increase in abuse and dependence. Currently, one user in five falls into a category of abuse or dependence. Many people now ingest cocaine by **free-basing**, a technique in which the pure cocaine basic alkaloid is chemically separated, or "freed," from processed cocaine, vaporized by heat from a flame, and inhaled through a pipe.

Smoking crack *Crack, a powerful form of free-base cocaine, is produced by boiling cocaine down into crystalline balls and is smoked with a special crack pipe.*

Millions more people use **crack**, a powerful form of free-base cocaine that has been boiled down into crystalline balls. It is smoked with a special pipe and makes a crackling sound as it is inhaled (hence the name). Crack is sold in small quantities at a fairly low cost, a practice that has resulted in crack epidemics among people who previously could not have afforded cocaine, primarily those in poor urban areas (OSAP, 1991). The crack epidemic is particularly disturbing because of the violent crime and risky sex-for-drugs behaviors reported in the crack-using population (Booth et al., 2000; Balshem et al., 1992). Approximately 3 percent of high school seniors report using crack within the past year, up from 1.5 percent in 1993 (Johnston et al., 1999).

WHAT ARE THE DANGERS OF COCAINE? Aside from cocaine's harmful effects on behavior, the drug poses serious physical dangers. Its growing use in powerful forms has caused the annual number of cocaine-related emergency room incidents in the United States to multiply 40 times since 1982, from around 4,000 cases to more than 160,000 (DAWN, 1998). In addition, cocaine has been linked to as many as 20 percent of all suicides by persons under 61 years of age (Marzuk et al., 1992).

The greatest danger of cocaine use is an overdose. Excessive doses have a strong effect on the respiratory center of the brain, at first stimulating it and then depressing it, to the point where breathing may stop. Cocaine can also create major, even fatal, heart problems (Mittleman et al., 1999). The heart beats rapidly and irregularly under the drug's influence and at the same time must work harder to pump blood through the vessels that have narrowed as a result of cocaine's effects (Kaufman et al., 1998). For some people, this strain on the heart causes a brain seizure that brings breathing or heart functioning to a sudden stop. In addition, pregnant women who use cocaine run the risk of having a miscarriage (Ness et al., 1999) and of having children with abnormalities in immune functioning, attention and learning, thyroid size, and dopamine and serotonin activity in the brain (Adler, 1992).

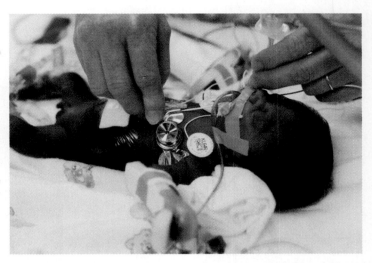

Prenatal concerns *This baby, born prematurely to a woman dependent on cocaine, lived only a few months. The use of cocaine, alcohol, or other drugs during pregnancy greatly increases the risk of miscarriage, premature birth, and child abnormalities.*

Amphetamines

The **amphetamines** are stimulant drugs that are manufactured in the laboratory. Some common examples are amphetamine (Benzedrine), dextroamphetamine (Dexedrine), and methamphetamine (Methedrine). First produced in the 1930s to help treat asthma, these drugs soon became popular among people trying to lose weight; athletes seeking an extra burst of energy; soldiers, truck drivers, and pilots trying to stay awake; and students studying for exams through the night. Physicians now know the drugs are far too dangerous to be used so casually, and they prescribe them much less freely (Fawcett & Busch, 1995). However, the illicit use of amphetamines seems to be increasing (Baberg, Nelesen, & Dimsdale, 1996).

Amphetamines are most often taken in pill or capsule form, although some people inject the drugs intravenously for a quicker, more powerful effect. Others take the drugs in such forms as "ice" and "crank," counterparts of free-base cocaine and crack, respectively. Like cocaine, amphetamines increase energy and alertness and reduce appetite when taken in small doses; produce a rush, intoxication, and psychosis in high doses; and cause an emotional letdown as they leave the body. Also like cocaine, amphetamines stimulate the central nervous system by increasing the release of the neurotransmitters dopamine, norepinephrine, and serotonin throughout the brain, although amphetamines do this by somewhat different actions than cocaine (Doweiko, 1999; Fawcett & Busch, 1995; Nestler et al., 1995).

Tolerance to amphetamines builds very quickly, so users are at great risk of becoming dependent. People who start using the drug to reduce their appetite and weight, for example, may soon find they are as hungry as ever, and increase their dose in response. Athletes who use amphetamines to increase their energy may also find before long that larger and larger amounts of the drug are needed. So-called "speed freaks," who pop pills all day for days at a time, have built a tolerance so high that they now take as much as 200 times their initial amphetamine dose. When people who depend on the drug stop taking it, they plunge into a deep depression and extended sleep identical to the withdrawal from cocaine. Around 1.5 to 2 percent of the population in the United States become dependent on amphetamines at some point in their lives (APA, 2000; Anthony et al., 1995).

Caffeine

Caffeine is the world's most widely used stimulant. People in the United States alone consume an estimated 30 million pounds of caffeine annually (Chou, 1992; Julien, 1988). Seventy-five percent of this caffeine is taken in the form of coffee (from the coffee bean); the rest is consumed in tea (from the tea leaf), cola (from the kola nut), chocolate (from the cocoa bean), and numerous prescription and over-the-counter medications, such as Excedrin (Chou, 1992; Johnson-Greene et al., 1988).

FREE-BASE A technique for ingesting cocaine in which the pure cocaine basic alkaloid is chemically separated from processed cocaine, vaporized by heat from a flame, and inhaled with a pipe.

CRACK A powerful, ready-to-smoke free-base cocaine.

AMPHETAMINE A stimulant drug that is manufactured in the laboratory.

CAFFEINE The world's most widely used stimulant, most often consumed in coffee.

BOX **12-2**

Tobacco, Nicotine, and Addiction

Almost 28 percent of all Americans over the age of 12 regularly smoke tobacco (NHSDA, 1998). Surveys also suggest that more than one-third of all high school seniors have smoked within the past month, at least half of them on a regular basis (Johnston et al., 1999). At the same time, 410,000 persons in the United States die each year as a result of smoking (Farley, 1994; Report of the Surgeon General, 1990, 1988). Smoking is directly tied to high blood pressure, coronary heart disease, lung disease, cancer, strokes, and other deadly medical problems. Nonsmokers who inhale cigarette smoke from their environment have a higher risk of lung cancer and other diseases (Report of the Surgeon General, 1987). And pregnant women who smoke are more likely than nonsmokers to deliver premature and underweight babies (Goldstein, 1994).

Research suggests that smoking may actually increase stress levels (Parrott, 1999), and most smokers know that smoking is unhealthful, so why do they continue to smoke? Because *nicotine,* the active substance in tobacco and a stimulant of the central nervous system, is as addictive as heroin, perhaps even more so (Report of the Surgeon General, 1988). Regular smokers develop a tolerance for nicotine and must smoke more and more in order to achieve the same results. When they try to stop smoking, they experience withdrawal symptoms—irritability, increased appetite, sleep disturbances, slower metabolism, cognitive difficulties, and a powerful desire to smoke (APA, 2000). Nicotine acts on the same neurotransmitters and reward center in the brain as amphetamines and cocaine (McGehee et al., 1995; Stolerman & Jarvis, 1995). Inhaling a puff of cigarette smoke delivers a dose of nicotine to the brain faster than it could be delivered by injection into the bloodstream.

The decline in the acceptability of smoking in our society has created a market for products and techniques to help people kick the habit. Most of these methods do not work very well. Self-help

An early start *An Albanian boy in Kosovo is already acquainted with the powers of nicotine.*

kits, informational pamphlets, commercial programs, and support groups are of limited help. Most people who stop smoking after receiving such interventions start smoking again within one year (Hall et al., 1985). Smokers who do quit permanently tend to be successful only after several failed attempts (Spanier et al., 1996).

One fairly successful behavioral treatment for nicotine addiction is *aversion therapy.* In one version of this approach, known as *rapid smoking,* the smoker sits in a closed room and puffs quickly on a cigarette, as often as once every six seconds, until he or she begins to feel ill and cannot take another puff. The feelings of illness become associated with smoking, and the smoker develops an aversion to cigarettes (Baker & Brandon, 1988).

Several biological treatments have also been developed. A common one is the use of *nicotine gum,* which contains a high level of nicotine that is released as the smoker chews. Theoretically, people who obtain nicotine by chewing will no longer feel a need to smoke (Moss, 1999; Fortmann & Killen, 1995). A similar approach is the *nicotine patch,* which is attached to the skin like a Band-Aid. Its nicotine is absorbed through the skin throughout the day, supposedly easing withdrawal and reducing the smoker's

need for nicotine. *Nicotine nasal spray,* a relatively new biological approach, delivers nicotine much more rapidly than other methods (Perkins et al., 1996). It can be used several times an hour, whenever the urge to smoke arises. While the spray may be as effective as the patch or gum, it is also potentially even more addictive than either of those methods (FDA, 1996), and smokers who use a nicotine nasal spray may be trading one habit for another (Hurt et al., 1995). And, finally, the antidepressant drug *bupropion* (brand names Zyban and Wellbutrin) has demonstrated some success as a treatment for cigarette smoking. Studies suggest that people who take this drug do better in their efforts to stop smoking than people who take placebos; and some have greater success than people who use a nicotine patch (Jorenby et al., 1999).

The more one smokes, the harder it is to quit. On the positive side, however, former smokers' risk of disease and death decreases steadily the longer they continue to abstain (Goldstein, 1994; Jaffe, 1985). This assurance may be a powerful motivator for many smokers, and, in fact, around 45 percent of regular smokers are eventually able to stop permanently (APA, 2000). In the meantime, more than 1,000 people die of smoking-related diseases each day.

Around 99 percent of ingested caffeine is absorbed by the body and reaches its peak concentration within an hour (Julien, 1988). It acts as a stimulant of the central nervous system, again producing a release of the neurotransmitters dopamine, serotonin, and norepinephrine in the brain (Benowitz, 1990). Thus it increases arousal and motor activity and reduces fatigue (Herz, 1999; Rees et al., 1999). It also disrupts the performance of motor tasks and may interfere with sleep (Chou, 1992; Jacobson & Thurman-Lacey, 1992). Finally, it increases respiration and gastric acid secretions in the stomach (Benowitz, 1990; Levitt, 1975).

More than two to three cups of brewed coffee (250 milligrams of caffeine) can produce caffeine intoxication, which may include such symptoms as restlessness, nervousness, anxiety, stomach disturbances, twitching, and increased heart rate (APA, 2000). Grand mal seizures and fatal respiratory failure or circulatory failure can occur at doses greater than 10 grams of caffeine (about 100 cups of coffee).

Many people who suddenly stop or cut back on their usual intake of caffeine experience withdrawal symptoms—even some individuals whose regular consumption was low (two and a half cups of coffee daily or seven cans of cola). One study had adult subjects consume their usual caffeine-filled drinks and foods for two days, then abstain from all caffeine-containing foods for two days while taking placebo pills that they thought contained caffeine, and then abstain from such foods for two days while taking actual caffeine pills (Silverman et al., 1992). More subjects experienced headaches (52 percent), depression (11 percent), anxiety (8 percent), and fatigue (8 percent) during the two-day placebo period than during the caffeine periods. In addition, subjects reported using more unauthorized medications (13 percent) and performed experimental tasks more slowly during the placebo period than during the caffeine periods.

Investigators often measure caffeine intake by coffee consumption, yet coffee also contains other chemicals that may be dangerous to one's health. Thus, although some studies hint at links between caffeine and cancer (particularly pancreatic cancer), the evidence is not conclusive. Similarly, studies demonstrating correlations between caffeine and heart rhythm irregularities (arrhythmias) or high cholesterol levels are not fully reliable (Hirsch et al., 1989; Rosmarin, 1989). Caffeine does, however, appear to cause at least a slight increase in blood pressure over time in regular users, and a larger but short-lived increase during the first few days of consumption by new users (Lane, 1999; Shi et al., 1993). As public awareness of these possible health risks has increased, caffeine consumption has declined. Around half of Americans now drink coffee, whereas 80 percent did so in 1983 (Chou, 1992).

FATAL CONSUMPTION

Because 10 grams of caffeine can be fatal, the substance is classified medically as a poison.

WAKE-UP CALL

Most coffee drinkers say they feel upset if they don't have a cup at their regular time (Carey & Mullins, 1995).

"Nowadays, Hal is ninety-nine percent caffeine-free."

Hallucinogens, Cannabis, and Substance Combinations

HALLUCINOGEN A substance that causes powerful changes primarily in sensory perception, including strengthening perceptions and producing illusions and hallucinations. Also called *psychedelic drug.*

LYSERGIC ACID DIETHYLAMIDE (LSD) A hallucinogenic drug derived from ergot alkaloids.

FLASHBACK LSD-induced sensory and emotional changes that recur long after the drug has left the body.

CANNABIS DRUGS Drugs produced from the different varieties of the hemp plant *Cannabis sativa.* They cause a mixture of hallucinogenic, depressant, and stimulant effects.

MARIJUANA One of the cannabis drugs, derived from the leaves and flowering tops of the hemp plant *Cannabis sativa.*

TETRAHYDROCANNABINOL (THC) The main active ingredient of cannabis substances.

Other kinds of substances may also cause problems for their users and for society. *Hallucinogens* produce delusions, hallucinations, and other sensory changes. *Cannabis substances* produce sensory changes, but they also have depressant and stimulant effects, and so they are considered apart from hallucinogens in DSM-IV. And many individuals compound their substance abuse problems by taking *combinations of drugs.*

Hallucinogens

Hallucinogens (from the Latin for "wander in mind") are substances that cause powerful changes in sensory perception, from strengthening a person's normal perceptions to inducing illusions and hallucinations. They produce sensations so out of the ordinary that they are sometimes called "trips." The trips may be exciting or frightening, enhancing or dangerous, depending on how a person's mind interacts with the drugs. Also called **psychedelic drugs**, the hallucinogens include LSD, mescaline, psilocybin, and MDMA ("ecstasy"). Many of these substances come from plants or animals; others are laboratory-produced rearrangements of natural psychedelics.

LSD (lysergic acid diethylamide), one of the most famous and most powerful hallucinogens, was derived by the Swiss chemist Albert Hoffman in 1938 from a group of naturally occurring drugs called *ergot alkaloids.* During the 1960s, a decade of social rebellion and experimentation, millions of persons turned to the drug as a way of expanding their experience. Within two hours of being swallowed, LSD brings on a state of *hallucinogen intoxication,* sometimes called *hallucinosis,* marked by a general strengthening of perceptions, particularly visual perceptions, along with psychological changes and physical symptoms. People may focus on small details—the pores of the skin, for example, or individual blades of grass. Colors may seem enhanced or take on a shade of purple. Illusions may be experienced in which objects seem distorted and may appear to move, breathe, or change shape. A person under the influence of LSD may also hallucinate—seeing people, objects, or forms that are not actually present.

Hallucinosis may also cause one to hear sounds more clearly, feel tingling or numbness in the limbs, or confuse the sensations of hot and cold. Some people have been badly burned after touching flames that felt cool to them under the influence of LSD. The drug may also cause different senses to cross, an effect called *synesthesia.* Colors, for example, may be "heard" or "felt."

LSD can also induce strong emotions, from joy to anxiety or depression. The perception of time may slow dramatically. Long-forgotten thoughts and feelings may resurface. Physical symptoms can include sweating, palpitations, blurred vision, tremors, and poor coordination. All these effects take place while the user is fully awake and alert, and they wear off in about six hours.

It seems that LSD produces these symptoms primarily by binding to some of the neurons that normally receive the neurotransmitter *serotonin,* altering the neurotransmitter's activity at those sites (Jacobs, 1994, 1984). These neurons ordinarily help the brain send visual information and control emotions (as we observed in Chapter 7); thus LSD's activity there produces various visual and emotional symptoms.

Inspired art *Psychedelic art seemed all-pervasive in the 1960s. Displayed on advertisements, clothing, record albums, and book covers, it was inspired by the kinds of images and sensations produced by psychedelic drugs such as LSD.*

More than 10 percent of all persons in the United States have used LSD or another hallucinogen at some point in their lives (APA, 2000; SAMHSA, 1996). Around 2 percent use such drugs currently (APA, 2000; NHSDA, 1998). Although people do not usually develop tolerance to LSD or have withdrawal symptoms when they stop taking it, the drug poses dangers for both one-time and long-term users. It is so powerful that any dose, no matter how small, is likely to produce enormous perceptual, emotional, and behavioral reactions. Sometimes the reactions are extremely unpleasant—an experience called a "bad trip." Reports of LSD users who injure themselves or others usually involve a reaction of this kind:

> A 21-year-old woman was admitted to the hospital along with her lover. He had had a number of LSD experiences and had convinced her to take it to make her less constrained sexually. About half an hour after ingestion of approximately 200 microgm., she noticed that the bricks in the wall began to go in and out and that light affected her strangely. She became frightened when she realized that she was unable to distinguish her body from the chair she was sitting on or from her lover's body. Her fear became more marked after she thought that she would not get back into herself. At the time of admission she was hyperactive and laughed inappropriately. Her stream of talk was illogical and affect labile. Two days later, this reaction had ceased.
>
> *(Frosch, Robbins, & Stern, 1965)*

Another danger is the long-term effect that LSD may have. Some users eventually develop psychosis or a mood or anxiety disorder. About one-quarter of users have **flashbacks**—a recurrence of the drug-induced sensory and emotional changes after the LSD has left the body (APA, 2000). Flashbacks may occur days or even months after the last LSD experience. Although they typically become less severe and disappear within several months, some people report flashbacks a year or more after taking the drug.

Cannabis

Cannabis sativa, the hemp plant, grows in warm climates throughout the world. The drugs produced from varieties of hemp are collectively called **cannabis**. The most powerful of them is *hashish;* the weaker ones include the best-known form of cannabis, **marijuana**, a mixture of the crushed leaves and flowering tops. Each of these drugs is found in various strengths because the potency of a cannabis drug is greatly affected by the climate in which the plant is grown, the way it was prepared, and the manner and duration of its storage. Of the several hundred active chemicals in cannabis, **tetrahydrocannabinol (THC)** appears to be the one most responsible for its effects. The greater the THC content, the more powerful the cannabis: hashish contains a large portion, while marijuana's is small.

When smoked, cannabis produces a mixture of hallucinogenic, depressant, and stimulant effects. At low doses, the smoker typically has feelings of joy and relaxation and may become either quiet or talkative. Some smokers, however, become anxious, suspicious, or irritated, especially if they have been in a bad mood or are smoking in an upsetting environment. Many smokers report sharpened perceptions and fascination with the intensified sounds and sights around them. Time seems to slow down, and distances and sizes seem greater than they actually are. This overall "high" is technically called *cannabis intoxication.* Physical changes include reddening of the eyes, fast heartbeat, increases in blood pressure and appetite, dryness in the mouth, and dizziness. Some people become drowsy and may fall asleep.

In high doses, cannabis produces odd visual experiences, changes in body image, and hallucinations (Mathew et al., 1993). Smokers may become confused or impulsive. Some worry that other people are trying to hurt them. Most of the effects of cannabis last three to six hours. The changes in mood, however, may continue longer (Chait, Fishman, & Schuster, 1985).

PARTY DRUG DU JOUR

In recent years, *methylene-dioxmethamphetamine,* or *MDMA,* known to the public as *Ecstasy,* has gained enormous popularity among teenagers and young adults as a "club drug," widely available at dance clubs, rock concerts, and raves (all-night social gatherings). Ingested by 4.4 percent of tenth-graders and 5.6 percent of twelfth-graders in 1998, this hallucinogen apparently can significantly impair memory (Reneman et al., 2000; Johnston et al., 1999; Bolla et al., 1998).

The source of marijuana *Marijuana is made from the leaves of the hemp plant,* Cannabis sativa. *The plant is an annual herb, reaches a height of between 3 and 15 feet, and is grown in a wide range of altitudes, climates, and soils.*

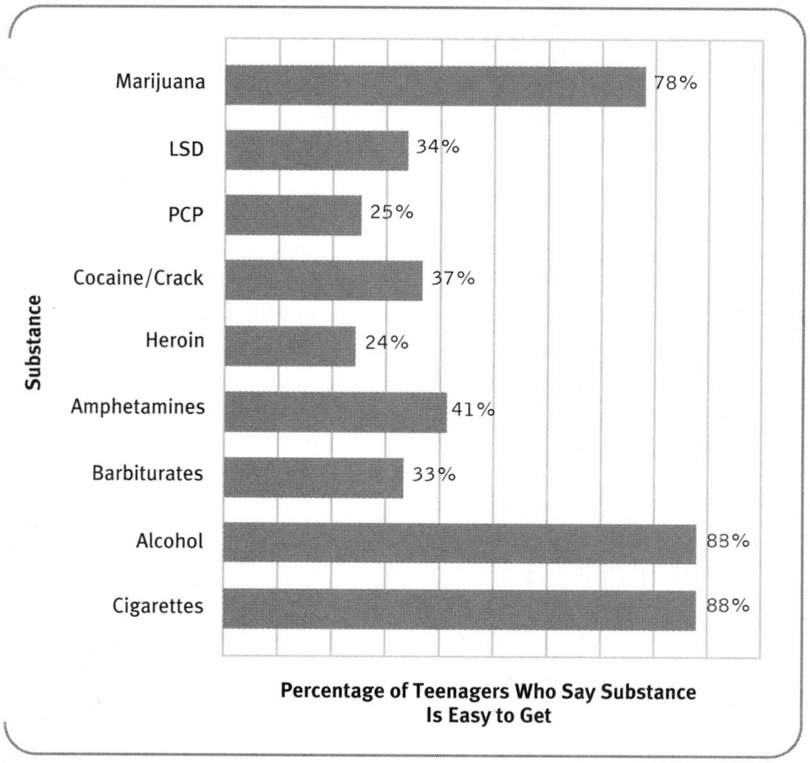
Marijuana
78%
LSD
34%
PCP
25%
Cocaine/Crack
37%
Heroin
24%
Amphetamines
41%
Barbiturates
33%
Alcohol
88%
Cigarettes
88%
Substance
Percentage of Teenagers Who Say Substance Is Easy to Get

FIGURE 12-3 How easy is it for teenagers to acquire substances? *Very easy in the case of cigarettes, alcohol, and marijuana. Fewer than 35 percent of surveyed tenth-graders, however, say it is easy to get LSD, PCP, heroin, or barbiturates (Johnston et al., 1999).*

MARIJUANA ABUSE AND DEPENDENCE Until the early 1970s, the use of marijuana, the weak form of cannabis, rarely led to a pattern of abuse or dependence. Today, however, many people, including large numbers of high school students, exhibit a pattern of marijuana abuse, getting high on marijuana regularly and finding their social and occupational or academic lives greatly affected. Many regular users also become physically dependent on marijuana. They develop a tolerance for it and may experience flulike symptoms, restlessness, and irritability when they stop smoking (Kouri, Pope, & Lukas, 1999; Ray & Ksir, 1993). Between 4 and 5 percent of all persons in the United States become dependent on marijuana at some point in their lives (APA, 2000; Anthony et al., 1995).

Why have patterns of marijuana abuse and dependence increased in the last three decades? Mainly because the drug has changed. The marijuana widely available in the United States today is two to ten times more powerful than that used in the early 1970s (see Figure 12-3). The THC content of today's marijuana is as high as 10 to 15 percent, compared to 1 to 5 percent in the late 1960s (APA, 2000). Marijuana is now grown in places with a hot, dry climate, which increases the THC content (Weisheit, 1990).

IS MARIJUANA DANGEROUS? As the strength and use of marijuana have increased, researchers have discovered that smoking it may pose certain dangers. It occasionally causes panic reactions similar to the ones caused by hallucinogens, and some smokers may fear they are losing their minds (APA, 2000; Ray & Ksir, 1993). Typically such reactions end in three to six hours, along with marijuana's other effects.

Because marijuana can interfere with the performance of complex sensorimotor tasks (Volkow et al., 1995; Goodman & Gilman, 1990) and with cognitive functioning (Hall & Solowiji, 1997; Pope & Yurgelun-Todd, 1996), it has been implicated in many automobile accidents. Furthermore, people on a marijuana high often fail to remember information, especially anything that has been recently learned, no matter how hard they try to concentrate; thus heavy marijuana smokers are at a serious disadvantage at school or work.

There are indications that regular marijuana smoking may also lead to long-term problems. It may, for example, contribute to lung disease. Studies show that marijuana smoking reduces the ability to expel air from the lungs even more than tobacco smoking does (Nahas et al., 1999). In addition, marijuana smoke contains significantly more tar and benzopyrene than tobacco smoke. Both of these substances have been linked to cancer (Ray & Ksir, 1993). Another concern is the effect of regular marijuana smoking on human reproduction. Studies since the late 1970s have discovered lower sperm counts in men who are chronic smokers of marijuana, and abnormal ovulation has been found in female smokers (Nahas et al., 1999; Nahas, 1984).

Efforts to educate the public about the growing dangers of regular marijuana use appeared to have paid off throughout the 1980s. The percentage of high school seniors who smoked the substance on a daily basis decreased from 11 percent in 1978 to 2 percent in 1992 (Johnston et al.,

Open for business *Cannabis use is legal in Holland, leading to an industry of marijuana shops. This man lights up a marijuana pipe in the "Cannabis Castle," where some of the drug's most potent strains are available.*

1993). Furthermore, in 1992 about 77 percent of high school seniors believed that regular marijuana smoking poses a serious health risk, a much higher percentage than that in earlier years (Johnston et al., 1993). However, marijuana use among the young jumped up again during the 1990s. Today 6 percent of high school seniors smoke marijuana daily, and fewer than 60 percent believe that regular use can be harmful (Johnston et al., 1999, 1996).

CANNABIS AND SOCIETY: A ROCKY RELATIONSHIP For centuries cannabis played a respected role in medicine. It was recommended as a surgical anesthetic by Chinese physicians 2,000 years ago and was used in other lands to treat cholera, malaria, coughs, insomnia, and rheumatism. When cannabis entered the United States in the early twentieth century, mainly in the form of marijuana, it was likewise used for various medical purposes. Soon, however, more effective medicines replaced it, and the favorable view of cannabis began to change. Marijuana began to be used as a recreational drug, and its illegal distribution became a law enforcement problem. Authorities assumed it was highly dangerous and outlawed the "killer weed." But marijuana didn't go away. During the 1960s, a time of disillusionment, protest, and self-exploration, young people discovered the pleasures of getting high from smoking marijuana. By the end of the 1970s, 16 million people reported using it at least once, and 11 percent of the population were recent users.

In the 1980s researchers developed precise techniques for measuring THC and for extracting pure THC from cannabis; they also developed laboratory forms of THC. These inventions opened the door to new medical applications for cannabis (Ray & Ksir, 1993), such as its use in treating glaucoma, a severe eye disease in which fluid from the eyeball is obstructed from flowing properly. Cannabis was also found to help patients with asthma and to reduce the nausea and vomiting of cancer patients in chemotherapy (Plasse et al., 1991). Some studies have also suggested that THC might improve the appetites of AIDS patients and so combat weight loss in people with that disorder (Johnson, 1996; Plasse et al., 1991).

In light of these findings, several interest groups campaigned during the late 1980s for the medical legalization of marijuana, which operates on the brain and body more quickly than the THC capsules developed in the laboratory. In 1992, however, the Drug Enforcement Administration opposed this measure, and the Food and Drug Administration stopped reviewing requests for the "compassionate use" of marijuana (Karel, 1992). They held that prescriptions for pure THC served all needed medical functions.

Advocates of the medical use of marijuana challenged this position again during the elections of 1996. Voter referendums, which have the force of law, were passed in California and Arizona, giving physicians the right to prescribe marijuana for "seriously ill" or "terminally ill" patients. Voters in the states of Alaska, Washington, Oregon, Colorado, and Nevada followed suit in 1998. The federal government countered by threatening to revoke the prescription-writing privilege of any physician who prescribed marijuana, and even to prosecute such physicians. Angered by the government's position on this complex issue, many more physicians have now openly joined the battle. In 1997 the *New England Journal of Medicine*, one of the world's most prestigious medical publications, published an editorial favoring the medical use of marijuana. The journal further called the government's threats "misguided, heavy-handed, and inhumane." And in 1999 an Institute of Medicine study, commissioned by the White House itself, concluded that marijuana can indeed serve medical functions. Clearly we have not heard the last of this issue.

> "Those addicted to marihuana, after an early feeling of exhilaration, soon lose all restraints, all inhibitions. They become bestial demoniacs, filled with the mad lust to kill."
>
> Kenneth Clark,
> social psychologist, 1936

Medicinal use *Suffering from severe arthritis and an eye condition similar to glaucoma, this woman puffs on a pipe filled with marijuana several times a day. It apparently eases her pain and helps clear her vision.*

FUTURE DIRECTIONS

A highly respected study by the Institute of Medicine concludes that the government and pharmaceutical firms should develop an *inhaler* to deliver cannabis to medical patients. This method would be safer than smoking marijuana, faster acting than THC capsules, and more precise than either technique (Benson & Watson, 1999).

Déjà vu *Polysubstance use, particularly a mixture of cocaine and opioids, proved fatal for performers John Belushi (left) and Chris Farley (right), each a featured actor on the television show* Saturday Night Live. *Farley had often stated his admiration for Belushi's talent and lifestyle.*

Combinations of Substances

Because people often take more than one drug at a time, a pattern called *polysubstance use,* researchers have studied the ways in which drugs interact with one another. Two important discoveries have emerged from this work: the phenomena of *cross-tolerance* and *synergistic effects.*

Sometimes two or more drugs are so similar in their actions on the brain and the body that as people build a tolerance for one drug, they are simultaneously developing a tolerance for the other, even if they have never taken the latter. Correspondingly, users who display such **cross-tolerance** can reduce the symptoms of withdrawal from one drug by taking the other. Alcohol and antianxiety drugs are cross-tolerant, for example, so it is sometimes possible to reduce the alcohol withdrawal reaction of delirium tremens by administering benzodiazepines, along with vitamins and electrolytes (Moss, 1999; Kosten & McCance-Katz, 1995).

When different drugs are in the body at the same time, they may multiply, or potentiate, each other's effects. The combined impact, called a **synergistic effect**, is often greater than the sum of the effects of each drug taken alone: a small dose of one drug mixed with a small dose of another can produce an enormous change in body chemistry. One kind of synergistic effect occurs when two or more drugs have *similar actions.* For instance, alcohol, benzodiazepines, barbiturates, and opioids—all depressants—may severely depress the central nervous system when mixed (Miller & Gold, 1990). Combining them, even in small doses, can lead to extreme intoxication, coma, and even death (Nishino et al., 1995). A young man may have just a few alcoholic drinks at a party, for example, and shortly afterward take a moderate dose of barbiturates to help him fall asleep. He believes he has acted with restraint and good judgment—yet he may never wake up.

A different kind of synergistic effect results when drugs have *opposite,* or *antagonistic, actions* (Braun, 1996). Stimulant drugs, for example, interfere with the liver's usual disposal of barbiturates and alcohol. Thus people who combine barbiturates or alcohol with cocaine or amphetamines may build up toxic, even lethal, levels of the depressant drugs in their systems. Students who take amphetamines to help them study late into the night and then take barbiturates to help them fall asleep are unwittingly placing themselves in serious danger.

Each year tens of thousands of people are admitted to hospitals with a multiple drug emergency, and several thousand of them die (DAWN, 1997). Sometimes the cause is carelessness or ignorance. Often, however, people use multiple drugs precisely because they enjoy the synergistic effects. In fact, **polysubstance-related disorders** are becoming as common as individual substance-related disorders in the United States, Canada, and Europe (Galanter & Castañeda, 1999; Newcomb, 1994). As many as 90 percent of persons who use one illegal drug are

VIOLATIONS OF THE LAW

The leading reasons for arrests in the United States include drug abuse violations (first place), driving under the influence (third), drunkenness (fifth), and violation of liquor laws (sixth) (Ash, 1998).

also using another to some extent (Cornish et al., 1995). A look-in on a group therapy session for users of crack reveals that several of the group members have used other substances in addition:

> **Therapist:** Okay. Now, can you give me a list of all the drugs you've used? Gary?
> **Gary:** Pot. Coke. Crack. Mescaline. Acid. Speed. Crystal meth. Smack. Base dust. Sometimes alcohol.
> **Dennis:** Alcohol. Pot. Coke. Mescaline. LSD. Amyl nitrate. Speed and Valium.
> **Davy:** Coke. Crack. Reefer. Alcohol. Acid. Mescaline. Mushrooms. Ecstasy. Speed. Smack.
> **Rich:** Alcohol. Pot. Ludes [Quaaludes]. Valium. Speed. Ups [amphetamines]. Downs [barbiturates]. Acid. Mescaline. Crack. Base. Dust. That's about it.
> **Carol:** Alcohol. Pot. Cocaine. Mescaline. Valium. Crack.
>
> *(Chatlos, 1987, pp. 30–31)*

Fans still mourn the deaths of many celebrities who have been the victims of polysubstance use. Elvis Presley's delicate balancing act of stimulants and depressants eventually killed him. Janis Joplin's mixtures of wine and heroin were ultimately fatal. And John Belushi's, River Phoenix's, and Chris Farley's liking for the combined effect of cocaine and opioids ("speedballs") also ended in tragedy.

What Causes Substance-Related Disorders?

Clinical theorists have developed sociocultural, psychological, and biological explanations for why people abuse or become dependent on various substances. No single explanation, however, has gained broad support. Like so many other disorders, excessive and chronic drug use is increasingly viewed as the result of a combination of these factors.

The Sociocultural View

A number of sociocultural theorists propose that people are most likely to develop patterns of substance abuse or dependence when they live under stressful socioeconomic conditions. In fact, studies have found that regions with higher levels of unemployment have higher rates of alcoholism (Linsky, Strauss, & Colby, 1985). Similarly, hunting societies, in which people presumably experience greater danger, uncertainty, and tension, have more alcohol problems than agrarian societies (Bacon, 1973; Horton, 1943); city dwellers have higher alcoholism rates than residents of small towns and rural areas (Cisin & Calahan, 1970); and lower socioeconomic classes have higher substance-abuse rates than other classes (Dohrenwend, 2000; Smith, North, & Spitznagel, 1993). Studies have also found higher rates of heroin addiction among people who live in stressful environments. About 40 percent of Army enlisted men used heroin at least once while serving in Vietnam, half of them so often that they had a withdrawal reaction when they stopped (Grinspoon & Bakalar, 1986).

Other sociocultural theorists propose that substance abuse and dependence are more likely to appear in families and social environments where substance use is valued, or at least accepted (see Table 12-4 and Box 12-3 on the next page). Researchers have, in fact, found that problem drinking is more common among teenagers whose parents and peers drink, as well as among teenagers whose family environments are stressful and unsupportive (Shucksmith,

CROSS-TOLERANCE Tolerance for a substance one has not taken before as a result of using another substance similar to it.

SYNERGISTIC EFFECT In pharmacology, an increase of effects that occurs when more than one substance is acting on the body at the same time.

POLYSUBSTANCE-RELATED DISORDER A long-term pattern of maladaptive behavior centered on abuse of or dependence on a combination of drugs.

Table 12-4

Annual Alcohol Consumption around the World*

	WINE	BEER	LIQUOR
France	63.5	40.1	2.5
Italy	58.0	25.1	0.9
Switzerland	46.0	65.0	1.7
Australia	15.7	102.1	1.2
Britain	12.2	100.0	1.5
U.S.A.	8.9	87.8	2.0
Russia	2.7	17.1	3.8
Czech Republic	1.7	140.0	1.0
Japan	1.0	55.0	2.1
Mexico	0.2	50.4	0.8

*Consumption in liters per capita.

Source: Shapiro, 1996; World Drink Trends, 1994; World Health Organization; Wine Market Council; Adams/Jobson Publishing Corp.

Chasing Highs Wherever They May Lead

Jonathan Melvoin, a backup keyboard player for the rock group Smashing Pumpkins, died of a heroin overdose in July 1996. Word soon spread that the brand of heroin he had taken was Red Rum, a strain smuggled in from Colombia. Its name—*murder* spelled backward—comes from the Stephen King novel *The Shining.*

Within hours the demand for Red Rum rose dramatically on the streets of Manhattan's Lower East Side. "It's kind of

Smashing aftermath *The Smashing Pumpkins, posing here for a studio photo a year prior to the Melvoin incident, fired the band's drummer after learning that he had been using drugs with the keyboardist Melvoin.*

sick," a narcotics officer told the *New York Times.* "But when people die from something or nearly die, all of a sudden there's this rush to get it."

ConsiderThis

⦿ Why might people actively seek drugs that are known to endanger their lives? • What effects might the use of drugs by some rock performers have on teenagers and young adults? • Who has the greater impact on the drug behaviors of teenagers and young adults: rock performers who speak out against drugs or rock performers who praise the virtues of drugs?

ConsiderThis

⦿ Different ethnic, religious, and national groups have different rates of alcohol abuse. What social factors might help explain this observation? • Can we be certain that biological factors are not involved?

Glendinning, & Hendry, 1997; Wills et al., 1996). Moreover, lower rates of alcohol abuse are found among Jews and Protestants, groups in which drinking is typically acceptable only as long as it remains within clear limits, whereas alcoholism rates are higher among the Irish and Eastern Europeans, who do not, on average, draw as clear a line (Kohn & Levav, 1995; Vaillant & Milofsky, 1982).

In sum, the sociocultural explanations of substance abuse and dependence are supported by studies that generally compare drug use among people of different environments or cultures. As with sociocultural explanations of other mental disorders, however, they fail to explain why only some people who live under unfavorable social conditions develop substance-related disorders. Psychological (psychodynamic and behavioral) and biological theorists have provided some insight into this issue.

The Psychodynamic View

Psychodynamic theorists believe that people who abuse substances have powerful *dependency needs* that can be traced to their early years (Shedler & Block, 1990; Abadi, 1984). They claim that when parents fail to satisfy a young child's need for nurturance, the child is likely to grow up depending excessively on others for help and comfort, trying to find the nurturance that was lacking during the early years. If this search for outside support includes experimentation with a drug, the person may well develop a dependent relationship with the substance.

Some psychodynamic theorists also believe that certain people respond to their early deprivations by developing a *substance abuse personality* that leaves them particularly prone to drug abuse. Personality inventories and patient interviews have in fact indicated that people who abuse or depend on drugs tend to be more dependent, antisocial, impulsive, novelty-seeking, and depressive than other people (Finn et al., 2000; Mâsse & Tremblay, 1997). These findings are correlational, however, and do not clarify whether such personality traits lead to drug use or whether drug use causes people to be dependent, impulsive, and the like (Galanter & Castañeda, 1999).

To better establish causation, one longitudinal study measured the personality traits of a large group of nonalcoholic young men and then kept track of each man's development (Jones, 1971, 1968). Years later, the traits of the men who developed alcohol problems in middle age were compared with the traits of those who did not. The men who developed alcohol problems had been more impulsive as teenagers and continued to be so in middle age, suggesting that impulsive men are indeed more prone to develop alcohol problems. Similarly, in one laboratory investigation, "impulsive" rats—those that generally had trouble delaying their rewards—were found to drink more alcohol when offered it than other rats (Poulos, Le, & Parker, 1995).

A major weakness of this line of argument is the very wide range of personality traits that has been linked to substance abuse and dependence. In fact, different studies point to different "key" traits. Inasmuch as some people with a drug addiction appear to be dependent, others impulsive, and still others antisocial, researchers cannot presently conclude that any one personality trait or group of traits stands out as a factor in substance-related disorders (Rozin & Stoess, 1993).

The Behavioral View

According to *operant conditioning* theorists, the temporary reduction of tension or raising of spirits produced by a drug has a rewarding effect, thus increasing the likelihood that the user will seek this reaction again (Carpenter & Hasin, 1998; Hughes et al., 1995). The rewarding effects of substances may also lead users to eventually try higher dosages or more powerful methods of ingestion (see Table 12-5). In support of this behavioral theory, studies have found that many subjects do in fact drink more alcohol or seek heroin when they feel tense (Cooney et al., 1997; Cooper, 1994). In one study, as subjects worked on a difficult anagram task, a confederate planted by the researchers unfairly criticized and belittled them (Marlatt, Kosturn, & Lang, 1975). The subjects were then asked to participate in an "alcohol taste task," ostensibly to compare and rate alcoholic beverages. The subjects who had been harassed drank more alcohol during the taste task than did the control subjects who had not been criticized. A third group of subjects were harassed while doing the anagrams but were given an opportunity to retaliate against their critics. These subjects drank relatively little during the tasting. Their retaliatory behavior had apparently reduced their tension and lessened their need for alcohol.

> "Water is the only drink for a wise man."
>
> Henry David Thoreau, *Walden*

> "When tempted, reach for a Lucky."
>
> Ad for Lucky Strikes cigarettes, 1930, targeting diet-conscious women

Table 12-5

Methods of Taking Substances

METHOD	ROUTE	TIME TO REACH BRAIN
Inhaling	Drug in vapor form is inhaled through mouth and lungs into circulatory system.	7 seconds
Snorting	Drug in powdered form is snorted into the nose. Some of the drug lands on the nasal mucous membranes, is absorbed by blood vessels, and enters the bloodstream.	4 minutes
Injection	Drug in liquid form directly enters the body through a needle. Injection may be intravenous or intramuscular (subcutaneous).	20 seconds (intravenous); 4 minutes (intramuscular)
Oral ingestion	Drug in solid or liquid form passes through esophagus and stomach and finally to the small intestines. It is absorbed by blood vessels in the intestines.	30 minutes
Other routes	Drugs can be absorbed through areas that contain mucous membranes. Drugs can be placed under the tongue, inserted anally and vaginally, and administered as eyedrops.	Variable

Source: Landry, 1994, p. 24.

Carrot juice on the rocks *Both public officials and clinical experts welcome the recent growth of juice bars (such as this one in New York City) and similar establishments, where substances other than alcohol are valued by patrons and help to trigger social interactions and activities.*

"Alcohol is like love. The first kiss is magic, the second is intimate, the third is routine."

Raymond Chandler,
The Long Good-bye

DRUGS AND CRIME

Fifty-seven percent of state prisoners and 45 percent of federal prisoners in the United States report using illicit drugs in the month before committing their offense (Bureau of Justice Statistics, 1999).

In a manner of speaking, the reward theorists are arguing that many people take drugs to "medicate" themselves when they feel tense (Anthony et al., 1995; Khantzian, 1985). If so, one would expect higher rates of drug abuse among people who suffer from anxiety, depression, or intense anger. In fact, substance abuse and dependence do appear to be fairly common among people with mood disorders (Swendsen & Merikangas, 2000). One study of 835 clinically depressed patients found that more than one-fourth abused drugs during episodes of depression (Hasin, Endicott, & Lewis, 1985). In another study, the negative thoughts and biases of depressed subjects were found to improve significantly after the subjects drank alcoholic beverages (Stephens & Curtin, 1995). Similarly, higher-than-usual rates of drug abuse have been found among people with posttraumatic stress disorder (Najavits et al., 1998), eating disorders (Higuchi et al., 1993), schizophrenia (Regier et al., 1990), antisocial personality disorder (Brooner et al., 1997), histories of being abused (Yama et al., 1993), and other psychological problems (Kessler et al., 1997).

Of course, not all drug users find drugs pleasurable or reinforcing when they first take them. Many people, for example, report that they did not get high the first time they smoked marijuana, and some opioid users were unaffected or sickened by their initial experiences with opioids. Moreover, even when drugs do initially produce pleasant feelings and rewards, a user's response to them tends to change over time. A number of people, for example, become anxious and depressed as they take more and more drugs (Roggla & Uhl, 1995; Vaillant, 1993). Why, then, do users keep on taking drugs?

Some behaviorists use Richard Solomon's *opponent-process theory* to answer this question. Solomon (1980) held that the brain is structured in such a way that pleasurable emotions, such as drug-induced euphoria, inevitably lead to opponent processes—negative aftereffects—that leave the person feeling worse than usual. People who continue to use pleasure-giving drugs inevitably develop opponent aftereffects, such as cravings for more of the drug, an increasing need for the drug, and withdrawal responses. According to Solomon, the opponent processes eventually dominate, and avoidance of the negative aftereffects replaces pursuit of pleasure as the primary motivation for taking drugs. Although a highly regarded theory, the opponent-process explanation has not received systematic research support (Peele, 1989).

Still other behaviorists have proposed that *classical conditioning* may play a role in drug abuse and dependence (Robbins et al., 2000; Remington et al., 1997; Childress et al., 1993, 1988). Objects present at the time drugs are taken may act as classically conditioned stimuli and come to produce some of the same pleasure brought on by the drugs themselves. Just the sight of a hypodermic needle or a regular supplier, for example, has been known to comfort people who abuse heroin or amphetamines and to relieve their withdrawal symptoms (Meyer, 1995).

In a similar manner, objects that are present during withdrawal distress may produce withdrawal-like symptoms (Meyer, 1995; Childress et al., 1993, 1984). One man who had formerly been dependent on heroin experienced nausea and other withdrawal symptoms when he returned to the neighborhood where he had gone through withdrawal in the past—a reaction that led him to start taking heroin again (O'Brien et al., 1975). Although this study demonstrates that withdrawal responses can be classically conditioned, other studies suggest that conditioning is not at work in most cases. Of forty persons who had gone through heroin withdrawal, only eleven reported having withdrawal symptoms during later encounters with environments and objects associated with their withdrawal, and only five of those people actually relapsed into heroin use (McAuliffe, 1982). In short, the classical conditioning explanations of drug abuse and dependence, like the operant conditioning explanations, have received at best mixed support (Powell, Bradley, & Gray, 1992).

The Biological View

In recent years researchers have come to suspect that drug misuse may have biological causes. Studies on genetic predisposition and specific biochemical processes have provided some support for these suspicions.

GENETIC PREDISPOSITION For years breeding experiments have been conducted to see whether certain animals are genetically predisposed to become dependent on drugs (Li, 2000; Kurtz et al., 1996). In several studies, for example, investigators have first identified animals that prefer alcohol to other beverages, and then mated them to one another. Generally, the offspring of these animals have been found to also display an unusual preference for alcohol (Melo et al., 1996).

Similarly, research with human twins has suggested that people may inherit a predisposition to abuse substances in response to unfavorable life circumstances (Kendler et al., 1994, 1992; Goodwin, 1984, 1976). One classic study found an alcohol-abuse *concordance* rate of 54 percent in a group of identical twins; that is, if one identical twin abused alcohol, the other twin also abused alcohol in 54 percent of the cases. In contrast, a group of fraternal twins had a concordance rate of only 28 percent (Kaij, 1960). As we have observed, however, such findings do not rule out other interpretations (Kendler & Gardner, 1998). For one thing, the parenting received by two identical twins may be more similar than that received by two fraternal twins.

A stronger indication that genetics may play a role in substance abuse and dependence comes from studies of alcoholism rates in people adopted shortly after birth (Cadoret, 1995; Goldstein, 1994). These studies have compared adoptees whose biological parents are dependent on alcohol with adoptees whose biological parents are not. By adulthood, the individuals whose biological parents are dependent on alcohol typically show higher rates of alcohol abuse than those with nonalcoholic biological parents.

Genetic linkage strategies and *molecular biology* techniques provide more direct evidence in support of the genetic hypothesis (Li, 2000; Rocha et al., 1998; Chen et al., 1996). One line of investigation has found an abnormal form of the so-called *dopamine-2 (D2) receptor gene* in a majority of subjects with alcohol dependence and half of subjects with cocaine dependence, but in less than 20 percent of nondependent subjects (Lawford et al., 1997; Blum & Noble, 1993; Blum et al., 1991). Some studies have also implicated other kinds of dopamine-linked genes to substance-related disorders (Nash, 1997).

BIOCHEMICAL FACTORS Over the past few decades, investigators have pieced together a general biological understanding of drug tolerance and withdrawal symptoms (Wise, 1996). As we have seen, when a particular drug is ingested, it increases the activity of certain neurotransmitters whose normal purpose is to sedate, reduce pain, lift mood, or increase alertness. When a person keeps on taking the drug, the brain apparently makes an adjustment and reduces its own production of the neurotransmitters (Goldstein, 1994). Because the drug is increasing neurotransmitter activity or efficiency, action by the brain is less necessary. As drug intake increases, the body's production of the neurotransmitters continues to decrease, leaving the person in need of more and more of the drug to achieve its effects. In this way, drug takers build tolerance for a drug, becoming more and more reliant on it rather than on their own biological processes to feel calm, comfortable, happy, or alert. If they suddenly stop taking the drug, their supply of neurotransmitters will be low for a time, producing the symptoms of withdrawal. Withdrawal continues until the brain resumes its normal production of the necessary neurotransmitters.

Which neurotransmitters are affected depends on the drug used. A chronic and excessive use of alcohol or benzodiazepines may lower the brain's production of the neurotransmitter GABA; regular use of opioids may reduce the brain's production of endorphins; and regular use of cocaine or amphetamines may lower

ANIMAL HIGHS
Animals sometimes use substances to get high or relieve stress. Llamas in Peru get frisky eating coca leaves (which contain cocaine). Grasshoppers that eat wild marijuana leaves jump unusually high. Elephants seek out fermented ripe fruit (Siegel, 1990).

Addicted to chocolate? *Recent studies suggest that the craving for chocolate may be more than just a state of mind. Apparently, some chemicals in chocolate may bind to the same neuron receptors that receive cannabis substances (di Tomaso, Beltramo, & Piomelli, 1996). At the same time, however, a person would have to eat 25 pounds of chocolate in one sitting to experience a cannabislike effect. Then again, for chocolate lovers . . . .*

REWARD CENTER A dopamine-rich pathway in the brain that produces feelings of pleasure when activated.

REWARD-DEFICIENCY SYNDROME A condition, suspected to be present in some individuals, in which the brain's reward center is not readily activated by the usual events in their lives.

AVERSION THERAPY A treatment in which clients are repeatedly presented with unpleasant stimuli while performing undesirable behaviors such as taking a drug.

the brain's production of dopamine (Volkow, Fowler, & Wang, 1999). In addition, researchers have identified neurotransmitters called *anandamides* (from the Sanskrit word for "bliss") that operate much like THC; excessive use of marijuana may reduce the production of these neurotransmitters (Lichtman & Martin, 1999; Biegon & Kerman, 1995).

This model helps explain why people who regularly take substances experience tolerance and withdrawal reactions. But why are drugs so rewarding, and why do certain people turn to them in the first place? A recent flurry of brain imaging studies suggest that many, perhaps all, drugs eventually activate a single **reward center**, or "pleasure pathway," in the brain (Volkow & Fowler, 2000; Bloom, 1998). This reward center apparently extends from the brain area called the *ventral tegmental area* (in the midbrain) to an area known as the *nucleus accumbens* and on to the *frontal cortex*. A key neurotransmitter in this pleasure pathway appears to be *dopamine*. When dopamine is activated there, a person experiences pleasure. Music may activate dopamine in the reward center. So may a hug or a word of praise. And so may drugs. Some researchers believe that other neurotransmitters may also play important roles in the reward center (Garris et al., 1999).

Certain drugs apparently stimulate the reward center directly. Remember that cocaine, amphetamines, and caffeine directly increase dopamine activity. Other drugs seem to stimulate it in roundabout ways. The biochemical reactions triggered by alcohol, opioids, and marijuana probably launch a series of chemical events that eventually lead to increased dopamine activity in the reward center (Volkow et al., 1997; Goldstein, 1994).

A number of theorists suspect that people who abuse drugs suffer from a **reward-deficiency syndrome**: their reward center is not readily activated by the usual events in their lives (Nash, 1997). So, they turn to drugs to stimulate this pleasure pathway, particularly at times of stress. Abnormal genes, such as the abnormal D2 receptor gene, have been cited as a possible cause of this syndrome (Lawford et al., 1997).

How Are Substance-Related Disorders Treated?

Many approaches have been used to treat substance-related disorders, including psychodynamic, behavioral, cognitive-behavioral, biological, and sociocultural therapies. Although these treatments sometimes meet with great success, more often they are only moderately helpful (Rabasca, 1998; Azrin et al., 1996). Today the treatments are typically used in combination (Galanter & Castañeda, 1999; Landry, 1994) on both an outpatient and an inpatient basis (Rychtarik et al., 2000).

The value of a treatment for substance abuse or dependence can be difficult to determine (Babor et al., 2000; Cornish et al., 1996). First, different substance-related disorders pose different treatment problems. Second, some people recover without any intervention at all, while others recover and then relapse, and still others fail to improve even after intensive treatment (Miller, 2000). Finally, different criteria are used by different clinical researchers. How long, for example, must a person refrain from substance use in order to be called a treatment success? And is total abstention the only criterion, or is a reduction of drug use acceptable?

Psychodynamic Therapies

Psychodynamic therapists try to help people with substance-related disorders become aware of and correct the psychological problems that they believe are at the root of the disorders. They first guide clients to uncover and work through their underlying conflicts, and then they try to help them change their substance-related styles of living (Hopper, 1995; Levinson, 1985). Although this approach has often been applied to substance-related disorders, research has not found it to be highly effective (Cornish et al., 1995; Holder et al., 1991). It may be that drug abuse or dependence, regardless of its primary causes, eventually becomes a

SPONTANEOUS REMISSION
Between 20 and 30 percent of all people with substance-related disorders apparently recover within 10 years without treatment (Schuckit, 1999).

ConsiderThis
◉ Only one-third of the $15 billion the U.S. government spends on drug abuse goes to prevention and treatment. Does the focus on the criminalization of drugs ultimately add to the stigma of drug abuse and, in turn, make effective treatment more difficult (Nash, 1997)?

stubborn independent problem that must be the direct target of treatment if people are to become drug-free. Psychodynamic therapy tends to be of greater help when combined with other approaches in a multidimensional treatment program. It has, for example, had some success when combined with behavioral and biological therapies (Carroll & Rounsaville, 1995; Galanter, 1993).

Behavioral Therapies

A widely used behavioral treatment for substance-related disorders is **aversion therapy**, an approach based on the principles of classical conditioning (Frawley & Smith, 1992). Individuals are repeatedly presented with an unpleasant stimulus (for example, an electric shock) at the very moment that they are taking a drug. After repeated pairings, they are expected to react negatively to the substance itself and to lose their craving for it.

Aversion therapy has been applied to alcohol abuse and dependence more than to other substance-related disorders. In one version of this therapy, drinking behavior is paired with drug-induced nausea and vomiting (Elkins, 1991; Cannon et al., 1986, 1981). Another version, *covert sensitization,* requires people with alcoholism to imagine extremely upsetting, repulsive, or frightening scenes while they are drinking (Kassel, Wagner, & Unrod, 1999). The pairing of the imagined scenes with liquor is expected to produce negative responses to liquor itself. Here are the kinds of scenes therapists may guide a client to imagine:

Downward spiral *Arrested for possession of cocaine and heroin in 1996, actor Robert Downey, Jr., was initially sent to a drug counseling program. However, Downey was unable to abstain from drugs and repeatedly violated the terms of his probation, leading to a three-year prison sentence.*

> I'd like you to vividly imagine that you are drinking and tasting (beer, whiskey, etc.). You are in a (restaurant, pub, etc.) where others are drinking. 'See' yourself there, having a drink. Capture the exact taste of it, the colour and the smell. Use all of your senses. Imagine that you are actually drinking it, tasting it, swallowing it, feel the glass in your hand; and be aware of its temperature, taste and smell, but especially the taste.
>
> As you swallow the drink, a man sitting not far from you gives a low groan, replaces his glass on the table and pushes it away. His head remains lowered as he grasps his stomach with both hands and continues moaning. His eyes are closed now as he grimaces and slowly shakes his head. His face has become a sickly pale colour, and his hands are trembling as he starts to make quick swallowing motions. He opens his eyes and claps both hands over his mouth, but he cannot hold it in and the vomit bursts out. You can see it so clearly. Pieces of food run down his face, soaking his clothes and even reaching his glass. He continues to throw up and particles of his last meal stick to his chin and the hot sticky smell of alcohol reaches you. He really is a disgusting sight. He's got the dry heaves now, there's nothing left to bring up, but his face is still pale and he continues moaning.
>
> I'd like you to vividly imagine that you are tasting the (beer, whiskey, etc.). See yourself tasting it, capture the exact taste, colour and consistency. Use all of your senses. After you've tasted the drink you notice that there is something small and white floating in the glass—it stands out. You bend closer to examine it more carefully, your nose is right over the glass now and the smell fills your nostrils as you remember exactly what the drink tastes like. Now you can see what's in the glass. There are several maggots floating on the surface. As you watch, revolted, one manages to get a grip on the glass and, undulating, creeps up the glass. There are even more of the repulsive creatures in the glass than you first thought. You realise that you have swallowed some of them and you're very aware of the taste in your mouth. You feel very sick and wish you'd never reached for the glass and had the drink at all.
>
> *(Clarke & Saunders, 1988, pp. 143-144)*

DRASTIC MEASURE

In one early form of aversion therapy, people with alcoholism were injected with *succinylcholine,* a drug that actually paralyzed their bodies while they tasted alcoholic beverages (Sanderson, Campbell, & Laverty, 1963). These clients did sometimes develop an aversion to alcohol, but concerns about the safety and ethics of this approach led to its discontinuation.

BEHAVIORAL SELF-CONTROL TRAINING (BSCT) A cognitive-behavioral approach to treating alcohol abuse and dependence in which clients are taught to keep track of their drinking behavior and to apply coping strategies in situations that typically trigger excessive drinking.

RELAPSE-PREVENTION TRAINING An approach to treating alcohol abuse that is similar to BSCT and also has clients plan ahead for risky situations and reactions.

DETOXIFICATION Systematic and medically supervised withdrawal from a drug.

ANTAGONIST DRUGS Drugs that block or change the effects of an addictive drug.

MOST VISIBLE SUBSTANCE

After analyzing 224 hours of prime-time television network programming, investigators from Cornell University concluded that alcohol is displayed on television programs more than any other food or drink.

Another behavioral approach focuses on teaching *alternative behaviors* to drug taking (Azrin et al., 1996). This approach, too, has been applied to alcohol abuse and dependence more than to other substance-related disorders. Problem drinkers may be taught to reduce their tensions with relaxation, meditation, or biofeedback instead of alcohol (Rohsenow, Smith, & Johnson, 1985). Some are also taught assertiveness or social skills to help them both express their anger more directly and withstand social pressures to drink (Kassel et al., 1999; Van Hasselt et al., 1993).

A behavioral approach that has been effective in the short-term treatment of people who abuse cocaine (a notoriously hard-to-treat group) and some other drugs is *contingency management*, which makes incentives (such as program privileges) contingent on the submission of drug-free urine specimens (Petry, 2000; Azrin et al., 1996; Carroll & Rounsaville, 1995). In one study, 68 percent of cocaine abusers who completed a six-month contingency training program achieved at least eight weeks of continuous abstinence (Higgins et al., 1993).

Behavioral interventions for substance abuse and dependence have usually had only limited success when they are the sole form of treatment (Carroll & Rounsaville, 1995). A major problem is that the approaches can be effective only when individuals are motivated to continue with them despite their unpleasantness or the amount of work that they require. Generally, behavioral treatments work best in combination with either biological or cognitive approaches (Kassel et al., 1999; Whorley, 1996).

Cognitive-Behavioral Therapies

Two popular approaches combine cognitive and behavioral techniques to help people gain *control* over their substance-related behaviors. In one, **behavioral self-control training (BSCT)**, applied to alcoholism in particular, therapists first have clients keep track of their own drinking behavior (Miller et al., 1992; Miller, 1983). Writing down the times, locations, emotions, bodily changes, and other circumstances of their drinking, they become more aware of the situations that place them at risk for excessive drinking. They are then taught coping strategies to use when such situations arise. They learn, for example, to set limits on their drinking (see Box 12-4 on page 380), to recognize when the limits are being approached, to control their rate of drinking (perhaps by spacing their drinks or by sipping them rather than gulping), and to practice relaxation techniques and other coping behaviors in situations in which they would otherwise be drinking. Approximately 70 percent of the people who complete this program apparently show some improvement, particularly those who are young and not physically dependent on alcohol (Hester, 1995; Miller et al., 1992).

In another cognitive-behavioral approach, **relapse-prevention training**, heavy drinkers are assigned many of the same tasks as clients in BSCT (Marlatt & Gordon, 1985, 1980). They are also taught to plan ahead of time how many drinks are appropriate, what to drink, and under what circumstances. The approach sometimes lowers the frequency of intoxication (Kassel et al., 1999). Like BSCT, it seems most effective for people who abuse alcohol but are not physically dependent on it (Meyer et al., 1989). The approach has also been used, with some success, in the treatment of marijuana and cocaine abuse (Carroll & Rounsaville, 1995; Wells et al., 1994).

Biological Treatments

Biological approaches may be used to help people withdraw from substances, abstain from them, or simply maintain their level of use without further increases (Moss, 1999). As with the other forms of treatment, biological approaches alone rarely bring long-term improvement, but they can be helpful when combined with other approaches (Cornish et al., 1995; Kleber, 1995).

DETOXIFICATION **Detoxification** is systematic and medically supervised withdrawal from a drug. Some detoxification programs are offered on an outpatient basis (Allan, Smith, & Mellin, 2000). Others are located in hospitals and clinics and may also offer individual and group therapy, a "full-service" institutional approach that has become popular. One detoxification approach is to have clients withdraw gradually from the substance, taking smaller and smaller doses until they are off it completely. A second detoxification strategy is to give clients other drugs that reduce the symptoms of withdrawal (Schuckit, 1999; Cornish et al., 1995). Antianxiety drugs, for example, are sometimes used to reduce severe alcohol withdrawal reactions such as delirium tremens and seizures (D'Onofrio et al., 1999). Detoxification programs seem to help motivated people withdraw from drugs (Allan et al., 2000). For people who fail to receive psychotherapy after withdrawal, however, relapse rates tend to be high (Pickens & Fletcher, 1991).

Forced detoxification *Abstinence does not always take place in a planned, medically supervised, or voluntary manner. This sufferer of alcoholism begins to experience symptoms of withdrawal soon after being imprisoned for public intoxication.*

ANTAGONIST DRUGS After successful cessation of drug use, people must avoid falling back into a pattern of abuse or dependence. As an aid to resisting temptation, some people with substance-related disorders are given **antagonist drugs**, which block or change the effects of the addictive drug. *Disulfiram (Antabuse)*, for example, is often given to people who are trying to stay away from alcohol (Moss, 1999; Landry, 1994). By itself a low dose of this drug seems to have few negative effects; but because disulfiram interferes with the body's metabolism of alcohol, a person who drinks alcohol while taking disulfiram will experience intense nausea, vomiting, blushing, faster heart rate, dizziness, and perhaps fainting. People taking disulfiram are less likely to drink alcohol because they know the terrible reaction that awaits them should they have even one drink. Disulfiram has proved helpful, but again only with people who are motivated to take it as prescribed (Cornish et al., 1995; Meyer et al., 1989).

Narcotic antagonists, such as *naloxone* and *naltrexone*, are sometimes used to treat people who are dependent on opioids. These drugs attach to endorphin receptor sites throughout the brain and make it impossible for the opioids to have their usual effect. Without the rush or high, continued drug use becomes pointless. Although narcotic antagonists have been helpful—particularly in emergencies, to rescue people from an overdose of opioids—some clinicians consider them too dangerous for regular treatment of opioid dependence. These antagonists must be administered carefully because of their ability to throw a person with an addiction into severe withdrawal (Rosen et al., 1996; Goldstein, 1994). In recent years, so-called *partial antagonists*, narcotic antagonists that produce less severe withdrawal symptoms, have been developed (Amass et al., 2000; Bickel & Amass, 1995).

Recent studies indicate that narcotic antagonists may also be useful in the treatment of alcohol and cocaine dependence (Schuckit, 1999; Nemecek, 1995). In some studies, for example, the narcotic antagonist naltrexone has helped reduce cravings for alcohol (O'Malley et al., 2000, 1996, 1992; Volpicelli et al., 1992). Why should narcotic antagonists, which operate at the brain's endorphin receptors, help with alcoholism, which has been tied largely to activity at GABA sites? The answer may lie in the reward center

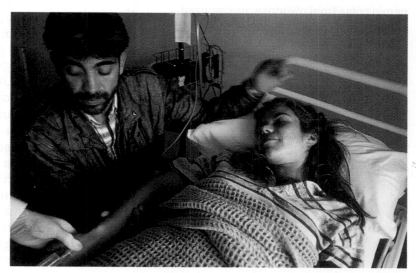

Rapid heroin detox *A number of clinics around the world, such as this one in Australia, now offer rapid detox programs in which heroin users receive general anesthesia to help them sleep through withdrawal and injections of narcotic antagonists that shorten the duration of detoxification to 5 or 6 hours.*

revealed that they are members of these programs and credit them with turning their lives around (Gleick, 1995; Galanter et al., 1990). Systematic studies of the programs have also had favorable findings, but they have been limited in number (Smart & Mann, 2000; Watson et al., 1997).

CULTURE-SENSITIVE PROGRAMS Many persons who abuse substances live in an impoverished and perhaps violent setting (NIDA, 1990). A growing number of today's treatment programs try to be sensitive to the special sociocultural pressures and problems faced by drug abusers who are poor, homeless, or members of ethnic minority groups (Gottfredson & Koper, 1996; Deitch & Solit, 1993). Therapists who are sensitive to their clients' life challenges can do more to address the stresses that often lead to relapse.

Similarly, therapists have become more aware that women often require treatment methods different from those designed for men (Knowlton, 1998; Lisansky-Gomberg, 1993). Women and men have different physical and psychological reactions to drugs, for example (Hamilton, 1991). In addition, treatment of women who abuse substances may be complicated by the impact of sexual abuse, the possibility that they may become pregnant while taking drugs, the stresses of raising children, and the fear of criminal prosecution for abusing drugs during pregnancy (Thompson & Kingree, 1998; Cornish et al., 1995). Thus many women with such disorders feel more comfortable seeking help at gender-sensitive clinics or residential programs; some such programs also allow children to live with their recovering mothers (Copeland & Hall, 1992; DeAngelis, 1992).

COMMUNITY PREVENTION PROGRAMS Perhaps the most effective approach to substance-related disorders is to prevent them (Schuckit, 2000; Kleber, 1995). The first drug-prevention efforts were conducted in schools. Today, prevention programs are also offered in workplaces, activity centers, and other community settings, and even through the media (Saunders & Lee, 2000; Guild & Lowe, 1998) (see Box 12-5). Some prevention programs argue for total abstinence from drugs, while others teach responsible use. Some seek to interrupt drug use; others try to delay the age at which people first experiment with drugs. Programs may also differ in whether they offer drug education, teach alternatives to drug use, try to change the psychological state of the potential user, attempt to change relationships with peers, or combine these techniques.

Prevention programs may focus on the *individual* (for example, by providing education about unpleasant drug effects), the *family* (by teaching parenting skills), the *peer group* (by teaching resistance to peer pressure), the *school* (by setting up firm enforcement of drug policies), or the *community* at large (by public service announcements such as the "Just say no" campaign). The most effective prevention efforts focus on several of these areas to provide a consistent message about drug abuse in all areas of individuals' lives (Wagenaar et al., 2000; NIDA, 1991). Some prevention programs have even been developed for preschool children (Hall & Zigler, 1997; Oyemade, 1989).

> "Outlawing drugs in order to solve the drug problem is much like outlawing sex in order to win the war against AIDS."
>
> Ronald Siegal, *Intoxication*, 1990

Before it begins *Community prevention programs for substance-related disorders often target very young children. Here children pledge abstinence from drug use on Red Ribbon Day by releasing balloons.*

CROSSROADS:
New Wrinkles to a Familiar Story

In some respects the story of the misuse of drugs is the same today as in the past. Substance use is still rampant, often creating damaging psychological disorders. New drugs keep emerging, and the public goes through periods of believing, naively, that they are "safe." Only gradually do people learn that these drugs, too,

BOX 12-5

"My Life's Great Big Secret"

On one of her shows in January 1995, the popular talk show host Oprah Winfrey revealed, with great emotion, that she had been physically dependent on cocaine in the mid-1970s. "That is my life's great big secret that has been held over my head," she said. "I understand the shame. I understand the guilt." Although surprised by this admission, her television audience responded with compassion and understanding, and thousands sent letters of support and appreciation for her candor.

ConsiderThis

⦿ What impact might admissions like Winfrey's have on people's willingness to seek treatment for substance abuse? • Does drug abuse by a middle-aged, highly regarded person conjure up a different image than drug abuse by a younger, less famous individual? • What different kinds of issues might be confronted by drug abusers of different genders or different races?

pose dangers. And treatments for substance-related disorders continue to have only limited effect.

Yet there are important new wrinkles in this familiar story. Researchers have begun to develop a clearer understanding of how drugs act on the brain and body. In the treatment domain, self-help groups and rehabilitation programs are flourishing. And preventive education to make people aware of the dangers of drug misuse is also expanding and seems to be having an effect. One reason for these improvements is that investigators and clinicians have stopped working in isolation and are instead looking for intersections between their own work and the contributions from other models. The same kind of integration that has helped with other psychological disorders has brought new promise to the study and treatment of substance-related disorders.

Perhaps the most important insight to be gained from these integrated efforts is that several of the models were already on the right track. Social pressures, personality characteristics, rewards, and genetic predispositions all seem to play a role in substance-related disorders, and in fact to operate together. For example, some people may inherit a malfunction of the biological reward center and so may need special doses of external stimulation—say, intense relationships, an abundance of certain foods, or drugs—to stimulate their reward center. Their behavior in pursuit of external rewards may thus acquire the earmarks of an addictive personality. Such individuals may be especially prone to experimenting with drugs, particularly when their social group makes the drugs available or when they are faced with heightened social and personal stress.

Just as each model has identified important factors in the development of substance-related disorders, each has made important contributions to treatment. As we have seen, the various forms of treatment seem to work best when they are combined with approaches from the other models, making integrated treatment the most productive approach.

These recent developments are encouraging. At the same time, however, enormous and increasing levels of drug use continue. New drugs and drug combinations are discovered almost daily, and with them come new problems, new questions, and needs for new research and new treatments. Perhaps the most valuable lesson is an old one. There is no free lunch. The pleasures derived from these substances come with high psychological and biological costs, some not yet even known.

MISUSE OF INHALANTS

In 1998 more than one-fourth of all eighth-graders and one-third of all tenth-graders in the United States tried to get high by inhaling the fumes of household products (such as colored markers, model glue, or spray paint), despite public warnings about the dangerous—sometimes fatal—effects of this practice (Johnston et al., 1999).

Sexual Disorders and Gender Identity Disorder

HARSH JUDGMENT

Two hundred years ago a Boston ship captain who publicly kissed his wife upon returning from a three-year voyage was made to sit two hours in stocks for the crime of "lewd and unseemly behavior" (Asimov, 1997).

Robert, a 57-year-old man, came to sex therapy with his wife because of his inability to get erections. He had not had a problem with erections until six months earlier, when they attempted to have sex after an evening out, during which he had had several drinks. They attributed his failure to get an erection to his being "a little drunk," but he found himself worrying over the next few days that he was perhaps becoming impotent. When they next attempted intercourse, he found himself unable to get involved in what they were doing because he was so intent on watching himself to see if he would get an erection. Once again he did not, and they were both very upset. His failure to get an erection continued over the next few months. Robert's wife was very upset and . . . frustrated, accusing him of having an affair, or of no longer finding her attractive. Robert wondered if he was getting too old, or if his medication for high blood pressure, which he had been taking for about a year, might be interfering with erection. . . . When they came for sex therapy, they had not attempted any sexual activity for over two months.

(LoPiccolo, 1992, p. 492)

Sexual behavior is a major focus of both our private thoughts and public discussions. Sexual feelings are a crucial part of our development and daily functioning, sexual activity is tied to the satisfaction of our basic needs, and sexual performance is linked to our self-esteem. Most people are fascinated by the abnormal sexual behavior of others and worry about the normality of their own sexuality.

Experts recognize two general categories of sexual disorders: sexual dysfunctions and paraphilias. People with *sexual dysfunctions* experience problems with their sexual responses. Robert, for example, had a dysfunction known as erectile disorder, a repeated failure to attain or maintain an erection during sexual activity. People with *paraphilias* have repeated and intense sexual urges or fantasies in response to objects or situations that society deems inappropriate, and they may behave inappropriately as well. They may be aroused by the thought of sexual activity with a child, for example, or of exposing their genitals to strangers, and they may act on those urges. In addition to the sexual disorders, DSM includes a diagnosis called *gender identity disorder*, a sex-related disorder in which people persistently feel that they have been assigned to the wrong sex and in fact identify with the other gender.

Sexual Dysfunctions

Sexual dysfunctions, disorders in which people cannot respond normally in key areas of sexual functioning, make it difficult or impossible to enjoy sexual intercourse. A large study suggests that as many as 31 percent of men and 43 percent of women in the United States suffer from such a dysfunction during their lives (Laumann et al., 1999, 1994). Sexual dysfunctions are typically very distressing, and they often lead to sexual frustration, guilt, loss of self-esteem, and interpersonal problems. Often these dysfunctions are interrelated, so that many patients with one experience

BOX **13-1**

Lifetime Patterns of Sexual Behavior

Sexual dysfunctions are, by definition, different from the usual patterns of sexual functioning. But in the sexual realm, what is "the usual"? Surprisingly, this question has not received much study until recently. In the mid-1980s, clinicians found their efforts to prevent the spread of AIDS hindered by a lack of available data and began to conduct large surveys on sexual behavior. Collectively, the studies of the past 15 years provide a wealth of useful, sometimes eye-opening information about sexual patterns in the "normal" populations of North America (Bortz, Wallace, & Wiley, 1999; Laumann et al., 1999, 1994; Seidman & Rieder, 1995; Janus & Janus, 1993).

Teenagers

More than 90 percent of boys masturbate by the end of adolescence, compared to 50 percent of girls. For the vast majority of them, masturbation began by age 14. Males report masturbating an average of one to two times a week, females once a month.

Around 20 percent of teenagers have heterosexual intercourse by the age of 15, and 80 percent by age 19. Today's teenagers are having intercourse younger than those of past generations. Most teens who are sexually experienced engage in only one sexual relationship at a time. Over the course of their teen years, however, most have at least two sex partners. Ten percent have five or more partners.

Extended periods without sex are still common, even for teenagers in a relationship. Half of sexually experienced adolescent girls have intercourse once a month or less. Sexually experienced teenage boys spend an average of six months of the year without intercourse.

Condom use by teenagers has increased somewhat during the past decade, partly because of warnings about AIDS. However, at most half of teenagers report having used a condom the last time they had sex. Less than a third of teenagers use condoms consistently and appropriately.

Early Adulthood (Ages 18–24)

More than 80 percent of unmarried young adults have intercourse in a given year. Of those who are sexually active, around a third have intercourse two or three times a month and another third engage in it two or three times a week. Masturbation remains common in young adulthood: close to 60 percent of men masturbate, a third of them at least once a week, and 36 percent of women masturbate, a tenth of them at least once a week.

Early interest *Sexual curiosity and feelings typically begin well before the teenage years. Children may first discover such feelings in unexpected places and may be confused and anxious about them for a while.*

Mid-Adulthood (Ages 25–59)

From the ages of 25 to 59, sexual relationships last longer and are more monogamous. More than 90 percent of people in this age range have sexual intercourse in a given year. Half of the unmarried men have two or more partners in a given year, compared to a quarter of the unmarried women.

Among sexually active adults, close to 60 percent of men have intercourse up to three times a week and around 60 percent of women once or twice a week. Middle-aged adults are still masturbating. Half of all middle-aged men masturbate at least monthly. Half of all women between 25 and 50 masturbate at least monthly, but only a third of those between 51 and 64 do so.

Old Age (Over Age 60)

More and more people stop having intercourse as the years go by—a total of 10 percent in their 40s, 15 percent in their 50s, 30 percent in their 60s, and 45 percent in their 70s. The decline in men's sexual activity usually comes gradually as they advance in age and their health fails. Sexual activity is more likely to drop off sharply for elderly women, commonly because of the death or illness of a partner. Elderly women also seem to lose interest in sex before elderly men do. Half of the women in their 60s report limited sexual interest, compared to fewer than 10 percent of the men.

Among elderly persons who remain sexually active, those in their 60s have intercourse an average of four times a month, those in their 70s two or three times a month. Around 70 percent of elderly men and 50 percent of elderly women continue to have sexual fantasies. Around half of men and a fourth of women continue to masturbate into their 90s.

Clearly sexual interests and behaviors remain an important part of life for large numbers of people, even as they grow older and as their sexual responses change to some degree.

them may reduce sexual desire (Beck, 1995; Rosen & Leiblum, 1995). Most cases of low sexual desire or sexual aversion are caused primarily by sociocultural and psychological factors, but biological conditions can also lower sex drive significantly (Kresin, 1993).

BIOLOGICAL CAUSES A number of hormones interact to produce sexual desire and behavior, and abnormalities in their activity can lower the sex drive (Warnock, Bundren, & Morris, 1997; Rosen & Leiblum, 1995). In both men and women, a high level of the hormone *prolactin,* a low level of the male sex hormone *testosterone,* and either a high or low level of the female sex hormone *estrogen* can lead to low sex drive. Low sex drive has been linked to the high levels of estrogen contained in some birth control pills, for example. Conversely, it has also been tied to the low level of estrogen found in many postmenopausal women or women who have recently given birth. Chronic physical illness can also lower the sex drive (Schiavi et al., 1995; Kresin, 1993). The low drive may be a direct result of the illness or an indirect result due to stress, pain, or depression brought on by the illness.

Sex drive can be lowered by some pain medications, certain psychotropic drugs, and a number of illicit drugs such as cocaine, marijuana, amphetamines, and heroin (Rosen, Lane, & Menza, 1999; Beck, 1995; Segraves, 1995). Low levels of alcohol may enhance the sex drive, by lowering a person's inhibitions, yet high levels will reduce it (Roehrich & Kinder, 1991).

PSYCHOLOGICAL CAUSES A general increase in anxiety or anger may reduce sexual desire in both men and women (Beck & Bozman, 1996; Bozman & Beck, 1991). Frequently, as cognitive theorists have noted, people with hypoactive sexual desire and sexual aversion have particular attitudes, fears, or memories that contribute to their dysfunction, such as a belief that sex is immoral or dangerous (LoPiccolo, 1995) (see Box 13-2). Other people are so afraid of losing control over their sexual urges that they try to resist them completely. And still others fear pregnancy.

A MATTER OF CHOICE

A number of people experience normal sexual interest and arousal but choose, as a matter of lifestyle, not to engage in sexual relations. These individuals would not be diagnosed as having hypoactive sexual desire.

BOX **13-2**

A Kiss Felt 'Round the World

In September 1996, 6-year-old Jonathan Prevette came home from school in Lexington, North Carolina, and admitted to his mother that he was in big trouble. His terrible deed? Not truancy, disrespect for the teacher, or fighting. To his mother's astonishment, the school had charged little Jonathan with *sexual harassment* for kissing another child on the cheek and suspended him for a day. The school later explained that by his kiss he had broken a rule against unwarranted and unwelcome touching of one student by another.

Within a day, Jonathan's photograph appeared in newspapers throughout the nation. People everywhere wondered how a 6-year-old child could be charged with so serious an offense. For his part, Jonathan seemed understandably confused by

his suspension—and more than a little saddened that he had missed an ice cream party at school.

ConsiderThis

⦿ Is a 6-year-old capable of understanding the implications of planting an uninvited kiss on another person?
• When school officials react so powerfully to behaviors that would be considered sexual in an adult, might they unintentionally be teaching the child and other young onlookers that sex is dirty, undesirable, and even dangerous?
• Does misapplying this label to the behavior of a young child trivialize the problem and implications of sexual harassment in the teenage and adult worlds?

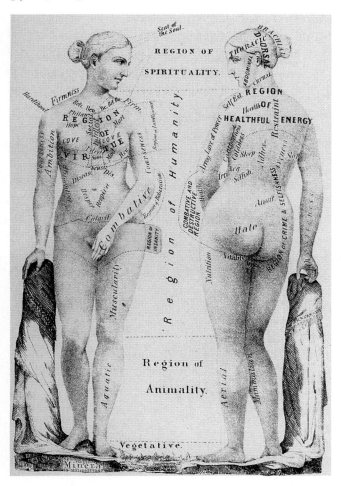

"The region of insanity" *Women of the nineteenth century were expected to experience limited sexual arousal. In fact, medical authorities described "excessive passion" in Victorian women as dangerous and as a possible cause of insanity (Gamwell & Tomes, 1995). This illustration from a nineteenth-century medical textbook even labels a woman's reproductive organs as her "region of insanity" (Buchanan, 1854).*

Certain psychological disorders may also contribute to hypoactive sexual desire and sexual aversion. Even a mild level of depression can interfere with sexual desire, and some people with obsessive-compulsive symptoms find contact with another person's body fluids and odors to be highly unpleasant (LoPiccolo, 1995).

SOCIOCULTURAL CAUSES The attitudes, fears, and psychological disorders that contribute to hypoactive sexual desire and sexual aversion occur within a social context, and thus certain sociocultural factors have also been linked to these dysfunctions. Many sufferers are feeling situational pressures—divorce, a death in the family, job stress, infertility difficulties, having a baby (Burns, 1995; Letourneau & O'Donohue, 1993). Others may be having problems in their relationships (LoPiccolo, 1997; Beck, 1995). People who are in an unhappy relationship, have lost affection for their partner, or feel powerless and dominated by their partner can lose interest in sex. Even in basically happy relationships, if one partner is a very unskilled, unenthusiastic lover, the other can begin to lose interest in sex. And sometimes partners differ in their needs for closeness. The one who needs more personal space may develop hypoactive sexual desire as a way of maintaining the necessary distance (LoPiccolo, 1997, 1995).

Cultural standards can also set the stage for hypoactive sexual desire and sexual aversion. Some men adopt our culture's double standard and thus cannot feel sexual desire for a woman they love and respect. A man may lose sexual interest in his wife when she has their first child, as he cannot think of a mother as a sexually exciting woman. More generally, because our society equates sexual attractiveness with youthfulness, many aging men and women lose interest in sex as their self-image or their attraction to their partner diminishes with age (LoPiccolo, 1995).

The trauma of sexual molestation or assault is especially likely to produce the fears, attitudes, and memories found in these sexual dysfunctions. Sexual aversion is very common in victims of sexual abuse and may persist for years, even decades (Jackson et al., 1990; McCarthy, 1990; Becker, 1989). In extreme cases, individuals may experience vivid flashbacks of the assault during adult sexual activity.

Disorders of Excitement

The **excitement phase** of the sexual response cycle is marked by changes in the pelvic region, general physical arousal, and increases in heart rate, muscle tension, blood pressure, and rate of breathing. In men, blood pools in the pelvis and leads to erection of the penis; in women, this phase produces swelling of the clitoris and labia, as well as lubrication of the vagina. Dysfunctions affecting the excitement phase are *female sexual arousal disorder* (once referred to as *frigidity*) and *male erectile disorder* (once called *impotence*).

FEMALE SEXUAL AROUSAL DISORDER Women with a **sexual arousal disorder** are persistently unable to attain or maintain proper lubrication or genital swelling during sexual activity (see Table 13-2). Understandably, many of them also experience an orgasmic disorder or other sexual dysfunction. In fact, this disorder is rarely diagnosed alone (Segraves & Segraves, 1991). Studies vary widely in their estimates of its prevalence, but most agree that more than 10 percent of women experience it (Laumann et al., 1999, 1994; Rosen et al., 1993). Because lack of sexual arousal in women is so often tied to an orgasmic disorder, researchers usually study and explain the two problems together. Correspondingly, we shall consider the causes of these problems together when we look at female orgasmic disorder.

> **Table 13-2** DSM-IV Checklist
>
> **FEMALE SEXUAL AROUSAL DISORDER**
>
> 1. Persistent or recurrent inability to attain, or to maintain until completion of the sexual activity, adequate lubrication or swelling response of sexual excitement.
> 2. Significant distress or interpersonal difficulty.
>
> **MALE ERECTILE DISORDER**
>
> 1. Persistent or recurrent inability to attain, or to maintain until completion of the sexual activity, an adequate erection.
> 2. Significant distress or interpersonal difficulty.
>
> *Based on APA, 2000, 1994.*

MALE ERECTILE DISORDER Men with **erectile disorder** persistently fail to attain or maintain an adequate erection during sexual activity (see again Table 13-2). This problem occurs in about 10 percent of the general male population, including Robert, the man whose difficulties opened this chapter (APA, 2000; Laumann et al., 1999). Carlos Domera also has erectile disorder:

> Carlos Domera is a 30-year-old dress manufacturer who came to the United States from Argentina at age 22. He is married to an American woman, Phyllis, also age 30. They have no children. Mr. Domera's problem was that he had been unable to have sexual intercourse for over a year due to his inability to achieve or maintain an erection. He had avoided all sexual contact with his wife for the prior five months, except for two brief attempts at lovemaking which ended when he failed to maintain his erection.
>
> The couple separated a month ago by mutual agreeement due to the tension that surrounded their sexual problem and their inability to feel comfortable with each other. Both professed love and concern for the other, but had serious doubts regarding their ability to resolve the sexual problem. . . .
>
> Mr. Domera conformed to the stereotype of the "macho Latin lover," believing that he "should always have erections easily and be able to make love at any time." Since he couldn't "perform" sexually, he felt humiliated and inadequate, and he dealt with this by avoiding not only sex, but any expression of affection for his wife.
>
> Ms. Domera felt "he is not trying; perhaps he doesn't love me, and I can't live with no sex, no affection, and his bad moods." She had requested the separation temporarily, and he readily agreed. However, they had recently been seeing each other twice a week. . . .
>
> During the evaluation he reported that the onset of his erectile difficulties was concurrent with a tense period in his business. After several "failures" to complete intercourse, he concluded he was "useless as a husband" and therefore a "total failure." The anxiety of attempting lovemaking was too much for him to deal with.
>
> He reluctantly admitted that he was occasionally able to masturbate alone to a full, firm erection and reach a satisfying orgasm. However, he felt ashamed and guilty about this, from both childhood masturbatory guilt and a feeling that he was "cheating" his wife. It was also noted that he had occasional firm erections upon awakening in the morning. Other than the antidepressant, the patient was taking no drugs, and he was not using much alcohol. There was no evidence of physical illness.
>
> *(Spitzer et al., 1983, pp. 105–106)*

"Erection is chiefly caused by scuraum, eringoes, cresses, crymon, parsnips, artichokes, turnips, asparagus, candied ginger, acorns bruised to powder and drank in muscadel, scallion, sea shell fish, etc."

Aristotle, *The Masterpiece,*
4th century B.C.

EXCITEMENT PHASE The phase of the sexual response cycle marked by changes in the pelvic region, general physical arousal, and increases in heart rate, muscle tension, blood pressure, and rate of breathing.

FEMALE SEXUAL AROUSAL DISORDER A female dysfunction marked by a persistent inability to attain sexual excitement, including adequate lubrication or genital swelling, during sexual activity.

MALE ERECTILE DISORDER A dysfunction in which a man repeatedly fails to attain or maintain an erection during sexual activity.

NOCTURNAL PENILE TUMESCENCE (NPT)
Erection during sleep.

PERFORMANCE ANXIETY The fear of performing inadequately and a related tension experienced during sex.

SPECTATOR ROLE A state of mind that some people experience during sex, focusing on their sexual performance to such an extent that their performance and their enjoyment are reduced.

ORGASM PHASE The phase of the sexual response cycle during which an individual's sexual pleasure peaks and sexual tension is released as muscles in the pelvic region contract rhythmically.

PREMATURE EJACULATION A dysfunction in which a man reaches orgasm and ejaculates before, on, or shortly after penetration and before he wishes to.

Unlike Mr. Domera, most men with an erectile disorder are over the age of 50, largely because so many cases are associated with ailments or diseases of older adults (Seidman & Rieder, 1995; Bancroft, 1989). The disorder is experienced by 5 to 9 percent of all men who are 40 years old and increases to at least 15 percent at age 60 (Laumann et al., 1999; Feldman et al., 1994). Moreover, according to surveys, half of all adult men experience erectile difficulty during intercourse at least some of the time (Feldman et al., 1994). Erectile dysfunction accounts for more than 400,000 visits to physicians and more than 30,000 hospital admissions in the United States each year (Ackerman & Carey, 1995).

Most cases of erectile disorder result from an interaction of biological, psychological, and sociocultural processes. Even minor physical impairment of the erection response may make a man vulnerable to the effects of psychosocial factors (Ackerman & Carey, 1995; Rosen et al., 1994). One study found that only ten of sixty-three cases of this disorder were caused by purely psychosocial factors, and only five were the result of physical impairment alone (LoPiccolo, 1991).

BIOLOGICAL CAUSES The same hormonal imbalances that can cause hypoactive sexual desire can also produce erectile disorder (Morales et al., 1991). More commonly, however, vascular problems—problems with the body's blood vessels—are the initiating factor (Althof & Seftel, 1995; Carey et al., 1993). An erection occurs when the chambers in the penis fill with blood, so any condition that reduces blood flow into the penis, such as heart disease or clogging of the arteries, may start the process that ultimately leads to the disorder (LoPiccolo, 1997; Feldman et al., 1994). It can also be caused by damage to the nervous system as a result of diabetes, spinal cord injuries, multiple sclerosis, kidney failure, or treatment with an artificial kidney machine (Newton, 1999; Leiblum & Segraves, 1995). In addition, as with hypoactive sexual desire, the use of certain medications and various forms of substance abuse, from alcohol abuse to cigarette smoking, may interfere with erections (Keene & Davies, 1999; Segraves, 1998).

Medical procedures, including ultrasound recordings and blood tests, have been developed for diagnosing biological causes of erectile disorder (Ackerman & Carey, 1995). Measuring **nocturnal penile tumescence (NPT)**, or erections during sleep, is particularly useful in assessing whether physical factors are responsible (Althof & Seftel, 1995; Schiavi et al., 1993). Men typically have erections during rapid eye movement (REM) sleep, the phase of sleep in which dreaming takes place. A healthy man is likely to have two to five REM periods each night, and perhaps two to three hours of penile erections (see Figure 13-3). Abnormal or absent nightly erections usually (but not always) indicate some physical basis for erectile failure (Mohr & Beutler, 1990). As a rough screening device, a patient may be instructed to fasten a simple "snap gauge" band around his penis before going to sleep and then check it the next morning. A broken band indicates that penile erection has occurred during the night. An unbroken band indicates a lack of nighttime erections and suggests that the person's general erectile problem may have a physical basis (Mohr & Beutler, 1990).

Psychological or organic? *The snap gauge, worn around the penis at night, is a fabric band with three plastic filaments. If the filaments are broken in the morning, the man knows that he has experienced normal erections during REM sleep and that erectile failures during intercourse are probably due to psychological factors.*

PSYCHOLOGICAL CAUSES Any of the psychological causes of hypoactive sexual desire can also interfere with arousal and lead to erectile disorder. As many as 90 percent of all men with severe depression, for example, experience some degree of erectile dysfunction (Leiblum & Segraves, 1995).

One well-supported psychological explanation for erectile disorder is a cognitive theory developed by William Masters and Virginia Johnson (1970). The explanation emphasizes **performance anxiety** and the **spectator role**. Once a man begins to experience erectile problems, for whatever reason, he becomes fearful about failing to have an erection and worries during each sexual encounter. Instead of relaxing and enjoying the sensations of sexual pleasure, he remains distanced from the activity, watching himself and focusing on the goal of reaching erection. Instead of being an aroused participant, he becomes a judge and spectator. Whatever the initial reason for the erectile dysfunction, the resulting spectator role becomes the reason for the ongoing problem. In this vicious cycle, the original cause of the erectile failure becomes less important than fear of failure.

SOCIOCULTURAL CAUSES Each of the sociocultural factors that contribute to hypoactive sexual desire has also been tied to erectile disorder. Men who have lost their jobs and are under financial stress, for example, are more likely to develop erectile difficulties than other men (Morokoff & Gillilland, 1993). Marital stress, too, has been tied to this dysfunction. Two relationship patterns in particular may contribute to it (LoPiccolo, 1991). In one, the wife provides too little physical stimulation for her aging husband, who, because of normal aging changes, now requires more intense, direct, and lengthy physical stimulation of the penis for erection to occur. In the second relationship pattern, a couple believes that only intercourse can give the wife an orgasm. This idea increases the pressure on the man to have an erection and makes him more vulnerable to erectile dysfunction. If the wife reaches orgasm manually or orally during their sexual encounter, his pressure to perform is reduced.

Disorders of Orgasm

During the **orgasm phase** of the sexual response cycle, an individual's sexual pleasure peaks and sexual tension is released as the muscles in the pelvic region contract, or draw together, rhythmically (see Figure 13-4 on the next page). The man's semen is ejaculated, and the outer third of the woman's vaginal wall contracts. Dysfunctions of this phase of the sexual response cycle are *premature ejaculation, male orgasmic disorder,* and *female orgasmic disorder.*

PREMATURE EJACULATION Eddie is typical of many men in his experience of premature ejaculation:

> Eddie, a 20-year-old student, sought treatment after his girlfriend ended their relationship because his premature ejaculation left her sexually frustrated. Eddie had had only one previous sexual relationship, during his senior year in high school. With two friends he would drive to a neighboring town and find a certain prostitute. After picking her up, they would drive to a deserted area and take turns having sex with her, while the others waited outside the car. Both the prostitute and his friends urged him to hurry up because they feared discovery by the police, and besides, in the winter it was cold. When Eddie began his sexual relationship with his girlfriend, his entire sexual history consisted of this rapid intercourse, with virtually no foreplay. He found caressing his girlfriend's breasts and genitals and her touching of his penis to be so arousing that he sometimes ejaculated before complete entry of the penis, or after at most only a minute or so of intercourse.
>
> *(LoPiccolo, 1995, p. 495)*

A man suffering from **premature ejaculation** persistently reaches orgasm and ejaculates with very little sexual stimulation before, on, or shortly after penetration, and before he wishes to (see Table 13-3 on the next page). Around

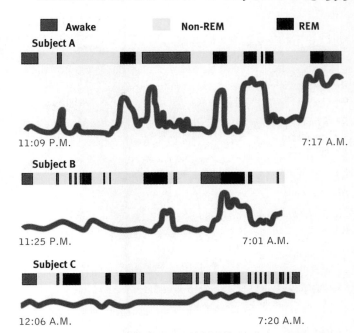

FIGURE 13-3 Measurements of erections during sleep *Subject A, a man without erectile problems, has normal erections during REM sleep. Subject B has erectile problems that seem to be at least partly psychogenic—otherwise he would not have any erections during REM sleep. Subject C's erectile disorder is related to organic problems, an interpretation supported by his lack of erections during REM sleep. (Adapted from Bancroft, 1985.)*

SEXUAL DURATION

In an extensive survey of people in the United States, respondents estimated that their average sexual experience lasts 39 minutes, including foreplay (Kanner, 1995).

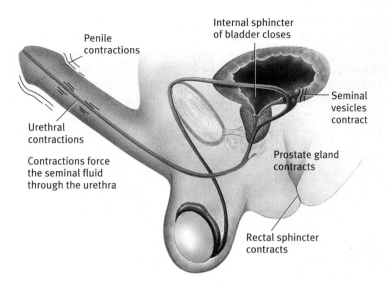

FIGURE 13-4 Normal male sexual anatomy *Changes in the male anatomy occur during the different phases of the sexual response cycle. (Adapted from Hyde, 1990, p. 199.)*

27 percent of men in the United States experience premature ejaculation at some time (Laumann et al., 1999, 1994; St. Lawrence & Madakasira, 1992). The typical duration of intercourse in our society has increased over the past several decades, in turn increasing the distress of men who suffer from premature ejaculation, typically men under the age of 30 (Bancroft, 1989).

Psychological, particularly behavioral, explanations of premature ejaculation have received more research support than other kinds of explanations. The dysfunction seems to be typical of young, sexually inexperienced men such as Eddie, who simply have not learned to slow down, control their arousal, and extend the pleasurable process of making love. In fact, premature ejaculation is very common when a young man has his first sexual encounter. With continued sexual experience, most men acquire greater control over their sexual responses. Men of any age who have sex only occasionally are also prone to ejaculate prematurely (LoPiccolo, 1985).

Clinicians have also suggested that premature ejaculation may be related to anxiety, hurried masturbation experiences during adolescence (in fear of being "caught" by parents), or poor recognition of one's own sexual arousal. However, these theories have only sometimes received clear research support (Dunn, Croft, & Hackette, 1999; Strassberg et al., 1990, 1987).

MALE ORGASMIC DISORDER A man with **male orgasmic disorder** repeatedly cannot reach orgasm or experiences long delays in reaching orgasm after normal sexual excitement (see again Table 13-3). The disorder occurs in 10 percent of the male population (APA, 2000; Laumann et al., 1999) and is typically a source of great frustration and upset, as in the case of John:

> John, a 38-year-old sales representative, had been married for 9 years. At the insistence of his 32-year-old wife, the couple sought counseling for their sexual problem— his inability to ejaculate during intercourse. During the early years of the marriage, his wife had experienced dif-

Table 13-3 DSM-IV Checklist

PREMATURE EJACULATION

1. Persistent or recurrent ejaculation with minimal sexual stimulation before, on, or shortly after penetration and before the person wishes it.
2. Significant distress or interpersonal difficulty.

MALE ORGASMIC DISORDER

1. Persistent or recurrent delay in, or absence of, orgasm following a normal sexual excitement phase during sexual activity.
2. Significant distress or interpersonal difficulty.

FEMALE ORGASMIC DISORDER

1. Persistent or recurrent delay in, or absence of, orgasm following a normal sexual excitement phase during sexual activity.
2. Significant distress or interpersonal difficulty.

Based on APA, 2000, 1994.

ficulty reaching orgasm until he learned to delay his ejaculation for a long period of time. To do this, he used mental distraction techniques and regularly smoked marijuana before making love. Initially, John felt very satisfied that he could make love for longer and longer periods of time without ejaculation and regarded his ability as a sign of masculinity.

About 3 years prior to seeking counseling, after the birth of their only child, John found that he was losing his erection before he was able to ejaculate. His wife suggested different intercourse positions, but the harder he tried, the more difficulty he had in reaching orgasm. Because of his frustration, the couple began to avoid sex altogether. John experienced increasing performance anxiety with each successive failure, and an increasing sense of helplessness in the face of his problem.

(Rosen & Rosen, 1981, pp. 317–318)

A low testosterone level, certain neurological diseases, and some head or spinal cord injuries can interfere with ejaculation (LoPiccolo, 1997, 1995, 1985). Drugs that slow down the sympathetic nervous system (such as alcohol, some medications for high blood pressure, certain antidepressants, and many antianxiety and antipsychotic medications) can also affect ejaculation (Segraves, 1998, 1995, 1993; LoPiccolo, 1997). For example, the antidepressant *fluoxetine,* or Prozac, appears to interfere with ejaculation in 15 to 25 percent of men who take it (Hirschfeld, 1999; Rosen et al., 1999; Buffum, 1992).

A leading psychological cause of male orgasmic disorder appears to be performance anxiety and the spectator role, the cognitive factors also involved in male erectile disorder. Once a man begins to focus on reaching orgasm, he may stop being an aroused participant in his sexual activity and instead become an unaroused, self-critical, and fearful observer (LoPiccolo, 1995). Finally, male orgasmic disorder may develop out of hypoactive sexual desire (Rosen & Leiblum, 1995; LoPiccolo & Friedman, 1988). A man who engages in sex primarily because of pressure from his partner, without any real desire for it, simply may not get aroused enough to reach orgasm.

FEMALE ORGASMIC DISORDER Stephanie and Bill, married for three years, came for sex therapy because of her total lack of orgasm.

Stephanie had never had an orgasm in any way, but because of Bill's concern, she had been faking orgasm during intercourse until recently. Finally she told him the truth, and they sought therapy together. Stephanie had been raised by a strictly religious family. She could not recall ever seeing her parents kiss or show physical affection for each other. She was severely punished on one occasion when her mother found her looking at her own genitals, at about age 7. Stephanie received no sex education from her parents, and when she began to menstruate, her mother told her only that this meant that she could become pregnant, so she mustn't ever kiss a boy or let a boy touch her. Her mother restricted her dating severely, with repeated warnings that "boys only want one thing." While her parents were rather critical and demanding of her (asking her why she got one B among otherwise straight A's on her report card, for example), they were loving parents and their approval was very important to her.

(LoPiccolo, 1995, p. 496)

Women with **female orgasmic disorder** rarely reach orgasm or generally experience a very delayed one (see again Table 13-3). Around 25 percent of women apparently have this problem—including more than a third of postmenopausal women (Laumann et al., 1999, 1994; Rosen & Leiblum, 1995). Studies indicate that 10 percent or more of women today have never had an orgasm, either alone

ConsiderThis

● Some theorists cite performance anxiety and the spectator role as contributing factors in certain sexual dysfunctions. Are there other important areas of dysfunction in life that might also be explained by performance anxiety and the spectator role?

MALE ORGASMIC DISORDER A male dysfunction characterized by a repeated inability to reach orgasm or long delays in reaching orgasm after normal sexual excitement.

FEMALE ORGASMIC DISORDER A dysfunction in which a woman rarely has an orgasm or repeatedly experiences a very delayed one.

VAGINISMUS A condition marked by involuntary contractions of the muscles around the outer third of the vagina, preventing entry of the penis.

NIGHTLY VISITS

Orgasms can sometimes occur during sleep. Ancient Babylonians said that such nocturnal orgasms were caused by a "maid of the night" who visited men in their sleep and a "little night man" who visited women (Kahn & Fawcett, 1993).

"When [masturbation] is discovered, it must in young children be put a stop to by such means as tying the hands, strapping the knees together with a pad between them, or some mechanical plan."

*From Cradle to School, a Book
for Mothers, 1902*

or during intercourse, and at least another 10 percent rarely have orgasms (LoPiccolo, 1995). At the same time, half of all women experience orgasm in intercourse at least fairly regularly (LoPiccolo & Stock, 1987). Women who are more sexually assertive (Hurlbert, 1991) and more comfortable with masturbation (Kelly, Stressberg, & Kircher, 1990) tend to have orgasms more regularly. Female orgasmic disorder appears to be more common among single women than among women who are married or cohabiting (Laumann et al., 1999, 1994).

Most clinicians agree that orgasm during intercourse is not a criterion of normal sexual functioning. Many women instead reach orgasm with their partners by direct stimulation of the clitoris (LoPiccolo, 1995). Although early psychoanalytic theory considered a lack of orgasm during intercourse to be pathological, evidence suggests that women who rely on stimulation of the clitoris for orgasm are entirely normal and healthy (Stock, 1993).

As we observed earlier, female orgasmic disorder typically is linked to female sexual arousal disorder, and the two tend to be studied, explained, and treated together (APA, 1995). Once again, biological, psychological, and sociocultural factors may combine to produce these disorders.

BIOLOGICAL CAUSES A variety of physiological conditions can affect a woman's arousal and orgasm. Diabetes can damage the nervous system in ways that interfere with arousal, lubrication of the vagina, and orgasm. Lack of orgasm has sometimes been linked to multiple sclerosis and other neurological diseases, to the same drugs and medications that interfere with ejaculation in men, and to postmenopausal changes in skin sensitivity and in the structure of the clitoris and of the vaginal walls (LoPiccolo, 1997; Segraves, 1995; Morokoff, 1993, 1988).

PSYCHOLOGICAL CAUSES The psychological causes of hypoactive sexual desire and sexual aversion may also lead to the female arousal and orgasmic disorders. In addition, as psychodynamic theorists might predict, memories of childhood traumas and relationships have sometimes been associated with these disorders. In one large study, memories of an unhappy childhood or loss of a parent during childhood were tied to lack of orgasm in adulthood (Raboch & Raboch, 1992). In another, childhood memories of a positive relationship with one's mother, affection between the parents, the mother's positive personality, and the mother's expression of positive emotions were all predictors of orgasm (Heiman et al., 1986).

SOCIOCULTURAL CAUSES For years many clinicians have believed that female arousal and orgasmic disorders may result from society's recurrent message to women that they should repress and deny their sexuality. And, in fact, many women with these problems report that they had a strict religious upbringing, were punished for childhood masturbation, received no preparation for the onset of menstruation, were restricted in their dating as teenagers, and were told that "nice girls don't" (LoPiccolo, 1997; Masters & Johnson, 1970).

A sexually restrictive history, however, is just as common among women who function well in sexual encounters (LoPiccolo, 1997; LoPiccolo & Stock, 1987). In addition, cultural messages about female sexuality have been more positive in recent years (see Figure 13-5), while the rate of female arousal and orgasmic disorders remains the same. Why, then, do some women and not others develop sexual arousal and orgasmic dysfunctions? Researchers suggest that unusually stressful events, traumas, or relationships may help produce the fears, memories, and attitudes that often characterize these dysfunctions. For example, more than half of women molested as children or raped as adults have arousal and orgasm dysfunctions (Browne & Finklehor, 1986).

Research has also related orgasmic behavior to certain qualities in a woman's intimate relationships. One study found that the likelihood of reaching orgasm was tied to how much emotional involvement each subject had during her first

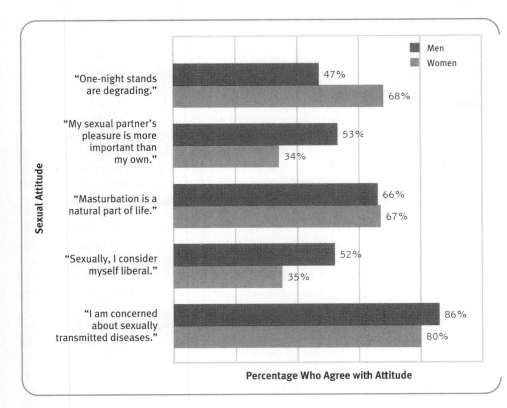

Percentage Who Agree with Attitude

FIGURE 13-5 **Sexual attitudes and gender** *According to surveys, women are more likely than men to consider "one-night stands" degrading, whereas, contrary to stereotypes, men are more likely than women to say that their sex partner's pleasure is more important than their own. (Adapted from Janus & Janus, 1993.)*

experience of intercourse and how long that relationship lasted, the pleasure the woman obtained during the experience, her current attraction to her partner's body, and her marital happiness (Heiman et al., 1986). Interestingly, the same study found that erotic fantasies during sex with their current partner were much more common in orgasmic than in nonorgasmic women.

Disorders of Sexual Pain

There are two sexual dysfunctions that do not fit neatly into a specific phase of the sexual response cycle. These are the sexual pain disorders, *vaginismus* and *dyspareunia,* each marked by enormous physical discomfort when sexual activity is attempted.

VAGINISMUS In **vaginismus**, involuntary contractions of the muscles around the outer third of the vagina prevent entry of the penis (see Table 13-4). Severe cases can prevent a couple from ever having intercourse. Women with severe cases typically avoid gynecological examinations, too (Rosen & Leiblum, 1993). Perhaps 20 percent of women occasionally experience pain during intercourse, but vaginismus probably occurs in less than 1 percent of all women (LoPiccolo, 1995).

Most clinicians agree with the cognitive-behavioral position that vaginismus is usually a conditioned fear response, set off by a woman's anticipation that intercourse will be painful and damaging. A variety of factors apparently can set the stage for this fear, including anxiety and ignorance about intercourse, exaggerated stories about how painful and bloody the first occasion of intercourse is for women, trauma caused by an unskilled lover who forces his penis into the vagina before the woman is aroused and lubricated, and, of course, the

Table 13-4 DSM-IV Checklist

VAGINISMUS

1. Recurrent or persistent involuntary spasm of the muscles of the outer third of the vagina that interferes with sexual intercourse.
2. Significant distress or interpersonal difficulty.

DYSPAREUNIA

1. Recurrent or persistent genital pain associated with sexual intercourse in either a male or female.
2. Significant distress or interpersonal difficulty.

Based on APA, 2000, 1994.

Rite of passage *A teenage girl in the Samburu highlands of Kenya has her genitals (clitoris and labia) cut so that she may be admitted into the society of mature women. Educated women across Africa are increasingly condemning this tradition, practiced by ethnic groups in 28 countries throughout the continent (Dugger, 1996). They argue that circumcision can lead to various sexual dysfunctions, deprives women of sexual pleasure, and also may create medical problems during childbirth.*

LATIN ORIGIN

"Coitus," a term for sexual intercourse, comes from the Latin *coire*, meaning "to go together."

UNEQUAL DISTRIBUTION

Sex is not distributed equally across the population of the United States. Half of all sexual activity is engaged in by 15 percent of adults (General Social Survey, 1998).

trauma of childhood sexual abuse or adult rape (Reissing, Binik, & Khalife, 1999; LoPiccolo, 1995).

Some women experience painful intercourse because of an infection of the vagina or urinary tract, a gynecological disease such as herpes simplex, or the physical effects of menopause. It may lead to their developing what is sometimes called "rational" vaginismus, in which the insertion of the penis will indeed cause them problems unless they receive medical treatment for these conditions (LoPiccolo, 1995). Most women who have vaginismus also have other sexual dysfunctions. Some, however, enjoy sex greatly, have a strong sex drive, and reach orgasm with stimulation of the clitoris. They just fear penetration of the vagina.

DYSPAREUNIA A person with **dyspareunia** (from Latin words meaning "painful mating") experiences severe pain in the genitals during sexual activity (see again Table 13-4). Surveys suggest that 15 percent of women and 3 percent of men suffer from this problem to some degree (APA, 2000; Laumann et al., 1999). Sufferers typically enjoy sex and get aroused but find their sex lives very limited by the pain that accompanies what used to be a positive event.

Dyspareunia in women usually has a physical cause (LoPiccolo, 1995; Steege & Ling, 1993). Among the most common are injury to the vagina, cervix, uterus, or pelvic ligaments during childbirth (Barrett et al., 1999). Similarly, the scar left by an episiotomy (a cut often made to enlarge the vaginal entrance and ease delivery) can cause pain. Dyspareunia has also been tied to collision of the penis with remaining parts of the hymen; infection of the vagina; wiry pubic hair that rubs against the labia during intercourse; pelvic diseases; tumors; cysts; and allergic reactions to the chemicals in vaginal douches and contraceptive creams, the rubber in condoms or diaphragms, or the protein in semen (LoPiccolo & Stock, 1987).

Although relationship problems or the psychological aftereffects of sexual abuse may contribute to this disorder, psychosocial factors alone are rarely responsible for it (LoPiccolo, 1995; LoPiccolo & Stock, 1987). In cases that are truly psychogenic, the woman is in fact likely to be suffering from hypoactive sexual desire (Steege & Ling, 1993). That is, penetration into an unaroused, unlubricated vagina is painful.

Treatments for Sexual Dysfunctions

The last 30 years have brought major changes in the treatment of sexual dysfunctions. For the first half of the twentieth century, the leading approach was long-term psychodynamic therapy. Clinicians assumed that sexual dysfunctioning was caused by failure to progress properly through the psychosexual stages of development, and they used techniques of free association and therapist interpretations to help clients gain insight about themselves and their problems. Although it was expected that broad personality changes would lead to improvement in sexual functioning, psychodynamic therapy was typically unsuccessful (Bergler, 1951).

In the 1950s and 1960s, behavioral therapists offered new treatments for sexual dysfunctions. Usually they tried to reduce the fears that they believed were causing the dysfunctions, by applying such procedures as relaxation training and systematic desensitization (Lazarus, 1965; Wolpe, 1958). These approaches had some success, but they failed to work in cases where the fundamental problems included misinformation, negative attitudes, and lack of effective sexual technique (LoPiccolo, 1995).

A revolution in the treatment of sexual dysfunctions occurred with the publication of William Masters and Virginia Johnson's landmark book *Human Sexual Inadequacy* in 1970. The *sex therapy* program they introduced has evolved into a complex approach, which now includes techniques from the various explanatory models, particularly cognitive, behavioral, couple, and family systems therapies (LoPiccolo, 1997).

WHAT ARE THE GENERAL FEATURES OF SEX THERAPY? Modern sex therapy is short-term and instructive, typically lasting 15 to 20 sessions. As the sex therapist and researcher Joseph LoPiccolo (1997, 1995) has explained, it centers on specific sexual problems rather than on broad personality issues. Carlos Domera, the Argentine man with an erectile disorder whom we met earlier, responded successfully to the multiple techniques of modern sex therapy:

> At the end of the evaluation session the psychiatrist reassured the couple that Mr. Domera had a "reversible psychological" sexual problem that was due to several factors, including his depression, but also more currently his anxiety and embarrassment, his high standards, and some cultural and relationship difficulties that made communication awkward and relaxation nearly impossible. The couple was advised that a brief trial of therapy, focused directly on the sexual problem, would very likely produce significant improvement within ten to fourteen sessions. They were assured that the problem was almost certainly not physical in origin, but rather psychogenic, and that therefore the prognosis was excellent.
>
> Mr. Domera was shocked and skeptical, but the couple agreed to commence the therapy on a weekly basis, and they were given a typical first "assignment" to do at home: a caressing massage exercise to try together with specific instructions not to attempt genital stimulation or intercourse at all, even if an erection might occur.
>
> Not surprisingly, during the second session Mr. Domera reported with a cautious smile that they had "cheated" and had had intercourse "against the rules." This was their first successful intercourse in more than a year. Their success and happiness were acknowledged by the therapist, but they were cautioned strongly that rapid initial improvement often occurs, only to be followed by increased performance anxiety in subsequent weeks and a return of the initial problem. They were humorously chastised and encouraged to try again to have sexual contact involving caressing and non-demand light genital stimulation, without an expectation of erection or orgasm, and to avoid intercourse.
>
> During the second and fourth weeks Mr. Domera did not achieve erections during the love play, and the therapy sessions dealt with helping him to accept himself with or without erections and to learn to enjoy sensual contact without intercourse. His wife helped him to believe genuinely that he could please her with manual or oral stimulation and that, although she enjoyed intercourse, she enjoyed these other stimulations as much, as long as he was relaxed.
>
> Mr. Domera struggled with his cultural image of what a "man" does, but he had to admit that his wife seemed pleased and that he, too, was enjoying the nonintercourse caressing techniques. He was encouraged to view his new lovemaking skills as a "success" and to recognize that in many ways he was becoming a better lover than many husbands, because he was listening to his wife and responding to her requests.
>
> By the fifth week the patient was attempting intercourse successfully with relaxed confidence, and by the ninth session he was responding regularly with erections. If they both agreed, they would either have intercourse or choose another sexual technique to achieve orgasm. Treatment was terminated after ten sessions....
>
> *(Spitzer et al., 1983, pp. 106–107)*

As Mr. Domera's treatment indicates, modern sex therapy includes a variety of principles and techniques. The following ones are applied in almost all cases, regardless of the dysfunction:

1. ***Assessment and conceptualization of the problem.*** Patients are initially given a medical examination and are interviewed concerning their "sex history" (Warren & Sampson, 1995) (see Figure 13-6 on the next page).

SEEKING TREATMENT

The single largest group of men who enter sex therapy consists of those with erectile difficulties (Spector & Carey, 1990).

ACCIDENTAL DISCOVERY

Viagra, the enormously popular drug for erectile problems, was discovered by accident. Testing it as a possible heart medication, researchers found that the drug increased blood flow to subjects' penises more effectively than to their hearts (Handy, 1998).

DYSPAREUNIA A disorder in which a person experiences severe pain in the genitals during sexual activity.

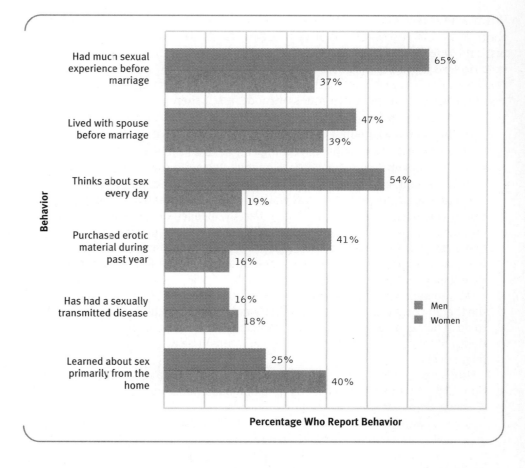

FIGURE 13-6   **Sexual behavior and gender**
According to questionnaires, men are much more likely than women to think about sex on a daily basis and to have purchased sexual material, such as erotic magazines, within the past year. Women are more likely to have learned about sex from the home. (Adapted from Michael et al., 1994; Janus & Janus, 1993.)

The therapist's focus during the interview is on gathering information about past life events and, in particular, current factors that are contributing to the dysfunction. In some cases, the client's partner is also interviewed (Ackerman & Carey, 1995). Various assessment tests may be given (Beck, 1995; Craig, Cannon, & Olson, 1995). Sometimes, proper assessment requires a team of specialists, perhaps including a psychologist, urologist, and neurologist.

2. ***Mutual responsibility.*** Therapists stress the principle of *mutual responsibility.* Both partners in the relationship share the sexual problem, regardless of who has the actual dysfunction, and treatment will be more successful when both are in therapy (Heiman et al., 1981).

3. ***Education about sexuality.*** Many patients who suffer from sexual dysfunctions know very little about the physiology and techniques of sexual activity. Thus sex therapists may discuss these topics and offer educational materials, including instructional books and videotapes.

4. ***Attitude change.*** Therapists help patients examine and change the beliefs about sexuality that are preventing sexual arousal and pleasure (Rosen, Leiblum, & Spector, 1994). Some of these mistaken beliefs are widely shared in our society (see Box 13-3 on page 405).

5. ***Elimination of performance anxiety and the spectator role.*** Therapists often teach couples *sensate focus,* or *nondemand pleasuring,* a series of sensual tasks, sometimes called "petting" exercises, in which the partners focus on the sexual pleasure that can be achieved by exploring and caressing each other's bodies at home, without demands to have intercourse or reach orgasm—demands that may be interfering with arousal. Couples are told at first to refrain from intercourse at home and to restrict their sexual activity to kissing, hugging, and sensual massage of

---

EYES OF THE BEHOLDER

In the movie *Annie Hall,* Annie's psychotherapist asks her how often she and her boyfriend, Alvie Singer, sleep together. Simultaneously, across town, Alvie's therapist asks him the same question. Alvie answers, "Hardly ever, maybe three times a week," while Annie responds, "Constantly, I'd say three times a week."

various parts of the body, but not of the breasts or genitals. Over time, they learn how to give and receive greater sexual pleasure and they build back up to the activity of sexual intercourse.

6. ***Increasing sexual communication skills.*** Couples are told to use their sensate-focus sessions at home to try sexual positions in which the person being caressed can guide the other's hands and control the speed, pressure, and location of the caressing. Couples are also taught to give instructions in a nonthreatening, informative manner ("It feels better over here, with a little less pressure"), rather than a threatening uninformative manner ("The way you're touching me doesn't turn me on").

7. ***Changing destructive lifestyles and marital interactions.*** A therapist may encourage a couple to change their lifestyle or take other steps to improve a situation that is having a destructive effect on their relationship—to distance themselves from interfering in-laws, for example, or to change or even quit a job that is too demanding. Similarly, if the couple's general relationship is marked by conflict, the therapist will try to help them improve it.

8. ***Addressing physical and medical factors.*** When sexual dysfunctions are caused by a medical problem, such as disease, injury, medication, or substance abuse, therapists try to address that problem. If antidepressant medications are causing a man's erectile disorder, for example, the clinician may reduce the dosage of the medication, change the time of day when the drug is taken, or prescribe a different antidepressant.

(Segraves, 1998, 1995; Shrivastava et al., 1995)

WHAT TECHNIQUES ARE APPLIED TO PARTICULAR DYSFUNCTIONS? In addition to the more or less universal components of sex therapy, specific techniques can help in each of the sexual dysfunctions.

HYPOACTIVE SEXUAL DESIRE AND SEXUAL AVERSION Hypoactive sexual desire and sexual aversion are among the most difficult dysfunctions to treat because of the many issues that may feed into them (LoPiccolo, 1997, 1995; Rosen & Leiblum, 1995). Thus therapists typically apply a combination of techniques (LoPiccolo & Friedman, 1988). In a technique called *affectual awareness*, patients visualize sexual scenes in order to discover any feelings of anxiety, vulnerability, and other negative emotions they may have concerning sex. In another technique, patients receive cognitive *self-instruction training* to help them change their negative

"If [a woman]... is normally developed mentally and well-bred, her sexual desire is small. If this were not so, the whole world would become a brothel and marriage and a family impossible."

Health and Longevity, 1909

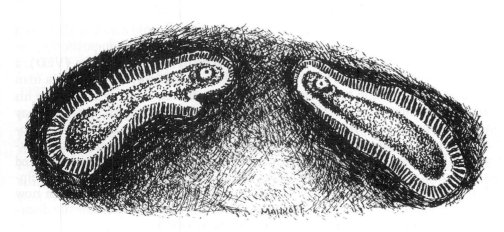

"You're wasting your time. I'm asexual."

DIRECTED MASTURBATION TRAINING A sex therapy approach that teaches women with female arousal or orgasmic disorders how to masturbate effectively and eventually to reach orgasm during sexual interactions.

"[Masturbation] produces seminal weakness, impotence, dysury, tabes dorsalis, pulmonary consumption, dyspepsia, dimness of sight, vertigo, epilepsy, hypochondriasis, loss of memory, manalgia, fatuity, and death."

Benjamin Rush, "the father of American psychiatry," 1812

A new message *Over the past several decades, Western society has increasingly viewed female sexual arousal and expression as normal and healthful and has sent this message to women through novels, movies, television shows, and magazines. This Diet Coke ad in which two women openly ogle a sexy construction worker was one of the most discussed television commercials of the 1990s.*

Some clinicians treat premature ejaculation with *fluoxetine* (Prozac) and other serotonin-enhancing antidepressant drugs. Because these drugs often reduce sexual arousal or orgasm, the reasoning goes, they may be helpful to men who experience premature ejaculation. Although some studies have reported positive results (Althof, 1995; Althof et al., 1994), researchers have yet to examine the long-term impact of these drugs on men with premature ejaculation. Nor have they determined whether such drugs may be combined effectively with psychological and interpersonal techniques (Rosen & Leiblum, 1995).

FEMALE AROUSAL AND ORGASMIC DISORDERS Specific treatment techniques for female arousal and orgasmic dysfunctions include self-exploration, enhancement of body awareness, and directed masturbation training (LoPiccolo, 1997; Heiman & LoPiccolo, 1988). These procedures are especially useful for women who have never had an orgasm under any circumstances. Hormone therapy is also being used increasingly (Warnock et al., 1999; Davis, 1998).

In **directed masturbation training**, a woman is taught step by step how to masturbate effectively and eventually to reach orgasm during sexual interactions (Hulbert & Apt, 1995; Hulbert et al., 1993). The training includes use of diagrams and reading material, private self-stimulation, erotic material and fantasies (see Box 13-4), "orgasm triggers" such as holding her breath or thrusting her pelvis, sensate focus with her partner, and sexual positioning that facilitates stimulation of the clitoris during intercourse. This training program appears to be highly effective: over 90 percent of women learn to have an orgasm during masturbation, about 80 percent during caressing by their partners, and about 30 percent during intercourse (LoPiccolo, 1997; Heiman & LoPiccolo, 1988).

Therapists may treat *situational* lack of orgasm, such as failure to reach orgasm only during intercourse with one's partner, by helping a client to identify and increasingly apply during intercourse some of those techniques that she is already using during masturbation (McCabe & Delaney, 1992). Efforts to treat situational orgasmic dysfunction have been less successful than efforts to treat generalized orgasmic dysfunction (Rosen & Leiblum, 1995; McCabe & Delaney, 1992). As we observed earlier, however, a lack of orgasm during intercourse is not necessarily a sexual dysfunction, provided the woman enjoys intercourse and can reach orgasm through caressing, either by her partner or by herself. For this reason some therapists believe that the wisest course is to simply educate women whose only concern is lack of orgasm during intercourse, informing them that they are quite normal.

VAGINISMUS Specific treatment for vaginismus, involuntary contractions of the muscles around the vagina, takes two approaches. First, a woman may practice tightening and relaxing her vaginal muscles until she attains more voluntary

control over them (LoPiccolo, 1995; Rosen & Leiblum, 1995). Second, she may receive gradual behavioral exposure treatment to help her overcome her fear of penetration, beginning by inserting increasingly large dilators in her vagina at home and at her own pace and eventually ending with the insertion of her partner's penis. Over 90 percent of the women treated for vaginismus eventually have pain-free intercourse (Beck, 1993; LoPiccolo, 1990). Many women with this problem, however, report that they received ineffective or inaccurate forms of treatment when they first sought help from their physicians (Ogden & Ward, 1995).

BOX 13-4

Surfing for Sex on the Internet

*I*n a given week, 62 million adults in the United States surf the Web (Maguire, 1998). Which topic is sought out most often in Internet searches? "Sex," by far. The second most-sought topic is "Erotica." Users search for these topics almost four times as often as "Games" and five times as often as "Music" (Foster, 1995).

ConsiderThis

◉ Why might sex be such a popular item on the Internet? • Is the ready availability of sex chat groups and other sexual material on the Internet psychologically healthy or damaging? • Might the spread of sexual material in our computerized world fuel abnormal sexual interests and behaviors, as some observers fear?

DYSPAREUNIA We saw earlier that the most common cause of dyspareunia, genital pain during intercourse, is physical, such as pain-causing scars or lesions. When the cause is known, a couple can learn intercourse positions that avoid putting pressure on the injured area. A medical intervention may also be tried (Meana & Binik, 1994), but it must still be combined with other sex therapy techniques to counteract the years of sexual anxiety and lack of arousal (Leiblum, 1996; Quevillon, 1993). Because many cases of dyspareunia are in fact caused by undiagnosed physical problems, it is very important that clients receive expert gynecological exams (Reid & Lininger, 1993).

WHAT ARE THE CURRENT TRENDS IN SEX THERAPY? Over the past 30 years, sex therapists have moved well beyond the approach first developed by Masters and Johnson (LoPiccolo, 1997; Rosen & Leiblum, 1995). For example, today's sex therapists regularly treat partners who are living together but not married. They also treat sexual dysfunctions that arise from psychological disorders such as depression, mania, schizophrenia, and certain personality disorders (Rowlands, 1995). In addition, sex therapists no longer screen out clients with severe marital discord, the elderly, the medically ill, or the physically handicapped (Dupont, 1995; Rosen & Leiblum, 1995) or clients with a homosexual orientation or those who have no long-term sex partner (Stravynski et al., 1997). Sex therapists are also paying more attention to excessive sexuality, sometimes called *sexual addiction* (Kafka & Hennen, 1999; Goodman, 1998; Rosen & Leiblum, 1995).

Many sex therapists currently worry about the sharp increase in the use of drugs and other medical interventions for sexual dysfunctions (see Box 13-5 on the next page), particularly for hypoactive sexual desire and male erectile disorder (Ackerman, 1995; Rosen & Leiblum, 1995). Their concern is that therapists will increasingly choose the biological interventions rather than integrating biological, psychological, and sociocultural interventions (Hartmann & Langer, 1993; Althof et al., 1991). In fact, narrow approaches of any kind probably cannot fully address the complex factors that cause most sexual problems (Ackerman & Carey, 1995). It took sex therapists years to recognize the considerable advantages of an integrated approach to sexual dysfunctions. The development of new medical interventions should not lead to its abandonment.

Masters and Johnson *The extensive research, theories, and clinical reports of William Masters and Virginia Johnson have dramatically changed the way clinicians understand and treat sexual functioning and dysfunctioning.*

BOX **13-5**

Improving a Dog's Life

A company in Buckner, Missouri, has developed a new product: artificial testicles for dogs. Called "neuticles," the testicle substitutes are slipped into a dog's scrotum immediately after neutering to protect the animal from emotional trauma. They are made of polypropylene, a material used to coat some human implants and surgical equipment. Over a thousand pairs were sold in 1996 alone. One dog owner explained, "A dog is like a kid. Same thing. Consideration for his feelings" (Steinberg, 1996). But many veterinarians have questioned "whether the plastic substitutes would improve a dog's esteem" (Uhlig, 1996).

ConsiderThis

◉ Why might some pet owners believe that this product is necessary or useful? • Are pet owners sometimes too quick to project human discomforts and fears onto animals? • On the other hand, why are other people often critical of the concern, kindness, and affection that many people lavish on their pets?

Paraphilias

Paraphilias are disorders in which individuals repeatedly have intense sexual urges or fantasies or display sexual behaviors that involve nonhuman objects, children, nonconsenting adults, or the experience of suffering or humiliation. Many people with a paraphilia can become aroused only when a paraphilic stimulus is present, fantasized about, or acted out. Others need the stimulus only occasionally, perhaps during times of stress.

According to DSM-IV, a diagnosis of paraphilia should be applied only when the urges, fantasies, or behaviors last at least six months (see Table 13-5). For most paraphilias, the urges, fantasies, or behaviors must also cause great distress or interfere with one's social life or job performance in order for a diagnosis to be applied (APA, 2000). For certain paraphilias, however, performance of the sexual behavior indicates a disorder even if the individual experiences no distress or impairment (APA, 2000). People who initiate sexual contact with children, for example, warrant a diagnosis of *pedophilia* regardless of how troubled the individuals may or may not be over their behavior.

Some people with one kind of paraphilia display others as well (Abel & Osborn, 1997). Relatively few people receive a formal diagnosis of paraphilia, but the large market in paraphilic pornography leads clinicians to suspect that the patterns may be quite common (APA, 2000). People whose paraphilias involve children or nonconsenting adults often come to the attention of clinicians when they get into legal trouble. Some experts argue that, with the exception of nonconsensual paraphilias, paraphilic activities should be considered a disorder only when they are the exclusive or preferred means of achieving sexual excitement and orgasm.

While theorists have proposed various explanations for paraphilias, there is little formal evidence to support them (Bradford, 1999). Moreover, none of the many treatments applied to paraphilias has

Table 13-5 DSM-IV Checklist

PARAPHILIA

1. Over a period of at least six months, recurrent, intense sexually arousing fantasies, sexual urges, or behaviors involving certain inappropriate stimuli or situations (nonhuman objects; the suffering or humiliation of oneself or one's partner; or children or other nonconsenting persons).

2. Significant distress or impairment over the fantasies, urges, or behaviors. (In some paraphilias—pedophilia, exhibitionism, voyeurism, frotteurism, and sexual sadism—the performance of paraphilic behaviors indicates a disorder, even in the absence of distress or impairment.)

Based on APA, 2000.

proved clearly effective (Bradford, 1999, 1998, 1995). Psychological and socio-cultural treatments for paraphilias have been available the longest, but today's professionals are also using biological interventions. Some clinicians administer drugs called *antiandrogens* that lower the production of testosterone, the male sex hormone, and reduce sex drive (Balon, 1998; Bradford, 1998, 1995). Although such drugs do indeed alter paraphilic patterns, several of them disrupt normal sexual feelings and behavior as well. Thus the drugs tend to be applied primarily when the paraphilias are of danger either to the individuals themselves or to other people (Bender, 1998). Clinicians have also become interested in the possible use of second-generation antidepressant medications to treat persons with paraphilias, hoping that the drugs will reduce these compulsion-like sexual behaviors just as they help reduce other kinds of compulsions (Balon, 1998; Leo & Kim, 1995).

Fetishism

The key features of **fetishism** are recurrent intense sexual urges, sexually arousing fantasies, or behaviors that involve the use of a nonliving object, often to the exclusion of all other stimuli. Usually the disorder begins in adolescence. Almost anything can be a fetish; women's underwear, shoes, and boots are particularly common (APA, 2000, 1994; Raphling, 1989). Some people with fetishism commit thievery in order to collect as many of the desired objects as possible. The objects may be touched, smelled, worn, or used in some other way while the person masturbates, or the individual may ask a partner to wear the object when they have sex. Several of these features are seen in the following case:

> A 32-year-old, single male . . . related that although he was somewhat sexually attracted by women, he was far more attracted by "their panties."
> To the best of the patient's memory, sexual excitement began at about age 7, when he came upon a pornographic magazine and felt stimulated by pictures of partially nude women wearing "panties." His first ejaculation occurred at 13 via masturbation to fantasies of women wearing panties. He masturbated into his older sister's panties, which he had stolen without her knowledge. Subsequently he stole panties from her friends and from other women he met socially. He found pretexts to "wander" into the bedrooms of women during social occasions, and would quickly rummage through their possessions until he found a pair of panties to his satisfaction. He later used these to masturbate into, and then "saved them" in a "private cache." The pattern of masturbating into women's underwear had been his preferred method of achieving sexual excitement and orgasm from adolescence until the present consultation.
>
> *(Spitzer et al., 1994, p. 247)*

Researchers have not been able to pinpoint the causes of fetishism (Wise, 1985). Psychodynamic theorists view fetishes as defense mechanisms that help people avoid the anxiety produced by normal sexual contact. Psychodynamic treatment for this problem, however, has met with little success (LoPiccolo, 1992).

Behaviorists propose that fetishes are acquired through classical conditioning. In one behavioral study, male subjects were shown a series of slides of nude women along with slides of boots (Rachman, 1966). After many trials, the subjects became aroused by the boot photos alone. If early sexual experiences similarly occur in the presence of particular objects, perhaps the stage is set for development of fetishes.

Behaviorists have sometimes treated fetishism with *aversion therapy* (Kilmann et al., 1982). In one study, an electric shock was administered to the arms or legs of subjects with fetishes while they imagined their objects of desire (Marks & Gelder, 1967). After two weeks of therapy all subjects in the study showed at least

CHEMICAL CASTRATION
In 1996 the California state legislature passed the first law in the United States allowing state judges to order antiandrogen drug treatments, often referred to as "chemical castration," for repeat sex crime offenders, such as men who repeatedly commit pedophiliac acts or rape.

"Man is the only animal that blushes. Or needs to."

Mark Twain

PARAPHILIAS Disorders characterized by recurrent and intense sexual urges, fantasies, or behaviors involving nonhuman objects, children, nonconsenting adults, or experiences of suffering or humiliation.

FETISHISM A paraphilia consisting of recurrent and intense sexual urges, fantasies, or behaviors that involve the use of a non-living object, often to the exclusion of all other stimuli.

Sex sells *Behaviorists explain fetishes and other paraphilias by pointing to classical conditioning, claiming that neutral stimuli often gain a sexual allure after they are associated with sexual objects or situations. Advertisers hope for a similar kind of effect when they present their products—mini discs, for example—in a sexually suggestive context.*

some improvement. In another aversion technique, *covert sensitization,* people with fetishism are guided to imagine the pleasurable object and repeatedly to pair this image with an *imagined* aversive stimulus, until the object of sexual pleasure is no longer desired.

Another behavioral treatment for fetishism is **masturbatory satiation** (Quinsey & Earls, 1990; Marshall & Lippens, 1977). In this method, the client masturbates to orgasm while fantasizing about a sexually appropriate object, then switches to fantasizing in detail about fetishistic objects while masturbating again and continues the fetishistic fantasy for an hour. The procedure is meant to produce a feeling of boredom, which in turn becomes linked to the fetishistic object.

Yet another behavioral approach to fetishism, also used for other paraphilias, is **orgasmic reorientation**, which teaches individuals to respond to more appropriate sources of sexual stimulation. People are shown conventional stimuli while they are responding to unconventional objects. A person with a shoe fetish, for example, may be instructed to obtain an erection from pictures of shoes and then to begin masturbating to a picture of a nude woman. If he starts to lose the erection, he must return to the pictures of shoes until he is masturbating effectively, then change back to the picture of the nude woman. When orgasm approaches, he must direct all attention to the conventional stimulus.

Transvestic Fetishism

Transvestic fetishism, also known as **transvestism** or **cross-dressing**, is a recurrent need or desire to dress in clothes of the opposite sex in order to achieve sexual arousal. In the following passage, a 42-year-old married father describes his pattern:

> I have been told that when I dress in drag, at times I look like Whistler's Mother [laughs], especially when I haven't shaved closely. I usually am good at detail, and I make sure when I dress as a woman that I have my nails done just so, and that my colors match. Honestly, it's hard to pin a date on when I began cross dressing. . . . If pressed, I would have to say it began when I was about 10 years of age, fooling around with and putting on my mom's clothes. . . . I was always careful to put everything back in its exact place, and in 18 years of doing this in her home, my mother never, I mean never, suspected, or questioned me about putting on her clothes. I belong to a transvestite support group . . . , a group for men who cross dress. Some of the group are homosexuals, but most are not. A true transvestite—and I am one, so I know—is not homosexual. We don't discriminate against them in the group at all; hey, we have enough trouble getting acceptance as normal people and not just a bunch of weirdos ourselves. They are a bunch of nice guys . . . , really. Most of them are like me.
>
>   Most of [the men in the group] have told their families about their dressing inclinations, but those that are married are a mixed lot; some wives know and some don't, they just suspect. I believe in honesty, and told my wife about this before we were married. We're separated now, but I don't think it's because of my cross dressing. . . . I have been asked many times why I cross dress, and it's hard to explain, other than it makes me feel good. There is something deep down that it gratifies. Some of my friends, when I was growing up, suggested psychotherapy, but I don't regard this as a problem. If it bothers someone else,

then they have the problem. . . . I function perfectly well sexually with my wife, though it took her some time to be comfortable with me wearing feminine underwear; yes, sometimes I wear it while making love, it just makes it more exciting.

(Janus & Janus, 1993, p. 121)

Like this man, the typical person with transvestism, almost always a heterosexual male, begins cross-dressing in childhood or adolescence (Docter & Prince, 1997; Bradley, 1995). He is the picture of characteristic masculinity in everyday life and is usually alone when he cross-dresses. A small percentage of such men cross-dress to visit bars or social clubs. Some wear a single item of women's clothing, such as underwear or hosiery, under their masculine clothes. Others wear makeup and dress fully as women. Many married men with transvestism involve their wives in their cross-dressing behavior (Kolodny, Masters, & Johnson, 1979). This pattern is often confused with *transsexualism*, but, as we shall see, they are two separate disorders.

The development of transvestic fetishism sometimes seems to follow the behavioral principles of operant conditioning. Parents or other adults have openly encouraged these individuals to cross-dress as children and even rewarded them for this behavior. In one case, a woman was delighted to discover that her young nephew enjoyed dressing in girls' clothes. She had always wanted a niece, and she proceeded to buy him dresses and jewelry and sometimes dressed him as a girl and took him out shopping.

A group approach *"Crossroads" is a self-help group for men with transvestic fetishism, a recurrent need to dress in women's clothing as a means to achieve sexual arousal.*

Exhibitionism

A person with **exhibitionism** has recurrent urges to expose his genitals to another person, almost always a member of the opposite sex, or has sexually arousing fantasies of doing so. He may also carry out those urges, but rarely attempts to initiate sexual activity with the person to whom he exposes himself (APA, 2000, 1994; Abel, 1989). More often, he wants to provoke shock or surprise. Sometimes a so-called flasher will expose himself in a particular neighborhood at particular hours. The urges typically intensify when the person has free time or is under significant stress (Abel, 1989).

Generally the disorder begins before age 18 and is most prevalent in males (APA, 2000, 1994). Persons with exhibitionism are typically immature in their dealings with the opposite sex and have difficulty in interpersonal relationships. Over half of them are married, but their sexual relations with their wives are not usually satisfactory (Blair & Lanyon, 1981; Mohr et al., 1964). Many have doubts or fears about their masculinity, and some apparently have a strong bond to a possessive mother.

As with other paraphilias, treatment generally includes aversion therapy and masturbatory satiation, possibly combined with orgasmic reorientation, social skills training, or psychodynamic therapy (LoPiccolo, 1992; McNally & Lukach, 1991). Clinicians have also reported some success with hypnotherapy (Epstein, 1983; Polk, 1983).

Voyeurism

A person who engages in **voyeurism** has recurrent and intense urges to secretly observe unsuspecting people as they undress or to spy on couples having intercourse. The person may also masturbate during the act of observing or when thinking about it afterward but does not generally seek to have sex with the person being spied on. This disorder usually begins before the age of 15 and tends to persist (APA, 2000, 1994).

MASTURBATORY SATIATION A behavioral treatment in which a client masturbates for a very long period of time while fantasizing in detail about a paraphilic object. The procedure is expected to produce a feeling of boredom that in turn becomes linked to the object.

ORGASMIC REORIENTATION A procedure for treating certain paraphilias by teaching clients to respond to new, more appropriate sources of sexual stimulation.

TRANSVESTIC FETISHISM A paraphilia consisting of repeated and intense sexual urges, fantasies, or behaviors that involve dressing in clothes of the opposite sex. Also known as *transvestism*.

EXHIBITIONISM A paraphilia in which persons have repeated sexually arousing urges or fantasies about exposing their genitals to another person, and may act upon those urges.

VOYEURISM A paraphilia in which a person has repeated and intense sexual desires to observe unsuspecting people in secret as they undress or to spy on couples having intercourse, and may act upon these desires.

Playful context *Dressing in clothes of the opposite sex does not necessarily convey a paraphilia. The context of sexual-like behaviors must be weighed. Here members of Harvard University's Hasty Pudding Theatricals Club, known for staging musicals in which male undergraduates dress like women, flank actor Samuel L. Jackson, the 1999 recipient of their Man of the Year award. Jackson's outfit is meant to spoof his famous "hamburger royal with cheese" discussion in the movie* Pulp Fiction.

The vulnerability of the people being observed and the probability that they would feel humiliated if they knew they were under observation are often part of the individual's enjoyment. In addition, the risk of being discovered often adds to the excitement, as we see in the following statement by a man with this disorder:

> Looking at a nude girlfriend wouldn't be as exciting as seeing her the sneaky way. It's not just the nude body but the sneaking out and seeing what you're not supposed to see. The risk of getting caught makes it exciting. I don't want to get caught, but every time I go out I'm putting myself on the line.
>
> *(Yalom, 1960, p. 316)*

Exhibitionism and voyeurism can play a role in normal sexuality, but in such cases they are engaged in with the consent or understanding of the partner. The defining characteristic of the disorder of voyeurism is the repeated invasion of other people's privacy. Some people with voyeurism are unable to have normal sexual relations; others, however, have a normal sex life apart from their voyeurism.

LEGAL REPERCUSSIONS

The majority of arrests for sexual offenses involve acts of exhibitionism, pedophilia, or voyeurism (APA, 2000).

Many psychodynamic clinicians propose that people with voyeurism are seeking by their actions to gain power over others, possibly because they feel inadequate or are sexually or socially shy. Others have explained voyeurism as an attempt to reduce fears of castration, originally produced by the sight of an adult's genitals. Theoretically, people with voyeurism are repeating the behavior that produced the original fright, to reassure themselves that there is nothing to fear (Fenichel, 1945). Behaviorists explain the disorder as a learned behavior that can be traced to a chance and secret observation of a sexually arousing scene. If such observations are repeated on several occasions while the onlooker masturbates, a voyeuristic pattern may develop.

Frotteurism

A person who develops **frotteurism** has repeated and intense sexual urges to touch and rub against a nonconsenting person, or has sexually arousing fantasies of doing so. The person may also act on the urges. Frottage (from French *frotter*, "to rub") is usually committed in a crowded place, such as a subway or a busy sidewalk (APA, 2000, 1994). The person, almost always a male, may rub his genitals against the victim's thighs or buttocks or fondle her genital area or breasts with his hands. Typically he fantasizes during the act that he is having a caring relationship with the victim. This paraphilia usually begins in the teenage years or earlier, often after the person observes others committing an act of frottage. After the person reaches the age of about 25, the acts gradually decrease and often disappear (APA, 2000, 1994).

Pedophilia

A person with **pedophilia**, literally "love of children," gains sexual gratification by watching, touching, or engaging in sexual acts with prepubescent children, usually 13 years or younger (see Box 13-6). Some people with this disorder are satisfied by child pornography or seemingly innocent material such as children's underwear ads; others are driven to actually watching, fondling, or engaging in sexual intercourse with children (Howitt, 1995; Barnard et al., 1989). Some people with pedophilia are attracted only to children; others are attracted to adults as well (APA, 2000, 1994). Both boys and girls can be pedophilia victims, but there is evidence suggesting that three-quarters of them are girls (Koss & Heslet, 1992).

People with pedophilia usually develop their disorder during adolescence. Many were themselves sexually abused as children (Howitt, 1995; McCormack et al., 1992). It is not unusual for them to be married and to have sexual difficulties or other frustrations in life that lead them to seek an arena in which they can be masters. Often these people are immature: their social and sexual skills may be underdeveloped, and thoughts of normal sexual relationships fill them with anxiety. Some people with pedophilia also exhibit faulty thinking, such as "It's all right to have sex with children as long as they agree" (Abel et al., 1984). A recent study of 45 men with this disorder found that 93 percent had at least one additional psychological disorder (Raymond et al., 1999). More than two-thirds of the men had a mood disorder at some time during their lives, 64 percent an anxiety disorder, 60 percent a substance-related disorder, 53 percent another paraphilia, and 24 percent a sexual dysfunction.

FROTTEURISM A paraphilia consisting of repeated and intense sexual urges, fantasies, or behaviors that involve touching and rubbing against a nonconsenting person.

PEDOPHILIA A paraphilia in which a person has repeated and intense sexual urges or fantasies about watching, touching, or engaging in sexual acts with prepubescent children, and may carry out these urges or fantasies.

DANGEROUS INTERACTIONS

A study of Internet chat rooms for children and teens estimated that two-thirds of the visitors were actually adults pretending to be children and seeking to engage in sex talk or to acquire or trade pornographic material (Lamb, 1998).

BOX 13-6

Serving the Public Good

As clinical practitioners and researchers conduct their work, should they consider the potential impact of their decisions on society? Many people, including a large number of clinicians, believe that the answer to this question is a resounding yes. Two clashes between the clinical field and the public interest in the 1990s—each centering on the disorder of pedophilia—brought this issue to life.

In 1994, the newly published DSM-IV ruled that people should receive a diagnosis of pedophilia only if their recurrent fantasies, urges, or behaviors involving sexual activity with children cause them significant distress or impairment in social, occupational, or other spheres of functioning. Critics worried that this criterion seemed to suggest that pedophilic behavior is acceptable, even normal, as long as it causes no distress or impair-

ment. Even the U.S. Congress condemned the DSM-IV definition.

In response to these criticisms, the American Psychiatric Association clarified its position in 1997, stating, "An adult who engages in sexual activity with a child is performing a criminal and immoral act which never can be considered moral or socially acceptable behavior." In 2000 the Association went further still and changed the DSM criteria for pedophilia, so that the disorder is now diagnosed if persons act on their sexual urges, regardless of whether they experience distress or impairment (APA, 2000). Similarly, acting on one's recurrent sexual urges or fantasies warrants a diagnosis in cases of exhibitionism, voyeurism, frotteurism, and sexual sadism.

Another clash between the clinical field and public sensibilities occurred in 1998 when a review article in the presti-

gious journal *Psychological Bulletin* concluded that the effects of child sexual abuse are not as long-lasting as usually believed. The study set off a firestorm, with critics arguing that the conclusion runs counter to evidence from a number of studies. Furthermore, many people worried that the article's conclusions could be used to legitimize pedophilia. After a groundswell of criticism, the American Psychological Association, publisher of the journal, acknowledged in 1999 that it should have given more thought to how the study would be received and should have either presented the article with an introduction outlining the Association's stance against child abuse or paired it with articles offering different viewpoints (Fowler, 1999). The association also said that in the future it will more carefully weigh the potential consequences of research publications.

SEXUAL MASOCHISM A paraphilia characterized by repeated and intense sexual urges, fantasies, or behaviors that involve being humiliated, beaten, bound, or otherwise made to suffer.

HYPOXYPHILIA A pattern in which people strangle or smother themselves, or ask their partner to strangle or smother them, to increase their sexual pleasure.

AUTOEROTIC ASPHYXIA A fatal lack of oxygen that persons may unintentionally produce while hanging, suffocating, or strangling themselves during masturbation.

SEXUAL SADISM A paraphilia characterized by repeated and intense sexual urges, fantasies, or behaviors that involve inflicting suffering on others.

"How strange would appear to be this thing that men call pleasure! And how curiously it is related to what is thought to be its opposite, pain! . . . Wherever the one is found, the other follows up behind."

Plato, *Phaedo,* 4th century B.C.

Most pedophilic offenders are imprisoned or forced into treatment if they are caught. After all, they are committing child sexual abuse when they take any steps toward sexual contact with a child. Treatments include those already mentioned for other paraphilias, such as aversion therapy, masturbatory satiation, and orgasmic reorientation (LoPiccolo, 1992; Enright, 1989). There is also a cognitive-behavioral treatment for pedophilia: *relapse-prevention training*, modeled after the relapse-prevention programs used in the treatment of substance dependence (see page 378). In this approach, clients identify the kinds of situations that typically trigger their pedophilic fantasies and actions (such as depressed mood or distorted thinking). They then learn strategies for avoiding the situations or coping with them more effectively (LoPiccolo, 1992; Pithers, 1990). Relapse-prevention training has apparently been of help in pedophilia and in certain other paraphilias as well. One study of 147 people with pedophilia found a low 4 percent relapse rate over a five-year period among the subjects who received this treatment (Pithers & Cumming, 1989).

Sexual Masochism

A person with **sexual masochism** is intensely sexually aroused by the act or thought of being humiliated, beaten, bound, or otherwise made to suffer. Many people have fantasies of being forced into sexual acts against their will, but only those who are very distressed or impaired by the fantasies receive this diagnosis (APA, 2000, 1994; Reik, 1989). Some people with the disorder act on the masochistic urges by themselves, perhaps tying, sticking pins into, or even cutting themselves. Others have their sexual partners restrain, bind, blindfold, spank, paddle, whip, beat, electrically shock, "pin and pierce," or humiliate them (APA, 2000, 1994).

An industry of products and services has arisen to satisfy the desires of people with sexual masochism. Here a 34-year-old woman describes her work as the operator of a sadomasochism house:

I get people here who have been all over looking for the right kind of pain they feel they deserve. Don't ask me why they want pain, I'm not a psychologist; but when they have found us, they usually don't go elsewhere. It may take some of the other girls an hour or even two hours to make these guys feel like they've had their treatment—I can achieve that in about 20 minutes. . . . Remember, these are businessmen, and they are not only buying my time, but they have to get back to work, so time is important.

Among the things I do, that work really quickly and well, are: I put clothespins on their nipples, or pins in their [testicles]. Some of them need to see their own blood to be able to get off. . . .

. . . All the time that a torture scene is going on, there is constant dialogue. . . . I scream at the guy, and tell him what a no-good rotten bastard he is, how this is even too good for him, that he knows he deserves worse, and I begin to list his sins. It works every time. Hey, I'm not nuts, I know what I'm doing. I act very tough and hard, but I'm really a very sensitive woman. But you have to watch out for a guy's health . . . you must not kill him, or have him get a heart attack. . . . I know of other places that have had guys die there. I've never lost a customer to death, though they may have wished for it during my "treatment." Remember, these are repeat customers. I have a clientele and a reputation that I value.

(Janus & Janus, 1993, p. 115)

In one form of sexual masochism, **hypoxyphilia**, people strangle or smother themselves (or ask their partner to strangle them) in order to enhance their sexual pleasure. There have, in fact, been a disturbing number of clinical reports of **autoerotic asphyxia**, in which individuals, usually males and as young as 10 years old, accidentally induce a fatal lack of oxygen by hanging, suffocating, or strangling themselves while masturbating. There is some debate as to whether the practice should be characterized as sexual masochism, but it is commonly accompanied by other acts of bondage (Blanchard & Hucker, 1991).

Most masochistic sexual fantasies begin in childhood. However, the person does not act out the urges until later, usually by early adulthood. The disorder typically continues for many years. Some people practice more and more dangerous acts over time or during times of particular stress (APA, 2000, 1994).

In many cases sexual masochism seems to have developed through the behavioral process of classical conditioning. One case study tells of a teenage boy with a broken arm who was caressed and held close by an attractive nurse as the physician set his fracture without anesthesia (Gebhard, 1965). The powerful combination of pain and sexual arousal he felt then may have been the cause of his later masochistic urges and acts.

Sexual Sadism

A person with **sexual sadism**, usually male, is intensely sexually aroused by the thought or act of inflicting physical or psychological suffering on others, by dominating, restraining, blindfolding, cutting, strangling, mutilating, or even killing the victim. The label is derived from the name of the famous Marquis de Sade (1740–1814), who tortured others in order to satisfy his sexual desires. People who fantasize about sadism typically imagine that they have total control over a sexual victim who is terrified by the sadistic act. Many carry out sadistic acts with a consenting partner, often a person with sexual masochism. Some, however, act out their urges on nonconsenting victims. A number of rapists, for example, exhibit sexual sadism. In all cases, the real or fantasized victim's suffering is the key to arousal.

S & M *People with sexual sadism and those with sexual masochism often achieve satisfaction with one another. Although many such relationships stay within safe bounds and are often portrayed with humor in photos, novels, and movies, they can cross the line and result in severe physical or psychological damage.*

Fantasies of sexual sadism, like those of sexual masochism, may first appear in childhood (Johnson & Becker, 1997); the sadistic acts, when they occur, develop by early adulthood (APA, 2000, 1994). The pattern is long-term. Sadistic acts sometimes stay at the same level of cruelty, but more often they increase in severity over the years. Obviously, people with severe forms of the disorder may be highly dangerous to others.

Some behaviorists believe that classical conditioning is at work in sexual sadism. While inflicting pain, perhaps unintentionally, on an animal or person, an adolescent may feel intense emotions and sexual arousal. The association between inflicting pain and being aroused sexually sets the stage for a pattern of sexual sadism. Behaviorists also propose that the disorder may result from modeling, when adolescents observe others achieving sexual satisfaction by inflicting pain. The many sexual magazines, books, and videotapes in our society make such models readily available (Lebegue, 1991).

Psychodynamic and cognitive theorists view people with sexual sadism as having underlying feelings of sexual inadequacy; they inflict pain in order to achieve a sense of power, which in turn increases their sexual arousal. In contrast, certain biological studies have found signs of possible abnormalities in the endocrine systems of persons with sadism (Langevin et al., 1988). None of these explanations, however, has been thoroughly investigated.

Sexual sadism has been treated by aversion therapy. The public's view of and distaste for this procedure has been influenced by Anthony Burgess's novel (later a movie) *A Clockwork Orange*, which describes simultaneous presentations of sadistic images and drug-induced stomach spasms to a sadistic young man until he is conditioned to feel nausea at the sight of such images. It is not

SEXUAL RULING

According to a narrow (5 to 4) Supreme Court decision in the 1997 case of *Kansas* v. *Hendricks*, convicted sex offenders may be removed from prison prior to release and subjected to involuntary civil commitment in a mental hospital if a court judges them likely to engage in further "predatory acts of sexual violence" as the result of a "mental abnormality" or "personality disorder." They must then remain institutionalized until their disorder and sexual dangerousness are rectified.

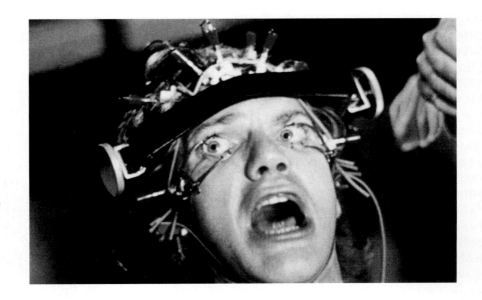

Cinematic introduction *In one of filmdom's most famous scenes, Alex, the sexually sadistic character in* A Clockwork Orange, *is forced to observe violent images while he experiences painful stomach spasms. Public attitudes toward aversion therapy were greatly influenced by this 1971 portrayal of the treatment approach.*

clear that aversion therapy is helpful in cases of sexual sadism. However, relapse-prevention training, used in some criminal cases, seems to be of value (Vaillant & Antonowicz, 1992; Pithers & Cumming, 1989).

A Word of Caution

The definitions of the paraphilias, like those of sexual dysfunctions, are strongly influenced by the norms of the particular society in which they occur (APA, 2000; Brown, 1983). Some clinicians argue that except when people are hurt by them, many paraphilic behaviors should not be considered disorders at all. Especially in light of the stigma associated with sexual disorders and the self-revulsion that many people experience when they believe they have such a disorder, we need to be very careful about applying these labels to others or to ourselves. Keep in mind that for years clinical professionals considered homosexuality a paraphilia, and their judgment was used to justify laws and even police actions against homosexual persons (King & Bartlett, 1999). Only when the gay rights movement helped change society's understanding of and attitudes toward homosexuality did clinicians stop considering it a disorder. In the meantime, the clinical field had unintentionally contributed to the persecution, anxiety, and humiliation of millions of people because of personal sexual behavior that differed from the conventional norms (see Box 13-7 on page 418).

Gender Identity Disorder

One of the most fascinating disorders related to sexuality is **gender identity disorder**, or **transsexualism**, a disorder in which people persistently feel that a vast mistake has been made—they have been assigned to the wrong sex (see Table 13-6). Such persons are preoccupied with getting rid of their primary and secondary sex characteristics—many of them find their own genitals repugnant—and acquiring the characteristics of the other sex (APA, 2000, 1994). Men with gender identity disorder outnumber women by around two to one. People with the problem often experience depression and may have thoughts of suicide (Bradley, 1995).

People with gender identity disorder usually feel uncomfortable wearing the clothes of their own sex and dress instead in clothes of the opposite sex. Their condition is not, however, transvestism. People with that paraphilia cross-dress in order to become sexually aroused; persons with transsexualism have much deeper reasons for cross-dressing, reasons of gender identity (Bradley, 1995). In

GENDER IDENTITY DISORDER A disorder in which a person persistently feels extremely uncomfortable about his or her assigned sex and strongly wishes to be a member of the opposite sex. Also known as *transsexualism*.

SEX-CHANGE SURGERY A surgical procedure that changes a person's sex organs and features, and, in turn, sexual identity.

PHALLOPLASTY A surgical procedure designed to create a functional penis.

addition to engaging in cross-dressing, individuals with transsexualism often take up roles and activities that are traditionally associated with the other sex (Brown et al., 1996).

Sometimes gender identity disorder emerges in children (Zucker, Bradley, & Sullivan, 1996; Sugar, 1995). Like adults with this disorder, they feel uncomfortable about their assigned sex and yearn to be members of the opposite sex. This childhood pattern usually disappears by adolescence or adulthood, but in some cases it develops into adult transsexualism (Bradley, 1995). Thus transsexual adults may have had a childhood gender identity disorder (Tsoi, 1992), but most children with a gender identity disorder do not become transsexual adults. Some adults with transsexualism do not develop any symptoms until mid-adulthood.

Various theories have been proposed to explain this disorder (Zucker et al., 1996; Sugar, 1995), but research to test the ideas has been limited and generally weak. Some clinicians suspect that biological factors play a key role in the disorder, and, in fact, one biological study has been hailed as a breakthrough (Zhou et al., 1995). Dutch investigators autopsied the brains of six people who had changed their sex from male to female. They found that a cluster of cells in the hypothalamus called the *bed nucleus of stria terminalis (BST)* was only half as large in these subjects as it was in a control group of normal men. Normally, a woman's BST is much smaller than a man's, so in effect the subjects with transsexualism were found to have a female-sized BST. Scientists do not know for certain what the BST does in humans, but they know that it helps regulate sexual behavior in male rats. Although other interpretations of these findings are possible, it may well be that men who develop transsexualism have a key biological difference that leaves them very uncomfortable with their assigned sex characteristics.

Some adults with transsexualism change their sexual characteristics by means of *hormone treatments* (Bradley, 1995). Physicians prescribe the female sex hormone *estrogen* for men with the disorder, causing breast development, loss of body and facial hair, and change in body fat distribution. Similar treatments with the male sex hormone *testosterone* are given to women with transsexualism.

Hormone therapy and psychotherapy enable many persons with transsexualism to lead a satisfactory existence in the gender role that they believe represents their true identity. For others, however, this is not enough, and their dissatisfaction leads them to undergo one of the most controversial practices in medicine: **sex-change surgery** (Liedl, 1999; Bradley, 1995). This surgery is preceded by one to two years of hormone therapy. The operation itself involves, for men, amputation of the penis, creation of an artificial vagina, and face-changing plastic surgery. For women, surgery may include bilateral mastectomy and hysterectomy. The procedure for creating a functioning penis, called **phalloplasty**, is performed in some cases, but it is not yet perfected. Doctors have, however, developed a silicone prosthesis that gives the patient the appearance of having male genitals (Hage & Bouman, 1992). Approximately 1,000 sex-change operations are performed each year in the United States. Studies

Table 13-6 DSM-IV Checklist

GENDER IDENTITY DISORDER

1. Strong and persistent cross-gender identification (for example, a stated desire to be the other sex, frequent passing as the other sex, desire to live or be treated as the other sex, or the conviction that one has the typical feelings and reactions of the other sex).
2. Persistent discomfort with one's sex or a sense of inappropriateness in the gender role of that sex (for example, preoccupation with getting rid of primary and secondary sex characteristics or belief that one was born the wrong sex).
3. Significant distress or impairment.

Based on APA, 2000, 1994.

James and Jan *Feeling like a woman trapped in a man's body, the British writer James Morris (left) underwent sex-change surgery, described in his 1974 autobiography,* Conundrum. *Today Jan Morris (right) is a successful author and seems comfortable with her change of gender.*

B O X **13-7**

Homosexuality and Society

In 1948, when Alfred Kinsey and his associates conducted one of the first extensive studies of male sexuality, they found that 4 percent of all men were exclusively homosexual and that 37 percent had had a homosexual experience that led to orgasm. In a later study they found the occurrence of homosexuality among women to be between one-half and one-third that of men (Kinsey et al., 1953). These findings shocked many people.

Homosexuality is not new; it has always existed in all cultures, as has the controversy that surrounds it. While most cultures do not openly advocate homosexuality, over the course of history few have condemned it so fiercely as Western culture does today. Nevertheless, research shows that a society's acceptance or rejection of people who engage in homosexual behavior does not affect the rate of the behavior.

Before 1973, the DSM listed homosexuality as a sexual disorder. Protests by gay activist groups and many psychotherapists eventually led to its elimination from the diagnostic manual as a sexual disorder. Most clinicians in the Western world now view homosexuality as a variant of normal sexual behavior, not a disorder (King & Bartlett, 1999).

Despite the growing acceptance of homosexuality by the clinical field, many people in Western society continue to hold antihomosexual attitudes and to spread myths about the lifestyles of homosexual persons. Contrary to these myths, research has shown that homosexual persons do not suffer from gender confusion; they are not more prone to psychopathology than others; and there is not an identifiable "homosexual personality."

To cope with the stress, discrimination, and even danger they face, many homosexual people have chosen to live on streets or in neighborhoods that are largely homosexual. Certain bars and restaurants serve as gathering places where gay people socialize and exchange information. In addition, organizations exist to support and lobby for homosexual people's rights, demanding equal treatment under the law and in society (Freiberg, 1994).

One of the key issues affecting support for homosexual rights has been the debate over whether homosexual people choose their lifestyle or whether it is an inherent part of their physiological makeup. This debate has been fueled by findings—pro and con—from the scientific community. Some research suggests that

homosexuality is not simply a lifestyle choice but linked to a physiological predisposition (Pillard & Bailey, 1995; Turner, 1995; Levay & Hamer, 1994). Such findings support the claim of the gay community that homosexuality is a naturally occurring phenomenon.

Some studies, for example, have suggested that homosexuality has a genetic component. In the early 1990s, two influential genetic linkage studies concluded that homosexuality may in some instances be passed on by the mother's genes (Hu et al., 1995; Hamer, 1993), although recent research has failed to support this particular conclusion (Rice et al., 1999). In addition, two studies found that when one identical twin was homosexual, his twin was also homosexual in more than 50 percent of the cases sampled. The number dropped to less than 20 percent when the siblings were fraternal twins or nontwins and to under 10 percent when the siblings were adopted and biologically unrelated (Bailey & Pillard, 1993). Although environmental factors also have a major impact on homosexuality—otherwise all persons with a homosexual identical twin would be homosexual—genetics may well play a key role in it.

Homosexual people are found in every socioeconomic group, every race,

---

LANDMARK CASE

The first sex-change operation took place in 1931, but the procedure did not gain acceptance in the medical world until 1952, when an operation converted an ex-soldier named George Jorgensen into a woman, renamed Christine Jorgensen. This transformation made headlines around the world.

in Europe suggest that one of every 30,000 men and one of every 100,000 women seek sex-change surgery (APA, 2000).

Clinicians have heatedly debated whether surgery is an appropriate treatment for gender identity disorder. Some consider it a humane solution, perhaps the most satisfying one to people with transsexualism (Cohen-Kettenis & Gooren, 1999; Cohen-Kettenis & van Goozen, 1997). Others argue that transsexual surgery is a "drastic nonsolution" for a largely psychological problem. The long-term psychological outcome of surgical sex reassignment is not clear. Some people seem to function well for years after such treatments (Rehman et al., 1999; Bradley, 1995), but others experience psychological difficulties. Without any form of treatment, gender identity disorder among adults is usually chronic, but some cases of spontaneous remission have reportedly occurred.

Our gender is so basic to our sense of identity that it is hard for most of us to imagine wanting to change it, much less to imagine the feelings of conflict and stress experienced by those who question their assigned gender. Whether the underlying cause is biological, psychological, or sociocultural, gender identity disorder is a dramatic dysfunction that shakes the foundations of the sufferer's existence.

Familiarity fosters acceptance *Although prejudice certainly remains, surveys indicate that the heterosexual public is growing more comfortable with displays of affection by homosexual couples—an important step toward the acceptance of differences in sexual orientation.*

and every profession. It is impossible to identify a characteristic that consistently separates them from the rest of the population other than their sexual orientation. The homosexual community argues that since sexual orientation is the only variable that consistently separates homosexual from heterosexual couples, gay couples should have the same rights as heterosexual ones. Today marriages are sometimes performed for same-sex couples. Furthermore, homosexual couples are increasingly asserting their rights to housing reserved for couples only and to spousal health insurance coverage; recent court decisions have supported such rights.

In the 1990s many controversies focused on the acceptance of homosexuality in the United States. Media coverage exposed episodes of gay-bashing in which homosexual men and women were beaten, even killed. The practice of "outing" increased—a practice in which gay activists expose public figures who have not themselves made their homosexuality known. In addition, President Bill Clinton reviewed the military's policy regarding homosexuality, an action that stirred an intense national debate and led the military to a "Don't ask, don't tell" policy. That is, the armed forces no longer try to identify homosexual persons, but, if faced with clear evidence, can discharge such individuals from the service.

One of the most important questions to be discussed during the debate on homosexuality and the military was whether Americans—those in the armed services specifically, but throughout the country as well—could overcome prejudice against homosexuality. Despite the high emotions this issue creates, research suggests that, through education and exposure, people of different sexual orientation can indeed learn to accept and work with one another (Beaty, 1999; Herek & Capitanio, 1993).

Now that clinical questions about homosexuality have been settled, a key issue remains: How will society deal with a significant proportion of its population that typically differs from the rest in but one way—their sexual orientation? So far, Western society cannot claim to have dealt very effectively or fairly with this question, but at least a trend toward understanding and equality seems to be emerging.

CROSSROADS:
A Private Topic Draws Public Attention

For all the public interest in sexual disorders, clinical theorists and practitioners have only recently begun to understand their nature and how to treat them. Although insights about the causes and treatment of paraphilias and gender identity disorder remain limited, 30 years of studying sexual dysfunctions are now paying dividends, and people with such dysfunctions are no longer doomed to a lifetime of sexual frustration (Rowland, 1999).

Studies of sexual dysfunctions have pointed to many psychological, sociocultural, and biological causes. Often, as we have seen in regard to so many disorders, the various causes may interact to produce a particular dysfunction, as in erectile disorder and female orgasmic disorder. For some dysfunctions, however, one cause alone is dominant, and integrated explanations may be inaccurate and unproductive. Premature ejaculation, for example, appears to have largely psychological causes, while dyspareunia usually has a physical cause.

The past three decades have also witnessed important progress in the treatment of sexual dysfunctions, and people with such problems are now often helped greatly by therapy. Sex therapy today is usually a complex program tailored to the particular problems of an individual or couple. Techniques from the various models may be combined, although in some instances the particular problem calls primarily for one approach.

One of the most important insights to emerge from all this work is that *education* about sexual dysfunctions can be as important as therapy. Sexual myths are still taken so seriously that they often lead to feelings of shame, self-hatred, isolation, and hopelessness—feelings that themselves contribute to sexual difficulty. Even a modest amount of education can help persons who are in treatment.

In fact, most people can benefit from a more accurate understanding of sexual functioning. Public education about sexual functioning—through books, television and radio, school programs, group presentations, and the like—has become a major clinical focus. It is important that these efforts continue and even increase in the coming years.

SUMMARY AND REVIEW

■ **Sexual dysfunctions** Sexual dysfunctions make it difficult or impossible for a person to have or enjoy sexual intercourse. *pp. 387–388*

■ **Disorders of desire** DSM-IV lists two disorders of the desire phase of the sexual response cycle: hypoactive sexual desire disorder, marked by a lack of interest in sex, and sexual aversion disorder, marked by a persistent revulsion to sexual activity. Biological causes for these disorders include abnormal hormone levels, certain drugs, and some medical illnesses. Psychological and sociocultural causes include specific fears, situational pressures, relationship problems, and the trauma of having been sexually molested or assaulted. *pp. 388–392*

■ **Disorders of excitement** Disorders of the excitement phase are female sexual arousal disorder, marked by a persistent inability to attain or maintain adequate lubrication or genital swelling during sexual activity, and male erectile disorder, a repeated inability to attain or maintain an erection during sexual activity. Biological causes of male erectile disorder include abnormal hormone levels, vascular problems, medical conditions, and certain medications. Psychological and sociocultural causes include the combination of performance anxiety and the spectator role; situational pressures such as job loss; and relationship problems. *pp. 392–395*

■ **Disorders of orgasm** Premature ejaculation, a persistent tendency to reach orgasm and ejaculate before or shortly after penetration, has been attributed to behavioral causes, such as inappropriate early learning and inexperience. Male orgasmic disorder, a repeated absence of or long delay in reaching orgasm, can have biological causes such as low testosterone levels, neurological diseases, and certain drugs, and psychological causes such as performance anxiety and the spectator role. The dysfunction may also develop from hypoactive sexual desire.

Female orgasmic disorder is a persistent absence of or long delay in orgasm in women. It, along with female sexual arousal disorder, has been tied to biological causes such as medical diseases and changes that occur after menopause, psychological causes such as memories of childhood traumas, and sociocultural causes such as relationship problems. Most clinicians agree that orgasm during intercourse is not critical to normal sexual functioning, provided a woman can reach orgasm with her partner during direct stimulation of the clitoris. *pp. 395–399*

■ **Sexual pain disorders** In vaginismus, involuntary contractions of the muscles around the outer third of the vagina prevent entry of the penis. In dyspareunia, the person experiences severe pain in the genitals during sexual activity. Dyspareunia usually occurs in women and typically has a physical cause such as injury resulting from childbirth. *pp. 399–400*

■ **Treatments for sexual dysfunctions** In the 1970s the work of William Masters and Virginia Johnson led to the development of sex therapy. Today sex therapy combines a variety of cognitive, behavioral, couple, and family systems therapies. It generally includes features such as careful assessment, education, acceptance of mutual responsibility, attitude changes, sensate focus exercises, improvements in communication, and couple therapy. In addition, specific techniques have been developed for each of the sexual dysfunctions. The use of biological treatments for sexual dysfunctions is also increasing. *pp. 400–407*

■ **Paraphilias** Paraphilias are disorders characterized by recurrent and intense sexual urges, fantasies, or behaviors involving either nonhuman objects, children, nonconsenting adults, or experiences of suffering or humiliation. The disorders are found primarily in men. The paraphilias include fetishism, transvestic fetishism (transvestism), exhibitionism, voyeurism, frotteurism, pedophilia, sexual masochism, and sexual sadism. Although various explanations have been proposed for these disorders, research has revealed little about their causes. A range of treatments have been tried, including aversion therapy, masturbatory satiation, orgasmic reorientation, and relapse-prevention training. *pp. 408–416*

■ **Gender identity disorder** People with gender identity disorder, or transsexualism, persistently feel that they have been assigned to the wrong sex and are preoccupied with acquiring the physical characteristics of the other sex. Men apparently outnumber females with this disorder by around two to one. Its causes are not well understood. Hormone treatments and psychotherapy have been used to help some people adopt the gender role they believe to be right for them. Sex-change operations have also been performed, but the appropriateness of surgery as a form of "treatment" has been hotly debated. *pp. 416–418*

○ **CYBER STUDY**

▲ *How do people with gender identity disorder feel about themselves and their bodies?* ▲ *How does gender identity disorder affect a person's life and functioning?* ▲ *Weigh the pros and cons of sex-change surgery.* ▲ *Observe the results of sex-change surgery.* ▲ *How might sexual feelings be expressed in dreams?*

SEARCH THE *ABNORMAL PSYCHOLOGY* CD-ROM FOR

▲ Chapter 13 video case and discussion
   "Brad"—Gender Identity Disorder

▲ Chapter 13 practice test and feedback

▲ Additional video case and discussion
   "Larry"—Psychoanalytic Therapy Session

LOG ON TO THE COMER WEB PAGE

[www.worthpublishers.com/comerabnormalpsychology4e] **FOR**

▲ Suggested Web links, research exercises, FAQ page, additional Chapter 13 practice test questions

CHAPTER

14

Schizophrenia

What . . . does schizophrenia mean to me? It means fatigue and confusion, it means trying to separate every experience into the real and the unreal and sometimes not being aware of where the edges overlap. It means trying to think straight when there is a maze of experiences getting in the way, and when thoughts are continually being sucked out of your head so that you become embarrassed to speak at meetings. It means feeling sometimes that you are inside your head and visualizing yourself walking over your brain, or watching another girl wearing your clothes and carrying out actions as you think them. It means knowing that you are continually "watched," that you can never succeed in life because the laws are all against you and knowing that your ultimate destruction is never far away.

(Rollin, 1980, p. 162)

Does it surprise you to see such a coherent firsthand description of how it feels to suffer from **schizophrenia**? People who have this disorder, though they previously functioned well or at least acceptably, deteriorate into an isolated wilderness of distorted perceptions, odd thoughts, disturbed emotions, and motor abnormalities. In Chapter 15 we shall see that schizophrenia is no longer the hopeless disorder of times past and that some sufferers, though certainly not all, now make remarkable recoveries. First, however, let us take a look at the symptoms of this disorder and at the theories that have been developed to explain them.

People with schizophrenia experience **psychosis**, a loss of contact with reality. Their ability to perceive and respond to environmental stimuli becomes so disturbed that they may not be able to function at home, with friends, in school, or at work. They may have hallucinations (false sensory perceptions) or delusions (false beliefs), or they may withdraw into a private world. As we observed in Chapter 12, taking LSD or abusing amphetamines or cocaine may produce psychosis. So may injuries or diseases of the brain. Most commonly, however, psychosis appears in the form of schizophrenia.

Schizophrenia appears to have been with us throughout history; it is one of the conditions commonly described as "madness" (Cutting, 1985). The Bible, for example, speaks of King Saul's mad rages and terrors, and of David feigning madness in order to escape his enemies. In 1865 a Belgian psychiatrist named Benedict Morel (1809–1873) applied the label *démence précoce* ("early dementia") to a 14-year-old-boy who showed the symptoms of this disorder, and in 1899 Emil Kraepelin introduced the use of the Latin form of Morel's label, *dementia praecox*. In 1911, however, the Swiss psychiatrist Eugen Bleuler (1857–1939) coined a new term, "schizophrenia," by combining Greek words that mean "split mind." Bleuler meant this name to imply (1) a fragmentation of thought processes, (2) a split between thoughts and emotions, and (3) a withdrawal from reality.

Approximately one of every 100 people in the world suffers from schizophrenia during his or her lifetime (APA, 2000). An estimated 2.5 million with this disorder are currently living in the United States (McGuire,

SCHIZOPHRENIA A psychotic disorder in which personal, social, and occupational functioning deteriorate as a result of strange perceptions, disturbed thought processes, unusual emotions, and motor abnormalities.

PSYCHOSIS A state in which a person loses contact with reality in key ways.

2000). Its financial cost is enormous—estimated by some at more than $100 billion annually, including the costs of hospitalization, lost wages, and disability benefits (Black & Andreasen, 1994). The emotional cost is even greater. In addition, sufferers have an increased risk of suicide and of physical—often fatal—illness (Meltzer, 1998; Brown, 1997). As we discussed in Chapter 9, it is estimated that up to 15 percent of persons with the disorder commit suicide (Andreasen, 1999; Peuskens et al., 1997).

Inner torment *Like this young woman, people with schizophrenia often appear to be trying to fight off the strange thoughts and perceptions that pervade their minds.*

Although schizophrenia appears in all socioeconomic groups, it is found more frequently in the lower levels (see Figure 14-1), leading some theorists to believe that the stress of poverty is itself a cause of the disorder. However, it could be that schizophrenia causes its victims to fall from a higher to a lower socioeconomic level or to remain poor because they are unable to function effectively (Munk & Mortensen, 1992). This is sometimes called the *downward drift* theory.

Equal numbers of men and women receive a diagnosis of schizophrenia. In men, however, the disorder often begins earlier and may be more severe (Gold, 1998; Castle et al., 1995). Almost 3 percent of all those who are divorced or separated suffer from schizophrenia sometime during their lives, compared to 1 percent of married people and 2 percent of people who remain single (Keith et al., 1991). Again, however, it is not clear whether marital problems are a cause or a result.

As many as 2.1 percent of African Americans receive a diagnosis of schizophrenia, compared with 1.4 percent of white Americans (Keith et al., 1991). However, according to census findings, African Americans are also more likely to be poor and to experience marital separation. When these factors are controlled for, the rates of schizophrenia are equal for the two racial groups.

People today, like those of the past, show great interest in schizophrenia, flocking to plays and movies (including the remarkably popular horror movies) that exploit or explore our fascination with the disorder. Yet, as we shall see, all too many people with schizophrenia are neglected in our country, their needs almost entirely ignored. Although effective interventions have been developed, most sufferers live without adequate treatment and without nearly fulfilling their potential as human beings (Torrey, 1997).

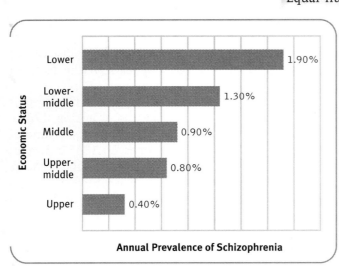

Economic Status

- Lower — 1.90%
- Lower-middle — 1.30%
- Middle — 0.90%
- Upper-middle — 0.80%
- Upper — 0.40%

Annual Prevalence of Schizophrenia

FIGURE 14-1 Socioeconomic class and schizophrenia *According to surveys, poor people in the United States are much more likely than wealthy people to experience schizophrenia. (Adapted from Keith et al., 1991.)*

The Clinical Picture of Schizophrenia

For years schizophrenia was a "wastebasket category" for diagnosticians, particularly in the United States, where the label might be assigned to anyone who acted unpredictably or strangely. Some clinicians were known to say that "even a trace of schizophrenia is schizophrenia" (Lewis & Piotrowski, 1954). The disorder is defined more precisely today, but still its symptoms vary greatly, and so do its triggers, course, and responsiveness to treatment (APA, 2000). In fact, a number of clinicians believe that schizophrenia is actually a group of distinct disorders that happen to have some features in common. To see the variety of forms schizophrenia may take, consider three people who were diagnosed as suffering from it. The cases are taken from the files of Silvano Arieti (1974), a famous theorist of the disorder.

> "To recover rationality after being irrational, to recover normal life, is a great thing."
>
> John Nash, 1994 recipient of Nobel Prize in Economics, after suffering from schizophrenia for 25 years

Ann, 26 years old

Ann graduated from high school and from a school for commercial art. . . . At the age of 18 she began going out with Henry. . . . They became engaged shortly thereafter and went out together frequently until their marriage. . . . Married life was considered a boring routine by both Ann and Henry. There was very little conversation between them. . . .

   Ann's disappointment in Henry increased. They had nothing in common; she was artistically inclined, whereas he had only an ordinary, conventional outlook toward life. It was at this time that she started to go dancing and then met Charles. Her interest in him increased, but . . . a divorce was not compatible with the precepts of the Catholic church. Her conflict grew and put her in a state of great agitation. . . .

   . . . One evening she came home from dancing and told her mother that she was going to give up her husband Henry, marry Charles, go to Brazil with him, and have twenty babies. She was talking very fast and saying many things, several of which were incomprehensible. At the same time she also told her mother that she was seeing the Virgin Mary in visions. She then went to her mother-in-law and told her to take back her son Henry, because he was too immature. The following day Ann went to work and tried to get the entire office down on their knees with her to recite the rosary. A few days later, her mother took her to a priest, whom she "told off" in no uncertain terms. She finally spit at him. A psychiatrist was consulted, and he recommended hospitalization.

(Arieti, 1974, pp. 173–177)

> "I feel cheated by having this illness."
>
> Individual with schizophrenia, 1996

Richard, 23 years old

In high school, Richard was an average student. After graduation from high school, he was drafted into the army. . . . Richard remembered [the] period . . . after his discharge from the army . . . as one of the worst in his life. . . . Any, even remote, anticipation of disappointment was able to provoke attacks of anxiety in him. . . .

   Approximately two years after his return to civilian life, Richard left his job because he became overwhelmed by these feelings of lack of confidence in himself, and he refused to go look for another one. He stayed home most of the day. His mother would nag him that he was too lazy and unwilling to do anything. He became slower and slower in dressing and undressing and taking care of himself. When he went out of the house, he felt compelled "to give interpretations" to everything he looked at. He did not know what to do outside the house, where to go, where to turn. If he saw a red light at a crossing, he would interpret it as a message that he should not go in that direction. If he saw an arrow, he would follow the arrow interpreting it as a sign sent by God that he should go in that direction. Feeling lost and horrified, he would go home and stay there, afraid to go out because going out meant making decisions or choices that he felt unable to make. He reached the point where he stayed home most of the time. But even at home, he was tortured by his symptoms. He could not act; any motion that he felt like making seemed to him an insurmountable obstacle, because he did not know whether he should make it or not. He was increasingly afraid of doing the wrong thing. Such fears prevented him from dressing, undressing, eating, and so forth. He felt paralyzed and lay motionless in bed. He gradually became worse, was completely motionless, and had to be hospitalized. . . .

Being undecided, he felt blocked, and often would remain mute and motionless, like a statue, even for days.

(Arieti, 1974, pp. 153–155)

LAURA, 40 YEARS OLD

Laura's desire was to become independent and leave home [in Austria] as soon as possible. . . . She became a professional dancer at the age of 20 . . . and was booked for vaudeville theaters in many European countries. . . .

It was during one of her tours in Germany that Laura met her husband. . . . They were married and went to live in a small provincial town in France where the husband's business was. . . . She spent a year in that town and was very unhappy. . . . [Finally] Laura and her husband decided to emigrate to the United States. . . .

They had no children, and Laura . . . showed interest in pets. She had a dog to whom she was very devoted. The dog became sick and partially paralyzed, and veterinarians felt that there was no hope of recovery. . . . Finally [her husband] broached the problem to his wife, asking her "Should the dog be destroyed or not?" From that time on Laura became restless, agitated, and depressed. . . .

. . . Later Laura started to complain about the neighbors. A woman who lived on the floor beneath them was knocking on the wall to irritate her. According to the husband, this woman had really knocked on the wall a few times; he had heard the noises. However, Laura became more and more concerned about it. She would wake up in the middle of the night under the impression that she was hearing noises from the apartment downstairs. She would become upset and angry at the neighbors. . . . Later she became more disturbed. She started to feel that the neighbors were now recording everything she said; maybe they had hidden wires in the apartment. She started to feel "funny" sensations. There were many strange things happening, which she did not know how to explain; people were looking at her in a funny way in the street; in the butcher shop, the butcher had purposely served her last, although she was in the middle of the line. During the next few days she felt that people were planning to harm either her or her husband. . . . In the evening when she looked at television, it became obvious to her that the programs referred to her life. Often the people on the programs were just repeating what she had thought. They were stealing her ideas. She wanted to go to the police and report them.

(Arieti, 1974, pp. 165–168)

"I shouldn't precisely have chosen madness if there had been any choice, but once such a thing has taken hold of you, you can't very well get out of it."

Vincent van Gogh, 1889

What Are the Symptoms of Schizophrenia?

Ann, Richard, and Laura all deteriorated from a normal level of functioning to become ineffective in dealing with the world. Each experienced some of the symptoms found in schizophrenia. The symptoms can be grouped into three categories: *positive symptoms* (excesses of thought, emotion, and behavior), *negative symptoms* (deficits of thought, emotion, and behavior), and *psychomotor symptoms*. Men with schizophrenia are more likely to display negative symptoms than women, but both sexes display positive symptoms to the same degree (Shtasel et al., 1992).

POSITIVE SYMPTOMS **Positive symptoms** are "patholological excesses," or bizarre additions, to a person's behavior. *Delusions, disorganized thinking and speech, heightened perceptions and hallucinations,* and *inappropriate affect* are the ones most often found in schizophrenia.

DELUSIONS Many people with schizophrenia develop **delusions**, ideas that they believe fervently but that have no basis in fact (see Box 14-1 on the next page). The deluded person may consider the ideas enlightening or may feel confused by them. Some people with schizophrenia hold a single delusion that dominates their lives and behavior, while others have many delusions. *Delusions of persecution* are the most common (APA, 2000). People with such delusions believe they are being plotted or discriminated against, spied on, slandered, threatened, attacked, or deliberately victimized. Laura believed that her neighbors were trying to irritate her and that other people were trying to harm her and her husband. Another woman with schizophrenia vividly recalled her delusions of persecution:

> I felt as if I was being put on a heavenly trial for misdeeds that I had done and was being held accountable by God. Other times I felt as if I was being pursued by the government for acts of disloyalty. . . . I felt that the government agencies had planted transmitters and receivers in my apartment so that I could hear what they were saying and they could hear what I was saying. I also felt as if the government had bugged my clothing, so that whenever I went outside my apartment I felt like I was being pursued. I felt like I was being followed and watched 24 hours a day.
>
> I would like to point out that these were my feelings then, and in hindsight I hold nothing against these government agencies. I now know that this constant monitoring was either punishment at the hands of God's servants for deeds I committed earlier in my life (sort of like being punished in hell but while I was still alive) or alternatively, but less likely, that I just imagined these things.
>
> *(Anonymous, 1996, p. 183)*

People with schizophrenia may also experience *delusions of reference*, in which they attach special and personal meaning to the actions of others or to various objects or events. Richard, for example, interpreted arrows on street signs as indicators of the direction he should take. People who experience *delusions of grandeur* believe themselves to be great inventors, religious saviors, or other specially empowered persons. And those with *delusions of control* believe their feelings, thoughts, and actions are being controlled by other people. This man hospitalized for schizophrenia imagined he was being controlled by telepathy:

> The inmates, here, hate me extremely because I am sane. . . . They talk to me telepathically, continuously and daily almost without cessation, day and night. . . . By the power of their imagination and daily and continuously, they create extreme pain in my head, brain, eyes, heart, stomach and in every part of my body. Also by their imagination and daily and continuously, they lift my heart and stomach and they pull my heart, and they stop it, move it, twist it and shake it and pull its muscles and tissues. . . . By telepathy and imagination, they force me to say orally whatever they desire, whenever they desire and as long as they desire. I never said a word of my own. I never created a thought or image of my own.
>
> *(Arieti, 1974, pp. 404–405)*

DISORGANIZED THINKING AND SPEECH People with schizophrenia may not be able to think logically and may speak in peculiar ways. These **formal thought disorders** can cause the sufferer great confusion

POSITIVE SYMPTOMS Symptoms of schizophrenia that seem to be excesses, or bizarre additions, to normal thoughts, emotions, or behaviors.

DELUSION A strange false belief firmly held despite evidence to the contrary.

FORMAL THOUGHT DISORDER A disturbance in the production and organization of thought.

Delusions of grandeur *In 1892, an artist who was a patient at a mental hospital claimed credit for this painting,* Self-Portrait as Christ. *Although few people with schizophrenia have his artistic skill, a number display similar delusions of grandeur.*

LOOSE ASSOCIATIONS A common thinking disturbance in schizophrenia, characterized by rapid shifts from one topic of conversation to another. Also known as *derailment*.

and make communication extremely difficult (Docherty, DeRosa, & Andreasen, 1996). Often they take the form of positive symptoms (pathological excesses), as in *loose associations*, *neologisms*, *perseveration*, and *clang*. (One formal thought disorder that belongs to the category of negative symptoms is described later on).

People who have **loose associations**, or **derailment**, the most common formal thought disorder, rapidly shift from one topic to another, believing that their incoherent statements make sense. A single, perhaps unimportant word in one sentence becomes the focus of the next. One man with schizophrenia, asked about his itchy arms, responded:

> The problem is insects. My brother used to collect insects. He's now a man 5 foot 10 inches. You know, 10 is my favorite number. I also like to dance, draw, and watch television.

NEOLOGISMS IN LITERATURE

In *Alice in Wonderland*, Lewis Carroll often combined two legitimate words to form a nonsensical word. Some such words are now part of the English language ("chortle," "galumph").

Some people with schizophrenia use *neologisms*, made-up words that typically have meaning only to the person using them. One individual stated, for example, "I am here from a foreign university . . . and you have to have a *plausity* of all acts of amendment to go through for the children's code . . . it is an *amorition* law . . . the children have to have this *accentuative* law so they don't go into the *mortite* law of the church" (Vetter, 1969, p. 189). Others may display the formal thought disorder of *perseveration,* in which they repeat their words and statements again and again (Capleton, 1996). Finally, some use *clang*, or rhyme, to think or express themselves. When asked how he was feeling, one man replied, "Well, hell, it's well to tell." Another described the weather as "So hot, you know it runs on a cot."

BOX 14-1

Relationships of the Mind

While playing in a professional tennis tournament in 1993, Monica Seles *(right)* was stabbed by a 38-year-old man from Germany. The attacker was obsessed with another tennis star, Steffi Graf, and believed that it was his responsibility to help Graf's career by striking down her rival. Seles did not return to professional tennis for two years.

In 1989 the actress Rebecca Shaeffer of the television show *My Sister Sam* was shot and killed outside her West Hollywood apartment by a fan. He had closely followed Shaeffer's career for months, and eventually he journeyed to her apartment building. When she failed to greet him warmly, he took her rebuff as a sign of arrogance and shot her.

At least 200,000 people are victimized by stalkers in the United States each year (Corwin, 1993). As many as 1 in 12 women and 1 in 50 men are stalked during their lifetimes (Abrams & Robinson, 1998; Klein, 1998). Some

stalkers suffer from *erotomanic delusions,* beliefs without any basis whatsoever that they are loved by someone who may actually be a casual acquaintance or a complete stranger (Silva et al., 2000; Anderson, 1993). Some people with such delusions, like Shaeffer's and Graf's pursuers, develop fantasies in which they feel driven to protect, harm, or even kill the object of their desire (Menzies et al., 1995).

ConsiderThis

⦿ Some experts believe that erotomanic delusions are more common today than they were in the past. Why might this be? • Do high-profile cases such as Seles's and Shaeffer's heighten or lower the probability that other cases of erotomanic delusions and stalking will emerge?

No, it's not "the King" *But surveys indicate that as many as one of every eight Americans believes that Elvis Presley is still alive—a belief that has led to numerous Elvis sightings at 7-Eleven stores around the country and encouraged an army of Elvis impersonators. Clinicians stop short of calling such beliefs delusions, however, noting that the Elvis loyalists do not hold on to their beliefs with a high degree of conviction. Most can be persuaded that Elvis has indeed "left the building."*

Formal thought disorders are not unique to schizophrenia. Loose associations and perseverations are common in cases of severe mania, for example. Even people who function normally may organize statements loosely or may on occasion use words that others fail to understand, especially when they are fatigued or feeling ill; but the instances of formal thought disorder in schizophrenia are much more common and severe (Holzman, 1986). Research suggests that some disorganized speech or thinking may appear long before a full pattern of schizophrenia unfolds (Amminger et al., 1999; Bilder et al., 1992).

HEIGHTENED PERCEPTIONS AND HALLUCINATIONS A deranged character in Edgar Allan Poe's "The Tell-Tale Heart" asks, "Have I not told you that what you mistake for madness is but the overacuteness of the senses?" Similarly, the perceptions and attention of some people with schizophrenia seem to intensify. They may feel that their senses are being flooded by all the sights and sounds that surround them. This makes it almost impossible for them to attend to anything important:

> Everything seems to grip my attention. . . . I am speaking to you just now, but I can hear noises going on next door and in the corridor. I find it difficult to shut these out, and it makes it more difficult for me to concentrate on what I am saying to you.
>
> *(McGhie and Chapman, 1961)*

Laboratory studies have repeatedly documented problems of perception and attention in schizophrenia (Kent & Turpin, 2000; Mass et al., 2000). In one study, subjects were instructed to listen for a particular syllable recorded against an ongoing background of speech (Harris et al., 1985). As long as the background speech was kept simple, subjects with and without schizophrenia were equally successful at picking out the syllable in question; but when the background speech was made more distracting, the subjects with schizophrenia became less able to identify the syllable. In many studies, subjects with this disorder have also demonstrated deficiencies in *smooth pursuit eye movement,* weaknesses that may be related again to attention problems. When asked to keep their head still and track a moving object back and forth with their eyes, subjects with schizophrenia tend to perform more poorly than those without schizophrenia (Nieman et al., 2000; Sereno & Holzman, 1995).

The various perception and attention problems in schizophrenia may develop years before the onset of the actual disorder (Cornblatt & Keilp, 1994; Cornblatt & Erlenmeyer-Kimling, 1985). Such problems also contribute to memory impairment, another difficulty found among many individuals with the disorder (APA, 2000; Nieman et al., 2000).

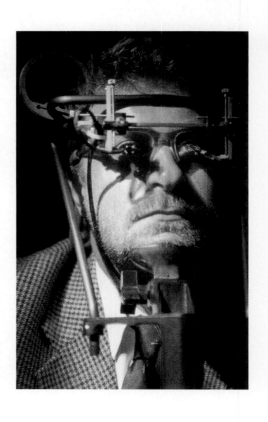

Poor tracking *Clinical researcher Michael Obuchowski demonstrates a device that reveals how well a person's eyes track a moving laser dot. People with schizophrenia tend to perform poorly on this and other eye pursuit tasks.*

"Last night I saw upon the stair
A little man who wasn't there.
He wasn't there again today.
Oh, how I wish he'd go away!"

Nursery rhyme

Another kind of perceptual problem in schizophrenia consists of **hallucinations**, perceptions that occur in the absence of external stimuli. People who have *auditory* hallucinations, by far the most common kind in schizophrenia, hear sounds and voices that seem to come from outside their heads (APA, 2000; Mueser, Bellack, & Brady, 1990). The voices may talk directly to the hallucinator, perhaps giving commands or warning of dangers, or they may be experienced as overheard:

> The voices . . . were mostly heard in my head, though I often heard them in the air, or in different parts of the room. Every voice was different, and each beautiful, and generally, speaking or singing in a different tone and measure, and resembling those of relations or friends. There appeared to be many in my head, I should say upwards of fourteen. I divide them, as they styled themselves, or one another, into voices of contrition and voices of joy and honour.
>
> *("Perceval's Narrative," in Bateson, 1974)*

Research suggests that people with auditory hallucinations actually produce the nerve signals of sound in their brains, "hear" them, and then believe that external sources are responsible. One study measured blood flow in *Broca's area,* the region of the brain that helps people produce speech (McGuire et al., 1996, 1995, 1993). The researchers found heightened blood flow in Broca's area while patients were experiencing auditory hallucinations. A related study instructed six men with schizophrenia to press a button whenever they experienced an auditory hallucination (Silbersweig et al., 1995). PET scans revealed increased activity near the surfaces of their brains, in the tissues of the brain's hearing center, when they pressed the button.

Hallucinations can also involve any of the other senses. *Tactile* hallucinations may take the form of tingling, burning, or electric-shock sensations. *Somatic* hallucinations feel as if something is happening inside the body, such as a snake crawling inside one's stomach. *Visual* hallucinations may produce vague perceptions of colors or clouds or distinct visions of people or objects. People with *gustatory* hallucinations regularly find that their food or drink tastes strange, and people with *olfactory* hallucinations smell odors that no one else does, such as the smell of poison or smoke.

Hallucinations and delusional ideas often occur together. A woman who hears voices issuing commands, for example, may have the delusion that the commands are being placed in her head by someone else. A man with delusions of persecution may hallucinate the smell of poison in his bedroom or the taste of poison in his coffee. Might one symptom cause the other? Whatever the cause and whichever comes first, the hallucination and delusion eventually feed into each other (see Box 14-2 on page 432):

> I thought the voices I heard were being transmitted through the walls of my apartment and through the washer and dryer and that these machines were talking and telling me things. I felt that the government agencies had planted transmitters and receivers in my apartment so that I could hear what they were saying and they could hear what I was saying.
>
> *(Anonymous, 1996, p. 183)*

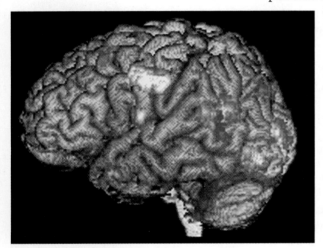

The human brain during hallucinations *This PET scan, taken at the moment a subject was experiencing auditory and visual hallucinations, shows heightened activity (yellow-orange) in hearing-related tissues at the brain's surface (Silbersweig et al., 1995). Conversely, the front of the brain, which is responsible for determining the source of sounds and other sensations, was quiet during the hallucinations. Thus, a person who is hallucinating seems to hear sounds produced by his or her own brain, but the brain cannot recognize that the sounds are actually coming from within.*

INAPPROPRIATE AFFECT Many people with schizophrenia display **inappropriate affect**, emotions that are unsuited to the situation. They may smile when making a somber statement or on being told terrible news, or appear upset in situations that should make them happy. They may also undergo inappropriate shifts in mood. During a tender conversation with his wife, for example, a man with schizophrenia suddenly started yelling obscenities at her and complaining about her inadequacies.

In at least some cases, these emotions may be merely a response to other features of the disorder. Consider a woman with schizophrenia who smiles when told of her husband's serious illness. She may not actually be happy about the news; in fact, she may not be understanding or even hearing it. She could, for example, be responding instead to another of the many stimuli flooding her senses, perhaps a joke coming from an auditory hallucination.

NEGATIVE SYMPTOMS **Negative symptoms** are those that seem to be "pathological deficits," characteristics that are lacking in an individual. *Poverty of speech, blunted and flat affect, loss of volition,* and *social withdrawal* are commonly found in schizophrenia. Such deficits greatly affect one's life and activities.

POVERTY OF SPEECH People with schizophrenia often display **alogia**, or **poverty of speech**, a reduction in speech or speech content. Some people with this negative kind of formal thought disorder think and say very little. Others say quite a bit but still manage to convey little meaning (Chen et al., 1996; Baltaxe & Simmons, 1995). Vaslav Nijinsky, one of the century's great ballet dancers, wrote the following diary entry on February 27, 1919, as his schizophrenia was becoming increasingly apparent:

> I do not wish people to think that I am a great writer or that I am a great artist nor even that I am a great man. I am a simple man who has suffered a lot. I believe I suffered more than Christ. I love life and want to live, to cry but cannot—I feel such a pain in my soul—a pain which frightens me. My soul is ill. My soul, not my mind. The doctors do not understand my illness. I know what I need to get well. My illness is too great to be cured quickly. I am incurable. Everyone who reads these lines will suffer—they will understand my feelings. I know what I need. I am strong, not weak. My body is not ill—it is my soul that is ill. I suffer, I suffer. Everyone will feel and understand. I am a man, not a beast. I love everyone, I have faults, I am a man—not God. I want to be God and therefore I try to improve myself. I want to dance, to draw, to play the piano, to write verses, I want to love everybody. That is the object of my life.
>
> *(Nijinsky, 1936)*

BLUNTED AND FLAT AFFECT Many people with schizophrenia have a *blunted affect*— they show less anger, sadness, joy, and other feelings than most people. And some show almost no emotions at all, a condition known as **flat affect**. Their faces are still, their eye contact poor, and their voices monotonous. In some cases, people with these problems may have *anhedonia,* a general lack of pleasure or enjoyment. In other cases, however, blunted or flat affect may reflect an inability to *express* emotions as others do. One study had subjects view very emotional film clips. Subjects with schizophrenia showed less facial expression than the others; however, they reported feeling just as much positive and negative emotion and in fact displayed greater skin arousal (Kring & Neale, 1996).

LOSS OF VOLITION Many people with schizophrenia experience **avolition**, or apathy, feeling drained of energy and of interest in normal goals and unable to start or follow through on a course of action (Lysaker & Bell, 1995). This problem is particularly common in people who have had schizophrenia for many years, as if they have been worn down by it. Similarly, individuals with the disorder may display *ambivalence,* or conflicting feelings, about most things. The avolition and ambivalence of Richard, the young man whose case was presented earlier, made eating, dressing, and undressing impossible ordeals for him.

HALLUCINATION The experiencing of sights, sounds, or other perceptions in the absence of external stimuli.

INAPPROPRIATE AFFECT A symptom of schizophrenia in which a person displays emotions that are unsuited to the situation.

NEGATIVE SYMPTOMS Symptoms of schizophrenia that seem to be deficits in normal thought, emotions, or behaviors.

ALOGIA A symptom of schizophrenia in which the person shows a decrease in speech or speech content. Also known as *poverty of speech*.

FLAT AFFECT A symptom of schizophrenia in which the person shows almost no emotions at all.

AVOLITION A symptom of schizophrenia marked by apathy and an inability to start or complete a course of action.

SOCIAL WITHDRAWAL People with schizophrenia may withdraw from their social environment and attend only to their own ideas and fantasies. Because their ideas are illogical and confused, the withdrawal has the effect of distancing them still further from reality. In fact, one study found that 75 percent of subjects with this disorder were less knowledgeable about everyday social issues than were people with other psychological disorders (Cutting & Murphy, 1990, 1988). The social withdrawal seems also to lead to a breakdown of social skills, including the ability to recognize other people's needs and emotions (Penn et al., 1997; Mueser et al., 1996).

PSYCHOMOTOR SYMPTOMS People with schizophrenia sometimes experience *psychomotor symptoms,* for example, awkward movements or repeated grimaces and odd gestures (Carnahan, Elliott, & Velamoor, 1996). The unusual gestures often seem to have a private purpose—perhaps ritualistic or magical.

The psychomotor symptoms of schizophrenia may take certain extreme forms collectively called **catatonia**. People in a *catatonic stupor* stop responding to their

---

BOX 14-2

Howling for Attention

❙ It's when I was bitten by a rabid dog. . . . When I'm emotionally upset, I feel as if I am turning into something else: my fingers go numb, as if I had pins and needles right in the middle of my hand; I can no longer control myself. . . . I get the feeling I'm becoming a wolf. I look at myself in the mirror and I witness my transformation. It's no longer my face; it changes completely. I stare, my pupils dilate, and I feel as if hairs are growing all over my body, as if my teeth are getting longer. . . . I feel as if my skin is no longer mine. ❙

(BENEZECH, DEWITTE, & BOURGEOIS, 1989)

*L*ycanthropy, the delusion of being an animal, is a rare psychological syndrome. The word "lycanthropy" comes from the Greek *lykos,* wolf, and *anthropos,* man. Accounts have been found all over the world of people who take on the characteristics and behavior of wolves or other animals. Belief in these tales has persisted for centuries. In the Middle Ages, lycanthropy was thought to be the result of demonic possession (Lehmann, 1985). In some societies it occurred after special ointments, probably hallucinogenic drugs, were applied, often for religious purposes (Lévi-Strauss, 1977). In other societies, cases

seem to have been closely linked to mental disorders, including schizophrenia, severe mood disorders, and certain forms of brain damage.

Mention of lycanthropy continues to produce an image of a werewolf baring its fangs at a terrified villager on a fog-shrouded moor. The legend was that the former had been bitten by another werewolf in an unbroken chain that passes on the legacy. But there are now more reasonable explanations for this type of behavior. One explanation is that some people afflicted with lycanthropy actually suffer from *congenital generalized hypertrichosis,* an extremely rare disease marked by excessive amounts of hair on the face and upper body (Maugh, 1995). Others may suffer from *porphyria,* an inherited blood disease whose victims sprout extra facial hair and are sensitive to sunlight. Still another current explanation ties lycanthropy to a disturbance in the activity of the temporal lobe of the brain, which is close to areas of the brain that may be responsible for visual hallucinations.

Despite these rational hypotheses, beliefs in werewolves as supernatural beings are likely to continue for the foreseeable future. Tales of demonic possession are more alluring than histories of congenital disease or temporal lobe abnormalities. Nor are publishers or movie producers likely to say good-bye to such good friends. Old explanations of lycanthropy may be flawed scientifically, but the profits they produce are far from a delusion.

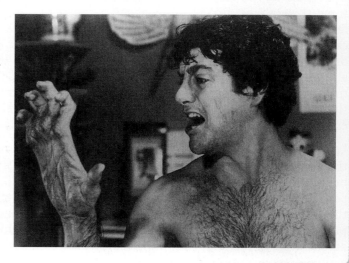

Crying wolf? *In the film* An American Werewolf in London, *a possessed man watches in terror as his hand stretches into the forepaw of a wolf.*

environment, remaining motionless and silent for long stretches of time. Recall how Richard would lie motionless and mute in bed for days. People who display *catatonic rigidity* maintain a rigid, upright posture for hours and resist efforts to be moved. Others exhibit *catatonic posturing,* assuming awkward, bizarre positions for long periods of time. They may spend hours holding their arms out at a 90-degree angle or balancing in a squatting position. They may also display *waxy flexibility,* indefinitely maintaining postures into which they have been placed by someone else. If a nurse raises a patient's arm or tilts the patient's head, for example, the individual will remain in that position until moved again. Finally, people who display *catatonic excitement,* a different form of catatonia, move excitedly, sometimes with wild waving of arms and legs.

A catatonic pose *These patients, photographed in the early 1900s, display features of catatonia, including catatonic posturing, in which they assume bizarre positions for long periods of time.*

What Is the Course of Schizophrenia?

Schizophrenia usually first appears between the person's late teens and mid-30s (APA, 2000). Although its course varies widely from case to case (Norman & Malla, 1995), many sufferers seem to go through three phases—prodromal, active, and residual. During the *prodromal phase,* schizophrenic symptoms, particularly positive symptoms, are not yet obvious, but the individual's ability to function is beginning to deteriorate. The person may withdraw socially, speak in vague or odd ways, develop strange ideas, or express little emotion. During the *active phase,* schizophrenic symptoms become apparent. Sometimes this phase is triggered by stress in the person's life. For Laura, the middle-aged woman described earlier, the immediate trigger was the loss of her cherished dog. Finally, many people with schizophrenia eventually enter a *residual phase,* in which they return to a prodromal-like level of functioning. The striking symptoms of the active phase lessen, but some negative symptoms, such as blunted emotions, may remain. Although one-quarter or more of patients recover completely from schizophrenia (McGuire, 2000), the majority continue to have at least some residual problems for the rest of their lives (Putnam et al., 1996).

Each of these phases may last for days or for years. A fuller recovery from schizophrenia is more likely in persons who functioned quite well before the disorder (had good *premorbid functioning*) or whose disorder was initially triggered by stress, came on abruptly, or developed during middle age (Lindström, 1996; Tolbert, 1996). Relapses are apparently more likely during times of stress (Hultman et al., 1997; Hirsch et al., 1996).

ConsiderThis

⊙ The philosopher F. W. Nietzsche said: "Insanity in individuals is something rare—but in groups, parties, nations, and epochs, it is the rule." What behaviors committed by groups might be considered psychotic if an individual were to perform them?

"And only you can hear this whistle?"

CATATONIA A pattern of extreme psychomotor symptoms found in some forms of schizophrenia, which may include catatonic stupor, rigidity, or posturing.

As we saw earlier, 1 percent of the general population develops schizophrenia. The prevalence rises to 3 percent among second-degree relatives with this disorder—that is, half-siblings, uncles, aunts, nephews, nieces, and grandchildren

mostly negative symptoms, such as flat affect, poverty of speech, and loss of volition.

CHAPTER

15

Treatments for
Schizophrenia

They call us insane—and in reality they are as inconsistent as we are, as flighty and changeable. This one in particular. One day he derides and ridicules me unmercifully; the next he talks to me sadly and this morning his eyes misted over with tears as he told me of the fate ahead. Damn him and all of his wisdom!

He has dinned into my ears a monotonous dirge—"Too Egotistical—too Egotistical—too Egotistical. Learn to think differently."—And how can I do it? How—how—can I do it? How the hell can I do it? I have tried to follow his suggestions but have not learned to think a bit differently. It was all wasted effort. Where has it got me?

(Jefferson, 1948)

With these words, Lara Jefferson, a young woman with schizophrenia, described her treatment experience in the 1940s. Her pain and frustration were typical of that experienced by hundreds of thousands of similar patients during that period of time. In fact, for much of human history, persons with schizophrenia were considered beyond help. They and their therapists faced the daunting task of trying to communicate while speaking virtually different languages. The disorder is still extremely difficult to treat, but clinicians are much more successful today than they were in the past (McGuire, 2000). Much of the credit goes to *antipsychotic drugs*, medications that help many people with schizophrenia think clearly and profit from therapies that previously would have had little effect on them (Lieberman et al., 1996).

As we shall see, each of the models offers treatments for schizophrenia, and all have been influential at one time or another. However, a mere description of the different approaches cannot convey the unhappiness suffered by the victims of this disorder as the various methods of treatment evolved over the years. People with schizophrenia have been subjected to more mistreatment and indifference than perhaps any other group of patients. Even today the majority of them do not receive adequate care, largely for reasons of economics and political priorities (Torrey, 1997). To better convey their plight, this chapter will depart from the usual format and discuss the treatments from a historical perspective. Ultimately, a look at how treatment has changed over the years will help us understand the nature, problems, and promise of today's approaches.

Institutional Care in the Past

For more than half of the twentieth century, most people with schizophrenia were *institutionalized* in a public mental hospital. Because patients with this disorder failed to respond to traditional therapies, the primary goals of these establishments were simply to restrain them and provide them with the most basic necessities—food, shelter, and clothing. Patients rarely saw therapists, and in fact were largely neglected and in many cases abused. Oddly enough, this state of affairs unfolded in an atmosphere of good intentions.

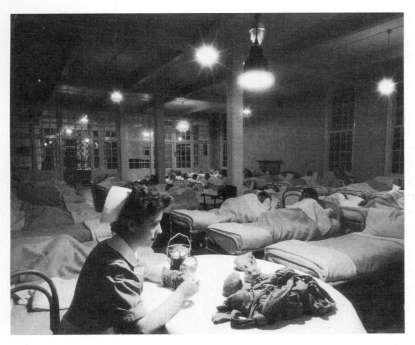

Overcrowded conditions *A night nurse sits in the ward of a public mental hospital in 1956 darning socks while the patients sleep. The beds in the ward are crammed close together, leaving no personal space of any kind for the patients.*

As we saw in Chapter 1, the move toward institutionalization in hospitals began in 1793, when the French physician Philippe Pinel "unchained the insane" at La Bicêtre asylum and began the practice of "moral treatment." For the first time in centuries, patients with severe disturbances were viewed as human beings who should be cared for with sympathy and kindness. As Pinel's ideas spread throughout Europe and the United States, they led to the creation of large mental hospitals rather than asylums to care for those with severe mental disorders (Goshen, 1967).

These new mental hospitals, typically located in isolated areas where land and labor were cheap, were meant to protect patients from the stresses of daily life and offer them a psychologically healthful environment in which they could work closely with therapists (Grob, 1966). States throughout the United States were even required by law to establish public mental institutions, **state hospitals**, for patients who could not afford private ones. Eventually, however, the state hospital system encountered serious problems.

BOX **15-1**

Lobotomy: How Could It Happen?

In 1949 a *New York Times* article reported on a medical procedure that appeared to offer hope to sufferers of severe mental disorders, people for whom no future had seemed possible outside of very overcrowded state mental institutions:

> ▌ Hypochondriacs no longer thought they were going to die, would-be suicides found life acceptable, sufferers from persecution complex forgot the machinations of imaginary conspirators. Prefrontal lobotomy, as the operation is called, was made possible by the localization of fears, hates, and instincts [in the prefrontal cortex of the brain]. It is fitting, then, that the Nobel Prize in medicine should be shared by Hess and Moniz. Surgeons now think no more of operations on the brain than they do of removing an appendix. ▌

We now know that the lobotomy was hardly a miracle treatment. Far from "curing" people with mental disorders, the procedure left thousands upon thousands extremely withdrawn, subdued, and even stuporous. The first lobotomy was performed by the Portuguese neuropsychiatrist Egas Moniz in 1935. His particular procedure, called a *prefrontal leukotomy,* consisted of drilling two holes in either side of the skull and inserting an instrument resembling an icepick into the brain tissue to cut or destroy nerve fibers. Moniz believed that severe abnormal thinking could be changed by cutting the nerve pathways that carried such thoughts from one part of the brain to another. In the 1940s Walter Freeman and his surgical partner, James Watts, developed a second kind of psychosurgery called the *transorbital lobotomy,* in which the surgeon inserted a needle into the brain through the eye socket and rotated it in order to destroy the brain tissue.

Why was the lobotomy so enthusiastically accepted by the medical community in the 1940s and 1950s? The neuroscientist Elliot Valenstein (1986) points first to the extreme overcrowding in mental hospitals at the time. This crowding was making it difficult to maintain decent standards in the hospitals. Valenstein also points to the personalities of the inventors of the procedure as important factors. Although these individuals were gifted and dedicated physicians, Valenstein also believes that their professional ambitions led them to move too quickly and boldly in applying the procedure.

The prestige and diplomatic skills of Moniz and Freeman were so great and the field of neurology was so small that their procedures drew little criticism. Physicians may also have been misled by the seemingly positive findings of early studies of the lobotomy, which, as it turned out, were not based on sound methodology (Swayze, 1995; Valenstein, 1986).

Wards became increasingly overcrowded, admissions kept rising, and state funding was unable to keep up. Too many aspects of treatment became the responsibility of nurses and attendants, whose knowledge and experience at that time were limited.

Between 1845 and 1955 nearly 300 state hospitals appeared in the United States, and the number of hospitalized patients on any given day rose from 2,000 in 1845 to nearly 600,000 in 1955. The priorities of the hospital administrators, and the quality of care, changed over those 110 years. In the face of overcrowding and understaffing, the emphasis shifted from giving humanitarian care to keeping order. In a throwback to the asylum period, unruly patients were restrained, isolated, and punished; individual attention disappeared. Patients were transferred to *back wards,* or chronic wards, if they failed to improve quickly (Bloom, 1984). Most of the patients on these wards suffered from schizophrenia (Hafner & an der Heiden, 1988). The back wards were in fact human warehouses filled with hopelessness. Staff members relied on straitjackets and handcuffs to deal with difficult patients. The often devastating lobotomy was among the more "advanced" treatments the field had to offer (see Box 15-1).

Many patients not only failed to improve under these conditions but developed additional symptoms, apparently as a result of institutionalization itself. The most common pattern of decline was called the *social breakdown syndrome:* extreme withdrawal, anger, physical aggressiveness, and loss of interest in personal appearance and functioning (Gruenberg, 1980). Often more troublesome than patients' original symptoms, this new syndrome made it impossible for them to return to society even if they somehow recovered from the symptoms that had first brought them to the hospital.

STATE HOSPITALS Public mental hospitals in the United States, run by each state.

Dubious Choice?

Egas Moniz was awarded the Nobel Prize in medicine and physiology in 1949 for his development of the lobotomy, the only treatment for mental disorders ever to be so honored.

By the 1950s, better studies revealed that in addition to having a fatality rate of 1.5 to 6 percent, lobotomies could cause serious problems such as brain seizures, huge weight gain, loss of motor coordination, partial paralysis, incontinence, endocrine malfunctions, and very poor intellectual and emotional responsiveness. When the public became concerned that the procedure might be used to control violent criminals, the lobotomy became a civil rights issue as well. Finally, the discovery of effective antipsychotic drugs put an end to this inhumane treatment for mental disorders.

Today's psychosurgical procedures are greatly refined and hardly resemble the lobotomies of 50 years back. Still, psychosurgery of any kind is now rare. It is, in fact, considered experimental and is used only as a last resort in the most severe cases of obsessive-compulsive disorder and depression (Goodman et al., 1992; Greist, 1992). Many professionals believe that any kind of surgery that destroys brain tissue is unethical and that it keeps alive one of the clinical field's most shameful and ill-advised efforts at cure.

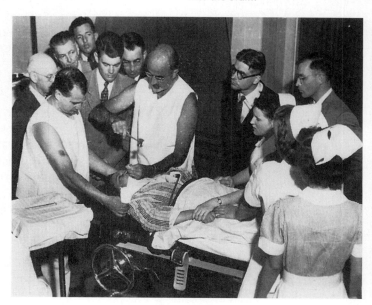

Lessons in psychosurgery *Neuropsychiatrist Walter Freeman performs a lobotomy in 1949 before a group of interested onlookers by inserting a needle through a patient's eye socket into the brain.*

Institutional Care Takes a Turn for the Better

In the 1950s, clinicians developed two institutional approaches that finally brought some hope to patients who had lived in institutions for years: *milieu therapy*, based on humanistic principles, and the *token economy program*, based on behavioral principles. These approaches particularly helped improve the personal care and self-image of patients, problem areas that had been worsened by institutionalization.

Milieu Therapy

In the opinion of humanistic theorists, institutionalized patients deteriorate because they are deprived of opportunities to exercise independence, responsibility, and positive self-regard, and to engage in meaningful activities. Thus the premise of **milieu therapy** is that institutions cannot be of help to patients unless they can somehow create a social climate, or milieu, that promotes productive activity, self-respect, and individual responsibility.

The pioneer of this approach was Maxwell Jones, a London psychiatrist who in 1953 converted a ward of patients with various psychological disorders into a *therapeutic community*. The patients were referred to as "residents," and were regarded as capable of running their own lives and making their own decisions. They participated in community government, working with staff members to establish rules and determine sanctions. In fact, patients and staff members alike were valued as important therapeutic agents. The atmosphere was one of mutual respect, support, and openness. Patients could also take on special projects, jobs, and recreational activities. In short, their daily schedule was designed to resemble life outside the hospital.

Milieu-style programs have since been set up in institutions throughout the Western world, often combined with other hospital approaches (Dobson et al., 1995; Ciompi et al., 1992). They vary from setting to setting but at a minimum are designed to encourage interactions (especially group interactions) between patients and staff, keep patients active, and raise expectations of what they can accomplish. Research over the years has shown that patients with schizophrenia in milieu hospital programs often improve and leave the hospital at higher rates than patients in programs offering primarily custodial care (Paul & Lentz, 1977; Cumming & Cumming, 1962). Many of these persons remain impaired, however, and must live in sheltered settings after their release. We shall see that many halfway houses and other community programs for individuals with schizophrenia are run in accordance with the same principles of resident self-government and work schedules that have proven effective in hospital milieu programs.

Hospital restraint *Prior to the advent of milieu therapy, token economies, and antipsychotic drugs, state hospitals across the United States became severely overcrowded and relied increasingly on mechanical restraints to control patients. At Byberry State Hospital in Philadelphia, for example, violent patients were often tied to their beds, a procedure that was employed as late as the 1950s.*

Leather cuffs for wrists and ankles

Straps from cuffs are locked to bed

The Token Economy

In the 1950s behaviorists had little status in mental institutions and were permitted to work only with patients whose problems seemed hopeless. Among the "hopeless" were many patients with schizophrenia. Through years of experimentation, behaviorists discovered that the systematic application of operant conditioning techniques could help change the behaviors of these individuals (Ayllon, 1963; Ayllon & Michael, 1959). Programs that apply these techniques are called **token economy programs**.

In token economy programs patients are rewarded when they behave acceptably and are not rewarded when they behave unacceptably. Typically, the immediate reward for acceptable behavior is a token that can later be exchanged for food, cigarettes, hospital privileges, and other desirable items, thus creating a "token economy." Acceptable behaviors likely to be targeted include caring for oneself and for one's possessions (making the bed, getting dressed), participating in a work program, speaking coherently, following ward rules, and exercising self-control.

HOW EFFECTIVE ARE TOKEN ECONOMY PROGRAMS? Researchers have found that token economies do help reduce psychotic and related behaviors (Emmelkamp, 1994; Belcher, 1988). In one very successful program, Gordon Paul and Robert Lentz (1977) set up a hospital token economy for 28 patients with chronic schizophrenia, most of whom improved greatly. After four and a half years, 98 percent of the subjects had been released, mostly to sheltered-care facilities, compared with 71 percent of patients treated in a milieu program and 45 percent of patients who received custodial care only.

WHAT ARE THE LIMITATIONS OF TOKEN ECONOMIES? Some clinicians have voiced reservations about the claims made for token economy programs (Kazdin, 1983). One problem is that many token economy studies, unlike Paul and Lentz's, are uncontrolled. When administrators set up a token economy, they usually bring all ward patients into the program rather than dividing the ward into a token economy group and a control group. As a result, patients' improvements can be compared only with their own past behaviors—a comparison that may be misleading. Changes in the physical setting, for example, or a general increase in staff attention could be causing patient improvements, rather than the token economy per se.

Many clinicians have also raised ethical and legal concerns. If token economy programs are to be effective, administrators need to control the important rewards in a patient's life, perhaps including such basic ones as food and a comfortable bed. But aren't there some things in life to which all human beings are entitled? Court decisions have now ruled that patients do indeed have certain basic rights that clinicians cannot violate, regardless of the positive goals of a treatment program. They have a right to food, storage space, and furniture, as well as freedom of movement (Emmelkamp, 1994).

Another question pertains to the quality of the improvements made under token economy programs. Are behaviorists having any effect on a patient's psychotic thoughts and perceptions or are they merely improving the person's ability to imitate normal behavior? This issue is illustrated by the case of a middle-aged man named John, who had the delusion that he was the U.S. government (Comer, 1973). Whenever he spoke, he spoke as the government. "We are happy to see you. . . . We need people like you in our service. . . . We are carrying out our activities in John's body." When John's hospital ward was converted into a token economy, the staff members targeted his delusional statements, and required him to identify himself properly to earn tokens. If he called himself John, he received tokens; if he insisted on describing himself as the government, he received nothing.

After a few months on the token economy program, John stopped referring to himself as the government. When asked his name, he would say, "John." Although staff members were understandably pleased with his improvement, John himself had a different view of the situation. In a private discussion he said:

The chain technique *Unimpressed by the success of milieu and token economy programs, some institutions around the world continue to use approaches that seem unenlightened at best. Despite constant criticism by the clinical establishment, the Longfa Tang Temple in southern Taiwan makes use of chains to "treat" the 700 patients who reside there. Often a severely disturbed patient is chained to a more stable patient and is led around to various activities and work assignments throughout the day.*

> We're tired of it. Every damn time we want a cigarette, we have to go through their bullshit. "What's your name? . . . Who wants the cigarette? . . . Where is the government?" Today, we were desperate for a smoke and went to Simpson, the damn nurse, and she made us do her bidding. "Tell me your name if you want a cigarette. What's your name?" Of course, we said, "John." We needed the cigarettes. If we told her the truth, no cigarettes. But we don't have time for this nonsense. We've got business to do, international business, laws to change, people to recruit. And these people keep playing their games.
>
> *(Comer, 1973)*

Critics of the behavioral approach would argue that John was still delusional and therefore as psychotic as before. Behaviorists, however, would argue that at the very least, John's judgment about the consequences of his behavior had improved. Learning to keep his delusion to himself might even be a step toward changing his private thinking.

Lastly, it has often been difficult for patients to make a satisfactory transition from hospital token economy programs to community living. In an environment where rewards are contingent on proper conduct, proper conduct becomes contingent on continued rewards. Some patients who find that the real world doesn't reward them so concretely abandon their newly acquired behaviors.

Nevertheless, token economy programs have had a most important effect on the treatment of people with schizophrenia. They were among the first hospital treatments that actually changed psychotic symptoms and got chronic patients moving again. These programs are no longer as popular as they once were (Glynn, 1990), but they are still used in many mental hospitals, usually along with medication, and in some community residences as well. The approach has also been applied to other clinical problems, including mental retardation, delinquency, and hyperactivity, as well as in other fields, such as education and business.

Antipsychotic Drugs

Milieu therapy and token economy programs helped improve the gloomy outlook for patients with schizophrenia, but it was the discovery of antipsychotic drugs in the 1950s that truly revolutionized treatment for this disorder. These drugs eliminate many of its symptoms and today are almost always a part of treatment. What is more, as we saw in Chapter 14, they have influenced the way clinicians now view schizophrenia.

The discovery of antipsychotic medications dates back to the 1940s, when researchers developed the first *antihistamine drugs* to combat allergies. Although antihistamines also produced considerable tiredness and drowsiness, they quickly became popular, and many such drugs were developed. The French surgeon Henri Laborit soon discovered that one group of antihistamines, *phenothiazines*, could also be used to help calm patients about to undergo surgery. After experimenting with several phenothiazine antihistamines and becoming most impressed with one called *chlorpromazine,* Laborit reported, "It provokes not any loss of consciousness, not any change in the patient's mentality but a slight tendency to sleep and above all 'disinterest' for all that goes on around him."

Laborit suspected that chlorpromazine might also have a calming effect on persons with severe psychological disorders. The psychiatrists Jean Delay and Pierre Deniker (1952) therefore tested the drug on six patients with psychotic symptoms and did indeed observe a sharp reduction in their symptoms. In 1954, chlorpromazine was approved for sale in the United States as an **antipsychotic drug** under the trade name Thorazine.

Since the discovery of the phenothiazines, other kinds of antipsychotic drugs have been developed (see Table 15-1). The ones developed throughout the 1960s,

PRIVATE NOTIONS
Surveys suggest that as many as 22 percent of people in the United States believe the Earth has been visited by aliens from outer space (Andrews, 1998).

ANTIPSYCHOTIC DRUGS Drugs that help correct grossly confused or distorted thinking.

NEUROLEPTIC DRUGS Conventional antipsychotic drugs, so called because they often produce undesired effects similar to the symptoms of neurological disorders.

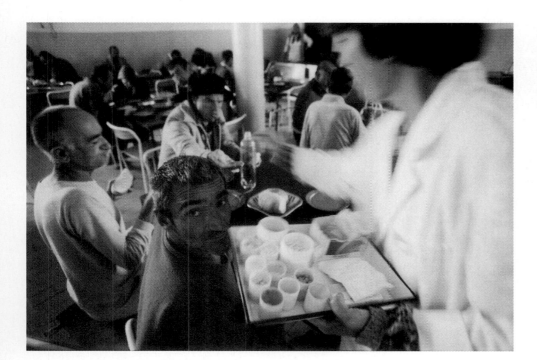

The drug revolution *Since the 1950s medications have become the center of treatment for patients hospitalized with schizophrenia and other severe mental disorders. The medications have resulted in shorter hospitalizations that last weeks rather than years.*

1970s, and 1980s are now referred to as "conventional" antipsychotic drugs in order to distinguish them from the "atypical" antipsychotics that have been developed in recent years. The conventional drugs are also known as **neuroleptic drugs**, because they often produce undesired movement effects similar to the symptoms of neurological diseases. Among the best known conventional drugs are thioridazine (Mellaril), fluphenazine (Prolixin), trifluoperazine (Stelazine) and haloperidol (Haldol).

As we saw in Chapter 14, antipsychotic drugs reduce the symptoms of schizophrenia at least in part by blocking excessive activity of the neurotransmitter dopamine, especially at the brain's dopamine D-2 receptors (Holcomb et al., 1996; Kusumi et al., 1995). Remember that some studies suggest that people with schizophrenia, particularly those with Type I schizophrenia, have excessive numbers of dopamine-receiving receptors, which may lead to heightened dopamine activity and to the symptoms of schizophrenia. After a patient takes antipsychotic drugs for a time, the dopamine-receiving neurons apparently grow more receptors (Strange, 1992; Burt et al., 1977; Seeman et al., 1976). It is as if the neurons recognize that dopamine transmission is being blocked by the drugs at the usual receptors and compensate by developing new ones. Now the patient has two groups of dopamine receptors—the excessive number of original ones, which are blocked, and a normal number of new ones, which ideally produce normal synaptic activity rather than schizophrenic symptoms.

How Effective Are Antipsychotic Drugs?

Research has repeatedly shown that antipsychotic drugs reduce schizophrenic symptoms in the majority of patients (Lieberman et al., 1996) (see Figure 15-1 on the next page). Moreover, in direct comparisons the drugs appear to be a more effective treatment for schizophrenia than any of the other approaches used alone, such as psychodynamic therapy, milieu therapy, and electroconvulsive therapy (May, Tuma, & Dixon, 1981; May & Tuma, 1964).

Table 15-1

Antipsychotic Drugs

CLASS/GENERIC NAME	TRADE NAME
Chlorpromazine	Thorazine
Risperidone	Risperdal
Triflupromazine	Vesprin
Thioridazine	Mellaril
Mesoridazine besylate	Serentil
Piperacetazine	Quide
Trifluoperazine	Stelazine
Fluphenazine	Prolixin, Permitil
Perphenazine	Trilafon
Acetophenazine maleate	Tindal
Chlorprothixene	Taractan
Thiothixene	Navane
Haloperidol	Haldol
Loxapine	Loxitane
Molindone hydrochloride	Moban, Lidone
Pimozide	Orap
Clozapine	Clozaril
Olanzapine	Zyprexa
Quetiapine	Seroquel

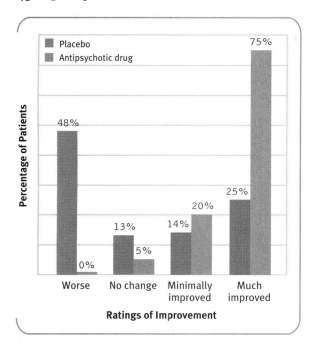

Placebo
Antipsychotic drug

75%

48%

13%
5%
14%
20%
25%

0%

Worse | No change | Minimally improved | Much improved

Ratings of Improvement

Percentage of Patients

FIGURE 15-1   The effectiveness of antipsychotic drugs *An early influential study found that after six weeks of treatment, 75 percent of patients with schizophrenia who had been given antipsychotic drugs were much improved, compared to only 25 percent of patients given placebos. In fact, close to half of those on the placebos worsened. (Adapted from Cole et al., 1964.)*

The drugs apparently produce the maximum level of improvement within the first six months of treatment (Szymanski et al., 1996); however, symptoms may return if patients stop taking the drugs too soon (Olfson et al., 2000) (see Box 15-2 on page 460). In one study, when the antipsychotic medications of people with chronic schizophrenia were changed to a placebo after five years, 75 percent of the patients relapsed within a year, compared to 33 percent of similar patients who continued to receive medication (Sampath et al., 1992).

As we observed in Chapter 14, antipsychotic drugs, particularly the conventional ones, reduce the positive symptoms of schizophrenia, such as hallucinations and delusions, more completely, or at least more quickly, than the negative symptoms, such as flat affect, poverty of speech, and loss of volition (Kirkpatrick et al., 2000; Szymanski et al., 1996). Correspondingly, people who display predominantly positive symptoms (Type I schizophrenia) generally have better rates of recovery from schizophrenia than those with predominantly negative symptoms (Type II schizophrenia) (Lindström, 1996; Lindström et al., 1992). Inasmuch as men with schizophrenia tend to have more negative symptoms than women, it is not surprising that they require higher doses and respond less readily to the antipsychotic drugs (Szymanski et al., 1996, 1995; Angermeyer et al., 1990; Seeman, 1982).

Although antipsychotic drugs are now prescribed for most cases of schizophrenia, patients often dislike their powerful effects—both intended and unintended—and some refuse to take them (Olfson et al., 2000). But like Edward Snow, a writer who overcame schizophrenia, many are greatly helped by the medications.

> In my case it was necessary to come to terms with a specified drug program. I am a legalized addict. My dose: 100 milligrams of Thorazine and 60 milligrams of Stelazine daily. I don't feel this dope at all, but I have been told it is strong enough to flatten a normal person. It keeps me—as the doctors agree—sane and in good spirits. Without the brain candy, as I call it, I would go—zoom—right back into the bin. I've made the institution scene enough already to be familiar with what it's like and to know I don't want to go back.
>
> *(Snow, 1976)*

The Unwanted Effects of Conventional Antipsychotic Drugs

In addition to reducing schizophrenic symptoms, the conventional antipsychotic drugs sometimes produce disturbing movement problems that may impair a patient's functioning (Gerlach & Peacock, 1995). These effects are called **extrapyramidal effects** because they appear to be caused by the drugs' impact on the extrapyramidal areas of the brain, which participate in the control of motor activity. These undesired effects are so common that they are listed as a separate category of disorders—*medication-induced movement disorders*—in DSM-IV (APA, 2000, 1994). They include *Parkinsonian and related symptoms, neuroleptic malignant syndrome,* and *tardive dyskinesia.*

PARKINSONIAN AND RELATED SYMPTOMS The most common extrapyramidal effects are *Parkinsonian symptoms,* reactions that closely resemble the features of the neurological disorder Parkinson's disease. At least half of patients on conventional antipsychotic drugs experience muscle tremors and muscle rigidity at some point in their treatment; they may shake, move slowly, shuffle their feet, and show little facial expression (APA, 2000). Common related symptoms are (1) *dystonia,* involuntary muscle contractions that produce bizarre and uncontrollable movements of the face, neck, tongue, and back (Khanna, Das, & Damodaran, 1992), and (2) *akathisia,* great restlessness, agitation, and discomfort in the

EXTRAPYRAMIDAL EFFECTS Unwanted movements, such as severe shaking, bizarre-looking grimaces, twisting of the body, and extreme restlessness, sometimes produced by conventional antipsychotic drugs.

TARDIVE DYSKINESIA Extrapyramidal effects that appear in some patients after they have taken conventional antipsychotic drugs for an extended time.

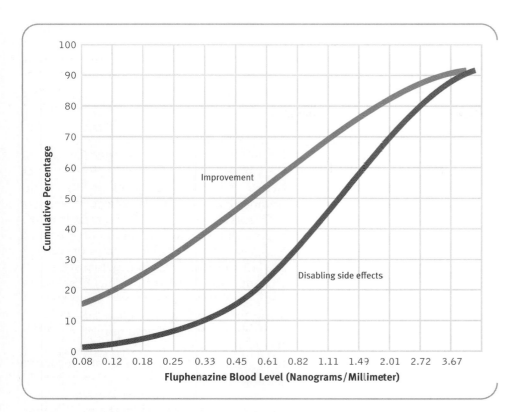

FIGURE 15-2 **The trade-off** *The reactions of patients with schizophrenia to the conventional antipsychotic drug fluphenazine (Prolixin) demonstrate the close relationship between drug dosage, patient improvement, and serious unwanted drug effects. As the blood level of the drug increases, patients improve, but disabling effects of the drug increase as well. At higher levels of the drug, the benefits-risk trade-off becomes questionable. (Adapted from Barondes, 1993, p. 162.)*

limbs, which causes individuals to move their arms and legs continually in search of relief. The Parkinsonian symptoms seem to be related to medication-induced reductions of dopamine activity in the *substantia nigra,* a part of the brain that coordinates movement and posture (Pickar et al., 1991). In most cases, they can be reversed if an anti-Parkinsonian drug is taken along with the antipsychotic drug (Silver et al., 1995). Alternatively, clinicians may have to reduce the dose of the antipsychotic drug or stop it altogether (see Figure 15-2).

NEUROLEPTIC MALIGNANT SYNDROME In as many as 2 percent of patients, particularly elderly ones, conventional antipsychotic drugs produce *neuroleptic malignant syndrome,* a severe, potentially fatal reaction consisting of muscle rigidity, fever, altered consciousness, and improper functioning of the autonomic nervous system (APA, 2000; Hermesh et al., 1992). As soon as the syndrome is recognized, drug use is discontinued and each neuroleptic symptom is treated medically (Velamoor et al., 1994; Levenson, 1985).

TARDIVE DYSKINESIA Whereas most of the undesired drug effects appear within days or weeks of the drug's introduction, a reaction called **tardive dyskinesia** (meaning "late-appearing movement disorder") does not usually appear until after a person has taken conventional antipsychotic drugs for more than a year. Sometimes it does not even appear until after the medications are stopped (Schultz et al., 1995; Wyatt, 1995). This syndrome may include involuntary writhing or ticlike movements of the tongue, mouth, face, or whole body; involuntary chewing, sucking, and lip smacking; and jerky, purposeless movements of the arms, legs, or entire body. It is sometimes accompanied by memory difficulties (Sorokin et al., 1988).

Most cases of tardive dyskinesia are mild and consist of a single symptom, such as tongue flicking; however, some are severe and include such features as continual rocking back and forth, irregular breathing, and grotesque twisting of the face and body. It is believed that over 20 percent of the people who take conventional drugs for an extended time develop tardive dyskinesia to some degree,

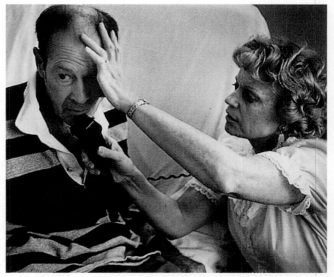

Unwanted effects *This man has a severe case of Parkinson's disease, a disorder caused by low dopamine activity, and his muscle tremors prevent him from shaving himself. The conventional antipsychotic drugs often produce similar Parkinsonian symptoms.*

B O X **15-2**

"The Monkeys Are Eating My Brain"

For much of the 1990s, Michael Laudor was an inspiration for anyone who had ever suffered from schizophrenia. In 1998 he became a cautionary note about the precarious nature of this disorder—a reminder that excessive stress or premature cessation of medications can lead to relapse and, in some instances, to dire consequences.

A brilliant young man who graduated *summa cum laude* from Yale University, Laudor developed schizophrenia at the age of 24 and was hospitalized for eight months. With antipsychotic medications, psychotherapy, and strong family support, he apparently overcame his many delusions and hallucinations and was accepted at Yale Law School. Still grappling with schizophrenia when he first learned of his acceptance, he screamed, "The monkeys are eating my brain." But he continued to recover during his years at Yale, and he became known for his brilliant mind, charismatic personality, and mastery of the jazz guitar (Morganthau, 1998).

Courageous and concerned about the plight of others with schizophrenia, Laudor openly discussed his disorder in a lengthy interview in the *New York Times* in 1995. "People with schizophrenia are negated constantly," he said then. "But I can . . . say I am a person with schizophrenia who has been a senior editor of *The Yale Law Review*, who is a reasonable candidate to be a law professor. And if I am not doing that, I will be doing something else of value to society."

The interview transformed his life. It led to a $600,000 advance for an autobiographical book and $1.5 million for the movie rights to it. He moved to a quiet New York suburb with his fiancée, Caroline Costello, the two of them prepared for the birth of a child, and Michael went to work on his book.

But on a summer day in 1998, Caroline was murdered—stabbed more than ten times with a chef's

IMPROPER DOSAGE

Recent interviews with over 700 people suffering from schizophrenia revealed that 39 percent of them were receiving too low a dosage of antipsychotic medication, 32 percent too high a dosage, and only 29 percent an appropriate dosage (PORT, 1998).

and the longer the drugs are taken, the greater the risk becomes (APA, 2000; Chakos et al., 1996). Patients over 45 years of age seem to be as much as six times more vulnerable than younger persons (Jeste et al., 1996).

Tardive dyskinesia can be difficult, sometimes impossible, to eliminate. If it is discovered early and the conventional drugs are stopped immediately, it will eventually disappear in most cases (APA, 2000; Pickar et al., 1991). Early detection, however, is elusive, because some of the symptoms are similar to schizophrenic symptoms. Clinicians may easily overlook them, continue to administer the drugs, and unintentionally create a more serious case of tardive dyskinesia (Fenn et al., 1996; McCreadie et al., 1996). The longer patients continue to take conventional antipsychotic drugs, the less likely it is that their tardive dyskinesia will disappear, even when the drugs are stopped. There is some evidence that treatment with vitamin E helps reduce or prevent tardive dyskinesia, but other research results conflict with that conclusion (Gattaz, 1995; Ricketts et al., 1995). Researchers do not fully understand why conventional antipsychotic drugs cause tardive dyskinesia; however, they suspect that, once again, the problem is related to the drugs' effect on dopamine receptors in the substantia nigra.

HOW SHOULD CONVENTIONAL ANTIPSYCHOTIC DRUGS BE PRESCRIBED? Today clinicians are more knowledgeable and more cautious about prescribing conventional antipsychotic drugs than they have been in the past. Previously, when patients did not improve with such a drug, their clinicians would keep increasing the dose (Kane, 1992); today a clinician will typically stop the drug (Coryell et al.,

knife. Soon after, Laudor was found on the campus of Cornell University, disheveled and spattered with blood. He confessed to attacking Caroline (Chua-Eoan, 1998). No one knew precisely what had caused Laudor to kill his fiancée, but few doubted that a return of psychotic functioning was generally responsible. The police reported that he seemed disoriented at the time of his arrest. His mother had detected delusional ideas in phone conversations that she had had with him during the days preceding the killing. Caroline herself had increasingly been expressing concerns to friends about his mental condition.

What triggered Laudor's relapse and out-of-character behavior (friends had never known him to be violent)? Some friends believe that he had stopped taking his antipsychotic medications; others suggest that the medications had stopped being effective. Then again, Laudor had been experiencing considerable stress in his life. He had not been able to find work as a law professor despite (or

perhaps because of) his fame, and writing the book seemed to place enormous pressure on him, given his perfectionistic ways. Some friends also pointed out that the death of Laudor's father in 1995 had left him without one of his most important sources of support: he had previously credited his father with saving his life.

Whatever the specific trigger, Laudor's fall was a tragedy not only for him and his fiancée but for everyone who saw him as evidence that schizophrenia can be conquered. Although numerous people with this disorder do recover, many without relapse, this highly publicized

Battle lost *(Facing page) Yale Law School student Michael Laudor, who described his inspirational battle against schizophrenia in a 1995 interview with the New York Times. (This page) Laudor is taken into custody in 1998 and charged with killing his fiancée in their garden apartment.*

case reminds us of how much the clinical field has yet to learn about the causes, course, and treatment of schizophrenia.

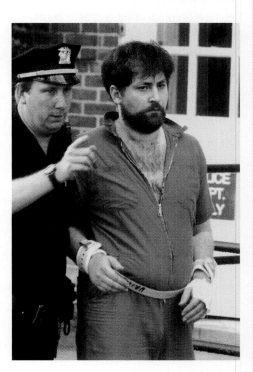

1998). Similarly, today's clinicians try to prescribe the lowest effective dose for each patient and to gradually reduce or stop medication weeks or months after the patient begins functioning normally (Gilbert et al., 1995). However, it turns out that many patients cannot function without these medications (Lerner et al., 1995), and they may be put back on the medications rather quickly, sometimes at doses that are higher than recommended (Remington et al., 1993).

New Antipsychotic Drugs

Chapter 14 noted that new "atypical" antipsychotic drugs have been developed in recent years (Schulz, 2000). As we have observed, these drugs are called atypical because their biological operation differs from that of the conventional antipsychotic medications: the former are received at fewer dopamine D-2 receptors and more D-1 and serotonin receptors than the latter (Worrel et al., 2000; Kasper et al., 1999). The most effective and widely used of these new drugs are **clozapine** (trade name Clozaril), **risperidone** (Risperdal), **olanzapine** (Zyprexa), and **quetiapine** (Seroquel). The atypical drugs appear to be more effective than the conventional drugs, helping as many as 85 percent of persons with schizophrenia, compared with the 65 percent helped by most of the earlier generation of drugs (Awad & Voruganti, 1999; Lieberman, 1998). It is particularly promising that the new drugs also help patients who experience primarily *negative symptoms* (Type II schizophrenia)—people who do not respond well to the conventional drugs (Remington & Kapur, 2000; Lieberman et al., 1996).

CLOZAPINE A commonly prescribed atypical antipsychotic drug. Other commonly prescribed atypical antipsychotic drugs are *risperidone, olanzapine,* and *quetiapine.*

Another major benefit of the atypical antipsychotic drugs is that they cause few extrapyramidal symptoms, apparently because they do not block as many D-2 receptors (APA, 2000; Remington & Kapur, 2000; Worrel et al., 2000). Most important, they do not seem to produce tardive dyskinesia (Casey, 1998). In fact, tardive dyskinesia and other extrapyramidal symptoms are sometimes reduced when patients with schizophrenia are switched from the conventional to the atypical drugs (Gerlach et al., 1996).

Yet the new drugs have serious drawbacks as well. With clozapine, for example, people run a 1 to 2 percent risk of developing **agranulocytosis**, a life-threatening reduction in white blood cells (Alvir, Lieberman, & Safferman, 1995). Patients who take this drug must therefore have frequent blood tests so that this effect can be detected early and the drug stopped (Perry, 2000; Honigfeld et al., 1998) (see Box 15-3). Moreover, there are some indications that combining clozapine with certain antidepressant drugs can produce serious medical problems for certain patients (Centorrino et al., 1996).

Psychotherapy

Before the discovery of antipsychotic drugs, psychotherapy was not really an option for people with schizophrenia. Most were simply too far removed from reality to profit from it. Only a handful of therapists, apparently blessed with extraordinary patience and skill, specialized in the psychotherapeutic treatment of this disorder and reported a measure of success (Will, 1967, 1961; Sullivan, 1962, 1953; Fromm-Reichmann, 1950, 1948, 1943). These therapists believed that the first task of such therapy was to win the trust of patients with schizophrenia and build a close relationship with them.

The well-known clinical theorist and therapist Frieda Fromm-Reichmann, for example, would initially tell her patients that they could continue to exclude her from their private world and hold onto their disorder as long as they wished. She reported that eventually, after much testing and acting out, the patients would accept, trust, and grow attached to her, and begin to talk to her about their problems. Case studies seemed to attest to the effectiveness of such approaches and to the importance of trust and emotional bonding in treatment. Here a recovered woman tells her therapist how she had felt during their early interactions:

> At the start, I didn't listen to what you said most of the time but I watched like a hawk for your expression and the sound of your voice. After the interview, I would add all this up to see if it seemed to show love. The words were nothing compared to the feelings you showed. I sense that you felt confident I could be helped and that there was hope for the future. . . .
>
> The problem with schizophrenics is that they can't trust anyone. They can't put their eggs in one basket. The doctor will usually have to fight to get in no matter how much the patient objects. . . .
>
> Loving is impossible at first because it turns you into a helpless little baby. The patient can't feel safe to do this until he is absolutely sure the doctor understands what is needed and will provide it.
>
> *(Hayward & Taylor, 1965)*

Today psychotherapy is successful in many more cases of schizophrenia, thanks to the assistance of antipsychotic drugs. By helping to relieve thought and perceptual disturbances, the drugs allow people with schizophrenia to learn about their disorder, participate actively in the therapeutic process, think more clearly about themselves and their relationships, and make changes in their behavior (Svensson, Hansson, & Nyman, 2000; Liberman et al., 1998; Atkinson et al., 1996). Although psychotherapy may be of little help during the earliest stages of treatment, it apparently becomes useful later on, particularly after medica-

AGRANULOCYTOSIS A life-threatening reduction in white blood cells. This condition is sometimes produced by clozapine, one of the atypical antipsychotic drugs.

BOX 15-3

Just Because You're Paranoid . . .

When *clozapine* (brand name Clozaril) was approved in 1990 for use as the first atypical antipsychotic drug in the United States, it opened the door to more effective and safer treatments for schizophrenia. However, the early use of this drug in the United States brought only frustration and heartache to hundreds of thousands of prospective users.

The problem with clozapine began with the discovery that a small percentage of people who take this drug develop *agranulocytosis,* a life-threatening drop in white blood cell count. The U.S. Food and Drug Administration (FDA) thus approved clozapine with the requirement that patients who take it must have their blood tested every week for signs of agranulocytosis.

Unfortunately, the drug's manufacturer decided to further require that all clozapine users in the United States had to purchase an entire treatment package consisting of the medication *and* weekly testing by the drug company's own subsidiaries. Most patients in the United States could not afford the company's

fee for this combination—a whopping $9,000 a year. What's more, their insurance companies refused to pay for it. Clearly patients were caught in the middle between big business and the health industry.

A flurry of lawsuits followed. So did federal investigations and hearings. After several years the drug's manufacturer finally agreed to sell clozapine separately, allowing patients to get blood tests elsewhere at lower cost. Moreover, the FDA reduced its requirement for such tests to every *two* weeks, rather than every week, after patients have received clozapine treatment for six months (Bender, 1998). Sadly, however, many patients had already lost valuable time.

ConsiderThis

◉ Why have people with schizophrenia been the victims of mistreatment (lobotomy or deinstitutionalization, for example) more often than people with other disorders? • Should companies in the private sector have so much control over the cost and distribution of a critical breakthrough drug, one that could improve millions of lives? • Clozapine was available in Europe fifteen years before its approval in the United States. Might the FDA be too cautious in its approach to new drugs?

tions have made an impact. The most helpful forms of psychotherapy include *insight therapy* and two sociocultural therapies—*family therapy* and *social therapy.* Often these approaches are combined and adjusted to a patient's particular needs (Jeffries, 1995; Prendergast, 1995).

Insight Therapy

Various kinds of insight therapies may be used in cases of schizophrenia (Scott & Wright, 1997; Chadwick & Trower, 1996). Studies suggest that the particular orientations of insight therapists are less important than their levels of experience with schizophrenia (Karon & Vandenbos, 1996). In addition, the therapists who are most successful tend to be those who take a relatively active role, setting limits, expressing opinions, challenging patients' statements, providing guidance, displaying empathy, and gaining trust (Fox, 2000; Whitehorn & Betz, 1975).

Family Therapy

Between 25 and 40 percent of people who are recovering from schizophrenia live with family: parents, siblings, spouses, or children (Torrey, Wolfe, & Flynn, 1988; Bocker, 1984). Such situations create special pressures, so that even if family stress was not a factor in the onset of the disorder, a patient's recovery may be greatly influenced by the behavior and reactions of the relatives at home.

DIFFERENCE OF OPINION

According to a survey in Australia, clinicians generally consider antipsychotic drugs and hospitalization to be very helpful approaches in cases of schizophrenia. The general population considers vitamins, herbal medicines, and self-help books to be of greater help (Jorm et al., 1997).

"I'M GLAD YOU CAME TO ME. VISIONS OF GHOSTS OF CHRISTMAS PAST, PRESENT AND FUTURE ARE CLEARLY DELUSIONS BASED ON UNDERLYING PSYCHOLOGICAL CONFLICTS."

(© 1998 Sidney Harris)

Generally speaking, persons with schizophrenia who feel positively toward their relatives do better in treatment (Lebell et al., 1993; Scott et al., 1993). As we observed in Chapter 14, recovered patients living with relatives who display high levels of *expressed emotion*—that is, relatives who are very critical, emotionally over-involved, and hostile—often have a higher relapse rate than those living with more positive and supportive relatives (Penn & Mueser, 1996; Fox, 1992; Vaughan et al., 1992).

For their part, family members may be greatly affected by the social withdrawal and unusual behaviors of a relative with schizophrenia (Bloch et al., 1995; Creer & Wing, 1974). One individual complained, for example, "In the evening you go into the sitting room and it's in darkness. You turn on the light and there he is just sitting there, staring in front of him."

To address such issues, clinicians now commonly incorporate family therapy into their treatment of schizophrenia, providing family members with guidance, training, practical advice, psychoeducation about the disorder, and emotional support and empathy (Baucom et al., 1998; Penn & Meuser, 1996). In family therapy, relatives establish more realistic expectations and become more tolerant, less guilt-ridden, and more willing to try new patterns of communication. Family therapy also helps the person with schizophrenia cope with the pressures of family life, interact more positively with family members, and benefit from the family environment. Research has found that family therapy—particularly when it is combined with drug therapy—helps reduce tensions within the family and so helps relapse rates go down (Cameron et al., 1999; Baucom et al., 1998). The principles of this approach are evident in the following description:

Mark was a 32-year-old single man living with his parents. He had a long and stormy history of schizophrenia with many episodes of psychosis, interspersed with occasional brief periods of good functioning. Mark's father was a bright but neurotically tormented man gripped by obsessions and inhibitions in spite of many years of psychoanalysis. Mark's mother appeared weary, detached, and embittered. Both parents felt hopeless about Mark's chances of recovery and resentful that needing to care for him would always plague their lives. They acted as if they were being intentionally punished. It gradually emerged that the father, in fact, was riddled with guilt and self-doubt; he suspected that his wife had been cold and rejecting toward Mark as an infant and that he had failed to intervene, due to his unwillingness to confront his wife and the demands of graduate school that distanced him from home life. He entertained the fantasy that Mark's illness was a punishment for this. Every time Mark did begin to show improvement—both in reduced symptoms and in increased functioning—his parents responded as if it were just a cruel torment designed to raise their hopes and then to plunge them into deeper despair when Mark's condition deteriorated. This pattern was especially apparent when Mark got a job. As a result, at such times, the parents actually became more critical and hostile toward Mark. He would become increasingly defensive and insecure, finally developing paranoid delusions, and usually would be hospitalized in a panicky and agitated state.

All of this became apparent during the psychoeducational sessions. When the pattern was pointed out to the family, they were able to recognize their self-fulfilling prophecy and were motivated to deal with it. As a result, the therapist decided to see the family together. Concrete instances of the pattern and its consequences were explored, and alternative responses by the parents were developed. The therapist encouraged both the parents and Mark to discuss their

SHORTER STAYS

In 1997 the average length of stay in a mental hospital in the United States was 10.2 days, down 11 percent from the previous year (NAPHS, 1999).

anxieties and doubts about Mark's progress, rather than to stir up one another's expectations of failure. The therapist had regular individual sessions with Mark as well as the family sessions. As a result, Mark has successfully held a job for an unprecedented 12 months.

(Heinrichs & Carpenter, 1983, pp. 284–285)

The families of people with schizophrenia may also turn to *family support groups* and *family psychoeducational programs* for assistance, encouragement, and advice (Herz et al., 2000; Zhang et al., 1998). In such programs, family members meet with others in the same situation to share their thoughts and emotions, provide mutual support, and learn about schizophrenia. Although research has yet to fully evaluate the usefulness of these groups, the approach is becoming quite popular.

"Her face was a solemn mask, and she could neither give nor receive affection."

Mother, 1991, describing her daughter who has schizophrenia

Social Therapy

Many clinicians believe that the treatment of people with schizophrenia should include techniques that address the social and other personal difficulties in the clients' lives. These clinicians offer practical advice; work with clients on problem solving, decision making, and social skills; make sure that the clients are taking their medications properly; and may even help them find work, financial assistance, and proper housing (McGuire, 2000; Penn & Mueser, 1996). This practical, active, and broad approach has been called at various times *social therapy* and *personal therapy* (Hogarty et al., 1997, 1986, 1974).

Research finds that social therapy does help keep patients with schizophrenia out of the hospital. One study compared the progress of four groups of chronic patients after their discharge from a state hospital (Hogarty et al., 1986, 1974). One group received both antipsychotic medications and social therapy in the community, while the other groups received medication only, social therapy only, or no treatment of any kind. The researchers' first finding was that chronic patients need to continue taking medication after being released in order to avoid rehospitalization. Over a two-year period, 80 percent of those who did not continue medication needed to be hospitalized again, compared to 48 percent of those who received medication. They also found that among the patients on medication, those who also received social therapy adjusted to the community and avoided rehospitalization most successfully. Clearly, social therapy played an important role in their recovery.

The Community Approach

The broadest approach for the treatment of schizophrenia is the *community approach*. In 1963, partly in response to the terrible conditions in public mental institutions, the U.S. government ordered many patients to be released and treated in their communities. Congress passed the Community Mental Health Act, which stipulated that patients with psychological disorders were henceforth to receive a range of mental health services—outpatient therapy, inpatient treatment, emergency care, preventive care, and aftercare—without leaving their communities, rather than being transported to institutions far from home. The act was meant to encompass a variety of psychological disorders, but patients with schizophrenia, especially those who had been institutionalized for years, were

Art that heals *Art and other creative activities can be therapeutic for people with schizophrenia and other severe mental disorders. More than 250,000 pieces of patient-produced art are on display at the Museum of the Unconscious in Rio de Janeiro, Brazil, where supervisors work closely with patients every day. One of the museum's most famous and talented patients, Fernando Diniz, poses with some of his extraordinary artwork.*

DEINSTITUTIONALIZATION The discharge of large numbers of patients from long-term institutional care so that they might be treated in community programs.

COMMUNITY MENTAL HEALTH CENTER A treatment facility that provides medication, psychotherapy, and emergency inpatient care for psychological problems and coordinates treatment in the community.

AFTERCARE A program of posthospitalization care and treatment out in the community.

affected most. Other countries around the world put similar sociocultural treatment programs into action shortly thereafter (Hafner & an der Heiden, 1988).

Thus began more than three decades of **deinstitutionalization**, an exodus of hundreds of thousands of patients with schizophrenia and other chronic mental disorders from state institutions into the community. On a given day in 1955 close to 600,000 patients were living in state institutions; today only around 70,000 patients reside in those settings (Lang, 1999; Torrey, 1997). Clinicians have learned that patients recovering from schizophrenia can profit greatly from community programs. However, as we shall see, the quality of community care for these people has been inadequate throughout the United States. The result is a "revolving door" syndrome: many patients have been released to the community, readmitted to an institution within months, released a second time, admitted yet again, and so on, over and over (Geller, 1992).

What Are the Features of Effective Community Care?

Today there is wide agreement that people recovering from schizophrenia need medication, psychotherapy, active monitoring of symptoms, help in handling daily pressures and responsibilities, guidance in making decisions, training in social skills, residential supervision, and vocational counseling, a combination of services sometimes called *assertive community treatment*. Those whose communities provide these services make greater progress than people whose communities do not (McGuire, 2000; Pickett et al., 1999; Peikin, 1998; Scott & Dixon, 1995). Some of the key features in effective community care programs are (1) coordination of patient services, (2) short-term hospitalization, (3) partial hospitalization, (4) halfway houses, and (5) occupational training.

COORDINATED SERVICES The writers of the Community Mental Health Act intended all community care to revolve around a **community mental health center**, a treatment facility that would provide medication, psychotherapy, and inpatient emergency care to people with severe disturbances, as well as coordinate the services offered by other community agencies. Each center was expected to serve a designated "catchment area," a geographic area with a population of 50,000 to 200,000 people.

When community mental health centers are available and provide this range of services, patients with schizophrenia often make significant progress (Scott & Dixon, 1995; Beiser et al., 1985). They are better integrated into the community and function more effectively than patients who receive only standard outpatient care (Madianos & Madianou, 1992). Coordination of services is particularly important for the so-called *mentally ill chemical abusers* (MICAs), patients with both schizophrenia and a substance-related disorder (see Box 15-4).

SHORT-TERM HOSPITALIZATION When people develop schizophrenic symptoms, today's clinicians first try to treat them on an outpatient basis, usually with a combination of antipsychotic medication and psychotherapy (Marder, 1996). If this approach fails, *short-term hospitalization* that lasts a few weeks (rather than months or years) may be tried. Soon after the patients improve in the hospital, they are released for **aftercare**, a general term for follow-up care and treatment in the community (Sederer, 1992). Short-term hospitalization usually leads to greater improvement and a lower rehospitalization rate than extended institutionalization (Caton, 1982). Countries throughout the world now favor this policy (Hafner & an der Heiden, 1988).

Community care in action *Clinicians have learned that people with schizophrenia and other severe disorders often make great progress in well-coordinated community treatment programs. Here patients begin their day with breakfast at New York City's Fountain House, a day center that provides daily activities and therapy, as well as extensive occupational training.*

BOX 15-4

Mentally Ill Chemical Abusers: A Challenge for Treatment

❙ A state appeals court yesterday ordered Larry Hogue, who has for years frightened residents of Manhattan's Upper West Side with his bizarre behavior, to remain in a state mental hospital until a hearing next week. . . . Before he was arrested, Mr. Hogue had attacked passers-by and cars in the area around West 96th Street and Amsterdam Avenue. . . .

. . . Mr. Hogue has been arrested 30 times and served at least six terms in prison, ranging from five days to a year, according to law-enforcement records. He now faces charges of criminal mischief for scraping the paint off a car last August. **❙**

(*NEW YORK TIMES,* February 9, 1993)

*D*uring the 1990s, Larry Hogue, nicknamed the "Wild Man of West 96th Street" by neighbors, became the best-known *mentally ill chemical abuser* (MICA) in the United States. MICAs are individuals who suffer from both a mental disorder (in his case schizophrenia) and a substance-related disorder. Between 20 and 50 percent of all people with chronic mental disorders may be MICAs (Blanchard et al., 2000; Buckley, 1998).

MICAs tend to be young and male. They often rate below average in social functioning and school achievement and above average in poverty, acting-out behavior, emergency room visits, and encounters with the criminal justice system (Bartels et al., 1993; O'Hare, 1992). MICAs commonly report greater distress and have poorer treatment outcomes than people with mental disorders who do not abuse substances (Carey et al., 1991).

The relationship between substance abuse and mental dysfunctioning is complex. A mental disorder may precede substance abuse, and the drug may be taken as a form of self-medication or as a result of impaired judgment (Ziedonis et al., 2000; Polcin, 1992). Conversely, substance abuse may cause or exacerbate psychopathology. Cocaine and amphetamines, for example, exacerbate the symptoms of psychosis and can quickly

intensify the symptoms of schizophrenia (Laruelle & Abi-Dargham, 1999; Shaner et al., 1993). Whichever begins first, substance abuse and mental disorders interact to create a unique problem that is, so to speak, greater than the sum of its parts (Boutros, Bonnet, & Mak, 1996). The course and outcome of one problem can be significantly influenced by the other.

Treatment of MICAs has been undermined by the tendency of patients to hide their drug abuse problems and for clinicians to underdiagnose them (Lehman et al., 1996). Unrecognized substance abuse may lead to misdiagnosis and misunderstanding of the disorders (Shaner et al., 1993). The treatment of MICAs is further complicated by the fact that many treatment facilities are designed and funded to treat *either* mental disorders or substance abuse; only some are equipped or willing to treat both. As a result, it is not uncommon for MICA patients to be rejected as inappropriate for treatment in both substance abuse and mental health programs. Many such individuals fall through the cracks in this way and find themselves in jail, like Larry Hogue, or in homeless shelters for want of the treatment they sought in vain (Blanchard et al., 2000).

Experts describe the ideal MICA treatment program as a safe and supportive therapeutic environment that offers techniques for treating both mental disorders

and substance abuse and takes into account the unique effects of both problems (Hellerstein, Rosenthal, & Miner, 1995; Fals & Schafer, 1992; Carey, 1989). One particularly inspiring development is the recent establishment of self-help groups for MICAs living in the community.

The problem of falling through the cracks is perhaps most poignantly seen in the case of homeless MICAs (Blanchard et al., 2000). Researchers estimate that 10 to 20 percent of the homeless population may be MICAs (Drake et al., 1991). MICAs typically are homeless longer than other homeless people and are more likely to experience extremely harsh conditions, such as living on the winter streets rather than in a homeless shelter. They are also more likely to be jailed, to trade sexual favors for food or money, to share needles, to engage in unprotected sex, and to be victimized in other ways (Susser et al., 1996). Homeless MICAs need programs committed to building trust and providing intensive case management and long-term practical assistance (Drake et al., 1991). In short, treatment programs must be tailored to MICAs' unique combination of problems rather than expecting them to adapt to traditional forms of care.

"Wild Man of West 96ᵗʰ Street" *The case of Larry Hogue, the so-called "Wild Man of West 96th Street," helped bring the plight of MICAs to public attention.*

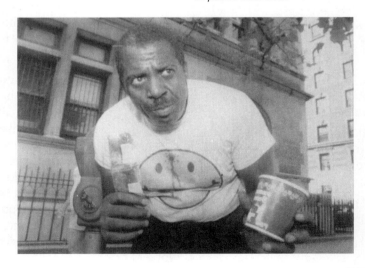

DAY CENTER A program that offers hospital-like treatment during the day only. Also known as *day hospital*.

HALFWAY HOUSE A residence for people with schizophrenia or other severe problems who cannot live alone or with their families, often staffed by paraprofessionals. Also known as *group home*.

SHELTERED WORKSHOP A supervised workplace for people who are not yet ready for competitive jobs.

PARTIAL HOSPITALIZATION For people who do not require full hospitalization but need more care than is supplied by outpatient therapy, some communities offer **day centers** or **day hospitals**, all-day programs in which patients return to their homes for the night (Clay, 1996; Goldberg, 1995). Such programs actually originated in Moscow in 1933, when a shortage of hospital beds necessitated the premature release of many patients. Today's day centers provide patients with daily supervised activities, therapy, and programs to improve social skills. People recovering from schizophrenia in day centers often do better than those who spend extended periods in a hospital or in traditional outpatient therapy (Takano et al., 1995).

HALFWAY HOUSES **Halfway houses,** also called **group homes** by clinicians, are homes for people who do not require hospitalization but cannot live alone or with their families. These residences, often large houses in areas where housing is inexpensive, may shelter between one and two dozen people. The live-in staff usually are *paraprofessionals*—lay people who receive training and ongoing supervision from outside mental health professionals. The houses are usually run with a *milieu therapy* philosophy that emphasizes mutual support, resident responsibility, and self-government.

Research indicates that halfway houses help many people recovering from schizophrenia adjust to community life and avoid rehospitalization (McGuire, 2000; Caton, 1982) (see Figure 15-3). Here is how one woman described living in a halfway house after ten hospitalizations in twelve years:

> The halfway house changed my life. First of all, I discovered that some of the staff members had once been clients in the program! That one single fact offered me hope. For the first time, I saw proof that a program could help someone, that it was possible to regain control over one's life and become independent. The house was democratically run; all residents had one vote and the staff members, outnumbered 5 to 22, could not make rules or even discharge a client from the program without majority sentiment. There was a house bill of rights that was strictly observed by all. We helped one another and gave support. When residents were in a crisis, no staff member hustled them off or increased their medication to calm them down. Residents could cry, be comforted and hugged until a solution could be found, or until they accepted that it was okay to feel bad. Even anger was an acceptable feeling that did not have to be feared, but could be expressed and turned into constructive energy. If you disliked some aspect of the program or the behavior of a staff member, you could change things rather than passively accept what was happening. Choices were real, and failure and success were accepted equally. . . . Bit by bit, my distrust faltered and the fears lessened. I slept better and made friends. . . . Other residents and staff members who had hallucinated for years and now were able to control their hallucinations shared with me some of the techniques that had worked for them. Things like diet . . . and interpersonal relationships became a few of my tools.
>
> *(Lovejoy, 1982, pp. 605–609)*

EMPLOYMENT NEEDS

Surveys indicate that 70 percent of people with severe psychological disorders rank work as an important goal (MRI, 1988).

OCCUPATIONAL TRAINING Paid employment provides income, independence, self-respect, and the stimulation of working with other people. It also brings companionship and order to one's daily life. For these reasons, occupational training and placement are important services for people with schizophrenia (McGuire, 2000; Bell, Lysaker, & Milstein, 1996).

Many people recovering from this disorder receive occupational training in a **sheltered workshop**—a supervised workplace for employees who are not ready for competitive or complicated jobs. The workshop replicates a typical work environment: products such as toys or simple appliances are manufactured and sold, workers are paid according to performance, and all are expected to be at work regularly and on time. For some, the sheltered workshop becomes a permanent

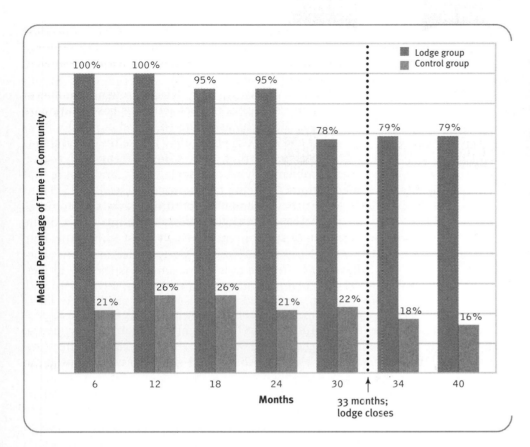

FIGURE 15-3 **The impact of halfway houses**
In a famous study by George Fairweather and his associates (1969), patients with schizophrenia who were released from a hospital to a "lodge" (halfway house and business program) adjusted better than patients who were released directly to a boardinghouse or apartment. They also remained in the community longer, avoided rehospitalization more successfully, and continued this trend even after the lodge closed.

workplace. For others, it is an important step toward better-paying and more demanding employment or a return to a previous job (Bell et al., 1996; Lehman, 1995). In the United States, occupational training is not universally available to people with severe mental disorders (Drake et al., 1996). Some studies find that only 25 percent of such people are employed, fewer than 10 percent outside of sheltered workplaces (MRI, 1998; Mulkern & Manderscheid, 1989).

How Has Community Treatment Failed?

There is no doubt that effective community programs promote the recovery of people with schizophrenia. However, fewer than half of all the people who need them receive appropriate community mental health services (McGuire, 2000; PORT, 1998). In fact, in any given year, almost 40 percent of all people with schizophrenia receive no treatment at all (Torrey, 1997; Regier et al., 1993). Two factors are primarily responsible: *poor coordination* of services and *shortage* of services.

POOR COORDINATION OF SERVICES In many communities, the various mental health agencies have no systematic procedures for communicating with one another (Leshner et al., 1992). Thus the local halfway house may have openings for people with schizophrenia but the therapist at the community mental health center may not know about it. Even within a single community agency, a patient may not have continuing contacts with the same staff members and is not assured of receiving consistent, methodical services.

Another problem is poor communication between state hospitals and community mental health centers (Torrey, 1997; Leshner et al., 1992). Sometimes community agencies are not even informed when patients are discharged from the hospital. This problem had its beginnings in the early days of deinstitutionalization, when hospitals were often forced to discharge patients before many community mental health centers were open and ready to serve them. The habits of independence that hospitals developed then have persisted to this day. Moreover,

"If it is possible to rehabilitate two-thirds of patients, why aren't we?"

Ronald Levant, 2000,
schizophrenia treatment researcher

Helping to meet the need *Because formal community services fall short for so many people with schizophrenia, the contributions of volunteers become especially important. Here, a young man with schizophrenia tries a mountain bike while his volunteer friend of 12 years looks on. The volunteer was enlisted by Compeer Inc., an organization in Rochester, New York, dedicated to befriending community residents who have psychological disorders.*

institutional care is now so expensive that institutions often feel pressured to release their patients before appropriate discharge plans have been devised and put in place (Leshner et al., 1992).

It is not surprising, then, that a growing number of community therapists now function as **case managers** for people with schizophrenia (Chan et al., 2000; Pickett et al., 1999; Wolff et al., 1997). Like the social therapists described earlier, they offer therapy and advice, teach problem-solving and social skills, and ensure that medications are being taken properly (see Box 15-5). In addition, they attempt to coordinate available community services, guide clients through the intricacies of the community system, and, perhaps most important, help protect clients' legal rights. Many professionals now believe that effective case management is the key to success for a community program (Dozier, 1996).

SHORTAGE OF SERVICES The number of community programs available to people with schizophrenia falls woefully short. The roughly 800 community mental health centers now operating in the United States are only one-third of the number projected in the early 1960s. Halfway houses and sheltered workshops are in similarly short supply.

Also disturbing is that the existing community mental health centers generally fail to provide adequate services for people with severe disorders. They tend to devote their efforts and money to people with less disabling problems, such as anxiety disorders or problems in social adjustment. Patients with schizophrenia therefore represent a small fraction of the people treated by community mental health centers (Torrey, 1997, 1988; Rosenstein et al., 1990, 1989).

Why is there such a shortage of services for people with schizophrenia? First, it appears that most mental health professionals simply prefer to work with people whose problems are less severe and long lasting (Lee et al., 1993; Harding et al., 1992). Second, neighborhood residents often object to the presence of community programs for patients recovering from schizophrenia, sometimes going so far as to picket, protest, and even vandalize community facilities (Leshner et al., 1992). This has been referred to as the "NIMBY" syndrome—an acronym for *not in my backyard.*

BOX 15-5

"I Miss Them, I Want Them to Come Back"

Scott Carrier (1966), a researcher in Utah, recalls his clinical interview with a woman who was suffering from schizophrenia:

I get to the question "Have you been worrying a lot?" And she says, yes, she has, she's been worrying a lot that the elders of the church, the Mormon Church, will take her daughter away from her. I ask her why, and she says because she stopped taking her medication. She says that the only reason she took it is because she told her bishop that she'd been visited by the archangel Gabriel and that she had had sex with him. And then she'd also been visited by the archangel Michael, and she'd had sex with both of them at once, and they'd ravished her almost every night since. So her bishop made her go to a doctor, and the doctor gave her some pills, and she took the pills, and the angels stopped coming. The bishop and the elders told her that if she had sex with any more angels they'd take her daughter away. So I ask her again why she stopped taking her medication, and she says, "I'm lonely, I miss them, I want them to come back." I

ConsiderThis

Why might some patients welcome delusions or hallucinations into their lives? • How might clinicians combat the resistance to treatment found in many persons with schizophrenia? • Was this woman totally free of schizophrenic symptoms even while she was on the medication?

Perhaps the primary reason for the shortage of community care is economic. On the one hand, more public funds are available for people with psychological disorders now than in the past. In 1963 a total of $1 billion was spent in this area, whereas today more than $61 billion is spent on people with mental disorders (Torrey, 1997, 1988; Redick et al., 1992). On the other hand, rather little of this new money is going to community treatment programs for people with severe disorders. Much of it goes to monthly income payments such as social security disability income, to services for persons with mental disorders in nursing homes and general hospitals, and to community services for people who are less disturbed (Torrey, 1997, 1988; Stein, 1993). Moreover, a considerable amount still goes to state hospitals (even though the populations of these hospitals have decreased more than 80 percent since 1963). Today the financial burden of providing community treatment for persons with long-term severe disorders often falls on local governments and nonprofit organizations rather than the federal or state government, and local resources cannot always meet this challenge.

WHAT ARE THE CONSEQUENCES OF INADEQUATE COMMUNITY TREATMENT? What happens to people with schizophrenia whose communities do not provide the services they need and whose families cannot afford private treatment? As we have observed, a large number receive no treatment at all; many others spend a short time in a state hospital and are then discharged prematurely, often without adequate follow-up treatment (Torrey, 1997; Torrey et al., 1988).

Many of the people with schizophrenia return to their families and receive medication and perhaps emotional and financial support, but little else in the way of treatment. Between 5 and 15 percent enter an alternative institution such as a nursing home or rest home, where they receive only custodial care and medication (Torrey, 1997; Smyer, 1989). As many as 35 percent are placed in single-room-occupancy hotels, boardinghouses, or rooming houses, typically in run-down inner-city neighborhoods. Many of these places offer only small rooms in conditions that are substandard and unsafe. The following newspaper account describes this situation:

> Hundreds of mentally ill patients throughout Dade County are being packed into aging hotels and homes that are little better than slums, according to health officials, who say the appalling living conditions virtually ensure patients will sink deeper into insanity.
>
> Florida's policy of emptying its mental institutions, a paucity of appropriate "halfway houses," and lax inspections of existing homes have left many mentally ill without the care that might ease them back into normal life.
>
> It also has left them without protection. Released from hospitals into overburdened halfway houses, the indigent patients eventually are shunted to landlords, some of whom jam them, perhaps three to a room, into decaying and dangerous buildings and then collect their welfare payments as rent.
>
> The worst buildings, found scattered throughout Little Havana and the dying hotel district in South Miami Beach, contain the stuff of nightmares. Piles of trash and feces litter the floors. Half-naked men wander purposelessly through hallways, and doors swing open into hot and fetid rooms where others, gazing vacantly at the ceiling, lie neglected on dirty cots. . . .
>
> In one instance, [the state Department of Health and Rehabilitative Services] released patients to a Little Havana house run by a landlord who three years earlier lost his state license to operate a group home because of its life-threatening conditions.
>
> The landlord . . . didn't apply for a license for his latest home at 218 SW Eighth Ave. Instead, he used plywood sheets to divide the coral rock house into

CASE MANAGER A community therapist who offers a full range of services for people with schizophrenia or other severe disorders, including therapy, advice, medication, guidance, and protection of patients' rights.

Lobbying for better care *In a creative form of protest, members of the Florida Alliance for the Mentally Ill chained together figures without faces in 1997 and placed them outside the state capitol building. The members were reminding state legislators about the needs of the tens of thousands of faceless patients who are held captive by their disorders.*

> 12-foot by 14-foot boxes and then told HRS workers he would take in the mentally ill.
>
> Each of the boxes, strung along trash-strewn passageways in the two-story house, contains a narrow bed, a fan and a chest of drawers. Hot meal containers and plastic forks fill waste bins. Most of the boxes also contained people like Vallant Garez, a timid 55-year-old whose bed sores attest to hours spent in bed, staring at a paint-chipped wall a foot from his pillow.
>
> *(Miami Herald, August 10, 1984)*

Most boardinghouse residents survive on government disability payments (Barker et al., 1992), and many spend their days wandering through neighborhood streets. Thus it is sometimes said that people with schizophrenia are now "dumped" in the community, just as they were once "warehoused" in institutions.

Finally, a great number of people with schizophrenia have become homeless (Herman et al., 2000; Susnick & Belcher, 1995). There are between 350,000 and 1 million homeless people in the United States, and approximately one-third apparently have a severe mental disorder, commonly schizophrenia (Torrey, 1997; Manderscheid & Rosenstein, 1992) (see Box 15-6). Many such persons have been released from hospitals. Others are young adults who were never hospitalized in the first place. Another 150,000 people with severe mental disorders end up in prisons because their disorders have led them to break the law (Torrey, 1997; DeAngelis, 1994). Certainly deinstitutionalization and the community mental health movement have failed these individuals, and many report actually feeling relieved if they are able to return to hospital life (Drake & Wallach, 1992).

The Promise of Community Treatment

Despite these very serious problems, proper community care has shown great potential for assisting in the recovery from schizophrenia and other severe disorders, and clinicians and many government officials continue to press to make it more available. In recent years government and professional agencies have created task forces whose purpose is to find more effective ways for the federal government, states, and local organizations to meet the needs of people with such disorders (Knowlton, 1997; Leshner et al., 1992).

Another important development has been the formation of *national interest groups* that push for better community treatment (McGuire, 2000; Torrey, 1997). One, the National Alliance for the Mentally Ill, began in 1979 with 300 members and has expanded to more than 208,000 members in 1,200 chapters (NAMI, 1999). Made up largely of relatives of people with severe mental disorders (particularly schizophrenia, bipolar disorders, and major depressive disorder), this group has become a powerful lobbying force in state legislatures and has pressured community mental health centers to treat more persons with schizophrenia and other severe disorders.

Today community care is a major feature of treatment for people recovering from schizophrenia in countries around the world (Dencker & Dencker, 1995; Fog, 1995). Some countries, learning from the mistakes of deinstitutionalization in the United States, have

THE NEW MENTAL INSTITUTIONS
The Los Angeles County Jail, where 3,300 of the 21,000 inmates require daily mental health services, is now de facto the largest mental institution in the United States (Torrey, 1997; Grinfeld, 1993).

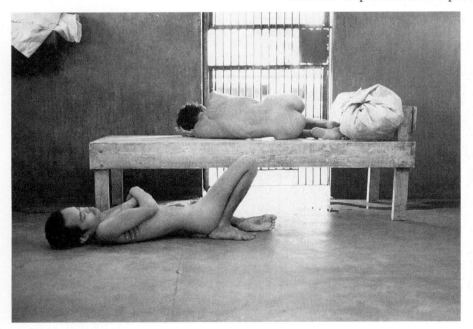

Hospital neglect *Even as countries around the world move away from long-term institutional care and toward community mental health, the horrors of asylums and overcrowded public mental hospitals continue to live in some locations. This heartwrenching scene inside a mental hospital in the southern Philippines clarifies the point.*

BOX **15-6**

Coming Full Circle

During the past three decades patients with schizophrenia have journeyed from mental hospitals, where they received poor care, into the community, where many receive no care at all. E. Fuller Torrey describes the ultimate irony in this tragic state of affairs:

> For three quarters of a century . . . part of Manhattan State Hospital [served] patients with severe mental illnesses. Then, as more and more beds became vacant in the 1970s, the building was no longer needed and it was turned over to the City of New York, which reopened it in 1981 as a public shelter [the Keener Shelter] for homeless men. . . .
>
> In 1990, the Keener Shelter housed 800 homeless men. At least 40 percent of them were mentally ill and many had previously been patients at Manhattan

State Hospital. One man with schizophrenia has been living in the Keener Shelter for seven years, the same period of time he had previously been there when it had been a hospital. . . . [The difference is] the Keener Shelter is

merely a shelter and cannot deliver the psychiatric care needed by many of its inhabitants. Nor is the Keener Shelter unique. . . . For many of these homeless, it is like returning home. ▮

(TORREY, 1997, pp. 23–24)

ConsiderThis

◉ How might patients react when they find themselves back in the same place where they were confined years earlier, under totally different circumstances?
• Might the Keener Shelter, which is run humanely and efficiently by the Volunteers of America, be more therapeutic than the old state hospitals?

organized their own community programs better and as a result have had more success with them (Perris, 1988). Both in the United States and abroad, varied and well-coordinated community treatment is seen as an important part of the solution to the problem of schizophrenia (Melle et al., 2000).

CROSSROADS:
An Important Lesson

After years of frustration and failure, clinicians now have an arsenal of weapons to use against schizophrenia—medication, institutional programs, psychotherapy, and community programs. It has become very clear that antipsychotic medications open the door for recovery from this disorder, but in most cases other kinds of treatment are also needed to help the recovery process along. The various approaches must be combined in different ways to meet each individual's specific needs.

Working with schizophrenia has taught therapists an important lesson: no matter how compelling the evidence for biological causation may be, a strictly biological approach to the treatment of psychological disorders is a mistake more often than not (McCabe et al., 1999). Largely on the basis of biological discoveries and pharmacological advances, hundreds of thousands of patients with schizophrenia and other severe mental disorders were released to their communities in the 1960s. Little attention was paid to the psychological and sociocultural needs of these individuals, and many of them have been trapped in their pathology ever since. Clinicians must remember this lesson, especially in today's climate, when managed care and government priorities often promote medication as the sole treatment for psychological problems.

"The city coroner of Liverpool . . . has lately drawn attention to the fact that there is no suitable provision for dealing with persons suffering from . . . mental aberration. . . . Such persons are frequently found to be unable to take care of themselves. . . . Latterly, however, the authorities of Mill Road Infirmary have declined to receive them, owing, it is stated, to there being no accommodation in the workhouse for the alleged lunatics; and there has been no alternative but . . . to bring them before the presiding magistrate [and] discharge them."

Journal of Mental Science, April 1898, pp. 449–450

When Kraepelin described schizophrenia at the turn of the twentieth century, he estimated that only 13 percent of its victims ever improved. Today, even with shortages in community care, many more such individuals show improvement (McGuire, 2000; Eaton et al., 1992). Twenty-five percent or more are believed to recover from schizophrenia completely, and an equal number return to relatively independent lives, although their occupational and social functioning may continue to fall short of earlier levels. These improvements notwithstanding, the clinical field still has far to go. Studies suggest that the recovery rates could be considerably higher (McGuire, 2000). It is unacceptable that the majority of people with this disorder receive few or none of the effective community interventions that have been developed, worse still that tens of thousands have become homeless. Although many factors have contributed to this state of affairs, neglect by clinical practitioners has certainly played a big role. It is now up to these professionals, along with public officials, to address the needs of all people with schizophrenia.

VOICE IN THE WILDERNESS

Suffering from delusions, a businessman named Clifford Beers spent two years in mental institutions during the early 1900s. His later description of conditions there in an autobiography, *A Mind That Found Itself*, spurred a widespread reform movement in the United States, called the "mental hygiene movement," which led to some key improvements in hospital conditions.

Consider This

◉ In the early years of antipsychotic drug use, patients who failed to respond to these drugs were likely to receive higher and higher dosages until many of them seemed to be walking zombies. Why might clinicians have used this medication strategy, even when the drugs failed to reduce symptoms?

SUMMARY AND REVIEW

▨ **Overview of treatment** For years all efforts to treat schizophrenia brought only frustration. The disorder is still difficult to treat, but today's therapies are more successful than those of the past. *p. 451*

▨ **Past institutional care** For more than half of the twentieth century, the main treatment for schizophrenia was institutionalization and custodial care. Because patients failed to respond to traditional therapies, they were usually placed in overcrowded public institutions (state hospitals in the United States), typically in back wards where the primary goal was to maintain and restrain them. Between 1845 and 1955 the number of state hospitals and mental patients rose steadily, while the quality of care declined. *pp. 451–453*

▨ **Improved institutional care** In the 1950s two in-hospital approaches were developed, milieu therapy and token economy programs. They often brought improvement and particularly helped patients to care for themselves and feel better about themselves. *pp. 454–456*

▨ **Antipsychotic drugs** The discovery of antipsychotic drugs in the 1950s revolutionized the treatment of schizophrenia. Today they are almost always a part of treatment. Theorists believe that the first generation of antipsychotic drugs operate by reducing excessive dopamine activity in the brain. These "conventional" antipsychotic drugs reduce the positive symptoms of schizophrenia more completely, or more quickly, than the negative symptoms.

The conventional antipsychotic drugs can also produce dramatic unwanted effects, particularly movement abnormalities called extrapyramidal effects, which include Parkinsonian and related symptoms, neuroleptic malignant syndrome, and tardive dyskinesia. Tardive dyskinesia apparently occurs in over 20 percent of the people who take conventional antipsychotic drugs for an extended time and can be difficult or impossible to eliminate, even when the drugs are stopped. Recently atypical antipsychotic drugs (such as clozapine and risperidone) have been developed, which seem to be more effective than the conventional drugs and to cause fewer or no extrapyramidal effects. *pp. 456–462*

▨ **Psychotherapy** Today psychotherapy is often employed successfully in combination with antipsychotic drugs. Helpful forms include insight therapy, family therapy, and social therapy. Family support groups and family psychoeducational programs are also growing in number. *pp. 462–465*

▨ **The community approach** A community approach to the treatment of schizophrenia began in the 1960s, when a policy of deinstitutionalization in the

United States brought about a mass exodus of hundreds of thousands of patients from state institutions into the community. Among the key elements of effective community care programs are coordination of patient services by a community mental health center, short-term hospitalization (followed by aftercare), day centers, halfway houses, and occupational training.

Unfortunately, the quality and funding of community care for people with schizophrenia and other severe disorders have been inadequate throughout the United States, often resulting in a "revolving door" syndrome. One consequence is that many people with such disorders are now homeless or in jail. Still others live in nursing homes or rest homes where they do not receive effective treatment, and many live in boardinghouses or single-room-occupancy hotels. *pp. 465–472*

■ **The promise of community treatment** The potential of proper community care to help people recovering from schizophrenia and other severe disorders continues to capture the interest of clinicians and policy makers. One major development has been the formation of national interest groups that are successfully promoting community treatment for people with these disorders. *pp. 472–474*

ALTERNATIVE PLACEMENT
Persons with severe mental disorders account for at least 10 percent of the jail populations in the United States (Torrey, 1999).

CYBER STUDY

▲ *See the dramatic impact of antipsychotic drugs.* ▲ *How do antipsychotic drugs open the door to other treatment approaches?* ▲ *How does successful treatment affect the outlook and goals of people with schizophrenia?* ▲ *Witness past hospital treatments for schizophrenia.* ▲ *Over the years, how might the various treatments for schizophrenia have harmed or set back patients?*

SEARCH THE *ABNORMAL PSYCHOLOGY* CD-ROM FOR

▲ Chapter 15 video case and discussion
  "Augustine"—Schizophrenia: Pharmacological Treatment

▲ Chapter 15 practice test and feedback

▲ Additional video cases and discussions
  "Steve"—Schizophrenia
  Early Procedures in Mental Hospitals

LOG ON TO THE COMER WEB PAGE

[www.worthpublishers.com/comerabnormalpsychology4e] **FOR**

▲ Suggested Web links, research exercises, FAQ page, additional Chapter 15 practice test questions

Disorders of Memory and Other Cognitive Functions

Brian was spending Saturday sailing with his wife, Helen. The water was rough but well within what they considered safe limits. They were having a wonderful time and really didn't notice that the sky was getting darker, the wind blowing harder, and the sailboat becoming more difficult to control. After a few hours of sailing, they found themselves far from shore in the middle of a powerful and dangerous storm.

The storm intensified very quickly. Brian had trouble controlling the sailboat amidst the high winds and wild waves. He and Helen tried to put on the safety jackets they had neglected to wear earlier, but the boat turned over before they were finished. Brian, the better swimmer of the two, was able to swim back to the overturned sailboat, grab the side, and hold on for dear life, but Helen simply could not overcome the rough waves and reach the boat. As Brian watched in horror and disbelief, his wife disappeared from view.

After a time, the storm began to lose its strength. Brian managed to restore the sailboat to its proper position and sail back to shore. Finally he reached safety, but the personal consequences of this storm were just beginning. The next days were filled with pain and further horror: the Coast Guard finding Helen's body . . . discussions with authorities . . . breaking the news to Helen's parents . . . conversations with friends . . . self-blame . . . grief . . . and more. On Wednesday, five days after that fateful afternoon, Brian collected himself and attended Helen's funeral and burial. It was the longest and most difficult day of his life. Most of the time, he felt like he was in a trance.

Soon after awakening on Thursday morning, Brian realized that something was terribly wrong with him. Try though he might, he couldn't remember the events of the past few days. He remembered the accident, Helen's death, and the call from the Coast Guard after they had found her body. But just about everything else was gone—right up through the funeral. At first he had even thought that it was now Sunday, and that his discussions with family and friends and the funeral were all ahead of him. But the newspaper, the funeral guest book, and a phone conversation with his brother soon convinced him that he had lost the past four days of his life.

Most of us experience a sense of wholeness and continuity as we interact with the world. We perceive ourselves as being more than a random collection of isolated sensory experiences, feelings, and behaviors. In other words, we have an *identity*, a sense of who we are—unique in our preferences, abilities, characteristics, and needs. Others recognize us and expect certain things of us. But more important, we recognize ourselves and have our own expectations, values, and goals. We have an awareness of where we fit in our environment.

Memory is a key to this sense of wholeness and identity, the link between our past, present, and future. Our recall of past experiences, although not always precisely accurate, determines how we react to present events and guides us in making decisions about the future. We recognize our friends and relatives, teachers and employers, and respond to them in

MEMORY The faculty for recalling past events and past learning.

appropriate ways. Without a memory we would always be starting over; with it, life moves forward.

People sometimes experience a major disruption of their memory—they lose the ability to remember new information they just learned or old information they once knew well. When, as in Brian's case, such changes in memory lack a clear physical cause, they are, by convention, called *dissociative disorders*. When the physical causes are apparent, the memory disorder is called *organic*. Some memory difficulties have both dissociative and organic elements (Cantagallo et al., 1999).

Dissociative Disorders

People with **dissociative disorders** experience major changes in memory without a clear physical cause. One part of the person's memory seems to be *dissociated*, or separated, from the rest. There are several different kinds of dissociative disorders. The primary symptom of *dissociative amnesia* is an inability to recall important personal events and information. A person with *dissociative fugue* not only forgets the past but travels to a new location and may assume a new identity. Individuals with *multiple personality disorder (dissociative identity disorder)* have two or more separate identities that may not always have a knowledge of each other's thoughts, feelings, and behavior.

Several memorable books and movies have portrayed dissociative disorders. Two of the best known are *The Three Faces of Eve* and *Sybil*, each about a woman with multiple personalities. The topic is so fascinating that most television drama series seem to include at least one case of dissociation every season, creating the impression that the disorders are very common. Many clinicians, however, believe that they are quite rare.

DSM-IV also lists *depersonalization disorder*, persistent feelings of being detached from one's own mental processes or body, as a dissociative disorder. People with this disorder feel as though they are observing themselves from the outside. Because memory problems are not the central feature of this disorder, it will not be discussed here.

ConsiderThis

⦿ Most people have had odd memory lapses such as forgetting why they are doing something, arriving at a destination without remembering any details of the drive there, forgetting an important appointment or occasion, having trouble remembering the name of a person or where they know someone from, or forgetting an event everyone else seems to remember. What kinds of explanations can you think of for each of these cases?

At risk *The stunned looks on the faces of these soldiers suggest confusion, shock, and exhaustion. Combat soldiers are particularly vulnerable to amnesia and other dissociative reactions. They may forget specific horrors, personal information, or even their identities.*

Dissociative Amnesia

People with **dissociative amnesia** are unable to recall important information, usually of a traumatic or stressful nature, about their lives (APA, 2000, 1994). The loss of memory is much more extensive than normal forgetting and is not caused by organic factors (see Table 16-1). Very often an episode of amnesia is directly triggered by a specific upsetting event (Gershuny & Thayer, 1999; Classen, Koopman, & Spiegel, 1993).

Dissociative amnesia may be *localized, selective, generalized,* or *continuous.* Any of these kinds of amnesia can be triggered by a traumatic experience such as Brian's, but each represents a particular pattern of forgetting. Brian was suffering from *localized,* or *circumscribed, amnesia,* the most common type of dissociative amnesia, in which a person loses all memory of events that transpired within a limited period of time, almost always beginning with some very disturbing occurrence. Recall that Brian awakened on the day after the funeral and could not recall any of the events of the past difficult days, beginning after the boating tragedy. He remembered everything that happened up to and including the accident. He could also recall everything from the morning after the funeral onward, but the days in between remained a total blank. The forgotten period is called the *amnestic episode.* During an amnestic episode, people may appear confused; in some cases they wander about aimlessly. They are already experiencing memory difficulties, but seem unaware of them. Brian, for example, felt like he was in a trance on the day of Helen's funeral.

People with *selective amnesia,* the second most common form of dissociative amnesia, remember some, but not all, events that occurred during a period of time. If Brian had selective amnesia, he might remember breaking the news to his in-laws and his conversations with friends, but perhaps not the funeral itself.

In some cases the loss of memory extends back to times long before the traumatic period. Brian might awaken after the funeral and find that, in addition to forgetting events of the past few days, he could not remember events that occurred earlier in his life. In this case, he would be experiencing *generalized amnesia.* In extreme cases, Brian might not even remember who he is and might fail to recognize relatives and friends.

In the forms of dissociative amnesia discussed so far, the period affected by the amnesia has an end. In *continuous amnesia,* however, forgetting continues into the present. Brian might forget new and ongoing experiences as well as what happened before and during the tragedy. Continuous forgetting of this kind is actually quite rare in cases of dissociative amnesia, but, as we shall see, not in cases of organic amnesia.

All of these forms of dissociative amnesia are similar in that the amnesia interferes primarily with *episodic memory*—one's autobiographical memory of personal material. *Semantic memory*—memory for abstract or encyclopedic information—remains intact. People with dissociative amnesia are as likely as anyone else to know the name of the president of the United States and how to write, read, drive a car, and so on.

Clinicians do not know the prevalence of dissociative amnesia, but they do know that many cases seem to begin during serious threats to health and safety, as in wartime and natural disasters (Karon & Widener, 1997; Kihlström et al., 1993). Combat veterans often report memory gaps of hours or days, and some forget personal information, such as their names and addresses (van der Hart, Brown, & Graafland, 1999; Bremner et al., 1993). In fact, at least 5 percent of all mental disorders that emerge during military combat are cases of dissociative amnesia. Close to half of these cases occur in soldiers who have endured enemy fire (Sargent & Slater, 1941).

The 1990s saw an explosion in the number of case reports of dissociative amnesia linked to child sexual abuse (see Box 16-1 on the next page). The illness

---

MARITAL OVERSIGHT

Surveys indicate that 16 percent of adults have forgotten their wedding anniversaries (22 percent of men and 11 percent of women). People married only a few years are as likely to forget as those married for many years (Kanner, 1995).

Table 16-1 DSM-IV Checklist

DISSOCIATIVE AMNESIA

1. One or more episodes of inability to recall important personal information, usually of a traumatic or stressful nature, that is too extensive to be explained by ordinary forgetfulness.
2. Significant distress or impairment.

Based on APA, 2000, 1994.

DISSOCIATIVE DISORDERS Disorders marked by major changes in memory that do not have clear physical causes.

DISSOCIATIVE AMNESIA A dissociative disorder marked by an inability to recall important personal events and information.

may also occur under more ordinary circumstances, such as the sudden loss of a loved one through rejection or death (Spiegel, 1994; Loewenstein, 1991) or guilt over behavior considered to be immoral (e.g., an extramarital affair).

BOX 16-1

Repressed Childhood Memories or False Memory Syndrome?

In recent years, reports of *repressed childhood memory of abuse* have attracted much public attention. Adults with this type of dissociative amnesia seem to recover buried memories of sexual and physical abuse from their childhood. A woman may claim, for example, that her father sexually molested her repeatedly between the ages of 5 and 7. Or a young man may remember that a family friend made sexual advances on several occasions when he was very young. Often the repressed memories surface during therapy for another problem, perhaps for an eating disorder or depression (Gudjonsson, 1997).

Early recall *Research suggests that our memories of early childhood may be influenced by the reminiscences of family members, our dreams, television and movie plots, and our present self-image.*

Experts are deeply split on this issue (Pope & Brown, 1996; Schooler, 1996, 1994). Some believe that recovered memories are just what they appear to be—horrible memories of abuse that have been buried for years in the person's mind. They point out that at least 200,000 to 300,000 children in the United States are victims of sexual abuse each year, terrible experiences that may leave the children vulnerable to dissociative amnesia. Some studies in fact suggest that 18 to 59 percent of sexual abuse victims have difficulty recalling at least some details of their traumas (Chu et al., 1999; Horn, 1993).

Other experts believe that the memories are actually *illusions*—false images created by a mind that is confused. In fact, an organization called the False Memory Syndrome Foundation now assists people who claim to be falsely charged with abuse. These theorists note that the details of childhood sexual abuse are usually remembered all too well, not completely wiped from memory (McNally et al., 1998; Loftus, 1993; APA, 1996). They also point out that memory in general is hardly foolproof (Schacter, 1999). Even when recalling events as dramatic as the explosion of the space shuttle *Challenger*, people give inaccurate accounts of where they were at the time of the event or who told them about it. If memory in general is so flawed, questions certainly can be raised about the validity of recovered memories.

If the alleged recovery of childhood memories is not what it appears to be, what is it? According to opponents of the concept, it may be a powerful case of suggestibility (Loftus, 2000, 1997). These theorists hold that both the clinical and public attention has led some therapists to make the diagnosis without sufficient evidence (Frankel, 1993). The therapists may actively search for signs of early sexual abuse in clients and even encourage clients to produce repressed memories (Ganaway, 1989). Certain therapists in fact use special *memory recovery techniques,* including hypnosis, regression therapy, journal writing, dream interpretation, and interpretation of bodily symptoms (Lindsay, 1996, 1994; Lindsay & Read, 1994). Perhaps some clients respond to the techniques by unknowingly forming false memories of abuse. The apparent memories may then become increasingly familiar to them as a result of repeated therapy discussions of the alleged incidents (Loftus, 1997; Belli et al., 1992). In short, recovered memories may actually be *iatrogenic*—unintentionally caused by the therapist.

Of course, repressed memories of childhood sexual abuse do not emerge only in clinical settings (Chu et al., 1999). Many individuals come forward on their own. Opponents of the repressed memory concept explain these cases by pointing to the many books, articles, and television shows that seem to validate repressed memories of childhood sexual abuse (Loftus, 1993). Several books even tell readers how to diagnose repression in themselves, often listing symptoms that are actually rather common—not clinical symptoms at all (Tavris, 1993). Readers who have a number of these symptoms may begin a search for repressed memories of childhood abuse.

It is important to recognize that the experts who question the recovery of repressed childhood memories do not in any way deny the problem of child sexual abuse (APA, 1996; Pope & Brown, 1996). In fact, proponents and opponents alike are greatly concerned that the public may take this debate to mean that clinicians have doubts about the scope of the problem of child sexual abuse. Whatever may be the outcome of the repressed memory debate, the problem of childhood sexual abuse appears to be all too real and all too common.

The personal impact of dissociative amnesia depends on how much is forgotten. Obviously, an amnestic episode of two years is more of a problem than one of two hours. Similarly, an amnestic episode during which a person's life changes in major ways causes more difficulties than one that is quiet and uneventful.

Dissociative Fugue

People with a **dissociative fugue** not only forget their personal identities and details of their past lives, but also flee to an entirely different location (see Table 16-2). Some individuals travel but a short distance, and make few social contacts in the new setting (APA, 2000, 1994). Although confused about their identity, they do not actually assume a new one. Their fugue is brief—a matter of hours or days—and ends suddenly. In other cases, however, the person travels far from home, takes a new name and establishes a new identity, develops new relationships, and even seeks a new line of work. Such people may even display new personality characteristics; often they are more outgoing (APA, 2000, 1994). Some have even been known to travel to foreign countries thousands of miles away. This more extensive kind of fugue is seen in the case of the Reverend Ansel Bourne, described by the famous psychologist William James at the end of the nineteenth century:

Table 16-2 DSM-IV Checklist

DISSOCIATIVE FUGUE

1. Sudden, unexpected travel away from home or one's customary place of work, with inability to recall one's past.
2. Confusion about personal identity, or the assumption of a new identity.
3. Significant distress or impairment.

Based on APA, 2000, 1994.

> On January 17, 1887, [the Reverend Ansel Bourne, of Greene, R.I.] drew 551 dollars from a bank in Providence with which to pay for a certain lot of land in Greene, paid certain bills, and got into a Pawtucket horsecar. This is the last incident which he remembers. He did not return home that day, and nothing was heard of him for two months. He was published in the papers as missing, and foul play being suspected, the police sought in vain his whereabouts. On the morning of March 14th, however, at Norristown, Pennsylvania, a man calling himself A. I. Brown who had rented a small shop six weeks previously, stocked it with stationery, confectionery, fruit and small articles, and carried on his quiet trade without seeming to any one unnatural or eccentric, woke up in a fright and called in the people of the house to tell him where he was. He said that his name was Ansel Bourne, that he was entirely ignorant of Norristown, that he knew nothing of shop-keeping, and that the last thing he remembered—it seemed only yesterday—was drawing the money from the bank, etc. in Providence. . . . He was very weak, having lost apparently over twenty pounds of flesh during his escapade, and had such a horror of the idea of the candy-store that he refused to set foot in it again.
>
> The first two weeks of the period remained unaccounted for, as he had no memory, after he had once resumed his normal personality, of any part of the time, and no one who knew him seems to have seen him after he left home. The remarkable part of the change is, of course, the peculiar occupation which the so-called Brown indulged in. Mr. Bourne has never in his life had the slightest contact with trade. "Brown" was described by the neighbors as taciturn, orderly in his habits, and in no way queer. He went to Philadelphia several times; replenished his stock; cooked for himself in the back shop, where he also slept; went regularly to church; and once at a prayer-meeting made what was considered by the hearers a good address, in the course of which he related an incident which he had witnessed in his natural state of Bourne.
>
> (James, 1890, pp. 391–393)

LINGUISTIC ROOTS

The term "fugue" comes from the Latin for "flee."

Approximately 0.2 percent of the population experience dissociative fugue. Like dissociative amnesia, a fugue usually follows a severely stressful event, such as a wartime experience or a natural disaster, though personal stress, such as financial or legal difficulties or episodes of depression, may also trigger it (APA,

DISSOCIATIVE FUGUE A dissociative disorder in which a person travels to a new location and may assume a new identity, simultaneously forgetting his or her past.

Lost and found *Cheryl Ann Barnes is helped off a plane by her grandmother and stepmother upon arrival in Florida in 1996. The 17-year-old high school honor student had disappeared from her Florida home and was found one month later in a New York City hospital listed as Jane Doe, apparently suffering from fugue.*

2000, 1994; Kihlström et al., 1993). Some adolescent runaways may be in a state of fugue (Loewenstein, 1991). Like cases of dissociative amnesia, fugues usually affect personal (episodic) memories from the past rather than encyclopedic or abstract (semantic) knowledge (Kihlström et al., 1993).

Fugues tend to end abruptly. In some cases, as with Reverend Bourne, the person "awakens" in a strange place, surrounded by unfamiliar faces, and wonders how he or she got there. In other cases, the lack of personal history may arouse suspicion. Perhaps a traffic accident or legal problem leads police to discover the false identity; at other times friends search for and find the missing person (Coons, 1999; Kihlström et al., 1993). When people are found before their state of fugue has ended, therapists may find it necessary to ask them many questions about the details of their lives, repeatedly remind them who they are, and even initiate psychotherapy before they recover their memories. As these people recover their past, some forget the events of the fugue period (APA, 2000, 1994).

The majority of people who experience dissociative fugue regain most or all of their memories and never have a recurrence. Since fugues are usually brief and totally reversible, individuals tend to experience few aftereffects (Keller & Shaywitz, 1986). People who have been away for months or years, however, often do have trouble adjusting to the family, social, or job changes that have occurred during their flights. In addition, some people commit illegal or violent acts in their fugue state and later must face the consequences.

Dissociative Identity Disorder (Multiple Personality Disorder)

Multiple personality disorder is both dramatic and disabling, as we see in the case of Eric:

> Dazed and bruised from a beating, Eric, 29, was discovered wandering around a Daytona Beach shopping mall on Feb. 9. . . . Transferred six weeks later to Daytona Beach's Human Resources Center, Eric began talking to doctors in two voices: the infantile rhythms of "young Eric," a dim and frightened child, and the measured tones of "older Eric," who told a tale of terror and child abuse. According to "older Eric," after his immigrant German parents died, a harsh stepfather and his mistress took Eric from his native South Carolina to a drug dealers' hideout in a Florida swamp. Eric said he was raped by several gang members and watched his stepfather murder two men.
>
> One day in late March an alarmed counselor watched Eric's face twist into a violent snarl. Eric let loose an unearthly growl and spat out a stream of obscenities. "It sounded like something out of *The Exorcist*," says Malcolm Graham, the psychologist who directs the case at the center. "It was the most intense thing I've ever seen in a patient." That disclosure of a new personality, who insolently demanded to be called Mark, was the first indication that Graham had been dealing with a rare and serious emotional disorder: true multiple personality. . . .
>
> Eric's other manifestations emerged over the next weeks: quiet, middle-aged Dwight; the hysterically blind and mute Jeffrey; Michael, an arrogant jock; the coquettish Tian, whom Eric considered a whore; and argumentative Phillip, the lawyer. "Phillip was always asking about Eric's rights," says Graham. "He was kind of obnoxious. Actually, Phillip was a pain."
>
> To Graham's astonishment, Eric gradually unfurled 27 different personalities, including three females. . . . They ranged in age from a fetus to a sordid old man

who kept trying to persuade Eric to fight as a mercenary in Haiti. In one therapy session, reports Graham, Eric shifted personality nine times in an hour. "I felt I was losing control of the sessions," says the psychologist, who has eleven years of clinical experience. "Some personalities would not talk to me, and some of them were very insightful into my behavior as well as Eric's."

(Time, *October 25, 1982, p. 70*)

A person with **multiple personality disorder**, or **dissociative identity disorder**, develops two or more distinct personalities, often called **subpersonalities** (or **alternate personalities**), each with a unique set of memories, behaviors, thoughts, and emotions (see Table 16-3). At any given time, one of the subpersonalities takes center stage and dominates the person's functioning. Usually one subpersonality, called the *primary,* or *host, personality,* appears more often than the others.

The transition from one subpersonality to another, called *switching,* is usually sudden and may be dramatic (APA, 2000, 1994; Dell & Eisenhower, 1990). Eric, for example, twisted his face, growled, and yelled obscenities while changing personalities. Switching is usually triggered by a stressful event, although clinicians can also bring about the change with hypnotic suggestion (APA, 2000, 1994; Smith, 1993; Brende & Rinsley, 1981) (see Box 16-2 on page 485).

Cases of multiple personality disorder were first reported almost four centuries ago (Bliss, 1985, 1980). Many clinicians consider the disorder to be rare, but recent reports suggest that it may be more common than was once thought (APA, 2000; Coons, 1998). Most cases are first diagnosed in late adolescence or early adulthood, but the symptoms usually begin in early childhood after episodes of abuse, typically before the age of 5 (Ross et al., 1991; Sachs, 1986). In fact, studies suggest that as many as 97 percent of patients have been physically, often sexually, abused during their early years (Ross et al., 1991, 1990, 1989; Dell & Eisenhower, 1990). Women receive this diagnosis at least three times as often as men (APA, 2000). In some cases, the parents of people with multiple personality disorder appear to have displayed some kind of dissociative disorder (Dell & Eisenhower, 1990; Ross et al., 1989).

HOW DO SUBPERSONALITIES INTERACT? How subpersonalities relate to or recall one another varies from case to case. Generally, however, there are three kinds of relationships. In *mutually amnesic* relationships, the subpersonalities have no awareness of one another (Ellenberger, 1970). Conversely, in *mutually cognizant* patterns, each subpersonality is well aware of the rest. They may hear one another's voices and even talk among themselves. Some are on good terms, while others do not get along at all. Eric's subpersonalities were mutually cognizant:

Most of the personalities interacted. Cye, a religious mystic, once left a comforting note for Eric. The pushy Michael, who loved rock music, hated Eric's classical records so much that he yanked the wires from a stereo. Eric defended the menacing Mark: "Mark never hurt anybody," he said one day. "He is just there to scare other people off when they get too close." Eric referred to his troupe of personalities as his "talking books." One of the characters was a librarian named Max who occasionally announced a sudden personality change by saying, "One of the books just fell off the shelf."

(Time, *October 25, 1982, p. 70*)

In *one-way amnesic* relationships, the most common relationship pattern, some subpersonalities are aware of others, but the awareness is not mutual. Those that are aware, called *co-conscious subpersonalities,* are "quiet observers"

Table 16-3 DSM-IV Checklist

MULTIPLE PERSONALITY DISORDER (DISSOCIATIVE IDENTITY DISORDER)

1. The presence of two or more distinct identities or personality states.
2. Control of the person's behavior recurrently taken by at least two of these identities or personality states.
3. An inability to recall important personal information that is too extensive to be explained by ordinary forgetfulness.

Based on APA, 2000, 1994.

ConsiderThis

Women are much more likely to receive a diagnosis of multiple personality disorder than men. What might be some reasons for this difference?

MULTIPLE PERSONALITY DISORDER A dissociative disorder in which a person develops two or more distinct personalities. Also known as *dissociative identity disorder.*

SUBPERSONALITIES The two or more distinct personalities found in individuals suffering from multiple personality disorder, each with a unique set of memories, behaviors, thoughts, and emotions. Also known as *alternate personalities.*

Movie madness *One of the cinema's best-known fictional sufferers of multiple personality disorder, Norman Bates, is horrified to discover that his mother (actually his subpersonality) has stabbed a woman to death in the shower in the movie* Psycho.

who watch the actions and thoughts of the other subpersonalities but do not interact with them. Sometimes while another subpersonality is dominating consciousness, the co-conscious personality makes itself known through indirect means, such as auditory hallucinations (perhaps a voice giving commands) or "automatic writing" (the current personality may find itself writing down words over which it has no control).

A one-way amnesic relationship was at work in the case of Miss Christine Beauchamp, one of the earliest reported and most famous examples of multiple personality (Prince, 1906). In therapy, this woman initially displayed three subpersonalities. Her therapist labeled them the Saint (a religious, even-tempered subpersonality), the Woman (irreligious and bad-tempered), and the Devil (mischievous and cheerful). The Saint, Miss Beauchamp's primary personality, knew nothing of the Woman or the Devil. The Woman knew of the Saint but not of the Devil. The Devil knew of both the Saint and the Woman but in different ways: she had direct access to the Saint's thoughts, but her knowledge of the Woman was based solely on her observations of the Woman's behavior.

Investigators used to believe that most cases of multiple personality disorder involved two or three subpersonalities. Studies now suggest, however, that the average number of subpersonalities per patient is much higher—fifteen for women and eight for men (APA, 2000; Ross et al., 1989). In fact, there have been cases in which 100 or more subpersonalities were observed (APA, 2000). Often the subpersonalities emerge in groups of two or three at a time.

In the case of "Eve White," made famous in the book and movie *The Three Faces of Eve,* a woman had three subpersonalities—Eve White, Eve Black, and Jane (Thigpen & Cleckley, 1957). Eve White, the primary personality, was quiet and serious; Eve Black was carefree and mischievous; and Jane was mature and intelligent. According to the book, these three subpersonalities eventually merged into Evelyn, a stable personality who was really an integration of the other three.

The book was mistaken, however; this was not to be the end of Eve's dissociation. In an autobiography 20 years later, she revealed that altogether twenty-two subpersonalities had come forth during her life, including nine subpersonalities after Evelyn. Usually they appeared in groups of three, and so the authors of *The Three Faces of Eve* apparently never knew about her previous or subsequent subpersonalities. She has now overcome her disorder, achieving a single, stable identity, and has been known as Chris Sizemore for over 25 years (Sizemore & Huber, 1988).

HOW DO SUBPERSONALITIES DIFFER? As in Chris Sizemore's case, subpersonalities often exhibit dramatically different characteristics. They may also have their own names and different *vital statistics, abilities and preferences,* and even *physiological responses* (Alpher, 1992; Dell & Eisenhower, 1990).

VITAL STATISTICS The subpersonalities may differ in features as basic as age, sex, race, and family history, as in the famous case of Sybil Dorsett. Sybil's multiple personality disorder has been described in fictional form (in the novel *Sybil*), but is based on a real case from the practice of the psychiatrist Cornelia Wilbur (Borch-Jacobsen, 1997; Schreiber, 1973). Sybil displayed seventeen subpersonalities, all with different identifying features. They included adults, a teenager, and a baby named Ruthie; two were male, named Mike and Sid. Sybil's subpersonalities each had particular images of themselves and of each other. The subpersonality named Vicky, for example, saw herself as an attractive blonde, while another, Peggy Lou, was described as a pixie with a pug nose. Mary was plump with dark hair, and Vanessa was a tall redhead with a willowy figure. Mike's olive skin and brown eyes stood in contrast to Sid's fair skin and blue eyes.

BOX **16-2**

Guilty and Not Guilty

In 1979, Kenneth Bianchi, one of two men known in the media as the Hillside Strangler, was accused of raping and murdering several women in the Los Angeles area. Bianchi denied the charges, but during an interview in which he underwent hypnosis, another person-

ality, named Steve, emerged. Steve claimed that he, not Kenneth, had committed the crimes.

Bianchi pleaded not guilty by reason of insanity, but the court refused to accept his claim of multiple personality disorder. The second personality, the prose-

cution pointed out, did not appear until Bianchi was hypnotized, and only after Bianchi was told by the examiner that the procedure would reveal another part of him. Bianchi was found guilty of the crimes.

ConsiderThis

⦿ What would have been an appropriate verdict had Bianchi's disorder been ruled genuine? • Might highly publicized trials such as this influence other people to believe that they have a multiple personality disorder? • More than one-quarter of all accused murderers claim to have no memory of their crimes (Noll & Turkington, 1994). Why might a murderer experience amnesia?

Courtroom tactic *Kenneth Bianchi tries to convince a judge that it was his subpersonality who committed the multiple rapes and murders of which he was accused.*

ABILITIES AND PREFERENCES Although memories of abstract or encyclopedic information are not usually affected by dissociative amnesia or fugue, they are often disturbed by multiple personality disorder. It is not uncommon for the different subpersonalities to have different areas of expertise or different abilities: one may be able to drive, speak a foreign language, or play a musical instrument, while the others cannot (Coons et al., 1988). Their handwritings can also differ (Coons, 1980). In addition, the subpersonalities usually have different tastes in food, friends, music, and literature, as in Sybil's case.

> Among outsiders Vanessa claimed to like everybody who wasn't a hypocrite. Peggy Lou vented her spleen against what she called "showoffs like Sybil's mother." Vicky favored intelligent and sophisticated persons. Both Mary and Sybil had a special fondness for children. Mary, indicating oneness rather than autonomy, remarked about a woman they all knew, "None of us liked her."
>
> Excited by conversations about music, Peggy Lou often shut her ears in the course of other conversations. Bored by female conversation in general, Mike and Sid sometimes succeeded in making Sybil break an engagement or nagged throughout the visit.
>
> . . . Marjorie told Dr. Wilbur, "I go with Sybil when she visits her friends, but they talk about things they like and I don't care about—houses, furniture, babies. But when Laura Hotchkins comes, they talk about concerts, and I like that."
>
> *(Schreiber, 1973, p. 288)*

THE BEGINNINGS OF SYBILIZATION

Several colleagues who worked closely with the author of *Sybil* and with the therapist claim that Sybil was actually a severe "hysteric," highly hypnotizable, extremely suggestible, and anxious to please her therapist, and that her disorder was in fact induced by the treatment techniques of hypnosis and sodium pentothal (Miller & Kantrowitz, 1999; Rieber, 1999).

"I'm Eve" *In 1975 Chris Sizemore revealed that she had been the subject of the book and the film* The Three Faces of Eve. *A fully integrated personality for more than 25 years, Ms. Sizemore is now an accomplished author, artist, and mental health spokesperson.*

"Memory isn't like reading a book; it's more like writing a book from fragmentary notes."

John F. Kihlström,
psychologist, 1994

IATROGENIC DISORDER A disorder that is unintentionally caused by a practitioner.

Chris Sizemore ("Eve") also displayed differences in abilities and preferences. She later pointed out, "If I had learned to sew as one personality and then tried to sew as another, I couldn't do it. Driving a car was the same. Some of my personalities couldn't drive" (1975, p. 4).

PHYSIOLOGICAL RESPONSES Researchers have discovered that subpersonalities may have physiological differences, such as differences in autonomic nervous system activity, blood pressure levels, and allergies (Putnam, Zahn, & Post, 1990). One study looked at the brain activities of different subpersonalities by measuring their *evoked potentials*—that is, brain response patterns recorded on an electroencephalograph (Putnam, 1984). The brain pattern a person produces in response to a specific stimulus (such as a flashing light) is usually unique and consistent. However, when an evoked potential test was administered to four subpersonalities of each of ten people with multiple personality disorder, the results were dramatic. The brain activity pattern of each subpersonality was unique, showing the kinds of variations usually found in totally different people.

The evoked potential study also used control subjects who *pretended* to have different subpersonalities. These normal individuals were instructed to create and rehearse alternate personalities. In contrast to real patients, the brain-reaction patterns of these subjects did not vary as they shifted from subpersonality to subpersonality, suggesting that simple faking cannot produce the brain reaction variations found in cases of multiple personality disorder.

HOW COMMON IS MULTIPLE PERSONALITY DISORDER? As we have seen, multiple personality disorder has traditionally been thought of as rare. Some researchers even argue that many or all cases are **iatrogenic**—that is, unintentionally produced by practitioners. They believe that therapists create this disorder by subtly suggesting the existence of other personalities during therapy or by explicitly asking a patient to produce different personalities while under hypnosis (Powell & Gee, 1999). In addition, they believe, a therapist who is looking for multiple personalities may reinforce these patterns by displaying greater interest when a patient displays symptoms of dissociation (Acocella, 1999; Frick, 1995; Merskey, 1995, 1992).

These arguments seem to be supported by the fact that many cases of multiple personality disorder first come to attention while the person is already in treatment for a less serious problem (Allison, 1978). But such is not true of all cases; many other people seek treatment because they have noticed time lapses throughout their lives or because relatives and friends have observed their subpersonalities (Schacter, 1989; Putnam, 1988, 1985).

The number of people diagnosed with multiple personality disorder has been increasing. By 1973 only 100 cases had ever been reported in professional journals. Although the disorder is still uncommon, thousands of cases have now been diagnosed in the United States and Canada alone (Merskey, 1995; Ross et al., 1989). Two factors may account for this increase. First, a growing number of today's clinicians believe that the disorder does exist and are willing to diagnose it (Foote, 1999; Pope et al., 1999). Second, diagnostic procedures tend to be more accurate today than in past years. For much of the twentieth century, schizophrenia was one of the clinical field's most commonly applied diagnoses (Rosenbaum, 1980). It was assigned, often incorrectly, to a wide range of unusual and mysterious patterns of abnormality, perhaps including multiple personality disorder. Under the stricter criteria of recent editions of the DSM, clinicians are now much more selective in diagnosing schizophrenia, allowing more cases of multiple personality disorder to be recognized (APA, 2000; Spiegel, 1994; French, 1987). In addition, several diagnostic tests have recently been developed to help detect multiple personality disorder (Steinberg & Hall, 1997; Mann, 1995). Despite such changes in professional perceptions, diagnostic practices, and assessment tools, however, many clinicians continue to question the legitimacy of this category and are reluctant to diagnose the disorder (Pope et al., 1999; Muller, 1998).

Explanations of Dissociative Disorders

A variety of theories have been proposed to explain dissociative disorders. Older explanations, such as those offered by psychodynamic and behavioral theorists, have not received much investigation. However, newer viewpoints, which combine cognitive, behavioral, and biological principles and highlight such factors as *state-dependent learning* and *self-hypnosis*, have begun to capture the interest of clinical scientists (Doan & Bryson, 1994).

THE PSYCHODYNAMIC VIEW Psychodynamic theorists believe that dissociative disorders are caused by *repression*, the most basic ego defense mechanism: people fight off anxiety by unconsciously preventing painful memories, thoughts, or impulses from reaching awareness. Everyone uses repression to a degree, but people with dissociative disorders are thought to repress their memories excessively (Brenner, 1999; Terr, 1988).

In the psychodynamic view, dissociative amnesia and fugue are *single* episodes of massive repression. In each of these disorders, a person unconsciously blocks the memory of an extremely upsetting event to avoid the pain of facing it (Noll & Turkington, 1994; Putnam, 1985). This reaction has its roots in childhood. When parents overreact to a child's expressions of id impulses (for example, to signs of sexual impulses), some children become excessively afraid of those impulses, defend against them, and develop a strict code prohibiting such "immoral" desires. Later in their lives, when they act in a manner that violates their moral code—by having an extramarital affair, for example—they are brought face to face with their unacceptable impulses. Repressing the whole situation may be their only protection from overwhelming anxiety.

In contrast, multiple personality disorder is thought to result from a *lifetime* of excessive repression (Brenner, 1999; Reis, 1993). Psychodynamic theorists believe that continuous use of repression is motivated by very traumatic childhood events, particularly abusive parenting. Young Sybil, for example, was repeatedly subjected to unspeakable tortures by her disturbed mother, Hattie:

> A favorite ritual . . . was to separate Sybil's legs with a long wooden spoon, tie her feet to the spoon with dish towels, and then string her to the end of a light bulb cord, suspended from the ceiling. The child was left to swing in space while the mother proceeded to the water faucet to wait for the water to get cold. After muttering, "Well, it's not going to get any colder," she would fill the adult-sized enema bag to capacity and return with it to her daughter. As the child swung in space, the mother would insert the enema tip into the child's urethra and fill the bladder with cold water. "I did it," Hattie would scream triumphantly when her mission was accomplished. "I did it." The scream was followed by laughter, which went on and on.
>
> *(Schreiber, 1973, p. 160)*

According to psychodynamic theorists, children who experience such traumas may come to fear the dangerous world they live in and take flight from it, by pretending to be another person who is safely looking on from afar. Abused children may also come to fear the impulses that they believe are the reasons for their excessive punishments. They may try to be "good" and "proper" all of the time by repressing the impulses they consider "bad" and "dangerous." Whenever "bad"

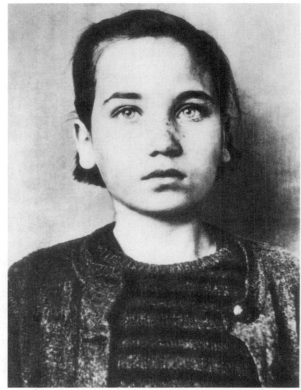

Early beginnings *Chris Sizemore's multiple personality disorder developed long before this photograph of her was taken at age 10. It emerged during her preschool years after she experienced several traumas (witnessing two deaths and a horrifying accident) within a three-month period.*

PROFIT DISTRIBUTIONS

Chris Sizemore received almost no revenues from the 1957 book and movie *The Three Faces of Eve*. In contrast, profits from *Sybil* were shared by the patient, her psychiatrist, and the book's author. Moreover, when the psychiatrist Cornelia Wilbur died in 1992, she left $25,000 and all *Sybil* royalties to the former patient (Miller & Kantrowitz, 1999).

STATE-DEPENDENT LEARNING Learning that becomes associated with the conditions under which it occurred, so that it is best remembered under the same conditions. That is, people may remember an event best when they return to the mental state they were in at the time of the event.

thoughts or impulses do break through, the children feel they must disown and deny them, and they unconsciously assign all unacceptable thoughts, impulses, and emotions to other personalities.

Most of the support for the psychodynamic position is drawn from case histories, which report such brutal childhood experiences as beatings, cuttings, burnings with cigarettes, imprisonment in closets, rape, and extensive verbal abuse. Yet some individuals with multiple personality disorder do not seem to have experiences of abuse in their background (Bliss, 1980). Moreover, child abuse appears to be far more common than multiple personality disorder. Why, then, do only a small fraction of abused children develop this disorder?

THE BEHAVIORAL VIEW Behaviorists believe that dissociation is a response learned through operant conditioning. People who experience a horrifying event may later find temporary relief when their minds drift to other subjects. For some, this momentary forgetting, leading to a drop in anxiety, increases the likelihood of future forgetting. In short, they are reinforced for the act of forgetting and learn—without being aware that they are learning—that such acts help them escape anxiety. Thus, like psychodynamic theorists, behaviorists see dissociation as escape behavior. But behaviorists believe that a reinforcement process rather than a hardworking unconscious is keeping the individuals unaware that they are using dissociation as a means of escape.

Like psychodynamic theorists, behaviorists have relied largely on case histories to support their view of dissociative disorders. Such descriptions do often support this view, but they are equally consistent with other kinds of explanations as well: a case that seems to show reinforcement of forgetting can usually also be interpreted as an instance of unconscious repression. In addition, the behavioral explanation fails to explain precisely how temporary and normal escapes from painful memories grow into a complex disorder (see Box 16-3) or why more people do not develop dissociative disorders. Theories that focus on state-dependent learning and self-hypnosis tackle some of the questions left unanswered by the psychodynamic and behavioral explanations.

STATE-DEPENDENT LEARNING If people learn something when they are in a particular situation or state of mind, they are likely to remember it best when they are again in that same condition. If they are given a learning task while under the influence of alcohol, for example, their later recall of the information may be strongest under the influence of alcohol (Overton, 1966). Similarly, if they smoke cigarettes while learning, they may later have better recall when they are again smoking.

This link between state and recall is called **state-dependent learning**. It was initially observed in experimental animals who were given certain drugs and then taught to perform certain tasks. Researchers repeatedly found that the animals' subsequent test performances were best in the same drug states (Arkhipov, 1999; Pusakulich & Nielson, 1976; Overton, 1966, 1964). Research with human subjects later showed that state-dependent learning can be associated with mood states as well: material learned during a happy mood is recalled best when the subject is again happy, and sad-state learning is recalled best during sad states (Eich, 1995; Bower, 1981) (see Figure 16-1).

What causes state-dependent learning? One possibility is that *arousal levels* are an important dimension of learning and memory. That is, a particular level of arousal will have a set of remembered events, thoughts, and skills attached to it. When a situation produces that particular level of arousal, the person is more likely to recall the memories linked to it.

Although people may remember certain events better in some arousal states than in others, most can recall events under a variety of states. However, perhaps people who are

FIGURE 16-1 **State-dependent learning** *In one study, subjects who learned a list of words while in a hypnotically induced happy state remembered the words better if they were in a happy mood when tested later than if they were in a sad mood. Conversely, subjects who learned the words when in a sad mood recalled them better if they were sad during testing than if they were happy (Bower, 1981).*

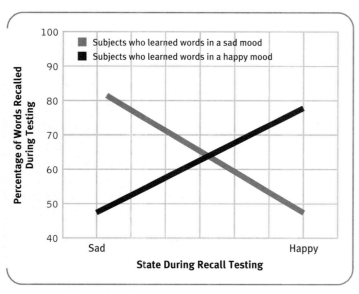

Legend: Subjects who learned words in a sad mood / Subjects who learned words in a happy mood

Y-axis: Percentage of Words Recalled During Testing (40–100)
X-axis: State During Recall Testing (Sad — Happy)

B O X **16-3**

Peculiarities of Memory

Usually memory problems must interfere greatly with a person's functioning before they are considered a sign of a disorder. *Peculiarities* of memory, on the other hand, fill our daily lives. The memory investigators Richard Noll and Carol Turkington (1994) have identified a number of these peculiarities—some familiar, some useful, some problematic, but none abnormal.

❖ **Absentmindedness** Often we fail to register information because our thoughts are focusing on other things. If we haven't absorbed the information in the first place, it is no surprise that later we can't recall it.

❖ **Déjà vu** Almost all of us have at some time had the strange sensation of recognizing a scene that we happen upon for the first time. We feel sure we have been there before.

❖ **Jamais vu** Sometimes we have the opposite experience: a situation or scene that is part of our daily life seems suddenly unfamiliar. "I knew it was my car, but I felt as if I'd never seen it before."

❖ **The tip-of-the-tongue phenomenon** To have something on the tip of the tongue is an acute "feeling of knowing": we are unable to recall some piece of information, but we know that we know it.

❖ **Eidetic images** Some people experience visual afterimages so vividly that they can describe a picture in detail after looking at it just once. The images may be memories of pictures, events, fantasies, or dreams.

❖ **Memory while under anesthesia** Some anesthetized patients may process enough of what is said in their presence during surgery to affect their recovery. In such cases, the ability to understand language has continued under anesthesia, even though the patient cannot explicitly recall it.

❖ **Memory for music** Even as a small child, Mozart could memorize and reproduce a piece of music after having heard it only once. While no one yet has matched the genius of Mozart, many musicians can mentally hear whole pieces of music, so that they can rehearse anywhere, far from their instruments.

❖ **Visual memory** Most people recall visual information better than other kinds of information: they can easily bring to their mind the appearance of places, objects, faces, or the pages of a book. They almost never forget a face, yet they may well forget the name attached to it. Other people have stronger verbal memories: they remember sounds or words particularly well, and the memories that come to their minds are often puns or rhymes.

❖ **Prenatal memory** Some North American medicine men claim to remember parts of a prenatal existence, an ability they believe is lost to "common" people. Many practicing Buddhists also claim to remember past lives. A few—as did Buddha himself—claim to remember their very first existence.

prone to develop dissociative disorders have state-to-memory links that are extremely rigid and narrow. Maybe each of their thoughts, memories, and skills is tied exclusively to a particular state of arousal, so that they recall a given event from the past only when they experience an arousal state almost identical to the state in which the memory was acquired. When such people are calm, for example, they may forget what occurred during stressful times, thus laying the groundwork for dissociative amnesia or fugue. Similarly, in multiple personality disorder, different arousal levels may produce entirely different groups of memories, thoughts, and abilities—that is, different subpersonalities (Putnam, 1992).

SUPPRESSED EMOTIONS,
SUPPRESSED MEMORY

In one study, subjects who were instructed to suppress their emotions
while viewing disturbing photographs
later displayed poorer recall of the photographs than did viewers who had
been allowed to wince, gasp, and otherwise respond with emotion (Richards
& Goss, 1999).

This could explain why personality transitions in multiple personality disorder tend to be sudden and stress-related.

SELF-HYPNOSIS As we first saw in Chapter 1, people who are *hypnotized* enter a sleeplike state in which they become very suggestible. While in this state, they can behave, perceive, and think in ways that would ordinarily seem impossible. They may, for example, become temporarily blind, deaf, or insensitive to pain (Fromm & Nash, 1992). Hypnosis can also help people remember events that occurred and were forgotten years ago, a capability used by many psychotherapists. Conversely, it can make people forget facts, events, and even their personal identities—an effect called *hypnotic amnesia* (Allen, Law, & Laravuso, 1996; Spanos & Coe, 1992).

Most studies of hypnotic amnesia follow similar formats. Subjects are asked to study a word list or other material until they are able to repeat it correctly. Under hypnosis, they are then directed to forget the material until they receive a *cancellation signal* (such as the snap of a finger), at which time they will suddenly recall the learned material. Repeatedly these experiments have found the sub-jects' memories to be poor during the period of hypnotic amnesia and then re-stored after the cancellation signal is given (Coe, 1989).

The parallels between hypnotic amnesia and dissociative disorders are striking (Bliss, 1980). Both are conditions in which people forget certain material for a period of time yet later remember it. And in both, the people forget without any insight into why they are forgetting or any awareness that something is being for-gotten. Finally, in both situations, personal and specific information is more readily forgotten than abilities or encyclopedic knowledge.

These parallels have led some theorists to conclude that dissociative disorders may be a form of **self-hypnosis** in which people hypnotize themselves to forget unpleasant events (Bliss, 1985, 1980; Hilgard, 1977). Dissociative amnesia, for example, may occur in people who, consciously or unconsciously, hypnotize themselves into forgetting horrifying experiences that have recently occurred in their lives. If the self-induced amnesia covers all memories of a person's past and identity, that person may undergo a dissociative fugue.

Self-hypnosis might also be used to explain multiple personality disorder. On the basis of several investigations, some theorists believe that multiple personal-ity disorder often begins between the ages of 4 and 6, a time when children are generally very suggestible and excellent hypnotic subjects (Kluft, 1987; Bliss, 1985, 1980) (see Figure 16-2). These theorists argue that some children who experience abuse or other horrifying events man-age to escape their threatening world by self-hypnosis, mentally separating themselves from their bodies and fulfilling their wish to become some other person or persons. One patient with multiple personality disorder observed, "I was in a trance often [during my childhood]. There was a little place where I could sit, close my eyes and imagine, until I felt very relaxed just like hypnosis" (Bliss, 1980, p. 1392).

There are different schools of thought about the nature of hypnosis. Some theorists see hypnosis as a *special process,* an out-of-the-ordinary kind of functioning (Bowers & Woody, 1996; Hilgard, 1992, 1987, 1977). Accordingly, these theorists contend that people with dissociative disorders place them-selves in internal trances during which their conscious func-tioning is significantly altered. Other theorists believe that hypnotic behaviors, and hypnotic amnesia in particular, are produced by *common social and cognitive processes,* such as high motivation, highly focused attention, role enactment, and self-fulfilling expectations (Spanos et al., 1995; Spanos & Coe, 1992). According to this point of view, hypnotized people are simply highly motivated individuals performing tasks that are

FIGURE 16-2 **Hypnotic susceptibility and age** *Multiple personality disorder often seems to begin between the ages of 4 and 6, when a child's hypnotic susceptibility is on the rise. A person's hypnotic susceptibility increases until just before adolescence, then generally de-clines. (Adapted from Morgan & Hilgard, 1973.)*

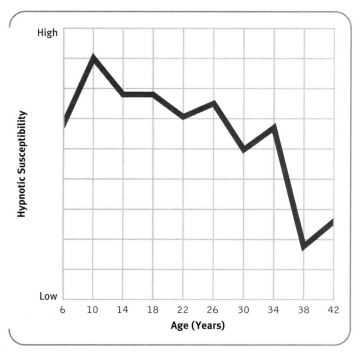

asked of them, while believing all along that the hypnotic state is doing the work for them. Common-process theorists hold that people with dissociative disorders provide themselves (or are provided by others) with powerful suggestions to forget, and that social and cognitive mechanisms then put the suggestions into practice (Lilienfeld et al., 1999). Whether hypnosis consists of special or common processes, hypnosis research effectively demonstrates the power of our normal thought processes, and so renders the notion of dissociative disorders somewhat less remarkable.

Treatments for Dissociative Disorders

As we have seen, people with dissociative amnesia and fugue often recover on their own. Only sometimes do their memory problems linger and require treatment (Lyon, 1985). In contrast, people with multiple personality disorder usually require treatment to regain their lost memories and develop an integrated personality. Treatments for dissociative amnesia and fugue tend to be more successful than those for multiple personality disorder.

HOW DO THERAPISTS HELP PEOPLE WITH DISSOCIATIVE AMNESIA AND FUGUE? The leading treatments for dissociative amnesia and fugue are psychodynamic therapy, hypnotic therapy, and drug therapy. *Psychodynamic therapists* ask patients with these disorders to free-associate and search their unconscious in the hope of bringing forgotten experiences back to consciousness (Loewenstein, 1991). The focus of psychodynamic therapy seems particularly well suited to the needs of people with these disorders. After all, the patients need to recover lost memories, and the general approach of psychodynamic therapists is to try to uncover memories—as well as other psychological processes—that have been repressed. Thus many theorists, including some who do not ordinarily favor psychodynamic approaches, believe that psychodynamic therapy may be the most appropriate and effective treatment for these disorders.

Another common treatment for dissociative amnesia and fugue is **hypnotic therapy**, or **hypnotherapy**. Therapists hypnotize patients and then guide them to recall the forgotten events (Spiegel, 1994; MacHovek, 1981; Bliss, 1980). Experiments have repeatedly indicated that hypnotic suggestion can successfully elicit forgotten memories, and experience has shown that people with dissociative disorders are usually highly susceptible to hypnosis (Frischholz et al., 1992; Putnam et al., 1986). Given the possibility that dissociative amnesia and fugue may each be a form of self-hypnosis, hypnotherapy may be a particularly appropriate intervention. It has been applied both alone and in combination with other approaches.

Sometimes intravenous injections of barbiturates such as *sodium amobarbital* (Amytal) or *sodium pentobarbital* (Pentothal) are used to help patients with dissociative amnesia and fugue regain lost memories (Ruedrich et al., 1985). The drugs are often called "truth serums," but the key to their success is their ability to sedate people and weaken their inhibitions, thus helping them to recall anxiety-producing events (Kluft, 1988; Perry & Jacobs, 1982). These drugs do not always work, however (Spiegel, 1994); and when they do help people recall past events, the individuals may forget upon wakening much of what they said under the drug's influence. For these reasons, the drugs, if used, are likely to be combined with other treatment approaches as well.

HOW DO THERAPISTS HELP INDIVIDUALS WITH MULTIPLE PERSONALITY DISORDER? Unlike victims of amnesia and fugue, people with multiple personality disorder rarely recover without treatment (Spiegel, 1994). Like the disorder itself, treatment for this pattern is complex and difficult. Therapists usually try to help the clients (1) recognize fully the nature of their disorder, (2) recover the gaps in their memory, and (3) integrate their subpersonalities into one functional personality (Kluft, 1999, 1992, 1991; Spiegel, 1994).

SELF-HYPNOSIS The process of hypnotizing oneself, sometimes for the purpose of forgetting unpleasant events.

HYPNOTIC THERAPY A treatment in which the patient undergoes hypnosis and is then guided to recall forgotten events or perform other therapeutic activities. Also known as *hypnotherapy*.

ConsiderThis

Hypnosis is often used by therapists to help uncover hidden memories, motives, and needs. But hypnotic therapists can also use this suggestive technique to create desires, emotions, and behaviors. How can hypnotists know when they are uncovering a person's state of mind as opposed to creating it?

Faulty recall *A forensic clinician uses a hypnotic procedure to help a witness recall the details of a crime. Research reveals, however, that such procedures are as capable of creating false memories as they are of uncovering real memories. Thus, recollections that initially emerge during hypnosis cannot be used as evidence in criminal cases.*

FUSION The final merging of two or more subpersonalities in multiple personality disorder.

SHORT-TERM MEMORY The memory system that collects new information. Also known as *working memory*.

LONG-TERM MEMORY The memory system that contains all the information that we have stored over the years.

RECOGNIZING THE DISORDER Once a diagnosis of multiple personality disorder is made, therapists typically try to bond with the primary personality and with each of the subpersonalities (Kluft, 1999, 1992). In general, such bonds are hard to achieve, given the patient's experience of abuse and consequent mistrust of others. As bonds are formed, therapists try to educate patients and help them to recognize fully the nature of their disorder (Allen, 1993). Some therapists actually introduce the subpersonalities to one another under hypnosis, and some have patients look at videotapes of their other personalities (Ross & Gahan, 1988; Sakheim, Hess, & Chivas, 1988). Many therapists have also found that group therapy helps to educate patients. Being with a group of people who all have multiple personality disorder helps relieve a person's feelings of isolation and fears of being "crazy" (Buchele, 1993; Becker & Comstock, 1992). Family therapy is often included in the treatment program to help educate spouses and children about the disorder and to gather helpful information about the patient (Porter, Kelly, & Grame, 1993).

RECOVERING MEMORIES To help patients recover the missing pieces of their past, therapists use many of the approaches applied in other dissociative disorders, including psychodynamic therapy, hypnotherapy, and sodium amobarbital (Kluft, 1999, 1991, 1985). These techniques work slowly for patients with multiple personality disorder, as some subpersonalities may keep denying experiences that the others recall (Lyon, 1992). One of the subpersonalities may even assume a "protector" role, to prevent the primary personality from suffering the pain of recollecting traumatic experiences. Some patients become self-destructive and violent during this phase of treatment (Kelly, 1993; Lamberti & Cummings, 1992; Young, Young, & Lehl, 1991).

INTEGRATING THE SUBPERSONALITIES The final goal of therapy is to merge the different subpersonalities into a single, integrated identity. Integration is a continuous process that occurs throughout treatment until patients "own" all of their behaviors, emotions, sensations, and knowledge. **Fusion** is the final merging of two or more subpersonalities. Many patients distrust this final treatment goal, and their subpersonalities are likely to see integration as a form of death (Kluft, 1999, 1991; Spiegel, 1994). As one subpersonality said, "There are too many advantages to being multiple. Maybe we're being sold a bill of goods by therapists" (Hale, 1983).

Therapists have used a range of approaches to help merge subpersonalities, including psychodynamic, supportive, cognitive, and drug therapies (Goldman, 1995; Fichtner et al., 1990; Caddy, 1985). One woman's primary personality was given assertiveness training: as she learned to express anger in more functional and satisfying ways, her aggressive and hostile subpersonality began to disappear.

Once the subpersonalities are integrated, further therapy is needed to solidify the complete personality and to teach social and coping skills that may help prevent later dissociations (Fink, 1992). In case reports, some therapists report high success rates (Kluft, 1999, 1993, 1984; Wilbur, 1984), but others find that patients continue to resist full and final integration. A few therapists have in fact questioned the need for full integration. The limited number of reported cases generally prevents researchers from gathering samples that are large enough to conduct enlightening research on the treatment of this disorder (Ross & Ellason, 1999).

Organic Memory Disorders

Some changes in memory have clear organic causes, such as brain injury, medical conditions, and substance misuse. Organic memory disorders are categorized as either *amnestic disorders,* which primarily affect memory, or *dementias,* which affect both memory and other cognitive functions. Before examining the organic memory disorders, we need to understand some basic information about the basic biology of memory.

The Biology of Memory

Much of what is known about the biology of memory has come from studies of people who have suffered injuries to specific locations of the brain. Important information has also been gained through experiments in which researchers surgically or chemically damage the brains of animals and then observe the effects on old memories and new learning. Additionally, molecular biology studies have shed light on specific changes that may occur in brain cells as memories form.

WHAT ARE THE DIFFERENT KINDS OF MEMORY? Scientists describe the human brain as having two memory systems that work together to help us learn and recall. **Short-term memory**, or **working memory**, gathers new information. **Long-term memory** is the accumulation of information that we have stored over the years, information that first made its way through the short-term memory system. The information held in short-term memory must be transformed, or *consolidated,* into long-term memory if we are to hold on to it. This transformation usually occurs in steps. When short-term information becomes part of our long-term memory, it is said to have been *encoded.* Remembering information that has been stored in long-term memory is called *retrieval* and is described as going into one's long-term memory to bring it out for use again in short-term, or working, memory (NIMH, 1996).

Information in long-term memory can be classified as either procedural or declarative. *Procedural memories* are learned skills we perform without needing to think about them, such as walking, cutting with scissors, or writing. *Declarative memory* consists of names, dates, and other facts that have been learned. Most organic memory disorders interfere far more with declarative memory than with procedural memory (see Table 16-4).

PEAK CONDITION

Research suggests that memory and other cognitive functions peak at approximately age 25 (McGaugh, 1999).

COMMON OCCURRENCE

In a 1997 survey, doctors reported that 80 percent of their patients over 30 years of age complained of memory loss (Muhammad, 1999).

Table 16-4

Comparison of Memory Disorders

	ANTEROGRADE (CONTINUOUS) AMNESIA	RETROGRADE (LOCALIZED, SELECTIVE, AND GENERALIZED) AMNESIA	DECLARATIVE MEMORY LOSS	PROCEDURAL MEMORY LOSS	ORGANIC CAUSES
Dissociative amnesia	Sometimes	Yes	Yes	Sometimes	No
Dissociative fugue	Sometimes	Yes	Yes	Sometimes	No
Multiple personality disorder	Yes	Yes	Yes	Yes	No
Amnestic disorders	Yes	Sometimes	Yes	Sometimes	Yes
Dementias	Yes	Yes	Yes	Yes	Yes

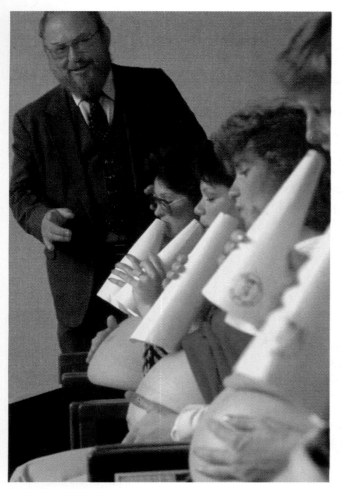

A bit too early *Each mother-to-be in this prenatal program talks to her fetus in order to establish an early relationship with the child. Memory studies suggest that the babies will not remember these early interventions, however; humans cannot intentionally recall events until sometime during their first or second year of life (Bauer, 1996; Mandler & McDonough, 1995).*

MEMORY BUSTERS

Substances that can temporarily impair memory include alcohol, sedative-hypnotic drugs, bromides, antidepressants, analgesics, blood pressure medications, insulin, seasickness patches, antihistamines, and antipsychotic drugs (Noll & Turkington, 1994).

WHAT IS THE ANATOMY OF MEMORY? Memories are difficult to locate. Researchers have searched for the place where the content of memory is stored, but they have concluded that no such storehouse exists. They now see memory as a *process* rather than a place, an activity that involves changes in cells throughout the brain. When the process is activated, a memory is triggered and comes forth. Occasionally this process leads to errors of memory (Schacter, 1999), but typically its operation is remarkably effective.

Certain brain structures appear to be especially important in memory (Rolls, 2000). Among the most important structures in short-term, or working, memory are the **prefrontal lobes**, located just behind the forehead (Goleman, 1995). When animals or humans acquire new information, their prefrontal lobes become more active (Haxby et al., 1996). Apparently this activity enables them to hold information temporarily and to continue working with the information as long as it is needed.

Among the brain areas most important to long-term memory are the **temporal lobes** (including the *hippocampus* and *amygdala*, key structures embedded under the temporal lobes) and the **diencephalon** (including the *mammillary bodies*, *thalamus*, and *hypothalamus*), which seem to help transform, or encode, short-term into long-term memory (Searleman & Hermann, 1994). Cases of organic memory loss involve damage to one or more of these areas (Aggleton & Shaw, 1996) (see Box 16-4 on page 496).

These brain regions also have numerous connections between them. A structure known as the *fornix,* for example, connects the hippocampus with the mammillary bodies. Damage to the fornix has effects on memory, suggesting that newly learned information travels along a circuit, and that disruption of the circuit may be the cause of some memory disorders (Aggleton & Shaw, 1996). There is also evidence, however, that memory circuits are redundant; if one pathway is disrupted, alternate routes may be available.

WHAT IS THE BIOCHEMISTRY OF MEMORY? What do the cells in these key areas of the brain do to create and store memories? Although no one has yet discovered the "engram"—the exact physical change in a cell that accounts for a memory—much is known about the electrical and chemical bases of learning and memory. One exciting finding is the role that *long-term potentiation (LTP)* may play (Martinez & Derrick, 1996; Bliss & Gardner, 1973). Apparently, repeated stimulation of nerve cells in the brain significantly increases the likelihood that the cells will respond—and respond strongly—to future stimulation. This effect can last quite a long time (hence the name "long-term potentiation"), long enough to be a key mechanism in the formation of memories. Think of many sleds ridden one after another down a snowy slope, creating a groove that later sledders can easily find. Perhaps LTP creates a kind of groove that helps memories form, so a person can more easily retrieve a memory later by following the well-worn path.

Memory researchers have also identified biochemical changes that occur in cells as memories form (Rosenzweig, 1996; Noll & Turkington, 1994). For example, when new information is acquired, *proteins* are produced in key brain cells. Several steps lead to this production of proteins. First, body organs receive new information and release neurotransmitters, particularly *acetylcholine* and *glutamate,* which carry the information to receptors on neurons located in key memory regions of the brain. Next the receptors trigger chemical changes—termed *second messengers*—within the receiving neurons. For example, *RNA (ribonucleic acid)* and *calcium* are produced in the cells, and these chemicals help manufacture the proteins.

If the activity of any of these chemicals is disturbed, the production of proteins may be prevented and the formation of memories interrupted (Martinez & Derrick, 1996; Rosenzweig, 1996). For example, by blocking the activity of glutamate, researchers have prevented both short-term memory and LTP. Similarly, by blocking the cellular production of RNA or of calcium, they have interrupted the formation of long-term memories. Such findings suggest that memory occurs as a result of changes within and between nerve cells.

Amnestic Disorders

Retrograde amnesia is an inability to remember events that occurred before the event that triggered amnesia. **Anterograde amnesia** is an ongoing inability to form new memories after the triggering event. As we have observed, people with dissociative amnesia typically suffer from retrograde amnesia and rarely suffer from anterograde amnesia. However, **amnestic disorders**, organic disorders in which memory loss is the primary symptom, are quite different (see Table 16-5). People with amnestic disorders *sometimes* suffer from retrograde amnesia, depending on the particular disorder, but they almost *always* experience anterograde amnesia.

In anterograde amnesia, it is as though information from short-term memory can no longer cross over into long-term memory. Not surprisingly, the anterograde amnesia observed in amnestic disorders is often the result of damage to the brain's temporal lobes or diencephalon, the areas largely responsible for transforming short-term memory into long-term memory.

In severe forms of anterograde amnesia, new acquaintances are forgotten almost immediately, and problems solved one day must be tackled again the next. The person may not remember anything that has happened since the organic problem first occurred. A middle-aged patient who suffered a physical trauma more than 20 years ago, for example, may still believe that Jimmy Carter is president of the United States. Sufferers of anterograde amnesia may continue to possess all their earlier verbal skills and many problem-solving abilities, however, and their IQ is not changed.

KORSAKOFF'S SYNDROME Fred, a 69-year-old man, was admitted to a mental hospital in a state of confusion, the result of **Korsakoff's syndrome**, an amnestic disorder that causes its victims to keep forgetting newly learned information (anterograde amnesia), although their general knowledge and intelligence remain intact:

Fred . . . had a history of many years of heavy drinking, although he denied drinking during the past several years. When seen in the admitting ward, the patient was neatly dressed, but there was some deterioration of his personal habits. Although pleasant and sociable with the interviewer and ward personnel, he was definitely confused. He wandered about the ward, investigating objects and trying on other people's clothing. He talked freely, though his speech tended to be rambling and at times incoherent. Most of his spontaneous conversation centered on himself, and there were a number of hypochondriacal complaints. Fred was disoriented for time and place, although he was able to give his name. He could not give his correct address, said his age was 91, and was unable to name the day, the month, or the year. He did not know where he was, although he said he was sent here by his landlord because he had been drinking. He admitted that he had been arrested for fighting and drinking, but he said that he had never had an attack of delirium tremens. [Fred] showed the characteristic symptom picture of Korsakoff's syndrome, with disorientation, confusion, and a strong tendency toward confabulation. When asked where he was, he said he was in a brewery. He gave the name of the brewery, but when asked the same question a few minutes later, he named another brewery. Similarly, he said that he knew the examiner, called him by an incorrect name, and a little later changed the name again. When leaving the examining room, he used still another name when he said politely, "Goodbye, Mr. Wolf!"

(Kisker, 1977, p. 308)

Table 16-5 DSM-IV Checklist

AMNESTIC DISORDER

1. Memory impairment.
2. Significant impairment in social or occupational functioning, and significant decline from a previous level of functioning.
3. Disturbance is the direct physiological result of a general medical condition or physical trauma.

Based on APA, 2000, 1994.

PREFRONTAL LOBES Regions of the brain that play a key role in short-term memory, among other functions.

TEMPORAL LOBES Regions of the brain that play a key role in transforming short-term to long-term memory, among other functions.

DIENCEPHALON A brain area (consisting of the mammillary bodies, thalamus, and hypothalamus) that plays a key role in transforming short-term to long-term memory, among other functions.

RETROGRADE AMNESIA A lack of memory about events that occurred before the event that triggered amnesia.

ANTEROGRADE AMNESIA The inability to remember new information that is acquired after the event that triggered amnesia.

AMNESTIC DISORDERS Organic disorders in which the primary symptom is memory loss.

KORSAKOFF'S SYNDROME An amnestic disorder caused by long-term alcoholism, an accompanying poor diet, and, in turn, a deficiency of vitamin B (thiamine).

BOX 16-4

"You Are the Music, While the Music Lasts"   Clayton S. Collins

Oliver Sacks [a well-known neurologist and writer] danced to the Dead. For three solid hours. At 60. And with "two broken knees." . . .

The power of music— . . . to "bring back" individuals rendered motionless and mute by neurological damage and disorders—is what's driving Sacks these days. The . . . author (*Migraine, A Leg to Stand On, The Man Who Mistook His Wife for a Hat, Seeing Voices* and *Awakenings*) . . . is working on another case-study book, one that deals in part with the role of music as a stimulus to minds that have thrown up stiff sensory barriers. . . .

"One sees how robust music is neurologically," Sacks says. "You can lose all sorts of particular powers but you don't tend to lose music and identity." . . .

Much of what he has encountered, particularly in working with patients at Beth Abraham Hospital, Bronx, N.Y., . . . relates to music.

"One saw patients who couldn't take a single step, who couldn't walk, but who could dance," he says. "There were patients who couldn't speak, but who could sing. The power of music in these patients was instantaneous . . . from a frozen Parkinsonian state to a freely flowing, moving, speaking state."

Sacks remembers a woman with Parkinson's who would sit perfectly still until "activated" by the music of Chopin, which she loved and knew by heart. She didn't have to hear a tune played. "It was sometimes sufficient to give her an opus number," Sacks says. "You would just say 'Opus 49,' and the F-minor 'Fantasy' would start playing in her mind. And she could move. . . ."

"Deeply demented people respond to music, babies respond to music, fetuses probably respond to music. Various animals respond to music," Sacks says. "There is something about the animal nervous system . . . which seems to respond to music all the way down. . . . ," Sacks says, citing the case of a patient with damage to the frontal lobes of his brain.

"When he sings, one almost has the strange feeling that [music] has given him his frontal lobes back, given him back, temporally, some function that has been lost on an organic basis," Sacks says, adding a quote from T. S. Eliot: "You are the music, while the music lasts."

The effects of music therapy may not always last. Sacks will take what he can get. "To organize a disorganized person for a minute is miraculous. And for half an hour, more so." . . .

The key, says Sacks, is for patients to "learn to be well" again. Music can restore to them, he says, the identity that predates the illness. "There's a health to music, a life to music." . . . Music's been healing for thousands of years, Sacks says. "It's just being looked at now more systematically and with these special populations."

"Greg" was an amnesiac with a brain tumor and no coherent memories of life since about 1969—but an encyclopedic memory of the years that came before, and a real love of Grateful Dead tunes.

Sacks took Greg to that night's [Grateful Dead] performance. "In the first half of the concert they were doing early music, and Greg was enchanted by everything," Sacks recalls. "I mean, he was not an amnesiac. He was completely oriented and organized and with it." Between sets Sacks went backstage and introduced Greg to band member Micky Hart, who was impressed with Greg's knowledge of the group but quite surprised when Greg asked after Pigpen. When told the former band member had died 20 years before, "Greg was very upset," Sacks recalls. "And then 30 seconds later he asked 'How's Pigpen?' "

During the second half, the band played its newer songs. And Greg's world began to fall apart. "He was bewildered and enthralled and frightened. Because the music for him—and this is an extremely musical man, who understands the idiom of the Grateful Dead—was both familiar and unfamiliar. . . . He said, 'This is like the music of the future.' "

Sacks tried to keep the new memories fresh. But the next day, Greg had no memory of the concert. It seemed as if all had been lost. "But—and this is strange—when one played some of the new music, which he had heard for the first time at the concert, he could sing along with it and remember it."

It is an encouraging development. . . . Children have been found to learn quickly lessons that are embedded in song. Sacks, the one-time quiet researcher, is invigorated by the possibilities. He wonders whether music could carry such information, to give his patient back a missing part of his life. To give Greg "some sense of what's been happening in the last 20 years, where he has no autobiography of his own."

That would have Sacks dancing in the aisles.

(Excerpted by permission from *Profiles,* the magazine of Continental Airlines, February 1994.)

Musical awakenings *Over the years, Oliver Sacks has treated neurological disorders with techniques ranging from medication to the music of the Grateful Dead.*

As we observed in Chapter 12, approximately 5 percent of people with chronic alcoholism develop Korsakoff's syndrome. A combination of excessive drinking and improper diet produce a deficiency of *vitamin B (thiamine)*, which leads to damage in portions of the diencephalon (Visser et al., 1999). Patients in the early stages of Korsakoff's syndrome, called *Wernicke's encephalopathy*, are extremely confused. Treated with large doses of thiamine, this milder syndrome subsides (APA, 2000, 1994). Untreated, it progresses to Korsakoff's syndrome.

Korsakoff's sufferers primarily lose memories of declarative knowledge; they are still able to incorporate new procedural knowledge, such as the way to solve a particular kind of puzzle, and they also maintain their language skills (Verfaellie et al., 1990). This may explain why Korsakoff's patients tend to *confabulate*. Like Fred, they use their general intellectual and language skills to make up elaborate stories and lies in an effort to replace the memories they keep losing.

In addition to severe anterograde amnesia, persons with Korsakoff's syndrome experience some retrograde amnesia. They have trouble remembering events from the years immediately before the onset of the syndrome, as opposed to more distant past events (Albert et al., 1979). The syndrome can also affect personality. Aggressive and loud individuals may become quieter and more passive as the disorder develops.

"The true art of memory is the art of attention."

Samuel Johnson

Missing pieces *These self-portraits by the German artist Anton Räderscheidt, following a stroke that temporarily damaged his right parietal lobe, show the importance of memory and attention. Shortly after his stroke, the artist omitted half of his face (upper left). Within nine months, he had recovered his cognitive skills and was able to complete all the details in his painting (lower right).*

HEAD INJURIES AND BRAIN SURGERY Both *head injuries* and *brain surgery* can cause amnestic disorders (Noll & Turkington, 1994). Either may destroy memory-related brain structures or cut the connections between memory-related areas of the brain. Second only in popularity to emotion-based amnesia as a theme in television shows and movies, bumps on the head are portrayed as a quick and easy way to lose one's memory. In fact, *mild* head injuries, such as a concussion that does not result in coma or a period of unconsciousness, rarely cause much memory loss, and what loss there is usually disappears within days or at most months (Levin et al., 1987; McLean et al., 1983). In contrast, almost half of all *severe* head injuries do cause some permanent learning and memory problems, both anterograde and retrograde. When memories do return, older ones typically return first (Searlemen & Herrmann, 1994).

Brain surgery may create more specific memory problems. The most famous case of memory loss as a result of brain surgery is that of H.M., a man whose identity has been protected for decades (Ogden & Corkin, 1991; Corkin, 1984, 1968; Milner, 1971). H.M. suffered from severe *epilepsy,* a disorder that produced seizures in his temporal lobes. To reduce his symptoms, doctors removed parts of both his temporal lobes, along with the amygdala and hippocampus. At that time, the involvement of these brain areas in the formation of memories was not known. (Today temporal lobe surgery is usually limited to either the right or left side of the brain). H.M. has experienced severe anterograde amnesia ever since his 1953 surgery. He is unable to recognize anyone he has met since the operation.

OTHER AMNESTIC DISORDERS Other biological events can also damage the brain areas that play key roles in memory. These include *vascular disease,* which affects the flow of blood to the brain (Gorelick et al., 1988); *heart attacks,* which interrupt the flow of oxygen to the brain (Volpe & Hirst, 1983); and certain infectious diseases (Hokkanen et al., 1995). Each may cause amnestic disorders of various kinds.

Dementias

Dementias, another group of syndromes marked by memory loss, are sometimes difficult to distinguish from the amnestic disorders. In dementia, however, severe memory problems combine with losses in at least one other cognitive function, such as abstract thinking or language (APA, 2000, 1994). People with certain forms of dementia may also undergo personality changes—they may begin to behave inappropriately, for example—and their symptoms may worsen steadily.

Most of us worry from time to time that we are losing our memory and other mental abilities. We rush out the door without our keys; we meet a familiar person and cannot remember her name; or in the middle of an important test our mind goes blank (Gallagher-Thompson & Thompson, 1995). At such times, we may well believe that we are on our way to dementia. Actually such mishaps are a common and quite normal feature of stress or of aging. As people move through middle age, these memory difficulties and lapses of attention increase, and may occur with regularity by the age of 60 or 70. Sometimes, however, people experience memory and other cognitive changes that are far more extensive and problematic. They, like Harry, are victims of dementia:

> Harry appeared to be in perfect health at age 58. . . . He worked in the municipal water treatment plant of a small city, and it was at work that the first overt signs of Harry's mental illness appeared. While responding to a minor emergency, he became confused

---

BRAIN TRAUMA

Two million people in the United States suffer traumatic brain injuries each year (Waxweiler et al., 1995). More than 20 percent of them experience lifelong aftereffects (NCIPC, 1999). The leading causes are car accidents and falls.

Losing one's mind *Because of their short-term memory problems, people with advanced cases of Alzheimer's disease, one source of dementia, are often unable to complete simple tasks such as painting a picture. In addition, their long-term memory deficits may prevent them from recognizing even close relatives or friends.*

about the correct order in which to pull the levers that controlled the flow of fluids. As a result, several thousand gallons of raw sewage were discharged into a river. Harry had been an efficient and diligent worker, so after puzzled questioning, his error was attributed to the flu and overlooked.

Several weeks later, Harry came home with a baking dish his wife had asked him to buy, having forgotten that he had brought home the identical dish two nights before. Later that week, on two successive nights, he went to pick up his daughter at her job in a restaurant, apparently forgetting that she had changed shifts and was now working days. A month after that, he quite uncharacteristically argued with a clerk at the phone company; he was trying to pay a bill that he had already paid three days before. . . .

Months passed and Harry's wife was beside herself. She could see that his problem was worsening. Not only had she been unable to get effective help, but Harry himself was becoming resentful and sometimes suspicious of her attempts. He now insisted there was nothing wrong with him, and she would catch him narrowly watching her every movement. . . . Sometimes he became angry— sudden little storms without apparent cause. . . . More difficult for his wife was Harry's repetitiveness in conversation: He often repeated stories from the past and sometimes repeated isolated phrases and sentences from more recent exchanges. There was no context and little continuity to his choice of subjects. . . .

Two years after Harry had first allowed the sewage to escape, he was clearly a changed man. Most of the time he seemed preoccupied; he usually had a vacant smile on his face, and what little he said was so vague that it lacked meaning. He had entirely given up his main interests (golf and woodworking), and he became careless about his person. More and more, for example, he slept in his clothes. Gradually his wife took over getting him up, toileted, and dressed each morning. . . .

Harry's condition continued to worsen slowly. When his wife's school was in session, his daughter would stay with him some days, and neighbors were able to offer some help. But occasionally he would still manage to wander away. On those occasions he greeted everyone he met—old friends and strangers alike— with "Hi, it's so nice." That was the extent of his conversation, although he might repeat "nice, nice, nice" over and over again. . . . When Harry left a coffee pot on a unit of the electric stove until it melted, his wife, desperate for help, took him to see another doctor. Again Harry was found to be in good health. [However] the doctor ordered a CAT scan [and eventually concluded] that Harry had "Pick-Alzheimer disease" and that there was no known cause and no effective treatment. . . .

Because Harry was a veteran . . . [he qualified for] hospitalization in a regional veterans' hospital about 400 miles away from his home. . . . Desperate, five years after the accident at work, [his wife] accepted with gratitude [this] hospitalization. . . .

At the hospital the nursing staff sat Harry up in a chair each day and, aided by volunteers, made sure he ate enough. Still, he lost weight and became weaker. He would weep when his wife came to see him, but he did not talk, and he gave no other sign that he recognized her. After a year, even the weeping stopped. Harry's wife could no longer bear to visit. Harry lived on until just after his sixty-fifth birthday, when he choked on a piece of bread, developed pneumonia as a consequence, and soon died.

(Heston, 1992, pp. 87–90)

DEMENTIAS Organic syndromes marked by major problems in memory and at least one other cognitive function.

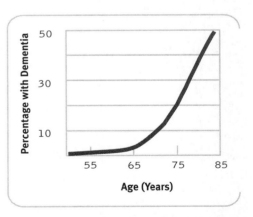

FIGURE 16-3 Dementia and age *The occurrence of dementia is closely related to age. Fewer than 1 percent of all 60-year-olds have dementia, compared to as many as 50 percent of those who are 85. After 60, the prevalence of dementia doubles every six years up to age 85 or so, then the increase tapers off. (Adapted from Cowley, 2000; Alzheimer's Association, 1997; Ritchie et al., 1992.)*

At any given time, around 3 percent of the world's adult population are suffering from dementia (Muir, 1997). Its occurrence is closely related to age (see Figure 16-3). Among people 65 years of age, the prevalence is around 1 to 2 percent, increasing to between 25 and 50 percent for those over the age of 85 (APA, 2000; Cowley, 2000; De Leon et al., 1996). Altogether, 4 million persons in the United States experience some form of dementia (Zal, 1999; Alzheimer's Association, 1996; Jenike, 1995). More than 70 forms have been identified (Noll &

Turkington, 1994). Some result from metabolic, nutritional, or other problems that can be corrected. Most forms of dementia, however, are caused by neurological problems, such as Alzheimer's disease and stroke, which are currently difficult or impossible to correct.

Table 16-6 DSM-IV Checklist

DEMENTIA OF THE ALZHEIMER'S TYPE

1. The development of multiple cognitive deficits manifested by both memory impairment and at least one of the following cognitive disturbances:
   a. Aphasia.
   b. Apraxia.
   c. Agnosia.
   d. Disturbance in executive functioning.
2. Significant impairment in social or occupational functioning, along with significant decline from a previous level of functioning.
3. Gradual onset and continuing cognitive decline.

Based on APA, 2000, 1994.

ALZHEIMER'S DISEASE **Alzheimer's disease**, named after Alois Alzheimer, the German physician who first identified it in 1907, is the most common form of dementia, accounting for at least half of the cases (Muir, 1997) (see Box 16-5). This gradually progressive disease sometimes appears in middle age (*early onset*), but most often it occurs after the age of 65 (*late onset*), and its prevalence increases markedly among people in their late 70s and early 80s (see Table 16-6).

The course of Alzheimer's disease ranges in duration from two to as many as twenty years. It usually begins with mild memory problems, lapses of attention, and difficulties in language and communication (Small, Kemper, & Lyon, 1997). As symptoms worsen, the person has trouble completing complicated tasks or remembering important appointments (Searleman & Herrmann, 1994). Harry, for example, had problems carrying out his responsibilities at the water treatment plant and repeatedly forgot when to pick up his daughter. Eventually sufferers also have difficulty with simple tasks, distant memories are forgotten, and changes in personality often become very noticeable. For example, a man may become uncharacteristically aggressive (Revetz, 1999).

People with Alzheimer's disease may at first deny that they have a problem (Sharkstein et al., 1997), but they soon become anxious or depressed about their state of mind; many also become agitated (Zal, 1999; Devanand et al., 1997). As the dementia progresses, however, they show less and less awareness of their limitations. As we saw in Harry's case, they may withdraw from others during the late stages of the disorder, become more confused about time and place, wander, and show very poor judgment (Gallagher-Thompson & Thompson, 1995). Eventually they become fully dependent on other people. They may lose almost all knowledge of the past and fail to recognize the faces of even close relatives. They also become increasingly uncomfortable at night and take frequent naps during the day. The late phase of the disorder can last from two to five years, with the individuals requiring constant care (Mace & Rabins, 1991).

"Our memory is our coherence, our reason, our feeling, even our action. Without it, we are nothing."

Luis Buñuel, Spanish filmmaker

BOX 16-5

To Know or Not to Know

For years the only way to diagnose Alzheimer's disease with certainty has been to wait for an autopsy. Today, however, scientists appear to be close to developing early, definitive tests for the disorder. In fact, diagnosticians may eventually be able to identify victims years or even decades before any noticeable decline in their memory or other cognitive functions (Jack et al., 1999; Small et al., 1999, 1995).

ConsiderThis

◉ Would people be better off not knowing that they will eventually be developing a disease that has no known cure? • How might the 1980 and 1984 presidential elections have turned out had people known that Ronald Reagan would eventually develop dementia?

Like Harry, Alzheimer's victims usually remain in fairly good health until the later stages of the disease. As their mental functioning declines, however, they become less active and spend much of their time just sitting or lying in bed. As a result, they are prone to develop illnesses such as pneumonia, which can result in death (Gallagher-Thompson & Thompson, 1995). Alzheimer's disease is responsible for 23,000 deaths each year in the United States, which makes it the eighth leading cause of death in elderly people (NCHS, 1999; Alzheimer's Association, 1997; Jenike, 1995).

In most cases, Alzheimer's disease can be diagnosed with certainty only after death (APA, 2000), when structural changes in the person's brain, such as excessive *neurofibrillary tangles* and *senile plaques,* can be fully examined (Iqbal & Grundke-Iqbal, 1996). **Neurofibrillary tangles**, twisted protein fibers found *within* the cells of the hippocampus and certain other brain areas, occur in all people as they age (see Figure 16-4), but people with Alzheimer's disease form an extraordinary number of them (Selkoe, 1992). **Senile plaques** are sphere-shaped deposits of a small molecule known as the *beta-amyloid protein* that form in the spaces *between* cells in the hippocampus, cerebral cortex, and certain other brain regions, as well as in some nearby blood vessels. The formation of plaques is also a normal part of aging, but again it is exceptionally high in people with Alzheimer's disease (Selkoe, 2000, 1999, 1992; Lorenzo & Yankner, 1996). Plaques may interfere with communications between cells, and so cause cell breakdown or cell death. Scientists do not fully understand why some people develop these problems and the disease. Research has suggested several possible causes, however, including *genetic* factors and *biochemical abnormalities.*

WHAT ARE THE GENETIC CAUSES OF ALZHEIMER'S DISEASE? It appears that Alzheimer's disease often has a genetic basis. Because many cases seem to run in families, clinicians now distinguish between *familial* Alzheimer's disease and *sporadic* Alzheimer's disease, which is not associated with a family history of the brain disease (Bergem et al., 1997). Studies have found that particular genes are responsible for the production of proteins called *beta-amyloid precursor protein (beta-APP)* and *presenilin. Mutations,* or abnormal forms, of these genes may lead to excessive accumulations of the beta-amyloid protein, or plaques, in certain

ALZHEIMER'S DISEASE The most common form of dementia, usually occurring after the age of 65.

NEUROFIBRILLARY TANGLES Twisted protein fibers that form within certain brain cells as people age.

SENILE PLAQUES Sphere-shaped deposits of beta-amyloid protein that form in the spaces between certain brain cells and in certain blood vessels as people age.

FIGURE 16-4 **The aging brain** *In old age, our brain undergoes changes that affect memory, learning, and reasoning to some degree. These same changes occur to an excessive degree in people with Alzheimer's disease. (Adapted from Selkoe, 1992, p. 136.)*

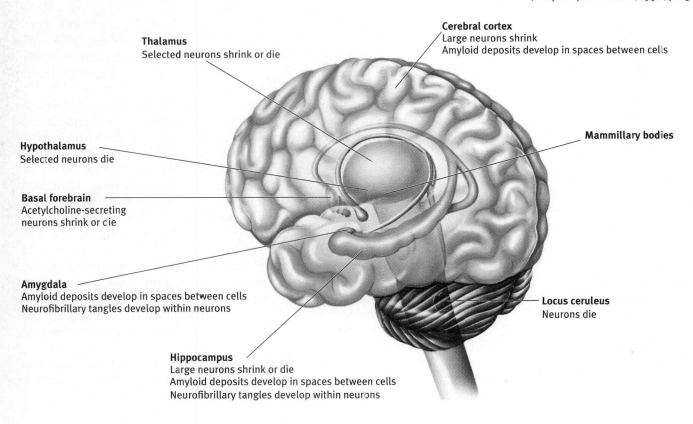

Thalamus
Selected neurons shrink or die

Cerebral cortex
Large neurons shrink
Amyloid deposits develop in spaces between cells

Hypothalamus
Selected neurons die

Mammillary bodies

Basal forebrain
Acetylcholine-secreting neurons shrink or die

Amygdala
Amyloid deposits develop in spaces between cells
Neurofibrillary tangles develop within neurons

Locus ceruleus
Neurons die

Hippocampus
Large neurons shrink or die
Amyloid deposits develop in spaces between cells
Neurofibrillary tangles develop within neurons

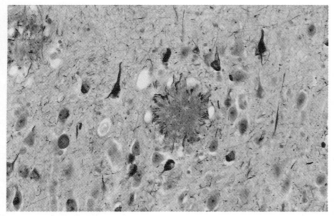

Biological culprits *Tissue from the brain of a 69-year-old man with Alzheimer's disease shows excessive amounts of* plaque *(large dark-gold sphere), the clusters of beta-amyloid protein that form outside cells, and of* neurofibrillary tangles, *the twisted fibers within cells that make the cells appear blackened (small dark blobs).*

areas of the brain (St. George-Hyslop, 2000; Saftig et al., 1999; Selkoe, 1999, 1998, 1996). Many theorists now believe that in some families genetically transmitted mutations of beta-APP and presenilin heighten the likelihood of plaque formation and, in turn, of Alzheimer's disease. Genetic studies have also linked certain kinds of Alzheimer's disease to defects on chromosomes 1, 14, 19, and 21 (Higgins et al., 1997; Roses et al., 1996). All of these discoveries are promising; but since the majority of people with Alzheimer's disease do not have a clear family history of the disorder, scientists cannot be certain about the influence of genetic mutations on the disease's development in the population as a whole (Gallagher-Thompson & Thompson, 1995).

WHAT ARE THE BIOCHEMICAL CAUSES OF ALZHEIMER'S DISEASE? Researchers have found that *acetylcholine* and *glutamate,* two of the neurotransmitters that play key roles in memory, are in low supply, or at least function erratically, in the brains of Alzheimer victims (Bissette et al., 1996; Lee et al., 1996). Thus some theorists believe that abnormal activity of these neurotransmitters contributes to the disorder. Other scientists believe that a slow-acting infection may help cause Alzheimer's disease (Prusiner, 1991), while still others point to dysfunction of the immune system (Hüll et al., 1996; McGeer & McGeer, 1996). High levels of zinc and aluminum have also been found in the brains of some Alzheimer's victims and have captured the interest of some investigators.

OTHER FORMS OF DEMENTIA A number of other disorders may also lead to dementia. **Vascular dementia**, also known as **multi-infarct dementia**, may follow a cerebrovascular accident, or *stroke,* during which blood flow to specific areas of the brain was cut off, thus damaging the areas. The patient may be aware of the stroke, or it may be "silent"—that is, the person may be unaware that anything has happened. Like Alzheimer's disease, vascular dementia is progressive, but its symptoms begin abruptly rather than gradually. Moreover, cognitive functioning may continue to be normal in areas of the brain that have not been affected by the stroke, in contrast to the broad cognitive impairment usually displayed by Alzheimer patients (Gallagher-Thompson & Thompson, 1995). Vascular dementia is the second most common type of dementia among the elderly, accounting for 8 to 29 percent of cases (Selkoe, 1992; Katzman, 1981). Inasmuch as men have a higher rate of cardiovascular disease and hypertension as they age, this form of disability occurs more often in men than in women (APA, 2000). Some people have both Alzheimer's disease and vascular dementia (Desmond et al., 2000).

Pick's disease, a rare disorder that affects the frontal and temporal lobes, is similar to Alzheimer's disease clinically, but the two diseases can be distinguished at autopsy. **Creutzfeldt-Jakob disease**, another source of dementia, whose symptoms often include spasmodic movements, is caused by a slow-acting virus that may live in the body for years before the disease develops (APA, 2000) (see Box 16-6). Once launched, however, the disease has a rapid course. **Huntington's disease** is an inherited progressive disease in which memory problems worsen over time, along with personality changes and mood difficulties (Scourfield et al., 1997). Huntington's victims have movement problems, too, such as severe twitching and spasms. Children of people with Huntington's disease have a 50 percent chance of developing it. And **Parkinson's disease**, the slowly progressive neurological disorder marked by tremors, rigidity, and unsteadiness, causes dementia in 20 to 60 percent of cases, particularly in older people or people whose cases are advanced (APA, 2000). As we observed in Chapters 14 and 15, Parkinson's disease is closely tied to low activity of the neurotransmitter dopamine in certain areas of the brain.

Lastly, cases of dementia may also be caused by viral and bacterial infectious disorders such as HIV and AIDs, meningitis, and advanced syphilis; by epilepsy; by drug abuse; or by toxins such as mercury, lead, or carbon monoxide.

VASCULAR DEMENTIA Dementia caused by a cerebrovascular accident, or stroke, which restricts blood flow to certain areas of the brain. Also known as *multi-infarct dementia.*

PICK'S DISEASE A neurological disease that affects the frontal and temporal lobes, causing dementia.

CREUTZFELDT-JAKOB DISEASE A form of dementia caused by a slow-acting virus that may live in the body for years before the disease appears.

HUNTINGTON'S DISEASE An inherited disease in which people develop progressive problems in cognition, emotion, and movement, and which results in dementia.

PARKINSON'S DISEASE A slowly progressive neurological disease, marked by tremors and rigidity, which may also cause dementia.

BOX 16-6

Mad Human Disease?

In the 1980s British farmers first became aware of *bovine spongiform encephalopathy,* or *mad cow disease.* Cows with this disease became disoriented, uncoordinated, and irritable, and eventually died. Autopsies revealed holes and tangles of protein in their brains. Researchers traced the disease to a particular feeding practice and officials promptly banned it. But symptoms of the disease do not appear until years after the infection is contracted, so a continuing epidemic unfolded. Some 173,000 cows have now died of the disease.

What does mad cow disease have to do with abnormal psychology in humans? Clinicians have noted that *Creutzfeldt-Jakob disease* (CJD), a form of human dementia, is somewhat similar, clinically and biologically, to mad cow disease. It is a rare progressive dementia—incurable and fatal—apparently caused by an infectious protein that stays in the body for decades before producing symptoms (APA, 2000; Prusiner, 1995). Normally, one out of a million people develops CJD each year (Pain, 1996). Yet in 1996, ten otherwise

healthy young adults in Britain died of a disease that appeared to be a new variant of CJD. Could those individuals have contracted their disease by eating the meat of infected cows?

In short order, panic swept across England and around the world. Most nations banned imports of British beef. Healthy cows could not be distinguished from infected ones, and so the United Kingdom agreed to destroy 4.5 million animals—almost half the nation's herd. By 2000, the number of slaughtered cows had reached 8 million.

ConsiderThis

Some scientists argue that mad cow disease cannot be transmitted from one species to another, while others counter that it is indeed possible (Aldhous, 1996). When scientists disagree, how should the public proceed? • If scientists were to suspect, without certainty, that large numbers of *human beings* were carrying a deadly contagious disease, how would public officials respond?

What Treatments Are Available for Organic Memory Disorders?

Treating amnestic disorders and dementias is a frustrating and difficult challenge. No single approach or set of approaches is effective in all cases, and treatment tends to offer modest help. However, recent research on the genetic, biochemical, and anatomical causes of these disorders has fostered hope that they may be treated more effectively or even prevented in the years to come (Kalb, 2000).

Currently the first step in treatment is to identify with as much certainty as possible the precise type and nature of the disease. Clinicians will typically take a complete history of the patient (knowing about a person's abuse of alcohol or a family history of Alzheimer's disease, for example, helps narrow the diagnosis), do extensive neuropsychological testing, and conduct brain scans to help pinpoint the biological causes of the patient's dysfunctioning (Pantano et al., 1999; Zal, 1999; Gonzalez, 1996).

A common approach to the treatment of organic memory disorders, particularly dementia, is the use of drugs that affect the neurotransmitters known to play important roles in memory. Two such drugs, *tacrine* (trade name Cognex) and *donepezil* (Aricept), prevent the breakdown of acetylcholine, the neurotransmitter that is in low supply in people with Alzheimer's disease. Some Alzheimer patients who take these drugs improve slightly in short-term memory and

DEMENTIA IN DOGS

In 1999 the Food and Drug Administration approved the use of the drug *selegiline* (trade name Anipril) to treat elderly dogs suffering from *canine cognitive dysfunction syndrome*—a disorder characterized by confusion, inability to recognize or respond to familiar household faces, and the loss of house training. Around 70 percent of canine subjects show some improvement with drug treatment.

Victim of Parkinson's disease *The world cheered when Muhammad Ali, considered the most skilled and influential athlete of his generation, lit the Olympic flame in 1996. At the same time, Ali's slow gait, halting verbal responses, and shaking hands and limbs demonstrated the impairment that Parkinson's disease can bring.*

Caregiver Stress

According to research, caring for a loved one with Alzheimer's disease takes an average of 69 to 100 hours per week. The major worries reported by caregivers are the monetary cost of help (54 percent), the effects of Alzheimer's-related stress within the family (49 percent), and lack of time for caregivers to attend to their own needs (49 percent) (Alzheimer's Association, 1997).

reasoning ability, as well as in their use of language and their ability to cope under pressure (Krall, Sramek, & Cutler, 1999; Lyketsos et al., 1996). Although the benefits of the drugs are limited and the risk of undesired effects (particularly for tacrine) is sometimes high, the drugs have been approved by the Food and Drug Administration. Most clinicians believe that they do not help every patient but may be of use to those in the early stages of Alzheimer's disease or those with a mild form of dementia (Krall et al., 1999; Hedaya, 1996). Other safer and more effective drugs are currently under development (Daly, 1999; Krall et al., 1999).

Tacrine, donepezil, and related drugs are prescribed *after* a person has developed Alzheimer's disease. A number of studies seem to suggest, however, that certain substances may actually help prevent or delay the onset of the disease. For example, one team of researchers concluded that women who take *estrogen,* the female sex hormone, for years after menopause cut their risk of developing Alzheimer's disease in half (Kawas et al., 1997). Similarly, long-term use of nonsteroid anti-inflammatory drugs such as *ibuprofen* and *naprosyn* (drugs found in Advil, Motrin, Nuprin, and other pain relievers) seems to greatly reduce the risk of Alzheimer's disease.

Behavioral and cognitive therapies have also been tried in cases of amnestic disorder and dementia, with modest success. Some people with amnestic disorders, particularly those whose amnesia is caused by a head injury, have successfully been taught special methods for remembering new information; in some cases the teachers have been computers (Schacter et al., 1990). The behavioral techniques applied to dementia typically focus on changing everyday patient behaviors that are stressful for the family, such as wandering at night, urinary incontinence, excessive demands for attention, and inadequate personal care (Fisher & Carstensen, 1990). In these techniques therapists use a combination of role-playing exercises, modeling, and practice to teach family members how and when to apply reinforcement in order to shape more positive behaviors (Pinkston & Linsk, 1984).

Caregiving can take a heavy toll on the close relatives of people with amnestic disorders or dementia, particularly the latter (Alspaugh et al., 1999; Kiecolt-Glaser et al., 1996). In fact, one of the most frequent reasons for the institutionalization of Alzheimer's victims is that overwhelmed caregivers can no longer cope with the difficulties of keeping them at home (Kaplan, 1998; Colerick & George, 1986). Many caregivers experience anger and depression, and their own physical and mental health often declines. Clinicians now recognize that one of the most important aspects of treating Alzheimer's disease and other forms of dementia is to focus on the emotional needs of the caregivers: their need for regular time-out, for education about the disease, and for psychotherapy when stress begins to build (Clyburn et al., 2000; Kalb, 2000). Some clinicians also provide caregiver support groups (Gallagher-Thompson et al., 1991).

In recent years, sociocultural approaches have begun to play an important role in the treatment of organic memory disorders, particularly the dementias (Kalb, 2000). A number of *day-care* facilities for patients with Alzheimer's disease have been developed, providing treatment programs and activities for outpatients throughout the day and returning them to their homes and families at night. In addition, many *assisted-living* facilities have been built, in which individuals suffering from dementia live in cheerful apartments, receive needed supervision, and take part in various activities that bring more joy and stimulation to their lives. These apartments are typically designed to meet the special needs of the residents—providing more light, for example, or enclosing gardens with circular paths so the individuals can go for strolls alone without getting lost (Kalb, 2000). Initial studies suggest that such facilities often help slow the cognitive decline of residents and enhance their enjoyment of life.

Day treatment *Two women go their separate ways in a New Jersey day-care facility for patients with Alzheimer's disease. Such facilities, which are growing in number, provide special programs and activities for patients. The individuals return to their families each night.*

Rather than being discouraged by the present limitations in the understanding and treatment of amnestic disorders and dementia, researchers are anticipating significant advances in the coming years. The neurological changes responsible for cognition are tremendously complex, but given the amount of research under way and present reports of progress, most investigators believe that exciting breakthroughs are indeed just over the horizon.

HOME CARE

Around 70 percent of people with Alzheimer's disease live at home. Around three-fourths of their caregivers are women (Kalb, 2000).

CROSSROADS:
Enormous Interest but Limited Knowledge

Sometimes scientists scoff at a phenomenon that captures the public's interest. Dissociative disorders elicited this response for many years. The public's interest in dissociative amnesia and fugue was enormous, but scientific attention was limited. Similarly, multiple personality disorder failed to spur much empirical research.

This scientific indifference has since made an about-face. The growing number of reported cases of dissociative disorders, particularly multiple personality disorder, over the past 25 years has convinced many researchers that these patterns do exist and may cause great dysfunctioning. Studies have also begun to suggest that the disorders may have their roots in long-familiar processes, such as state-dependent learning and self-hypnosis.

Still, we do not yet have comprehensive theories about the causes of dissociative disorders—or fully developed, systematic treatment programs. And some clinicians worry that the pendulum may, in fact, be swinging too far—that the current degree of interest in dissociative disorders may be creating a false impression of their prevalence or importance. They argue that many current diagnoses are based less on a careful assessment of symptoms than on the increasing popularity of these disorders in the field. They also worry that at least some of the legal defenses based on dissociative disorders may be contrived or inaccurate. Of course, such possibilities only highlight the need for continuing investigation.

Less controversial, but equally fascinating, are the disorders of memory that have organic causes. The complexity of the brain makes amnestic disorders and

THE LAW OF DISUSE

In the early 1900s many scientists believed in the law of disuse, the principle that unused memories naturally deteriorate over time. Studies later revealed, however, that it is not time or disuse per se that causes forgetting but biological changes in the brain or intervening events that occur over the passage of time (Noll & Turkington, 1994).

dementias difficult to understand, diagnose, and treat. However, researchers announce exciting new discoveries almost daily. Because of the organic nature of these disorders, the research is largely biological; but the disorders have such a powerful impact on patients and their families that psychological and sociocultural investigations will not lag behind for long.

A common message derived from the many studies of dissociative disorders and organic memory disorders is the importance of memory for the human mind. Memory is so central to the continuity of our lives and to our self-concept that research in this area is of potential value to every person's well-being. Thus we can expect that studies into the nature of memory and memory disorders will continue to proliferate in the years to come.

POWER OF THE WRITTEN WORD

According to a story told by Socrates, the Egyptian god Thamus was horrified at the invention of the alphabet. Thamus predicted that it would increase forgetfulness by encouraging people to rely on written words rather than their memory (Noll & Turkington, 1994).

MEMORY BOOSTERS

Popular natural supplements that supposedly boost memory include products named "Brain Fuel," "Brain-Storm," "Food for Thought," and "Brain Gum" (Muhammad, 1999). The Chinese herb *Ginkgo biloba* is the most popular memory-enhancing supplement on the market, with sales of over $100 million each year.

SUMMARY AND REVIEW

■ **Dissociative disorders** Memory plays a key role in our functioning by linking our past, present, and future. People with dissociative disorders experience major changes in memory that are not due to clear physical causes. Typically, one part of the memory is dissociated, or separated, from the rest. People with dissociative amnesia are suddenly unable to recall important personal information or past events in their lives. Those with dissociative fugue not only fail to remember their personal identities but flee to a different location and may establish a new identity.

In another dissociative disorder, multiple personality disorder, people display two or more distinct subpersonalities. The subpersonalities often have complex relationships with one another and usually differ in vital statistics, abilities and preferences, and even physiological responses. A primary personality appears more often than the others. The number of people diagnosed with multiple personality disorder has increased in recent years. *pp. 478–487*

■ **Explanations of dissociative disorders** The dissociative disorders are not yet well understood. Among the processes that have been cited to explain them are extreme repression, operant conditioning, state-dependent learning, and self-hypnosis. The latter two phenomena, in particular, have excited the interest of clinical scientists. The state-dependent learning explanation suggests that the thoughts, memories, and skills of people who develop dissociative disorders are tied exclusively to specific states of arousal; that is, to whatever emotion or mental state the people were experiencing when they first acquired the thoughts, memories, or skills. The self-hypnosis explanation proposes that people with these disorders have hypnotized themselves to forget horrifying experiences in their lives. *pp. 487–491*

■ **Treatments for dissociative disorders** Dissociative amnesia and fugue may end on their own or may require treatment. Multiple personality disorder typically requires treatment. Approaches commonly used to help people with dissociative amnesia and fugue recover their lost memories are psychodynamic therapy, hypnotic therapy, and sodium amobarbital or sodium pentobarbital. Therapists who treat people with multiple personality disorder use the same approaches but focus on trying to help the clients recognize the nature and scope of their disorder, recover the gaps in their memories, and integrate their subpersonalities into one functional personality. *pp. 491–492*

■ **Organic memory disorders** Amnestic disorders and dementias are organic disorders that cause major problems in short-term memory, long-term memory, or both. Often the disorders are caused by abnormalities in key brain structures, such as the prefrontal lobes, the temporal lobes (including the hippocampus and amygdala embedded under them), and the diencephalon (including the mammillary bodies, thalamus, and hypothalamus). Amnestic disorders, disorders that primarily affect memory, may be the result of Korsakoff's syndrome, head injury, brain surgery, or certain other problems. Dementias, conditions that affect both memory and other cognitive functions, include Alzheimer's disease and vascular dementia. Alzheimer's disease has been linked to an unusually high number of neurofibrillary tangles and senile plaques in the brain. A number of causes have been proposed for this disease, including genetic factors, abnormal neurotransmitter activity, slow-acting infections, immune system problems, and high levels of zinc or aluminum in the brain. Both drug and behavioral therapies have been applied to organic memory disorders, with limited success. Addressing the needs of caregivers is now also recognized as a key part of treatment. In addition, sociocultural approaches such as day-care facilities are on the rise. The coming years are expected to see major treatment breakthroughs. *pp. 493–505*

DIAGNOSTIC CONFUSION

One out of ten people who seem to have dementia may actually be suffering from depression (Backmon, 1998; Noll & Turkington, 1994).

CYBER STUDY

▲ *Observe an individual with multiple personality disorder.* ▲ *See "switches" from subpersonality to subpersonality.* ▲ *How do therapists treat multiple personality disorder?* ▲ *What problems are faced by sufferers of Alzheimer's disease and their caregivers?* ▲ *Observe the special memory skills of savant functioning in action.*

SEARCH THE *ABNORMAL PSYCHOLOGY* CD-ROM FOR

▲ Chapter 16 video cases and discussions
  "Tony"—Multiple Personality Disorder
  "Walter"—Alzheimer's Disease

▲ Chapter 16 practice test and feedback

▲ Additional video case and discussion
  "George & Charles"—Savant Syndrome

LOG ON TO THE COMER WEB PAGE

[www.worthpublishers.com/comerabnormalpsychology4e] **FOR**

▲ Suggested Web links, research exercises, FAQ page, additional Chapter 16 practice test questions

While interviewing for the job of editor, Frederick said, "This may sound self-serving, but I am extraordinarily gifted. I am certain that I will do great things in this position, that I and the newspaper will soon set the standard for journalism in this city." The committee was impressed. Certainly, Frederick's credentials were strong, but even more importantly, his self-confidence and boldness had wowed them.

A year later, many of the same individuals were describing Frederick differently—arrogant, self-serving, cold, ego-maniacal, draining. He had performed well as editor (though not as spectacularly as he seemed to think), but that performance could not outweigh his impossible personality. Colleagues below and above him had grown weary of his manipulations, his emotional outbursts, his refusal to ever take the blame, his nonstop boasting, and his grandiose plans. Once again Frederick had outworn his welcome.

To be sure, Frederick had great charm, and he knew how to make others feel important, when it served his purpose. Thus he always had his share of friends and admirers. But in reality they were just passing through, until Frederick would tire of them or feel betrayed by their lack of enthusiasm for one of his self-serving interpretations or grand plans. Or until they simply could take Frederick no longer.

Bright and successful though he was, Frederick always felt entitled to more than he was receiving—to higher grades at school, greater compensation at work, more attention from girlfriends. If criticized even slightly, he reacted with fury, and was certain that the critic was jealous of his superior intelligence, skill, or looks. At first glance, Frederick seemed to have a lot going for him socially. Typically, he could be found in the midst of a deep, meaningful, romantic relationship—one in which he might be tender, attentive, and seemingly devoted to his partner. But Frederick would always tire of his partner within a few weeks or months and would turn cold or even mean. Often he started affairs with other women while still involved with the current partner. The breakups—usually unpleasant and sometimes ugly—rarely brought sadness or remorse to him, and he would almost never think about his former partner again. He always had himself.

Each of us has a **personality**—a unique and enduring pattern of inner experience and outward behavior. We tend to react in our own predictable and consistent ways. These consistencies, often called *personality traits,* may be the result of inherited characteristics, learned responses, or a combination of the two (Millon, 1999; Watson, Clark, & Harkness, 1994). Yet our personalities are also flexible. We learn from experience. As we interact with our surroundings, we try out various responses to see which are more effective. This is a flexibility that people who suffer from a personality disorder usually do not have.

A **personality disorder** is an inflexible pattern of inner experience and outward behavior. The pattern is seen in most of the person's interactions, continues for years, and differs markedly from the experiences and behaviors usually expected of people (see Table 17-1 on the next page). Frederick

Table 17-1 DSM-IV Checklist

PERSONALITY DISORDER

1. An enduring pattern of inner experience and behavior that deviates markedly from the expectations of the individual's culture, with at least two of the following areas affected: • cognition • affectivity • interpersonal functioning • impulse control.
2. Pattern is inflexible and pervasive across a broad range of personal and social situations.
3. Pattern is stable and long-lasting, and its onset can be traced back at least to adolescence or early adulthood.
4. Significant distress or impairment.

Based on APA, 2000, 1994.

Early notions of personality *Scientists have long suspected that biological factors help account for personality and personality disorders. In the theory of* phrenology, *Franz Joseph Gall (1758–1828) held that the brain consists of distinct portions, each responsible for some aspect of personality. Phrenologists tried to assess personality by feeling bumps and indentations on a person's head.*

PERSONALITY A unique and long-term pattern of inner experience and outward behavior, which leads to consistent reactions across various situations.

PERSONALITY DISORDER A very rigid pattern of inner experience and outward behavior that differs from the expectations of one's culture and leads to dysfunctioning.

seems to display such a disorder. For most of his life, his narcissism, grandiosity, outbursts, and insensitivity to others have been excessive and have dominated his functioning. The rigid traits of people with personality disorders often lead to psychological pain for the individual and social or occupational difficulties. The disorders may also bring pain to others. Witness the upset and turmoil experienced by Frederick's co-workers and girlfriends.

Personality disorders typically become recognizable in adolescence or early adulthood, although some start during childhood (APA, 2000, 1994). These are among the most difficult psychological disorders to treat. Many sufferers are not even aware of their personality problems and fail to trace their difficulties to their inflexible style of thinking and behaving. It has been estimated that between 4 and 15 percent of all adults may have a personality disorder (Kessler & Zhao, 1999; Lenzenweger et al., 1997; Links, 1997).

As we saw in Chapter 4, DSM-IV distinguishes Axis II disorders, disorders of long standing that usually begin well before adulthood and continue into adult life, from the Axis I disorders, the more acute disorders, which often begin as a noticeable change in a person's usual behavior and are, in many cases, of limited duration. The personality disorders are Axis II disorders; these patterns are not typically marked by changes in intensity or periods of clear improvement.

It is common for a person with a personality disorder to suffer from an acute (Axis I) disorder simultaneously, a relationship called *comorbidity* (Flick et al., 1993). Perhaps personality disorders predispose people to develop certain Axis I disorders. For example, people with avoidant personality disorder, who fearfully shy away from all relationships, may be prone to develop a social phobia. Then again, certain Axis I disorders may set the stage for a personality disorder. Or perhaps some biological factor creates a predisposition to both (Hirschfeld, 1999; Koenigsberg et al., 1999). Whatever the reason for the relationship, research indicates that the presence of a personality disorder complicates and reduces a person's chances for a successful recovery from psychological problems (Costello, 1996).

DSM-IV identifies ten personality disorders and separates them into three groups, called *clusters* (APA, 2000, 1994). One cluster, marked by odd or eccentric behavior, consists of the *paranoid, schizoid,* and *schizotypal* personality disorders. A second group features dramatic behavior and consists of the *antisocial, borderline, histrionic,* and *narcissistic* personality disorders. The final cluster features a high degree of anxiety, and includes the *avoidant, dependent,* and *obsessive-compulsive* personality disorders.

The various personality disorders overlap so much that it can be difficult to distinguish one from the other (Zimmerman, 1994) (see Figure 17-1). In fact,

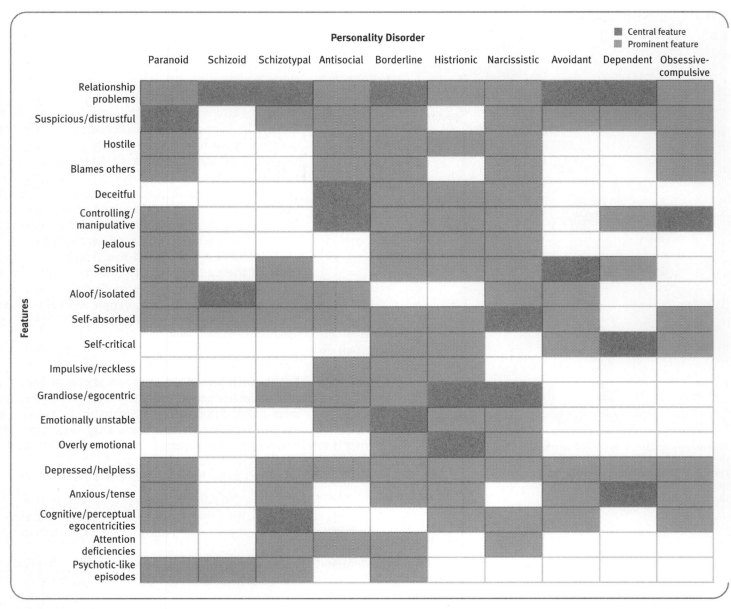

FIGURE 17-1   Prominent and central features of DSM-IV's ten personality disorders
The symptoms of the various disorders often overlap greatly, leading to frequent misdiagnosis or to multiple diagnoses for a given client.

diagnosticians sometimes determine that particular individuals have more than one personality disorder (Grove & Tellegen, 1991). In addition, clinicians often disagree as to the correct diagnosis for people with personality disorders. This lack of consensus has raised serious questions about the validity (accuracy) and reliability (consistency) of the present DSM categories, a concern that we shall return to later (O'Connor & Dyce, 1998; Costello, 1996).

Finally, the diagnosis of personality disorder can easily be overapplied. We may catch glimpses of ourselves or of people we know in the descriptions of these disorders, and we may be tempted to conclude that we or they have a personality disorder (Maher & Maher, 1994; Widiger & Costa, 1994). In the vast majority of instances, such interpretations are incorrect. We all display personality traits. Only rarely are they so inflexible, maladaptive, and distressful that they can be considered disorders.

"Odd" Personality Disorders

The cluster of *"odd" personality disorders* consists of the *paranoid, schizoid,* and *schizotypal* personality disorders. People with these disorders typically display odd or eccentric behaviors that are similar to but not as extensive as those seen in schizophrenia, including extreme suspiciousness, social withdrawal, and peculiar ways of thinking and perceiving things. Such behaviors often leave the person isolated. Some clinicians believe that these personality disorders are actually related to schizophrenia, and they call them *schizophrenia-spectrum disorders* (Battaglia et al., 1997; Siever, 1992). In support of this idea, people with these personality disorders often qualify for an additional diagnosis of schizophrenia or have close relatives with schizophrenia (APA, 2000, 1994; Battaglia et al., 1991). Of course, such findings may simply reflect the difficulty of distinguishing these personality disorders from schizophrenia, rather than some kind of direct relationship between them.

Clinicians have learned much about the symptoms of the odd personality disorders but have not been so successful in determining their causes or how to treat them. In fact, people with these disorders rarely seek treatment (Fabrega et al., 1991).

Paranoid Personality Disorder

People with **paranoid personality disorder** deeply distrust other people and are suspicious of their motives (APA, 2000, 1994). Because they believe that everyone intends them harm, they shun close relationships. Their trust in their own ideas and abilities can be excessive, though, as we see in the case of Charles:

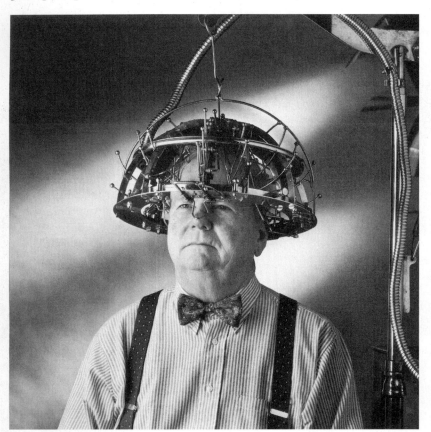

Phrenology update *It appears that old ideas die hard. A 1930 device called the* psychograph *carried on the tradition of phrenology, studying and measuring bumps on the head in order to assess an individual's personality.*

> Charles, an only child of poorly educated parents, had been recognized as a "child genius" in early school years. He received a Ph.D. degree at 24, and subsequently held several responsible positions as a research physicist in an industrial firm.
>
> His haughty arrogance and narcissism often resulted in conflicts with his superiors; it was felt that he spent too much time working on his own "harebrained" schemes and not enough on company projects. Charles . . . began to feel that both his superiors and his subordinates were "making fun of him" and not taking him seriously. To remedy this attack upon his status, Charles began to work on a scheme that would "revolutionize the industry," a new thermodynamic principle which, when applied to his company's major product, would prove extremely efficient and economical. After several months . . . he presented his plans to the company president. Brilliant though it was, the plan overlooked certain obvious simple facts of logic and economy.
>
> Upon learning of its rejection, Charles withdrew to his home where he became obsessed with "new ideas," proposing them in intricate schematics and formulas to a number of government officials and industrialists. These resulted in new rebuffs which led to further efforts at self inflation.
>
> *(Millon, 1969, pp. 329–330)*

EARNED DISTRUST?

Two and a half million telephone conversations were secretly wiretapped by the U.S. government in 1997 (Administrative Office of the U.S. Courts, 1998).

Ever on guard and cautious, and seeing threats everywhere, people like Charles continually expect to be the targets of some trickery (see Figure 17-2). They find "hidden" meanings in everything, which are usually belittling or threatening. In a study that required individuals to role-play, subjects with paranoia were more likely than control subjects to read hostile intentions into the actions of others. In addition, they more often chose anger as the appropriate role-play response (Turkat et al., 1990).

Quick to challenge the loyalty or trustworthiness of acquaintances, people with paranoid personality disorder remain cold and distant. A woman might avoid confiding in anyone, for example, for fear of being hurt; or a husband might, without any justification, persist in questioning his wife's faithfulness. Although inaccurate and inappropriate, their suspicions are not usually *delusional*; the ideas are not so bizarre or so firmly held as to clearly remove the individuals from reality (Fenigstein, 1996).

People with this disorder are critical of weakness and fault in others, particularly at work. They are unable to recognize their own mistakes, however, and are extremely sensitive to criticism. Argumentative and rigid, they often blame others for the things that go wrong in their lives, and they persistently bear grudges (Fenigstein, 1996; Vaillant, 1994). Between 0.5 and 2.5 percent of adults are believed to experience this disorder, apparently more men than women (APA, 2000, 1994).

EXPLANATIONS OF PARANOID PERSONALITY DISORDER The proposed explanations of paranoid personality disorder, like those of most other personality disorders, have received little systematic research. Psychodynamic theories, the oldest of the explanations for this disorder, trace the pattern to early interactions with demanding parents, particularly distant, rigid fathers and overcontrolling, rejecting mothers (Manschreck, 1996). (We shall see that psychodynamic explanations for almost all the personality disorders begin the same way—with repeated mistreatment during childhood and lack of love.) According to one psychodynamic view, some individuals come to view their environment as hostile as a result of their parents' persistently unreasonable demands. They must always be on the alert because they cannot trust others, and they are likely to develop feelings of extreme anger (Cameron, 1974). They also project these feelings onto others, and as a result feel increasingly persecuted (Garfield & Havens, 1991). Similarly, some cognitive theorists suggest that people with paranoid personality disorder, in their efforts to bear up under the demanding expectations of others and to cope with feelings of humiliation, shame, and inadequacy, generally adopt broad maladaptive assumptions such as "People are evil" and "People will attack you if given the chance" (Beck & Freeman, 1990; Freeman et al., 1990).

Biological theorists propose that paranoid personality disorder has genetic causes (Fenigstein, 1996). A study that looked at self-reports of suspiciousness in 3,810 Australian twin pairs found that if one twin was excessively suspicious, the other had an increased likelihood of also being suspicious (Kendler et al., 1987). Once again, however, it is important to note that such similarities between twins might also be the result of common environmental experiences.

TREATMENTS FOR PARANOID PERSONALITY DISORDER People with paranoid personality disorder do not typically consider themselves in need of help, and few come to treatment willingly (Millon, 1999). Furthermore, many who are in treatment view the role of patient as subordinate (and therefore highly objectionable) and distrust and rebel against their therapists (Fenigstein, 1996; Sparr et al., 1986). It is not surprising, then, that therapy for this disorder, as for most other personality disorders, has limited effect and progresses very slowly (Quality Assurance Project, 1990).

Object relations therapists, the psychodynamic therapists who give center stage to relationships, try to see past the patient's anger and work on what they view as his or her deep wish for a satisfying relationship (Auchincloss & Weiss, 1992). Behavioral and cognitive therapists, for their part, try to help these

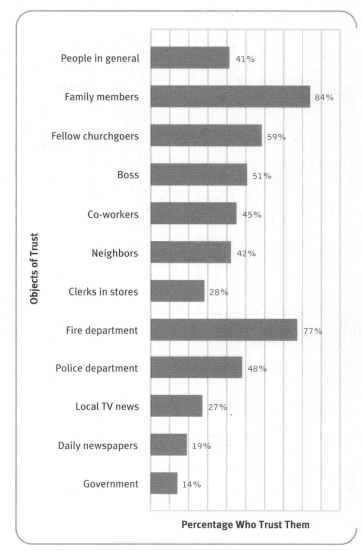

FIGURE 17-2 **Whom do you trust?** *Although distrust and suspiciousness are the hallmarks of paranoid personality disorder, even persons without this disorder are surprisingly untrusting. In a recent survey of a broad sample of society, only 41 percent of respondents said that they generally trust people. Most do trust their family members and local fire department; however, few trust clerks in stores, daily newspapers, or the government. (Adapted from Pew Research Center for the People and the Press, 1997.)*

PARANOID PERSONALITY DISORDER A personality disorder marked by a pattern of distrust and suspiciousness of others.

individuals control their anxiety and improve their skills at solving interpersonal problems. Cognitive therapists also try to guide the clients to develop more realistic interpretations of other people's words and actions and to become more aware of other people's points of view (Beck & Freeman, 1990). Drug therapy is generally ineffective (Block & Pristach, 1992).

Schizoid Personality Disorder

People with **schizoid personality disorder** persistently avoid and are detached from social relationships and demonstrate little in the way of emotion (APA, 2000, 1994). Like people with paranoid personality disorder, these individuals do not have close ties with others. The reason they avoid social contact, however, has nothing to do with paranoia—it is that they genuinely prefer to be alone. Take Roy:

> Roy was a successful sanitation engineer involved in the planning and maintenance of water resources for a large city; his job called for considerable foresight and independent judgment but little supervisory responsibility. In general, he was appraised as an undistinguished but competent and reliable employee. There were few demands of an interpersonal nature made of him, and he was viewed by most of his colleagues as reticent and shy and by others as cold and aloof.
>
> Difficulties centered about his relationship with his wife. At her urging they sought marital counseling for, as she put it, "he is unwilling to join in family activities, he fails to take an interest in the children, he lacks affection and is disinterested in sex."
>
> The pattern of social indifference, flatness of affect and personal isolation which characterized much of Roy's behavior was of little consequence to those with whom a deeper or more intimate relationship was not called for; with his immediate family, however, these traits took their toll.
>
> *(Millon, 1969, p. 224)*

People like Roy, often described as "loners," make no effort to start or keep friendships, take little interest in having sexual relationships, and even seem indifferent to their families. They seek out jobs that require little or no contact with others. When necessary, they can form functional, if distant, work relations, but they prefer to keep to themselves. Many live by themselves as well. Not surprisingly, their social skills tend to be weak (Birtchnell, 1996). If they marry, their lack of interest in intimacy may create marital or family problems, as it did for Roy.

People with schizoid personality disorder are self-absorbed and generally unaffected by praise or criticism. They rarely show any feelings, expressing neither joy nor anger. They seem to have no need for attention or acceptance; are typically viewed as cold, humorless, or dull; and generally succeed in being ignored. The prevalence of this disorder is not known, although it is estimated to be present in fewer than 1 percent of the population (Weissman, 1993). It is slightly more likely to occur in men than in women, and men may also be more impaired by it (APA, 2000).

EXPLANATIONS OF SCHIZOID PERSONALITY DISORDER Many psychodynamic theorists, particularly object relations theorists, propose that schizoid personality disorder has its roots, paradoxically, in an unsatisfied need for human contact (Carstairs, 1992; Horner, 1991, 1975). The parents of people with this disorder, like those of people with paranoid personality disorder, are believed to have been unaccepting or even abusive of their children. Whereas individuals with paranoid symptoms react to such parenting chiefly with a sense of distrust, those with schizoid personality disorder become hampered in their ability to give or receive

---

"In most of us, by the age of thirty, the character has set like plaster, and will never soften again."

William James, *Principles of Psychology,* 1890

SCHIZOID PERSONALITY DISORDER A personality disorder in which a person persistently avoids social relationships and shows little emotional expression.

SCHIZOTYPAL PERSONALITY DISORDER A personality disorder in which a person displays a pattern of interpersonal problems marked by extreme discomfort in close relationships, odd forms of thinking and perceiving, and behavioral eccentricities.

love. They cope by avoiding all relationships. Another psychodynamic view, self theory, describes this personality pattern as a "self disorder," in which the sufferer lacks self-esteem and the ability to comfort her- or himself (Cirese, 1993; Gabbard, 1990). Because such individuals are unsure of who they are, they cannot relate to others.

Cognitive theorists propose, not surprisingly, that people with schizoid personality disorder suffer from deficiencies in their thinking. Their thoughts tend to be vague and empty, and they have trouble scanning the environment to arrive at accurate perceptions (Beck & Freeman, 1990). Unable to pick up emotional cues from others, they simply cannot respond to emotions. As this theory might predict, children with schizoid personality disorder develop language and motor skills very slowly, whatever their level of intelligence (Wolff, 1991).

TREATMENTS FOR SCHIZOID PERSONALITY DISORDER Their social withdrawal prevents most people with schizoid personality disorder from entering therapy unless some other disorder, such as alcoholism, makes treatment necessary. These clients are likely to remain emotionally distant from the therapist, seem not to care about their treatment, and make limited progress at best (Millon, 1999; Quality Assurance Project, 1990).

Cognitive therapists have sometimes been able to help people with this disorder experience more positive emotions and more satisfying social interactions (Beck & Freeman, 1990). Their techniques include presenting clients with lists of emotions to think about or having them write down and remember pleasurable experiences. Behavioral therapists have sometimes had success teaching social skills to such clients, using role playing, exposure techniques, and homework assignments as tools (Millon, 1999). Group therapy is apparently useful when it offers a safe setting for social contact (Vaillant & Perry, 1985), although people with this disorder may resist any pressure to take part (Gabbard, 1990). As with paranoid personality disorder, drug therapy has offered little help (Liebowitz et al., 1986).

Alone, either way *Different personality disorders often yield similar behaviors. People with either schizoid or avoidant personality disorder spend much of their time alone. The former, however, truly want to be alone, whereas the latter yearn for but fear social relationships.*

Schizotypal Personality Disorder

People with **schizotypal personality disorder** display a range of interpersonal problems marked by extreme discomfort in close relationships, very odd patterns of thinking and perceiving, and behavioral eccentricities (APA, 2000, 1994). Anxious around others, they seek isolation and have few close friends. Many feel intensely lonely. The disorder is more severe than the paranoid and schizoid personality disorders, as we see in the case of Harold:

Harold was the fourth of seven children. . . . "Duckie," as Harold was known, had always been a withdrawn, frightened and "stupid" youngster. The nickname "Duckie" represented a peculiar waddle in his walk; it was used by others as a term of derogation and ridicule. Harold rarely played with his sibs or neighborhood children; he was teased unmercifully because of his "walk" and his fear of pranksters. Harold was a favorite neighborhood scapegoat; he was intimidated even by the most innocuous glance in his direction. . . .

Harold's family was surprised when he performed well in the first few years of schooling. He began to falter, however, upon entrance to junior high school. At about the age of 14, his schoolwork became extremely poor, he refused to go to classes and he complained of a variety of vague, physical pains. By age 15 he had totally withdrawn from school, remaining home in the basement room that he shared with two younger brothers. Everyone in his family began to speak of him as "being touched." He thought about "funny religious things that didn't make sense"; he also began to draw "strange things" and talk to himself. When he was 16, he once ran out of the house screaming "I'm gone, I'm gone, I'm gone . . . ," saying that his "body went to heaven" and that he had to run outside to recover it; rather interestingly, this event occurred shortly after his father had been committed by the courts to a state mental hospital. By age 17, Harold was ruminating all day, often talking aloud in a meaningless jargon; he refused to come to the family table for meals.

(Millon, 1969, pp. 347–348)

As with Harold, the thoughts and behaviors of people with schizotypal personality disorder can be noticeably disturbed (Birtchnell, 1996). These symptoms may include *ideas of reference*—beliefs that unrelated events pertain to them in some important way—and *bodily illusions*—such as sensing an external "force" or presence. A number of people with this disorder see themselves as having special extrasensory abilities, and some believe that they have magical control over others. Examples of schizotypal eccentricities include repeatedly arranging cans to align their labels, organizing closets extensively, or wearing an odd assortment of clothing. The emotions of these individuals may be inappropriate, flat, or humorless.

People with schizotypal personality disorder often have great difficulty keeping their attention focused (Lenzenwerger et al., 1991). This problem may help explain one of their key characteristics—*digressive speech*. Their conversation is typically vague, yet far too elaborate, and they often use loose associations (Caplan et al., 1990). Similar features are seen in schizophrenia, but in schizotypal personality disorder, these problems in attention and thought do not represent a complete break from reality.

Sometimes the perceptual distortions and magical thinking found in schizotypal personality disorder reflect creative ability (Schuldberg et al., 1988). Most often, however, people with this disorder drift aimlessly and lead an idle, unproductive life (Millon, 1990). They are likely to choose undemanding jobs in which they can work below their capacity and are not required to interact with other people.

It has been estimated that around 3 percent of all people—slightly more males than females—may have a schizotypal personality disorder (APA, 2000; Weissman, 1993). The symptoms they display often differ along gender lines. The "positive" symptoms (that is, the excesses), such as magical thinking and ideas of reference, seem to be more common in women, whereas the "negative" symptoms (the deficits), such as limited emotions and lack of friends, appear to be more common among men (Raine, 1992).

EXPLANATIONS OF SCHIZOTYPAL PERSONALITY DISORDER Because the symptoms of schizotypal personality disorder so often resemble schizophrenia, researchers have hypothesized that similar factors are at work in both disorders (Raine et al., 1997). They have in fact found that schizotypal symptoms, like schizophrenic patterns, are often linked to poor family communication and to psychological disorders in parents (Asarnow et al., 1991; Nagy & Szatmari, 1986). Moreover, they have learned that defects in attention may contribute to schizotypal personality disorder, just as they apparently do to schizophrenia (Cadenhead et al., 2000; Roitman et al., 1997). For example, subjects with either disorder perform poorly on *backward masking,* a laboratory test of attention that requires subjects to identify a visual stimulus immediately after a previous stimulus has flashed on and off the screen. People with these disorders have a hard time shutting out the first stimulus in order to focus on the second (Weston & Siever, 1993; Braff & Saccuzzo, 1985). Finally, researchers have begun to link schizotypal personality disorder to some of the same biological factors found in schizophrenia, such as high activity of the neurotransmitter dopamine and enlarged brain ventricles (Trestman et al., 1996; Weston & Siever, 1993). As we saw in Chapter 14, there are indications that these biological factors may have a genetic base (Carey & DiLalla, 1994; Kendler et al., 1991).

A COMMON BELIEF

People who think that they have extrasensory abilities are not necessarily suffering from schizotypal personality disorder. In fact, according to one large survey, half of all people believe in ESP (Kanner, 1995).

CHARACTER INGESTION

As late as the Victorian era, many English parents believed babies absorbed personality and moral uprightness as they took in milk. Thus, if a mother could not nurse, it was important to find a wetnurse of good character (Asimov, 1997).

Although these findings do suggest a close relationship between schizotypal personality disorder and schizophrenia, the personality disorder has also been linked to mood disorders. Relatives of people with depression have a higher than usual rate of schizotypal personality disorder, and vice versa. Thus, at the very least, this personality disorder is not tied exclusively to schizophrenia (Schulz et al., 1986).

TREATMENTS FOR SCHIZOTYPAL PERSONALITY DISORDER Therapy is as difficult in cases of schizotypal personality disorder as it is in cases of paranoid and schizoid personality disorders (Millon, 1999; Stone, 1989; McGlashan, 1986). Most therapists agree on the need to help these clients "reconnect" with the world and recognize the limits of their thinking and their powers. The therapists may thus try to set clear limits—for example, by requiring punctuality—and work on helping the clients recognize where their views end and those of the therapist begin (Stone, 1989). Other therapy goals are to increase positive social contacts, ease loneliness, reduce overstimulation, and help the individuals become more aware of their personal feelings (Millon, 1999; Quality Assurance Project, 1990).

Cognitive therapists further try to teach clients to evaluate their unusual thoughts or perceptions objectively and to ignore the inappropriate ones (Beck & Freeman, 1990). A therapist may keep track of a person's odd or magical predictions, for example, and later point out their inaccuracy. When a client is speaking and begins to digress, the therapist might ask the individual to sum up what he or she is trying to say. On occasion, specific behavioral methods, such as speech lessons, social skills training, and tips on appropriate dress and manners, have helped clients learn to blend in better and be more comfortable around others (Liebowitz et al., 1986).

Antipsychotic drugs have been given to people with schizotypal personality disorder, again because of the disorder's similarity to schizophrenia. In low doses the drugs appear to have helped some people, usually by reducing certain of their thought problems (Coccaro, 1998; Weston & Siever, 1993).

"Dramatic" Personality Disorders

The cluster of *"dramatic" personality disorders* includes the antisocial, borderline, histrionic, and narcissistic personality disorders. The behaviors of people with these problems are so dramatic, emotional, or erratic that it is almost impossible for them to have relationships that are truly nurturing and satisfying.

These personality disorders are more commonly diagnosed than the others (Fabrega et al., 1991). However, only the antisocial and borderline personality disorders have been studied extensively, partly because they create so many problems for other people. The causes of the disorders, like those of the odd personality disorders, are not well understood. Treatments range from ineffective to moderately effective.

Antisocial Personality Disorder

Sometimes described as *"psychopaths"* or *"sociopaths,"* people with **antisocial personality disorder** persistently disregard and violate others' rights (APA, 2000, 1994). Aside from substance-related disorders, this is the disorder most closely linked to adult criminal behavior (see Box 17-1 on the next page). DSM-IV stipulates that a person must be at least 18 years of age to receive this diagnosis; however, most with antisocial personality disorder displayed some patterns of misbehavior before they were 15, including truancy, running away, physical cruelty to animals or people, destruction of property, and setting fires.

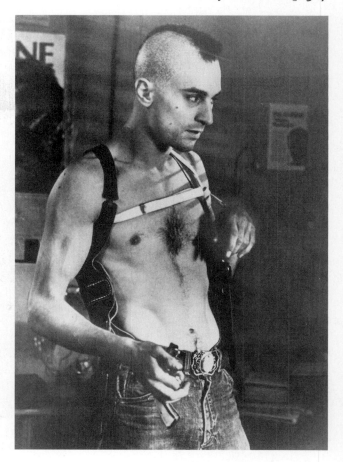

Taxi Driver *Some of film's most memorable characters have displayed personality disorders. Travis Bickle, of* Taxi Driver *fame, seemed to manifest the symptoms of schizotypal personality disorder, including social discomfort and a reduced capacity for interpersonal relationships. He also displayed self-referential interpretations of various events, cognitive distortions, a highly suspicious nature, grandiosity, emotional flatness, and temporary psychotic episodes.*

ANTISOCIAL PERSONALITY DISORDER A personality disorder marked by a general pattern of disregard for and violation of other people's rights.

BOX 17-1

When Life Imitates Art

Oliver Stone's 1994 movie *Natural Born Killers* tells the tale of two sociopathic thrill seekers, Mickey and Mallory, who grow world-famous as they travel the countryside committing brutal murders. Stone meant to satirize our culture's appetite for violence, but the film itself inspired more copycat killings than any other movie ever made (Shnayerson, 1996). Numerous young people went on similar killing sprees, citing *Natural Born Killers* as their inspiration.

The copycat phenomenon is not new. When Stanley Kubrick's film *A Clockwork Orange* was released in 1971, critics praised its powerful social statement. But when some British youths copied the actions of the movie's gang leader

and raped a woman to the tune of "Singin' in the Rain," Kubrick had the film banned in Britain (Shnayerson, 1996). It remains so today.

ConsiderThis

◉ Must individuals already be antisocial in order to be influenced by films such as these, or do the films confuse people who are not antisocial by glorifying criminal and violent behavior?
• Should filmmakers and writers consider the possible psychological influence of their work on suggestible individuals before they undertake such projects?

Robert Hare (1993), a leading researcher of antisocial personality disorder, recalls an early professional encounter with a prison inmate named Ray:

"Society prepares the crime; the criminal commits it."

Buckle

In the early 1960s, I found myself employed as the sole psychologist at the British Columbia Penitentiary. . . . I wasn't in my office for more than an hour when my first "client" arrived. He was a tall, slim, dark-haired man in his thirties. The air around him seemed to buzz, and the eye contact he made with me was so direct and intense that I wondered if I had ever really looked anybody in the eye before. That stare was unrelenting—he didn't indulge in the brief glances away that most people use to soften the force of their gaze.

Without waiting for an introduction, the inmate—I'll call him Ray—opened the conversation: "Hey, Doc, how's it going? Look, I've got a problem. I need your help. I'd really like to talk to you about this."

Eager to begin work as a genuine psychotherapist, I asked him to tell me about it. In response, he pulled out a knife and waved it in front of my nose, all the while smiling and maintaining that intense eye contact.

Once he determined that I wasn't going to push the button, he explained that he intended to use the knife not on me but on another inmate who had been making overtures to his "protégé," a prison term for the more passive member of a homosexual pairing. Just why he was telling me this was not immediately clear, but I soon suspected that he was checking me out, trying to determine what sort of a prison employee I was. Following our session, in which he described his "problem" not once or twice but many times, I kept quiet about the knife. To my relief, he didn't stab the other inmate, but it soon became evident that Ray had caught me in his trap: I had shown myself to be a soft touch who would overlook clear violations of fundamental prison rules in order to develop "professional" rapport with the inmates.

From that first meeting on, Ray managed to make my eight-month stint at the prison miserable. His constant demands on my time and his attempts to manipulate me into doing things for him were unending. On one occasion, he convinced me that he would make a good cook . . . and I supported his request for a transfer from the machine shop (where he had apparently made the knife). What I didn't consider was that the kitchen was a source of sugar, potatoes, fruit, and other ingredients that could be turned into alcohol. Several months after I had recommended the transfer, there was a mighty eruption below the floorboards directly under the warden's table. When the commotion died down, we found an elaborate system for distilling alcohol below the floor. Something had gone wrong and one of the pots had exploded. There was nothing unusual about the presence of a still in a maximum-security prison, but the audacity of placing one under the warden's seat shook up a lot of people. When it was discovered that Ray was the brains behind the bootleg operation, he spent some time in solitary confinement.

Once out of "the hole," Ray appeared in my office as if nothing had happened and asked for a transfer from the kitchen to the auto shop—he really felt he had a knack, he saw the need to prepare himself for the outside world, if he only had the time to practice he could have his own body shop on the outside. . . . I was still feeling the sting of having arranged the first transfer, but eventually he wore me down.

Soon afterward I decided to leave the prison to pursue a Ph.D. in psychology, and about a month before I left Ray almost persuaded me to ask my father, a roofing contractor, to offer him a job as part of an application for parole.

Ray had an incredible ability to con not just me but everybody. He could talk, and lie, with a smoothness and a directness that sometimes momentarily disarmed even the most experienced and cynical of the prison staff. When I met him he had a long criminal record behind him (and, as it turned out, ahead of him); about half his adult life had been spent in prison, and many of his crimes had been violent. . . . He lied endlessly, lazily, about everything, and it disturbed him not a whit whenever I pointed out something in his file that contradicted one of his lies. He would simply change the subject and spin off in a different direction. Finally convinced that he might not make the perfect job candidate in my father's firm, I turned down Ray's request—and was shaken by his nastiness at my refusal.

Before I left the prison for the university, I took advantage of the prison policy of letting staff have their cars repaired in the institution's auto shop—where Ray still worked, thanks (he would have said no thanks) to me. The car received a beautiful paint job and the motor and drivetrain were reconditioned.

With all our possessions on top of the car and our baby in a plywood bed in the backseat, my wife and I headed for Ontario. The first problems appeared soon after we left Vancouver, when the motor seemed a bit rough. Later, when we encountered some moderate inclines, the radiator boiled over. A garage mechanic discovered ball bearings in the carburetor's float chamber; he also pointed out where one of the hoses to the radiator had clearly been tampered with. These problems were repaired easily enough, but the next one, which arose while we were going down a long hill, was more serious. The brake pedal became very spongy and then simply dropped to the floor—no brakes, and it was a long hill. Fortunately, we made it to a service station, where we found that the brake line had been cut so that a slow leak would occur. Perhaps it was a coincidence that Ray was working in the auto shop when the car was being tuned up, but I had no doubt that the prison "telegraph" had informed him of the owner of the car.

(Hare, 1993)

Antisocial and homicidal *Charles Manson, who directed his followers to kill nine people in 1969, fits many of the criteria of antisocial personality disorder, including disregard for and violation of others' rights, impulsivity, disregard for truth, and lack of remorse. In a recent interview Manson bragged, "I was crazy when crazy meant something."*

FAULTY LIE DETECTORS

One study found that supposed experts on lying were not very effective at detecting falsehoods. When viewing videotaped statements and evaluating their truth or falsehood, police identified only 51 percent of the lies and clinical psychologists and federal judges identified only 62 percent of them (Ekman, O'Sullivan, & Frank, 1999).

Like Ray, people with antisocial personality disorder lie incessantly (Seto et al., 1997). Many cannot work consistently at a job; they are absent frequently and are likely to quit their jobs altogether (Bland et al., 1988). Usually they are also careless with money and frequently fail to pay their debts. They are often impulsive, taking action without thinking of the consequences (Lykken, 1995).

Correspondingly, they may be irritable, aggressive, and quick to start fights (Vaillant, 1994). Many travel from place to place.

Recklessness is another common trait: people with antisocial personality disorder have little regard for their own safety or for that of others, even their children. They are egocentric, as well, and likely to have difficulty maintaining close relationships (Birtchnell, 1996; Whitely, 1994). Usually they develop a knack for gaining personal profit at the expense of other people. The pain or damage they cause seldom concerns them, so clinicians commonly say that they lack a moral conscience (Lykken, 1995). They think of their victims as weak and deserving of being conned or robbed.

Surveys indicate that up to 3 percent of people in the United States meet the criteria for antisocial personality disorder (APA, 2000; Kessler et al., 1994). White Americans are somewhat more likely than African Americans to receive the diagnosis (Robins et al., 1991), and the disorder is as much as four times more common among men than women (Kessler & Zhao, 1999).

Because people with this disorder are often arrested, researchers frequently look for people with antisocial patterns in prison populations (Lish et al., 1996; Kaplan et al., 1994; Parker, 1991). Among men in urban jails, the antisocial personality pattern has been strongly linked to past arrests for crimes of violence (Abram & Teplin, 1990). For many people with this disorder, criminal behavior declines after the age of 40; some, however, continue their criminal activities throughout their lives (Arboleda-Florez & Holley, 1991).

Studies and clinical observations also indicate higher rates of alcoholism and other substance-related disorders among people with antisocial personality disorder than in the rest of the population (Myers, Stewart, & Brown, 1998; Sher & Trull, 1994). Perhaps intoxication and substance abuse help trigger the development of antisocial personality disorder by loosening a person's inhibitions (Kaminer, 1991). Or perhaps this personality disorder somehow makes a person more prone to develop a pattern of substance abuse (Bukstein et al., 1989). Then again, perhaps antisocial personality disorder and substance abuse both have the same cause, such as a deep-seated need to take risks (Sher & Trull, 1994). Interestingly, drug users with the personality disorder often cite the recreational aspects of drug use as their reason for starting and maintaining it (Mirin & Weiss, 1991).

Finally, children with conduct disorder and an accompanying attention-deficit hyperactivity disorder apparently have a heightened risk of developing antisocial personality disorder (APA, 2000, 1994). These two childhood disorders, which we shall examine in Chapter 18, often bear similarities to antisocial personality disorder. Like adults with antisocial personality disorder, children with a conduct disorder persistently lie and violate rules and other people's rights; and children with attention-deficit hyperactivity disorder lack foresight and judgment and fail to learn from experience (Bloomingdale & Bloomingdale, 1989). Intriguing as these observations may be, however, the precise connection between the childhood disorders and the personality disorder has been difficult to pinpoint.

EXPLANATIONS OF ANTISOCIAL PERSONALITY DISORDER Explanations of antisocial personality disorder come from the psychodynamic, behavioral, cognitive, and biological models. As with many other personality disorders, psychodynamic theorists propose that this one, too, begins with an absence of parental love during infancy, leading to a lack of basic trust (Gabbard, 1990). In this view, some children—the ones who develop antisocial personality disorder—respond to the early inadequacies by becoming emotionally distant. The only way they have of bonding with others is through the use of power and destructiveness.

In support of the psychodynamic explanation, researchers have found that people with this disorder are more likely than others to have had significant stress in their childhoods, particularly in such forms as family

PREVIOUS IDENTITY
Antisocial personality disorder was referred to as "moral insanity" during the nineteenth century.

The making of a sociopath? *In 1974 the newspaper heiress Patty Hearst was kidnapped by a terrorist group called the Symbionese Liberation Army. After being locked in a closet for months and experiencing other tortures, the young woman participated with the group in various antisocial activities. A jury ruled in 1976 that Hearst, shown here during a bank robbery, had acted with free will and in accordance with her own personality, and sentenced her to seven years in prison for grand theft. She was released after two years when President Jimmy Carter commuted her sentence.*

poverty, family violence, and parental conflict or divorce (Marshall & Cooke, 1999; Luntz & Widom, 1994; Farrington, 1991). Many of them have also grown up with parents who themselves had antisocial personality disorder (Lahey et al., 1988). Having such a parent could certainly impair one's trust in others.

Many behavioral theorists have suggested that antisocial symptoms may be learned through *modeling*, or imitation. As evidence, they too point to the higher rate of antisocial personality disorder among the parents of people with this disorder. Other behaviorists have suggested that some parents unintentionally teach antisocial behavior by regularly reinforcing a child's aggressive behavior (Capaldi & Patterson, 1994; Patterson, 1986, 1982). When the child misbehaves or becomes violent in reaction to the parents' requests or orders, for example, the parents may give in to restore peace. Without meaning to, they may be teaching the child to be stubborn and perhaps even violent.

The cognitive view says that people with antisocial personality disorder hold attitudes that trivialize the importance of other people's needs (Levenson, 1992). Such a philosophy of life, some theorists suggest, may be far more common in our society than people recognize (see Figure 17-3). Cognitive theorists further propose that people with this disorder have genuine difficulty recognizing a point of view other than their own.

Finally, a number of studies suggest that biological factors may play an important role in antisocial personality disorder. Research reveals that people with this disorder often experience less anxiety than other people, and so may lack a key ingredient for learning (Zuckerman, 1996; Lykken, 1995; Patrick, 1994). This would help explain why they have so much trouble learning from negative life experiences or tuning in to the emotional cues of others.

Several studies have found that subjects with antisocial personality disorder are less able than control subjects to learn laboratory tasks, such as finding their way out of a maze, when the key reinforcements are punishments such as shock or loss of money (Newman et al., 1992, 1987; Lykken, 1995, 1957). When experimenters make the punishments very apparent or force subjects to pay attention to them, learning improves; however, left to their own devices, subjects with this disorder are not influenced much by punishments. Perhaps they simply do not react as anxiously as other people to negative events.

Why should people with antisocial personality disorder experience less anxiety than other people? The answer may lie in the biological realm (Raine et al., 2000). Subjects with the disorder are likely to respond to warnings or expectations of stress with low brain and bodily arousal, such as slow autonomic arousal and slow EEG waves (Patrick et al., 1993, 1990; Hare, 1982, 1978). Perhaps because of the low arousal, the individuals easily tune out threatening or emotional situations, and so are unaffected by them.

It could also be argued that because of their physical underarousal people with antisocial personality disorder will be more likely than other people to take risks and seek thrills. That is, they may be drawn to antisocial activity precisely because it meets an underlying biological need for more excitement and arousal. In support of this idea, as we observed earlier, antisocial personality disorder often goes hand in hand with sensation-seeking behavior (Hasselbrock & Hasselbrock, 1992; Zuckerman, 1989, 1978) (see Box 17-2 on the next page).

TREATMENTS FOR ANTISOCIAL PERSONALITY DISORDER Approximately one-quarter of all people with antisocial personality disorder receive treatment for it (Regier et al., 1993), yet no treatment appears to be effective (Mannuzza & Klein,

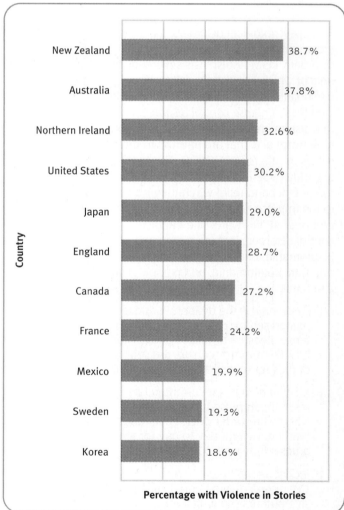

FIGURE 17-3 **Are some cultures more antisocial than others?** *In a cross-cultural study, teenagers were asked to write stories describing how imaginary characters would respond to various conflicts. About one-third of the respondents from New Zealand, Australia, Northern Ireland, and the United States described violent responses, compared to less than one-fifth of the subjects from Korea, Sweden, and Mexico. (Adapted from Archer & McDaniel, 1995.)*

1991). A major obstacle is the individuals' lack of conscience or desire to change (Millon, 1999; Widiger, Corbitt, & Millon, 1992). Most of those in therapy have been forced to participate by an employer, their school, or the law, or else they come to the attention of therapists when they also develop another psychological disorder (Fulwiler & Pope, 1987). Not surprisingly, one study found that 70 percent of these patients left treatment prematurely (Gabbard & Coyne, 1987).

Some cognitive-behavioral therapists try to induce clients with antisocial personality disorder to think about moral issues and about the needs of other people (Beck & Freeman, 1990). In a similar vein, a number of hospitals and prisons have tried to create a therapeutic community for people with this disorder, a

BOX 17-2

Gambling and Other Impulse Problems

Impulsivity is a symptom of many psychological disorders, including the antisocial and borderline personality disorders. DSM-IV also lists several disorders of which impulsivity, rather than personality, is the central feature. People with these *impulse-control disorders* fail to resist an impulse, drive, or temptation to perform acts that are harmful to themselves or others (APA, 2000, 1994). Usually they experience growing tension before the act and relief when they give in to the impulse. Some, but not all, feel regret or guilt afterward. The impulse-control disorders include pyromania, kleptomania, intermittent explosive disorder, trichotillomania, and pathological gambling.

❖ *Pyromania* is the deliberate and repeated setting of fires to achieve intense pleasure or relief from tension. It is different from *arson*, the setting of fires for revenge or financial gain.

❖ *Kleptomania* is a recurrent failure to resist the impulse to steal. People with this disorder often have more than enough money to pay for the articles they steal.

❖ Individuals with *intermittent explosive disorder* have periodic aggressive outbursts in which they may seriously attack people and destroy property. Their explosiveness far exceeds any provocation.

❖ People with *trichotillomania* repeatedly pluck hair from various parts of their bodies, particularly the scalp, eyebrows, and eyelashes (Stein, Christenson, & Hollander, 1999; McElroy et al., 1994).

❖ The most common of the impulse-control disorders is *pathological gambling*, persistent and repeated gambling behavior that disrupts one's life at home or at work (APA, 2000, 1994).

It is estimated that as many as 3.4 percent of adults and 3 to 8 percent of teenagers and college students suffer from pathological gambling (APA, 2000; Buckley, 1995). Clinicians are careful, however, to distinguish between pathological and social gambling. Pathological gambling is defined less by the amount of time or money spent in gambling than by the addictive nature of the behavior. People with this disorder cannot walk away from a bet and are restless and irritable if gambling is denied them. Repeated losses of money lead to more gambling in an effort to win the money back, and the gambling continues even

in the face of financial, social, and health problems. Many people go through four progressive phases during episodes of pathological gambling: winning, losing, desperation, and hopelessness (Rosenthal, 1992).

A great deal of attention has recently been directed toward the treatment of pathological gambling. Treatments that combine cognitive, behavioral, and other approaches and that help build coping skills tend to be the most effective (Echeburúa, Báez, & Fernandez-Montalvo, 1996; Bujold et al., 1994). People who join self-help support groups, such as Gamblers Anonymous, a network patterned after Alcoholics Anonymous, seem to have a higher recovery rate, perhaps in part because they have admitted that they have a problem and are seeking to conquer it.

Recently journalists and others have asked whether the "medicalization" of gambling has the effect of somehow excusing an irresponsible, often illegal pattern of behavior (Vatz & Weinberg, 1993). However, several recent studies suggest that pathological gambling and other impulse-control disorders are complex problems that often involve a variety of causes, including even biochemical factors (Stein et al., 1993; McElroy et al., 1992).

structured environment that teaches responsibility toward others (Reid & Burke, 1989; Salama, 1988). Still another popular approach uses physically challenging wilderness programs to build self-confidence, self-esteem, and commitment to others in a group (Reid & Burke, 1989). Some patients seem to profit from these programs. Generally, however, most of today's treatment approaches have little or no impact on people with antisocial personality disorder.

Borderline Personality Disorder

People with **borderline personality disorder** exhibit great instability, including major shifts in mood, an unstable self-image, and impulsivity. These characteristics combine to make their relationships very unstable as well (APA, 2000, 1994; Barratt & Stanford, 1996). Some of Ellen Farber's difficulties are typical:

> Ellen Farber, a 35-year-old, single insurance company executive, came to a psychiatric emergency room of a university hospital with complaints of depression and the thought of driving her car off a cliff. . . . Ms. Farber appeared to be in considerable distress. She reported a 6-month period of increasingly persistent dysphoria and lack of energy and pleasure. Feeling as if she were "made of lead," Ms. Farber had recently been spending 15–20 hours a day in her bed. She also reported daily episodes of binge eating, when she would consume "anything I can find," including entire chocolate cakes or boxes of cookies. She reported problems with intermittent binge eating since adolescence, but these had recently increased in frequency. . . .
>
> She attributed her increasing symptoms to financial difficulties. Ms. Farber had been fired from her job two weeks before coming to the emergency room. She claimed it was because she "owed a small amount of money." When asked to be more specific, she reported owing $150,000 to her former employers and another $100,000 to various local bank. . . . From age 30 to age 33, she had used her employer's credit cards to finance weekly "buying binges," accumulating the $150,000 debt. [To relieve feelings of distress,] every few days she would impulsively buy expensive jewelry, watches, or multiple pairs of the same shoes. . . .
>
> In addition to lifelong feelings of emptiness, Ms. Farber described chronic uncertainty about what she wanted to do in life and with whom she wanted to be friends. She had many brief, intense relationships with both men and women, but her quick temper led to frequent arguments and even physical fights. Although she had always thought of her childhood as happy and carefree, when she became depressed, she began to recall [being abused verbally and physically by her mother].
>
> *(Spitzer et al., 1994, pp. 395–397)*

Like Ellen Farber, people with borderline personality disorder swing in and out of very depressive, anxious, and irritable states that last anywhere from a few hours to a few days or more (see Table 17-2 on the next page). Their emotions seem to be always in conflict with the world around them (Perry & Cooper, 1986). They are prone to bouts of anger (Gardner et al., 1991), which sometimes result in physical aggression and violence (Lish et al., 1996). Just as often, however, they direct their impulsive anger inward and inflict bodily harm on themselves. Many seem troubled by deep feelings of emptiness (Koenigsberg et al., 1999).

Many of the patients who come to mental health emergency rooms are individuals with borderline personality disorder who have intentionally hurt themselves (Bongar et al., 1990; Margo & Newman, 1989). Their impulsive, self-destructive activities may range from alcohol and substance abuse to delinquency, unsafe sex, reckless driving, and cutting themselves (Trull et al., 2000; Morgenstern et al., 1997; Garfinkel & Gallop, 1992). Suicidal threats and actions are also common. Studies suggest that 70 percent of people with this disorder attempt

BORDERLINE PERSONALITY DISORDER A personality disorder in which an individual displays repeated instability in interpersonal relationships, self-image, and mood, as well as impulsive behavior.

EXPRESSION OF ANGER

Only 23 percent of adults in the United States report openly expressing their anger (Kanner, 1998). Around 39 percent say that they hide or contain their anger, and 23 percent walk away to try to collect themselves.

Table 17-2

Comparison of Personality Disorders

	DSM-IV CLUSTER	SIMILAR DISORDERS ON AXIS I	RESPONSIVENESS TO TREATMENT
Paranoid	Odd	Schizophrenia; delusional disorder	Modest
Schizoid	Odd	Schizophrenia; delusional disorder	Modest
Schizotypal	Odd	Schizophrenia; delusional disorder	Modest
Antisocial	Dramatic	Conduct disorder	Poor
Borderline	Dramatic	Mood disorders	Moderate
Histrionic	Dramatic	Somatoform disorders; mood disorders	Modest
Narcissistic	Dramatic	Cyclothymic disorder (mild bipolar disorder)	Poor
Avoidant	Anxious	Social phobia	Moderate
Dependent	Anxious	Separation anxiety disorder; dysthymic disorder (mild depressive disorder)	Moderate
Obsessive-compulsive	Anxious	Obsessive-compulsive anxiety disorder	Moderate

suicide at least once in their lives; around 6 to 9 percent actually commit suicide (Davis, Gunderson, & Myers, 1999). Many, like Ellen, try to hurt themselves as a way of dealing with their chronic feelings of emptiness, boredom, and identity confusion. A common pattern is for people with the disorder to enter clinical treatment by way of the emergency room, after a suicide attempt or episode of self-mutilation (Sansone, Wiederman, & Sansone, 2000; Moskovitz, 1996).

People with borderline personality disorder frequently form intense, conflict-ridden relationships in which their feelings are not necessarily shared by the other person (Modestin & Villiger, 1989). They often violate the boundaries of a relationship (Gunderson, 1996; Melges & Swartz, 1989). Thinking in dichotomous (black-and-white) terms, they quickly become furious when their expectations are not met; yet they remain very attached to the relationships, paralyzed by a fear of being left alone. Sometimes they cut themselves or carry out other self-destructive acts to prevent partners from leaving.

Around 2 percent of the general population are thought to suffer from borderline personality disorder. Close to 75 percent of the patients who receive this diagnosis are women (APA, 2000; Grilo et al., 1996). The course of the disorder varies from person to person. In the most common pattern, the instability and risk of suicide reach a peak during young adulthood and then gradually wane with advancing age (APA, 2000).

EXPLANATIONS OF BORDERLINE PERSONALITY DISORDER Because a fear of abandonment tortures so many people with borderline personality disorder, psychodynamic theorists have looked once again to early parental relationships to explain the disorder (Gunderson, 1996). Object relations theorists, for example,

REASONS FOR SELF-MUTILATION
In one study of persons who admitted to regularly cutting, burning, or otherwise mutilating themselves, the individuals said that they performed such acts to see whether they were still alive or real; to quiet negative feelings such as anger, fear, or guilt; to block painful memories; or to cry out for help (Bower, 1995).

propose that an early lack of acceptance by parents may lead to a loss of self-esteem, increased dependence, and an inability to cope with separation (Cardasis, Hochman, & Silk, 1997; Richman & Sokolove, 1992).

Research has found that the early childhoods of many people with borderline personality disorder are consistent with this psychodynamic view. The parents of these individuals often neglected or rejected them or otherwise behaved inappropriately (Ludolph et al., 1990; Paris et al., 1988). Similarly, their childhoods were often marked by multiple parent substitutes, divorce, or death (Plakun, 1991; Wilson et al., 1986). Many studies have also found instances of great trauma in the early lives of people with borderline symptoms, including physical and sexual abuse, sometimes even incest (Spoont, 1996; Atlas, 1995). In fact, some theorists believe that the disorder may be an extended form of posttraumatic stress disorder, triggered by early horrors (Gunderson & Sabo, 1993).

Some features of borderline personality disorder have also been linked to biological abnormalities. Sufferers who are particularly impulsive, as demonstrated by a suicide attempt or aggression against others, apparently have lower brain serotonin activity (Gurvits et al., 2000; Spoont, 1996). People with the disorder also experience abnormalities in sleep that are similar to those of depressed persons (Siever & Davis, 1991). In accord with these biological findings, close relatives of those with borderline personality disorder are five times more likely than the general population to have the disorder (Torgersen, 2000, 1984; Kendler et al., 1991).

Finally, some sociocultural theorists suggest that cases of borderline personality disorder are particularly likely to emerge in cultures that change rapidly. As a culture loses its stability, they argue, it inevitably leaves many of its members with problems of identity, a sense of emptiness, heightened anxiety, and fears of abandonment (Paris, 1991). Family units may disintegrate, leaving people with little sense of belonging. Changes of this kind in society today may explain growing reports of the disorder.

TREATMENTS FOR BORDERLINE PERSONALITY DISORDER It appears that psychotherapy can eventually lead to some degree of improvement for people with borderline personality disorder (APA, 2000; Links & Heslegrave, 2000). It is not easy, however, for a therapist to strike an effective balance between empathizing with the patient's dependency and anger and challenging his or her way of thinking (Beck, 1997; Horton, 1992). Furthermore, when such a person does make progress in treatment, termination is sometimes difficult because of the patients' remaining problems with relationships and abandonment (Sansone et al., 1991).

Psychodynamic therapy has been somewhat successful when it focuses on the patient's central relationship disturbance, poor sense of self, and pervasive loneliness and emptiness (Gunderson, 1996; Michels, 1992). This treatment has sometimes been combined with cognitive-behavioral approaches designed to help people recognize the perspectives of others (Koerner & Linehan, 2000; Scheel, 2000; Linehan, 1993, 1992). For example, the therapist may model alternative ways of interpreting and reacting to situations (Westen, 1991). Group therapy has also been of help to some people with borderline personality disorder (Stone, 2000; Moskovitz, 1996). It offers them an opportunity to form close attachments to a number of persons rather than focusing all their emotions and hopes on one or two "chosen" relationships.

Finally, antidepressant, antibipolar, antianxiety, and antipsychotic drugs have helped some individuals with this disorder to calm their emotional and aggressive storms (Davis et al., 2000, 1999; Benedetti et al., 1998). Given the heightened risk of suicide attempts by these patients, however, their use of drugs on an outpatient basis is controversial. Some individuals have benefited from a combination of drug therapy and psychotherapy (Koenigsberg, 1993).

An unthinkable act *People around the world felt angry and betrayed in 1994 when they learned that Susan Smith had murdered her two sons by buckling them into the family car and pushing it into a nearby river. For days the woman from South Carolina had tearfully told a story of forced abduction and had begged for the boys' safe return, fooling everyone, including her ex-husband. Some clinicians believe that Smith's impulsive and violent act, her shallow motives, her shifting moods and unstable self-image, and her capacity to convincingly deceive reflect a borderline or antisocial personality disorder.*

THE MYTH OF VENTING

Contrary to the notion that "letting off steam" reduces anger, angry subjects in one study acted much *more* aggressively after hitting a punching bag than did angry subjects who first sat quietly for a while (Bushman et al., 1999).

Histrionic Personality Disorder

People with **histrionic personality disorder**, once called **hysterical personality disorder**, are extremely emotional—they are typically described as "emotionally charged"—and continually seek to be the center of attention (APA, 2000, 1994). Their exaggerated, rapidly changing moods can complicate life considerably, as we see in the case of Suzanne:

> Suzanne, an attractive and vivacious woman, sought therapy in the hope that she might prevent the disintegration of her third marriage. The problem she faced was a recurrent one, her tendency to become "bored" with her husband and increasingly interested in going out with other men. She was on the brink of "another affair" and decided that before "giving way to her impulses again" she had "better stop and take a good look" at herself. . . .
>
> Suzanne was quite popular during her adolescent years. . . . Rather than going on to college, Suzanne attended art school where she met and married a fellow student—a "handsome, wealthy ne'er-do-well." Both she and her husband began "sleeping around" by the end of the first year, and she "wasn't certain" that her husband was the father of her daughter. A divorce took place several months after the birth of this child.
>
> Soon thereafter she met and married a man in his forties who gave both Suzanne and her daughter a "comfortable home, and scads of attention and love." It was a "good life" for the four years that the marriage lasted. . . . In the third year of this marriage she became attracted to a young man, a fellow dancing student. The affair was brief, but was followed by a quick succession of several others. Her husband learned of her exploits, but accepted her regrets and assurances that they would not continue. They did continue, and the marriage was terminated after a stormy court settlement.
>
> Suzanne "knocked about" on her own for the next two years until she met her present husband, a talented writer who "knew the scoop" about her past. . . . She had no inclination to venture afield for the next three years. She enjoyed the titillation of "playing games" with other men, but she remained loyal to her husband, even though he was away on reportorial assignments for periods of one or two months. The last trip, however, brought forth the "old urge" to start an affair. It was at this point that she sought therapy.
>
> *(Millon, 1969, p. 251)*

People with histrionic personality disorder are always "on stage," using theatrical gestures and mannerisms and the most grandiose language to describe ordinary everyday events. Like a chameleon, they keep changing—but not for protection. Their goal is to attract and impress an audience, and in their pursuit they change not only their surface characteristics—according to the latest fads—but also their opinions and beliefs. In fact, their speech is actually rather scanty in detail and substance, and they seem to lack a sense of who they really are.

Approval and praise are the life's blood of these individuals; they must have others present to witness their exaggerated emotional states. Vain, self-centered, demanding, and unable to delay gratification for long, they overreact to any minor event that gets in the way of their quest for attention. Some make suicide attempts, largely to manipulate others (APA, 2000; Guillard & Guillard, 1987).

People with this disorder may draw attention to themselves by exaggerating their physical illnesses or fatigues (Morrison, 1989). They may also behave very provocatively and try to achieve their goals through sexual seduction. Most obsess over how they look and how others will perceive them, often wearing bright, eye-catching clothes. They exaggerate the depth of their relationships (see Box 17-3), considering themselves to be the intimate friends of people who see them as no more than casual acquaintances. Often, they become involved with romantic partners who may be exciting but who do not treat them well.

STOLEN GLANCES

Up to a point, concern about one's appearance is quite normal. One-fourth of adults in the United States regularly check their reflections in store windows and mirrors; two-thirds steal glances at least occasionally (Kanner, 1995).

BOX 17-3

"Oh, What a Tangled Web . . ."

One of the most popular movies of 1997 was *Liar, Liar,* starring Jim Carrey. The movie's plot—a notorious liar loses his capacity to deceive—struck a chord in most viewers.

Almost everyone lies from time to time. In fact, in one large survey 91 percent of people admitted that they lie regularly (Kanner, 1995). For example, almost 80 percent of adults have given a false name or phone number on occasion. However, many of us know people who, like Carrey's character, lie habitually, almost as if driven to do so. They are not necessarily trying to protect themselves, and their lies often get them in trouble (Ford et al., 1988). Interestingly, compulsive lying is not considered a disorder, although it is sometimes characteristic of people with antisocial, histrionic, or narcissistic personality disorder. Nor has lying received much attention from clinical theorists or researchers.

ConsiderThis

● What might be the differences between "normal" lying and "pathological" lying? ● If lying is sometimes pathological, why is it not studied more extensively? ● How do various institutions in our society—business, government, academia, science, religion—view lying, and how might these views affect the prevalence and nature of individual lies? ● Why do people often admire someone who deceives—a flatterer, an art forger, a jewel thief?

Until recently, this disorder was believed to be more common in women than in men, and clinicians long described profiles of the "hysterical wife" (Reich, 1987; Char, 1985). Research, however, has revealed gender bias in past diagnoses. When evaluating case studies of people with a mixture of histrionic and antisocial traits, clinicians in several studies gave a diagnosis of histrionic personality disorder to women more than men (Ford & Widiger, 1989; Hamilton et al., 1986). The latest statistics suggest that 2 to 3 percent of adults have this personality disorder, with males and females equally affected (APA, 2000; Nestadt et al., 1990).

EXPLANATIONS OF HISTRIONIC PERSONALITY DISORDER The psychodynamic perspective was originally developed to help explain cases of hysteria (see Chapter 10), so it is no surprise that these theorists continue to have a strong interest in histrionic personality disorder today. Most psychodynamic theorists believe that as children, people with this disorder experienced unhealthy relationships in which cold and controlling parents left them feeling unloved and afraid of abandonment (Gunderson, 1988). To defend against deep-seated fears of loss, the individuals learned to behave dramatically, inventing crises that would require other people to act protectively (Kuriansky, 1988).

Some psychodynamic theories focus exclusively on female patients. They suggest that an early lack of maternal nurturance causes some daughters to develop an intense need for their father's attention and to seek it through displays of affection and dependence that go far beyond the usual behavior of young girls toward their fathers. These highly flirtatious and dramatic displays of emotion establish the histrionic pattern that governs later relationships in their lives (Phillips & Gunderson, 1994; Gabbard, 1990). Such individuals enter adulthood as "unhappy little girls," looking at men as idealized fathers and always trying to manipulate them (Char, 1985).

Cognitive explanations look instead at the lack of substance and extreme suggestibility found in people with histrionic personality disorder. These theories see

"Personality disorders . . . are the only things left in psychiatry where people think you are bad."

Gary M. Flaxenberg, psychiatrist, 1998

NARCISSISTIC PERSONALITY DISORDER
A personality disorder marked by a broad pattern of grandiosity, need for admiration, and lack of empathy.

the individuals as becoming increasingly self-focused and emotional, and less and less interested in knowing about the world at large. With no detailed memories of what they never learned, they must rely on hunches or on other people to provide them with direction in life (Hollander, 1988). Some cognitive theorists also propose that people with this disorder hold a general assumption that they are helpless to care for themselves, and so they constantly seek out others who will meet their needs (Beck & Freeman, 1990).

Finally, sociocultural theorists believe that histrionic personality disorder is produced in part by society's norms and expectations. Until recently, our society encouraged girls to hold on to childhood and dependency as they grew up (Hollander, 1988). The vain, dramatic, and selfish behavior of the histrionic person may actually be an exaggeration of femininity as our culture once defined it (Beck & Freeman, 1990).

TREATMENTS FOR HISTRIONIC PERSONALITY DISORDER Unlike people with most other personality disorders, those with histrionic personality disorder often seek out treatment on their own (Nestadt et al., 1990). Working with them can be very difficult, however, because of the demands, tantrums, and seductiveness they are likely to deploy (Millon, 1999; Phillips & Gunderson, 1994). Another problem is that these individuals may pretend to have important insights or to experience change during treatment, merely to please the therapist. To avoid becoming embroiled in such problems, therapists must remain objective and maintain strict professional boundaries (Gabbard, 1990).

Cognitive therapists have tried to help people with this disorder to change their belief that they are helpless and also to develop better, more deliberate ways of thinking and solving problems. Psychodynamic therapy and group therapy have also been applied (Phillips & Gunderson, 1994; Beck & Freeman, 1990). In all these approaches, therapists aim to help the clients recognize their excessive dependency, find inner satisfaction, and become more self-reliant (Chodoff, 1989). Clinical case reports suggest that each of the approaches can be useful. Drug therapy is less successful, however, except as a means of relieving the depressive symptoms experienced by some patients (Liebowitz et al., 1986).

Narcissistic Personality Disorder

"To love oneself is the beginning of a life-long romance."

Oscar Wilde, *An Ideal Husband,* 1895

People with **narcissistic personality disorder** are generally grandiose in manner, need much admiration, and feel no empathy with others (APA, 2000, 1994). Convinced of their own great success, power, or beauty, they expect constant attention and admiration from those around them. Frederick, the man whom we met at the beginning of this chapter, was one such person. So is Steven, a 30-year-old artist, married, with one child:

> Steven came to the attention of a therapist when his wife insisted that they seek marital counseling. According to her, Steve was "selfish, ungiving and preoccupied with his work." Everything at home had to "revolve about him, his comfort, moods and desires, no one else's." She claimed that he contributed nothing to the marriage, except a rather meager income. He shirked all "normal" responsibilities and kept "throwing chores in her lap," and she was "getting fed up with being the chief cook and bottlewasher, tired of being his mother and sleep-in maid."
>
> On the positive side, Steven's wife felt that he was basically a "gentle and good-natured guy with talent and intelligence." But this wasn't enough. She wanted a husband, someone with whom she could share things. In contrast, he wanted, according to her, "a mother, not a wife"; he didn't want "to grow up, he didn't know how to give affection, only to take it when he felt like it, nothing more, nothing less."
>
> Steve presented a picture of an affable, self-satisfied and somewhat disdainful young man. He was employed as a commercial artist, but looked forward to

his evenings and weekends when he could turn his attention to serious painting. He claimed that he had to devote all of his spare time and energies to "fulfill himself," to achieve expression in his creative work. . . .

His relationships with his present co-workers and social acquaintances were pleasant and satisfying, but he did admit that most people viewed him as a "bit self-centered, cold and snobbish." He recognized that he did not know how to share his thoughts and feelings with others, that he was much more interested in himself than in them and that perhaps he always had "preferred the pleasure" of his own company to that of others.

(Millon, 1969, pp. 261–262)

The Greek myth has it that Narcissus died enraptured by the beauty of his own reflection in a pool, pining away with longing to possess his own image. His name has come to be synonymous with extreme self-involvement, and indeed people with narcissistic personality disorder have a grandiose sense of self-importance. They exaggerate their achievements and talents, expecting others to recognize them as superior, and often appear arrogant. They are very choosy about their friends and associates, believing that their problems are unique and can be appreciated only by other "special," high-status people. Because of their charm, they often make favorable first impressions. Yet they can rarely maintain long-term relationships.

Like Steven, people with narcissistic personality disorder are seldom interested in the feelings of others. Many take advantage of others to achieve their own ends, perhaps partly out of envy; at the same time they believe others envy them (Wink, 1996). Though grandiose, some of these individuals react to criticism or frustration with bouts of rage or humiliation (Gramzow & Tangney, 1992). Others may react with cold indifference (Messer, 1985). And still others become extremely pessimistic and filled with depression. Periods of zest may alternate with periods of disappointment (Wink, 1996; Svrakic, 1990, 1987).

Probably less than 1 percent of adults display narcissistic personality disorder, up to 75 percent of them men (APA, 2000; Grilo et al., 1996). Narcissistic-type behaviors and thoughts are common and normal among teenagers and do not usually lead to adult narcissism (APA, 1994).

EXPLANATIONS OF NARCISSISTIC PERSONALITY DISORDER Psychodynamic theorists more than others have theorized about narcissistic personality disorder, and, again, they propose that the problem begins with cold, rejecting parents. They argue that some people with this background spend their lives defending against feeling unsatisfied, rejected, unworthy, and wary of the world (Wink, 1996). They do so by repeatedly telling themselves that they are actually perfect and desirable, and also by seeking admiration from others (Vaillant, 1994). Object relations theorists, the psychodynamic theorists who emphasize relationships, interpret the grandiose self-image as a way for these people to convince themselves that they are totally self-sufficient and without need of warm relationships with their parents or anyone else (Kernberg, 1989; Siomopoulos, 1988).

Another group of psychodynamic theorists, self theorists, argue that rejecting parents deprive their children of *mirroring*, which self theory considers one of the most important processes in the development of a healthy sense of self (Wink, 1996; Fiscalini, 1993; Kohut, 1971). That is, the parents fail to empathize with and confirm the child's innate sense of vigor and uniqueness. As a result, the child's "grandiose" self and "reality-based" self, which normally

EGOIST VS. EGOTIST

An *egoist* is a person concerned primarily with his or her own interests. An *egotist* has an inflated sense of self-worth. A boastful egotist is not necessarily a self-absorbed egoist.

"Call it vanity, call it narcissism, call it egomania. I love you."

would merge, remain split throughout life, and the grandiose self, with its inflated sense of desirability and power, becomes dominant (Svrakic, 1989; Kohut, 1984). In support of the various psychodynamic theories, research has found that abused children and children of divorce are at particular risk for the development of narcissistic personality disorder. So are children who have been given up for adoption or whose mothers or fathers have died (Kernberg, 1989).

A number of behavioral and cognitive theorists propose that narcissistic personality disorder may develop when people are treated too *positively* rather than too negatively in early life. They hold that certain individuals acquire a superior and grandiose attitude when their "admiring or doting parents" teach them to "overvalue their self worth" (Millon, 1987). In support of this explanation, firstborn and only children, who are often viewed by their parents as having special talents or intelligence, score higher than other children on measures of narcissism (Curtis & Cowell, 1993).

Finally, many sociocultural theorists see a link between narcissistic personality disorder and "eras of narcissism" in society (Cooper & Ronningstam, 1992). They suggest that family values and social ideals in certain societies periodically break down, producing generations of youth who are self-centered and materialistic, and have short attention spans. Western cultures in particular, which encourage self-expression, individualism, and competitiveness, are considered likely to produce such generations of narcissism.

TREATMENTS FOR NARCISSISTIC PERSONALITY DISORDER Narcissistic personality disorder is one of the most difficult personality patterns to treat (Lawrence, 1987). The patients who consult therapists usually do so because of a related disorder, most commonly depression (Millon, 1999; Beck & Freeman, 1990). Once in treatment, the individuals may try to manipulate the therapist into supporting their sense of superiority. Some also seem to project their grandiose attitudes onto their therapists and develop a love-hate stance toward them (Uchoa, 1985).

Psychodynamic therapists seek to help people with this disorder recognize and work through their basic insecurities and defenses (Adler, 2000; Masterson, 1990; Kernberg, 1989). Cognitive therapists, focusing primarily on the self-centered thinking of such clients, redirect the clients' focus onto the opinions of others, teach them to interpret criticism more rationally, increase their ability to empathize, and change their all-or-nothing notions (Beck & Freeman, 1990). None of the approaches has had much success, however.

"Anxious" Personality Disorders

The cluster of *"anxious" personality disorders* includes the *avoidant, dependent,* and *obsessive-compulsive* personality disorders. People with these patterns typically display anxious and fearful behavior. Although many of the symptoms of these disorders are similar to those of the anxiety and depressive disorders (Skodol et al., 1999), researchers have not found direct links between this cluster and those Axis I patterns (Weston & Siever, 1993). As with most of the other personality disorders, research support for the various explanations is very limited. At the same time, treatments for these disorders appear to be modestly to moderately helpful—significantly better than for other personality disorders.

Avoidant Personality Disorder

People with **avoidant personality disorder** are very uncomfortable and inhibited in social situations, overwhelmed by feelings of inadequacy, and extremely sensitive to negative evaluation (APA, 2000, 1994). They are so fearful of being rejected that they give no one an opportunity to reject them—or to accept them either:

Consider This

Some people believe that the past 15 years have witnessed an increase in narcissistic behavior and thinking in Western society. What features of Western society during this span of time (for example, child-rearing philosophies, advertising campaigns, sports heroes, book topics, and television) may be contributing to a rise in narcissistic functioning?

AVOIDANT PERSONALITY DISORDER A personality disorder in which an individual is consistently uncomfortable and restrained in social situations, overwhelmed by feelings of inadequacy, and extremely sensitive to negative evaluation.

James was a bookkeeper for nine years, having obtained his position upon graduation from high school. He spoke of himself as a shy, fearful and quiet boy ever since early childhood. . . .

James was characterized by his supervisor as a loner, a peculiar young man who did his work quietly and efficiently. They noted that he ate alone in the company cafeteria and never joined in coffee breaks or in the "horsing around" at the office. . . .

As far as his social life was concerned, James had neither dated nor gone to a party in five years. . . . He now spent most of his free time reading, watching TV, daydreaming and fixing things around the house.

James experienced great distress when new employees were assigned to his office section. Some 40 people worked regularly in this office and job turnover resulted in replacement of four or five people a year. . . . In recent months, a clique formed in his office. Although James very much wanted to be a member of this "in-group," he feared attempting to join them because "he had nothing to offer them" and thought he would be rejected. In a short period of time, he, along with two or three others, became the object of jokes and taunting by the leaders of the clique. After a few weeks of "being kidded," he began to miss work, failed to complete his accounts on time, found himself unsure of what he was doing and made a disproportionate number of errors. . . .

(Millon, 1969, pp. 231–232)

People like James actively avoid occasions for social contact. At the center of this withdrawal lies not so much poor social skills as a dread of criticism, disapproval, or rejection. They are timid and hesitant in social situations, afraid of saying something foolish or of embarrassing themselves by blushing or acting nervous. Even in intimate relationships they express themselves very carefully, afraid of being shamed or ridiculed.

People with this disorder believe themselves to be unappealing or inferior to others. They exaggerate the potential difficulties of new situations, so they seldom take risks or try out new activities. They usually have few or no close friends, though they actually yearn for intimate relationships, and frequently feel depressed and lonely. As a substitute, some take refuge in an inner world of fantasy and imagination (Millon, 1990).

Avoidant personality disorder is similar to a *social phobia* (see Chapter 5), and many people with one of these disorders also experience the other (Boone et al., 1999; Fahlen, 1995). The similarities include a fear of humiliation and low confidence. A key difference between the two conditions is that people with a social phobia primarily fear social *circumstances,* while people with the personality disorder tend to fear close social *relationships* (Turner et al., 1986).

Between 0.5 and 1.0 percent of adults have avoidant personality disorder, men as frequently as women (APA, 2000). Many children and teenagers are also painfully shy and avoid other people, but this is usually just a normal part of their development.

EXPLANATIONS OF AVOIDANT PERSONALITY DISORDER Theorists often assume that avoidant personality disorder has the same causes as anxiety disorders—such as early traumas, conditioned fears, upsetting beliefs, or biochemical abnormalities. However, research has not yet tied the personality disorder directly to the anxiety disorders (Weston & Siever, 1993). In the meantime, psychodynamic and cognitive explanations are the most popular among clinicians.

Psychodynamic theorists focus mainly on the general sense of shame felt by people with avoidant personality disorder. Some trace the shame to childhood experiences such as early bowel and bladder accidents (Gabbard, 1990). If parents repeatedly punish or ridicule a child for having such accidents, the child may develop a negative self-image. This may lead to the individual's feeling unlovable

SELF-ASSESSMENT
According to various surveys, approximately 48 percent of people in the United States consider themselves to be shy to some degree (Carducci, 2000).

throughout life and distrusting the love of others (Liebowitz et al., 1986). Similarly, cognitive theorists believe that harsh criticism and rejection in early childhood may lead certain people to assume that others in their environment will always judge them negatively. These individuals come to expect rejection, misinterpret the reactions of others to fit that expectation, discount positive feedback, and generally fear social involvements—setting the stage for avoidant personality disorder. In one study, subjects with this disorder were asked to recall their childhood, and their descriptions supported both the psychodynamic and cognitive theories. They remembered, for example, receiving little encouragement from their parents and few displays of parental love or pride (Arbel & Stravynski, 1991).

TREATMENTS FOR AVOIDANT PERSONALITY DISORDER People with avoidant personality disorder come to therapy in the hope of finding acceptance and affection. Keeping them in treatment can be a challenge, however, for many of them soon begin to avoid the sessions (Millon, 1999; Beck & Freeman, 1990). Often they distrust the therapist's sincerity and start to fear his or her rejection. Thus, as with several of the other personality disorders, a key task of the therapist is to gain the individual's trust (Millon, 1999; Gabbard, 1990).

Beyond building trust, therapists tend to treat people with avoidant personality disorder much as they treat people with social phobias and other anxiety disorders. Such approaches have had at least modest success. Psychodynamic therapists try to help clients recognize and resolve the unconscious conflicts that may be operating (Hurt et al., 1991). Cognitive therapists help them change their distressing beliefs and thoughts, carry on in the face of painful emotions, and improve their self-image (Beck & Freeman, 1990; Alden, 1989). Behavioral therapists provide social skills training, as well as exposure treatments that require people to gradually increase their social contacts (Quality Assurance Project, 1991; Stravynski et al., 1987). Group therapy may also be recommended, to provide practice in social interactions (Azima, 1993; Renneberg et al., 1990). Antianxiety and antidepressant drugs are sometimes useful in reducing the social anxiety of people with avoidant personality disorder, although the symptoms may return when medication is stopped (Liebowitz et al., 1991, 1990; Mattick & Newman, 1991).

Just a stage *Many children and teenagers are painfully shy, easily embarrassed, and uncomfortable with people other than their parents, siblings, or close friends. Such reactions are a common and normal part of development, and do not, by themselves, indicate an avoidant or dependent personality disorder.*

Dependent Personality Disorder

People with **dependent personality disorder** have a pervasive, excessive need to be taken care of (APA, 2000, 1994). As a result, they are clinging and submissive, fearing separation from their parent, spouse, or other close relationship. They rely on others to such an extent that they cannot make the smallest decision for themselves. Mr. G. is a case in point.

DEPENDENT PERSONALITY DISORDER A personality disorder characterized by a pattern of clinging and obedience, fear of separation, and an ongoing need to be taken care of.

> Mr. G.['s] . . . place of employment for the past 15 years had recently closed and he had been without work for several weeks. He appeared less dejected about the loss of his job than about his wife's increasing displeasure with his decision to "stay at home until something came up." She thought he "must be sick" and insisted that he see a doctor. . . .
>
> Mr. G. was born in Europe, the oldest child and only son of a family of six children. . . . His mother kept a careful watch over him, prevented him from engaging in undue exertions and limited his responsibilities; in effect, she precluded his developing many of the ordinary physical skills and competencies that most youngsters learn in the course of growth. . . .
>
> A marriage was arranged by his parents. His wife was a sturdy woman who worked as a seamstress, took care of his home, and bore . . . four children. Mr. G.

performed a variety of odds-and-ends jobs in his father's tailoring shop. His mother saw to it, however, that he did no "hard or dirty work," just helping about and "overlooking" the other employees. As a consequence, Mr. G. learned none of the skills of the tailoring trade.

Shortly before the outbreak of World War II, Mr. G. came to visit two of his sisters who previously had emigrated to the United States; when hostilities erupted in Europe he was unable to return home. All members of his family, with the exception of a young son, perished in the war.

During the ensuing years, he obtained employment at a garment factory owned by his brothers-in-law. Again he served as a helper, not as a skilled workman. Although he bore the brunt of essentially good-humored teasing by his co-workers throughout these years, he maintained a friendly and helpful attitude, pleasing them by getting sandwiches, coffee and cigarettes at their beck and call.

He married again to a hard-working, motherly type woman who provided the greater portion of the family income. Shortly thereafter, the son of his first wife emigrated to this country. Although the son was only 19 at the time, he soon found himself guiding his father's affairs, rather than the other way around.

(Millon, 1969, p. 242)

> "The deepest principle of human nature is the craving to be appreciated."
>
> William James

It is normal and healthy to depend on others, but those with dependent personality disorder constantly need assistance with even the most mundane matters and demonstrate extreme feelings of inadequacy and helplessness. Afraid that they cannot care for themselves, they cling desperately to friends or relatives (see Box 17-4 on the next page).

We observed earlier that people with avoidant personality disorder have difficulty *initiating* relationships. In contrast, people with dependent personality disorder have difficulty with *separation*. The individuals feel completely helpless and devastated when a close relationship ends, and they quickly seek out another relationship to fill the void. Many cling persistently to relationships with partners who physically or psychologically abuse them.

Lacking confidence in their own ability and judgment, people with this disorder seldom disagree with others and allow even important decisions to be made for them. They may depend on a parent or spouse to decide where to live, what job to have, and which neighbors to befriend (APA, 2000, 1994; Overholser, 1996). Because they so fear rejection, they are overly sensitive to disapproval and exert themselves to meet other people's wishes and expectations, even if it means volunteering for unpleasant or demeaning tasks.

Detachment and separation *One child gazes fearfully out the bus window and another hides his eyes as they cross the border into a refugee camp during Serbia's attempted purge of 850,000 ethnic Albanians from Kosovo in 1999. Clinicians worry that the abrupt and traumatic separations from home and family experienced by thousands of Kosovar children may have produced lingering insecurities and fears of abandonment, leaving them particularly vulnerable to such problems as dependent personality disorder, depression, and anxiety.*

BOX **17-4**

Internet Dependence: A New Kind of Problem

The computer age has apparently brought with it a new psychological problem—an uncontrollable need to be *on-line* (Orzack, 1998). Some clinicians consider it a kind of substance-related disorder. Others think it has the qualities of an impulse-control disorder. And many note that the pattern resembles dependent personality disorder, except that in this new pattern the individual is excessively dependent on a cyberbeing and on numerous fellow users, ever seeking their company, guidance, and reassurance, and fearing separation. For some people, the *Internet*, the conglomeration of computer networks that spans the world, has become a black hole. Sufferers spend up to 60 hours a week surfing the Net, participating in chat groups, e-mailing acquaintances, or playing complex computer games (Black, Belsare, & Schlosser, 1999; Murray, 1996). They describe their need to be on-line as an obsession for which they have unintentionally sacrificed their jobs, education, friends, even spouses. University students seem especially prone to the problem:

I was first introduced while I was studying at the university in '91. . . . I discovered by accident one day that you could send little messages to people in other universities and even people in America and other exotic places like Mexico and Finland! Well, that was the point of no return for me and I began spending inordinately large periods of time on-line. That was at the beginning of my final year. . . . [My] attendance record got worse and worse [and] predictably enough I failed in spectacular fashion. But I didn't mind so much because I had the Net to catch me, I'd made many friends on and offline through it, including my then girlfriend, so life wasn't that bad really, was it? . . .

I've [since] learned to censor out some things, and not to get entwined up to my arse in endless threads of chat. Okay, so this is bad in some ways, but I feel a little more in control of my life. I don't find myself involuntarily glued to my screen at 4 A.M. talking about something that isn't even interesting, begging myself to go to bed. I

(ANONYMOUS, 1996)

Like the person quoted in this excerpt, growing numbers of users have become absorbed in the social world of the Internet. Chat rooms allow them to "talk" with other computer users around the world 24 hours a day, 365 days a year; news groups allow them to post messages and receive responses. These services have allowed people to create social worlds, replete with acquaintanceship, friendship, and romance.

One study of 18,000 Internet users found that as many as 16 percent of respondents were overly dependent on it (Greenfield, 1999). In other research, the investigator Kimberly S. Young (1998, 1996) classified subjects as dependent on the Internet if they met four or more of the following criteria over a 12-month period:

1. Felt preoccupied with the Internet.

2. Needed to spend increasing amounts of time on the Internet to achieve satisfaction.

3. Were unable to control their Internet use.

4. Felt restless or irritable when they tried to cut down or stop Internet use.

Many people with dependent personality disorder feel distressed, lonely, and sad; often, they dislike themselves (Overholser, 1996, 1992). Thus they are at risk for depression and anxiety disorders (Skodol et al., 1999; Reich, 1996; Bornstein, 1995). Their fear of separation and their feelings of helplessness may leave them particularly susceptible to suicidal thoughts, especially when they believe that a relationship is about to end (Kiev, 1989).

The exact prevalence of dependent personality disorder is not known, although some studies suggest that around 2 percent of the population may experience it (Zimmerman & Coryell, 1989). For years clinicians have believed that more women than men display this pattern (Overholser, 1992), but some research suggests that the disorder is just as common in men (APA, 2000; Reich, 1990). Several studies have found the close relatives of male subjects with this disorder to have higher-than-usual rates of depressive disorders, while the relatives of female subjects have higher rates of panic disorders. Perhaps different factors predispose men and women to the personality disorder (Reich, 1990).

EXPLANATIONS OF DEPENDENT PERSONALITY DISORDER Psychodynamic explanations for dependent personality disorder are very similar to those for depression. Freudian theorists argue, for example, that unresolved conflicts during the oral stage of psychosexual development can evolve into a lifelong need for nurturance, thus heightening the likelihood of a dependent personality disorder (Greenberg & Bornstein, 1988). Similarly, object relations theorists say that early parental loss or rejection may prevent normal experiences of *attachment* and *separation*, leaving some children with fears of abandonment that persist through-

5. Used the Internet as a way of escaping from problems or of improving their mood.

6. Lied to family members or friends to conceal the extent of their involvement with the Internet.

7. Risked the loss of a significant relationship, job, or educational or career opportunity because of the Internet.

8. Kept returning to the Internet even after spending an excessive amount of money on on-line fees.

9. Went through withdrawal when off-line.

10. Stayed on-line longer than they originally intended.

Given the apparent size of this problem, counseling programs and workshops are increasing in number, particularly on college campuses. Among the most popular treatment approaches are support groups similar to Alcoholics Anonymous—some of them, ironically, operating on the Internet. The Internet Addiction Support Group, for example, has attracted many subscribers who admit to the problem, provide support for each other, and swap methods for reducing their use of the Internet (Murray, 1996). This sounds to some clinicians "like having an Alcoholics Anonymous meeting in a bar" (Orzack, 1996). Others point out, however, that many dependent Internet users cannot tear themselves away from their computers long enough to visit a traditional treatment center (Belluck, 1996).

(Randy Jones/The New York Times)

out their lives. Still other psychodynamic theorists suggest that, to the contrary, many parents of people with this disorder were overinvolved and overprotective, thus increasing their children's dependency, insecurity, and separation anxiety (Bornstein, 1996, 1992).

Behaviorists propose that parents of people with dependent personality disorder unintentionally rewarded their children's clinging and "loyal" behavior, while at the same time punishing acts of independence, perhaps through the withdrawal of love. Alternatively, some parents' own dependent behaviors may have served as models for their children.

Finally, cognitive theorists identify two maladaptive attitudes as helping to produce and maintain this disorder: (1) "I am inadequate and helpless to deal with the world," and (2) "I must find a person to provide protection so I can cope" (Beck, 1997; Beck & Freeman, 1990). *Dichotomous* (black-and-white) *thinking* may also play a key role: "If I am to be dependent, I must be completely helpless," or "If I am to be independent, I must be alone." Such thinking prevents sufferers of this disorder from making efforts to be autonomous.

TREATMENTS FOR DEPENDENT PERSONALITY DISORDER In therapy, people with this personality disorder usually place all responsibility for their treatment and well-being on the clinician (Beck, 1997; Perry, 1989). Accordingly, a central task of therapy is to help patients accept responsibility for themselves. Because the domineering behaviors of a spouse or parent may help foster a patient's symptoms, some clinicians propose couple or family therapy as well, or even separate therapy for the partner or parent (Millon, 1999; Liebowitz et al., 1986).

Dysfunctional toons *As the technology of film animation has become more complex over time, so have the personality problems of animated characters. (Left) Troubled characters of the past were usually defined by a single undesirable personality trait, as demonstrated by Snow White's friend Grumpy, second from left. (Right) Today's characters have groups of self-defeating traits. Beavis and Butt-Head, for example, display poor control of impulses, disregard for others' rights, disturbed relationships, emotional and cognitive shallowness, and, in Beavis's case, submissive and clinging behavior.*

Treatment for dependent personality disorder can be at least modestly helpful. Psychodynamic therapy for this pattern focuses on many of the same issues as therapy for depressed people, including the transference of dependency needs onto the therapist (Perry, 1989). Behavioral therapists often provide assertiveness training to help clients better express their own wishes in relationships. Cognitive therapists try to help clients challenge and change their assumptions of incompetence and helplessness (Beck & Freeman, 1990).

Finally, as with avoidant personality disorder, a group therapy format is often beneficial because it provides opportunities for the client to receive support from a number of peers rather than from a single dominant person (Azima, 1993; Perry, 1989). In addition, group members serve as models for one another as they practice better ways to express feelings and solve problems (Beck & Freeman, 1990).

Obsessive-Compulsive Personality Disorder

People with **obsessive-compulsive personality disorder** are so preoccupied with order, perfection, and control that they lose all flexibility, openness, and efficiency. Their insistence on doing everything "right" impairs their productivity, as in the case of Wayne:

OBSESSIVE-COMPULSIVE PERSONALITY DISORDER A personality disorder marked by such an intense focus on orderliness, perfectionism, and control that the individual loses flexibility, openness, and efficiency.

> Wayne was advised to seek assistance from a therapist following several months of relatively sleepless nights and a growing immobility and indecisiveness at his job. When first seen, he reported feelings of extreme self-doubt and guilt and prolonged periods of tension and diffuse anxiety. It was established early in therapy that he always had experienced these symptoms. They were now merely more pronounced than before.
>
> The precipitant for this sudden increase in discomfort was a forthcoming change in his academic post. New administrative officers had assumed authority at the college, and he was asked to resign his deanship to return to regular departmental instruction. In the early sessions, Wayne spoke largely of his fear of facing classroom students again, wondered if he could organize his material well, and doubted that he could keep classes disciplined and interested in his lectures. It was his preoccupation with these matters that he believed was preventing him from concentrating and completing his present responsibilities.
>
> At no time did Wayne express anger toward the new college officials for the "demotion" he was asked to accept. He repeatedly voiced his "complete confidence" in the "rationality of their decision." Yet, when face-to-face with them, he observed that he stuttered and was extremely tremulous.
>
> Wayne was the second of two sons, younger than his brother by three years. His father was a successful engineer, and his mother a high school teacher. Both

were "efficient, orderly and strict" parents. Life at home was "extremely well planned," with "daily and weekly schedules of responsibilities posted" and "vacations arranged a year or two in advance." Nothing apparently was left to chance. . . . Wayne adopted the "good boy" image. Unable to challenge his brother either physically, intellectually or socially, he became a "paragon of virtue." By being punctilious, scrupulous, methodical and orderly, he could avoid antagonizing his perfectionistic parents, and would, at times, obtain preferred treatment from them. He obeyed their advice, took their guidance as gospel and hesitated making any decision before gaining their approval. Although he recalled "fighting" with his brother before he was six or seven, he "restrained his anger from that time on and never upset his parents again."

(Millon, 1969, pp. 278–279)

In Wayne's preoccupation with rules and order and doing things right, he has trouble seeing the larger picture. When faced with a task, he and others with obsessive-compulsive disorder may become so focused on organization and details that they fail to grasp the point of the activity. As a result, their work is often behind schedule (some seem unable to finish any job), and they may neglect leisure activities and friendships.

People with obsessive-compulsive personality disorder set unreasonably high standards for themselves and others. They can never be satisfied with their performance, but they refuse to delegate responsibility or to work with a team, convinced that others are too careless or incompetent to do the job right. Because they are so afraid of making mistakes, they may be reluctant to make decisions.

These individuals also tend to be rigid and stubborn, particularly in their morals, ethics, and values. They live by a strict personal code and use it as a yardstick for measuring others. They may have trouble expressing much affection, and their relationships are often stiff and superficial. In addition, they are rarely generous with their time or money. Some cannot even throw away objects that are worn out or useless (APA, 2000, 1994; Warren & Ostrom, 1988).

Around 1 to 2 percent of the general population has obsessive-compulsive personality disorder, with white, educated, married, and employed individuals receiving the diagnosis most often (APA, 2000; Weissman, 1993; Nestadt et al., 1991). Men are twice as likely as women to exhibit the disorder (APA, 2000).

Many clinicians believe that obsessive-compulsive personality disorder and obsessive-compulsive disorder (the anxiety disorder) are closely related. Certainly, the two disorders share a number of features (Pollack, 1987). Moreover, many people who suffer from the anxiety disorder qualify for the personality disorder diagnosis as well (APA, 2000; Jenike, 1991). However, other personality disorders (avoidant, histrionic, schizotypal, and dependent) may be even more common among those with the anxiety disorder (Steketee, 1990). In fact, researchers have not found a specific link between obsessive-compulsive personality disorder and the obsessive-compulsive anxiety disorder (Mavissakalian et al., 1990).

EXPLANATIONS OF OBSESSIVE-COMPULSIVE PERSONALITY DISORDER Most explanations of obsessive-compulsive personality disorder borrow heavily from those of obsessive-compulsive anxiety disorder, despite the doubts concerning a link between the two disorders. As with so many of the personality disorders, psychodynamic explanations dominate and research evidence is limited.

Freudian theorists suggest that people with obsessive-compulsive personality disorder are *anal regressive*. That is, because of overly harsh toilet training during the anal stage, they become filled with

"An obstinate man does not hold opinions, but they hold him."

Alexander Pope

Toilet rage *According to Freud, toilet training often produces rage in a child. If parents are too harsh in their approach, the child may become fixated at the anal stage and prone to obsessive-compulsive functioning later in life.*

anger, and they remain *fixated* at this stage. To keep their anger under control, they persistently resist both their anger and their instincts to have bowel movements. In turn, they become extremely orderly and restrained; many become passionate collectors. Other psychodynamic theorists suggest that any early struggles with parents over control and independence may ignite the aggressive impulses at the root of this personality disorder (Kuriansky, 1988; Mollinger, 1980).

Cognitive theorists have little to say about the origins of obsessive-compulsive personality disorder, but they do propose that illogical thinking processes help keep it going. They point, for example, to dichotomous thinking, which may produce rigidity and perfectionism. Similarly, they note, people with this disorder tend to misread or exaggerate the potential outcomes of mistakes or errors.

TREATMENTS FOR OBSESSIVE-COMPULSIVE PERSONALITY DISORDER People with obsessive-compulsive personality disorder do not usually believe there is anything wrong with them. They therefore are not likely to seek treatment unless they are also suffering from anxiety or depression (or some other Axis I disturbance) or unless someone close to them insists that they get treatment (Beck & Freeman, 1990). Whereas drug therapy and behavioral therapy have been highly effective for people with obsessive-compulsive anxiety disorder, individuals with the personality disorder often appear to respond better to psychodynamic or cognitive therapy (Primac, 1993; Jenike, 1991, 1990). Psychodynamic therapists typically try to help them recognize, experience, and accept their feelings and underlying insecurities, and perhaps to take risks and accept their personal limitations (Millon, 1999; Salzman, 1989). Cognitive therapists focus on helping clients to change their dichotomous thinking, perfectionism, indecisiveness, procrastination, and chronic worrying.

> **A CRITICAL DIFFERENCE**
> People with obsessive-compulsive anxiety disorder typically do not want or like their symptoms; those with obsessive-compulsive personality disorder often embrace their symptoms and rarely wish to resist them (Zohar & Pato, 1991).

What Problems Are Posed by the DSM Categories?

Most of today's clinicians acknowledge that personality disorders are significant and troubling patterns. Yet these disorders are particularly hard to diagnose and easy to misdiagnose, difficulties that indicate serious problems with the *validity* (accuracy) and *reliability* (consistency) of the DSM categories (O'Connor & Dyce, 1998; Costello, 1996). One problem is that some of the criteria used to diagnose personality disorders cannot be observed directly. To distinguish paranoid from schizoid personality disorder, for example, clinicians must ask not only whether people avoid forming close relationships, but also why. In other words, the diagnoses often rely heavily on the interpretations of the individual clinician. A related problem is that clinicians differ widely in their judgments about when a normal personality style crosses the line and deserves to be called a disorder (Widiger & Costa, 1994). Some even believe that it is wrong ever to think of personality styles as mental disorders, however troublesome they may be.

The similarity of personality disorders within a cluster, or even between clusters, poses yet another problem. Within the "anxious" cluster, for example, there is considerable overlap between the symptoms of avoidant personality disorder and those of dependent personality disorder (Bornstein, 1998). Faced with similar feelings of inadequacy, fear of disapproval, and the like, is it reasonable for clinicians to consider them separate disorders (Livesley et al., 1994)? Also, the many borderline traits ("dramatic" cluster) found among some people with dependent personality disorder ("anxious" cluster) may indicate that these two disorders are but different versions of one basic pattern (Dolan, Evans, & Norton, 1995; Flick et al., 1993).

Another problem is that people with quite different personalities may be given the same personality disorder diagnosis (Costello, 1996; Widiger, 1993, 1992). Individuals must meet a certain number of criteria from DSM-IV to receive a given diagnosis, but no single feature is necessary for any diagnosis (Millon, 1999).

> **PASSIVE-AGGRESSIVE PERSONALITY DISORDER** A category of personality disorder listed in past versions of the DSM, marked by a pattern of negative attitudes and resistance to the demands of others.

Partly because of these problems, diagnosticians keep changing the criteria used to assess each of the personality disorders. In fact, the diagnostic categories themselves have changed more than once, and they will no doubt change again. For example, DSM-IV dropped a past category, **passive-aggressive personality disorder**, a pattern of negative attitudes and passive resistance to the demands of others, because research failed to show that this was more than a single trait. The pattern is now being studied more carefully and may be included once again in future editions of the DSM, perhaps within a broader category called *negativistic personality disorder*.

Given these problems, some theorists believe that the personality disorders actually differ more in *degree* than in type of dysfunction and have proposed that the disorders be organized according to the severity of certain key traits rather than by the presence or absence of specific traits (APA, 2000; Westen & Shedler, 2000; Costello, 1996). It is not yet clear where these arguments will lead, but at the very least, the growing intensity of the debate is another indication that most clinicians consider personality disorders to be important categories in the understanding and treatment of human behavior.

ConsiderThis

Try to invent a way of organizing and defining personality disorders that improves upon the present diagnostic system. • How would the current DSM categories fit into your new scheme?

CROSSROADS:
Disorders of Personality Are Rediscovered

During the first half of the twentieth century, clinicians believed deeply in the unique, enduring patterns we call personality, and they tried to define important personality traits. They then discovered how readily people can be shaped by transient situations, and a backlash developed. The concept of personality seemed to lose legitimacy, and for a while it became almost an obscene word in some circles. The diagnostic category of personality disorders experienced a similar rejection. When psychodynamic and humanistic theorists dominated the clinical field, *neurotic character disorders,* a set of diagnoses similar to today's personality disorders, were considered useful clinical categories (Millon et al., 2000). But their popularity declined as other models grew in influence.

During the past decade, serious interest in personality and personality disorders has rebounded. In case after case, clinicians have concluded that rigid personality traits do seem to pose special problems, and they have developed new objective tests and interview guides to assess these disorders, setting in motion a wave of systematic research (Langbehn et al., 1999; Scarpa et al., 1999). So far, only the antisocial and, to a lesser extent, the borderline personality disorders have received much study. As other personality disorders attract research attention as well, however, clinicians should be better able to answer some pressing

Personality au naturel *As suggested by the varied reactions of these polar bears to events at Canada's Hudson Bay, human beings are not the only creatures who demonstrate differences in personality, mood, and lifestyle. Natural data of this kind have led many theorists to suspect that inborn, biological factors contribute, at least in part, to personality differences and personality disorders.*

ConsiderThis

○ It is common for people outside the clinical field to mistakenly diagnose mental disorders in themselves, relatives, or acquaintances, and the personality disorders are among the most favored diagnoses. Why do you think these disorders are particularly subject to such efforts at amateur psychology?

DISTRUSTING SOULS

According to surveys, the people who tend to be the most distrustful in the United States are those who were repeatedly warned by their parents against trusting strangers. Other characteristics: they are under 30 years of age; are socially isolated; live in the city; live in poor or crime-ridden neighborhoods; and report having no religious affiliation (Pew Research Center, 1997).

questions: How common are the various personality disorders? How useful are the present categories? How are the disorders related? And what treatments are most effective?

One of the most important questions is, Why do people develop these patterns? As we have seen, psychological, as opposed to biological and sociocultural, theories have offered the most suggestions so far, but these proposed explanations are not very precise, and they do not have strong research support. Given the current enthusiasm for biological explanations, genetic and biological factors are likely to receive more study in the coming years, helping researchers determine their possible interaction with psychological causes. Hopefully, sociocultural factors will receive investigation as well. As we have seen, sociocultural theorists have only occasionally offered explanations for personality disorders. However, sociocultural factors may well play an important role in these disorders and should be examined more carefully, especially since, by definition, each of the patterns diagnosed as a personality disorder differs markedly from the expectations of a person's culture.

The future will undoubtedly bring major changes to the explanations and treatments for personality disorders, and the categories of personality disorders will probably undergo change as well. Such changes, however, are now more likely to be based on research rather than on clinical intuitions and impressions. For the many people caught in the web of rigid and maladaptive personality traits, these changes should make an important, and overdue, difference.

SUMMARY AND REVIEW

▨ **Personality disorders** A personality disorder is an inflexible pattern of inner experience and outward behavior. Such patterns are wide-ranging and enduring, differ markedly from social norms, and lead to distress or impairment. Explanations for most of the personality disorders have received only limited research support. DSM-IV distinguishes ten personality disorders and separates them into three clusters. *pp. 509–511*

▨ **"Odd" personality disorders** Three of the personality disorders are marked by the kinds of *odd or eccentric behavior* often seen in the Axis I disorder schizophrenia. People with paranoid personality disorder display a broad pattern of distrust and suspiciousness. Those with schizoid personality disorder persistently avoid social relationships, have little or no social interests, and show little emotional expression. Individuals with schizotypal personality disorder display a range of interpersonal problems marked by extreme discomfort in close relationships, very odd forms of thinking and behavior, and behavioral eccentricities. People with these three kinds of disorders usually are resistant to treatment, and treatment gains tend to be modest at best. *pp. 511–517*

▨ **"Dramatic" personality disorders** Four of the personality disorders are marked by highly *dramatic, emotional, or erratic symptoms*. People with antisocial personality disorder display a pattern of disregard for and violation of the rights of others. No known treatment is notably effective. People with borderline personality disorder display a pattern of instability in interpersonal relationships, self-image, and mood, along with extreme impulsivity. Treatment apparently can be helpful and lead to some improvement. People with histrionic personality disorder (once called hysterical personality disorder) display a pattern of extreme emotionality and attention seeking. Clinical case reports suggest that treatment is helpful on occasion. Finally, people with narcissistic personality disorder display a pattern of grandiosity, need for admiration, and lack of empathy. It is one of the most difficult disorders to treat. *pp. 517–530*

■ **"Anxious" personality disorders** Three of the personality disorders are marked by the kinds of symptoms found in the Axis I anxiety and depressive disorders. People with avoidant personality disorder are consistently uncomfortable and inhibited in social situations, overwhelmed by feelings of inadequacy, and extremely sensitive to negative evaluation. People with dependent personality disorder have a persistent need to be taken care of, are submissive and clinging, and fear separation. Individuals with obsessive-compulsive personality disorder are so preoccupied with order, perfection, and control that they lose their flexibility, openness, and efficiency. A variety of treatment strategies have been used for people with these disorders and apparently have been modestly to moderately helpful. *pp. 530–538*

■ **Problems posed by the DSM categories** It appears that personality disorders are commonly misdiagnosed, an indication of serious problems in the validity and reliability of the diagnostic categories. *pp. 538–539*

CYBER STUDY

▲ *How might obsessive-compulsive personality disorder and obsessive-compulsive anxiety disorder overlap?* ▲ *What roles do orderliness, perfection, and the tendency to collect things play in each of these disorders?* ▲ *How do clinicians assess psychopathy, or antisocial personality disorder?* ▲ *Does treatment help people with psychopathy?*

SEARCH THE *ABNORMAL PSYCHOLOGY* CD-ROM FOR

▲ Chapter 17 video case and discussion
  "Bill"—Obsessive-Compulsive Disorder

▲ Chapter 17 practice test and feedback

▲ Additional video cases and discussions
  "Jennifer"—Obsessive-Compulsive Disorder
  The Mind of the Psychopath
  "Pat"—Psychopathy

LOG ON TO THE COMER WEB PAGE

[www.worthpublishers.com/comerabnormalpsychology4e] **FOR**

▲ Suggested Web links, research exercises, FAQ page, additional Chapter 17 practice test questions

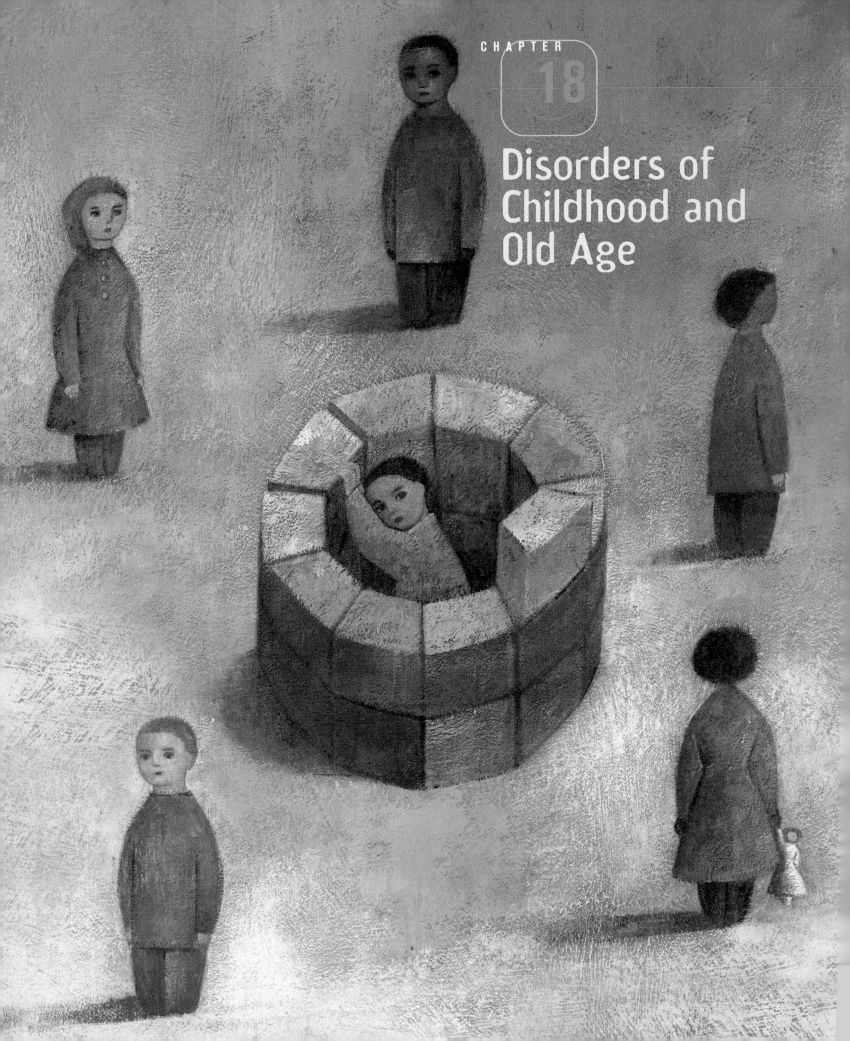

Disorders of Childhood and Old Age

Billy, a 7-year-old . . . child, was brought to a mental health clinic by his mother because "he is unhappy and always complaining about feeling sick." . . . His mother describes Billy as a child who has never been very happy and never wanted to play with other children. From the time he started nursery school, he has complained about stomachaches, headaches, and various other physical problems. . . .

Billy did well in first grade, but in second grade he is now having difficulty completing his work. He takes a lot of time to do his assignments and frequently feels he has to do them over again so that they will be "perfect." Because of Billy's frequent somatic complaints, it is hard to get him off to school in the morning. If he is allowed to stay home, he worries that he is falling behind in his schoolwork. When he does go to school, he often is unable to do the work, which makes him feel hopeless about his situation. . . .

His worries have expanded beyond school, and frequently he is clinging and demanding of his parents. He is fearful that if his parents come home late or leave and go somewhere without him that something may happen to them. . . .

Although Billy's mother acknowledges that he has never been really happy, in the last 6 months, she feels, he has become much more depressed. He frequently lies around the house, saying that he is too tired to do anything. He has no interest or enjoyment in playing. His appetite has diminished. He has trouble falling asleep at night and often wakes up in the middle of the night or early in the morning. Three weeks ago, he talked, for the first time, about wanting to die. . . .

(Spitzer et al., 1994, pp. 333–334)

[Oscar] was an 83-year-old married man with an episode of major depressive disorder. . . . He said that about one and one-half years prior to beginning treatment, his brother had died. In the following months, two friends whom he had known since childhood died. Following these losses, he became increasingly anxious [and] grew more and more pessimistic. Reluctantly, he acknowledged, "I even thought about ending my life." Review of his symptoms indicated that while [generalized] anxiety was a prominent part of his clinical picture, so was depression. . . .

During . . . treatment, [Oscar] discussed his relationship with his brother. He discussed how distraught he was to watch his brother's physical deterioration from an extended illness. He described the scene at his brother's deathbed and the moment "when he took his final breath." He experienced guilt over the failure to carry out his brother's funeral services in a manner he felt his brother would have wanted. While initially characterizing his relationship with his brother as loving and amiable, he later acknowledged that he disapproved of many ways in which his brother acted. Later in therapy, he also reviewed different facets of his past relationships with his two deceased friends. He expressed sadness that the long years had ended. . . . [Oscar's] life had been organized around visits to his brother's home and outings with

OPPOSITIONAL DEFIANT DISORDER A childhood disorder in which children argue repeatedly with adults, lose their temper, and swear, feeling intense anger and resentment.

CONDUCT DISORDER A childhood disorder in which the child repeatedly violates the basic rights of others, displaying aggression and sometimes destroying others' property, lying, cheating, or running away from home.

that he didn't like school because he didn't have any friends, and he wasn't good at playing games like baseball and soccer like the other kids were, stating "I'm not really very good at anything." . . . When asked what he would wish for if he could have any three wishes granted he indicated, "I would wish that I was the type of boy my mother and father want, I would wish that I could have friends, and I would wish that I wouldn't feel sad so much."

In speaking with the parents, the mother reported that she and her husband had become increasingly concerned about their son during the past year. She indicated that he always seemed to look sad and cried a lot for no apparent reason and that he appeared to have lost interest in most of the things that he used to enjoy doing. The mother confirmed Bobby's statements that he had no friends, indicating that he had become more and more of a loner during the past 6 to 9 months. She stated that his schoolwork had also suffered in that he is unable to concentrate on school assignments and seems to have "just lost interest." The mother notes, however, that her greatest concern is that he has recently spoken more and more frequently about "killing himself," saying that the parents would be better off if he wasn't around.

(Schwartz & Johnson, 1985, p. 214)

Approximately 2 percent of children under 17 years of age experience major depressive disorder (Kazdin, 1994). The rate for teenagers alone is about 7 percent (Petersen et al., 1993, 1991). The symptoms in young sufferers are likely to include physical discomfort (for example, stomachaches or headaches), irritability, and social withdrawal (APA, 2000, 1994). There appears to be no difference in the rates of depression in boys and girls before the age of 11, but by the age of 16, girls are twice as likely as boys to be depressed (Hankin & Abramson, 1999; Angold & Rutter, 1992).

Explanations of childhood depression are similar to those of adult depression. Theorists have pointed, for example, to factors such as loss, learned helplessness, negative cognitions, and low serotonin or norepinephrine activity (Stark et al., 2000; Todd et al., 1996). Also, like adult depression, many cases of childhood depression seem to be triggered by a negative life event, major change, rejection, or ongoing abuse.

Like depression among adults, childhood depression often is helped by cognitive therapy or interpersonal approaches such as social skills training. In addition, family therapy can be effective (Beardslee et al., 1996; Vostanis et al., 1996). Antidepressant medications have not proved consistently useful in cases involving children (Geller et al., 1999, 1993), but they do seem to help depressed adolescents (Sallee et al., 1997).

How could you? *Childhood anxieties may be the result of developmental upsets, such as the increasingly common experience of having to share a parent's affection with a new stepparent. The face of this boy after his mother's remarriage says it all.*

Disruptive Behavior Disorders

Children often flout rules or misbehave (see Figure 18-1 and Box 18-3). If they consistently display extreme hostility and defiance, however, they may qualify for a diagnosis of oppositional defiant disorder or conduct disorder. Those with **oppositional defiant disorder** argue repeatedly with adults, lose their temper, and feel great anger and resentment. They often ignore adult rules and requests, deliberately annoy other people, and blame others for their own mistakes and problems. The disorder is more common in boys than in girls before puberty, but equal in both sexes after puberty. Between 2 and 16 percent of children display this pattern (APA, 2000).

Children with **conduct disorder**, a more severe problem, go further and repeatedly violate the basic rights of others. They are often aggressive and may in fact be physically cruel to people or animals, deliberately destroy other people's

BOX 18-3

Power Play among Kids

Every few years children around the world turn to a new fantasy hero or heroine. Often their fascination with the character arouses adults' concern and interest. The Mighty Morphin Power Rangers—both male and female—have been the center of controversy ever since the television show of the same name became popular several years back (Hellmich, 1995).

Many of today's clinical theorists and parents worry that the Power Rangers are far too violent and teach children that violence solves problems. Others are concerned that aggressive action heroes such as these may create confusion between fantasy and reality.

ConsiderThis

⦿ Could violent action heroes help produce oppositional defiant disorder and conduct disorder? • Some experts suggest that superhero play is actually a healthy activity. How might this be so? • Might concerns about action figures be overblown?

See and do *A four-year-old flexes his muscles in front of the Red Ranger during a Power Rangers Rocket Tour.*

---

property, lie and cheat, skip school, or run away from home (see Table 18-1 on the next page). Many steal from, threaten, or harm their victims, committing such crimes as shoplifting, forgery, breaking into buildings or cars, mugging, and armed robbery. As they get older their acts of physical violence may include rape or, in rare cases, homicide (APA, 2000, 1994).

Conduct disorder usually begins between 7 and 15 years of age (APA, 2000). Between 1 and 10 percent of children display this pattern, boys more than girls. Children with a mild conduct disorder may improve over time, but severe cases frequently continue into adulthood and may develop into *antisocial personality disorder* or other psychological problems (Myers, Stewart, & Brown, 1998).

Many children with conduct disorder are suspended from school, placed in foster homes, or incarcerated. When children between the ages of 8 and 18 break the law, the legal system often labels them *juvenile delinquents.* More than half of the juveniles who are arrested each year are *recidivists,* meaning they have records of previous arrests. Boys are much more involved in juvenile crime than girls, although rates for girls are on the increase. Girls are most likely to be arrested for drug use, sexual offenses, and running away, boys for drug use and crimes against property. Arrests of teenagers for serious crimes have at least tripled during the past 20 years: the juvenile crime rate jumped almost 50 percent just between 1988 and 1992 (U.S. Department of Justice, 1994).

Cases of conduct disorder have been linked to genetic and biological factors, drug abuse, poverty, and exposure to community violence (Steiner & Wilson, 1999; Needleman et al., 1996). However, they have most often been tied to troubled parent-child relationships, family conflict, and family hostility

FIGURE 18-1   Early misbehavior *Teachers' evaluations of more than 700 preschoolers indicated that the rates of both noncompliant and aggressive behavior dropped as the children grew older. (Adapted from Crowther et al., 1981.)*

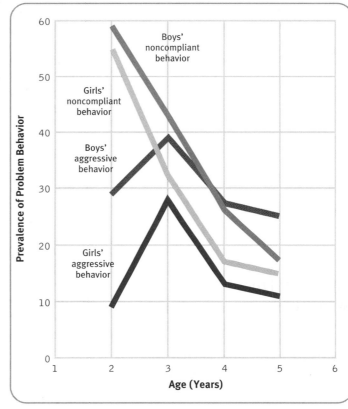

Table 18-2 DSM-IV Checklist

ATTENTION-DEFICIT/HYPERACTIVITY DISORDER

1. Either of the following groups:
   A. At least six of the following symptoms of *inattention,* persisting for at least six months to a degree that is maladaptive and inconsistent with development level:
      a. Frequent failure to give close attention to details, or making careless mistakes.
      b. Frequent difficulty in sustaining attention.
      c. Frequent failure to listen when spoken to directly.
      d. Frequent failure to follow through on instructions and failure to finish work.
      e. Difficulty organizing tasks and activities.
      f. Avoidance of, dislike of, and reluctance to engage in tasks that require sustained mental effort.
      g. Frequent loss of items necessary for tasks or activities.
      h. Easy distraction by irrelevant stimuli.
      i. Forgetfulness in daily activities.
   B. At least six of the following symptoms of *hyperactivity-impulsivity,* persisting for at least six months to a degree that is maladaptive and inconsistent with developmental level:
      a. Fidgeting with hands or feet, or squirming in seat.
      b. Frequent wandering from seat in classroom or similar situation.
      c. Frequent running about or climbing excessively in situations in which it is inappropriate.
      d. Frequent difficulty playing or engaging in leisure activities quietly.
      e. Frequent "on the go" activity or acting as if "driven by a motor."
      f. Frequent excessive talking.
      g. Frequent blurting out of answers before questions have been completed.
      h. Frequent difficulty awaiting turn.
      i. Frequent interrupting of or intruding on others.
2. The presence of some symptoms before the age of 7.
3. Impairment from the symptoms in at least two settings.
4. Significant impairment.

Based on APA, 2000, 1994.

symptoms is much more pronounced than the other (Gaub & Carlson, 1997). About half of the children with ADHD also have learning or communication problems, many perform poorly in school, a number have difficulty interacting with other children, and about 80 percent misbehave, often quite seriously (Mariani & Barkley, 1997; Greene et al., 1996). It is also common for the children to have mood or anxiety problems (Spencer, Biederman, & Wilens, 2000, 1999).

Around 5 percent of schoolchildren display ADHD, as many as 90 percent of them boys. The disorder usually persists throughout childhood (APA, 2000, 1994; Ross & Ross, 1982). Many children show a marked lessening of symptoms as they move into late adolescence, but others continue to have problems (Wilson & Marcotte, 1996). One-third of affected children have ADHD as adults (Trollor, 1999; Lie, 1992). Those whose parents have had ADHD are more likely than others to develop it, and the prevalence of the disorder is higher than usual among relatives of people with the disorder (APA, 2000, 1994; Faraone et al., 1996, 1994).

METHYLPHENIDATE A stimulant drug, known better by the trade name Ritalin, commonly used to treat ADHD.

Today's clinicians generally consider ADHD to have several interacting causes, including biological causes (the disorder was, in fact, once referred to as *minimal brain damage*), high levels of stress, and family dysfunctioning (Baird et al., 2000; Mostofsky, 1999; Needleman et al., 1996). However, none of these suggested causes, examined in isolation, has received clear and consistent research support (Anastopoulos & Barkley, 1992). Sociocultural theorists point out that ADHD symptoms and a diagnosis of ADHD may themselves create interpersonal problems and produce additional symptoms in the child. That is, children who are hyperactive tend to be viewed particularly negatively by their peers and by their parents, and they often view themselves quite negatively as well (APA, 2000; McCormick, 2000; King & Young, 1981).

Behavioral intervention *Educational and treatment programs for children with ADHD use behavioral principles that clearly spell out target behaviors and program rewards and systematically reinforce appropriate behaviors by the children.*

There is heated disagreement about the most effective treatment for ADHD (Hoagwood et al., 2000; Jadad et al., 2000; Spencer et al., 2000, 1999). The most common approach has been the use of stimulant drugs, such as **methylphenidate (Ritalin)** (see Figure 18-3 and Box 18-4 on the next page). These drugs sometimes have a quieting effect on children with ADHD and increase their ability to solve problems, perform academically, and control aggression. However, some clinicians worry about the possible long-term effects of the drugs (Bennett et al., 1999). Behavioral therapy, also applied widely, teaches parents and teachers how to reward attentiveness or self-control in the children. Such operant conditioning treatments have often been helpful, especially when combined with drug therapy (Klassen et al., 1999; Du Paul & Barkley, 1993).

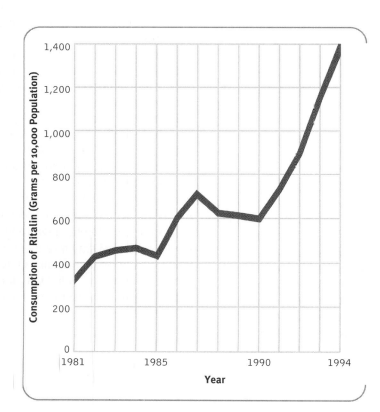

FIGURE 18-3 **The rise of Ritalin** *The use of Ritalin has been increasing since the early 1980s, when researchers discovered that it helped people with ADHD. Sales almost tripled during the 1990s alone. (Adapted from Drug Enforcement Administration, 1996.)*

> Table **18-5** DSM-IV Checklist

AUTISTIC DISORDER

1. A total of at least six items from the following groups of symptoms:
   A. *Impairment in social interaction,* as manifested by at least two of the following:
      a. Marked impairment in the use of multiple nonverbal behaviors such as eye-to-eye gaze, facial expression, body postures, and gestures to regulate social interaction.
      b. Failure to develop peer relationships appropriately.
      c. Lack of spontaneous seeking to share enjoyment, interests, or achievements with other people.
      d. Lack of social or emotional reciprocity.
   B. *Impairment in communication,* as manifested by at least one of the following:
      a. Delay in, or total lack of, the development of spoken language.
      b. In individuals with adequate speech, marked impairment in the ability to start or sustain a conversation with others.
      c. Stereotyped and repetitive use of language, or idiosyncratic language.
      d. Lack of varied, spontaneous make-believe play or social imitative play.
   C. *Restricted repetitive and stereotyped patterns of behavior, interests, and activities,* as manifested by at least one of the following:
      a. Abnormal preoccupation with one or more stereotyped and restricted patterns of interest.
      b. Inflexible adherence to specific nonfunctional routines or rituals.
      c. Stereotyped and repetitive motor mannerisms (e.g., hand or finger flapping or twisting).
      d. Persistent preoccupation with parts of objects.
2. Prior to 3 years of age, delay or abnormal functioning in either social interaction, language, or symbolic or imaginative play.

Based on APA, 2000, 1994.

"No two people with autism are the same. Its precise form of expression is different in every case."

Oliver Sacks, 2000

"97X Bam. The Future of Rock and Roll . . .
97X Bam. The Future of Rock and Roll . . .
97X Bam. The Future of Rock and Roll . . .
97X Bam. The Future of Rock and Roll . . ."

Raymond Babbit, *Rain Man,* 1988
(echolalic response to a
radio advertisement)

Several other disorders are similar to autism but differ to some degree in symptoms or time of onset. Properly speaking, these different disorders are categorized as *pervasive developmental disorders,* but most clinicians refer to them in general as "autism," and this chapter will do the same.

WHAT ARE THE FEATURES OF AUTISM? The individual's *lack of responsiveness,* including extreme aloofness and lack of interest in other people, has long been considered the central feature of autism (Volkmar et al., 1993). Like Mark, children with this disorder typically do not reach for their parents during infancy. Instead they may arch their backs when they are held and appear not to recognize or care about those around them.

Language and communication problems take various forms in autism. Approximately half of all sufferers fail to speak or develop language skills (Dawson & Castelloe, 1992; Rutter, 1966). Those who do talk may show peculiarities in their speech. One of the most common speech problems is *echolalia,* the exact echoing of phrases spoken by others. The individuals repeat the words with the same accent or inflection, but with no sign of understanding. Some even repeat a sentence days after they have heard it (*delayed echolalia*). People with autism may also display other speech oddities, such as *pronominal reversal,* or confusion of pronouns—the use of "you" instead of "I." When Mark was hungry, he would say, "Do you want dinner?" In addition, individuals may have problems naming objects (*nominal aphasia*), using abstract language, employing a proper tone when speaking, speaking spontaneously, or understanding speech.

Autism is also marked by *limited imaginative play* and *very repetitive and rigid behavior*. Affected children may be unable to play in a varied, spontaneous way or to include others in their play. Typically they become very upset at minor changes of objects, persons, or routine and resist any impediment to their repetitive behaviors. Mark, for example, lined things up and screamed if they were disturbed. Similarly, children with autism may react with tantrums if a parent wears an unfamiliar pair of glasses, a chair is moved to a different part of the room, or a word in a song is changed. Kanner (1943) labeled such reactions a *perseveration of sameness*. Furthermore, many sufferers become strongly attached to particular objects—plastic lids, rubber bands, buttons, water. They may collect these objects, carry them, or play with them constantly. Some are fascinated by movement and may watch spinning objects, such as fans, for hours.

The *motor movements* of people with this disorder may also be unusual. Mark would jump, flap his arms, twist his hands and fingers, and make faces. These acts are called *self-stimulatory behaviors*. Some individuals perform *self-injurious behaviors*, such as repeatedly lunging into or banging their head against a wall, pulling their hair, or biting themselves.

These symptoms suggest a very disturbed and contradictory pattern of reactions to stimuli (Wing, 1976; Wing & Wing, 1971) (see Box 18-5 on the next page). Sometimes the individuals seem *overstimulated* by sights and sounds and to be trying to block them out, while at other times they seem *understimulated* and to be performing self-stimulatory actions. They may fail to react to loud noises, for example, yet turn around when they hear soda being poured. Similarly, they may fail to recognize that they have reached the edge of a dangerous high place, yet immediately spot a small object that is out of position in their room.

WHAT CAUSES AUTISM?   A variety of explanations have been offered for autism. This is one disorder for which sociocultural explanations have probably been overemphasized and initially led investigators in the wrong direction. More recent work in the psychological and biological spheres has persuaded clinical theorists that cognitive limitations and brain abnormalities are the primary causes of autism.

SOCIOCULTURAL CAUSES   At first, theorists thought that family dysfunction and social stress were the primary causes of autism. When he first identified autism, for example, Leo Kanner (1954, 1943) argued that particular *personality characteristics of the parents* created an unfavorable climate for development and contributed to the child's disorder. He saw these parents as very intelligent yet cold— "refrigerator parents." These claims had enormous influence on the public and on the self-image of the parents themselves, but research has totally failed to support a picture of rigid, cold, rejecting, or disturbed parents (Roazen, 1992).

Similarly, some other clinicians have proposed that a high degree of *social and environmental stress* is a factor in autism. Once again, however, research has not supported this notion. Investigators who have compared children with autism to children without the disorder have found no differences in the rate of parental death, divorce, separation, financial problems, or environmental stimulation (Cox et al., 1975).

PSYCHOLOGICAL CAUSES   According to some theorists, people with autism have a primary perceptual or cognitive disturbance that makes normal communication and interactions impossible. One influential explanation holds that individuals with this disorder fail to develop a **theory of mind**—an awareness that other people base their behaviors on their own beliefs, intentions, and other mental states, not on information that they have no way of knowing (Frith, 2000; Happé, 1997, 1995; Leslie, 1997).

"Autism is . . . *genetically lethal* [for researchers]. That means people who have it don't usually have children. If it is not passed on, the genetics are difficult to study."

Marvin Schwalb, molecular geneticist, 1999

THEORY OF MIND   Awareness that other people base their behaviors on their own beliefs, intentions, and other mental states, not on information they have no way of knowing.

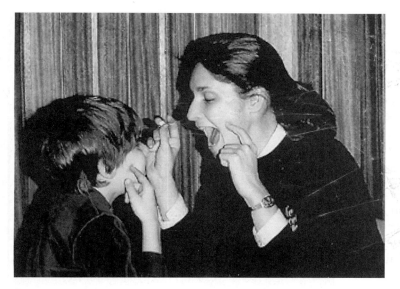

Learning to speak *Behaviorists have had success teaching many children with autism to speak. The therapist systematically models how to position the mouth and how to make appropriate sounds, and then rewards the child's accurate imitations.*

classrooms. The gains continued into the subjects' teenage years. In light of such findings, many clinicians now consider early behavioral programs to be the preferred treatment for autism (Harris, 2000, 1995).

Therapies for people with autism, particularly the behavioral therapies, are ideally applied in school while they are young. The children attend special classes, often at special schools, where education and therapy can be combined. Specially trained teachers help the children improve their skills, behaviors, and interactions with the world. Higher-functioning persons with this disorder may spend at least part of their school day in normal classrooms, developing social and academic skills in the company of nonautistic students (Simpson & Sasso, 1992; Tomchek et al., 1992).

COMMUNICATION TRAINING Even when given intensive behavioral treatment, half of the people with autism remain speechless. As a result, many therapists also teach other forms of communication, including *sign language* and *simultaneous communication,* a method combining sign language and speech. They may also turn to **augmentative communication systems**, such as "communication boards" or computers that use pictures, symbols, or written words to represent objects or needs. A child may point to a picture of a fork to give the message "I am hungry," for example, or point to a radio for "I want music."

PARENT TRAINING Today's treatment programs involve parents in a variety of ways. Behavioral programs, for example, often train parents so that they can apply behavioral techniques at home (Erba, 2000; Love, Matson, & West, 1990). Instruction manuals for parents and home visits by teachers and other professionals are often included in such programs. In addition, individual therapy and support groups are becoming more available to help parents deal with their own emotions and needs. A number of parent associations and lobbies also offer emotional support and practical help.

COMMUNITY INTEGRATION Many of today's school-based and home-based programs for autism teach self-help, self-management, and living, social, and work skills as early as possible, to help the children function better in their communities (Koegel et al., 1992; Stahmer & Schreibman, 1992). In addition, greater numbers of carefully run *group homes* and *sheltered workshops* are now available for teenagers and young adults with autism (Van Bourgondien & Schopler, 1990). These and related programs help the individuals become a part of their community; they also reduce the concerns of aging parents whose children will always need supervision (Pfeiffer & Nelson, 1992).

Mental Retardation

Ed Murphy, aged 26, can tell us what it's like to be diagnosed as retarded:

> What is retardation? It's hard to say. I guess it's having problems thinking. Some people think that you can tell if a person is retarded by looking at them. If you think that way you don't give people the benefit of the doubt. You judge a person by how they look or how they talk or what the tests show, but you can never really tell what is inside the person.
>
> *(Bogdan & Taylor, 1976, p. 51)*

AUGMENTATIVE COMMUNICATION SYSTEM A method for enhancing the communication skills of individuals with autism, mental retardation, or cerebral palsy by teaching them to point to pictures, symbols, letters, or words on a communication board or computer.

MENTAL RETARDATION A disorder marked by intellectual functioning and adaptive behavior that are well below average.

INTELLIGENCE QUOTIENT (IQ) A score derived from intelligence tests that theoretically represents a person's overall intellectual capacity.

For much of his life Ed was labeled mentally retarded and was educated and cared for in special institutions. During his adult years, clinicians discovered that Ed's intellect was in fact higher than had been assumed. In the meantime, however, he had lived the childhood and adolescence of a person labeled retarded, and his statement reveals the kinds of difficulties often faced by people with this disorder.

The term "mental retardation" has been applied to a varied population, including children in institutional wards who rock back and forth, young people who work in special job programs, and men and women who raise and support their families by working at undemanding jobs. Approximately one of every 100 persons receives this diagnosis (APA, 2000). Around three-fifths of them are male and the vast majority are considered *mildly* retarded.

According to DSM-IV, people should receive a diagnosis of **mental retardation** when they display general *intellectual functioning* that is well below average, in combination with poor *adaptive behavior* (APA, 2000, 1994; AAMR, 1992). That is, in addition to having a low IQ (a score of 70 or below), a person with mental retardation must have great difficulty in areas such as communication, home living, self-direction, work, or safety (APA, 2000, 1994). The symptoms must also appear before the age of 18 (see Table 18-6). Although these DSM-IV criteria may seem straightforward, they are in fact hard to apply.

ASSESSING INTELLIGENCE Educators and clinicians administer intelligence tests to measure intellectual functioning (see Chapter 4). These tests consist of a variety of questions and tasks that rely on different aspects of intelligence, such as knowledge, reasoning, and judgment. Having difficulty in one or two of these subtests or areas of functioning does not necessarily reflect low intelligence (see Box 18-6 on the next page). It is an individual's overall test score, or **intelligence quotient (IQ)**, that is thought to indicate general intellectual ability.

Many theorists have questioned whether IQ tests are indeed valid. Do they actually measure what they are supposed to measure? The correlation between IQ and school performance is rather high—around .50—indicating that many children with lower IQs do, as one might expect, perform poorly in school, while many of those with higher IQs perform better (Ceci & Williams, 1997). At the same time, the correlation also suggests that the relationship is far from perfect. That is, a particular child's school performance is often higher or lower than his or her IQ might predict. Correlations between IQ and job performance or social effectiveness, other areas that might be expected to reflect intellectual ability, are even lower (Neisser et al., 1996).

Intelligence tests also appear to be socioculturally biased, as we observed in Chapter 4 (Lee, 1999; Neisser et al., 1996). Children reared in households at the middle and upper socioeconomic levels tend to have an advantage on the tests because they are regularly exposed to the kinds of language and thinking that the tests evaluate. The tests rarely measure the "street sense" needed for survival by people who live in poor, crime-ridden areas—a kind of know-how that certainly requires intellectual skills. Similarly, members of cultural minorities and people for whom English is a second language often appear to be at a disadvantage in taking these tests.

If IQ tests do not always measure intelligence accurately and objectively, then the diagnosis of mental retardation also may be biased (Baroff & Olley, 1999; Wilson, 1992). That is, some people may receive the diagnosis partly because of cultural differences, discomfort with the testing situation, or the bias of a tester.

ASSESSING ADAPTIVE FUNCTIONING Diagnosticians cannot rely solely on a cutoff IQ score of 70 to determine whether a person suffers from mental retardation. Some people with a low IQ are

---

> **Table 18-6 DSM-IV Checklist**
>
> **MENTAL RETARDATION**
>
> 1. Significantly subaverage intellectual functioning: an IQ of approximately 70 or below on an individually administered IQ test.
> 2. Concurrent deficits or impairments in present adaptive functioning in at least two of the following areas:
>   a. Communication.
>   b. Self-care.
>   c. Home living.
>   d. Social/interpersonal skills.
>   e. Use of community resources.
>   f. Self-direction.
>   g. Functional academic skills.
>   h. Work.
>   i. Leisure.
>   j. Health.
>   k. Safety.
> 3. Onset before the age of 18.
>
> Based on APA, 2000, 1994.

Getting a head start *Studies suggest that IQ scores and school performances of children from poor neighborhoods can be improved by enriching their daily environments at a young age through programs such as "Head Start," thus revealing the powerful effect of the environment on IQ scores and intellectual performance.*

BOX **18-6**

Reading and 'Riting and 'Rithmetic

Over 20 percent of children, boys more often than girls, develop slowly and function poorly compared to their peers in an area such as learning, communication, or coordination (APA, 2000). The children do not suffer from mental retardation, and, in fact, they are often very bright, yet their problems may interfere with school performance, daily living, and, in some cases, social interactions (Geisthardt & Munsch, 1996). Similar difficulties may be seen in the children's close biological relatives. According to DSM-IV, these children may be suffering from a learning disorder, a communication disorder, or a developmental coordination disorder.

In *learning disorders,* children's arithmetic skill, written expression skill, or reading performance is well below their intellectual capacity and causes academic and personal dysfunctioning (APA, 2000, 1994). One learning disorder is called *mathematics disorder* and is diagnosed in children who have markedly impaired mathematical skills. Children with *disorder of written expression* make extreme and persistent errors in spelling, grammar, punctuation, and paragraph organization. And children with *reading disorder,* also known as *dyslexia,* have great difficulty recognizing words and comprehending as they read. They typically read slowly and haltingly and may omit, distort, or substitute words as they go.

The *communication disorders* take various forms as well (APA, 2000, 1994). Children with *phonological disorder* consistently fail to make correct speech sounds at an appropriate age, so that many of them seem to be talking baby talk. Those with *expressive language disorder* have trouble using language to express themselves. They may struggle at learning new words; confine their speech to short simple sentences; or show a general lag in language development. Children with *mixed receptive/expressive language disorder* have difficulty comprehending and expressing language. And those who suffer from *stuttering* display a disturbance in the fluency and timing

Dyslexic impairment *A student with dyslexia has trouble copying words. His mistakes reflect the difficulties he experiences when reading.*

of their speech. They may repeat, prolong, or interject sounds, pause before finishing a word, or experience excessive tension in the muscles used for speech.

Finally, children with *developmental coordination disorder* perform coordinated motor activities at a level well below that of others their age (APA, 2000, 1994). Younger children with this disorder are clumsy and are slow to master skills such as tying shoelaces, buttoning shirts, and zipping pants. Older children with the disorder may have great difficulty assembling puzzles, building models, playing ball, and printing or writing.

Studies have linked these developmental disorders to genetic defects, birth injuries, lead poisoning, inappropriate diet, sensory or perceptual dysfunction, and poor teaching (Erickson, 1997; Gelfand et al., 1982). Research implicating each of these factors has been quite limited, however, and the precise causes of the disorders remain unclear.

Some of the disorders respond to special treatment approaches (Merzenich et al., 1996). Reading therapy, for example, is very helpful in mild cases of reading disorder, and speech therapy brings about complete recovery in most cases of phonological disorder (Merzenich et al., 1996). Furthermore, learning, communication, and developmental coordination disorders often disappear before

adulthood, even without any treatment (APA, 2000).

The inclusion of learning, communication, and coordination problems in the DSM is controversial. Many clinicians view them as strictly educational or social problems, best addressed at school or at home. The framers of DSM-IV have reasoned, however, that the additional problems created by these disorders and the frequent links to other psychological problems justify their clinical classifications (Mishna, 1996). Of special concern are studies that have found an increased risk of depression and even suicide in adolescents with certain of these problems, particularly the learning disorders (Huntington & Bender, 1993).

ConsiderThis

⊙ In past times, a child with one of these problems might simply be called a "weak" reader, "clumsy," or the like. What are the advantages to the child of affixing clinical names to the patterns? • Might there be disadvantages to such labels? • Should these patterns be listed in DSM-IV as psychological disorders?

quite capable of managing their lives and functioning independently, while others are not. The cases of Brian and Jeffrey show the range of adaptive abilities.

> Brian comes from a lower-income family. He always has functioned adequately at home and in his community. He dresses and feeds himself and even takes care of himself each day until his mother returns home from work. He also plays well with his friends. At school, however, Brian refuses to participate or do his homework. He seems ineffective, at times lost, in the classroom. Referred to a school psychologist by his teacher, he received an IQ score of 60.

> Jeffrey comes from an upper-middle-class home. He was always slow to develop, and sat up, stood, and talked late. During his infancy and toddler years, he was put in a special stimulation program and given special help and attention at home. Still Jeffrey has trouble dressing himself today and cannot be left alone in the backyard lest he hurt himself or wander off into the street. Schoolwork is very difficult for him. The teacher must work slowly and provide individual instruction for him. Tested at age 6, Jeffrey received an IQ score of 60.

Brian seems well adapted to his environment outside of school. However, Jeffrey's limitations are pervasive. In addition to his low IQ score, Jeffrey has difficulty meeting challenges at home and elsewhere. Thus, a diagnosis of mental retardation may be more appropriate for Jeffrey than for Brian.

Several scales, such as the *Vineland* and *AAMR adaptive behavior scales,* have been developed to assess adaptive behavior (Leland, 1991; Britton & Eaves, 1986). Here again, however, some people function better in their lives than the scales predict, while others fall short. Thus to properly diagnose mental retardation, clinicians should observe the functioning of each individual in his or her everyday environment, taking both the person's background and the community's standards into account. Even then, such judgments can be subjective, and clinicians are not always familiar with the standards of a particular culture or community.

WHAT ARE THE CHARACTERISTICS OF MENTAL RETARDATION? The most consistent sign of mental retardation is that the person learns very slowly (Baroff & Olley, 1999; Kail, 1992; Hale & Borkowski, 1991). Other areas of difficulty are attention, short-term memory, planning, and language. Those who are institutionalized with mental retardation are particularly likely to have these limitations. It may be that the unstimulating environment and minimal interactions with staff in many institutions contribute to such difficulties.

"The IQ test was invented to predict academic performance, nothing else. If we wanted something that would predict life success, we'd have to invent another test completely."

Robert Zajonc, psychologist, 1984

Artistic development *Clinicians have come to recognize that people with mental retardation can benefit from instruction in the arts as well as academic and vocational training. Individuals enrolled in this creative arts course at the center of the Association for Retarded Persons develop greater self-confidence and better communication skills along with improved artistic ability.*

DSM-IV describes four levels of mental retardation: *mild* (IQ 50–70), *moderate* (IQ 35–49), *severe* (IQ 20–34), and *profound* (IQ below 20). In contrast, the American Association of Mental Retardation (1992) prefers to distinguish different kinds of mental retardation according to the level of support the person needs—*intermittent, limited, extensive,* or *pervasive.*

MILD RETARDATION Approximately 85 percent of all people with mental retardation fall into the category of **mild retardation** (IQ 50–70) (APA, 2000). They are sometimes called "educably retarded" because they can benefit from schooling and can support themselves as adults. Still, they typically need assistance when they are under stress. Their jobs tend to be unskilled or semiskilled. Mild mental retardation is not usually recognized until a child enters school and is assessed there. Interestingly, the intellectual performance of individuals in this category often seems to improve with age; some even seem to leave the label behind when they leave school, and they go on to function well in the community.

Research has linked mild mental retardation mainly to sociocultural and psychological causes (Stromme & Magnus, 2000), particularly poor and unstimulating environments, inadequate parent-child interactions, and insufficient learning experiences during a child's early years. These relationships have been observed in studies comparing deprived and enriched environments (see Figure 18-4). In fact, some community programs have sent workers into the homes of young children with low IQ scores to help enrich the environment there, and their interventions have often improved the children's functioning. When continued, programs of this kind also help improve the children's later performance in school (Ramey & Ramey, 1999, 1998, 1992).

Although these factors seem to be the leading causes of mild mental retardation, at least some biological factors also may be operating. Studies suggest, for example, that a mother's moderate drinking, drug use, or malnutrition during pregnancy may lower her child's intellectual potential (Neisser et al., 1996; Stein et al., 1972). Similarly, malnourishment hurts the intellectual development of young children, although this effect can be reversed at least partly if a child's diet is improved before too much time has gone by (Baroff & Olley, 1999; Brown & Pollitt, 1996; Neisser et al., 1996).

MODERATE, SEVERE, AND PROFOUND RETARDATION Approximately 10 percent of persons with mental retardation function at a level of **moderate retardation** (IQ 35–49). They can learn to care for themselves and can benefit from vocational training, and many can work in unskilled or semiskilled jobs, usually under supervision. Most persons with moderate retardation also function well in the community if they have supervision (APA, 2000, 1994).

Approximately 4 percent of people with mental retardation display **severe retardation** (IQ 20–34). They usually require careful supervision, profit somewhat from vocational training, and can perform only basic work tasks in structured and sheltered settings. Their understanding of communication is usually better than their speech. Most are able to function well in the community if they live in group homes, community nursing homes, or with their families (APA, 2000, 1994).

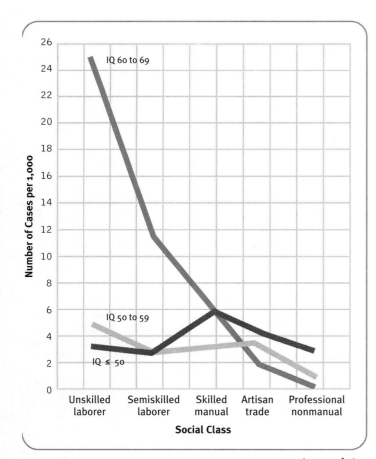

FIGURE 18-4 Mental retardation and socio-economic class *The prevalence of mild mental retardation is much higher in the lower socio-economic classes than in the upper classes. In contrast, the forms of mental retardation that result in greater impairment are evenly distributed. (Adapted from Popper, 1988; Birch et al., 1970.)*

Around 1 percent of all people with mental retardation fall into the category of **profound retardation** (IQ below 20). With training they may learn or improve basic skills such as walking, some talking, and feeding themselves. They need a very structured environment, with close supervision and considerable help, including a one-to-one relationship with a caregiver, in order to develop to the fullest (APA, 2000, 1994). Severe and profound levels of mental retardation often appear as part of larger syndromes that include severe physical handicaps.

In many cases these physical problems are even more limiting than an individual's low intellectual functioning.

WHAT ARE THE CAUSES OF MENTAL RETARDATION? The primary causes of moderate, severe, and profound retardation are biological, although people who function at these levels are also greatly affected by their family and social environment (Baroff & Olley, 1999; Bruce et al., 1996). Sometimes genetic factors are at the root of these biological problems, in the form of chromosomal or metabolic disorders. In fact, researchers have identified 1,000 genetic causes of mental retardation, although few of them have undergone much study (Azar, 1995). Other biological causes of these kinds of mental retardation come from unfavorable conditions that occur before, during, or after birth.

CHROMOSOMAL CAUSES The most common of the chromosomal disorders leading to mental retardation is **Down syndrome**, named after Langdon Down, the British physician who first identified it. Fewer than 1 of every 1,000 live births result in Down syndrome, but this rate increases greatly when the mother's age is over 35. Many older expectant mothers are now encouraged to undergo *amniocentesis* (testing of the amniotic fluid that surrounds the fetus) during the fourth month of pregnancy to identify Down syndrome and other chromosomal abnormalities.

Individuals with Down syndrome may have a small head, flat face, slanted eyes, high cheekbones, and, in some cases, a protruding tongue. The latter may affect their pronunciation and clarity of speech (Mahoney et al., 1981). They are often very affectionate with family members, but in general display the same range of personality characteristics as people in the general population (Carr, 1994).

Several types of chromosomal abnormalities may cause Down syndrome. The most common type (94 percent of cases) is *trisomy 21,* in which the individual has three free-floating twenty-first chromosomes instead of two (Pueschel & Thuline, 1991). In a second type, *translocation,* the person has two normal twenty-first chromosomes and a third twenty-first chromosome fused with another chromosome (the fifteenth or thirteenth). And in a third extremely rare type, *mosaicism,* cells with two and cells with three twenty-first chromosomes are found in the same person. Most people with Down syndrome range in IQ from 35 to 55. The individuals appear to age early, and many even show signs of dementia as they approach 40 (Zigman et al., 1995; Carr, 1994). Studies suggest that Down syndrome and early dementia often occur together because the genes that produce them are located close to each other on chromosome 21 (Selkoe, 1991).

Fragile X syndrome is the second most common chromosomal cause of mental retardation (Zigler & Hodapp, 1991). Children born with a fragile X chromosome (that is, an X chromosome with a genetic abnormality that leaves it prone to breakage and loss) generally have mild to moderate degrees of intellectual dysfunctioning, language impairment, and, in some cases, behavioral problems (Baroff & Olley, 1999).

METABOLIC CAUSES In metabolic disorders, the body's breakdown or production of chemicals is disturbed. The metabolic disorders that affect intelligence and development are typically caused by the pairing of two defective *recessive genes,* one from each parent. Although one such gene would have no influence if it were paired with a normal gene, its pairing with another defective gene leads to major problems for the child.

MILD RETARDATION A level of mental retardation (IQ between 50 and 70) at which people can benefit from education and support themselves as adults.

MODERATE RETARDATION A level of mental retardation (IQ between 35 and 49) at which people can learn to care for themselves and benefit from vocational training.

SEVERE RETARDATION A level of mental retardation (IQ between 20 and 34) at which individuals require careful supervision and can learn to perform basic work in structured and sheltered settings.

PROFOUND RETARDATION A level of mental retardation (IQ below 20) at which individuals need a very structured environment with close supervision.

DOWN SYNDROME A form of mental retardation caused by an abnormality in the twenty-first chromosome.

Reaching higher *Prior to the 1970s, clinicians were pessimistic about the potential of people with Down syndrome. Today they are viewed as individuals who can learn and accomplish many things in their lives. Derek Finstad, a 16-year-old with this disorder, celebrates with his football teammates after the team's 56–0 season-opening victory.*

The most common metabolic disorder to cause mental retardation is *phenylketonuria (PKU)*, which strikes 1 of every 17,000 children. Babies with PKU appear normal at birth but cannot break down the amino acid *phenylalanine*. The chemical accumulates and is converted into substances that poison the system, causing severe retardation and several other symptoms. Today infants can be screened for PKU, and if started on a special diet before 3 months of age, they may develop normal intelligence.

In *Tay-Sachs disease*, another metabolic disorder resulting from a pairing of recessive genes, children progressively lose their mental functioning, vision, and motor ability over the course of two to four years, and eventually die. One of every 30 persons of Eastern European Jewish ancestry carries the recessive gene responsible for this disorder, so that one of every 900 Jewish couples is at risk for having a child with Tay-Sachs disease.

PRENATAL AND BIRTH-RELATED CAUSES As a fetus develops, major physical problems in the pregnant mother can threaten the child's prospects for a normal life (Baroff & Olley, 1999; Neisser et al., 1996). When a pregnant woman has too little iodine in her diet, for example, her child may develop *cretinism,* characterized by an abnormal thyroid gland, slow development, mental retardation, and a dwarflike appearance. The disorder is rare today because the salt in most diets now contains supplemental iodine. Also, any infant born with this disorder may quickly be given thyroid extract to bring about a normal development.

Other prenatal problems may also cause mental retardation. As we observed in Chapter 12, children whose mothers drink too much alcohol during pregnancy may be born with **fetal alcohol syndrome**, a group of very serious problems that includes lower intellectual functioning (CDC, 1998). In fact, a generally safe level of alcohol consumption during pregnancy has not been established by research. In addition, certain maternal infections during pregnancy—*rubella* (German measles) and *syphilis,* for example—may cause childhood problems that include mental retardation.

Birth complications can also lead to mental retardation. A prolonged period without oxygen (*anoxia*) during or after delivery can cause brain damage and retardation in a baby (Erickson, 1992). Similarly, although premature birth does not necessarily lead to long-term problems for children, researchers have found that a birth weight of less than 3.5 pounds is associated with a heightened risk of retardation (Neisser et al., 1996).

CHILDHOOD PROBLEMS After birth, particularly up to age 6, certain injuries and accidents can affect intellectual functioning and in some cases lead to mental retardation. Poisonings, serious head injuries caused by accident or abuse, excessive exposure to X rays, and excessive use of certain drugs pose special dangers. For example, a serious case of *lead poisoning,* from eating lead-based paints or inhaling high levels of automobile fumes, can cause retardation in children. Mercury, radiation, nitrite, and pesticide poisoning may do the same. In addition, certain infections, such as *meningitis* and *encephalitis,* can lead to mental retardation if they are not diagnosed and treated in time (Baroff & Olley, 1999; Berney, 1993).

INTERVENTIONS FOR PEOPLE WITH MENTAL RETARDATION The quality of life attained by people with mental retardation depends largely on sociocultural factors: where they live and with whom, how they are educated, and the growth opportunities available at home and in the community. Thus intervention programs for these individuals direct their primary efforts toward providing comfortable and stimulating residences, social and economic opportunities, and a proper education. Once these needs are met, psychological or biological treatments are also of help in some cases.

Environmental danger *Children such as this toddler who scrape and eat lead-based paint chips may experience lead poisoning, which can cause mental retardation.*

WHAT IS THE PROPER RESIDENCE? Until recent decades, parents of children with mental retardation would send them to live in public institutions—**state schools**—as early as possible. These overcrowded institutions provided basic care, but residents were neglected, often abused, and isolated from society.

> They had me scheduled to go to P-8—a back ward—when just one man looked at me. I was a wreck. I had a beard and baggy State clothes on. I had just arrived at the place. I was trying to understand what was happening. I was confused. What I looked like was P-8 material. There was this supervisor, a woman. She came on the ward and looked right at me and said: "I have him scheduled for P-8." An older attendant was there. He looked over at me and said, "He's too bright for that ward. I think we'll keep him." . . .
>
> Of course I didn't know what P-8 was then, but I found out. I visited up there a few times on work detail. That man saved my life. Here was a woman that I had never known who they said was the building supervisor looking over me. At that point I'm pretty positive that if I went there I would have fitted in and I would still be there.
>
> *(Bogdan & Taylor, 1976, p. 49)*

During the 1960s and 1970s, the public became more aware of these sorry conditions, and, as part of the broader *deinstitutionalization* movement (see Chapter 15), demanded that many people with mental retardation be released from the state schools (Beyer, 1991). In many cases, the releases occurred without adequate preparation or supervision. Like deinstitutionalized people suffering from schizophrenia, the individuals were virtually dumped into the community. Often they failed to adjust and had to be institutionalized once again.

Since that time, reforms have led to the creation of small institutions that teach self-sufficiency, devote more staff time to patient care, and offer educational and medical services. Many of these institutions and other community residences emulate the principles of **normalization** first started in Denmark and Sweden—they attempt to provide living conditions comparable to those enjoyed by the rest of society, flexible routines, and normal developmental experiences, including opportunities for self-determination, sexual fulfillment, and economic freedom (Baroff & Olley, 1999; Wolfensberger, 1983, 1972). Growing numbers of group homes, halfway houses, small local branches of larger institutions, and independent residences now apply these principles, teaching clients with retardation to get along in the community.

Today the vast majority of children with mental retardation live at home rather than in an institution (Erickson, 1992). As they approach adulthood and as their parents age, however, the family may no longer be able to provide the kinds of assistance and experiences these individuals require (Krauss et al., 1992), and a community residence becomes an appropriate alternative for some. Most people with mental retardation, including almost all with mild mental retardation, now spend their adult lives either in the family home or in a community residence (Blacher & Baker, 1994, 1992; Jacobson & Schwartz, 1991).

WHICH EDUCATIONAL PROGRAMS WORK BEST? Because early intervention seems to offer such great promise, educational programs for individuals with mental retardation may begin during the earliest years. The appropriate education depends on the individual's degree of retardation (Cipani, 1991). Educators hotly debate whether special classes or mainstreaming is most effective once the children enter school (Freeman & Alkin, 2000; Gottlieb et al., 1991). In **special education**, children with mental retardation are grouped together in a separate, specially designed educational program. **Mainstreaming**, in contrast, places them in regular classes with nonretarded students. Neither approach seems consistently superior (Gottlieb, 1981). It may well be that mainstreaming is better for some areas of learning and for some children, special classes for others.

FETAL ALCOHOL SYNDROME A group of problems in a child, including lower intellectual functioning, low birth weight, and irregularities in the hands and face, that result from excessive alcohol intake by the mother during pregnancy.

STATE SCHOOL A state-supported institution for individuals with mental retardation.

NORMALIZATION The principle that institutions and community residences should expose people with mental retardation to living conditions and opportunities similar to those found in the rest of society.

SPECIAL EDUCATION An approach to educating children with mental retardation in which they are grouped together and given a separate, specially designed education.

MAINSTREAMING The placement of children with mental retardation in regular school classes with children who are not mentally retarded.

ConsiderThis

◉ Those who support special classes for people with mental retardation believe that such programs allow the participants to experience feelings of success and to receive needed special attention, while those who favor mainstreaming argue that this format offers a more normal educational experience and increased interaction between children with and without mental retardation. What are the merits and flaws of each position?

Computer classes *In recent years, educators have developed stimulating and interactive computer programs to help teach academic, social, and other skills to people with mental retardation. The programs complement classroom instruction and can be tailored to the individual abilities and needs of each student.*

Normal needs *The interpersonal and sexual needs of people with mental retardation are normal, and many, such as this engaged couple, demonstrate considerable ability to express intimacy.*

Many teachers use operant conditioning principles to improve the self-help, communication, social, and academic skills of individuals with mental retardation (Erickson, 1992). They break learning tasks down into small steps, giving positive reinforcement as each increment is accomplished. In addition, many institutions, schools, and private homes have set up *token economy programs*—the operant conditioning programs that have also been used to treat institutionalized patients suffering from schizophrenia.

WHEN IS THERAPY NEEDED? Like anyone else, people with mental retardation sometimes experience emotional and behavioral problems (Olley & Baroff, 1999; Pearson et al., 1996). At least 10 percent of them have a diagnosable psychological disorder other than mental retardation (Grizenko et al., 1991). Furthermore, some suffer from low self-esteem, interpersonal problems, and difficulties adjusting to community life. These problems are helped to some degree by either individual or group therapy (Baroff & Olley, 1999). In addition, large numbers of people with retardation are given psychotropic medications (Madrid et al., 2000). Many clinicians suggest, however, that too often the medications are used simply for the purpose of making the individuals easier to manage (Erickson, 1992).

HOW CAN OPPORTUNITIES FOR PERSONAL, SOCIAL, AND OCCUPATIONAL GROWTH BE INCREASED? People need to feel effective and competent in order to move forward in life. Those with mental retardation are most likely to achieve these feelings if their communities allow them to grow and to make many of their own choices (Wehmeyer, 1992). Denmark and Sweden, where the normalization movement originated, are again leaders in this area, developing youth clubs that encourage those with mental retardation to take risks and function independently (Perske, 1972).

Socializing, sex, and marriage are difficult issues for people with mental retardation and their families, but with proper training and practice, the individuals can usually learn to use contraceptives and carry out responsible family planning (Bakken et al., 1993; Dowdney & Skuse, 1993). The National Association for Retarded Citizens offers guidance in these matters, and some clinicians have developed *dating skills programs* (Valenti-Hein et al., 1994).

Some states restrict marriage for people with mental retardation (Levesque, 1996). These laws are rarely enforced, however, and in fact between one-quarter and half of all people with mild mental retardation eventually marry (Grinspoon et al., 1986). Contrary to popular myths, the marriages can be very successful. Moreover, while some individuals may be incapable of raising children, many are quite able to do so, either on their own or with special help and community services (Levesque, 1996; Bakken et al., 1993).

Finally, adults with mental retardation—whatever the severity—need the personal and financial rewards that come with holding a job (Faubion & Andrew, 2000; AAMR, 1992). Many work in **sheltered workshops**, protected and supervised workplaces that train them at a pace and level tailored to their abilities. After training in the workshops, many with mild or moderate retardation move on to hold regular jobs.

Although training programs for people with mental retardation have improved greatly in quality over the past 30 years, they are insufficient in number. Consequently, most of these individuals fail to receive a complete range of educational and occupational training services. Additional programs are required so that more people with mental retardation may achieve their full potential, as workers and as human beings.

Disorders of Later Life

Old age is usually defined in our society as the years past age 65. By this account more than 35 million people in the United States are "old," representing around 15 percent of the total population; this is an eleven-fold increase since 1900 (Hobbs, 1997) (see Figure 18-5). Older women outnumber older men by 3 to 2.

Like childhood, old age brings special pressures, unique upsets, and profound biological changes. People become more prone to illness and injury as they age, and they are likely to experience the stress of loss—the loss of spouses, friends, and adult children, and the loss of former activities and roles. Many lose their sense of purpose after they retire. Even favored pets and possessions are sometimes lost (Gallagher-Thompson & Thompson, 1995).

The stresses of elderly people need not necessarily result in psychological problems (Schultz & Heckhausen, 1996). In fact, some older persons use the changes that come with aging as opportunities for learning and growth (see Box 18-7 on the next page). For others, however, the stresses of old age do lead to psychological difficulties (Banerjee & Macdonald, 1996). Studies indicate that as many as 50 percent of elderly people would benefit from mental health services (MacDonald & Schnur, 1987), yet fewer than 20 percent actually receive them. **Geropsychology**, the field of psychology dedicated to the mental health of elderly people, has developed almost entirely within the last 30 years, and at present fewer than 4 percent of all clinicians work primarily with elderly patients (Birren & Schroots, 2000; Sleek, 1996).

The psychological problems of elderly persons may be divided into two groups. One group consists of disorders that are found in people of all ages but that often prove to be connected to the process of aging when they occur in an elderly person. These include depression and anxiety and substance-related disorders. The other group consists of disorders that are most likely to be found in the elderly, such as delirium and dementia.

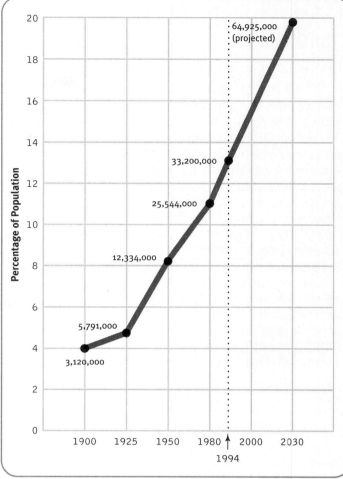

FIGURE 18-5 **On the rise** *The population of people aged 65 and older in the United States increased eleven-fold during the twentieth century. The percentage of elderly people in the population increased from 4 percent in 1900 to 12.5 percent in 1994 and is expected to be 20 percent in 2030 (Hobbs, 1997; AARP, 1990).*

Mood, Anxiety, and Substance-Related Disorders

Depression is the most common mental health problem of older adults. As with Oscar, the man whose case description opened this chapter, depression is particularly common among elderly persons who have recently experienced a trauma, such as the loss of a spouse or close friend or the development of a serious physical illness. Overall, as many as 20 percent of the elderly experience some form of this disorder (Lyness et al., 1999; Koenig & Blazer, 1992). The rate is highest in older women (Fernandez et al., 1995).

Several studies suggest that depression among older people raises their chances of developing significant medical problems. For example, older depressed people with high blood pressure are almost three times as likely to suffer a stroke as older nondepressed people with the same condition (Simonsick et al., 1995). Similarly, elderly people who are depressed recover more slowly and less completely from heart attacks, hip fractures, pneumonia, and other infections and illnesses (Goleman, 1995).

Like younger adults, older individuals who are depressed may be helped by cognitive therapy, interpersonal therapy, antidepressant medications, or a combination of these approaches (Katz & Oslin, 2000; Coon et al., 1999; Hinrichsen, 1999). Between half and 65 percent of older patients with depression improve with such treatments. At the same time, it is sometimes difficult to use

SHELTERED WORKSHOP A protected and supervised workplace that offers job opportunities and training at a pace and level tailored to people with various psychological disabilities.

GEROPSYCHOLOGY The field of psychology concerned with the mental health of elderly people.

BOX **18-7**

The Oldest Old

Clinicians suggest that aging need not inevitably lead to psychological problems. Nor apparently does it always lead to physical problems. When researchers recently studied people over 95 years of age—often called the "oldest old"—they were surprised to find that these individuals are on average more healthy, clear-headed, and agile than those in their 80s and early 90s (Perls, 1995). Many, in fact, are still employed, sexually active, and able to enjoy the outdoors and the arts.

Some scientists believe that individuals who live this long carry "longevity" genes that make them resistant to disabling or terminal infections (Perls, 1995). The individuals themselves often credit a good frame of mind or regular behaviors that they have maintained for many years—eating healthful food, pursuing regular exercise, not smoking.

ConsiderThis

• The "oldest old" often seem particularly well adjusted. Does their positive frame of mind lead to longevity, or does outstanding health produce greater happiness? • Why do many in this age group attribute their longevity to psychological factors, while scientists seem to prefer biological explanations?

John Parrish, a 104-year-old medicine man living in Monument Valley, Arizona.

antidepressant drugs effectively and safely with older persons because the body breaks the drugs down differently in later life (Bell, 1999; Bender, 1999). Finally, group therapy can be a useful approach for older people who are depressed (Finkel, 1991).

Anxiety is also common among elderly people (Fuentes & Cox, 2000; Krasucki, Howard, & Mann, 1998). Surveys indicate that generalized anxiety disorder and agoraphobia are particularly common, experienced by up to 7 percent and 5 percent, respectively (Flint, 1994). In fact, these numbers may be low, as anxiety in the elderly tends to be underreported (Sleek, 1996). Both the elderly individual and the clinician may interpret physical symptoms of anxiety, such as heart palpitations and sweating, as symptoms of a medical condition.

Older adults with anxiety disorders have been treated with psychotherapy of various kinds, particularly cognitive therapies (Stanley & Averill, 1999; McCarthy et al., 1991). Many also receive benzodiazepines or other antianxiety medications, although more and more of those with obsessive-compulsive disorder are, like younger sufferers, being treated with serotonin-enhancing antidepressant drugs such as *fluoxetine (Prozac)* (Calamari & Cassiday, 1999; Jenike, 1991). Again, however, all such drugs must be used cautiously with people over 60 years of age.

Alcohol abuse and other forms of *substance abuse* are another problem for many older persons, although the prevalence of these disorders actually declines among people over 60 (Graham et al., 1996). Nonetheless, 4 to 6 percent of older people, particularly men, experience alcohol-related disorders in any given year (Adams & Cox, 1997). Researchers often distinguish between older problem drinkers who have experienced significant alcohol-related problems for many years, perhaps since their 20s or 30s, and those who do not start the pattern until their 50s or 60s. The latter group typically begin their abusive drinking as a reaction to the negative events and

A dream fulfilled *Staying active, pursuing goals, and seeking stimulation are keys to coping with and enjoying life, particularly old age. In 1997, former president George Bush fulfilled his dream of skydiving from a plane 12,500 feet above the desert. He had wanted to do this since World War II when he had been forced to bail out of his torpedo bomber. After the dive, an excited Bush said that it was "something I'll carry with me for the rest of my life."*

pressures of growing older, such as the death of a spouse or unwanted retirement. Alcohol abuse and dependence in elderly people are treated much as in younger adults (see Chapter 12), with such approaches as detoxification, Antabuse, Alcoholics Anonymous (AA), and cognitive-behavioral therapy (Dupree & Schonfeld, 1999).

A leading kind of substance problem in the elderly is the misuse of prescription drugs (Graham et al., 1996). Most often it is unintentional. Older people receive twice as many prescriptions on average as younger persons, and one-quarter take three or more drugs daily (Patterson et al., 1999; Lipton, 1988). Thus their risk of confusing medications or skipping doses is high (Salzman et al., 1995). Physicians and pharmacists are now trying to simplify medication regimens and to educate older patients about their prescriptions, clarifying directions and teaching them to watch for undesired effects (Gallagher-Thompson & Thompson, 1995).

Delirium and Dementia

Delirium is a clouding of consciousness. As the person's awareness of the environment becomes less clear, he or she has great difficulty concentrating, focusing attention, and thinking sequentially, which leads to misinterpretations, illusions, and, on occasion, hallucinations (APA, 2000, 1994). Sufferers may believe that it is morning in the middle of the night or that they are home when actually they are in a hospital room.

This state of massive confusion typically develops over a short period of time, usually hours or days. It may occur in any age group, including children, but is most common in elderly persons. In fact, when elderly people enter a hospital to be treated for a general medical condition, one in ten of them shows the symptoms of delirium (APA, 2000, 1994). At least another 10 percent develop delirium during their stay in the hospital (APA, 2000; Inouye et al., 1999; Inouye, 1998).

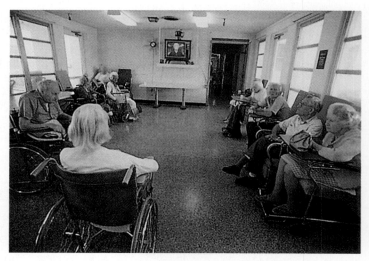

Dreary setting *Most aging persons fear that they will eventually be forced by poor health to reside in a nursing home, separated from their families, friends, and homes. An additional concern is that many of today's nursing homes are unstimulating settings in which residents may be neglected, mistreated, and overmedicated.*

Fever, metabolic disorders, infections, poor nutrition, head injuries, certain brain diseases, and stress (including the trauma of surgery) may all cause delirium. So may intoxication by certain substances, such as prescription drugs. Partly because older people face so many of these problems, they are more likely than younger ones to experience delirium. If a clinician accurately identifies delirium, it can often be easy to correct—by treating the underlying infection, for example, or changing the patient's drug prescription. However, delirium is not always recognized for what it is (Inouye, 1999, 1998). One study on a medical ward found that admission doctors detected only one of fifteen consecutive cases of delirium (Cameron et al., 1987). Incorrect diagnosis of this kind may contribute to a high death rate for older people with delirium (Rabins & Folstein, 1982).

As we saw in Chapter 16, **dementia** is a syndrome marked by severe problems in memory and in at least one other cognitive function, such as abstract thinking, judgment, or language. All people experience some cognitive decline as they age, but only a minority develop dementia. People with this syndrome may also undergo extreme personality and behavioral changes, and their symptoms may worsen progressively. Some also react to their disorder with agitation, anxiety, or depression (Thorpe, 1999; Krishnan et al., 1996; Mintzer & Brawman-Mintzer, 1996). As we have seen, the occurrence of dementia is closely related to age. Around 1 to 2 percent of people 65 years of age experience it, compared to more than one-quarter of those over the age of 85 (Cowley, 2000; DeLeon et al., 1996). Dementia is sometimes confused with delirium, and in fact the two may occur together.

Like delirium, dementia sometimes has a cause that is reversible. Some sufferers, for example, have nutritional disorders that can be corrected. Similarly,

DELIRIUM A rapidly developing clouding of consciousness in which a person has great difficulty concentrating, focusing attention, and following an orderly sequence of thought.

DEMENTIA A syndrome marked by severe problems in memory and in at least one other cognitive function.

improving vision and hearing can substantially improve the cognitive functioning of some individuals (Evenhuis, 1999). However, most cases of dementia are caused by neurological problems, such as Alzheimer's disease and stroke, that currently are difficult or impossible to address (see pp. 498–505).

Issues Affecting the Mental Health of the Elderly

As the study and treatment of elderly people have progressed, three issues have raised concern among clinicians: the problems faced by elderly members of ethnic minority groups, the serious inadequacies of long-term care, and the need for a health-maintenance approach to medical care in an aging world (Gallagher-Thompson & Thompson, 1995).

Discrimination due to ethnicity has long been a problem in the United States (see Chapter 2), and many people suffer as a result, particularly those who are old (Cavanaugh, 1990). To be both old and a member of a minority group is considered a kind of "double jeopardy" by many observers. For older women in minority groups, the difficulties are sometimes termed "triple jeopardy," as many more older women than older men live alone, are widowed, and are poor. Clinicians must take into account their older patients' ethnicity as they try to diagnose and treat their mental health problems (Kelty et al., 2000; Bazargan, 1996) (see Figure 18-6).

Some elderly people from ethnic minority groups face language barriers that interfere with their medical and mental health care. Others may hold cultural beliefs that prevent them from consulting a therapist. Moreover, many members of minority groups do not trust the majority establishment or do not know about medical and mental health services that are sensitive to their culture and their particular needs (Ralston, 1991; Jackson, 1988). As a result, it is common for elderly members of ethnic minority groups to rely solely on family members or friends for remedies and health care.

Many older people require *long-term care,* a general term that refers variously to the services offered in a partially supervised apartment, in a senior housing complex for mildly impaired elderly persons, or in a nursing home where skilled medical and nursing care are available around the clock. The quality of care in such residences varies widely.

At any given time in the United States, only about 5 percent of the elderly population actually live in nursing homes, but most older adults live in fear of being "put away" (NCHS, 1999; Hobbs, 1997). They fear having to move, losing independence, and living in a medical environment. Many elderly people know someone who died shortly after being admitted to a long-term care facility, and this increases their fears and pessimism about life in such settings (Gallagher-Thompson & Thompson, 1995).

Many also worry about the cost of long-term care facilities. Families today are trying to keep elderly relatives at home longer, and so most older people enter nursing homes only in the last stages of a disease and in need of almost total care. Around-the-clock nursing care is expensive, and nursing home costs continue to rise. The health insurance plans available today do not even begin to cover the costs of long-term or permanent placement (Gallagher-Thompson & Thompson, 1995). Worry over these issues can significantly harm the mental health of older adults, perhaps leading to depression and anxiety as well as family conflict (Banerjee & Macdonald, 1996).

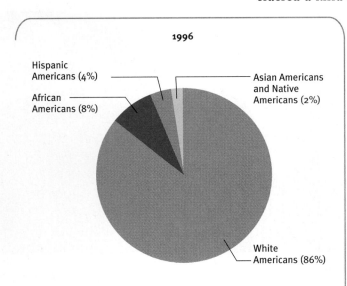

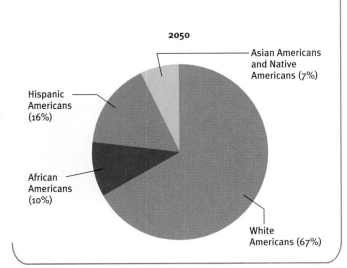

FIGURE 18-6 Ethnicity and old age *The elderly population is becoming racially and ethnically more diverse. In the United States today, 86 percent of all people over the age of 65 are white Americans. By 2050, only 67 percent of the elderly will be in this group. (Adapted from Hobbs, 1997; NIA, 1996.)*

Stimulating effects *When long-term-care institutions offer stimulating programs (such as this exercise class for people with Alzheimer's disease), allow patients to control their lives, and involve family members and friends, elderly persons are generally happier and show relatively better cognitive functioning.*

Finally, gerontologists suggest that the current generation of young adults should take a *health-maintenance,* or *wellness,* approach to their own aging process. In other words, they should do things that promote physical and mental health—avoid smoking, eat well-balanced and healthful meals, exercise regularly, and take advantage of psychoeducational, stress management, and other mental health programs. There is a growing belief that older adults will adapt more readily to changes and negative events if their physical and psychological health is reasonably good (Gallagher-Thompson & Thompson, 1995).

CROSSROADS:
Clinicians Discover the Young and the Elderly

Early in this century, mental health professionals virtually ignored children and the elderly. Today the problems of these groups have caught the attention of researchers and clinicians (Jellinek, 1999). Although all of the leading models have been used to help explain and treat these problems, the sociocultural perspective—especially the family perspective—is considered to play a special role.

Because both children and the elderly have limited control over their lives, they are particularly affected by the attitudes and reactions of family members. Clinicians must therefore deal with those attitudes and reactions as they try to address the problems of the young and the old. Treatments for conduct disorder, ADHD, mental retardation, and other problems of childhood typically fall short unless clinicians educate and work with the family as well. Similarly, clinicians who treat elderly patients with dementia are most successful when they also consider the concerns and needs of the family caregivers.

At the same time, clinicians who work with children, adolescents, and the elderly have learned that a narrow focus on any one model can lead to problems. For years autism was explained exclusively by family factors, misleading theorists and therapists alike, and adding to the pain of parents already devastated by their child's disorder. In the past, too, the sociocultural model often led professionals wrongly to accept the depression and anxiety of elderly people as inevitable, given the many losses suffered in old age.

The increased clinical focus on the young and the elderly has been accompanied by increased attention to their human and legal rights. More and more, clinicians have called on government agencies to protect the rights and safety of these sometimes powerless groups. In doing so, they hope to fuel the fight against child abuse and neglect, sexual abuse, malnourishment, and fetal alcohol syndrome, and to better address the health and financial needs of the elderly.

AGING AND RELIGION

On average, the death rate of elderly people who regularly attend religious services is 46 percent lower than the rate of those who attend infrequently (Koenig et al., 1999).

ConsiderThis
● Need aging lead to depression and other psychological problems? What kinds of attitudes, preparations, and activities might help an individual enter old age with peace of mind and even anticipation?

"What an amount of good nature and humor it takes to endure the gruesome business of growing old."

Sigmund Freud, 1937

As the mistreatment of young people receives greater attention and as the elderly population grows larger, the special needs of these groups are becoming more visible. Thus the study and treatment of their psychological problems are likely to continue at an rapid pace. Now that clinicians and public officials have "discovered" these populations, they are not likely to underestimate their needs and importance again.

SUMMARY AND REVIEW

■ **Disorders of childhood and old age** Certain psychological problems are particularly likely to emerge during childhood and old age. Such problems may be caused by the special pressures of those stages of life, by unique experiences, or by biological factors. *pp. 543-545*

■ **Disorders of childhood and adolescence** Emotional and behavioral problems are common in childhood and adolescence, but in addition, one-fifth of all children and adolescents in the United States experience a diagnosable psychological disorder. Anxiety disorders are particularly common among children. This group of problems includes adult-like disorders, such as social phobia and generalized anxiety disorder, and the unique childhood pattern of separation anxiety disorder, which is characterized by excessive anxiety, often panic, whenever a child is separated from a parent. Depression is found in 2 percent of all children under 17 years of age and in 7 percent of adolescents.

Children with disruptive behavior disorders exceed the normal breaking of rules and act very aggressively. In one such disorder, oppositional defiant disorder, they argue repeatedly with adults, lose their temper, and feel intense anger and resentment. In conduct disorder, a more severe pattern, they repeatedly violate the basic rights of others. Children with conduct disorders often are violent and cruel, and may lie, cheat, steal, and run away.

Children who display attention-deficit/hyperactivity disorder (ADHD) attend poorly to tasks or behave overactively and impulsively, or both. Ritalin and other stimulant drugs and behavioral programs are often effective treatments. Children with an elimination disorder—enuresis or encopresis—repeatedly urinate or pass feces in inappropriate places. The behavioral bell-and-battery technique is an effective treatment for enuresis. *pp. 545-558*

■ **Long-term disorders that begin in childhood** Autism and mental retardation are problems that emerge early and typically continue throughout a person's life. People with autism are extremely unresponsive to others, have poor communication skills (including echolalia and pronominal reversal), and behave in a very rigid and repetitive manner (displaying perseveration of sameness, strong attachments to objects, self-stimulatory behaviors, and self-injurious behaviors). The leading explanations of autism point to cognitive deficits, such as failure to develop a theory of mind, and biological abnormalities, such as abnormal development of the cerebellum, as causal factors. Although no treatment totally reverses the autistic pattern, significant help is available in the form of behavioral treatments, communication training, treatment and training for parents, and community integration.

People with mental retardation are significantly below average in intelligence and adaptive ability. Approximately one of every 100 people receives this diagnosis. Mild retardation, by far the most common level of mental retardation, has been linked primarily to environmental factors such as understimulation, inadequate parent-child interactions, and insufficient early learning experiences. Moderate, severe, and profound mental retardation are caused primarily by biological factors, although individuals who function at these levels are also enormously affected by their family and social environment. The leading biological causes are chromosomal abnormalities (as in Down syndrome), metabolic disorders that typically are caused by the pairing

ACADEMIC BATTLEFIELD

One of every ten students in the United States carried a weapon (such as a gun, knife, or club) to school within the past month (CDC, 1998).

of two defective recessive genes (for example, phenylketonuria, or PKU, and Tay-Sachs disease), disorders resulting from prenatal problems (cretinism and fetal alcohol syndrome), disorders resulting from birth complications, such as anoxia or extreme prematurity, and childhood disease and injuries.

Today intervention programs for people with mental retardation emphasize the importance of a comfortable and stimulating residence, either the family home or a small institution or group home that follows the principles of normalization. Other important interventions include proper education, therapy for psychological problems, and programs offering training in socializing, sex, marriage, parenting, and occupational skills. One of the most intense debates in the field of education centers on whether individuals with mental retardation profit more from special classes or from mainstreaming. Research has not consistently favored one approach over the other. *pp. 558–572*

■ **Disorders of later life** The problems of elderly people are often linked to the losses and other stresses and changes that accompany advancing age. As many as 50 percent of the elderly would benefit from mental health services, yet fewer than 20 percent receive them. Depression is the most common mental health problem among this age group. Older people may also suffer from generalized anxiety disorder, agoraphobia, or other anxiety disorders. In addition, between 4 and 6 percent exhibit alcohol-related problems in any given year, and many others misuse prescription drugs.

Older people are more likely than people of other age groups to experience delirium, a clouding of consciousness in which a person has great difficulty concentrating, focusing attention, and following an orderly sequence of thought. Dementia, a syndrome characterized by severe memory loss and other cognitive disturbances, becomes increasingly common in older age groups.

In studying and treating the problems of old age, clinicians have become concerned about three issues: the problems of elderly members of ethnic minority groups, inadequacies of long-term care, and the need for health maintenance by young adults. *pp. 573–577*

RESIDENTIAL SHIFT

Around 200,000 people with mental retardation lived in large state institutions in 1967, compared to 60,000 today (Lakin et al., 1999, 1996).

EYE OF THE BEHOLDER

People under the age of 30 were asked when "old" age begins. Their average answer was 67 years. The average answer given by people over the age of 60 was 77 years (*Roper Reports*, 1998).

CYBER STUDY

▲ *Observe the symptoms of ADHD in action.* ▲ *When do a child's behaviors call for a clinical diagnosis and treatment?* ▲ *Observe the educational mainstreaming of a young man with autism.* ▲ *Witness savant skills.* ▲ *Observe the symptoms and impact of dementia.*

SEARCH THE *ABNORMAL PSYCHOLOGY* CD-ROM FOR

▲ Chapter 18 video cases and discussions
  "Michael"—ADHD
  "Joseph"—Autism
  "George & Charles"—Savant Syndrome

▲ Chapter 18 practice test and feedback

▲ Additional video case and discussion
  "Walter"—Alzheimer's Disease

LOG ON TO THE COMER WEB PAGE

[www.worthpublishers.com/comerabnormalpsychology4e] **FOR**

▲ Suggested Web links, research exercises, FAQ page, additional Chapter 18 practice test questions

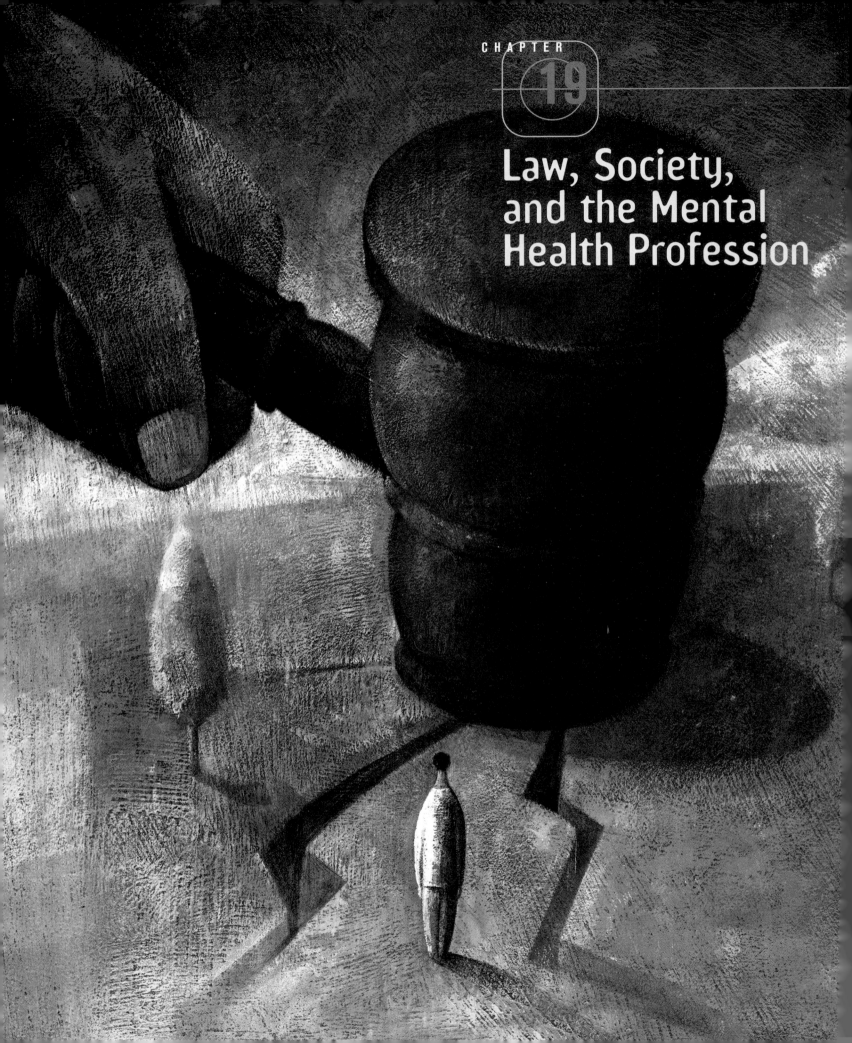

Law, Society, and the Mental Health Profession

Dear Jodie:

There is a definite possibility that I will be killed in my attempt to get Reagan. It is for this very reason that I am writing you this letter now. As you well know by now, I love you very much. The past seven months I have left you dozens of poems, letters and messages in the faint hope you would develop an interest in. . . . Jodie, I would abandon this idea of getting Reagan in a second if I could only win your heart and live out the rest of my life with you, whether it be in total obscurity or whatever. I will admit to you that the reason I'm going ahead with this attempt now is because I just cannot wait any longer to impress you. I've got to do something now to make you understand in no uncertain terms that I am doing all of this for your sake. By sacrificing my freedom and possibly my life I hope to change your mind about me. This letter is being written an hour before I leave for the Hilton Hotel. Jodie, I'm asking you please to look into your heart and at least give me the chance with this historical deed to gain your respect and love. I love you forever.

JOHN HINCKLEY

John W. Hinckley Jr. wrote this letter to the actress Jodie Foster in March 1981. Soon after writing it, he stood waiting, pistol ready, outside the Washington Hilton Hotel. Moments later, President Ronald Reagan came out of the hotel, and the popping of pistol fire was heard. As Secret Service men pushed Reagan into the limousine, a policeman and the president's press secretary fell to the pavement. The president had been shot, and by nightfall most of America had seen the face and heard the name of the disturbed young man from Colorado.

We have observed throughout this book that the psychological dysfunctioning of an individual does not occur in isolation. It is influenced—sometimes caused—by societal and social pressures, and it affects the lives of relatives, friends, and acquaintances. The case of John Hinckley demonstrates in powerful terms that individual dysfunction may, in some cases, also affect the well-being and rights of people the person does not know.

By the same token, clinical scientists and practitioners do not conduct their work in isolation. As they study and treat people with psychological problems, they are affecting and being affected by other institutions of society. We have seen, for example, how the government has regulated clinicians' use of electroconvulsive therapy, how clinicians have helped carry out the government's policy of deinstitutionalization, and how clinicians have called the psychological ordeal of Vietnam veterans to the attention of society.

In short, like their clients, clinical professionals operate within a complex social system, and in fact, it is the system that defines and regulates their professional responsibilities. Just as we must understand the social context in which abnormal behavior occurs in order to understand the behavior, so must we understand the context in which this behavior is studied and treated.

Two social institutions have a particularly strong impact on the mental health profession—the legislative and judicial systems. These institutions—

collectively, the legal field—have long been responsible for promoting and protecting both the public good and the rights of individuals. Sometimes the relationship between the legal field and the mental health field has been harmonious (Bersoff et al., 1997), and they have worked together to protect the rights and meet the needs of troubled individuals and of society at large. At other times, they have clashed, and one field has imposed its will on the other.

This relationship has two distinct aspects. On the one hand, mental health professionals often play a role in the criminal justice system, as when they are called upon to help the courts assess the mental stability of people accused of crimes, for example. They responded to this call in the Hinckley case, as we shall see, and in thousands of other cases. On the other hand, the legislative and judicial systems are responsible for regulating certain aspects of mental health care. The courts may, for example, force some individuals to enter treatment, even against their will. In addition, the law protects the rights of patients.

How Do Clinicians Influence the Criminal Justice System?

To be able to mete out just and appropriate punishments, the courts need to know whether defendants are *responsible* for the crimes they commit and *capable* of defending themselves in court. If not, it would be inappropriate to find individuals guilty or punish them in the usual manner. The courts have decided that in some instances people who suffer from severe *mental instability* may not be responsible for their actions or may not be able to defend themselves in court, and so should not be punished in the usual way. Although the courts make the final judgment as to mental instability, their decisions are guided to a large degree by the opinions of mental health professionals.

When people accused of crimes are judged to be mentally unstable, they are usually sent to a mental institution for treatment, a process called **criminal commitment**. Actually there are several forms of criminal commitment. In one, individuals are judged mentally unstable *at the time of their crimes* and so innocent of wrongdoing. They may plead **not guilty by reason of insanity** and bring mental health professionals into court to support their claim. When people are found not guilty on this basis, they are committed for treatment until they improve enough to be released.

In a second form of criminal commitment, individuals are judged mentally unstable *at the time of their trial* and so are considered unable to understand the trial procedures and defend themselves in court. They are committed for treatment until they are competent to stand trial. Once again, the testimony of mental health professionals helps determine the defendant's psychological functioning.

These judgments of mental instability have generated many arguments. Some people consider the judgments to be "loopholes" in the legal system that allow criminals to escape proper punishment for wrongdoing. Others argue that a legal system simply cannot be just unless it allows for extenuating circumstances, such as mental instability. The practice of criminal commitment differs from country to country. In this chapter we shall observe primarily how it operates in the United States. Although the specific principles and procedures of each country may differ, most countries grapple with the same issues, concerns, and decisions that we shall be examining.

Criminal Commitment and Insanity during Commission of a Crime

Consider once again the case of John Hinckley. Was he insane at the time he shot the president? If insane, should he be held responsible for his actions? On June 21, 1982, fifteen months after he shot four men in the nation's capital, a jury pronounced Hinckley not guilty by reason of insanity. Hinckley thus joined

CRIMINAL COMMITMENT A legal process by which people accused of a crime are instead judged mentally unstable and sent to a mental health facility for treatment.

NOT GUILTY BY REASON OF INSANITY (NGRI) A verdict stating that defendants are not guilty of committing a crime because they were insane at the time of the crime.

M'NAGHTEN TEST A widely used legal test for insanity which holds people to be insane at the time they committed a crime if, because of a mental disorder, they did not know the nature of the act or did not know right from wrong.

IRRESISTIBLE IMPULSE TEST A legal test for insanity that holds people to be insane at the time they committed a crime if they were driven to do so by an uncontrollable "fit of passion."

DURHAM TEST A legal test for insanity that holds people to be insane at the time they committed a crime if their act was the result of a mental disorder or defect.

AMERICAN LAW INSTITUTE TEST A legal test for insanity that holds people to be insane at the time they committed a crime if, because of a mental disorder, they did not know right from wrong or they could not resist an uncontrollable impulse to act.

Richard Lawrence, a house painter who shot at Andrew Jackson in 1835, and John Schrank, a saloonkeeper who shot former president Teddy Roosevelt in 1912, as a would-be assassin who was found not guilty by reason of insanity.

Although most Americans were shocked by the Hinckley verdict, those familiar with the insanity defense were not so surprised. In this case, as in other federal court cases at that time, the prosecution had the burden of proving that the defendant was sane beyond a reasonable doubt. Many state courts placed a similar responsibility on the prosecution. To present a clear-cut demonstration of sanity can be difficult, especially when the defendant has exhibited bizarre behavior in other areas of life. In fact, a few years later, Congress passed a law making it the defense's burden in federal cases to prove that defendants are insane, rather than the prosecution's burden to prove them sane. The majority of state legislatures have since followed suit (Steadman et al., 1993).

It is important to recognize that "insanity" is a *legal* term. That is, the definition of "insanity" used in criminal cases was written by legislators, not by clinicians. Defendants may have mental disorders but not necessarily qualify for a legal definition of insanity. Modern Western definitions of insanity can be traced to the murder case of Daniel M'Naghten in England in 1843. M'Naghten shot and killed Edward Drummond, the secretary to British Prime Minister Robert Peel, while trying to shoot Peel. Because of M'Naghten's apparent delusions of persecution, the jury found him to be not guilty by reason of insanity. The public was appalled by this decision, and their angry outcry forced the British law lords to define the insanity defense more clearly. This legal definition has come to be known as the **M'Naghten rule**:

> To establish a defense of insanity, it must be proved that at the time of committing the act, the party accused was laboring under such a defect of reason, from disease of the mind, as not to know the nature and quality of the act he was doing, or if he did know it, that he did not know he was doing what was wrong.

In essence, the M'Naghten test held that experiencing a mental disorder at the time of a crime does not by itself mean that the person was insane; the defendant also had to be *unable to know right from wrong*. The state and federal courts in the United States adopted this test as well.

In the late nineteenth century some state and federal courts in the United States, dissatisfied with the M'Naghten rule, adopted a different test—the **irresistible impulse test**. This test, which had first been used in Ohio in 1834, emphasized the inability to control one's actions. A person who committed a crime during an uncontrollable "fit of passion" was considered insane and not guilty under this test.

For years, state and federal courts chose between the M'Naghten test and the irresistible impulse test to determine the sanity of criminal defendants. For a while a third test, called the **Durham test**, also became popular, but it was soon replaced in most courts. This test, based on a decision handed down by the Supreme Court in 1954 in the case of *Durham v. United States,* stated simply that people are not criminally responsible if their "unlawful act was the product of mental disease or mental defect." This test was meant to offer more flexibility in court decisions, but it proved too flexible. Insanity defenses could point to such problems as alcoholism or other forms of substance dependence, and conceivably even headaches or ulcers, which were listed as psychophysiological disorders in DSM-I.

In 1955 the American Law Institute (ALI) formulated a test that combined aspects of the M'Naghten, irresistible impulse, and Durham tests. The **American Law Institute test** held that people are not criminally responsible if they had a

Would-be assassin *Few courtroom decisions have spurred as much debate or legislative action as the jury's verdict that John Hinckley, having been captured in the act of shooting President Ronald Reagan, was not guilty by reason of insanity.*

M'Naghten's Fate

After being judged not guilty by reason of insanity, Daniel M'Naghten lived in a mental hospital until his death twenty-two years later (Slovenko, 1995).

ConsiderThis

⚫ In some states, the defense must prove that a defendant was not guilty by reason of insanity, while in other states the prosecution must prove that a defendant making this plea was not insane. Which burden of proof is more appropriate?

"[John Hinckley suffers from] schizophrenia."

Expert defense witness, June 7, 1982

"Hinckley does not suffer from schizophrenia."

Expert prosecution witness, June 7, 1982

"[Hinckley had] a very severe depressive disorder."

Expert defense witness, May 20, 1982

"There is little to suggest he was seriously depressed [the day of the shootings]."

Expert prosecution witness, June 4, 1982

mental disorder or defect at the time of a crime that prevented them from knowing right from wrong *or* from being able to control themselves and to follow the law. The ALI test also established that repeated criminal or antisocial behavior itself could not be cited to demonstrate mental disease or "irresistable impulse." There had to be independent indicators of mental instability.

For a time the new test became the most widely accepted legal test of insanity. After the Hinckley verdict, however, there was a public uproar over the "liberal" ALI guidelines, and people called for tougher standards. Partly in response to this uproar, the American Psychiatric Association recommended in 1983 that people should be found not guilty by reason of insanity *only if* they did not know right from wrong at the time of the crime; an inability to control themselves and to follow the law should no longer be sufficient grounds for a judgment of insanity. In short, the association was calling for a return to the M'Naghten standard. This test now is used in all cases tried in federal courts and in about half of the state courts (Steadman et al., 1993). The more liberal ALI standard is still used in the remaining state courts, except in Idaho, Montana, and Utah, which have done away with the insanity plea altogether. Research has not found, however, that the stricter M'Naghten definition actually reduces the likelihood of verdicts of not guilty by reason of insanity (Ogloff et al., 1992; Finkel, 1991, 1990, 1989).

People suffering from severe mental disorders in which confusion is a major feature may not be able to tell right from wrong or to control their behavior (Nestor & Haycock, 1997; Elliott, 1996). It is therefore not surprising that approximately two-thirds of defendants who are acquitted of a crime by reason of insanity qualify for a diagnosis of schizophrenia (Steadman et al., 1993). The vast majority of these acquitted defendants have a history of past hospitalization, arrest, or both. About half who successfully plead insanity are white, and 86 percent are male. Their mean age is 32 years. The crimes for which defendants are found not guilty by reason of insanity vary greatly. However, approximately 65 percent are violent crimes of some sort (Steadman et al., 1993). Close to 15 percent of those acquitted are accused specifically of murder (see Figure 19-1 and Box 19-1).

WHAT CONCERNS ARE RAISED BY THE INSANITY DEFENSE? Despite the changes in the insanity tests, criticism of the insanity defense continues (Slovenko, 1995). One concern is the fundamental difference between the law and the science of human behavior. The law assumes that individuals have free will and are generally responsible for their actions. Several models of human behavior, in contrast, assume that physical or psychological forces act to determine the individual's behavior (Winslade, 1983). Inevitably, then, legal definitions of insanity and responsibility will differ from those suggested by clinical research.

A second criticism pertains to the uncertainty of scientific knowledge about abnormal behavior. During a typical insanity defense trial, the testimony of defense clinicians conflicts with that of clinicians hired by the prosecution, requiring the jury to weigh the claims of "experts" who disagree in their assessments. Some people see this lack of professional agreement as evidence that the state of clinical knowledge in some areas may be too incomplete to be allowed to influence important legal proceedings (Golding et al., 1999; Slovenko, 1995; Szasz, 1963). Others counter that the field has made great strides—for example, developing several psychological scales to help clinicians discriminate more consistently between the sane and insane as defined by the M'Naghten standard (Rogers & Shuman, 2000; Rogers & Sewell, 1999). In addition, the Council on Psychiatry and the Law (1992) has recommended a system of peer review, to ensure that clinicians consulted in legal cases adhere to professional standards.

Even with helpful scales in hand, however, clinicians making judgments of legal insanity face a problem that is difficult to overcome: they must evaluate the

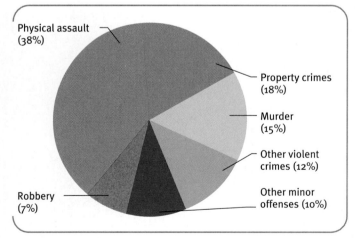

Physical assault (38%)

Property crimes (18%)

Murder (15%)

Other violent crimes (12%)

Other minor offenses (10%)

Robbery (7%)

FIGURE 19-1 **Crimes for which persons are found not guilty by reason of insanity (NGRI)** *A review of NGRI verdicts in eight states revealed that most people who were acquitted on this basis had been charged with a crime of violence. (Based on Steadman et al., 1993; Callahan et al., 1991.)*

BOX 19-1

Famous Insanity Defense Cases

1977 In Michigan, Francine Hughes poured gasoline around the bed where her husband, Mickey, lay in a drunken stupor. Then she lit a match and set him on fire. At her trial she explained that he had beaten her repeatedly for 14 years, and he had threatened to kill her if she tried to leave him. The jury found her not guilty by reason of temporary insanity, making her into a symbol for many abused women across the nation. Some people saw the decision as confirmation of a woman's right to self-defense in her own home.

1978 David "Son of Sam" Berkowitz, a serial killer in New York City, explained that a barking dog had sent him demonic messages to kill. Although two psychiatrists assessed him as psychotic, he was found guilty of his crimes. Long after his trial, he said that he had actually made up the delusions.

1979 Kenneth Bianchi, one of the pair known as the Hillside Stranglers, entered a plea of not guilty by reason of insanity but was found guilty along with his cousin of sexually assaulting and murdering women in the Los Angeles area in late 1977 and early 1978. He claimed that he had multiple personality disorder.

1980 In December, Mark David Chapman murdered John Lennon. Chapman later explained that he had killed the rock music legend because he believed Lennon to be a "sell-out." He also described hearing the voice of God, considered himself his generation's "catcher in the rye" (from the J. D. Salinger novel), and compared himself to Moses. Despite clinical testimony that supported Chapman's plea of not guilty by reason of insanity, he was ultimately convicted of murder.

1981 In an attempt to prove his love for the actress Jodie Foster, John Hinckley, Jr., tried to assassinate President Ronald Reagan. Hinckley was found not guilty by reason of insanity and was committed to St. Elizabeths Hospital for the criminally insane in Washington, where he remains today.

1992 Jeffrey Dahmer, a 31-year-old mass murderer in Milwaukee, was tried for the killings of 15 young men. Dahmer apparently drugged some of his victims and performed crude lobotomies on them in an attempt to create zombielike companions for himself. He also dismembered his victims' bodies and stored their parts to be eaten. Although his defense attorney argued that Dahmer was not guilty by reason of insanity, the jury found him guilty as charged. He was beaten to death by another inmate in 1995.

1994 On June 23, 1993, 24-year-old Lorena Bobbitt cut off her husband's penis with a 12-inch kitchen knife while he slept. During her trial, defense attorneys argued that after years of abuse by John Bobbitt, his wife suffered a brief psychotic episode and was seized by an "irresistible impulse" to cut off his penis after he came home drunk and raped her. In 1994, the jury acquitted her of the charge of malicious wounding by reason of temporary insanity. She was committed to a state mental hospital for further assessment and treatment and released a few months later.

1997 John E. Du Pont, 57-year-old heir to his family's chemical fortune, shot and killed the Olympic wrestling champion Dave Schultz in January 1995. The murder took place on Du Pont's 800-acre estate, where he had built a sports center for amateur athletes. Schultz, his close friend, had coached wrestlers at the center. In 1997 Du Pont was found guilty of third-degree murder, but mentally ill, and he was sentenced to prison for 13 to 30 years. He is currently receiving treatment at the mental health unit of a correctional institution.

Guilty and not insane *Theodore Kaczynski, the so-called Unabomber who sent mail bombs to unsuspecting victims for 18 years, refused all legal efforts to have himself judged mentally incompetent to stand trial or not guilty by reason of insanity. Preferring a conviction for murder to a label of insanity, he pleaded guilty in a federal court in 1998 and is now serving a life sentence without parole.*

Legal experts *Each segment of the clinical field has its own "forensic" specialists who represent it in the courts and houses of legislature. Forensic psychologists, psychiatrists, and social workers typically receive special training in such duties as evaluating the functioning of criminal defendants, making recommendations concerning patients' rights, and assessing the psychological trauma experienced by crime victims (Ladds, 1997).*

ConsiderThis

🔘 After a patient has been criminally committed to an institution, why might a clinician be reluctant to declare that the person is mentally stable and unlikely to commit the same crime again, even if the patient shows significant improvement?

GUILTY BUT MENTALLY ILL A verdict stating that defendants are guilty of committing a crime, but are also suffering from a mental illness that should be treated during their imprisonment.

state of mind a defendant was in during an event that occurred weeks, months, or years earlier. Because mental states can and do change over time and across situations, clinicians can never be entirely certain that their assessments of mental instability at the time of the crime are accurate.

Perhaps the criticism of the insanity defense most often heard is that it allows dangerous criminals to escape punishment. Granted, some people who successfully plead insanity are released from treatment facilities just months after their acquittal. Yet the number of such cases is quite small. According to surveys, the public dramatically overestimates the percentage of defendants who plead insanity, guessing it to be 30 to 40 percent, when in fact it is less than 1 percent (Steadman et al., 1993). Moreover, only a minority of these fake or exaggerate their psychological symptoms (Fauteck, 1995), and only one-quarter of defendants who plead insanity are actually found not guilty on this basis (Callahan et al., 1991). In the end, less than 1 of every 400 defendants in the United States is found not guilty by reason of insanity.

During most of U.S. history, a successful insanity plea achieved the equivalent of a long-term prison sentence (Callahan & Silver, 1998). Treatment in a mental hospital often amounted to a longer sentence than a verdict of guilty would have brought (Lymburner & Roesch, 1999; Ogloff et al., 1992). Because hospitalization resulted in little, if any, improvement, clinicians were reluctant to predict that the offenders would not repeat their crimes. Moreover, tragic cases would occasionally call into question clinicians' ability to make such judgments and to predict dangerousness. In Idaho, for example, a young man raped two women and was found not guilty by reason of insanity. He was released after less than a year of treatment, shot a nurse, and this time was convicted of assault with intent to kill. The uproar over this 1981 case led the Idaho state legislature to abolish the insanity plea.

Today, however, offenders are being released from mental hospitals earlier and earlier. This trend is the result of the increasing effectiveness of drug therapy in institutions, the growing reaction against extended institutionalization, and a greater emphasis on patients' rights (Blackburn, 1993). In 1992, in the case of *Foucha v. Louisiana*, the U.S. Supreme Court clarified that the *only* acceptable basis for determining the release of hospitalized offenders is whether or not they are still "insane"; they cannot be kept indefinitely in mental hospitals solely because they are dangerous. Some states maintain control of offenders even after their release from hospitals (Hilday, 1999). The states may insist on community treatment, monitor the patients closely, and rehospitalize them if necessary.

WHAT OTHER VERDICTS ARE AVAILABLE? In recent years 13 states have added another verdict option—**guilty but mentally ill** (Slovenko, 1995). Defendants who receive this verdict are found to have had a mental illness at the time of their crimes, but the illness was not fully related to or responsible for the crime. The guilty-but-mentally-ill option enables jurors to convict a person they view as dangerous while also suggesting that the individual receive needed treatment. Defendants found to be guilty but mentally ill are given a prison term with the added recommendation that they also undergo treatment if necessary.

In Georgia, juries given the option of finding a person guilty but mentally ill have delivered fewer insanity acquittals (Callahan et al., 1992). Studies with mock juries have found that many jurors prefer having this third option, seeing it as "moral, just and an adequate means of providing for the treatment needs of mentally ill offenders" (Boudouris, 2000; Roberts, Golding, & Fincham, 1987). However, those who criticize this option point out that appropriate mental health care is supposed to be available to all prisoners anyway, regardless of the verdict.

Justice served? *Mass protests took place in San Francisco after Dan White was convicted of voluntary manslaughter rather than premeditated murder in the killings of Mayor George Moscone and Supervisor Harvey Milk, one of the nation's leading gay activists. For many, the 1979 verdict highlighted the serious pitfalls of the "diminished capacity" defense.*

They argue that the new option differs from a guilty verdict in name only (Slovenko, 1995; Tanay, 1992). Critics also argue that the option may confuse jurors already faced with an enormously complex task (APA, 1983; Morris, 1983).

Some states allow still another kind of defense, *guilty with diminished capacity*. Here a defendant's mental dysfunctioning is viewed as an extenuating circumstance that the court should take into consideration when determining the precise crime of which he or she is guilty (Clark, 1999). The defense lawyer argues that because of mental dysfunctioning, the defendant could not have *intended* to commit a particular crime. The person can then be found guilty of a lesser crime—of manslaughter (unlawful killing without intent), say, instead of murder in the first degree (planned murder). The case of Dan White, who shot and killed Mayor George Moscone and City Supervisor Harvey Milk of San Francisco in 1978, illustrates the use of this verdict.

> On the morning of November 27, 1978, Dan White loaded his .38 caliber revolver. White had recently resigned his position as a San Francisco supervisor because of family and financial pressures. Now, after a change of heart, he wanted his job back. When he asked Mayor George Moscone to reappoint him, however, the mayor refused. Supervisor Harvey Milk was among those who had urged Moscone to keep White out, for Milk was America's first openly gay politician, and Dan White had been an outspoken opponent of measures supporting gay rights.
>
> White avoided the metal detector at City Hall's main entrance by climbing through a basement window after telling construction workers who recognized him that he had forgotten his keys. After they unlocked the window for him, he went straight to the mayor's office. . . . White pulled out his gun and shot the mayor once in the arm and once in the chest. As Moscone lay bleeding on the floor, White walked over to him and, from only inches away, fired twice into Moscone's head.
>
> White then reloaded his gun, ran down the hall, and spotted Harvey Milk. White asked to talk with him. Right after the two men went into White's former office, three more shots rang out. Milk crumpled to the floor. Once again White from point-blank range fired two more bullets into his victim's head. Shortly afterward he turned himself in to the police. Several months later the jury rendered its verdict: Dan White was not guilty of murder, only voluntary manslaughter.

"I feel the insanity defense should be retained. I bear no grudge against John Hinckley, but I sure don't hope he wins the Irish Sweepstakes."

James Brady, presidential news secretary shot by John Hinckley

Murder is the illegal killing of a human being with malice aforethought, that is, with the intent to kill. Manslaughter is the illegal killing of a human being without malice aforethought. The attacker may intend to harm the victim, but not to kill. If the victim nonetheless dies, the crime is voluntary manslaughter. Involuntary manslaughter is an illegal killing from negligence rather than intentional harm. . . .

. . . Defense attorney Douglas Schmidt argued that a patriotic, civic-minded man like Dan White—high school athlete, decorated war veteran, former fireman, policeman, and city supervisor—could not possibly have committed such an act unless something had snapped inside him. The brutal nature of the two final shots to each man's head only proved that White had lost his wits. White was not fully responsible for his actions because he suffered from "diminished capacity." Although White killed Mayor George Moscone and Supervisor Harvey Milk, he had not planned his actions. On the day of the shootings, White was mentally incapable of planning to kill, or even of wanting to do such a thing.

Well known in forensic psychiatry circles, Martin Blinder, professor of law and psychiatry at the University of California's Hastings Law School in San Francisco, brought a good measure of academic prestige to White's defense. White had been, Blinder explained to the jury, "gorging himself on junk food: Twinkies, Coca-Cola. . . . The more he consumed, the worse he'd feel and he'd respond to his ever-growing depression by consuming ever more junk food." Schmidt later asked Blinder if he could elaborate on this. "Perhaps if it were not for the ingestion of this junk food," Blinder responded, "I would suspect that these homicides would not have taken place." From that moment on, Blinder became known as the author of the Twinkie defense. . . .

Dan White was convicted only of voluntary manslaughter, and was sentenced to seven years, eight months. (He was released on parole January 6, 1984.) Psychiatric testimony convinced the jury that White did not wish to kill George Moscone or Harvey Milk.

The angry crowd that responded to the verdict by marching, shouting, trashing City Hall, and burning police cars was in good part homosexual. Gay supervisor Harvey Milk had worked well for their cause, and his loss was a serious setback for human rights in San Francisco. Yet it was not only members of the gay community who were appalled at the outcome. Most San Franciscans shared their feelings of outrage.

(Coleman, 1984, pp. 65–70)

DAN WHITE: THE AFTERMATH
Dan White was released from prison in 1984 and spent a year on parole. He committed suicide in 1985.

Because of possible miscarriages of justice, many legal experts have argued against the "diminished capacity" defense (Slovenko, 1992; Coleman, 1984), and a number of states have eliminated it. Some studies find, however, that jurors are often capable of using the option in careful and appropriate ways (Finkel & Duff, 1989; Finkel et al., 1985).

WHAT ARE SEX OFFENDER STATUTES? Since 1937, when Michigan passed the first "sex psychopath" law, some states have placed sex offenders in a special legal category (Bumby & Maddox, 1999; Monahan & Davis, 1983). These states believe that people who are repeatedly found guilty of certain sex crimes have a mental disorder, and so the states categorize them as *mentally disordered sex offenders*.

People classified in this way have been convicted of a criminal offense and are thus judged to be responsible for their actions. Nevertheless, like people found not guilty by reason of insanity, mentally disordered sex offenders are committed to a mental health facility (Small, 1992). In part, such laws reflect a belief held by some legislators that sex offenders are psychologically disturbed. On a practical level, the laws help protect sex offenders from the physical abuse that they often receive in prison society.

Over the last two decades, a growing number of states have been changing or abolishing these sex-offender laws. There are several reasons for this trend. First, some states have found the laws difficult to apply. Some state laws, for example,

MENTAL INCOMPETENCE A state of mental instability that leaves defendants unable to understand the legal charges and proceedings they are facing and unable to prepare an adequate defense with their attorney.

require that the offender be found "sexually dangerous beyond a reasonable doubt"—a judgment that is often beyond the reach of the clinical field's expertise (Szasz, 1991). Furthermore, there is evidence that racial bias can significantly affect the use of the sex-offender classification (Sturgeon & Taylor, 1980). White Americans are twice as likely to be granted sex-offender status as African Americans or Hispanic Americans who have been convicted of similar crimes.

Criminal Commitment and Incompetence to Stand Trial

Regardless of their state of mind at the time of a crime, defendants may be judged to be **mentally incompetent** to stand trial. The competence requirement is meant to ensure that defendants understand the charges they are facing and can work with their lawyers to prepare and conduct an adequate defense (Gutheil, 1999; Roesch et al., 1999). This minimum standard of competence was specified by the Supreme Court in the case of *Dusky v. United States* (1960).

The issue of competence is most often raised by the defendant's attorney, although prosecutors, arresting police officers, and even the judge may raise it as well (Meyer, 1992). They prefer to err on the side of caution, because some convictions have been reversed on appeal when a defendant's competence was not established at the beginning. When the issue of competence is raised, the judge orders a psychological evaluation, usually on an inpatient basis. Approximately 20 percent of defendants who receive such an evaluation are in fact found to be incompetent to stand trial (Hiday, 1999). If the court decides that the defendant is incompetent, the person is assigned to a mental health facility until competent to stand trial (Bennett & Kish, 1990).

Many more cases of criminal commitment result from decisions of mental incompetence than from verdicts of not guilty by reason of insanity (Roesch et al., 1999). However, the majority of criminals currently institutionalized for psychological treatment in the United States are not from either of these two groups. Rather, they are convicted inmates whose psychological problems have led prison officials to decide they need treatment—either in mental health units within the prison or in mental hospitals (Monahan & Steadman, 1983; Steadman et al., 1982).

It is possible that an innocent defendant, ruled incompetent to stand trial, could spend years in a mental health facility with no opportunity to disprove the criminal accusations. Some defendants have, in fact, served longer "sentences" in mental health facilities awaiting a ruling of competence than they would have

ASSESSING COMPETENCE

Each year in the United States an estimated 25,000 defendants are assessed for their mental competence to stand trial (Winick, 1995).

Population unserved *The majority of people who receive treatment under criminal commitment procedures are inmates who develop psychological problems while they are in prison, not defendants who are found not guilty by reason of insanity or deemed mentally incompetent to stand trial. Given the overcrowded and unsafe conditions in most prisons, the prevalence of psychological problems among prisoners is extraordinarily high, and only a fraction of those who need treatment are afforded mental health services.*

served in prison had they been convicted (Meyer, 1992). Such a possibility was reduced when the Supreme Court ruled, in the case of *Jackson v. Indiana* (1972), that an incompetent defendant cannot be indefinitely committed. After a reasonable amount of time, he or she should either be found competent and tried, set free, or transferred to a mental health facility under *civil* commitment procedures.

Until the early 1970s, most states required the commitment of mentally incompetent defendants to maximum-security institutions for the "criminally insane" (Winick, 1983). Under current law, the courts have greater flexibility. In some cases, particularly when the charge is a minor one, the defendant may even be treated on an outpatient basis.

How Do the Legislative and Judicial Systems Influence Mental Health Care?

Just as clinical science and practice have influenced the legal system, so has the legal system had a major impact on clinical practice. First, courts and legislatures have developed the process of **civil commitment**, which allows certain people to be forced into mental health treatment. Although many people who show signs of mental disturbance seek treatment voluntarily, a large number are not aware of their problems or are simply not interested in undergoing therapy. What are clinicians to do for these people? Should they force treatment upon them? Or do people have the right to feel miserable and function ineffectively? The law has answered this question by developing civil commitment guidelines under which certain people can be required to submit to treatment.

Second, the legal system, on behalf of the state, has taken on the responsibility for protecting patients' rights during treatment. This protection extends not only to patients who have been involuntarily committed but also to those who seek treatment voluntarily, even on an outpatient basis.

Civil Commitment

Every year in the United States large numbers of people with mental disorders are involuntarily committed to mental institutions. These civil commitments have long caused controversy and debate. In some ways the law provides greater protection for suspected criminals than for people suspected of psychosis (Burton, 1990).

WHY COMMIT? Generally our legal system permits involuntary commitment of individuals when they are considered to be *in need of treatment* and *dangerous to themselves or others*. People may be dangerous to themselves if they are suicidal or if they act recklessly (for example, drinking Drano to prove that they are immune to such a poison). They may be dangerous to others if they seek to harm them or if they unintentionally place others at risk. The state's authority to commit disturbed individuals rests on its duties to protect the interests of the individual and of society: the principles of *parens patriae* and police power (Wettstein, 1988). Under *parens patriae* ("parent of the country"), the state can make decisions that promote the patient's best interests and provide protection from self-harm, including the decision to impose hospitalization. Conversely, *police power* allows the state to take steps to protect society from a person who is violent or otherwise dangerous (see Box 19-2).

WHAT ARE THE PROCEDURES FOR CIVIL COMMITMENT? Civil commitment laws vary from state to state. Some basic procedures, however, are common to most of these laws.

Often, family members begin commitment proceedings. In response to a son's psychotic behavior and repeated assaults on other people, for example, his

> "When a man says that he is Jesus or Napoleon . . . he is labeled psychotic and locked up in the madhouse. Freedom of speech is only for normal people."
>
> Thomas S. Szasz, *The Second Sin*

CIVIL COMMITMENT A legal process by which an individual can be forced to undergo mental health treatment.

BOX 19-2

Serial Murderers: Madness or Badness?

I A shy, brilliant boy, he skipped two grades in school and entered Harvard at age 16. He went on to receive a Ph.D. in mathematics from the University of Michigan in 1967. Securing a highly prestigious position at the University of California, Berkeley, he seemed destined for fame and success. But . . . two years into his stint at Berkeley, he decided to drop out of society—opting instead for a grubby . . . existence in rural Montana.

It was here, alone in a 10-foot-by-12-foot shack, that this reclusive eccentric produced his most renowned works: sixteen bombs, three deaths, twenty-three maimings, several taunting letters to *The New York Times*, and a 35,000-word antitechnology manifesto. By the end of his eighteen-year rampage, "Unabomber"—his FBI code name—had become a household word. On April 3, 1996, federal agents raided Theodore Kaczynski's Montana cabin, and his reign of mail bomb terror, which had captured the attention of a nation, was finally put to an end. I

(DUFFY, 1996; THOMAS, 1996)

Theodore Kaczynski has joined a growing list of serial killers who have fascinated and horrified Americans over the years: Ted Bundy, David Berkowitz ("Son of Sam"), Albert DeSalvo, John Wayne Gacy, Jeffrey Dahmer. Serial murderers seem to kill for the sheer thrill of the experience. Clinical theorists do not yet understand these individuals, but they are beginning to use the information that has been gathered about them to speculate on the psychology behind their violence.

Although each follows his own pattern, serial killers appear to have some characteristics in common. Most are white males between 25 and 34 years old, of average to high intelligence, generally clean-cut, smooth-talking, attractive, and skillful manipulators. For the most part, these men have no permanent ties to any community and move from place to place in pursuit of the kill. They typically select their victims carefully. Many are fascinated by police work and the popular media and follow their crimes closely in the news (Ressler & Schactman, 1992; Holmes & DeBurger, 1985).

Many serial killers have mental disorders, but they do not typically fit the legal criteria of insanity (Fox & Levin, 1999). Park Dietz, a psychiatrist and highly regarded expert on the subject, offers this explanation:

I None of the serial killers I've had the occasion to study or examine has been legally insane, but none has been normal, either. They've all been people who've got mental disorders. But despite their mental disorders, which have to do with their sexual interests and their character, they've been people who knew what they were doing, knew what they were doing was wrong, but chose to do it anyway. I

(DOUGLAS, 1996, PP. 344–345)

As a result, the plea of not guilty by reason of insanity is generally unsuccessful for serial killers. This outcome may also be influenced by the concern of communities that a defendant found not guilty by reason of insanity may be released too quickly (Gresham, 1993).

Richard Chase, a serial murderer who believed that he needed to drink human blood to stop his own from turning to powder, is one of the few serial killers who are clearly psychotic (Ressler & Schactman, 1992). More often, serial killers seem to display severe *personality disorders* (Scarf, 1996). Lack of conscience and an utter disregard for people and the rules of society—key features of antisocial personality disorder—are typical. Narcissistic thinking is quite common as well. The feeling of being special may even give the killer an unrealistic belief that he will not get caught (Scarf, 1996). Often it is this sense of invincibility that leads to his capture.

Sexual dysfunction and fantasy also seem to play a part (Ressler & Schactman, 1992). Studies have found that vivid fantasies, often sexual and sadistic, may help drive the killer's behavior (Lachmann & Lachmann, 1995; Ressler & Schactman, 1992). Some clinicians also believe that the killers may be trying to overcome general feelings of powerlessness by controlling, hurting, or eliminating those who are momentarily weaker (Fox & Levin, 1999; Levin & Fox, 1985). Studies show that the majority of serial killers were abused as children—physically, sexually, and emotionally (Ressler & Schactman, 1992).

Despite such profiles and suspicions, clinical theorists do not yet understand why serial killers behave as they do. Thus, most agree with Dietz when he asserts, "It's hard to imagine any circumstance under which they should be released to the public again" (Douglas, 1996, p. 349).

This 1994 artist's sketch of the Unabomber has become a powerful symbol of serial murder and terror.

parents may try to persuade him to seek admission to a mental institution. If the son refuses, the parents may go to court and seek an involuntary commitment order. If the son is a minor, the process is simple. The Supreme Court, in the case of *Parham v. J. R.* (1979), ruled that a hearing is not necessary in such cases, as long as a mental health professional considers commitment necessary. If the son is an adult, however, the process is more involved. The court will usually order a mental examination and allow the person to contest the commitment in court, often represented by a lawyer (Holstein, 1993).

Although the Supreme Court has provided few guidelines concerning specific procedures of civil commitment, one important decision, in the case of *Addington v. Texas* (1979), outlined the *minimum standard of proof* needed for commitment. Here the Court ruled that before an individual can be committed, there must be "clear and convincing" proof that he or she is mentally ill and has met the state's criteria for involuntary commitment. The ruling does not suggest what criteria should be used. That matter is still left to each state. But, whatever the state's criteria, clinicians must offer clear and convincing proof that the individual meets those criteria. When is proof clear and convincing, according to the Court? When it provides 75 percent certainty that the criteria of commitment have been met. This is far less than the near-total certainty ("beyond a reasonable doubt") required to convict people of committing a crime.

EMERGENCY COMMITMENT Many situations require immediate action; no one can wait for commitment proceedings when a life is at stake. Consider, for example, an emergency room patient who is suicidal or hearing voices demanding hostile actions against others. He or she may need immediate treatment and round-the-clock supervision. If treatment could not be given in such situations without the patient's full consent, the consequences could be tragic (Currier, 1999).

Therefore, many states give clinicians the right to certify that certain patients need temporary commitment and medication. In past years, these states required certification by two *physicians* (not necessarily psychiatrists in some of the states). Today states may allow certification by nonphysician mental health professionals as well. The clinicians must declare that the state of mind of the patients makes them dangerous to themselves or others. By tradition, the certifications are often referred to as *two-physician certificates,* or "*2 PCs.*" The length of such emergency commitments varies from state to state, but three days is often the limit (Holstein, 1993). Should clinicians come to believe that a longer stay is necessary, formal commitment proceedings may be initiated during the period of emergency commitment.

WHO IS DANGEROUS? In the past, people with mental disorders were actually less likely than others to commit violent or dangerous acts (see Box 19-3). This low rate of violence was apparently related to the fact that so many such individuals lived in institutions. As a result of deinstitutionalization, however, hundreds of thousands of people with severe disturbances now live in the community and receive little, if any, treatment. Some of these individuals are indeed dangerous to themselves or others (Hiday, 1999).

Although approximately 90 percent of people with mental disorders are in no way violent or dangerous (Swanson et al., 1990), studies now suggest at least a small relationship between severe mental disorders and violent behavior (Taylor et al., 1998; Hodgins et al., 1996). After reviewing a number of studies, John Monahan (1993, 1992), a law and psychology professor, concluded that the rate of violent behavior among persons with severe mental disorders, particularly psychotic disorders, is at least somewhat higher than that of people without such disorders:

- Approximately 15 percent of patients in mental hospitals have assaulted another person prior to admission.

INVOLUNTARY COMMUNITY TREATMENT

Thirty-seven states and Washington, D.C., now have involuntary-outpatient laws, in which outpatients who are considered dangerous can be institutionalized if they fail to keep regular outpatient appointments and take their medications (Warner, 1999). Few of the states, however, impose the laws very often.

- Around 25 percent of patients in mental hospitals assault another person during hospitalization.

- Approximately 12 percent of all people with schizophrenia, major depression, or bipolar disorder have assaulted other people, compared with 2 percent of persons without a mental disorder. Between 25 and 35 percent of people who display a substance-related disorder have assaulted others.

- Approximately 4 percent of people who report having been violent during the past year suffer from schizophrenia, whereas 1 percent of nonviolent persons suffer from schizophrenia.

Monahan cautions that the findings do not suggest that people with mental disorders are generally dangerous. Nor do they justify the "caricature of the mentally disordered" that is often portrayed by the media, the "shunning of former patients by employers and neighbors," or the "lock 'em up" laws proposed by some politicians. But they do indicate that a severe mental disorder may be more of a risk factor for violence than mental health experts have generally believed.

A judgment of *dangerousness* is often required for involuntary civil commitment. But can mental health professionals accurately predict who will commit violent acts? Research suggests that psychiatrists and psychologists are wrong more often than right when they make *long-term* predictions of violence (Buchanan, 1999, 1997; Limandri & Sheridan, 1995). Most often they overestimate the likelihood that a patient will eventually be violent. On the other hand, studies suggest that *short-term* predictions—that is, predictions of imminent violence—can be more accurate (Binder, 1999; McNiel & Binder, 1991). Researchers are now working, with some success, to develop new assessment techniques that use statistical approaches and are more objective in their long-term and short-term predictions of dangerousness than the subjective judgments of clinicians (Cunningham & Reidy, 1999; Duggan, 1997; Borum, 1996).

SUBSTANCE USE MAY BE THE KEY

A large study of patients discharged from mental hospitals within the previous year found that only 5 percent of those who remained on medication and stayed away from drugs and alcohol committed violent acts, the same percentage as nonpatients who lived in the same neighborhood. In contrast, 10 percent of patients who used drugs or alcohol committed violent acts after discharge from the hospital (Steadman et al., 1998).

BOX 19-3

The Violence of Mice and Men and Women

Is the tendency to be violent inherited? Fascinating evidence comes from the laboratories of Johns Hopkins University. Scientists investigating the role of *nitric oxide* in the brain damage suffered by stroke victims created mice who lacked the gene necessary to produce this neurotransmitter (Nelson et al., 1995). The unexpected result: male mice who lacked nitric oxide became violent rapists and mouse murderers. The "monster mice," as they were nicknamed, attacked, bit, wrestled, and chased other mice. Female mice were not affected by a lack of nitric oxide. The researchers theorized that nitric oxide probably plays a key role in the regulation of male aggressive behavior.

Consider This

⊙ If it turns out that gene abnormalities leave some humans prone to violent acts, should those people be held responsible for their criminal acts the same as other people are? • If abnormal genes found in humans were clearly linked to aggression, could people with these genes be forced into treatment under the present standards of civil commitment?

"GO RIGHT AHEAD. I KNOW YOU'RE BRED TO BE MEAN AND VICIOUS, JUST AS I'm BRED TO BE ALTRUISTIC."

(© 1992 Sidney Harris, *American Scientist* magazine)

Failure to predict *The 1990s witnessed the growth of a new form of dangerousness—children and adolescents who shoot family members, schoolmates, and teachers. A school-cafeteria surveillance camera captures Dylan Klebold and Eric Harris in the midst of their killing rampage at Columbine High School in Littleton, Colorado, on April 20, 1999. Earlier videos made by the two boys suggest that they had planned their attack for more than a year. Despite building a violent Web site, threatening other students, having problems with the law, and, in the case of one boy, receiving treatment for mental health problems, professionals were not able to predict or prevent their violent behavior.*

"This is how we live [in Russia]: without any arrest warrant or any medical justification four policemen and two doctors come to a healthy man's house. The doctors declare that he is crazy, the police Major shouts: 'We are an Organ of Coercion! Get up!' They twist his arms and drive him off to the mad house."

Aleksandr Solzhenitsyn, Russian
novelist and political dissident, 1971

WHAT ARE THE PROBLEMS WITH CIVIL COMMITMENT? Civil commitment has been criticized on several grounds. Foremost is the difficulty of assessing a person's dangerousness. If judgments of dangerousness are often inaccurate, how can one justify their being used to deprive people of liberty (Ennis & Emory, 1978)? Second, the legal definitions of "mental illness" and "dangerousness" are vague. The terms may be defined so broadly that they could be applied to almost anyone the evaluators view as undesirable. Indeed, it is not unheard of for mental illness to be imputed to people whose primary offenses were bouncing checks, spending "too much" money, living unconventional lives, or holding unpopular political opinions (Wexler, 1983) (see Box 19-4). Indeed, many civil libertarians worry about involuntary commitment being used to control people, as it has been in the former Soviet Union and certain other countries where mental hospitals have routinely housed people with dissenting political views (Morse, 1982; Ennis & Emory, 1978). A third problem is the sometimes questionable therapeutic value of civil commitment. Research suggests that many people committed involuntarily do not respond well to therapy (Wanck, 1984). It may be that people often need a sense of choice or control in order to succeed in treatment (Langer, 1983).

On the basis of these and other arguments, some clinicians suggest that involuntary commitment should be abolished (Szasz, 1977, 1963). Others, however, advocate finding a more systematic way to evaluate dangerousness when decisions are to be made about commitment. They suggest instituting a process of *risk assessment* that would arrive at statements such as, "The patient is believed to have X likelihood of being violent to the following people or under the following conditions over Y period of time." Proponents argue that this would be a more useful and appropriate way of deciding where and how people with psychological disorders should be treated (Snowden, 1997; Monahan & Steadman, 1996; Steadman et al., 1993).

TRENDS IN CIVIL COMMITMENT The flexibility of the involuntary commitment laws probably reached a peak in 1962. That year, in the case of *Robinson v. California*, the Supreme Court ruled that imprisoning people who suffered from drug addictions might violate the Constitution's ban on cruel and unusual punishment, and it recommended involuntary civil commitment to a mental hospital as a more reasonable action. This ruling encouraged the civil commitment of many kinds of "social deviants." In the years immediately following, civil commitment procedures granted far fewer rights to "defendants" than the criminal courts did (Holstein, 1993). In addition, involuntarily committed patients found it particularly difficult to obtain release.

During the late 1960s and early 1970s, reporters, novelists, civil libertarians, and others spoke out against the ease with which so many people were being unjustifiably committed to mental hospitals. As the public became more aware of these issues, state legislatures started to pass stricter standards for involuntary commitment (Arben, 1999; Holstein, 1993). Some states, for example, spelled out specific types of behavior that had to be observed before an assessment of dangerousness could be made. Rates of involuntary commitment then declined and release rates rose (Wanck, 1984).

Today fewer people are institutionalized through civil commitment procedures than in the past. The lower commitment rate has not led to more criminal behavior or more arrests of people who would have been committed under more

ConsiderThis

⊙ Today how are people who have been institutionalized viewed and treated by others? • Is the stigma of hospitalization a legitimate argument against civil commitment?

BOX 19-4

The Separation of Mind and State

During the presidential campaigns of 1992 and 1996, the independent candidate Ross Perot was branded "emotionally unbalanced" by some of his detractors. Perot reacted with good humor and even adopted singer Willie Nelson's "Crazy" as his theme song. The strategy of questioning the psychological stability of political opponents was taken to the extreme in the former Soviet Union, particularly under the rule of Josef Stalin, when many political opponents were placed in mental hospitals to get them out of the way.

Politically motivated labeling was at work during the mid-nineteenth-century debate over slavery in the United States, when those who favored slavery attacked Abraham Lincoln in the press as "insane" for his antislavery stance (Gamwell & Tomes, 1995). Many people, even among those who were against slavery, feared radical abolitionists and called them mentally unbalanced, blaming them for the nation's turmoil.

The trial of the abolitionist John Brown brought the issue out front for all to see. Brown, a white opponent of slavery, organized a small force of African Americans and white Americans to attack the federal armory at Harpers Ferry in Virginia. He was captured after two

days and tried for murder and treason. Many of Brown's supporters, including his own defense attorneys, urged him to plead not guilty by reason of insanity to avoid the death penalty (Gamwell & Tomes, 1995). Some fellow abolitionists, however, were offended by the suggestion that Brown's actions represented insanity, and Brown himself proudly maintained that he was mentally stable. In the end, Brown was convicted and executed.

As the historians Lynn Gamwell and Nancy Tomes (1995) point out, it was in the interests of both sides of the case to have Brown declared legally insane. Many people who opposed slavery believed that an insanity verdict would distance Brown's radical behavior from their own efforts in the public's mind and would calm public fears of violence by abolitionists. Many of those who defended slavery believed that a judgment of insanity would hurt Brown's reputation and prevent him from becoming a martyr for the abolitionist cause—as in fact he did become. Obviously, the verdict pleased neither side.

Clinical labels have been used for political gain throughout the ages. We may not always be able to stop the practice, but we should at least be aware of it. As

we read about historical events, we must be careful to weigh the available evidence and separate mental health labels that are used correctly from those that seek merely to further a political cause.

"Last Moments of John Brown" *The Abolitionist John Brown's journey to execution is portrayed in Thomas Hovenden's painting,* Last Moments of John Brown, *1884.*

flexible criteria (Teplin, Abram, & McClelland, 1994; Hiday, 1992). Nevertheless, some states are concerned that commitment criteria are now too strict, and they are moving toward broadening the criteria once again (Beck & Parry, 1992; Belcher & Blank, 1990). It is not yet clear whether this broadening will lead to a return to the vague commitment procedures of the past.

Protecting Patients' Rights

> "What . . . are you talking about—68 days? That's in jail, sucker. . . . You're with us, and you're gonna stay with us until we let you go."
>
> Hospital attendant, *One Flew Over the Cuckoo's Nest* (1975), informing patient R. P. McMurphy that his criminal commitment could extend beyond his original jail term

Over the past two decades, court decisions and state and federal laws have significantly expanded the rights of patients with mental disorders, in particular the *right to treatment* and the *right to refuse treatment*.

HOW IS THE RIGHT TO TREATMENT PROTECTED? When people are committed to mental institutions and do not receive treatment, the institutions become, in effect, prisons for the unconvicted. To many patients in the late 1960s and the 1970s, large state mental institutions were just that. Thus some patients and their attorneys began to demand that the state honor their **right to treatment**. In the landmark case of *Wyatt v. Stickney,* a suit on behalf of institutionalized patients in Alabama in 1972, a federal court ruled that the state was constitutionally obligated to provide "adequate treatment" to all people who had been committed involuntarily. Because conditions in the state's hospitals were so deplorable, the judge laid out goals that state officials had to meet, including more therapists, better living conditions, more privacy, more social interactions and physical exercise, and a more ethical use of physical restraint and medication. Other states have since adopted many of these standards.

Another important decision was handed down in 1975 by the Supreme Court in the case of *O'Connor v. Donaldson.* After being held in a Florida mental institution for more than 14 years, Kenneth Donaldson sued for release. Donaldson had repeatedly sought release and had been overruled by the institution's psychiatrists. He argued that he and his fellow patients were receiving inadequate treatment, being largely ignored by the staff, and allowed minimal personal freedom. The Supreme Court ruled in his favor, fined the hospital's superintendent, and said that such institutions must review patients' cases periodically. The justices also ruled that the state cannot continue to institutionalize against their will people who are not dangerous and who are capable of surviving on their own or with the willing help of responsible family members or friends. In a later case of importance, *Youngberg v. Romeo* (1982), the Supreme Court further ruled that people committed involuntarily have a right to "reasonably nonrestrictive confinement conditions" as well as "reasonable care and safety."

To help protect the rights of patients, Congress passed the Protection and Advocacy for Mentally Ill Individuals Act in 1986 (Woodside & Legg, 1990). This law set up *protection and advocacy systems* in all states and U.S. territories and gave public advocates who worked for patients the power to investigate possible abuse and neglect, and to address those problems legally.

Environmental change *During the past two decades, court decisions have set minimum standards for mental health care and for treatment environments. Some older facilities have been closed or redesigned to meet these standards. Shortly after this photograph was taken, this wing of a mental hospital closed.*

In recent years public advocates have argued that the right to treatment should also be extended to the tens of thousands of people with severe mental disorders who are repeatedly released from hospitals into ill-equipped communities. Many such people have no place to go and are unable to care for themselves, often winding up homeless or in prisons, where the percentage of inmates who receive treatment is quite low (Torrey, 1997; SAMHSA, 1993). A number of advocates are now suing federal and state agencies throughout the country, demanding that they fulfill the promises of the community mental health movement (see Chapter 15).

HOW IS THE RIGHT TO REFUSE TREATMENT PROTECTED? During the past two decades the courts have also decided that patients, particularly those in institutions, have the **right to**

refuse treatment (Wysoker, 1999). The courts have been reluctant to make a single general ruling on this right because there are so many different kinds of treatment, and a general ruling based on one of them might have unintended effects. Therefore, rulings usually target one specific treatment at a time.

Most of the right-to-refuse-treatment rulings pertain to *biological treatments* (Wettstein, 1999). These treatments are easier to impose on patients without their cooperation than psychotherapy, and they often seem more aversive and hazardous. For example, state rulings have consistently granted patients the right to refuse *psychosurgery,* the most irreversible form of physical treatment—and therefore the most dangerous.

Some states have also acknowledged a patient's right to refuse *electroconvulsive therapy (ECT),* the treatment used in many cases of severe depression (see Chapter 8). However, the right-to-refuse issue is more complex with regard to ECT than to psychosurgery. ECT is very effective for many people with severe depression; yet it can cause emotional trauma and can also be misused.

> When her private psychiatrist told her to enter a psychiatric hospital for shock treatment, she reluctantly agreed. After entering the hospital, however, she changed her mind. Despite her protests, she was given shock treatment and experienced the usual effects of confusion and memory loss. After a few shocks, however, her wish to stop the treatment became so strong that she said to a nurse, "I just have to get out of here. I'm leaving no matter what you say." It was then that she escaped.
>
> When the psychiatrist who had sent her to the hospital found out that Nan had run away, he telephoned her at home and said he would call the police if she did not return to the hospital. Under this pressure she returned, telling the nurses, "I really don't want to be here; I feel like I'm being forced to have shock. The doctor said if I didn't come back he'd send the police after me." Despite these events, her readmission was called voluntary, with no mention of her documented fear of shock treatment, of her desire not to be in the hospital, or of the threat of police intervention. She received more shock treatment during her second hospitalization, until she fled once more.
>
> *(Coleman, 1984, pp. 166-167)*

Today many states grant patients—particularly voluntary patients—the right to refuse ECT. Usually a patient must be informed fully about the nature of the treatment and must give written consent to it. A number of states continue to permit ECT to be forced on committed patients, whereas others require the consent of a close relative or other third party in such cases.

In the past, patients did not have the right to refuse *psychotropic medications.* States viewed the drugs as a benign form of treatment that often helped and rarely hurt. As we have seen, however, many psychotropic drugs are exceedingly powerful, and some produce effects that are unwanted and dangerous, such as tardive dyskinesia. As these harmful effects have become more apparent, some states have granted patients the right to refuse medication.

Two leading federal cases have led the way in strengthening this right—*Rennie v. Klein* (1979, 1981) in New Jersey and *Rogers v. Okin* (1979, 1980, 1981) in Massachusetts. Typically, states that recognize a patient's right to refuse medication require physicians to explain the purpose of the medication to patients and obtain their written consent. If a patient's refusal is considered incompetent, dangerous, or irrational, many states allow it to be overturned by an independent psychiatrist, medical committee, or local court (Wettstein, 1999, 1988; Prehn, 1990). However, the refusing patient is supported in this process by a lawyer or other patient advocate.

WHAT OTHER RIGHTS DO PATIENTS HAVE? Court decisions have safeguarded still other patient rights over the past several decades. Patients who perform work

---

RIGHT TO TREATMENT The legal right of patients, particularly those who are involuntarily committed, to receive adequate treatment.

RIGHT TO REFUSE TREATMENT The legal right of patients to refuse certain forms of treatment.

"Many insane persons . . . refuse all medications. We may triumph over this repugnance by causing them to take, without their knowledge, some substance which . . . provokes [stomach] pains, and even [bowel movements]. These accidents, by causing uneasiness in the mind of the patient respecting his health, render him docile."

Jean Esquirol, French mental health reformer, 1845

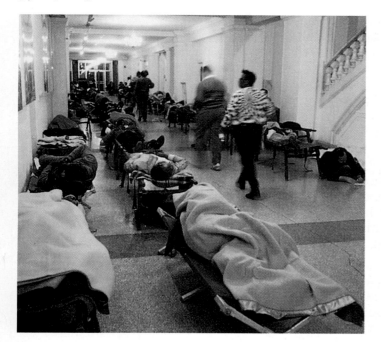

The right to an appropriate community residence *Although "guaranteed" the right to live in community adult homes, many people with chronic and severe mental disorders receive no treatment or guidance and wind up on the streets or in public shelters, such as this shelter for the homeless in Washington, D.C.*

in mental institutions, particularly private institutions, are now guaranteed at least a minimum wage. In addition, a district court ruled in the 1974 case of *Stoner v. Miller* that patients released from state mental hospitals have a right to aftercare and to an appropriate community residence, such as a halfway house. And in the 1975 case of *Dixon v. Weinberger*, another district court ruled that people with psychological disorders should receive treatment in the least restrictive facility available. If an inpatient program at a community mental health center is available, for example, then that is the facility to which they should be assigned, not a mental hospital. In the 1999 case of *Olmstead v. L.C. et al.* the Supreme Court again confirmed that patients have a right to community treatment.

THE "RIGHTS" DEBATE Few would argue with the intent of the patients' rights that are guaranteed today. Certainly, people with psychological disorders have civil rights that must be protected at all times. However, many clinicians express concern that the patients' rights rulings and laws may unintentionally deprive these patients of opportunities for recovery. Consider the right to refuse medication (Appelbaum & Grisso, 1995; Grisso & Appelbaum, 1995). If medications can help a patient with schizophrenia to recover, does not the patient have the right to that recovery? If confusion causes the patient to refuse medication, can clinicians in good conscience delay medication while legal channels are cleared? The psychologist Marilyn Whiteside raises similar concerns in her description of a 25-year-old patient with mental retardation:

> He was 25 and severely retarded. And after his favorite attendant left, he became self-abusive. He beat his fists against the side of his head until a football helmet had to be ordered for his protection. Then he clawed at his face and gouged out one of his eyes.
>
> The institution psychologists began a behavior program that had mildly aversive consequences: they squirted warm water in his face each time he engaged in self-abuse. When that didn't work, they requested permission to use an electric prod. The Human Rights Committee vetoed this "excessive and inhumane form of correction" because, after all, the young man was retarded, not criminal.
>
> Since nothing effective could be done that abridged the rights and negated the dignity of the developmentally disabled patient, he was verbally reprimanded for his behavior—and allowed to push his thumb through his remaining eye. He is now blind, of course, but he has his rights and presumably his dignity.
>
> (Whiteside, 1983, p. 13)

NO RIGHT TO VOTE

Forty-two states deny voting privileges to people judged variously as "incompetent," "insane," "incapacitated," "idiot," "lunatic," and of "unsound mind" (Moore, 1997).

Similar questions can even be raised about the right of patients to a minimum wage. Although the court ruling correctly tries to protect patients from being taken advantage of by institutions, it may also disrupt helpful token economy programs (Glynn, 1990). As we saw in Chapter 15, these behavioral programs reinforce patients' desirable behavior with hospital privileges, social rewards, and the like. While monetary reinforcement may be effective for some patients, nonmonetary rewards may be more effective for others. By depriving such programs of flexibility in determining rewards, a court-ordered minimum wage may reduce a patient's chances for recovery.

On the other side of the argument, the clinical field has not always done an effective job of protecting patients' rights. Over the years, many patients have been overmedicated and received improperly administered treatments (Crane,

1973). Similarly, some institutions have misused patients' labor. Furthermore, one must ask whether the field's present state of knowledge justifies clinicians' overriding of patients' rights. Can clinicians confidently say that a given treatment will help a patient? Can they predict when a treatment will have harmful effects? Since clinicians themselves often disagree, it seems appropriate for patients, their advocates, and outside evaluators to play key roles in decision making.

MALPRACTICE SUIT A legal suit charging a therapist with improper conduct in the course of treatment.

In What Other Ways Do the Clinical and Legal Fields Interact?

Mental health and legal professionals may influence each other's work in other ways as well. During the past two decades, their paths have crossed in three new areas: *malpractice suits, jury selection,* and *professional boundaries.*

Malpractice Suits

The number of **malpractice lawsuits** against therapists has risen so sharply in recent years that clinicians have coined terms for the fear of being sued—"litigaphobia" and "litigastress." Claims have been made against clinicians in response to a patient's attempted suicide, sexual activity with a patient, failure to obtain informed consent for a treatment, negligent drug therapy, omission of drug therapy that would speed improvement, improper termination of treatment, and wrongful commitment (Malley & Reilly, 1999; Smith, 1991; Wettstein, 1989).

Improper termination of treatment was at issue in one highly publicized case in 1985. A man being treated for alcohol-related depression was released from a state hospital in Alabama. Two and a half months later, he shot and killed a new acquaintance in a motel lounge. He was convicted of murder and sentenced to life in prison. The victim's father, claiming negligence, filed a civil suit against a psychologist, physician, and social worker at the state hospital, and after two years of legal action a jury awarded him a total of almost $7 million. The state supreme court later overturned the verdict, saying that a state hospital is entitled to a certain degree of immunity in such cases.

Two investigators who studied the effects of this case found that the hospital had released 11 percent of its patients during the six months before the lawsuit was filed, 10 percent during the two years it was being litigated, but only 7 percent of its patients during the six months after the verdict (Brodsky & Poythress, 1990). Although judgments about a patient's improvement are supposed to be made on their own merits, they were apparently being affected by a heightened fear of litigation at this hospital. Clearly a malpractice suit, or the fear of one, can have significant effects on clinical decisions and practice, for better or for worse.

A JUDGMENT OF MALPRACTICE

After firing a rifle on a busy street and killing two men in 1995, the delusional law student Wendell Williamson was found not guilty by reason of insanity. From his room in a mental hospital, Williamson later sued the psychiatrist who had seen him a handful of times 8 months prior to the killings, contending that the therapist had not made a correct diagnosis or followed up after the sessions. In 1998, a jury awarded Williamson a judgment of $500,000.

Jury Selection

During the past 20 years, more and more lawyers have turned to clinicians for psychological advice in conducting trials (Strier, 1999; Gottschalk, 1981). A new breed of clinical specialists, known as "jury specialists," has evolved. They advise lawyers about which jury candidates are likely to favor their side and which strategies are likely to win jurors' support during trials. The jury specialists make their suggestions on the basis of surveys, interviews, analyses of jurors' backgrounds and attitudes, and laboratory simulations of upcoming trials. However, it is not clear that a clinician's advice is more valid than a lawyer's instincts or that either's judgments are particularly accurate. Because some lawyers believe that clinical advice is useful, however, clinical professionals are influencing these legal procedures and decisions.

Professional Boundaries

During the past several years the legislative and judicial systems have helped to change the *boundaries* that distinguish one clinical profession from another. In particular, they have given more authority to psychologists and blurred the lines that once separated psychiatry from psychology. Congress, for example, has passed a group of bills that permit psychologists to receive direct reimbursements from Medicare for treating elderly and disabled people. Until recently, only psychiatrists received such payments. Similarly, a growing number of states are ruling that psychologists can admit patients to the state's hospitals, a power previously held only by psychiatrists (Cullen, 1993).

In 1991, with the blessings of Congress, the Department of Defense (DOD) started to reconsider the biggest difference of all between the practices of psychiatrists and psychologists—the authority to prescribe drugs, a role heretofore denied to psychologists. The DOD set up a trial training program for Army psychologists, initially called *Cutting Edge* (later changed to the *Psychopharmacology Demonstration Project*), in which the psychologists prescribed drugs for psychological problems under the supervision of physicians (DeLeon, 1992). By 1997 ten psychologists had graduated from the program, which consisted of one year of formal medical school and pharmacological training followed by a one-year residency.

The issue of prescription privileges for psychologists is of particular interest to the military, which suffers from a shortage of mental health services. From the beginning, however, everyone in the clinical field recognized the much larger implications of the trial program. In 1996 the American Psychological Association recommended that *all* psychologists be allowed to attend a postdoctoral educational program in prescription services and receive certification to prescribe medications if they pass. And in recent years, several states have introduced legislation regarding the expansion of prescription privileges (Hanson et al., 1999).

As the action by the American Psychological Association suggests, the legislative and judicial systems do not simply take it upon themselves to interfere in the affairs of clinical professionals. In fact, professional associations of psychologists, psychiatrists, and social workers lobby in state legislatures across the country for laws and decisions that may increase the authority of their members. In each instance, clinicians seek the involvement of other institutions as well, demonstrating again how the mental health system interacts with other sectors of our society.

ConsiderThis

◉ Most psychiatrists do not want psychologists to be granted the authority to prescribe psychotropic medications. Surprisingly, many psychologists oppose the idea as well. Why might they take this position?

What Ethical Principles Guide Mental Health Professionals?

Discussions of the legal and mental health systems may sometimes give the impression that clinicians as a group are uncaring and are considerate of patients' rights and needs only when forced. This, of course, is not true. Most clinicians care greatly about their clients and strive to help them and, at the same time, respect their rights and dignity.

But clinicians do face difficult obstacles in the pursuit of these goals. First, patients' rights and proper care raise complex questions that do not have simple or obvious answers. Different clients and therapists, all guided by their diverse perspectives, may arrive at different answers to such questions. Second, clinicians, like other professionals, often have difficulty appreciating the full impact of their actions or changing the system in which they work. Indeed, thousands of conscientious and caring clinicians contributed to the appalling system of institutional care that marked the first half of the twentieth century—partly because they did not appreciate how misguided the system was and partly because they felt helpless to change it. A third problem is that, like other professions, the clinical field

CODE OF ETHICS A body of principles and rules for ethical behavior, designed to guide decisions and actions by members of a profession.

includes at least a few practitioners who place their own needs and wishes before others'. For the integrity of the profession and the protection of individual clients, such professionals need to be monitored and regulated.

Clinicians do not rely exclusively on the legislative and court systems to ensure proper and effective clinical practice. They also regulate themselves by continually developing and revising ethical guidelines for members of the clinical field (Bersoff, 1995). Many legal decisions do nothing more than convert these already-existing professional guidelines into laws.

Each profession within the mental health field has its own **code of ethics** (Malley & Reilly, 1999). The code of the American Psychological Association is typical (Nagy, 2000). This code, highly respected by other mental health professionals and public officials, begins with the basic principle that the goal of psychologists "is to broaden knowledge of behavior and, where appropriate, to apply it pragmatically to improve the conditions of both the individual and society" (APA, 1995, 1992). Moreover, because their "judgments and actions may affect the lives of others," the code calls for psychologists to guard against "factors that might lead to misuse of their influence." Some specific guidelines in the current code are the following:

The ethics of giving professional advice *Like John Gray, author of* Men Are From Mars, Women Are From Venus, *many of today's clinicians offer advice to millions of people in books, at workshops, on television and radio programs, and in tape packages. Their presentations often affect people greatly, and so they, too, are bound by the field's ethics codes to act responsibly and professionally and to base their presentations on appropriate psychological literature.*

1. *Psychologists are permitted to offer advice* in self-help books, on television and radio programs, in newspaper and magazine articles, through mailed material, and in other places, provided they do so responsibly and professionally and base their advice on appropriate psychological literature and practices.

2. *Psychologists may not conduct fraudulent research, plagiarize the work of others, or publish false data.* During the past two decades cases of scientific fraud or misconduct have been discovered in all of the sciences, including psychology. These acts have led to misunderstandings of important issues, taken scientific research in the wrong direction, and damaged public trust. Unfortunately, the effects of research misconduct are hard to undo even after a retraction. The impressions created by false findings may continue to influence the thinking of both the public and other scientists for years (Pfeifer & Snodgrass, 1990).

3. *Psychologists must acknowledge their limitations* with regard to patients who are disabled or whose gender, ethnicity, language, socioeconomic status, or sexual orientation differs from that of the therapist. This guideline often requires psychotherapists to obtain additional training or supervision, consult with more knowledgeable colleagues, or refer clients to more appropriate professionals.

4. *Psychologists who make evaluations and testify in legal cases must base their assessments on sufficient information and substantiate their findings appropriately.* If an adequate examination of the individual in question is not possible, psychologists must make clear the limited nature of their testimony.

5. *Psychologists may not take advantage of clients and students, sexually or otherwise.* This guideline pertains to the widespread social problem of sexual harassment, as well as the problem of therapists who take sexual advantage of clients in therapy. The code specifically forbids a sexual relationship with a present or former therapy client for at least two years after the end of treatment; and even then such a relationship is permitted only in "the most unusual circumstances." Furthermore, psychologists may not accept as clients people with whom they have previously had a sexual relationship.

THE LIMITS OF EXPERTISE

When mental health experts testify at trials, they must base their opinions only on firsthand observations that they have collected outside of court and on information presented at the trial (Federal Rules of Evidence 702).

The past two decades have seen an increase in the number of clients who have told state licensing boards of sexual misconduct by their therapist or sued their therapist for such behavior (Zamichow, 1993). These increases may reflect not a greater prevalence of such cases but clients' heightened awareness of and anger over the inappropriateness of such behavior. Some cases in point:

> Two women patients brought claims against the same male psychologist in the mid-1980s for having sex during treatment, which he claimed was for "therapeutic benefit." In the first case . . . the patient sued for sexual misconduct, emotional distress, pain and loss of self-esteem. . . . In the second case, the patient sued the therapist for sexual misconduct, breach of contract and assault and battery. The cases were settled out of court.
>
> A woman sued a husband-and-wife psychotherapy team for sexual misconduct and mental and physical discomfort. The patient said sex with the male therapist resulted in a pregnancy and subsequent abortion, and that the woman therapist also inappropriately cuddled her. The case was settled out of court.
>
> *(Youngstrom, 1990, p. 21)*

"Society is built on trust."

Robert South

Clients may suffer great emotional damage from such betrayals of trust (Malley & Reilly, 1999; Lazarus, 1995). In fact, a number of therapists are now treating clients whose primary problem is that they previously experienced some form of sexual misconduct by a therapist (Bloom et al., 1999; Wincze et al., 1996; Pope & Vetter, 1991). Many such clients experience the symptoms of posttraumatic stress disorder or major depressive disorder (Luepker, 1999; Hankins et al., 1994).

How many therapists actually have a sexual relationship with a client? A 1977 study found that 12.1 percent of male and 2.6 percent of female psychologists admitted having sexual contact with patients (Holroyd & Brodsky, 1977). A more recent survey revealed that 0.9 percent of male therapists and 0.2 percent of female therapists had had sexual contact with patients (Borys & Pope, 1989). The decline shown by these studies may indicate that fewer therapists are in fact having sexual relationships with patients, either because of a growing recognition of the inappropriateness of such behavior or because of growing fear of its consequences. Or it may be that today's therapists are simply less willing to admit, even anonymously, misbehavior that is a felony in a growing number of states. Thus several reviewers estimate that some form of sexual misconduct with patients is still engaged in by around 8 percent of today's male therapists and 2 percent of female therapists (Malley & Reilly, 1999; Illingworth, 1995; Hankins et al., 1994).

Although the vast majority of therapists keep their sexual behavior within appropriate professional bounds, their ability to control private feelings is apparently another matter. In one survey, 72 percent of therapists reported having a sexual fantasy about a client, although most said that this was a rare occurrence (Pope, 2000; Pope & Brown, 1996; Pope et al., 1987). In other surveys, close to 90 percent reported having been sexually attracted to a client, at least on occasion (Pope, 2000; Pope & Brown, 1996; Pope & Tabachnick, 1993). Although few of these therapists acted on their feelings, 63 percent felt guilty, anxious, or concerned about the attraction (Pope et al., 1986).

ConsiderThis

● Although more than two-thirds of therapists have felt sexually attracted to a client on at least one occasion, only around one-third have ever felt sexually attracted to their own therapist (Pope & Brown, 1996). How might these different reactions be explained?

In recent years sexual ethics training has been given high priority in many clinical training programs (Housman & Stake, 1999). In addition, consumer-oriented brochures on sexual misconduct in psychotherapy have been developed to help clients evaluate the appropriateness of their therapists' behavior (Thorn, Shealy, & Briggs, 1993). Indeed, many clinicians believe it imperative that clients learn to identify and respond assertively to early warning signs of therapist sexual misconduct.

6. *Psychologists must adhere to the principle of confidentiality.* All of the state courts abide by laws protecting therapist **confidentiality**, and in the 1996 case of *Jaffee v. Redmond,* the Supreme Court applied this principle to federal courts as well. For peace of mind and to ensure effective therapy, clients must be able to trust that their private exchanges with a therapist will not be repeated to others (Smith-Bell & Winslade, 1994). Thus the code of ethics states that psychologists "must take reasonable precautions to respect the confidentiality rights" of clients.

There are times, however, when the principle of confidentiality must be compromised. A therapist in training, for example, must discuss cases on a regular basis with a supervisor. Clients, in turn, must be informed when such discussions are occurring.

A second exception arises in cases of outpatients who are clearly dangerous. The 1976 case of *Tarasoff v. Regents of the University of California,* one of the most important cases to affect client-therapist relationships, concerned an outpatient at a University of California hospital. He had confided to his therapist that he wanted to harm his former girlfriend, Tanya Tarasoff. Several days after ending therapy, the former patient fulfilled his promise. He stabbed Tanya Tarasoff to death.

Should confidentiality have been broken in this case? The therapist, in fact, felt that it should. Campus police were notified, but the patient was released after some questioning. In their suit against the hospital and therapist, the victim's parents argued that the therapist should have also warned them and their daughter that the patient intended to harm Ms. Tarasoff. The California Supreme Court agreed: "The protective privilege ends where the public peril begins." In addition to ordering a breach of confidentiality, this ruling requires the therapist to perform an extremely difficult feat: to determine when "a patient poses a serious danger of violence to others."

The current code of ethics for psychologists thus declares that therapists have a **duty to protect**—a responsibility to break confidentiality, even without the client's consent, when it is necessary "to protect the client or others from harm." Since the *Tarasoff* ruling, California's courts have further held that therapists are obligated to protect people who are close to a client's intended victim and thus in danger. A child, for example, is likely to be at risk when a client plans to assault the child's mother. The California courts have stipulated, however, that the duty to protect applies only when the intended victim is readily identifiable, as opposed to the public at large, and only when the intended object of violence is a person, as opposed to property. Many, but not all, states have adopted the California court rulings or similar ones (Bloom, 1990; Pietrofesa et al., 1990), and a number have passed "duty to protect bills," that clarify the rules of confidentiality for therapists and protect them from certain civil suits (Bersoff, 1999; Monahan, 1993).

Most of today's therapists agree that it is often appropriate to breach confidentiality. In one survey, almost 80 percent of the therapists reported having broken confidentiality when a client was suicidal, 62 percent when child abuse was occurring, and 58 percent when a client was homicidal (Pope et al., 1987).

CONFIDENTIALITY The principle that certain professionals will not divulge the information they obtain from a client.

DUTY TO PROTECT The principle that therapists must break confidentiality in order to protect a person who may be the intended victim of a client.

"Anyhow we are getting tired of making bombs. It's no fun having to spend all your evenings and weekends preparing dangerous mixtures."

Letter from the Unabomber (later identified as Ted Kaczynski) to *The New York Times,* April 1995

Mental Health, Business, and Economics

The legislative and judicial systems are not the only social institutions with which mental health professionals interact. The business and economic fields are two other sectors that influence and are influenced by clinical practice and study. To be sure, health care in all its varieties is itself a business, and many decisions in the clinical field are based on economic considerations (see Box 19-5), but the mental health field in turn influences the conduct of business and economic programs.

Bringing Mental Health Services to the Workplace

Collectively, psychological disorders are among the ten leading categories of work-related disorders and injuries in the United States. In fact, almost 12 per-

---

B O X **19-5**

The Itemized Statement in Clinical Psychiatry: A New Concept in Billing

▌ (In this article, by Robert S. Hoffman, M.D., which originally appeared in *The Journal of Irreproducible Results,* 1980, the psychiatrist's biting wit is equaled only by his sense of outrage over the growing demands made by insurance companies.) ▌

*D*ue to the rapidly escalating costs of health care delivery, there has been increasing pressure on physicians to document and justify their charges for professional services. This has created a number of serious problems, particularly in the field of psychiatry. Chief among these is the breach of confidentiality that arises when sensitive clinical information is provided to third-party insurance carri-

ers, e.g. the patient's diagnosis or related details about his/her psychiatric disorder. Even when full disclosure of such information is made, insurance carriers frequently deny benefits because the description of the treatment appears imprecise or inadequate. There also has been some criticism of the standard hourly fee-for-service, the argument being that psychiatrists, like other medical specialists, should be required to adjust their fees depending upon the particular treatment offered.

In view of these considerations, a method is required which will bring psychiatric billing in line with accepted medical practice. The procedure illustrated below, which we have successfully em-

ployed in our clinic for the past two years, achieves this goal. It requires only a modest investment in time and effort: the tape-recording of all psychotherapy sessions, transcription of tapes, tabulation of therapeutic interventions, and establishment of a relative value scale for the commonly used maneuvers. This can easily be managed by two full-time medical billing personnel per psychiatrist. The method, in our hands, has been found to increase collections from third-party carriers by 65% and to raise a typical psychiatrist's annual net income almost to the level of a municipal street sweeper or plumber's assistant.

Below is a specimen monthly statement illustrating these principles:

CALVIN L. SKOLNIK, M.D., INC.
A Psychiatry Corporation

Jan. 5, 1978

Mr. Sheldon Rosenberg
492 West Maple Dr.
East Orange, N.J.

Dear Mr. Rosenberg:

In response to the request by your insurer, Great Lakes Casualty and Surety Co., for more precise documentation of professional services rendered, I have prepared the enclosed itemization for the month of December. I trust that this will clarify the situation sufficiently for your benefit payments to be resumed.

Until next Tuesday at 11:00, I remain

Cordially,

CALVIN L. SKOLNIK, M.D.

cent of all employees are said to experience psychological problems that are serious enough to affect their work. Psychological problems contribute to 60 percent of all absenteeism from work, up to 90 percent of industrial accidents, and 65 percent of work terminations (Kemp, 1994). Alcohol abuse and other substance-related disorders are particularly damaging, increasing absenteeism by as much as six times, accidents by four times, and workers' compensation claims by five times (Martin, Kraft, & Roman, 1994; Wright, 1984). The business world has often turned to clinical professionals to help prevent and correct such problems (Schott, 1999; Hantula & Reilly, 1996; Millar, 1990, 1984). Two common means of providing mental health care in the workplace are employee assistance programs and problem-solving seminars.

DANGER IN THE WORKPLACE

Six percent of all rapes, 8 percent of all robberies, and 16 percent of all assaults occur at work (Bureau of Justice Statistics, 1994).

Charges				
140	clarifications		@ .25	35.00
157	restatements		@ .25	39.25
17	broad-focus questions		@ .35	5.95
42	narrow-focus questions		@ .30	12.60
86	reflections of dominant emotional theme		@ .35	30.10
38	resolutions of inconsistencies		@ .45	17.10
22	pointings out of nonverbal communications		@ .40	8.80
187	encouragements to say more		@ .15	28.05
371	sympathetic nods with furrowed brow		@ .10	37.10
517	acknowledgments of information reception (Uh-huhs, Umhmmm, etc.)		@ .08	41.36
24	interpretations of unconscious defense configurations		@ .30	7.20
16	absolutions for evil deeds		@ .50	8.00
2	pieces of advice		@ .75	1.50
6	expressions of personal feelings		@ .50	3.00
2	personal reminiscences		@ .65	1.30
35	misc. responses (sighs, grunts, belches, etc.)		@ .20	7.00
7	listening to remarks disparaging therapist's appearance, personal habits, or technique		@1.75	12.25
12	listening to sarcastic remarks about psychiatry		@ 1.00	12.00
3	listening to psychiatrist jokes		@ .80	2.40
3	telephone calls to therapist		@ .15	.45
1	telephone call to therapist at especially inopportune moment		@ 10.50	10.50
22	Kleenex tissues		@ .005	.11
1	ashtray		@ 3.50	3.50
1	filling and repainting of 1 ashtray-size dent in wall		@ 27.50	27.50
1	shampooing of soft drink stain on carpet		@ 15.00	15.00
1	letter of excuse from work		@ 2.50	2.50
2	surcharges for unusually boring or difficult sessions		@ 35.00	70.00
	Subtotal: charges			$438.52
Credits				
4	unusually interesting anecdotes		@ .45	1.80
3	good jokes		@ .50	1.50
1	item of gossip about another patient which was found useful in her therapy		@ 3.50	3.50
1	apology for sarcastic remark		@ 1.00	1.00
1	use of case history at American Psychiatric Association convention			10.00
1/2	chicken salad sandwich on whole wheat w/mayo		@ 1.75	.88
7	bummed cigarettes (65¢/pack)			.23
1	damaged Librium tablet, returned unused			.10
	Subtotal: credits			$18.99
Total: PLEASE REMIT—				$419.53

Employee assistance programs, mental health services made available by a place of business, are run either by mental health professionals who work directly for a company or by outside mental health agencies (Oher, 1999; Canty, 1996). Companies publicize such programs at the work site, educate workers about psychological dysfunctioning, and teach supervisors how to identify workers who are having psychological problems. Businesses believe that employee assistance programs save them money in the long run by preventing psychological problems from interfering with work performance and by reducing employee insurance claims (Dickens, 1999; Miller, 1998), although these beliefs have yet to undergo extensive testing (Kemp, 1994).

Stress-reduction and **problem-solving seminars** are workshops or group sessions in which mental health professionals teach employees techniques for coping, solving problems, and handling and reducing stress (Kagan et al., 1995). Programs of this kind are just as likely to be aimed at high-level executives as at assembly-line workers. Often employees are required to attend such workshops, which may run for several days, and are given time off from their jobs to do so. Again, the businesses expect these programs to save money by helping workers to achieve a healthier state of mind, suffer less dysfunction on the job, and improve their performance.

The Economics of Mental Health

We have already seen how economic decisions by the government may influence the clinical field's treatment of people with severe mental disorders. For example, the desire of the state and federal governments to reduce costs was an important consideration in the country's deinstitutionalization movement, which contributed to the premature release of hospital patients into the community. Economic decisions by government agencies may affect other kinds of clients and treatment programs as well (see Figure 19-2).

FIGURE 19-2 **Mental health spending** *The average amount of money spent for mental health services annually per person in the United States increased sevenfold, from $16.53 in 1969 to $116.69 in 1992. However, the amount spent actually stopped increasing during the 1990s. Moreover, when adjustments are made for inflation and expenditures are stated in 1969 dollars, the amount spent per person actually fell in the 1990s from $22.81 to $19.83, close to the amount back in 1969. (Adapted from Redick et al., 1996, 1992.)*

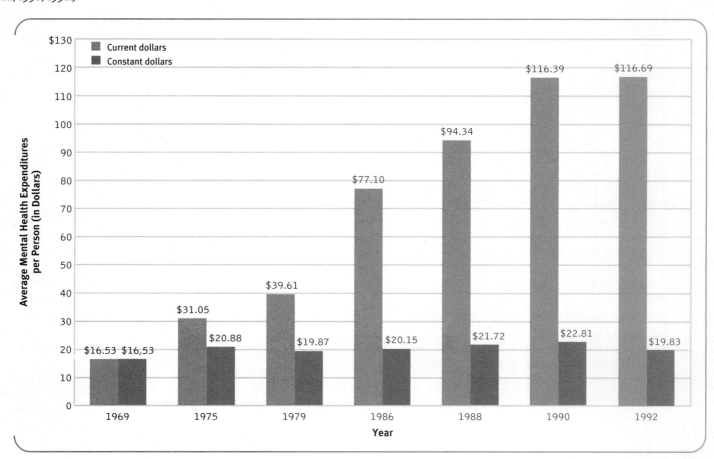

"I wish I could help you. The problem is that you're too sick for managed care."

On the one hand, government funding for people with psychological disorders has risen sharply over the past three decades, from $3 billion in 1969 to $61 billion today (Torrey, 1997; Redick et al., 1992). On the other hand, much of that money is spent on income support, housing subsidies, and other such expenses, rather than directly on mental health services. Government funding for services actually appears to be decreasing. It currently covers less than half the cost of all mental health services, leaving most of the expense to individual patients and their private insurance companies (Taube, 1990).

The growing economic role of private insurance companies has had a significant effect on the way clinicians go about their work. In an effort to reduce their expenditures and to keep track of the payments they are making, many of these companies have developed **managed care programs**, in which the insurance company decides such questions as which therapists clients may choose, the cost of sessions, and the number of sessions for which a client may be reimbursed (Manderscheid et al., 1999). These and other insurance plans may also control expenses through the use of **peer review systems**, in which clinicians who work for the insurance company periodically review a client's treatment program and recommend that insurance benefits be either continued or stopped. Typically, insurers require detailed reports or session notes from the therapist, often including intimate personal information about the patient (Stoline & Sharfstein, 1996; Appelbaum, 1993).

As we observed in Chapter 1, many therapists and clients dislike managed care programs and peer reviews. They believe that the reports required of therapists breach confidentiality, even when efforts are made to protect anonymity, and that the value of therapy in a given case is sometimes difficult to convey in a brief report. They also argue that the priorities of managed care programs inevitably shorten therapy, even if longer-term treatment would be advisable in particular cases. The priorities may also favor treatments that offer short-term results (for example, drug therapy) over more costly approaches that might achieve a more promising long-term improvement. As in the medical arena, disturbing stories are often heard about patients who are prematurely cut off from mental health services by their managed care programs. In short, many clinicians fear that the current system amounts to regulation of therapy by insurance companies rather than by therapists.

A PUBLIC VIEW

In a 1999 survey of 1000 people across the United States, 67 percent of respondents said the government should spend more money to treat people with mental disorders who cannot afford to pay (Time/CNN, 1999).

EMPLOYEE ASSISTANCE PROGRAM A mental health program offered by a business to its employees.

STRESS-REDUCTION SEMINAR A workshop or series of group sessions offered by a business in which mental health professionals teach employees how to cope with and solve problems and reduce stress.

MANAGED CARE PROGRAM An insurance program in which the insurance company decides the cost, method, provider, and length of treatment.

PEER REVIEW SYSTEM A system by which clinicians paid by an insurance company may periodically review a patient's progress and recommend the continuation or termination of insurance benefits.

The Person within the Profession

The actions of clinical researchers and practitioners not only influence and are influenced by other institutions but are closely tied to their personal needs and goals (see Box 19-6). We have seen that the human strengths, imperfections, wisdom, and clumsiness of clinical professionals may affect their theoretical orientations, their interactions with clients, and the kinds of clients with whom they choose to work. We have also looked at how personal leanings may sometimes override professional standards and scruples and, in extreme cases, lead clinical scientists to commit research fraud and clinical practitioners to engage in sexual misconduct with clients.

A national survey of the mental health of therapists found that 84 percent reported being in therapy at least once (Pope & Brown, 1996; Pope & Tabachnick, 1994). Their reasons were largely the same as those of other clients, with emotional problems, depression, and anxiety topping the list. In fact, 61 percent of the therapists reported having experienced depression, 29 percent reported having had suicidal feelings, and 4 percent said they had attempted suicide (Pope & Tabachnick, 1994). In related research a number of therapists in treatment reported being raised in dysfunctional families, where some experienced physical or sexual abuse, parental alcoholism, institutionalization of a parent in a mental hospital, death of a family member, or other early traumas (Elliot & Guy, 1993). Still another survey revealed that all therapists feel like imposters at some point in their career. Some 87 percent feel like fakes at least occasionally, and 18 percent feel that way frequently (Gibbs & DeVries, 1987).

It is not clear why so many therapists report having psychological problems. Perhaps their jobs are highly stressful; perhaps therapists are simply more aware of their own negative feelings or are more likely to pursue treatment for their problems; or perhaps individuals with personal concerns are more inclined to choose clinical work as a profession. Whatever the reason, clinicians bring a set of psychological issues and emotions to their work that may, along with other important factors, affect how they listen and respond to clients.

COUNTERTRANSFERENCE

In a national survey of 285 therapists, 87 percent reported having been angry at a client on at least one occasion, and 57 percent have raised their voice at a client (Pope & Tabachnick, 1993).

BOX 19-6

Therapists under Attack

A number of therapists have found out that their rights—including the right to a safe practice—may be violated (Flannery et al., 2000; Brasic & Fogelman, 1999). Between 12 and 14 percent of therapists have been attacked by their patients at least once in private therapy, and an even larger percentage have been assaulted in mental hospitals (Tryon, 1987; Bernstein, 1981). One study found that 40 percent of psychiatrists had been assaulted at least once during their careers (Menninger, 1993). Patients have used a variety of weapons in their attacks, including such common objects as shoes, lamps, fire extinguishers, and canes. Some have used guns or knives and have severely wounded or even killed a therapist.

Many therapists who have been attacked continue to feel anxious and insecure in their work for a long time after. Some try to be more selective in accepting patients and look for cues that signal impending violence. One therapist even studied karate for a year and a half (Tryon, 1987).

ConsiderThis

How might lingering anxiety affect the behavior and effectiveness of clinicians who have been attacked? • What do these attacks suggest about therapists' ability to predict dangerousness? • Such attacks seem to be on the rise. Why?

"STOP TRYING TO PSYCHOANALYZE ME WHEN I'M TRYING TO PSYCHOANALYZE YOU."

(© 2000 Sidney Harris)

The science and profession of abnormal psychology seeks to understand, predict, and change abnormal functioning. But we must not lose sight of the broader context in which its activities are conducted. Mental health researchers and clinicians are human beings, living within a society of human beings, working to serve human beings. The mixture of discovery, misdirection, promise, and frustration that we have encountered throughout this book is thus to be expected. When one thinks about it, could the study and treatment of human behavior really proceed in any other way?

"You must look into people as well as at them."

Chesterfield (1694–1773)

CROSSROADS:
Operating within a Larger System

At one time, clinical researchers and professionals conducted their work largely in isolation. Today, however, their activities have numerous ties to the legislative, judicial, economic, and other established systems. One reason for this growing interconnectedness is that the clinical field has achieved a high level of respect and acceptance in our society. Clinicians now serve millions of people in many ways. They contribute to almost every endeavor of society, from education to ecology, and are widely looked to as sources of expertise. When a field achieves such prominence, it inevitably affects how other institutions are run. It also attracts public scrutiny and a desire by the public to monitor its activities.

Today, when people with psychological problems seek help from a therapist, they are entering a complex system consisting of numerous interconnected parts. Just as their personal problems have evolved within a social structure, so will their treatment be affected by the various parts of a larger system—the therapist's values and needs, legal and economic forces, societal attitudes, and yet other forces. These many forces influence clinical research as well.

The effects of this larger system on an individual's psychological needs can be positive or negative, like a family's impact on each of its members. When the system protects a client's rights and confidentiality, for example, it is serving the client well. When economic, legal, or other societal forces limit treatment options, cut off treatment prematurely, or stigmatize a person, the system is adding to the person's problems.

"I spent . . . two hours chatting with Einstein. . . . He is cheerful, assured and likable, and understands as much about psychology as I do about physics, so we got on together very well."

Sigmund Freud, 1927

Because of the enormous growth and impact of the mental health profession in our society, it is essential that we understand its strengths and weaknesses. As we have seen throughout this book, the field has made impressive advancements in knowledge, especially during the past several decades. What mental health professionals do not know and cannot do, however, still outweighs what they do know and can do. Everyone who turns to the clinical field—directly or indirectly—must recognize that it is young and imperfect. Society is vastly curious about behavior and often in need of information and help. What we as a society must remember, however, is that the field is truly at a *crossroads*.

SUMMARY AND REVIEW

- **The legal system and the mental health field** The mental health profession interacts with the legislative and judicial systems in two key ways. First, clinicians help assess the mental stability of people accused of crimes. Second, the legislative and judicial systems help regulate mental health care. *pp. 581–582*

- **Criminal commitment** The punishment of persons convicted of crimes depends on the assumption that individuals are responsible for their acts and are capable of defending themselves in court. Evaluations by clinicians may help judges and juries decide the culpability of defendants and sometimes result in criminal commitment.

  If defendants are judged to have been mentally unstable at the time they committed a crime, they may be found not guilty by reason of insanity and placed in a treatment facility rather than a prison. "Insanity" is a legal term, defined by legislators, not by clinicians. In federal courts and about half the state courts, insanity is judged in accordance with the M'Naghten test, which holds that defendants were insane at the time of a criminal act if they did not know the nature or quality of the act or did not know right from wrong at the time they committed it. Other states use the broader American Law Institute test.

  The insanity defense has been criticized on several grounds, and some states have added an additional option, guilty but mentally ill. Defendants who receive this verdict are sentenced to prison with the proviso that they will also receive psychological treatment. Still another verdict option is guilty with diminished capacity. A related category consists of convicted sex offenders, who are considered in some states to have a mental disorder and are therefore assigned to treatment in a mental health facility.

  Regardless of their state of mind at the time of the crime, defendants may be found mentally incompetent to stand trial, that is, incapable of fully understanding the charges or legal proceedings that confront them. If so, they are typically sent to a mental hospital until they are competent to stand trial. *pp. 582–590*

- **Civil commitment** The legal system also influences the clinical profession. First, courts may be called upon to commit noncriminals to mental hospitals for treatment, a process called civil commitment. Society allows involuntary commitment of people considered to be in need of treatment and dangerous to themselves or others. Laws governing civil commitment procedures vary from state to state, but a minimum standard of proof—clear and convincing evidence of the necessity of commitment—has been defined by the Supreme Court. *pp. 590–596*

- **Protecting patients' rights** The courts and legislatures significantly affect the mental health profession by specifying legal rights to which patients are entitled. The rights that have received the most attention are the right to treatment and the right to refuse treatment. *pp. 596–599*

JOHN HINCKLEY, 1999

In 1999, a U.S. Court of Appeals ruled that John Hinckley may make supervised day trips away from Washington, DC's St. Elizabeth's hospital, where he is currently confined.

ARRESTING THE HOMELESS

Many homeless people with severe mental disorders currently wind up in jail rather than in treatment. Most of them are charged with such infractions as disorderly conduct, trespassing, not paying for a meal, menacing, panhandling, loitering, or "lewd and lascivious behavior" (for example, urinating on a street corner) (Mulhern, 1990; Valdiserri, Carroll, & Harti, 1986).

■ **Other clinical-legal interactions** Mental health and legal professionals also cross paths in three other areas. First, malpractice suits against therapists have increased in recent years. Second, lawyers may solicit the advice of mental health professionals regarding the selection of jurors and case strategies. Third, the legislative and judicial systems help define professional boundaries. *pp. 599–600*

■ **Ethical principles** Each clinical profession has a code of ethics. The psychologists' code includes prohibitions against engaging in fraudulent research and against taking advantage of clients and students, sexually or otherwise. It also establishes guidelines for respecting patient confidentiality. The case of *Tarasoff v. Regents of the University of California* helped to determine the circumstances in which therapists have a duty to protect the client or others from harm and must break confidentiality. *pp. 600–603*

■ **Mental health, business, and economics** Clinical practice and study also intersect with the business and economic worlds. Clinicians often help to address psychological problems in the workplace, for example, through employee assistance programs and stress-reduction and problem-solving seminars.

Reductions in government funding of clinical services have left much of the expense for these services to be paid by insurance companies. Private insurance companies are setting up managed care programs whose structure and reimbursement procedures influence, and often reduce, the duration and focus of therapy. Their procedures, which include peer review systems, may also compromise patient confidentiality and the quality of therapy services. *pp. 604–607*

DECLINING COSTS

Mental health expenditures by insurance companies fell 54 percent during the 1990s. Total health care spending fell just 7 percent during the same decade (*Wall Street Journal*, 1998).

■ **The person within the profession** Mental health activities are affected by the personal needs, values, and goals of the human beings who provide the clinical services. These factors inevitably affect the choice, direction, and even quality of their work. *pp. 608–609*

CYBER STUDY

▲ *When might people not be responsible for aggressive or violent acts?* ▲ *Can clinicians predict antisocial acts, dangerousness, and violence?* ▲ *Did the hospital treatments of past times violate patients' rights?* ▲ *Is it appropriate to commit people who are experiencing suicidal thoughts, depression, or hallucinations?*

SEARCH THE *ABNORMAL PSYCHOLOGY* CD-ROM FOR

▲ Chapter 19 video cases and discussions
   "Mark"—Aggression, Violence, and the Brain
   The Mind of the Psychopath
   "Pat"—Psychopathy

▲ Chapter 19 practice test and feedback

▲ Additional video cases and discussions
   Early Procedures in Mental Hospitals
   Early Electroconvulsive Therapies
   "Andy"—Suicide
   "Steve"—Schizophrenia

LOG ON TO THE COMER WEB PAGE

[www.worthpublishers.com/comerabnormalpsychology4e] **FOR**

▲ Suggested Web links, research exercises, FAQ page, additional Chapter 19 practice test questions

glossary

Abnormal psychology The scientific study of abnormal behavior in order to describe, predict, explain, and change abnormal patterns of functioning.

Acetylcholine A neurotransmitter that has been implicated in depression and in dementia.

Acute stress disorder An anxiety disorder in which fear and related symptoms are experienced soon after a traumatic event and last less than a month.

Addiction Physical dependence on a substance, marked by such features as tolerance, withdrawal symptoms during abstinence, or both.

Affect A subjective experience of emotion or mood.

Affectual awareness One component of sexual therapy for hypoactive sexual desire or sexual aversion in which the client becomes aware of his or her negative emotions regarding sex.

Aftercare A program of posthospitalization care and treatment out in the community.

Agoraphobia An anxiety disorder in which a person is afraid to be in places or situations from which escape might be difficult (or embarrassing) or help unavailable if paniclike symptoms were to occur.

Agoraphobia without history of panic disorder An agoraphobic pattern that does not have its origin in a panic attack.

Agranulocytosis A life-threatening reduction in white blood cells. This condition is sometimes produced by clozapine, one of the atypical antipsychotic drugs.

Akathisia A Parkinsonian symptom consisting of a very high degree of restlessness and agitation and great discomfort in the limbs.

Alarm stage An increase of activity in the sympathetic nervous system in the presence of a perceived threat. See also *General adaptation syndrome*.

Alcohol Any beverage containing ethyl alcohol, including beer, wine, and liquor.

Alcohol dehydrogenase An enzyme that breaks down alcohol in the stomach before it enters the blood. Women have significantly less of this enzyme than men and therefore tend to become more intoxicated after ingesting an equal dose of alcohol.

Alcohol withdrawal delirium A dramatic reaction experienced by some people who are alcohol-dependent. It occurs within three days of cessation or reduction of drinking and consists of mental confusion, clouded consciousness, and terrifying visual hallucinations. Also known as *delirium tremens* (DTs).

Alcoholics anonymous (AA) A self-help organization that provides support and guidance for persons with alcohol abuse or dependence.

Alcoholism A pattern of behavior in which a person abuses or develops a dependence on alcohol.

Alogia A symptom of schizophrenia in which the person shows a decrease in speech or speech content. Also known as *poverty of speech*.

Alpha waves Brain waves characteristic of relaxed wakefulness.

Alprazolam (Xanax) A benzodiazepine drug, also shown to be effective in the treatment of panic disorder.

Altruistic suicide Suicide committed by people who intentionally sacrifice their lives for the well-being of society.

Alzheimer's disease The most common form of dementia, usually occurring after the age of 65.

Amenorrhea The absence of menstrual cycles.

American Law Institute Test A legal test for insanity that holds people to be insane at the time they committed a crime if, because of a mental disorder, they did not know right from wrong or they could not resist an uncontrollable impulse to act.

Amnesia Loss of memory. See also *Anterograde, Dissociative,* and *Retrograde Amnesia.*

Amnestic disorders Organic disorders in which the primary symptom is memory loss.

Amniocentesis A prenatal procedure used to test the amniotic fluid that surrounds the fetus, in order to detect the possibility of birth defects.

Amphetamine A stimulant drug that is manufactured in the laboratory.

Amphetamine-induced psychotic disorder A syndrome caused by a high dose of amphetamines that closely mimics schizophrenia and includes hallucinations and motor hyperactivity.

Amygdala The structure in the brain's limbic system that gives rise to emotional behavior and that may also regulate the link between arousal and memory.

Anaclitic depression A pattern of depressed behavior—found among very young children—that is caused by separation from one's mother.

Anal stage In psychoanalytic theory, the second 18 months of life, during which the child's focus of pleasure shifts to the anus, and libidinal gratification comes from retaining and passing feces.

Analogue experiment A research method in which the experimenter produces abnormal-like behavior in laboratory subjects and then conducts experiments on the subjects.

Anatomical brain disorders Problems stemming from abnormal size or shape of certain brain regions.

Anesthesia A lessening or loss of sensation for touch or pain.

Anomic suicide Suicide committed by individuals whose social environment fails to provide stability, thus leaving them without a sense of belonging.

Anorexia nervosa A disorder marked by the pursuit of extreme thinness and by an extreme loss of weight.

Anoxia A complication of birth in which the baby is deprived of oxygen.

Antabuse (Disulfiram) A drug that is relatively benign when taken by itself, but causes intense nausea, vomiting, increased heart rate, and dizziness when taken with alcohol. It is often taken by people who are trying to refrain from drinking alcohol.

Antagonist drugs Drugs that block or change the effects of an addictive drug.

Anterograde amnesia The inability to remember new information that is acquired after the event that triggered amnesia.

Anthropology The study of human cultures and institutions.

Antianxiety drugs Psychotropic drugs that help reduce tension and anxiety.

Antibipolar drugs Psychotropic drugs that help stabilize the moods of people suffering from a bipolar mood disorder.

Antibodies Bodily chemicals that seek out and destroy antigens such as bacteria or viruses.

Antidepressant drugs Psychotropic drugs that improve the moods of people with depression.

Antigen A foreign invader of the body, such as a bacterium or virus.

Antipsychotic drugs Psychotropic drugs that help correct the confusion, hallucinations, and delusions found in psychotic disorders.

Antisocial personality disorder A personality disorder characterized by a pervasive pattern of disregard for and violation of other people's rights.

Anxiety The central nervous system's physiological and emotional response to a vague sense of threat or danger.

Anxiety disorders Disorders in which anxiety is a central symptom.

Anxiety sensitivity A tendency to focus on one's bodily sensations, assess them illogically, and interpret them as harmful.

Anxiolytics Drugs that reduce anxiety (from "anxiety" and the Greek *lytikos,* able to loosen or dissolve). Also known as *Antianxiety drugs.*

Aphasia A common symptom in some kinds of dementia, characterized by difficulty producing the names of individuals and objects.

Aphrodisiac A substance that is thought to increase the sex drive. Over the centuries people have considered many substances to be aphrodisiacs, but none has been proven to increase the sex drive.

Arbitrary inference An error in logic in which a person draws negative conclusions on the basis of little or even contrary evidence. It may contribute to some cases of depression.

Assertiveness training A cognitive-behavioral approach to increasing assertive behavior that is socially desirable.

Assessment The process of collecting and interpreting relevant information about a client or subject.

Asthma A medical problem marked by narrowing of the trachea and bronchi, which results in shortness of breath, wheezing, coughing, and a choking sensation.

Asylum A type of institution that first became popular in the sixteenth century to provide care for persons with mental disorders. Most became virtual prisons.

Attention-deficit/hyperactivity disorder (ADHD) A disorder marked by either inability to focus attention or by overactive and impulsive behavior, or both.

Attribution An explanation of events as resulting from particular causes.

Atypical antipsychotic drugs A new group of antipsychotic drugs whose biological action is different from that of the traditional antipsychotic drugs.

Auditory hallucination A hallucination in which a person hears sounds and voices that are not actually present.

Augmentative communication system A method for enhancing the communication skills of individuals with autism, mental retardation, or cerebral palsy by teaching them to point to pictures, symbols, letters, or words on a communication board or computer.

Aura A warning sensation that may precede a migraine headache.

Autism A pervasive developmental disorder characterized by extreme unresponsiveness to others, poor communication skills, and behavior that is highly restricted and repetitive.

Autistic disorder A long-term disorder marked by extreme unresponsiveness to others, poor communication skills, and highly repetitive and rigid behavior.

Autoerotic asphyxia A fatal lack of oxygen that persons may unintentionally produce while hanging, suffocating, or strangling themselves during masturbation.

Automatic thoughts Numerous unpleasant thoughts that help to cause or maintain depression, anxiety, or other forms of psychological dysfunction.

Autonomic learning The inadvertent conditioning of particular responses in the autonomic nervous system.

Autonomic nervous system (ANS) The network of nerve fibers that connects the central nervous system to all the other organs of the body.

Aversion therapy A treatment based on the principles of classical conditioning in which clients are repeatedly presented with shocks or another unpleasant stimulus while they are performing undesirable behaviors such as taking a drug.

Avoidance behavior Behavior that removes or avoids anxiety-producing objects or situations.

Avoidant personality disorder A personality disorder in which an individual is consistently uncomfortable and restrained in social situations, overwhelmed by feelings of inadequacy, and extremely sensitive to negative evaluation.

Avolition A symptom of schizophrenia marked by apathy and an inability to start or complete a course of action.

Axon The long fiber that extends from the body of the neuron. Messages, or impulses, travel down it to the nerve endings.

B-cell Lymphocyte that produces antibodies.

Barbiturates Addictive sedative-hypnotic drugs used to reduce anxiety or to help people fall asleep.

Baroreceptors Sensitive nerves in the arteries responsible for alerting the brain when blood pressure becomes too high.

Baseline data An individual's initial response level on a test or scale.

Basic irrational assumptions The inaccurate and inappropriate beliefs held by people with various psychological problems, according to Albert Ellis.

Battery A series of tests, each of which produces a different kind of data.

Behavioral assessment The collection of information about specific dysfunctional behaviors a person engages in.

Behavioral medicine A field of treatment that combines psychological and physical interventions to treat or prevent medical problems.

Behavioral model A theoretical perspective that emphasizes ingrained behavior and the ways in which it is learned.

Behavioral self-control training (BSCT) A cognitive-behavioral approach to treating alcohol abuse and dependence in which clients are taught to keep track of their drinking behavior and to apply coping strategies in situations that typically trigger excessive drinking.

Behavioral therapy (Behavior modification) A therapeutic approach that views the goal of therapy as identifying the client's specific problem-causing behaviors and either modifying them or replacing them with more appropriate ones.

Behaviors The responses that an organism makes to its environment.

Bender Visual-Motor Gestalt Test A neuropsychological test in which a subject is asked to copy a set of nine simple designs and later reproduce the designs from memory.

Benzodiazepines The most common group of antianxiety drugs, which includes Valium and Xanax.

Bereavement The process of working through the grief that one feels when a loved one dies.

Beta-amyloid protein A small molecule that forms sphere-shaped deposits called senile plaques. These deposits collect in excessive numbers in the spaces between neurons in people with Alzheimer's disease, interfering with memory and learning.

Beta blocker A drug that reduces the physical symptoms of anxiety by blocking the reception of norepinephrine in the brain.

Bilateral electroconvulsive therapy (ECT) A form of electroconvulsive therapy in which one electrode is applied to each side of the forehead, and electrical current is passed through the brain's frontal lobes.

Binge An episode of uncontrollable eating during which a person ingests a very large quantity of food.

Binge-eating disorder A type of eating disorder in which a person displays a pattern of binge eating without any accompanying compensatory behaviors.

Binge-eating/purging-type anorexia nervosa A type of anorexia nervosa in which people engage in eating binges but still lose excessive weight by forcing themselves to vomit after meals or by abusing laxatives or diuretics.

Biofeedback A treatment technique in which a client is given information about physiological reactions as they occur and learns to control the reactions voluntarily.

Biofeedback training A treatment technique in which a client is given information about physiological reactions as they occur and learns to control the reactions voluntarily.

Biological challenge A procedure used to produce panic in subjects or clients by having them exercise vigorously or perform some other potentially panic-inducing task in the presence of a researcher or therapist.

Biological model The theoretical perspective that cites organic processes as the key to human behavior.

Biological therapy The use of physical and chemical procedures to help people overcome psychological difficulties.

Biopsychosocial theories Explanations that explain abnormality as resulting from an interaction of genetic, biological, developmental, emotional, behavioral, cognitive, social, and societal influences.

Bipolar disorder A mood disorder marked by alternating or intermixed periods of mania and depression.

Bipolar I disorder A type of bipolar disorder marked by full manic and major depressive episodes.

Bipolar II disorder A type of bipolar disorder marked by mildly manic (hypomanic) episodes and major depressive episodes.

Birth complications Biological conditions during birth, including anoxia and extreme prematurity, that can compromise the physical and psychological well-being of the child.

Blind design An experiment in which subjects do not know whether they are in the experimental or the control condition.

Blocking A symptom associated with schizophrenia in which thoughts seem to disappear from memory and statements end in silence before they can be completed.

Blunted affect A symptom of schizophrenia in which a person displays less emotion—anger, sadness, joy—than other people.

Body dysmorphic disorder A somatoform disorder marked by excessive worry that some aspect of one's physical appearance is defective. Also known as *dysmorphobia*.

Borderline personality disorder A personality disorder in which an individual displays repeated instability in interpersonal relationships, self-image, and mood, as well as impulsive behavior.

Brain stem The region of the central nervous system that connects the spinal cord with the cerebrum.

Brain wave The oscillations of electrical potential, as measured by an electroencephalogram, that are created by neurons in the brain.

Breathing-related sleep disorder A sleep disorder in which sleep is frequently disrupted by a breathing problem, causing excessive sleepiness or insomnia.

Brief psychotic disorder Psychotic symptoms that appear suddenly after a very stressful event or a period of emotional turmoil and last anywhere from a few hours to a month.

Briquet's syndrome See *Somatization disorder*.

Bulimia nervosa A disorder marked by frequent eating binges that are followed by forced vomiting or other extreme compensatory behaviors to avoid gaining weight.

Caffeine The world's most widely used stimulant, most often consumed in coffee.

Cannabis drugs Drugs produced from the different varieties of the hemp plant *Cannabis sativa*. They cause a mixture of hallucinogenic, depressant, and stimulant effects.

Case management A full-service form of community treatment that seems to be particularly helpful for persons with schizophrenia. In addition to offering therapy and advice, teaching problem-solving and social skills, and making sure that medications are taken properly, case managers help coordinate community services, guide clients through the community system, and, perhaps most important, act as advocates for the clients.

Case manager A community therapist who offers a full range of services for people with schizophrenia or other severe disorders, including therapy, advice, medication, guidance, and protection of patients' rights.

Case study A detailed account of a person's life and psychological problems.

Catatonia A pattern of extreme psychomotor symptoms found in some forms of schizophrenia, which may include catatonic stupor, rigidity, or posturing.

Catatonic excitement A form of catatonia in which a person moves excitedly, sometimes with wild waving of the arms and legs.

Catatonic stupor A symptom associated with schizophrenia in which a person becomes almost totally unresponsive to the environment, remaining motionless and silent for long stretches of time.

Catatonic type of schizophrenia A type of schizophrenia dominated by severe psychomotor disturbances.

Catecholamine theory The view that unipolar depression is related to low activity of norepinephrine (a catecholamine).

Catharsis The reliving of past repressed feelings in order to settle internal conflicts and overcome problems.

Caudate nuclei Structures in the brain, within the region known as the basal ganglia, that help convert sensory information into thoughts and actions.

Central nervous system The brain and spinal cord.

Cerebellum An area of the brain that coordinates movement in the body and perhaps helps control a person's ability to shift attention rapidly.

Cerebral cortex The outer layer of the cerebrum, or upper portion of the brain, also known as the *gray matter*. It is associated with higher cognitive functions.

Checking compulsion A compulsion in which people feel compelled to check the same things over and over.

Child abuse The intentional, nonaccidental use of physical or psychological force by an adult on a child, often aimed at hurting, injuring, or destroying the child.

Chlorpromazine A phenothiazine drug commonly used for treating schizophrenia. Marketed as Thorazine.

Chromosomes The structures within a cell that contain genes.

Circadian rhythm sleep disorder A sleep disorder in which people experience excessive sleepiness or insomnia as the result of a mismatch between the sleep-wake cycle in their environment and their own circadian sleep-wake cycle.

Circadian rhythms Internal "clocks" consisting of recurrent biological fluctuations.

Cirrhosis A disease of the liver, often caused by excessive drinking, in which the liver becomes scarred, forms fibrous tissue, and begins to change its anatomy and functioning.

Civil commitment A legal process by which an individual can be forced to undergo mental health treatment.

Clang A rhyme used by individuals with schizophrenia as a guide to formulating thoughts and statements.

Classical conditioning A process of learning in which two events that repeatedly occur close together in time become tied together in a person's mind and so produce the same response.

Classification system A list of disorders, along with descriptions of symptoms and guidelines for making appropriate diagnoses.

Cleaning compulsion A common compulsion in which people feel compelled to keep cleaning themselves, their clothing, their homes, or anything they might touch.

Client-centered therapy The humanistic therapy developed by Carl Rogers in which clinicians try to help clients by conveying acceptance, accurate empathy, and genuineness.

Clinical interview A face-to-face encounter in which clinicians ask questions of clients, weigh their responses and reactions, and learn about them and their psychological problems.

Clinical psychologist A professional who earns a doctorate in clinical psychology by completing four years of graduate training in abnormal functioning and its treatment as well as a one-year internship at a mental hospital or mental health agency.

Clinical psychology The study, assessment, treatment, and prevention of abnormal behavior.

Clitoris The female sex organ located in front of the urinary and vaginal openings. It becomes enlarged during sexual arousal.

Clozapine A commonly prescribed atypical antipsychotic drug. Other commonly prescribed atypical antipsychotic drugs are risperidone, olazapine, and quetiapine.

Cocaine An addictive stimulant obtained from the coca plant. It is the most powerful natural stimulant known.

Code of ethics A body of principles and rules for ethical behavior, designed to guide decisions and actions by members of a profession.

Cognition The intellectual capacity to think, remember, and anticipate.

Cognitive behavior Thoughts and beliefs, many of which remain private.

Cognitive-behavioral model A theoretical perspective that attributes psychological problems to cognitive behaviors.

Cognitive model A theoretical perspective that emphasizes the process and content of the thinking that underlies an individuals behavior.

Cognitive therapy A therapy that helps people recognize and change their faulty thinking processes.

Cognitive triad The three forms of negative thinking that Aaron Beck theorizes lead people to feel depressed. The triad consists of a negative view of one's experiences, oneself, and the future.

Cohort A group of people who are born in the same time period or year—that is, people of the same generation.

Coitus Sexual intercourse.

Community mental health A sociocultural treatment approach emphasizing community care, particularly for people with severe psychological disturbances.

Community mental health center A treatment facility that provides medication, psychotherapy, and emergency inpatient care for psychological problems and coordinates treatment in the community.

Community mental health treatment A treatment approach that emphasizes community care.

Comorbidity The occurrence of two or more psychological problems in the same individual.

Compulsion A repetitive and rigid behavior or mental act that a person feels driven to perform in order to prevent or reduce anxiety.

Computerized axial tomography (CAT scan) A composite image of the brain created by compiling X-ray images taken from many angles.

Concordance A statistical measure of the frequency with which family members (often both members of a pair of twins) have the same particular characteristic.

Conditioned response (CR) A response previously associated with an unconditioned stimulus that comes to be elicited by a conditioned stimulus.

Conditioned stimulus (CS) A previously neutral stimulus that comes to be associated with a nonneutral stimulus, and can then elicit responses similar to those elicited by the nonneutral stimulus.

Conditioning A simple form of learning.

Conditions of worth According to client-centered theorists, the internal standards by which a person judges his or her own lovability and acceptability, determined by the standards (i.e., conditions of worth) to which the person was held as a child.

Conduct disorder A childhood disorder in which the child repeatedly violates the basic rights of others, displaying aggression and sometimes destroying others' property, lying, cheating, or running away from home.

Confabulation A spontaneously made-up event fabricated to fill in a gap in one's own memory. Characteristic of persons with alcoholism suffering from Korsakoff's syndrome.

Confederate An experimenter's accomplice who plays a role in creating a believable counterfeit situation in an experiment.

Confidentiality The principle that certain professionals will not divulge the information they obtain from a client.

Confound In an experiment a variable other than the independent variable that is also acting on the dependent variable.

Conjoint family therapy A family therapy approach in which the therapist focuses primarily on communication within the family system, helping members to recognize harmful patterns of communication, to appreciate the impact of such patterns on other family members, and to change the patterns.

Contingency training A short-term behavioral treatment for drug abuse in which clients receive incentives contingent on submitting drug-free urine samples.

Continuous amnesia A disturbance of memory in which forgetting continues into the present, and new and ongoing experiences fail to be retained.

Control group In an experiment, a group of subjects who are not exposed to the independent variable.

Conversion disorder A somatoform disorder in which a psychosocial need or conflict is converted into dramatic physical symptoms that affect voluntary motor or sensory function.

Coronary heart disease Illness of the heart caused by a blocking of the coronary arteries.

Correlation The degree to which events or characteristics vary along with each other.

Correlational coefficient (r) A statistical expression of the direction and the magnitude of a correlation, ranging from $+1.00$ to -1.00.

Correlational method A research procedure used to determine how much events or characteristics vary along with each other.

Corticosteroids A group of hormones, including cortisol, released by the adrenal glands at times of stress.

Counseling psychology A mental health specialty similar to clinical psychology that requires completion of its own graduate training program.

Countertransference A phenomenon of psychotherapy in which therapists' own feelings, history, and values subtly influence the way they interpret a patient's problems.

Couple therapy A therapy format in which the therapist works with two people who share a long-term relationship. Also called *marital therapy.*

Covert desensitization Desensitization training that focuses on imagining confrontations with the frightening objects or situations while in a state of relaxation. See also *In vivo desensitization.*

Covert sensitization A behavioral treatment for eliminating unwanted behavior by pairing the behavior with unpleasant mental images.

Crack A powerful, ready-to-smoke free-base cocaine.

Cretinism A congenital disorder characterized by mental retardation and physical abnormalities and caused by low levels of iodine in a pregnant woman's diet.

Creutzfeldt-Jakob disease A form of dementia caused by a slow-acting virus that may live in the body for years before the disease appears.

Criminal commitment A legal process by which people accused of a crime are instead judged mentally unstable and sent to a mental health facility for treatment.

Crisis intervention A treatment approach that tries to help people in a psychological crisis to view their situation more accurately, make better decisions, act more constructively, and overcome the crisis.

Critical incident stress debriefing Training in how to help victims talk about their feelings and reactions to traumatic incidents.

Cross-tolerance Tolerance for a substance one has not taken before as a result of using another substance similar to it.

Culture A people's common history, values, institutions, habits, skills, technology, and arts.

Cyclothymic disorder A disorder marked by numerous periods of hypomanic symptoms and mild depressive symptoms.

D-2 receptors The subgroup of dopamine receptors that have been linked most often to schizophrenia. Other subgroups—D-1, D-3, D-4, and D-5 receptors—may, however, turn out to play just as important a role in the disorder.

Date rape Rape by a date or close acquaintance.

Day center A program that offers hospital-like treatment during the day only. Also known as *day hospital*.

Death darer A person who is ambivalent about the wish to die even as he or she attempts suicide.

Death ignorer A person who attempts suicide without recognizing the finality of death.

Death initiator A person who attempts suicide believing that the process of death is already under way and that he or she is simply hastening the process.

Death seeker A person who clearly intends to end his or her life at the time of a suicide attempt.

Declarative memory Memory for information that is directly accessible to consciousness, such as names, dates, and other learned facts.

Defense mechanisms See *Ego defense mechanisms*.

Deinstitutionalization The practice, begun in the 1960s, of releasing hundreds of thousands of patients from public mental hospitals.

Déjà vu The haunting sense of having previously seen or experienced a new scene or situation.

Delirium A rapidly developing clouding of consciousness in which a person has great difficulty concentrating, focusing attention, and following an orderly sequence of thought.

Delirium tremens (DTs) A dramatic withdrawal reaction experienced by some people who are alcohol-dependent. It consists of mental confusion, clouded consciousness, and terrifying visual hallucinations. Also called *alcohol withdrawal delirium*.

Delusion A strange false belief firmly held despite evidence to the contrary.

Delusion of control The belief that one's impulses, feelings, thoughts, and actions are being controlled by other people.

Delusion of grandeur The belief that one is a great inventor, historical figure, religious savior, or other specially empowered person.

Delusion of persecution The belief that one is being plotted or discriminated against, spied on, slandered, threatened, attacked, or deliberately victimized.

Delusion of reference A belief that attaches special and personal significance to the actions of others or to various objects or events.

Delusional disorder A disorder consisting of persistent, nonbizarre delusions that are not part of a schizophrenic disorder.

Dementia An organic syndrome marked by severe problems in memory and at least one other cognitive function.

Demonology The belief that abnormal behavior results from supernatural causes such as evil spirits.

Dendrite The extensions, or antennae, located at one end of a neuron that receive impulses from other neurons.

Denial An ego defense mechanism in which a person fails to acknowledge unacceptable thoughts, feelings, or actions.

Dependent personality disorder A personality disorder characterized by a pattern of clinging and obedience, fear of separation, and an ongoing need to be taken care of.

Dependent variable The variable in an experiment that is expected to change as the independent variable is manipulated.

Depersonalization disorder A disorder characterized by a persistent and recurrent feeling of being detached from one's own mental processes or body; that is, one feels unreal and alien.

Depression A low, sad state marked by significant levels of sadness, lack of energy, low self-worth, guilt, or related symptoms.

Derailment (Loose associations) A common formal thought disorder of schizophrenia, characterized by rapid shifts from one topic of conversation to another.

Derealization The feeling that the external world is unreal and strange.

Desire phase The phase of the sexual response cycle consisting of an urge to have sex, sexual fantasies, and sexual attraction to others.

Desynchronization An imbalance between the body's circadian rhythms and the rhythms of the environment.

Detoxification Systematic and medically supervised withdrawal from a drug.

Deviance Variance from accepted patterns of behavior.

Diagnosis A determination that a person's problems reflect a particular disorder.

Diathesis-stress explanation The view that a person must first have a predisposition to a disorder and then be subjected to episodes of severe stress in order to develop the disorder.

Diazepam A benzodiazepine drug marketed as Valium.

Dichotomous thinking Viewing problems and solutions in rigid "either/or" terms.

Diencephalon A brain area (consisting of the mammillary bodies, thalamus, and hypothalamus) that plays a key role in transforming short-term to long-term memory, among other functions.

Directed masturbation A sex therapy approach that teaches women with female arousal or orgasmic disorders how to masturbate effectively and eventually to reach orgasm during sexual interactions.

Disaster response network A network of thousands of volunteer mental health professionals who mobilize to provide free emergency mental health services at disaster sites throughout North America.

Disorganized type of schizophrenia A type of schizophrenia marked primarily by confusion, incoherence, and flat or inappropriate affect.

Displacement An ego defense mechanism that channels unacceptable id impulses toward another, safer substitute.

Disregulation model A theory that explains psychophysiological disorders as breakdowns in the body's negative feedback loops, which lead to interruption of the body's smooth, self-regulating operation.

Dissociative amnesia A dissociative disorder marked by an inability to recall important personal events and information.

Dissociative disorders Disorders marked by major changes in memory that do not have clear physical causes.

Dissociative fugue A dissociative disorder in which a person travels to a new location and may assume a new identity, simultaneously forgetting his or her past.

Dissociative identity disorder (Multiple personality disorder) A disorder in which a person displays two or more distinct personalities.

Dizygotic twins Twins who develop from separate eggs.

Dopamine The neurotransmitter whose high activity has been shown to be related to schizophrenia.

Dopamine hypothesis The theory that schizophrenia results from excessive activity of the neurotransmitter dopamine.

Double depression A sequence in which dysthymic disorder leads to a major depressive disorder.

Double-bind communication Simultaneous messages that are mutually contradictory.

Double-bind hypothesis A theory that some parents repeatedly communicate pairs of messages that are mutually contradictory, helping to produce schizophrenia in their children.

Double-blind design Experimental procedure in which neither the subject nor the experimenter knows whether the subject has received the experimental treatment or a placebo.

Down syndrome A form of mental retardation caused by an abnormality in the twenty-first chromosome.

Drapetomania According to a nineteenth-century diagnostic category, an obsessive desire for freedom that drove some slaves to try to flee from captivity.

Dream A series of ideas and images that form during sleep.

Drug abuse The ongoing excessive intake of a substance that results in emotional, social, occupational, or functional impairment.

Drug maintenance therapy An approach to treating substance dependence in which clients are given legally and medically supervised doses of a substitute drug with which to satisfy their addiction.

Drug therapy The use of psychotropic drugs to alleviate the symptoms of psychological disorders.

DSM-IV The fourth, and current, edition of the Diagnostic and Statistical Manual of Mental Disorders.

Durham test A legal test for insanity that holds people to be insane at the time they committed a crime if their act was the result of a mental disorder or defect.

Duty to protect The principle that therapists must break confidentiality in order to protect a person who may be the intended victim of a client.

Dyslexia (Reading disorder) A disorder characterized by a marked impairment in the ability to recognize words and to comprehend what one reads, not caused by visual or hearing defects, poor schooling, or intellectual deficit.

Dyspareunia A disorder in which a person experiences severe pain in the genitals during sexual activity.

Dyssomnias Sleep disorders in which the amount, quality, or timing of sleep is disturbed.

Dysthymic disorder A mood disorder that is similar to but longer-lasting and less disabling than a major depressive disorder.

Dystonia A Parkinsonian symptom in which involuntary muscle contractions cause bizarre and uncontrollable movements of the face, neck, tongue, and back.

Eccentric A person who deviates from an established behavioral pattern, or exhibits odd or whimsical behavior.

Echolalia A symptom of autism or schizophrenia in which a person responds to being spoken to by repeating some of the other person's words.

Educational psychology A mental health specialty that focuses on behavior and problems, particularly in educational settings.

Ego According to Freud, the psychological force that employs reason and operates in accordance with the reality principle.

Ego defense mechanisms According to psychoanalytic theory, strategies developed by the ego to control unacceptable id impulses and to avoid or reduce the anxiety they arouse.

Ego ideal A composite image of the values one has acquired—the kind of person one believes in striving to become.

Ego psychology A psychodynamic theory that focuses on the importance of the ego.

Ego theory The psychodynamic theory that emphasizes the role of the ego and considers it an independent force.

Ego-dystonic homosexuality A past DSM category indicating a homosexual orientation accompanied by extreme distress.

Egoistic suicide Suicide committed by people over whom society has little or no control, people who are not inhibited by the norms or rules of society.

Eidetic imagery A strong visual image of an object or scene that persists in some persons long after the object or scene is removed.

Ejaculation Contractions of the muscles at the base of the penis that cause sperm to be ejected.

Electra complex According to Freud, the pattern of desires all girls experience in which they develop a sexual attraction to their father.

Electroconvulsive therapy (ECT) A form of biological treatment, used primarily on depressed patients, in which a brain seizure is triggered as an electric current passes through electrodes attached to the patient's forehead.

Electroencephalograph (EEG) A device that records electrical impulses in the brain.

Electromyograph (EMG) A device that provides feedback about the level of muscular tension in the body.

Electrooculograph A device that records the movement of the eyes.

Emergency commitment Temporary commitment to a mental hospital of a patient who is behaving in a bizarre or violent way. See also *Two-physician certificates.*

Employee assistance program A mental health program offered by a business to its employees.

Encephalitis An early-childhood disease that can sometimes cause serious brain damage if untreated.

Encopresis A childhood disorder characterized by repeated defecating in inappropriate places, such as one's clothing.

Encounter group A small group guided by a leader through intensive experiences designed to develop participants' self-awareness and, as a consequence, their skills in human relationships.

Endogenous depression A depression that appears to develop without antecedents and is assumed to be caused by internal factors.

Endorphins Neurotransmitters that help relieve pain and reduce emotional tension. They are sometimes referred to as the body's own opioids.

Enmeshed family pattern A family system in which members are overinvolved with each other's affairs and overconcerned about each other's welfare.

Enuresis A childhood disorder marked by repeated bed-wetting or wetting of one's clothes.

Epidemiological study A study that measures the incidence and prevalence of a disorder in a given population.

Epilepsy (Brain seizure disorder) A disorder of the brain characterized by seizures; alterations in consciousness; and impairment of sensory, mental, or motor skills.

Episodic memory A person's autobiographical memory of personal experiences and other highly personal material.

Ergot alkaloid A naturally occurring compound from which LSD is derived.

Erogenous zones Body areas that Freud considered representative of the child's sexual drives and conflicts at each of the normal stages of development.

Essential hypertension Chronic high blood pressure brought about by a combination of psychological and physiological factors.

Estrogen The primary female sex hormone.

Ethyl alcohol The chemical compound in all alcoholic beverages that is rapidly absorbed into the blood and immediately begins to affect the person's functioning.

Evoked potentials The brain response patterns recorded on an electroencephalograph.

Excitement phase The phase of the sexual response cycle marked by changes in the pelvic region, general physical arousal, and increases in heart rate, muscle tension, blood pressure, and rate of breathing.

Exhaustion stage The failure of the parasympathetic nervous system to resist a sustained response of the sympathetic nervous system. It leads to a breakdown in the control of the autonomic nervous system over the organs of the body. See also *General adaptation syndrome.*

Exhibitionism A paraphilia in which persons have repeated sexually arousing urges or fantasies about exposing their genitals to another person, and may act upon those urges.

Existential anxiety A universal fear of the limits and responsibilities of one's existence.

Existential model The theoretical perspective that human beings are born with the total freedom to either face up to one's existence and give meaning to one's life or to shrink from that responsibility.

Existential therapy A therapy that encourages clients to accept responsibility for their lives and to live with greater meaning and values.

Exorcism The practice in early societies of treating abnormality by coaxing evil spirits to leave the person's body.

Experiment A research procedure in which a variable is manipulated and the effect of the manipulation is observed.

Experimental group In an experiment, the subjects who are exposed to the independent variable under investigation.

Exposure and response prevention A behavioral treatment for obsessive-compulsive disorder that exposes clients to anxiety-arousing thoughts or situations and then prevents them from performing their compulsive acts.

Exposure treatments Behavioral treatments in which persons are exposed to the objects or situations they dread.

Expressed emotion The general level of criticism, disapproval, and hostility expressed in a family. People recovering from schizophrenia are considered more likely to relapse if their families rate high in expressed emotion.

External validity The degree to which the results of a study may be generalized beyond that study.

Extinction The decrease in responding that occurs when an unconditioned stimulus is no longer paired with the conditioned stimulus, or when a response is no longer rewarded.

Extrapyramidal effects Unwanted movements, such as severe shaking, bizarre-looking grimaces, twisting of the body, and extreme restlessness, sometimes produced by traditional antipsychotic drugs.

Eye movement desensitization and reprocessing A behavioral exposure treatment in which clients move their eyes in a saccadic (rhythmic) manner from side to side while flooding their minds with images of phobic objects and situations.

Facilitated communication A controversial method for teaching individuals with autism to communicate. The therapist or "facilitator" provides physical assistance as the individual types or points to letters on a keyboard or communication board.

Factitious disorder An illness with no identifiable physical cause, in which the patient is believed to be intentionally producing or faking symptoms in order to assume a sick role.

Family pedigree study A research design in which investigators determine how many and which relatives of a person with a disorder have the same disorder.

Family systems theory A theory that views the family as a system of interacting parts whose interactions exhibit consistent patterns and unstated rules.

Family therapy A therapy format in which the therapist meets with all members of a family and helps them to change in therapeutic ways.

Fantasy An ego defense mechanism in which a person uses imaginary events to satisfy unacceptable impulses.

Fear The central nervous system's physiological and emotional response to a serious threat to one's well-being.

Fear hierarchy A list of objects or situations that frighten a person, starting with those that are slightly feared and ending with those that are feared greatly.

Female orgasmic disorder A dysfunction in which a woman rarely has an orgasm or repeatedly experiences a very delayed one.

Female sexual arousal disorder A female dysfunction marked by a persistent inability to attain sexual excitement, including adequate lubrication or genital swelling, during sexual activity.

Fetal alcohol syndrome A group of problems in a child, including lower intellectual functioning, low birth weight, and irregularities in the hands and face, that result from excessive alcohol intake by the mother during pregnancy.

Fetishism A paraphilia consisting of recurrent and intense sexual urges, fantasies, or behaviors that involve the use of a nonliving object, often to the exclusion of all other stimuli.

Fixation According to Freud, a condition in which the id, ego, and superego do not mature properly and are frozen at an early stage of development.

Flashback LSD-induced sensory and emotional changes that recur long after the drug has left the body.

Flat affect A symptom of schizophrenia in which the person shows almost no emotions at all.

Flooding A treatment for phobias in which clients are exposed repeatedly and intensively to a feared object and made to see that it is actually harmless.

Folie à deux (Shared psychotic disorder) A psychotic disorder in which a delusion is shared by two people.

Forebrain The top area of the brain, consisting of the cerebrum, thalamus, and hypothalamus.

Forensic science The study of legal issues relating to medicine or psychology.

Formal thought disorder A disturbance in the production and organization of thought.

Fragile X syndrome A chromosomal disorder characterized by moderate to severe degrees of mental handicaps, language impairments, and behavioral problems.

Free association A psychodynamic technique in which the patient describes any thought, feeling, or image that comes to mind, even if it seems unimportant.

Free-base A technique for ingesting cocaine in which the pure cocaine basic alkaloid is chemically separated from processed cocaine, vaporized by heat from a flame, and inhaled with a pipe.

Free-floating anxiety Chronic and persistent feelings of nervousness and agitation that are not clearly attached to a specific, identifiable threat.

Frontal lobe The region of each cerebral hemisphere that helps govern motor function and abstract thinking.

Frotteurism A paraphilia consisting of repeated and intense sexual urges, fantasies, or behaviors that involve touching and rubbing against a nonconsenting person.

Fugue See *Dissociative fugue*.

Functional mental disorders A term used in the past to indicate abnormal behavior patterns that have no clear link to physical abnormalities in the brain.

Fusion The final merging of two or more subpersonalities in multiple personality disorder.

GABA The neurotransmitter gamma-aminobutyric acid, whose low activity has been linked to generalized anxiety disorder.

Galvanic skin response (GSR) Changes in the electrical resistance of the skin.

Ganja A recreational drug of at least intermediate strength derived from varieties of the hemp plant.

Gender identity disorder A disorder in which a person persistently feels extremely uncomfortable about his or her assigned sex and strongly wishes to be a member of the opposite sex. Also known as *transsexualism*.

Genes The segments of a chromosome that control the characteristics and traits we inherit.

General adaptation syndrome A three-stage reaction to stress proposed by theorist Hans Selye to describe the relationship between stress and the autonomic nervous system.

General paresis An irreversible, progressive disorder with both physical and mental symptoms, including paralysis and delusions of grandeur.

Generalized amnesia A pattern in which a person forgets both the period beginning with a traumatic event and all other events before the onset of this period.

Generalized anxiety disorder A disorder marked by persistent and excessive feelings of anxiety and worry about numerous events and activities.

Genetic linkage study A research approach in which extended families with high rates of a disorder over several generations are observed in order to determine whether the disorder closely follows the distribution pattern of other family traits.

Genital stage In Freud's theory, the stage beginning at approximately 12 years old, when the child begins to find sexual pleasure in heterosexual relationships.

Geropsychology The field of psychology concerned with the mental health of elderly people.

Gestalt therapy The humanistic therapy developed by Fritz Perls in which clinicians actively move clients toward self-recognition and self-acceptance by using techniques such as role-playing and self-discovery exercises.

Glia Brain cells that support the neurons.

Glutamate A common neurotransmitter that is apparently depleted in the brains of Alzheimer's victims.

Grief The reaction one experiences when a loved one is lost.

Group home Special homes where people with disorders or disabilities are taught self-help, living, and working skills.

Group therapy A therapy format in which a group of people with similar problems meet together with a therapist to work on those problems.

Guided participation A modeling technique in which the therapist and client first construct a fear hierarchy and the client then observes and imitates the therapist experiencing the least feared item in the hierarchy, a more feared item, and so on.

Guilty but mentally ill A verdict stating that defendants are guilty of committing a crime, but are also suffering from a mental illness that should be treated during their imprisonment.

Habituation training A therapeutic technique in which a therapist tries to call forth a client's obsessive thoughts again and again, with the expectation that the thoughts will eventually lose their power to frighten and thus to cause anxiety.

Halcion (Triazolam) An antianxiety drug that is quickly metabolized in the body.

Halfway house A residence for people with schizophrenia or other severe problems who cannot yet live alone or with their families, often staffed by paraprofessionals.

Hallucination The experiencing of sights, sounds, or other perceptions in the absence of external stimuli.

Hallucinogen A substance that causes powerful changes primarily in sensory perception, including strengthening of perceptions and producing illusions and hallucinations. Also called *psychedelic drug.*

Hallucinogen persisting perception disorder (Flashback) The recurrence of drug-induced sensory and emotional changes long after a hallucinogenic drug has left the body.

Hallucinosis A state of perceptual distortion and hallucination.

Hardiness A set of positive attitudes in response to stress that enables a person who has been exposed to life-threatening situations to carry on with a sense of fortitude, control, and commitment.

Hashish The most powerful drug produced from varieties of the hemp plant.

Hebephrenic schizophrenia See *Disorganized type of schizophrenia.*

Helper T-cell A lymphocyte that identifies antigens and then both multiplies and triggers the production of other kinds of immune cells.

Helplessness See *Learned helplessness.*

Heroin One of the most addictive substances derived from opium, illegal in the United States under all circumstances.

High The pleasant feeling of relaxation and euphoria that follows the rush from certain recreational drugs.

High-risk study A study in which people hypothesized to be at greater risk for developing a disorder are followed throughout their childhood and compared with controls who are considered not to be at risk.

Hindbrain The lower rearward portion of the brain comprised of the medulla, pons, and cerebellum.

Hippocampus Part of the limbic system, located below the cerebral cortex, that is involved in the memory system. Damage to this area can result in severe memory difficulties.

Histrionic personality disorder A personality disorder in which an individual displays a pattern of excessive emotionality and attention seeking. Once called *hysterical personality disorder.*

Homeostasis A state in which the parts of a system interact in ways that enable the system to maintain itself and survive.

Homosexuality Sexual preference for a person of one's own gender.

Hopelessness A pessimistic belief that one's present circumstances, problems, or mood will not change.

Hormones The chemicals released by glands into the bloodstream.

Humanistic model The theoretical perspective that human beings are born with a natural inclination to be friendly, cooperative, and constructive, and are driven to self-actualize.

Humanistic therapy A system of therapy that tries to help clients look at themselves accurately and acceptingly so that they can fulfill their positive inborn potential.

Humanistic-existential model A theoretical point of view that stresses the roles of values and choices in determining human individuality and fulfillment.

Humanistic-existential therapy A system of therapy that tries to help clients view themselves and their situations more ac-

curately and acceptingly and move toward actualizing their full potential as human beings.

Humors According to Greek and Roman physicians, bodily chemicals that influence mental and physical functioning.

Huntington's disease An inherited disease in which people develop progressive problems in cognition, emotion, and movement, and which results in dementia.

Hydrocephalus A disease characterized by an increase in cerebrospinal fluid and resultant head enlargement.

Hypertension Chronic high blood pressure.

Hypnosis A sleeplike suggestible state during which a person can be directed to act in unusual ways, to experience unusual sensations, to remember seemingly forgotten events, or to forget remembered events.

Hypnotic amnesia A condition in which a person forgets facts, events, and even his or her identity in obedience to an instruction received under hypnosis.

Hypnotic therapy A treatment in which the patient undergoes hypnosis and is then guided to recall forgotten events or perform other therapeutic activities. Also known as *hypnotherapy.*

Hypnotism The inducing of a trancelike mental state in which a person becomes extremely suggestible.

Hypoactive sexual desire disorder A disorder marked by a lack of interest in sex and hence a low level of sexual activity.

Hypochondriasis A somatoform disorder in which people mistakenly fear that minor changes in their physical functioning indicate a serious disease.

Hypomanic pattern A pattern in which a person experiences symptoms of mania, but the symptoms are less severe and cause less impairment than a manic episode.

Hypothalamus A part of the brain that helps regulate various bodily functions, including eating and hunger.

Hypothesis A tentative explanation advanced to provide a basis for an investigation.

Hypoxyphilia A pattern in which people strangle or smother themselves, or ask their partner to strangle or smother them, to increase their sexual pleasure.

Hysteria A term once used to describe what are now known as conversion disorder, somatization disorder, and pain disorder associated with psychological factors.

Hysterical disorder A type of somatoform disorder in which physical functioning is altered or lost.

Hysterical somatoform disorders Somatoform disorders in which people suffer actual changes in their physical functioning.

Iatrogenic disorder A disorder that is unintentionally caused by a practitioner.

Id According to Freud, the psychological force that produces instinctual needs, drives, and impulses.

Identification The unconscious incorporation of parental values and feelings and fusing them with one's identity. Also an ego defense mechanism in which persons take on the values and feelings of the person who is causing them anxiety.

Idiographic understanding An understanding of the behavior of a particular individual.

Imipramine A tricyclic drug that has been found to be effective in treating unipolar depression.

Immune system The body's network of activities and cells that identify and destroy antigens and cancer cells.

Imposter phenomenon A persistent feeling that one does not deserve one's success because it is based solely on hard work or manipulation of others rather than competence.

Impulse-control disorders Disorders in which people repeatedly fail to resist an impulse, drive, or temptation to perform an act that is harmful to themselves or to others.

In vivo desensitization Desensitization training that makes use of actual physical situations, as opposed to imagined ones. See also *Covert desensitization.*

Inappropriate affect A symptom of schizophrenia in which a person displays emotions that are unsuited to the situation.

Incest Sexual relations between close relatives.

Incidence The number of new cases of a disorder occurring in a population over a specific period of time.

Independent variable The variable in an experiment that is manipulated to determine whether it has an effect on another variable.

Individual therapy A therapeutic approach in which a therapist sees a client alone for sessions that may last from fifteen minutes to two hours.

Indoleamine theory The view that unipolar depression is caused by deficiencies in the activity of serotonin (an indoleamine).

Informed consent A person's consent to participate in an experiment or procedure, given with full knowledge of the potential benefits and risks.

Inhibited power motive style A personality style characterized by a strong but inhibited need for power. It is linked to a tendency to develop physical illness.

Insanity defense A legal defense in which persons charged with a criminal offense claim to be not guilty by reason of insanity and try to show that, as a result of mental dysfunctioning, they were not legally responsible for their conduct at the time of their offense.

Insight therapy Psychotherapeutic approach that helps the patient primarily achieve a greater understanding of his or her problem and key aspects of his or her functioning.

Insomnia Difficulty falling or staying asleep.

Instrumental conditioning See *Operant conditioning.*

Integrity test A test that seeks to measure whether the test taker is generally honest or dishonest.

Intelligence quotient (IQ) A general score derived from intelligence tests that is considered to represent a person's overall level of intelligence.

Intelligence test A test designed to measure a person's intellectual ability.

Intermittent explosive disorder An impulse-control disorder in which people periodically fail to resist aggressive impulses, leading to the performance of serious assaults on people or destruction of property.

Internal validity The accuracy with which a study can pinpoint one out of various possible factors as being the cause of a phenomenon.

Interpersonal psychotherapy (IPT) A treatment for unipolar depression that is based on the belief that clarifying and changing one's interpersonal problems will help lead to recovery.

Intoxication A temporary substance-induced state in which a person exhibits impaired judgment, mood changes, irritability, slurred speech, and loss of coordination.

Introjection The unconscious incorporation of parental values that leads to the development of the superego in the child. Also, according to psychodynamic theory, people who have lost a loved one may introject, or fuse, their own identity with that of the person they have lost.

Irresistible impulse test A legal test for insanity that holds people to be insane at the time they committed a crime if they were driven to do so by an uncontrollable "fit of passion."

Isolation An ego defense mechanism in which people unconsciously isolate and disown undesirable and unwanted thoughts, experiencing them as foreign intrusions.

Jamais vu The experience of not recognizing a scene or situation that one has previously experienced.

Juvenile delinquents Term often used by the legal system to describe children between the ages of 8 and 18 who break the law.

Killer T-cell A lymphocyte that seeks out and destroys body cells that have been infected by viruses.

Kleptomania An impulse-control disorder characterized by the recurrent failure to resist impulses to steal objects not needed for personal use or monetary value.

Koro A pattern of anxiety found in Southeast Asia in which a man suddenly becomes intensely fearful that his penis will withdraw into his abdomen and that he will die as a result.

Korsakoff's syndrome An alcohol-related amnestic disorder marked by extreme confusion, memory impairment, and other neurological symptoms.

L-dopa A precursor of dopamine, given to patients suffering from Parkinson's disease, a disease in which dopamine is low.

Latency stage In psychoanalytic theory, the stage children enter at 6 years of age in which their sexual desires apparently subside and their libidinal energy is devoted to developing new interests, activities, and skills.

Latent content The symbolic meaning of a dream.

Lateral hypothalamus (LH) The region of the hypothalamus that, when activated, produces hunger.

Learned helplessness The perception, based on past experiences, that one has no control over one's reinforcements.

Learning disorder A developmental disorder marked by impairments in cognitive skills such as reading, mathematics, or language.

Lesion Localized damage to tissue.

Lethality scale A scale used by crisis prevention centers to estimate a caller's potential for suicide.

Leveled programs A token economy system that incorporates different levels of difficulty.

Libido In Freudian theory, the sexual energy that fuels the id and other forces of personality.

Life change units (LCUs) A system for measuring the stress associated with various life events.

Light therapy (Phototherapy) A treatment for seasonal affective disorder in which patients are exposed to extra light for several hours.

Limbic system Region of the brain at the lower part of the cerebrum that controls bodily changes associated with emotions.

Lithium A metallic element that occurs in nature as a mineral salt and is an effective treatment for bipolar disorders.

Lobotomy Psychosurgery that severs the connections between the cortex of the brain's frontal lobes and the lower centers of the brain.

Localized (circumscribed) amnesia In this, the most common form of dissociative amnesia, a person forgets all events that occurred over a limited period of time.

Locus ceruleus A small area of the brain that seems to be active in the regulation of emotions. Many of its neurons use norepinephrine.

Logotherapy A treatment that focuses on changing clients' attitudes toward their existence. Developed by Viktor Frankl.

Long-term memory The memory system that contains all the information that we have stored over the years.

Longitudinal study A study that observes the same subjects on many occasions over a long period of time.

Loose associations A common thinking disturbance in schizophrenia, characterized by rapid shifts from one topic of conversation to another. Also known as *derailment*.

Lycanthropy A condition in which a person believes himself or herself to be possessed by wolves or other animals.

Lymphocytes White blood cells that circulate through the lymph system and bloodstream, helping the body identify and destroy antigens and cancer cells.

Lysergic acid diethylamide (LSD) A hallucinogenic drug derived from ergot alkaloids.

M'Naghten test A widely used legal test for insanity that holds people to be insane at the time they committed a crime if, because of a mental disorder, they did not know the nature of the act or did not know right from wrong.

Magnetic resonance imaging (MRI) The use of the magnetic property of certain atoms in the brain to create a detailed picture of the brain's structure.

Mainstreaming The placement of children with mental retardation in regular school classes with children who are not mentally retarded.

Major depressive disorder A mood disorder marked by the symptoms of depression that is disabling and is not caused by such factors as drugs or a general medical condition.

Major depressive episode A severe episode of depressed mood that is significantly disabling and is not caused by such factors as drugs or a general medical condition.

Male erectile disorder A dysfunction in which a man repeatedly fails to attain or maintain an erection during sexual activity.

Male orgasmic disorder A male dysfunction characterized by a repeated inability to reach orgasm or long delays in reaching orgasm after normal sexual excitement.

Malingering Intentionally feigning illness to achieve some external gains, such as financial compensation or military deferment.

Malpractice suit A legal suit charging a therapist with improper conduct in the course of treatment.

Managed care program An insurance program in which the insurance company decides the cost, method, provider, and length of treatment.

Mania A state or episode of euphoria or frenzied activity in which people may have an exaggerated belief that the world is theirs for the taking.

Manic-depressive disorder See *Bipolar disorder*.

Manifest content The consciously remembered features of a dream.

Mantra A sound, uttered or thought, used to focus one's attention and to turn away from ordinary thoughts and concerns during meditation.

MAO inhibitor An antidepressant drug that prevents the action of the enzyme monoamine oxidase.

Marijuana One of the cannabis drugs, derived from the leaves and flowering tops of the hemp plant *Cannabis sativa*.

Marital schism A family situation in which the father and mother are in open conflict, with each trying to undercut the other and compete for the loyalty of the child. Some theorists believe this conflict can lead to schizophrenic behavior in the daughter.

Marital skew A family situation in which a so-called schizophrenogenic mother dominates the family, and the father keeps peace by continually yielding to her wishes. Some theorists believe this conflict can lead to schizophrenic behavior in the son.

Marital therapy A therapeutic approach in which the therapist works with two people who share a long-term relationship. It focuses on the structure and communication patterns in the relationship.

Masochism See *Sexual masochism*.

Masturbation Self-stimulation of the genitals to achieve sexual arousal.

Masturbatory satiation A behavioral treatment in which a client masturbates for a very long period of time while fantasizing in detail about a paraphilic object. The procedure is expected to produce a feeling of boredom that in turn becomes linked to the object.

Mean The average of a group of scores.

Medication-induced movement disorders Disturbing movement abnormalities that are sometimes a side effect of antipsychotic drugs. They include Parkinsonian symptoms, neuroleptic malignant syndrome, and tardive dyskinesia.

Meditation A technique of turning one's concentration inward and achieving a slightly changed state of consciousness.

Melancholia A condition described by early Greek and Roman philosophers and physicians as consisting of unshakable sadness. Today it is known as *depression*.

Melatonin A hormone that appears to have a role in regulating mood. It is secreted when a person's surroundings are dark, but not when they are light.

Memory The faculty for recalling past events and past learning.

Meningitis A childhood disease marked by inflammation of the meninges of the brain. It can lead to brain damage and mental retardation if not treated.

Mental age The age level at which a person performs on a test of intellectual skill, independent of his or her chronological age.

Mental incompetence A state of mental instability that leaves defendants unable to understand the legal charges and proceedings they are facing and unable to prepare an adequate defense with their attorney.

Mental retardation A disorder marked by intellectual functioning and adaptive behavior that are well below average.

Mental status exam A set of interview questions and observations designed to reveal the degree and nature of a client's abnormal functioning.

Mentally ill chemical abuser (MICA) A person with a chronic mental disorder who also abuses alcohol or other drugs.

Mescaline A hallucinogenic drug.

Mesmerism The method employed by Austrian physician F. A. Mesmer to treat hysterical disorders. It was a precursor of hypnotism.

Metabolism The chemical and physical processes that go on in any living organism that break down food and convert it into energy. Also, the biochemical transformation of substances in the cells of living things, as when the liver breaks down alcohol into acetylaldehyde.

Metacommunication The context, tone, and gestures attached to any message. See also *Primary communication*.

Methadone A laboratory-made substitute drug for heroin. See also *Drug maintenance therapy*.

Methadone maintenance program An approach to treating heroin dependence in which clients are given legally and medically supervised doses of a substitute drug, methadone.

Methylphenidate A stimulant drug, known better by the trade name Ritalin, commonly used to treat ADHD.

Microencephaly A biological disorder characterized by a small, unusually shaped head, resulting from a combination of hereditary, prenatal, birth, and postnatal factors.

Midbrain The middle region of the brain.

Migraine headache An extremely severe headache that occurs on one side of the head, often preceded by a warning sensation and sometimes accompanied by dizziness, nausea, or vomiting.

Mild retardation A level of mental retardation (IQ between 50 and 70) at which people can benefit from education and support themselves as adults.

Milieu therapy A humanistic approach to institutional treatment based on the belief that institutions can help patients recover by creating a climate that promotes self-respect, responsible behavior, and meaningful activity.

Mind-body dualism René Descartes's position that the mind is separate from the body.

Minnesota Multiphasic Personality Inventory (MMPI) A widely used personality inventory consisting of a large number of statements that subjects mark as being true or false for them.

Minor tranquilizers See *Antianxiety drugs*.

Mitral valve prolapse (MVP) A cardiac malfunction marked by periodic episodes of heart palpitations.

Mixed design A research design in which a correlational analysis is mixed with an experimental analysis. See also *Quasi-experiment*.

Model A set of assumptions and concepts that help scientists explain and interpret observations.

Modeling A process of learning in which a person observes and then imitates others. Also, a therapy approach based on the same principle.

Moderate retardation A level of mental retardation (IQ between 35 and 49) at which people can learn to care for themselves and benefit from vocational training.

Monoamine oxidase (MAO) A body chemical that destroys the neurotransmitter norepinephrine.

Monoamine oxidase (MAO) inhibitors Antidepressant drugs that lower MAO activity and thus increase the level of norepinephrine activity in the brain.

Monozygotic twins Twins who have developed from a single egg.

Mood disorder Disorder affecting one's emotional state, including major depressive disorder and bipolar disorders.

Moral anxiety According to Freud, anxiety that results from being punished or threatened for expressing id impulses

rather than following superego standards. A person eventually comes to perceive the id impulses themselves as threatening.

Moral treatment A nineteenth-century approach to treating people with mental dysfunction that emphasized moral guidance and humane and respectful treatment.

Morphine A highly addictive substance derived from opium that is particularly effective in relieving pain.

Multiaxial system A classification system in which different "axes," or branches of information, are required from the diagnostician. DSM-IV is a multiaxial system.

Multidimensional risk perspective A theory that identifies several kinds of risk factors that are thought to combine to help cause a disorder. The more factors present, the greater the risk of developing the disorder.

Multiple personality disorder A dissociative disorder in which a person develops two or more distinct personalities. Also known as *dissociative identity disorder*.

Multiple-baseline design An experimental design in which several behaviors of a single subject are measured and then the experimenter observes the effect that the manipulation of an independent variable has on each of the behaviors.

Munchausen syndrome The extreme and chronic form of factitious disorder in which a person induces symptoms, gains admission to a hospital, and receives treatment.

Munchausen syndrome by proxy A disorder in which parents make up or induce physical illnesses in their children.

Muscle-contraction headache A headache caused by the narrowing of muscles surrounding the skull. Also known as *tension headache*.

Narcissistic personality disorder A personality disorder marked by a broad pattern of grandiosity, need for admiration, and lack of empathy.

Narcolepsy A dyssomnia characterized by sudden onsets of REM sleep during waking hours, generally brought on by strong emotion.

Narcotic Any natural or synthetic derivative of opium.

Narcotic antagonist A substance that counteracts the effects of opioids. See *Antagonist drugs*.

Natural experiment An experiment in which nature, rather than an experimenter, manipulates an independent variable.

Naturalistic observation A method for observing behavior in which clinicians or researchers observe people in their everyday environments.

Negative correlation A statistical relationship in which the value of one variable increases while the other variable decreases.

Negative feedback loops A physiological process in which the brain receives information about external events from the environment, processes this information, and then stimulates body organs into action. Mechanisms in the organs then provide negative feedback, telling the brain that its stimulation has been sufficient and should now stop.

Negative symptoms Symptoms of schizophrenia that seem to be deficits in normal thought, emotions, or behaviors.

Neologism A made-up word that has meaning only to the person using it.

Nerve ending The region at the neuron's terminus from which an impulse that has traveled through the neuron is transmitted to a neighboring neuron.

Neurofibrillary tangles Twisted protein fibers that form within certain brain cells as people age.

Neuroleptic drugs Traditional antipsychotic drugs, so called because they often produce undesired effects similar to the symptoms of neurological disorder.

Neuroleptic malignant syndrome A severe, potentially fatal reaction to antipsychotic drugs, marked by muscle rigidity, fever, altered consciousness, and autonomic dysfunction.

Neurological Relating to the structure or activity of the brain.

Neurological test A test that directly measures brain structure or activity.

Neuron A nerve cell.

Neuropsychological test A test that detects brain impairment by measuring a person's cognitive, perceptual, and motor performances.

Neurosis Freud's term for disorders characterized by intense anxiety, attributed to failure of a person's ego defense mechanisms to cope with his or her unconscious conflicts.

Neurotic anxiety In Freudian theory, anxiety experienced by people who are repeatedly and excessively prevented, by their parents or by circumstances, from expressing their id impulses.

Neurotransmitter A chemical that, released by one neuron, crosses the synaptic space to be received at receptors on the dendrites of neighboring neurons.

Neutralizing A person's attempt to eliminate unwanted thoughts by thinking or behaving in ways that put matters right internally, that make up for the unacceptable thoughts.

Nicotine patch A patch attached to the skin like an adhesive bandage; its nicotine content is absorbed through the skin, supposedly easing the withdrawal reaction brought on by quitting cigarette smoking.

Nightmare disorder A common parasomnia in which a person experiences chronic distressful, frightening dreams.

Nocturnal penile tumescence (NPT) Erection during sleep.

Nomothetic understanding A general understanding of the nature, causes, and treatments of abnormal psychological functioning in the form of laws or principles.

Nonpurging-type bulimia nervosa A type of bulimia nervosa in which an individual displays compensatory behaviors other than self-induced vomiting or the misuse of laxatives, such as fasting or exercising frantically.

Nootropics Drugs designed to help enhance memory.

Norepinephrine A neurotransmitter whose abnormal activity is linked to depression and panic disorder.

Normalization The principle that institutions and community residences should expose people with mental retardation to living conditions and opportunities similar to those found in the rest of society.

Normalization program A treatment program for persons with mental retardation, which provides everyday conditions that closely resemble life in the mainstream of society.

Norms A society's stated and unstated rules for proper conduct.

Not guilty by reason of insanity (NGRI) A verdict stating that defendants are not guilty of committing a crime because they were insane at the time of the crime.

Object loss The loss of a significant person in one's life. According to psychodynamic theory, the risk of object loss during the oral stage (the loss of the mother who provides food and comfort) makes a child anxious and triggers defense mechanisms.

Object relations theory The psychodynamic theory that views the desire for relationships as the key motivating force in human behavior.

Observer drift The tendency of an observer who is rating subjects in an experiment to gradually and involuntarily change criteria, thus making the data unreliable.

Obsession A persistent thought, idea, impulse, or image that is experienced repeatedly, feels intrusive, and causes anxiety.

Obsessive-compulsive disorder A disorder in which a person has recurrent and unwanted thoughts, a need to perform repetitive and rigid actions, or both.

Obsessive-compulsive personality disorder A personality disorder marked by

such an intense focus on orderliness, perfectionism, and control that the individual loses flexibility, openness, and efficiency.

Oedipus complex In Freudian theory, the pattern of desires in which boys become attracted to their mother as a sexual object and see their father as a rival they would like to push aside.

Operant conditioning A process of learning in which behavior that leads to satisfying consequences is likely to be repeated.

Operationalization The translating of an abstract variable into discrete, observable entities or events.

Opioid Opium or any of the drugs derived from opium, including morphine, heroin, and codeine.

Opium A highly addictive substance made from the sap of the opium poppy.

Opponent-process theory An explanation for drug addiction based on the interplay of positive, pleasurable emotions that come from ingesting the drug and negative aftereffects that leave a person feeling even worse than usual.

Oppositional defiant disorder A childhood disorder in which children argue repeatedly with adults, lose their temper, and swear, feeling intense anger and resentment.

Oral stage In this earliest developmental stage in Freud's conceptualization of psychosexual development, the infant's main libidinal gratification comes from feeding and from the body parts involved in it.

Orbital frontal cortex A region of the brain in which impulses involving excretion, sexuality, violence, and other primitive activities normally arise.

Organic mental disorders A term used in the past to distinguish mental disorders that have clear physical causes.

Orgasm A peaking of sexual pleasure, consisting of rhythmic muscular contractions in the pelvic region. A man's semen is ejaculated, and the outer third of a woman's vaginal wall contracts.

Orgasm phase The phase of the sexual response cycle during which an individual's sexual pleasure peaks and sexual tension is released as muscles in the pelvic region contract rhythmically.

Orgasmic reorientation A procedure for treating certain paraphilias by teaching clients to respond to new, more appropriate sources of sexual stimulation.

Outpatient A setting for treatment in which persons visit a therapist's office as opposed to remaining in a hospital.

Overt behavior Observable actions or clear verbalizations.

Pain disorder associated with psychological factors A somatoform disorder marked by pain, with psychosocial factors playing a central role in the onset, severity, or continuation of the pain.

Panic attack Periodic, discrete bouts of panic that occur abruptly and reach a peak within minutes.

Panic disorder An anxiety disorder marked by recurrent and unpredictable panic attacks.

Panic disorder with agoraphobia A panic disorder in which panic attacks lead to agoraphobic patterns of behavior.

Panic disorder without agoraphobia A panic disorder in which agoraphobia is absent.

Paradigm An implicit theoretical framework that arises out of an explicit set of basic assumptions. A scientist's paradigm affects the way he or she interprets observations and other data.

Paranoid personality disorder A personality disorder marked by a pattern of distrust and suspiciousness of others.

Paranoid type of schizophrenia A type of schizophrenia in which the person has an organized system of delusions and hallucinations.

Paraphilias Disorders characterized by recurrent and intense sexual urges, fantasies, or behaviors involving nonhuman objects, children, nonconsenting adults, or experiences of suffering or humiliation.

Paraprofessional A person without previous professional training who provides services under the supervision of a mental health professional.

Parasomnias Sleep disorders characterized by the occurrence of abnormal events during sleep.

Parasuicide A suicide attempt that does not result in death.

Parasympathetic nervous system The group of nerve fibers of the autonomic nervous system that helps maintain normal organ functioning. It also slows organ functioning after stimulation and returns other body processes to normal.

Parens patriae The principle by which the state can make decisions—such as to hospitalize a person against his or her wishes—that are believed to promote the individual's best interests and protect him or her from self-harm or neglect.

Parkinsonian symptoms Dystonia, akathisia, tardive dyskinesia, and other symptoms similar to those found in Parkinson's disease. Patients with schizophrenia who take traditional antipsychotic medications may display one or more of these symptoms.

Parkinson's disease A slowly progressive neurological disease, marked by tremors and rigidity, which may also cause dementia.

Passive-aggressive personality disorder A category of personality disorder listed in past versions of the DSM, marked by a pattern of negative attitudes and resistance to the demands of others.

Pathological gambling An impulse-control disorder characterized by recurrent and persistent maladaptive gambling behavior that disrupts personal, family, or vocational pursuits.

Pedophilia A paraphilia in which a person has repeated and intense sexual urges or fantasies about watching, touching, or engaging in sexual acts with prepubescent children, and may carry out these urges or fantasies.

Peer review system A system by which clinicians paid by an insurance company may periodically review a patient's progress and recommend the continuation or termination of insurance benefits.

Penile prosthesis A surgical implant consisting of a semirigid rod made of rubber and wire that produces an artificial erection.

Penis envy The Freudian theory that girls wish to overcome their feelings of inferiority during the phallic phase by having a penis.

Performance anxiety The fear of performing inadequately and a related tension experienced during sex.

Perseveration The persistent repetition of words and statements often seen in autism or schizophrenia.

Personality A unique and long-term pattern of inner experience and outward behavior, which leads to consistent reactions across various situations.

Personality assessment The gathering of information about the components of someone's personality and any unconscious conflicts he or she may be experiencing.

Personality disorder A very rigid pattern of inner experience and outward behavior that differs from the expectations of one's culture and leads to dysfunctioning.

Personality inventory A test designed to measure broad personality characteristics, consisting of statements about behaviors, beliefs, and feelings that people evaluate as either characteristic or uncharacteristic of them.

Personality trait An enduring consistency with which a person reacts to and acts upon his or her surroundings.

Pervasive developmental disorders A broad category of disorders beginning in early childhood, characterized by severe and pervasive impairments in reciprocal social interaction skills, communication skills, or the presence of stereotyped behavior, interests, and activities.

Phallic stage In psychoanalytic theory, the period between the third and fourth years when the focus of sexual pleasure shifts to the genitals.

Phalloplasty A surgical procedure designed to create a functional penis.

Pharmacotherapist A psychiatrist who primarily prescribes medications. Also known as a *psychopharmacologist*.

Phenomenology One's personal experiences and perspective on the world.

Phenothiazines A group of antihistamine drugs that became the first group of effective antipsychotic medications.

Phenylketonuria (PKU) A metabolic disorder in which the body is unable to metabolize the amino acid phenylalanine into tyrosine. If untreated, the phenylalanine accumulates and is converted into substances that poison the system and cause mental retardation.

Phobia A persistent and unreasonable fear of a particular object, activity, or situation.

Phototherapy See *Light therapy*.

Pick's disease A neurological disease that affects the frontal and temporal lobes, causing dementia.

Placebo A sham treatment that the subject believes to be genuine.

Play therapy An approach to treating childhood disorders that helps children express their conflicts and feelings indirectly by drawing, playing with toys, and making up stories.

Pleasure principle In Freudian theory, the pursuit of gratification that motivates the id.

Plethysmograph A device used to measure sexual arousal.

Polygraph A test that seeks to determine whether or not the test taker is telling the truth by measuring physiological responses such as respiration level, perspiration level, and heart rate.

Polysubstance use The misuse of combinations of drugs to achieve a synergistic effect.

Polysubstance-related disorder A long-term pattern of maladaptive behavior centered on abuse of or dependence on a combination of drugs.

Positive correlation A statistical relationship in which the values of two variables increase together or decrease together.

Positive symptoms Symptoms of schizophrenia that seem to be excesses, or bizarre additions, to normal thoughts, emotions, or behaviors.

Positron emission tomography (PET scan) A computer-produced motion picture showing rates of metabolism throughout the brain.

Postpartum depression An episode of depression that may begin for some new mothers within four weeks after childbirth. It is different from the more common "baby blues" and the less common postpartum psychosis.

Posttraumatic stress disorder An anxiety disorder in which fear and related symptoms continue to be experienced long after a traumatic event.

Poverty of content A lack of meaning in spite of high emotion that is often found in the speech of people with schizophrenia who display loose associations.

Predisposition An inborn or acquired vulnerability (or inclination or diathesis) for developing certain symptoms.

Prefrontal lobes Regions of the brain that play a key role in short-term memory, among other functions.

Premature ejaculation A dysfunction in which a man reaches orgasm and ejaculates before, on, or shortly after penetration and before he wishes to.

Premenstrual dysphoric disorder A pattern characterized by markedly depressed mood, anxiety, and marked mood changes, and a decreased interest in activities during the last week of the luteal phase. These symptoms remit within a few days after the onset of menses. This pattern is listed in the appendix of DSM-IV as a category provided for further study.

Premorbid The period prior to the onset of an illness.

Preoccupation somatoform disorders Somatoform disorders in which people misinterpret and overreact to minor, even normal, bodily symptoms or features.

Preparedness A predisposition to develop certain fears.

Presenile Occurring in middle age.

Presenile dementia Dementia occurring in middle age. See also *Dementia*.

Prevalence The total number of cases of a disorder occurring in a population over a specific period of time.

Prevention A key aspect of community mental health programs, which strive to prevent or at least minimize psychological disorders.

Primary communication The semantic content in any message. See also *Metacommunication*.

Primary gain In psychodynamic theory, the gain achieved when hysterical symptoms keep internal conflicts out of awareness.

Primary hypersomnia A sleep disorder in which the predominant problem is excessive sleepiness for at least a month. It takes the form of prolonged sleep episodes or daytime sleep that occurs almost daily.

Primary insomnia A sleep disorder in which the predominant complaint is an inability to initiate or maintain sleep.

Primary personality The subpersonality that appears more often than the others in individuals with multiple personality disorder.

Primary process In Freudian theory, a source of id gratification that consists of activating a memory or image of a desired object.

Primary process gratification In Freudian theory, an indirect source of id gratification. The child receives gratification by activating a memory or image of a desired object. Also called *wish fulfillment.*

Private psychotherapy An arrangement in which a person directly pays a therapist for counseling services.

Proband The person who is the focus of a genetic study.

Procedural memory Memory of learned physical or cognitive skills we perform without needing to think about them. These memories are not directly accessible to consciousness.

Prodromal phase The period during which symptoms of schizophrenia are not yet prominent, but the person has begun to deteriorate from previous levels of functioning.

Profound retardation A level of mental retardation (IQ below 20) at which individuals need a very structured environment with close supervision. They may learn and improve basic skills such as walking, some talking, and feeding themselves.

Prognosis A prediction of the course and outcome of a disorder.

Projection An ego defense mechanism in which a person attributes to others undesirable characteristics or impulses in himself or herself.

Projective test A test consisting of ambiguous material that people interpret or respond to.

Prolactin A pituitary hormone that can interfere with the sex drive.

Prophylactic drug A drug that actually helps prevent symptoms from developing.

Prospective study A study that predicts future changes on the basis of past and present events.

Protection and advocacy system The system by which lawyers and advocates who work for patients may investigate possible cases of patient abuse and neglect and then address any problems they find.

Prozac (Fluoxetine) A second-generation antidepressant that appears to have fewer undesired side effects than MAO inhibitors and tricyclics. It also appears to be an effective treatment for eating disorders and obsessive-compulsive disorder.

Psychedelic drugs Substances, such as LSD, that cause profound perceptual changes. Also called *hallucinogenic drugs.*

Psychiatric social worker A mental health specialist who is qualified to conduct psy-

chotherapy upon earning a master's degree or doctorate in social work.

Psychiatrist A physician who in addition to medical school has completed three to four years of residency training in the treatment of abnormal mental functioning.

Psychoanalysis Either the theory or the treatment of abnormal mental functioning that emphasizes unconscious psychological forces as the cause of psychopathology.

Psychodrama A group therapy technique that calls for group members to act out dramatic roles as if they were participating in an improvised play. They express their feelings and thoughts, explore new behaviors and attitudes, and empathize with the feelings and perspectives of others.

Psychodynamic model The theoretical perspective that sees all human functioning as being shaped by dynamic (interacting) psychological forces and looks at people's unconscious internal conflicts in order to explain their behavior.

Psychodynamic therapy A system of therapy whose goals are to help clients uncover past traumatic events and the inner conflicts that have resulted from them; resolve, or settle, those conflicts; and resume interrupted personal development.

Psychogenesis The development of abnormal functioning from psychological causes.

Psychogenic illness An illness caused primarily by psychosocial factors such as worry, family stress, and unconscious needs.

Psychogenic perspective The view that the chief causes of abnormal functioning are psychological.

Psychological autopsy A procedure used to analyze information about a deceased person in order to determine whether the person's death was self-inflicted.

Psychoneuroimmunology The study of the connections among stress, the body's immune system, and illness.

Psychopathology Any abnormal pattern of functioning that may be described as deviant, distressful, dysfunctional, or dangerous.

Psychopathy See *Antisocial personality disorder.*

Psychopharmacologist A psychiatrist who primarily prescribes medications. Also known as a *pharmacotherapist.*

Psychophysiological disorders Illnesses that result from an interaction of psychosocial and organic factors. Also known as *psychosomatic disorders* or *psychological factors affecting medical condition.*

Psychophysiological test A test that measures physical responses (such as heart rate and muscle tension) as possible indicators of psychological problems.

Psychosexual stages The developmental stages defined by Freud in which the id, ego, and superego interact. Each stage is marked by a different source of libidinal pleasure.

Psychosis A state in which a person loses contact with reality in key ways.

Psychosomatic (psychophysiological) illnesses Illnesses believed to result from an interaction of both physical and psychosocial causes. DSM-IV labels these illnesses "psychological factors affecting medical condition."

Psychosurgery Brain surgery for mental disorders.

Psychotherapy A treatment system in which words and acts are used by a client (patient) and therapist to overcome psychological difficulties.

Psychotropic medications Drugs that primarily affect the brain and reduce many symptoms of mental dysfunctioning.

Purging-type bulimia nervosa A type of bulimia nervosa in which an individual regularly induces vomiting or misuses laxatives or diuretics.

Pyromania An impulse-control disorder characterized by a pattern of fire setting for pleasure, gratification, or relief from tension.

Quasi-experiment An experiment in which investigators make use of control and experimental groups that already exist in the world at large. Also called a *mixed design.*

Quinine A drug that is often added to heroin to counteract the dangers of infection.

Random assignment A selection procedure that ensures that subjects are randomly placed either in the control group or in the experimental group.

Rap group A group that meets to talk about and explore members' problems in an atmosphere of mutual support.

Rape Forced sexual intercourse or another sexual act upon a nonconsenting person or intercourse with an underage person.

Rapid eye movement (REM) sleep The period of the sleep cycle during which the eyes move quickly, back and forth, indicating that the person is dreaming.

Rapprochement movement An effort to identify a set of common strategies that run through the work of all effective therapists.

Rational-emotive therapy A cognitive therapy developed by Albert Ellis that helps clients to identify and change the irrational assumptions and thinking that help cause their psychological disorder.

Rationalization An ego defense mechanism in which one creates acceptable reasons for unwanted or undesirable behavior.

Reaction formation An ego defense mechanism whereby a person suppresses an unacceptable desire by taking on a lifestyle that expresses the opposite desire.

Reactive depression A depression that appears to follow on the heels of clear-cut precipitating events.

Reactivity The extent to which the very presence of an observer affects a person's behavior.

Reality principle In Freudian theory, the knowledge we acquire through experience and from the people around us that it can be dangerous or unacceptable to express our id impulses outright.

Receptor A site on a neuron that receives a neurotransmitter.

Reciprocal effects explanation The view that key factors produce abnormality by increasing the likelihood or intensity of other key factors.

Reflex gratification In Freudian theory, a direct source of id gratification, as when an infant seeks and receives milk from the mother's breast to satisfy its hunger.

Regression An ego defense mechanism in which a person returns to a more primitive mode of interacting with the world.

Reinforcement The desirable or undesirable stimuli that follow as a result of an organism's behavior.

Relapse-prevention training An approach to treating alcohol abuse that is similar to BSCT and also has clients plan ahead for risky situations and reactions.

Relaxation training A treatment procedure that teaches clients to relax at will.

Reliability A measure of the consistency of test or research results.

Repression An ego defense mechanism that prevents unacceptable impulses from reaching consciousness.

Reserpine A drug originally used to treat high blood pressure but later discovered to cause depression in some people.

Residential treatment center A place where people formerly dependent on drugs live, work, and socialize in a drug-free environment. Also called a *therapeutic community*.

Residual type of schizophrenia A type of schizophrenia in which the acute symptoms of the disorder have lessened in strength and number, yet remain in residual form.

Resistance An unconscious refusal to participate fully in therapy.

Resistance stage The parasympathetic nervous system's attempt to counteract the response of the sympathetic nervous system in the presence of a threat. See also *General adaptation syndrome*.

Resolution phase The fourth phase in the sexual response cycle, characterized by relaxation and a decline in arousal following orgasm.

Resperidone (Risperdole) A commonly prescribed atypical antipsychotic drug.

Response inventories Tests designed to measure a person's responses in one specific area of functioning, such as affect, social skills, or cognitive processes.

Response prevention See *Exposure and response prevention*.

Response set A particular way of responding to questions or statements on a test, such as always selecting "true" regardless of the content of the questions.

Restricting type anorexia nervosa A type of anorexia nervosa in which people reduce their weight by restricting their food intake.

Reticular formation The body's arousal center, located in the brain.

Retrograde amnesia A lack of memory about events that occurred before the event that triggered amnesia.

Retrospective study (1) A kind of psychological autopsy in which clinicians and researchers piece together data from the past. This type of study is common for studying the past of a person who committed suicide. (2) Also, a kind of research study in which subjects are asked to recall past events.

Reversal design (ABAB) A single-subject experimental design in which behavior is measured to achieve a baseline (A), then again after the treatment has been applied (B), then again after the conditions during baseline have been reintroduced (A), and then once again after the treatment is reintroduced (B).

Reward A dopamine-rich pathway in the brain that produces feelings of pleasure when activated.

Reward-deficiency syndrome A condition, suspected to be present in some individuals, in which the brain's reward center is not readily activated by the usual events in their lives.

Right to refuse treatment The legal right of patients to refuse certain forms of treatment.

Right to treatment The legal right of patients, particularly those who are involuntarily committed, to receive adequate treatment.

Ritalin Trade name for methylphenidate, a stimulant drug that is helpful in many cases of attention-deficit/hyperactivity disorder (ADHD).

Role play A therapy technique in which clients are instructed to act out roles assigned to them by the therapist.

Rorschach test A projective test using a subject's reactions to inkblots to help reveal psychological features of the subject.

Rosenthal effect The general finding that the results of any experiment often conform to the expectations of the experimenter. It is attributed to the effects of bias.

Ruminative response Dwelling repeatedly on one's depressive symptoms.

Rush A spasm of warmth and ecstasy that occurs when certain drugs, such as heroin, are ingested.

Sample A group of subjects representative of the larger population about which a researcher wishes to make a statement.

Savant A person with a major mental disorder or intellectual handicap who has some extraordinary ability despite his or her handicaps.

Schizoaffective disorder A disorder in which symptoms of both schizophrenia and a mood disorder are prominent.

Schizoid personality disorder A personality disorder in which a person persistently avoids social relationships and shows little emotional expression.

Schizophrenia A psychotic disorder in which personal, social, and occupational functioning deteriorate as a result of strange perceptions, disturbed thought processes, unusual emotions, and motor abnormalities.

Schizophreniform disorder A disorder in which all of the key features of schizophrenia are present but last between one and six months.

Schizophrenogenic mother A type of mother—supposedly cold, domineering, and uninterested in the needs of others—who was once thought to cause schizophrenia in her child.

Schizotypal personality disorder A personality disorder in which a person displays a pattern of interpersonal problems marked by extreme discomfort in close relationships, odd forms of thinking and perceiving, and behavioral eccentricities.

School phobia A childhood pattern in which children fear going to school and often stay home for a long period of time.

School refusal See *School phobia*.

Scientific method The process of systematically gathering and evaluating information through careful observations to gain an understanding of a phenomenon.

Seasonal affective disorder (SAD) A mood disorder in which mood episodes are related to changes in season.

Second messengers Chemical changes within a neuron just after the neuron receives a neurotransmitter message and just before it responds.

Second-generation antidepressants New antidepressant drugs that differ structurally from tricyclics and MAO inhibitors.

Secondary gain In psychodynamic theory, the gain achieved when hysterical symptoms elicit kindness from others or provide an excuse to avoid unpleasant activities.

Secondary process In Freudian theory, the ego's mode of operation, consisting of assessing new situations, weighing in past experiences, anticipating consequences, and planning how best to obtain gratification.

Sedative-hypnotic drug A psychotropic drug used in low doses to reduce anxiety and in higher doses to help people sleep. Also called *anxiolytic drug.*

Selective amnesia A disorder in which the person remembers some but not all events occurring over a circumscribed period of time.

Selective serotonin reuptake inhibitors (SSRIs) A group of second-generation antidepressant drugs that increase serotonin activity specifically, without affecting other neurotransmitters.

Self psychology A psychodynamic theory developed by Heinz Kohut that focuses on the role of the self.

Self theory The psychodynamic theory that emphasizes the role of the self—our unified personality.

Self-actualization The humanistic process by which people fulfill their potential for goodness and growth.

Self-efficacy The belief that one can master and perform needed behaviors whenever necessary.

Self-help group A group made up of people with similar problems who help and support one another without the direct leadership of a clinician.

Self-hypnosis The process of hypnotizing oneself, sometimes for the purpose of forgetting unpleasant events.

Self-instruction training A cognitive treatment that teaches clients to use coping self-statements at times of stress or discomfort.

Self-monitoring A technique for observing behavior in which clients observe themselves.

Self-statements According to some cognitive theorists, statements about oneself, sometimes counterproductive, that come to mind during stressful situations.

Semantic memory A person's memory for abstract, encyclopedic, or categorical information.

Senile Typical of or occurring in people over the age of 65.

Senile dementia See *Dementia.*

Senile plaques Sphere-shaped deposits of beta-amyloid protein that form in the spaces between certain brain cells and in certain blood vessels as people age.

Sensate focus A treatment for sexual disorders that instructs couples to take the focus away from intercourse and instead spend time concentrating on mutual massage, kissing, and hugging. This approach reduces the pressure to achieve erection and orgasm.

Separation anxiety disorder A childhood disorder marked by excessive anxiety, even panic, whenever the child is separated from home or a parent.

Serotonin A neurotransmitter whose abnormal activity is linked to depression, obsessive-compulsive disorder, and eating disorders.

Severe retardation A level of mental retardation (IQ between 20 and 34) at which individuals require careful supervision and can learn to perform basic work in structured and sheltered settings.

Sex-change surgery A surgical procedure that changes a person's sex organs and features, and, in turn, sexual identity.

Sex-offender statute The presumption by some state legislators that people who are repeatedly found guilty of certain sex crimes have a mental disorder and should be categorized as "mentally disordered sex offenders."

Sexual aversion disorder A disorder characterized by an aversion to and avoidance of genital sexual interplay.

Sexual dysfunction A disorder marked by an inability to function normally in some area of the human sexual response cycle.

Sexual masochism A paraphilia characterized by repeated and intense sexual urges, fantasies, or behaviors that involve being humiliated, beaten, bound, or otherwise made to suffer.

Sexual pain disorder A dysfunction in which a person experiences pain during arousal or intercourse. See also *Dyspareunia* and *Vaginismus.*

Sexual response cycle The generalized sequence of behavior and feelings that occurs during sexual intercourse, consisting of desire, excitement, orgasm, and resolution.

Sexual sadism A paraphilia characterized by repeated and intense sexual urges, fantasies, or behaviors that involve inflicting suffering on others.

Shaping A learning procedure in which successive approximations of the desired behavior are rewarded.

Shared psychotic disorder (Folie à deux) A disorder in which a person embraces delusions held by another individual.

Sheltered workshop A protected and supervised workplace that offers job opportunities and training at a pace and level tailored to people with various disabilities.

Short-term memory The memory system that collects new information. Also known as *working memory.*

Shuttle box A box partitioned by a barrier that an animal can jump over in order to escape or avoid shock.

Single-subject experimental design A research method in which a single subject is observed and measured both before and after the manipulation of an independent variable.

Situation anxiety The various levels of anxiety produced in a person by different situations.

Sleep apnea A disorder in which the person actually stops breathing for up to thirty or more seconds while asleep.

Sleep terror disorder A parasomnia in which persons awaken suddenly during the first third of their major sleep episode, screaming out in extreme fear and agitation.

Sleepwalking disorder A parasomnia in which people repeatedly leave their beds and walk around without being conscious of the episode or remembering it later.

Social breakdown syndrome A pattern of deterioration resulting from institutionalization and characterized by extreme withdrawal, anger, physical aggressiveness, and loss of interest in personal appearance.

Social phobia A severe and persistent fear of social or performance situations in which embarrassment may occur.

Social skills training A therapy approach that helps people learn or improve social skills and assertiveness through role playing and rehearsing of desirable behaviors.

Social therapy An approach to therapy in which the therapist makes practical advice and life adjustment a central focus of treatment for schizophrenia. Therapy also focuses on problem solving, decision making, development of social skills, and management of medications. Also known as *sociotherapy.*

Sociocultural model The theoretical perspective that emphasizes the effect of society and culture on individual behavior.

Sociology The study of human relationships and social groups.

Sociopathy See *Antisocial personality disorder.*

Sociotherapy See *Social therapy.*

Sodium amobarbital (Amytal) A drug used to put people into a near-sleep state during which they may recall forgotten events.

Sodium pentobarbital (Pentothal) See *Sodium amobarbital.*

Somatization disorder A somatoform disorder marked by numerous recurring physical ailments without an organic basis. Also known as *Briquet's syndrome.*

Somatoform disorder A physical illness or ailment that is explained largely by psychosocial causes, in which the patient experiences no sense of wanting or guiding the symptoms.

Somatogenesis The development of abnormal functioning from physical causes.

Somatogenic perspective The view that abnormal psychological functioning has physical causes.

Special education An approach to educating children with mental retardation in which they are grouped together and given a separate, specially designed education.

Specific phobia A severe and persistent fear of a specific object or situation (excluding agoraphobia and social phobia).

Spectator role A state of mind that some people experience during sex, focusing on their sexual performance to such an extent that their performance and their enjoyment are reduced.

Standardization The process in which a test is administered to a large group of persons whose performance then serves as a common standard or norm against which any individual's score can be measured.

State hospitals State-run public mental institutions in the United States.

State school A state-supported institution for individuals with mental retardation.

State-dependent learning Learning that becomes associated with the conditions under which it occurred, so that it is best remembered under the same conditions. That is, people may remember an event best when they return to the mental state they were in at the time of the event.

Statistical analysis The application of principles of probability to the findings of a study in order to learn how likely it is that the findings have occurred by chance.

Statistical significance A measure of the probability that an observed event occurred by chance rather than as the result of a particular relationship or an experimental manipulation.

Statutory rape Sexual intercourse with a minor, under any condition.

Stimulant drug A drug that increases the activity of the central nervous system.

Stimulus generalization A phenomenon in which responses to one stimulus are also produced by similar stimuli.

Stress management program An approach to treating generalized and other anxiety disorders that teaches clients techniques for reducing and controlling stress.

Stress reduction seminar A workshop or series of group sessions offered by a business in which mental health professionals teach employees how to cope with and solve problems and reduce stress.

Stress response A person's particular reactions to stress.

Stressor An event that creates a sense of threat by confronting a person with a demand or opportunity for change.

Structural family therapy A family systems treatment approach in which the therapist pays particular attention to family structure, including power issues, the role each member plays within the family, and the alliances between family members.

Structured interview An interview format in which clinicians ask prepared questions.

Structured observation A method for observing behavior in which people are observed in artificial settings such as clinicians' offices or laboratories.

Stutter A disturbance in the normal fluency and timing of speech. Persons may repeat, prolong, or interject sounds; pause within a word; or experience excessive physical tension when they produce words.

Subintentional death A death in which the victim plays an indirect, hidden, partial, or unconscious role.

Subject An individual chosen to participate in a study.

Sublimination In psychoanalytic theory, the rechanneling of impulses into endeavors that are both socially acceptable and personally gratifying. It can also be used as an ego defense mechanism.

Subpersonalities The two or more distinct personalities found in individuals suffering from multiple personality disorder, each with a unique set of memories, behaviors, thoughts, and emotions. Also known as *alternate personalities*.

Substance abuse A pattern of behavior in which people rely on a drug excessively and regularly, bringing damage to their relationships, functioning poorly at work, or putting themselves or others in danger.

Substance dependence A pattern of behavior in which people organize their lives around a drug, possibly building a tolerance to it or experiencing withdrawal symptoms when they stop taking it, or both.

Substance-related disorder A pattern of maladaptive behavior centered around the use of, abuse of, or dependence on certain substances.

Suicide A self-inflicted death in which the person acts intentionally, directly, and consciously.

Suicide prevention program A program that tries to identify people who are at risk of killing themselves and to offer them crisis intervention.

Superego According to Freud, the psychological force that represents a person's values and ideals.

Support group A therapy-like group of people with a common psychological problem who meet and work on their difficulties together.

Supportive nursing care A treatment, applied to anorexia nervosa in particular, in which well-trained nurses conduct a day-to-day hospital program.

Symbolic loss According to Freudian theory, the loss of a valued object (for example, a loss of employment) which is unconsciously interpreted as the loss of a loved one. Also called *imagined loss*.

Sympathetic nervous system The nerve fibers of the autonomic nervous system that quicken the heartbeat and produce other changes experienced as fear or anxiety.

Symptom A physical or psychological sign of a disorder.

Symptom substitution The belief held by some psychodynamic therapists that quick symptom reduction is likely to result in the replacement of the old symptoms by new ones.

Synapse The tiny space between the nerve ending of one neuron and the dendrite of another.

Syndrome A cluster of symptoms that usually occur together.

Synergistic effect In pharmacology, an increase of effects that occurs when more than one substance is acting on the body at the same time.

Synesthesia A crossing over of sensory perceptions, caused by LSD and other hallucinogenic drugs. For example, a loud sound may be experienced as visible fluctuation in the air.

Systematic desensitization A behavioral treatment that uses relaxation training and a fear hierarchy to help clients with phobias react calmly to the objects or situations they dread.

Tarantism Also known as St. Vitus's dance, this was a disorder that occurred throughout Europe between A.D. 900 and 1800 in which groups of people would suddenly start to jump around, dance, and go into convulsions.

Tardive dyskinesia Extrapyramidal effects that appear in some patients after they have taken traditional antipsychotic drugs for an extended time.

Tay-Sachs disease A metabolic disorder resulting from a pairing of recessive genes that causes mental deterioration, loss of visual functioning, and death.

Temporal lobes Regions of the brain that play a key role in transforming short-term to long-term memory, among other functions.

Tension headache See *Muscle-contraction headache*.

Test A device for gathering information about a few aspects of a person's psychological functioning from which broader information about the person can be inferred.

Testosterone The principal male sex hormone.

Tetrahydrocannabinol (THC) The main active ingredient of cannabis substances.

Thalamus The region of the brain that acts as a relay station for sensory information, sending it to the cerebrum.

Thanatos According to the Freudian view, thanatos is the basic death instinct that functions in opposition to the life instinct.

Thematic Apperception Test A projective test using pictures that depict people in somewhat unclear situations.

Theory of mind Awareness that other people base their behaviors on their own beliefs, intentions, and other mental states, not on information they have no way of knowing.

Therapist A person who implements a system of therapy to help a person overcome psychological difficulties.

Therapy A special, systematic process for helping people overcome their psychological difficulties. The process may consist primarily of discussion or action (psychotherapy) or of biological intervention.

Token economy program A behavioral program in which a person's desirable behaviors are reinforced systematically throughout the day by the awarding of tokens that can be exchanged for goods or privileges.

Tolerance The adjustment that the brain and the body make to the regular use of certain drugs so that ever larger doses are needed to achieve the earlier effects.

Trait anxiety The general level of anxiety that a person brings to the various events in his or her life.

Tranquilizer A drug that reduces anxiety.

Transference According to psychodynamic theorists, a process that occurs during psychotherapy, in which patients act toward the therapist as they did or do toward important figures in their lives.

Transsexualism (Gender identity disorder) A disorder in which persons feel uncomfortable about their assigned sex and strongly wish to be a member of the opposite sex. They are often preoccupied with getting rid of their primary and secondary sex characteristics, and many find their own genitals repugnant.

Transvestic fetishism A paraphilia consisting of repeated and intense sexual urges, fantasies, or behaviors that involve dressing in clothes of the opposite sex. Also known as *transvestism*.

Treatment A procedure designed to help change abnormal behavior into more normal behavior. Also called *therapy*.

Trephination An ancient operation in which a stone instrument was used to cut away a circular section of the skull, perhaps to treat abnormal behavior.

Trichotillomania An extremely painful and upsetting impulse-control disorder or compulsion in which people repeatedly pull at and even yank out their hair, eyelashes, and eyebrows.

Tricyclic An antidepressant drug such as imipramine that has three rings in its molecular structure.

Trisomy A chromosomal aberration in which an individual has three chromosomes of one kind rather than the usual two.

Tube and intravenous feeding Forced nourishment sometimes provided to sufferers of anorexia nervosa when their condition becomes life-threatening.

Two-physician certificates (2 PCs) A method of emergency involuntary commitment used in some states, marked by certification by two clinicians that a person is in such a state of mind as to be dangerous to himself or herself or to others and may be committed involuntarily.

Type A personality style A personality pattern characterized by hostility, cynicism, drivenness, impatience, competitiveness, and ambition.

Type B personality style A personality pattern in which persons are more relaxed, less aggressive, and less concerned about time.

Type I schizophrenia A type of schizophrenia characterized mainly by positive symptoms, such as delusions, hallucinations, and certain formal thought disorders.

Type II schizophrenia A type of schizophrenia in which the person experiences mostly negative symptoms, such as flat affect, poverty of speech, and loss of volition.

Tyramine A chemical that, if allowed to accumulate, can raise blood pressure dangerously. It is found in many common foods and is broken down by MAO. See also *MAO inhibitor*.

Tyrosine The chemical that most people produce by metabolizing the amino acid phenylalanine, a process that fails to occur in children with phenylketonuria.

Ulcer A lesion that forms in the wall of the stomach or of the duodenum.

Unconditional positive regard Full, warm acceptance of a person regardless of what he or she says, thinks, or feels; a critical component of client-centered therapy.

Unconditioned response (UCR) The natural, automatic response elicited by an unconditioned stimulus.

Unconditioned stimulus (UCS) A stimulus that elicits an automatic, natural response.

Unconscious The deeply hidden mass of memories, experiences, and impulses that is viewed in Freudian theory as the wellspring of most behavior.

Undifferentiated type of schizophrenia A type of schizophrenia in which no single set of psychotic symptoms (incoherence, psychomotor disturbances, delusions, or hallucinations) dominates.

Undoing An ego defense mechanism whereby a person unconsciously cancels out an unacceptable desire or act by performing another act.

Unilateral electroconvulsive therapy (ECT) A form of electroconvulsive therapy in which electrodes are attached to the head so that electrical current passes through only one side of the brain.

Unipolar depression Depression without a history of mania.

Unstructured interview An interview format in which the clinician asks questions spontaneously, based on issues that emerge during the interview.

Vacuum erection device (VED) A nonsurgical device that can be used to produce an erection. It consists of a hollow cylinder that is placed over the penis and connected to a hand pump.

Vaginismus A condition marked by involuntary contractions of the muscles around the outer third of the vagina, preventing entry of the penis.

Validity The accuracy of a test's or study's results; that is, the extent to which the test or study actually measures or shows what it claims.

Valium (Diazepam) An antianxiety drug.

Variable Any characteristic or event that can vary, whether from time to time, from place to place, or from person to person.

Vascular dementia Dementia caused by a cerebrovascular accident, or stroke, which restricts blood flow to certain areas of the brain.

Ventromedial hypothalamus (VMH) The region of the hypothalamus that, when activated, depresses hunger.

Vicarious conditioning Acquiring fear or other reactions through modeling.

Visual hallucinations Hallucinations in which a person may either experience vague perceptions, perhaps of colors or clouds, or have distinct visions of people, objects, or scenes that are not there.

Voyeurism A paraphilia in which a person has repeated and intense sexual desires to observe unsuspecting people in secret as they undress or to spy on couples having intercourse, and may act upon these desires.

Waxy flexibility A type of catatonia in which a person will maintain a posture into which he or she has been placed by someone else.

Weight set point The weight level that a person is predisposed to maintain, controlled in part by the hypothalamus.

Wernicke's encephalopathy (Alcohol-induced persisting amnestic disorder) A neurological disease characterized by confusion, excitement, delirium, double vision, and other eye-movement abnormalities, and caused by an alcohol-related deficiency of vitamin B. If untreated it progresses into Korsakoff's syndrome.

Windigo An intense fear of being turned into a cannibal by a flesh-eating monster. The disorder was once found among Algonquin Indian hunters.

Wish fulfillment In psychodynamic theory, the gratification of id instincts by primary process thinking.

Withdrawal Unpleasant, sometimes dangerous reactions that may occur when people who use a drug regularly stop taking or reduce their dosage of the drug.

Working through The psychoanalytic process of facing conflicts, reinterpreting feelings, and overcoming one's problems.

references

Journal Abbreviations

Acta Psychiatr. Scandin. *Acta Psychiatrica Scandinavica*
Addic. Behav. *Addictive Behaviors*
Adol. Psychiat. *Adolescent Psychiatry*
Adv. Behav. Res. Ther. *Advances in Behavior Research and Therapy*
Adv. Drug React. Toxicol. Rev. *Advanced Drug Reaction and Toxcology Review*
Adv. Mind-Body Med. *Advances in Mind-Body Medicine*
Alcohol Alcoholism *Alcohol and Alcoholism*
Amer. Hlth. *American Health*
Amer. J. Addict. *American Journal on Addictions*
Amer. J. Cardiol. *American Journal of Cardiology*
Amer. J. Clin. Hyp. *American Journal of Clinical Hypnosis*
Amer. J. Clin. Hypnother. *American Journal of Clinical Hypnotherapy*
Amer. J. Clin. Nutr. *American Journal of Clinical Nutrition*
Amer. J. Comm. Psych. *American Journal of Community Psychology*
Amer. J. Criminal Justice *American Journal of Criminal Justice*
Amer. J. Forens. Psychol. *American Journal of Forensic Psychology*
Amer. J. Ger. Psychiat. *American Journal of Geriatric Psychiatry*
Amer. J. Hlth. Sys. Pharmacol. *American Journal of Health Systems and Pharmacology*
Amer. J. Med. Genet. *American Journal of Medical Genetics*
Amer. J. Ment. Def. *American Journal of Mental Deficiency*
Amer. J. Ment. Retard. *American Journal on Mental Retardation*
Amer. J. Obstet. Gynecol. *American Journal of Obstetrics and Gynecology*
Amer. J. Orthopsychiat. *American Journal of Orthopsychiatry*
Amer. J. Psychiat. *American Journal of Psychiatry*
Amer. J. Psychother. *American Journal of Psychotherapy*
Amer. J. Pub. Hlth. *American Journal of Public Health*
Amer. Psychologist *American Psychologist*
Amer. Sci. *American Scientist*
Amer. Sociol. Rev. *American Sociological Review*
Ann. Behav. Med. *Annals of Behavioral Medicine*
Ann. Clin. Psychiat. *Annals of Clinical Psychiatry*
Ann. Internal Med. *Annals of Internal Medicine*
Ann. Med. *Annals of Medicine*
Ann. Neurol. *Annals of Neurology*
Ann. Pharmacother. *Annals of Pharmacotherapy*
Annu. Rev. Neurosci. *Annual Review of Neuroscience*
Annu. Rev. Psychol. *Annual Review of Psychology*
Appl. Cog. Psychol. *Applied Cognitive Psychology*
Appl. Neuropsychol. *Applied Neuropsychology*
Appl. Prev. Psychol. *Applied and Preventive Psychology*
Appl. Psychophysiol. Biofeedback *Applied Psychophysiology and Biofeedback*
Arch. Fam. Med. *Archives of Family Medicine*
Arch. Gen. Psychiat. *Archives of General Psychiatry*
Arch. Internal Med. *Archives of Internal Medicine*
Arch. Neurol. *Archives of Neurology*
Arch. Pediatr. Adoles. Medicine *Archives of Pediatric Adolescent Medicine*
Arch. Psychiatr. Nursing *Archives of Psychiatric Nursing*
Arch. Sex. Behav. *Archives of Sexual Behavior*
Arch. Suic. Res. *Archives of Suicide Research*
Austral. J. Clin. Exp. Hyp. *Australian Journal of Clinical and Experimental Hypnosis*
Austral. New Zeal. J. Psychiat. *Australian and New Zealand Journal of Psychiatry*
Austral. Psychologist *Australian Psychologist*

Basic Appl. Soc. Psychol. *Basic and Applied Social Psychology*
Behav. Brain Res. *Eehavioral Brain Research*
Behav. Change *Behaviour-Change*
Behav. Cog. Psychother. *Behavioral and Cognitive Psychotherapy*
Behav. Genet. *Behavioral Genetics*
Behav. Med. *Behavioral Medicine*
Behav. Mod. *Behavior Modification*
Behav. Neurosci. *Behavioral Neuroscience*
Behav. Psychother. *Behavioural Psychotherapy*
Behav. Res. Meth. Instru. *Computers Behavioral Research Methods, Instruments and Computers*
Behav. Res. Ther. *Behavior Research and Therapy*
Behav. Sci. *Behavioral Science*
Behav. Sci. Law. *Behavioral Science and the Law*
Behav. Ther. *Behavior Therapy*
Biofeed. Self-Reg. *Biofeedback and Self-Regulation*
Biol. Psychiat. *Biological Psychiatry*
Biol. Psychol. *Biological Psychology*
Brain Behav. Immun. *Brain, Behavior and Immunity*
Brain Inj. *Brain Injury*
Brain Res. *Brain Research*
Brit. J. Cog. Psychother. *British Journal of Cognitive Psychotherapy*
Brit. J. Dev. Psychol. *British Journal of Developmental Psychology*
Brit. J. Med. Psychol. *British Journal of Medicinal Psychology*
Brit. J. Psychiat. *British Journal of Psychiatry*
Brit. J. Urol. *British Journal of Urology*
Brit. Med. J. *British Medical Journal*
Bull. Amer. Acad. Psychiat. Law *Bulletin of the American Academy of Psychiatry Law*
Bull. Menninger Clin. *Bulletin of the Menninger Clinic*
Bull. Psychol. *Bulletin de Psychologie*
Bull. Psychosom. Scc. *Bulletin of the Psychosomatic Society*

Canad. J. Neurol. Sci. *Canadian Journal of Neurological Science*
Canad. J. Psychiat. *Canadian J. Psychiatry*
Canad. Psychol. *Canadian Psychology*
Child Abuse Negl. *Child Abuse and Neglect*
Child Adol. Psychiat. Clin. N. Amer. *Child and Adolescent Psychiatric Clinics of North America*
Child Dev. *Child Development*
Child Maltreat: J. Amer. Profess. Soc. Abuse Child. *Child Maltreatment: Journal of the American Professional Society on the Abuse of Children*
Child Psychiat. Human Dev. *Child Psychiatry and Human Development*
Chron. Higher Educ. *Chronicle of Higher Education*
Clin. Child Psychol. Psychiat. *Clinical Child Psychology and Psychiatry*
Clin. Electroencephalogr. *Clinical Electroencephalography*
Clin. Pediatr. *Clinical Pediatrics*
Clin. Pharmacol. Ther. *Clinical and Pharmacological Therapy*
Clin. Psychol. Rev. *Clinical Psychology Review*
Clin. Psychol.: Sci. Prac. *Clinical Psychology: Science and Practice*
Clin. Rehab. *Clinical Rehabilitation*
Clin. Soc. Work J. *Clinical Social Work Journal*
Clin. Ther.: Inter. J. Drug Ther. *Clinical Therapeutics: The International Journal of Drug Therapy*
Cog. Emot. *Cognition & Emotion*
Cog. Ther. Res. *Cognitive Therapy and Research*
Communic. Res. *Communication Research*
Comprehen. Psychiat. *Comprehensive Psychiatry*
Comprehen. Ther. *Comprehensive Therapy*
Contemp. Hyp. *Contemporary Hypnosis*
Contemp. Psychol. *Contemporary Psychology*
Criminal Justice Behav. *Criminal Justice and Behavior*

Cult. Div. Ethnic Minority Psychol. *Cultural Diversity and Ethnic Minority Psychology*
Cult. Med. Psychiat. *Culture, Medicine and Psychiatry*
Curr. Direct. Psychol. Sci. *Current Directions in Psychological Science*
Curr. Probl. Pediatr., *Current Problems in Pediatrics*

Death Stud. *Death Studies*
Dement. Ger. Cogn. Disord. *Dementia and Geriatric Cognitive Disorders*
Depress. Anx. *Depression and Anxiety*
Dev. Neuropsychol. *Developmental Neuropsychology*
Dev. Psychol. *Developmental Psychology*
Dev. Psychopathol. *Developmental Psychopathology*
Dis. Nerv. Syst. *Diseases of the Nervous System*
Diss. Abstr. Inter.: Sect. A: Human Soc. Sci. *Dissertation Abstracts International: Section A: Humanities and Social Sciences*
Diss. Abstr. Inter.: Sect. B: Sci. Eng. *Dissertation Abstracts International: Section B: The Sciences and Engineering*
Dissociat. Prog. Dissociat. Disorders *Dissociation Progress in the Dissociative Disorders*
Drug. Alc. Dep. *Drug and Alcohol Dependence*

Eat. Disord.: J. Treat. Prev. *Eating Disorders: The Journal of Treatment and Prevention*
Empir. Stud. Arts *Empirical Studies of the Arts*
Endocrine Res. *Endocrine Research*
Ethics Behav. *Ethics & Behavior*
Eur. Arch. Psychiat. Clin. Neurosci. *European Archives of Psychiatry and Clinical Neuroscience*
Eur. Arch. Psychiat. Neurol. Sci. *European Archives of Psychiatry and Neurological Science*
Eur. J. Med. Res. *European Journal of Medical Research*
Eur. J. Pers. *European Journal of Personality*
Eur. J. Psychiat. *European Journal of Psychiatry*
Eur. J. Psychol. Assess. *European Journal of Psychological Assessment*
Eur. Neurol. *European Neurology*
Eur. Neuropsychopharmacology *European Neuropsychopharmacology*
Eur. Psychiat. *European Psychiatry*
Eur. Urol. *European Urology*
Exp. Clin. Psychopharmacol. *Experimental and Clinical Pharmacology*

Fam. Process *Family Process*
Fed. Probation *Federal Probation*

G. Ital. Suic. *Giornale Italiano di Suicidologia*
Gen. Hosp. Psychiat. *General Hospital Psychiatry*
Gender Soc. *Gender and Society*

Hlth. Care Women Inter. *Health Care for Women International*
Hlth. Psychol. *Health Psychology*
Homeostasis Hlth. Dis. *Homeostasis Health and Disease*
Hosp. Comm. Psychiat. *Hospital and Community Psychiatry*
Human Mutat. *Human Mutation*
Human Psychopharmacol. Clin. Exp. *Human Psychopharmacology Clinical and Experimental*

Imag. Cog. Pers. *Imagination, Cognition and Personality*
Indian J. Clin. Psychol. *Indian Journal of Clinical Psychology*
Indiv. Psychol. J. Adlerian Theory Res. Prac. *Individual Psychology: A Journal of Adlerian Theory, Research and Practice*
Injury Prev. *Injury Prevention*
Integ. Physiol. Behav. Sci. *Integrative Physiological and Behavioral Science*

Integ. Psychiat. *Integrated Psychiatry*
Inter. Clin. Psychopharmacology *International Clinical Psychopharmacology*
Inter. Forum Psychoanal. *International Forum of Psychoanalysis*
Inter. J. Addic. *International Journal of Addiction*
Inter. J. Aging Human Dev. *International Journal of Aging and Human Development*
Inter. J. Behav. Dev. *International Journal of Behavioral Development*
Inter. J. Behav. Med. *International Journal of Behavioral Medicine*
Inter. J. Clin. Exp. Hyp. *International Journal of Clinical and Experimental Hypnosis*
Inter. J. Eat. Disorders *International Journal of Eating Disorders*
Inter. J. Ger. Psychiat. *International Journal of Geriatric Psychiatry*
Inter. J. Group Psychother. *International Journal of Group Psychotherapy*
Inter. J. Ment. Hlth. *International Journal of Mental Health*
Inter. J. Methods Psychiatr. Res. *International Journal of Methods in Psychiatric Research*
Inter. J. Obesity *International Journal of Obesity*
Inter. J. Offend. Ther. Compar. Crimin. *International Journal of Offender Therapy and Comparative Criminology*
Inter. J. Psychiat. Clin. Prac. *International Journal of Psychiatry in Clinical Practice*
Inter. J. Psychoanal. *International Journal of Psychoanalysis*
Inter J. Psychoanal.-Psychother. *International Journal of Psycho analytic-Psychotherapy*
Inter. J. Psychol. Religion *International Journal for the Psychology of Religion*
Inter. J. Psychophysiol. *International Journal of Psychophysiology*
Inter. J. Psychosom. *International Journal of Psychosomatics*
Inter. J. Soc. Psychiat. *International Journal of Social Psychiatry*
Inter. J. Stress Manag. *International Journal of Stress Management*
Inter. Med. J. *International Medical Journal*
Inter. Psychoger. *International Psychogeriatrics*
Irish J. Psychol. Med. *Irish Journal of Psychological Medicine*
Issues Ment. Hlth. Nurs. *Issues in Mental Health Nursing*
Ital. J. Neurol. Sci. *Italian Journal of Neurological Sciences*

J. Abnorm. Child Psychol. *Journal of Abnormal Child Psychology*
J. Abnorm. Psychol. *Journal of Abnormal Psychology*
J. Abnorm. Soc. Psychol. *Journal of Abnormal and Social Psychology*
J. Adol. Hlth. *Journal of Adolescent Health*
J. Adolescence *Journal of Adolescence*
J. Adv. Nurs. *Journal of Advanced Nursing*
J. Affect. Disorders *Journal of Affective Disorders*
J. Alcohol Drug Educ. *Journal of Alcohol and Drug Education*
J. Amer. Acad. Child Adol. Psychiat. *Journal of the American Academy of Child and Adolescent Psychiatry*
J. Amer. Acad. Psychiat. Law *Journal of the American Academy of Psychiatry and the Law*
J. Amer. Acad. Psychoanal. *Journal of the American Academy of Psychoanalysis*
J. Amer. Board Fam. Pract. *Journal of American Board of Family Practitioners*
J. Amer. Coll. Hlth. *Journal of American College Health*
J. Amer. Ger. Soc. *Journal of the American Geriatric Society*

J. Amer. Osteopath. Assoc. *Journal of American Osteopath Associates*
J. Amer. Psychiat. Nurs. Assoc. *Journal of the American Psychiatric Nurses Association*
J. Amer. Psychoanal. Assoc. *Journal of the American Psychoanalytical Association*
J. Anx. Dis. *Journal of Anxiety Disorders*
J. Appl. Behav. Anal. *Journal of Applied Behavior Analysis*
J. Appl. Behav. Sci. *Journal of Applied Behavioral Sciences*
J. Appl. Physiol. *Journal of Applied Physiology*
J. Appl. Soc. Psychol. *Journal of Applied Social Psychology*
J. Appl. Soc. Sci. *Journal of Applied Social Sciences*
J. Asthma *Journal of Asthma*
J. Autism Child. Schizo. *Journal of Autism and Childhood Schizopherenia*
J. Autism Dev. Disorders *Journal of Autism and Developmental Disorders*
J. Behav. Decis. Making *Journal of Behavioral Decision Making*
J. Behav. Ther. Exp. Psychiat. *Journal of Behavior Therapy and Experimental Psychiatry*
J. Cardiovasc. Pharmacol. Ther. *Journal of Cardiovascular Pharmacology and Therapy*
J. Child Adol. Psychopharmacol. *Journal of Child and Adolescent Psychopharmacology*
J. Child Psychol. Psychiat. Allied Disc. *Journal of Child Psychology, Psychiatry and Allied Disciplines*
J. Child Psychol. Psychiat. *Journal of Child Psychology and Psychiatry*
J. Child Sex. Abuse *Journal of Child Sexual Abuse*
J. Clin. Child Psychol. *Journal of Clinical Child Psychology*
J. Clin. Geropsychol. *Journal of Clinical Geropsychology*
J. Clin. Psychiat. *Journal of Clinical Psychiatry*
J. Clin. Psychol. *Journal of Clinical Psychology*
J. Clin. Psychol. Med. Settings *Journal of Clinical Psychology in Medical Settings*
J. Clin. Psychopharmacol. *Journal of Clinical Psychopharmacology*
J. Cog. Psychother. *Journal of Cognitive Psychotherapy*
J. Coll. Student Dev. *Journal of College Student Development*
J. Comm. Psychol. *Journal of Community Psychology*
J. Cons. Clin. Psychol. *Journal of Consulting and Clinical Psychology*
J. Couns. Dev. *Journal of Counseling & Development*
J. Couns. Psychol. *Journal of Counseling Psychology*
J. Cross-Cult. Psychol. *Journal of Cross-Cultural Psychology*
J. Early Adolescence *Journal of Early Adolescence*
J. Epidemiol. Comm. Hlth. *Journal of Epidemiology and Community Health*
J. Exp. Anal. Behav. *Journal of Experimental Analysis of Behavior*
J. Exp. Child Psychol. *Journal of Experimental Child Psychology*
J. Exp. Psychol. Gen. *Journal of Experimental Psychology General*
J. Exp. Psychol. *Journal of Experimental Psychology*
J. Exp. Soc. Psychol. *Journal of Experimental Social Psychology*
J. Fam. Issues *Journal of Family Issues*
J. Fam. Prac. *Journal of Family Practice*
J. Fam. Psychother. *Journal of Family Psychotherapy*
J. Gamb. Stud. *Journal of Gambling Studies*
J. Gen. Internal Med. *Journal of General Internal Medicine*
J. Gen. Psychol. *Journal of Genetic Psychology*
J. Ger. A Biol. Sci. Med. Sci. *Journal of Gerontology, A: Biological Science and Medical Science*
J. Ger. B Psychol. Sci. Soc. Sci. *Journal of Gerontology, B. Psychological Science and Social Science*
J. Geriat. Psychiat. Neurol. *Journal of Geriatric Psychiatry and Neurology*

J. Hlth. Care Poor Underserved. *Journal of Health Care for the Poor and Underserved*
J. Hlth. Soc. Behav. *Journal of Health and Social Behavior*
J. Human. Psychol. *Journal of Humanistic Psychology*
J. Interpers. Violence *Journal of Interpersonal Violence*
J. Learn. Dis. *Journal of Learning Disorders*
J. Marital Fam. Ther. *Journal of Marital and Family Therapy*
J. Med. Genet. *Journal of Medical Genetics*
J. Ment. Hlth. Admin. *Journal of Mental Health Administration*
J. Ment. Hlth. Couns. *Journal of Mental Health Counseling*
J. Ment. Hlth. UK *Journal of Mental Health UK*
J. Nerv. Ment. Dis. *Journal of Nervous and Mental Diseases*
J. Neurochem. *Journal of Neurochemistry*
J. Neurol. Neurosurg. Psychiat. *Journal of Neurology and Neurosurgical Psychiatry*
J. Neuropsych. Clin. Neurosci. *Journal of Neuropsychiatry and Clinical Neurosciences*
J. Neurotrauma *Journal of Neurotrauma*
J. Occup. Hlth. Psychol. *Journal of Occupational Health Psychology*
J. Perinat. Med. *Hournal of Perinatal Medicine*
J. Pers. Assess. *Journal of Personality Assessment*
J. Pers. Disorders *Journal of Personality Disorders*
J. Pers. Soc. Psychol. *Journal of Personality and Social Psychology*
J. Pharmacol. Exp. Ther. *Journal of Pharmacology and Experimental Therapeutics*
J. Pineal Res. *Journal of Pineal Research*
J. Primary Prev. *Journal of Primary Prevention*
J. Psychiat. Neurosci. *Journal of Psychiatry & Neuroscience*
J. Psychiatr. Res. *Journal of Psychiatric Research*
J. Psychol. *Journal of Psychology*
J. Psychopharmacol. *Journal of Psychopharmacology*
J. Psychosom. Med. *Journal of Psychosomatic Medicine*
J. Psychosom. Res. *Journal of Psychosomatic Research*
J. Psychother. Prac. Res. *Journal of Psychotherapy Practice and Research*
J. Rat.-Emot. & Cog.-Behav. Ther. *Journal of Rational-Emotive & Cognitive-Behavior Therapy*
J. Rehab. *Journal of Rehabilitation*
J. Sci. Study Religion *Journal for the Scientific Study of Religion*
J. Sex Educ. Ther. *Journal of Sex Education and Therapy*
J. Sex Marital Ther. *Journal of Sex and Marital Therapy*
J. Sex Res. *Journal of Sex Research*
J. Soc. Behav. Pers. *Journal of Social Behavior and Personality*
J. Soc. Clin. Psychol. *Journal of Social and Clinical Psychology*
J. Soc. Pers. Relationships *Journal of Social and Personal Relationships*
J. Soc. Psychol. *Journal of Social Psychology*
J. Sociol. Soc. Welfare *Journal of Sociology and Social Welfare*
J. Sport Exercise Psychol. *Journal of Sport and Exercise Psychology*
J. Stud. Alc. *Journal of Studies on Alcohol*
J. Substance Abuse. *Journal of Substance Abuse*
J. Traum. Stress. *Journal of Traumatic Stress*
J. Urology *Journal of Urology*
J. Youth Adolescence *Journal of Youth and Adolescence*
JAMA *Journal of the American Medical Association*
Jap. J. Hyp. *Japanese Journal of Hypnosis*

Law Human Behav. *Law and Human Behavior*
Law Psychol. Rev. *Law and Psychology Review*

Marriage Fam. Rev. *Marriage and Family Review*
Med. Aspects Human Sex. *Mental Aspects of Human Sexuality*
Med. J. Austral. *Medical Journal of Australia*

Military Med. *Military Medicine*
MMW Fortschr. Med. *MMW Fortschritte der Medizin*
Mol. Psychiat. *Molecular Psychiatry.*

N. Engl. J. Med. *New England Journal of Medicine*
Ned. Tijdschr. Geneeskd. *Nederlands Tijdschrift voor Geneeskunde*
Neurol. Clin. *Neurologic Clinics*
Neuropsychiat., Neuropsychol., Behav. Neurol. *Neuropsychiatry, Neuropsychology, and Behavioral Neurology*
New Zeal. Med. J. *New Zealand Medical Journal*
NY St. J. Med. *New York State Journal of Medicine*

Obesity Hlth. *Obesity and Health*
Omega: J. Death Dying *Omega: Journal of Death and Dying*

Pediatr. Clin. N. Amer. *Pediatric Clinics of North America*
Percept. Motor Skills *Perceptual and Motor Skills*
Pers. Individ. Diff. *Personality and Individual Differences*
Pers. Soc. Psychol. Bull. *Personality and Social Psychology Bulletin*
Pharmacol. Biochem. Behav. *Pharmacological Biochemical Behavior*
Pharmacol. Rev. *Pharmacological Reviews*
Philos. Psychiat. Psychol. *Philosophy, Psychiatry, and Psychology*
Physiol. Behav. *Physiology and Behavior*
Postgrad. Med. J. *Postgraduate Medical Journal*
Proc. Natl. Acad. Sci. USA *Proceedings of the National Academy of Science*
Profess. Psychol.: Res. Pract. *Professional Psychology: Research and Practice*
Profess. Psychologist *Professional Psychologist*
Profess. School Couns. *Professional School Counseling*
Prog. Neuropsychopharmacol. Biol. Psychiat. *Progressive Neuropsychopharmacological Biological Psychiatry*
Prog. Neuropsychopharmacol. *Progressive Neuropsychopharmacology*
Psychiat. Genet. *Psychiatry and Genetics*
Psychiat. Res. *Psychiatry Research*
Psychiatr. Serv. *Psychiatric Services*
Psychiatr. Times *Psychiatric Times*
Psychiatr. Ann. *Psychiatric Annals*
Psychiatr. Clin. N. Amer. *Psychiatric Clinics of North America*
Psychiatr. Hosp. *Psychiatric Hospital*
Psychiatr. J. Univ. Ottawa *Psychiatric Journal of the University of Ottawa*
Psychiatr. Quart. *Psychiatric Quarterly*
Psychoanal. Psychol. *Psychoanalytic Psychology*
Psychol. Addict. Behav. *Psychology of Addictive Behavior*
Psychol. Aging *Psychology and Aging*
Psychol. Assess. *Psychological Assessment*
Psychol. Bull. *Psychological Bulletin*
Psychol. Med. *Psychological Medicine*
Psychol. Rec. *Psychological Record*
Psychol. Rep. *Psychological Reports*
Psychol. Rev. *Psychological Review*
Psychol. Schools *Psychology in the Schools*
Psychol. Sci. *Psychological Science*
Psychol. Women Quart. *Psychology of Women Quarterly*
Psychopharmacol. Bull. *Psychopharmacology Bulletin*
Psychopharmacology (Berl) *Psychopharmacology (Berlin)*
Psychosom. Med. *Psychosomatic Medicine*
Psychosomatics *Psychosomatics*
Psychother. Priv. Prac. *Psychotherapy in Private Practice*
Psychother. Res. *Psychotherapy Research*

Psychother. Theory Res. Prac. *Psychotherapy: Theory, Research and Practice*
Public Pers. Manag. *Public Personnel Management*

Quart. J. Stud. Alcohol. *Quarterly Journal on the Studies of Alcoholism*

Rehab. Couns. Bull. *Rehabilitation Counseling Bulletin*
Rehab. Nursing *Rehabilitation Nursing*
Rehab. Psychol. *Rehabilitation Psychology*
Remed. Spec. Educ. *Remedial and Special Education*
Reprod. Nutr. Dev. *Reproductive and Nutritional Development*
Res. Nursing Hlth. *Research in Nursing and Health*
Res. Soc. Work Prac. *Research on Social Work Practice*

S. Afr. J. Psychol. *South African Journal of Psychology*
Scand. J. Work Envir. Hlth. *Scandinavian Journal of Work and Environment Health*
Schizo. Bull. *Schizophrenic Bulletin*
Schizo. Res. *Schizophrenia Research*
Scientif. Amer. *Scientific American*
Sem. in Neuro. *Seminars in Neurology*
Sex. Abuse J. Res. Treat. *Sexual Abuse Journal of Research and Treatment*
Sex. Disability *Sexual Disability*
Sex. Marital Ther. *Sexual and Marital Therapy*
Soc. Behav. Pers. *Social Behavior and Personality*
Soc. Forces *Social Forces*
Soc. Psychiat. *Social Psychiatry*
Soc. Psychiat. Psychiatr. Epidemiol. *Social Psychiatry and Psychiatric Epidemiology*
Soc. Sci. Med. *Social Science and Medicine*
Soc. Work Hlth. Care *Social Work Health Care*
Substance Use Misuse *Substance Use and Misuse*
Suic. Life-Threat. Behav. *Suicide and Life-Threatening Behavior*

Topics Early Childhood Spec. Ed. *Topics in Early Childhood Special Education*
Trends Cell Biol. *Trends in Cell Biology*
Trends Neurosci. *Trends in Neuroscience*

Women Hlth. *Women & Health*

References

AA (Alcoholics Anonymous) World Services. (2000).

AA [Alcoholics Anonymous] World Services. (1998). Personal communication. Statistics branch. New York.

AAMR (American Association on Mental Retardation). (1992). *Mental retardation: Definition, classification, and systems of supports* (9th ed.). Washington, DC: Author.

AAPC (American Association for Protecting Children). (1992). *Highlights of official child neglect and abuse reporting.* Denver, CO: American Humane Society.

AARP (American Association. of Retired Persons). (1990). *A profile of older Americans.* Washington, DC: Author.

ADVTP (Alaska Domestic Violence Training Project). (1996). Training the Trainers Workshop.

APA. (1983). APA statement on the insanity defense: Insanity defense work group. *Amer. J. Psychiat., 140*(6), 681–688.

APA. (1993). *Practice guideline for major depressive disorder in adults.* Washington, DC: Author.

APA. (1995). *Ethical principles of psychologists and code of conduct.* Washington, DC: Author.

APA. (1996). Interim report of the working group on investigation of memories of childhood abuse. In K. Pezdek & W. P. Banks (Eds.), *The recovered memory/false memory debate.* San Diego: Academic Press.

APA (American Psychiatric Association). (1994). *Diagnostic and statistical manual of mental disorders* (4th ed.). Washington, DC: Author.

APA (American Psychiatric Association). (1995). Survey: Healthy mind over matter. In *USA Today,* May 23, 1995, p. 1D.

APA. (2000). *DSM-IV text revision.* Washington, DC: Author.

Abadi, S. (1984). Adiccion: la eterna repeticion de un desencuentro (Acerca de la dependencia humana) [Addiction: The endless repetition of a disencounter]. *Revista de Psicoanalisis, 41*(6), 1029–1044.

Abel, E. L., & Zeidenberg, P. (1985). Age, alcohol and violent death: A postmortem study. *J. Stud. Alc., 46,* 228–231.

Abel, G. G. (1989). Paraphilias. In H. I. Kaplan & B. J. Sadock (Eds.), *Comprehensive textbook of psychiatry* (5th ed., Vol. 1). Baltimore: Williams & Wilkins.

Abel, G. G., & Osborn, C. (1992). The paraphilias: The extent and nature of sexually deviant and criminal behavior. *Psychiatr. Clin. N. Amer., 15*(3), 675–687.

Abel, G. G., Becker, J. V., & Cunningham-Rathner, J. (1984). Complications, consent, and cognitions in sex between children and adults. *Inter. J. Law Psychiat., 7,* 89–103.

Abou-Saleh, M. T. (1992). Lithium. In E. S. Paykel (Ed.), *Handbook of affective disorders.* New York: Guilford.

Abou-Saleh, M. T., Ghubash, R., Karim, L., Krymski, M., & Anderson, D. N. (1999). The role of pterins and related factors in the biology of early postpartum depression. *Eur. Neuropsychopharmacology, 9*(4), 295–300.

Abraham, K. (1911). Notes on the psychoanalytic investigation and treatment of manic-depressive insanity and allied conditions. In *Selected papers on psychoanalysis* (pp. 137–156). New York: Basic Books, 1960.

Abraham, K. (1916). The first pregenital stage of the libido. In *Selected papers on psychoanalysis* (pp. 248–279). New York: Basic Books, 1960.

Abraham, S., & Llewellyn-Jones, D. (1984). *Eating disorders: The facts.* New York: Oxford University Press.

Abram, K. M., & Teplin, L. A. (1990). Drug disorder, mental illness, and violence. *Nat. Inst. Drug Abuse Res. Monogr. Ser., 103,* 222–238.

Abrams, K. M., & Robinson, G. E. (1998). Stalking: Part I. An overview of the problem. *Canad. J. Psychiat., 43*(5), 473–476.

Abramson, E. E., & Valene, P. (1991). Media use, dietary restraint, bulimia and attitudes towards obesity: A preliminary study. *Brit. Rev. of Bulimia Anorexia Nervosa, 5*(2), 73–76.

Abramson, L. Y., Alloy, L. B., Hogan, M. E., Whitehouse, W. G., Donovan, P., Rose, D. T., Panzarella, C., & Raniere, D. (1999). Cognitive vulnerability to depression: Theory and evidence. *J. Cog. Psychother., 13*(1), 5–20.

Abramson, L. Y., Metalsky, G. I., & Alloy, L. B. (1989). Hopelessness depression: A theory-based subtype of depression. *Psychol. Rev., 96*(2), 358–372.

Abramson, L. Y., Seligman, M. E., & Teasdale, J. D. (1978). Learned helplessness in humans: Critique and reformulation. *J. Abnorm. Psychol., 87*(1), 49–74.

Ackerman, M. D., & Carey, M. P. (1995). Psychology's role in the assessment of erectile dysfunction: Historical precedents, current knowledge, and methods. *J. Cons. Clin. Psychol., 63*(6), 862–876.

Acocella, J. (1999). *Creating hysteria: Women and multiple personality disorder.* San Francisco: Jossey-Bass.

Adam, K. S., Bouckoms, A., & Streiner, D. (1982). Parental loss and family stability in attempted suicide. *Arch. Gen. Psychiat., 39*(9), 1081–1085.

Adams, C. E., Pantelis, C., Duke, P. J., & Barnes, T. R. E. (1996). Psychopathology, social, and cognitive functioning in a hostel for homeless women. *Brit. J. Psychiat., 168,* 82–86.

Adams, P. R., & Adams, G. R. (1984). Mount Saint Helen's ashfall: Evidence for a disaster stress reaction. *Amer. Psychologist, 39,* 252–260.

Adams, W. L., & Cox, N. S. (1997). Epidemiology of problem drinking among elderly people. In A. Gurnack (Ed.), *Older adults' misuse of alcohol, medicines, and other drugs.* New York: Springer.

Addington, D. (1995). The use of placebos in clinical trials for acute schizophrenia. *Canad. J. Psychiat., 40*(4), 171–176.

Ader, R., Felten, D., & Cohen, N. (1991). *Psychoneuroimmunology* (2nd ed.). New York: Academic Press.

Adler, G. (2000). The alliance and the more disturbed patient. In S. T. Levy et al. (Eds.), *The therapeutic alliance. Workshop series of the American Psychoanalytic Association, Monograph 9.* Madison, CT: International Universities Press.

Adler, J. (1998, May 4). Take a pill and call me tonight. *Newsweek,* 48.

Adler, N. E., Boyce, T., Chesney, M. A., Cohen, S., Folkman, S., Kahn, R. L., & Syme, S. L. (1994). Socioeconomic status and health: The challenge of the gradient. *Amer. Psychologist, 49*(1), 15–24.

Adler, T. (1992). Prenatal cocaine exposure has subtle, serious effects. *APA Monitor, 23*(11), 17.

Administrative Office of the U.S. Courts. (1998). Statistics. Cited in *Time,* May 25, 1998, 33.

Advokat, C. P., & Kutlesic, V. (1995). Pharmacotherapy of the eating disorders: A commentary. *Neurosci. and Biobehav. Rev., 19*(1), 59–66.

Aggleton, J. P., & Shaw, C. (1996). Amnesia and recognition memory: A re-analysis of psychometric data. *Neuropsychology, 34*(1), 51–62.

Agid, O., Shapira, B., Zislin, J., Ritsner, M., Hanin, B., Murad, H., Troudart, T., Bloch, M., Heresco-Levy, U., & Lerer, B. (1999). Environment and vulnerability to major psychiatric illnesses: A case control study of early parental loss in major depression, bipolar disorder and schizophrenia. *Mol. Psychiat., 4*(2), 163–172.

Agras, W. S. (1984). Behavioral medicine: An overview. In A. J. Frances & R. E. Hales (Eds.), *American Psychiatric Association annual review* (Vol. 5). Washington, DC: American Psychiatric Press.

Agras, W. S. (1984). The behavioral treatment of somatic disorders. In W. D. Gentry (Ed.), *Handbook of behavioral medicine.* New York: Guilford.

Agras, W. S. (1995). Treatment of eating disorders. In A.F. Schatzberg & C.B. Nemeroff (Eds.), *The American Psychiatric Press textbook of psychopharmacology.* Washington, DC: American Psychiatric Press.

Agras, W. S., Rossiter, E. M., Arnow, B., Telch, C. F., et al. (1994). One-year follow-up of psychosocial and pharmacologic treatments for bulimia nervosa. *J. Clin. Psychiat., 55* (5), 179–183.

Agras, W. S., Sylvester, D., & Oliveau, D. (1969). The epidemiology of common fears and phobias. *Comprehen. Psychiat., 10*(2), 151–156.

Aiken, L. R. (1985). *Psychological testing and assessment* (5th ed.). Boston: Allyn & Bacon.

Akhtar, S., Wig, N. H., Verma, V. K., Pershod, D., & Verma, S. K. (1975). A phenomenological analysis of symptoms in obsessive-compulsive neuroses. *Brit. J. Psychiat., 127,* 342–348.

Albert, M. S., Butters, N., & Levin, J. (1979). Temporal gradients in the retrograde amnesia of patients with alcoholic Korsakoff's disease. *Arch. Neurol., 36,* 211–216.

Albertini, R. S., & Phillips, K. A. (1999). Thirty-three cases of body dysmorphic disorder in children and adolescents. *J. Amer. Acad. Child Adol. Psychiat., 38*(4), 453–459.

Albucher, R. C., Abelson, J. L., & Nesse, R. (1998). Defense mechanism changes in successfully treating patients with obsessive-compulsive disorder. *Amer. J. Psychiat., 155*(4), 558–559.

Alden, L. (1989). Short-term structured treatment for avoidant personality disorder. *J. Cons. Clin. Psychol., 57*(6), 756–764.

Aldhous, P. (1996, April 27). Matching proteins raise CJD fears. *New Scientist,* p. 21.

Aldridge, D. (1998). *Suicide: The tragedy of hopelessness.* London: Jessica Kingsley Pub.

Aldwin, C. M., Sutton, K. J., Chiara, G., & Spiro, A. (1996). Age differences in stress, coping, and appraisal: Findings from the normative aging study. *Journal of Gerontology, 51B*(4), 179–188.

Alexander, B. (1981). Behavioral approaches to the treatment of bronchial asthma. In C. K. Prokop & L. A. Bradley (Eds.), *Medical psychology: Contributions to behavioral medicine.* New York: Academic Press.

Allan, C., Smith, I., & Mellin, M. (2000). Detoxification from alcohol: A comparison of home detoxification and hospital-based day patient care. *Alcohol Alcoholism, 35*(1), 66–69.

Allard, R., Marshall, M., & Plante, M. C. (1992). Intensive follow-up does not decrease the risk of repeat suicide attempts. *Suic. Life-Threat. Behav., 22,* 303–314.

Allaz, A. F., Vannotti, M., Desmeules, J., Piguet, V., Celik, Y., Pyroth, O., Guex, P., & Dayer, P. (1998). Use of the label "litigation neurosis" in patients with somatoform pain disorder. *Gen. Hosp. Psychiat., 20*(2), 91–97.

Allderidge, P. (1979). Hospitals, madhouses and asylums: Cycles in the care of the insane. *Brit. J. Psychiat., 134,* 321–334.

Allen, J. G. (1993). Dissociative processes: Theoretical underpinnings of a working model for clinician and patient. *Bull. Menninger Clin., 57*(3), 287–308.

Allen, J. J. B., Law, H., & Laravvso, J. J. (1996). Items for assessing posthypnotic recognition amnesia with the HGSHS:A and the SHSS:C[1]. *Inter. J. Clin. Exp. Hyp., 44*(1), 52–65.

Allison, R. B. (1978). A rational psychotherapy plan for multiplicity. *Svensk Tidskrift Hyp., 3,* 9–16.

Alloy, L. B., Kelly, K. A., Mineka, S., & Clements, C. M. (1990). Comorbidity of anxiety and depressive disorders: A helplessness-hopelessness perspective. In J. D. Maser & R. Cloninger (Eds.), *Comorbidity of mood and anxiety disorders.* Washington, DC : American Psychiatric Press.

Allsop, S., Saunders, B., & Phillips, M. (2000). The process of relapse in severely dependent male problem drinkers. *Addiction, 95*(1), 95–106.

Allumbaugh, D. L., & Hoyt, W. T. (1999). Effectiveness of grief therapy: A meta-analysis. *J. Couns. Psychol., 46*(3), 370–380.

Alpher, V. S. (1992). Introject and identity: Structural-interpersonal analysis and psychological assessment of multiple personality disorder. *J. Pers. Assess., 58*(2), 347–367.

Alspaugh, M. E. L., Stephens, M. A. P., Townsend, A. L., Zarit, S. H., & Greene, R. (1999). Longitudinal patterns of risk for depression in dementia caregivers: Objective and subjective primary stress as predictors. *Psychol. Aging, 14*(1), 34–43.

Althof, S. E. (1995). Pharmacologic treatment of rapid ejaculation. Special issue: Clinical sexuality. *Psychiat. Clin. N. Amer., 18*(1), 85–94.

Althof, S. E., & Seftel, A. D. (1995). The evaluation and management of erectile dysfunction. *Psychiat. Clin. N. Amer., 18*(1), 171–191.

Althof, S. E., Levine, S. B., Corty, E., Risen, C., & Stern, E. (1994, March). *The role of clomipramine in the treatment of premature ejaculation.* Paper presented at the 16th annual meeting of the Society for Sex Therapy and Research.

Altshuler, L. L., Post, R. M., Leverich, G. S., Mikalauskas, K., Rosoff, A., & Ackerman, L. (1995). Antidepressant-induced mania and cycle acceleration: A controversy revisited. *Amer. J. Psychiat., 152* (8), 1130–1138.

Alvir, J. J., Lieberman, J. A., & Safferman, A. Z. (1995). Do white-cell count spikes predict agranulocytosis in clozapine recipients? *Psychopharmacol. Bull., 31* (2), 311–314.

Alzheimer's Association. (1997, February 17). Survey: Stress on Alzheimer caregivers. Cited in *USA Today,* p. 1D.

Aman, M. G., & Singh, N. N. (1991). Pharmacological intervention. In J. L. Matson & J. A. Mulick (Eds.), *Handbook of mental retardation.* New York: Pergamon Press.

Amass, L., Kamien, J. B., & Mikulich, S. K. (2000). Efficacy of daily and alternate-day dosing regimens with the combination buprenorphine-naloxone tablet. *Drug Alc. Dep., 58*(1–2), 143–152.

Ambrosini, P. J., Bianchi, M. D., Rabinovich, H., & Elia, J. (1993). Antidepressant treatments in child and adolescents: I. Affective disorders. *J. Amer. Acad. Child Adol. Psychiat., 32*(1), 1–6.

Amenson, C., & Lewinsohn, P. (1981). An investigation into the observed sex difference in prevalence of unipolar depression. *J. Abnorm. Psychol., 90,* 1–13.

American Academy of Pediatrics. (1999). Media alert: AAP addresses Colorado shooting.

American Medical Association. (1992). *Diagnostic treatment guidelines on domestic violence.* Washington, DC: Author.

American Use of Time Project. (1995). Survey. As cited in J.P. Robinson & G. Godbey, The great American slowdown. *American Demographics, 13*(6), 34–41

Amir, M., Kaplan, Z., Efroni, R., & Kotler, M. (1999). Suicide risk and coping styles in posttraumatic stress disorder patients. *Psychother. Psychosomat., 68*(2), 76–81.

Amminger, G. P., Pape, S., Rock, D., Roberts, S. A., Ott, S. L., Squires-Wheeler, E., Kestenbaum, C., & Erlenmeyer, K. L. (1999). Relationship between childhood behavioral disturbance and later schizophrenia in the New York High-Risk Project. *Amer. J. Psychiat., 156*(4), 525–530.

Anastasi, A. (1982). *Psychological testing* (5th ed.). New York: Macmillan.

Anastopoulos, A. D., & Barkley, R. A. (1992). Attention deficit-hyperactivity disorder. In C. E. Walker & M. C. Roberts (Eds.), *Handbook of clinical child psychology* (2nd ed.). New York: Wiley.

Andersen, A. E. (1985). *Practical comprehensive treatment of anorexia nervosa and bulimia.* Baltimore: Johns Hopkins University Press.

Andersen, A. E. (1990). Diagnosis and treatment of males with eating disorders. In A. E. Andersen (Ed.), *Males with eating disorders.* New York: Brunner/Mazel.

Andersen, A. E. (1992). Eating disorders in males: A special case? In K. D. Brownell, J. Rodin, & J. H. Wilmore (Eds.), *Eating, body weight, and performance in athletes: Disorders of modern society.* Philadelphia: Lea & Febiger.

Andersen, A. E. (1992). Eating disorders in males: Critical questions. In R. Lemberg (Ed.), *Controlling eating disorders with facts, advice, and resources*. Phoenix, AZ: Oryx Press.

Andersen, A. E. (1995). Sequencing treatment decisions: Cooperation or conflict between therapist and patient. In G. Szmukler, C. Dare, & J. Treasure (Eds.), *Handbook of eating disorders: Theory, treatment and research*. Chichester, England: Wiley.

Andersen, B. L., Kiecolt-Glaser, J. K., & Glaser, R. (1994). A biobehavioral model of cancer stress and disease course. *Amer. Psychologist, 49*(5), 389–404.

Anderson, D. (1994). *Breaking the tradition on college campuses: Reducing drug and alcohol misuse*. Fairfax, VA.: George Mason University Press.

Anderson, N. B., & Scott, P. A. (1999). Making the case for psychophysiology during the era of molecular biology. *Psychophysiology, 36*(1), 1–13.

Andersen, R. E., Bartlett, S. J., Morgan, G. D., & Brownell, K. D. (1995). Weight loss, psychological, and nutritional patterns in competitive male body builders. *Inter. J. Eat. Disorders, 18*, 49–57.

Anderson, S. C. (1993). Anti-stalking laws: Will they curb the erotomanic's obsessive pursuit? *Law Psychol. Rev., 17*, 171–191.

Anderson, S. R., Avery, D. L., DiPietro, E. K., Edwards, G. L., et al. (1989). Intensive home-based early intervention with autistic children. *Educ. Treatment Children, 10*(4), 352–366.

Anderson, W. P., Reid, C. M., & Jennings, G. L. Pet ownership and risk factors for cardiovascular disease. *Med. J. Austral., 157*(5), 298–301.

Andrade, V. M. (1996). Superego, narcissism and culture. *Revista Brasileira de Psicanalise, 30*(2), 385–405.

Andrasik, F., Blanchard, E. B., Neff, D. F., & Rodichok, L. D. (1984). Biofeedback and relaxation training for chronic headache: A controlled comparison of booster treatments and regular contacts for long-term maintenance. *J. Cons. Clin. Psychol, 52*(4), 609–615.

Andreasen, N. C. (1980). Mania and creativity. In R. H. Belmaker & H. M. van Praag (Eds.), *Mania: An evolving concept*. New York: Spectrum.

Andreasen, N. C. (1999). Understanding the causes of schizophrenia [editorial; comment]. *N. Engl. J. Med., 340*(8), 645–647.

Andreasen, N. C. (2000, February). Interviewed in P. A. McGuire, New hope for people with schizophrenia. *Monitor on Psychology, 31*(2), p. 24–28.

Andreasen, N. C., Hoffman, R. E., & Grove, W. M. (1985). Mapping abnormalities in language and cognition. In M. Alpert (Ed.), *Controversies in schizophrenia: Changes and constancies*. New York: Guilford.

Andreasen, N. C., Rezai, K., Alliger, R., Swayze, V. W., Flaum, M., Kirchner, P., Cohen, G., & O'Leary, D. S. (1992). Hypofrontality in neuroleptic-naïve patients and in patients with chronic schizophrenia: Assessment with xenon 133 single-photon emission computed tomography with the Tower of London. *Arch. Gen. Psychiat., 49*, 943–958.

Andrews, V. (1998, December 14). Abducted by aliens? Or just a little schizoid? *HealthScout*.

Andrulonis, P. A. (1991). Disruptive behavior disorders in boys and the borderline personality disorder in men. *Ann. Clin. Psychiat., 3*(1), 23–26.

Angermeyer, K. C., Kuhn, L., & Goldstein, J. M. (1990). Gender and the course of schizophrenia: Differences in treated outcomes. *Schizo. Bull., 16* (2), 293–307.

Angold, A., & Rutter, M. (1992). Effects of age and pubertal status on depression in a large clinical sample. *Development and Psychopathology, 4*(1), 5–28.

Angst, J. (1995). The epidemiology of depressive disorders. *Eur. Neuropsychopharmacology* (Suppl.), pp. 95–98.

Angst, J. (1999). Major depression in 1998: Are we providing optimal therapy? *J. Clin. Psychiat., 60*(Suppl. 6), 5–9.

Annas, G. J. (1993). Physician-assisted suicide—Michigan's temporary solution. *N. Engl. J. Med., 328*(21), 1573–1574.

Anonymous. (1996). First person account: Social, economic, and medical effects of schizophrenia. *Schizo. Bull., 22* (1), 183.

Anooshian, J., Streltzer, J., & Goebert, D. (1999). Effectiveness of a psychiatric pain clinic. *Psychosomatics, 40*(3), 226–232.

Anthony, J. C., Arria, A. M., & Johnson, E. O. (1995). Epidemiological and public health issues for tobacco, alcohol, and other drugs. In J. M. Oldham & M. B. Riba (Eds.), *American Psychiatric Press review of psychiatry* (Vol. 14). Washington, DC: American Psychiatric Press.

Anthony, J. C., Warner, L. A., & Kessler, R. C. (1994). Comparative epidemiology of dependence on tobacco, alcohol, controlled substances and inhalants: Basic findings from the National Comorbidity Survey. *Clin. Exp. Psychopharmacol., 2*, 244–268.

Antoni, M. H., Baggett, L., Ironson, G., LaPerriere, A., August, S., Klimas, N., Schneiderman, N., & Fletcher, M. A. (1991). Cognitive-behavioral stress management intervention buffers distress responses and immunologic changes following notification of HIV-1 seropositivity. *J. Cons. Clin. Psychol., 59*(6), 906–915.

Antony, M. M., Brown, T. A., & Barlow, D. H. (1997). Heterogeneity among specific phobia types in DSM-IV. *Behav. Res. Ther., 35*, 1089–1100.

Apelle, S., Lynn S. J., & Newman, L. (1998, December 14). Cited in V. Andrews, Abducted by aliens? Or just a little schizoid? *HealthScout*.

Appelbaum, P. S. (1993). Legal liability and managed care. *Amer. Psychologist, 48*, 251–257.

Appelbaum, P. S., & Grisso, T. (1995). The MacArthur treatment competence study: I. Mental illness and competence to consent to treatment. *Law Human Behav., 19* (2), 105–126.

Arata, C. M. (1999). Repeated sexual victimization and mental disorders in women. *J. Child Sex. Abuse, 7*(3), 1–17.

Arbel, N., & Stravynski, A. (1991). A retrospective study of separation in the development of adult avoidant personality disorder. *Acta Psychiatr. Scandin., 83*(3), 174–178.

Arben, P. D. (1999). A commentary: Why civil commitment laws don't work the way they're supposed to. *J. Sociol. Soc. Welfare, 26*(3), 61–70.

Arboleda-Florez, J., & Holley, H. L. (1991). Antisocial burnout: An exploratory study. *Bull. Amer. Acad. Psychiatr. Law, 19*(2), 173–183.

Archer, D., & McDaniel, P. (1995). Violence and gender: Differences and similarities across societies. In R. B. Ruback & N. A. Weiner (Eds.), *Interpersonal violent behaviors: Social and cultural aspects*. New York: Springer.

Archer, R. P. (1997). Future directions for the MMPI-A: Research and clinical issues. *J. Pers. Assess., 68* (1), 95–109.

Arieti, S. (1974). *Interpretation of schizophrenia*. New York: Basic Books.

Arieti, S., & Bemporad, J. (1978). *Severe and mild depression: The psychotherapeutic approach*. New York: Basic Books.

Aring, C. D. (1974). The Gheel experience: Eternal spirit of the chainless mind! *JAMA, 230*(7), 998–1001.

Aring, C. D. (1975). Gheel: The town that cares. *Fam. Hlth., 7*(4), 54–55, 58, 60.

Arkhipov, V. I. (1999). Memory dissociation: The approach to the study of retrieval processes. *Behav. Brain Res., 106*(1–2), 39–46.

Arkin R., Hermann, A., & Leonardelli, G. (1999). Study on thinking pattern of chronic self-doubters. Paper presented at the annual meeting of the American Psychological Society, Denver, CO.

Arnett, J. J. (1999). Adolescent storm and stress, reconsidered. *Amer. Psychologist, 54*(5), 317–326.

Arnette, J. (1996). Physiological effects of chronic grief: A biofeedback treatment approach. *Death Stud., 20*, 59–72.

Arnold, L. E. (1973, October). Is this label necessary? *J. School Hlth., 43*, 510–514.

Asarnow, J. R., Asarnow, R. F., Hornstein, N., & Russell, A. (1991). Childhood-onset schizophrenia: Developmental perspectives on schizophrenic disorders. In E. F. Walker (Ed.), *Schizophrenia: A life-course developmental perspective*. San Diego: Academic Press.

Asberg, M., Traskman, L., & Thoren, P. (1976). 5 HIAA in the cerebrospinal fluid: A biochemical suicide predictor? *Arch. Gen. Psychiat., 33*(10), 1193–1197.

Aserinsky, E., & Kleitman, N. (1953). Eye movements during sleep. *Fed. Process, 13*, 6–7.

Ash, R. (1998). *The top 10 of everything 1999*. New York: DK Publishing.

Ash, R. (1999). *Fantastic book of 1001 facts*. New York: DK Publishing.

Ashton, H. (1995). Toxicity and adverse consequences of benzodiazepine use. *Psychiatr. Ann., 25* (3), 158–165.

Ashton, J. R., & Donnan, S. (1981). Suicide by burning as an epidemic phenomenon: An analysis of 82 deaths and inquests in England and Wales in 1978–9. *Psychol. Med., 11*(4), 735–739.

Asimov, I. (1997). *Isaac Asimov's book of facts*. New York: Random House (Wings Books).

Atkinson, D. R., Brown, M. T., Parham, T. A., Matthews, L. G., et al. (1996). African American client skin tone and clinical judgments of African American and European American psychologists. *Profess. Psychol.: Res. Pract., 27* (5), 500–505.

Atlas, J. A. (1995). Association between history of abuse and borderline personality disorder for hospitalized adolescent girls. *Psychol. Rep., 77*, 1346.

Attie, I., & Brooks-Gunn, J. (1992). Developmental issues in the study of eating problems and eating disorders. In J. H. Crowther, D. L. Tennenbaum, S. E. Hobfoll, & M. A. P. Stephens (Eds.), *The etiology of bulimia nervosa: The individual and familial context*. Washington, DC: Hemisphere.

Auchincloss, E. L., & Weiss, R. W. (1992). Paranoid character and the intolerance of indifference. *J. Amer. Psychoanal. Assoc., 40*(4), 1013–1037.

Auge, W. K., III, & Auge, S. M. (1999). Naturalistic observation of athletic drug-use patterns and behavior in professional-caliber bodybuilders. *Substance Use Misuse, 34*(2), 217–249.

Austin, J. B., & Dankwort, J. (1999). Standards for batterer programs: A review and analysis. *J. Interpers. Violence, 14*(2), 152–168.

Avery, D., & Lubrano, A. (1979). Depression treated with imipramine and ECT: The DeCarolis study reconsidered. *Amer. J. Psychiat., 136*, 559–569.

Avia, M. D., Ruiz, M. A., Olivares, E., Crespo, M., et al. (1996). Shorter communications. The meaning of psychological symptoms: Effectiveness of a group intervention with hypochondriacal patients. *Behav. Res. Ther., 34*(1), 23–31.

Awad, A. G., & Voruganti, L. N. (1999). Quality of life and new antipsychotics in schizophrenia: Are patients better off? *Inter. J. Soc. Psychiat., 45*(4), 268–275.

Ayd, F. J., Jr. (1956). A clinical evaluation of Frenquel. *J. Nerv. Ment. Dis., 124*, 507–509.

Ayd, F. J., & Palma, J. M. (1999, May). Suicide: Risk recognition and prevention. *Psychiat. Times, XVI*(5).

Ayllon, T. (1963). Intensive treatment of psychotic behavior by stimulus satiation and food reinforcement. *Behav. Res. Ther., 1*, 53–62.

Ayllon, T., & Michael, J. (1959). The psychiatric nurse as a behavioural engineer. *J. Exp. Anal. Behav., 2*, 323–334.

Ayres, J. J. B. (1998). Fear conditioning and avoidance. In W. T. O'Donohue et al. (Eds.), *Learning and behavior therapy*. Boston: Allyn & Bacon.

Azar, B. (1995). Mental disabilities and the brain-gene link. *APA Monitor, 26* (12), 18.

Azar, B. (1996). Intrusive thoughts proven to undermine our health. *APA Monitor, 27* (10), 34.

Azar, S. T., & Siegal, B. R. (1990). Behavioral treatment of child abuse: A developmental perspective. *Behav. Mod., 14* (3), 279–300.

Azar, S. T., & Wolfe, D. A. (1989). Child abuse and neglect. In E. J. Mash & R. Barkley (Eds.), *Treatment of childhood disorders*. New York: Guilford.

Azar, S. T., Robinson, D. R., Hekimian, E. E., & Twentyman, C. T. (1984). Unrealistic expectations and problem solving ability in maltreating and comparison mothers. *J. Cons. Clin. Psychol., 52*, 687–691.

Azima, F. J. C. (1993). Group psychotherapy with personality disorders. In H. I. Kaplan & B. J. Sadock (Eds.), *Comprehensive group psychotherapy* (3rd ed.). Baltimore: Williams & Wilkins.

Azrin, N. H., Acierno, R., Kogan, E. S., Donohue, B., Besalel, V. A., & McMahon, P. T. (1996). Follow-up results of supportive versus behavioral therapy for illicit drug use. *Behav. Res. Ther., 34*(1), 41–46.

Baberg, H. T., Nelesen, R. A., & Dimsdale, J. E. (1996). Amphetamine use: Return of an old scourge in a consultation psychiatry setting. *Amer. J. Psychiat., 153*(6), 789–793.

Babor, T. F., Aguirre-Molina, M., Marlatt, G. A., & Clayton, R. (1999). Managing alcohol problems and risky drinking. *American Journal of Health Promotion, 14*(2), 98–103.

Babor, T. F., Steinberg, K., Anton, R., & Del Bocca, F. (2000). Talk is cheap: Measuring drinking outcomes in clinical trials. *J. Stud. Alc., 61*(1), 55–63.

Bacon, S. D. (1973). The process of addiction to alcohol: Social aspects. *Quart. J. Stud. Alcohol., 34*(1, Pt. A), 1–27.

Baer, L., Platman, S. R., Kassir, S., & Fieve, R. R. (1971). Mechanisms of renal lithium handling and their relationship to mineralcorticoids: A dissociation between sodium and lithium ions. *J. Psychiatr. Res., 8*(2), 91–105.

Baer, R. A., Kroll, L. S., Rinaldo, J., & Ballenger, J. (1999). Detecting and discriminating between random responding and overreporting on the MMPI-A. *J. Pers. Assess., 72*(2), 308–320.

Bagby, E. (1922). The etiology of phobias. *J. Abnorm. Psychol., 17*, 16–18.

Bagley, C. (1991). Poverty and suicide among Native Canadians: A replication. *Psycho. Rep., 69*(1), 149–150.

Bahrick, H. (1996, January). Cited in G. Neimeyer, Anecdotes for education. *Newsletter for Abnormal Psychology*.

Bailey, J. M., Pillard, R. C., Neale, M. C., et al. (1993). Heritable factors influence sexual orientation in women. *Arch. Gen. Psychiat., 50*(3), 217–223.

Bailine, S. H., Rifkin, A., Kayne, E., Selzer, J. A., Vital-Herne, J., Blieka, M., & Pollack, S. (2000). Comparison of bifrontal and bitemporal ECT for major depression. *Amer. J. Psychiat., 157*(1), 121–123.

Baird, J., Stevenson, J. C., & Williams, D. C. (2000). The evolution of ADHD: A disorder of communication? *Q. Rev. Biol., 75*(1), 17–35.

Baker, D., Roberts, R., & Towell, T. (2000). Factors predictive of bone mineral density in eating-disordered women: A longitudinal study. *Inter. J. Eat. Disorders, 27*(1), 29–35.

Baker, D. G., West, S. A., Nicholson, W. E., Ekhator, N. N., Kasckow, J. W., Hill, K. K., Bruce, A. B., Orth, D. N., & Geracioti, T. D. (1999). Serial CSF corticotropin-releasing hormone levels and adrenocortical activity in combat veterans with posttraumatic stress disorder. *Amer. J. Psychiat., 156*(4), 585–588.

Baker, F. M., & Bell, C. C. (1999). Issues in the psychiatric treatment of African Americans. *Psychiat. Serv., 50*(3), 362–368.

Baker, T., & Brandon, T. H. (1988). Behavioral treatment strategies. In *A report of the Surgeon General: The health consequences of smoking: Nicotine addiction*. Rockville, MD: U. S. Dept. of Health and Human Services.

Bakish, D. (1999). The patient with comorbid depression and anxiety: The unmet need. *J. Clin. Psychiat., 60*(Suppl. 6), 20–24.

Bakken, J., Miltenberger, R. G., & Schauss, S. (1993). Teaching parents with mental retardation: Knowledge versus skills. *Amer. J. Ment. Retard., 97*(4), 405–417.

Baldessarini, R. J., Tondo, L., & Hennen, J. (1999). Effects of lithium treatment and its discontinuation on suicidal behavior in bipolar manic-depressive disorders. *J. Clin. Psychiat., 60*(Suppl. 2), 77–84.

Baldwin, D. S. (1998). Depression and panic: Comorbidity. *Eur. Psychiat., 13*(Suppl. 2), 65s–70s.

Baldwin, D. S. (1998). Depression and panic: Comorbidity. *Eur. Psychiat., 13*(Suppl. 2), 65s–70s.

Balk, D. F. (1995). Bereavement research using control groups: Ethical obligations and questions. [Special issue: Ethics and bereavement research]. *Death Stud. 19* (2), 123–138.

Ball, S. G., Baer, L., & Otto, M. W. (1996). Symptom subtypes of obsessive-compulsive disorder in behavioral treatment studies: A quantitative review. *Behav. Res. Ther., 34*(1), 47–51.

Ballenger, J. C. (1988). The clinical use of carbamazepine in affective disorders. *J. Clin. Psychiat., 49*(Suppl.), 13–19.

Ballenger, J. C. (1995). Benzodiazepines. In A. F. Schatzberg & C. B. Nemeroff (Eds.), *The American Psychiatric Press textbook of psychopharmacology*. Washington, DC: American Psychiatric Press.

Ballenger, J. C. (1997). Panic disorder in the medical setting. *J. Clin. Psychiatr., 38* (Suppl. 2), 13–17.

Ballenger, J. C. (1998). Treatment of panic disorder in the general medical setting. *J. Psychosom. Res., 44*(1), 5–15.

Ballenger, J. C. (1999). Current treatments of the anxiety disorders in adults. *Biol. Psychiat., 46*(11), 1579–1594.

Ballinger, S. E. (1987). Uses and limitations of hypnosis in treating a conversion overlay following somatic trauma. *Austral. J. Clin. Exp. Hyp., 15*(1), 29–37.

Balon, R. (1998). Pharmacological treatment of paraphilias with a focus on antidepressants. *J. Sex Marital Ther., 24*(4), 241–254.

Balshem, M., Oxman, G., Van Rooyen, D., & Girod, K. (1992). Syphilis, sex, and crack cocaine: Images of risk and morality. *Soc. Sci. Med., 35*(2), 147–160.

Baltaxe, C. A. M., & Simmons J. Q., III. (1995). Speech and language disorders in children and adolescents with schizophrenia. *Schizo. Bull., 21* (4), 677–692.

Bancroft, J. (1971). A comparative study of aversion and desensitization in the treatment of homosexuality. In L. Burns & J. Worsley (Eds.), *Behaviour therapy in the 1970s*. Bristol, UK: Wright.

Bancroft, J. (1989). *Human sexuality and its problems*. New York: Churchill-Livingstone.

Bandura, A. (1971). Psychotherapy based upon modeling principles. In A. E. Bergin & S. L. Garfield (Eds.), *Handbook of psychotherapy and behavior change*. New York: Wiley.

Bandura, A. (1971). Vicarious and self-reinforcement processes. In R. Glaser (Ed.), *The nature of reinforcement*. New York: Academic Press.

Bandura, A. (1977). Self-efficacy: Toward a unifying theory of behavioral change. *Psychol. Rev., 84*(2), 191–215.

Bandura, A., & Rosenthal, T. (1966). Vicarious classical conditioning as a function of arousal level. *J. Pers. Soc. Psychol., 3*, 54–62.

Bandura, A., Adams, N. E., & Beyer, J. (1977). Cognitive processes mediating behavioral change. *J. Pers. Soc. Psychol., 35*(3), 125–139.

Banister, P., Burman, E., Parker, I., Taylor, M., & Tindall, C. (1994). *Qualitative methods in psychology: A research guide*. Buckingham, UK: Open University Press.

Banner, B. (1998, April). Are you normal? It's a laugh. *American Demographics*.

Barak, A. (1999). Psychological applications on the Internet: A discipline on the threshold of a new millenium. *Appl. Prev. Psychol., 8*(4), 231–245.

Barak, Y., Kimhi, R., & Weizman, R. (2000). Is selectivity for serotonin uptake associated with a reduced emergence of manic episodes in depressed patients? *Inter. Clin. Psychopharmacology, 15*(1), 53–56.

Barber, A. (1999, March). HerZines. Some yet-to-be exploited niches in the women's magazine market. *American Demographics*.

Barber, T. X. (1984). Hypnosis, deep relaxation, and active relaxation: Data, theory and clinical applications. In F. L. Woolfolk & P. M. Lehrer (Eds.), *Principles and practice of stress management*. New York: Guilford.

Barber, T. X. (1993). Hypnosuggestive approaches to stress reduction: Data, theory, and clinical applications. In P. M. Lehrer & R. L. Woolfolk (Eds.), *Principles and practice of stress management* (2nd ed.). New York: Guilford.

Bardenstein, K. K., McGlashan, T. H., & McGlashan, T. H. (1988). The natural history of a residentially treated borderline sample: Gender differences. *J. Pers. Disorders, 2*(1), 69–83.

Barker, C., Pistrang, N., & Elliott, R. (1994). *Research methods in clinical and counseling psychology*. Chichester, England: Wiley.

Barker, J. G., & Howell, R. J. (1992). The plethysmograph: A review of recent literature. *Bull. Amer. Acad. Psychiat. Law, 20*(1), 13–25.

Barker, P. R., Manderscheid, R. W., Hendershot, G. E., Jack, S. S., Schoenborn, C. A., & Goldstrom, I. (1992). Serious mental illness and disability in the adult household population: United States, 1989. In R. W. Manderscheid & M. A. Sonnenschein (Eds.), *Mental health, United States, 1992*. Washington, DC: U. S. Department of Health and Human Services.

Barker, S. B. (1999, February). Therapeutic aspects of the human-companion animal interaction. *Psychiat. Times, XVI*(2).

Barlow, D. H. (1988). Current models of panic disorder and a view from emotion theory. In A. J. Frances & R. E. Hales (Eds.), *American Psychiatric*

Press review of psychiatry (Vol. 7). Washington, DC: American Psychiatric Press.

Barlow, D. H. (1989). Treatment outcome evaluation methodology with anxiety disorders: Strengths and key issues. *Adv. Behav. Res. Ther., 11*(3), 121-132.

Barnard, G. W., Fuller, A. K., Robbins, L., & Shaw, T. (1989). *The child molester: An integrated approach to evaluation and treatment.* New York: Brunner/Mazel.

Barnes, G. E., & Prosen, H. (1985). Parental death and depression. *J. Abnorm. Psychol., 94*(1), 64-69.

Barnett, P. A., & Gotlib, I. H. (1990). Cognitive vulnerability to depressive symptoms among men and women. *Cog. Ther. Res., 14*(1), 47-61.

Baroff, G. S., & Olley, J. G. (1999). *Mental retardation: Nature, cause, and management (3rd ed.).* Philadelphia: Brunner/Mazel.

Baron, M., Barkai, A., Gruen, R., Peselow, E., et al. (1987). Platelet sup 3H imipramine binding and familial transmission of affective disorders. *Neuropsychobiology, 17*(4), 182-186.

Barondes, S. H. (1993). *Molecules and mental illness.* New York: Scientific American Library.

Barraclough, B. M., Bunch, J., Nelson, B., et al. (1974). A hundred cases of suicide: Clinical aspects. *Brit. J. Psychiat., 125,* 355-373.

Barratt, E. S., & Stanford, M. S. (1996). Impulsiveness. In C. G. Costello (Ed.), *Personality characteristics of the personality disordered.* New York: Wiley.

Barrett, G., Pendry, E., Peacock, J., Victor, C., Thakar, R., & Manyonda, I. (1999). Women's sexuality after childbirth: A pilot study. *Arch. Sex Behav., 28*(2), 179-191.

Barrett, P. M., Dadds, M. R., & Rapee, R. M. (1996). Family treatment of childhood anxiety: A controlled trial. *J. Cons. Clin. Psychol., 64*(2), 333-342.

Barrett, P. M., Rapee, R. M., Dadds, M. M., & Ryan, S. M. (1996). Family enhancement of cognitive style in anxious and aggressive children. *J. Abnorm. Child Psychol., 24*(2), 187-203.

Barrington, M. R. (1980). Apologia for suicide. In M. P. Battin & D. J. Mayo (Eds.), *Suicide: The philosophical issues.* New York: St. Martin's Press.

Barron, J. W. (Ed.). (1998). *Making diagnosis meaningful: Enhancing evaluation and treatment of psychological disorders.* Washington, DC: American Psychological Association.

Barroso, J. (1999). Long-term nonprogressors with HIV disease. *Nurs.*

Barsky, A. J., & Klerman, G. L. (1983). Overview: Hypochondriasis, bodily complaints and somatic styles. *Amer. J. Psychiat., 140,* 273-283.

Barta, P. E., Pearlson, G. D., Brill, L. B., II, Royall, R., et al. (1997). Planum temporale asymmetry reversal in schizophrenia: Replication and relationship to gray matter abnormalities. *Amer. J. Psychiat., 154* (5), 661-667.

Bartels, S., Teague, G., Drake, R., Clark, R., Bush, P., & Noordsy, D. (1993). Substance abuse in schizophrenia: Service utilization and costs. *J. Nerv. Ment. Dis., 181*(4), 227-232.

Bartrop, R. W., Lockhurst, E., Lazarus, L., Kiloh, L. G., & Penny, R. (1977). Depressed lymphocyte function after bereavement. *Lancet, 1,* 834-836.

Bass, C., Bond, A., Gill, D., & Sharpe, M. (1999). Frequent attenders without organic disease in a gastroenterology clinic: Patient characteristics and health care use. *Gen. Hosp. Psychiat., 21*(1), 30-38.

Bassett, A. S. (1992). Chromosomal aberrations and schizophrenia: Autosomes. *Brit. J. Psychiat., 161,* 323-334.

Bastiani, A. M., Altemus, M., Pigott, T. A., Rubenstein, C., et al. (1996). Comparison of obsessions and compulsions in patients with anorexia nervosa and obsessive compulsive disorder. *Biol. Psychiat., 39,* 966-969.

Bastiani, A. M., Rao, R., Weltzin, T., & Kaye, W. H. (1995). Perfectionism in anorexia nervosa. *Inter. J. Eat. Disorders, 17*(2), 147-152.

Batchelor, W. F. (1988). AIDS 1988. *Amer. Psychologist, 43*(11), 853-858.

Bates, G. W., Thompson, J. C., & Flanagan, C. (1999). The effectiveness of individual versus group induction of depressed mood. *J. Psychol., 133*(3), 245-252.

Bateson, G. (1978, April 21). The double-bind theory—Misunderstood? *Psychiatr. News,* p. 40.

Bateson, G., Jackson, D., Haley, J., & Weakland, J. (1956). Toward a theory of schizophrenia. *Behav. Sci., 1,* 251-264.

Battaglia, M., Cavallini, M. C., Macciardi, F., & Bellodi, L. (1997). The structure of DSM-III-R schizotypal personality disorder diagnosed by direct interviews. *Schizo. Bull., 23*(1), 83-92.

Battaglia, M., Gasperini, M., Sciuto, G., Scherillo, P., et al. (1991). Psychiatric disorders in the families of schizotypal subjects. *Schizo. Bull., 17*(4), 659-668.

Battin, M. P. (1980). Manipulated suicide. In M. P. Battin & D. J. Mayo (Eds.), *Suicide: The philosophical issues.* New York: St. Martin's Press.

Battin, M. P. (1980). Suicide: A fundamental human right? In M. P. Battin & D. J. Mayo (Eds.), *Suicide: The philosophical issues.* New York: St. Martin's Press.

Battin, M. P. (1982). *Ethical issues in suicide.* Englewood Cliffs, NJ: Prentice Hall.

Battin, M. P. (1998, December 11). Interviewed in V. Andrews, Beyond Kevorkian: What others say about "last rights." *HealthScout.*

Battin, M.P. (1999) Can suicide be rational? Yes, sometimes. In J. L. Werth, Jr. (Ed.), *Contemporary perspectives on rational suicide.* Philadelphia: Brunner/Mazel.

Battle, E. K., & Brownell, K. D. (1996). Confronting a rising tide of eating disorders and obesity: Treatment vs. prevention and policy. *Addic. Behav., 32*(6), 755-765.

Battle, Y. L., Martin, B. C., Dorfman, J. H., & Miller, L. S. (1999). Seasonality and infectious disease in schizophrenia: The birth hypothesis revisited. *J. Psychiatr. Res., 33*(6), 501-509.

Baucom, D. H., Shoham, V., Mueser, K. T., Daiuto, A. D., & Stickle, T. R. (1998). Empirically supported couple and family interventions for marital distress and adult mental health problems. *J. Cons. Clin. Psychol., 66*(1), 53-88.

Bauer, M., & Boegner, F. (1996). Neurological syndromes in factitious disorder. *J. Nerv. Ment. Dis., 184*(5), 281-288.

Bauer, P. J. (1996). What do infants recall of their lives? Memory for specific events by one- to two-year-olds. *Amer. Psychologist, 51*(1), 29-41.

Bauer, R. M. (2000). The flexible battery approach to neuropsychological assessment. In R. D. Vanderploeg et al. (Eds.), *Clinician's guide to neuropsychological assessment.* Mahwah, NJ: Erlbaum.

Baum, A. (1990). Stress, intrusive imagery, and chronic stress. *Hlth. Psychol., 9,* 653-675.

Baum, A., Gatchel, R. J., & Schaeffer, M. (1983). Emotional, behavioural and physiological effects of chronic stress at Three Mile Island. *J. Cons. Clin. Psychol., 51,* 565-572.

Baxter, L. R., Schwartz, J. M., Bergman, K. S., Szuba, M. P., Guze, B. H., Mazziotta, J. C., Alazraki, A., Selin, C. E., Ferng, H. K., Munford, P., & Phelps, M. E. (1992). Caudate glucose metabolic rate changes with both drug and behavior therapy for obsessive-compulsive disorder. *Arch. Gen. Psychiat., 49,* 681-689.

Baxter, L. R., Schwartz, J. M., Guze, B. H., Bergman, K., et al. (1990). PET imaging in obsessive compulsive disorder with and without depression. Symposium: Serotonin and its effects on human behavior (1989, Atlanta, GA). *J. Clin. Psychiat., 51*(Suppl.), 61-69.

Bazargan, M. (1996). Self-reported sleep disturbance among African-American elderly: The effects of depression, health status, exercise, and social support. *Inter. J. Aging Human Dev., 42*(2), 143-160.

Beach, S. R. H., Sandeen, E. E., & O'Leary, K. D. (1990). Depression in marriage: A model for etiology and treatment. In D. H. Barlow (Ed.), *Treatment manuals for practitioners.* New York: Guilford.

Beamish, P. M., Granello, P. F., Granello, D. H., McSteen, P. B., et al. (1996). Outcome studies in the treatment of panic disorder: A review. *J. Couns. Dev., 74,* 460-467.

Beardslee, W. R., Wright, E., Rothberg, P. C., Salt, P., & Versage, E. (1996). Response of families to two preventive intervention strategies: Long-term differences in behavior and attitude change. *J. Amer. Child Adol. Psychiat., 35*(6), 774-782.

Beaty, L. A. (1999). *Identity development of homosexual youth and parental and familial influences on the coming out process.* Chicago: Northeastern Illinois University Press.

Beautrais, A., Joyce, P., & Mulder, R. (2000). Unmet need following serious suicide attempt: Follow-up of 302 individuals for 30 months. In G. Andrews, S. Henderson, et al. (Eds.), *Unmet need in psychiatry: Problems, resources, responses.* New York: Cambridge University Press.

Beauvais, F. (1992). The consequences of drug and alcohol use for Indian youth. *Amer. Indian Alaska Native Ment. Hlth. Res., 5*(1), 32-37.

Bebbington, P. E. (1998). Epidemiology of obsessive-compulsive disorder. *Brit. J. Psychiat., 173*(Suppl. 35), 2-6.

Bebbington, P., & Ramana, R. (1995). The epidemiology of bipolar affective disorder. *Soc. Psychiat. Psychiatr. Epidemiol., 30,* 279-292.

Beck, A. T. (1967). *Depression: Clinical, experimental and theoretical aspects.* New York: Harper & Row.

Beck, A. T. (1976). *Cognitive therapy and the emotional disorders.* New York: International University Press.

Beck, A. T. (1985). Theoretical perspectives on clinical anxiety. In A. H. Tuma & J. D. Maser (Eds.), *Anxiety and the anxiety disorders.* Hillsdale, NJ: Erlbaum.

Beck, A. T. (1988). Cognitive approaches to panic disorder: Theory and therapy. In S. Rachman & J. Maser (Eds.), *Panic: Psychological perspectives.* Hillsdale, NJ: Erlbaum.

Beck, A. T. (1991). Cognitive therapy: A 30-year retrospective. *Amer. Psychologist, 46*(4), 368-375.

Beck, A. T. (1993). Cognitive approaches to stress. In P. M. Lehrer & R. L. Woolfolk (Eds.), *Principles and practice of stress management (2nd ed.).* New York: Guilford.

Beck, A. T. (1997). Cognitive therapy: Reflections. In J. K. Zeig (Ed.), *The evolution of psychotherapy: The third conference.* New York: Brunner/Mazel.

Beck, A. T., & Weishaar, M. E. (1995). Cognitive therapy. In R. J. Corsini & D. Wedding (Eds.), *Current psychotherapies (5th ed.).* Itasca, IL: Peacock.

Beck, A. T., Emery, G., & Greenberg, R. (1985). *Anxiety disorders and phobias: A cognitive perspective.* New York: Basic Books.

Beck, A. T., & Emery, G., with Greenberg, R. L. (1985). Differentiating anxiety and depression: A test of the cognitive content-specificity hypothesis. *J. Abnorm. Psychol., 96,* 179-183.

Beck, A. T., Freeman, A., & Assoc. (1990). *Cognitive therapy of personality disorders.* New York: Guilford.

Beck, A. T., Laude, R., & Bohnert, M. (1974). Ideational components of anxiety neurosis. *Arch. Gen. Psychiat., 31,* 319–325.

Beck, A. T., Resnik, H., & Lettieri, D. (Eds.). (1974). *The prediction of suicide.* Philadelphia: Charles Press.

Beck, A. T., Rush, A. J., Shaw, B. F., & Emery, G. (1979). *Cognitive therapy of depression.* New York: Guilford.

Beck, A. T., Ward, C. H., Mendelson, M., Mock, J. E., & Erbaugh, J. (1962). Reliability of psychiatric diagnosis: 2. A study of consistency of clinical judgments and ratings. *Amer. J. Psychiat., 119,* 351–357.

Beck, A. T., Weissman, A., Lester, D., et al. (1974). The measurement of pessimism: The hopelessness scale. *J. Cons. Clin. Psychol. 42,* 861–865.

Beck, A. T., et al. (1985). Treatment of depression with cognitive therapy and amitriptyline. *Arch. Gen. Psychiat., 42*(2), 142–148.

Beck, J. C., & Parry, J. W. (1992). Incompetence, treatment refusal, and hospitalization. *Bull. Amer. Acad. Psychiatr. Law, 20*(3), 261–267.

Beck, J. G. (1995). Hypoactive sexual desire disorder: An overview. *J. Cons. Clin. Psychol., 63*(6), 919–927.

Beck, J. G., & Bozman, A. (1996). Gender differences in sexual desire: The effects of anger and anxiety. *Arch. Sex. Behav., 24*(6), 595–612.

Becker, A. (1999, May 31). Fat-phobia in the Fijis: TV-thin is in. *Newsweek,* p. 70.

Becker, E. S., Rinck, M., Roth, W. T., & Margraf, J. (1998). Don't worry and beware of white bears: Thought suppression in anxiety patients. *J. Anx. Dis., 12*(1), 39–55.

Becker, J. V. (1989). Impact of sexual abuse on sexual functioning. In S. R. Leiblum & R. C. Rosen (Eds.), *Principles and practice of sex therapy* (2nd ed.). New York: Guilford.

Becker, P., & Comstock, C. (1992, October). *A retrospective look at one MPD/DD group: Recommendations for future MPD/DD groups.* Paper presented at the Ninth International Conference of the International Society for the Study of Multiple Personality and Dissociative Disorders, Chicago.

Becvar, D. S., & Becvar, R. J. (1993). *Family therapy: A systemic integration* (2nd ed.). Boston: Allyn & Bacon.

Bednar, R. L., & Kaul, T. J. (1994). Experiential group research: Can the canon fire? In A. E. Bergin & S. L. Garfiel (Eds.), *Handbook of psychotherapy and behavior change* (4th ed.). New York: Wiley.

Beebe, D. K. (1991). Emergency management of the adult female rape victim. *Amer. Fam. Physician, 43,* 2041–2046.

Begley, S. (1989, August 14). The stuff that dreams are made of. *Newsweek,* p. 40.

Begley, S. (1995, October 9). Promises, promises. *Newsweek,* pp. 60–62.

Begley, S. (2000, May 8). A world of their own. *Newsweek,* pp. 52–63.

Beidel, D. C., Turner, S. M., & Morris, T. L. (1995). A new inventory to assess childhood social anxiety and phobia: The social phobia and anxiety inventory for children. *Psychol. Assess., 7*(1), 73–79.

Bein, E. (1998). How well does long-term psychoanalytically oriented inpatient treatment work? A review of a study by Blatt and Ford. *Psychother. Res., 8*(1), 30–34.

Beiser, M., Shore, J. H., Peters, R., & Tatum, E. (1985). Does community care for the mentally ill make a difference? A tale of two cities. *Amer. J. Psychiat., 142,* 1047–1052.

Beitman, B. D. (1993). Afterword to Section IV. In J. M. Oldham, M. B. Riba, & A. Tasman (Eds.), *Review of psychiatry* (Vol. 12). Washington, DC: American Psychiatric Press.

Beitman, B. D. (1993). Pharmacotherapy and the stages of psychotherapeutic change. In J. M. Oldham, M. B. Riba, & A. Tasman (Eds.), *Review of psychiatry* (Vol. 12). Washington, DC: American Psychiatric Press.

Beitman, B. D. (1996). Integrating pharmacotherapy and psychotherapy: An emerging field of study. *Bull. Menninger Clin., 60*(2), 160–173.

Belcher, J. R. (1988). Defining the service needs of homeless mentally ill persons. *Hosp. Comm. Psychiat., 39*(11), 1203–1205.

Belcher, J. R. (1988). The future role of state hospitals. *Psychiatr. Hosp., 19*(2), 79–83.

Belcher, J. R., & Blank, H. (1990). Protecting the right to involuntary commitment. *J. Appl. Soc. Sci., 14*(1), 95–115.

Belkin, L. (1990, June 6). Doctor tells of first death using his suicide device. *New York Times,* A1, p. 3.

Bell, I. R. (1999). A guide to current psychopharmacological treatments for affective disorders in older adults: Anxiety, agitation, and depression. In M. Duffy (Ed.), *Handbook of counseling and psychotherapy with older adults.* New York: Wiley.

Bell, M. D., Lysaker, P. H., & Milstein, R. M. (1996). Clinical benefits of paid work activity in schizophrenia. *Schizo. Bull., 22*(1), 51–67.

Belle, D. (1990). Poverty and women's mental health. *Amer. Psychologist., 45*(3), 385–389.

Belli, R. F., Windschitl, P. D., McCarthy, T. T., & Winfrey, S. E. (1992). Detecting memory impairment with a modified test procedure: Manipulating retention interval with centrally presented event items. *J. Exp. Psychol.: Learn., Memory, Cog., 18,* 356–367.

Bellinger, D. L., Madden, K. S., Felten, S. Y., & Felten, D. L. (1994). Neural and endocrine links between the brain and the immune system. In C. S. Lewis, C. O'Sullivan, & J. Barraclough (Eds.), *The psychoimmunology of cancer: Mind and body in the fight for survival.* Oxford, England: Oxford University Press.

Bellivier, F., Leboyer, M., Courtet, P., Feingold, J., Buresi, C., & Malafosse, A. (1999). "Association between the tryptophane hydroxylase gene and manic-depressive illness": Reply. *Arch. Gen. Psychiat., 56*(1), 101.

Belluck, P. (1996, December 1). The symptoms of Internet addiction. *New York Times,* p. 5.

Belmaker, R. H., Bersudsky, Y., Genjamin, J., Agam, G., Levine, J., & Kofman, O. (1995). Manipulation of Inositol-linked second messenger systems as a therapeutic strategy in psychiatry. In G. Gessa, W. Fratta, L. Pani, & G. Serra (Eds.), *Depression and mania: From neurobiology to treatment.* New York: Raven Press.

Bemporad, J. R. (1992). Psychoanalytically orientated psychotherapy. In E. S. Paykel (Ed.), *Handbook of affective disorders.* New York: Guilford.

Bemporad, J. R., & Vasile, R. G. (1999). Dynamic psychotherapy. In M. Hersen & A.S. Bellack (Eds.), *Handbook of comparative interventions for adult disorders* (2nd ed.). New York: Wiley.

Ben Shakhar, G., Bar Hillel, M., Bilu, Y., & Shefler, G. (1998). Seek and ye shall find: Test results are what you hypothesize they are. *J. Behav. Decis. Making, 11*(4), 235–249.

Bender, K. J. (1998). FDA approves reduced clozapine monitoring; increased patient access versus increased risk. *Psychiatr. Times, XV*(5).

Bender, K. J. (1998). New prescription for paraphilia? *Psychiatr. Times, XV*(4).

Bender, K. J. (1999). Assessing antidepressant safety in the elderly. *Psychiatr. Times, XVI*(1).

Bender, L. (1938). *A visual motor gestalt test and its clinical use.* New York: American Orthopsychiatric Assoc.

Bender, R., Jockel, K. H., Trautner, C., Spraul, M., & Berger, M. (1999). Effect of age on excess mortality in obesity. *JAMA, 281*(16), 1498–1504.

Benedetti, F., Sforzini, L., Colombo, C., Maffei, C., & Smeraldi, E. (1998). Low-dose clozapine in acute and continuation treatment of severe borderline personality disorder. *J. Clin. Psychiat., 59,* 103–107.

Benezech, M., DeWitte, J. J. E., & Bourgeois, M. (1989). A lycanthropic murderer [Letter to the editor]. *Amer. J. Psychiat., 146*(7), 942.

Bennett, F. C., Brown, R. T., Craver, J., & Anderson, D. (1999). Stimulant medication for the child with attention-deficit/hyperactivity disorder. *Pediatr. Clin. N. Amer., 46*(5), 929–944, vii.

Bennett, G. T., & Kish, G. R. (1990). Incompetency to stand trial: Treatment unaffected by demographic variables. *J. Forensic Sci., 35*(2), 403–412.

Bennett, M. B. (1987). Afro-American women, poverty and mental health: A social essay. *Women Hlth., 12*(3–4), 213–228.

Bennett, M. E., Miller, J. H., & Woodall, W. G. (1999). Drinking, binge drinking and other drug use among southwestern undergraduates: Three-year trends. *American Journal of Drug and Alcohol Abuse, 25*(2), 331–350.

Bennett, M. P. (1998). The effect of mirthful laughter on stress and natural killer cell cytotoxicity. *Diss. Abstr. Inter.: Sect. B: Sci. Eng., 58*(7–B), 3553.

Benowitz, N. (1990). Clinical pharmacology of caffeine. *Annu. Rev. Med., 41,* 277–288.

Bensley, L. S., Spieker, S. J., Van Eenwyk, J., & Schoder, J. (1999). Self-reported abuse history and adolescent problem behaviors: II. Alcohol and drug use. *J. Adol. Hlth., 24*(3), 173–180.

Bensley, L. S., Van Eenwyk, J., Spieker, S. J., & Schoder, J. (1999). Self-reported abuse history and adolescent problem behaviors: I. Antisocial and suicidal behaviors. *J. Adol. Hlth., 24*(3), 163–172.

Benson, J. (1996, January 15). Crime: Law and order. *Newsweek,* pp. 48–54.

Benson, J., & Watson, S. (1999). *Marijuana and medicine: Assessing the science base.* Washington, DC: National Academy Press.

Bergem, A. L., Engedal, K., & Kringlen, E. (1997). The role of heredity in late-onset Alzheimer disease and vascular dementia: A twin study. *Arch. Gen. Psychiat., 54,* 264–270.

Berger, F. M. (1970). The discovery of meprobamate. In F. Ayd & B. Blackwell (Eds.), *Discoveries in biological psychiatry.* Philadelphia: Lippincott.

Bergler, E. (1951). *Neurotic counterfeit sex.* New York: Grune & Stratton.

Berk, S. N., & Efran, J. S. (1983). Some recent developments in the treatment of neurosis. In C. E. Walker et al. (Eds.), *The handbook of clinical psychology: Theory, research, and practice* (Vol. 2). Homewood, IL: Dow Jones-Irwin.

Berlin, I. N. (1987). Suicide among American Indian adolescents: An overview. *Suic. Life-Threat. Behav., 17,* 218–232.

Berliner, R., Solomon, S., Newman, L. C., & Lipton, R. B. (1999). Migraine: Clinical features and diagnosis. *Comprehen. Ther., 25*(8–10), 397–402.

Berman, A. L. (1986). Helping suicidal adolescents: Needs and responses. In C. A. Corr & J. N. McNeil (Eds.), *Adolescence and death.* New York: Springer.

Berman, A. L., & Jobes, D. A. (1991). *Adolescent suicide: Assessment and intervention.* Washington, DC: American Psychological Association.

Berman, A. L., & Jobes, D. A. (1995). Suicide prevention in adolescents (age 12–18). [Special issue:

Suicide prevention: Toward the year 2000.] *Suic. Life-Threat. Behav., 25*(1), 143–154.

Berman, S., Delaney, N., Gallagher, D., Atkins, P., & Graeber, M. (1987). Respite care: A partnership between a Veterans Administration nursing home and families to care for frail elders at home. *Gerontologist, 27*, 581–584.

Berney, B. (1993). Round and round it goes: The epidemiology of childhood lead poisoning, 1950–1990. *Milbank Quarterly, 71*(1), 3–39.

Bernstein, H. A. (1981). Survey of threats and assaults directed toward psychotherapists. *Amer. J. Psychother., 35*, 542–549.

Berrettini, W. H. (2000). Susceptibility loci for bipolar disorder: Overlap with inherited vulnerability to schizophrenia. *Biol. Psychiat., 47*(3), 245–251.

Bersoff, D. M., & Bersoff, D. N. (1999). Ethical perspectives in clinical research. In P. C. Kendall, J. N. Butcher, et al. (Eds.), *Handbook of research methods in clinical psychology* (2nd ed.). New York: Wiley.

Bersoff, D. N. (Ed.). (1995). *Ethical conflicts in psychology.* Washington, DC: American Psychological Association.

Bersoff, D. N. (Ed.). (1999). *Ethical conflicts in psychology* (2nd ed.). Washington, DC: American Psychological Association.

Bersoff, D. N., Goodman-Delahunty, J. G., Grisso, J. T., Hans, V. P., Poythress, N. G., Jr., & Roesch, R. G. (1997). Training in law and psychology. *Amer. Psychologist., 52*(12), 1301–1310.

Bertani, A., Perna, G., Arancio, C., Caldirola, D., & Bellodi, L. (1997). Pharmacologic effect of imipramine, paroxetine, and sertraline on 35% carbon dioxide hypersensitivity in panic patients: A double-blind, random, placebo-controlled study. *J. Clin. Psychopharmacol., 17*(2), 97–101.

Beutel, M., Deckardt, R., Von Rad, M., & Weiner, H. (1995). Grief and depression after miscarriage: Their separation, antecedents, and course. *Psychosom. Med., 57*, 517–526.

Beutler, L. E. (1979). Toward specific psychological therapies for specific conditions. *J. Cons. Clin. Psychol., 47*, 882–892.

Beutler, L. E. (1991). Have all won and must all have prizes? Revisiting Luborsky et al.'s verdict. *J. Cons. Clin. Psychol., 59*, 226–232.

Beutler, L. E. (1998). Identifying empirically supported treatments: What if we didn't? *J. Cons. Clin. Psychol., 66*(1), 113–120.

Beutler, L. E., Machado, P. P. P., & Neufeldt, S. A. (1994). Therapist variables. In A. E. Bergin & S. L. Garfield (Eds.), *Handbook of psychotherapy and behavior change.* New York: Wiley.

Beutler, L. E., Williams, R. E., Wakefield, P. J., & Entwistle, S. R. (1995). Bridging scientist and practitioner perspectives in clinical psychology. *Amer. Psychologist., 50*(12), 984–994.

Beyer, H. A. (1991). Litigation involving people with mental retardation. In J. L. Matson & J. A. Mulick (Eds.), *Handbook of mental retardation* (2nd ed.). New York: Pergamon Press.

Bickel, W. K., & Amass, L. (1995). Buprenorphine treatment of opioid dependence: A review. *Exp. Clin. Psychopharmacol., 3*(4), 477–489.

Bickel, W. K., Amass, L., Crean, J. P., & Badger, G. J. (1999). Buprenorphine dosing every 1, 2, or 3 days in opioid-dependent patients. *Psychopharmacology, 146*(2), 111–118.

Bickman, L., & Dokecki, P. (1989). Public and private responsibility for mental health services. *Amer. Psychologist., 44*(8), 1133–1137.

Biddle, S., Akande, D., Armstrong, N., Ashcroft, M., Brooke, R., & Goudes, M. (1996). The self-motivation inventory modified for children: Evidenced on psychometric properties and its use in physical exercise. *International Journal of Sport Psychology, 27*(3), 237–250.

Biederman, J., Rosenbaum, J. F., Hirshfeld, D. R., Farone, S. V., Bolduc, E. A., Gersten, M., Meminger, S. R., Kagan, J., Snidman, N., & Reznick, J. S. (1990). Psychiatric correlates of behavioral inhibition in young children of parents with and without psychiatric disorders. *Arch. Gen. Psychiat., 47*, 21–16.

Biegon, A., & Kerman, I. (1995). Quantitative autoradiography of cannabinoid receptors in the human brain post-mortem. In A. Biegon & N. D. Volkow (Eds.), *Sites of drug action in the human brain.* Boca Raton, FL: CRC Press.

Biegon, A., Dillon, K., Volkow, N. D., & Fowler, J. S. (1995). Quantitative autoradiographic localization and characterization of cocaine binding sites in the human brain post-mortem. In A. Biegon & N. D. Volkow (Eds.), *Sites of drug action in the human brain.* Boco Raton, FL: CRC Press, Inc.

Bienvenu, O. J., & Eaton, W. W. (1998). The epidemiology of blood-injection-injury phobia. *Psychol. Med., 28*(5), 1129–1136.

Bijl, R. V., Ravelli, A., & van Zessen, G. (1998). Prevalence of psychiatric disorder in the general population: Results of the Netherlands Mental Health Survey and Incidence Study (NEMESIS). *Soc. Psychiat. Psychiat. Epidemiol., 33*(12), 587–595.

Bilder, R. M., Lipschutz-Broch, L., Reiter, G., Geisler, S. H., et al. (1992). Intellectual deficits in first-episode schizophrenia: Evidence for progressive deterioration. *Schizo. Bull., 18*(3), 437–448.

Binder, R. L. (1999). Are the mentally ill dangerous? *J. Amer. Acad. Psychiat. Law, 27*(2), 189–201.

Binet, A., & Simon, T. (1916). *The development of intelligence in children (The Binet-Simon Scale).* Baltimore: Williams & Wilkins.

Binik, Y. M., Servan-Schreiber, D., Freiwald, S., & Hall, K. S. (1988). Intelligent computer-based assessment and psychotherapy: An expert system for sexual dysfunction. *J. Nerv. Ment. Dis., 176*(7), 387–400

Birch, H. G., Richardson, S. A., Baird, D., et al. (1970). *Mental subnormality in the community—A clinical and epidemiological study.* Baltimore: Williams & Wilkins.

Bird, J. (1979). The behavioral treatment of hysteria. *Brit. J. Psychiat., 134*, 129–137.

Birtchnell, J. (1996). Detachment. In C. G. Costello (Ed.), *Personality characteristics of the personality disordered.* New York: Wiley.

Bissette, G., Seidler, F. J., Nemeroff, C. B., & Slotkin, T. A. (1996). High affinity choline transporter status in Alzheimer's disease tissue from rapid autopsy. In R. J. Wurtman, S. Corkin, J. H. Growdon & R. M. Nitsch (Eds.), *The neurobiology of Alzheimer's disease.* New York: New York Academy of Sciences.

Bisson, J. I. & Deahl, M. P. (1994). Psychological debriefing and prevention of post-traumatic stress: More research is needed. *Brit. J. Psychiat., 165*(6), 717–720.

Blacher, J., & Baker, B. L. (1992). Toward meaningful involvement in out-of-home placement settings. *Ment. Retard., 30*(1), 35–43.

Blacher, J., & Baker, B. L. (1994). Family involvement in residential treatment of children with retardation: Is there evidence of detachment? *J. Child Psychol. Psychiat. Allied Disc., 35*(3), 505–520.

Black, D. W., & Andreasen, N. C. (1994). Schizophrenia, schizophreniform disorder, and delusional (paranoid) disorder. In R. E. Hales, S. C. Yudofsky, & J. A. Talbott (Eds.), *The American Psychiatric Press textbook of psychiatry* (2nd ed.). Washington, DC: American Psychiatric Press.

Black, D. W., Belsare, G., & Schlosser, S. (1999). Clinical features, psychiatric comorbidity, and health-related quality of life in persons reporting compulsive computer use behavior. *J. Clin. Psychiat., 60*(12), 839–844.

Black, D. W., Kehrberg, L. L. D., Flumerfelt, D. L., & Schlosser, S. S. (1997). Characteristics of 36 subjects reporting compulsive sexual behavior. *Amer. J. Psychiat., 154*, 243–249.

Black, D. W., Monahan, P., & Gabel, J. (1997). Fluvoxamine in the treatment of compulsive buying. *J. Clin. Psychiat., 58*(4), 159–163.

Black, S. T. (1993). Comparing genuine and simulated suicide notes: A new perspective. *J. Cons. Clin. Psychol., 61*(4), 699–702.

Black, S. T. (1995). Comparing genuine and simulated suicide notes: Response to Diamond et al. (1995.) *J. Cons. Clin. Psychol., 63*(1), 49–51.

Blackburn, R. (1993). *The psychology of criminal conduct: Theory, research, and practice.* New York: Wiley.

Blackman, S. (1998). Is it depression or is it dementia? *Psychiatr. Times., XV*(2).

Blackmun, S. (1998). From Mars to Venus—Couples sex therapy. *Psychiatr. Times, XV*(9).

Blair, C. D., & Lanyon, R. I. (1981). Exhibitionism: Etiology and treatment. *Psychol. Bull., 89*(3), 439–463.

Blanchard, E. B. (1994). Behavioral medicine and health psychology. In A. E. Bergin & S. L. Garfield (Eds.), *Handbook of psychotherapy and behavior change.* New York: Wiley.

Blanchard, E. B., & Andrasik, F. (1982). Psychological assessment and treatment of headache: Recent developments and emerging issues. *J. Cons. Clin. Psychol., 50*(6), 859–879.

Blanchard, E. B., Buckley, T. C., Hickling, E. J., & Taylor, A. E. (1998). Posttraumatic stress disorder and comorbid major depression: Is the correlation an illusion? *J. Anx. Dis., 12*(1), 21–37.

Blanchard, E. B., Schwarz, S. P., Suls, J. M., Gerardi, M., et al. (1992). Two controlled evaluations of multicomponent psychological treatment of irritable bowel syndrome. *Behav. Res. Ther., 30*(2), 175–189.

Blanchard, J. J., Brown, S.A., Horan, W. P., & Sherwood, A. R. (2000). Substance use disorders in schizophrenia: Review, integration, and a proposed model. *Clinical Psychology Review, 20*(2), 207–234.

Blanchard, R., & Hucker, S. J. (1991). Age, transvestism, bondage, and concurrent paraphilic activities in 117 fatal cases of autoerotic asphyxia. *Brit. J. Psychiat., 159*, 371–377.

Bland, R., & Harrison, C. (2000). Developing and evaluating a psychoeducation program for caregivers of bipolar affective disorder patients: Report of a pilot project. *Res. Soc. Work Prac., 10*(2), 209–228.

Bland, R. C., Orn, H., & Newman, S. C. (1988). Lifetime prevalence of psychiatric disorders in Edmonton. *Acta Psychiatr. Scandin., 77*(Suppl. 338), 24–32.

Blank, A. S. (1982). Apocalypse terminable and interminable: Operation Outreach for Vietnam veterans. *Hosp. Comm. Psychiat., 33*(11), 913–918.

Blaser, M. J. (1996, February). The bacteria behind ulcers. *Scientif. Amer.,* pp. 104–107.

Blasko, D. G., Kazmerski, V. A., Corty, E. W., & Kallgren, C. A. (1998). Courseware for observational research (COR): A new approach to teaching naturalistic observation. *Behav. Res. Meth. Instru. Computers, 30*(2), 217–222.

Blatt, S. J. (1995). The destructiveness of perfectionism. Implications for the treatment of depression. *Amer. Psychologist., 50*(12), 1003–1020.

Blatt, S. J. (1999). Personality factors in brief treatment of depression: Further analyses of the NIMH-sponsored Treatment for Depression Collaborative Research Program. In D. S. Janowsky et al. (Eds.),

Psychotherapy indications and outcomes. Washington, DC: American Psychiatric Press.

Blazer, D. G., George, L. K., & Hughes, D. (1991). The epidemiology of anxiety disorders: An age comparison. In C. Salzman & B. D. Lebowitz (Eds.), *Anxiety in the elderly.* New York: Springer.

Blazer, D. G., Hughes, D., George, L. K., Swartz, M., & Boyer, R. (1991). Generalized anxiety disorder. In L. N. Robins & D. A. Regier (Eds.), *Psychiatric disorders in America: The epidemiologic catchment area study.* New York: Maxwell Macmillan International.

Blehar, M. C., & Oren, D. A. (1995). Women's increased vulnerability to mood disorders: Integrating psychobiology and epidemiology. *Depression, 3,* 3–12.

Blier, P., & de Montigny, C. (1994, July). Current advances and trends in the treatment of depression. *TIPS, 15,* 220–226.

Blinder, B. J., Blinder, M. C., & Sanathara, V. A. (1998, December). Eating disorders and addiction. *Psychiatr. Times, XV*(12).

Bliss, E. L. (1980). Multiple personalities: A report of 14 cases with implications for schizophrenia and hysteria. *Arch. Gen. Psychiat., 37*(12), 1388–1397.

Bliss, E. L. (1980). *Multiple personality, allied disorders and hypnosis.* New York: Oxford University Press.

Bliss, E. L. (1985). "How prevalent is multiple personality?": Dr. Bliss replies. *Amer. J. Psychiat., 142*(12), 1527.

Bliss, T., & Gardner, M. A. (1973). Long-lasting potentiation of synaptic transmission in the dentate area of unanesthetized rabbit following stimulation of the prerforant path. *J. Physiol., 232,* 357–374.

Bloch, S., Crouch, E., & Reibstein, J. (1982). Therapeutic factors in group psychotherapy: A review. *Arch. Gen. Psychiat., 27,* 216–324.

Bloch, S., Szmukler, G. I., Herrman, H., Benson, A., & Colussa, S. (1995). Counseling caregivers of relatives with schizophrenia: Themes, interventions, and caveats. *Fam. Process, 34,* 413–425.

Block, B., & Pristach, C. A. (1992). Diagnosis and management of the paranoid patient. *Amer. Fam. Physician, 45*(6), 2634–2640.

Bloom, B. L. (1984). *Community mental health: A general introduction* (2nd ed.). Monterey, CA: Brooks/Cole.

Bloom, C., Gitter, A., Gutwill, S., Kogel, L., & Zaphiropoulos, L. (1994). *Eating problems: A feminist psychoanalytic treatment model.* New York: Basic Books.

Bloom, F. (1998, June). *Substance abuse and reward systems in the brain.* Lecture presented at the 151st Annual Meeting of the American Psychiatric Association, Toronto.

Bloom, F., Lazerson, A., & Hofstadter, L. (1985). *Brain, mind, and behavior.* New York: W. H. Freeman.

Bloom, J. D. (1990). The *Tarasoff* decision & gun control legislation. *Inter. J. Offend. Ther. Compar. Criminol., 34*(1), v–viii.

Bloom, J. D., Nadelson, C. C., & Notman, M. T. (Eds.). (1999). *Physician sexual misconduct.* Washington, DC: American Psychiatric Press.

Bloomfield, H. H., Nordfors, M., & McWilliams, P. (1996). *Hypericum & depression.* Los Angeles: Prelude Press.

Bloomingdale, L., & Bloomingdale, E. (1989). Childhood identification and prophylaxis of antisocial personality disorder. In R. Rosner & H. I. Schwartz (Eds.), *Juvenile psychiatry and the law.* New York: Plenum.

Blum, K., & Noble, E. (1993). Drug dependence and the A1 allele gene. *Drug Alc. Dep., 33*(5).

Blum, K., Noble, E., Sheridan, P., Finley, O., et al. (1991). Association of the A1 allele of the D2 dopamine receptor gene with severe alcoholism. *Alcohol, 8*(5), 409–416.

Bocker, F. M. (1984). Soziale Integration und Kontakte zu Bezugspersonen des gewohnten sozialen Umfeldes wahrend stationarer Behandlung im psychiatrischen Krankenhaus. Eine prospective katamnestische Untersuchung an erstmals aufgenommenen Patienten mit schizophrenen und cyclothymen Psychosen [Social integration and contact with people in the normal social environment during treatment in a psychiatric hospital: A follow-up of first-admission inpatients with schizophrenia and affective disorders]. *Eur. Arch. Psychiat. Neurol. Sci., 234*(4), 250–257.

Bockoven, J. S. (1963). *Moral treatment in American psychiatry.* New York: Springer.

Boergers, J., Spirito, A., & Donaldson, D. (1998). Reasons for adolescent suicide attempts: Associations with psychological functioning. *J. Amer. Acad. Child Adol. Psychiat., 37*(12), 1287–1293.

Bogdan, R., & Taylor, S. (1976, January). The judged, not the judges: An insider's view of mental retardation. *Amer. Psychologist., 31*(1), 47–52.

Bogerts, B. (1999). The neuropathology of schizophrenic diseases: Historical aspects and present knowledge. *Eur. Arch. Psychiat. Clin. Neurosci., 249*(Suppl. 4), 2–13.

Bolgar, H. (1965). The case study method. In B. B. Wolman (Ed.), *Handbook of clinical psychology.* New York: McGraw-Hill.

Bolla, K. I., McCann, U. D., & Ricaurte, G. A. (1998). Memory impairment in abstinent MDMA ("Ecstasy") users. *Neurology, 51*(6), 1532–1537.

Bolton, D., Luckie, M., & Steinberg, D. (1995). Long-term course of obsessive-compulsive disorder treated in adolescence. *J. Amer. Acad. Child Adol. Psychiat., 34*(11), 1441–1450.

Bolund, C. (1985). Suicide and cancer: II. Medical and care factors in suicides by cancer patients in Sweden, 1973–1976. *J. Psychol. Oncology, 3*(1), 31–52.

Bondolfi, G., Dufour, H., Patris, M., May, J. P., Billeter, U., Eap, C. B., & Baumann, P. (1998). Risperidone versus clozapine in treatment-resistant chronic schizophrnia: A randomized double-blind study. *Amer. J. Psychiat., 155*(4), 499–504.

Bongar, B., Peterson, L. G., Golann, S., & Hardiman, J. J. (1990). Self-mutilation and the chronically suicidal patient: An examination of the frequent visitor to the psychiatric emergency room. *Ann. Clin. Psychiat., 2*(3), 217–222.

Bonn, D. (1996). Melatonin's multifarious marvels: Miracle or myth: *Lancet, 347,* 184.

Bonner, R. L. (1992). Isolation, seclusion, and psychosocial vulnerability as risk factors for suicide behind bars. In R. W. Maris, A. L. Berman, J. T. Maltsberger, & R. I. Yufit (Eds.), *Assessment and prediction of suicide.* New York: Guilford.

Boone, M. L., McNeil, D. W., Masia, C. L., Turk, C. L., Carter, L. E., Ries, B. J., & Lewin, M. R. (1999). Multimodal comparisons of social phobia subtypes and avoidant personality disorder. *J. Anx. Dis., 13*(3), 271–292.

Booth, R. E., Kwiatkowski, C. F., & Chitwood, D. D. (2000). Sex related HIV risk behaviors: Differential risks among injection drug users, crack smokers and injection drug users who smoke crack. *Drug Alc. Dep., 58*(3), 219–226.

Borch-Jacobsen, M. (1997). Sybil – The making of a disease: An interview with Dr. Herbert Spiegel. *The New York Review of Books, 44*(7), 60–64.

Borison, R. L. (1995). Clinical efficacy of serotonin-dopamine antagonists relative to classic neuroleptics. *J. Clin. Psychopharmacol., 15*(1, Suppl. 1), 24S–29S.

Bornstein, R. A., Schwarzkopf, S. B., Olson, S. C., & Nasrallah, H. A. (1992). Third-ventricle enlargement and neuropsychological deficit in schizophrenia. *Bio. Psychiat., 31*(9), 954–961.

Bornstein, R. F. (1992). The dependent personality: Developmental, social, and clinical perspectives. *Psychol. Bull., 112*(1), 3–23.

Bornstein, R. F. (1995). Comorbidity of dependent personality disorder and other psychological disorders: An integrative review. *J. Pers. Disorders, 9*(4), 286–303.

Bornstein, R. F. (1996). Dependency. In C. G. Costello (Ed.), *Personality characteristics of the personality disordered.* New York: Wiley.

Bornstein, R. F. (1998). Dependency in the personality disorders: Intensity, sight, expression, and defense. *J. Clin. Psychol., 54*(2), 175–189.

Bornstein, R. F. (1999). Criterion validity of objective and projective dependency tests: A meta-analytic assessment of behavioral prediction. *Psychol. Assess., 11*(1), 48–57.

Boros, S., Ophoven, J., Anderson, R., & Brubaker, L. (1995). Munchausen syndrome by proxy: A profile for medical child abuse. *Austral. Fam. Physician, 24*(5), 768–773.

Bortz, W. M., II, Wallace, D. H., & Wiley, D. (1999). Sexual function in 1,202 aging males: Differentiating aspects. *J. Ger. A Biol. Sci. Med. Sci., 54*(5), M237–241.

Borum, R. (1996). Improving the clinical practice of violence risk assessment. Technology, guidelines, and training. *Amer. Psychologist., 51*(9), 945–956.

Borys, D. S., & Pope, K. S. (1989). Dual relationships between therapist and client: A national study of psychologists, psychiatrists and social workers. *Profess. Psychol., 20,* 283–293.

Bosc, M. (2000). Assessment of social functioning in depression. *Comprehen. Psychiat., 41*(1), 63–69.

Bose, J. (1995). Depression. In M. Lionells, J. Fiscalini, C. H. Mann, & D. B. Stern (Eds.), *Handbook of interpersonal psychoanalysis.* Hillsdale, NJ: Analytic Press.

Bott, E. (1928). Teaching of psychology in the medical course. *Bull. Assoc. Amer. Med. Colleges, 3,* 289–304.

Bouchard, C., Rheaume, J., & Ladouceur, R. (1999). Responsibility and perfectionism in OCD: An experimental study. *Behav. Res. Ther., 37*(3), 239–248.

Boudewyns, P. A. (1996). Posttraumatic stress disorder: Conceptualization and treatment. In M. Hersen, R. M. Eisler, & P. M. Miller (Eds.), *Progress in behavior modification* (Vol. 30). Pacific Grove, CA: Brooks/Cole.

Boudewyns, P. A., Stwertka, S. A., Hyer, L. A., Albrecht, J. W., & Sperr, E. V. (1991). *Eye movement desensitization for PTSD of combat: A treatment outcome pilot study.* Paper presented at the convention of the American Psychological Association, San Francisco.

Boudouris, J. (2000). The insanity defense in Polk County, Iowa. *Amer. J. Forens. Psychol., 18*(1), 41–79.

Bourgeois, M. (1991). Serotonin, impulsivity and suicide. *Human Psychopharmacol. Clin. Exp., 6*(Suppl.), 31–36.

Bourgeois, M. (1995, December). [Importance of DSM IV (APA) and ICD-10 (WHO) in diagnosis and treatment of mood disorders.] *Encephale* (Spec. No. 5), 47–52. [French.]

Bourin, M., Malinge, M., & Guitton, B. (1995). [Provocative agents in panic disorder.] *Therapie 50*(4), 301–306. [French]

Bourne, P. G. (1970). *Men, stress & Vietnam.* Boston: Little, Brown.

Boutros, N., Bonnet, K., & Mak, T. (1996). Drug abuse: A significant variable in schizophrenia research. *Biol. Psychiat., 39,* 1053–1054.

Bowen, K. (2000). Child abuse and domestic violence in families of children seen for suspected sexual abuse. *Clin. Pediatr., 39*(1), 33–40.

Bowen, M. A. (1960). A family concept of schizophrenia. In D. D. Jackson (Ed.), *The etiology of schizophrenia*. New York: Basic Books.

Bower, B. (1995). Moods and the muse. *Sci. News, 147,* 378–380.

Bower, B. (1995). Deceptive appearances: Imagined physical defects take an ugly personal toll. *Sci. News, 148,* 40–41.

Bower, G. H. (1981). Mood and memory. *Amer. Psychologist, 36*(2), 129–148.

Bowers, K. S., & Woody, E. Z. (1996). Hypnotic amnesia and the paradox of intentional forgetting. *J. Abnorm. Psychol., 105*(3), 381–390.

Bowman, E. S., & Markand, O. N. (1996). Psychodynamics and psychiatric diagnoses of pseudoseizure subjects. *Amer. J. Psychiat., 153*(1), 57–63.

Boyce, W. T., Chesney, M., Alkon, A., Tschann, J. M., et al. (1995). Psychobiologic reactivity to stress and childhood respiratory illnesses: Results of two prospective studies. *Psychosom. Med., 57,* 411–422.

Boyd, J. H., Rae, D. S., Thompson, J. W., Burns, B. J., et al. (1990). Phobia: Prevalence and risk factors. *Soc. Psychiat. Psychiatr. Epidemio., 25*(6), 314–323.

Bozman, A., & Beck, J. G. (1991). Covariation of sexual desire and sexual arousal: The effects of anger and anxiety. *Arch. Sex. Behav., 20,* 47–60.

Braatvedt, G. D. (1999). Outcome of managing impotence in clinical practice. *New Zeal. Med. J., 112*(1092), 272–274.

Bradbury, T. N., & Karney, B. R. (1993). Longitudinal study of marital interaction and dysfunction: Review and analysis. *Clin. Psychol. Rev., 13*(1), 15–27.

Bradford, J. M. W. (1995). Pharmacological treatment of the paraphilias. In J. M. Oldham & M. B. Riba (Eds.), *American Psychiatric Press review of psychiatry* (Vol. 14). Washington, DC: American Psychiatric Press.

Bradford, J. M. (1999). The paraphilias, obsessive compulsive spectrum disorder, and the treatment of sexually deviant behaviour. *Psychiatr. Quart., 70*(3), 209–219.

Bradley, B. P., Mogg, K., Falla, S. J., & Hamilton, L. R. (1998). Attentional bias for threatening facial expressions in anxiety: Manipulation of stimulus duration. *Cog. Emot., 12*(6), 737–753.

Bradley, S. J. (1995). Psychosexual disorders in adolescence. In J. M. Oldham & M. B. Riba (Eds.), *American Psychiatric Press review of psychiatry,* (Vol. 14). Washington, DC: American Psychiatric Press.

Brady, J. P., & Lind, D. L. (1961). Experimental analysis of hysterical blindness: Operant conditioning techniques. *Arch. Gen. Psychiat., 4,* 331–339.

Braff, D. L., & Saccuzzo, D. P. (1985). The time course of information-processing deficits in schizophrenia. *Amer. J. Psychiat., 142*(2), 170–174.

Braginsky, B. M., Braginsky, D. D., & Ring, K. (1969). *Methods of madness: The mental hospital as a last resort.* New York: Holt.

Brandon, S. (1981). The history of shock treatment. In *Electroconvulsive therapy: An appraisal.* Oxford: Oxford University Press.

Brandon, S., Boakes, J., Glaser, D., & Green, R. (1998). Recovered memories of childhood sexual abuse: Implications for clinical practice. *Brit. J. Psychiat., 172,* 296–307.

Brannen, S. J., Bradshaw, R. D., Hamlin, E. R., II, Fogarty, J. P., & Colligan, T. W. (1999). Spouse abuse: Physician guidelines to identification, diagnosis and management in the uniformed services. *Military Med., 164*(1), 30–36.

Brasic, J. R., & Fogelman, D. (1999). Clinician safety. *Psychiar. Clin. N. Amer., 22*(4), 923–940.

Brauer, A. (1999). Biofeedback and anxiety. *Psychiatr. Times, XVI*(2).

Braun, D. L. (1995, July 28). Interview. In S. Gilbert, More men may seek eating-disorder help. *New York Times.*

Brawman-Mintzer, O., & Lydiard, R. B. (1997). Biological basis of generalized anxiety disorder. *J. Clin. Psychiat., 58*(Suppl. 3), 16–25.

Bray, G. A., Dahms, W. T., Atkinson, R. L., et al. (1980). Factors controlling food intake: A comparison of dieting and intestinal bypass. *Amer. J. Clin. Nutr., 33,* 376–382.

Bray, J. W., Zarkin, G. A., Dennis, M. L., & French, M. T. (2000). Symptoms of dependence, multiple substance use, and labor market outcomes. *American Journal of Drug and Alcohol Abuse, 26*(1), 77–95.

Breggin, P. R. (1998). *Talking back to Ritalin: What doctors aren't telling you about stimulants for children.* Monroe, ME: Common Courage Press.

Breier, A. (1995). Serotonin, schizophrenia and antipsychotic drug action. *Schizo. Res., 14*(3), 187–202.

Breitbart, W., Rosenfeld, B., & Passik, S. (1996). Interest in physician-assisted suicide among ambulatory HIV-infected patients. *Amer. J. Psychiat., 153*(2), 238–242.

Bremner, J. D. (1999). Does stress damage the brain? *Biol. Psychiat., 45*(7), 797–805.

Bremner, J. D., Southwick, S. M., & Charney, D. S. (1999). The neurobiology of posttraumatic stress disorder: An integration of animal and human research. In P. A. Saigh, J. D. Bremner, et al. (Eds.), *Posttraumatic stress disorder: A comprehensive text.* Boston: Allyn & Bacon.

Bremner, J. D., Southwick, S. M., Johnson, D. R., Yehuda, R., & Charney, D. S. (1993). Childhood physical abuse and combat-related posttraumatic stress disorder in Vietnam veterans. *Amer. J. Psychiat , 150*(2), 235–239.

Bremner, J. D., Steinberg, M., Southwick, S. M., Johnson, D. R., & Charney, D. S. (1993). Use of the structured clinical interview for DSM-IV dissociative disorders for systematic assessment of dissociative symptoms in posttraumatic stress disorder. *Amer. J. Psychiat., 150*(7), 1101–1014.

Brems, C. (1995). Women and depression: A comprehensive analysis. In W. Beckham & W. Leber (Eds.), *Handbook of depression* (2nd ed.). New York: Guilford.

Brende, J. O., & Parson, E. R. (1985). *Vietnam veterans.* New York: Plenum.

Brende, J. O., & Rinsley, D. B. (1981). A case of multiple personality with psychological automatisms. *J. Amer. Acad. Psychoanal., 9*(1), 129–151.

Brenner, I. (1999). Deconstructing DID. *Amer. J. Psychother., 53*(3), 344–360.

Brent, D.A. & Kolko, D.J. (1998). Psychotherapy: Definitions, mechanisms of action, and relationship to etiological models. *J. Abnorm. Child Psychol., 26*(1), 17–25.

Brent, D. A., Bridge, J., Johnson, B. A., & Connolly, J. (1996). Suicidal behavior runs in families. A controlled family study of adolescent suicide victims. *Arch. Gen. Psychiat., 53,* 1145–1152.

Brent, D. A., Bridge, J., Johnson, B. A., & Connolly, J. (1998). Suicidal behavior runs in families: A controlled family study of adolescent suicide victims. In R. J. Kosky, H. S. Eshkevari, & R. Hassan (Eds.), *Suicide prevention: The global context.* New York: Plenum Press.

Brent, D. A., Kupfer, D. J., Bromet, E. J., & Dew, M. A. (1988). The assessment and treatment of patients at risk for suicide. In A. J. Frances & R. E. Hales (Eds.), *American Psychiatric Press review of psychiatry* (Vol. 7). Washington, DC: American Psychiatric Press.

Brent, D. A., Moritz, G., Liotus, L., Schweers, J., Balach, L., Roth, C., & Perper, J. A. (1998).

Familial risk factors for adolescent suicide: A case-control study. In R. J. Kosky, H. S. Eshkevari, & R. Hassan (Eds.), *Suicide prevention: The global context.* New York: Plenum Press.

Breslau, N., Chilcoat, H. D., Kessler, R. C., & Davis, G. C. (1999). Previous exposure to trauma and PTSD effects of subsequent trauma: Results from the Detroit Area Survey of Trauma. *Amer. J. Psychiat., 156*(6), 902–907.

Breton, J. J., Bergeron, L., Valla, J. P., Berthiaume, C., Gaudet, N., Lambert, J., St. Georges, M., Houde, L., & Lepine, S. (1999). Quebec child mental health survey: Prevalence of DSM-III-R mental health disorders. *J. Child Psychol. Psychiat. Allied Disc., 40*(3), 375–384.

Brew, B. J. (1999). AIDS dementia complex. *Neurol. Clin., 17*(4), 861–881.

Brewerton, T. D., Lydiard, R. B., Herzog, D. B., Brotman, A. W., et al. (1995). Comorbidity of Axis I psychiatric disorders in bulimia nervosa. *J. Clin. Psychiat., 56*(2), 77–80.

Brewin, C. R., Andrews, B., Rose, S., & Kirk, M. (1999). Acute stress disorder and posttraumatic stress disorder in victims of violent crime. *Amer. J. Psychiat., 156*(3), 360–366.

Brisman, J. (1992). Bulimia in the older adolescent: An analytic perspective to a behavioral problem. In J. D. O'Brien, D. J. Pilowsky, & O. W. Lewis, (Eds.), *Psychotherapies with children and adolescents: Adapting the psychodynamic process.* Washington, DC: American Psychiatric Press.

Bristow, M., & Bright, J. (1995). Group cognitive therapy in chronic depression: Results from two intervention studies. *Behav. Cog. Psychother., 23,* 373–380.

Britton, W. H., & Eaves, R. C. (1986). Relationship between the Vineland Adaptive Behavior Scales-Classroom Edition of the Vineland Social Maturity Scales. *Amer. J. Ment. Def., 91*(1), 105–107.

Brodsky, S., & Pothyress, N. (1990). Presentation. American Psychological Association Convention, Boston.

Bromet, E. J., Hough, L., & Connell, M. (1984). Mental health of children near the Three Mile Island reactor. *J. Prev. Psychiat., 2,* 275–301.

Bromet, E. J., Schulberg, H. C., & Dunn, L. (1982). Reactions of psychiatric patients to the Three Mile Island nuclear accident. *Arch. Gen. Psychiat., 39*(6), 725–730.

Brooks, G. R., & Richardson, F. C. (1980). Emotional skills training: A treatment program for duodenal ulcer. *Behav. Ther., 11*(2), 198–207.

Brooner, R. K., King, V. L., Kidorf, M., Schmidt, C. W., & Bigelow, G. E. (1997). Psychiatric and substance use comorbidity among treatment-seeking opioid abusers. *Arch. Gen. Psychiat., 54,* 71–80.

Brown, A. S., Susser, E. S., Butler, P. D., Andrews, R. R., Kaufmann, C. A., & Gorman, J. M. (1996). Neurobiological plausibility of prenatal nutritional deprivation as a risk factor for schizophrenia. *J. Nerv. Ment. Dis., 184*(2), 71–85.

Brown, B. S. (1983). The impact of political and economic changes upon mental health. *Amer. J. Orthopsychiat., 53*(4), 583–592.

Brown, E. (1972). Assessment from a humanistic perspective. *Psychother. Theory Res. Prac., 9,* 103–106.

Brown, G. L., Ebert, M., Goyer, P., Jimerson, D. C., Klein, W. J., Bunney, W. E., & Goodwin, F. K. (1982). Aggression, suicide, and serotonin: Relationships to CSF amine metabolites. *Amer. J. Psychiat., 139,* 741–746.

Brown, G. L., Goodwin, F. K., Ballenger, J. C., Goyer, P. F., & Major, L. F. (1979). Aggression in humans correlates with cerebrospinal fluid metabolites. *Psychiatr. Res., 1,* 131–139.

Brown, G. L., Linnoila, M. I., & Goodwin, F. K. (1992). Impulsivity, aggression, and associated affects: Relationship to self-destructive behavior and suicide. In R. W. Maris, A. L. Berman, J. T. Maltsberger, & R. I. Yufit (Eds.), *Assessment and prediction of suicide.* New York: Guilford.

Brown, G. W. (1988). Early loss of parent and depression in adult life. In S. Fisher & J. Reason (Eds.), *Handbook of life stress, cognition and health.* Chichester, England: Wiley.

Brown, G. W., & Harris, T. O. (1978). *Social origins of depression: A study of psychiatric disorder in women.* London: Tavistock.

Brown, G. W., Monck, E. M., Carstairs, G. M., & Wing, J. K. (1962). Influence on family life on the course of schizophrenic illness. *Brit. J. Prev. Soc. Med., 16,* 55–68.

Brown, J. H., Henteleff, P., Barakat, S., & Rowe, C. J. (1986). Is it normal for terminally ill patients to desire death? *Amer. J. Psychiat., 143*(2), 208–211.

Brown, J. L., & Pollitt, E. (1996, February.). Malnutrition, poverty and intellectual development. *Scientif. Amer.,* pp. 38–43.

Brown, L. (1993). Enrollment of drug abusers in HIV clinical trials: A public health imperative for communities of color. *J. Psychoactive Drugs, 25*(1), 45–48.

Brown, M. W., & Massaro, S. (1998, February 3). *Study identifies mechanism for cocaine-induced stroke and other brain damage.* Washington, DC: National Institutes of Health/National Institute on Drug Abuse. [NIH news release]

Brown, P. J., Stout, R. L., & Mueller, T. (1996). Posttraumatic stress disorder and substance abuse relapse among women: A pilot study. *Psychol. Addict. Behav., 10*(2), 124–128.

Brown, S. (1997). Excess mortality of schizophrenia: A meta-analysis. *Brit. J. Psychiat., 171,* 502–508.

Brown, W. A. (1998, January). The placebo effect. *Scientif. Amer.,* pp. 90–95.

Browne, A., & Finklehor, D. (1986). Impact of child sexual abuse: A review of the research. *Psychol. Bull., 99*(1), 66–77.

Brownell, K. D. (1991). Dieting and the search for the perfect body. Where physiology and culture collide. *Behav. Ther., 22,* 1–12.

Brownell, K. D., & Napolitano, M. A. (1995). Distorting reality for children: Body size proportions of Barbie and Ken dolls. *Inter. J. Eat. Disorders, 18*(3), 295–298.

Brownell, K. D., & O'Neil, P. M. (1993). Obesity. In D. H. Barlow (Ed.), *Clinical handbook of psychological disorders: A step-by-step treatment manual* (2nd ed.). New York: Guilford.

Brownell, K. D., & Wadden, T. A. (1992). Etiology and treatment of obesity: Understanding a serious, prevalent, and refractory disorder. *J. Cons. Clin. Psychol., 60*(4), 505–517.

Bruce, E. J., Schultz, C. L., & Smyrnios, K. X. (1996). A longitudinal study of the grief of mothers and fathers of children with intellectual disability. *Brit. J. Med. Psychol., 69,* 33–45.

Bruce, M. L., & Kim, K. M. (1992). Differences in the effects of divorce on major depression in men and women. *Amer. J. Psychiat., 149*(7), 914–917.

Bruce, T. J., & Saeed, S. A. (1999). Social anxiety disorder: A common, underrecognized mental disorder. *Amer. Fam. Phys., 60*(8), 2311–2320, 2322.

Bruch, H. (1962). Perceptual and conceptual disturbances in anorexia nervosa. *Psychosom. Med., 24,* 187–194.

Bruch, H. (1973). *Eating disorders: Obesity, anorexia nervosa and the person within.* New York: Basic Books.

Bruch, H. (1973). Psychiatric aspects of obesity. *Psychiatr. Ann., 3*(7), 6–10.

Bruch, H. (1978). *The golden cage: The enigma of anorexia nervosa.* Cambridge, MA: Harvard University Press.

Bruch, H. (1981). Developmental considerations of anorexia nervosa and obesity. *Canad. J. Psychiat., 26,* 212–217.

Bruch, H. (1982). Anorexia nervosa: Therapy and theory. *Amer. J. Psychiat., 139,* 1531–1538.

Bruch, H. (1991). The sleeping beauty: Escape from change. In S. I. Greenspan & G. H. Pollock (Eds.), *The course of life: Vol. 4. Adolescence.* Madison, CT: International Universities Press.

Brumberg, J. J. (1988). *Fasting girls: The history of anorexia nervosa.* New York: Penguin Books.

Bruni, F. (1998, November 22). Behind the jokes, a life of pain and delusion; For Letterman stalker, mental illness was family curse and scarring legacy. *New York Times,* Sect. 1, p. 45.

Bryant, R. A., & Harvey, A. G. (1995). Posttraumatic stress in volunteer firefighters: Predictors of stress. *J. Nerv. Ment. Dis., 183*(4), 267–271.

Buchan, H., Johnstone, E. C., McPherson, K., Palmer, R. L., et al. (1992). Who benefits from electroconvulsive therapy? Combined results of the Leicester and Northwick Park trials. *Brit. J. Psychiat., 160,* 355–359.

Buchanan, A. (1997). The investigation of acting on delusions as a tool for risk assessment in the mentally disordered. *Brit. J. Psychiat., 170*(Suppl. 32), 12–14.

Buchanan, A. (1999). Risk and dangerousness. *Psychol. Med., 29*(2), 465–473.

Buchanan, R. W., & Carpenter, W.T. (1997). The neuroanatomies of schizophrenia. *Schizo. Bull., 23*(3), 367–372.

Buchele, B. J. (1993). Group psychotherapy for persons with multiple personality and dissociative disorders. *Bull. Menninger Clin., 57*(3), 362–370.

Buchkremer, G., Monking, H. S., Holle, R., & Hornung, W. P. (1995). The impact of therapeutic relatives' groups on the course of illness of schizophrenic patients. *Eur. Psychiat., 10*(1), 17–27.

Buchsbaum, M. S., & Haier, R. J. (1987). Functional and anatomical brain imaging: Impact on schizophrenia research. *Schizo. Bull., 13*(1), 115–132.

Buchwald, A. M., & Rudick-Davis, D. (1993). The symptoms of major depression. *J. Abnorm. Psychol., 102*(2), 197–205.

Buckley, J. T. (1995) Nation raising "a generation of gamblers." *USA Today,* pp. 1A–2A.

Buckley, P. F. (1998). Substance abuse in schizoophrenia: A review. *J. Clin. Psychiat., 59*(Suppl. 3), 26–30.

Buffum, J. (1992). Prescription drugs and sexual function. *Psychiatric Med., 10*(2), 181–198.

Bugental, J. F. (1965). The existential crisis in intensive psychotherapy. *Psychother. Theory Res. Prac., 2*(1), 16–20.

Bugental, J. F. T. (1992). The betrayal of the human: Psychotherapy's mission to reclaim our lost identity. In J. K. Zeig (Ed.), *The evolution of psychotherapy: The second conference.* New York: Brunner/Mazel.

Bugental, J. F. T. (1997). There is a fundamental division in how psychotherapy is conceived. In J. K. Zeig (Ed.), *The evolution of psychotherapy: The third conference.* New York: Brunner/Mazel.

Bujold, A., Ladouceur, R., Sylvain, C., & Boisvert J. M. (1994). Treatment of pathological gamblers: An experimental study. *J. Behav. Ther. Exp. Psychiat., 25*(4), 275–282.

Bukstein, O. G., Brent, D. A., & Kaminer, Y. (1989). Comorbidity of substance abuse and other psychiatric disorders in adolescents. *Amer. J. Psychiat., 146*(9), 1131–1141.

Bulik, C. M., Sullivan, P. F., Carter, F. A., McIntosh, V. V., & Joyce, P. R. (1998). The role of exposure with response prevention in the cognitive-behavioural therapy for bulimia nervosa. *Psychol. Med., 28*(3), 611–623.

Bumby, K. M., & Maddox, M. C. (1999). Judges' knowledge about sexual offenders, difficulties presiding over sexual offense cases, and opinions on sentencing, treatment, and legislation. *Sex. Abuse J. Res. Treat., 11*(4), 305–315.

Bunney, W. E., & Bunney, B. G. (2000). Molecular clock genes in man and lower animals: Possible implications for circadian abnormalities in depression. *Neuropsychopharmacology, 22*(4), 335–345.

Bunney, W. E., & Davis, J. M. (1965). Norepinephrine in depressive reactions: A review. *Arch. Gen. Psychiat., 13*(6), 483–493.

Bunney, W. E., & Garland, B. L. (1984). Lithium and its possible modes of actions. In R. M. Post & J. C. Ballenger (Eds.), *Neurobiology of mood disorders: Vol. I. Frontiers of Clinical Neuroscience.* Baltimore: Williams & Wilkins.

Burd, L., Severud, R., Kerbeshian, J., & Klug, M. G. (1999). Prenatal and perinatal risk factors for autism. *J. Perinat. Med., 27*(6), 441–450.

Bureau of Justice Statistics. (1999). *Report on U.S. prison population.*

Bureau of Justice Statistics. (1999). *Substance abuse and treatment, state and federal prisoners, 1997.* Washington, DC: U.S. Department of Justice.

Burgess, E., & Haaga, D. A. (1994). The Positive Automatic Thoughts Questionnaire (ATQ-P) and the Automatic Thoughts Questionnaire-Revised (ATQ-RP): Equivalent measures of positive thinking? *Cog. Ther. Res., 18*(1), 15–23.

Burnett, R., Mallett, R., Bhugra, D., Hutchinson, G., Der., G., & Leff, J. (1999). The first contact of patients with schizophrenia with psychiatric services: Social factors and pathways to care in a multi-ethnic population. *Psychol. Med., 29*(2), 475–483.

Burnette, E. (1996). Urban activists call for hands-on community work. *APA Monitor, 27*(10), 30.

Burnette, E., & Murray, B. (1996). Conduct disorders need early treatment. *APA Monitor, 27*(10), 40.

Burney, J., & Irwin, H. J. (2000). Shame and guilt in women with eating-disorder symptomatology. *J. Clin. Psychol., 56*(1), 51–61.

Burns, L. H. (1995). An overview of sexual dysfunction in the infertile couple. *J. Fam. Psychother., 6*(1), 25–46.

Burns, T. P., & Crisp, A. H. (1985). Factors affecting prognosis in male anorexics. *J. Psychiatr. Res., 19*(2–3), 323–328.

Burr, J. A., Hartman, J. T., & Matteson, D. W. (1999). Black suicide in U.S. metropolitan areas: An examination of the racial inequality and social integration-regulation hypotheses. *Soc. Forces, 77*(3), 1049–1080.

Burt, D. R., Creese, I., & Snyder, S. H. (1977). Anti-schizophrenic drugs: Chronic treatment elevates dopamine receptor binding in brain. *Science, 196*(4287), 326–328.

Burton, V. S. (1990). The consequences of official labels: A research note on rights lost by the mentally ill, mentally incompetent, and convicted felons. *Comm. Ment. Hlth. J., 26*(3), 267–276.

Burvill, P. W. (1998). Migrant suicide rates in Australia and in country of birth. *Psychol. Med., 28*(1), 201–208.

Busatto, G. F., Pilowsky, L. S., Costa, D. C., Ell, P. J., David, A. S., et al. (1997). Correlation between reduced in vivo benzodiazepine receptor binding and severity of psychotic symptoms in schizophrenia. *Amer. J. Psychiat., 154*(1), 56–63.

Bushman, B. J., Baumeister, R. F., & Stack, A. D. (1999). Catharsis, aggression, and persuasive influence: Self-fulfilling or self-defeating prophecies? *J. Pers. Soc. Psychol., 76*(3), 367–376.

Bustillo, J. R., Thaker, G., Buchanan, R. W., Moran, M., et al. (1997). Visual information-processing impairments in deficit and nondeficit schizophrenia. *Amer. J. Psychiat., 154*(5), 647–654.

Butcher, J. N. (1999). *A beginner's guide to the MMPI-2.* Washington, DC: American Psychological Assoc.

Butcher, J. N., Lim, J., & Nezami, E. (1998). Objective study of abnormal personality in cross-cultural settings: The Minnesota Multiphasic Personality Inventory (MMPI-2). *J. Cross-Cult. Psychol., 29*(1), 189–211.

Butler, G., Fennel, M., Robson, P., & Gelder, M. (1991). A comparison of behavior therapy and cognitive behavior therapy in the treatment of generalized anxiety disorder. *J. Cons. Clin. Psychol., 59*(1), 167–175.

Butler, R. N. (1975). Psychiatry and the elderly: An overview. *Amer. J. Psychiat., 132,* 893–900.

Button, E. (1993). *Eating disorders: Personal construct therapy and change.* Chichester, England: Wiley.

Buttross, S. (2000). Attention deficit-hyperactivity disorder and its deceivers. *Curr. Probl. Pediatr., 30*(2), 37–50.

Buysse, D. J., Frank, E., Lowe, K. K., Cherry, C. R., & Kupfer, D. J. (1997). Electroencephalographic sleep correlates to episode and vulnerability to recurrence in depression. *Depression, 41,* 406–418.

Buysse, D. J., Reynolds, C. F., & Kupfer, D. J. (1993). Depression. In M. A. Carsakadon (Ed.), *The Encyclopedia of Sleep and Dreaming.* New York: Macmillan.

Buysse, D. J., Tu, X. M., Cherry, C. R., Begley, A. E., Kowalski, J., Kupfer, D. J., & Frank, E. (1999). Pretreatment REM sleep and subjective sleep quality distinguish depressed psychotherapy remitters and nonremitters. *Biol. Psychiat., 45*(2), 205–213.

Byrnes, G., & Kelly, I. W. (1992). Crisis calls and lunar cycles: A twenty-year review. *Psychol. Rep., 71*(3, Pt.1), 779–785.

CDC (Centers for Disease Control and Prevention). (1996, December 20). *What CDC is doing to prevent fetal alcohol syndrome and other alcohol-related developmental disabilities.* National Center for Environmental Health (NCEH), Division of Birth Defects and Developmental Disabilities (DBDDD).

CDC (Centers for Disease Control and Prevention). (1997). Cited in NCIPC (National Center for Injury Prevention and Control), Impaired driving fact sheet.

CDC (Centers for Disease Control and Prevention). (1998, March 20). *Suicide among black youths.* Office of Communications, Division of Medicine.

CDC (Centers for Disease Control and Prevention). (1998, May 21). *Facts about violence among youth and violence in schools.* Office of Communications, Division of Medicine.

CDC (Centers for Disease Control and Prevention). (1998, December 11). *Impaired driving.* Office of Communications, Division of Medicine.

CPC (Centers for Disease Control and Prevention). (1999, June 29). Cited in S. Uretsky, The world will end tomorrow, *HealthScout.*

Cacciola, J. S., Rutherford, M. J., Alterman, A. I., McKay, J. R., & Snider, E. C. (1996). Personality disorders and treatment outcomes in methadone maintenance patients. *J. Nerv. Ment. Dis., 184*(4), 234–239.

Caces, F., & Harford, T. (1998). Time series analysis of alcohol consumption and suicide mortality in the United States, 1934–1987. *J. Stud. Alc., 59*(4), 455–461.

Caddy, G. R. (1985). Cognitive behavior therapy in the treatment of multiple personality. *Behav. Mod., 9*(3), 267–292.

Cadenhead, K. S., Light, G. A., Geyer, M. A., & Braff, D. L. (2000). Sensory gating deficits assessed by the P50 event-related potential in subjects with schizotypal personality disorder. *Amer. J. Psychiat., 157*(1), 55–59.

Cadoret, R. J., Yates, W. R., Troughton, E., Woodworth, G., & Stewart, M. A. (1995). Adoption study demonstrating two genetic pathways to drug abuse. *Arch. Gen. Psychiat., 52,* 42–52.

Cage, M. C. (1992). 42% of college students engage in "binge drinking," survey shows. *Chron. Higher Educ., 39*(6), S30.

Cahill, S. P., Carrigan, M. H., & Frueh, B. C. (1999). Does EMDR work? and if so, why?: A critical review of controlled outcome and dismantling research. *J. Anx. Dis., 13*(1–2), 5–33.

Calamari, J. E., & Cassiday, K. L. (1999). Treating obsessive-compulsive disorder in older adults: A review of strategies. In M. Duffy (Ed.), *Handbook of counseling and psychotherapy with older adults.* New York: Wiley.

Calev, A., Gaudino, E. A., Squires, N. K., Zervas, I. M., & Fink, M. (1995). ECT and non-memory cognition: A review. *Brit. J. Clin. Psychol., 34,* 505–515.

Calev, A., Kochav-Lev, E., Tubi, N., Nigal, D., et al. (1991). Change in attitude toward electroconvulsive therapy: Effects of treatment, time since treatment, and severity of depression. *Convulsive Therapy, 7*(3), 184–189.

Calev, A., Nigal, D., Shapira, B., Tubi, N., et al. (1991). Early and long-term effects of electroconvulsive therapy and depression on memory and other cognitive functions. *J. Nerv. Ment. Dis., 179*(9), 526–533.

Callahan, C. M., Wolinsky, F. D., Stump, T. E., Nienaber, N. A., Hui, S. L., & Tierney, W. M. (1998). Mortality, symptoms, and functional impairment in late-life depression. *J. Gen. Internal Med., 13*(11), 746–752.

Callahan, L. A., & Silver, E. (1998). Factors associated with the conditional release of persons acquitted by reason of insanity: A decision tree approach. *Law Human Behav., 22*(2), 147–163.

Callahan, L. A., McGreevy, M. A., Cirincione, C., & Steadman, H. J. (1992). Measuring the effects of the GBMI verdict: Georgia's 1982 GBMI reform. *Law Human Behav., 16*(4), 447–461.

Callahan, L. A., Steadman, H. J., McGreevy, M. A., & Robbins, P. C. (1991). The volume and characteristics of insanity defense pleas: An eight-state study. *Bull. Amer. Acad. Psychiat. Law, 19*(4), 331–338.

Calsyn, D. A., Fleming, C., Wells, E. A., & Saxon, A. J. (1996). Personality disorder subtypes among opiate addicts in methadone maintenance. *Psychol. Addict. Behav., 10*(1), 3–8.

Camara, W. J., & Schneider, D. L. (1994). Integrity tests: Facts and unresolved issues. *Amer. Psychologist., 49*(2), 112–119.

Cameron, D. J., Thomas, R. I., Mulvhill, M., & Bronheim, H. (1987). Delirium: A test of the Diagnostic and Statistical Manual III criteria on medical inpatients. *J. Amer. Ger. Soc., 35,* 1007–1010.

Cameron, N. (1974). Paranoid conditions and paranoia. In S. Arieti & E. Brody (Eds.), *American handbook of psychiatry.* New York: Basic Books.

Cameron, P. M., Leszcz, M., Bebchuk, W., Swinson, R. P., Antony, M. M., Azim, H. F., Doidge, N., Korenblum, M. S., Nigam, T., Perry, J. C., & Seeman, M. V. (1999). The practice and roles of the psychotherapies: A discussion paper. *Canad. J. Psychiat., 44*(Suppl 1), 18S–31S.

Campbell, J. C. (1995). Prediction of homicide of and by battered women. In J. C. Campbell (Ed.), *Assessing dangerousness: Violence by sexual offenders, batterers, and child abusers.* Thousand Oaks, CA: Sage.

Campbell, R. V., O'Brien, S., Bickett, A. D., & Lutzker, J. R. (1983). In-home parent training of migraine headaches and marital counseling as an ecobehavioral approach to prevent child abuse. *J. Behav. Ther. Exp. Psychiat., 14,* 147–154.

Campbell, T. L., & Patterson, J.M. (1995). The effectiveness of family interventions in the treatment of physical illness. Special Issue: The effectiveness of marital and family therapy. *J. Marital Fam. Ther., 21*(4), 545–583.

Campbell, T. W. (1999). Challenging the evidentiary reliability of DSM-IV. *Amer. J. Forens. Psychol., 17*(1), 47–68.

Canetto, S. S. (1995). Elderly women and suicidal behavior. In S. S. Canetto & D. Lester (Eds.), *Women and suicidal behavior.* New York: Springer.

Canetto, S. S. (1995). Suicidal women: Prevention and intervention strategies. In S. S. Canetto & D. Lester (Eds.), *Women and suicidal behavior.* New York: Springer.

Canetto, S. S., & Lester, D. (1995). Gender and the primary prevention of suicide mortality. [Special issue]. *Suic. Life-Threat. Behav., 25*(1), 58–69.

Canetto, S. S., & Lester, D. (1995). The epidemiology of women's suicidal behavior. In S. S. Canetto & D. Lester (Eds.), *Women and suicidal behavior.* New York: Springer.

Canino, E., Cardona, R., Monsalve, P., Perez, A. F., Lopez, B., & Fragachan, F. (1994). A behavioral treatment program as a therapy in the control of primary hypertension. *Acta Cient. Venez., 45*(1), 23–30.

Cannon, D. S., Baker, T. B., Gino, A., & Nathan, P. E. (1986). Alcohol-aversion therapy: Assessment of conditioning. *J. Cons. Clin. Psychol., 54,* 825–830.

Cannon, D. S., Baker, T. B., & Wehl, W. K. (1981). Emetic and electric shock alcohol aversion therapy: Six- and twelve-month follow-up. *J. Cons. Clin. Psychol., 49,* 360–368.

Cannon, T. D., & Marco, E. (1994). Structural brain abnormalities as indicators of vulnerability to schizophrenia. *Schizo. Bull., 20*(1), 89–102.

Cantagallo, A., Grassi, L., & Della Sala, S. (1999). Dissociative disorder after traumatic brain injury. *Brain Inj., 13*(4), 219–228.

Cantor, C. H., & Baume, P. J. M. (1998). Access to methods of suicide: What impact? *Austral. New Zeal. J. Psychiat., 32*(1), 8–14.

Canty, G. F. (1996). A heart to heart on depression. *The Institute Notebook, 5*(3), 1,4.

Canty, G. F. (1996). Therapists at work. *The Institute Notebook, 5*(2), 1,4.

Capaldi, D. M., & Patterson, G. R. (1994). Interrelated influences of contextual factors on antisocial behavior in childhood and adolescence for males. In D. C. Fowles, P. Sutker, & S. H. Goodman (Eds.), *Progress in experimental personality and psychopathology research.* New York: Springer.

Caplan, R., Perdue, S., Tanguay, P. E., & Fish, B. (1990). Formal thought disorder in childhood onset schizophrenia and schizotypal personality disorder. *J. Child Psychol. Psychiat. Allied Disc., 31*(7), 1103–1114.

Capleton, R. A. (1996). Cognitive function in schizophrenia: Association with negative and positive symptoms. *Psychol. Rep., 78,* 123–128.

Capps, L., Sigman, M., Sena, R., Henker, B., & Whalen, C. (1996). Fear, anxiety and perceived control in children of agoraphobic parents. *J. Child Psychol. Psychiat., 37*(4), 445–452.

Cardasis, W., Hochman, J. A., & Silk, K. R. (1997). Transitional objects and borderline personality disorder. *Amer. J. Psychiat, 154*(2), 250–255.

Carducci, B. (2000, March 13). Taking the pain out of painfully shy. *Los Angeles Times,* Part E, p. 2.

Carek, P. J., & Dickerson, L. M. (1999). Current concepts in the pharmacological management of obesity. *Drugs, 57*(6), 883–904.

Carels, R. A., Baucom, D. H., Leone, P. & Rigney, A. (1998). Psychosocial factors and psychological symptoms: HIV in a public health setting. *J. Comm. Psychol., 26*(2), 145–162.

Carey, A. R., & Mullins, M.E. (1995, July 31). Survey: Caffeine and baby boomers. Cited in *USA Today,* p. 1D.

Carey, G., & DiLalla, D. L. (1994). Personality and psychopathology: Genetic perspectives. *J. Abnorm. Psychol., 103*(1), 32–43.

Carey, G., & Gottesman, I. I. (1981). Twin and family studies of anxiety, phobic, and obsessive disorders. In D. K. Klein & J. Rabkin (Eds.), *Anxiety: New research and changing concepts.* New York: Raven Press.

Carey, K. (1989). Emerging treatment guidelines for mentally ill chemical abusers. *Hosp. Comm. Psychiat., 40*(4), 341–342.

Carey, K. B. & Carey, M. P. (1995). Reasons for drinking among psychiatric outpatients: Relationship to drinking patterns. *Psychol. Addict. Behav., 9*(4), 251–257.

Carey, M., Carey, K., & Meisler, A. (1991). Psychiatric symptoms in mentally ill chemical abusers. *J. Nerv. Ment. Dis., 179*(3), 136–138.

Carey, M. P., Wincze, J. P., & Meisler, A. W. (1993). Sexual dysfunction: Male erectile disorder. In D. H. Barlow (Ed.), *Clinical handbook of psychological disorders: A step-by-step treatment manual* (2nd ed.). New York: Guilford.

Carey, R. J., Pinheiro-Carrera, M., Dai, H., Tomaz, C., & Huston, J. P. (1995). L-Dopa and psychosis: Evidence for L-dopa-induced increases in prefrontal cortex dopamine and in serum corticosterone. *Biol. Psychiat., 38,* 669–676.

Carlson, G. A., Rich, C. L., Grayson, P., & Fowler, R. C. (1991). Secular trends in psychiatric diagnoses of suicide victims. *J. Affect. Disorders, 21,* 127–132.

Carnahan, H., Elliott, D., & Velamoor, V. R. (1996). Influence of object size on prehension in leukotomized and unleukotomized individuals with schizophrenia. *J. Clin. Exp. Neuropsychol., 18*(1), 136–147.

Carpenter, K.M., & Hasin, D. (1998). A prospective evaluation of the relationship between reasons for drinking and DSM-IV alcohol-use disorders. *Addic. Behav., 23*(1), 41–46.

Carper, R. A., & Courchesne, E. (2000). Inverse correlation between frontal lobe and cerebellum sizes in children with autism. *Brain, 123*(Pt. 4), 836–844.

Carr, J. (1994). Annotation: Long term outcome for people with Down syndrome. *J. Child Psychol. Psychiat. Allied Disc, 35*(3), 425–439.

Carr, R. E. (1998). Panic disorder and asthma: Causes, effects and research implications. *J. Psychosom. Res., 44*(1), 43–52.

Carrasco, J. L., Diaz-Marsa, M., Hollander, E., Cesar, J., & Saiz-Ruiz, J. (2000). Decreased platelet monoamine oxidase activity in female bulimia nervosa. *Eur. Neuropsychopharmacology., 10*(2), 113–117.

Carrey, N. J., Butter, H. J., Persinger, M. A., & Bialik, R. J. (1995). Physiological and cognitive correlates of child abuse. *J. Amer. Acad. Child Adol. Psychiat., 34*(8), 1067–1075.

Carrier, S. (1996, December). The test. *Harper's Magazine,* pp. 31–33.

Carrington, P. (1978). *Clinically standardized meditation (CSM) instructors kit.* Kendall Park, NJ: Pace Educational Systems.

Carrington, P. (1993). Modern forms of meditation. In P. M. Lehrer & R. L. Woolfolk (Eds.), *Principles and practice of stress management* (2nd ed.). New York: Guilford.

Carris, M. J., Sheeber, L., & Howe, S. (1998). Family rigidity, adolescent problem-solving deficits, and suicidal ideation: A mediational model. *J. Adolescence., 21*(4), 459–472.

Carroll, K. M., & Rounsaville, B. J. (1995). Psychosocial treatments. In J. M. Oldham & M. B. Riba (Eds.), *American Psychiatric Press review of psychiatry,* (Vol. 14). Washington, DC: American Psychiatric Press.

Carstairs, K. (1992). Paranoid-schizoid or symbiotic? *Inter. J. Psychoanal., 73*(1), 71–85.

Carter, C. S., Servan-Schreiber, D., & Perlstein, W. M. (1997). Anxiety disorders and the syndrome of chest pain with normal coronary arteries: Prevalence and pathophysiology. *J. Clin. Psychiat., 58* (Suppl. 3), 70–73.

Cartwright, R. D., & Lamberg, L. (1992). *Crisis dreaming: Using your dreams to solve your problems.* New York: HarperCollins.

Casey, D.E. (1998). Effects of clozapine therapy in schizophrenic individuals at risk for tardive dyskinesia. *J. Clin. Psychiat., 59* (Suppl. 3), 13–37.

Cash, T. F., & Henry, P. E. (1995). Women's body images: The results of a national survey in the U. S. A. *Sex Roles, 33*(1/2), 19–28.

Casper, R. C. (1995). Biology of eating disorders. In A. F. Schatzberg & C. B. Nemeroff (Eds.), *The American Psychiatric Press textbook of psychopharmacology.* Washington, DC: American Psychiatric Press.

Cassem, N. H., & Hyman, S. E. (1995). Psychological management of grief and serious illness. In *Scientific American Series: Vol. 13, Psychiatry.* New York: Scientific American.

Castle, D. J., Abel, K., Takei, N., & Murray, R. M. (1995). Gender differences in schizophrenia: Hormonal effect or subtypes? *Schizo. Bull., 21*(1), 1–12.

Castrogiovanni, P., Pieraccini, F., & Di Muro, A. (1998). Suicidality and aggressive behavior. *Acta Psychiat. Scandin., 97*(2), 144–148.

Catherall, D. R. (1999). Family as a group treatment for PTSD. In B. H. Young & D. D. Blake (Eds.), *Group treatments for post-traumatic stress disorder.* Philadelphia: Brunner/Mazel.

Caton, C. L. (1982). Effect of length of inpatient treatment for chronic schizophrenia. *Amer. J. Psychiat., 139*(7), 856–861.

Cattell, H., & Jolley, D. J. (1995). One hundred cases of suicide in elderly people. *Brit. J. Psychiat., 166*(4), 451–457.

Cauchon, D. (1995, December 6). Patients often aren't informed of full danger. *USA Today,* pp. 1A–2A.

Cauchon, D. (1999, February). Patients often aren't informed of danger. *USA Today.*

Cautela, J. R. (1966). Treatment of compulsive behavior by covert sensitization. *Psychol. Rec., 16*(1), 33–41.

Cauwels, J. M. (1983). *Bulimia: The binge-purge compulsion.* New York: Doubleday.

Cavanaugh, J. C. (1990). *Adult development and aging.* Belmont, CA: Wadsworth.

Ceci, S. J., & Williams, W. M. (1997). Schooling, intelligence, and income. *Amer. Psychologist, 52*(10), 1051–1058.

Centorrino, F., Baldessarini, R. J., Frankenburg, F. R., Kando, J., Volpicelli, S. A., & Flood, J. G. (1996). Serum levels of clozapine and norclozapine in patients treated with selective serotonin reuptake inhibitors. *Amer. J. Psychiat., 153*(6), 820–822.

Cerf, C., & Navasky, V. (1998). *The experts speak.* New York: Villard.

Cerletti, U., & Bini, L. (1938). L'elettroshock. *Arch. Gen. Neurol. Psychiat. & Psychoanal., 19,* 266–268.

Chabra, A., Chavez, G. F., Harris, E. S., & Shah, R. (1999). Hospitalization for mental illness in adolescents: Risk groups and impact on the health care system. *J. Adol. Hlth., 24*(5), 349–356.

Chadwick, P., & Trower, P. (1996). Cognitive therapy for punishment paranoia: A single case experiment. *Behav. Res. Ther., 34*(4), 351–356.

Chaika, E. O. (1990). *Understanding psychotic speech: Beyond Freud and Chomsky.* Springfield, IL: Thomas.

Chait, L. D., Fishman, M. W., & Schuster, C. R. (1985). "Hangover" effects the morning after marijuana smoking. *Drug Alc. Dep., 15*(3), 229–238.

Chakos, M. H., Alvir, J. M. J., Woerner, M. G., Koreen, A., Geisler, S., Mayerhoff, D., Sobel, S., Kane, J. M., Borenstein, M., & Lieberman, J. A. (1996). Incidence and correlates of tardive dyskinesia in first episode of schizophrenia. *Arch. Gen. Psychiat., 53,* 313–319.

Chamberlain, P. (1985). Increasing the attention span of five mentally handicapped children using their parents as agents of change. *Behav. Psychother., 13*(20), 142–153.

Champion, L. A., & Power, M. J. (1995). Social and cognitive approaches to depression: Towards a new synthesis. *Brit. J. Clin. Psychol., 34,* 485–503.

Chan, S., MacKenzie, A., Ng, D. T., & Leung, J. K. (2000). An evaluation of the implementation of case management in the community psychiatric nursing service. *J. Adv. Nurs., 31*(1), 144–156.

Chang, Y., & Gates, D. (1997, March 10). The piano man. *Newsweek,* pp. 62–66.

Char, W. F. (1985). The hysterical spouse. *Med. Aspects Human Sex., 19*(9), 123–133.

Charney, D. S., Heninger, G. R., & Redmond, D. E. (1983). Yohimbine induced anxiety and increased noradrenergic function in humans: Effects of diazepam and clonidine. *Life Science, 33,* 19–29.

Charney, D. S., Heninger, G. R., & Redmond, D. E. (1984, May). Neurobiological mechanism. From Abstracts of the APA Annual Meeting (Abstract 30C). Los Angeles.

Charney, D. S., Heninger, G. R., & Sternberg, D. E. (1984). The effect of mianserin on alpha 2 adrenergic receptor function in depressed patients. *Brit. J. Psychiat., 144,* 407–418.

Charney, D. S., Woods, S. W., Goodman, W. K., & Heninger, G. R. (1987). Neurobiological mechanisms of panic anxiety: Biochemical and behavioral correlates of yohimbine-induced anxiety. *Amer. J. Psychiat., 144*(8), 1030–1036.

Charney, D. S., Woods, S. W., Krystal, J. H., Nagy, L. M., & Heninger, G. R. (1992). Noradrenergic neuronal dysregulation in panic disorder: The effects of intravenous yohimbine and clonidine in panic disorder patients. *Acta Psychiatr. Scandin., 86,* 273–282.

Charney, D. S., Woods, S. W., Price, L. H., Goodman, W. K., Glazer, W. M., & Heninger, G. R. (1990). Noradrenergic dysregulation in panic disorder. In J. C. Ballenger (Ed.), *Neurobiology of panic disorder.* New York: Wiley-Liss.

Chase, M. (1993, May 28). Psychiatrists declare severe PMS a depressive disorder. *Wall Street Journal,* pp. B1, B6.

Chase, M. (1996, April 15). If you're considering melatonin, weigh facts against all the hype. *Wall Street Journal,* pp. B1–B2.

Chastang, F., Rioux, P., Dupont, I., Baranger, E., Kovess, V., & Zarifian, E. (1998). Suicide attempts and job insecurity: A complex association. *Eur. Psychiat., 13*(7), 359–364.

Chatlos, C. (1987). *Crack: What you should know about the cocaine epidemic.* New York: Perigee Books.

Chen, E. Y. H., Lam, L. C. W., Chen, R. Y. L., & Nguyen, D. G. H. (1996). Negative symptoms, neurological signs and neuropsychological impairments in 204 Hong Kong Chinese patients with schizophrenia. *Brit. J. Psychiat., 168,* 227–233.

Chen, W. J., Loh, E. W., Hsu, Y. P., Chen, C., Yu, J., & Cheng, A. T. A. (1996). Alcohol-metabolising genes and alcoholism among Taiwanese Han men: Independent effect of ADH2, ADH3, and ALDH2. *Brit. J. Psychiat., 168,* 762–767.

Chen, X., & Cui, Q. (1995). Effect of biofeedback and relaxation training on patients with 1st or 2nd period primary hypertension. *Chin. Ment. Hlth. J., 9*(3), 126, 125.

Chen, X., Rubin, R. H., & Li, B. (1995). Depressed mood in Chinese children: Relations with school performance and family environment. *J. Cons. Clin. Psychol., 63*(6), 938–947.

Chen, Y. R., Swann, A. C., & Burt, D. B. (1996). Stability of diagnosis in schizophrenia. *Amer J. Psychiat., 153*(5), 682–686.

Cherland, E., & Fitzpatrick, R. (1999). Psychotic side effects of psychostimulants: A 5-year review. *Canad. J. Psychiat., 44*(8), 811–813.

Childress, A. R., Hole, A. V., Ehrman, R. N., et al. (1993). Cue reactivity and cue reactivity interventions in drug dependence. In L. S. Onken, J. D. Blaine, & J. J. Boren (Eds.), *Behavioral treatments for drug abuse and dependence* (NIDA Research Monograph Series No. 137). Rockville, MD: National Institute on Drug Abuse.

Childress, A. R., McLellan, A. T., & O'Brien, C. P. (1984). Assessment and extinction of conditioned withdrawal-like responses in an integrated treatment for opiate dependence. In L. S. Harris (Ed.), *Problems of drug dependence* (NIDA Research Monograph Series No. 55). Rockville, MD: National Institute on Drug Abuse.

Childress, A. R., McLellan, A. T., & O'Brien, C. P. (1988). Classically conditioned responses in cocaine and opioid dependence: A role in relapse? In B. A. Ray (Ed.), *Learning factors in substance abuse* (NIDA Research Monograph Series No. 84). Rockville, MD: National Institute on Drug Abuse.

Chiu, L. H. (1971). Manifested anxiety in Chinese and American children. *J. Psychol., 79,* 273–284.

Chochinov, H., Wilson, K., Enns, M., Mowchum, N., Lander, S., Levitt, M., & Clinch, J. (1995). Desire for death in the terminally ill. *Amer. J. Psychiat., 152,* 1185–1191.

Chodoff, P. (1989). Histrionic personality disorder. In American Psychiatric Association (Ed.), *Treatments of psychiatric disorders: A task force report of the American Psychiatric Association.* Washington, DC: American Psychiatric Press.

Chorpita, B. F., & Lilienfeld, S. O. (1999). Clinical assessment of anxiety sensitivity in children and adolescents: Where do we go from here? *Psychol. Assess., 11*(2), 212–224.

Christensen, A., & Heavey, C.L. (1999). Interventions for couples. *Annu. Rev. Psychol., 50,* 165–190.

Christensen, A. J., Dornick, R., Ehlers, S. L., & Schultz, S. K. (1999). Social environment and longevity in schizophrenia. *Psychosom. Med., 61*(2), 141–145.

Christenson, G. A., & Mackenzie, T. B. (1995). Trichotillomania, body dysmorphic disorder, and obsessive-compulsive disorder. *J. Clin. Psychiat., 56*(5), 211–212.

Chu, J. A., Frey, L. M., Ganzel, B. L., & Matthews, J. A. (1999). Memories of childhood abuse: Dissociation, amnesia, and corroboration. *Amer. J. Psychiat., 156*(5), 749–755.

Chua-Eoan, H. (1998, June 29). A precarious genius. *Time,* p. 42.

Chynoweth, R. (1977). Significance of suicide notes. *Austral. New Zeal. J. Psychiat., 11,* 197–200.

Ciccocioppo, R. (1999). The role of serotonin in craving: From basic research to human studies. *Alcohol Alcoholism, 34*(2), 244–253.

Cimons, M. (1999, June 10). Some drugs affect men, women differently, but why? *Miami Herald.*

Ciompi, L., Dauwalder, H., Maier, C., Aebi, E., Trutsch, K., Kupper, Z., & Rutishauser, C. (1992). The pilot project 'soteria berne': Clinical experiences and results. *Brit. J. Psychiat., 161*(Suppl. 18), 145–153.

Cipani, E. (1991). Educational classification and placement. In J. L. Matson & J. A. Mulick (Eds.), *Handbook of mental retardation.* New York: Pergamon Press.

Cirese, S. (1993). Personal communication.

Cisin, I. H., & Calahan, D. (1970, July 6). The big drinkers. *Newsweek,* p. 57.

Clark, A. J. (1995). Projective techniques in the counseling process. *J. Counc. Dev., 73*(3), 311–316.

Clark, C. R. (1999). Specific intent and diminished capacity. In A. K. Hess, I. B. Weiner, et al. (Eds.), *The handbook of forensic psychology* (2nd ed.). New York: Wiley.

Clark, D. A. (1992). Depressive, anxious and intrusive thoughts in psychiatric inpatients and outpatients. *Behav. Res. Ther., 30,* 93–102.

Clark, D. A., & Purdon, C. (1993). New perspectives for a cognitive theory of obsessions. *Austral. Psychologist.*

Clark, D. A., Beck, A. T., & Alford, B. A. (1999). *Scientific foundations of cognitive theory and therapy of depression.* New York: Wiley.

Clark, D. C. (1999). The puzzle of suicide in later life. In M. T. Stimming, M. Stimming, et al. (Eds.), *Before their time: Adult children's experiences of parental suicide.* Philadephia: Temple University Press.

Clark, D. M. (1993). Cognitive mediation of panic attacks induced by biological challenge tests. *Adv. Behav. Res. Ther., 15,* 75–84.

Clark, D. M. (1999). Anxiety disorders: Why they persist and how to treat them. *Behav. Res. Ther., 37*(Suppl. 1), S5–S27.

Clark, D. M., & Wells, A. (1997). Cognitive therapy for anxiety disorders. In L. J. Dickstein, M. B. Riba, & J. M. Oldham (Eds.), *Review of psychiatry* (Vol. 16). Washington, D.C.: American Psychiatric Press, Inc.

Clark, D.M., Salkovskis, P.M., Hackmann, A., Middleton, H., Anastasiades, P., & Gelder, M. (1994). A comparison of cognitive therapy, applied relaxation and imipramine in the treatment of panic disorder. *Brit. J. Psychiat., 164*(6). 759–769.

Clark, R., Anderson, N. B., Clark, V. R., & Williams, D. R. (1999). Racism as a stressor for African Americans: A biopsychosocial model. *Amer. Psychologist., 54*(10), 805–816.

Clarke, G. N., Rohde, P., Lewinsohn, P. M., Hops, H., & Seeley, J. R. (1999). Cognitive-behavioral treatment of adolescent depression: Efficacy of acute group treatment and booster sessions. *J. Amer. Acad. Child Adol. Psychiat., 38*(3), 272–279.

Clarke, J., Stein, M. D., Sobota, M., Marisi, M., & Hanna, L. (1999). Victims as victimizers: Physical aggression by persons with a history of childhood abuse. *Arch. Internal Med., 159*(16), 1920–1924.

Clarke, J. C., & Saunders, J. B. (1988). *Alcoholism and problem drinking: Theories and treatment.* Sydney: Pergamon Press.

Classen, C., Koopman, C., & Spiegel, D. (1993). Trauma and dissociation. *Bull. Menninger Clin., 57*(2), 178–194.

Clay, R. A. (1996). Day treatment helps empower patients. *APA Monitor, 26*(5), 31.

Clay, R. A. (1996). Modern hypnosis wins clinical respect, praise. *APA Monitor, 26*(5), 31.

Clay, R. A. (1996). Psychologists' faith in religion begins to grow. *APA Monitor, 27*(8), 1, 48.

Clay, R. A. (1997). Is assisted suicide ever a rational choice? *APA Monitor, 28*(4), 1, 43.

Clay, R. A. (1999, July/August). Psychologists rush to help kosovar refugees. *APA Monitor, 30*(7), 12.

Clements, R. (1999). Prevalence of alcohol-use disorders and alcohol-related problems in a college student sample. *J. Amer. Col. Hlth., 48*(3), 111–118.

Clifford, J. S., Norcross, J. C., & Sommer, R. (1999). Autobiographies of mental health clients: Psychologists' uses and recommendations. *Profess. Psychol.: Res. Pract., 30*(1), 56–59.

Clum, G., & Yang, B. (1995). Additional support for the reliability and validity of the Modified Scale for Suicide Ideation. *Psychol. Assess., 7*(1), 122–125.

Clyburn, L. D., Stones, M. J., Hadjistavropoulos, T., & Tuokko, H. (2000). Predicting caregiver burden and depression in Alzheimer's disease. *J. Ger. B Psychol. Sci. Soc. Sci., 55*(1), S2–S13.

Coambs, R. B., & McAndrews, M. P. (1994). The effects of psychoactive substances on workplace performance. In S. Macdonald & P. Roman (Eds.), *Research advances in alcohol and drug problems: Vol. 11. Drug testing in the workplace.* New York: Plenum Press.

Cobb, J. M. T., & Steptoe, A. (1998). Psychosocial influences on upper respiratory infectious illness in children. *J. Psychosom. Res., 45*(4), 319–330.

Coccaro, E. F. (1998). Clinical outcome of psychopharmacologic treatment of borderline and schizotypal personality disordered subjects. *J. Clin. Psychiat., 59*(Suppl. 1), 30–35.

Coe, C. L. (1999). Psychosocial factors and psychoneuroimmunology within a lifespan perspective. In D. P. Keating, C. Hertzman, et al. (Eds.), *Developmental health and the wealth of nations: Social, biological, and educational dynamics.* New York: Guilford.

Coe, W. C. (1989). Posthypnotic amnesia: Theory and research. In N. P. Spanos & J. F. Chaves (Eds.), *Hypnosis: The cognitive-behavioral perspective.* Buffalo, NY: Prometheus Books.

Cohen, D., Llorente, M., & Eisendorfer, C. (1998). Homicide-suicide in older persons. *Amer. J. Psychiat., 155,* 390–396.

Cohen, L., Ardjoen, R. C., & Sewpersad, K. S. M. (1997). Type A behaviour pattern as a risk factor after myocardial infarction: A review. *Psychology and Health, 12,* 619–632.

Cohen, M. B., Baker, G., Cohen, R. A., Fromm-Reichmann, F., & Weigert, E. V. (1954). An intensive study of twelve cases of manic-depressive psychosis. *Psychiatry, 17,* 103–137.

Cohen, R. M., Semple, W. E., Gross, M., & Nordahl, T. E. (1988). From syndrome to illness: Delineating the pathophysiology of schizophrenia with PET. *Schizo. Bull., 14*(2), 169–176.

Cohen, S., & Herbert, T. B. (1996). Health psychology: Psychological factors and physical disease from the perspective of human psychoneuroimmunology. In J. T. Spence, J. M. Darley, & D. J. Foss (Eds.), *Annual review of psychology* (Vol. 47). Palo Alto, CA: Annual Reviews.

Cohen-Kettenis, P. T., & Gooren, L. J. (1999). Transsexualism: A review of etiology, diagnosis and treatment. *J. Psychosom. Res., 46*(4), 315–333.

Cohen-Kettenis, P. T., & van Goozen, S. H. M. (1997). Sex reassignment of adolescent transsexuals: A follow-up study. *J. Amer. Acad. Child Adol. Psychiat., 36*(2), 263–271.

Cohen-Sandler, R., Berman, A. L., & King, R. A. (1982). A follow-up study of hospitalized suicidal children. *J. Amer. Acad. Child Psychiat., 214,* 398–403.

Cohl, H. A. (1997). *The book of mosts.* New York: St. Martin's Press.

Colahan, M. (1995). Being a therapist in eating disorder treatment trials: Constraints and creativity. Special Issue: Eating disorders. *J. Fam. Ther., 17*(1), 79–96.

Colahan, M., & Senior, R. (1995). Family patterns in eating disorders: Going round in circles, getting nowhere fasting. In G. Szmukler, C. Dare, & J. Treasure (Eds.), *Handbook of eating disorders: Theory, treatment and research.* Chichester, England: Wiley.

Colbach, E. M. (1987). Hysteria again and again and again. *Inter. J. Offend. Ther. Compar. Crimin., 31*(1), 41–48.

Colburn, D. (1996, November 19). Singer's suicide doesn't lead to "copycat" deaths. *Washington Post Health,* p. 5

Colby, K. M., Faught, W. S., & Parkison, R. C. (1979). Cognitive therapy of paranoid conditions: Heuristic suggestions based on a computer simulation model. *Cog. Ther. Res., 3*(1) 55–60.

Cole, D. A., & Turner, J. E., Jr. (1993). Models of cognitive mediation and moderation in child depression. *J. Abnorm. Psychol., 102*(2), 271–281.

Cole, J. O., & Yonkers, K. A. (1995). Nonbenzodiazepine anxiolytics. In A. F. Schatzberg & C. B. Nemeroff (Eds.), *The American Psychiatric Press textbook of psychopharmacology.* Washington, DC: American Psychiatric Press.

Cole, J. O., Klerman, G. L., Goldberg, S. C., et al. (1964). Phenothiazine treatment in acute schizophrenia. *Arch. Gen. Psychiat., 10,* 246–261.

Coleman, L. (1984). *The reign of error: Psychiatry, authority, and law.* Boston: Beacon.

Colerick, E. J., & George, L. K. (1986). Predictors of institutionalization among caregivers of patients with Alzheimer's disease. *J. Amer. Ger. Soc., 34,* 493–498.

Collier, D. A., Arranz, M. J., Li, T., et al. (1997). Association between the 5-HT2A gene promoter polymorphism and anorexia nervosa [letter]. *Lancet, 351,* 499.

Comer, R. (1973). *Therapy interviews with a schizophrenic patient.* Unpublished manuscript.

Compas, B. E., Haaga, D. A. F., Keefe, F. J., Leitenberg, H., & Williams, D. A. (1998). Sampling of empirically supported psychological treatments from health psychology: Smoking, chronic pain, cancer, and bulimia nervosa. *J. Cons. Clin. Psychol., 66*(1), 89–112.

Compton, W. M., Helzer, J. E., Hwu, H., Yeh, E., McEvoy, L., Tipp, J. E., & Spitznagel, E. L. (1991). New methods in cross-cultural psychiatry: Psychiatric illness in Taiwan and the United States. *Amer. J. Psychiat., 148*(12), 1697–1704.

Coney, N. S., & Mackey, W. C. (1998). On whose watch? The silent separation of American children from their fathers. *J. Sociol. Soc. Welfare, 25*(3), 143–178.

Connelly, S. (1999, February 4). The end of Sybilization. *Daily News* (New York), p. 55.

Conrad, N. (1992). Stress and knowledge of suicidal others as factors in suicidal behavior of high school adolescents. *Issues in Ment. Hlth. Nurs., 13*(2), 95–104.

Constantino, G., Malgady, R. G., & Vazquez, C. (1981). A comparison of Murray's TAT and a new thematic apperception test for urban Hispanic children. *Hispanic Journal of Behavioral Sciences, 3,* 291–300.

Conwell, Y., Caine, E. D., & Olsen, K. (1990). Suicide and cancer in late life. *Hosp. Comm. Psychiat., 43,* 1334–1338.

Conwell, Y., Duberstein, P. R., Cox, C., Herrmann, J., Forbes, N., & Caine, E. D. (1998). Age differences in behaviors leading to completed suicide. *Amer. J. Ger. Psychiat., 6*(2), 122–126.

Cook, C. E., Jeffcoat, A. R., & Perez-Reyes, M. (1985). Pharmacokinetic studies of cocaine and phencyclidine in man. In G. Barnett & C. N. Chiang (Eds.), *Pharmacokinetics and pharmacodynamics of psychoactive drugs.* Foster City, CA: Biomedical Publications.

Cook, E. H., Rowlett, R., Jaselskis, C., Leventhal, B. L. (1992). Fluoxetine treatment of children and adults with autistic disorder and mental retardation. *J. Amer. Acad. Child Adol. Psychiat., 31*(4), 739–745.

Coon, D. W., Rider, K., Gallagher-Thompson, D., & Thompson, L. (1999). Cognitive-behavioral therapy for the treatment of late-life distress. In M. Duffy (Ed.), *Handbook of counseling and psychotherapy with older adults.* New York: Wiley.

Cooney, N. L., Litt, M. D., Morse, P. A., Bauer, L. O., & Gaupp, L. (1997). Alcohol cue reactivity, negative-mood reactivity, and relapse in treated alcoholic men. *J. Abnorm. Psychol., 106*(2), 243–250.

Coons, P. M. (1980). Multiple personality: Diagnostic considerations. *J. Clin. Psychiat., 41*(10), 330–336.

Coons, P. M. (1998). The dissociative disorders. Rarely considered and underdiagnosed. *Psychiat. Clin. N. Amer., 21*(3), 637–648.

Coons, P. M. (1999). Psychogenic or dissociative fugue: A clinical investigation of five cases. *Psychol. Rep., 84*(3, Pt. 1), 881–886.

Coons, P. M., Bowman, E. S., & Milstein, V. (1988). Multiple personality disorder: A clinical investigation of 50 cases. *J. Nerv. Ment. Dis., 176*(9), 519–527.

Cooper, A. M., & Ronningstam, E. (1992). Narcissistic personality disorder. In A. Tasman & M. B. Riba (Eds.), *American Psychiatric Press review of psychiatry* (Vol. 11). Washington, DC: American Psychiatric Press.

Cooper, A., Scherer, C. R., Boies, S. C., & Gordon, B. L. (1999). Sexuality on the Internet: From sexual exploration to pathological expression. *Profess. Psychol.: Res. Pract., 30*(2), 154–164.

Cooper, M. L. (1994). Motivations for alcohol use among adolescents: Development and validation of a four-factor model. *Psychol. Assess., 6*(2), 117–128.

Cooper, P. J., & Eke, M. (1999). Childhood shyness and maternal social phobia: A community study. *Brit. J. Psychiat., 174,* 439–443.

Copeland, J., & Hall, W. (1992). A comparison of women seeking drug and alcohol treatment in a specialist women's and two traditional mixed-sex treatment services. *Brit. J. Addic., 87*(9), 1293–1302.

Coppen, A. (1994). Depression as a lethal disease: Prevention strategies. *J. Clin. Psychiat., 55*(Suppl. 4), 37–45.

Cordova, J. V., & Jacobson, N. S. (1993). Couple distress. In D. H. Barlow (Ed.), *Clinical handbook of psychological disorders: A step-by-step treatment manual* (2nd ed.). New York: Guilford.

Corey-Bloom, J., Jernigan, T., Archibald, S., Harris, M. J., et al. (1995). Quantitative magnetic resonance imaging of the brain in late-life schizophrenia. *Amer. J. Psychiat., 152*(3), 447–449.

Corkin, S. (1968). Acquisition of motor skill after bilateral medial temporal-lobe excision. *Neuropsychologia, 6,* 255–264.

Corkin, S. (1984). Lasting consequences of bilateral medial temporal lobectomy: Clinical course and experimental findings in H.M. *Sem. in Neuro., 4,* 249–259.

Cornblatt, B. A., & Erlenmeyer-Kimling, L. (1985). Global attentional deviance as a marker of risk for schizophrenia: Specificity and predictive validity. *J. Abnorm. Psychol., 94*(4), 31–46.

Cornblatt, B. A., & Keilp, J. G. (1994). Impaired attention, genetics, and the pathophysiology of schizophrenia. *Schizo. Bull., 20*(1), 31–46.

Cornelius, J. R., Salloum, I. M., Mezzich, J., Cornelius, M. D., Fabrega, H., Ehler, J. G., Ulrich, R. F., Thase, M. E., & Mann, J. J. (1995). Disproportionate suicidality in patients with comorbid major depression and alcoholism. *Amer. J. Psychiat., 152*(3), 358–364.

Cornell, C. P., & Gelles, R. J. (1983). *Intimate violence in families.* Beverly Hills, CA: Sage.

Cornish, J. W., McNicholas, L. F., & O'Brien, C. P. (1995). Treatment of substance-related disorders. In A. F. Schatzberg & C. B. Nemeroff (Eds.), *The American Psychiatric Press textbook of psychopharmacology.* Washington, DC: American Psychiatric Press.

Corrigan, P. W., & Penn, D. L. (1999). Lessons from social psychology on discrediting psychiatric stigma. *Amer. Psychologist., 54*(9), 765–776.

Corwin, M. (1993, May 8). When the law can't protect. *Los Angeles Times,* p. A1.

Coryell, W., Leon, A., Winokur, G., Endicott, J., et al. (1996). Importance of psychotic features to long-term course in major depressive disorder. *Amer. J. Psychiat., 153,* 483–489.

Coryell, W., Miller, D. D., & Perry, P. J. (1998). Haloperidol plasma levels and dose optimization. *Amer. J. Psychiat., 155,* 48–53.

Costa, E. (1983). Are benzodiazepine recognition sites functional entities for the action of endogenous effectors or merely drug receptors? *Adv. in Biochem. & Psychopharm., 38,* 249–259.

Costa, E. (1985). Benzodiazepine-GABA interactions: A model to investigate the neurobiology of anxiety. In A. H. Tuma & J. Maser (Eds.), *Anxiety and the anxiety disorders.* Hillsdale, NJ: Erlbaum.

Costa, E., Guidotti, A., Mao, C. C., & Suria, A. (1975). New concepts on the mechanism of action of benzodiazepines. *Life Sciences, 17*(2), 167–185.

Costa, E., Guidotti, A., & Toffano, G. (1978). Molecular mechanisms mediating the action of benzodiazepines on GABA receptors. *Brit. J. Psychiat., 133,* 239–248.

Costantino, G., Malgady, R.G., & Rogler, L. H. (1986). Cuento therapy: A culturally sensitive modality for Puerto Rican children. *J. Cons. Clin. Psychol., 54*(5), 639–645.

Costanzo, P. R., Musante, G. J., Friedman, K. E., Kern, L. S., & Tomlinson, K. (1999). The gender specificity of emotional, situational, and behavioral indicators of binge eating in a diet-seeking obese population. *Inter. J. Eat. Disorders, 26*(2), 205–210.

Costello, C. G. (1996). The advantages of focusing on the personality characteristics of the personality disordered. In C. G. Costello (Ed.), *Personality characteristics of the personality disordered.* New York: Wiley.

Council on Psychiatry and the Law. (1992). Peer review of psychiatric testimony. *Bull. Amer. Acad. Psychiat. Law, 20*(3), 343–352.

Courchesne, E. (1997, May 23). *The developmental neurobiological approach to understanding autism: From behavioral symptoms to biological explanations.* Keynote address at the Eden Institute Foundation Princeton Lecture Series on Autism.

Courchesne, R., & Courchesne, E. (1997). From impasse to insight in autism research: From behavioral symptoms to biological explanations. *Dev. Psychopathol.,* Special Issue.

Cowan, D., & Brunero, S. (1997). Group therapy for anxiety disorders using rationale emotive behaviour therapy. *Austral. New Zeal. J. Ment. Hlth. Nurs.*, 6(4), 164–168.

Cowen, E. L. (1991). In pursuit of wellness. 98th Annual Convention of the American Psychological Association Distinguished Contributions to Psychology in the Public Interest Award Address (1990, Boston, MA). *Amer. Psychologist.*, 46, 404–408.

Cowley, G. (2000, January 31). Alzheimer's: Unlocking the mystery. *Newsweek*, pp. 46–51.

Cox, A., Rutter, M., Newman, S., & Bartak, L. (1975). A comparative study of infantile autism and specific developmental receptive language disorder: II. Parental characteristics. *Brit. J. Psychiat.*, 126, 146–159.

Cox, B. J. (1996). The nature and assessment of catastrophic thoughts in panic disorder. *Behav. Res. Ther.*, 34(4), 363–374.

Cox, B. J., Borger, S. C., & Enns, M. W. (1999). Anxiety sensitivity and emotional disorders: Psychometric studies and their theoretical implications. In S. Taylor et al. (Eds.), *Anxiety sensitivity: Theory, research, and treatment of the fear of anxiety.* The LEA series in personality and clinical psychology. Mahwah, NJ: Erlbaum.

Cox, B. J., Endler, N. S., & Swinson, R. P. (1995). An examination of levels of agoraphobic severity in panic disorder. *Behav. Res. Ther.*, 33(1), 57–62.

Cox, B. J., Endler, N. S., & Swinson, R. P. (1995). Anxiety sensitivity and panic attack symptomatology. *Behav. Res. Ther.*, 33(7), 833–836.

Cox, B. J., Enns, M. W., Borger, S. C., & Parker, J. D. A. (1999). The nature of the depressive experience in analogue and clinically depressed samples. *Behav. Res. Ther.*, 37(1), 15–24.

Cox, D. J., Sutphen, J., Borowitz, S., Kovatchev, B., & Ling, W. (1998). Contribution of behavior therapy and biofeedback to laxative therapy in the treatment of pediatric encopresis. *Ann. Behav. Med.*, 20(2), 70–76.

Cox, R. H., Robb, M., & Russell, W. D. (1999). Order of scale administration and concurrent validity of the Anxiety Rating Scale. *Percept. Motor Skills*, 88(1), 271–272.

Coy, T. V. (1998). The effect of repressive coping style on cardiovascular reactivity and speech disturbances during stress. *Diss. Abstr. Inter.: Sect. B: Sci. Eng.*, 58(8-B), 4512.

Coyne, J. C. (1976). Depression and the response of others. *J. Abnorm. Psychol.*, 85(2), 186–193.

Coyne, J. C., Schwenk, T. L., & Fechner-Bates, S. (1995). Nondetection of depression by primary care physicians reconsidered. *Gen. Hosp. Psychiat.*, 17(1), 3–12.

Craddock, N., & Jones, I. (1999). Genetics of bipolar disorder. *J. Med. Genet.*, 36(8), 585–594.

Craig, R. J., Cannon, B., & Olson, R. E. (1995). Psychological screening of impotence with Finney's MMPI-derived impotence scale. *Psychol. Rep.*, 77, 1019–1026.

Cramer, P. (1996). *Storytelling, narrative, and the Thematic Apperception Test.* New York: Guilford.

Crandall, C. S., Preisler, J. J., & Aussprung, J. (1992). Measuring life events stress in the lives of college students: The Undergraduate Stress Questionnaire (USQ). *Journal of Behavioral Medicine*, 15(6), 627–662.

Crane, G. E. (1973). Persistent dyskinesia. *Brit. J. Psychiat.*, 122, 395–405.

Craske, M. G., & Rowe, M. K. (1997). Nocturnal panic. *Clin. Psychol.:Sci. Prac.*, 4, 153–174.

Craske, M. G., Rowe, M., Lewin, M., & Noriega-Dimitri, R. (1997). Interoceptive exposure versus breathing retraining within cognitive-behavioural therapy for panic disorder with agoraphobia. *Brit. J. Clin. Psychol.*, 36, 85–99.

Cravatta, M. J. (1998, January). Looking for luck. *American Demographics.*

Creer, C., & Wing, J. K. (1974). *Schizophrenia at home.* London: National Schizophrenia Fellowship.

Creese, I., Burt, D. R., & Snyder, S. H. (1977). Dopamine receptor binding enhancement accompanies lesion-induced behavioral supersensitivity. *Science*, 197, 596–598.

Crijnen, A. A., Achenbach, T. M., & Verhulst, F. C. (1999). Problems reported by parents of children in multiple cultures: The Child Behavior Checklist syndrome constructs. *Amer. J. Psychiat.*, 156(4), 569–574.

Crino, R. D., & Andrews, G. (1996). Obsessive-compulsive disorder and Axis I comorbidity. *J. Anx. Dis.*, 10(1), 37–46.

Crisp, A. H. (1981). Anorexia nervosa at a normal weight?: The abnormal-normal weight control syndrome. *Inter. J. Psychiat. Med.*, 11, 203–233.

Crits, C. P., Connolly, M. B., Azarian, K., Crits-Cristoph, K., & Shappell, S. (1996). An open trial of brief supportive-expressive psychotherapy in the treatment of generalized anxiety disorder. *Psychotherapy*, 33(3), 418–430.

Crits-Christoph, P. (1992). The efficacy of brief dynamic psychotherapy: A meta-analysis. *Amer. J. Psychiat.*, 149, 151–158.

Crits-Christoph, P., Baranackie, K., Kurcias, J. S., Beck, A. T., Carroll, K., Perry, K., Luborsky, L., McLellan, A. T., Woody, G. E., Thompson, L., Gallagher, D., & Zitrin, C. (1991). Meta-analysis of therapist effects in psychotherapy outcome studies. *Psychother. Res.*, 1(2), 81–91.

Crits-Christoph, P., Crits-Christoph, K., Wolf-Palacio, D., Fichter, M., & Rudick, D. (1995). Brief supportive-expressive psychodynamic therapy for generalized anxiety disorder. In J. P. Barber, P. Crits-Cristoph, et al. (Eds.), *Dynamic therapies for psychiatric disorders.* New York: Basic Books.

Crocker, P. R. (1989). A follow-up of cognitive-affective stress management training. *J. Sport Exercise Psychol.*, 11, 236–242.

Crompton, M. R. (1985). Alcohol and violent accidental and suicidal death. *Med. Sci. Law*, 25, 59–62.

Crosby, A. E., Cheltenham, M. P., & Sacks, J. J. (1999). Incidence of suicidal ideation and behavior in the United States, 1994. *Suic. Life-Threat. Behav.*, 29(2), 131–140.

Crow, T. J. (1980). Positive and negative schizophrenic symptoms and the role of dopamine: II. *Brit. J. Psychiat.*, 137, 383–386.

Crow, T. J. (1982). Positive and negative symptoms and the role of dopamine in schizophrenia. In G. Hemmings (Ed.), *Biological aspects of schizophrenia and addiction.* New York: Wiley.

Crow, T. J. (1985). The two-syndrome concept: Origins and current status. *Schizo. Bull.*, 11(3), 471–486.

Crowley, T. J., Macdonald, M. J., Whitmore, E. A., & Mikulich, S. K. (1998). Cannabis dependence, withdrawal, and reinforcing effects among adolescents with conduct symptoms and substance use disorder. *Drug Alc. Dep.*, 50(1), 27–37.

Crowther, J. H., Bond, L. A., & Rolf, J. E. (1981). The incidence, prevalence, and severity of behavior disorder among preschool-age children in day care. *J. Abnorm. Child Psychol.*, 9, 23–42.

Cruise, K.R., & Rogers, R. (1998). An analysis of competency to stand trial: An integration of case law and clinical knowledge. *Behav. Sci. Law*, 16, 35–50.

Crystal, S., & Schlosser, L. R. (1999). The HIV-mental health challenge. In A. V. Horwitz, T. L. Scheid, et al. (Eds.), *A handbook for the study of mental health: Social contexts, theories, and systems.* New York: Cambridge University Press.

Culbertson, F. M. (1997). Depression and gender: An international review. *Amer. Psychologist*, 52(1), 25–31.

Cullen, E. A. (1993, August). Iowa becomes the tenth state with a hospital privileges statute for psychologists. *Practitioner Focus*, 6(2), p. 6.

Culp, A. M., Clyman, M. M., & Culp, R. E. (1995). Adolescent depressed mood, reports of suicide attempts, and asking for help. *Adolescence*, 30(120), 827–837.

Cumming, J., & Cumming, E. (1962). *Ego and milieu: Theory and practice of environmental therapy.* New York: Atherton.

Cunningham, J. (1999, February 16). Health: Hex marks the spot; Many people with mental problems would rather see this man than their GP. John Cunningham on why the NHS is studying voodoo. *The Guardian* (London), p. 16.

Cunningham, M. D., & Reidy, T. J. (1999). Don't confuse me with the facts: Common errors in violence risk assessment at capital sentencing. *Criminal Justice Behav.*, 26(1), 20–43.

Currier, G. W. (Ed.). (1999). *New developments in emergency psychiatry: Medical, legal, and economic.* San Francisco: Jossey-Bass.

Curtis, G. C., Magee, W. J., Eaton, W. W., Wittchen, H.-U., & Kessler, R. C. (1998). Specific fears and phobias: Epidemiology and classification. *Brit. J. Psychiat.*, 173, 212–217.

Curtis, J. M., & Cowell, D. R. (1993). Relation of birth order and scores on measures of pathological narcissism. *Psychol. Rep.*, 72(1), 311–315.

Cuticchia, A. J. (2000). Future vision of the GDB human genome database. *Human Mutat.*, 15(1), 62–67.

Cutmore, T. R. H., & James, D. A. (1999). Identifying and reducing noise in psychophysiological recordings. *Inter. J. Psychophysiol.*, 32(2), 129–150.

Cutting, J. (1985). *The psychology of schizophrenia.* Edinburgh, UK: Churchill-Livingstone.

Cutting, J., & Murphy, D. (1988). Schizophrenic thought disorder: A psychological and organic interpretation. *Brit. J. Psychiat.*, 152, 310–319.

Cutting, J., & Murphy, D. (1990). Impaired ability of schizophrenics, relative to manics or depressives, to appreciate social knowledge about their culture. *Brit. J. Psychiat.*, 157, 355–358.

Cyr, J. J., & Kalpin, R. A. (1988). Investigating the lunar-lunacy relationship: A reply to Rotton and Kelly. *Psychol. Rep.*, 62(1), 319–322.

Cyranowski, J. M., Frank, E., Young, E., & Shear, K. (2000). Adolescent onset of the gender differences in lifetime rates of major depression. *Arch. Gen. Psychiat.*, 57(1), 21–27.

Cytryn, L., & McKnew, D. H., Jr. (1996). *Growing up sad: Childhood depression and its treatment.* New York: Norton.

DAWN (Drug Abuse Warning Network). (1997). *Highlights from 1996 Report.* Drug Abuse Warning Network.

DAWN (Drug Abuse Warning Network). (1998). *Highlights from 1998 Report.* Drug Abuse Warning Network.

DHM (Discovery Health Media). (1999, August 2). How America measures up. *Newsweek*, pp. 50–53.

D'Onofrio, G., Rathlev, N. K., Ulrich, A. S., Fish, S. S., & Freedland, E. S. (1999). Lorazepam for the prevention of recurrent seizures related to alcohol. *N. Engl. J. Med.*, 340(12), 915–919.

Dalby, J. T. (1997). Elizabethan madness: On London's stage. *Psychol Rep.*, 81, 1331–1343.

Daly, M. P. (1999). Diagnosis and management of Alzheimer disease. *J. Amer. Board Fam. Pract.*, 12(5), 375–385.

Dalzell, H. J. (2000). Whispers: The role of family secrets in eating disorders. *Eat. Disord.: J. Treat. Prev.*, 8(1), 43–61.

Dana, R. H. (1999). Projective assessment of Latinos in the United States: Current realities, problems, and prospects. *Cult. Div. Ethnic Minority Psychol.,* 4(3), 165–184.

Dare, C., & Crowther, C. (1995). Living dangerously: Psychoanalytic psychotherapy of anorexia nervosa. In G. Szmukler, C. Dare, & J. Treasure (Eds.), *Handbook of eating disorders: Theory, treatment and research.* Chichester, England: Wiley.

Dare, C., & Crowther, C. (1995). Psychodynamic models of eating disorders. In G. Szmukler, C. Dare, & J. Treasure (Eds.), *Handbook of eating disorders: Theory, treatment and research.* Chichester, England: Wiley.

Dare, C., & Eisler, I. (1992). Family therapy for anorexia nervosa. In P. J. Cooper & A. Stein (Eds.), *Feeding problems and eating disorders in children and adolescents.* Philadelphia: Harwood Academic Publishers.

Dare, C., & Eisler, I. (1995). Family therapy. In G. Szmukler, C. Dare, & J. Treasure (Eds.), *Handbook of eating disorders: Theory, treatment and research.* Chichester, England: Wiley.

Dare, C., & Eisler, I. (1995). Family therapy. In G.I. Szmukler & C.Dare (Eds.), *Handbook of treatment for eating disorders* (2nd ed.). New York: Guilford.

Darvres-Bornoz, J., Lemperiere, T., Degiovanni, A., & Gaillard, P. (1995). Sexual victimization in women with schizophrenia and bipolar disorder. *Soc. Psychiat. Psychiat. Epidemiol.,* 30(2), 78–84.

Davanloo, H. (Ed.). (1980). *Short-term dynamic psychotherapy.* New York: Jason Aronson.

Davey, G. C. L., & Levy, S. (1999). Internal statements associated with catastrophic worrying. *Pers. Individ. Diff.,* 26(1), 21–32.

Davidson, J. R. T. (1997). Use of benzodiazepines in panic disorder. *J. Clin. Psychiat.,* 58(Suppl. 2), 26–28.

Davidson, J. R. T. (1998). Pharmacotherapy of social anxiety disorder. *J. Clin. Psychiat.,* 59(Suppl. 17), 47–53.

Davidson, J. R., Hughes, D., Blazer, D. G., & George, L. K. (1991). Posttraumatic stress disorder in the community: An epidemiological study. *Psychol. Med.,* 21(3), 713–721.

Davidson, J., Hughes, D., George, L., & Blazer, D. (1996). The association of sexual assault and attempted suicide within the community. *Arch. Gen. Psychiat.,* 53, 550–555.

Davis, J. D., Kane, J. M., Marder, S. R., Brauzer, B., Gierl, B., Schooler, N., Casey, D. E., & Hassan, M. (1993). Dose response of propheylatic antipsychotics. *J. Clin. Psychiat.,* 54(Suppl. 3), 24–30.

Davis, J. M., Comaty, J. E., & Janicak, P. G. (1988). The psychological effects of antipsychotic drugs. In C. N. Stefanis & A. D. Rabavilis (Eds.), *Schizophrenia: Recent biosocial developments.* New York: Human Sciences Press.

Davis, J. O., & Phelps, J. A. (1995). Twins with schizophrenia: Genes or germs? *Schizo. Bull.,* 21(1), 13–18.

Davis, L. L., Ryan, W., Adinoff, B., & Petty, F. (2000). Comprehensive review of the psychiatric uses of valproate. *J. Clin. Psychopharmacol.,* 20(Suppl 1), 1S–17S.

Davis, M. (1992). Analysis of aversive memories using the fear potentiated startle paradigm. In N. Butters & L. R. Squire (Eds.), *The neuropsychology of memory* (2nd ed.). New York: Guilford.

Davis, P. J. (1999). Gender differences in autobiographical memory for childhood emotional experiences. *J. Pers. Soc. Psychol.,* 76(3), 498–510.

Davis, R., Olmsted, M., Rockert, W., Marques, T., & Dolhanty, J. (1997). Group psychoeducation for bulimia nervosa with and without addi-tional psychotherapy process sessions. *Inter. J. Eat. Disorders,* 22, 25–34.

Davis, R. C., Brickman, E., & Baker, T. (1991). Supportive and unsupportive responses of others to rape victims: Effects on concurrent victim adjustment. *Amer. J. Comm. Psychol.,* 19, 443–451.

Davis, S. F. (1992). Report to the American Psychological Association. Reported in *Psychol. Today,* 25(6), 9.

Davis, S. R. (1998). The clinical use of androgens in female sexual disorders. *J. Sex Marital Ther.,* 24(3), 153–163.

Davis, T., Gunderson, J. G., & Myers, M. (1999). Borderline personality disorder. In D.G. Jacobs (Ed.), *The Harvard Medical School guide to suicide assessment and intervention.* San Francisco: Jossey-Bass.

Davison, A. N., & Dobbing, J. (1966). Myelination as a vulnerable period in brain development. *Brit. Med. Bull.,* 22, 40–44.

Dawson, G., & Castelloe, P. (1992). Autism. In C. E. Walker (Ed.), *Clinical psychology: Historical and research foundations.* New York: Plenum Press.

DeAngelis, T. (1992, December). Illness linked with repressive style of coping. *APA Monitor,* 23(12) 14.

DeAngelis, T. (1992, November). Best psychological treatment for many men: Group therapy. *APA Monitor,* 23(11), 31.

DeAngelis, T. (1992, November). Program embodies feminist values to aid women with addictions. *APA Monitor,* 23(11), 29.

DeAngelis, T. (1993, September). Controversial diagnosis is voted into latest DSM. *APA Monitor,* 24(9), 32–33.

DeAngelis, T. (1994, March). Poor kids are focus of asthma studies. *APA Monitor,* 25(3), 26–27.

DeAngelis, T. (1994, May). Vets, minorities, single moms make up homeless population. *APA Monitor,* 25(5), 39.

DeAngelis, T. (1996, October). New interventions address teen-age behavior problems. *APA Monitor,* p. 42.

Dearwater, S. R., Coben, J. H., Campbell, J. C., Nah, G., Glass, N., McLoughlin, E., & Bekemeier, B. (1998). Prevalence of intimate partner abuse in women treated at community hospital emergency departments. *JAMA,* 280, 433–438.

Deaton, A. V. (1998). Treating conversion disorders: Is a pediatric rehabilitation hospital the place? *Rehab. Psychol.,* 43(1), 56–62.

deBeurs, E., van Balkom. A. J. L. M., Lange, A., Koele, P., et al. (1995). Treatment of panic disorder with agoraphobia: Comparison of fluvoxamine, placebo, and psychological panic management combined with exposure and of exposure in vivo alone. *Amer. J. Psychiat.,* 152(5), 683–691.

de Castro, J. M., & Pearcey, S. M. (1995). Lunar rhythms of the meal and alcohol intake of humans. *Physiol. Behav.,* 57(3), 439–444.

DeCubas, M., & Field, T. (1993). Children of methadone-dependent women: Developmental outcomes. *Amer. J. Orthopsychiat.,* 63(2), 266–269.

de Groot, J. M., & Kennedy, S. H. (1995). Integrating clinical and research psychiatry. *J. Psychiat. Neurosci.,* 20(2), 150–154.

Deitch, D., & Solit, R. (1993). International training for drug abuse treatment and the issue of cultural relevance. *J. Psychoactive Drugs,* 25(1), 87–92.

Deitz, S. M. (1977). An analysis of programming DRL schedules in educational settings. *Behav. Res. Ther.,* 15(1), 103–111.

Dekker, J. (1993). Inhibited male orgasm. In W. O'Donohue and J. Geer (Eds.), *Handbook of sexual dysfunctions.* Boston: Allyn & Bacon.

Del Monte, M. (1995). Silence and emptiness in the service of healing: Lessons from meditation. *Brit. J. Psychother.,* 11(3), 368–378.

Delay, J., & Deniker, P. (1952). Le traitement des psychoses par une methode neurolytique derivee d'hibernotherapie: Le 4560 RP utilise seul en cure prolongee et continuee. *Congres des Medicins Alienistes et Neurologistes de France et des Pays du Langue Francaise,* 50, 503–513.

DeLeon (1992) Cited in Youngstrom, N. Training brings psychologists closer to prescribing drugs. *APA Monitor,* 23(10).

DeLeon, M. J., Convit, A., George, A. E., Golomb., J., De Santi, S., Tarshish, C., Rusinek, H., Bobinski, M., Ince, C., Miller, D., & Wisniewski, H. (1996). *In vivo* structural studies of the hippocampus in normal aging and in incipient Alzheimer's disease. In R. J. Wurtman, S. Corkin, J. H. Growdon, & R. M. Nitsch (Eds.), *The neurobiology of Alzheimer's disease.* New York: New York Academy of Sciences.

DeLeon, P. H., & Wiggins, J. G., Jr. (1996). Prescription privileges for psychologists. *Amer. Psychologist,* 51(3), 225–229.

Delgado, P. L., & Moreno, F. A. (2000). Role of norepinephrine in depression. *J. Clin. Psychiat.,* 61(Suppl.), 5–12.

Delisle, J. R. (1986). Death with honors: Suicide among gifted adolescents [Special issue]. *J. Couns. Dev.,* 64(9), 558–560.

Dell, P. F., & Eisenhower, J. W. (1990). Adolescent multiple personality disorder: A preliminary study of eleven cases. *J. Amer. Acad. Child Adol. Psychiat.,* 29(3), 359–366.

de Man, A. F., Ludec, C. P., & Labreche-Gauthier, L. (1992). Parental control in child rearing and multidimensional locus of control. *Psychol. Rep.,* 70(1), 320–322.

Dencker, S. J., & Dencker, K. (1995). The need for quality assurance for a better compliance and increased quality of life in chronic schizophrenic patients. XIIth AEP Congress: Improvement of compliance: Quality assurance: Increased quality of life in community care in schizophrenia. *Inter. Clin. Psychopharmacology,* 9(Suppl 5), 35–40.

DeNelsky, G. Y. (1996). The case against prescription privileges for psychologists. *Amer. Psychologist,* 51(3), 207–212.

DeRubeis, R. J., & Crits-Christoph, P. (1998). Empirically supported individual and group psychological treatments for adult mental disorders. *J. Cons. Clin. Psychol.,* 66(1), 37–52.

DeRubeis, R. J., Tang, T. Z., Gelfand, L. A., & Feeley, M. (2000). Recent findings concerning the processes and outcomes of cognitive therapy for depression. In S. L. Johnson, A. M. Hayes, et al. (Eds.), *Stress, coping, and depression.* Mahwah, NJ: Erlbaum.

De Silva, P. (1995). Cognitive-behavioural models of eating disorders. In G. Szmukler, C. Dare, & J. Treasure (Eds.), *Handbook of eating disorders: Theory, treatment and research.* Chichester, England: Wiley.

Desmond, D. W., Morony, J. T., Paik, M. C., Sano, M., Mohr, J. P., Aboumatar, S., Tseng, C. L., Chan, S., Williams, J. B., Remien, R. H., Hauser, W. A., & Stern, Y. (2000). Frequency and clinical determinants of dementia after ischemic stroke. *Neurology,* 54(5), 1124–1131.

Devanand, D. P., Jacobs, D. M., Tang, M. X., Del Castillo-Castaneda, C., et al. (1997). The course of psychopathologic features in mild to moderate Alzheimer disease. *Arch. Gen. Psychiat.,* 54, 257–263.

DeVeaugh-Geiss, J., Moroz, G., Biederman, J., Cantwell, D. P., et al. (1992). Clomipramine hydrochloride in childhood and adolescent obsessive compulsive disorder. A multicenter trial. *J. Amer. Acad. Child Adol. Psychiat.,* 31(1), 45–49.

DeVita, E. (1996, January-February). Melatonin: The hottest hormone of all. *Amer. Hlth.*, pp. 72-73.

Dew, M. A., Bromet, E. J., Brent, D., & Greenhouse, J. B. (1987). A quantitative literature review of the effectiveness of suicide prevention centers. *J. Cons. Clin. Psychol., 55*, 239-244.

de Wilde, E. J., & Kienhorst, I. C. W. M. (1998). Life events and adolescent suicidal behavior. In T. W. Miller et al. (Eds.), *Children of trauma: Stressful life events and their effects on children and adolescents.* International Universities Press stress and health series, Monograph 8. Madison, CT: International Universities Press.

de Wilde, E. J., Kienhorst, I. C. W. M., Diekstra, R. F. W., & Wolters, W. H. G. (1992). The relationship between adolescent suicidal behavior and life events in childhood and adolescence. *Amer. J. Psychiat, 149*, 45-51.

Diamond, D. (1987). Psychotherapeutic approaches to the treatment of panic attacks, hypochondriasis and agoraphobia. *Brit. J. Med. Psychol., 60*, 85-90.

Dickens, R. S. (1999). The alignment of EAP and business unit goals. In J. M. Oher, et al. (Eds.), *The employee assistance handbook.* New York: Wiley.

Diekstra, R. F. W. (1989). Suicidal behavior in adolescents and young adults: The international picture. *Crisis, 10*, 16-35.

Diekstra, R. F. W. (1989). Suicide and attempted suicide: An international perspective. *Acta Psychiatr. Scandin., 80*(Suppl. 354), 1-24.

Diekstra, R. F., Kienhorst, C. W. M., & de Wilde, E. J. (1995). Suicide and suicidal behaviour among adolescents. In M. Rutter & D. J. Smith, *Psychosocial disorders in young people.* Chichester, England: Wiley.

Diener, E. (2000, January). Subjective well-being: The science of happiness and a proposal for a national index. *Amer. Psychologist, 55*(1), 34-43.

Diener, E., & Diener, C. (1996). Most people are happy. *Psychol. Sci., 7*(3), 181-185.

Diener, E., Sandvik, E., Pavot, W., & Fujita, F. (1992). Extraversion and subjective well-being in a U. S. national probability sample. *J. Res. Pers., 26*(3), 205-215.

Diener, E., Sandvik, E., Seidlitz, L., & Diener, M. (1993). The relationship between income and subjective well-being: Relative or absolute? *Soc. Indicators Res., 28*(3), 195-223.

Dilsaver, S. C. (1990). Onset of winter depression earlier than generally thought? *J. Clin. Psychiat., 51*(6), 258.

Dilsaver, S. C., & Swann, A. C. (1995). Mixed mania: Apparent induction by a tricyclic antidepressant in five consecutively treated patients with bipolar depression. *Biol. Psychiat., 37*(1), 60-62.

Dinwiddie, S. H., Heath, A. C., Dunne, M. P., Bucholz, K. K., Madden, P. A. F., Slutske, W. F., Bierut, L. J., Statham, D. B., & Martin, N. G. (2000). Early sexual abuse and lifetime psychopathology: A co-twin-control study. *Psychol. Med., 30*(1), 41-52.

Dircks, P., Grimm, F., Tausch, A., & Wittern, O. (1980). Förderung der seelischen Lebensqualität von Krebspatienten durch personenzentrierte Gruppengespräche. *Z. Klin. Psychol., 9*, 241-251.

di Tomaso, E., Beltramo, M., & Piomelli, D. (1996, August 22). Brain cannabinoids in chocolate. *Nature, 382*, pp. 677-678.

Dixon, L. B., & Lehman, A. F. (1995). Family interventions for schizophrenia. *Schizo. Bull., 21*(4), 631-643.

Dixon, W. A., Heppner, P. P., Burnett, J. W., & Lips, B. J. (1993). Hopelessness and stress: Evidence for an interactive model of depression. *Cog. Ther. Res., 17*(1), 39-52.

Doan, B. D., & Bryson, S. E. (1994). Etiological and maintaining factors in multiple personality disorder: A critical review. In R.M. Klein & B.K. Doane (Eds.), *Psychological concepts and dissociative disorders.* Hillsdale, NJ: Erlbaum.

Dobson, D. J. G., McDougall, G., Busheikin, J., & Aldous, J. (1995). Effects of social skills training and social milieu treatment on symptoms of schizophrenia. *Psychiat. Serv., 46*(4), 376-380.

Docherty, N. M., DeRosa, M., & Andreasen, N. C. (1996). Communication disturbances in schizophrenia and mania. *Arch. Gen. Psychiat., 53*, 358-364

Docter, R. F., & Prince, V. (1997). Transvestism: A survey of 1032 cross-dressers. *Arch. Sex. Behav., 26*(6), 589-605.

Doherty, W. (1999, July 1). Interviewed in P. Tucker, Marital therapy field splitting up. *HealthScout.*

Dohrenwend, B. P. (2000). The role of adversity and stress in psychopathology: Some evidence and its implications for theory and research. *J. Hlth. Soc. Behav., 41*(1), 1-19.

Dohrmann, R. J., & Laskin, D. M. (1978). An evaluation of electromyographic feedback in the treatment of myofascial pain-dysfunction syndrome. *JAMA, 96*, 656-662.

Doka, K. J. (1999). A primer on loss and grief. In J. D. Davidson & K. J. Doka (Eds.), *Living with grief at work, at school, at worship.* Philadelphia: Brunner/Mazel.

Dolan, B., Evans, C., & Norton, K. (1995). Multiple Axis-II diagnoses of personality disorder. *Brit. J. Psychiat., 166*, 107-112.

Dole, V. P., & Nyswander, M. (1965). A medical treatment for heroin addiction. *JAMA, 193*, 646-650.

Dole, V. P., & Nyswander, M. (1967). Heroin addiction, a metabolic disease. *Arch. Internal Med., 120*, 19-24.

Dolinski, D., & Nawrat, R. (1998). "Fear-then-relief" procedure for producing compliance: Beware when the danger is over. *J. Exp. Soc. Psychol., 34*(1), 27-50.

Domino, G., & Swain, B. J. (1986). Recognition of suicide lethality and attitudes toward suicide in mental health professions. *Omega: J. Death Dying, 16*(4), 301-308.

Domino, G., & Takahashi, Y. (1991). Attitudes toward suicide in Japanese and American medical students. *Suic. Life-Threat. Behav., 21*(4), 345-359.

Donaldson, S. K., Klein, D. N., Riso, L. P., & Schwartz, J. E. (1997). Comorbidity between dysthymic and major depressive disorders: A family study analysis. *J. Affect. Disorders, 42*, 103-111.

Donohue, B., Thevenin, D. M., & Runyon, M. K. (1997). Behavioral treatment of conversion disorder in adolescence. *Behav. Mod. 21*(2), 231-251.

Donohue, J., & Gebhard, P. (1995). The Kinsey Institute/Indiana University report on sexuality and spinal cord injury. *Sex. Disability, 13*(1), 7-85.

Donovan, S. J., Susser, E. S., Nunes, E. V., Stewart, J. W., et al. (1997). Divalproex treatment of disruptive adolescents: A report of 10 cases. *J. Clin Psychiat, 58*(1), 12-15.

Dorpat, T. L. (1998). Self psychology: An overview. In R. Langs et al. (Eds.), *Current theory of psychoanalysis.* Madison, CT: International Universities Press, Inc.

Dorr, N. C. (1999). Blood pressure in African Americans: Examining the role of coping with discrimination. *Diss. Abstr. Inter.: Sect. B: Sci. Eng., 59*(7-B), 3769.

Dorwart, R. A., & Ostacher, M. J. (1999). A community psychiatry approach to preventing suicide. In D. G. Jacobs (Ed.), *The Harvard Medical School guide to suicide assessment and intervention.* San Francisco: Jossey-Bass.

Double, D. B. (1991). A cluster analysis of manic states. *Comprehen. Psychiat., 32*(3), 187-194.

Dougher, M. J. (1997). Cognitive concepts, behavior analysis, and behavior therapy. *J. Behav. Ther. Exp. Psychiat., 28*(1), 65-70.

Douglas, J. (1996). *Mind hunter: Inside the FBI's elite serial crime unit.* New York: Pocket Star.

Douglas, V. I., Barr, R. G., Amin, K., O'Neill, M. E., & Britton, B. G. (1988). Dosage effects and individual responsivity to methylphenidate in attention deficit disorder. *J. Child Psychol. Psychiat. Allied Disc., 29*, 453-475.

Dowdney, L., & Skuse, D. (1993). Parenting provided by adults with mental retardation. *J. Child Psychol. Psychiat. Allied Disc., 34*(1), 25-47.

Doweiko, H. E. (1999). *Concepts of chemical dependency* (4th ed.). Pacific Grove, CA: Brooks/Cole.

Downey, A. M. (1991). The impact of drug abuse upon adolescent suicide. *Omega: J. Death Dying, 22*(4), 261-275.

Downey, R. G., Sinnett, E. R., & Seeberger, W. (1998). The changing face of MMPI practice. *Psychol. Rep., 83*(3, Pt. 2), 1267-1272.

Doyle, A. C. (1938). The sign of the four. In *The complete Sherlock Holmes.* Garden City, NY: Doubleday.

Dozier, M. (1996). Personal correspondence. University of Delaware, Newark.

Drake, R. E., & Wallach, M. A. (1992). Mental patients' attraction to the hospital: Correlates of living preference. *Comm. Ment. Hlth. J., 28*(1), 5-12.

Drake, R. E., McHugo, G. J., Becker, D. R., Anthony, W. A., & Clark, R. E. (1996). The New Hampshire study of supported employment for people with severe mental illness. *J. Cons. Clin. Psychol., 64*(2), 391-399.

Drake, R. E., Osher, F., & Wallach, M. (1991). Homelessness and dual diagnosis. *Amer. Psychologist, 46*(11), 1149-1158.

Drane, J. (1995). Physician-assisted suicide and voluntary active euthanasia: Social ethics and the role of hospice. *Amer. J. Hospice & Palliative Care, 12*(6), 3-10.

Drug Enforcement Administration. (1996). *Consumption of ritalin.* Washington, DC: Author.

Druss, B. G., & Rosenheck, R. A. (1998). Mental disorders and access to medical care in the United States. *Amer. J. Psychiat., 155*(12), 1775-1777.

Dubbert, P. M. (1995). Behavioral (life-style) modification in the prevention and treatment of hypertension. *Clin. Psychol. Rev., 15*(3), 187-216.

Duberstein, P. R., Conwell, Y., & Cox, C. (1998). Suicide in widowed persons: A psychological autopsy comparison of recently and remotely bereaved older subjects. *Amer. J. Ger. Psychiat., 6*(4), 328-334.

Duberstein, P., Conwell, Y., Cox, C., Podgorski, C., Glazer, R., & Caine, E. (1995). Attitudes toward self-determined death: A survey of primary care physicians. *J. Amer. Ger. Soc., 43*, 395-400.

Dubner, A. E., & Motta, R. W. (1999). Sexually and physically abused foster care children and posttraumatic stress disorder. *J. Cons. Clin. Psychol., 67*(3), 367-373.

Duffy, B. (1996, April 15). The mad bomber? *U. S. News & World Report*, pp. 29-36.

Dugas, M. J., Freeston, M. H., Ladouceur, R., Rheaume, J., Provencher, M., & Boisvert, J. M. (1998). Worry themes in primary GAD, secondary GAD, and other anxiety disorders. *J. Anx. Dis., 12*(3), 253-261.

Duggan, C. (1997). Introduction. *Brit. J. Psychiat., 170*(Suppl. 32), 1-3.

Duggan, J. P., & Booth, D. A. (1986). Obesity, overeating, and rapid gastric emptying in rats with ventromedial hypothalamic lesions. *Science, 231*(4738), 609-611.

Dugger, C. W. (1996, October 5). Genital ritual is unyielding in Africa. *New York Times*, pp. 1, 6-7.

Dunbar, F. (1948). *Synopsis of psychosomatic diagnosis and treatment.* St. Louis: Mosby.

Duncan, R. M., & Cheyne, J. A. (1999). Incidence and functions of self-reported private speech in young adults: A self-verbalization. *Canadian Journal of Behavioral Science, 31*(2), 133–136.

Dunn, K. M., Croft, P. R., & Hackett, G. I. (1999). Association of sexual problems with social, psychological, and physical problems in men and women: A cross sectional population survey. *J. Epidemiol. Comm. Hlth., 53*(3), 144–148.

Dunner, D. L., & Hall, K. S. (1980). Social adjustment and psychological precipitants in mania. In R. H. Belmaker & H. M. van Praag (Eds.), *Mania: An evolving concept.* New York: Spectrum.

Du Paul, G. J., & Barkley, R. A. (1993). Behavioral contributions to pharmacotherapy: The utility of behavioral methodology in medication treatment of children with attention-deficit hyperactivity disorder. *Behav. Ther., 24,* 47–65.

Dupont, S. (1995). Multiple sclerosis and sexual functioning: A review. *Clin. Rehab. 9*(2), 135–141.

Dupree, L. W., & Schonfeld, L. (1999) Management of alcohol abuse in older adults. In M. Duffy (Ed.), *Handbook of counseling and psychotherapy with older adults.* New York: Wiley.

Durkheim, E. (1951). *Suicide.* New York: Free Press. (Original work published in 1897)

Dweck, C. S. (1976). Children's interpretation of evaluative feedback: The effect of social cues on learned helplessness. *Merrill Palmer Quart., 22*(2), 105–109.

Dwyer, J. T., Feldman, J. J., Seltzer, C. C., & Mayer, J. (1969). Body image in adolescents: Attitudes toward weight and perception of appearance. *Amer. J. Clin. Nutr., 20,* 1045–1056.

Eakes, G. G. (1995). Chronic sorrow: The lived experience of parents of chronically mentally ill individuals. *Arch. Psychiatr. Nursing, 9*(2), 77–84.

Eaton, W. W., & Muntaner, C. (1999). Socioeconomic stratification and mental disorder. In A. V. Horwitz, T. L. Scheid, et al. (Eds.), *A handbook for the study of mental health: Social contexts, theories, and systems.* New York: Cambridge University Press.

Eaton, W. W., Bilker, W., Haro, J. M., & Herman, H. (1992). Long-term course of hospitalization for schizophrenia: II. Change with passage of time. *Schizo. Bull., 18*(2), 229–241.

Eaton, W. W., Dryman, A., & Weissman, M. M. (1991). Panic and phobia. In L. N. Robins & D. A. Regier (Eds.), *Psychiatric disorders in America: The Epidemiologic Catchment Area Study.* New York: Maxwell Macmillan International.

Eaves, L., Schultz, S. C., et al. (1988). Genetics, immunology, and virology. *Schizo. Bull., 14*(3), 365–382.

Ebihara, S., Marks, T., Hudson, D. J., & Menaker, M. (1986). *Science, 231,* 491–493.

Echeburúa, E., Báez, C., & Fernández-Montalvo, J. (1996). Comparative effectiveness of three therapeutic modalities in the psychological treatment of pathological gambling: Long-term outcome. *Behav. Cog. Psychother., 24,* 51–72.

Eckenrode, J., Laird, M., & Doris, J. (1993). School performance and disciplinary problems among abused and neglected children. *Dev. Psychol., 29*(1), 54–62.

Edelman, R. E., & Chambless, D. L. (1995). Adherence during sessions and homework in cognitive-behavioral group treatment of social phobia. *Behav. Res. Ther., 33*(5), 573–577.

Edelstein, B. A., & Semenchuk, E. M. (1996). Interviewing older adults. In L. L. Carstensen, B. A. Edelstein, et al. (Eds.), *The practical handbook of clinical gerontology.* Thousand Oaks, CA: Sage.

Editors of Roper Reports. (1998, January). Partying like it's 1999. Source: Roper Starch Worldwide, NY. *American Demographics.*

Edwards, T. M. (1998, November 9). What the cutters feel. *Behavior, 152*(19).

Egan, B. M. (1992). Vascular reactivity, sympathetic tone, and stress. In E. H. Johnson, E. D. Gentry, & S. Julius (Eds.), *Personality, elevated blood pressure, and essential hypertension.* Washington, DC: Hemisphere.

Egeland, B. (1991, February). Presentation. American Association for the Advancement of Science.

Ehrman, M. (1995, June 25). Reaching out for virtual therapy. *Los Angeles Times,* pp. E1, E4.

Eich, E. (1995). Mood as a mediator of place dependent memory. *J. Exp. Psychol. Gen. 124*(3), 293–308.

Eigan, L. (1991, February) Alcohol practices, policies, and potentials of American colleges and universities. An OSAP White Paper, Office for Substance Abuse Prevention, Rockville, MD.

Einarson, T. R., Arikian, S. R., Casciano, J., & Doyle, J. J. (1999). Comparison of extended-release venlafaxine, selective serotonin reuptake inhibitors, and tricyclic antidepressants in the treatment of depression: A meta-analysis of randomized controlled trails. *Clin Ther.: Inter. J. Drug Ther., 21*(2), 296–308.

Eisen, J. L., Goodman, W. K., Keller, M. B., Warshaw, M. G., DeMarco, L. M., Luce, D. D., & Rasmussen, S. A. (1999). Patterns of remission and relapse in obsessive-compulsive disorder: A 2-year prospective study. *J. Clin. Psychiat., 60*(5), 346–351.

Eisen, M. R. (1993). The victim's burden: Guilt, shame and abuse. *Imag. Cog. Pers., 12*(1), 69–88.

Eisenberg, L. (1958). School phobia: A study in the communication of anxiety. *Amer. J. Psychiat., 114,* 712–718.

Eisendrath, S. J. (1995). Psychiatric aspects of chronic pain. *Neurology, 45*(Suppl 9), S26–S34.

Eisenthal, S., Koopman, C., & Lazare, A. (1983). Process analysis of two dimensions of the negotiated approach in relation to satisfaction in the initial interview. *J. Nerv. Ment. Dis., 171,* 49–54.

Eisler, I. (1995). Family models of eating disorders. In G. Szmukler, C. Dare, & J. Treasure (Eds.), *Handbook of eating disorders: Theory, treatment and research.* Chichester, UK: Wiley.

Eitinger, L. (1964). *Concentration camp survivors in Norway and Israel.* New York: Humanities Press.

Eitinger, L. (1969). Psychosomatic problems in concentration camp survivors. *J. Psychosom. Res., 13,* 183–190.

Eitinger, L. (1973). A follow-up study of the Norwegian concentration camp survivors: Mortality and morbidity. *Isr. Ann. Psychiat. Relat. Disciplines, 11,* 199–210.

Ekman, P., O'Sullivan, M., & Frank, M. G. (1999). A few can catch a liar. *Psychol. Sci., 10*(3), 263–266.

Elias, M. (1993, July 15). Poor odds for heroin recovery. *USA Today,* p. 1D.

Elias, M. (1995, April 18). Therapist's program to go on-line. *USA Today,* p. 1D.

Elias, M. (2000, March 7). Online mental-health therapy in its formative years. *USA Today,* p. 3D.

Elkin, I. (1994). The NIMH Treatment of Depression Collaborative Research Program: Where we began and where we are. In A. E. Bergin & S. L. Garfiel (Eds.), *Handbook of psychotherapy and behavior change* (4th ed.). New York: Wiley.

Elkin, I., Shea, M. T., Watkins, J. T., Imber, S. D., et al. (1989). National Institute of Mental Health Treatment of Depression Collaborative Research Program: General effectiveness of treatments. *Arch. Gen. Psychiat., 46*(11), 971–982.

Elkins, D. N. (1999, October). Spirituality: It's what's missing in mental health. *Psychol. Today,* pp. 45–48.

Elkins, I. J., & Cromwell, R. L. (1994). Priming effects in schizophrenia: Associative interference and facilitation as a function of visual context. *J. Abnorm. Psychol., 103*(4), 791–800.

Elkins, R. L. (1991). An appraisal of chemical aversion (emetic therapy) approaches to alcoholism treatment. *Behav. Res. Ther., 29,* 387–414.

Ellenberger, H. F. (1970). *The discovery of the unconscious.* New York: Basic Books.

Ellenberger, H. F. (1972). The story of "Anna O.": A critical review with new data. *J. History Behav. Sci., 8,* 267–279.

Elliot, D. M., & Guy, J. D. (1993). Mental health professionals vs. non-mental health professionals: Childhood trauma and adult functioning. *Profess. Psychol.: Res. and Prac., 24*(1), 83–90.

Elliott, C. (1996). *The rules of insanity: Moral responsibility and the mentally ill offender.* Albany: State University of New York Press.

Ellis, A. (1962). *Reason and emotion in psychotherapy.* Secaucus, NJ: Lyle Stuart.

Ellis, A. (1977). The basic clinical theory of rational-emotive therapy. In A. Ellis & R. Grieger (Eds.), *Handbook of rational-emotive therapy.* New York: Springer.

Ellis, A. (1979). A note on the treatment of agoraphobics with cognitive modification versus prolonged exposure in vivo. *Behav. Res. Ther., 17,* 162–164.

Ellis, A. (1979). The theory of rational-emotive therapy. In A. Ellis & J. M. Whitely (Eds.), *Theoretical and empirical foundations of rational-emotive therapy.* Monterey, CA: Brooks/Cole.

Ellis, A. (1995). Rational emotive behavior therapy. In R. J. Corsini & D. Wedding (Eds.), *Current psychotherapies* (5th ed.). Itasca, IL: Peacock.

Ellis, A. (1997). The evolution of Albert Ellis and rational emotive behavior therapy. In J. K. Zeig (Ed.), *The evolution of psychotherapy: The third conference.* New York: Brunner/Mazel.

Ellis, A. (1999). *How to make yourself happy and remarkably less disturbable.* Atascadero, CA: Impact Publishers.

Ellison, C. G., & Levin, J. S. (1998). The religion-health connection: Evidence, theory, and future directions. *Health Education and Behavior, 25*(6), 700–720.

Ellison, J. M. (1998). SSRIs and sexual dysfunction. *Psychiat. Times, XV*(8).

Elsesser, K., Sartory, G., & Maurer, J. (1996). The efficacy of complaints management training in facilitating benzodiazepine withdrawal. *Behav. Res. Ther., 34*(2), 149–156.

Emmanuel, N. P., Ware, M. R., Brawman-Mintzer, O., Ballenger, J. C., & Lydiard, R. B. (1999). Once-weekly dosing of fluoxetine in the maintenance of remission in panic disorder. *J. Clin. Psychiat., 60*(5), 299–301.

Emmelkamp, P. M. (1982). Exposure in vivo treatments. In A. Goldstein & D. Chambless (Eds.), *Agoraphobia: Multiple perspectives on theory and treatment.* New York: Wiley.

Emmelkamp, P. M. (1982). *Phobic and obsessive-compulsive disorders.* New York: Plenum Press.

Emmelkamp, P. M. (1994). Behavior therapy with adults. In A. E. Bergin & S. L. Garfiel (Eds.), *Handbook of psychotherapy and behavior change* (4th ed.). New York: Wiley.

Emrick, C. D., & Hansen, J. (1983). Assertions regarding effectiveness of treatment for alcoholism: Fact or fantasy? *Amer. Psychologist, 38,* 1078–1088.

Engel, G. L. (1968). A life setting conducive to illness: The giving-up-given-up complex. *Ann. Internal Med., 69,* 293.

Ennis, B. J., & Emery, R. D. (1978). *The rights of patients* (ACLU Handbook Series). New York: Avon.

Enoch, M. A., Kaye, W. H., Rotondo, A., et al. (1998). 5-HT2A promoter polymorphism - 1438G/A, anorexia nervosa, and obsessive-compulsive disorder [letter]. *Lancet, 351,* 1785–1786.

Enright, S. J. (1989). Paedophilia: A cognitive/behavioural treatment approach in a single case. *Brit. J. Psychiat., 155,* 399–401.

Ensminger, M. E. (1995, December). Welfare and psychological distress: A longitudinal study of African American urban mothers. *J. Hlth. Soc. Behav., 36,* 346–359.

Epstein, S. (1983). Hypnotherapeutic control of exhibitionism: A brief communication. *Inter. J. Clin. Exp. Hyp., 31*(2), 63–66.

Erba, H. W. (2000). Early intervention programs for children with autism: Conceptual frameworks for implementation. *Amer. J. Orthopsychiat., 70*(1), 82–94.

Erdelyi, M. H. (1985). *Psychoanalysis: Freud's cognitive psychology.* New York: W. H. Freeman.

Erdelyi, M. H. (1992). Psychodynamics and the unconscious. *Amer. Psychologist, 47*(6), 784–787.

Ereshefsky, L. (1995). Treatment strategies for schizophrenia. New Antipsychotic Treatments for Schizophrenia Symposium. *Psychiat. Ann., 25*(5), 285–296.

Erickson, M. T. (1992). *Behavior disorders of children and adolescents.* Englewood Cliffs, NJ: Prentice Hall.

Erikson, E. (1963). *Childhood and society.* New York: Norton.

Ernst, N. D., & Harlan, W. R. (1991). Obesity and cardiovascular disease in minority populations: Executive summary. Conference highlights, conclusions, and recommendations. *Amer. J. Clin. Nutr., 53*(Suppl.), 1507–1511.

Escobar, J. I., Gara, M., Waitzkin, H., Silver, R. C., Holman, A., & Compton, W. (1998). DSM-IV hypochondriasis in primary care. *Gen. Hosp. Psychiat., 20*(3), 155–159.

Eser, A. (1981). "Sanctity" and "quality" of life in a historical comparative view. In S. E. Wallace & A. Eser (Eds.), *Suicide and euthanasia: The rights of personhood.* Knoxville: University of Tennessee Press.

Essau, C. A., Conradt, J., & Petermann, F. (1999). Frequency of panic attacks and panic disorder in adolescents. *Depress. Anx., 9*(1), 19–26.

Etzersdorfer, E., & Sonneck, G. (1998). Preventing suicide by influencing mass-media reporting. The Viennese experience 1980–1996. *Arch. Suic. Res., 4*(1), 67–74.

Evans, G. & Farberow, N. L. (1988). *The encyclopedia of suicide.* New York: Facts on File.

Evenhuis, H. M. (1999). Associated medical aspects. In M. P. Janicki & A. P. Dalton (Eds.), *Dementia, aging, and intellectual disabilities: A handbook.* Philadelphia: Brunner/Mazel.

Everson, S. A., Goldberg, D. E., Kaplan, G. A., Cohen, R. D., et al. (1996). Hopelessness and risk of mortality and incidence of myocardial infarction and cancer. *Psychosom. Med., 58,* 113–121.

Exner, J. E. (1993). *The Rorschach: A comprehensive system: Vol. 1. Basic foundations* (3rd ed.). New York: Wiley.

Exner, J. E. (1997). The future of Rorschach in personality assessment. *J. Pers. Assess., 68*(1), 37–46.

Exner, J. E., Jr. (1999). The Rorschach measurement concepts and issues of validity. In S. E. Embretson, S. L. Herschberger, et al. (Eds.), *The new rules of measurement: What every psychologist and educator should know.* Mahwah, NJ: Erlbaum.

Express Scripts, Inc. (1999, June 29). *1998 Express Scripts Trend Report.* St. Louis: Author.

FDA (Food and Drug Administration) (1996, March 26). Press release. Cited in A. Manning, Quitter's new tool: Nicotine nasal spray. *USA Today,* p. 1A.

FDA (Food and Drug Administration). (1999, January 13). Bedwetting may be more widespread than thought. *HealthScout.*

Fabrega, H., Ulrich, R., Pilkonis, P., & Mezzich, J. (1991). On the homogeneity of personality disorder clusters. *Comprehen. Psychiat., 32*(5), 373–386.

Faedda, G. L., Tondo, L., Teichner, M. H., Baldessarini, R. J., Gelbard, H. A., & Floris, G. F. (1993). Seasonal mood disorders: Patterns of seasonal recurrence in mania and depression. *Arch. Gen. Psychiat., 50*(1), 17–23.

Fahlen, T. (1995). Personality traits in social phobia I: Comparisons with healthy controls. *J. Clin. Psychiat., 56*(12), 560–568.

Fahrenberg, J., Foerster, F., & Wilmers, F. (1995). Is elevated blood pressure level associated with higher cardiovascular responsiveness in laboratory tasks and with response specificity? *Psychophysiology, 32*(1), 81–91.

Fahrenberg, J., Franck, M., Baas, U., & Jost, E. (1995). Awareness of blood pressure: Interoception or contextual judgement? *J. Psychosom. Res., 39*(1), 11–18.

Fairbairn, G. J. (1998). Suicide, language, and clinical practice. *Philos. Psychiat. Psychol., 5*(2), 157–169.

Fairbank, J. A., & Keane, T. M. (1982). Flooding for combat-related stress disorders: Assessment of anxiety reduction across traumatic memories. *Behav. Ther., 13,* 499–510.

Fairburn, C. G. (1985). Cognitive-behavioural treatment for bulimia. In D. M. Garner & P. E. Garfinkel (Eds.), *Handbook of psychotherapy for anorexia nervosa and bulimia.* New York: Guilford.

Fairburn, C. G. (1985). The management of bulimia nervosa. *J. Psychiat. Res., 19,* 465–472.

Fairburn, C. G., Jones, R., Peveler, R. C., Hope, R. A., & O'Connor, M. (1993). Psychotherapy and bulimia nervosa: Longer-term effects of interpersonal psychotherapy behavior therapy, and cognitive behavior therapy. *Arch. Gen. Psychiat., 50,* 419–428.

Fairburn, C. G., Norman, P. A., Welch, S. L., O'Connor, M. E., et al. (1995). A prospective study of outcome in bulimia nervosa and the long-term effects of three psychological treatments. *Arch. Gen. Psychiat., 52*(4), 304–312.

Fairweather, G. W., Danders, D. H., Maynard, H., & Cressler, D. L. (1969). *Community life for the mentally ill: An alternative to institutional care.* Chicago: Aldine.

Falloon, I. R. H., Coverdale, J. H., & Brooker, C. (1996). Psychosocial interventions in schizophrenia: A review. *Inter. J. Ment. Hlth., 25*(1), 3–21.

Fals, S. W., & Schafer, J. (1992). The treatment of substance abusers diagnosed with obsessive-compulsive disorder: An outcome study. *J. Substance Abuse Treatment, 9*(4), 365–370.

Famy, C., Streissguth, A. P., & Unis, A. S. (1998). Mental illness in adults with fetal alcohol syndrome or fetal alcohol effects. *Amer. J. Psychiat., 155*(4), 552–554.

Faraone, S. V., Biederman, J., Mick, E., Wozniak, J., et al. (1996). Attention deficit hyperactivity disorder in a multigenerational pedigree. *Biol. Psychiat., 39,* 906–908.

Faraone, S. V., Biederman, J., & Milberger, S. (1994). An exploratory study of ADHD among second-degree relatives of ADHD children. *Biol. Psychiat., 35*(6), 398–402.

Faraone, S.V., Tsuang, M.T., & Tsuang, D.W. (1999). *Genetics of mental disorders: A guide for students, clinicians, and researchers.* New York: Guilford.

Farley, C. J. (1994, April 18). The butt stops here. *Time,* pp. 58–64.

Farrington, D. P. (1991). Psychological contributions to the explanations of offending. *Issues Criminol. & Legal Psychol., 1*(17), 7–19.

Fasko, S. N., & Fasko, D. (1991). Suicidal behavior in children. *Psychology: J. of Human Behav., 27*(4)-28(1), 10–16.

Fauber, R. L., & Long, N. (1992). Parenting in a broader context: A reply to Emery, Finchman, and Cummings. *J. Cons. Clin. Psychol., 60*(6), 913–915.

Faubion, C. W., & Andrew, J. (2000). A systems analysis of the case coordinator model and an outcomes analysis in supported employment. *Rehab. Couns. Bull., 43*(2), 75–83, 96.

Fausel, D. F. (1995). Stress inoculation training for stepcouples. *Marriage Fam. Rev., 21*(1–2), 137–155.

Fauteck, P. K. (1995). Detecting the malingering of psychosis in offenders: No easy solutions. *Criminal Justice Behav., 22*(1), 3–18.

Fava, M. (2000). New approaches to the treatment of refractory depression. *J. Clin. Psychiat., 61*(Suppl.), 26–32.

Fava, M., Bless, E., Otto, M. W., Pava, J. A., & Rosenbaum, J. F. (1994). Dysfunctional attitudes in major depression. *J. Nerv. Ment. Dis., 182*(1), 45–49.

Fava, M., Rankin, M. A., Wright, E. C., Alpert, J. E., Nierenberg, A. A., Pava, J., & Rosenbaum, J. F. (2000). Anxiety disorders in major depression. *Comprehen. Psychiat., 41*(2), 97–102.

Favaro, A., Maiorani, M., Colombo, G., & Santonastaso, P. (1999). Traumatic experiences, posttraumatic stress disorder, and dissociative symptoms in a group of refugees from former Yugoslavia. *J. Nerv. Ment. Dis., 187*(5), 306–308.

Fawcett, J. (1999). Profiles of completed suicides. In D.G. Jacobs (Ed.), *The Harvard Medical School guide to suicide assessment and intervention.* San Francisco: Jossey-Bass.

Fawcett, J., & Busch, K. A. (1995). Stimulants in psychiatry. In A. F. Schatzberg & C. B. Nemeroff (Eds.), *The American Psychiatric Press textbook of psychopharmacology.* Washington, DC: American Psychiatric Press.

Fawcett, J., Scheftner, W., Clark, D., Hedeker, D., et al. (1987). Clinical predictors of suicide in patients with major affective disorders: A controlled prospective study. *Amer. J. Psychiat., 144*(1), 35–40.

Fawzy, F. I., Fawzy, N. W., Hyun, C. S., Elashoff, R., Guthrie, D., et al. (1993). Malignant melanoma: Effects of an early structured psychiatric intervention, coping, and affective state on recurrence and survival six years later. *Arch. Gen. Psychiat., 50,* 681–689.

Fehre, K., & White, B. J. (Eds.). (1996). *The self-help group directory* (14th ed.). Denville, NJ: Northwest Convenant Medical Center.

Feighner, J. P. (1999). Overview of antidepressants currently used to treat anxiety disorders. *J. Clin. Psychiat., 60*(Suppl. 22), 18–22.

Feinberg, M. (1999). Pharmacotherapy. In M. Hersen & A. S. Bellack (Eds.), *Handbook of comparative interventions for adult disorders* (2nd ed.). New York: Wiley.

Feinstein, R. E., & Brewer, A. A. (Eds.). (1999). *Primary care psychiatry and behavioral medicine: Brief office treatment and management pathways.* New York: Springer.

Feldman, H. A., Goldstein, I., Hatzichristou, D. G., Krane, R. J., & McKinlay, J. B. (1994). Impotence and its medical and psychosocial correlates: Results of the Massachusetts Male Aging Study. *J. Urology, 151,* 54–61.

Feldman, M. D., & Feldman, J. M. (1995). Tangled in the web: Countertransference in the therapy of factitious disorders. *Inter. J. Psychiat. Med.*, 25(4), 389–399.

Feldman, M. D., Ford, C.V., & Reinhold, T. (1994). *Patient or pretender: Inside the strange world of factitious disorders.* New York: Wiley.

Fenichel, O. (1945). *The psychoanalytic theory of neurosis.* New York: Norton.

Fenigstein, A. (1996). Paranoia. In C. G. Costello (Ed.), *Personality characteristics of the personality disordered.* New York: Wiley.

Fenn, D. S., Moussaoui, D., Hoffman, W. F., Kadri, N., Bentounssi, B., Tilane, A., Khomeis, M., & Casey, D. E. (1996). Movements in never-medicated schizophrenics: A preliminary study. *Psychopharmacology, 123,* 206–210.

Fennig, S., Schwartz, J. E., & Bromet, E. J. (1994). Are diagnostic criteria, time of episode and occupational impairment important determinants of the female:male ration for major depression? *J. Affect. Disorders, 30,* 147–154.

Fenton, W. S., & McGlashan, T. H. (1994). Antecedents, symptom progression, and long-term outcome of the deficit syndrome in schizophrenia. *Amer. J. Psychiat., 151*(3), 351–356.

Fenton, W. S., Mosher, L. R., Herrell, J. M., & Blyler, C. R. (1998). Randomized trial of general hospital and residential alternative care for patients with severe and persistent mental illness. *Amer. J. Psychiat., 155*(4), 516–522.

Fergusson, D. M., Woodward, L. J., & Horwood, L. J. (2000). Risk factors and life processes associated with the onset of suicidal behavior during adolescence and early adulthood. *Psychol. Med., 30*(1), 23–39.

Fernandez, F., Levy, J. K., Lachar, B. L., Small, G. W., et al. (1995). The management of depression and anxiety in the elderly. *J. Clin. Psychiat., 56* (Suppl. 2), 20–29.

Fernandez-Guasti, A., & Lopez-Rubalcava, C. (1998). Modification of the anxiolytic action of 5-HT-sub(1A) compounds by GABA-benzodiazepine agents in rats. *Pharmacol. Biochem. Behav., 60*(1), 27–32.

Ferrada, N. M., Asberg, M., Ormstad, K., & Nordstrom, P. (1995). Definite and undetermined forensic diagnoses of suicide among immigrants in Sweden. *Acta Psychiatr. Scandin., 91*(2), 130–135.

Ferrier, I. N. (1999). Treatment of major depression: Is improvement enough? *J. Clin. Psychiat., 60*(Suppl. 6), 10–14.

Fichter, M. (1990). Psychological therapies in bulimia nervosa. In M. M. Fichter (Ed.), *Bulimia nervosa: Basic research, diagnosis and therapy.* Chichester, England: Wiley.

Fichter, M. M., & Pirke, K. M. (1995). Starvation models and eating disorders. In G. Szmukler, C. Dare, & J. Treasure (Eds.), *Handbook of eating disorders: Theory, treatment and research.* Chichester, England: Wiley.

Fichtner, C. G., Kuhlman, D. T., Gruenfeld, M. J., & Hughes, J. R. (1990). Decreased episodic violence and increased control of dissociation in a carbamazepine-treated case of multiple personality. *Biol. Psychiat., 27*(9), 1045–1052.

Field, T. M. (1977). Effects of early separation, interactive deficit, and experimental manipulations on infant-mother face-to-face interaction. *Child Dev., 48*(3), 763–771.

Fieve, R. R. (1975). *Moodswing.* New York: Morrow.

Figley, C. R. (1978). Symptoms of delayed combat stress among a college sample of Vietnam veterans. *Military Med., 143*(2), 107–110.

Figley, C. R., & Leventman, S. (1990). Introduction: Estrangement and victimization. In C. R. Figley & S. Leventman (Eds.), *Strangers at home: Vietnam veterans since the war.* New York: Praeger.

Fink, D. (1992). The psychotherapy of multiple personality disorder. A case study. *Psychoanalytic Inquiry, 12*(1), 49–70.

Fink, M. (1988). Convulsive therapy: A manual of practice. In A. J. Frances & R. Hales (Eds.), *Review of psychiatry* (Vol. 7). Washington, DC: American Psychiatric Press.

Fink, M. (1992). Electroconvulsive therapy. In E. S. Paykel (Ed.), *Handbook of affective disorders.* New York: Guilford.

Fink, M. (1995). Recognizing NMS as a type of catatonia. *Neuropsychiat., Neuropsychol., Behav. Neurol., 8*(1), 75–76.

Fink, P. (1995). Psychiatric illness in patients with persistent somatisation. *Brit. J. Psychiat., 166,* 93–99.

Fink, P., Ewald, H., Jensen, J., Sorensen, L., Engberg, M., Holm, M., & Munk-Jorgensen, P. (1999). Screening for somatization and hypochondriasis in primary care and neurological in-patients: A seven-item scale for hypochondriasis and somatization. *J. Psychosom. Res., 46*(3), 261–273.

Fink, P., Sorensen, L., Engberg, M., Holm, M., & Munk-Jorgensen, P. (1999). Somatization in primary care: Prevalence, health care utilization, and general practitioner recognition. *Psychosomatics, 40*(4), 330–338.

Finkel, N. J. (1988). *Insanity on trial.* New York: Plenum Press.

Finkel, N. J. (1989). The Insanity Defense Reform Act of 1984: Much ado about nothing. *J. Behav. Sci. Law, 7*(3), 403–419.

Finkel, N. J. (1990). De facto departures from insanity instructions. *Law Human Behav., 14*(2), 105–122.

Finkel, N. J. (1991). The insanity defense. *Law Human Behav., 15*(5), 533–555.

Finkel, N. J., & Duff, K. (1989). The insanity defense: Giving jurors a third option. *Forensic Reports, 1,* 65–70.

Finkel, N. J., Shaw, R., Bercaw, S., & Koch, J. (1985). Insanity defenses: From the juror's perspective. *Law Psychol. Rev., 9,* 97–92.

Finkel, S. (1991). Group psychotherapy in later life. In W. A. Myers (Ed.), *New techniques in the psychotherapy of older patients.* Washington, DC: American Psychiatric Press.

Finkelhor, D., Asdigian, N., & Dziuba-Leatherman, J. (1995). Victimization prevention programs for children: A follow-up. *Amer. J. Pub. Hlth., 85*(12), 1684–1689.

Finkelstein, J. R. J., Cannon, T. D., Gur, R. E., Gur, R. C., & Moberg, P. (1997). Attentional dysfunctions in neuroleptic-naive and neuroleptic-withdrawn schizophrenic patients and their siblings. *J. Abnorm. Psychol., 106*(2), 203–212.

Finn, P. R., Sharkansky, E. J., Brandt, K. M., & Turcotte, N. (2000). The effects of familial risk, personality, and expectancies on alcohol use and abuse. *J. Abnorm. Psychol., 109*(1), 122–133.

First, M. B., Spitzer, R. L., Gibbon, M., & Williams, J. B. W. (1995). The structured clinical interview for DSM-III-R personality disorders (SCID-II): I. Description. *J. Pers. Disorders, 9*(2), 83–91.

Fiscalini, J. (1993). Interpersonal relations and the problem of narcissism. In J. Fiscalini & A. L. Grey (Eds.), *Narcissism and the interpersonal self.* New York: Columbia University Press.

Fishbain, D. A. (2000). Re: The meeting of pain and depression: Comorbidity in women. *Canad. J. Psychiat., 45*(1), 88.

Fishbain, D. A., Cutler, R. B., Rosomoff, H. L., & Rosomoff, R. S. (1998). Do antidepressants have an analgesic effect in psychogenic pain and somatoform pain disorder? A meta-analysis. *Psychosom. Med., 60*(4), 503–509.

Fisher, J. E., & Carstensen, L. L. (1990). Behavior management of the dementias. *Clin. Psychol. Rev., 10,* 611–629.

Fisher, J. O., & Birch, L. L. (1999). Restricting access to palatable foods affects children's behavioral response, food selection, and intake. *Amer. J. Clin. Nutr., 69*(6), 1264–1272.

Fisher, P. L., & Durham, R. C. (1999). Recovery rates in generalized anxiety disorder following psychological therapy: An analysis of clinically significant change in the STAI-T across outcome studies since 1990. *Psychol. Med., 29*(6), 1425–1434.

Fitz, A. (1990). Religious and familial factors in the etiology of obsessive-compulsive disorder: A review. *J. Psychol. Theol., 18*(2), 141–147.

Flaherty, J. A., & Adams, S. (1998). Therapist-patient race and sex matching: Predictors of treatment duration. *Psychiat. Times., XV*(1).

Flament, M. F., Koby, E., Rapoport, J. L., Berg, C. J., et al. (1991). Childhood obsessive-compulsive disorder: A prospective follow-up study. *Annu. Progr. Child Psychiat. Child Dev.,* 373–394.

Flanagan, O. (2000). *Dreaming souls: Sleep, dreams, and the evolution of the conscious mind.* New York: Oxford University Press.

Flanagan, R., & di Guiseppe, R. (1999). Critical review of the TEMAS: A step within the development of thematic apperception instruments. *Psychol. Schools, 36*(1), 21–30.

Flannery, R. B., Jr., Fisher, W., Walker, A., Kolodziej, K., & Spillane, M. J. (2000). Assaults on staff by psychiatric patients in community residences. *Psychiat. Serv., 51*(1), 111–113.

Flaskerud, J. H. (2000). Ethnicity, culture, and neuropsychiatry. *Issues Ment. Hlth. Nurs., 21*(1), 5–29.

Flaskerud, J. H., & Hu, L. (1992). Racial/ethnic identity and amount and type of psychiatric treatment. *Amer. J. Psychiat., 149*(3), 379–384.-

Flaskerud, J. H., & Hu, L. (1992). Relationship of ethnicity to psychiatric diagnosis. *J. Nerv. Ment. Dis., 180*(5), 296–303.

Flavin, D. K., Franklin, J. E., & Frances, R. J. (1990). Substance abuse and suicidal behavior. In S. J. Blumenthal & D. J. Kupfer (Eds.), *Suicide over the life cycle: Risk factors, assessment, and treatment of suicidal patients.* Washington, DC: American Psychiatry Press.

Fleer, J., & Pasewark, R. A. (1982). Prior public health agency contacts of individuals committing suicide. *Psychol. Rep., 50*(3, Pt. 2), 1319–1324.

Fleishman, J. A., & Fogel, B. (1994). Coping and depressive symptoms among people with AIDS. *Hlth. Psychol., 13*(2), 156–169.

Flett, G. L., Vredenburg, K., & Krames, L. (1997). The continuity of depression in clinical and nonclinical samples. *Psychol. Bull., 121*(3), 395–416.

Flick, S. N., Roy-Byrne, P. P., Cowley, D. S., Shores, M. M., & Dunner, D. L. (1993). DSM-III-R personality disorders in a mood and anxiety disorders clinic: Prevalence, comorbidity, and clinical correlates. *J. Affect. Disorders, 27,* 71–79.

Flint, A. J. (1994). Epidemiology and comorbidity of anxiety disorders in the elderly. *Amer. J. Psychiat., 151*(5), 640–649.

Flint, J., Corley, R., DeFries, J. C., Fulker, D. W., Gray, J. A., Miller, S., & Collins, A. C. (1995). Chromosomal mapping of three loci determining quantitative variation of susceptibility to anxiety in the mouse. *Science, 268,* 1432–1435.

Floyd, F. J., O'Farrell, T. J., & Goldberg, M. (1987). Comparison of marital observational measures: The Marital Interaction Coding System and the Communications Skills Test. *J. Cons. Clin. Psychol., 55*(3), 2200.

Foa, E. B., & Franklin, M. E. (1999). Cognitive behavior therapy. In M. Hersen, A. S. Bellack, et al. (Eds.), *Handbook of comparative interventions for adult disorders* (2nd ed.). New York: Wiley.

Foa, E. B., & Kozak, M. J. (1995). DSM-IV field trial: Obsessive compulsive disorder. *Amer. J. Psychiat., 152*(1), 90–96.

Foderaero, L. W. (1993, August 12). Electroshock therapy makes a comeback. *Anchorage Daily News,* p. D3.

Foderaro, L. (1994, March 6). Got problems? Dial a shrink. *New York Times,* p. B4.

Foderaro, L. (1995, June 16). The mentally ill debate what to call themselves. *New York Times,* p. B1.

Fog, R. (1995). New diagnostic vistas. XIIth AEP Congress: Improvement of compliance: Quality assurance: Increased quality of life in community care in schizophrenia. *Inter. Clin. Psychopharmacology, 9*(Suppl. 5), 71–73.

Fogel, B. S. (1986). ECT versus tricyclic antidepressants. *Amer. J. Psychiat., 143*(1), 121.

Fombonne, E. (1995). Eating disorders: Time trends and possible explanatory mehanisms. In M. Rutter & D. J. Smith, *Psychosocial disorders in young people.* Chichester, England: Wiley.

Fombonne, E. (1999). The epidemiology of autism: A review. *Psychol. Med., 29*(4), 769–786.

Fonagy, P. (1999). Psychcanalytic theory from the viewpoint of attachment theory and research. In J. Cassidy, P. R. Shaver, et al. (Eds.), *Handbook of attachment: Theory, research, and clinical applications.* New York: Guilford Press.

Fondacaro, K. M., & Butler, W. M. (1995). Suicidality in female survivors of child sexual abuse. In S. S. Canetto & D. Lester (Eds.), *Women and suicidal behavior.* New York: Springer.

Fong, M. L., & Silien, K. A. (1999). Assessment and diagnosis of DSM-IV anxiety disorders. *J. Couns. Dev., 77*(2), 209–217.

Foote, B. (1999). Dissociative identity disorder and pseudo-hysteria. *Amer. J. Psychother., 53*(3), 320–343.

Ford, C. E., & Hamerton, J. L. (1956). The chromosomes of man. *Nature, 178,* 1020–1023.

Ford, C. V., King, B. H., & Hollender, M. H. (1988). Lies and liars: Psychiatric aspects of prevarication. *Amer. J. Psychiat., 145*(5), 554–562.

Ford, J. D., & Stewart, J. (1999). Group psychotherapy for war-related PTSD with military veterans. In B. H. Young & D. D. Blake (Eds.), *Group treatments for post-traumatic stress disorder.* Philadelphia: Brunner/Mazel.

Foreyt, J. P., Poston, W. S. C., & Goodrick, G. K. (1996). Future directions in obesity and eating disorders. *Addic. Behav., 21*(6), 767–778.

Fortmann, S., & Killen, J. (1995). Nicotine gum and self-help behavioral treatment for smoking relapse prevention: Results from a trial using population-based recruitment. *J. Cons. Clin. Psychol., 63*(3), 460–468.

Foster, P. S., Smith, E. W. L., & Webster, D. G. (1999). The psychophysiological differentiation of actual, imagined, and recollected anger. *Imag. Cog. Pers., 18*(3), 189–203.

Foster, S. L., & Cone, J. D. (1986). Design and use of direct observation. In A. R. Ciminero, K. S. Calhoun, & H. E. Adams (Eds.), *Handbook of behavioral assessment* (2nd ed.). New York: Wiley.

Foster-Higgins. (1991, June 8) Cited in L. Block, Mental health expenses make employers anxious. *Business Insurance,* p. 3.

Fowler, J. S., Volkow, N. D., & Wolf, A. P. (1995). PET studies of cocaine in human brain. In A. Biegon & N. D. Volkow (Eds.), *Sites of drug action in the human brain.* Boca Raton, FL: CRC Press.

Fowler, R. (1999, June 10). Cited in Associated Press release (Philadelphia), Outrage over sex abuse study.

Fox, J. A., & Levin, J. (1999). Serial murder: Popular myths and empirical realities. In M. D. Smith, M.

A. Zahn, et al. (Eds.), *Homicide: A sourcebook of social research.* Thousand Oaks, CA: Sage.

Fox, P. (1992). Implications for expressed emotion therapy within a family therapeutic context. *Hlth. Soc. Work, 17*(3), 207–213.

Fox, V. (2000). Empathy: The wonder quality of mental health treatment. *Psychiatric Rehabilitation Journal, 23*(3), 292–293.

Frances, A. J., & Egger, H. L. (1999). Whither psychiatric diagnosis. *Austral. New Zeal. J. Psychiat., 33*(2), 161–165.

Frances, R. J., & Franklin, J. E. (1988). Alcohol and other psychoactive substance use disorders. In J. A. Talbott, R. E. Hales, & S. C. Yudofsky (Eds.), *Textbook of psychiatry.* Washington, DC: American Psychiatric Press.

Franchini, L., Gasperini, M., Perez, J., Smeraldi, E., & Zanardi, R. (1997). A double-blind study of long-term treatment with sertraline or fluvoxamine for prevention of highly recurrent unipolar depression. *J. Clin. Psychiat., 58*(3), 104–107.

Francis, L. J. (1999). Happiness is a thing called stable extraversion: A further examination of the relationship between the Oxford Happiness Inventory and Eysenck's dimensional model of personality and gender. *Pers. Individ. Diff., 26*(1), 5–11.

Francis, M. E., & Pennebaker, J. W. (1992). Putting stress into words: The impact of writing on physiological, absentee, and self-reported emotional well-being measures. *Amer. J. Hlth. Promotion, 6*(4), 280–287.

Frank, E. (1997). Enhancing patient outcomes: Treatment adherence. *J. Clin. Psychiat., 58*(Suppl. 1), 11–14.

Frank, E. (1999). Paper on bipolar disorder therapy presented at the Third International Conference on Bipolar Disorder, Pittsburgh, PA.

Frank, E., Grochocinski, V. J., Spanier, C. A., Buysse, D. J., Cherry, C. R., Houck, P. R., Stapf, D. M., & Kupfer, D. J. (2000). Interpersonal psychotherapy and antidepressant medication: Evaluation of a sequential treatment strategy in women with recurrent major depression. *J. Clin. Psychiat., 61*(1), 51–57.

Frank, E., Kupfer, D. J., Perel, J. M., Cornes, C., Jarrett, D. B., Mallinger, A. G., et al. (1990). Three-year outcomes for maintenance therapies in recurrent depression. *Arch. Gen. Psychiat., 47*(12), 1093–1099.

Frank, E., Kupfer, D. J., Wagner, E. F., McEachran, A. B., & Cornes, C. (1991). Efficacy of interpersonal therapy as a maintenance treatment of recurrent depression: Contributing factors. *Arch. Gen. Psychiat., 48,* 1053–1059.

Frank, J. D. (1973). *Persuasion and healing* (rev. ed.). Baltimore: Johns Hopkins University Press.

Frankel, F. H. (1993). Adult reconstruction of childhood events in the multiple personality literature. *Amer. J. Psychiat., 150*(6), 954–958.

Frankish, C. J. (1994). Crisis centers and their role in treatment: Suicide prevention versus health promotion. In A. A. Leenaars, J. T. Maltsberger, & R. A. Neimeyer (Eds.), *Treatment of suicidal people.* Washington, DC: Taylor & Francis.

Frankl, V. E. (1963). *Man's search for meaning.* New York: Washington Square.

Frankl, V. E. (1975). Paradoxical intention and dereflection. *Psychother. Theory Res. Prac., 12*(3), 226–237.

Franklin, M. E., Jaycox, L. H., & Foa, E. B. (1999). Social skills training. In M. Hersen & A. S. Bellack (Eds.), *Handbook of comparative interventions for adult disorders* (2nd ed.). New York: Wiley.

Frasciello, L. M., & Willard, S. G. (1995). Anorexia nervosa in males: A case report and review of the literature. *Clin. Soc. Work J., 23*(1), 47–58.

Frawley, P., & Smith, J. (1992). One-year follow-up after multimodal inpatient treatment for cocaine and methamphetamine dependencies. *J. Substance Abuse Treatment, 9,* 271–286.

Frayn, D. H. (1991). The incidence and significance of perceptual qualities in the reported dreams of patients with anorexia nervosa. *Canad. J. Psychiat., 36*(7), 517–520.

Frederick, C. J. (1969). Suicide notes: A survey and evaluation. *Bull. Suicidol., 8,* 17–26.

Fredrikson, M., Annas, P., Fischer, H., & Wik, G. (1996). Gender and age differences in the prevalence of specific fears and phobias. *Behav. Res. Ther., 34*(1), 33–39.

Freeman, A., & Oster, C. (1999). Cognitive behavior therapy. In M. Hersen & A.S. Bellack (Eds.), *Handbook of comparative interventions for adult disorders* (2nd ed.). New York: Wiley.

Freeman, A., Pretzer, J., Fleming, B., & Simon, K. M. (1990). *Clinical applications of cognitive therapy.* New York: Plenum Press.

Freeman, C. (1995). Cognitive therapy. In G. Szmukler, C. Dare, & J. Treasure (Eds.), *Handbook of eating disorders: Theory, treatment and research.* Chichester, England: Wiley.

Freeman, L. J., Templer, D. I., & Hill, C. (1999). The relationship between adult happiness and self-appraised childhood happiness and events. *J. Gen. Psychol., 160*(1), 46–54.

Freeman, M. P., & Stoll, A. L. (1998). Mood stabilizer combinations: A review of safety and efficacy. *Amer. J. Psychiat., 155*(1), 12–21.

Freeman, S. F. N., & Alkin, M. C. (2000). Academic and social attainments of children with mental retardation in general education and special education settings. *Remed. Spec. Educ., 21*(1), 3–18.

Freeston, M. H., & Ladouceur, R. (1997). What do patients do with their obsessive thoughts? *Behav. Res. Ther., 35*(4), 335–348.

Freeston, M. H., Ladouceur, R., Gagnon, F., & Thibodeau, N. (1992). *Beliefs about obsessional thoughts.* Unpublished manuscript, Laval University, Quebec City, Quebec.

Freeston, M. H., Rhéaume, J., & Ladouceur, R. (1996). Correcting faulty appraisals of obsessional thoughts. *Behav. Res. Ther., 34*(5/6), 433–446.

Freiberg, P. (1994, April). Gay-rights position takes on significance. *APA Monitor, 25*(4), 40.

French, O. (1987). More on multiple personality disorder. *Amer. J. Psychiat., 144*(1), 123–124.

Freud, S. (1885). On the general effects of cocaine. *Medicinisch-chirurgisches Centralblatt, 20,* 373–375.

Freud, S. (1894). The neuropsychoses of defense. In J. Strachey (Ed.), *The standard edition of the complete psychological works of Sigmund Freud* (Vol. 3). London: Hogarth Press, 1962.

Freud, S. (1900). *The interpretation of dreams* (J. Strachey, Ed. & Trans.). New York: Wiley.

Freud, S. (1909). Analysis of a phobia in a five-year-old boy. In *Sigmund Freud: Collected Papers* (Vol. 3). New York: Basic Books.

Freud, S. (1915). A case of paranoia counter to psychoanalytic theory. In *Complete psychological works* (Vol. 14). London: Hogarth, 1957.

Freud, S. (1917). *A general introduction to psycho-analysis* (J. Riviere, Trans.). New York: Liveright, 1963.

Freud, S. (1917). Mourning and melancholia. In *Collected Papers* (Vol. 4), pp. 152–172. London: Hogarth Press and the Institute of Psychoanalysis, 1950.

Freud, S. (1924). The loss of reality in neurosis and psychosis. In *Sigmund Freud's collected papers,* (Vol. 2), pp. 272–282. London: Hogarth Press.

Freud, S. (1933). *New introductory lectures on psychoanalysis.* New York: Norton.

Freud, S. (1957). Mourning and melancholia. In J. Strachey (Ed. & Trans.), *The standard edition of complete psychological works* (Vol. 14). London: Hogarth Press. (Originally published 1917).

Frey, K. A., Koeppe, R. A., & Holthoff, V. A. (1995). *In vivo* imaging of benzodiazepine receptors with positron emission tomography. In A. Biegon & N. D. Volkow (Eds.), *Sites of drug action in the human brain.* Boca Raton, FL: CRC Press.

Frick, P. J., Christian, R. E., & Wooton, J. M. (1999). Age trends in association between parenting practices and conduct problems. *Behav. Mod., 23*(1), 106–128.

Frick, W. B. (1995). The subpersonalities controversy: A reply to my critics. *J. Human Psychol., 35*(1), 97–101.

Fride, F. (1995). Anandamides: Tolerance and cross-tolerance to delta 9-tetrahydrocannabinol. *Brain Res., 697*(1–2), 83–90.

Friedman, M., & Rosenman, R. (1959). Association of specific overt behavior pattern with blood and cardiovascular findings. *JAMA, 169*, 1286.

Friedman, M., Thoresen, C., Gill, J., et al. (1984). Alteration of type A behavior and reduction in cardiac recurrences in postmyocardial infarction patients. *Amer. Heart J., 108*(2), 653–665.

Friedman, M. J. (1999). Pharmacotherapy for posttraumatic stress disorder. In M. J. Horowitz et al., (Eds.), *Essential papers on posttraumatic stress disorder.* Essential papers in psychoanalysis. New York: New York University Press.

Friend, T. (1996, March 4). Alzheimer's deaths "underestimated". *USA Today,* Section D, p. 1.

Friman, P. C., & Warzak, W. J. (1990). Nocturnal enuresis: A prevalent, persistent, yet curable parasomnia. *Pediatrician, 17*(1), 38–45.

Friman, P. C., Allen, K. D., Kerwin, M. L. E., & Larzelere, R. (1993). Changes in modern psychology: A citation analysis of the Kuhnian displacement thesis. *Amer. Psychologist, 48*(6), 658–664.

Frischholz, E. J., Lipman, L. S., Braun, B. G., & Sachs, R. G. (1992). Psychopathology, hypnotizability, and dissociation. *Amer. J. Psychiat., 149*(11), 1521–1525.

Frith, U. (2000). Cognitive explanations of autism. In K. Lee et al. (Eds.), *Childhood cognitive development: The essential readings.* Essential readings in development psychology. Malden, MA: Blackwell.

Frith, U., Morton, J., & Leslie, A. M. (1991). The cognitive basis of a biological disorder: Autism. *Trends Neurosci., 14*, 433–438.

Fritz, C., Farver, T. B., & Kass, P. H. (1997). Correlation among three psychological scales used in research of caregivers for patients with Alzheimer's disease. *Psychol. Rep., 80*, 67–80.

Fromm, E., & Nash, M. R., (Eds.) (1992). *Contemporary hypnosis research.* New York: Guilford.

Fromm-Reichmann, F. (1943). Psychotherapy of schizophrenia. *Amer. J. Psychiat., 111*, 410–419.

Fromm-Reichmann, F. (1948). Notes on the development of treatment of schizophrenia by psychoanalytic psychotherapy. *Psychiatry, 11*, 263–273.

Fromm-Reichmann, F. (1950). *Principles of intensive psychotherapy.* Chicago: University of Chicago.

Fromme, K., Katz, E., & D'Amico, E. (1997). Effects of alcohol intoxication on the perceived consequences of risk taking. *Exp. Clin. Psychopharmacol., 5*(1), 14–23.

Frosch, W. A., Robbins, E. S., & Stern, M. (1965). Untoward reactions to lysergic acid diethylamide (LSD) resulting in hospitalization. *N. Engl. J. Med., 273*, 1235–1239.

Fry, R. (1993). Adult physical illness and childhood sexual abuse. *J. Psychosom. Res., 37*(2), 89–103.

Fuentes, K., & Cox, B. (2000). Assessment of anxiety in older adults: A community-based survey and comparison with younger adults. *Behav. Res. Ther., 38*(3), 297–309.

Fukunishi, I. (1998). Eating attitudes in female college students with self-reported alexithymic characteristics. *Psychol. Rep., 82*, 35–41.

Fukunishi, I., Hosaka, T., Negishi, M., Moriya, H., Hayashi, M., & Matsumoto, T. (1996). Subclinical depressive symptoms in HIV infection are related to avoidance coping responses: A comparison with end-stage renal failure and breast cancer. *Psychol. Rep., 78*, 483–488.

Fuller, R. C. (1982, Fall). Carl Rogers, religion, and the role of psychology in American culture. *J. Human. Psychol., 22*, 21–32.

Fulwiler, C., & Pope, H. G., Jr. (1987). Depression in personality disorder. In O. G. Cameron (Ed.), *Presentations of depression: Depressive symptoms in medical and other psychiatric disorders.* New York: Wiley.

Funari, D. J., Piekarski, A. M., & Sherwood, R. J. (1991). Treatment outcomes of Vietnam veterans with posttraumatic stress disorder. *Psychol. Rep., 68*(2), 571–578.

Furukawa, T. A., Ogura, A., Hirai, T., Fujihara, S., Kitamura, T., & Takahashi, K. (1999). Early parental separation experiences among patients with bipolar disorder and major depression: A case-control study. *J. Affect. Disorders, 52*(1–3), 85–91.

Fyer, A. J., Mannuzza, S., Gallops, M. S., Martin, L. Y., Aaronson, C., Gorman, J. M., Liebowitz, M. R., & Klein, D. F. (1990). Familial transmission of simple phobias and fears: A preliminary report. *Arch. Gen. Psychiat., 47*, 252–256.

Gabbard, G. O. (1990). *Psychodynamic psychiatry in clinical practice.* Washington, DC: American Psychiatric Press.

Gabbard, G. O. (1998, September). The impact of psychotherapy on the brain. *Psychiatr. Times, XV*(9).

Gabbard, G. O., & Coyne, L. (1987). Predictors of response of antisocial patients to hospital treatment. *Hosp. Comm. Psychiat., 38*(11), 1181–1185.

Gabbard, G. O., & Goodwin, F. K. (1996). Integrating biological and psychosocial perspectives. In L. J. Dickstein, M. B. Riba, & J. M. Oldham (Eds.), *Review of psychiatry* (Vol. 15). Washington, DC: American Psychiatric Press.

Gable, S. L., & Shean, G. D. (2000). Perceived social competence and depression. *J. Soc. Pers. Relationships, 17*(1), 139–150.

Gaboriau, H., & Graham, H. D. (1999, April). *The desire for cosmetic facial plastic surgery may result from a personality disorder, not vanity.* Paper presented at meeting of American Academy of Facial Plastic and Reconstructive Surgery. Palm Desert, CA.

Galanter, M. (1993). Network therapy for addiction: A model for office practice. *Amer. J. Psychiat., 150*(1), 28–35.

Galanter, M., & Castañeda, R. (1999). Psychotherapy and family network therapy. In M. Hersen & A. S. Bellack (Eds.), *Handbook of comparative interventions for adult disorders* (2nd ed.). New York: Wiley.

Galanter, M., Talbott, D., Gallegos, K., & Rubenstone, E. (1990). Combined Alcoholics Anonymous and professional care for addicted physicians. *Amer. J. Psychiat., 147*(1), 64–68.

Gallacher, J. E., Yarnell, J. W. G., Sweetnam, P. M., Elwood, P. C., & Stansfeld, S. A. (1999). Anger and incident heart disease in the Caerphilly study. *Psychosom. Med., 61*(4), 446–453.

Gallagher, R. (1998, December 17). Interviewed in R. Vigoda, More college students showing signs of stress. *The Seattle Times.*

Gallagher-Thompson, D., & Thompson, L. W. (1995). Problems of aging. In R. J. Comer (Ed.), *Abnormal psychology.* New York: W. H. Freeman.

Gallagher-Thompson, D., Lovett, S., & Rose, J. (1991). Psychotherapeutic interventions for stressed family caregivers. In W. A. Myers (Ed.), *New techniques in the psychotherapy of older patients.* Washington, DC: American Psychiatric Press.

Galper, J. (1998, June). Population update for June. *American Demographics.*

Gamwell, L., & Tomes, N. (1995). *Madness in America: Cultural and medical perceptions of mental illness before 1914.* Ithaca, NY: Cornell University Press.

Ganaway, G. K. (1989). Historical versus narrative truth: Clarifying the role of exogenous trauma in the etiology of MPD and its variants. *Dissociation, 2,* 205–222.

Ganley, A. (1981). *A participant and trainer's manual for working with men who batter.* Washington, DC: Center for Women Policy Studies.

Gannon, L., Luchetta, T., Rhodes, K., Pardie, L., & Segrist, D. (1992). Sex bias in psychological research: Progress or complacency? *Amer. Psychologist, 47*(3), 389–396.

Ganzach, Y. (1995). Nonlinear models of clinical judgment: Meehl's data revisited. *Psychol. Bull., 118*(3), 422–429.

Ganzini, L., Leong, G. B., Fenn, D. S., Silva, J. A., & Weinstock, R. (2000). Evaluation of competence to consent to assisted suicide: Views of forensic psychiatrists. *Amer. J. Psychiat., 157*(4), 595–600.

Garb, H. N., Florio, C. M., & Grove, W. M. (1998). The validity of the Rorschach and the Minnesota Multiphasic Personality Inventory: Results from meta-analyses. *Psychol. Sci., 9*(5), 402–404.

Garber, J., Weiss, B., & Shanley, N. (1993). Cognitions, depressive symptoms, and development in adolescents. *J. Abnorm. Psychol., 102*(1), 47–57.

Gardner, D. L., Leibenluft, E., O'Leary, K. M., & Cowdry, R. W. (1991). Self-ratings of anger and hostility in borderline personality disorder. *J. Nerv. Ment. Dis., 179*(3), 157–161.

Gardner, F. L., McGowan, L. P., DiGiuseppe, R., & Sutton-Simon, K. (1980, November). *A comparison of cognitive and behavioral therapies in the reduction of social anxiety.* Paper presented to the American Association of Behavior Therapy, New York.

Gardner, J. P. (1996). *The effects of sleep deprivation on serotonergic neuronal activity in the dorsal raphe nucleus of the cat.* Unpublished doctoral dissertation, Princeton University, Princeton, NJ.

Gardner, R. (1984, July 12). Full moon lunacy: Fact or fiction. *Trenton Times,* p. B1.

Garety, P. (1991). Reasoning and delusions. *Brit. J. Psychiat., 159*(Suppl. 14), 14–18.

Garfield, D. A., & Havens, L. (1991). Paranoid phenomena and pathological narcissism. *Amer. J. Psychother., 45*(2), 160–172.

Garfield, S. L. (1998). Some comments on empirically supported treatments. *J. Cons. Clin. Psychol., 66*(1), 121–125.

Garfield, S. L., & Bergin, A. E. (1994). Introduction and historical overview. In A. E. Bergin & S. L. Garfield (Eds.), *Handbook of psychotherapy and behavior change* (4th ed.). New York: Wiley.

Garfinkel, P. E., & Gallop, R. (1992). Eating disorders and borderline personality disorder. In D. Silver & M. Rosenbluth (Eds.), *Handbook of borderline disorders.* Madison, CT: International Universities Press.

Garfinkel, P. E., & Garner, D. M. (1982). *Anorexia nervosa: A multidimensional perspective.* New York: Brunner/Mazel.

Garfinkel, P. E., Lin, E., Goering, P., Spegg, C., Goldbloom, D. S., Kennedy, S., Caplan, A. S.,

& Woodside, D. B. (1995). Bulimia nervosa in a Canadian community sample: Prevalence in comparison of subgroups. *Amer. J. Psychiat., 152,* 1052–1058.

Garland, A. F., Shaffer, D., & Whittle, B. (1989). A national survey of adolescent suicide prevention programs. *J. Amer. Acad. Child Adol. Psychiat., 28,* 931–934.

Garnefski, N., & Diekstra, R. F. W. (1997). Adolescents from one parent, stepparent and intact families: Emotional problems and suicide attempts. *J. Adolescence, 20,* 201–208.

Garner, D. M., & Bemis, K. M. (1982). A cognitive-behavioral approach to anorexia nervosa. *Cog. Ther. Res., 6*(2), 123–150.

Garner, D. M., & Bemis, K. M. (1985). Cognitive therapy for anorexia nervosa. In D. M. Garner & P. E. Garfinkel (Eds.), *Handbook of psychotherapy for anorexia nervosa and bulimia.* New York: Guilford.

Garner, D. M., & Fairburn, C. G. (1988). Relationship between anorexia nervosa and bulimia nervosa: Diagnostic implications. In D. M. Garner & P. E. Garfinkel (Eds.), *Diagnostic issues in anorexia nervosa and bulimia nervosa.* Brunner/Mazel eating disorders monograph series, No. 2. New York: Brunner/Mazel.

Garner, D. M., Cooke, A. K., & Marano, H. E. (1997). The 1997 body image survey results. *Psychol. Today,* pp. 30–44.

Garner, D. M., Garfinkel, P. E., & O'Shaughnessy, M. (1985). The validity of the distinction between bulimia with and without anorexia nervosa. *Amer. J. Psychiat., 142,* 581–587.

Garner, D. M., Garfinkel, P. E., Schwartz, D., & Thompson, M. (1980). Cultural expectations of thinness in women. *Psychol. Rep., 47,* 483–491.

Garner, D. M., Olmsted, M. P., & Polivy, J. (1984). *The EDI.* Odessa, FL: Psychological Assessment Resources.

Garner, D. M., Rockert, W., Davis, R., Garner, M. V., Olmsted, M. P., & Eagle, M. (1993). Comparison of cognitive-behavioral and supportive-expressive therapy for bulimia nervosa. *Amer. J. Psychiat., 150*(1), 37–46.

Garralda, M. E. (1996). Somatisation in children. *J. Child Psychol. Psychiat., 37*(1), 13–33.

Garris, P. A., Kilpatrick, M., Bunin, M. A., Michael, D., Walker, Q. D., & Wightman, R. M. (1999). Dissociation of dopamine release in the nucleus accumbens from intracranial self-stimulation. *Nature, 398*(6722), 67–69.

Garrison, C. Z., McKeown, R. E., Valois, R. F., & Vincent, M. L. (1993). Aggression, substance use, and suicidal behaviors in high school students. *Amer. J. Pub. Hlth., 83*(2), 179–184.

Garssen, B., & Goodkin, K. (1999). On the role of immunological factors as mediators between psychosocial factors and cancer progression. *Psychiat. Res., 85*(1), 51–61.

Gatchel, R. J., & Baum, A. (1983). *An introduction to health psychology.* New York: Random House.

Gattaz, W. F. (1995). Does vitamin E prevent tardive dyskinesia? *Biol. Psychiat., 37*(12), 896–897.

Gaub, M., & Carlson, C. L. (1997). Behavioral characteristics of DSM-IV ADHD subtypes in a school-based population. *J. Abnorm. Child Psychol., 25*(2), 103–111.

Gawin, F. H., & Ellinwood, E. H. (1988). Cocaine and other stimulants: Actions, abuse, and treatment. *N. Eng. J. Med., 318,* 1173–1182.

Gay, P. (1999, March 29). Psychoanalyst Sigmund Freud. *Time,* pp. 66–69.

Gaynes, B. N., Magruder, K. M., Burns, B. J., Wagner, H. R., Yarnall, K. S. H., & Broadhead, W. E. (1999). Does a coexisting anxiety disorder predict persistence of depressive illness in primary care patients with major depression? *Gen. Hosp. Psychiat., 21*(3), 158–167.

Gearty, R. (1999, February 27). Exorcist mom who killed daughter judged insane. *New York Daily News,* p. 40.

Gebhard, P. H. (1965). Situational factors affecting human sexual behavior. In F. Beach (Ed.), *Sex and behavior.* New York: Wiley.

Gebhard, P. H., Gagnon, J. H., Pomeroy, W. B., & Christenson, C. V. (1965). *Sex offenders: An analysis of types.* New York: Harper & Row.

Geist, R., Heinmaa, M., Stephens, D., Davis, R., & Katzman, D. K. (2000). Comparison of family therapy and family group psychoeducation in adolescents with anorexia nervosa. *Canad. J. Psychiat., 45*(2), 173–178.

Geisthardt, C., & Munsch, J. (1996). Coping with school stress: A comparison of adolescents with and without learning disabilities. *J. Learn. Disabilities, 29*(3), 287–296.

Gelfand, D. M., Jenson, W. R., & Drew, C. J. (1982). *Understanding child behavior disorders.* New York: Holt, Rinehart & Winston.

Geller, B., Fox, L. W., & Fletcher, M. (1993). Effect of tricyclic antidepressants on switching to mania and on the onset of bipolarity in depressed 6- to 12-year-olds. *J. Amer. Acad. Child. Adol. Psychiat., 32*(1), 43–50.

Geller, B., Reising, D., Leonard, H. L., Riddle, M. A., Walsh, B. T. (1999). Critical review of tricyclic antidepressant use in children and adolescents. *J. Amer. Acad. Child Adol. Psychiat., 38*(5), 513–528.

Geller, J. L. (1992). A historical perspective on the role of state hospitals viewed from the era of the "revolving door." *Amer. J. Psychiat., 149,* 1526–1533.

Gelles, R. J. (1992). Poverty and violence toward children. *Amer. Behav. Scientist, 35*(3), 258–274.

Gelles, R. J., & Straus, M. A. (1987). Is violence toward children increasing? A comparison of 1975 and 1985 national survey rates. *J. Interpers. Violence, 2,* 212–222.

Gelman, D. (1983, November 7). A great emptiness. *Newsweek,* pp. 120–126.

Gelman, D., & Katel, P. (1993, April 5). The trauma after the storm. *Newsweek.*

General Social Survey, University of Chicago (GSS). (1998, February). Cited in J. Student, *American Demographics.*

George, E. L., Friedman, J. C., & Miklowitz, D. J. (2000). Integrated family and individual therapy for bipolar disorder. In S. L. Johnson, A. M. Hayes, et al. (Eds.), *Stress, coping, and depression.* Mahwah, NJ: Erlbaum.

Gerlach, J., & Hansen, L. (1992). Clozapine and D1/D2 antagonism in extrapyramidal functions. *Brit. J. Psychiat., 160*(Suppl.), 34–37.

Gerlach, J., & Peacock, L. (1995). Intolerance to neuroleptic drugs: The art of avoiding extrapyramidal syndromes: Treatment-resistant schizophrenia in perspective: Assessment and management. *Eur. Psychiat., 10*(Suppl. 1), 27S–31S.

Gerlach, J., Lublin, H., & Peacock, L. (1996). Extrapyramidal symptoms during long-term treatment with antipsychotics: Special focus on clozapine and D1 and D2 dopamine antagonists. *Neuropsychopharmacology, 14,* 35S–39S.

Gernsbacher, L. M. (1985). *The suicide syndrome.* New York: Human Sciences Press.

Gershon, E. S. (2000). Bipolar illness and schizophrenia as oligogenic diseases: Implications for the future. *Biol. Psychiat., 47*(3), 240–244.

Gershon, E. S., & Nurnberger, J. I. (1995). Bipolar illness. In J. M. Oldham & M. B. Riba (Eds.), *American Psychiatric Press review of psychiatry* (Vol. 14). Washington, DC: American Psychiatric Press.

Gershon, E. S., & Rieder, R. O. (1992). Major disorders of mind and brain. *Scientif. Amer., 127–133.*

Gershuny, B. S., & Thayer, J. F. (1999). Relations among psychological trauma, dissociative phenomena, and trauma-related distress: A review and integration. *Clin. Psychol. Rev., 19*(5), 631–657.

Ghaemi, S. N., Boiman, E. E., & Goodwin, F. K. (1999). Kindling and second messengers: An approach to the neurobiology of recurrence in bipolar disorder. *Biol. Psychiat., 45*(2), 137–144.

Gheorghiu, V. A., & Orleanu, P. (1982). Dental implant under hypnosis. *Amer. J. Clin. Hyp., 25*(1), 68–70.

Gibbs, M. S. (1989). Factors in the victim that mediate between disaster and psychopathology: A review. *J. Traum. Stress, 2,* 489–514.

Gidron, Y., Davidson, K. & Bata, I. (1999). The short-term effects of a hostility-reduction intervention on male coronary heart disease patients. *Hlth. Psychol., 18*(4), 416–420.

Gilbert, K. (1996). "We've had the same loss, why don't we have the same grief?" Loss and differential grief in families. *Death Stud., 20,* 269–283.

Gilbert, P. L., Harris, M. J., McAdams, L. A., & Jeste, D. V. (1995). Neuroleptic withdrawal in schizophrenic patients: Review of the literature. *Arch. Gen. Psychiat., 52*(3), 173–188.

Gilbert, S. (1996, May 1). Estrogen patch appears to lift severe depression in new mothers. *New York Times,* p. C12.

Gilbert, S. (1996, July 28). More men may seek eating-disorder help. *New York Times.*

Gill, A. D. (1982). Vulnerability to suicide. In E. L. Bassuk, S. C. Schoonover, & A. D. Gill (Eds.), *Lifelines: Clinical perspectives on suicide.* New York: Plenum Press.

Gillberg, C. (1992). Subgroups in autism: Are there behavioral phenotypes typical of underlying medical conditions? *J. Intellectual Disability Res., 36*(3), 201–214.

Gillham, J. E., Reivich, K. J., Jaycox, L. H., & Seligman, M. E. (1995). Prevention of depressive symptoms in schoolchildren: Two-year follow-up. *Psychol. Sci., 6*(6), 343–351.

Ginsberg, B. G. (1984). Beyond behavior modification: Client-centered play therapy with the retarded. *Acad. Psychol. Bull., 6*(3), 321–334.

Girón, M., Manjón-Arce, P., Puerto-Barber, J., Sánchez-García, E., & Gómez-Beneyto, M. (1998). Clinical interview skills and identification of emotional disorders in primary care. *Amer. J. Psychiat., 155*(4), 530–535.

Gist, R., & Woodall, S. J. (1999). There are no simple solutions to complex problems: The rise and fall of critical incident stress debriefing as a response to occupational stress in the fire service. In R. Gist & B. Lubin (Eds.), *Response to disaster.* Philadelphia: Brunner/Mazel.

Given, C. W., Given, B. A., Stommel, M., & Azzouz, F. (1999). The impact of new demands for assistance on caregiver depression: Tests using an inception cohort. *Gerontologist, 39*(1), 76–85.

Gladis, M. M., Wadden, T. A., Vogt, R., Foster, G., Kuehnel, R. H., & Barlett, S. J. (1998). Behavioral treatment of obese binge eaters: Do they need different care? *J. Psychosom. Res., 44*(3/4), 375–384.

Glaser, R., Kiecolt-Glaser, J. K., Bonneau, R. H., Malarkey, W., Kennedy, S., & Hughes, J. (1992). Stress-induced modulation of the immune response to recombinant hepatitis B vaccine. *Psychosom. Med., 54,* 22–29.

Glass, C. R., & Merluzzi, T. V. (2000). Cognitive and behavioral assessment. In C. E. Watkins, Jr., V. L. Campbell, et al. (Eds.), *Testing and assessment in counseling practice* (2nd ed). Mahwah, NJ: Erlbaum.

Glass, C. R., Arnkoff, D. B., & Rodriquez, B. F. (1998). An overview of directions in psychotherapy integration research. *Journal of Psychotherapy Integration, 8*(4), 187–209.

Glassman, A. H., & Shapiro, P. A. (1998). Depression and the course of coronary artery disease. *Amer. J. Psychiat., 155*(1), 4–11.

Glausiusz, J. (1996, January). The genes of 1995. *Discover,* p. 36.

Glausiusz, J. (1997, January). The genes of 1996. *Discover,* p. 36.

Glazer, S. (1993, February 26). Violence against women: Is the problem more serious than statistics indicate? *CQ Researcher, 3*(8), 169–192.

Gleaves, D. H., Williamson, D. A., & Barker, S. E. (1993). Confirmatory factor analysis of a multidimensional model of bulimia nervosa. *J. Abnorm. Psychol., 102*(1), 173–176.

Gleick, E. (1995, July 10). Sobering times for A. A. *Time,* pp. 49–50.

Glick, I. D. (1999). Family therapies: Efficacy, indications, and treatment outcomes. In D.S. Janowsky et al. (Eds.), *Psychotherapy indications and outcomes.* Washington, DC: American Psychiatric Press.

Globisch, J., Hamm, A. O., Esteves, F., & Oehman, A. (1999). Fear appears fast: Temporal course of startle reflex potentiation in animal fearful subjects. *Psychophysiology, 36*(1), 66–75.

Glogower, F. D., Fremouw, W. J., & McCroskey, J. C. (1978). A component analysis of cognitive restructuring. *Cog. Ther. Res., 2*(3), 209–223.

Glynn, S. M. (1990). Token economy approaches for psychiatric patients: Progress and pitfalls of chronic psychiatric illness. *Behav. Mod., 14*(4), 383–407.

Glynn, S. M., Eth, S., Randolph, E. T., Foy, D. W., et al. (1995). Behavioral family therapy for Vietnam combat veterans with posttraumatic stress disorder. *J. Psychother. Prac. Res., 4*(3), 214–223.

Goate, A., Chartier, H. M., Mullan, M., et al. (1991). Segregation of a missense mutation in the amyloid precursor protein gene with familial Alzheimer's disease. *Nature, 349*(6311), 704–706.

Godding, V., Kruth, M., & Jamart, J. (1997). Joint consultation for high-rish asthmatic children and their families with pediatrician and child psychiatrist as co-therapists: Model and evaluation. *Fam. Process,* 36, 265–280.

Goetzel, R. Z., Anderson, D. R., Whitmer, R. W., Ozminkowski, R. J., Dunn, R. L., & Wasserman, J. (1998). The relationship between modifiable health risks and health care expenditures. An analysis of the multi-employer HERO health risk and cost database. The Health Enhancement Research Organization (HERO) Research Committee. *Journal of Occupational and Environmental Medicine, 40*(10), 843–854.

Goisman, R. M., Goldenberg, I., Vasile, R. G., & Keller, M. B. (1995). Comorbidity of anxiety disorders in a multicenter anxiety study. *Comprehen. Psychiat., 36*(4), 303–311.

Goisman, R. M., Warshaw, M. G., & Keller, M. B. (1999). Psychosocial treatment prescriptions for generalized anxiety disorder, panic disorder, and social phobia, 1991–1996. *Amer. J. Psychiat., 156*(11), 1819–1821.

Goisman, R. M., Warshaw, M. G., Steketee, G. S., Fierman, E. J., et al. (1995). DSM-IV and the disappearance of agoraphobia without a history of panic disorder: New data on a controversial diagnosis. *Amer. J. Psychiat., 152*(10), 1438–1443.

Gold, E. R. (1986). Long-term effects of sexual victimization in childhood: An attributional approach. *J. Cons. Clin. Psychol.,* 54, 471–475.

Gold, J. H. (1998). Gender differences in psychiatric illness and treatments: A critical review. *J. Nerv. Ment. Dis., 186*(12), 769–775.

Goldberg, C. (1999, March 7). Interviewed in M. Jurkowitz, I'm OK; you're OK; Y2K? Does all the worry about deadly computer bugs express our primal fear of entering 2000? *Boston Globe,* p. C1.

Goldberg, D. (1995). Cost effectiveness studies in the evaluation of mental health services in the community: Current knowledge and unsolved problems. XIIth AEP Congress: Improvement of the quality of life in community care in schizophrenia. *Inter. Clin. Psychopharmacology, 9*(Suppl. 5), 29–34.

Goldberg, J. F., Harrow, M., & Grossman, L. S. (1995). Recurrent affective syndromes in bipolar and unipolar mood disorders at follow-up. *Brit. J. Psychiat.,* 166, 382–385.

Goldbloom, D. S., Hicks, L. K., & Garkinfel, P. E. (1990). Platelet serotonin uptake in bulimia nervosa. *Biol. Psychiat., 28*(7), 644–647.

Golden, M. (1964). Some effects of combining psychological tests on clinical inferences. *J. Cons. Clin. Psychol.,* 28, 440–446.

Golden, R. N., & Gilmore, J. H. (1990). Serotonin and mood disorders. *Psychiatr. Ann., 20*(10), 580–588.

Goldfried, M. R., & Wolfe, B. E. (1996). Psychotherapy practice and research. Repairing a strained alliance. *Amer. Psychologist, 51*(10), 1007–1016.

Goldfried, M. R., & Wolfe, B. E. (1998). Toward a more clinically valid approach to therapy research. *J. Cons. Clin. Psychol., 66*(1), 143–150.

Goldiamond, I. (1965). Self-control procedures in personal behavior problems. *Psychol. Rep.,* 17, 851–868.

Golding, S. L., Skeem, J. L., Roesch, R., & Zapf, P. A. (1999). The assessment of criminal responsibility: Current controversies. In A. K. Hess, I. B. Weiner, et al. (Eds.), *The handbook of forensic psychology* (2nd ed.). New York: Wiley.

Goldman, B. D. (1999). The circadian timing system and reproduction in mammals. *Steroids, 64*(9), 679–685.

Goldman, J. G. (1995). A mutual story-telling technique as an aid to integration after abreaction in the treatment of MPD. *Dissociat. Prog. Dissociat. Disorders 8*(1), 53–60.

Goldman, S., & Beardslee, W.R. (1999). Suicide in children and adolescents. In D.G. Jacobs (Ed.), *The Harvard Medical School guide to suicide assessment and intervention.* San Francisco: Jossey-Bass.

Goldney, R. D. (1998). Suicide prevention is possible: A review of recent studies. *Arch. Suic. Res., 4*(4): 329–339.

Goldstein, A. (1994). *Addiction: From biology to drug policy.* New York: W. H. Freeman.

Goldstein, G. (1990). Comprehensive neuropsychological assessment batteries. In G. Goldstein & M. Hersen (Eds.), *Handbook of psychological assessment* (2nd ed.). New York: Pergamon Press.

Goldstein, G., & Hersen, M. (1990). Historical perspectives. In G. Goldstein & M. Hersen (Eds.), *Handbook of psychological assessment* (2nd ed.). New York: Pergamon Press.

Goleman, D. (1995, May 2). Biologists find site of working memory. *New York Times,* pp. C1, C9.

Goleman, D. (1995, June 13). Provoking a patient's worst fears to determine the brain's role. *New York Times,* pp. C1, C10.

Goleman, D. (1995, September 6). Depression in the old can be deadly, but the symptoms are often missed. *New York Times,* p. C10.

Goleman, D. (1995, October 4). Eating disorder rates surprise the experts. *New York Times,* p. C11.

Goleman, D. (1996, May 1). Higher suicide risk for perfectionists. *New York Times,* p. C12.

Goleman, D., & Gurin, J. (1993). Mind/body medicine-At last. *Psychol. Today, 26*(2), 16, 80.

Gonzalez, R. G. (1996). Molecular and functional magnetic resonance neuroimaging for the study of dementia. In R. J. Wurtman, S. Corkin, J. H. Growdon, & R. M. Nitsch (Eds.), *The neurobiology of Alzheimer's disease.* New York: New York Academy of Sciences.

Good, M. (1995). A comparison of the effects of jaw relaxation and music on postoperative pain. *Nursing Res., 44*(1), 52–57.

Good, M., Stanton-Hicks, M., Grass, J. A., Anderson, G. C., Choi, C., Schoolmeesters, L. J., & Salman, A. (1999). Relief of postoperative pain with jaw relaxation, music and their combination. *Pain, 81*(1–2), 163–172.

Goodman, A. (1998). Sexual addiction: Diagnosis and treatment. *Psychiatr. Times, XV*(10).

Goodman, D. (1992). NIMH grantee finds drug responses differ among ethnic groups. *ADAMHA News, 18*(1), p. 5.

Goodman, L. S., & Gilman, A. (Eds.). (1990). *The pharmacological basis of therapeutics* (8th ed.). New York: Pergamon Press.

Goodman, R. (1990). Technical note: Are perinatal complications causes or consequences of autism? *J. Child Psychol. Psychiat. Allied Disc., 31*(5), 809–812.

Goodman, W. K., McDougle, C., & Price, L. H. (1992). Pharmacotherapy of obsessive compulsive disorder. *J. Clin. Psychiat., 53*(Suppl. 4), 29–37.

Goodwin, C. J. (1995). *Research in psychology: Methods and design.* New York: Wiley.

Goodwin, D. W. (1976). Adoption studies of alcoholism. *J. Operational Psychiat., 7*(1), 54–63.

Goodwin, D. W. (1984). Studies of familial alcoholism: A review. *J. Clin. Psychiat., 45*(12, Sect. 2), 14–17.

Goodwin, F. K., & Jamison, K. R. (1984). The natural course of manic-depressive illness. In R. M. Post & J. C. Ballenger (Eds.), *Neurobiology of mood disorders.* Baltimore: Williams & Wilkins.

Goodwin, F. K., & Jamison, K. R. (1990). *Manic-depressive illness.* New York: Oxford University Press.

Goodyer, I. M., Herbert, J., Tamplin, A., Secher, S. M., & Pearson, J. (1997). Short-term outcome of major depression: II. Life events, family dysfunction, and friendship difficulties as predictors of persistent disorder. *J. Amer. Acad. Child Adol. Psychiat., 36*(4), 474–480.

Gordis, E. (1991). *Alcohol research: Promise for the decade.* Rockville, MD: National Institute of Alcohol Abuse and Alcoholism.

Gordon, R. A. (1990). *Anorexia and bulimia.* Cambridge, England: Basil Blackwell.

Gordon, R. A. (2000). *Eating disorders: Anatomy of a social epidemic* (2nd ed.). Malden, MA: Blackwell.

Gore, S. M. (1999). Suicide in prisons: Reflection of communities served, or exacerbated risk? *Brit. J. Psychiat.,* 175, 50–55.

Gorelick, P. B., Amico, L. L., Ganellen, R., et al. (1988). Transient global amnesia and thalamic infarction. *Neurology,* 38, 496–499.

Gorman, C. (1995, November 13). Trapped in the body of a man? *Time,* pp. 94–95.

Gorman, C. (1998, August 17). E-mail your doctor. *Time.*

Gorman, J. M., & Kent, J. M. (1999). SSRIs and SNRIs: Broad spectrum of efficacy beyond major depression. *J. Clin. Psychiat., 60*(Suppl. 4), 33–39.

Gorman, J. M., Papp, L. A., & Coplan, J. D. (1995). Neuroanatomy and neurotransmitter function in panic disorder. In S. P. Roose & R. A. Glick (Eds.), *Anxiety as symptom and signal.* Hillsdale, NJ: Analytic Press.

Gorwood, P., Bouvard, M., Mouren-Simeoni, et al. (1998). Genetics and anorexia nervosa: A review of candidate genes. *Psychiat. Genet.,* 8, 1–12.

Goshen, C. E. (1967). *Documentary history of psychiatry: A source book on historical principles.* New York: Philosophy Library.

Gotlib, I. H., & Neubauer, D. L. (2000). Information-processing approaches to the study of cognitive biases in depression. In S. L. Johnson, A. M. Hayes, et al. (Eds.), *Stress, coping, and depression.* Mahwah, NJ: Erlbaum.

Gotlib, I. H., & Robinson, L. A. (1982). Responses to depressed individuals: Discrepancies between self-report and observer-related behavior. *J. Abnorm. Behav., 91*(4), 231–240.

Gottesman, I. I. (1991). *Schizophrenia genesis.* New York: W. H. Freeman.

Gottfredson, D. C., & Koper, C. S. (1996). Race and sex differences in the prediction of drug use. *J. Cons. Clin. Psychol., 54*(2), 305–313.

Gottlieb, J. (1981). Mainstreaming: Fulfilling the promise? *Amer. J. Ment. Def., 86*(2), 115–126.

Gottlieb, J., Alter, M., & Gottlieb, B. W. (1991). Litigation involving people with mental retardation. In J. L. Matson & J. A. Mulick (Eds.), *Handbook of mental retardation.* New York: Pergamon Press.

Gottschalk, E. C. (1981, April 3). While more firms try jury consultants, debate grows over how much they help. *Wall St. Journal.*

Gould, M. S., Shaffer, D., & Davies, M. (1990). Truncated pathways from childhood to adulthood: Attrition in follow-up studies due to death. In L. Robins & M. Rutter (Eds.), *Straight and devious pathways from childhood to adulthood.* Cambridge, England: Cambridge University Press.

Gowers, S. G., North, C. D., & Byram, V. (1996). Life event precipitants of adolescent anorexia nervosa. *J. Child Psychol. Psychiat., 37*(4), 469–477.

Graham, J., & Gaffan, E. A. (1997). Fear of water in children and adults: Etiology and familial effects. *Behav. Res. Ther., 35*(2), 91–108.

Graham, J. R. (1977). *The MMPI: A practical guide.* New York: Oxford University Press.

Graham, J. R. (1987). *The MMPI: A practical guide* (2nd ed.). New York: Oxford University Press.

Graham, K., Clarke, D., Bois, C., Carver, V., et al. (1996). Addictive behavior of older adults. *Addic. Behav., 21*(3), 331–346.

Gramzow, R., & Tangney, J. P. (1992). Proneness to shame and the narcissistic personality. *Pers. Soc. Psychol. Bull., 18*(3), 369–376.

Grant, B. F., & Dawson, D. A. (1997). Age at onset of alcohol use and its association with DSM-IV alcohol abuse and dependence: Results from the National Longitudinal Alcohol Epidemiologic Survey. *J. Substance Abuse, 9,* 103–110.

Grant, I., Marcotte, T. D., & Heaton, R. K. (1999). Neurocognitive complications of HIV disease. *Psychol. Sci., 10*(3), 191–195.

Grassi, M. P., Perin, C., Borella, M., & Mangoni, A. (1999). Assessment of cognitive function in asymptomatic HIV-positive subjects. *Eur. Neurol., 42*(4), 225–229.

Graves, J. S. (1993). Living with mania: a study of outpatient group psychotherapy for bipolar patients. *Amer. J. Psychother., 47*(1), 113–126.

Gray, H. (1959). *Anatomy of the human body* (27th ed.). Philadelphia: Lea & Febiger.

Gray, J., Nielsen, D. R., Wood, L. E., Andresen, M., & Dolce, K. (2000). Academic progress of children who attended a preschool for abused children: A follow-up of the Keepsafe Project. *Child Abuse Negl. 24*(1), 25–32.

Gray, J. A. (1982). *The neuropsychology of anxiety.* New York: Oxford University Press.

Gray, J. A. (1985). Issues in the neuropsychology of anxiety. In A. H. Tuma & J. D. Maser (Eds.), *Anxiety and the anxiety disorders.* Hillside, NJ: Erlbaum.

Gray, J. A. (1995) Neural systems, emotion and personality. In J. Madden, S. Matthysse, & J. Barchas (Eds.), *Adaptation, learning and affect.* New York: Raven Press.

Gray, J. A., & McNaughton, N. (1996). The neuropsychology of anxiety: Reprise. In D. A. Hope (Ed.), *The Nebraska Symposium on Motivation* (Vol. 43). Lincoln: University of Nebraska Press.

Greeley, A. M. (1991). *Faithful attraction.* New York: Tor Books.

Green, S. A. (1985). *Mind and body: The psychology of physical illness.* Washington, DC: American Psychiatric Press.

Greenberg, D. M. (1998). Sexual recidivism in sex offenders. *Canad. J. Psychiat., 43*(5), 459–465.

Greenberg, I., Chan, S., & Blackburn, G. L. (1999). Nonpharmacologic and pharmacologic management of weight gain. *J. Clin Psychiat., 60*(Suppl. 21), 31–36.

Greenberg, L., Elliott, R., & Lietaer, G. (1994). Research on experiential psychotherapies. In A. E. Bergin & S. L. Garfield (Eds.), *Handbook of psychotherapy and behavior change.* New York: Wiley.

Greenberg, L. S., Watson, J. C., & Lietaer, G. (Eds.) (1998). *Handbook of experiential psychotherapy.* New York: Guilford.

Greenberg, P. E., Sisitsky, T., Kessler, R. C., Finkelstein, S. N., Berndt., E. R., Davidson, J. R., Ballenger, J. C., & Fyer, A. J. (1999). The economic burden of anxiety disorders in the 1990s. *J. Clin. Psychiat., 60*(7), 427–435.

Greenberg, R. P., & Bornstein, R. F. (1988). The dependent personality: II. Risk for psychological disorders. *J. Pers. Disorders, 2*(2), 136–143.

Greene, R. W., Biederman, J., Faraone, S. V., Ouellette, C., et al. (1996). Toward a new psychometric definition of social disability in children with attention-deficit hyperactivity disorder. *J. Amer. Acad. Child Adol. Psychiat., 35*(5), 571–578.

Greenfield, D. (1999, April 1). Virtual addiction survey. Cited in P. Tucker, Are you addicted to the Net? *HealthScout.*

Greenhill, L. L. (1992). Pharmacologic treatment of attention deficit hyperactivity disorder. *Psychiatr. Clin. N. Amer., 15*(1), 1–27.

Greer, S. (1999). Mind-body research in psychooncology. *Adv. Mind-Body Med., 15*(4), 236–244.

Gregoire, A. J. P., Kumar, R., Everitt, B., Henderson, A. F., & Studd, J. W. W. (1996, April 6). Transdermal oestrogen for treatment of severe post-natal depression. *Lancet, 347,* pp. 930–933.

Greist, J. H. (1990). Treatment of obsessive compulsive disorder: Psychotherapies, drugs, and other somatic treatment. *J. Clin. Psychol., 51*(Suppl. 8), 44–50.

Greist, J. H. (1992). An integrated approach to treatment of obsessive-compulsive disorder. *J. Clin. Psychiat., 53*(Suppl. 4), 38–41.

Greist, J. H., & Klein, M. H. (1980). Computer programs for patients, clinicians, and researchers in psychiatry. In J. B. Sidowski, J. H. Johnson, & T. A. Williams (Eds.), *Technology in mental health care delivery systems.* Norwood, NJ: Ablex.

Gresham, A. C. (1993). The insanity plea: A futile defense for serial killers. *Law Psychol. Rev., 17,* 193–208.

Griffiths, R., Gross, G., Russell, J., Thornton, C., Beumont, P. J. V., Schotte, D., & Touyz, S. W. (1998). Perceptions of bed rest of anorexic patients. *Inter. J. Eat. Disorders, 23,* 443–447.

Grigg, J. R. (1988). Imitative suicides in an active duty military population. *Military Med., 153*(2), 79–81.

Grilo, C. M., Becker, D. F., Fehon, D. C., Walker, M. L., et al. (1996). Gender differences in personality disorders in psychiatrically hospitalized adolescents. *Amer. J. Psychiat., 153*(8), 1089–1091.

Grinfield, M. J. (1993, July). Report focuses on jailed mentally ill. *Psychiatr. Times,* pp. 1–3.

Grinfeld, M. J. (1997). Mysterious brain disease defies easy solution. *Psychiatr. Times., XIV*(11).

Grinfield, M. J. (1998, February). "Patient dumping"—Mentally ill get shortchanged. *Psychiatr. Times, XV* (2).

Grinspoon, L., & Bakalar, J. B. (1986). Can drugs be used to enhance the psychotherapeutic process? *Amer. J. Psychother., 40*(3), 393–404.

Grinspoon, L., et al. (Eds.). (1986). Paraphilias. *Harvard Med. School Ment. Hlth. Newsletter, 3*(6), 1–5.

Grisso, T., & Appelbaum, P. S. (1995). The MacArthur treatment competence study: III. Abilities of patients to consent to psychiatric and medical treatments. *Law Human Behav., 19*(2), 149–174

Grizenko, N., Cvejic, H., Vida, S., & Sayegh, L. (1991). Behaviour problems of the mentally retarded. *Canad. J. Psychiat., 36*(10), 712–717.

Grob, G. N. (1966). *State and the mentally ill: A history of Worcester State Hospital in Massachusetts, 1830-1920.* Chapel Hill: University of North Carolina Press.

Grossman, F., Manji, H. K., & Potter, W. Z. (1993). Platelet $x2$-adrenoreceptors in depression: A critical examination. *J. Psychopharmacol., 7*(1), 4–18.

Grossman, S. P. (1990). Brain mechanisms concerned with food intake and body-weight regulation. In M. M. Fichter (Ed.), *Bulimia nervosa: Basic research, diagnosis and therapy.* Chichester, England: Wiley.

Grotstein, J. C. (1996). Object relations theory. In E. Nersessian, & R. G. Kopff (Eds.), *Textbook of psychoanalysis.* Washington, DC: American Psychiatric Press.

Grove, W. M., & Tellegen, A. (1991). Problems in the classification of personality disorders. *J. Pers. Disorders, 5,* 31–42.

Gruenberg, E. M. (1980). Mental disorders. In J. M. Last (Ed.), *Maxcy-Rosenau public health and preventive medicine* (11th ed.). New York: Appleton-Century-Crofts.

Gruneberg, M. M., & Sykes, R. N. (1993). The generalisability of confidence—accuracy studies in eyewitnessing. *Memory, 1*(3), 185–189.

Guastello, S. J., & Reike, M. L. (1991). A review and critique of honesty test research. *Behav. Sci. Law, 9*(4), 501–523.

Gudjonsson, G. H. (1997). Accusations by adults of childhood sexual abuse: A survey of the members of the British False Memory Society (BFMS). *Appl. Cog. Psychol., 11,* 3–18.

Guidotti, A., & Costa, E. (1998). Can the antidysphoric and anxiolytic profiles of selective serotonin reuptake inhibitors be related to their ability to increase brain 3alpha, 5alpha-tetrahydroprogesterone (allopregnanolone) availability? *Biol. Psychiat., 44*(9), 865–873.

Guild, T., & Lowe, G. (1998). Media messages and alcohol education: A school-based study. *Psychol. Rep., 82,* 124–126.

Guillard, P., & Guillard, C. (1987). Suicide and attempted suicide in Martinique. *Psychol. Med., 19*(5), 629–630.

Gunderson, J. G. (1988). Personality disorders. In A. M. Nicholi, Jr. (Ed.), *The new Harvard guide to psychiatry.* Cambridge, MA: Belknap Press.

Gunderson, J. G. (1996). The borderline patient's intolerance of aloneness: Insecure attachments and therapist availability. *Amer. J. Psychiat., 153*(6), 752–758.

Gunderson, J. G., & Sabo, A. N. (1993). The phenomenological and conceptual interface between borderline personality disorder and PTSD. *Amer. J. Psychiat., 150,* 19–27.

Gupta, M. A., & Johnson, A. M. (2000). Nonweight-related body image concerns among female eating-disordered patients and nonclinical controls: Some preliminary observations. *Inter. J. Eat. Disorders, 27*(3), 304–309.

Gur, R. E., & Pearlson, G. D. (1993). Neuroimaging in schizophrenia research. *Schizo. Bull., 19,* 337–353.

Guralnick, M. J. (1998). Effectiveness of early intervention for vulnerable children: A developmental perspective. *Amer. J. Ment. Retard., 102*(4), 319–345.

Gurvits, I. G., Koenigsberg, H. W., & Siever, L. J. (2000). Neurotransmitter dysfunction in patients with borderline personality disorder. *Psychiat. Clin. N. Amer., 23*(1), 27–40.

Gutheil, T. G. (1999). A confusion of tongues: Competence, insanity, psychiatry, and the law. *Psychiat. Serv., 50*(6), 767–773.

HEW (Health Education and Welfare). (1976). *Even my kids didn't know I was an alcoholic: An interview with Dick Van Dyke* (ADM 76–348). Washington, DC: U.S. Government Printing Office.

Haaga, D. A. F., & Beck, A. T. (1992). Cognitive therapy. In E. S. Paykel (Ed.), *Handbook of affective disorders.* New York: Guilford.

Hackenberg, T. D. (1998). Laboratory methods in human behavioral ecology. In K. A. Lattal, M. Perone, et al. (Eds.), *Handbook of research methods in human operant behavior. Applied clinical psychology.* New York: Plenum Press.

Hackerman, F., Buccino, D., Gallucci, G., & Schmidt, C. W., Jr. (1996). The effect of a split in WAIS-R VIQ and PIQ scores on patients with cognitive impairment and psychiatric illness. *J. Neuropsych. Clin. Neurosci. 8,* 85–87.

Hackman, R. M., Stern, J. S., & Gerschwin, M. E. (2000). Hypnosis and asthma: A critical review. *J. Asthma, 37*(1), 1–15.

Hadley, S. W., & Strupp, H. H. (1976). Contemporary views of negative effects in psychotherapy: An integrated account. *Arch. Gen. Psychiat., 33*(1), 1291–1302.

Hafner, H., & an der Heiden, W. (1988). The mental health care system in transition: A study in organization, effectiveness, and costs of complementary care for schizophrenic patients. In C. N. Stefanis & A. D. Rabavilis (Eds.), *Schizophrenia: Recent biosocial developments.* New York: Human Sciences Press.

Hage, J. J., & Bouman, F. G. (1992). Silicone genital prosthesis for female-to-male transsexuals. *Plastic Reconstructive Surgery, 90*(3), 516–519.

Haight, B. K., Michel, Y., & Hendrix, S. (1998). Life review: Preventing despair in newly relocated nursing home residents: Short- and long-term effects. *Inter. J. Aging Human Dev., 47*(2), 119–142.

Halaas, J. L., Gajiwala, K. F., Maffei, M., Cohen, S. L., et al. (1995). Weight-reducing effects of the plasma protein encoded by the obese gene. *Science, 269,* 543–546.

Hale, C. A., & Borkowski, J. G. (1991). Attention, memory and cognition. In J. L. Matson & J. A. Mulick (Eds.), *Handbook of mental retardation.* New York: Pergamon Press.

Hale, E. (1983, April 17). Inside the divided mind. *New York Times Magazine,* pp. 100–106.

Haliburn, J. (2000). Reasons for adolescent suicide attempts. *J. Amer. Acad. Child Adol. Psychiat., 39*(1), 13–14.

Hall, C. (1997, March 17). It's not only the string section that's highly strung. *Electronic Telegraph.*

Hall, L., with L. Cohn. (1980). *Eat without fear.* Santa Barbara, CA: Gurze.

Hall, N. W., & Zigler, E. (1997). Drug-abuse prevention efforts for young children: A review and critique of existing programs. *Amer. J. Orthopsychiat., 67*(1), 134–143.

Hall, S. M., Tunstall, C., Rugg, D., et al. (1985). Nicotine gum and behavioral treatment in smoking cessation. *J. Cons. Clin. Psychol., 53,* 256–258.

Hall, W., & Solowij, N. (1997). Long-term cannabis use and mental health. *Brit. J. Psychiat., 171,* 107–108.

Hallam, R. S., & Rachman, S. (1976). Current status of aversion therapy. In M. Hersen, R. Eisler, & P. Miller (Eds.), *Progress in behavior modification* (Vol. 2). New York: Academic Press.

Halmi, K. A. (1985). Behavioral management for anorexia nervosa. In D. M. Garner & P. E. Garfinkel (Eds.), *Handbook of psychotherapy for anorexia nervosa and bulimia.* New York: Guilford.

Halmi, K. A. (1985). Classification of the eating disorders. *J. Psychiatr. Res., 19,* 113–119.

Halmi, K. A. (1995). Current concepts and definitions. In G. Szmukler, C. Dare, & J. Treasure (Eds.), *Handbook of eating disorders: Theory, treatment and research.* Chichester, England: Wiley.

Halmi, K. A., Agras, W. S., Kaye, W. H., & Walsh, B. T. (1994). Evaluation of pharmacologic treatments in eating disorders. In R. F. Prien & D. S. Robinson (Eds.), *Clinical evaluation of psychotropic drugs: Principles and guidelines.* New York: Raven Press, Ltd.

Halmi, K. A., Eckert, E., Marchik, P. A., et al. (1991). Comorbidity of psychiatric diagnoses in anorexia nervosa. *Arch. Gen. Psychiat., 48,* 712–718.

Halmi, K. A., Sunday, S. R., Puglisi, A., et al. (1989). Hunger and satiety in anorexia and bulimia nervosa. *Ann. NY Acad. Sci., 575,* 431–445.

Halperin, J. M., & McKay, K. E. (1998). Psychological testing for child and adolescent psychiatrists: A review of the past 10 years. *J. Amer. Acad. Child Adol. Psychiat., 37*(6), 575–584.

Halstead, W. C. (1947). *Brain and intelligence: A quantitative study of the frontal lobes.* Chicago: University of Chicago.

Hamer, D. H., Hu, S., Magnuson, V. L., Hu, N., et al. (1993). A linkage between DNA markers on the X chromosome and male sexual orienation. *Science, 261,* 321–327.

Hamilton, N. (1991). Intake and diagnosis of drug-dependent women. In *National Conference on Drug Abuse Research and Practice Conference highlights.* Rockville, MD: National Institute on Drug Abuse.

Hamilton, S., Rothbart, M., & Dawes, R. N. (1986). *Sex Roles, 15*(5–6), 269–274.

Hammen, C. (1999). The emergence of an interpersonal approach to depression. In T. Joiner, J. C. Coyne, et al. (Eds.), *The interactional nature of depression: Advances in interpersonal approaches.* Washington, DC: American Psychological Association.

Hammen, C. L., & Glass, D. R. (1975). Expression, activity, and evaluation of reinforcement. *J. Abnorm. Psychol., 84*(6), 718–721.

Hammen, C. L., & Krantz, S. (1976). Effect of success and failure on depressive cognitions. *J. Abnorm. Psychol., 85*(8), 577–588.

Hammen, C., Gitlin, M., & Altshuler, L. (2000). Predictors of work adjustment in bipolar I patients: A naturalistic longitudinal follow-up. *J. Cons. Clin. Psychol., 68*(2), 220–225.

Hammond, K. R., & Summers, D. A. (1965). A cognitive dependence on linear and non-linear cues. *Psychol. Rev., 72,* 215–224.

Hancock, L. N. (1996, March 18). Mother's little helper. *Newsweek,* pp. 51–56.

Handler, L. (1998). Teaching and learning the interpretation of the Wechsler Intelligence Tests as personality instruments. In L. Handler, M. J. Hilsenroth, et al. (Eds.), *Teaching and learning personality assessment.* The LEA series in personality and clinical psychology. Mahwah, NJ: Erlbaum.

Hankin, B. L., & Abramson, L. Y. (1999). Development of gender differences in depression: Description and possible explanations. *Ann. Med., 31*(6), 372–379.

Hankin, B. L., Abramson, L. Y., Moffitt, T. E., Silva, P. A., McGee, R., & Angell, K. E. (1998). Development of depression from preadolescence to young adulthood: Emerging gender differences in a 10-year longitudinal study. *J. Abnorm. Psychol., 197*(1), 128–140.

Hankins, G. C., Vera, M. I., Barnard, G. W., & Herkov, M. J. (1994). Patient-therapist sexual involvement: A review of clinical and research data. *Bull. Amer. Acad. Psychiat. Law., 22*(1), 109–126.

Hanson, K. M., Louie, C. E., Van Male, L. M., Pugh, A. O., Karl, C., Muhlenbrook, L., Lilly, R. L., & Hagglund, K. J. (1999). Involving the future: The need to consider the views of psychologists-in-training regarding prescription privileges for psychologists. *Profess. Psychol.: Res. Pract., 30*(2), 203–208.

Hantula, D. A., & Reilly, N. A. (1996). Reasonable accommodation for employees with mental disabilities: A mandate for effective supervision? *Behav. Sci. Law, 14,* 107–120.

Happé, F. G. E. (1995). The role of age and verbal ability in the theory of mind task performance of subjects with autism. *Child Dev., 66,* 843–855.

Happé, F. G. E. (1997). Central coherence and theory of mind in autism: Reading homographs in context. *Brit. J. Dev. Psychol., 15,* 1–12.

Harding, C. M., Zubin, J., & Strauss, J. S. (1992). Chronicity in schizophrenia: Revisited. *Brit. J. Psychiat., 161*(Suppl. 18), 27–37.

Hare, R. D. (1978). Electrodermal and cardiovascular correlates of sociopathy. In R. D. Hare & D. Shalling (Eds.), *Psychopathic behaviour: Approaches to research.* New York: Wiley.

Hare, R. D. (1980). A research scale for the assessment of psychopathy in criminal populations. *Pers. Individ. Diff., 1*(2), 111–119.

Hare, R. D. (1982). Psychopathy and physiological activity during anticipation of an aversive stimulus in a distraction paradigm. *Psychophysiology, 19*(3), 266–271.

Hare, R. D. (1993). *Without conscience: The disturbing world of the psychopaths among us.* New York: Pocket Books.

Hargrave, G. E., Hiatt, D., Ogard, E. M., & Karr, C. (1994). Comparison of MMPI and MMPI-2 for a sample of peace officers. *Psychol. Assess., 6,* 27–32.

Hargreaves, R. J., & Shepheard, S. L. (1999). Pathophysiology of migraine—New insights. *Canad. J. Neurol. Sci., 26*(Suppl. 3), S12–S19.

Harkavy, J. M., & Asnis, G. (1985). Suicide attempts in adolescence: Prevalence and implications. *N. Engl. J. Med., 313,* 1290–1291.

Harlow, H. F., & Harlow, M. K. (1965). The affectional systems. In A. Schrier, H. Harlow, & F. Stollnitz, *Behavior of nonhuman primates* (Vol. 2). New York: Academic Press.

Harrington, R. C., Fudge, H., Rutter, M. L., Bredenkamp, D., Groothues, C., & Pridham, J. (1993). Child and adult depression: A test of continuities with data from a family study. *Brit. J. Psychiat., 162,* 627–633.

Harris, A., Ayers, T., & Leek, M. R. (1985). Auditory span of apprehension deficits in schizophrenia. *J. Nerv. Ment. Dis., 173*(11), 650–657.

Harris, E. C., & Barraclough, B. (1997). Suicide as an outcome for mental disorders. *Brit. J. Psychiat., 170,* 205–228.

Harris, E. C., & Barraclough, B. (1998). Excess mortality of mental disorder. *Brit. J. Psychiat., 173,* 11–53.

Harris, F. C., & Lahey, B. B. (1982). Subject reactivity in direct observation assessment: A review and critical analysis. *Clin. Psychol. Rev., 2,* 523–538.

Harris, G., Rice, M., & Cormier, C. (1991). Length of detention in matched groups of insanity acquittees and convicted offenders. *International Journal of Law and Psychiatry, 14,* 223–236.

Harris, L. M., & Menzies, R. G. (1996). Origins of specific fears: A comparison of associative and non-associative accounts. *Anxiety, 2,* 248–250.

Harris, S. (1999, June 22). Schizophrenia drugs often out of reach. *USA Today.*

Harris, S. L. (1995). Autism. In M. Hersen & R. T. Ammerman, *Advanced abnormal psychology.* Hillsdale, NJ: Erlbaum.

Harris, S. L. (2000). Pervasive developmental disorders: The spectrum of autism. In M. Hersen, R. T. Ammerman, et al. (Eds.), *Advanced abnormal child psychology* (2nd ed.). Mahwah, NJ: Erlbaum.

Harris, S. L., & Milch, R. E. (1981). Training parents as behavior modifiers for their autistic children. *Clin. Psychol. Rev., 1,* 49–63.

Harrow, M., et al. (1988). A longitudinal study of thought disorder in manic patients. *Arch. Gen. Psychiat., 43*(8), 781–785.

Hart, B. (1993). Battered women and the criminal justice system. Special Issue: The impact of arrest on domestic assault. *Amer. Behav. Sci., 36*(5), 624–638.

Hart, B. (1993). The legal road to freedom. In M. Hansen & M. Harway (Eds.), *Battering and family therapy: A feminist perspective.* Newbury Park, CA: Sage.

Hart, K., & Kenny, M. E. (1995, August). *Adherence to the superwoman ideal and eating disorder symptoms among college women.* Paper presented at the American Psychological Association, New York.

Hart, S. N., & Brassard, M. R. (1987). A major threat to children's mental health: Psychological maltreatment. *Amer. Psychologist, 42*(2), 160–165.

Hart, S. N., & Brassard, M. R. (1991). Psychological maltreatment: Progress achieved. *Developmental Psychopathology, 3*(1), 61–70.

Harter, S., & Marold, D. B. (1994). Psychosocial risk factors contributing to adolescent suicidal ideation. In G. G. Naom & S. Borst (Eds.), *Children, youth, and suicide: Developmental perspectives.* New directions for child development, No. 64. San Francisco: Jossey-Bass.

Hartmann, U., & Langer, D. (1993). Combination of psychosexual therapy and intrapenile injections in the treatment of erectile dysfunctions: Rationale and predictors of outcome. *J. Sex Educ. Ther., 19,* 1–12.

Hartung, C. M., & Widiger, T. A. (1998). Gender differences in the diagnosis of mental disorders: Conclusions and controversies of the DSM-IV. *Psychol. Bull., 123*(3), 260–278.

Harvard School of Public Health (1995). *Binge drinking on American college campuses: A new look at an old problem.* Boston.

Harvey, E. (1999). Short-term and long-term effects of early parental employment on children of the National Longitudinal Survey of Youth. *Dev. Psychol., 35*(2), 445–459.

Hasin, D., Endicott, J., & Lewis, C. (1985). Alcohol and drug abuse in patients with affective syndromes. *Comprehen. Psychiat., 26,* 283–295.

Hassan, R. (1998). One hundred years of Emile Durkheim's Suicide: A Study in Sociology. *Austral. New Zeal. J. Psychiat., 32*(2), 168–171.

Hatonen, T., Alila, A., & Laakso, M. L. (1996). Exogenous melatonin fails to counteract the light-induced phase delay of human melatonin rhythm. *Brain Res., 710*(1–2), 125–130.

Haworth-Hoeppner, S. (2000). The critical shapes of body image: The role of culture and family in the production of eating disorders. *J. Marr. Fam., 62*(1), 212–227.

Hawton, K. (1986). *Suicide and attempted suicide among children and adolescents.* Beverly Hills, CA: Sage.

Hawton, K. (1998). Why has suicide increased in young males? *Crisis, 19*(3), 119–124.

Hawton, K., Appleby, L., Platt, S., Foster, T., Cooper, J., Malmberg, A., & Simkin, S. (1998). The psychological autopsy approach to studying suicide: A review of methodological issues. *J. Affect. Disorders, 50*(2–3), 269–276.

Hawton, K., Fagg, J., Simkin, S., Bale, E., & Bond, A. (2000). Deliberate self-harm in adolescents in Oxford, 1985–1995. *J. Adolescence, 23*(1), 47–55.

Haxby, J. V., Ungerleider, L. G., Horwitz, B., Maisog, J. M., Rapoport, S. I., & Grady, C. L. (1996). Face encoding and recognition in the human brain. *Proc. Nat. Acad. Sci. USA, 93*(2), 922–927.

Hay, L. R., Hay, W. R., & Angle, H. V. (1977). The reactivity of self-recording: A case report of a drug abuser. *Behav. Ther., 8*(5), 1004–1007.

Hayes, L. M., & Rowan, J. R. (1988). *National study of jail suicides: Seven years later.* Alexandria, VA: National Center for Institutions and Alternatives.

Haynes, S. G., Feinleib, M., & Kannel, W. B. (1980). The relationship of psychosocial factors to coronary heart disease in the Framingham study: III. Eight-year incidence of coronary heart disease. *Amer. J. Epidemiol., 111,* 37–58.

Haynes, S. N., & O'Brien, W. H. (2000). *Principles and practice of behavioral assessment.* New York: Kluwer Academic/Plenum Press.

Haynes, S. N., Nelson, K., & Blaine, D. D. (1999). Psychometric issues in assessment research. In P. C. Kendall, J. N. Butcher, et al. (Eds.), *Handbook of research methods in clinical psychology* (2nd ed.). New York: Wiley.

Hayward, C., Killen, J. D., Hammer, L. D., Litt, I. F., Wilson, D. M., Simmonds, B., & Taylor, C. B. (1992). Pubertal stage and panic attack history in sixth- and seventh-grade girls. *Amer. J. Psychiat., 149,* 1239–1243.

Hayward, M. D., & Taylor, J. E. (1965). A schizophrenic patient describes the action of intensive psychotherapy. *Psychiat. Quart., 30.*

Haywood, T. W., Kravitz, H. M., Grossman, L. S., Cavanaugh, J. L., et al. (1995). Predicting the "revolving door" phenomenon among patients with schizophrenia, schizoaffective, and affective disorders. *Amer. J. Psychiat., 152*(6), 856–861.

Hazell, P., & Lewin, T. (1993). Friends of adolescent suicide attempters and completers. *J. Amer. Acad. Child Adol. Psychiat., 32*(1), 76–81.

He, H., & Richardson, J. S. (1995). A pharmacological, pharmacokinetic and clinical overview of risperidone, a new antipsychotic that blocks serotonin 5-HT2 and dopamine D2 receptors. *Inter. Clin. Psychopharmacology, 10*(1), 19–30.

Healy, D., & Williams, J. M. (1988). Dysrhythmia, dysphoria, and depression: The interaction of learned helplessness and circadian dysrhythmia in the pathogenesis of depression. *Psychol. Bull., 103*(2), 163–178.

Heather, N., Winton, M., & Rollnick, S. (1982). An empirical test of "a cultural delusion of alcoholics." *Psychol. Rep., 50*(2), 379–382.

Heaton, R. K., Baade, L. E., & Johnson, K. L. (1978). Neuropsychological test results associated with psychiatric disorders in adults. *Psychol. Bull., 85,* 141–162.

Hedaya, R. J. (1996). *Understanding biological psychiatry.* New York: Norton.

Heflinger, C. A., Cook, V. J., & Thackrey, M. (1987). Identification of mental retardation by the System of Multicultural Pluralistic Assessment: Nondiscriminatory or nonexistent? *J. School Psychol., 25*(2), 177–183.

Heilbrun, A. B., & Witt, N. (1990). Distorted body image as a risk factor in anorexia nervosa: Replication and clarification. *Psychol. Rep., 66*(2), 407–416.

Heiman, J. R. (1977). A psychophysiological exploration of sexual-arousal patterns in females and males. *Psychophysiology, 14,* 266–274.

Heiman, J. R., & Grafton-Becker, V. (1989). Orgasmic disorders in women. In S. R. Leiblum & R. C. Rosen (Eds.), *Principles and practice of sex therapy: Update for the 1990's.* New York: Guilford.

Heiman, J. R., & LoPiccolo, J. (1988). *Becoming orgasmic: A personal and sexual growth program for women.* New York: Prentice Hall.

Heiman, J. R., Gladue, B. A., Roberts, C. W., & LoPiccolo, J. (1986). Historical and current factors discriminating sexually functional from sexually dysfunctional married couples. *J. Marital Fam. Ther., 12*(2), 163–174.

Heiman, J. R., LoPiccolo, L., & LoPiccolo, J. (1981). Treatment of sexual dysfunction. In A. S. Gurman & D. P. Kniskern (Eds.), *Handbook of family therapy.* New York: Brunner/Mazel.

Heimberg, R. G., Dodge, C. S., Hope, D. A., Kennedy, C. R., et al. (1990). Cognitive behavioral group treatment for social phobia: Comparison with a credible placebo control. *Cog. Ther. Res., 14*(1), 1–23.

Heimberg, R. G., Liebowitz, M. R., Hope, D. A., & Schneier, F. R. (1995). *Social phobia: Diagnosis, assessment, and treatment.* New York: Guilford.

Heimberg, R. G., Liebowitz, M. R., Hope, D. A., Schneier, F. R., Holt, C. S., Welkowitz, L. A., Juster, H. R., Campeas, R., Bruch, M. A., Cloitre, M., Fallon, B., & Klein, D. F. (1998). Cognitive behavioral group therapy vs. phenelzine therapy for social phobia: 12–week outcome. *Arch. Gen. Psychiat., 55*(12), 1133–1141.

Heimberg, R. G., Salzman, D. G., Holt, C. S., & Blendall, K. (1991). *Cognitive behavioral treatment for social phobia: Effectiveness at five-year follow-up.* Manuscript submitted for publication.

Heimberg, R. G., Salzman, D. G., Holt, C. S., & Blendall, K. A. (1993). Cognitive-behavioral group treatment for social phobia: Effectiveness at five-year follow-up. *Cog. Ther. Res., 17,* 325–339.

Heinrichs, D. W., & Carpenter, W. T., Jr. (1983). The coordination of family therapy with other treatment modalities for schizophrenia. In W. McFarlane (Ed.), *Family therapy in schizophrenia.* New York: Guilford.

Heise, L., & Chapman, J. R. (1990). Reflections on a movement: The U.S. battle against women abuse. In M. Schuler (Ed.), *Freedom from violence: Women's strategies round the world.* OEF International.

Heller, K. (1996). Coming of age of prevention science: Comments on the 1994 National Institute of Mental Health–Institute of Medicine Prevention Reports. *Amer. Psychologist, 51*(11), 1123–1127.

Hellerstein, D. J., Rosenthal, R. N., & Miner, C. R. (1995). A prospective study of integrated outpatient treatment for substance-abusing schizophrenic patients. *Amer. J. Addict., 4*(1), 33–42.

Hellmich, N. (1995, July 21). Power rangers: Negative or empowering? *USA Today,* p. 4D

Hellström, K., & Öst, L.-G. (1996). Prediction of outcome in the treatment of specific phobia. A cross validation study. *Behav. Res. Ther., 34*(5/6), 403–411.

Helms, J. E. (1992). Why is there no study of cultural equivalence in standardized cognitive ability testing? *Amer. Psychologist, 47*(9), 1083–1101.

Helzer, J. E., Burnam, A., & McEvoy, L. T. (1991). Alcohol abuse and dependence. In L. N. Robins & D. S. Regier (Eds.), *Psychiatric disorders in America: The Epidemiological Catchment Area Study.* New York: Free Press.

Hendin, H. (1995). Assisted suicide, euthanasia, and suicide prevention: The implications of the Dutch experience. *Suic. Life-Threat. Behav., 25*(1), 193–205.

Hendin, H. (1999). Suicide, assisted suicide, and euthanasia. In D.G. Jacobs (Ed.), *The Harvard Medical School guide to suicide assessment and intervention.* San Francisco: Jossey-Bass.

Hendin, H. (1999). Suicide, assisted suicide, and medical illness. *J. Clin. Psychiat., 60*(Suppl. 2), 46–50.

Hendren, J. (1999, April 15). Prescription errors blamed on pharmaceutical name game. *Nando Times.*

Henning, C. W., Crabtree, C. R., & Baum, D. (1998). Mental health CPR: Peer contracting as a response to potential suicide in adolescents. *Arch. Suic. Res., 4*(2), 169–187.

Henriksson, M. M., Isometsa, E. T., Hietanen, P. S., Aro, H. M., & Lonnqvist, J. K. (1995). Research report. Mental disorders in cancer suicides. *J. Affect. Disorders, 36,* 11–20.

Hepple, J., & Quinton, C. (1997). One hundred cases of attempted suicide in the elderly. *Brit. J. Psychiat., 171,* 42–46.

Herek, G. M., & Capitanio, J. P. (1993). Public reaction to AIDS in the U.S.: A 2nd generation of stigma. *Amer. J. Pub. Hlth., 83*(4), 574–577.

Herek, G. M., & Glunt, E. K. (1988). An epidemic of stigma: Public reactions to AIDS. *Amer. Psychologist, 43*(11), 886–891.

Herman, D., Opler, L., Felix, A., Valencia, E., Wyatt, R. J., & Susser, E. (2000). A critical time intervention with mentally ill homeless men: Impact on psychiatric symptoms. *J. Nerv. Ment. Dis., 188*(3), 135–140.

Hermann, C., Kim, M., & Blanchard, E. B. (1995). Behavioral and prophylactic pharmacological intervention studies of pediatric migraine: An exploratory meta-analysis. *Pain, 60*(3), 239–255.

Hermesh, H., Aizenberg, D., Weizman, A., Lapidot, M., Mayor, C., & Munitz, H. (1992). Risk for definite neuroleptic malignant syndrome: A prospective study in 223 consecutive inpatients. *Brit. J. Psychiat., 161,* 254–257.

Hersen, M., Bellack, A. S., Himmelhoch, J. M., & Thase, M. E. (1984). Effects of social skill training, amitriptyline, and psychotherapy in unipolar depressed women. *Behav. Ther., 15,* 21–40.

Hersen, M., & Van Hasselt, V. B. (Eds.) (1998). *Basic interviewing: A practical guide for counselors and clinicians.* Mahwah, NJ: Erlbaum.

Hershman, D. J., & Lieb, J. (1998). *Manic depression and creativity.* Amherst, NY: Prometheus Books.

Hertel, P. (1998). Relation between rumination and impaired memory in dysphoric moods. *J. Abnorm. Psychol., 107*(1), 166–172.

Herz, L. R., Volicer, L., Ross, V., & Rhéaume, Y. (1992). A single-case-study method for treating resistiveness in patients with Alzheimer's disease. *Hosp. Comm. Psychiat., 43*(7), 720–724.

Herz, M .I., Lamberti, J. S., Mintz, J., Scott, R., O'Dell, S. P., McCartan, L., & Nix, G. (2000). A program for relapse prevention in schizophrenia: A controlled study. *Arch. Gen. Psychiat., 57*(3), 277–283.

Herz, R. S. (1999). Caffeine effects on mood and memory. *Behav. Res. Ther., 37*(9), 869–879.

Herzog, D. B., Dorer, D. J., Keel, P. K., Selwin, S. E., Ekeblad, E. R., Flores, A. T., Greenwood, D. N., Burwell, R. A., & Keller, M. B. (1999). Recovery and relapse in anorexia and bulimia nervosa: A 7.5-year follow-up study. *J. Amer. Acad. Child Adol. Psychiat., 38*(7), 829–837.

Hess, N. (1995). Cancer as a defence against depressive pain. University College Hospital/Middlesex Hospital Psychotherapy Department. *Psychoanalytic Psychother., 9*(2), 175–184.

Hester, R. K. (1995). Behavioral self-control training. In R. K. Hester & W. R. Miller (Eds.), *Handbook of alcoholism treatment approaches: Effective alternatives* (2nd ed.). Boston: Allyn & Bacon.

Heston, L. L. (1992). *Mending minds: A guide to the new psychiatry of depression, anxiety, and other serious mental disorders.* New York: W. H. Freeman.

Hewitt, P. L., Newton, J., Flett, G. L., & Callander, L. (1997). Perfectionism and suicide ideation in adolescent psychiatric patients. *J. Abnorm. Child Psychol., 25*(2), 95–101.

Hibma, M., & Griffin, J. F. T. (1994). Brief communication: The influence of maternal separation on humoral and cellular immunity in farmed deer. *Brain, Behav., Immun. 8,* 80–85.

Hickie, I., Pols, R. G., Koschera, A., & Davenport, T. (2000). Why are somatoform disorders so poorly recognized and treated? In G. Andrews, S. Henderson, et al. (Eds.), *Unmet need in psychiatry: Problems, resources, responses.* New York: Cambridge University Press.

Hiday, V. A. (1992). Coercion in civil commitment: Process, preferences, and outcome. *Inter. J. Law Psychiat., 15*(4), 359–377.

Hiday, V. A. (1999). Mental illness and the criminal justice system. In A. V. Horwitz & T. L. Scheid (Eds.), *A handbook for the study of mental health: Social contexts, theories, and systems.* Cambridge, England: Cambridge University Press.

Higgins, G. A., Large, C. H., Rupniak, H. T., & Barnes, J. C. (1997). Apolipoprotein E and Alzheimer's disease: A review of recent studies. *Pharmacol. Biochem. Behav., 56*(4), 675–685.

Higgins, S. T., Budney, A. J., Bickel, W. K., Hughes, J., Foerg, F., & Badger, G. (1993). Achieving cocaine abstinence with a behavioral approach. *Amer. J. Psychiat., 150*(5), 763–769.

Higuchi, S., Suzuki, K., Yamada, K., Parrish, K., & Kono, H. (1993). Alcoholics with eating disorders: Prevalence and clinical course, A study from Japan. *Brit. J. Psychiat., 162,* 403–406.

Hilgard, E. R. (1977). Controversies over consciousness and the rise of cognitive psychology. *Austral. Psychologist, 12*(1), 7–26.

Hilgard, E. R. (1987). Research advances in hypnosis: Issues and methods. *Inter. J. Clin. Exp. Hyp., 35,* 248–264.

Hilgard, E. R. (1992). Dissociation and theories of hypnosis. In E. Fromm & M. R. Nash (Eds.), *Contemporary hypnosis research.* New York: Guilford.

Hill, A. J., & Franklin, J. A. (1998). Mothers, daughters and dieting: Investigating the transmission of weight control. *Brit. J. Clin. Psychol., 37,* 3–13.

Hill, A. J., & Robinson, A. (1991). Dieting concerns have a functional effect on the behaviour of nine-year-old girls. *Brit. J. Clin. Psychol., 30*(3), 265–267.

Hill, S. Y., & Muka, D. (1996). Childhood psychopathology in children from families of alcoholic female probands. *J. Amer. Acad. Child. Adol. Psychiat., 35*(6), 725–733.

Hiller, W., Rief, W., & Fichter, M. M. (1995). Further evidence for a broader concept of somatization disorder using the Somatic Symptom Index. *Psychosomatics, 36*(3), 285–294.

Hinrichsen, G.A. (1999). Interpersonal psychotherapy for late-life depression In M. Duffy (Ed.), *Handbook of counseling and psychotherapy with older adults.* New York: Wiley.

Hinshaw, S. P. (1991). Stimulant medication and the treatment of aggression in children with attentional deficits. *J. Clin. Child Psychol., 20,* 301–312.

Hiroto, D. S. (1974). Locus of control and learned helplessness. *J. Exp. Psychol., 102*(2), 187–193.

Hirsch, S., & Leff, J. (1975). *Abnormalities in parents of schizophrenics.* Oxford: Oxford University Press.

Hirsch, S., Adams, J. K., Frank, L. R., Hudson, W., Keene, R., Krawitz-Keene, G., Richman, D., & Roth, R. (Eds.). (1974). *Madness: Network news reader.* San Francisco: Glide Publications.

Hirsch, S., Bowen, J., Emami, J., Cramer, P., Jolley, A., Haw, C., & Dickinson, M. (1996). A one year prospective study of the effect of life events and medication in the aetiology of schizophrenic relapse. *Brit. J. Psychiat., 168,* 49–56.

Hirschfeld, D. R., Rosenbaum, J. F., Biederman, J., Bolduc, E. A., Farone, S. V., Snidman, N., Reznick, J. S., & Kagan, J. (1992). Stable behavioral inhibition and its association with anxiety disorder. *J. Amer. Acad. Child Adol. Psychiat., 31,* 103–111.

Hirschfeld, R. M. (1992). The clinical course of panic disorder and agoraphobia. In G. D. Burrows, S. M. Roth, & R. Noyes, Jr. (Eds.), *Handbook of anxiety* (Vol. 5). Oxford: Elsevier.

Hirschfeld, R. M. (1996). Placebo response in the treatment of panic disorder. *Bull. Menninger Clin., 60*(2, Suppl. A), A76–A86.

Hirschfeld, R. M. (1999). Efficacy of SSRIs and newer antidepressants in severe depression: Comparison with TCAs. *J. Clin. Psychiat., 60*(5), 326–335.

Hirschfeld, R. M. (1999). Management of sexual side effects of antidepressant therapy. *J. Clin. Psychiat., 60*(Suppl. 14), 27–30.

Hirschfeld, R. M. (1999). Personality disorders and depression: Comorbidity. *Depress. Anx., 10*(4), 142–146.

Hirschfeld, R. M., & Davidson, L. (1988). Clinical risk factors for suicide. [Special issue]. *Psychiatr. Ann., 18*(11), 628–635.

Hirschfeld, R. M., & Davidson, L. (1988). Risk factors for suicide. In A. J. Frances & R. E. Hales (Eds.), *American Psychiatric Press review of psychiatry* (Vol. 7). Washington, DC: American Psychiatric Press.

Hirschfeld, R. M., & Russell, J. M. (1997). Assessment and treatment of suicidal patients. *N. Engl. J. Med., 337,* 910–915.

Hlastala, S. A., Frank, E., Mallinger, A. G., Thase, M. E., Ritenour, A. M., & Kupfer, D. J. (1997). Bipolar depression: An underestimated treatment challenge. *Depress. Anx., 5,* 73–83,

Ho, T. P., Hung, S. F., Lee, C. C., Chung, K. F., et al. (1995). Characteristics of youth suicide in Hong Kong. *Soc. Psychiat. Psychiatr. Epidemiol., 30*(3), 107–112.

Hoagwood, K., Kelleher, K. J., Feil, M., & Comer, D. M. (2000). Treatment services for children with ADHD: A national perspective. *J. Amer. Acad. Child Adol. Psychiat., 39*(2), 198–206.

Hobbs, F. B. (1997). The elderly population. *U.S. Census Bureau: The official statistics.* Washington, DC: U.S. Census Bureau.

Hobson, C. J., Kamen, J., Szostek, J., Nethercut, C. M., Tiedmann, J. W., & Wojnarowicz, S. (1998). Stressful life events: A revision and update of the Social Readjustment Rating Scale. *Inter. J. Stress Manag., 5*(1), 1–23.

Hobson, J. A., & McCarley, R. W. (1977). The brain as a dream state generator: An activation-synthesis hypothesis of the dream process. *Amer. J. Psychiat., 134*(12), 1335–1348.

Hochhauser, M. (1999). Informed consent and patient's rights documents: A right, a rite, or a rewrite? *Ethics Behav., 9*(1), 1–20.

Hodgins, S., Mednick, S. A., Brennan, P. A., Schulsinger, F., & Engberg, M. (1996). Mental disorder and crime. *Arch. Gen. Psychiat., 53,* 489–496.

Hodgson, R. J., & Rachman, S. (1972). The effects of contamination and washing in obsessional patients. *Behav. Res. Ther., 10,* 111–117.

Hoebel, B. G., & Teitelbaum, P. (1966). Weight regulation in normal and hypothalamic hyperphagic rats. *J. Compar. Physiol. Psychol., 61*(2), 189–193.

Hoehn-Saric, R. (1998). Generalized anxiety disorder: Guidelines for diagnosis and treatment. *CNS Drugs, 9*(2), 85–98.

Hogan, R. A. (1968). The implosive technique. *Behav. Res. Ther., 6,* 423–431.

Hogarty, G. E., Greenwald, D., Ulrich, R. F., Kornblith, S. J., DiBarry, A. L., Cooley, S., Carter, M., & Flesher, S. (1997). Three-year trials of personal therapy among schizophrenic patients living with or independent of family: II. Effects on adjustment of patient. *Amer. J. Psychiat., 154*(11), 1514–1524.

Hogarty, G. E., et al. (1974). Drug and sociotherapy in the aftercare of schizophrenic patients: II. Two-year relapse rates. *Arch. Gen. Psychiat., 31*(5), 609–618.

Hogarty, G. E., et al. (1986). Family psychoeducation, social skills training, and maintenance chemotherapy in the aftercare treatment of schizophrenia: I. One-year effects of a controlled study on relapse and expressed emotion. *Arch. Gen. Psychiat., 43*(7), 633–642.

Hoge, R. D., Andrews, D. A., & Leschied, A. W. (1996). An investigation of risk and protective factors in a sample of youthful offenders. *J. Child Psychiat., 37*(4), 419–424.

Hohagen, F., Winkelmann, G., Rasche-Raeuchle, H., Hand, I., Koenig, A., Muenchau, N., Hiss, H., Geiger-Kabisch, C., Kaeppler, C., Schramm, P., Rey, E., Aldenhoff, J., & Berger, M. (1998). Combination of behaviour therapy with fluvoxamine in comparison with behaviour therapy and placebo: Results of a multicentre study. *Brit. J. Psychiat., 173*(Suppl. 35), 71–78.

Hokkanen, L., Launes, J., Vataja, R., Valanne, L., et al. (1995). Isolated retrograde amnesia for autobiographical material associated with acute left temporal lobe encephalitis. *Psychol. Med., 25*(1), 203–208.

Holcomb, H. H., Cascella, N. G., Thaker, G. K., Medoff, D. R., Dannals, R. F., & Tamminga, C. A. (1996). Functional sites of neuroleptic drug action in the human brain: PET/FDG studies with and without Haloperidol. *Amer. J. Psychiat., 153,* 41–49.

Holder, H., Longabaugh, R., Miller, W., et al. (1991). The cost effectiveness of treatment for alcoholism: A first approximation. *J. Stud. Alc., 52,* 517–540.

Holinger, P. C., & Offer, D. (1982). Prediction of adolescent suicide: A population model. *Amer. J. Psychiat., 139,* 302–307.

Holinger, P. C., & Offer, D. (1991). Sociodemographic, epidemiologic, and individual attributes. In L. Davidson & M. Linnoila (Eds.), *Risk factors for youth suicide.* New York: Hemisphere.

Holinger, P. C., & Offer, D. (1993). *Adolescent suicide.* New York: Guilford.

Holland, J. C. (1996, September). Cancer's psychological challenges. *Scientif. Amer.,* pp. 158–160.

Holland, R. L., Musch, B. C., & Hindmarch, I. (1999). Specific effects of benzodiazepines and tricyclic antidepressants in panic disorder: Comparisons of clomipramine with alprazolam SR and adinazolam SR. *Human Psychopharmacol. Clin. Exp., 14*(2), 119–124.

Hollander, E., & Aronowitz, B. R. (1999). Comorbid social anxiety and body dysmorphic disorder: Managing the complicated patient. *J. Clin. Psychiat., 60*(Suppl. 9), 27–31.

Hollander, E., Simeon, D., & Gorman, J. M. (1994). Anxiety disorders. In R. E. Hales, S. C. Yudofsky, & J. A. Talbott (Eds.), *The American Psychiatric Press textbook of psychiatry* (2nd ed.). Washington, DC: American Psychiatric Press.

Hollander, M. H. (1988). Hysteria and memory. In H. M. Pettinati (Ed.), *Hypnosis and memory.* New York: Guilford.

Hollifield, M., Paine, S., Tuttle, L., & Kellner, R. (1999). Hypochondriasis, somatization, and perceived health and utilization of health care services. *Psychosomatics, 40*(5), 380–386.

Hollifield, M., Tuttle, L., Paine, S., & Kellner, R. (1999). Hypochondriasis and somatization related to personality and attitudes toward self. *Psychosomatics, 40*(5), 387–395.

Hollon, S. D., & Beck, A. T. (1986). Research on cognitive therapies. In S. L. Garfield & A. E. Bergin (Eds.), *Handbook of psychotherapy and behavior change.* New York: Wiley.

Hollon, S. D., & Beck, A. T. (1994). Cognitive and cognitive-behavioral therapies. In A. E. Bergin & S. L. Garfiel (Eds.), *Handbook of psychotherapy and behavior change* (4th ed.). New York: Wiley.

Hollon, S. D., Shelton, R. C., & Davis, D. D. (1993). Cognitive therapy for depression: Conceptual issues and clinical efficacy. *J. Cons. Clin. Psychol., 61*(2), 270–275.

Holmes, R. M., & DeBurger, J. E. (1985). Profiles in terror: The serial murderer. *Fed. Probation, 49,* 29–34.

Holmes, T. H., & Rahe, R. H. (1967). The Social Readjustment Rating Scale. *J. Psychosom. Res., 11,* 213–218.

Holmes, T. H., & Rahe, R. H. (1989). The Social Readjustment Rating Scale. In T. H. Holmes & E. M. David (Eds.), *Life change, life events, and illness: Selected papers.* New York: Praeger.

Holmes, V. F., & Rich, C. L. (1990). Suicide among physicians. In S. J. Blumenthal & D. J. Kupfer (Eds.), *Suicide over the life cycle: Risk factors, assessment, and treatment of suicidal patients.* Washington, DC: American Psychiatry Press.

Holmes, W. C., & Slap, G. B. (1998). Sexual abuse of boys: Definition, prevalence, correlates, sequelae, and management. *JAMA, 280*(21), 1855–1862.

Holroyd, J. (1996). Hypnosis treatment of clinical pain: Understanding why hypnosis is useful. *Inter. J. Clin. Exp. Hyp., 54*(1), 33–51.

Holroyd, J. C., & Brodsky, A. M. (1977). Psychologists' attitudes and practices regarding erotic and nonerotic physical contact with patients. *Amer. Psychologist, 32,* 843–849.

Holstein, J. A. (1993). *Court-ordered insanity: Interpretive practice and involuntary commitment.* New York: Aldine de Gruyter.

Holzman, P. S. (1986). Quality of thought disorder in differential diagnosis. *Schizo. Bull., 12,* 360–372.

Honig, A., Hofman, A., Hilwig, M., Noorthoorn, E., & Ponds, R. (1995). Psychoeducation and expressed emotion in bipolar disorder: Preliminary findings. *Psychiat. Res., 56*(3), 299–301.

Honig, P. (2000). Family work. In B. Lask, R. Bryant-Waugh, et al. (Eds.), *Anorexia nervosa and related eating disorders in childhood and adolescence* (2nd ed.). Hove, England: Psychology Press/Taylor & Francis.

Honigfeld, G., Arellano, F., Sethi, J., Bianchini, A., & Schein, J. (1998). Reducing clozapine-related morbidity and mortality: 5 years of experience with the clozaril national registry. *J. Clin. Psychiat., 59*(Suppl. 3), 3–7.

Honikman, J. I. (1999). Role of self-help techniques for postpartum mood disorders. In L. J. Miller et al. (Eds.), *Postpartum mood disorders.* Washington, DC: American Psychiatric Press.

Hooley, J. M., & Hiller, J. B. (2000). Personality and expressed emotion. *J. Abnorm. Psychol., 109*(1), 40–44.

Hooley, J. M., & Teasdale, J. D. (1989). Predictors of relapse in unipolar depressives: Expressed emotions, marital distress, and perceived critcism. *J. Abnorm. Psychol., 98*(3), 229–235.

Hooley, J. M., Orley, J., & Teasdale, J. D. (1986). Levels of expressed emotion and relapse in depressed patients. *Brit. J. Psychiat., 148,* 642–647.

Hope, D. A., & Heimberg, R. G. (1993). Social phobia and social anxiety. In D. H. Barlow (Ed.), *Clinical handbook of psychological disorders: A step-by-step treatment manual* (2nd ed.). New York: Guilford.

Hopkins, J., Marcus, M., & Campbell, S. (1984). Postpartum depression: A critical review. *Psychol. Bull., 95*(3), 498–515.

Hopper, E. (1995). A psychoanalytical theory of 'drug addiction': Unconscious fantasies of homosexuality, compulsions and masturbation within the context of traumatogenic processes. *Inter. J. Psychoanal., 76*(6), 1121–1142.

Horesh, N., Apter, A., Lepkifker, E., Ratzoni, G., et al. (1995). Life events and severe anorexia nervosa in adolescence. *Acta Psychiatr. Scandin., 91*(1), 5–9.

Horgan, J. (1995, November). Gay genes, revisited. *Scientif. Amer.,* p. 26.

Horn, M. (1993, November). Memories lost and found. *U.S. News & World Report,* pp. 52–63.

Horner, A. J. (1975). Stages and processes in the development of early object relations and their associated pathologies. *Inter. Rev. Psychoanal., 2,* 95–105.

Horner, A. J. (1991). *Psychoanalytic object relations therapy.* Northvale, NJ: Jason Aronson.

Horney, K. (1937). *The neurotic personality of our time.* New York: Norton.

Hornyak, L. M., Green, J. P., et al. (Eds.). (2000). *Healing from within: The use of hypnosis in women's health care.* Dissociation, trauma, memory, and hypnosis book series. Washington, DC: American Psychological Association.

Horowitz, B. (1996, February 20). Portion sizes and fat content "out of control." *USA Today,* pp. 1A–2A.

Horowitz, J., Damato, E., Solon, L., Metzsch, G., & Gill, V. (1995). Postpartum depression: Issues in clinical assessment. *J. Perinatol., 15*(4), 268–278.

Horton, D. (1943). The functions of alcohol in primitive societies: A cross-cultural study. *Quart. J. Stud. Alcohol., 4,* 199–320.

Horton, P. C. (1992). A borderline treatment dilemma: To solace or not to solace. In D. Silver & M. Rosenbluth (Eds.), *Handbook of borderline disorders.* Madison, CT: International Universities Press.

Hou, C., Miller, B. L., Cummings, J. L., Goldberg, M., Mychack, P., Bottino, V., & Benson, D. F. (2000). Artistic savants. *Neuropsychiat. Neuropsychol. Behav. Neurol., 13*(1), 29–38.

Housman, L. M., & Stake, J. E. (1999). The current state of sexual ethics training in clinical psychology: Issues of quantity, quality and effectiveness. *Profess. Psychol.: Res. Pract., 30*(3), 302–311.

Howe, A., & Walker, C. E. (1992). Behavioral management of toilet training enuresis, encopresis. *Pediat. Clin. N. Amer., 39*(3), 413–432.

Howe, R., & Nugent, T. (1996, April 22). The gory details. *People,* pp. 91–92.

Howells, J. G., & Guirguis, W. R. (1985). *The family and schizophrenia.* New York: International Universities Press.

Howitt, D. (1995). *Paedophiles and sexual offences against children.* Chichester, England: Wiley.

Hsu, L. K. G. (1980). Outcome of anorexia nervosa: A review of literature (1954–1978). *Arch. Gen. Psychiat., 37,* 1041–1046.

Hsu, L. K. G., & Holder, D. (1986). Bulimia nervosa: Treatment and short-term outcome. *Psychol. Med., 16,* 65.

Hsu, L. K. G., Crisp, A. H., & Callender, J. S. (1992). Psychiatric diagnoses in recovered and unrecovered anorectics 22 years after onset of illness: A pilot study. *Comprehen. Psychiat., 33*(2), 123-127.

Hsu, L. K. G., Crisp, A. H., & Harding, B. (1979). Outcome of anorexia nervosa. *Lancet, 1*, 61-65.

Hu, S., Pattatucci, A. M. L., Patterson, C., Li, L., et al. (1995, November). Linkage between sexual orientation and chromosome Xq28 in males but not in females. *Nature Genetics, 11*, 248-256.

Huff, C. O. (1999). Source, recency, and degree of stress in adolescence and suicide ideation. *Adolescence, 34*(133), 81-89.

Hugdahl, K. (1995). *Psychophysiology: The mind-body perspective.* Cambridge, MA: Harvard University Press.

Hughes, J. R., Oliveto, A. H., Bickel, W. K., Higgins, S. T., & Badger, G. J. (1995). The ability of low doses of caffeine to serve as reinforcers in humans: A replication. *Exp. Clin. Psychopharmacol., 3*(4), 358-363.

Hull, J. D., et al. (1995, January 30). Special Report: The State of the Union. *Time*, pp. 53-74

Hüll, M., Berger, M., Volk, B., & Bauer, J. (1996). Occurrence of interleukin-6 in cortical plaques of Alzheimer's disease patients may precede transformation of diffuse into neuritic plaques. In R. J. Wurtman, S. Corkin, J. H. Growdon, & R. M. Nitsch (Eds.), *The neurobiology of Alzheimer's disease.* New York: New York Academy of Sciences.

Hultman, C. M., Wieselgren, I.-M., & Öhman, A. (1997). Relationships between social support, social coping and life events in the relapse of schizophrenic patients. *Scand. J. Psychol., 38*, 3-13.

Humphrey, D. H., & Dahlstrom, W. G. (1995). The impact of changing from the MMPI to the MMPI-2 on profile configurations. *J. Pers. Assess., 64*(3), 428-439.

Humphreys, K. (1996). Clinical psychologists as psychotherapists. History, future, and alternatives. *Amer. Psychologist, 51*(3), 190-197.

Humphreys, K., & Rappaport, J. (1993). From the community mental health movement to the war on drugs: A study in the definition of social problems. *Amer. Psychologist, 48*(8), 892-901.

Humphry, D., & Wickett, A. (1986). *The right to die: Understanding euthanasia.* New York: Harper & Row.

Hunicutt, C. P., & Newman, I. A. (1993). Adolescent dieting practices and nutrition knowledge. Health values. *Journal of Health Behavior, Education and Promotion, 17*(4), 35-40.

Hunt, C., & Andrews, G. (1995). Comorbidity in the anxiety disorders: The use of a life-chart approach. *J. Psychiat. Res., 29*(6), 467-480.

Huntington, D. D., & Bender, W. N. (1993). Adolescents with learning disabilities at risk: Emotional well-being, depression, suicide. *J. Learn. Disabilities, 26*(3), 159-166.

Hurlbert, D. F. (1991). The role of assertiveness in female sexuality: A comparative study between sexually assertive and sexually nonassertive women. *J. Sex Marital Ther., 17*, 183-190.

Hurlbert, D. F. (1993). A comparative study using orgasm consistency training in the treatment of women reporting hypoactive sexual desire. *J. Sex Marital Ther., 19*, 41-55.

Hurlbert, D. F., & Apt, C. (1995). The coital alignment technique and directed masturbation: A comparative study on female orgasm. *J. Sex Marital Ther., 21*(1), 21-29.

Hurlbert, D. F., White, L. C., Powell, R. D., & Apt, C. (1993). Orgasm consistency training in the treatment of women reporting hypoactive sexual desire: An outcome comparison of women-only groups and couples-only groups. *J. Behav. Ther. Exp. Psychiat., 24*(1), 3-13.

Hurley, A. D., & Hurley, F. L. (1986). Counseling and psychotherapy with mentally retarded clients: I. The initial interview. *Psych. Aspects Ment. Retard. Rev., 5*(5), 22-26.

Hurley, J. D., & Meminger, S. R. (1992). A relapse-prevention program: Effects of electromyographic training on high and low levels of state and trait anxiety. *Percept. Motor Skills, 74*(3, Pt. 1), 699-705.

Hurt, R., Offord, K., Lauger, G., Marusic, Z., et al. (1995). Cessation of long-term nicotine gum use: A prospective, randomized trial. *Addiction, 90*(3), 407-413.

Hurt, S. W., Reznikoff, M., & Clarkin, J. F. (1991). *Psychological assessment, psychiatric diagnosis, and treatment planning.* New York: Brunner/Mazel.

Husaini, B. A. (1997, January). Predictors of depression among the elderly: Racial differences over time. *Amer. J. Orthopsychiat., 67*(1), 48-58.

Hutchinson, R. L., & Little, T. J. (1985). A study of alcohol and drug usage by nine- through thirteen-year-old children in central Indiana. *J. Alcohol Drug Educ., 30*(3), 83-87.

Hwu, H. G., Yeh, E. K., & Chang, L. Y. (1989). Prevalence of psychiatric disorders in Taiwan defined by the Chinese Diagnostic Interview Schedule. *Acta Psychiatr. Scandin., 79*, 136-147.

Hyde, A. P., & Goldman, C. R. (1992). Use of a multi-modal family group in the comprehensive treatment and rehabilitation of people with schizophrenia. *Psychosoc. Rehab. J., 15*(4), 77-86.

Hyde, J. S. (1990). *Understanding human sexuality* (4th ed.). New York: McGraw-Hill.

Hyler, S. E., & Spitzer, R. T. (1978). Hysteria split asunder. *Amer. J. Psychiat., 135*, 1500-1504.

Hyman, S. E. (1999). Looking to the future: The role of genetics and molecular biology in research on mental illness. In S. Weissman, M. Sabshin, et al. (Eds.), *Psychiatry in the new millennium.* Washington, DC: American Psychiatric Press.

Iacono, W. G., & Patrick, C. J. (1997). Polygraphy and integrity testing. In R. Rogers et al. (Eds.), *Clinical assessment of malingering and deception* (2nd ed.). New York: Guilford.

Ichikawa, J., & Meltzer, H. Y. (1999). Relationship between dopaminergic and serotonergic neuronal activity in the frontal cortex and the action of typical and atypical antipsychotic drugs. *Eur. J. Psychiat. Clin. Neurosci., 249*(Suppl. 4), 90-98.

Iga, M. (1993). Japanese suicide. In A. A. Leenaars (Ed.), *Suicidology.* Northvale, NJ: Jason Aronson.

Iketani, T., Kiriike, N., Nakanishi, S., & Nakasuji, T. (1995). Effects of weight gain and resumption of menses on reduced bone density in patients with anorexia nervosa. *Biol. Psychiat., 37*(80), 521-527.

Illingworth, P. M. L. (1995). Patient-therapist sex: Criminalization and its discontents. *J. of Contemporary Health Law and Policy, 11*, 389-416.

Inouye, S. K. (1998). Delirium in hospitalized older patients: Recognition and risk factors. *J. Ger. Psychiat., 11*(3), 118-125.

Inouye, S. K. (1999). Predisposing and precipitating factors for delirium in hospitalized older patients. *Dement. Ger. Cogn. Disord., 10*(5), 393-400.

Inouye, S. K., Bogardus, S. T., Jr., Charpentier, P. A., Leo-Summers, L., Acampora, D., Holford, T. R., & Cooney, L. M., Jr. (1999). A multicomponent intervention to prevent delirium in hospitalized older patients. *N. Engl. J. Med., 340*(9), 669-676.

Inouye, S. K., Schlesinger, M. J., & Lydon, T. J. (1999). Delirium: A symptom of how hospital care is failing older persons and a window to improve quality of hospital care. *Amer. J. Med.,*

106(5), 565-573.

Inskip, H. M., Harris, E. C., & Barraclough, B. (1998). Lifetime risk of suicide for affective disorder, alcoholism and schizophrenia. *Brit. J. Psychiat., 172*, 35-37.

International Narcotics Control Board. (1999, February 23). Annual report. Cited in *Washington Post.*

Iqbal, K., & Grundke-Iqbal, I. (1996). Molecular mechanism of Alzheimer's neurofibrillary degeneration and therapeutic intervention. In R. J. Wurtman, S. Corkin, J. H. Growdon, & R. M. Nitsch (Eds.), *The neurobiology of Alzheimer's disease.* New York: New York Academy of Sciences.

Ironson G., Friedman, A., Klimas, N., Antoni, M., Fletcher, M. A., LaPerriere, A., Simoneau, J., & Schneiderman, N. (1994). Distress, denial, and low adherence to behavioral interventions predict faster disease progression in gay men infected with human immunodeficiency virus. *Inter. J. Behav. Med., 1*, 90-105.

Ironson, G., Taylor, C. B., Boltwood, M., et al. (1992). Effects of anger on left ventricular ejection fraction in coronary artery disease. *Amer. J. Cardiol., 70*(3), 281-285.

Isometsae, E. T., & Loennqvist, J. K. (1998). Suicide attempts preceding completed suicide. *Brit. J. Psychiat., 173*, 531-535.

Ito, A., Ichihara, M., Hisanaga, N., Ono, Y., et al. (1992). Prevalence of seasonal mood changes in low latitude area: Seasonal Pattern Assessment Questionnaire score of Quezon City workers. *Jpn. J. of Psychiat., 46*, 249.

Iversen, L. L. (1975). Dopamine receptors in the brain. *Science, 188*, 1084-1089.

Iverson, G. L., & Barton, E. (1999). Interscorer reliability of the MMPI-2: Should TRIN and VRIN be computer scored? *J. Clin. Psychol., 55*(1), 65-69.

Jablensky, A. (1995). Kraepelin's legacy: Paradigm or pitfall for modern psychiatry? [Special issue: Emil Kraepelin and 20th century psychiatry]. *Eur. Arch. Psychiat. Clin. Neurosci., 245*(4-5), 186-188.

Jack, C. R., Jr., Petersen, R. C., Xu, Y. C., O'Brien, P. C., Smith, G. E., Ivnik, R. J., Boeve, B. F., Waring, S. C., Tangalos, E. G., & Kokmen, E. (1999). Prediction of AD with MRI-based hippocampal volume in mild cognitive impairment. *Neurology, 52*(7), 1397-1403.

Jackson, J. L., Calhoun, K. S., Amick, A. A., Madever, H. M., & Habif, V. L. (1990). Young adult women who report childhood intrafamilial sexual abuse: Subsequent adjustment. *Arch. Sex. Behav., 19*(3), 211-221.

Jackson, J. S. (Ed.). (1988). *The black American elderly: Research on physical and psychosocial health.* New York: Springer.

Jacobs, B. L. (Ed.). (1984). *Hallucinogens: Neurochemical, behavioral, and clinical perspectives.* New York: Raven Press.

Jacobs, B. L. (1994). Serotonin, motor activity and depression-related disorders. *Amer. Sci., 82*, 456-463.

Jacobs, D. G. (Ed.). (1999). *The Harvard Medical School guide to suicide assessment and intervention.* San Francisco: Jossey-Bass.

Jacobs, D. G., Brewer, M., & Klein-Benheim, M. (1999). Suicide assessment: An overview and recommended protocol. In D. G. Jacobs (Ed.), *The Harvard Medical School guide to suicide assessment and intervention.* San Francisco: Jossey-Bass.

Jacobs, R. (1993). AIDS communication: College students' AIDS knowledge and information sources. *Hlth. Values, J. Hlth., Behav., Educ., Promotion, 17*(3), 32-41.

Jacobs, S.C. (1999) *Traumatic grief: Diagnosis, treatment, and prevention.* Philadelphia: Brunner/Mazel.

Jacobs, L. K., Rabinowitz, I., Popper, M. S., Solomon, R. J., Sokol, M. S., & Pfeffer, C. R. (1994). Interviewing prepubertal children about suicidal ideation and behavior. *J. Amer. Acad. Child Adol. Psychiat., 33*(4), 439–452.

Jacobson, B., & Thurman-Lacey, S. (1992). Effect of caffeine on motor performance by caffeine-naive and -familiar subjects. *Percept. Motor Skills, 74,* 151–157.

Jacobson, G. (1999). The inpatient management of suicidality. In D.G. Jacobs (Ed.), *The Harvard Medical School guide to suicide assessment and intervention.* San Francisco: Jossey-Bass.

Jacobson, J. W., & Schwartz, A. A. (1991). Evaluating living situations of people with development disabilities. In J. L. Matson & J. A. Mulick (Eds.), *Handbook of mental retardation.* New York: Pergamon Press.

Jacobson, N. S. (1989). The maintenance of treatment gains following social learning-based marital therapy. *Behav. Ther., 20*(3), 325–336.

Jacobson, N. S., & Gortner, E. T. (2000). Can depression be de-medicalized in the 21st century: Scientific revolutions, counter-revolutions and the magnetic field of normal science. *Behav. Res. Ther., 38*(2), 103–117.

Jacobson, N. S., Dobson, K. S., Truax, P. A., Addis, M. E., et al. (1996). A component analysis of cognitive-behavioral treatment for depression. *J. Cons. Clin. Psychol., 64*(2), 295–304.

Jadad, A. R., Booker, L., Gauld, M., Kakuma, R., Boyle, M., Cunningham, C. E., Kim, M., & Schachar, R. The treatment of attention-deficit hyperactivity disorder: An annotated bibliography and critical appraisal of published systematic reviews and metaanalyses. *Canad. J. Psychiat., 44*(10), 1025–1035.

Jaffe, J. H. (1985). Drug addiction and drug abuse. In Goodman & Gilman (Eds.), *The pharmacological basis of therapeutic behavior.* New York: Macmillan.

Jahangir, F., ur-Rehman, H., & Jan., T. (1998). Degree of religiosity and vulnerability to suicidal attempt/plans in depressive patients among Afghan refugees. *Inter. J. Psychol. Religion, 8*(4), 265–269.

James, W. (1890). *Principles of psychology* (Vol. 1). New York: Holt, Rinehart & Winston.

Jamison, K. R. (1987). Psychotherapeutic issues and suicide prevention in the treatment of bipolar disorders. In R. E. Hales & A. J. Frances (Eds.), *Psychiatric update: American Psychiatric Association annual review* (Vol. 6). Washington, DC: American Psychiatric Press.

Jamison, K. (1995, February). Manic-depressive illness and creativity. *Scientif. Amer.,* pp. 63–67.

Jamison, K. R. (1995). *An unquiet mind.* New York: Vintage Books.

Janca, A., Isaac, M., & Costa-e-Silva, J. A. (1995). World Health Organization International Study of Somatoform Disorders: Background and rationale. *Eur. J. Psychiat., 9*(2), 100–110.

Janowsky, D. S., & Davis, J. M. (1976). Methylphanidate, dextroamphetamine, and levamfetamine: Effects on schizophrenic symptoms. *Arch. Gen. Psychiat., 33*(3), 304–308.

Janowsky, D. S., El-Yousef, M. K., Davis, J. M., & Sekerke, H. J. (1973). Provocation of schizophrenic symptoms by intravenous administration of methylphenidate. *Arch. Gen. Psychiat., 28,* 185–191.

Janus, S. S., & Janus, C. L. (1993). *The Janus report on sexual behavior.* New York: Wiley.

Jarrett, R. B., Schaffer, M., McIntire, D., Witt-Browder, A., Kraft, D.. & Risser, R. C. (1999). Treatment of atypical depression with cognitive therapy or phenelzine: A double-blind, placebo-controlled trial. *Arch. Gen. Psychiat., 56*(5), 431–437.

Jefferson, J. W., & Greist, J. H. (1994). Mood disorders. In R. E. Hales, S. C. Yudofsky, & J. A. Talbott (Eds.), *The American Psychiatric Press textbook of psychiatry* (2nd ed.). Washington, DC: American Psychiatric Press.

Jefferson, L. (1948). *These are my sisters.* Tulsa, OK: Vickers.

Jeffries, J. J. (1995). Working with schizophrenia: A clinician's personal experience. *Canad. J. Psychiat., 40*(3, Suppl. 1), S22–S25.

Jellinek, M. S. (1999). Changes in the practice of child and adolescent psychiatry: Are our patients better served? *Journal of Developmental and Behavioral Pediatrics, 20*(5), 378–380.

Jemmott, J. B. (1987). Social motives and susceptibility to disease: Stalking individual differences in health risks. *J. Pers., 55*(2), 267–298.

Jemmott, J. B., Borysenko, J. Z., Borysenko, M., McClelland, D. C., et al. (1983). Academic stress, power motivation and decrease in secretion rate of salivary immunoglobulin. *Lancet, 12,* 1400–1402.

Jencks, C. (1998). Racial bias in testing. In C. Jencks, M. Phillips, et al. (Eds.), *The black-white test score gap.* Washington, DC: Brookings Institution.

Jenike, M. A. (1990). Approaches to the patient with treatment-refractory obsessive compulsive disorder. *J. Clin. Psychiat., 51*(Suppl. 2), 15–21.

Jenike, M. A. (1991). Geriatric obsessive-compulsive disorder. *J. Geriat. Psychiat. Neurol., 4,* 34–39.

Jenike, M. A. (1991). Management of patients with treatment-resistant obsessive-compulsive disorder. In M. T. Pato & J. Zohar (Eds.), *Current treatments of obsessive-compulsive disorder.* Washington, DC: American Psychiatric Press.

Jenike, M. A. (1991). Obsessive-compulsive disorders: A clinical approach. In W. Coryell & G. Winokur (Eds.), *The clinical management of anxiety disorders.* New York: Oxford University Press.

Jenike, M. A. (1992). New developments in treatment of obsessive-compulsive disorder. In A. Tasman & M. B. Riba (Eds.), *Review of psychiatry* (Vol. 11). Washington, DC: American Psychiatric Press.

Jenike, M. A. (Ed.). (1994, October). *J. Geriat. Psychiat. Neurol.*

Jenike, M. A. (1995). Alzheimer's disease. In *Scientific American Series: Vol. 13. Psychiatry.* New York: Scientific American.

Jenike, M. A., Baer, L., Ballantine, H. T., Martuza, R. L., Tynes, S., Giriunas, I., Buttolph, M. L., & Cassem, N. H. (1991). Cingulotomy for refractory obsessive-compulsive disorder: A long-term follow-up of 33 patients. *Arch. Gen. Psychiat., 48,* 548–555.

Jenkins, R., Lewis, G., Bibbington, P., Brugha, T., et al. (1997). The National Psychiatric Morbidity Surveys of Great Britain: Initial findings from the household survey. *Psychol. Med., 27*(4), 775–789.

Jenkins, R. L. (1968). The varieties of children's behavioral problems and family dynamics. *Amer. J. Psychiat., 124*(10), 1440–1445.

Jenkins-Hall, K., & Sacco, W. P. (1991). Effect of client race and depression on evaluations by white therapists. *J. Soc. Clin. Psychol., 10*(3), 322–333.

Jensen, G. M. (1998). The experience of injustice: Health consequences of the Japanese American internment. *Diss. Abstr. Inter.: Sect. A: Human Soc. Sci., 58*(7-A), 2718.

Jessen, G., Jensen, B. F., Arensman, E., Bille-Brahe, U., Crepet, P., De Leo, D., Hawton, K., Haring, C., Hjelmeland, H., Michel, K.,

Ostamo, A., Salander-Renberg, E., Schmidtke, A., Temesvary, B., & Wasserman, D. (1999). Attempted suicide and major public holidays in Europe: Findings from the WHO/EURO multicentre study on parasuicide. *Acta Psychiat. Scandin., 99*(6), 412–418.

Jeste, D. V., Eastham, J. H., Lacro, J. P., Gierz, M., Field, M. G., & Harris, M. J. (1996). Management of late-life psychosis. *J. Clin. Psychiat., 57*(Suppl 3), 39–45.

Joffe, R. T., Singer, W., Levitt, A. J., & MacDonald, C. (1993). A placebo-controlled comparison of lithium and triiodothyronine augmentation of tricyclic antidepressants in unipolar refractory depression. *Arch. Gen. Psychiat., 50,* 387–393.

Johnsen, F. (1994). *The encyclopedia of popular misconceptions.* New York: Citadel Press.

Johnson, B. R., & Becker, J. V. (1997). Natural born killers?: The development of the sexually sadistic serial killer. *J. Amer. Acad. Psychiat. Law., 25*(3), 335–348.

Johnson, C. (1995, February 8). National Collegiate Athletic Association study. In *The Hartford Courant.*

Johnson, C., & Wonderlich, S. A. (1992). Personality characteristics as a risk factor in the development of eating disorders. In J. H. Crowther, D. L. Tennenbaum, S. E. Hobfoll, & M. A. P. Stephens (Eds.), *The etiology of bulimia nervosa: The individual and familial context.* Washington, DC: Hemisphere.

Johnson, D. R., Feldman, S., & Lubin, H. (1995). Critical interaction therapy: Couples therapy in combat-related posttraumatic stress disorder. *Fam. Process, 34,* 401–412.

Johnson, D. R., Rosenheck, R., Fontana, A., Lubin, H., et al. (1996). Outcome of intensive inpatient treatment for combat-related posttraumatic stress disorder. *Amer. J. Psychiat., 153,* 771–777.

Johnson, E. H., Gentry, W. D., & Julius, S. (Eds.). (1992). *Personality, elevated blood pressure, and essential hypertension.* Washington, DC: Hemisphere.

Johnson, F. A. (1991). Psychotherapy of the elderly anxious patient. In C. Salzman & B. D. Lebowitz (Eds.), *Anxiety in the elderly.* New York: Springer.

Johnson, J. G., Cohen, P., Brown, J., Smailes, E. M., & Bernstein, D. P. (1999). Childhood maltreatment increases risk for personality disorders during early adulthood. *Arch. Gen. Psychiat., 56*(7), 600–606.

Johnson, K. (1996, December 31). Medical marijuana rejected as "hoax." *USA Today,* p. 4A.

Johnson, M. E., Jones, G., & Brems, C. (1996). Concurrent validity of the MMPI-2 feminine gender role (*GF*) and masculine gender role (*GM*) scales. *J. Pers. Assess., 66*(1), 153–168.

Johnson, M. R., & Lydiard, R. B. (1998). Comorbidity of major depression and panic disorder. *J. Clin. Psychol., 54*(2), 201–210.

Johnson, N. R. (1987). Panic at "The Who concert stampede." An empirical assessment. *Social Problems, 34,* 362–373.

Johnson, S. K., DeLuca, J., & Natelson, B. H. (1996). Assessing somatization disorder in the chronic fatigue syndrome. *Psychosom. Med., 58,* 50–57.

Johnson, W. D. (1991). Predisposition to emotional distress and psychiatric illness amongst doctors: The role of unconscious and experiential factors. *Brit. J. Med. Psychol., 64*(4), 317–329.

Johnson, W. G., Schlundt, D. G., Barclay, D. R., Carr-Nangle, R. E., et al. (1995). A naturalistic functional analysis of binge eating. Special Series: Body dissatisfaction, binge eating, and dieting as interlocking issues in eating disorders research. *Behav. Ther. 26*(1), 101–118.

Johnson-Greene, D., Fatis, M., Sonnek, K., & Shawchuck, C. (1988). A survey of caffeine use and associated side effects in a college population. *J. Drug Educ., 18*(3), 211–219.

Johnston, D. W. (1992). The management of stress in the prevention of coronary heart disease. In S. Maes, H. Levental, & M. Johnston (Eds.), *International review of health psychology* (Vol. 1). New York: Wiley.

Johnston, J. (1999, April 9). "Cyber-shrinks" a click away: Traditional therapy too costly for insurers. *HealthScout.*

Johnston, L. D., Bachman, J., & O'Malley, P. (1996). *Monitoring the Future study.* Rockville, MD.: National Institute on Drug Abuse (NIDA).

Johnston, L. D., Bachman, J. G., & O'Malley, P. M. (1998). *Monitoring the Future Study.* Rockville, MD: National Institute on Drug Abuse (NIDA).

Johnston, L. D., O'Malley, P. M., & Bachman, J. G. (1993). *National survey results on drug use from the Monitoring the Future Study, 1975–1992.* Rockville, MD: National Institute on Drug Abuse.

Johnston, L. D., O'Malley, P. M., & Bachman, J. G. (1998). Cited in press release, Drug use by American young people begins to turn downward. Ann Arbor: University of Michigan News and Information Services.

Johnston, L. D., O'Malley, P. M., & Bachman, J. G. (1998). Cited in press release, Smoking among American teens declines some. Ann Arbor: University of Michigan News and Information Services.

Johnston, L. D., O'Malley, P. M., & Bachman, J. G. (1999). Cited in press release, Drug trends in 1999 among American teens are mixed. Ann Arbor: Univ. of Michigan News and Information Services.

Johnston, L. D., O'Malley, P. M., & Bachman, J. G. (1999). Cited in press release, Cigarette smoking among American teens continues gradual decline. Ann Arbor: University of Michigan News and Information Services.

Joiner, T. E. (1995). The price of soliciting and receiving negative feedback: Self-verification theory as a vulnerability to depression theory. *J. Abnorm. Psychol., 104*(2), 364–372.

Joiner, T. E., Jr. (1999). A test of interpersonal theory of depression in youth psychiatric inpatients. *J. Abnorm. Child Psychol., 27*(1), 77–85.

Joiner, T. E., Jr. (1999). The clustering and contagion of suicide. *Curr. Direct. Psychol. Sci., 8*(3), 89–92.

Joiner, T. E., Coyne, J. C., et al. (Eds.). (1999). *The interactional nature of depression: Advances in interpersonal approaches.* Washington, DC: American Psychological Association.

Joiner, T. E., Heatherton, T. F., Rudd, M. D., & Schmidt, N. B. (1997). Perfectionism, perceived weight status, and bulimic symptoms: Two studies testing a diathesis-stress model. *J. Abnorm. Psychol., 106*(1), 145–153.

Joiner, T. E., Jr., Katz, J., & Heatherton, T. F. (2000). Personality features differentiate late adolescent females and males with chronic bulimic symptoms. *Inter. J. Eat. Disorders, 27*(2), 191–197.

Joiner, T. E., Metalsky, G. I., & Wonderlich, S. A. (1995). Bulimic symptoms and the development of depressive symptoms: The moderating role of attributional style. *Cog. Ther. Res, 19*(6), 651–666.

Joiner, T. E., Jr., Vohs, K. D., & Heatherton, T. F. (2000). Three studies on the factorial distinctiveness of binge eating and bulimic symptoms among nonclinical men and women. *Inter. J. Eat. Disorders, 27*(2), 198–205.

Joiner, T. E., Wonderlich, S. A., Metalsky, G. I., & Schmidt, N. B. (1995). Body dissatisfaction: A feature of bulimia, depression, or both? *J. Soc. Clin. Psychol., 14*(4), 339–355.

Jones, A., & Schechter, S. (1992). *When love goes wrong.* New York: HarperCollins.

Jones, G. D. (1997). The role of drugs and alcohol in urban minority adolescent suicide attempts. *Death Stud., 21,* 189–202.

Jones, M. C. (1968). Personality correlates and antecedants of drinking patterns in males. *J. Cons. Clin. Psychol., 32,* 2–12.

Jones, M. C. (1971). Personality antecedents and correlates of drinking patterns in women. *J. Cons. Clin. Psychol., 36,* 61–69.

Jordan, D. (1993). *1001 facts somebody screwed up.* Atlanta, GA: Longtreet Press.

Jordan, D. (1997). *1001 more facts somebody screwed up.* Atlanta, GA: Longtreet Press.

Jorenby, D. E., Leischow, S. J., Nides, M. A., Rennard, S. I., Johnston, J. A., Hughes, A. R., Smith, S. S., Muramoto, M. L., Daughton, D. M., Doan, K., Fiore, M. C., & Baker, T. B. (1999). A controlled trial of sustained-release bupropion, a nicotine patch, or both for smoking cessation. *N. Engl. J. Med., 340*(9), 685–691.

Jorm, A. F., Korten, A. E., Jacomb, P. A., Rodgers, B., Pollitt, P., Christensen, H., & Henderson, S. (1997). Helpfulness of interventions for mental disorders: Beliefs of health professionals compared with the general public. *Brit. J. Psychiat., 171,* 233–237.

Joyner, C. D., & Swenson, C. C. (1993). Community-level intervention after a disaster. In C. F. Saylor (Ed.), *Children and disasters.* New York: Plenum Press.

Judd, L. L. (1995). Depression as a brain disease. *Depression, 3,* 121–124.

Juel-Nielsen, N., & Videbech, T. (1970). A twin study of suicide. *Acta Genet. Med. Gemellol., 19,* 307–310.

Julien, R. M. (1988). *A primer of drug action* (5th ed.). New York: W. H. Freeman.

Julius, S. (1992). Relationship between the sympathetic tone and cardiovascular responsiveness in the course of hypertension. In E. H. Johnson, E. D. Gentry, & S. Julius (Eds.), *Personality, elevated blood pressure, and essential hypertension.* Washington, DC: Hemisphere.

Jung, W., & Irwin, M. (1999). Reduction of natural killer cytotoxic activity in major depression: Interaction between depression and cigarette smoking. *Psychosom. Med., 61*(3), 263–270.

Jurkowitz, M. (1999, March 7). I'm OK; you're OK; Y2K? Does all the worry about deadly computer bugs express our primal fear of entering 2000? *Boston Globe,* p. C1.

Just, N., & Alloy, L. B. (1997). The response styles theory of depression: Tests and an extension of the theory. *J. Abnorm. Psychol., 106*(2), 221–229.

Juster, H. R., Heimberg, R. G., & Holt, C. S. (1996). Social phobia: Diagnostic issues and review of cognitive behavioral treatment strategies. In M. Hersen, R. M. Eisler, & P. M. Miller (Eds.), *Progress in behavior modification* (Vol. 30). Pacific Grove, CA: Brooks/Cole.

Kabat-Zinn, J., Massion, A. O., Kristeller, J., Peterson, L. G., et al. (1992). Effectiveness of a meditation-based stress reduction program in the treatment of anxiety disorders. *Amer. J. Psychiat., 149*(7), 936–943.

Kafha, M. P., & Hennen, J. (1999). The paraphilia-related disorders: An empirical investigation of nonparaphilic hypersexuality disorders in outpatient males. *J. Sex Marital Ther., 25*(4), 305–319.

Kagan, J., & Snidman, N. (1991). Infant predictors of inhibited and uninhibited profiles. *Psychol. Sci., 2,* 40–44.

Kagan, J., & Snidman, N. (1999). Early childhood predictors of adult anxiety disorders. *Biol. Psychiat., 46*(11), 1536–1541.

Kagan, N. I., Kagan, H., & Watson, M. G. (1995). Stress reduction in the workplace: The effectiveness of psychoeducational progams. *J. Couns. Psychol., 42*(1), 71–78.

Kahn, A. P., & Fawcett, J. (1993). *The encyclopedia of mental health.* New York: Facts on File.

Kaij, L. (1960). *Alcoholism in twins: Studies on the etiology and sequels of abuse of alcohol.* Stockholm: Almquist & Wiksell.

Kail, R. (1992). General slowing of information-processing by persons with mental retardation. *Amer. J. Ment. Retard., 97*(3), 333–341.

Kalafat, J., & Elias, M. J. (1995). Suicide prevention in an educational context: Broad and narrow foci [Special issue: Suicide prevention: Toward the year 2000]. *Suic. Life-Threat. Behav., 25*(1), 123–133.

Kalafat, J., & Ryerson, D. M. (1999). The implementation and institutionalization of a school-based youth suicide prevention program. *J. Primary Prev., 19*(3), 157–175.

Kalb, C. (2000, January 31). Coping with the darkness: Revolutionary new approaches in providing care for helping people with Alzheimer's stay active and feel productive. *Newsweek,* pp. 52–54.

Kalin, N. H. (1993, May). The neurobiology of fear. *Scientif. Amer.,* pp. 94–101.

Kalska, H., Punamaeki, R. L., Maekinen-Pelli, T., & Saarinen, M. (1999). Memory and metamemory functioning among depressed patients. *Appl. Neuropsychol., 6*(2), 96–107.

Kaminer, Y. (1991). Adolescent substance abuse. In R. J. Frances & S. I. Miller (Eds.), *Clinical textbook of addictive disorders.* New York: Guilford.

Kanakis, D. M., & Thelen, M. H. (1995, July/August). Parental variables associated with bulimia nervosa. *Addic. Behav., 20,* 491–500.

Kandel, E. R. (1998). A new intellectual framework for psychiatry. *Amer. J. Psychiat., 155*(4), 457–469.

Kane, J. M. (1992). Clinical efficacy of clozapine in treatment-refractory schizophrenia: An overview. *Brit. J. Psychiat., 160*(Suppl. 17), 41–45.

Kanner, B. (1995). *Are you normal?: Do you behave like everyone else?* New York: St. Martin's Press.

Kanner, B. (1998, February). Are you normal? Turning the other cheek. *American Demographics.*

Kanner, B. (1998, May). Are you normal? Creatures of habit. *American Demographics.*

Kanner, B. (1998, August). Are you normal? Summertime. *American Demographics.*

Kanner, B. (1999, January). Hungry, or just bored? *American Demographics.*

Kanner, L. (1943). Autistic disturbances of affective contact. *Nerv. Child. 2,* 217.

Kanner, L. (1954). To what extent is early infantile autism determined by constitutional inadequacies? *Proceedings of the Assoc. Res. Nerv. Ment. Dis., 33,* 378–385.

Kaplan, A. (1998, September). Caring for the caregivers: Family interventions and Alzheimer's disease. *Psychiat. Times, XV*(9).

Kaplan, A. (1999). China's suicide patterns challenge depression theory. *Psychiatr. Times, XVI*(1).

Kaplan, A. S., & Garfinkel, P. E. (1999). Difficulties in treating patients with eating disorders: A review of patient and clinician variables. *Canad. J. Psychiatr., 44*(7), 665–670.

Kaplan, H. I., Sadock, B. J., & Greb, J. A. (1994). *Synopsis of psychiatry* (7th ed.). Baltimore: Williams & Wilkins.

Kaplan, H. S. (1974). *The new sex therapy: Active treatment of sexual dysfunction.* New York: Brunner/Mazel.

Kaplan, M. D. (1999). Developmental and psychiatric evaluation in the preschool context. *Child Adol. Psychiat. Clin. N. Amer., 8*(2), 379–393.

Kaplan, M. S., Marks, G., & Mertens, S. B. (1997). Distress and coping among women with HIV infection: Preliminary findings from a multiethnic sample. *Amer. J. Orthopsychiat., 67*(1), 80–91.

Kaplan, W. (1984). *The relationship between depression and anti-social behavior among a court-referred adolescent population.* Paper presented to the American Academy of Child Psychiatry, Toronto.

Kapur, S., & Remington, G. (1996). Serotonin-dopamine interaction and its relevance to schizophrenia. *Amer. J. Psychiat., 153*(4), 466–476.

Karasu, T. B. (1992). The worst of times, the best of times. *J. Psychother. Prac. Res., 1,* 2–15.

Karel, R. (1992, May 1). Hopes of many long-term sufferers dashed as FDA ends medical marijuana program. *Psychiatr. News.*

Karel, R. (1998, December 18). Journals issue mixed verdict on popular alternative therapies. *Psychiatr. News.*

Karlberg, L., Unden, A. L., Elofsson, S., & Krakau, I. (1998). Is there a connection between car accidents, near accidents, and Type A drivers? *Behav. Med., 24*(3), 99–106.

Karon, B. P. (1985). Omission in review of treatment interactions. *Schizo. Bull., 11*(1), 16–17.

Karon, B. P., & Vandenbos, G. R. (1996). *Psychotherapy of schizophrenia: The treatment of choice.* Northvale, NJ: Jason Aronson.

Karon, B. P., & Widener, A. J. (1997). Repressed memories and World War II: Lest we forget. *Profess. Psychol.: Res. Pract., 28*(4), 338–340.

Karp, D.A. (1996). *Speaking of sadness: Depression, disconnection, and the meanings of illness.* New York: Oxford University Press.

Karp, J. F., & Frank, E. (1995). Combination therapy and the depressed woman. *Depression, 3,* 91–98.

Kashani, J. H., Suarez, L., Luchene, L., & Reid, J. C. (1998). Family characteristics and behavior problems of suicidal and non-suicidal children and adolescents. *Child Psychiat. Human Dev., 29*(2), 157–168.

Kaslow, N. J., Reviere, S. L., Chance, S. E., Rogers, J. H., Hatcher, C. A., Wasserman, F., Smith, L., Jessee, S., James, M. E., & Seelig, B. (1998). An empirical study of the psychodynamics of suicide. *J. Amer. Psychoanal. Assoc., 46*(3), 777–796.

Kasper, S., Kauscher, J., Kufferle, B., Barnas, C., Pezawas, L., & Quiner, S. (1999). Dopamine- and serotonin-receptors in schizophrenia: Results of imaging-studies and implications for pharmacotherapy in schizophrenia. *Eur. Arch. Psychiat. Clin. Neurosci., 249*(Suppl. 4), 83–89.

Kassel, J. D., Wagner, E. F., & Unrod, M. (1999). Alcoholism-behavior therapy. In M. Hersen & A. S. Bellack (Eds.), *Handbook of comparative interventions for adult disorders* (2nd ed.). New York: Wiley.

Kate, N. T. (1998, March). How many children? *American Demographics.*

Kate, N. T. (1998, April). Two careers, one marriage. *American Demographics.*

Kate, N. T. (1998, May). Freshmen get wholesome. *American Demographics.*

Katel, P., & Beck, M. (1996, March 29). Sick kid or sick Mom? *Newsweek,* p. 73.

Kato, T., Takahashi, S., Shioiri, T., & Inubushi, T. (1993). Alterations in brain phosphorous metabolism in bipolar disorder detected by in vivo 31 P and 7 Li magnetic resonance spectroscopy. *J. Affect. Disorders, 27,* 53–60.

Katon, W. J., & Walker, E. A. (1998). Medically unexplained symptoms in primary care. *J. Clin. Psychiat., 59*(Suppl. 20), 15–21.

Katona, C. L. E. (1995). Refractory depression: A review with particular reference to the use of lithium augmentation. *Eur. Neuropsychopharmacology* (Suppl.), 109–113.

Katz, I., & Oslin, D. (Eds.). (2000). *Annual review of gerontology and geriatrics: Focus on psychopharmacologic interventions in late life* (Vol. 19). New York: Springer.

Katz, R. J., Lott, M., Landau P., & Waldmeier, P. (1993). A clinical test of noradrenergic involvement in the therapeutic mode of action of an experimental antidepressant. *Biol. Psychiat., 33,* 261–266.

Katzman, R. (1981, June). Early detection of senile dementia. *Hosp. Practitioner,* pp. 61–76.

Kaufman, M. (1999, June 8). White House decries stigma: "A health issue—no more and no less." *Washington Post,* p. Z07.

Kaufman, M. J., Levin, J. M., Maas, L. C., Rose, S. L., Lukas, S. E., Mendelson, J. H., Cohen, B. M., & Renshaw, P. F. (1998). Cocaine decreases relative cerebral blood volume in humans: A dynamic susceptibility contrast magnetic resonance imaging study. *Psychopharmacology (Berl), 138*(1), 76–81.

Kaufman, M. J., Siegel, A. J., Mendelson, J. H., Rose, S. L., Kukes, T. J., Sholar, M. B., Lukas, S. E., & Renshaw, P. F. (1998). Cocaine administration induces human splenic constriction and altered hematologic parameters. *J. Appl. Physiol., 85*(5), 1877–1883.

Kawas, C., Resnick, S., Morrison, A., Brookmeyer, R., Corrada, M., Zonderman, A., Bacal, C., Lingle, D. D., & Metter, E. J. (1997). A prospective study of estrogen replacement therapy and the risk of developing Alzheimer's disease: The Baltimore Longtitudinal Study of Aging. *Neurology, 48*(6), 1517–1521.

Kaye, W. H., Gendall, K. A., Fernstrom, M. H., Fernstrom, J. D., McConaha, C. W., & Weltzin, T. E. (2000). Effects of acute tryptophan depletion on mood in bulimia nervosa. *Biol. Psychiat., 47*(2), 151–157.

Kaye, W. H., Gendall, H., & Strober, M. (1998). Serotonin neuronal function and selective serotonin reuptake inhibitor treatment in anorexia and bulimia nervosa. *Biol. Psychiat., 44*(9), 825–838.

Kaye, W. H., Greeno, C. G., Moss, H., Fernstrom, J., Fernstrom, M., Lilenfeld, L. R., Weltzin, T. E., & Mann, J. J. (1998). Alterations in serotonin activity and psychiatric symptoms after recovery from bulimia nervosa. *Arch. Gen. Psychiat., 55*(10), 927–935.

Kazdin, A. E. (1983). Failure of persons to respond to the token economy. In E. B. Foa & P. M. G. Emmelkamp (Eds.), *Failures in behavior therapy.* New York: Wiley.

Kazdin, A. E. (1990). Childhood depression. *J. Child Psychol. Psychiat. Allied Disc., 31,* 121–160.

Kazdin, A. E. (1993). Psychotherapy for children and adolescents: Current progress and future research directions. *Amer. Psychologist, 48*(6), 644–657.

Kazdin, A. E. (1994). Methodology, design, and evaluation in psychotherapy research. In A. E. Bergin & S. L. Garfiel (Eds.), *Handbook of psychotherapy and behavior change* (4th ed.). New York: Wiley.

Kazdin, A. E. (1994). Psychotherapy for children and adolescents. In A. E. Bergin & S. L. Garfiel (Eds.), *Handbook of psychotherapy and behavior change* (4th ed.). New York: Wiley.

Kazdin, A. E., & Wassell, G. (1999). Barriers to treatment participation and therapeutic change among children referred for conduct disorder. *J. Clin. Child Psychol., 28*(2), 160–172.

Kazdin, A. E. & Weisz, J. R. (1998). Identifying and developing empirically supported child and adolescent treatments. *J. Cons. Clin. Psychol., 66*(1), 19–36.

Kazes, M., Danion, J. M., Grange, D., Pradignac, A., et al. (1994). Eating behaviour and depression before and after antidepressant treatment: A prospective, naturalistic study. *J. Affect. Disorders, 30,* 193–207.

Kearney, C. A., & Silverman, W. K. (1998). A critical review of pharmacotherapy for youth with anxiety disorders: Things are not as they seem. *J. Anx. Dis., 12*(2), 83–102.

Kearney-Cooke, & Steichen-Asch, P. (1990). Men, body image, and eating disorders. In A. E. Andersen (Ed.), *Males with eating disorders.* New York: Brunner/Mazel.

Kebabian, J. W., Petzold, G. L., & Greengard, P. (1972). Dopamine-sensitive adenylate cyclase in caudate nucleus of rat brain and its similarity to the "dopamine receptor." *Proc. Natl. Acad. Sci. USA, 69,* 2145–2149.

Keel, P. K., & Mitchell, J. E. (1997). Outcome in bulimia nervosa. *Amer. J. Psychiat., 154,* 313–321.

Keel, P. K., Mitchell, J. E., Miller, K. B., Davis, T. L., & Crow, S. J. (1999). Long-term outcome of bulimia nervosa. *Arch. Gen. Psychiat., 56*(1), 63–69.

Keel, P. K., Mitchell, J. E., Miller, K. B., David, T. L., & Crow, S. J. (2000). Predictive validity of bulimia nervosa as a diagnostic category. *Amer. J. Psychiat., 157*(1), 136–138.

Keel, P. K., Mitchell, J. E., Miller, K. B., Davis, T. L., & Crow, S. J. (2000). Social adjustment over 10 years following diagnosis with bulimia nervosa. *Inter. J. Eat. Disorders, 27*(1), 21–28.

Keen, E. (1970). *Three faces of being: Toward an existential clinical psychology.* By the Meredith Corp. Reprinted by permission of Irvington Publishers.

Keene, L. C., & Davies, P. H. (1999). Drug-related erectile dysfunction. *Adv. Drug React. Toxicol. Rev., 18*(1), 5–24.

Keesey, R. E., & Corbett, S. W. (1983). Metabolic defense of the body weight set-point. In A. J. Stunkard & E. Stellar (Eds.), *Eating and its disorders.* New York: Raven Press.

Keilman, J. (1999, June 24). E-therapy; affordable counseling is now a click away. *The Times-Picayune,* p. E1.

Keith, S. J., Regier, D. A., & Rae, D. S. (1991). Schizophrenic disorders. In L. N. Robins & D. S. Regier (Eds.), *Psychiatric disorders in America: The Epidemiological Catchment Area Study.* New York: Free Press.

Kelleher, M. J., Chambers, D., Corcoran, P., Williamson, E., & Keeley, H. S. (1998). Religious sanctions and rates of suicide worldwide. *Crisis, 19*(2), 78–86.

Kelleher, M. J., Hynes, F., Kelleher, M. J. A., & Keeley, H. (1998). Suicide as a complication of schizophrenia. *Irish J. Psychol. Med., 15*(1), 24–25.

Keller, M. B. (1988). Diagnostic issues and clinical course of unipolar illness. In A. J. Frances & R. E. Hales (Eds.), *Review of psychiatry* (Vol. 7). Washington, DC: American Psychiatric Press.

Keller, M. B. (1999, May). *Chronic depression: Psychotherapy and pharmacotherapy: Additive or synergistic?* Paper presented at the annual meeting of the American Psychiatric Association, Washington, DC.

Keller, R., & Shaywitz, B. A. (1986). Amnesia or fugue state: A diagnostic dilemma. *J. Dev. Behav. Pediatr., 7*(8), 131–132.

Kellner, C. (1999, February 2). Interviewed in D. Cauchon, How shock therapy works. *USA Today.*

Kellner, M., & Yehuda, R. (1999). Do panic disorder and posttraumatic stress disorder share a common psychoneuroendocrinology? *Psychoneuroendocrinology, 24*(5), 485–504.

Kelly, K. A. (1993). Multiple personality disorders: Treatment coordination in a partial hospital setting. *Bull. Menninger Clin., 57*(3), 390–398.

Kelly, M. J., Mufson, M. J., & Rogers, M. P. (1999). Medical settings and suicide. In D.G.

Jacobs (Ed.), *The Harvard Medical School guide to suicide assessment and intervention.* San Francisco: Jossey-Bass.

Kelly, M. P., Strassberg, D. S., & Kircher, J. R. (1990). Attitudinal and experiental correlates of anorgasmia. *Arch. Sex. Behav., 19,* 165–172.

Kelly, V. A., & Myers, J. E. (1996). Parental alcoholism and coping: A comparison of female children of alcoholics with female children of nonalcoholics. *J. Couns. Dev., 74*(5), 501–504.

Kelty, M. F., Hoffman, R. R., III, Ory, M. G., & Harden, J. T. (2000). Behavioral and sociocultural aspects of aging, ethnicity, and health. In R. M. Eisler, M. Hersen, et al. (Eds.), *Handbook of gender, culture, and health.* Mahwah, NJ: Erlbaum.

Kemeny, M. E., & Laudenslager, M. L. (1999). Beyond stress: The role of individual difference factors in psychoneuroimmunology. *Brain Behav. Immun., 13*(2), 73–75.

Kemp, A., Green, B. L., Hovanitz, C., & Rawlings, E. I. (1995). Incidence and correlates of posttraumatic stress disorder in battered women: Shelter and community samples. *J. Interpers. Violence, 10*(1), 43–55.

Kemp, D. R. (1994). *Mental health in the workplace: An employer's and manager's guide.* Westport, CT: Quorum Books.

Kemper, T. L., & Bauman, M. (1998). Neuropathology of infantile autism. *Journal of Neuropathology and Experimental Neurology, 57*(7), 645–652.

Kendall, P. C. (1990). Behavioral assessment and methodology. In C. M. Franks, G. T. Wilson, P. C. Kendall, & J. P. Foreyt (Eds.), *Review of behavior therapy: Theory and practice* (Vol. 12). New York: Guilford.

Kendall, P. C. (Ed.). (1990). *Child and adolescent therapy: Cognitive-behavioral procedures.* New York: Guilford.

Kendall, P. C. (1990). Cognitive processes and procedures in behavior therapy. In C. M. Franks, G. T. Wilson, P. C. Kendall, & J. P. Foreyt (Eds.), *Review of behavior therapy: Theory and practice* (Vol. 12). New York: Guilford.

Kendall, P. C. (1998). Empirically supported psychological therapies. *J. Cons. Clin. Psychol., 66*(1), 3–6.

Kendall, P. C. (2000). *Childhood disorders.* Hove, England: Psychology Press/Taylor & Francis.

Kendler, K. S. (1997). The diagnostic validity of melancholic major depression in a population-based sample of female twins. *Arch. Gen. Psychiat., 54,* 299–304.

Kendler, K. S., & Gardner, C. O., Jr. (1998). Twin studies of adult psychiatric and substance dependence disorders: Are they biased by differences in the environmental experiences of monozygotic and dizygotic twins in childhood and adolescence? *Psychol. Med., 28*(3), 625–633.

Kendler, K. S., Heath, A., & Martin, N. G. (1987). A genetic epidemiologic study of self-report suspiciousness. *Comprehen. Psychiat., 28*(3), 187–196.

Kendler, K. S., Heath, A., Neale, M., Kessler, R., & Eaves, L. (1992). A population-based twin study of alcoholism in women. *JAMA, 268*(14), 1877–1882.

Kendler, K. S., Karkowski, L. M., & Prescott, C. A. (1998). Stressful life events and major depression: Risk period, long-term contextual threat and diagnostic specificity. *J. Nerv. Ment. Dis., 186*(11), 661–669.

Kendler, K. S., Karkowski, L. M., & Prescott, C. A. (1999). Causal relationship between stressful life events and the onset of major depression. *Amer. J. Psychiat., 156*(6), 837–848.

Kendler, K. S., Kessler, R. C., Walters, E. E., MacLean, C., Neale, M. C., Heath, A. C., &

Eaves, L. J. (1995). Stressful life events, genetic liability, and onset of an episode of major depression in women. *Amer. J. Psychiat., 152,* 833–842.

Kendler, K. S., McGuire, M., Gruenberg, A. M., O'Hare, A., Spellman, M., & Walsh, D. (1993). The Roscommon Family Study. *Arch. Gen. Psychiat., 50,* 527–540.

Kendler, K. S., McGuire, M., Gruenberg, A. M., & Walsh, D. (1994). An epidemiological, clinical, and family study of simple schizophrenia in County Roscommon, Ireland. *Amer. J. Psychiat., 151*(1), 27–34.

Kendler, K. S., Myers, J. M., O'Neill, F. A., Martin, R., Murphy, B., MacLean, C. J., Walsh, D., & Straub, R. E. (2000). Clinical features of schizophrenia and linkage to chromosomes 5q, 6p, 8p, and 10p in the Irish study of high-density schizophrenia families. *Amer. J. Psychiat., 157*(3), 402–408.

Kendler, K. S., Neale, M. C., Heath, A. C., Kessler, R. C., & Eaves, L. J. (1994). A twin-family study of alcoholism in women. *Amer. J. Psychiat., 151*(5), 707–715.

Kendler, K. S., Neale, M. C., Kessler, R. C., Heath, A. C., & Eaves, L. J. (1993). Panic disorder in women: A population-based twin study. *Psychol. Med., 23,* 397–406.

Kendler, K. S., Neale, M. C., Kessler, R. C., Heath, A. C., et al. (1992). Generalized anxiety disorder in women: A population-based twin study. *Arch. Gen. Psychiat., 49*(4), 267–272.

Kendler, K. S., Ochs, A. L., Gorman, A. M., Hewitt, J. K., Ross, D. E., & Mirsky, A. F. (1991). The structure of schizotypy: A pilot multi-trait twin study. *Psychiat. Res., 36*(1), 19–36.

Kendler, K. S., Walters, E. E., Neale, M. C., Kessler, R. C., et al. (1995). The structure of the genetic and environmental risk factors for six major psychiatric disorders in women: Phobia, generalized anxiety disorder, panic disorder, bulimia, major depression, and alcoholism. *Arch. Gen. Psychiat., 52*(5), 374–383.

Kendler, K. S., Walters, E. E., Truett, K. R., Heath, A. C., et al. (1995). A twin-family study of self-report symptoms of panic-phobia and somatization. *Behav. Genet. 25*(6), 499–515.

Kennedy, S. H., Katz, R., Neitzert, C. S., Ralevski, E., et al. (1995). Exposure with response prevention treatment of anorexia nervosa-bulimic subtype and bulimia nervosa. *Behav. Res. Ther., 33*(6), 685–689.

Kent, D. A., Tomasson, K., & Coryell, W. (1995). Course and outcome of conversion and somatization disorders: A four-year follow-up. *Psychosomatics, 36*(2), 138–144.

Kent, G., & Turpin, G. (2000). Attention and information processing: Applications to schizophrenia. In D. Gupta & R.M. Gupta (Eds.), *Psychology for psychiatrists.* London: Whurr Publishers, Ltd.

Kernberg, O. F. (1976). *Object-relations theory and clinical psychoanalysis.* New York: Jason Aronson.

Kernberg, O. F. (1997). Convergences and divergences in contemporary psychoanalytic technique and psychoanalytic psychotherapy. In J. K. Zeig (Ed.), *The evolution of psychotherapy: The third conference.* New York: Brunner/Mazel.

Kernberg, P. F. (1989). Narcissistic personality disorder in childhood. *Psychiatr. Clin. N. Amer., 12*(3), 671–694.

Kessing, L. V., Andersen, P. K., Mortensen, P. B., & Bolwig, T. G. (1998). Recurrence in affective disorder: I. Case register study. *Brit. J. Psychiat, 172,* 23–28.

Kessler, R. C., & Zhao, S. (1999). The prevalence of mental illness. In A. V. Horwitz & T. L. Scheid (Eds.), *A handbook for the study of mental health: Social contexts, theories, and systems.* Cambridge, England: Cambridge University Press.

Kessler, R. C., Berglund, P. A., Zhao, S., Leaf, P. J. et al. (1996).The 12–month prevalence and correlates of serious mental illness (SMI). In R. W. Manderscheid & M. A. Sonnenschein (Eds.), *Mental health, United States, 1996.* (DHHS Pub. No. SMA 96–3098). Washington, DC: U.S. Department of Health and Human Services.

Kessler, R. C., Crum, R. M., Warner, L. A., Nelson, C. B., et al. (1997). Lifetime co-occurrence of DSM-III-R alcohol abuse and dependence with other psychiatric disorders in the National Comorbidity Survey. *Arch. Gen. Psychiat., 54,* 313–321.

Kessler, R. C., DuPont, R. L., Berglund, P., & Wittchen, H. U. (1999). Impairment in pure and comorbid generalized anxiety disorder and major depression at 12 months in two national surveys. *Amer. J. Psychiat., 156*(12), 1915–1923.

Kessler, R. C., McGonagle, K. A., Zhao, S., Nelson, C. B., Hughes, M., Eshleman, S., Wittchen, H. U., & Kendler, K. S. (1994). Lifetime and 12–month prevalence of DSM-III-R psychiatric disorders among persons aged 15–54 in the United States: Results from the National Comorbidity Survey. *Arch. Gen. Psychiat., 51*(1), 8–19.

Kessler, R. C., Olfson, M., & Berglund, P. A. (1998). Patterns and predictors of treatment contact after first onset of psychiatric disorders. *Amer. J. Psychiat., 155*(1), 62–69.

Kessler, R. C., Sonnega, A., Bromet, E., Hughes, M., & Nelson, C. B. (1995). Posttraumatic stress disorder in the National Comorbidity Survey. *Arch. Gen. Psychiat., 52,* 1048–1060.

Kessler, R. C., Stang, P. E., Wittchen, H.-U., Ustun, T. B., Roy-Burne, P. P., & Walters, E. E. (1998). Lifetime panic-depression comorbidity in the National Comorbidity Survey. *Arch. Gen. Psychiat., 55,* 801–808.

Kessler, R. C., et. al. (1999). The economic burden of anxiety isorders in the 1990s. *J. Clin. Psychiat., 60*(7), 427–435.

Ketter, T. A., George, M. S., Kimbrell, T. A., Benson, B. E., & Post, R. (1996). Functional brain imaging, limbic function, and affective disorders. *Neuroscientist, 2*(1), 55–65.

Kettl, P. (1998). Alaska native suicide: Lessons for elder suicide. *Inter. Psychoger., 110*(2), 205–211.

Kety, S. S. (1974). From rationalization to reason. *Amer. J. Psychiat., 131*(9), 957–963.

Kety, S. S. (1988). Schizophrenic illness in the families of schizophrenic adoptees: Findings from the Danish national sample. *Schizo. Bull., 14*(2), 217–222.

Kety, S. S., Rosenthal, D., Wender, P. H., Schulsinger, F., & Jacobsen, B. (1978). The biologic and adoptive families of adopted individuals who become schizophrenic: Prevalence of mental illness and other characteristics. In L. C. Wynne, R. L. Cromwell, & S. Matthysse (Eds.), *The nature of schizophrenia: New approaches to research and treatment.* New York: Wiley.

Kety, S. S., Rosenthal, D., Wender, P. H., et al. (1968). The types and prevalence of mental illness in the biological and adoptive families of schizophrenics. *J. Psychiatr. Res., 6,* 345–362.

Kety, S. S., Rosenthal, D., Wender, P. H., et al. (1975). Mental illness in the biological and adoptive families of adopted individuals who became schizophrenic: A preliminary report based on psychiatric interviews. In R. R. Fieve, D. Rosenthal, & H. Brill (Eds.), *Genetic research in psychiatry.* Baltimore: Johns Hopkins University Press.

Kewman, D. G., & Tate, D. G. (1998). Suicide in SCI: A psychological autopsy. *Rehab. Psychol., 43*(2), 143–151.

Keys, A., Brozek, J., Henschel, A., Mickelson, O., & Taylor, H. L. (1950). *The biology of human starvation.* Minneapolis: University of Minnesota Press.

Khanna, R., Das, A., & Damodaran, S. S. (1992). Prospective study of neuroleptic-induced dystonia in mania and schizophrenia. *Amer. J. Psychiat.*, 149(4), 511–513.

Khantzian, E. J. (1985). The self-medication hypothesis of addictive disorders: Focus on heroin and cocaine dependence. *Amer. J. Psychiat.*, 142(11), 1259–1264.

Kheriaty, E., Kleinknecht, R. A., & Hyman, I. E., Jr. (1999). Recall and validation of phobic origins as a function of a structured interview versus the Phobia Origins Questionnaire. *Behav. Mod.*, 23(1), 61–78.

Kiecolt-Glaser, J. K., & Glaser, R. (1988). Methodological issues in behavioral immunology research with humans. *Brain Behav. Immun.*, 2, 67–68.

Kiecolt-Glaser, J. K., & Glaser, R. (1988). Psychological influences on immunity: Implications for AIDS. *Amer. Psychologist*, 43(11), 892–898.

Kiecolt-Glaser, J. K., & Glaser, R. (1999). Psychoneuroimmunology and immunotoxicology: Implications for carcinogenesis. *Psychosom. Med.*, 61(3), 271–272.

Kiecolt-Glaser, J. K., Dura, J. R., Speicher, C. E., Trask, O. J., & Glaser, R. (1991). Spousal caregivers of dementia victims: Longitudinal changes in immunity and health. *Psychosom. Med.*, 53, 345–362.

Kiecolt-Glaser, J. K., Fisher, L., Ogrocki, P., Stout, J. C., Speicher, C. E., & Glaser, R. (1987). Marital quality, marital disruption, and immune function. *Psychosom. Med.*, 49, 13–34.

Kiecolt-Glaser, J. K., Garner, W., Speicher, C., Penn, G. M., Holliday, J., & Glaser, R. (1984). Psychosocial modifiers of immunocompetence in medical students. *Psychosom. Med.*, 46, 7–14.

Kiecolt-Glaser, J. K., Glaser, R., Gravenstein, S., Malarkey, W. B., & Sheridan, J. (1996). Chronic stress alters the immune response to influenza virus vaccine in older adults. *Proc. Natl. Acad. Sci. U.S.A.*, 93, 3043–3047.

Kiecolt-Glaser, J. K., Glaser, R., Shuttleworth, E. C., Dyer, C. S., Ogrocki, P., & Speicher, C. E. (1987). Chronic stress and immunity in family caregivers of Alzheimer's disease victims *Psychsom. Med.*, 49, 523–535.

Kiecolt-Glaser, J. K., Kennedy, S., Malkoff, S., Fisher, L., Speicher, C. E., & Glaser, R. (1988). Marital discord and immunity in males. *Psychosom. Med.*, 50, 213–229.

Kiecolt-Glaser, J. K., Page, G. G., Marucha, P. T., MacCallum, R. C., & Glaser, R. (1998). Psychological influences on surgical recovery. Perspectives from psychoneuroimmunology. *Amer. Psychologist*, 53(11), 1209–1218.

Kiecolt-Glaser, J. K., et al. (1991). Spousal caregivers of dementia victims: Longitudinal changes in immunity and health. *Psychosom. Med.*, 53(4), 345–362.

Kienhorst, C. W. M., Wolters, W. H. G., Diekstra, R. F. W., & Otte, E. (1987). A study of the frequency of suicidal behaviour in children aged 5 to 14. *J. Child Psychol. Psychiat. Allied Disc.*, 28(1), 151–165.

Kienhorst, I. C., de Wilde, E. J., Diekstra, R. F. W., & Wolters, W. H. G. (1995). Adolescents' image of their suicide attempt. *J. Amer. Acad. Child Adol. Psychiat.*, 34(5), 523–628.

Kiesler, C. A. (1992). U.S. mental health policy: Doomed to fail. *Amer. Psychologist*, 47(9), 1077–1082.

Kiesler, D. J. (1966). Some myths of psychotherapy research and the search for a paradigm. *Psychol. Bull.*, 65, 110–136.

Kiesler, D. J. (1995). Research classic: "Some myths of psychotherapy research and the search for a

paradigm": Revisited. *Psychother. Res.*, 5(2), 91–101.

Kiev, A. (1989). Suicide in adults. In J. G. Howells (Ed.), *Modern perspectives in the psychiatry of the affective disorders.* New York: Brunner/Mazel.

Kihlström, J. F., Tataryn, D. J., & Hoyt, I. P. (1993). Dissociative disorders. In P. B. Sucker & H. E. Adams (Eds.), *Comprehensive handbook of psychopathology* (2nd ed.), New York: Plenum Press.

Killen, J. D. (1996). Development and evaluation of a school-based eating disorder symptoms prevention program. In L. Smolak, M. P. Levine, & R. Striegel-Moore (Eds.), *The developmental psychopathology of eating disorders: Implications for research, prevention, and treatment.* Mahwah, NJ: Erlbaum.

Killen, J. D., Taylor, C. B., Hayward, C., Wilson, D. M., Hammer, L. D., Robinson, T. N., Litt, I., Simmonds, B. A., Varady, A., & Kraemer, H. (1994). The pursuit of thinness and onset of eating disorder symptoms in a community sample of adolescent girls: A three-year prospective analysis. *Inter. J. Eat. Disorders*, 16, 227–238.

Kilmann, P. R., Sabalis, R. F., Gearing, M. L., Bukstel, L. H., & Scovern, A. W. (1982). The treatment of sexual paraphilias: A review of outcome research. *J. Sex Res.*, 18, 193–252.

Kilmann, P. R., Wagner, M. K., & Sotile, W. M. (1977). The differential impact of self-monitoring on smoking behavior: An exploratory study. *J. Clin. Psychol.*, 33(3), 912–914.

Kim, J. J., Mohamed, S., Andreasen, N. C., O'Leary, D. S., Watkins, G. L., Ponto, L. L. B., & Hichwa, R. D. (2000). Regional neural dysfunctions in chronic schizophrenia studied with positron emission tomography. *Amer. J. Psychiat.*, 157(4), 542–548.

Kimball, A. (1993). Nipping and tucking. In Skin deep: Our national obsession with looks. *Psychol. Today*, 26(3), 96.

Kimzey, S. L. (1975). The effects of extended spaceflight on hematologic and immunologic systems. *J. Amer. Med. Women's Assoc.*, 30(5), 218–232.

Kimzey, S. L., Johnson, P. C., Ritzman, S. E., & Mengel, C. E. (1976, April). Hematology and immunology studies: The second manned Skylab mission. *Aviat., Space, Envir. Med.*, pp. 383–390.

Kinard, E. M. (1982). Child abuse and depression: Cause or consequence? *Child Welfare*, 61, 403–413.

Kinderman, P., & Bentall, R. P. (1997). Causal attributions in paranoia and depression: Internal, personal, and situational attributions for negative events. *J. Abnorm. Psychol.*, 106(2), 341–345.

King, C. A., & Young, R. D. (1981). Peer popularity and peer communication patterns: Hyperactive vs. active but normal boys. *J. Abnorm. Child Psychol.*, 9(4), 465–482.

King, D. W., King, L. A., Foy, D. W., & Gudanowski, D. M. (1996). Prewar factors in combat related posttraumatic stress disorder: Structural equation modeling with a national sample of female and male Vietnam veterans. *J. Cons. Clin. Psychol.*, 64, 520–531.

King, D. W., King, L. A., Foy, D. W., Keane, T. M., & Fairbank, J. A. (1999). Posttraumatic stress disorder in a national sample of female and male Vietnam veterans: Risk factors, war-zone stressors, and resilience-recovery variables. *J. Abnorm. Psychol.*, 108(1), 164–170.

King, G. A., Polivy, J., & Herman, C. P. (1991). Cognitive aspects of dietary restraint: Effects on person memory. *Inter. J. Eat. Disorders*, 10(3), 313–321.

King, L. W., Liberman, R. P., & Roberts, J. (1974). *An evaluation of personal effectiveness training (assertive training): A behavior group therapy.*

Paper presented at the 31st annual conference of American Group Psychotherapy Association, New York.

King, M., & Bartlett, A. (1999). British psychiatry and homosexuality. *Brit. J. Psychiat.*, 175, 106–113.

King, M. B., & Mezey, G. (1987). Eating behaviour of male racing jockeys. *Psychol. Med.*, 17, 249–253.

King, M. K., Schmaling, K. B., Cowley, D. S., & Dunner, D. L. (1995). Suicide attempt history in depressed patients with and without a history of panic attacks. *Comprehen. Psychiat.*, 36(1), 25–30.

King, M. P., & Tucker, J. A. (2000). Behavior change patterns and strategies distinguishing moderation drinking and abstinence during the natural resolution of alcohol problems without treatment. *Psychol. Addict. Behav.*, 14(1), 48–55.

King, N. J. (1993). Simple and social phobias. In T. H. Ollendick & R. J. Prinz (Eds.), *Advances in clinical child psychology* (Vol. 15). New York: Plenum Press.

King, N. J., Eleonora, G., & Ollendick, T. H. (1998). Etiology of childhood phobias: Current status of Rachman's three pathways theory. *Behav. Res. Ther.*, 36(3), 297–309.

Kinsey, A. C., Pomeroy, W. B., Martin, C. E., & Gebhard, P. H. (1953). *Sexual behavior in the human female.* Philadelphia: Saunders.

Kinzie, J., Leung, P., Boehnlein, J., & Matsunaga, D. (1992). Psychiatric epidemiology of an Indian village: A 19-year replication study. *J. Nerv. Ment. Dis.*, 180(1), 33–39.

Kirk, S. A., & Kutchins, H. (1992). *The selling of DSM: The rhetoric of science in psychiatry.* New York: Aldine de Gruyter.

Kirkpatrick, B., Kopelowicz, A., Buchanan, R.W., & Carpenter, W. T., Jr. (2000). Assessing the efficacy of treatments for the deficit syndrome of schizophrenia. *Neuropsychopharmacology*, 22(3), 303–310.

Kirmayer, L. J., Robbins, J. M., & Paris, J. (1994). Somatoform disorders: Personality and the social matrix of somatic distress. *J. Abnorm. Psychol.*, 103(1), 125–136.

Kirn, W. (1997, August 18). The ties that bind. *Time*, pp. 48–50.

Kisker, G. W. (1977). *The disorganized personality.* New York: McGraw-Hill.

Klassen, A., Miller, A., Raina, P., Lee, S. K., & Olsen, L. (1999). Attention-deficit hyperactivity disorder in children and youth: A quantitative systematic review of the efficacy of different management strategies. *Canad. J. Psychiat.*, 44(10), 1007–1016.

Klausner, J. D., Sweeney, J. A., Deck, M. D., Haas, G. L., et al. (1992). Clinical correlates of cerebral ventricular enlargement in schizophrenia: Further evidence for frontal lobe disease. *J. Nerv. Ment. Dis.*, 180(7), 407–412.

Kleber, H. D. (1981). Detoxification from narcotics. In J. H. Lowinson & P. Ruiz (Eds.), *Substance abuse: Clinical problems and perspectives.* Baltimore: William & Wilkins.

Kleber, H. D. (1995). Afterword to section I. In J. M. Oldham & M. B. Riba (Eds.), *American Psychiatric Press review of psychiatry* (Vol. 14). Washington, DC: American Psychiatric Press.

Klein, D. F. (1964). Delineation of two drug-responsive anxiety syndromes. *Psychopharmacologia*, 5, 397–408.

Klein, D. F., & Fink, M. (1962). Psychiatric reaction patterns to imipramine. *Amer. J. Psychiat.*, 119, 432–438.

Klein, E., Kreinin, I., Chistyakov, A., Koren, D., Mecz, L., Marmur, S., Ben-Shachar, D., & Feinsod, M. (1999). Therapeutic efficacy of right prefrontal slow repetitive transcranial magnetic stimulation in major depression. *Arch. Gen. Psychiat., 56*(4), 315–320.

Klein, K., Forehand, R., Armistead, L., & Long, P. (1997). Delinquency during the transition to early adulthood: Family and parenting predictors from early adolescence. *Adolescence, 32*(125), 61–80.

Klein, M. (1998, January). Suicidal states. *American Demographics.*

Klein, M. (1998, March). Looking out for Fido. *American Demographics.*

Klein, M. (1998, March). Moving experiences. *American Demographics.*

Klein, M. (1998, March). Stalking situations. *American Demographics.*

Klein, R. G., Koplewicz, H. S., & Kaner, A. (1992). Imipramine treatment of children with separation anxiety disorder: Special section: New developments in pediatric psychopharmacology. *J. Amer. Acad. Child Adol. Psychiat., 31*(1), 21–28.

Kleinman, A., & Cohen, A. (1997, March). Psychiatry's global challenge. *Scientif. Amer.,* pp. 86–89.

Klerman, G. L. (1984). Characterologic manifestations of affective disorders: Toward a new conceptualization: Commentary. *Integ. Psychiat., 2*(3), 94–96.

Klerman, G. L., & Weissman, M. M. (1992). Interpersonal psychotherapy. In E. S. Paykel (Ed.), *Handbook of affective disorders.* New York: Guilford.

Klerman, G. L., Weissman, M. M., Rounsaville, B., & Chevron, E. (1984). *Interpersonal psychotherapy of depression.* New York: Basic Books.

Klerman, G. L., Weissman, M. M., Markowitz, J., Glick, I., Wilner, P. J., Mason, B., & Shear, M. K. (1994). Medication and psychotherapy. In A. E. Bergin & S. L. Garfiel (Eds.), *Handbook of psychotherapy and behavior change* (4th ed.). New York: Wiley.

Kliewer, W., Lepore, S. J., Oskin, D., & Johnson, P. D. (1998). The role of social and cognitive processes in children's adjustment to community violence. *J. Cons. Clin. Psychol., 66*(1), 199–209.

Klimes-Dougan, B., Free, K., Ronsaville, D., Stilwell, J., Welsh, C. J., & Radke-Yarrow, M. (1999). Suicidal ideation and attempts: A longitudinal investigation of children of depressed and well mothers. *J. Amer. Acad. Child Adol. Psychiat., 38*(6), 651–659.

Kline, N. S. (1958). Clinical experience with iproniazid (Marsilid). *J. Clin. Exp. Psychopathol., 19*(1, Suppl.), 72–78.

Kline, P. (1993). *The handbook of psychological testing.* New York: Routledge.

Kling, K. C., Hyde, J. S., Showers, C. J., & Buswell, B. N. (1999). Gender differences in self-esteem: A meta-analysis. *Psychol. Bull., 125*(4), 470–500.

Klocek, J. W., Oliver, J. M., & Ross, M. J. (1997). The role of dysfunctional attitudes, negative life events, and social support in the prediction of depressive dysphoria: A prospective longitudinal study. *Soc. Behav. Pers., 25*(2), 123–136.

Klopfer, B., & Davidson, H. (1962). *The Rorschach technique.* New York: Harcourt, Brace.

Kluft, R. P. (1983). Hypnotherapeutic crisis intervention in multiple personality. *Amer. J. Clin. Hyp., 26*(2), 73–83.

Kluft, R. P. (1984). Treatment of multiple personality disorder: A study of 33 cases. *Psychiat. Clin. N. Amer., 7*(1), 9–29.

Kluft, R. P. (1985). Hypnotherapy of childhood multiple personality disorder. *Amer. J. Clin. Hyp., 27*(4), 201–210.

Kluft, R. P. (1987). The simulation and dissimulation of multiple personality disorder. *Amer. J. Clin. Hyp., 30*(2), 104–118.

Kluft, R. P. (1988). The dissociative disorders. In J. Talbott, R. Hales, & S. Yudofsky (Eds.), *Textbook of psychiatry.* Washington, DC: American Psychiatric Press.

Kluft, R. P. (1991). Multiple personality disorder. In A. Tasman & S. M. Goldfinger (Eds.), *American Psychiatric Press review of psychiatry* (Vol. 10). Washington, DC: American Psychiatric Press.

Kluft, R. P. (1992). Discussion: A specialist's perspective on multiple personality disorder. *Psychoanalyt. Inquiry, 12*(1), 139–171.

Kluft, R. P. (1993). Basic principles in conducting the psychotherapy of multiple personality disorder. In R. P. Kluft & C. G. Fine (Eds.), *Clinical perspectives on multiple personality disorder.* Washington, DC: American Psychiatric Press.

Kluft, R. P. (1999). An overview of the psychotherapy of dissociative identity disorder. *Amer. J. Psychother., 53*(3), 289–319.

Knesper, D. J., Pagnucco, D. J., & Wheeler, J. R. (1985). Similarities and differences across mental health services providers and practice settings in the United States. *Amer. Psychologist, 40*(12), 1352–1369.

Knowlton, L. (1995, August 29). Licensed to heal. *Los Angeles Times,* p. E3.

Knowlton, L. (1997, May). Outreach Program aids homeless mentally ill. *Psychiatr. Times, XIV*(5).

Knowlton, L. (1998). "Women Healing" conference examines women in recovery. *Psychiatr. Times, XV*(7).

Knox, L. S., Albano, A. M., & Barlow, D. H. (1996). Parental involvement in the treatment of childhood obsessive compulsive disorder: A multiple-baseline examination incorporating parents. *Behav. Ther., 27,* 93–115.

Knutson, B., Wolkowitz, O. M., Cole, S. W., Chan, T., Moore, E. A., Johnson, R. C., Terpstra, J., Turner, R. A., & Reus, V. I. (1998). Selective alteration of personality and social behavior by serotonergic intervention. *Amer. J. Psychiat., 155,* 373–379.

Knutson, J. F. (1995). Psychological characteristics of maltreated children. In J. T. Spence, J. M. Darley, & D. J. Foss (Eds.), *Annu. Rev. Psychol., 46,* 401–431.

Kobasa, S. C. (1979). Stressful life events, personality, and health: An inquiry into hardiness. *J. Pers. Soc. Psychol., 37*(1), 1–11.

Kobasa, S. C. (1982). Commitment and coping in stress resistance among lawyers. *J. Pers. Soc. Psychol., 42,* 707–717.

Kobasa, S. C. (1982). The hardy personality: Towards a social psychology of stress and health. In J. Suls & G. Sanders (Eds.), *Social psychology of health and illness.* Hillsdale, NJ: Erlbaum.

Kobasa, S. C. (1984). Barriers to work stress: II. The "hardy" personality. In W. D. Gentry, H. Benson, & C. J. de Wolff (Eds.), *Behavioral medicine: Work, stress and health.* The Hague: Martinus Nijhoff.

Kobasa, S. C. (1987). Stress responses and personality. In R. C. Barnett, L. Biener, & G. K. Baruch (Eds.), *Gender and stress.* New York: Free Press.

Kobasa, S. C. (1990). Stress resistant personality. In R. E. Ornstein & C. Swencionis (Eds.), *The healing brain: A scientific reader.* Oxford, England: Pergamon Press.

Kocsis, J. H., Friedman, R. A., Markowitz, J. C., Miller, N., Gniwesch, L., & Bram, J. (1995). Stability of remission during tricyclic antidepressant continuation therapy for dysthymia. *Psychopharmacol. Bull., 31*(2), 213–216.

Koegel, L. K., Koegel, R. L., Hurley, C., & Frea, W. D. (1992). Improving social skills and disruptive behavior in children with autism through self-management. *J. Appl. Behav. Anal., 25*(2), 341–353.

Koenig, H. G., & Blazer, D. (1992). Epidemiology of geriatric affective disorders. *Clin. Geriatr. Med., 8,* 235–251.

Koenig, H. G., George, L. K., & Peterson, B. L. (1998). Religiosity and remission of depression in medically ill older patients. *Amer. J. Psychiat., 155*(4), 536–542.

Koenig, H. G., Hays, J. C., Larson, D. B., George, L. K., Cohen, H. J., McCullough, M. E., Meador, K. G., & Blazer, D. G. (1999). Does religious attendance prolong survival? A six-year-follow-up study of 3,968 older adults. *J. Ger. A Biol. Sci Med. Sci., 54*(7), M370–M376.

Koenigsberg, H. W. (1993). Combining psychotherapy and pharmacotherapy in the treatment of borderline patients. In J. M. Oldham, M. B. Riba, & A. Tasman (Eds.), *Review of psychiatry.* Washington, DC: American Psychiatric Press.

Koenigsberg, H. W., Anwunah, I., New, A. S., Mitropoulou, V., Schopick, F., & Siever, L. J. (1999). Relationship between depression and borderline personality disorder. *Depress. Anx., 10*(4), 158–167.

Koerner, K., & Linehan, M. M. (2000). Research on dialectical behavior therapy for patients with borderline personality disorder. *Psychiatr. Clin. N. Amer., 23*(1), 151–167.

Kohn, R., & Levav, I. (1995, May 23). Jewish depression study. Cited in *USA Today,* p. 1D.

Kohut, H. (1971). *The analysis of the self.* New York: International Universities Press.

Kohut, H. (1977). *The restoration of the self.* New York: International Universities Press.

Kohut, H. (1984). *How does analysis cure?* Chicago: University of Chicago Press.

Kohut, H., & Wolf, E. S. (1978). The disorders of the self and their treatment: An outline. *Inter. J. Psychoanal., 59*(4), 413–425.

Kolata, G. (1998, January 11). The fat's in the fire, again. *New York Times,* Section 4, p. 4.

Kolbert, E. (1998, January 19). Housing hope of mentally ill is fading away. *New York Times,* p. B1.

Kolff, C. A., & Doan, R. N. (1985). Victims of torture: Two testimonies. In E. Stover & E. O. Nightingale (Eds.), *The breaking of bodies and minds: Torture, psychiatric abuse, and the health professions.* New York: W. H. Freeman.

Kolodny, R., Masters, W. H., & Johnson, J. (1979). *Textbook of sexual medicine.* Boston: Little, Brown.

Komara, F. A. (1999). Management of behavioral problems in elderly patients with dementia. *J. Amer. Osteopath Assoc., 99*(Suppl. 9), S9–12.

Komaroff, A. L., Masuda, M., & Holmes, T. H. (1986). The Social Readjustment Rating Scale: A comparative study of Negro, white, and Mexican Americans. *J. Psychosom. Res., 12,* 121–128.

Komaroff, A. L., Masuda, M., & Holmes, T. H. (1989). The Social Readjustment Rating Scale: A comparative study of Black, white, and Mexican Americans. In T. H. Holmes and E. M. David (Eds.), *Life change, life events, and illness.* New York: Praeger.

Kong, D. (1998, November 18). Still no solution in the struggle on safeguards—Doing harm: Research on the mentally ill. *Boston Globe,* p. A1.

Koopman, C., Classen, C., Cardena, E., & Spiegel, D. (1995). When disaster strikes, acute stress disorder may follow. *J. Traum. Stress., 8*(1), 29–46.

Koopman, C., Hermanson, K., Diamond, S., Angell, K., & Spiegel, D. (1998). Social support, life stress, pain and emotional adjustment to advanced breast cancer. *Psycho-Oncology, 7*(2), 101–111.

Kopelman, M. D. (1995). The Korsakoff syndrome. *Brit. J. Psychiat., 166*(2), 154–173.

Korchin, S. J., & Sands, S. H. (1983). Principles common to all psychotherapies. In C. E. Walker et al. (Eds.), *The handbook of clinical psychology.* Homewood, IL: Dow Jones-Irwin.

Koren, D., Arnon, I., & Klein, E. (1999). Acute stress response and posttraumatic stress disorder in traffic accident victims: A one-year prospective, follow-up study. *Amer. J. Psychiat.*, 156(3), 367–373.

Kosik, K. S. (1992). Alzheimer's disease: A cell biological perspective. *Science, 256*, 780–783.

Kosky, R. J., Eshkevari, H. S., Goldney, R. D., & Hassan, R. (1998). *Suicide prevention: The global context.* New York: Plenum Press.

Koss, M. P. (1992). The underdetection of rape: Methodological choices influence incidence estimates. *J. Soc. Issues*, 48(1), 61–75.

Koss, M. P. (1993). Rape: Scope, impact, interventions, and public policy responses. *Amer. Psychologist*, 48(10), 1062–1069.

Koss, M. P., & Heslet, L. (1992). Somatic consequences of violence against women. *Arch. Fam. Med.*, 1(1), 53–59.

Koss, M. P., Koss, P., & Woodruff, W. J. (1991). Deleterious effects of criminal victimization on women's health and medical utilization. *Arch. Internal Med.*, 151, 342–357.

Koss, M. P., Woodruff, W. J., & Koss, P. (1991). Criminal victimization among primary care medical patients: Prevalence, incidence, and physician usage. *Behav. Sci. Law*, 9, 85–96.

Kosten, T. R., & McCance-Katz, E. (1995). New pharmacotherapies. In J. M. Oldham & M. B. Riba (Eds.), *American Psychiatric Press review of psychiatry* (Vol. 14). Washington, DC: American Psychiatric Press.

Kouri, E. M., Pope, H. G., Jr., & Lukas, S. E. (1999). Changes in aggressive behavior during withdrawal from long-term marijuana use. *Psychopharmacology (Berl)*, 143(3), 302–308.

Kovacs, M. (1996). Presentation and source of major depression disorder during childhood and later years of the life span. *J. Amer. Child Adol. Psychiat.*, 35(6), 705–715.

Kovacs, M. (1997). Depressive disorders in childhood: An impressionistic landscape. *J. Child Psychol. Psychiat.*, 38(3), 287–298.

Kovacs, M., Goldston, D., & Gatsonis, C. (1993). Suicidal behaviors and childhood-onset depressive disorders: A longitudinal investigation. *J. Amer. Acad. Child Adol. Psychiat.*, 32, 8–20.

Krabbendam, L., Visser, P. J., Derix, M. M. A., Verhey, F., Hofman, P., Verhoeven, W., Tuinier, S., & Jolles, J. (2000). Normal cognitive performance in patients with chronic alcoholism in contrast to patients with Korsakoff's syndrome. *J. Neuropsych. Clin. Neurosci.*, 12(1), 44–50.

Kraines, S. H., & Thetford, E. S. (1972). *Help for the depressed.* Springfield, IL: Thomas.

Krall, W. J., Sramek, J. J., & Cutler, N. R. (1999). Cholinesterase inhibitors: A therapeutic strategy for Alzheimer disease. *Ann. Pharmacother.*, 33(4), 441–450.

Kramer, M. (1989, August 14). Cited in S. Begley, "The stuff that dreams are made of." *Newsweek*, p. 40.

Kramer, M. (1992). Cited in R. D. Cartwright & L. Lamberg, *Crisis dreaming: Using your dreams to solve your problems.* New York: HarperCollins.

Krantz, L. (1992). *What the odds are.* New York: Harper Perennial.

Krasucki, C., Howard, R., & Mann, A. (1998). The relationship between anxiety disorders and age. *Inter. J. Ger. Psychiat.*, 13(2), 79–99.

Kratochwill, T. R. (1992). Single-case research design and analysis: An overview. In T. R. Kratochwill & J. R. Levin (Eds.), *Single-case research design and analysis: New directions for psychology and education.* Hillsdale, NJ: Erlbaum.

Kratzer, L., & Hodgins, S. (1997). Adult outcomes of child conduct problems: A cohort study. *J. Abnorm. Child Psychol.*, 25(1), 65–81.

Krauss, M. W., Seltzer, M. M., & Goodman, S. J. (1992). Social support networks of adults with mental retardation who live at home. *Amer. J. Ment. Retard.*, 96(4), 432–441.

Krausz, M., Muller-Thomsen, T., & Haasen, C. (1995). Suicide among schizophrenic adolescents in the long-term course of illness. *Psychopathology*, 28(2), 95–103.

Kresin, D. (1993). Medical aspects of inhibited sexual desire disorder. In W. O'Donohue & J. Geer (Eds.), *Handbook of sexual dysfunctions.* Boston: Allyn & Bacon.

Kring, A. M., & Neale, J. M. (1996). Do schizophrenic patients show a disjunctive relationship among expressive, experiential, and psychophysiological components of emotion? *J. Abnorm. Psychol.*, 105(2), 249–257.

Krishnan, K. R. R., Swartz, M. S., Larson, M. J., & Santo-Liquido, G. (1984). Funeral mania in recurrent bipolar affective disorders: Reports of three cases. *J. Clin. Psychiat.*, 45, 310–311.

Krishnan, K. R. R., Tupler, L. A., Ritchie, J. C., McDonald, W. M., et al. (1996). Brief reports. Apolipoprotein E-ε4 frequency in geriatric depression. *Biol. Psychiat.*, 40, 69–71.

Krug, E. G., Kresnow, M. J., Peddicord, J. P., Dahlberg, L. L., Powell, K. E., Crosby, A. E., & Annest, J. L. (1998). Suicide after natural disasters. *N. Eng. J. Med.*, 338(6), 373–378.

Krupinski, J., Tiller, J. W. G., Burrows, G. D., & Mackenzie, A. (1998). Predicting suicide risk among young suicide attempters. In R. J. Kosky, H. S. Eshkevari, & R. Hassan (Eds.), *Suicide prevention: The global context.* New York: Plenum Press.

Kuch, K., & Cox, B. J. (1992). Symptoms of PTSD in 124 survivors of the Holocaust. *Amer. J. Psychiat.*, 149(3), 337–340.

Kuczmarski, R., Fiegal, K., Campbell, S., & Johnson, C. (1994). Increasing prevalence of overweight among U.S. adults: The National Health and Nutrition Examination Surveys, 1960–1991. *JAMA, 272*, 205–211.

Kuhn, R. (1958). The treatment of depressive states with G-22355 (imipramine hydrochloride). *Amer. J. Psychiat.*, 115, 459–464.

Kuhn, T. S. (1962). *The structure of scientific revolutions.* Chicago: University of Chicago Press.

Kulhara, P., Basu, D., Mattoo, S. K., Sharan, P., & Chopra, R. (1999). Lithium prophylaxis of recurrent bipolar affective disorder: Long-term outcome and its psychosocial correlates. *J. Affect. Disorders*, 54(1–2), 87–96.

Kulisevsky, J., Berthier, M. L., Avila, A., Gironell, A., & Escartin, A. E. (1998). Unrecognized Tourette syndrome in adult patients referred for psychogenic tremor. *Arch. Neurol.*, 55(3), 409–414.

Kupeli, S., Aydos, K., & Budak, M. (1999). Penile implants in erectile impotence. The importance of clinical experience on outcome. *Eur. Urol.*, 36(2), 129–135.

Kuperman, S., Schlosser, S. S., Lidral, J., & Reich, W. (1999). Relationship of child psychopathology to parental alcoholism and antosicla personality disorder. *J. Amer. Acad. Child Adol. Psychiat.*, 38(6), 686–692.

Kupfer, D. J. (1995). Acute continuation and maintenance treatment of mood disorders. *Depression*, 3, 137–138.

Kupfer, D. L. (1999). Cited in L. Rabasca, I'm okay and you're okay, but not so sure about Y2K. *APA Monitor*, 30(1), 1,18.

Kuriansky, J. B. (1988). Personality style and sexuality. In R. A. Brown & J. R. Field (Eds.), *Treatment of sexual problems in individual and couples therapy.* Costa Mesa, CA: PMA Publishing.

Kurtz, D. L., Stewart, R. B., Zweifel, M., Li, T.-K., & Froehlich, J. C. (1996). Genetic differences in tolerance and sensitization to the sedative/hypnotic effects of alcohol. *Pharmacol. Biochem. Behav.*, 53(3), 585–591.

Kushner, H. I. (1995). Women and suicidal behavior: Epidemiology, gender and lethality in historical perspective. In S. S. Canetto & D. Lester (Eds.), *Women and suicidal behavior.* New York: Springer.

Kushner, M. G., Riggs, D. S., Foa, E. B., & Miller, S. M. (1992). Perceived controllability and the development of posttraumatic stress disorder (PTSD) in crime victims. *Behav. Res. Ther.*, 31(1), 105–110.

Kusumi, I., Ishikane, T., Matsubara, S., & Koyama, T. (1995). Long-term treatment with haloperidol or clozapine does not affect dopamine D^4 receptors in rat frontal cortex. *J. Neural Transmission, 101*, 231–235.

LEMAS (Law Enforcement Management and Administrative Statistics Survey). (1990). Cited in U.S. Dept. of Justice (1994), Violence between inmates (Special report).

Labbate, L. A., & Snow, M. P. (1992). Posttraumatic stress symptoms among soldiers exposed to combat in the Persian Gulf. *Hosp. Comm. Psychiat.*, 43(8), 831–833.

Labbé, E. E. (1995). Treatment of childhood migraine with autogenic training and skin temperature biofeedback: A component analysis. *Headache*, 35(1), 10–13.

Labellarte, M. J., Ginsburg, G. S., Walkup, J. T., & Riddle, M. A. (1999). The treatment of anxiety disorders in children and adolescents. *Biol. Psychiat.*, 46(11), 1567–1578.

Labott, S. M., Preisman, R. C., Popovich, J., & Iannuzzi, M. C. (1995). Health care utilization of somatizing patients in a pulmonary subspecialty clinic. *Psychosomatics*, 36(2), 122–128.

Lachmann, A., & Lachmann, F. M. (1995). The personification of evil: Motivations and fantasies of the serial killer. *Inter. Forum Psychoanal.*, 4(1), 17–23.

Lachner, G., & Engel, R. R. (1994). Differentiation of dementia and depression by memory tests: A meta-analysis. *J. Nerv. Ment. Dis.*, 182(1), 34–39.

Lacks, P. (1999). *Bender Gestalt screening for brain dysfunction* (2nd ed.). New York: Wiley.

Ladds, B. (1997). Forensic treatment and rehabilitation: The growing need for more services and more research. *Inter. J. Ment. Hlth.*, 25(4), 3–10.

Lader, M., & Scotto, J. C. (1998). A multicentre double-blind comparison of hydroxyzine, buspirone and placebo in patients with generalized anxiety disorder. *Psychopharmacology* 139(4), 402–406.

Ladouceur, R., Blais, F., Freeston, M. H., & Dugas, M. J. (1998). Problem solving and problem orientation in generalized anxiety disorder. *J. Anx. Dis.*, 12(2), 139–152.

Ladouceur, R., Freeston, M. H., Gagnon, F., Thibodeau, N., et al. (1995). Cognitive-behavioral treatment of obsessions. *Behav. Mod.* 19(2), 247–257.

Lahey, B. B., Hartdagen, S. E., Frick, P. J., McBurnett, K., et al. (1988). Conduct disorder: Parsing the confounded relation to parental divorce and antisocial personality. *J. Abnorm. Psychol.*, 97(3), 334–337.

Lahiri, A., et. al. (1998, November). Study on blood pressure. *Circulation.*

Laing, R. D. (1959). *The divided self: An existential study in sanity and madness.* London: Tavistock.

Laing, R. D. (1964). *The divided self* (2nd ed.). London: Pelican.

Laing, R. D. (1967). *The politics of experience.* New York: Pantheon.

Lakin, K. C., Anderson, L., Prouty, R., & Polister, B. (1999). State institution populations less than one third of 197, residents older with more impairments. *Mental Retardation, 37,* 85–86.

Lakin, K. C., Prouty, B., Smith, G., & Braddock, D. (1996). Nixon goal surpassed: Two-fold . *Mental Retardation, 34,* 67.

Lakin, M. (1998). Carl Rogers and the culture of psychotherapy. In G. A. Kimble, M. Wertheimer, et al. (Eds.), *Portraits of pioneers in psychology* (Vol. 3). Washington, DC: American Psychological Association.

Lam, R. W., Tam, E. M., Shiah, I.-S., Yatham, L. N., & Zis, A. P. (2000). Effects of light therapy on suicidal ideation in patients with winter depression. *J. Clin. Psychiat., 61*(1), 30–32.

Lamb, H. R. (1994). Public psychiatry and prevention. In R. E. Hales, S. C. Yudofsky, & J. A. Talbott, (Eds.), *The American Psychiatric Press textbook of psychiatry* (2nd ed.). Washington, DC: American Psychiatric Press.

Lamb, M. (1998). Cybersex: Research notes on the characteristics of the visitors to online chat rooms. *Deviant Behavior: An Interdisciplinary Journal, 19,* 121–135.

Lambert, M. J., & Bergin, A. E. (1994). The effectiveness of psychotherapy. In A. E. Bergin & S. L. Garfield (Eds.), *Handbook of psychotherapy and behavioral change* (4th ed.). New York: Wiley.

Lambert, M. J., Shapiro, D. A., & Bergin, A. E. (1986). The effectiveness of psychotherapy. In S. L. Garfield & A. E. Bergin (Eds.), *Handbook of psychotherapy and behavioral change* (3rd ed.). New York: Wiley.

Lambert, M. J., Weber, F. D., & Sykes, J. D. (1993, April). *Psychotherapy versus placebo.* Poster presented at the annual meeting of the Western Psychological Association, Phoenix, AZ.

Lambert, M. T., & Silva, P. S. (1998). An update on the impact of gun control legislation on suicide. *Psychiatr. Quart., 69*(2), 127–134.

Lamberti, J. S., & Cummings, S. (1992). Hands-on restraints in the treatment of multiple personality disorder. *Hosp. Comm. Psychiat., 43*(3), 283–284.

Landes, R. (1999, March 7). Interviewed in M. Jurkowitz, I'm OK; you're OK; Y2K? Does all the worry about deadly computer bugs express our primal fear of entering 2000? *Boston Globe,* p. C1.

Landsbergis, P. A., Schnall, P. L., Warren, K., Pickering, T. G., & Schwartz, J. E. (1994). Association between ambulatory blood pressure and alternative formulations of job strain. *Scand. J. Work Envir. Hlth., 20,* 349–363.

Lane, J. (1999). *Habitual moderate caffeine consumption elevates blood pressure and levels of stress hormones.* Paper presented at 1999 meeting of the Society of Behavioral Medicine, San Diego, CA.

Lang, J. (1999, April 16). Local jails dumping grounds for mentally ill. *Detroit News.*

Langbehn, D. R., Pfohl, B. M., Reynolds, S., Clark, L. A., Battaglia, M., Bellodi, L., Cadoret, R., Grove, W., Pilkonis, P., & Links, P. (1999). The Iowa Personality Disorder Screen: Development and preliminary validation of a brief screening interview. *J. Pers. Disorders, 13*(1), 75–89.

Langer, E. J. (1983). *The psychology of control.* Beverly Hills, CA: Sage.

Langer, S. Z., & Raisman, R. (1983). Binding of (3H) imipramine and (3H) desipramine as biochemical tools for studies in depression. *Neuropharmacology, 22,* 407–413.

Langevin, R., Bain, J., Wortzman, G., Hucker, S., et al. (1988). Sexual sadism: Brain, blood, and behavior. *Ann. NY Acad. of Sci., 528,* 163–171.

Langlois, F., Freeston, M. H., & Ladouceur, R. (2000). Differences and similarities between obsessive intrusive thoughts and worry in a nonclinical population: Study 2. *Behav. Res. Ther., 38*(2), 175–189.

Langlois, F., Freeston, M. H., & Ladouceur, R. (2000). Differences and similarities between obsessive intrusive thoughts and worry in a nonclinical population: Study 1. *Behav. Res. Ther., 38*(2), 157–173.

Langwieler, G., & Linden, M. (1993). Therapist individuality in the diagnosis and treatment of depression. *J. Affect. Disorders, 27,* 1–12.

Lara, M. E., & Klein, D. N. (1999). Psychosocial processes underlying the maintenance and persistence of depression: Implications for understanding chronic depression. *Clin. Psychol. Rev., 19*(5), 553–570.

Larsson, B., & Ivarsson, T. (1998). Clinical characteristics of adolescent psychiatric inpatients who have attempted suicide. *Eur. Child Adol. Psychiat., 7*(4), 201–208.

Laruelle, M., & Abi-Dargham, A. (1999). Dopamine as the wind of the psychotic fire: New evidence from brain imaging studies. *J. Psychopharmacol., 13*(4), 358–371.

Lask, B. (2000). Aetiology. In B. Lask, R. Bryant-Waugh, et al. (Eds.), *Anorexia nervosa and related eating disorders in childhood and adolescence* (2nd ed.). Hove, England: Psychology Press/Taylor & Francis.

Lask, B., & Bryant-Waugh, R. (Eds.). (2000). *Anorexia nervosa and related eating disorders in childhood and adolescence* (2nd ed.). Hove, England: Psychology Press/Taylor & Francis.

Lask, B., Bryant-Waugh, R., et al. (Eds.) *Anorexia nervosa and related eating disorders in childhood and adolescence* (2nd ed.) Hove, England: Psychology Press/Taylor & Francis.

Laumann, E. O., Gagnon, J. H., Michael, R. T., & Michaels, S. (1994). *The social organization of sexuality.* Chicago: University of Chicago Press.

Laumann, E. O., Paik, A., & Rosen, R. C. (1999). Sexual dysfunction in the United States: Prevalence and predictors. *JAMA, 281*(13), 1174.

Laumann, E. O., Paik, A., & Rosen, R. C. (1999). Sexual dysfunction in the United States: Prevalence and predictors. *JAMA, 281*(6), 537–544.

Lautenbacher, S., & Rollman, G. B. (1999). Somatization, hypochondriasis, and related conditions. In A. R. Block, E. F. Kremer, et al. (Eds.), *Handbook of pain syndromes: Biopsychosocial perspectives.* Mahwah, NJ: Erlbaum.

Lawford, B. R., Young, R. McD., Rowell, J. A., Gibson, J. N., et al. (1997). Association of the D² dopamine receptor A1 allele with alcoholism: Medical severity of alcoholism and type of controls. *Biol. Psychiat., 41,* 386–393.

Lawrence, C. (1987). An integrated spiritual and psychological growth model in the treatment of narcissism. *J. Psychol. Theol., 15*(3), 205–213.

Lawrence, E., Eldridge, K., Christensen, A., & Jacobson, N. S. (1999). Integrative couple therapy: The dyadic relationship of acceptance and change. In J. Donovan et al. (Eds.), *Short-term couple therapy.* New York: Guilford Press.

Lawrence, G. H. (1986). Using computers for the treatment of psychological problems. *Comput. Human Behav., 2*(1), 43–62.

Lazarus, A. A. (1965). The treatment of a sexually inadequate man. In L. P. Ullman & L. Krasner (Eds.), *Case studies in behavior modification.* New York: Holt, Rinehart & Winston.

Lazarus, J. A. (1995). Ethical issues in doctor-patient sexual relationships. [Special issue: Clinical sexuality]. *Psychiat. Clin. N. Amer., 18*(1), 55–70.

Lazarus, R. S., & Folkman, S. (1984). *Stress, appraisal, and coping.* New York: Springer.

Lean, M. E., Han, T. S., & Seidell, J. C. (1999). Impairment of health and quality of life using new US federal guidelines for the identification of obesity. *Arch. Internal Med., 159*(8), 837–843.

Leane, W., & Shute, R. (1998). Youth suicide: The knowledge and attitudes of Australian teachers and clergy. *Suic. Life-Threat. Behav., 28*(2), 165–173.

Lebegue, B. (1991). Paraphilias in U.S. pornography titles: "Pornography made me do it" (Ted Bundy). *Bull. Amer. Acad. Psychiat. Law, 19*(1), 43–48.

Lebell, M. B., Marder, S. R., Mintz, J., Mintz, L. I., Tompson, M., Wirshing, W., Johnston-Cronk, K., & McKenzie, J. (1993). Patients' perceptions of family emotional climate and outcome in schizophrenia. *Brit. J. Psychiat., 162,* 751–754.

Lebow, J. L., & Gurman, A. S. (1995). Research assessing couple and family therapy. In J. T. Spence, J. M. Darley, & D. J. Foss (Eds.), *Annual review of psychology* (Vol. 46). Palo Alto, CA: Annual Reviews.

Lecrubier, Y. (1995). Pharmacotherapy and the role of new and classic antidepressants. *Depression, 3,* 134–136.

Lecrubier, Y., Bakker, A., Dunbar, G., and the collaborative paroxetine panic study investigators. (1997). A comparison of paroxetine, clomipramine and placebo in the treatment of panic disorder. *Acta Psychiatr. Scandin, 95,* 145–152.

Ledoux, S., Choquet, M., & Manfredi, R. (1993). Associated factors for self-reported binge eating among male and female adolescents. *J. Adolescence, 16,* 75–91.

Lee, D. E. (1985). Alternative self-destruction. *Percept. Motor Skills, 61*(3, Part 2), 1065–1066.

Lee, D. Y., Uhlemann, M. R., & Barak, A. (1999). Effects of diagnostic suggestion on the clinical judgments and recall memories of autobiography. *J. Soc. Clin. Psychol., 18*(1), 35–46.

Lee, J. K., Lee, C. H., Park, D. B., Kee, B. S., Na, C., Lee, Y. S., Cho, J. Y., Nam, B. W., Lee, K. H., & Chang, D. S. (1998). Circulating natural killer cell in neurotic patients. *Inter. Med. J., 5*(2), 121–126.

Lee, P. W. H., Lieh-Mak, Tu, K. K., & Spinks, J. A. (1993). Coping strategies of schizophrenic patients and their relationship to outcome. *Brit. J. Psychiat., 163,* 177–182.

Lee, R. K. K., Jimenez, J., Cox, A. J., & Wurtman, R. J. (1996). Metabotropic glutamate receptors regulate APP processing in hippocampal neurons and cortical astrocytes derived from fetal rats. In R. J. Wurtman, S. Corkin, J. H. Growdon, & R. M. Nitsch (Eds.), *The neurobiology of Alzheimer's disease.* New York: New York Academy of Sciences.

Lee, T., & Seeman, P. (1980). Elevation of brain neuroleptic/dopamine receptors in schizophrenia. *Amer. J. Psychiat., 137,* 191–197.

Lee, W. M. L. (1999). *An introduction to multicultural counseling.* Philadelphia: Taylor & Francis.

Leenaars, A. A. (1989). *Suicide notes: Predictive clues and patterns.* New York: Human Sciences Press.

Leenaars, A. A. (1991). Suicide in the young adult. In A. A. Leenaars (Ed.), *Life span perspectives of suicide: Time-lines in the suicide process.* New York: Plenum Press.

Leenaars, A. A. (1992). Suicide notes, communication, and ideation. In R. W. Maris, A. L. Berman, J. T. Maltsberger, & R. I. Yufit (Eds.), *Assessment and prediction of suicide.* New York: Guilford.

Leenaars, A. A., & Lester, D. (1992). Facts and myths of suicide in Canada and the United States. *J. Soc. Psychol., 132*(6), 787–789.

Leenaars, A. A., & Lester, D. (1998). The impact of gun control on suicide: Studies from Canada. *Arch. Suic. Res., 4*(1), 25–40.

Leenaars, A. A., & Lester, D. (1999). Domestic integration and suicide in the provinces of Canada. *Crisis, 20*(2), 59–63.

Leenaars, A. A., & Wenckstern, S. (1998). Principles of postvention: Applications to suicide and trauma in schools. *Death Stud., 22*(4), 357–391.

Leenstra, A. S., Ormel, J., & Giel, R. (1995). Positive life change and recovery from depression and anxiety: A three-stage longitudinal study of primary care attenders. *Brit. J. Psychiat., 166*(3), 333–343.

Lehman, A. F. (1995). Vocational rehabilitation in schizophrenia. *Schizo. Bull., 21*(4), 645–656.

Lehman, A. F., Myers, C. P., Dixon, L. B., & Johnson, J. L. (1996). Detection of substance use disorders among psychiatric inpatients. *J. Nerv. Ment. Dis., 184*(4), 228–233.

Lehman, R. S. (1991). *Statistics and research design in the behavioral sciences.* Belmont, CA: Wadsworth.

Lehmann, H. E. (1985). Current perspectives on the biology of schizophrenia. In M. N. Menuck & M. V. Seeman. *New perspectives in schizophrenia.* New York: Macmillan.

Lehoux, P. M., Steiger, H., & Jabalpurlawa, S. (2000). State/trait distinctions in bulimic syndromes. *Inter. J. Eat. Disorders, 27*(1), 36–42.

Lehrer, P. M. (1998). Emotionally triggered asthma: A review of research literature and some hypotheses for self-regulation. *Appl. Psychophysiol. Biofeedback, 23*(1), 13–41.

Leibbrand, R., Hiller, W., & Fichter, M. M. (2000). Hypochondriasis and somatization: Two distinct aspects of somatoform disorders? *J. Clin. Psychol., 56*(1), 63–72.

Leibenluft, E. (1996). Women with bipolar illness: Clinical and research issues. *Amer. J. Psychiat., 153*(2), 163–173.

Leibenluft, E. (2000). Women and bipolar disorder: An update. *Bull. Menninger Clin., 64*(1), 5–17.

Leiblum, S. R., (1996). Sexual pain disorders. In *Treatment of psychiatric disorders: The DSM-IV edition.* Washington, DC: American Psychiatric Press.

Leiblum, S. R., & Segraves, R. T. (1995). Sex and aging. In J. M. Oldham & M. B. Riba (Eds.), *American Psychiatric Press review of psychiatry* (Vol. 14). Washington, DC: American Psychiatric Press.

Leipsic, J. S., Abraham, H. D., & Halperin, P. (1995). Neuroleptic malignant syndrome in the elderly. *J. Geriat. Psychiat. Neurol., 8*(1), 28–31.

Leitenberg, H., Yost, L. W., & Carroll-Wilson, M. (1986). Negative cognitive errors in children: Questionnaire development, normative data, and comparisons between children with and without self-reported symptoms of depression, low self-esteem, and evaluation anxiety. *J. Cons. Clin. Psychol., 54*, 528–536.

Leland, H. (1991). Adaptive behavior scales. In J. L. Matson & J. A. Mulick (Eds.), *Handbook of mental retardation.* New York: Pergamon Press.

Lenderking, W. R., Tennen, H., Nackley, J. F., Hale, M. S., Turner, R. R., & Testa, M. A. (1999). The effects of venlafaxine on social activity level in depressed outpatients. *J. Clin. Psychiat., 60*(3), 157–163.

Lennkh, C., & Simhandl, C. (2000). Current aspects of valproate in bipolar disorder. *Inter. Clin. Psychopharmacology, 15*(1), 1–11.

Lenox, R. H., McNamara, R. F., Papke, R. L., & Manji, H. K. (1998). Neurobiology of lithium: An update. *J. Clin. Psychiat., 59*(Suppl. 6), 37–47.

Lenzenweger, M. F., Cornblatt, B. A., & Putnick, M. (1991). Schizotypy and sustained attention. *J. Abnorm. Psychol., 100*(1), 84–89.

Lenzenweger, M. F., Loranger, A. W., Korfine, L., & Neff, C. (1997). Detecting personality disorders in a non-clinical population: Application of a two-stage procedure for case identification. *Arch. Gen. Psychiat., 54*, 345–351.

Leo, R. J., & Kim, K. Y. (1995). Clomipramine treatment of paraphilias in elderly demented patients. *J. Geriatr. Psychiat. Neurol., 8*(2), 123–124.

Leon, G. R. (1977). *Case histories of deviant behavior* (2nd ed.). Boston: Allyn & Bacon.

Leon, G. R. (1984). *Case histories of deviant behavior* (3rd ed.). Boston: Allyn & Bacon.

Leonard, B. E. (1997). Neurotransmitters in depression: Noradrenaline and serotonin and their interactions. *J. Clin. Psychopharmacol., 17*(2, Suppl. 1), 1S.

Leonard, B. E. (1999). Therapeutic applications of benzodiazepine receptor ligands in anxiety. *Human Psychopharmacol. Clin. Exp. 14*(2), 125–135.

Lerer, B., Shapira, B., Calev, A., Tubi, N., Drexler, H., Kindler, S., Lidsky, D., & Schwartz, J. E. (1995). Antidepressant and cognitive effects of twice- versus three-times-weekly ECT. *Amer. J. Psychiat., 152*(4), 564–570.

Lerner, H. D. (1936). Current developments in the psychoanalytic psychotherapy of anorexia nervosa and bulimia nervosa. *Clin. Psychologist, 39*(2), 39–43.

Lerner, P. M. (1998). *Psychoanalytic perspectives on the Rorschach.* Hillsdale, NJ: Analytic Press.

Lerner, V., Fotyanov, M., Liberman, M., Shlafman, M., & Bar-El, Y. (1995). Maintenance medication for schizophrenia and schizoaffective patients. *Schizo. Bull., 21*(4), 693–701.

Leroux, J. A. (1986). Suicidal behavior and gifted adolescents. *Roeper Rev., 9*(2), 77–79.

Lesch, K. P., Bengel, D., Heils, A., Sabol, S. Z., Greenberg, B. D., Petri, S., Benjamin, J., Muller, C. R., Hamer, D. H., & Murphy, D. L. (1996). Association of anxiety-related traits with a polymorphism in the serotonin transporter gene regulatory region. *Science, 24*(5292), 1527–1531.

Lesch, K.-P., Bengel, D., Heils, A., Sabol, S. Z., Greenberg, B. D., Petri, S., Benjamin, J., Müller, C. R., Hamer, D. H., & Murphy, D. L. (1996, November 29). Association of anxiety-related traits with a polymorphism in the serotonin transporter gene regulatory region. *Science, 274*, 1527–1531.

Leserman, J., Drossman, D. A., Li, Z., Toomey, T. C., et al. (1996). Sexual and physical abuse history in gastroenterology practice: How types of abuse impact health status. *Psychosom. Med., 58*(1), 4–15.

Leshner, A. I., et al. (1992). *Outcasts on the main street: Report of the Federal Task Force on Homelessness and Severe Mental Illness.* Washington, DC: Interagency Council on the Homeless.

Leslie, A. (1997, May 23). *Theory of mind impairment in autism: Its nature and significance.* Keynote address at The Eden Institute Foundation Princeton Lecture Series on Autism.

Lester, D. (1972). Myth of suicide prevention. *Comprehen. Psychiat., 13*(6), 555–560.

Lester, D. (1974). The effects of suicide prevention centers on suicide rates in the United States. *Pub. Hlth. Rep., 89*, 37–39.

Lester, D. (1985). Accidental deaths as disguised suicides. *Psychol. Rep., 56*(2), 626.

Lester, D. (1985). The quality of life in modern America and suicide and homicide rates. *J. Soc. Psychol., 125*(6), 779–780.

Lester, D. (1989). *Can we prevent suicide?* New York: AMS Press.

Lester, D. (1991). Do suicide prevention centers prevent suicide? *Homeostasis Hlth. Dis., 33*(4), 190–194.

Lester, D. (1991). The etiology of suicide and homi-cide in urban and rural America. *J. Rural Commun. Psychol., 12*(1), 15–27.

Lester, D. (1992). Alcoholism and drug abuse. In R. W. Maris, A. L. Berman, J. T. Maltsberger, & R. I. Yufit (Eds.), *Assessment and prediction of suicide.* New York: Guilford.

Lester, D. (1992). Is there a need for suicide prevention? *Crisis, 2*, 94.

Lester, D. (1992). Suicide and disease. *Loss, Grief & Care, 6*(2–3), 173–181.

Lester, D. (1997). Effect of suicide prevention centers in Ireland and Great Britain. *Psychol. Rep., 81*, 1186.

Lester, D. (1998). Differences in content of suicide notes by age and method. *Percept. Motor Skills, 87*(2), 530.

Lester, D. (1998). Experience of loss in famous suicides. *Psychol. Rep., 82*(3, Pt. 1), 1090.

Lester, D. (1998). Judging the sex and age of suicide note writers. *Percept. Motor Skills, 86*(3, Pt. 2), 1218.

Lester, D. (1998). Preventing suicide by restricting access to methods for suicide. *Arch. Suic. Res., 4*(1), 7–24.

Lester, D. (1998). Suicidal behavior in African-American slaves. *Omega: J. Death Dying, 37*(1), 1–13.

Lester, D. (1998). Suicide and homicide after the fall of communist regimes. *Eur. Psychiat., 13*(2), 98–100.

Lester, D. (1998). The association of alcohol use, abuse and treatment with suicide and homicide rates. *G. Ital. Suic., 8*(1), 23–24.

Lester, D., & Linn, M. (1998). Joseph Richman's signs for distinguishing genuine from simulated suicide notes. *Percept. Motor Skills, 87*(1), 242.

Lester, D., & Linn, M. (1998). The content of suicide notes written by those using different methods for suicide. *Percept. Motor Skills, 87*(2), 722.

Lester, D., & Saito, Y. (1999). The reasons for suicide in Japan. *Omega: J. Death Dying, 38*(1), 65–68.

Leszcz, M. (1992). Group psychotherapy of the borderline patient. In D. Silver & M. Rosenbluth (Eds.), *Handbook of borderline disorders.* Madison, CT: International Universities Press.

Letourneau, E., & O'Donohue, W. (1993). Sexual desire disorders. In W. O'Donohue & J. Geer (Eds.), *Handbook of sexual dysfunctions.* Boston: Allyn & Bacon.

Le Unes, A. D., Nation, J. R., & Turley, N. M. (1980). Male-female performance in learned helplessness. *J. Psychol., 104*, 255–258.

Leung, N., Waller, G., & Thomas, G. (2000). Outcome of group cognitive-behavior therapy for bulimia nervosa: The role of core beliefs. *Behav. Res. Ther., 38*(2), 145–156.

Leutwyler, K. (1996). Paying attention: The controversy over ADHD and the drug Ritalin is obscuring a real look at the disorder and its underpinnings. *Scientif. Amer., 272*(2), 12–13.

Leutwyler, K. (1996, February). Schizophrenia revisited: New studies focus on malfunctions in the brain. *Scientif. Amer., 22–23.*

Levant, R. F. (2000, February). Interviewed in P. A. McGuire. New hope for people with schizophrenia. *Monitor on Psychology, 31*(2), pp. 24–28.

LeVay, S., & Hamer, D. H. (1994). Evidence for a biological influence in male homosexuality. [Review]. *Scientif. Amer., 270*(5), 44–49.

Levenson, J. L. (1985). Neuroleptic malignant syndrome. *Amer. J. Psychiat., 142*, 1137–1145.

Levenson, M. R. (1992). Rethinking psychopathy. *Theory Psychol., 2*(1), 51–71.

Levesque, R. J. R. (1996). Regulating the private relations of adults with mental disabilities: Old laws, new policies, hollow hopes. *Behav. Sci. Law, 14*, 83–106.

Levin, B. L. (1992). Managed health care: A national perspective. In R. W. Manderscheid & M. A. Sonnenschein (Eds.), *Mental health, United States, 1992*. Washington, DC: U.S. Department of Health and Human Services.

Levin, H. S., Mattis, S., Ruff, R. M., Eisenberg, H. M., Marshall, L. F., Tabaddor, K., High, W. M., Jr., & Frankowski, R. F. (1987). Neurobehavioral outcome following minor head injury: A three-center study. *J. Neurosurg., 66*, 234–243.

Levin, J., & Fox, J. A. (1985). *Mass murder*. New York: Plenum Press.

Levine, M. D. (1975). Children with encopresis: A descriptive analysis. *Pediatrics, 56*, 412–416.

Levine, M. D. (1987). *How schools can help combat student eating disorders: Anorexia nervosa and bulimia*. Washington, DC: National Education Assoc.

Levinson, V. R. (1985). The compatibility of the disease concept with a psychodynamic approach in the treatment of alcoholism. [Special issue: Psychosocial issues in the treatment of alcoholism.] *Alcohol. Treatment Quart., 2*, 7–24.

Levitan, H. L. (1981). Implications of certain dreams reported by patients in a bulimic phase of anorexia nervosa. *Canad. J. Psychiat., 26*(4), 228–231.

Levitt, E. E. (1989). *The clinical application of MMPI Special Scales*. Hillsdale, NJ: Erlbaum.

Levitt, R. (1975). *Psychopharmacology: A biological approach*. New York: Wiley.

Levy, D., Kimhi, R., Barak, Y., Demmer, M., et al. (1996). Brainstem auditory evoked potentials of panic disorder patients. *Neuropsychobiology 33*, 164–167.

Levy, N. B. (1985). The psychophysiological disorders: An overview. In R. C. Simons (Ed.), *Understanding human behavior in health and illness* (3rd ed.). Baltimore: Williams & Wilkins.

Levy, R. L., Cain, K. C., Jarrett, M., & Heitkemper, M. M. (1997). The relationship between daily life stress and gastrointestinal symptoms in women with irritable bowel syndrome. *J. Behav. Med., 20*(2), 177–197.

Levy, S. R., Jurkovic, G. L., & Spirito, A. (1995). A multisystems analysis of adolescent suicide attempters. *J. Abnorm. Child Psychol., 23*(2), 221–234.

Lewin, B. D. (1950). *The psychoanalysis of elation*. New York: Norton.

Lewinsohn, P. M. (1988). A prospective study of risk factors for unipolar depression. *J. Abnorm. Psychol., 97*(3), 251–284.

Lewinsohn, P. M., & Clarke, G. N. (1999). Psychosocial treatment for adolescent depression. *Clin. Psychol. Rev., 19*(3), 329–342.

Lewinsohn, P. M., Antonuccio, D. O., Steinmetz, J. L., & Teri, L. (1984). *The coping with depression course*. Eugene, OR: Castalia.

Lewinsohn, P. M., Clarke, G. N., Hops, H., & Andrews, J. (1990). Cognitive-behavioral treatment for depressed adolescents. *Behav. Ther., 21*, 385–401.

Lewinsohn, P. M., Rohde, P., Teri, L., & Tilson, M. (1990, April). Presentation. Western Psychological Association.

Lewinsohn, P. M., Sullivan, J. M., & Grosscup, S. J. (1982). Behavioral therapy: Clinical applications. In A. T. Rush (Ed.), *Short-term psychotherapies for the depressed patient*. New York: Guilford.

Lewinsohn, P. M., Youngren, M. A., & Grosscup, S. J. (1979). Reinforcement and depression. In R. A. Depue (Ed.), *The psychobiology of the depressive disorders*. New York: Academic Press.

Lewis, O., & Chatoor, I. (1994). Eating disorders. In J. M. Oldham & M. B. Riba (Eds.), *Review of psychiatry* (Vol. 13). Washington, DC: American Psychiatric Press.

Lewis-Harter, S. (2000). Psychosocial adjustment of adult children of alcoholics: A review of the recent empirical literature. *Clin. Psychol. Rev., 20*(3), 311–337.

Li, G., Chanmugam, A., Rothman, R., DiScala, C., Paidas, C. N., & Kelen, G. D. (1999). Alcohol and other psychoactive drugs in trauma patients aged 10–14 years. *Injury Prev., 5*(2), 94–97.

Li, T. K. (2000). Pharmacogenetics of responses to alcohol and genes that influence alcohol drinking. *J. Stud. Alc., 61*(1), 5–12.

Liberman, R. P. (1982). Assessment of social skills. *Schizo. Bull., 8*(1), 82–84.

Liberman, R. P., & Raskin, D. E. (1971). Depression: A behavioral formulation. *Arch. Gen. Psychiat., 24*, 515–523.

Liberman, R., Marder, S., Marshall, B. D., Jr., Mintz, J., & Kuehnel, T. (1998). Biobehavioral therapy: Interactions between pharmacotherapy and behavior therapy in schizophrenia. In T. Wykes, N. Tarrier, et al. (Eds.), *Outcome and innovation in psychological treatment of schizophrenia*. Chicester, England: Wiley.

Libow, J. A. (1995). Munchausen by proxy victims in adulthood: A first look. *Child Abuse Negl., 19*(9), 1131–1142.

Libow, J. A., & Schreirer, H. A. (1998) Factitious disorder by proxy. In R. T. Ammerman & J. V. Campo (Eds.), *Handbook of pediatric psychology and psychiatry: Vol. 1. Psychological and psychiatric issues in the pediatric setting*. Boston: Allyn & Bacon.

Lichtenberg, J. W., & Kalodner, C. (1997, February 28). *The science-based practice of counseling psychology: A case for empirically-validated interventions*. Paper presented at the midwinter meeting of the Council of Counseling Psychology Training Programs, La Jolla, CA.

Lichtman, A. H., & Martin, B. R. (1999). Analgesic properties of THC and its synthetic derivatives. In G. G. Nahas, K. M. Sutin, et al. (Eds.), *Marihuana and medicine*. Clifton, NJ: Humana Press.

Lickey, M. E., & Gordon, B. (1991). *Medicine and mental illness: The use of drugs in psychiatry*. New York: W. H. Freeman.

Lidz, T. (1963). *The family and human adaptation*. New York: International Universities Press.

Lidz, T. (1973). *The origin and treatment of schizophrenic disorders*. New York: Basic Books.

Lidz, T., Cornelison, A., & Fleck, S. (1965). *Schizophrenia and the family*. New York: International Universities Press.

Lidz, T., Cornelison, A., Fleck, S., & Terry, D. (1957). The intra-familial environment of the schizophrenic patient: II. Marital schism and marital skew. *Amer. J. Psychiat., 114*, 241–248.

Lie, N. (1992). Follow-ups of children with attention deficit hyperactivity disorder. *Acta Psychiatr. Scandin., 85*, 40.

Lieberman, J. A. (1995). Signs and symptoms: What can they tell us about the clinical course and pathophysiologic processes of schizophrenia. *Arch. Gen. Psychiat., 52*(5), 361–363.

Lieberman, J. A. (1998). Maximizing Clozapine therapy: Managing side effects. *J. Clin. Psychiat., 59*(Suppl. 3), 38–43.

Lieberman, J. A., Alvir, J. Ma., Koreen, A., Geisler, S., Chakos, M., Scheitman, B., & Woerner, M. (1996). Psychobiologic correlates of treatment response in schizophrenia. *Neuropsychopharmacology, 14*, 13S–21S.

Liebowitz, M. R. (1992). Diagnostic issues in anxiety disorders. In A. Tasman & M. B. Riba (Eds.), *Review of psychiatry* (Vol. 11). Washington, DC: American Psychiatric Press.

Liebowitz, M. R., Heimberg, R. G., Schneier, F. R., Hope, D. A., Davies, S., Holt, C. S., Goetz, D., Juster, H. R., Lin, S. H., Bruch, M. A.,

Marshall, R. D., & Klein, D. F. (1999). Cognitive-behavioral group therapy versus phenelzine in social phobia: Long-term outcome. *Depress. Anx., 10*(3), 89–98.

Liebowitz, M. R., Hollander, E., Schneier, F., Campeas, R., et al. (1990). Reversible and irreversible monoamine oxidase inhibitors in other psychiatric disorders. *Acta Psychiatr. Scandin., 82*(Suppl. 360), 29–34.

Liebowitz, M. R., Schneier, F. R., Hollander, E., & Welkowitz, L. A., et al. (1991). Treatment of social phobia with drugs other than benzodiazepines. *J. Clin. Psychiat., 52*(Suppl.), 10–15.

Liebowitz, M. R., Stone, M., & Turkat, I. D. (1986). Treatment of personality disorders. In A. Frances & R. Hales (Eds.), *American Psychiatric Association annual review* (Vol. 5). Washington, DC: American Psychiatric Press.

Liebowitz, S. F., & Hoebel, B. G. (1998). Behavioral neuroscience of obesity. In G. A. Bray, C. Bouchard, & P. T. James (Eds.), *The handbook of obesity*. New York: Dekker.

Liedl, B. (1999). Sex-adjusting surgery in transsexualism. [Article in German] *MMW Fortschr Med., 141*(23), 41–45.

Lifton, R. J. (1973). *Home from the war: Vietnam veterans, neither victims nor executioners*. New York: Simon & Schuster.

Lilienfeld, S. O., Lynn, S. J., Kirsch, I., Chaves, J. F., Sarbin, T. R., Ganaway, G. K., & Powell, R. A. (1999). Dissociative identity disorder and the sociocognitive model: Recalling the lessons of the past. *Psychol. Bull., 125*(5), 507–523.

Limandri, B. J., & Sheridan, D. J. (1995). Prediction of intentional interpersonal violence: An introduction. In J. C. Campbell (Ed.), *Assessing dangerousness: Violence by sexual offenders, batterers, and child abusers*. Thousand Oaks, CA: Sage.

Lindner, M. (1968). *Hereditary and environmental influences upon resistance to stress*. Unpublished doctoral dissertation, University of Pennsylvania, Philadelphia.

Lindsay, D. S. (1994). Contextualizing and clarifying criticisms of memory work in psychotherapy. *Consciousness Cog., 3*, 426–437.

Lindsay, D. S. (1996). Contextualizing and clarifying criticisms of memory work in psychotherapy. In K. Pezdek & W. P. Banks (Eds.), *The recovered memory/false memory debate*. San Diego: Academic Press.

Lindsay, D. S., & Read, J. D. (1994). Psychotherapy and memories of childhood sexual abuse: A cognitive perspective. *J. App. Cog. Psychol. 8*, 281–338.

Lindstrom, E. M., Ohlund, L. S., Lindstrom, L. H., & Ohman, A. (1992). Symptomatology and electrodermal activity as predictors of neuroleptic response in young male schizophrenic inpatients. *Psychiat. Res., 42*(2), 145–158.

Lindström, L. H. (1996). Clinical and biological markers for outcome in schizophrenia: A review of a longitudinal follow-up study in Uppsala schizophrenia research project. *Neuropsychopharmacology, 14*, 23S–26S.

Linehan, M. M. (1992). Behavior therapy, dialectics, and the treatment of borderline personality disorder. In D. Silver & M. Rosenbluth (Eds.), *Handbook of borderline disorders*. Madison, CT: International Universities Press.

Linehan, M. M. (1993). *Cognitive-behavioral therapy of borderline personality disorder*. New York: Guilford.

Linehan, M. M. (1998, June 7). Cited in G. Hochman, On the Edge. *Inquirer Magazine*, p. 36.

Linehan, M. M., & Nielsen, S. L. (1981). Assessment of suicide ideation and parasuicide: Hopelessness and social desirability. *J. Cons. Clin. Psychol., 49*(5), 773–775.

Links, P. S. (1996). *Clinical assessment and management of severe personality disorders*. Washington, DC: American Psychiatric Press.

Links, P. S., & Heslegrave, R. J. (2000). Prospective studies of outcome. Understanding mechanisms of change in patients with borderline personality disorder. *Psychiat. Clin. N. Amer., 23*(1), 137–150.

Linsky, A. S., Strauss, M. A., & Colby, J. P. (1985). Stressful events, stressful conditions and alcohol problems in the United States: A partial test of Bales's theory. *J. Stud. Alc., 46*(1), 72–80.

Linszen, D. H., Dingemans, P. M., Nugter, M. A., Willem, A. J., et al. (1997). Patient attributes and expressed emotion as risk factors for psychotic relapse. *Schizo. Bull., 23*(1), 119–130.

Linz, T. D., Hooper, S. R., Hynd, G. W., Isaac, W., et al. (1990). Frontal lobe functioning in conduct disordered juveniles: Preliminary findings. *Arch. Clin. Neuropsychol., 5*(4), 411–416.

Lipke, H. J., & Botkin, A. L. (1992). Brief case studies of eye movement desensitization and reprocessing (EMD/R) with chronic post-traumatic stress disorder. *Psychotherapy, 29*, 591–595.

Lipowski, Z. J. (1987). Somatization: Medicine's unsolved problem. *Psychosomatics, 28*(6), 294–297.

Lipschitz, A. (1995). Suicide prevention in young adults (age 18–30). [Special issue: Suicide prevention: Toward the year 2000.] *Suic. Life-Threat. Behav., 25*(1), 155–170.

Lipsky, M. J., Kassinove, H., & Miller, N. J. (1980). Effects of rational-emotive therapy, rational role reversal, and rational-emotive imagery on the emotional adjustment of community mental health center patients. *J. Cons. Clin. Psychol., 48*(3), 366–374.

Lipton, A. A., & Simon, F. S. (1985). Psychiatric diagnosis in a state hospital: Manhattan State revisited. *Hosp. Comm. Psychiat., 36*(4), 368–373.

Lipton, H. L. (1988). A prescription for change. *Generations, 12*(4), 74–79.

Lisansky-Gomberg, E. (1993). Women and alcohol: Use and abuse. *J. Nerv. Ment. Dis., 181*(4), 211–216.

Lish, J. D., Kavoussi, R. J., & Coccaro, E. F. (1996). Aggressiveness. In C. G. Costello (Ed.), *Personality characteristics of the personality disordered*. New York: Wiley.

Liss, M., & Stahly, G. (1993). Domestic violence and child custody. In M. Hansen & M. Harway (Eds.), *Battering and family therapy. A feminist perspective*. Newbury Park, CA: Sage.

Lissner, L., Odell, P. M., D'Agostino, R. B., Stokes, J., Kreger, B. E., Bélanger, A. J., & Brownell, K. D. (1991). Variability of body weight and health outcomes in the Farmingham population. *N. Engl. J. Med., 324*, 1839–1844.

Litinsky, A. M., & Haslam, N. (1998). Dichotomous thinking as a sign of suicide risk on the TAT. *J. Pers. Assess., 71*(3), 368–378.

Litman, R. E. (1995). Suicide prevention in a treatment setting. [Special issue: Suicide prevention: Toward the year 2000.] *Suic. Life-Threat. Behav., 25*(1), 134–142.

Litt, M. D. (1996). A model of pain and anxiety associated with acute stressors: Distress in dental procedures. *Behav. Res. Ther., 34*(5/6), 459–476.

Little, K. B., & Shneidman, E. S. (1959). Congruences among interpretations of psychological test and amamnestic data. *Psychol. Monog., 73*(476).

Liu, L. (1999, March 19). Before you pop that pill... Something to know if you're over 65.

Livesley, W. J. (Ed.). (1995). *The DSM-IV personality disorders*. New York: Guilford.

Livesley, W. J., Schroeder, M. L., Jackson, D. N., & Jang, K. L. (1994). Categorical distinctions in the study of personality disorder: Implications for classification. *J. Abnorm. Psychol., 103*(1), 6–17.

Livingston, R., Witt, A., & Smith, G. R. (1995). Families who somatize. *J. Dev Behav. Pediat., 16*(1), 42–46.

Lloyd, G. G., & Lishman, W. A. (1975). Effect of depression on the speed of recall of pleasant and unpleasant experiences. *Psychol. Med., 5*, 173–180.

Lloyd, G. K., Fletcher, A., & Minchin, M. C. W. (1992). GABA agonists as potential anxiolytics. In G. D. Burrows, S. M. Roth, & R. Noyes, Jr., *Handbook of Anxiety* (Vol. 5). Oxford, England: Elsevier.

Lloyd, R. M. (1992). Negotiating child sexual abuse: The interactional character of investigative practices. *Social Problems, 39*(2), 109–124.

Lock, J., & Giammona, A. (1999). Severe somatoform disorder in adolescence: A case series using a rehabilitation model for intervention. *Clin. Child Psychol. Psychiat., 4*(3), 341–351.

Loebel, J. P., Loebel, J. S., Dager, S. R., Centerwall, B. S., et al. (1991). Anticipation of nursing home placement may be a precipitant of suicide among the elderly. *J. Amer. Ger. Soc., 39*(4), 407–408.

Loerch, B., Graf-Morgenstern, M., Hautzinger, M., & Schlegel, S. (1999). Randomised placebo-controlled trial of moclobemide, cognitive-behavioural therapy and their combination in panic disorder with agoraphobia. *Brit. J. Psychiat., 174*, 205–212.

Loewenstein, R. J. (1991). Psychogenic amnesia and psychogenic fugue: A comprehensive review. In A. Tasman & S. M. Goldfinger (Eds.), *American Psychiatric Press review of psychiatry* (Vol. 10). Washington, DC: American Psychiatric Press.

Loftus, E. F. (1993). The reality of repressed memories. *Amer. Psychologist, 48*, 518–537.

Loftus, E. F. (1997). Repressed memory accusations: Devastated families and devastated patients. *Appl. Cog. Psychol., 11*. 25–30.

Loftus, E.F. (2000). Remembering what never happened. In E. Tulving et al. (Eds.), *Memory, consciousness, and the brain: The Tallinn Conference*. Philadelphia: Psychology Press/Taylor & Francis.

Loge, J. H., Ekeberg, O., & Kaasa, S. (1998). Fatigue in the general Norwegian population: Normative data and associations. *J. Psychosom. Res., 56*(1), 53–65.

Logue, A. W. (1991). *The psychology of eating and drinking*. New York: W. H. Freeman.

LoLordo, A., & Sun Foreign Staff. (1998, September 13). Holocaust continues to take toll; Trauma: A portion of Israel's survivors have had to be institutionalized as the horrors they lived through have overwhelmed them. (Baltimore) *Sun*, p. 2A.

Longo, L. P. (1998). Non-benzodiazepine pharmacotherapy of anxiety and panic in substance abusing patients. *Psychiat. Ann., 28*(3), 14–153.

Lonigan, C. J., Shannon, M. P., Taylor, C. M., et al. (1994). Children exposed to disaster: II. Risk factors for the development of post-traumatic symptomatology. *J. Amer. Acad. Child Adol. Psychiat., 33*, 94–105.

Loomer, H. P., Saunders, J. C., & Kline, N. S. (1957). A clinical and phamacodynamic evaluation of iproniazid as a psychic energizer. *Amer. Psychiat. Assoc. Res. Rep., 8*, 129.

LoPiccolo, C. J., Goodkin, K., & Baldewicz, T. T. (1999). Current issues in the diagnosis and management of malingering. *Ann. Med., 31*(3), 166–173.

LoPiccolo, J. (1985). Advances in diagnosis and treatment of male sexual dysfunction. *J. Sex Marital Ther., 11*(4), 215–232.

LoPiccolo, J. (1990). Treatment of sexual dysfunction. In A. S. Bellak, M. Hersen, & A. E. Kazdin (Eds.), *International handbook of behavior modification and therapy* (2nd ed.). New York: Plenum Press.

LoPiccolo, J. (1991). Post-modern sex therapy for erectile failure. In R. C. Rosen & S. R. Leiblum (Eds.), *Erectile failure: Diagnosis and treatment*. New York: Guilford.

LoPiccolo, J. (1992). Paraphilias. *Nord. Sex., 10*(1), 1–14.

LoPiccolo, J. (1995). Sexual disorders and gender identity disorders. In R. J. Comer, *Abnormal psychology* (2nd ed.). New York: W. H. Freeman.

LoPiccolo, J. (1997). Sex therapy: A post-modern model. In S. J. Lynn & J. P. Garske (Eds.), *Contemporary psychotherapies: Models and methods* (2nd ed.).

LoPiccolo, J., & Friedman, J. R. (1988). Broad spectrum treatment of low sexual desire: Integration of cognitive, behavioral, and systemic treatment. In S. Leiblum & R. Rosen (Eds.), *Sexual desire disorders*. New York: Guilford.

LoPiccolo, J., & Stock, W. E. (1987). Sexual function, dysfunction, and counseling in gynecological practice. In Z. Rosenwaks, F. Benjamin, & M. L. Stone (Eds.), *Gynecology*. New York: Macmillan.

Lorand, S. (1950). *Clinical studies in psychoanalysis*. New York: International Universities Press.

Lorand, S. (1968). Dynamics and therapy of depressive states. In W. Gaylin (Ed.), *The meaning of despair*. New York: Jason Aronson.

Loranger, A. W., Sartoruis, N., Andreoli, A., Berger, P., et al. (1994). The International Personality Disorder Examination. *Arch. Gen. Psychiat., 51*, 215–224.

Lorenzo, A., & Yankner, B. A. (1996). Amyloid fibril toxicity in Alzheimer's disease and diabetes. In R. J. Wurtman, S. Corkin, J. H. Growdon, & R. M. Nitsch (Eds.), *The neurobiology of Alzheimer's disease*. New York: New York Academy of Sciences.

Losonczy, M. F., et al. (1986). Correlates of lateral ventricular size in chronic schizophrenia: I. Behavioral and treatment response measures. *Amer. J. Psychiat., 143*(8), 976–981.

Lotufo-Neto, F., Trivedi, M., & Thase, M. E. (1999). Meta-analysis of the reversible inhibitors of monoamine oxidase type A moclobemide and brofaromine for the treatment of depression. *Neuropsychopharmacology, 20*(3), 226–247.

Love, S. R., Matson, J. L., & West, D. (1990). Mothers as effective therapists for autistic children's phobias. *J. Appl. Behav. Anal., 23*(3), 379–385.

Lovejoy, M. (1982). Expectations and the recovery process. *Schizo. Bull., 8*(4), 605–609.

Low, P., Jeffries, J., Jr., & Bonnie, R. (1986). *The trial of John W. Hinkley, Jr.: A case study in the insanity defense*. Mineola, NY: Foundation Press.

Lowe, M. R., Gleaves, D. H., DiSimone-Weiss, R. T., Forgueson, C., et al. (1996). Restraint, dieting, and the continuum model of bulimia nervosa. *J. Abnorm. Psychol., 105*(4), 508–517.

Lu, L. (1999). Personal or environmental causes of happiness: A longitudinal analysis. *J. Soc. Psychol., 139*(1), 79–90.

Lubetsky, M. J. (1986). The psychiatrist's role in the assessment and treatment of the mentally retarded child. *Child Psychiat. Human Dev., 16*(4), 261–273.

Luborsky, L. (1973). Forgetting and remembering (momentary forgetting) during psychotherapy. In M. Mayman (Ed.), *Psychoanalytic research and psychological issues* (Monograph 30). New York: International Universities Press.

Luborsky, L., Diguer, L., Luborsky, E., & Schmidt, K. A. (1999). The efficacy of dynamic versus other psychotherapies: Is it true that "everyone has won and all must have prizes"?—An Update. In D. S. Janowsky et al. (Eds.), *Psychotherapy indications and outcomes*. Washington, DC: American Psychiatric Press.

Luborsky, L., Singer, B., & Luborsky, L. (1975). Comparative studies of psychotherapies. *Arch. Gen. Psychiat., 32*, 995–1008.

Ludolph, P. S., Westen, D., Misle, B., Jackson, A., et al. (1990). The borderline diagnosis in adolescents: Symptoms and developmental history. *Amer. J. Psychiat., 147*(4), 470–476.

Ludwig, A. (1994). Creative activity and mental illness in female writers. *Amer. J. Psychiat., 151,* 1650–1656.

Ludwig, A. M. (1995). *The price of greatness: Resolving the creativity and madness controversy.* New York: Guilford.

Luechken, L. J. (1998). Childhood attachment and loss experiences affect adult cardiovascular and cortisol function. *Psychosom. Med., 60*(6), 765–772.

Luepker, E. T. (1999). Effects of practitioners' sexual misconduct: A follow-up study. *J. Amer. Acad. Psychiat. Law, 27*(1), 51–63.

Lundberg, U., Dohns, I. E., Medlin, B., Sandsjoe, L., Palmerud, G., Kadefors, R., Ekstroem, M., & Parr, D. (1999). Psychophysiological stress responses, muscle tension, and neck and shoulder pain among supermarket cashiers. *J. Occup. Hlth. Psychol., 4*(3), 245–255.

Lundholm, J. K., & Waters, J. E. (1991). Dysfunctional family systems: Relationship to disordered eating behaviors among university women. *J. Substance Abuse, 3*(1), 97–106.

Luntz, B. K., & Widom, C. S. (1994). Antisocial personality disorder in abused and neglected children grown up. *Amer. J. Psychiat., 151*(5), 670–674.

Lutgendorf, S. K., Antoni, M. H., Ironson, G., Klimas, N., Kumar, M., Starr, K., McCabe, P., Cleven, K., Fletcher, M. A., & Schneiderman, N. (1997). Cognitive-behavioral stress management decreases dysphoric mood and herpes simplex virus-type 2 antibody titers in symptomatic HIV-seropositive gay men. *J. Cons. Clin. Psychol., 65,* 31–43.

Lydiard, R. B., & Brawman-Mintzer, O. (1998). Anxious depression. *J. Clin. Psychiat., 59*(Suppl. 18), 10–17.

Lyketsos, C. G., Hoover, D. R., Guccione, M., Dew, M. A., et al. (1996). Changes in depressive symptoms as AIDS develops. *Amer. J. Psychiat., 153*(11), 1430–1437.

Lykken, D. T. (1995). *The antisocial personalities.* Hillsdale, NJ: Erlbaum.

Lykken, D. T. (1998). *A tremor in the blood: Uses and abuses of the lie detector.* New York: Plenum Press.

Lykken, D. T,., & Tellegen, A. (1996). Happiness is a stochastic phenomenon. *Psychol. Sci., 7*(3), 186–189.

Lyman, B. (1982). The nutritional values and food group characteristics of foods preferred during various emotions. *J. Psychol., 112,* 121–127.

Lymburner, J. A., & Roesch, R. (1999). The insanity defense: Five years of research (1993–1997). *Inter. J. Law Psychiat., 22*(3–4), 213–240.

Lynch, G. (1998). The application of self-psychology to short-term counselling. *Psychodynamic Counselling, 4*(4), 473–485.

Lyness, J. M., Caine, E. D., King, D. A., Cox, C., & Yoediono, Z. (1999). Psychiatric disorders in older primary care patients. *J. Gen. Internal Med., 14*(4), 249–254.

Lyness, J. M., King, D. A., Cox, C., Yoediono, Z., & Caine, E. D. (1999). The importance of subsyndromal depression in older primary care patients: Prevalenced and associated functional disability. *J. Amer. Ger. Soc., 47*(6), 647–652.

Lyon, K. A. (1992). Shattered mirror: A fragment of the treatment of a patient with multiple personality disorder. *Psychoanal. Quarter., 12*(1), 71–94.

Lyon, L. S. (1985). Facilitating telephone number recall in a case of psychogenic amnesia. *J. Behav. Ther. Exp. Psychiat., 16*(2), 147–149.

Lyon, M., Chatoor, I., Atkins, D., Silber, T., et al. (1997, Spring). Testing the hypothesis of the multidimensional model of anorexia nervosa in adolescents. *Adolescence, 32*(125), 101–111.

Lysaker, P., & Bell, M. (1995). Work and meaning: Disturbance of volition and vocational dysfunction in schizophrenia. *Psychiatry, 58*(4), 392–400.

MORI (Market Opinion Research International). (1999, May 22) Poll on animal experimentation. *New Scientist.*

MRI (Matrix Research Institute). (1998). *The facts about mental illness and work.* Philadelphia, PA: Author.

MacDonald, M. L., & Schnur, R. E. (1987). Anxieties and American elders: Proposals for assessment and treatment. In L. Michelson & L. M. Ascher (Eds.), *Anxiety and stress disorders: Cognitive behavioral assessment and treatment.* New York: Guilford.

MacDonald, W. L. (1998). The difference between blacks' and whites' attitudes toward voluntary euthanasia. *J. Sci. Study Religion, 37*(3), 411–426.

Mace, N., & Rabins, P. (1991). *The 36-hour day* (2nd ed.). Baltimore: Johns Hopkins University Press.

MacHovek, F. J. (1981). Hypnosis to facilitate recall in psychogenic amnesia and fugue states: Treatment variables. *Amer. J. Clin. Hyp., 24*(1), 7–13.

Machover, K. (1949). *Personality projection in the drawing of the human figure.* Springfield, IL: Thomas.

MacIntyre, D., & Carr. A. (1999). Evaluation of the effectiveness of the stay safe primary prevention program for child sexual abuse. *Child Abuse Negl., 23*(12), 1307–1325.

MacIntyre, D., & Carr, A. (1999). Helping children to the other side of silence: A study of the impact of the stay safe program on Irish children's disclosures of sexual victimization. *Child Abuse Negl., 23*(12), 1327–1340.

Madge, N., & Harvey, J. G. (1999). Suicide among the young: The size of the problem. *J. Adolescence, 22*(1), 145–155.

Madianos, M. G., & Madianou, D. (1992). The effects of long-term community care on relapse and adjustment of persons with chronic schizophrenia. *Inter. J. Ment. Hlth., 21*(1), 37–49.

Madrid, A. L., State, M. W., & King, B. H. (2000). Pharmacologic management of psychiatric and behavioral symptoms in mental retardation. *Child Adol. Psychiat. Clin. N. Amer., 9*(1), 225–243.

Magee, W. J., Eaton, W. W., Wittchen, H.-U., McGonagle, K. A., & Kessler, R. C. (1996). Agoraphobia, simple phobia, and social phobia in the National Comorbidity Survey. *Arch. Gen. Psychiat., 53,* 159–168.

Magherini, G., & Biotti, V. (1998). Madness in Florence in the 14th–18th centuries: Judicial inquiry and medical diagnosis, care, and custody. *International Journal of Law and Psychiatry, 21*(4), 355–368.

Maguire, T. (1998, December). Web nets the masses. *American Demographics.*

Maguire, T. (1999, January). The skinny on Zzzzzzs. *American Demographics.*

Maher, B. A. (1974). Delusional thinking and perceptual disorder. *J. Individ. Psychol., 30*(1), 98–113.

Maher, B. A., & Maher, W. B. (1994). Personality and psychopathology: A historical perspective. *J. Abnorm. Psychol., 103*(1), 72–77.

Maher, W. B., & Maher, B. A. (1985). Psychopathology: I. From ancient times to the eighteenth century. In G. A. Kimble & K. Schlesinger (Eds.), *Topics in the history of psychology* (Vol. 2). Hillsdale, NJ: Erlbaum.

Mahoney, G., Glover, A., & Finger, I. (1981). Relationship between language and sensorimotor development of Down syndrome and nonretarded children. *Amer. J. Ment. Def., 86*(1), 21–27.

Maier, S. F. (1997, September). *Stressor controllability, anxiety, and serotonin.* Paper presented at the National Institute of Mental Health Workshop on Cognition and Anxiety, Rockville, MD.

Maier, W., Gaensicke, M., Gater, R., Rezaki, M. Tiemens, B., & Urzua, R. F. (1999). Gender differences in the prevalence of depression: A survey in primary care. *J. Affect. Disorders, 53*(3), 241–252.

Maier, W., Gansicke, M., Freyberger, H. J., Linz, M., Heun, R., & Lecrubier, Y. (2000). Generalized anxiety disorder (ICD-10) in primary care from a cross-cultural perspective: A valid diagnostic entity? *Acta Psychiatr. Scandin., 101*(1), 29–36.

Maier, S. F., Watkins, L. R., & Fleshner, M. (1994). Psychoneuroimmunology. The interface between behavior, brain and immunity. *Amer. Psychologist, 49*(12), 1004–1017.

Maj, M., Pirozzi, R., Magliano, L., & Bartoli, L. (1998). Long-term outcome of lithium prophylaxis in bipolar disorder: A 5-year prospective study of 402 patients at a lithium clinic. *Amer. J. Psychiat., 155*(1), 30–35.

Maj, M., Satz, P., Janssen, R., Zaudig, M., et al. (1994). WHO neuropsychiatric AIDS study, Cross-sectional phase II. *Arch. Gen. Psychiat., 51,* 51–61.

Malcolm, A. H. (1990, Jun. 9). Giving death a hand. *New York Times,* p. A6.

Maller, R. G., & Reiss, S. (1992). Anxiety sensitivity in 1984 and panic attacks in 1987. *J. Anx. Dis., 6*(3), 241–247.

Malley, P. B., & Reilly, E. P. (1999). *Legal and ethical dimensions for mental health professionals.* Philadelphia: Taylor & Francis.

Malone, K. M, Corbitt, E. M., Li, S., & Mann, J. J. (1996). Prolactin response to fenfluramine and suicide attempt lethality in major depression. *Brit. J. Psychiat., 168:*324–329.

Maltsberger, J. T. (1999). The psychodynamic understanding of suicide. In D. G. Jacobs et al. (Eds.), *The Harvard Medical School guide to suicide assessment and intervention.* San Francisco: Jossey-Bass.

Mandell, A. J., & Knapp, S. (1979). Asymmetry and mood, emergent properties of seratonin regulation: A proposed mechanism of action of lithium. *Arch. Gen. Psychiat., 36*(8), 909–916.

Manderscheid, R. W., & Rosenstein, M. (1992). Homeless persons with mental illness and alcohol or other drug abuse: Current research, policy, and prospects. *Curr. Opin. Psychiat., 5,* 273–278.

Manderscheid, R. W., Henderson, M. J., Witkin, M. J., & Atay, J. E. (1999). Contemporary mental health systems and managed care. In A. V. Horwitz & T. L. Scheid (Eds.), *A handbook for the study of mental health: Social contexts, theories, and systems.* Cambridge, England: Cambridge University Press.

Mandler, J. M., & McDonough, L. (1995). Long-term recall of event sequences in infancy. *J. Exp. Child Psychol., 59,* 457–474.

Manji, H. K., Bebchuk, J. M., Moore, G. J., Glitz, D., Hasanat, K. A., & Chen, G. (1999). Modulation of CNS signal transduction pathways and gene expression by mood-stabilizing agents: Therapeutic implications. *J. Clin. Psychiat., 60*(Suppl. 2), 27–39.

Manley, R. S., & Needham, L. (1995). An anti-bulimia group for adolescent girls. *J. Child Adol. Group Ther., 5*(1), 19–33.

Mann, B. J. (1995). The North Carolina Dissociation Index: A measure of dissociation using items from the MMPI-2. *J. Pers. Assess.*, 64(2), 349–359.

Mann, J. J., & Arango, V. (1999). The neurobiology of suicidal behavior. In D.G. Jacobs (Ed.), *The Harvard Medical School guide to suicide assessment and intervention.* San Francisco: Jossey-Bass.

Mann, J. J., Malone, K. M., Diehl, D. J., Perel, J., Cooper, T. B., & Mintun, M. A. (1996). Demonstration in vivo of reduced serotonin responsivity in the brain of untreated depressed patients. *Amer. J. Psychiat.*, 153(2), 174–182.

Mann, J. J., Oquendo, M., Underwood, M. D., & Arango, V. (1999). The neurobiology of suicide risk: A review for the clinician. *J. Clin. Psychiat.*, 60(Suppl. 2), 7–11.

Manning, A. (1996, January 16). New alcohol programs turn focus to moderation. *USA Today*, p. 6D.

Mannuzza, S., Klein, R. G., Bessler, A., Malloy, P., & LaPadula, M. (1993). Adult outcome of hyperactive boys. *Arch. Gen. Psychiat.*, 50, 565–576.

Mannuzza, S., Klein, R. G., Bressler, A., Malloy, P., LaPadula, M. (1998). Adult psychiatric status of hyperactive boys grown up. *Amer. J. Psychiat.*, 155(4), 493–498.

Manschreck, T. C. (1996). Delusional disorder: The recognition and management of parancia. *J. Clin. Psychiat.*, 57(Suppl. 3), 32–38.

Manson, J. E., Willett, W. C., Stampfer, M. J., Colditz, G. A., et al. (1995). Body weight and mortality among women. *N. Engl. J. Med.*, 333(11), 677–685.

Manson, S. M., & Good, B. J. (1993). *Cultural considerations in the diagnosis of DSM-IV mood disorders. Cultural proposals and supporting papers for DSM-IV.* Submitted to the DSM-IV Task Force by the Steering Committee, NIMH-Sponsored Group on Culture and Diagnosis.

Manuck, S. B., Cohen, S., Rabin, B. S., Muldoon, M. F., & Bachen, E. A. (1991). Individual differences in cellular immune responses to stress. *Psychol. Sci.*, 2, 1–5.

Marazitti, D., Akiskal, H. S., Rossi, A., & Cassano, G. B. (1999). Alteration of the platelet serotonin transporter in romantic love. *Psychol. Med.*, 29(3), 741–745.

March, J. S., & Curry, J. F. (1998). Predicting the outcome of treatment. *J. Abnorm. Child Psychol.*, 26(1), 39–51.

Marcus, D. K. (1999). The cognitive-behavioral model of hypochondriasis: Misinformation and triggers. *J. Psychosom. Res.*, 47(1), 79–91.

Marder, S. R. (1996). Management of schizophrenia. *J. Clin. Psychiat.*, 57(Suppl. 3), 9–13.

Margo, G. M., & Newman, J. S. (1989). Venesection as a rare form of self-mutilation. *Amer. J. Psycother.*, 43(3), 427–432.

Margo, J. L. (1985). Anorexia nervosa in adolescents. *Brit. J. Med. Psychol.*, 58(2), 193–195.

Margraf, J., Barlow, D. H., Clark, D. M., & Telch, M. J. (1993). Psychological treatment of panic: Work in progress on outcome, active ingredients, and follow-up. *Behav. Res. Ther.*, 31(1), 1–8.

Margraf, J., Ehlers, A., Roth, W. T., Clark, D. B., et al. (1991). How "blind" are double-blind studies? *J. Cons. Clin. Psychol.*, 59(1), 184–187.

Mariani, M. A., & Barkley, R. A. (1997). Neuropsychological and academic functioning in preschool boys with attention deficit hyperactivity disorder. *Dev. Neuropsychol.*, 13(1), 111–129.

Maris, R. W. (1992). How are suicides different? In R. W. Maris, A. L. Berman, J. T. Maltsberger, & R. I. Yufit (Eds.), *Assessment and prediction of suicide.* New York: Guilford.

Maris, R. W. (1992). Methods of suicide. In R. W. Maris, A. L. Berman, J. T. Maltsberger, & R. I. Yufit (Eds.), *Assessment and prediction of suicide.* New York: Guilford.

Maris, R. W. (1992). Overview of the study of suicide assessment and prediction. In R. W. Maris, A. L. Berman, J. T. Maltsberger, & R. I. Yufit (Eds.), *Assessment and prediction of suicide.* New York: Guilford.

Maris, R. W., & Silverman, M. M. (1995). Postscript: Summary and synthesis [Special issue: Suicide prevention: Toward the year 2000.] *Suic. Life-Threat. Behav.*, 25(1), 205–209.

Markman, H. J., & Hahlweg, K. (1993). The prediction and prevention of marital distress: An international perspective. *Clin. Psychol. Rev.*, 13(1), 29–43.

Marks, I. M. (1986). Genetics of fear and anxiety disorders. *Brit. J. Psychiat.*, 149, 406–418.

Marks, I. M. (1987). Comment on S. Lloyd Williams' "On anxiety and phobia." *J. Anx. Dis.*, 1(2), 181–196.

Marks, I. M. (1987). *Fears, phobias and rituals: Panic, anxiety and their disorders.* New York: Oxford University Press.

Marks, I. M., & Gelder, M. G. (1967). Transvestism and fetishism: Clinical and psychological changes during faradic aversion. *Brit. J. Psychiat.*, 113, 711–730.

Marks, I. M., & Swinson, R. (1992). Behavioral and/or drug therapy. In G. D. Burrows, S. M. Roth, & R. Noyes, Jr., *Handbook of anxiety* (Vol. 5). Oxford, England: Elsevier.

Marks, J. (1998, October 12). Mayor vs. drug czar. *U.S. News.*

Marlatt, G. A. (1985). Controlled drinking: The controversy rages on. *Amer. Psychologist*, 40(3), 374–375.

Marlatt, G. A., & Gordon, J. (Eds.). (1980). Determinants of relapse: Implications for the maintenance of behavior change. In P. Davidson & S. Davidson (Eds.), *Behavioral medicine.* New York: Brunner/Mazel.

Marlatt, G. A., & Gordon, J. R. (1985). *Relapse prevention: Maintenance strategies in the treatment of addictive behaviors.* New York: Guilford.

Marlatt, G. A., Kosturn, C. F., & Lang, A. R. (1975). Provocation to anger and opportunity for retaliation as determinants of alcohol consumption in social drinkers. *J. Abnorm. Psychol.*, 84(6), 652–659.

Marmar, C. R., Foy, D., Kagan, B., & Pynoos, R. S. (1993). An integrated approach for treating posttraumatic stress. In J. M. Oldham, M. B. Riba, & A. Tasman (Eds.), *Review of psychiatry* (Vol. 12). Washington, DC: American Psychiatric Press.

Marquis, J. N., & Morgan, W. G. (1969). *A guidebook for systematic desensitization.* Palo Alto, CA: Veterans Administration Hospital.

Marsella, A. J. (1980). Depressive experience and disorder across cultures. In H. C. Triandis & J. Draguns (Eds.), *Handbook of cross-cultural psychology* (Vol. 6). Boston: Allyn & Bacon.

Marshall, J. J. (1997). Personal communication.

Marshall, J. R. (1997). Alcohol and substance abuse in panic disorder. *J. Clin. Psychiat.*, 58(Suppl. 2), 46–49.

Marshall, L. A., & Cooke, D. J. (1999). The childhood experiences of psychopaths: A retrospective study of familial and societal factors. *J. Pers. Disorders*, 13(3), 211–225.

Marshall, W. L., & Lippens, K. (1977). The clinical value of boredom: A procedure for reducing inappropriate sexual interests. *J. Nerv. Ment. Dis.*, 165, 283–287.

Marston, W. M. (1917). Systolic blood pressure changes in deception. *J. Exp. Physiol.*, 2, 117–163.

Martin, G. (1998). Media influence to suicide: The search for solutions. *Arch. Suic. Res.*, 4(1), 51–66.

Martin, G., & Pear, J. (1999). *Behavior modification: What it is and how to do it* (6th ed.). Upper Saddle River, NJ: Prentice-Hall.

Martin, J. K., Kraft, J. M., & Roman, P. M. (1994). Extent and impact of alcohol and drug use problems in the workplace: A review of the empirical evidence. In S. Macdonald & P. Roman (Eds.), *Research advances in alcohol and drug problems: Vol. 11. Drug testing in the workplace.* New York: Plenum Press.

Martin, S. (1996). Improving lives, not just infrastructures. *APA Monitor*, 27(10), 24.

Martin, W. T. (1984). Religiosity and U.S. suicide rates, 1972–1978. *J. Clin. Psychol.*, 40(5), 1166–1169.

Martineau, J., Barthelemy, C., Jouve, J., & Muh, J. P. (1992). Monoamines (serotonin and catecholamines) and their derivatives in infantile autism: Age-related changes and drug effects. *Dev. Med. Child Neurol.*, 34(7), 593–603.

Martinez, J. L., Jr., & Derrick, B. E. (1996). Longterm potentiation and learning. In J. T. Spence, J. M. Darley, & D. J. Foss (Eds.), *Annual review of psychology* (Vol. 47). Palo Alto, CA: Annual Reviews.

Martinez, P., & Richters, J. E. (1993). The NIMH community violence project: II. Children's distress symptoms associated with violence exposure. *Psychiatry*, 56, 22–35.

Marzuk, P. M., Tardiff, K., Leon, A. C., Stajic, M., Morgan, E. B., & Mann, J. J. (1992). Prevalence of cocaine use among residents of New York City who committed suicide during a one-year period. *Amer. J. Psychiat.*, 149(3), 371–375.

Maslow, A. H. (1970). *Motivation and personality* (2nd ed.). New York: Harper & Row.

Mass, R., Wolf, K., Wagner, M., & Haasen, C. (2000). Differential sustained attention/vigilance changes over time in schizophrenics and controls during a degraded stimulus continuous performance test. *European Archives of Psychiatry and Clinical Neuroscience*, 250(1), 24–30.

Mâsse, L. C., & Tremblay, R. E. (1997). Behavior of boys in kindergarten and the onset of substance use during adolescence. *Arch. Gen. Psychiat.*, 54, 62–68.

Masters, W. H., & Johnson, V. E. (1966). *Human sexual response.* Boston: Little, Brown.

Masters, W. H., & Johnson, V. E. (1970). *Human sexual inadequacy.* Boston: Little, Brown.

Masterson, J. F. (1990). Psychotherapy of borderline and narcissistic disorders: Establishing a therapeutic alliance. *J. Pers. Disorders*, 4(2), 182–191.

Matarazzo, J. D. (1984). Behavioral health: A 1990 challenge for the health sciences professions. In J. D. Matarazzo, S. M. Weiss, J. A. Herd, N. E. Miller, & S. M. Weiss (Eds.), *Behavioral health: A handbook of health enhancement and disease prevention.* New York: Wiley.

Mathew, R., Wilson, W., Blazer, D., & George, L. (1993). Psychiatric disorders in adult children of alcoholics: Data from the epidemiologic catchment area project. *Amer. J. Psychiat.*, 150(5), 793–796.

Mathew, S. J., Yudofsky, S. C., McCullough, L. B., Teasdale, T. A., & Jankovic, J. (1999). Attitudes toward neurosurgical procedures for Parkinson's disease and obsessive-compulsive disorder. *J. Neuropsych. Clin. Neurosci.*, 11(2), 259–267.

Mathews, A. (1984). Anxiety and its management. In R. N. Gaind, F. I. Fawzy, B. L. Hudson, & R. O. Pasnau (Eds.), *Current themes in psychiatry* (Vol. 3). New York: Spectrum..

Mathews, A., Whitehead, A., & Hellett, J. (1983). Psychological and hormonal factors in the treatment of female sexual dysfunction. *Psychol. Med.*, 13, 83–92.

Mathias, J. L., Mertin, P., & Murray, A. (1995). The psychological functioning of children from backgrounds of domestic violence. *Austral. Psychologist*, 30(1), 47–56.

Matsunaga, H., Kaye, W. H., McConaha, C., Plotnicov, K., Pollice, C., & Rao, R. (2000). Personality disorders among subjects recovering from eating disorders. *Internat. J. Eat. Disorders, 27*(3), 353–357.

Matthews, A., & Mackintosh, B. (1998). A cognitive model of selective processing in anxiety. *Cog. Ther. Res., 22*(6), 539–560.

Matthys, W., Walterbos, W., Njio, L., & Van Engeland, H. (1988). Person perception of children with conduct disorders. *Tijdskr. voor Psychiatr., 30*(5), 302–314.

Mattick, R. P., & Newman, C. R. (1991). Social phobia and avoidant personality disorder. *Inter. Rev. Psychiat., 3*(2), 163–173.

Mattis, S., & Wilson, B. C. (1997). Psychological assessment in a managed care climate: The neuropsychological evaluation. In L. J. Dickstein, M. B. Riba, & J. M. Oldham (Eds.), *Review of psychiatry* (Vol. 16). Washington, DC: American Psychiatric Press.

Maugh, T. H., II (1995, May 31). Researchers hone in on gene that may cause "werewolf" disorder. *Los Angeles Times*, p. A3.

Mauk, G. W., & Sharpnack, J. D. (1998). A light unto the darkness: The psychoeducational imperative of school-based suicide postvention. In A. H. Esman, L. T. Flaherty, et al. (Eds.), *Adolescent psychiatry: Developmental and clinical studies* (Vol. 23). Annals of the American Society for Adolescent Psychiatry. Hillsdale, NJ: Analytic Press.

Maurer, D. W., & Vogel, V. H. (1978). *Narcotics and narcotic addiction.* Springfield, IL: Thomas.

Mavissakalian, M. R., Hamann, M. S., & Jones, B. (1990). Correlates of DSM III personality disorder in obsessive-compulsive disorder. *Comprehen. Psychiat., 31*(6), 481–489.

Max, J. E., Smith, W. L., Lindgren, S. D., Robin, D. A., et al. (1995). Case study: Obsessive-compulsive disorder after severe traumatic brain injury in an adolescent. *J. Amer. Acad. Child. Adol. Psychiat., 34*(1), 45–49.

May, P. R. A., & Tuma, A. H. (1964). Choice of criteria for the assessment of treatment outcome. *J. Psychiat. Res., 2*(3), 16–527.

May, P. R. A., Tuma, A. H., & Dixon, W. J. (1981). Schizophrenia: A follow-up study of the results of five forms of treatment. *Arch. Gen. Psychiat., 38*, 776–784.

May, R. (1961). *Existential psychology.* New York: Random House.

May, R. (1967). *Psychology and the human dilemma.* New York: Van Nostrand-Reinhold.

May, R. (1987). Therapy in our day. In J. K. Zeig (Ed.), *The evolution of psychotherapy.* New York: Brunner/Mazel.

May, R., & Yalom, I. (1989). Existential psychotherapy. In R. J. Corsini & D. Wedding (Eds.), *Current psychotherapies.* Itasca, IL: Peacock.

May, R., & Yalom, I. (1995). Existential psychotherapy. In R. J. Corsini & D. Wedding (Eds.), *Current psychotherapies* (5th ed.). Itasca, IL: Peacock.

May, R., Angel, E., & Ellenberger, H. F. (1958). *Existence: A new dimension in psychiatry and psychology.* New York: Basic Books.

Mays, D. T., & Franks, C. M. (1985). *Negative outcome in psychotherapy and what to do about it.* New York: Springer.

Mazo, E. (1999, March 23). Studying St. John's wort; Pitt participating in examination of popular herbal anti-depressant. *Pittsburgh Post-Gazette*, p. G5.

McCabe, M. P., & Delaney, S. M. (1992). An evaluation of therapeutic programs for the treatment of secondary inorgasmia in women. *Arch. Sex. Behav., 21*(1), 69–89.

McCabe, R., Roder-Wanner, U. U., Hoffmann, K., & Priebe, S. (1999). Therapeutic relationships and quality of life: Association of two subjective constructs in schizophrenia patients. *Inter. J. Soc. Psychiat., 45*(4), 276–283.

McCarroll, J. E., Fullerton, C. S., Ursano, R. J., & Hermsen, J. M. (1996). Posttraumatic stress symptoms following forensic dental identification: Mt. Carmel, Waco, Texas. *Amer. J. Psychiat., 153*, 778–782.

McCarthy, M. (1990). The thin ideal, depression and eating disorders in women. *Behav. Res. Ther., 28*(3), 205–215.

McCarthy, P. R., Katz, I. R., & Foa, E. B. (1991). Cognitive-behavioral treatment of anxiety in the elderly: A proposed model. In C. Salzman & B. D. Leibowitz (Eds.), *Anxiety in the elderly.* New York: Springer.

McClelland, D. C. (1993). Motives and health. In G. G. Brannigan & M. R. Merrens (Eds.), *The undaunted psychologist.* New York: McGraw-Hill.

McClelland, S. (1998, September 21). Grief crisis counsellors under fire: Trauma teams were quick to descend on Peggy's Cove. Susan McClelland asks whether they do more harm than good. *Ottawa Citizen*, p. A4.

McCormack, A., Rokous, F. E., Hazelwood, R. R., & Burgess, A. W. (1992). An exploration of incest in the childhood development of serial rapists. *J. Fam. Violence, 7*(3), 219–228.

McCormick, L. H. (2000). Improving social adjustment in children with attention-deficit/hyperactivity disorder. *Arch. Fam. Med., 9*(2), 191–194.

McCoy, S. A. (1976). Clinical judgments of normal childhood behavior. *J. Cons. Clin. Psychol., 44*(5), 710–714.

McCreadie, R. G., Thara, R., Kamath, S., Padmavathy, R., Latha, S., Mathrubootham, N., & Menon, M. S. (1996). Abnormal movements in never-medicated Indian patients with schizophrenia. *Brit. J. Psychiat., 168*, 221–226.

McCurdy, K., & Daro, D. (1993). *Current trends: A fifty state survey.* Washington, DC: National Committee for the Prevention of Child Abuse.

McDaniel, J. S., Moran, M. G., Levenson, J. L., & Stoudemire, A. (1994). Psychological factors affecting medical conditions. In R. E. Hales, S. C. Yudofsky, & J. A. Talbott, (Eds.), *The American Psychiatric Press textbook of psychiatry* (2nd ed.). Washington, DC: American Psychiatric Press.

McEachin, J. J., Smith, T., & Lovaas, O. I. (1993). Long-term outcome for children with autism who received early intensive behavioral treatment. *Amer. J. Ment. Retard., 97*(4), 359–372.

McElroy, S. L., Hudson, J. L., Pope, H. G., & Keck, P. E. (1991). Kleptomania: Clinical characteristics and associated psychopathology. *Psychol. Med., 21*(1), 93–108.

McElroy, S. L., Hudson, J. I., Pope, H. G., Keck, P. E., et al. (1992). The DSM-III—R impulse control disorders not elsewhere classified: Clinical characteristics and relationship to other psychiatric disorders. *Amer. J. Psychiat., 149*(3), 318–327.

McEvoy, J. (1992). Fragile X syndrome: A brief overview. *Educ. Psychol. Prac., 8*(3), 146–149.

McFarlane, A.C. (1999). Risk factors for the acute biological and psychological response to trauma. In R. Yehuda (Ed.), *Risk factors for posttraumatic stress disorder.* Washington, DC: American Psychiatric Press.

McGaugh, J. (1999, March 30). Interviewed in L. Muhammad. Experts brainstorming over memory loss. *USA Today*, p. 6D.

McGeer, P. L., & McGeer, E. G. (1996). Anti-inflammatory drugs in the fight against Alzheimer's disease. In R. J. Wurtman, S. Corkin, J. H. Growdon, & R. M. Nitsch (Eds.), *The neurobiology of Alzheimer's disease.* New York: New York Academy of Sciences.

McGehee, D. S., Heath, M. J. S., Gelber, S., Devay, P., & Role, L. W. (1995). Nicotine enhancement of fast excitatory synaptic transmission in CNS by presynaptic receptors. *Science, 269*, 1692–1696.

McGhie, A., & Chapman, J. S. (1961). Disorders of attention and perception in early schizophrenia. *Brit. J. Med. Psychol., 34*, 103–116.

McGlashan, T. H. (1986). Schizotypal personality disorder: Chestnut Lodge follow-up study: VI. Long-term follow-up perspectives. *Arch. Gen. Psychiat., 43*(4), 329–334.

McGlynn, F. D., & Bates, L. W. (1999). Cognitive behavior therapy. In M. Hersen & A.S. Bellack (Eds.), *Handbook of comparative interventions for adult disorder* (2nd ed.). New York: Wiley.

McGlynn, F. D., Moore, P. M., Lawyer, S., & Karg, R. (1999). Relaxation training inhibits fear and arousal during in vivo exposure to phobia-cue stimuli. *J. Behav. Ther. Exp. Psychiat., 30*(3), 155–168.

McGoldrick, M., Gerson, R., & Shellenberger, S. (1999). *Genograms: Assessment and intervention* (2nd ed.). New York: Norton.

McGrady, A., Lynch, D., Nagel, R., & Zsembik, C. (1999). Application of the High Risk Model of Threat Perception to a primary care patient population. *J. Nerv. Ment. Dis., 187*(6), 369–375.

McGrath, P. H. (1999). Clinical psychology issues in migraine headaches. *Canad. J. Neurol. Sci., 26*(Suppl. 3), S33–S36.

McGuffin, P., Katz, R., Watkins, S., & Rutherford, J. (1996). A hospital-based twin register of the heritability of DSM-IV unipolar depression. *Arch. Gen. Psychiat., 53*, 129–136.

McGuire, D. (1982). The problem of children's suicide: Ages 5–14. *Inter. J. Offend. Ther. Compar. Crimin., 26*(1), 10–17.

McGuire, P. A. (2000, February). New hope for people with schizophrenia. *Monitor on Psychology, 31*(2), 24–28.

McGuire, P. K., Shah, G. M. S., & Murray, R. M. (1993). Increased blood flow in Broca's area during auditory hallucinations in schizophrenia. *Lancet, 342*, 703–706.

McGuire, P. K., Silbersweig, D. A., Wright, I., Murray, R. M., Frackowiak, R. S., & Frith, C. D. (1996). The neural correlates of inner speech and auditory verbal imagery in schizophrenia: Relationship to auditory verbal hallucinations. *Brit. J. Psychiat., 169*(2), 148–159.

McGuire, P. K., Silbersweig, D. A., Wright, I., Murray, R. M., et al. (1995). Abnormal monitoring of inner speech: A physiological basis for auditory hallucinations. *Lancet, 346*, 596–600.

McIntosh, J. L. (1987). Suicide: Training and education needs with an emphasis on the elderly. *Gerontol. Geriat. Educ., 7*, 125–139.

McIntosh, J. L. (1991). Epidemiology of suicide in the U.S. In A. A. Leenaars (Ed.), *Life span perspectives of suicide.* New York: Plenum Press.

McIntosh, J. L. (1992). Epidemiology of suicide in the elderly. *Suic. Life-Threat. Behav., 22*(1), 15–35.

McIntosh, J. L. (1992). Methods of suicide. In R. W. Maris, A. L. Berman, J. T. Maltsberger, & R. I. Yufit (Eds.), *Assessment and prediction of suicide.* New York: Guilford.

McIntosh, J. L. (1995). Suicide prevention in the elderly (age 65–99) [Special issue: Suicide prevention: Toward the year 2000.] *Suic. Life-Threat. Behav., 25*(1), 180–192.

McIntosh, J. L. (1996). *U. S. suicide rates 1932–1992.* Washington, DC: National Center for Health Statistics.

McIntosh, J. L. (1999). Arguments against rational suicide: A gerontologist's perspective. In J. L.

Werth, Jr., et al. (Eds.), *Contemporary perspectives on rational suicide.* Series in death, dying, and bereavement. Philadelphia: Brunner/Mazel.

McIntosh, J. L. (1999). Research on survivors of suicide. In M. T. Stimming, M. Stemming, et al. (Eds.), *Before their time: Adult children's experiences of parental suicide.* Philadelphia: Temple University Press.

McIntosh, J. L., & Santos, J. F. (1982). Changing patterns in methods of suicide by race and sex. *Suic. Life-Threat. Behav., 12,* 221–233.

McIntosh, J. L., Hubbard, R. W., & Santos, J. F. (1985). Suicide facts and myths: A study of prevalence. *Death Stud., 9,* 267–281.

McKay, J. R., Alterman, A. I., McLellan, A. T., Snider, E. C., & O'Brien, C. P. (1995). Effect of random versus nonrandom assignment in a comparison of inpatient and day hospital rehabilitation for male alcoholics. *J. Cons. Clin. Psychol., 63*(1), 70–78.

McKee, G. R. (1998). Lethal vs. nonlethal suicide attempts in jail. *Psychol. Rep., 82*(2), 611–614.

McKenzie, S. J., Williamson, D. A., & Cubic, B. A. (1993). Stable and reactive body image disturbances in bulimia nervosa. *Behav. Ther., 24,* 195–207.

McKisack, C., & Waller, G. (1997). Factors influencing the outcome of group psychotherapy for bulimia nervosa. *Inter. J. Eat. Disorders, 22,* 1–13.

McLean, A., Temkin, N. R., Dikmen, S., & Wyler, A. R. (1983). The behavioral sequelae of head injury. *J. Clin. Neuropsychol., 5,* 361–376.

McLean, P. D., & Hakstian, A. R. (1979). Clinical depression: Comparative efficacy of outpatient treatments. *J. Cons. Clin. Psychol., 47*(5), 818–836.

McLeer, S. V., Dixon, J. F., Henry, D., Ruggiero, K., Escovitz, K., Niedda, T., & Scholle, R. (1998). Psychopathology in non-clinically referred sexually abused children. *J. Amer. Acad. Child Adol. Psychiat., 37*(12), 1326–1333.

McLellan, A. T., Arndt, I. O., Metzger, D. S., et al. (1993). The effects of psychosocial services in substance abuse treatment. *JAMA, 269,* 1953–1959.

McLoyd, V. C. (1998). Socioeconomic disadvantage and child development. *Amer. Psychologist, 53*(2), 185–204.

McNally, R. J. (1999). Anxiety sensitivity and information-processing biases for threat. In S. Taylor et al. (Eds.), *Anxiety sensitivity: Theory, research, and treatment of the fear of anxiety.* The LEA series in personality and clinical psychology. Mahwah, NJ: Erlbaum.

McNally, R. J. (1999). Theoretical approaches to the fear of anxiety. In S. Taylor et al. (Eds.), *Anxiety sensitivity: Theory, research, and treatment of the fear of anxiety.* The LEA series in personality and clinical psychology. Mahwah, NJ: Erlbaum.

McNally, R. J., & Lukach, B. M. (1991). Behavioral treatment of zoophilic exhibitionism. *J. Behav. Ther. Exp. Psychiat., 22*(4), 281–284.

McNally, R. J., Hornig, C. D., & Donnell, C. D. (1995). Clinical versus nonclinical panic: A test of suffocation false alarm theory. *Behav. Res. Ther., 33*(2), 127–131.

McNally, R. J., Metzger, L. J., Lasko, N. B., Clancy, S. A., & Pitman, R. K. (1998). Directed forgetting of trauma cues in adult survivors of childhood sexual abuse with and without post-traumatic stress disorder. *J. Abnorm. Psychol., 107*(4), 596–601.

McNeal, E. T., & Cimbolic, P. (1986). Antidepressants and biochemical theories of depression. *Psychol. Bull., 99*(3), 361–374.

McNeil, E. B. (1967). *The quiet furies.* Englewood Cliffs, NJ: Prentice Hall.

McNiel, D. E., & Binder, R. L. (1991). Clinical assessment of the risk of violence among psychiatric inpatients. *Amer. J. Psychiat., 148*(10), 1317–1321.

Meana, M., & Binik, Y. M. (1994). Painful coitus: A review of female dyspareunia. *J. Nerv. Ment. Dis., 182,* 264–272.

Mechanic, D. (1999). Mental health and mental illness: Definitions and perspectives. In A. V. Horwitz & T. L. Scheid (Eds.), *A handbook for the study of mental health: Social contexts, theories, and systems.* Cambridge, England: Cambridge University Press.

Mednick, S. A. (1971). Birth defects and schizophrenia. *Psychol. Today, 4,* 48–50.

Mednick, S. A., Gabrielli, W. F., Jr., & Hutchings, B. (1987). Genetic factors in the etiology of criminal behavior. In S. A. Mednick, T. E. Moffitt, & S. A. Stack (Eds.), *The causes of crime: New biological approaches.* Cambridge, England: Cambridge University Press..

Meehl, P. E. (1960). The cognitive activity of the clinician. *Amer. Psychologist, 15,* 19–27.

Meehl, P. E. (1996). *Clinical versus statistical prediction: A theoretical analysis and a review of the evidence.* Northvale, NJ: Jason Aronson.

Mehlum, L., Hytten, K., & Gjertsen, F. (1999). Epidemiological trends of youth suicide in Norway. *Arch. Suic. Res., 5*(3), 193–205.

Mehta, U., & Bedient, L. (1999). Update on ECT. *Carrier Clinic Medical Education Letter, 200,* 1–4.

Meibach, R. C., Mullane, J. F., & Binstok, G. (1987). A placebo-controlled multicenter trial of propranolol and chlordiazepoxide in the treatment of anxiety. *Curr. Ther. Res., 41,* 65–76.

Meichenbaum, D. H. (1972). Cognitive modification of test-anxious college students. *J. Cons. Clin. Psychol., 39,* 370–380.

Meichenbaum, D. H. (1972). Examination of model characteristics in reducing avoidance behavior. *J. Behav. Ther. Exp. Psychiat., 3,* 225–227.

Meichenbaum, D. H. (1975). A self-instructional approach to stress management: A proposal for stress inoculation training. In I. Sarason & C. D. Spielberger (Eds.), *Stress and anxiety* (Vol. 2). New York: Wiley.

Meichenbaum, D. H. (1975). Enhancing creativity by modifying what subjects say to themselves. *Amer. Educ. Res. J., 12*(2), 129–145.

Meichenbaum, D. H. (1975). Theoretical and treatment implications of development research on verbal control of behavior. *Canad. Psychol. Rev., 16*(1), 22–27.

Meichenbaum, D. H. (1975). Toward a cognitive of self-control. In G. Schwartz & D. Shapiro (Eds.), *Consciousness and self-regulation: Advances in research.* New York: Plenum Press.

Meichenbaum, D. H. (1977). *Cognitive-behavior modification: An integrative approach.* New York: Plenum Press.

Meichenbaum, D. H. (1977). Dr. Ellis, please stand up. *Couns. Psychologist, 7*(1), 43–44.

Meichenbaum, D. H. (1992). Evolution of cognitive behavior therapy: Origins, tenets, and clinical examples. In J. K. Zeig (Ed.), *The evolution of psychotherapy: The second conference.* New York: Brunner/Mazel.

Meichenbaum, D. H. (1993). Stress inoculation training: A 20-year update. In P. M. Lehrer & R. L. Woolfolk (Eds.), *Principles and practice of stress management* (2nd ed.). New York: Guilford.

Meichenbaum, D. H. (1993). The personal journey of a psychotherapist and his mother. In G. G. Brannigan & M. R. Merrens (Eds.), *The undaunted psychologist: Adventures in research.* New York: McGraw-Hill.

Meichenbaum, D. H. (1997). The evolution of a cognitive-behavior therapist. In J. K. Zeig (Ed.), *The evolution of psychotherapy: The third conference.* New York: Brunner/Mazel.

Meilman, P., Leichliter, J. S., & Presley, C. A. (1999). Greeks and athletes: Who drinks more? *J. Amer. Coll. Hlth., 47*(4), 187–190

Melfi, C. A., Croghan, T. W., & Hanna, M. P. (1999). Access to treatment for depression in a Medicaid population. *J. Hlth. Care Poor Underserved, 10*(2), 201–215.

Melges, F. T., & Swartz, M. S. (1989). Oscillations of attachment in borderline personality disorder. *Amer. J. Psychiat., 146*(9), 1115–1120.

Melle, I., Friis, S., Hauff, E., & Vaglum, P. (2000). Social functioning of patients with schizophrenia in high-income welfare societies. *Psychiat. Serv., 51*(2), 223–228.

Melo, J. A., Shendure, J., Pociask, K., & Silver, L. M. (1996, June). Identification of sex-specific quantiative trait loci controlling alcohol preference in C57BL/6 mice. *Nature Genetics, 13,* 147–153.

Meltzer, H. Y. (1991). The mechanism of action of novel antipsychotic drugs. *Schizo. Bull., 17*(2), 263–287.

Meltzer, H. Y. (1992). Dimensions of outcome with clozapine. *Brit. J. Psychiat., 160*(Suppl. 17), 46–53.

Meltzer, H. Y. (1992). Treatment of the neuroleptic-nonresponsive schizophrenic patient. *Schizo. Bull., 18*(3), 515–542.

Meltzer, H. Y. (1995). Neuroleptic withdrawal in schizophrenic patients: An idea whose time has come. *Arch. Gen. Psychiat., 52*(3), 200–202.

Meltzer, H. Y. (1998). Suicide in schizophrenia: Risk factors and clozapine treatment. *J. Clin. Psychiat., 59*(Suppl. 3), 15–20.

Meltzer, H. Y. (2000). Genetics and etiology of schizophrenia and bipolar disorder. *Biol. Psychiat., 47*(3), 171–173.

Melville, J. (1978). *Phobias and obsessions.* New York: Penguin.

Mendels, J. (1970). *Concepts of depression.* New York: Wiley.

Mendelson, W., Hatoum, H. T., Kong, S. X., Wong, J. M., & Kania, C. M. (1999). Insomnia and its impact. *Psychiat. Times, XVI*(3).

Mendlewicz, J., Fleiss, J. L., & Fieve, R. R. (1972). Evidence for X-linkage in the transmission of manic-depressive illness. *JAMA, 222,* 1624–1627.

Mendlewicz, J., Linkowski, P., & Wilmotte, J. (1980). Linkage between glucose-6-phosphate dehydrogenase deficiency in manic depressive psychosis. *Brit. J. Psychiat., 137,* 337–342.

Mendlewicz, J., Simon, P., Sevy, S., Charon, F., Brocas, H., Legros, S., & Vassart, G. (1987). Polymorphic DNA marker on X chromosome and manic depression. *Lancet, 1,* 1230–1232.

Menke, J. A., McClead, R. E., & Hansen, N. B. (1991). Perspectives on perinatal complications associated with mental retardation. In J. L. Matson & J. A. Mulick (Eds.), *Handbook of mental retardation.* New York: Pergamon Press.

Menninger, K. (1938). *Man against himself.* New York: Harcourt.

Menninger, W. W. (1993). Management of the aggressive and dangerous patient. *Bull. Menninger Clin., 57,* 209.

Menzies, R. G., & Clarke, J. C. (1993). A comparison of in vivo and vicarious exposure in the treatment of childhood water phobia. *Behav. Res. Ther., 31*(1), 9–15.

Menzies, R. G., & Clarke, J. C. (1995). The etiology of phobias: A non-associative account. *Clin. Psychol. Rev., 15,* 23–48.

Menzies, R. P. D., Federoff, J. P., Green, C. M., & Isaacson, K. (1995). Prediction of dangerous behaviour in male erotomania. *Brit. J. Psychiat.*, 116(4), 529–536.

Merikangas, K. R., Stevens, D. E., & Angst, J. (1994). Psychopathology and headache syndromes in the community. *Headache*, 34(8), S17–S22.

Mersch, P. P., Emmelkamp, P. M., & Lips, C. (1991). Social phobia: Individual response patterns and the long-term effects of behavioural and cognitive interventions. A follow-up study. *Behav. Res. Ther.*, 29(4), 357–362.

Merskey, H. (1986). Classification of chronic pain: Descriptions of chronic pain syndromes and definitions of pain terms. *Pain, 3*, 226.

Merskey, H. (1992). The manufacture of personalities: The production of multiple personality disorder. *Brit. J. Psychiat.*, 160, 327–340.

Merskey, H. (1995). Multiple personality disorder and false memory syndrome. *Brit. J. Psychiat.*, 166(3), 281–283.

Merzenich, M. M., Jenkins, W. M., Johnston, P., Schreiner, C., et al. (1996). Temporal processing deficits of language-learning impaired children ameliorated by training. *Science*, 271, 77–84.

Messer, A. A. (1985). Narcissistic people. *Med. Aspects Human Sex.*, 19(9), 169–184.

Messer, S. B., Tishby, O., & Spillman, A. (1992). Taking context seriously in psychotherapy research: Relating therapist interventions to patient progress in brief psychodynamic therapy. *J. Cons. Clin. Psychol.*, 60(5), 678–688.

Mesulam, M. M., Hyman, S. E., Hobson, J. A., & Silvestri, R. (1999). Brain and behavior. In A. M. Nicholi et al. (Eds.), *The Harvard guide to psychiatry* (3rd ed.). Cambridge, MA: Belknap Press/Harvard University Press.

Metalsky, G. I., Joiner, T. E., Jr., Hardin, T. S., & Abramson, L. Y. (1993). Depressive reactions to failure in a naturalistic setting: A test of the hopelessness and self-esteem theories of depression. *J. Abnorm. Psychol.*, 102(1), 101–109.

Metha, A., Weber, B., & Webb, L. D. (1998). Youth suicide prevention: A survey and analysis of policies and efforts in the 50 states. *Suic. Life-Threat. Behav.*, 28(2), 150–164.

Meyer, R. E. (1995). Biology of psychoactive substance dependence disorders: Opiates, cocaine, and ethanol. In A. F. Schatzberg & C. B. Nemeroff (Eds.), *The American Psychiatric Press textbook of psychopharmacology*. Washington, DC: American Psychiatric Press.

Meyer, R. E., Murray, R. F., Jr., Thomas, F. B., et al. (1989). *Prevention and treatment of alcohol problems: Research opportunities*. Washington, DC: National Academy Press.

Meyer, R. G. (1992). *Abnormal behavior and the criminal justice system*. New York: Lexington Books.

Michael, R. T., Gagnon, J. H., Laumann, E. O., & Kolata, G. (1994). *Sex in America: A definitive survey*. Boston: Little, Brown.

Michaelson, R. (1993). Flood volunteers build emotional levees. *APA Monitor*, 24(10), 30.

Michels, R. (1992). The borderline patient: Shifts in theoretical emphasis and implications for treatment. In D. Silver & M. Rosenbluth (Eds.), *Handbook of borderline disorders*. Madison, CT: International Universities Press.

Mickalide, A. D. (1990). Sociocultural factors influencing weight among males. In A. E. Andersen (Ed.), *Males with eating disorders*. New York: Brunner/Mazel.

Miklowitz, D. J., Goldstein, M. J., & Nuechterlein, K. H. (1995). Verbal interactions in the families of schizophrenic and bipolar affective patients. *J. Abnorm. Psychol.*, 104(2), 268–276.

Miles, C. P. (1977). Conditions predisposing to suicide: A review. *J. Nerv. Ment. Dis.*, 164(4), 231–246.

Millar, J. D. (1984). The NIOSH-suggested list of the ten leading work-related diseases and injuries. *J. Occup. Med.*, 26, 340–341.

Millar, J. D. (1990). Mental health and the workplace: An interchangeable partnership. *Amer. Psychologist*, 45(10), 1165–1166.

Millar, M. G., & Millar, K. U. (1996). Effects of message anxiety on disease detection and health promotion behaviors. *Basic Appl. Soc. Psychol.*, 18(1), 61–74.

Miller, A. (1998, August 30). Special report: Managed care and mental health; Employee assistance programs. *Atlanta Journal and Constitution*, p. 07R.

Miller, A. (1999). Appropriateness of psychostimulant prescription to children: Theoretical and empirical perspectives. *Canad. J. Psychiat.*, 44(10), 1017–1024.

Miller, G. A. (1999, January 6). Cited in Gap widening between genetic and behavioral research. *Science Daily News Release*.

Miller, I. W., Norman, W. H., & Keitner, G. I. (1999). Combined treatment for patients with double depression. *Psychother. Psychosom.*, 68(4), 180–185.

Miller, K. J., Gleaves, D. H., Hirsch, T. G., Green, B. A., Snow, A. C., & Corbett, C. C. (2000). Comparisons of body image dimensions by race-ethnicity and gender in a university population. *Inter. J. Eat. Disorders*, 27(3), 310–316.

Miller, L. S., Wasserman, G. A., Neugebauer, R., Gorman-Smith, D., & Kambookos, D. (1999). Witnessed community violence and antisocial behavior in high-risk, urban boys. *J. Clin. Child Psychol.*, 28(1), 2–11.

Miller, M., & Kantrowitz, B. (1999, January 25). Unmasking Sybil: A re-examination of the most famous psychiatric patient in history. *Newsweek*, pp. 66–68.

Miller, M. A., & Rahe, R. H. (1997). Life changes scahling for the 1990s. *J. Psychosom. Res.*, 43(3), 297–292.

Miller, M. N., & Pumariega, A. (1999). Culture and eating disorders. *Psychiatr. Times*, XVI(2).

Miller, N. E. (1948). Studies of fear as an acquirable drive: I. Fear as motivation and fear-reduction as reinforcement in the learning of new responses. *J. Exp. Psychol.*, 38, 89–101.

Miller, N. S. (1999). Benzodiazepines: Behavioral and pharmacologic basis of addiction, tolerance, and dependence. In *The Hatherleigh guide to psychopharmacology*. The Hatherleigh guides series, Vol. 11. New York: Hatherleigh Press.

Miller, N. S., & Gold, M. S. (1990). Benzodiazepines: Tolerance, dependence, abuse, and addiction. *J. Psychoactive Drugs*, 22(1), 23–33.

Miller, N. S., Klamen, D. L., & Costa, E. (1998). Medications of abuse and addiction: Benzodiazepines and other sedatives/hypnotics. In R. E. Tarter, R. T. Ammerman, et al. (Eds.), *Handbook of substance abuse: Neurobehavioral pharmacology*. New York: Plenum Press.

Miller, N. S., Mahler, J. C., & Gold, M. S. (1991). Suicide risk associated with drug and alcohol dependence. *J. Addic. Dis.*, 10(3), 49–61.

Miller, P. M. (1996). Redefining success in eating disorders. *Addic. Behav.*, 21(6), 745–754.

Miller, P. M., Ingham, J. G., & Davidson, S. (1976). Life events, symptoms, and social support. *J. Psychiatr. Res.*, 20(6), 514–522.

Miller, W. R. (1983). Controlled drinking, *Quart. J. Stud. Alcohol*, 44, 68–83.

Miller, W. R. (1998). Researching the spiritual dimensions of alcohol and other drug problems. *Addiction*, 93(7), 979–990.

Miller, W. R. (2000). Rediscovering fire: Small interventions, large effects. *Psychol. Addict. Behav.*, 14(1), 6–18.

Miller, W. R., & Seligman, M. E. (1975). Depression and learned helplessness in man. *J. Abnorm. Psychol.*, 84(3), 228–238.

Miller, W. R., Leckman, A. L., Delaney, H. D., & Tinchom, M. (1992). Long-term follow-up of behavioral self-control training. *J. Stud. Alc.*, 51, 108–115.

Millon, T. (1969). *Modern psychopathology: A biosocial approach to maladaptive learning and functioning*. Philadelphia: Saunders.

Millon, T. (1987). *Millon Clinical Multiaxial Inventory-II: Manual for the MCMI-II* (2nd ed.). Minneapolis, MN: National Computer Systems.

Millon, T. (1990). The disorders of personality. In L. A. Pervin (Ed.), *Handbook of personality theory and practice*. New York: Guilford.

Millon, T. (1990). *Toward a new personology*. New York: Wiley.

Millon, T. (1999). *Personality-guided therapy*. New York: Wiley.

Millon, T., Davis, R., Millon, C., Escovar, L., & Meagher, S. (2000). *Personality disorders in modern life*. New York: Wiley.

Millward, D. (1996, June 3). Beware of the dog that is being prescribed Prozac. *Electronic Telegraph*, Issue 397.

Milner, B. (1971). Interhemispheric difference in the localization of psychological processes in man. *Brit. Med. Bull.*, 27, 272–277.

Mineka, S. (1985). Animal models of anxiety-based disorders: Their usefulness and limitations. In A. H. Tuma & J. Maser (Eds.), *Anxiety and the anxiety disorders*. Hillsdale, NJ: Erlbaum.

Mineka, S., Davidson, M., Cook, M., & Keir, R. (1984). Observational conditioning of snake fear in rhesus monkeys. *J. Abnorm. Psychol.*, 93(4), 355–372.

Miner, I. D., & Feldman, M. D. (1998). Factitious deafblindness: An imperceptible variant of factitious disorder. *Gen. Hosp. Psychiat.*, 20(1), 48–51.

Mintzer, J. E., & Brawman-Mintzer, O. (1996). Agitation as a possible expression of generalized anxiety disorder in demented elderly patients toward a treatment approach. *J. Clin. Psychiat.*, 57(Suppl. 7), 55–63.

Minuchin, S. (1974). *Families and family therapy*. Cambridge, MA: Harvard University Press.

Minuchin, S. (1987). My many voices. In J. K. Zeig (Ed.), *The evolution of psychotherapy*. New York: Brunner/Mazel.

Minuchin, S. (1997). The leap to complexity: Supervision in family therapy. In J. K. Zeig (Ed.), *The evolution of psychotherapy: The third conference*. New York: Brunner/Mazel.

Minuchin, S., Rosman, B. L., & Baker, L. (1978). *Psychosomatic families: Anorexia nervosa in context*. Cambridge, MA: Harvard University Press.

Mirabella, R. F., Frueh, B. C., & Fossey, M. D. (1995). Exposure therapy and antidepressant medication for treatment of chronic PTSD. *Amer. J. Psychiat.*, 152(6), 955–956.

Miranda, J., & Persons, J. D. (1988). Dysfunctional attitudes are mood state dependent. Meetings of the Assoc. for Advancement of Behavior Therapy. *J. Abnorm. Psychol.*, 97(1), 76–79.

Mirin, S. M., & Weiss, R. D. (1991). Substance abuse and mental illness. In R. J. Frances & S. I Miller (Eds.), *Clinical textbook of addictive disorders*. New York: Guilford.

Mirowsky, J., & Ross, C. (1995). Sex differences in distress: Real of artifact? *Amer. Sociol. Rev.*, 60, 449–468.

Mirsky, I. A. (1958). Physiologic, psychologic, and social determinants of the etiology of duodenal ulcer. *Amer. J. Digestional Dis.*, 3, 285–314.

Mishara, B. L. (1998). Suicide, euthanasia and AIDS. *Crisis*, 19(2), 87–96.

Mishna, F. (1996). Clinical report. In their own words: Therapeutic factors for adolescents who have learning disabilities. *Inter. J. Group Psychother., 46*(2), 265–273.

Mitchel, J. E., & Peterson, C. B. (1997). Cognitive-behavioral treatment of eating disorder. In L. J. Dickstein, M. B. Riba, & J. M. Oldham (Eds.), *Review of psychiatry* (Vol. 16). Washington, D.C.: American Psychiatric Press.

Mitchell, J. E., & de Zwaan, M. (1993). Pharmacological treatments of binge eating. In C. G. Fairburn & G. T. Wilson (Eds.), *Binge eating: Nature, assessment, and treatment.* New York: Guilford.

Mitchell, J. E., Pyle, R. L., & Miner, R. A. (1982). Gastric dilation as a complication of bulimia. *Psychosomatics, 23,* 96–97.

Mittleman, M. A., Mintzer, D., Maclure, M., Tofler, G. H., Sherwood, J. B., & Muller, J. E. (1999). Triggering of myocardial infarction by cocaine. *Circulation, 99*(21), 2737–2741.

Mizes, J. S. (1995). Eating disorders. In M. Hersen & R. T. Ammerman (Eds.), *Advanced abnormal child psychology.* Hillsdale, NJ: Erlbaum.

Modestin, J., & Villiger, C. (1989). Follow-up study on borderline versus nonborderline personality disorders. *Comprehen. Psychiat., 30*(3), 236–244.

Modrow, J. (1992). *How to become a schizophrenic: The case against bio. psychiatry.* Everett, WA: Apollyon Press.

Moen, P. (1999, January). *The time squeeze: Work/family strategies in the next century.* Panel presentation at the annual meeting of the American Association for the Advancement of Science, Anaheim, CA.

Moene, F. C., & Hoogduin, K. A. L. (1999). The creative use of unexpected responses in the hypnotherapy of patients with conversion disorders. *Inter. J. Clin. Exp. Hyp., 47*(3), 209–226.

Moffitt, T. E., Brammer, G. L., Caspi, A., et al. (1998). Whole blood serotonin relates to violence in an epidemiological study. *Biol. Psychiat., 43*(6), 446–457.

Mogale, C. C. (1999). "Moriti wa letswele" (the shadow of the breast)—a stress-related somatoform pain disorder. *S. Afr. J. Psychol., 29*(2), 72–75.

Mogg, K., & Bradley, B. P. (1998). A cognitive motivational analysis of anxiety. *Behav. Res. Ther., 36*(9), 809–848.

Mogg, K., Bradley, B. P., Millar, N., & White, J. (1995). A follow-up study of cognitive bias in generalized anxiety disorder. *Behav. Res. Ther., 33*(8), 927–935.

Mohler, H., & Okada, T. (1977). Benzodiazepine receptor: Demonstration in the central nervous system. *Science, 198*(4319), 849–851.

Mohler, H., Richards, J. G., & Wu, J.-Y. (1981). Autoradiographic localization of benzodiazepine receptors in immunocytochemically identified Y-aminobutyric synapses. *Proc. Natl. Acad. Sci., U.S.A., 78,* 1935–1938.

Mohr, D. C., & Beutler, L. E. (1990). Erectile dysfunction: A review of diagnostic and treatment procedures. *Clin. Psychol. Rev., 10*(1), 123–150.

Mohr, J. W., Turner, R. E., & Jerry, M. B. (1964). *Pedophilia and exhibitionism.* Toronto: University of Toronto Press.

Moilanen, I., Tirkkonen, T., Jarvelin, M. R., Linna, S. L., Almqvist, F., Piha, J., Rasanen, E., & Tamminen, T. (1998). A follow-up of enuresis from childhood to adolescence. *Brit. J. Urol., 81*(Suppl. 3), 94–97.

Moldin, S. O., & Gottesman, I. I. (1997). At issue: Genes, experience, and chance in schizophrenia – positioning for the 21st century. *Schizo. Bull., 23*(4), 547–561.

Moller, H. J. (1999). Effectiveness and safety of benzodiazepines. *J. Clin. Psychopharmacol., 19*(6 Suppl. 2), 2S–11S.

Mollerstrom, W. W., Patchner, M. A., & Milner, J. S. (1992). Family violence in the Air Force: A look at offenders and the role of the Family Advocacy Program. *Mil. Med., 157*(7), 371–374.

Mollinger, R. N. (1980). Antithesis and the obsessive-compulsive. *Psychoanal. Rev., 67*(4), 465–477.

Monahan, J. (1992). Mental disorder and violent behavior: Perceptions and evidence. *Amer. Psychologist, 47*(4), 511–521.

Monahan, J. (1993). Limiting therapist exposure to *Tarasoff* liability: Guidelines for risk containment. *Amer. Psychologist, 48*(3), 242–250.

Monahan, J. (1993). Mental disorder and violence: Another look. In S. Hodgins (Ed.), *Mental disorder and crime.* Newbury Park, CA: Sage.

Monahan, J., & Davis, S. K. (1983). Mentally disordered sex offenders. In J. Monahan & H. J. Steadman (Eds.), *Mentally disordered offenders.* New York: Plenum Press.

Monahan, J., & Steadman, H. J. (1996). Violent storms and violent people. How meteorology can inform risk communication in mental health law. *Amer. Psychologist, 51*(9), 931–938.

Monahan, J., & Steadman, H. J. (Eds.). (1983). *Mentally disordered offenders.* New York: Plenum Press.

Moncrieff, J. (1997). Lithium: Evidence reconsidered. *Brit. J. Psychiat., 171,* 113–119.

Moncrieff, J., Drummond, C., Candy, B., Checinski, K., & Farmer, R. (1996). Sexual abuse in people with alcohol problems: A study of the prevalence of sexual abuse and its relationship to drinking behavior. *Brit. J. Psychiat., 169,* 355–360.

Montgomery, S. A. (1999). Managing the severely ill and long-term depressed. *Inter. J. Psychiat. Clin. Prac., 3*(Suppl. 1), S13–S17.

Montgomery, S. A. (1999). Social phobia: Diagnosis, severity and implications for treatment. *Eur. Arch. Psychiat. Clin. Neurosci., 249*(Suppl. 1), S1–S6.

Montgomery, S. A., & Kasper, S. (1995). Comparison of compliance between serotonin reuptake inhibitors and tricyclic antidepressants: A meta-analysis. *Inter. Clin. Psychopharmacology, 9*(Suppl. 4), 33–40.

Montgomery, S. A., Bebbington, P., Cowen, P., Deakin, W., et al. (1993). Guidelines for treating depressive illness with antidepressants. *J. Psychopharmacol., 7*(1), 19–23.

Montgomery, S. A., Dufour, H., Brion S., Gailledreau, J., et al. (1988). The prophylactic efficacy of fluoxetine in unipolar depression. *Brit. J. Psychiat., 153*(Suppl. 3), 69–76.

Moore, M. T. (1997, October 30). Maine initiative would give the vote to all mentally ill. *USA Today,* p. 12A.

Moore, N. C. (2000). A review of EEG biofeedback treatment of anxiety disorders. *Clin. Electroencephalogr., 31*(1), 1–6.

Moos, R. H., & Cronkite, R. C. (1999). Symptom-based predictors of a 10-year chronic course of treated depression. *J. Nerv. Ment. Dis., 187*(6), 360–368.

Morales, A., Condra, M., Heaton, J. P. W., & Varrin, S. (1991). Impotence: Organic factors and management approach. *Sex. Marital Ther., 6*(2), 97–106.

Morgan, A. H., & Hilgard, E. R. (1973). Age differences in susceptibility to hypnosis. *Inter. J. Clin. Exp. Hyp., 21,* 73–85.

Morgan, C. D., & Murray, H. A. (1935). A method of investigating fantasies: The Thematic Apperception Test. *Arch. Neurol. Psychiat., 34,* 289–306.

Morgan, M. J., & London, E. D. (1995). The use of positron emission tomography to study the acute effects of addictive drugs on cerebral metabolism. In A. Biegon & N. D. Volkow (Eds.), *Sites of drug action in the human brain.* Boca Raton, FL: CRC Press.

Morganthaler, A. (1999). Male impotence. *Lancet, 354*(9191), 1713–1718.

Morganthau, T. (1998, June 29). Descent into darkness. *Newsweek,* pp. 54–55.

Morgenstern, J., Langenbucher, J., Labouvie, E., & Miller, K. J. (1997). The comorbidity of alcoholism and personality disorders in a clinical population: Prevalence rates and relation to alcohol typology variables. *J. Abnorm. Psychol., 106*(1), 74–84.

Morin, C. M., Colecchi, C., Brink, D., Astruc, M., et al. (1995). How "blind" are double-blind placebo-controlled trials of benzodiazepine hypnotics? *Sleep, 18*(4), 240–245.

Morokoff, P. J. (1988). Sexuality in premenopausal and postmenopausal women. *Psychol. Women Quart., 12,* 489–511.

Morokoff, P. J. (1993). Female sexual arousal disorder. In W. O'Donohue & J. Geer (Eds.), *Handbook of sexual dysfunctions.* Boston: Allyn & Bacon.

Morokoff, P. J., & Gillilland, R. (1993). Stress, sexual functioning, and marital satisfaction. *J. Sex Res., 30*(1), 43–53.

Morral, A. R., McCaffrey, D., & Iguchi, M. Y. (2000). Hardcore drug users claim to be occasional users: Drug use frequency underreporting. *Drug Alc. Dep., 57*(3), 193–202.

Morren, M. (1998). Hostility as a risk factor for coronary heart disease. *Psycholoog, 33*(3), 101–108.

Morris, G. (1983). Acquittal by reason of insanity: Developments in the law. In J. Monahan & H. J. Steadman (Eds.), *Mentally disordered offenders.* New York: Plenum Press.

Morrison, J. (1989). Histrionic personality disorder in women with somatization disorder. *Psychosomatics, 30*(4), 433–437.

Morse, S. J. (1982). A preference for liberty: The case against involuntary commitment of the mentally disordered. *Calif. Law Rev., 70,* 55–106.

Mortensen, P. B., Pedersen, C. B., Westergaard, T., Wohlfahrt, J., Ewald, H., Mors, O., Andersen, P. K., & Melbye, M. (1999). Effects of family history and place and season of birth on the risk of schizophrenia. *N. Engl. J. Med., 340*(8), 603–608.

Mosak, H. H., & Goldman, S. E. (1995). An alternative view of the purpose of psychoses. *Indiv. Psychol. J. Adlerian Theory, Res. Prac., 51*(1), 46–49.

Moscicki, E. K. (1999). Epidemiology of suicide. In D. G. Jacobs (Ed.), *The Harvard Medical School guide to suicide assessment and intervention.* San Francisco: Jossey-Bass.

Moshinsky, D. (1995). *Things you know that are not so.* Voorhees, NJ: Russet Press.

Moskovitz, R. A. (1996). *Lost in the mirror: An inside look at borderline personality disorder.* Dallas, TX: Taylor Publishing.

Moss, D. (1999). Biofeedback, mind-body medicine, and the higher limits of human nature. In D. Moss et al. (Eds.), *Humanistic and transpersonal psychology: A historical and biographical sourcebook.* Westport, CT: Greenwood.

Moss, H. B. (1999). Pharmacotherapy. In M. Hersen & A. S. Bellack (Eds.), *Handbook of comparative interventions for adult disorders* (2nd ed.). New York: Wiley.

Mostofsky, S. (1999, April). Brain abnormalities in children with ADHD. Paper presented at 51st annual meeting of American Academy of Neurology, Toronto.

Motto, J. (1967). Suicide and suggestibility: The role of the press. *Amer. J. Psychiat., 124,* 252–256.

Mowrer, O. H. (1939). A stimulus-response analysis of anxiety and its role as a reinforcing agent. *Psychol. Rev., 46,* 553–566.

Mowrer, O. H. (1939). *An experimentally produced "social problem" in rats* [Film]. Bethlehem, PA: Lehigh University, Psychological Cinema Register.

Mowrer, O. H. (1947). On the dual nature of learning: A reinterpretation of "conditioning" and "problem-solving." *Harvard Educ. Rev., 17,* 102–148.

Mowrer, O. H., & Mowrer, W. M. (1938). Enuresis: A method for its study and treatment. *Amer. J. Orthopsychiat., 8,* 436–459.

Mueller, R. A., & Courchesne, E. (2000). Autism's home in the brain: Reply. *Neurology, 54*(1), 270.

Mueser, K. T., Bellack, A. S., & Brady, E. U. (1990). Hallucinations in schizophrenia. *Acta Psychiatr. Scandin., 82*(1), 29–36.

Mueser, K. T., Doonan, R., Penn, D. L., Blanchard, J. J., Bellack, A. S., Nishith, P., & DeLeon, J. (1996). Emotion recognition and social competence in chronic schizophrenia. *J. Abnorm. Psychol., 105*(2), 271–275.

Mufson, L., Weissman, M. M., Moreau, D., & Garfinkel, R. (1999). Efficacy of interpersonal psychotherapy for depressed adolescents. *Arch. Gen. Psychiat., 57*(6), 573–579.

Muhammad, L. (1999, March 30). Experts brainstorming over memory loss. *USA Today,* p. 6D.

Muir, J. L. (1997). Acetylcholine, aging, and Alzheimer's disease. *Pharmacol. Biochem. Behav., 56*(4), 687–696.

Mulder, A. (1996). *Prevention of suicidal behaviour in adolescents: The development and evaluation of a teacher's education programme.* Leiden, The Netherlands: University of Leiden Press.

Mulhern, B. (1990, December 15–18). Everyone's problem, no one's priority. *Capital Times.*

Mulkern, V. M., & Manderscheid, R. W. (1989). Characteristics of community support program clients in 1980 and 1984. *Hosp. Comm. Psychiat., 40*(2), 165–172.

Muller, R. J. (1998). A patient with dissociative identity disorder "switches" in the emergency room. *Psychiatr. Times., XV*(11).

Mullins, L. L., Olson, R. A., & Chaney, J. M. (1992). A social learning/family systems approach to the treatment of somatoform disorders in children and adolescents. *Fam. Sys. Med., 10*(2), 201–212.

Munk, J. P., & Mortensen, P. B. (1992). Social outcome in schizophrenia: A 13-year follow-up. *Soc. Psychiat. Psychiat. Epidemiol., 27*(3), 129–134.

Muris, P., Merckelbach, H., & Clavan, M. (1997). Abnormal and normal compulsions. *Behav. Res. Ther. 35*(3), 249–252.

Murphy, C. M., Meyer, S. L., & O'Leary, K. D. (1994). Dependency characteristics of partner assaultive men. *J. Abnorm. Psychol., 103*(4), 729–735.

Murphy, G. E. (1998). Why women are less likely than men to commit suicide. *Comprehen. Psychiat., 39*(4), 165–175.

Murphy, J. B., & Lipshultz, L. I. (1988). Infertility in the paraplegic male. In E. A. Tanagho, T. F. Lue, & R. D. McClure (Eds.), *Contemporary management of impotence and infertility.* Baltimore: Williams & Wilkins.

Murphy, S. M. (1990). Rape, sexually transmitted diseases and human immunodeficiency virus infection. *Inter. J. STD AIDS, 1,* 79–82.

Murray, B. (1996). Computer addictions entangle students. *APA Monitor, 27*(6), 38–39.

Murray, B. (1996). Hypnosis helps children address their many fears. *APA Monitor, 27*(10), 46.

Murray, H. A. (1938). *Explorations in personality.* Fairlawn, NJ: Oxford University Press.

Murray, K. (1993, May 9). When the therapist is a computer. *New York Times,* Section 3, p. 25.

Murray, R. M., & Fearon, P. (1999). The developmental "risk factor" model of schizophrenia. *J. Psychiat. Res., 33*(6), 497–499.

Murstein, B. I., & Fontaine, P. A. (1993). The public's knowledge about psychologists and other mental health professionals. *Amer. Psychologist, 48*(7), 839–845.

Mussell, M. P., Mitchell, J. E., de Zwaan, M., Crosby, R. D., et al. (1996). Clinical characteristics associated with binge eating in obese females: A descriptive study. *Inter. J. Obesity, 20,* 324–331.

Mustaine, E. E., & Tewksbury, R. (1998). Specifying the role of alcohol in predatory victimization. *Deviant Behavior: An Interdisciplinary Journal, 19,* 173–199.

Muuss, R. E. (1986). Adolescent eating disorder: Bulimia. *Adolescence, 21*(82), 257–267.

Myatt, R. J., & Greenblatt, M. (1993). Adolescent suicidal behavior. In A. A. Leenaars (Ed.), *Suicidology.* Northvale, NJ: Jason Aronson.

Mydans, S. (1996, October 19). New Thai tourist sight: Burmese "giraffe women." *New York Times,* p. C1.

Myers, D., & Diener, E. (1995). Who is happy? *Psychol. Sci., 6*(1), 10–19.

Myers, D., & Diener, E. (1996, May). The pursuit of happiness. *Scientif. Amer.,* pp. 70–72.

Myers, D. G. (2000). The funds, friends, and faith of happy people. *Amer. Psychologist, 55*(1), 56–67.

Myers, M. G., Stewart, D. G., & Bown, S. A. (1998). Progression from conduct disorder to antisocial personality disorder following treatment for adolescent substance abuse. *Amer. J. Psychiat., 155*(4), 479–485.

NAMHC (National Advisory Mental Health Council). (1996). Basic behavioral science research for mental health. *Amer. Psychologist, 51*(3), 181–189.

NAMHC. (1996). Basic behavioral science research for mental health. Sociocultural and environmental processes. *Amer. Psychologist, 51*(7), 722–731.

NAMHC (National Advisory Mental Health Council). (1996). Basic behavioral science research for mental health. Perception, attention, learning, and memory. *Amer. Psychol. 51*(2), 133–142.

NAMHC Basic Behavioral Science Task Force. (1996). Basic behavioral science research for mental health: Vulnerability and resilience. *Amer. Psychologist, 51*(1), 22–28.

NAMI (National Alliance for the Mentally Ill). (1994). Personal communication.

NAMI (National Alliance for the Mentally Ill). (1996, February 7). Survey on mental health insurance. Cited in *USA Today,* p. 4D.

NAMI (National Alliance for the Mentally Ill). (1999). Testimony before House committee on Ways and Means Subcommittee on Social Security, March 11.

NAPHS (National Association of Psychiatric Health Systems). (1999). *The NAPHS 1998 annual survey report—trends in psychiatric health systems: A benchmarking report.* Washington, DC: Author.

NCHS (National Center for Health Statistics). (1990). *Vital statistics of the United States, 1987,* Vol. 2. Mortality. Washington, DC: Government Printing Office.

NCHS (National Center for Health Statistics). (1994). *Advance report of final mortality statistics, 1992.* (Monthly vital statistics report, 43.) Hyattsville, MD: Public Health Service.

NCHS (National Center for Health Statistics). (1995). *Advance report of final divorce statistics.* (Monthly vital statistics report, 43.) (9, Suppl). Hyattsville, MD: Public Health Service.

NCHS (National Center for Health Statistics). (1999). *Fastats A to Z. Alzheimer's disease.* Washington, DC: Center for Disease Control.

NCHS (National Center for Health Statistics). (1999). *Fastats A to Z. Chronic liver disease/cirrhosis.* Washington, DC: Center for Disease Control.

NCHS (National Center for Health Statistics). (1999). *Fastats A to Z. Divorce.* Washington, DC: Center for Disease Control.

NCHS (National Center for Health Statistics). (1999). *Fastats A to Z. Health of the elderly.* Washington, DC: Center for Disease Control.

NCHS (National Center for Health Statistics). (1999). *Fastats A to Z. Overweight prevalence.* Washington, DC: Center for Disease Control.

NCHS (National Center for Health Statistics). (1999). *National Center for Health Statistics, Health, United States, 1996-1997* (DHHS Publ. No. PHS 97-1232).Hyattsville, MD: Center for Disease Control.

NCHS (National Center for Health Statistics). (1999). *Fastats. Asthma.* September 24.

NCHS (National Center for Health Statistics). (1999). *Fastats. Hypertension.* September 9.

NCHS (National Center for Health Statistics). (2000). *Births, marriages, divorces, and deaths: Provisional data for January 1999.* Centers for Disease Control and Prevention (National Vital Statistics Reports, vol. 48, no. 1).

NCIPC (National Center for Injury Prevention and Control). (1999, February 20). *Suicide in the United States.*

NCIPC (National Center for Injury Prevention and Control). (1999, October 25). *Epidemiology of traumatic brain injury in the United States.* Centers for Disease Control and Prevention.

NCVS (National Crime Victimization Survey). (1993). *Highlights from 20 years of surveying crime victims: The National Crime Victimization Survey, 1973-1992.* Washington, DC: Bureau of Justice Statistics.

NCVS (National Crime Victimization Survey). (1996). Washington, DC: Bureau of Justice Statistics.

NHSDA (National Household Survey on Drug Abuse). (1998). *1998 national estimates of rates of use and other measures related to drugs, alcohol, cigarettes, and other forms of tobacco.* Washington, DC: U.S. Department of Health and Human Services.

NIA (National Institute on Aging). (1996). *Aging America poses unprecendented challenge. 65+.* Washington, DC: Office of the Demography of Aging.

NIAAA (National Institute on Alcohol Abuse and Alcoholism). (1992). *Alcohol alert #15. Alcohol and AIDA.* Rockville, MD: Author.

NIAAA (National Institute on Alcohol Abuse and Alcoholism). (1992). *Alcohol alert #16. Moderate drinking.* Rockville, MD: Author.

NIDA (National Institute on Drug Abuse). (1990). *Substance abuse among blacks in the U. S.* Rockville, MD: Author.

NIDA (National Institute on Drug Abuse). (1990). *Substance abuse among Hispanic Americans.* Rockville, MD: Author.

NIDA (National Institute on Drug Abuse). (1991). *Annual emergency room data, 1991.* Rockville, MD: Author.

NIDA (National Institute on Drug Abuse). (1991). *Annual medical examiner data, 1991.* Rockville, MD: Author.

NIDA (National Institute on Drug Abuse). (1991). *Third triennial report to Congress on drug abuse and drug abuse research.* Rockville, MD: Author.

NIDA (National Institute on Drug Abuse). (1995). *Facts about teenagers and drug abuse. NIDA Capsule.* Rockville, MD: Author.

NIDA (National Institute on Drug Abuse). (1996). *Monitoring the future study, 1975-1996.* Rockville, MD: Author.

NIDA (National Institute on Drug Abuse). (1998). *Economic costs of alcohol and drug abuse.* Washington, DC: Author.

NIH (National Institutes of Health). (1999, February 19). American Indian: Facts-at-a-glance for women's health.

NIH (National Institutes of Health). (1998, October 7). New "gene map" doubles number of genes. *NIH News Advisory.*

NIMH (National Institute of Mental Health). (1999, June 7). National Institute of Mental Health launches landmark study. Press release.

NMHA (National Mental Health Association). (1999, June 5). Poll. *U.S. Newswire.*

Nagle, D. L., McGrail, S. H., Vitale, J., Woolf, E. A., Dussault, B. J., Jr., DiRocco, L., Holmgren, L., Montagno, J., Bork, P., Huszar, D., Fairchild-Huntress, V., Ge, P., Keilty, J., Ebeling, C., Baldini, L., Gilchrist, J., Voen, P., Carlson, G. A., & Moore, K. J. (1999). The mahogany protein is a receptor involved in suppression of obesity. *Nature, 398*(6723), 148-152.

Nagy, J., & Szatmari, P. (1986). A chart review of schizotypal personality disorders in children. *J. Autism Dev. Disorders, 16*(3), 351-367.

Nagy, L. M., Krystal, J. H., Charney, D. S., Merikangas, K. R., & Woods, S. W. (1993). Long-term outcome of panic disorder after short-term imipramine and behavioral group treatment: 2.9-year naturalistic follow-up study. *J. Clin. Psychopharmacol., 13*(1), 16-24.

Nagy, L. M., Morgan, C. A., III, Southwick, S. M., & Charney, D. S. (1993). Open prospective trial of fluoxetine for posttraumatic stress disorder. *J. Clin. Psychopharmacol., 13*(2), 107-113.

Nagy, T. F. (2000). *Ethics in plain English: An illustrative casebook for psychologists.* Washington, DC: American Psychological Association.

Nahas, G. G. (1984). Toxicology and pharmacology. In G. G. Nahas (Ed.), *Marijuana in science and medicine.* New York: Raven Press.

Nahas, G. G., Sutin, K. M., Harvey, D., Agurell, S., Pace, N., & Cancro, R. (Eds.). (1999). *Marihuana and medicine.* Clifton, NJ: Humana Press.

Najavitis, L. M., Gastfriend, D. R., Barber, J. P., Reif, S., Muenz, L. R., Blaine, J., Frank, A., Crits-Christoph, P., Thase, M., & Weiss, R. D. (1998). Cocaine dependence with and without PTSD among subjects in the National Institute on Drug Abuse collaborative cocaine treatment study. *Amer. J. Psychiat., 155*(2), 214-219.

Najman, J. M., Andersen, M. J., Bor, W., O'Callaghan, M. J., & Williams, G. M. (2000). Postnatal depression—Myth and reality: Maternal depression before and after the birth of a child. *Soc. Psychiat. Psychiat. Epidemiol., 35*(1), 19-27.

Nakao, M., Nomura, S., Shimosawa, T., Fujita, T., & Kuboki, T. (2000). Blood pressure biofeedback treatment of white-coat hypertension. *J. Psychosom. Res., 48*(2), 161-169.

Narrow, W. E., Regier, D. A., Rae, D. S., Manderscheid, R. W., & Locke, B. Z. (1993). Use of services by persons with mental and addictive disorders: Findings from the National Institute of Mental Health Epidemiologic Catchment Area Program. *Arch. Gen. Psychiat., 50,* 95-107.

Nash, J. M. (1997, May 5). Addicted. *Time,* p. 68-76.

Nash, J. M. (1997). Special report: Fertile minds. *Newsweek, 149*(5), 48-56.

Nathan, P. E., & Lagenbucher, J. W. (1999). Psychopathology: Description and classification. *Annu. Rev. Psychol., 50,* 79-107.

National Commission on Children (1991). *Speaking of kids: A national survey of children and parents.* Washington, DC: Author.

National Mental Health Association. (1983). *Myths and realities: A report of the National Commission on the insanity defense.* Arlington VA: Author.

National Opinion Research Center. (1994). *Survey on extramarital relationships.* Washington, DC: Author.

Needleman, H. O., Riess, J. A., Tobin, M. J., Biesecker, G. E., et al. (1996). Bone lead levels and delinquent behavior. *JAMA, 275*(5), 363-369.

Needleman, L. D. (1999). *Cognitive case conceptualization: A guidebook for practitioners.* Mahwah, NJ: Erlbaum.

Neel, J. V. (1994). *Physician to the gene pool.* New York: Wiley.

Neeleman, J., & Farrell, M. (1997). Suicide and substance misuse. *Brit. J. Psychiat., 171,* 303-304.

Neeleman, J., & Persaud, R. (1995). Why do psychiatrists neglect religion? *Brit. J. Med. Psychol., 68*(2), 169-178.

Neeleman, J., Wessely, S., & Lewis, G. (1998). Suicide acceptability in African- and white Americans: The role of religion. *J. Nerv. Ment. Dis., 186*(1), 12-16.

Neimeyer, G. (1996). Glossary of therapists. In R. Comer (Ed.), *Abnormal psychology newsletter* (Issue No. 6).

Neimeyer, R. A., & Bonnelle, K. (1997). The suicide intervention response inventory: A revision and validation. *Death Stud., 21,* 59-81.

Neisser, U., Boodoo, G., Bouchard, T. J., Jr., Boykin, A. W., et al. (1996). Intelligence: Knowns and unknowns. *Amer. Psychologist, 51*(2), 77-101.

Nelson, R. O. (1977). Assessment and therapeutic functions of self-monitoring. In M. Hersen, R. M. Eisler, & P. M. Miller (Eds.), *Progress in behavior modification.* New York: Academic Press.

Nelson, R. O. (1981). Realistic dependent measures for clinical use. *J. Cons. Clin. Psychol., 49,* 168-182.

Nelson, R., Demas, G., Huang, P., Fishman, M., Dawson, V., Dawson, T., & Snyder, S. (1995). Behavioral abnormalities in male mice lacking neuronal nitric oxide synthase. *Nature, 378,* 383-386.

Nemecek, S. (1995, April). I get no kick from CH_3CH_2OH: A new treatment for alcoholism receives FDA approval. *Scientif. Amer.,* pp. 24,26.

Ness, R. B., Grisso, J. A., Herschinger, N., Markovic, N., Shaw, L. M., Day, N. L., & Kline, J. (1999). Cocaine and tobacco use and the risk of spontaneous abortion. *N. Engl. J. Med., 340*(5), 333-339.

Nesse, R. M. (2000). Is depression an adaptation? *Arch. Gen. Psychiat., 57*(1), 14-20.

Nestadt, G., Romanoski, A. J., Brown, C. H., Chahal, R., et al. (1991). DSM-III compulsive personality disorder: An epidemiological survey. *Psychol. Med., 21*(2), 461-471.

Nestadt, G., Romanoski, A. J., Chahal, R., Merchant, A., Folstein, M. F., Gruenberg, E. M., & McHugh, P. R. (1990). An epidemiological study of histrionic personality disorder. *Psychol. Med., 29,* 413-422.

Nestler, E. J., Fitzgerald, L. W., & Self, D. W. (1995). Neurobiology. In J. M. Oldham & M. B. Riba (Eds.), *American Psychiatric Press review of psychiatry* (Vol. 14). Washington, DC: American Psychiatric Press.

Nestor, P. G., & Haycock, J. (1997). Not guilty by reason of insanity of murder: Clinical and neuropsychological characteristics. *J. Amer. Acad. Psychiat. Law., 23*(2), 161-171.

Neugebauer, R. (1978). Treatment of the mentally ill in medieval and early modern England: A reappraisal. *J. Hist. Behav. Sci., 14,* 158-169.

Neugebauer, R. (1979). Medieval and early modern theories of mental illness. *Arch. Gen. Psychiat., 36,* 477-483.

Neumaier, J. F., Petty, F., Kramer, G. L., Szot, P., & Hamblin, M. W. (1997). Learned helplessness increases 5-hydroxytryptamine$_{1B}$ receptor mRNA levels in the rat dorsal raphe nucleus. *Biol. Psychiat., 41,* 668-674.

Neuman, P. A., & Halvorson, P. A. (1983). *Anorexia nervosa and bulimia: A handbook for counselors and therapists.* New York: Van Nostrand-Reinhold.

Neumarker, K. J. (1997). Mortality and sudden death in anorexia nervosa. *Inter. J. Eat. Disorders, 21*(3), 205-212.

Newcomb, M. D. (1994). Predictors of drug use and implications for the workplace. In S. Macdonald & P. Roman (Eds.), *Research advances in alcohol and drug problems: Vol. 11. Drug testing in the workplace.* New York: Plenum Press.

Newman, D. L., Moffitt, T. E., Caspi, A., & Silva, P. A. (1998). Comorbid mental disorders: Implications for treatment and sample selection. *J. Abnorm. Psychol., 107*(2), 305-311.

Newman, J. D., & Farley, M. J. (1995). An ethologically based, stimulus and gender-sensitive non-human primate model for anxiety. *Prog. Neuropsychopharmacol. Biol. Psychiat., 19*(4), 677-685.

Newman, J. P., Kosson, D. S., & Patterson, C. M. (1987). Response perseveration in psychopaths. *J. Abnorm. Psychol., 96,* 145-149.

Newman, J. P., Kosson, D. S., & Patterson, C. M. (1992). Delay of gratification in psychopathic and nonpsychopathic offenders. *J. Abnorm. Psychol., 101*(4), 630-636.

Newman, R., et al. (1996). State leadership conference mobilizes practitioners for community outreach. *Practitioner Update, 4*(1), 1.

Newsweek Poll (1995). *The state of shame and the union.* Princeton, NJ: Princeton Survey Research Associates.

Newton, J. T. O., Spence, S. H., & Schotte, D. (1995). Cognitive-behavioral therapy versus EMG biofeedback in the treatment of chronic low back pain. *Behav. Res. Ther., 33*(6), 691-697.

Newton, S. E. (1999). Sexual dysfunction in men on chronic hemodialysis: A rehabilitation nursing concern. *Rehab. Nursing, 24*(1), 24-29.

Neziroglu, F. (1998, January). Body dysmorphic disorder: A common but underdiagnosed clinical entity. *Psychiatr. Times, XV*(1).

Neziroglu, F., McKay, D., Todaro, J., & Yaryura-Tobias, J. A. (1996). Effect of cognitive behavior therapy on persons with body dysmorphic disorder and comorbid Axis II diagnoses. *Behav. Ther., 27,* 67-77.

Nezlek, J. B., Hampton, C. P., & Shean, G. D. (2000). Clinical depression and day-to-day social interaction in a community sample. *J. Abnorm. Psychol., 109*(1), 11-19.

Nichols, M. P. (1984). *Family therapy: Concepts and methods.* New York: Gardner Press.

Nichols, M. P. (1992). *The power of family therapy.* New York: Gardner Press.

Nichols, M. P., & Minuchin, S. (1999). Short-term structural family therapy with couples. In J. Donovan et al. (Eds.), *Short-term couple therapy.* New York: Guilford Press.

Nicholson, P. (1999). Loss, happiness and postpartum depression: The ultimate paradox. *Canad. Psychol., 40*(2), 162-178.

Nichter, M., & Nichter, M. (1991). Hype and weight. *Med. Anthropol., 13*(3), 249–284.

Nichter, M., & Vuckovic, N. (1994). Fat talk: Body image among adolescent females. In N. Sault (Ed.), *Mirror, mirror: Body image and social relations.* New Brunswick, NJ: Rutgers University Press.

Nicoli, A. M., Jr. (1999). History and mental status. In A. M. Nicoli, Jr. (Ed.), *The Harvard guide to psychiatry* (3rd ed.). Cambridge, MA: Belknap Press/Harvard University Press.

Nie, N. (1999, July). Tracking our techno future. What are the social consequences of innovation? *American Demographics.*

Nielson, S., Møller-Madsen, S., Isager, T., Jørgensen, J., Pagsberg, K., & Theander, S. (1998). Standardized mortality in eating disorders—A quantitative summary of previously published and new evidence. *J. Psychosom. Res., 14*(3/4), 413–434.

Nieman, D. H., Bour, L. J., Linszen, D. H., Goede, J., Koelman, J. H. T. M., Gersons, B. P. R., & Ongerboer de Visser, B. W. (2000). Neuropsychological and clinical correlates of anti-saccade task performance in schizophrenia. *Neurology, 54*(4), 866–871.

Nietzel, M. T., Bernstein, D. A., & Milich, R. (1994). *Introduction to clinical psychology* (4th ed.). Englewood Cliffs, NJ: Prentice Hall.

Nijinsky, V. (1936). *The diary of Vaslav Nijinsky.* New York: Simon & Schuster.

Nock, M. K., & Marzuk, P. M. (1999) Murder-suicide: Phenomenology and clinical implications. In D.G. Jacobs (Ed.), *The Harvard Medical School guide to suicide assessment and intervention.* San Francisco: Jossey-Bass.

Nolen, W. A. (1999). Pharmacotherapy in bipolar disorder. *Ned Tijdschr Geneeskd 143*(25), 1299–1305. [Dutch.]

Nolen-Hoeksema, S. (1987). Sex differences in unipolar depression: Evidence and theory. *Psychol. Bull., 101*(2), 259–282.

Nolen-Hoeksema, S. (1990). *Sex differences in depression.* Stanford, CA: Stanford University Press.

Nolen-Hoeksema, S. (1995). Gender differences in coping with depression across the lifespan. *Depression, 3,* 81–90.

Nolen-Hoeksema, S. (1998). The other end of the continuum: The costs of rumination: *Psychological Inquiry, 9*(3), 216–219.

Nolen-Hoeksema, S., & Girgus, J. (1995). Explanatory style and achievement, depression, and gender differences in childhood and early adolescence. In G. Buchanan & M. Seligman (Eds.), *Explanatory style.* Hillsdale, NJ: Erlbaum.

Noll, R., & Turkington, C. (1994). *The encyclopedia of memory and memory disorders.* New York: Facts on File.

Nonacs, R., & Cohen, L. S. (1998). Postpartum mood disorders: Diagnosis and treatment guidelines. *J. Clin. Psychiat., 59*(Suppl. 2), 34–40.

Noonan, J. R. (1971). An obsessive-compulsive reaction treated by induced anxiety. *Amer. J. Psychother., 25*(2), 293–299.

Norcross, J. C., & Prochaska, J. O. (1984). Where do behavior (and other) therapists take their troubles? II. *Behav. Therapist, 7*(2), 26–27.

Norcross, J. C., & Prochaska, J. O. (1986). Psychotherapist heal thyself: I. The psychological distress and self-change of psychologists, counselors, and laypersons. *Psychotherapy, 23,* 102–114.

Norcross, J. C., Prochaska, J. O., & Farber, J. A. (1993). Psychologists conducting psychotherapy: New findings and historical comparisons on the psychotherapy division membership. *Psychotherapy, 30*(4), 692–697.

Norcross, J. C., Beutler, L. E., & Clarkin, J. F. (Eds.). (1998). Prescriptive eclectic psychotherapy. In R. A. Dorfman et al. (Eds.), *Paradigms of*

clinical social work (Vol. 2). Philadelphia: Brunner/Mazel.

Norcross, J. C., Strausser, D. J., & Missar, C. D. (1988). The process and outcomes of psychotherapists' personal treatment experiences. *Psychotherapy, 25,* 36–43.

Nordenberg, L. (1998). *Dealing with the depths of depression.* Washington, DC: U.S. Food and Drug Administration.

Nordstrom, P., Samuelsson, M., & Asberg, M. (1995). Survival analysis of suicide risk after attempted suicide. *Acta Psychiatr. Scandin., 91*(5), 336–340.

Norman, R. M. G., & Malla, A. K. (1995). Prodromal symptoms of relapse in schizophrenia: A review. *Schizo. Bull., 21*(4), 527–539.

North, C. S., Nixon, S. J., Shariat, S., Mallonee, S., McMillen, J. C., Spitznagel, E. L., & Smith, E. M. (1999). Psychiatric disorders among survivors of the Oklahoma City bombing. *JAMA, 282*(8), 755–762.

Norton, G. R., Cox, B. J., Asmundson, G. J. G., & Maser, J. D. (1995). The growth of research on anxiety disorders during the 1980s. *J. Anx. Dis., 9*(1), 75–85.

Norton, G. R., Cox, B. J., Hewitt, P. L., & McLeod, L. (1997). Personality factors associated with generalized and non-generalized social anxiety. *Pers. Individ. Diff., 22*(5), 655–660.

Nott, K. H., & Vedhara, K. (1999). Nature and consequences of stressful life events in homosexual HIV-positive men: A review. *AIDS Care, 11*(2), 235–243.

Novaco, R. W. (1977). A stress inoculation approach to anger management in the training of law enforcement officers. *Amer. J. Comm. Psych., 5*(3), 327–346.

Novaco, R. W. (1977). Stress innoculation: A cognitive therapy for anger and its application to a case of depression. *J. Cons. Clin. Psychol., 45*(4), 600–608.

Noyes, R., Jr. (1999). The relationship of hypochondriasis to anxiety disorders. *Gen. Hosp. Psychiat., 21*(1), 8–17.

Nurnberger, J. I., Jr., & Gershon, E. S. (1984). Genetics of affective disorders. In R. M. Post & J. C. Ballenger (Eds.), *Neurobiology of mood disorders: Vol. 1. Frontiers of clinical neuroscience.* Baltimore: Williams & Wilkins.

Nurnberger, J. I., Jr., & Gershon, E. S. (1992). Genetics. In E. S. Paykel (Ed.), *Handbook of affective disorders.* New York: Guilford.

OSAP (Office for Substance Abuse Prevention). (1991). *Children of alcoholics: Alcoholism tends to run in families.* Rockville, MD: Author.

OSAP (Office for Substance Abuse Prevention). (1991). *College youth.* Rockville, MD: Author.

OSAP (Office for Substance Abuse Prevention). (1991). *Crack cocaine: A challenge for prevention.* Rockville, MD: Author.

OSAP (Office for Substance Abuse Prevention). (1991). *Impaired driving.* Rockville, MD: Author.

O'Brien, C. P., O'Brien, T. J., Mintz, J., & Brady, J. P. (1975). Conditioning of narcotic abstinence symptoms in human subjects. *Drug. Alc. Dep., 1,* 115–123.

O'Carroll, R. (1991). Sexual desire disorders: A review of controlled treatment studies. *J. Sex Res., 28,* 607–624.

O'Connor, B. P., & Dyce, J. A. (1998). A test of models of personality disorder configuration. *J. Abnorm. Psychol., 107*(1), 3–16.

O'Connor, S., Deeks, J. J., Hawton, K., Simkin, S., Keen, A., Altman, D. G., Philo, G., & Bulstrode, C. (1999). Effects of a drug overdose in a television drama on knowledge of specific

dangers of self poisoning: Population based surveys. *Brit. Med. J., 318*(7189), 955–956.

O'Hare, T. (1992). The substance-abusing chronically mentally ill client: Prevalence, assessment, treatment and policy concerns. *Soc. Work, 37*(2), 185–187.

O'Leary, D., Gill, D., Gregory, S., & Shawcross, C. (1995). Which depressed patients respond to ECT? The Nottingham results. *J. Affect. Disorders, 33*(4), 245–250.

O'Leary, K. D., & Kent, R. (1973). Behavior modification for social action: Research tactics and problems. In L. A. Hamerlynck, L. C. Handy, & E. J. Mash (Eds.), *Behavior change: Methodology, concepts, and practice.* Champaign, IL: Research Press.

O'Leary, K. M., Brouwers, P., Gardner, D. L., & Cowdry, R. W. (1991). Neuropsychological testing of patients with borderline personality disorder. *Amer. J. Psychiat., 148*(1), 106–111.

O'Leary, K. M., Turner, E. R., Gardner, D., & Cowdry, R. W. (1991). Homogeneous group therapy of borderline personality disorder. *Group, 15*(1), 56–64.

O'Malley, S. S., Jaffe, A., Chang, G., Schottenfeld, R., Meyer, R., & Rounsaville, B. (1992). Naltrexone and coping skills therapy for alcohol dependence. *Arch. Gen. Psychiat., 49,* 881–888.

O'Malley, S. S., Jaffe, A. J., Rode, S., & Rounsaville, B. J. (1996). Experience of a "slip" among alcoholics treated with naltrexone or placebo. *Amer. J. Psychiat., 153,* 281–283.

O'Malley, S. S., Krishnan-Sarin, S., Farren, C., & O'Connor, P. G. (2000). Naltrexone-induced nausea in patients treated for alcohol dependence: Clinical predictors and evidence for opioid-mediated effects. *J. Clin. Psychopharmacol., 20*(1), 69–76.

O'Neill, S. (1997). Therapy for "bereaved" toy owners. *Electronic Telegraph,* p. 728.

Oei, T. P., Lim, B., & Hennessy, B. (1990). Psychological dysfunction in battle: Combat stress reactions and posttraumatic stress disorder. *Clin. Psychol. Rev., 10*(3), 355–388.

Oei, T. P. S., Llamas, M., & Devilly, G. J. (1999). The efficacy and cognitive processes of cognitive behaviour therapy in the treatment of panic disorder with agoraphobia. *Behav. Cog. Psychother., 27*(1), 63–88.

Offer, D., Ostrov, E., & Howard, K. I. (1981). The mental health professional's concept of the normal adolescent. *Arch. Gen. Psychiat., 38*(2), 140–152.

Ogden, J. A., & Corkin, S. (1991). Memories of H. M. In W. C. Abraham, M. C. Corballis, & K. G. White (Eds.), *Memory mechanisms: A tribute to G. V. Goddard.* Hillsdale, NJ: Erlbaum.

Ogden, J., & Ward, E. (1995). Help-seeking behavior in suffers of vaginismus. *Sex Marital Ther., 10*(1), 23–30.

Ogloff, J. R. P., Schweighofer, A., Turnbull, S. D., & Whittemore, K. (1992). Empirical research regarding the insanity defense: How much do we really know? In J. R. P. Ogloff (Ed.), *Law and psychology: The broadening of the discipline.*

Ohayon, M. M. (1997). Prevalence of DSM-IV diagnostic criteria of insomnia: Distinguishing insomnia related to mental disorders from sleep disorders. *J. Psychiat. Res., 31*(3), 333–346.

Ohayon, M. M., Cualet, M., & Lemoine, P. (1998). Comorbidity of mental and insomnia disorders in the general population. *Comprehen. Psychiat., 39*(4), 185–197.

Ohberg, A., Penttila, A., & Lonnqvist, J. (1997). Driver suicides. *Brit. J. Psychiat., 171,* 468–472.

Oher, J. M. (1999). *The employee assistance handbook.* New York: Wiley.

Ohman, A., & Soares, J. J. F. (1993). On the automatic nature of phobic fear: Conditioned electrodermal responses to masked fear-relevant stimuli. *J. Abnorm. Psychol., 102*(1), 121–132.

Ohman, A., Erixon, G., & Lofberg, I. (1975). Phobias and preparedness: Phobic versus neutral pictures as continued stimuli for human autonomic responses. *J. Abnorm. Psychol., 84,* 41–45.

Okasha, A., Ismail, M. F., Khalil, A. H., El-Fiki, R., Soliman, A., & Okasha, T. (1999). A psychiatric study of nonorganic chronic headache patients. *Psychosomatics, 40*(3), 233–238.

Oldenburg, D. (1995, August 18). Miserable? Check out self-analysis. *Washington Post,* p. G5.

Olfson, M., & Klerman, G. L. (1993). Trends in the prescription of antidepressants by office based psychiatrists. *Amer. J. Psychiat., 150*(4), 571–577.

Olfson, M., Mechanic, D., Hansell, S., Boyer, C.A., Walkup, J., & Weiden, P.J. (2000). Predicting medication noncompliance after hospital discharge among patients with schizophrenia. *Psychiatr. Serv., 51*(2), 216–222.

Olfson, M., Pincus, H. A., & Dial, T. H. (1994). Professional practice patterns of U. S. psychiatrists. *Amer. J. Psychiat., 151*(1), 89–95.

Oliver, J. E. (1993). Intergenerational transmission of child abuse: Rates, research and clinical implications. *Amer. J. Psychiat., 150*(9).

Ollendick, T. H., & King, N. J. (1998). Empirically supported treatments for children with phobic and anxiety disorders: Current status. *J. Clin. Child Psychol., 27*(2), 156–167.

Olley, J. G., & Baroff, G. S. (1999). Psychiatric disorders in mental retardation. In G. S. Baroff & J. G. Olley (Eds.), *Mental retardation: Nature, cause, and management* (3rd ed.). Philadelphia: Brunner/Mazel.

Olmos de Paz, T. (1990). Working-through and insight in child psychoanalysis. *Melanie Klein & Object Relations, 8*(1), 99–112.

Olmsted, M. P., Kaplan, A. S., & Rockert, W. (1994). Rate and prediction of relapse in bulimia nervosa. *Amer. J. Psychiat., 151*(5), 738–743.

Olsson, G. I., & von Knorring, A. L. (1999). Adolescent depression: Prevalence in Swedish high-school students. *Acta Psychiatr. Scandin., 99*(5), 324–331.

Open Minds. (1997). Cited in *The NAMI Advocate, 19*(3), 19.

Oppenheim, S., & Rosenberger, J. (1991). Treatment of a case of obsessional disorder: Family systems and object relations approaches. *Amer. J. Fam. Ther., 19*(4), 327–333.

Orsillo, S. M., Weathers, F. W., Litz, B. T., Steinberg, H. R., et al. (1996). Current and lifetime psychiatric disorders among veterans with war zone-related posttraumatic stress disorder. *J. Nerv. Ment. Dis., 184,* 307–313.

Orzack, M. H. (1996, December 1). Interview in P. Belluck, The symptoms of Internet addiction. *New York Times,* p. 5.

Orzack, M.H. (1998). Computer addiction: What is it? *Psychiatr. Times, XV*(8).

Öst, L.G. (1989). *Blood phobia: A specific phobia subtype in DSM-IV.* Paper requested by the Simple Phobia Subcommittee of the DSM-IV Anxiety Disorders Work Group.

Öst, L.-G., & Westling, B. E. (1995). Applied relaxation vs. cognitive behavior therapy in the treatment of panic disorder. *Behav. Res. Ther., 33*(2), 145–158.

Osterweis, M., & Townsend, J. (1988). *Understanding bereavement reactions in adults and children: A booklet for lay people.* Rockville, MD: U. S. Department of Health and Human Services.

Ostrow, D. G., Kalichman, S. C., et al. (Eds.). (1999). *Psychosocial and public health impacts of new HIV therapies.* New York: Kluwer Academic/Plenum.

Oswalt, R., & Finkelberg, S. (1995). College depression: Causes, duration, and coping. *Psychol. Rep., 77,* 858.

Otto, M. W. (1999). Cognitive-behavioral therapy for social anxiety disorder: Model, methods, and outcome. *J. Clin. Psychiat., 60*(Suppl. 9), 14–19.

Overbeek, T., Rikken, J., Schruers, K., & Griez, E. (1998). Suicidal ideation in panic disorder patients. *J. Nerv. Ment. Dis., 186*(9), 577–580.

Overholser, J. C. (1992). Interpersonal dependency and social loss. *Pers. Individ. Diff., 13*(1), 17–23.

Overholser, J. C. (1996). The dependent personality and interpersonal problems. *J. Nerv. Ment. Dis., 184*(1), 8–16.

Overmeyer, S., Taylor, E., Blanz, B., & Schmidt, M. H. (1999). Psychosocial adversities underestimated in hyperkinetic children. *J. Child Psychol. Psychiat., 40*(2), 259–263.

Overmier, J. B. (1992). On the nature of animal models of human behavioral dysfunction. In J. B. Overmier & P. D. Burke (Eds.), *Animal models of human pathology: A bibliography of a quarter century of behavioral research 1967-1992.* Washington, DC: American Psychological Association.

Overstreet, D. H. (1993). The Flinders sensitive line rats: A genetic animal model of depression. *Neurosci. Biobehav. Rev., 17,* 51–68.

Overton, D. (1964). State-dependent or "dissociated" learning produced with pentobarbital. *J. Compar. Physiol. Psychol., 57,* 3–12.

Overton, D. (1966). State-dependent learning produced by depressant and atropine-like drugs. *Psychopharmacologia, 10,* 6–31.

Owen, F., Crow, T. J., & Poulter, M. (1987). Central dopaminergic mechanisms in schizophrenia. *Acta Psychiatr. Belg., 87*(5), 552–565.

Owen, F., Crow, T. J., Poulter, M., et al. (1978). Increased dopamine receptor sensitivity in schizophrenia. *Lancet, 2,* 223–226.

Owen, M. K., Lancee, W. J., & Freeman, S. J. (1986). Psychological factors and depressive symptoms. *J. Nerv. Ment. Dis., 174*(1), 15–23.

Oyemade, U. J. (1989). *Parents and children getting a head start against drugs. Fact Sheet 1989.* Alexandria, VA: National Head Start Association.

Ozden, A., & Canat, S. (1999). Factitious hemoptysis. *J. Amer. Acad. Child Adol. Psychiat., 38*(4), 356–357.

PORT (Patient Outcomes Research Team) (1998). Cited in S. Barlas, Patient outcome research team study on schizophrenia offers grim indictment. *Psychiatr. Times, XV*(6).

Pace, T. M., & Dixon, D. N. (1993). Changes in depressive self-schemata and depressive symptoms following cognitive therapy. *J. Couns. Psychol., 40*(3), 288–294.

Padma, N. H. (1999). A new era in the treatment of erectile dysfunction. *Amer. J. Cardiol., 84*(5B), 18N–23N.

Page, S. (1996, February 21). Nationwide hot line to aid abuse victims. *USA Today,* p. 1D.

Pain, S. (1996, March). Ten deaths that may tell a shocking tale. *New Scientist,* p. 6.

Painter, K. (1992, March 25). Drunken-driving casualties aren't the only victims of alcohol abuse. *USA Today,* p. 5D.

Pajer, K. (1995). New strategies in the treatment of depression in women. *J. Clin. Psychiat., 56*(Suppl. 2), 30–37.

Palmore, E. B. (1999). Suicide can be rational for senescent or terminal patients. In J. L. Werth, Jr., et al. (Eds.), *Contemporary perspectives on rational suicide.* Series in death, dying, and bereavement. Philadelphia: Brunner/Mazel.

Panikkar, G.P. (1999). Cocaine addiction: Neurobiology and related current research in pharmacotherapy. *Substance Abuse, 20*(3), 149–166.

Pankratz, L. (1999). Factitious disorders and factitious disorders by proxy. In S. D. Netherton, D. Holmes, et al. (Eds.), *Child and adolescent psychological disorders: A comprehensive textbook.* New York: Oxford University Press.

Pantano, P., Caramia, F., & Pierallini, A. (1999). The role of MRI in dementia. *Ital. J. Neurol. Sci., 20*(8), S250–S253.

Paradis, C. M., Freidman, S., Hatch, M., & Lazar, R. M. (1992). Obsessive-compulsive disorder onset after removal of a brain tumor. *J. Nerv. Ment. Dis., 180*(8), 535–536.

Paris, J. (1991). Personality disorders, parasuicide, and culture. *Transcult. Psychiatr. Res. Rev., 28*(1), 25–39.

Paris, J., Nowlis, D., & Brown, R. (1988). Developmental factors in the outcome of borderline personality disorder. *Comprehen. Psychiat., 29*(2), 147–150.

Park, A. (1996). Health roundup: The human condition. *Time,* p. 82.

Parker, G. (1983). Parental "affectionless control" as an antecedent to adult depression. *Arch. Gen. Psychiat., 48,* 956–960.

Parker, G. (1992). Early environment. In E. S. Paykel (Ed.), *Handbook of affective disorders.* New York: Guilford.

Parker, G., Hadzi-Pavlovic, D., Brodaty, H., Boyce, P., Mitchell, P., Wilhelm, K., Hickie, I., & Eyers, K. (1993). Psychomotor disturbance in depression: Defining the constructs. *J. Affect. Disorders, 27,* 255–265.

Parker, G., Hadzi-Pavlovic, D., Greenwald, S., & Weissman, M. (1995). Low parental care as a risk factor to lifetime depression in a community sample. *J. Affect. Disorders, 33*(3), 173–180.

Parker, G., Roussos, J., Mitchell, P., Wilhelm, K., et al. (1997). Distinguishing psychotic depression from melancholia. *J. Affect. Dis., 42,* 155–167.

Parker, G., Wilhelm, K., Mitchell, P., Austin, M. P., Roussos, J., & Gladstone, G. (1999). The influence of anxiety as a risk to early onset depression. *J. Affect. Disorders, 52*(1–3), 11–17.

Parker, N. (1991). The Gary David case. *Austral. New Zeal. J. Psychiat., 25*(3), 371–374.

Parker, P. E. (1993). A case report of Munchausen syndrome with mixed psychological features. *Psychosomatics, 34*(4), 360–364.

Parker, S., Nichter, M., Vuckovic, N., Sims, C., & Ritenbaugh, C. (1995). Body image and weight concerns among African American and white adolescent females: Differences that make a difference. *Human Organization, 54*(2), 103–114.

Parnas, J. (1988). Assortative mating in schizophrenia: Results from the Copenhagen high-risk study. *Psychiatry, 51*(1), 58–64.

Parnell, T. F. (1998). Defining Munchausen by proxy syndrome. In T. F. Parnell, D. O. Day, et al. (Eds.), *Munchausen by proxy syndrome: Misunderstood child abuse.* Thousand Oaks, CA: Sage Publications.

Parrott, A. C. (1999). Does cigarette smoking cause stress? *Amer. Psychologist, 54*(10), 817–820.

Parry, B. L. (1999). Postpartum depression in relation to other reproductive cycle mood changes. In L. J. Miller et al. (Eds.), *Postpartum mood disorders.* Washington, DC: American Psychiatric Press.

Partonen, T., Vakkuri, O., Lamberg-Allardt, C., & Lönnqvist, J. (1996). Effects of bright light on sleepiness, melatonin, and 25-hydroxyvitamin D_3 in winter seasonal affective disorder. *Biol. Psychiat., 39,* 865–872.

Pato, M. T., & Pato, C. N. (1997). Obsessive-compulsive disorder in adults. In L. J. Dickstein, M. B. Riba, & J. M. Oldham (Eds.), *Review of psychiatry* (Vol. 16). Washington, DC: American Psychiatric Press.

Patrick, C. J. (1994). Emotion and psychopathy: Startling new insights. *Psychophysiology, 31*(4), 319–330.

Patrick, C. J., Bradley, M. M., & Lang, P. J. (1993). Emotion in the criminal psychopath: Startle reflex modulation. *J. Abnorm. Psychol., 102*(1), 82–92.

Patrick, C. J., Cuthbert, B. N., & Lang, P. J. (1990). Emotion in the criminal psychopath: Fear imagery. *Psychophysiology, 27*(Suppl.), 55.

Patronek, G. (1999, January 13). Interviewed in A. Marcus, Portrait of a pet-o-pile: Animal hoarding often signals mental illness, experts say. *HealthScout.*

Patterson, G. R. (1982). *Coercive family process.* Eugene, OR: Castalia.

Patterson, G. R. (1986). Performance models for antisocial boys. *Amer. Psychologist, 41*, 432–444.

Patterson, T. L., Lacro, J. P., & Jeste, D. V. (1999). Abuse and misuse of medications in the elderly. *Psychiatr. Times, XVI*(4).

Patton, G.C., Johnson-Sabine, E., Wood, K., Mann, A.H., & Wakeling, A. (1990). Abnormal eating attitudes in London school girls—A prospective epidemiological study: Outcome at twelve month followup. *Psychol. Med., 20,* 383–394.

Patton, G. C., Selzer, R., Coffee, C., Carlin, J. B., & Wolfe, R. (1999). Onset of adolescent eating disorders: Population based cohort study over 3 years. *Brit. Med. J., 318*(7186), 765–768.

Paul, G. L. (1967). The strategy of outcome research in psychotherapy. *J. Cons. Psychol., 31,* 109–118.

Paul, G. L., & Lentz, R. (1977). *Psychosocial treatment of the chronic mental patient.* Cambridge, MA: Harvard University Press.

Paurohit, N., Dowd, E. T., & Cottingham, H. F. (1982). The role of verbal and nonverbal cues in the formation of first impressions of black and white counselors. *J. Couns. Psychol., 4,* 371–378.

Paxton, S. J., & Diggens, J. (1997). Avoidance coping, binge eating, and depression: An examination of the escape theory of binge eating. *Inter. J. Eat. Disorders, 22,* 83–87.

Paykel, E. S. (Ed.). (1982). *Handbook of affective disorders.* New York: Guilford.

Paykel, E. S. (1991). Stress and life events. In L. Davidson & M. Linnoila (Eds.), *Risk factors for youth suicide.* New York: Hemisphere.

Paykel, E. S. (1995). Clinical efficacy of reversible and selective inhibitors of monoamine oxidase A in major depression. *Acta Psychiatr. Scandin. Suppl., 91*(386), 22–27.

Paykel, E. S. (1995). Psychotherapy, medication combinations, and compliance. Compliance strategies to optimize antidepressant treatment outcomes. *J. Clin. Psychiat., 56*(1), 24–30.

Paykel, E. S., & Cooper, Z. (1992). Life events and social stress. In E. S. Paykel (Ed.), *Handbook of affective disorders.* New York: Guilford.

Paykel, E. S., Rao, B. M., & Taylor, C. N. (1984). Life stress and symptom pattern in outpatient depression. *Psychol. Med., 14*(3), 559–568.

Payne, A. F. (1928). *Sentence completion.* New York: New York Guidance Clinics.

Payte, T. J. (1989). Combined treatment modalities: The need for innovative approaches. Third National Forum on AIDS and Chemical Dependency of the American Society of Addiction Medicine. *J. Psychoactive Drugs, 21*(4), 431–434.

Pearlin, L. I. (1999). Stress and mental health: A conceptual overview. In A. V. Horwitz & T. L. Scheid (Eds.), *A handbook for the study of mental health: Social contexts, theories, and systems.* Cambridge, England: Cambridge University Press.

Pearson, D. A., Yaffee, L. S., Loveland, K. A., & Lewis, K. R. (1996). Comparison of sustained and selective attention in children who have mental retardation with and without attention deficit hyperactivity disorder. *Amer. J. Ment. Retard., 100*(6), 592–607.

Pearson, J. L. (2000). Suicidal behavior in later life: Research update. In R. W. Maris, S. S. Canetto, et al. (Eds.), *Review of suicidology, 2000.* New York: Guilford.

Peele, S. (1989). *Diseasing of America: Addiction treatment out of control.* Lexington, MA: Lexington Books/D.C. Heath.

Peele, S. (1992). Alcoholism, politics, and bureaucracy: The consensus against controlled-drinking therapy in America. *Addic. Behav., 17,* 49–62.

Peikin, D. (1998, December). Advocacy group promotes unique treatment model for severe illness. *APA Monitor,* p. 8

Pekrun, R. (1992). Expectancy-value theory of anxiety: Overview and implications. In D. G. Forgays, T. Sosnowski, & K. Wrzesniewski (Eds.), *Anxiety: Recent developments in cognitive, psychophysiological, and health research.* Washington, DC: Hemisphere.

Pekrun, R. (1992). The impact of emotions on learning and achievement: Towards a theory of cognitive/motivational mediators. *Appl. Psychol.: Inter. Rev., 41*(4), 359–376.

Penava, S. J., Otto, M. W., Maki, K. M., & Pollack, M. H. (1998). Rate of improvement during cognitive-behavioral group treatment for panic disorder. *Behav. Res. Ther., 36*(7–8), 665–673.

Pendery, M. L., Maltzman, I. M., & West, L. J. (1982). Controlled drinking by alcoholics? New findings and a reevaluation of a major affirmative study. *Science, 217*(4555), 169–175.

Penn, D. L., & Mueser, K. T. (1996). Research update on the psychosocial treatment of schizophrenia. *Amer. J. Psychiat., 153,* 607–617.

Penn, D. L., Corrigan, P. W., Bentall, R. P., Racenstein, J. M., & Newman, L. (1997). Social cognition in schizophrenia. *Psychol. Bull., 121*(1), 114–132.

Pennebaker, J. W. (1997). *Opening up: The healing power of expressing emotions* (rev. ed.) New York: Guilford Press.

Pennebaker, J. W. (1997). Writing about emotional experiences as a therapeutic process. *Psychol. Sci., 8*(3), 162–166.

Penninx, B. W., Guralnik, J. M., Ferrucci, L., Simonsick, E. M., Deeg, D. J., & Wallace, R. B. (1998). Depressive symptoms and physical decline in community-dwelling older persons. *JAMA, 279*(21), 1720–1726.

Pentz, M. A. (1999). Prevention in the community. In R. T. Ammerman, P. J. Ott, et al. (Eds.), *Prevention and societal impact of drug and alcohol abuse.* Mahwah, NJ: Erlbaum.

Perkins, K., Grobe, J., DiAmico, D., Fonte, C., Wilson, A., & Stiller, R. (1996). Low-dose nicotine nasal spray use and effects during initial smoking cessation. *Exp. Clin. Psychopharmacol., 4*(2), 191–197.

Perls, F. S. (1969). *Gestalt therapy verbatim.* Moab, UT: Real People.

Perls, F. S. (1973). *The Gestalt approach.* Palo Alto, CA: Science Behavior.

Perls, T. T. (1995, January). The oldest old. *Scientif. Amer.,* pp. 70–75.

Perrez, M., Horner, M., & Morval, M. (1998). How do we measure stress: A new approach: Systematic self-observation using a pocket computer. *Bull. Psychol., 51*(436), 427–439.

Perris, C. (1988). Decentralization, sectorization, and the development of alternatives to institutional care in a northern county in Sweden. In C. N. Stefanis & A. D. Rabavilis (Eds.), *Schizophrenia: Recent biosocial developments.* New York: Human Sciences Press.

Perry, J. C. (1989). Dependent personality disorder. In American Psychiatric Association (Eds.), *Treatments of psychiatric disorders: A task force report of the American Psychiatric Association.* Washington, DC: American Psychiatric Press.

Perry, J. C. (1992). Problems and considerations in the valid assessment of personality disorders. *Amer. J. Psychiat., 149,* 1645–1653.

Perry, J. C. (1993). Longitudinal studies of personality disorders. *J. Pers. Disorders, 7,* 63–85.

Perry, J. C., & Cooper, S. H. (1986). A preliminary report on defenses and conflicts associated with borderline personality disorder. *J. Amer. Psychoanal. Assoc., 34*(4), 863–893.

Perry, J. C., & Jacobs, D. (1982). Overview: Clinical applications of the amytal interview in psychiatric emergency settings. *Amer. J. Psychiat., 139*(5), 552–559.

Perry, P. J. (2000). Therapeutic drug monitoring of atypical antipsychotics: Is it of potential clinical value? *CNS Drugs, 13*(3), 167–221.

Perske, R. (1972). The dignity of risk and the mentally retarded. *Ment. Retard., 10,* 24–27.

Persons, J. B., & Silberschatz (1998). Are results of randomized controlled trials useful to psychotherapists? *J. Cons. Clin. Psychol., 66*(1), 126–135.

Petersen, A. C., Compas, B., & Brooks-Gunn, J. (1991). *Depression in adolescence: Implications of current research for programs and policy.* Report prepared for the Carnegie Council on Adolescent Development, Washington, DC

Petersen, A. C., Compas, B. E., Brooks-Gunn, J., Ey, S., & Grant, K. E. (1993). Depression in adolescence. *Amer. Psychologist, 48*(2), 155–168.

Petersen, A. L., Talcott, G. W., Kelleher, W. J., & Haddock, C. K. (1995). Site specificity of pain and tension in tension-type headaches. *Headache, 35*(2), 89–92.

Peterson, B. D., West, J., Pincus, H. A., Kohout, J., et al. (1996). An update on human resources in mental health. In R. W. Manderscheid & M. A. Sonnenschein (Eds.)., *Mental health, United States, 1996* (DHHS Publication No. SMA 96–3098). Washington, DC: U. S. Department of Health and Human Services.

Peterson, B. S., Leckman, J. F., Arnsten, A., Anderson, G. M., Staib., L. H., Gore, J. C., Bronen, R. A., Malison, R., Scahill, L., & Cohen, D. J. (1998). Neuroanatomical circuitry. In J. F. Leckman, D. J. Cohen, et al. (Eds.), *Tourette's syndrome—Tics, obsessions, compulsions: Developmental psychopathology and clinical care.* New York: Wiley.

Peterson, C. (1993). Helpless behavior. *Behav. Res. Ther., 31*(3), 289–295.

Peterson, J. (1996). Healing continues a year after bombing. *APA Monitor, 27*(6), 22.

Peterson, K. S. (1996, February 21). Harm of domestic strife lingers. *USA Today,* p. 3D.

Peterson, L., & Roberts, M. C. (1991). Treatment of children's problems. In C. E. Walker (Ed.), *Clinical psychology: Historical and research foundations.* New York: Plenum Press.

Petry, N. M. (2000). A comprehensive guide to the application of contingency management procedures in clinical settings. *Drug Alc. Dep., 58*(1–2), 9–25.

Peuskens, J., De Hert, M., Cosyns, P., Pieters, G., et al. (1997). Suicide in young schizophrenic patients during and after inpatient treatment. *Inter. J. Ment. Hlth., 25*(4), 39–44.

Pew Research Center for the People and the Press. (1997). *Trust and citizen engagement in metropolitan Philadelphia: A case study.* Washington, DC: Author.

Pfeffer, C. R. (1986). *The suicidal child.* New York: Guilford.

Pfeffer, C. R. (1993). Suicidal children. In A. A. Leenaars (Ed.), *Suicidology.* Northvale, NJ: Jason Aronson.

Pfeffer, C. R. (2000). Suicidal behavior in prepubertal children: From the 1980s to the new millennium. In R. W. Maris, S. S. Canetto, et al. (Eds.), *Review of suicidology, 2000.* New York: Guilford.

Pfeffer, C. R., Klerman, G. L., Hurt, S. W., Kakuma, T., et al. (1993). Suicidal children grow up: Rates and psychosocial risk factors for suicide attempts during follow-up. *J. Amer. Acad. Child Adol. Psychiat., 30,* 106–113.

Pfeffer, C. R., Normandin, L., & Kakuma, T. (1998). Suicidal children grow up: Relations between family psychopathology and adolescents' lifetime suicidal behavior. *J. Nerv. Ment. Dis., 186*(5), 269–275.

Pfeffer, C. R., Zuckerman, S., Plutchik, R., & Mizruchi, M. S. (1984). Suicidal behavior in normal school children: A comparison with child psychiatric inpatients. *J. Amer. Acad. Child Adol. Psychiat., 23,* 416–423.

Pfeifer, M. P., & Snodgrass, G. L. (1990). The continued use of retractable invalid scientific literature. *JAMA, 263*(10), 1420–1427.

Pfeiffer, S. I., & Nelson, D. D. (1992). The cutting edge in services for people with autism. *J. Autism Dev. Disorders, 22*(1), 95–105.

Phares, E. J. (1979). *Clinical psychology: Concepts, methods, and profession.* Homewood, IL: Dorsey.

Phelps, L., & Grabowski, J. (1993). Fetal alcohol syndrome: Diagnostic features and psychoeducational risk factors. *School Psychol. Quart., 7*(2), 112–128.

Phillips, D. P. (1974). The influence of suggestion on suicide: Substantive and theoretical implications of the *Werther* effect. *Amer. Sociol. Rev., 39,* 340–354.

Phillips, D. P., & Ruth, T. E. (1993). Adequacy of official suicide statistics for scientific research and public policy. *Suic. Life-Threat. Behav., 23*(4), 307–319.

Phillips, D. P., Christenfeld, N., Glynn, L. M., & Steinberg, A. (1999). The influence of medical and legal authorities on deaths facilitated by physicians. *Suic. Life-Threat. Behav., 29*(1), 48–57.

Phillips, D. P., Lesyna, K., & Paight, D. J. (1992). Suicide and the media. In R. W. Maris, A. L. Berman, J. T. Maltsberger, & R. I. Yufit (Eds.), *Assessment and prediction of suicide.* New York: Guilford.

Phillips, K. A. (2000). Body dysmorphic disorder: Diagnostic controversies and treatment challenges. *Bull. Menninger Clin., 64*(1), 18–35.

Phillips, K. A. (2000). Connection between obsessive-compulsive disorder and body dysmorphic disorder. In W. K. Goodman & M. V. Rudorfer (Eds.), *Obsessive-compulsive disorder: Contemporary issues in treatment.* Personality and clinical psychology series. Mahwah, NJ: Erlbaum.

Phillips, K. A., & Gunderson, J. G. (1994). Personality disorders. In R. E. Hales, S. C. Yudofsky, & J. A. Talbott (Eds.), *The American Psychiatric Press textbook of psychiatry* (2nd ed.). Washington, DC: American Psychiatric Press.

Phillips, K. A., Kim, J. M., & Hudson, J. I. (1995). Body image disturbance in body dysmorphic disorder and eating disorders: Obsessions or delusions? *Psychiat. Clin. N. Amer., 18*(2), 317–334.

Phillips, K. A., McElroy, S. L., Keck, P. E., Pope, H. G., et al. (1993). Body dysmorphic disorder: 30 cases of imagined ugliness. *Amer. J. Psychiat., 150*(2), 302–308.

Phillips, M. R., Liu, H., & Zhang, Y. (1999). Suicide and social change in China. *Cult. Med. Psychiat., 23*(1), 25–50.

Philpot, V. D., Holliman, W. B., & Madonna, S., Jr. (1995). Self-statements, locus of control, and depression in predicting self-esteem. *Psychol. Rep., 76*(3, Pt 1), 1007–1010.

Piacentini, J., Rotheram-Bors, M. J., Gillis, J. R., Graae, F., et al. (1995). Demographic predictors of treatment attendance among adolescent suicide attempters. *J. Cons. Clin. Psychiat., 63*(3), 469–473.

Pickar, D., Owen, R. R., & Litman, R. E. (1991). New developments in pharmacotherapy of schizophrenia. In A. Tasman & S. M. Goldfinger (Eds.), *American Psychiatric Press review of psychiatry* (Vol. 10). Washington, DC: American Psychiatric Press.

Pickens, J., Field, T., Prodromidis, M., Pelaez-Nogueras, M., et al. (1995). Posttraumatic stress, depression and social support among college students after Hurricane Andrew. *J. Coll. Student Dev., 36*(2), 152–161.

Pickens, R., & Fletcher, B. (1991). Overview of treatment issues. In R. Pickens, C. Leukefeld, & C. Schuster (Eds.), *Improving drug abuse treatment.* Rockville, MD: National Institute on Drug Abuse.

Pickett, S. A., Cook, J. A., & Razzano, L. (1999). Psychiatric rehabilitation services and outcomes: An overview. In A. V. Horwitz & T. L. Scheid (Eds.), *A handbook for the study of mental health: Social contexts, theories, and systems.* Cambridge, England: Cambridge University Press.

Pietrofesa, J. J., et al. (1990). The mental health counselor and "duty to warn." *J. Ment. Hlth. Couns., 12*(2), 129–137.

Pike, K. M., & Rodin, J. (1991). Mothers, daughters, and disordered eating. *J. Abnorm. Psychol., 100*(2), 198–204.

Pillard, R. C., & Bailey, J. M. (1995). A biologic perspective on sexual orientation. [Special issue: Clinical sexuality.] *Psychiat. Clin. N. Amer., 18*(1), 71–84.

Pincus, H. A., Henderson, B., Blackwood, D., & Dial, T. (1993). Trends in research in two general psychiatric journals in 1969–1990: Research on research. *Amer. J. Psychiat., 150*(1), 135–142.

Pine, D. S. (1999). Pathophysiology of childhood anxiety disorders. *Biol. Psychiat., 46*(11), 1555–1566.

Pinhas, L., Toner, B. B., Ali, A., Garfinkel, P. E., & Stuckless, N. (1999). The effects of the ideal of female beauty on mood and body satisfaction. *Inter. J. Eat. Disorders, 25*(2), 223–226.

Pinkston, E. M., & Linsk, N. L. (1984). Behavioral family intervention with the impaired elderly. *Gerontologist, 24,* 576–583.

Piotrowski, C., Belter, R. W., & Keller, J. W. (1998). The impact of "managed care" on the practice of psychological testing: Preliminary findings. *J. Pers. Assess., 70*(3), 441–447.

Pirke, K. M., Kellner, M., Philipp, E., Laessle, R., Krieg, J. C., & Fichter, M. M. (1992). Plasma norepinephrine after a standardized test meal in acute and remitted patients with anorexia nervosa and in healthy controls. *Biol. Psychiat., 31,* 1074–1077.

Pirkis, J., & Burgess, P. (1998). Suicide and recency of health care contacts: A systematic review. *Brit. J. Psychiat., 173,* 462–474.

Pirkola, S. P., Isometsae, E. T., Heikkinen, M. E., & Loennqvist, J. K. (2000). Suicides of alcohol misusers and non-misusers in a nationwide population. *Alcohol Alcoholism, 35*(1), 70–75.

Pithers, W. D. (1990). Relapse prevention with sexual aggressors. In W. L. Marshall, D. R. Laws, & H. E. Barbaree (Eds.). *Handbook of sexual assault.* New York: Plenum Press.

Piven, J., Palmer, P., Jacobi, D., Childress, D., & Arndt, S. (1997). Broader autism phenotype: Evidence from a family history study of multiple-incidence autism families. *Amer. J. Psychiat., 154*(2), 185–190.

Plakun, E. M. (1991). Prediction of outcome in borderline personality disorder. *J. Pers. Disorders, 5*(2), 93–101.

Plasse, T. F., et al. (1991). Recent clinical experience with dronabinol. *Pharmacol. Biochem. Behav., 40,* 695.

Plomin, R., DeFries, J. C., McClearn, G. E., & Rutter, M. (1997). *Behavioral genetics: A primer* (3rd ed.). New York: W. H. Freeman.

Plous, S. (1996). Attitudes toward the use of animals in psychological research and education: Results from a national survey of psychologists. *Amer. Psychologist, 51*(11), 1167–1180.

Podoll, K., & Robinson, D. (1999). Lewis Carroll's migraine experiences. *Lancet, 353*(9161), 1366.

Polcin, D. (1992). Issues in the treatment of dual diagnosis clients who have chronic mental illness. *Profess. Psychol.: Res. Prac., 23*(1), 30–37.

Polk, W. M. (1983). Treatment of exhibitionism in a 38-year-old male by hypnotically assisted covert sensitization. *Inter. J. Clin. Exp. Hyp., 31,* 132–138.

Pollack, J. M. (1987). Relationship of obsessive-compulsive personality to obsessive-compulsive disorder: A review of the literature. *J. Psychol., 121*(2), 137–148.

Pollack, M. H. (1999). Social anxiety disorder: Designing a pharmacologic treatment strategy. *J. Clin. Psychiat., 60*(Suppl. 9), 20–25.

Pollack, W. (1989). Schizophrenia and the self: Contributions of psychoanalytic self-psychology. *Schizo. Bull., 15*(2), 311–322.

Pollock, M. H., Kradin, R., Otto, M. W., Worthington, J., et al. (1996). Prevalence of panic in patients referred for pulmonary function testing at a major medical center. *Amer. J. Psychiat., 153,* 110–113.

Polonsky, D. (1998). Interviewed in S. Blackmun, From Mars to Venus—Couples sex therapy. *Psychiatr. Times, XV*(9).

Polster, E. (1992). The self in action: A Gestalt outlook. In J. K. Zeig (Ed.), *The evolution of psychotherapy: The second conference.* New York: Brunner/Mazel.

Pope, B. (1983). The initial interview. In C. E. Walker (Ed.), *The handbook of clinical psychology: Theory, research, and practice.* Homewood, IL: Dow Jones-Irwin.

Pope, H. G., & Hudson, J. I. (1984). *New hope for binge eaters: Advances in the understanding and treatment of bulimia.* New York: Harper & Row.

Pope, H. G., & Hudson, J. I. (1992). Is childhood sexual abuse a risk factor for bulimia nervosa? *Amer. J. Psychiat., 149,* 455–463.

Pope, H. G., & Yurgelun-Todd, D. (1996). The residual cognitive effects of heavy marijuana use in college students. *JAMA, 275*(7), 521–527.

Pope, H. G., Jr., Oliva, P. S., Hudson, J. I., Bodkin, J. A., & Gruber, A. J. (1999). Attitudes toward DSM-IV dissociative disorders diagnoses among board-certified American psychiatrists. *Amer. J. Psychiat., 156*(2), 321–323.

Pope, K. S. (2000). Therapists' sexual feelings and behaviors: Research, trends, and quandaries. In L. T. Szuchman, F. Muscarella, et al. (Eds.), *Psychological perspectives on human sexuality.* New York: Wiley.

Pope, K. S., & Bouhoutsos, J. (1986). *Sexual intimacy between therapists and patients.* New York: Praeger.

Pope, K. S., & Brown, L. S. (1996). *Recovered memories of abuse: Assessment, therapy, forensics.* Washington, DC: American Psychological Association.

Pope, K. S., & Tabachnick, B. G. (1993). Therapists' anger, hate, fear, and sexual feelings:

National survey of therapist responses, client characteristics, critical events, formal complaints, and training. *Profess. Psychol.: Res. Pract., 24*(2), 142–152.

Pope, K. S., & Tabachnick, B. G. (1994). Therapists as patients: A national survey of psychologists' experiences, problems, and beliefs. *Profess. Psychol.: Res. Prac., 25*(3), 247–258.

Pope, K. S., & Vetter, V. A. (1991). Prior therapist-patient sexual involvement among patients seen by psychologists. *Psychotherapy, 28*(3), 429–438.

Pope, K. S., Tabachnick, B. G., & Keith-Spiegel, P. (1986). Sexual attraction to clients: The human therapist and the (sometimes) inhuman training system. *Amer. Psychologist, 41*(2), 147–158.

Pope, K. S., Tabachnick, B. G., & Keith-Spiegel, P. (1987). Ethics of practice: The beliefs and behaviors of psychologists as therapists. *Amer. Psychologist, 42*(11), 993–1166.

Popenhagen, M. P., & Qualley, R. M. (1998). Adolescent suicide: Detection, intervention, and prevention. *Profess. School Couns., 1*(4), 30–36.

Popper, C. W. (1988). Disorders usually first evident in infancy, childhood, or adolescence. In J. Talbott, R. S. Hales, & S. C. Yudofsky (Eds.), *Textbook of psychiatry.* Washington, DC: American Psychiatric Press.

Poretz, M., & Sinrod, B. (1991). *Do you do it with the lights on?* New York: Ballantine Books.

Porter, S., Kelly, K. A., & Grame, C. J. (1993). Family treatment of spouses and children of patients with multiple personality disorder. *Bull. Menninger Clin., 57*(3), 371–379.

Porzelius, L. K., Berel, S., & Howard, C. (1999). Cognitive behavior therapy. In M. Hersen & A. S. Bellack (Eds.), *Handbook of comparative interventions for adult disorders* (2nd ed.). New York: Wiley.

Post, R. M., et al. (1978). Cerebrospinal fluid norepinephrine in affective illness. *Amer. J. Psychiat., 135*(8), 907–912.

Post, R. M., Ballenger, J. C., & Goodwin, F. K. (1980). Cerebrospinal fluid studies of neurotransmitter function in manic and depressive illness. In J. H. Wood (Ed.), *The neurobiology of cerebrospinal fluid* (Vol. 1). New York: Plenum Press.

Poulos, C. X., Le, A. D., & Parker, J. L. (1995). Impulsivity predicts individual susceptibility to high levels of alcohol self-administration. *Behav. Pharmacol., 6*(8), 810–814.

Poulton, R. G., & Andrews, G. (1996). Change in danger cognitions in agoraphobia and social phobia during treatment. *Behav. Res. Ther., 34*(5/6), 413–421.

Poulton, R., Thomson, W. M., Davies, S., Kruger, E., et al. (1997). Good teeth, bad teeth and fear of the dentist. *Behav. Res. Ther., 35*(4), 327–334.

Powell, J., Bradley, B., & Gray, J. (1992). Classical conditioning and cognitive determinants of subjective craving for opiates: An investigation of their relative contributions. *Brit. J. Addic., 87*(8), 1133–1144.

Powell, R. A., & Gee, T. L. (1999). The effects of hypnosis on dissociative identity disorder: A reexamination of the evidence. *Canad. J. Psychiat., 44*(9). 914–916.

Powers, P. S. (1999). The last word: Athletes and eating disorders. *Eat. Disord.: J. Treat. Prev., 7*(3), 249–255.

Powis, T. (1990, March 19). Paying for the past: A brainwashing victim seeks compensation. *Macleans.*

Prange, A. J., et al. (1970). Enhancement of imipramine by thyroid stimulating hormone: Clinical and theoretical implications. *Amer. J. Psychiat., 127*(2), 191–199.

Prange, A. J., et al. (1970). Use of a thyroid hormone to accelerate the action of imipramine. *Psychosomatics, 11*(5), 442–444.

Prange, A. J., et al. (1974). L tryptophan in mania: Contribution to a permissive hypothesis of affective disorders. *Arch. Gen. Psychiat., 30*(1), 56–62.

Prehn, R. A. (1990). Medication refusal: Suggestions for intervention. *Psychiatr. Hosp., 21*(1), 37–40.

Prendergast, P. J. (1995). Integration of psychiatric rehabilitation in the long-term management of schizophrenia. *Canad. J. Psychiat., 40*(3, Suppl. 1), S18–S21.

Preti, A., & Miotto, P. (1998). Seasonality in suicides: The influence of suicide method, gender and age on suicide distribution in Italy. *Psychiat. Res., 81*(2), 219–231.

Preti, A., & Miotto, P. (2000). Influence of method on seasonal distribution of attempted suicides in Italy. *Neuropsychobiology, 41*(2), 62–72.

Price, L. H. (1990). Serotonin reuptake inhibitors in depression and anxiety: An overview. *Ann. Clin. Psychiat., 2*(3), 165–172.

Price, R. W., Brew, B., Sidtis, J., Rosenblum, M., Scheck, A. C., & Cleary, P. (1988). The brain in AIDS: Central nervous system HIV-1 infection and AIDS dementia complex. *Science, 239*, 586–592.

Prien, R. F. (1992). Maintenance treatment. In E. S. Paykel (Ed.), *Handbook of affective disorders.* New York: Guilford.

Prien, R. F., Caffey, E. M., Jr., & Klett, C. J. (1974). Factors associated with treatment success in lithium carbonate prophylaxis. *Arch. Gen. Psychiat., 31*, 189–192.

Primac, D. W. (1993). Measuring change in a brief therapy of a compulsive personality. *Psychol. Rep., 72*(1), 309–310.

Prince, M. (1906). *The dissociation of a personality.* New York: Longmans, Green.

Princeton Survey Research Associates. (1996). Adultery in the '90s. In *Newsweek Poll.* New York: Author.

Princeton Survey Research Associates. (1996). *Healthy steps for young children: Survey of parents.* Princeton: Author.

Prochaska, J. O. (1984). *Systems of psychotherapy.* Chicago: Dorsey.

Prochaska, J. O., & Norcross, J. C. (1994). *Systems of psychotherapy: A transtheoretical analysis* (3rd ed.). Pacific Grove, CA: Brooks/Cole.

Prothrow-Stith, D., & Spivak, H. (1999). America's tragedy. *Psychiat. Times, XVI*(6).

Provini, C., Everett, J. R., & Pfeffer, C. R. (2000). Adults mourning suicide: Self-reported concerns about bereavement, needs for assistance, and help-seeking behavior. *Death Stud., 24*(1), 1–19.

Prudic, J., & Sackeim, H. A. (1999). Electroconvulsive therapy and suicide risk. *J. Clin. Psychiat., 60*(Suppl. 2), 104–110.

Prusiner, S. (1995, January). The prion diseases. *Scientif. Amer.,* pp. 48–57.

Prusiner, S. B. (1991). Molecular biology of prion diseases. *Science, 252*, 1515–1522.

Prusoff, B. A., Weissman, M. M., Klerman, G. L., & Rounsaville, B. J. (1980). Research diagnostic criteria subtypes of depression: Their role as predictors of differential response to psychotherapy and drug treatment. *Arch. Gen. Psychiat., 37*(7), 796–801.

Pueschel, S. M., & Thuline, H. C. (1991). Chromosome disorders. In J. L. Matson & J. A. Mulick (Eds.), *Handbook of mental retardation.* New York: Pergamon.

Puk, G. (1991). Treating traumatic memories: A case report on the eye movement desensitization procedure. *J. Behav. Ther. Exp. Psychiat., 22*, 149–151.

Pulver, A. E. (2000). Search for schizophrenia susceptibility genes. *Biol. Psychiat., 47*(3), 221–230.

Purnell, L. A. (1999). Youth violence and post-traumatic stress disorder: Assessment, implications, and promising school-based strategies. In C. W. Branch et al. (Eds.), *Adolescent gangs: Old issues, new approaches.* Philadelphia: Charles Press.

Pusakulich, R. L., & Nielson, H. C. (1976). Cue use in state-dependent learning. *Physiol. Psychol., 4*(4), 421–428.

Putnam, F. W. (1984). The psychophysiologic investigation of multiple personality disorder. *Psychiatr. Clin. N. Amer., 7*, 31–40.

Putnam, F. W. (1985). Dissociation as a response to extreme trauma. In R. P. Kluft, *Childhood antecedents of multiple personality.* Washington, DC: American Psychiatric Press.

Putnam, F. W. (1985). Multiple personality disorder. *Med. Aspects Human Sex., 19*(6), 59–74.

Putnam, F. W. (1988). The switch process in multiple personality disorder and other state-change disorders. *Dissociation, 1,* 24–32.

Putnam, F. W. (1992). Are alter personalities fragments of figments? *Psychoanaly. Inquiry, 12*(1), 95–111.

Putnam, F. W. (1996). Posttraumatic stress disorder in children and adolescents. In L. J. Dickstein, M. B. Riba, & J. M. Oldham (Eds.), *Review of psychiatry* (Vol. 15). Washington, DC: American Psychiatric Press.

Putnam, F. W., Guroff, J. J., Silberman, E. K., Barban, L., et al. (1986). The clinical phenomenology of multiple personality disorder: Review of 100 recent cases. *J. Clin. Psychol., 47*(6), 285–293.

Putnam, F. W., Zahn, T. P., & Post, R. M. (1990). Differential autonomic nervous system activity in multiple personality disorder. *J. Psychiatr. Res., 31*(3), 251–260.

Putnam, K. M., Harvey, P. D., Parrella, M., White, L., Kincaid, M., Powchik, P., & Davidson, M. (1996). Symptom stability in geriatric chronic schizophrenic inpatients: A one-year follow-up study. *Biol. Psychiat., 39,* 92–99.

Pyle, R. L. (1999). Dynamic psychotherapy. In M. Hersen & A. S. Bellack (Eds.), *Handbook of comparative interventions for adult disorders* (2nd ed.). New York: Wiley.

Quality Assurance Project. (1990). Treatment outlines for paranoid, schizotypal and schizoid personality disorders. *Austral. New Zeal. J. Psychiat., 24,* 339–350.

Quality Assurance Project. (1991). Treatment outlines for antisocial personality disorder. *Austral. New Zeal. J. Psychiat., 25,* 541–547.

Quality Assurance Project. (1991). Treatment outlines for avoidant, dependent and passive-aggressive personality disorders. *Austral. New Zeal. J. Psychiat., 25*(3), 311–313.

Quality Assurance Project. (1991). Treatment outlines for borderline, narcissistic and histrionic personality disorders. *Austral. New Zeal. J. Psychiat., 25,* 392–403.

Quevillon, R. P. (1993). Vaginismus. In W. O'Donohue & J. Geer (Eds.), *Handbook of sexual dysfunctions.* Boston: Allyn & Bacon.

Quinsey, V. L., & Earls, G. M. (1990). The modificator of sexual preferences. In W. L. Marshall, D. R. Laws, & H. E. Barbaree (Eds.), *Handbook of sexual assault.* New York: Plenum.

Quitkin, F. M. (1999). Placebos, drug effects, and study design: A clinician's guide. *Amer. J. Psychiat., 156*(6), 829–836.

Rabasca, L. (1998). Substance abuse treatment works. *APA Monitor, 29*(11), 7.

Rabasca, L. (1999). I'm okay and you're okay, but not so sure about Y2K. *APA Monitor, 30*(1), 1,18.

Rabins, P. V., & Folstein, M. F. (1982). Delirium and dementia: Diagnostic criteria and fatality rates. *Brit. J. Psychiat.*, 140, 149– 153.

Raboch, J., & Raboch, J. (1992). Infrequent orgasm in women. *J. Sex Marital Ther.*, 18(2), 114–120.

Rachman, S. (1966). Sexual fetishism: An experimental analog. *Psychol. Rec.*, 18, 25–27.

Rachman, S. (1985). A note on the conditioning theory of fear acquisition. *Behav. Ther.*, 16(4), 426–428.

Rachman, S. (1985). Obsessional-compulsive disorders. In B. P. Bradley & C. T. Thompson (Eds.), *Psychological applications in psychiatry.* Chicester, England: Wiley.

Rachman, S. (1985). The treatment of anxiety disorders: A critique of the implications for psychopathology. In A. Tuma & J. Maser (Eds.), *Anxiety and the anxiety disorders.* Hillsdale, NJ: Erlbaum.

Rachman, S. (1993). Obsessions, responsibility and guilt. *Behav. Res. Ther.*, 31(2), 149–154.

Rachman, S., & Hodgson, R. (1980). *Obsessions and compulsions.* Englewood Cliffs, NJ: Prentice Hall.

Rachman, S., Hodgson, R., & Marzillier, J. (1970). Treatment of an obsessional-compulsive disorder by modelling. *Behav. Res. Ther.*, 8, 385–392.

Ragin, A. B., Pogue-Geile, M. F., & Oltmanns, T. F. (1989). Poverty of speech in schizophrenia and depression during inpatient and post-hospital periods. *Brit. J. Psychiat.*, 154, 52–57.

Ragland, J. D., & Berman, A. L. (1991). Farm crisis and suicide: Dying on the vine? *Omega: J. Death Dying*, 22(3), 173–185.

Raguram, R., Weiss, M. G., Channabasavanna, S. M., & Devins, G. M. (1996). Stigma, depression, and somatization in south India. *Amer. J. Psychiat.*, 153, 1043–1049.

Rahe, R. H. (1968). Life-change measurement as a predictor of illness. *Proc. R. Soc. Med.*, 61, 1124–1126.

Raine, A. (1989). Evoked potentials and psychopathy. *Inter. J. Psychophysiol.*, 8(1), 1–16.

Raine, A. (1992). Sex differences in schizotypal personality in a nonclinical population. *J. Abnorm. Psychol.*, 101(2), 361–4.

Raine, A., Benishay, D., Lencz, T., & Scarpa, A. (1997). Abnormal orienting in schizotypal personality disorder. *Schizo. Bull.*, 23(1), 75–82.

Raine, A., Lencz, T., Bihrle, S., LaCasse, L., & Colletti, P. (2000). Reduced prefrontal gray matter volume and reduced autonomic activity in antisocial personality disorder. *Arch. Gen. Psychiat.*, 57(2), 119–127.

Raison, C. L., Klein, H. M., & Steckler, M. (1999). The moon and madness reconsidered. *J. Affect. Disorders*, 53(1), 99–106.

Raja, M., & Miti, G. (1995). Neuroleptic malignant syndrome. *Neuropsychiat., Neuropsychol., Behav. Neurol.*, 8(1), 74.

Raloff, J. (1995). Drug of darkness: Can a pineal hormone head off everything from breast cancer to aging? *Sci. News*, 147, 300– 301.

Ralston, P. A. (1991). Senior centers and minority elders: A critical review. *Gerontologist*, 31, 325–331.

Ram, R., Bromet, E. J., Eaton, W. W., & Pato, C. (1992). The natural course of schizophrenia: A review of first-admission studies. *Schizo. Bull.*, 18(2), 185–207.

Ramey, C. T., & Ramey, S. L. (1992). Effective early intervention. *Ment. Retard.*, 30(6), 337–345.

Ramey, C. T., & Ramey, S. L. (1998). Early intervention and early experience. *Amer. Psychologist*, 53, 109–120.

Ramey, C. T., & Ramey, S. L. (1999). *Right from birth: Building your child's foundation for life (birth to 18 months).* New York: Goddard Press.

Ramirez, E., Maldonado, A., & Martos, R. (1992). Attributions modulate immunization against learned helplessness in humans. *J. Pers. Soc. Psychol.*, 62(1), 139–146.

Ramirez, S. Z., Wassef, A., Paniagua, F. A., & Linskey, A. O. (1996). Mental health providers' perceptions of cultural variables in evaluating ethnically diverse clients. *Profess. Psychol.: Res. Pract.*, 27, 284–288.

Ramm, E., Marks, I. M., Yuksel, S., & Stern, R. S. (1981). Anxiety management training for anxiety states: Positive compared with negative self-statements. *Brit. J. Psychiat.*, 140, 397–373.

Rampello, L., Nicoletti, F., & Nicoletti, F. (2000). Dopamine and depression: Therapeutic implications. *CNS Drugs*, 13(1), 35–45.

Rand, C. S., & Kuldau, J. M. (1991). Restrained eating (weight concerns) in the general population and among students. *Inter. J. Eat. Disorders*, 10(6), 699–708

Randall, L. O. (1982). Discovery of benzodiazepines. In E. Usdin, P. Skolnick, J. F. Tallman, Jr., et al. (Eds.), *Pharmacology of benzodiazepines.* London: Macmillan.

Rao, S. M. (2000). Neuropsychological evaluation. In B. S. Fogel, R. B. Schiffer, et al. (Eds.), *Synopsis of neuropsychiatry.* Philadelphia: Lippincott-Raven.

Rapee, R. M. (1993). Psychological factors in panic disorder. *Adv. Behav. Res. Ther.*, 15(1), 85–102.

Rapee, R. M., & Hayman, K. (1996). The effects of video feedback on the self-evaluation of performance in socially anxious subjects. *Behav. Res. Ther.*, 34(4), 315–322.

Raphling, D. L. (1989). Fetishism in a woman. *J. Amer. Psychoanal. Assoc.*, 37(2), 465–491.

Rapoport, J. L. (1989, March). The biology of obsessions and compulsions. *Scientif. Amer.*, pp. 82–89.

Rapoport, J. L. (1991). Recent advances in obsessive-compulsive disorder. *Neuropsychopharmacology*, 5(1), 1–10.

Raskin, D. C. (1982). The scientific basis of polygraph techniques and their uses in the judicial process. In A. Trankell (Ed.), *Reconstructing the past: The role of psychologists in criminal trials.* Stockholm: Norstedt & Soners.

Raskin, M., Peeke, H. V. S., Dickman, W., & Pinkster, H. (1982). Panic and generalized anxiety disorders: Developmental antecedents and precipitants. *Arch. Gen. Psychiat.*, 39, 687–689.

Raskin, N. J., & Rogers, C. R. (1995). Person-centered therapy. In R. J. Corsini & D. Wedding (Eds.), *Current psychotherapies* (5th ed.). Itasca, IL: Peacock.

Rassin, E., Merckelbach, H., Muris, P., & Spaan, V. (1999). Thought-action fusion as a causal factor in the development of intrusions. *Behav. Res. Ther.*, 37(3), 231–237.

Ravetz, R. S. (1999). Psychiatric disorders associated with Alzheimer's disease. *J. Amer. Osteopath Assoc.*, 99(Suppl. 9), S13–S16.

Ravizza, L., Maina, G., Bogetto, F., Albert, U., Barzega, G., & Bellino, S. (1998). Long term treatment of obsessive-compulsive disorder. *CNS Drugs*, 10(4), 247–255.

Ray, O., & Ksir, C. (1993). *Drugs, society, and human behavior.* St. Louis: Mosby.

Raymond, N. C., Coleman, E., Ohlerking, F., Christenson, G. A., & Miner, M. (1999). Psychiatric comorbidity in pedophilic sex offenders. *Amer. J. Psychiat.*, 156(5), 786–788.

Razali, S. M., Hasanah, C. I., Aminah, K., & Subramaniam, M. (1998). Religious-sociocultural psychotherapy in patients with anxiety and depression. *Austral. New Zeal. J. Psychiat.*, 32(6), 867–872.

Rebert, W. M., Stanton, A. L., & Schwarz, R. M. (1991). Influence of personality attributes and

daily moods on bulimic eating patterns. *Addic. Behav.* 16(6), 497–505.

Redick, R. W., Witkin, M. J., Atay, J. E., & Manderscheid, R. W. (1992). Specialty mental health system characteristics. In R. W. Manderscheid & M. A. Sonnenschein (Eds.), *Mental health, United States, 1992.* Washington, DC: U. S. Department of Health and Human Services.

Redick, R. W., Witkin, M. J., Atay, J. E., & Manderscheid, R. W. (1996). Highlights of organized mental health services in 1992 and major national and state trends. In R. W. Manderscheid & M. A. Sonnenschein (Eds.), DHHS Publication No. SMA 96-3098. Washington, DC: U. S. Department of Health and Human Services.

Redmond, D. E. (1977). Alterations in the function of the nucleus locus coeruleus: A possible model for studies of anxiety. In I. Hanin & E. Usdin (Eds.), *Animal models in psychiatry and neurology.* New York: Pergamon Press.

Redmond, D. E. (1979). New and old evidence for the involvement of a brain norepinephrine system in anxiety. In W. E. Fann, I. Karacan, A. D. Pokorny, & R. L. Williams (Eds.), *Phenomenology and treatment of anxiety.* New York: Spectrum.

Redmond, D. E. (1981). Clonidine and the primate locus coeruleus: Evidence suggesting anxiolytic and anti-withdrawal effects. In H. Lal & S. Fielding (Eds.), *Psychopharmacology of clonidine.* New York: Alan R. Liss.

Redmond, D. E. (1985). Neurochemical basis for anxiety and anxiety disorders: Evidence from drugs which decrease human fear or anxiety. In A. H. Tuma & J. Maser (Eds.), *Anxiety and the anxiety disorders.* Hillsdale, NJ: Erlbaum.

Reed, L. J. (Eds.). (1998). *Webster's new world pocket book of facts.* New York: Macmillan.

Rees, K., Allen, D., & Lader, M. (1999). The influences of age and caffeine on psychomotor and cognitive function. *Psychopharmacology*, 145(2), 181–188.

Rees, L. (1964). The importance of psychological, allergic and infective factors in childhood asthma. *J. Psychosom. Res.*, 7(4), 253–262.

Rees, W. D., & Lutkin, S. G. (1967). Mortality of bereavement. *Brit. Med. J.*, 4, 13–16.

Reese, S. (1998, January). Get it together, do-gooders. *American Demographics*

Regehr, C., Cadell, S., & Jansen, K. (1999). Perceptions of control and long-term recovery from rape. *Amer. J. Orthopsychiat.*, 69(1), 110–115.

Regier, D. A., Narrow, W. E., Rae, D. S., Manderscheid, R. W., Locke, B. Z., & Goodwin, F. K. (1993). The de facto US Mental and Addictive Disorders Service System: Epidemiologic Catchment Area prospective 1-year prevalence rates of disorders in services. *Arch. Gen. Psychiat.*, 50, 85–94.

Regier, D. A., Rae, D. S., Narrow, W. E., Kaelber, C. T., & Schatzberg, A. F. (1998). Prevalence of anxiety disorders and their comorbidity with mood and addictive disorders. *Brit. J. Psychiat.*, 173(Suppl. 34), 24–28.

Rehman, J., Lazer, S., Benet, A. E., Schaefer, L. C., & Melman, A. (1999). The reported sex and surgery satisfactions of 28 postoperative male-to-female transsexual patients. *Arch. Sex Behav.*, 28(1), 71–89.

Reich, J. H. (1987). Sex distribution of DSM-III personality disorders in psychiatric outpatients. *Amer. J. Psychiat.*, 144(4), 485–488.

Reich, J. H. (1990). Comparisons of males and females with DSM-III dependent personality disorder. *Psychiatr. Res.*, 33(2), 207–214.

Reich, J. (1996). The morbidity of DSM-III-R dependent personality disorder. *J. Nerv. Ment. Dis.*, 184(1), 22–26.

Reid, A. H. (1997). Mental handicap or learning disability: A critique of political correctness. *Brit. J. Psychiat., 170*, 1.

Reid, J. B., Eddy, J. M., Fetrow, R. A., & Stoolmiller, M. (1999). Description and immediate impacts of a preventive intervention for conduct problems. *Amer. J. Comm. Psych., 27*(4), 483–517.

Reid, R., & Lininger, T. (1993). Sexual pain disorders in the female. In W. O'Donohue & J. Geer (Eds.), *Handbook of sexual dysfunctions*. Boston: Allyn & Bacon.

Reid, S. (1998). Suicide in schizophrenia: A review of the literature. *J. Ment. Hlth. UK, 7*(4), 345–353.

Reid, W. H., & Burke, W. J. (1989). Antisocial personality disorder. In American Psychiatric Association (Eds.), *Treatments of psychiatric disorders: A task force report of the American Psychiatric Association*. Washington, DC: American Psychiatric Press.

Reik, T. (1989). The characteristics of masochism. *Amer. Imago, 46*(2-3), 161–195.

Reis, B. E. (1993). Toward a psychoanalytic understanding of multiple personality disorder. *Bull. Menninger Clin., 57*(3), 309–318.

Reisch, T., Schlatter, P., & Tschacher, W. (1999). Efficacy of crisis intervention. *Crisis, 20*(2), 78–85.

Reiss, S. (1985). The mentally retarded, emotionally disturbed adult. In M. Sigman (Ed.), *Children with emotional disorders and developmental disabilities*. New York: Grune & Stratton.

Reiss, S., Peterson, R. A., Gursky, D. M., & McNally, R. J. (1986). Anxiety sensitivity, anxiety frequency, and the prediction of fearfulness. *Behav. Res. Ther., 24*, 1–8.

Reissing, E. D., Binik, Y. M., & Khalife, S. (1999). Does vaginismus exist? A critical review of the literature. *J. Nerv. Ment. Dis., 187*(5), 261–274.

Reitan, R. M., & Wolfson, D. (1985). *The Halstead-Reitan Neuropsychological Test Battery: Theory and clinical interpretation*. Tucson, AZ: Neuropsychology.

Remafedi, G., French, S., Story, M., Resnick, M. D., & Blum, R. (1998). The relationship between suicide risk and sexual orientation: Results of a population-based study. *Amer. J. Pub. Hlth., 88*(1), 57–60.

Remington, B., Roberts, P., & Glautier, S. (1997). The effect of drink familiarity on tolerance to alcohol. *Addic. Behav., 22*(1), 45–53.

Remington, G., & Kapur, S. (2000). Atypical antipsychotics: Are some more typical than others? *Psychopharmacology, 148*(1), 3–15.

Remington, G., Pollock, B., Voineskos, G., Reed, K., & Coulter, K. (1993). Acutely psychotic patients receiving high-dose Haloperidol therapy. *J. Clin. Psychopharmacol., 13*(1), 41–45.

Reneman, L., Booij, J., Schmand, B., van den Brink, W., & Gunning, B. (2000). Memory disturbances in "ecstasy" users are correlated with an altered brain serotonin neurotransmission. *Psychopharmacology, 148*(3), 322–324.

Renneberg, G., Goldstein, A. J., Phillips, D., & Chambless, D. L. (1990). Intensive behavioral group treatment of avoidant personality disorder. *Behav. Ther., 21*(3), 363–377.

Reppucci, N. D., Woolard, J. L., & Fried. C. S. (1999). Social, community, and preventive interventions. *Annu. Rev. Psychol., 50*, 387–418.

Ressler, R. K., & Schactman, T. (1992). *Whoever fights monsters*. New York: St. Martin's Press.

Rey, J. M., & Walter, G. (1997). Half a century of ECT use in young people. *Amer. J. Psychiat., 154*(5), 595–602.

Reyna, L. J. (1989). Behavior therapy, applied behavior analysis, and behavior modification. In J. Hobson (Ed.), *Abnormal states of brain and mind*. Boston: Birkhauser.

Reynolds, A. J. (1998, January). Resilience among black urban youth: Prevalence, intervention effects, and mechanisms of influence. *Amer. J. Orthopsychiat., 68*(1), 84–100.

Reynolds, C. F., III, Frank, E., Perel, J. M., Imber, S. D., Cornes, C., Miller, M. D., Mazumdar, S., Houck, P. R., Dew, M. A., Stack, J. A., Pollock, B. G., & Kupfer, D. J. (1999). Nortriptyline and interpersonal psychotherapy as maintenance therapies for recurrent major depression: A randomized controlled trial in patients older than 59 years. *JAMA, 281*(1), 39–45.

Rhodes, A. E., & Links, P. S. (1998). Suicide and suicidal behaviours: Implications for mental health services. *Canad. J. Psychiat., 43*(8), 785–791.

Rhodes, R. (1999). Cited in L. Rabasca, I'm okay and you're okay, but not so sure about Y2K. *APA Monitor, 30*(1), 18.

Ricca, V., Mannucci, E., Moretti, S., Di Bernardo, M., Zucchi, T., Cabras, P. L., & Rotella, C. M. (2000). Screening for binge eating disorder in obese outpatients. *Comprehen. Psychiat., 41*(2), 111–115.

Rice, D. P., & Miller, L. S. (1998). Health economics and cost implications of anxiety and other mental disorders in the United States. *Brit. J. Psychiat., 173*(Suppl. 34), 4–9.

Rice, G., Anderson, C., Risch, N., & Ebers, G. (1999). Male homosexuality: Absence of linkage to microsatellite markers at Xq28. *Science, 284*(5414), 665–667.

Rice, K. M., Blanchard, E. B., & Purcell, M. (1993). Biofeedback treatments of generalized anxiety disorder: Preliminary results. *Biofeedback Self Regul., 18*(2), 93–105.

Rich, C. L., Dhossche, D. M., Ghani, S., & Isacsson, G. (1998). Suicide methods and presence of intoxicating abusable substances: Some clinical and public health implications. *Ann. Clin. Psychiat., 10*(4), 169–175.

Richards, J. M., & Gross, J. J. (1999). Composure at any cost? The cognitive consequences of emotion suppression. *Pers. Soc. Psychol. Bull., 25*(8), 1033–1044.

Richards, P. S., & Bergin, A. E. (Eds.) (2000). *Handbook of psychotherapy and religious diversity*. Washington, DC: American Psychological Association.

Richardson, S. (1997, January). An ancient immunity. *Discover*, p. 30.

Richardson, S. (1997, January). The second key. *Discover*, pp. 29–30.

Richman, J. (1999). Similarities and differences between younger and older suicidal people. *J. Clin. Geropsychol., 5*(1), 1–17.

Richman, N. E., & Sokolove, R. L. (1992). The experience of aloneness, object representation, and evocative memory in borderline and neurotic patients. *Psychoanalyt. Psychiat., 9*(1), 77–91.

Richter, P., Werner, J., Heerlein, A., Kraus, A., & Sauer, H. (1998). On the validity of the Beck Depression Inventory: A review. *Psychopathology, 31*(3), 160–168.

Richters, J. E., & Martinez, P. (1993). The NIMH community violence project: I. Children as victims of and witnesses to violence. *Psychiatry, 56*, 7–21.

Rickels, K., DeMartinis, N., & Aufdembrinke, B. (2000). A double-blind, placebo-controlled trial of abecarnil and diazepam in the treatment of patients with generalized anxiety disorder. *J. Clin. Psychopharmacol., 20*(1), 12–18.

Rickels, K., Schweizer, E., Weiss, S., & Zavodnick, S. (1993). Maintenance drug treatment for panic disorder: II. Short- and long-term outcome after drug taper. *Arch. Gen. Psychiat., 50*, 61–68.

Ricketts, R. W., Singh, N. N., Ellis, C. R., Chambers, S., et al. (1995). Calcium channel blockers and vitamin E for tardive dyskinesia in adults with mental retardation. [Special issue: Pharmacotherapy III.] *J. Dev. Phys. Disabilities, 7*(2), 161–174.

Riddle, M. (1998). Obsessive-compulsive disorder in children and adolescents. *Brit. J. Psychiat., 173*(Suppl. 35), 91–96.

Riddle, M. A., Bernstein, G. A., Cook, E. H., Leonard, H. L., March, J. S., & Swanson, J. S. (1999). Anxiolytics, adrenergic agents, and naltrexone. *J. Amer. Acad. Child Adol. Psychiat., 38*(5), 546–556.

Rieber, R. W. (1999, March). Hypnosis, false memory, and multiple personality: A trinity of affinity. *History Psychiat.*

Riggs, D. S., & Foa, E. B. (1993). Obsessive compulsive disorder. In D. H. Barlow (Ed.), *Clinical handbook of psychological disorders: A step-by-step treatment manual* (2nd ed.). New York: Guilford.

Rihmer, Z., Rutz, W., & Pihlgren, H. (1995). Depression and suicide on Gotland. An intensive study of all suicides before and after a depression-training programme for general practitioners. *J. Affect. Disorders, 35*, 147–152.

Rimland, B. (1988). Vitamin B6 (and magnesium) in the treatment of autism. *Autism Research Review International, 1*(4).

Rimland, B. (1992). *Form letter regarding high dosage vitamin B6 and magnesium therapy for autism and related disorders*. Autism Research Institute, publication 39E.

Rimland, B. (1992). Leominster: Is pollution a cause of autism? *Autism Res. Rev. Inter., 6*(2), 1.

Rimm, D. C., & Litvak, S. B. (1969). Self-verbalization and emotional arousal. *J. Abnorm. Psychol., 74*(2), 181–187.

Rimm, D. C., & Masters, J. C. (1979). *Behavior therapy: Techniques and empirical findings* (2nd ed.). New York: Academic Press.

Ringuette, E., & Kennedy, T. (1966). *J. Abnorm. Psychol., 71*, 136–141.

Risch, S. C., & Janowsky, D. S. (1984). Cholinergic-adrenergic balance in affective illness. In R. M. Post & J. C. Ballenger (Eds.), *Neurobiology of mood disorders: Vol. 1. Frontiers cf clinical neuroscience*. Baltimore: Williams & Wilkins.

Ritchie, K., Kildea, D., & Robine, J. M. (1992). The relationship between age and the prevalence of senile dementia: A meta-analysis of recent data. *Inter. J. Epidemiol., 21*, 763–769

Roan, S. (1995, September 19) A poor state of mind. *Los Angeles Times*, pp. E1, E7.

Roazen, P. (1992). The rise and fall of Bruno Bettelheim. *Psychohist. Rev., 20*(3), 221–250.

Robbins, S. J., Ehrman, R. N., Childress, A. R., Cornish, J. W., & O'Brien, C. P. (2000). Mood state and recent cocaine use are not associated with levels of cocaine cue reactivity. *Drug Alc. Dep., 59*(1), 33–42.

Robert, P. H., Aubin, B. V., & Darcourt, G. (1999). Serotonin and the frontal lobes. In B. L. Miller, J. L. Cummings, et al. (Eds.), *The human frontal lobes: Functions and disorders*. The science and practice of neuropsychology series. New York: Guilford.

Roberts, A. R. (1979). Organization of suicide prevention agencies. In L. D. Hankoff & B. Einsidler (Eds.), *Suicide: Theory and clinical aspects*. Littleton, MA: PSG Publishing.

Roberts, C. F., Golding, S. L., & Fincham, F. D. (1987). Implicit theories of criminal responsibility. *Law Human Behav., 11*(3), 297–232.

Robertson, E. (1992). The challenge of dual diagnosis. *J. Hlth. Care Poor Underserved, 3*(1), 198–207.

Robertson, M. (1992). *Starving in the silences: An exploration of anorexia nervosa.* New York: New York University Press.

Robin, A. L., Siegel, P. T., & Moye, A. (1995). Family versus individual therapy for anorexia: Impact on family conflict. Topical Section: Treatment and therapeutic processes. *Inter. J. Eat. Disorders, 17*(4), 313–322.

Robins, L. N., & Regier, D. S. (1991). *Psychiatric disorders in America: The Epidemiological Catchment Area Study.* New York: Free Press.

Robins, L. N., Locke, B. Z., & Regier, D. A. (1991). An overview of psychiatric disorders in America. In L. N. Robins & D. A. Regier (Eds.), *Psychiatric disorders in America: The Epidemiological Catchment Area Study.* New York: Free Press.

Robison, L. M., Sclar, D. A., Skaer, T. L., & Galin, R. S. (1999). National trends in the prevalence of attention-deficit/hyperactivity disorder and the prescribing of methylphenidate among school children: 1990–1995. *Clin. Pediatr., 38*(4), 209–217.

Rocha, B. A., Scearce-Levie, K., Lucas, J. J., Hiroi, N., Castanon, N., Crabbe, J. C., Nestler, E. J., & Hen, R. (1998). Increased vulnerability to cocaine in mice lacking the serotonin-1B receptor. *Nature, 393*(6681), 175–178.

Rodgers, L. N. (1995). Prison suicide: Suggestions from phenomenology. *Deviant Behav., 16*(2), 113–126.

Rodier, P. M. (2000, February). The early origins of autism. *Scientif. Amer.,* pp. 56–63.

Rodin, J. (1992). Sick of worrying about the way you look? Read this. *Psychol. Today, 25*(1), 56–60.

Roedema, T. M., & Simons, R. F. (1999). Emotion-processing deficit in alexithymia. *Psychophysiology, 36*(3), 379–387.

Roehrich, L., & Kinder, B. N. (1991). Alcohol expectancies and male sexuality: Review and implications for sex therapy. *J. Sex Marital Ther., 17*(1), 45–54.

Roemer, L., Borkovec, M., Posa, S., & Borkovec, T. D. (1995). A self-report diagnostic measure of generalized anxiety disorder. *J. Behav. Ther. Exp. Psychiat., 26*(4), 345–350.

Roesch, R. (1991). *The encyclopedia of depression.* New York: Facts on File.

Roesch, R., Zapf, P. A., Golding, S. L., & Skeem, J. L. (1999). Defining and assessing competence to stand trial. In A. K. Hess, I. B. Weiner, et al. (Eds.), *The handbook of forensic psychology* (2nd ed.). New York: Wiley.

Roesler, T. A., & McKenzie, N. (1994). Effects of childhood trauma on psychological functioning of adults sexually abused as children. *J. Nerv. Ment. Dis., 182*(3), 145–150.

Rogers, C. R. (1951). *Client-centered therapy.* Boston: Houghton Mifflin.

Rogers, C. R. (1961). *On becoming a person.* Boston: Houghton Mifflin.

Rogers, C. R. (1987). Rogers, Kohut, and Erickson: A personal perspective on some similarities and differences. In J. K. Zeig (Ed.), *The evolution of psychotherapy.* New York: Brunner/Mazel.

Rogers, C. R., & Dymond, R. (1954). *Psychotherapy and personality change.* Chicago: University of Chicago.

Rogers, C. R., & Sanford, R. C. (1989). Client-centered psychotherapy. In H. I. Kaplan & B. J. Sadock (Eds.), *Comprehensive textbook of psychiatry* (5th ed., Vol 1). Baltimore: Williams & Wilkins.

Rogers, J. C., & Holloway, R. L. (1990). Assessing threats to the validity of experimental and observational designs. *Fam. Pract. Res. J., 10*(2), 81–95.

Rogers, R. (1987). Assessment of criminal responsibility: Empirical advances and unanswered questions. *J. Psychiat. Law, 51*(1), 73–82.

Rogers, R., & Ewing, C. P. (1992). The measurement of insanity: Debating the merits of the R-CRAS and its alternatives. *Inter. J. Law Psychiat., 15,* 113–123.

Rogers, R., & Sewell, K. W. (1999). The R-CRAS and insanity evaluations: A re-examination of construct validity. *Behav. Sci. Law, 17*(2), 181–194.

Rogers, R., & Shuman, D. W. (2000). *Conducting insanity evaluations* (2nd ed.) New York: Guilford.

Roggla, H., & Uhl, A. (1995). Depression and relapses in treated chronic alcoholics. *Inter. J. Addic., 30*(3), 337–349.

Rogler, L. H. (1999). Methodological sources of cultural insensitivity in mental health research. *Amer. Psychologist, 54*(6), 424–433.

Rogler, L. H., Malgady, R. G., & Rodriguea, O. (1989). *Hispanics and mental health: A framework for research.* Malabar, FL: Krieger Publishing.

Rohsenow, D. J., Smith, R. E., & Johnson, S. (1985). Stress management training as a prevention program for heavy social drinkers: Cognition, affect, drinking, and individual differences. *Addic. Behav., 10*(1), 45–54.

Roitman, S. E. L., Cornblatt, B. A., Bergman, A., Obuchowski, M., et al. (1997). Attention functioning in schizotypal personality disorder. *Amer. J. Psychiat., 154*(5), 655–660.

Rolland, J. S., & Walsh, F. (1994). Family therapy: Systems approaches to assessment and treatment. In R. E. Hales, S. C. Yudofsky, & J. A. Talbott, (Eds.), *The American Psychiatric Press textbook of psychiatry* (2nd ed.). Washington, DC: American Psychiatric Press.

Rollin, H. R. (1980). *Coping with schizophrenia.* London: Burnett.

Rolls, B. J., Fedroff, I. C., & Guthrie, J. F. (1991). Gender differences in eating behavior and body weight regulation. *Hlth. Psychol., 10*(2), 133–142.

Rolls, E. T. (2000). Memory systems in the brain. *Annu. Rev. Psychol., 51,* 599–630.

Ronen, T. (1993). Intervention package for treating encopresis in a 6-year-old boy: A case study. *Behav. Psychother., 21,* 127–135.

Roper, G., Rachman, S., & Hodgson, R. (1973). An experiment on obsessional checking. *Behav. Res. Ther., 11,* 271–277.

Roper Reports. (1998, February). Marriage: The art of compromise. *American Demographics*

Roper Reports. (1998, August). How old is old? *American Demographics.*

Rosen, E. F., Anthony, D. L., Booker, K. M., Brown, T. L., et al. (1991). A comparison of eating disorder scores among African American and white college females. *Bull. Psychon. Soc., 29*(1), 65–66.

Rosen, J. C., & Leitenberg, H. (1982). Bulimia nervosa: Treatment with exposure and response prevention. *Behav. Ther., 13*(1), 117–124.

Rosen, J. C., & Leitenberg, H. (1985). Exposure plus response prevention treatment of bulimia. In D. M. Garner & P. E. Garfinkel (Eds.), *Handbook of psychotherapy for anorexia nervosa and bulimia.* New York: Guilford.

Rosen, J. C., Orosan, P., & Reiter, J. (1995). Cognitive behavior therapy for negative body image in obese women. *Behav. Ther., 26,* 25–42.

Rosen, L. W., & Hough, D. O. (1988). Pathogenic weight-control behaviors of female college gymnasts. *Physician Sports Med., 16*(9), 141–144.

Rosen, L. W., McKeag, D. B., Hough, D. O., & Curley, V. (1986). Pathogenic weight-control behavior in female athletes. *The Physician and Sports Medicine, 14*(1), 79–86.

Rosen, M. I., McMahon, T. J., Hameedi, F. A., Pearsall, H. R., Woods, S. W., Kreek, M. J., & Kosten, T. R. (1996). Effect of clonidine pretreatment on naloxone-precipitated opiate withdrawal. *J. Pharmacol. Exp. Ther., 276,* 1128–1135.

Rosen, R. C., & Leiblum, S. R. (1993). Treatment of male erectile disorder: Current options and dilemmas. *J. Sex. Marital Ther., 8*(1), 5–8.

Rosen, R. C., & Leiblum, S. R. (1995). Hypoactive sexual desire. *Psychiat. Clin. N. Amer., 13*(1), 107–121.

Rosen, R. C., & Leiblum, S. R. (1995). Hypoactive sexual desire. [Special issue: Clinical sexuality.] *Psychiat. Clin. N. Amer., 18*(1), 107–121.

Rosen, R. C., & Leiblum, S. R. (1995). Treatment of sexual disorders in the 1990s: An integrated approach. *J. Cons. Clin. Psychol., 63*(6), 877–890.

Rosen, R. C., & Rosen, L. R. (1981). *Human sexuality.* New York: Knopf.

Rosen, R. C., Lane, R. M., & Menza, M. (1999). Effects of SSRIs on sexual function: A critical review. *J. Clin. Psychopharmacol., 19*(1), 67–85.

Rosen, R. C., Leiblum, S. R., & Spector, I. (1994). Psychologically based treatment for male erectile disorder: A cognitive-interpersonal model. *J. Sex Marital Ther., 20,* 78–85.

Rosen, R. C., Taylor, J. F., Leiblum, S. R., & Bachmann, G. A. (1993). Prevalence of sexual dysfunction in women: Results of a survey study of 329 women in an outpatient gynecological clinic. *J. Sex Marital Ther., 19,* 171–188.

Rosenbaum, M. (1980). The role of the term schizophrenia in the decline of diagnoses of multiple personality. *Arch. Gen. Psychiat., 37*(12), 1383–1385.

Rosenberg, H. (1993). Prediction of controlled drinking by alcoholics and problem drinkers. *Psychol. Bull., 113*(1), 129–139.

Rosenfarb, I. S., Goldstein, M. J., Mintz, J., & Nuechterlein, K. H. (1995). Expressed emotion and subclinical psychopathology observable within the transactions between schizophrenic patients and their family members. *J. Abnorm. Psychol., 104*(2), 259–267.

Rosenfeld, M. (1998, November 22). Van Gogh's madness: Long after the painter's death, the diagnosis debate lives on. *Washington Post,* p. G1.

Rosenhan, D. L. (1973). On being sane in insane places. *Science, 179*(4070), 250–258.

Rosenman, R. H. (1990). Type A behavior pattern: A personal overview. *J. Soc. Behav. Pers., 5,* 1–24.

Rosenstein, D. S., & Horowitz, H. A. (1996). Adolescent attachment and psychopathology. *J. Cons. Clin. Psychol., 64*(2), 244–253.

Rosenstein, M. J., Milazzo-Sayre, L. J., & Manderscheid, R. W. (1989). Care of persons with schizophrenia: A statistical profile. *Schizo. Bull., 15*(1), 45–58.

Rosenstein, M. J., Milazzo-Sayre, L. J., & Manderscheid, R. W. (1990). Characteristics of persons using specialty inpatient, outpatient, and partial care programs in 1986. In R. W. Manderscheid & M. A. Sonnenschein (Eds.), *Mental health, United States, 1990* (DHHS Publication No. ADM 90-1708). Washington DC: U. S. Department of Health &Human Services.

Rosenthal, D. A., & Berven, N. L. (1999). Effects of client race on clinical judgment. *Rehab. Couns. Bull., 42*(3), 243–264.

Rosenthal, N. E., & Blehar, M. C. (Eds.). (1989). *Seasonal affective disorders and phototherapy.* New York: Guilford.

Rosenthal, R. (1966). *Experimenter effects in behavioral research.* New York: Appleton-Century-Crofts.

Rosenthal, R. J. (1992). Pathological gambling. *Psychiatr. Ann., 22*(2), 72–78.

Rosenzweig, M. R. (1996). Aspects of the search for neural mechanisms of memory. In J. T. Spence, J.

M. Darley, & D. J. Foss (Eds.), *Annual review of psychology* (Vol. 47). Palo Alto, CA: Annual Reviews.

Rosenzweig, S. (1933). The recall of finished and unfinished tasks as affected by the purpose with which they were performed. *Psychol. Bull., 30,* 698.

Rosenzweig, S. (1943). An experimental study of repression with special reference to need-persistive and ego-defensive reactions to frustration. *J. Exp. Psychol., 32,* 64–74.

Roses, A. D., Einstein, G., Gilbert, J., Goedert, M., Han, S. H., Huang, D., Hulette, C., Masliah, E., Pericak-Vance, M. A., Saunders, A. M., Schmechel, D. E., Strittmatter, W. J., Weisgraber, K. H., & Xi, P. T. (1996). Morphological, biochemical, and genetic support for an apolipoprotein E effect on microtubular metabolism. In R. J. Wurtman, S. Corkin, J. H. Growdon, & R. M. Nitsch (Eds.), *The neurobiology of Alzheimer's disease.* New York: New York Academy of Sciences.

Ross, A. O. (1981). *Child behavior therapy: Principles, procedures and empirical basis.* New York: Wiley.

Ross, C. A., & Ellason, J. (1999). Comment on the effectiveness of treatment for dissociative identity disorder. *Psychol. Rep., 84*(3, Pt. 2), 1109–1110.

Ross, C. A., & Gahan, P. (1988). Techniques in the treatment of multiple personality disorder. *Amer. J. Psychother., 42*(1), 40–52.

Ross, C. A., Miller, S. D., Reagor, P., & Bjornson, L., et al. (1990). Structured interview data on 102 cases of multiple personality disorder from four centers. *Amer. J. Psychiat., 147*(5), 596–601.

Ross, C. A., Miller, S. D., Bjornson, L., Reagor, P., Fraser, G. A., & Anderson, G. (1991). Abuse histories in 102 cases of multiple personality disorder. *Canad. J. Psychiat., 36,* 97–101.

Ross, C. A., Norton, G. R., & Wozney, K. (1989). Multiple personality disorder: An analysis of 236 cases. *Canad. J. Psychiat., 34*(5), 413–418.

Ross, D. M., & Ross, S. A. (1982). *Hyperactivity: Current issues, research and theory* (2nd ed.). New York: Wiley.

Rosse, R., Fay-McCarthy, M., Collins, J., Risher-Flowers, D., Alim, T., & Deutsch, S. (1993). Transient compulsive foraging behavior associated with crack cocaine use. *Amer. J. Psychiat., 150*(1), 155–156.

Rosselli, M., & Ardila, A. (1996). Cognitive effects of cocaine and polydrug abuse. *J. Clin. Exp. Neuropsychol., 18*(1), 122–135.

Rossi, A., Bustini, M., Prosperini, P., Marinangeli, M. G., Splendiani, A., Daneluzzo, E., & Stratta, P. (2000). Neuromorphological abnormalities in schizophrenic patients with good and poor outcome. *Acta Psychiatr. Scandin., 101*(2), 161–166.

Rossor, M. N., Kennedy, A. M., & Frackowiak, R. S. J. (1996). Clinical and neuroimaging features of familial Alzheimer's disease. In R. J. Wurtman, S. Corkin, J. H. Growdon & R. M. Nitsch (Eds.), *The neurobiology of Alzheimer's disease.* New York: New York Academy of Sciences.

Rossow, I., & Amundsen, A. (1995). Alcohol abuse and suicide: A 40-year prospective study of Norwegian conscripts. *Addiction, 90*(5), 685–691.

Rotenberg, V., Kayumov, L., Indursky, P., Kimhi, R., Venger, A., Melamed, Y., & Elizur, A. (1999). Slow wave sleep redistribution and REM sleep eye movement density in depression: Towards the adaptive function of REM sleep. *Homeostatis Hlth. Dis., 39*(3–4), 81–89.

Rothbaum, B. O., Foa, E. B., Riggs, D. S., Murdock, T., & Walsh, W. (1992). A prospective examination of posttraumatic stress disorder in rape victims. *J. Traum. Stress, 5*(3), 455–475.

Rothblum, E. D. (1992). The stigma of women's weight: Social and economic realities. *Feminism Psychol., 2*(1), 61–73.

Rowland, D. L. (1999). Issues in the laboratory study of human sexual response: A synthesis for the nontechnical sexologist. *J. Sex Res., 36*(1), 3–15.

Rowlands, P. (1995). Schizophrenia and sexuality. *J. Sex. Marital Ther. 10*(1), 47–61.

Roy, A. (1982). Suicide in chronic schizophrenics. *Brit. J. Psychiat., 141,* 171–177.

Roy, A., Nielsen, D., Rylander, G., Sarchiapone, M., & Segal, N. (1999). Genetics of suicide in depression. *J. Clin. Psychiat., 60*(Suppl. 2), 12–17.

Rozin, P., & Stoess, C. (1993). Is there a general tendency to become addicted? *Addic. Behav., 18,* 81–87.

Rubinstein, S., & Caballero, B. (2000). Is Miss America an undernourished role model? *JAMA, 283*(12), 1569.

Rudd, M. D. (1998). An integrative conceptual and organizational framework for treating suicidal behavior. *Psychotherapy, 35*(3), 346–360.

Rudd, M. D. (2000). Integrating science into the practice of clinical suicidology: A review of the psychotherapy literature and a research agenda for the future. In R. W. Maris, S. S. Canetto, et al. (Eds.), *Review of suicidology, 2000.* New York: Guilford.

Rudolph, J., Langer, I., & Tausch, R. (1980). An investigation of the psychological affects and conditions of person-centered individual psychotherapy. *Z. Klin. Psychol.: Forsch. Praxis, 9,* 23–33.

Ruedrich, S. L., Chu, C., & Wadle, C. V. (1985). The amytal interview in the treatment of psychogenic amnesia [Special issue]. *Hosp. Comm. Psychiat., 36*(10), 1045–1046.

Rush, A. J., Weissenburger, J., & Eaves, G. (1986). Do thinking patterns predict depressive symptoms? *Cog. Ther. Res., 10*(2), 225–235.

Rushford, N., & Ostermeyer, A. (1997). Body image disturbances and their change with videofeedback in anorexia nervosa. *Behav. Res. Ther., 35*(5), 389–398.

Rushton, J. L. (1999). *Prescribing of SSRIs in child and adolescent populations.* Paper presented at the Pediatric Academic Societies Annual Meeting, San Francisco.

Russell, G. (1979). Bulimia nervosa: An ominous variant of anorexia nervosa. *Psychol. Med., 9*(3), 429–448.

Russell, G. F. M. (1995). Anorexia nervosa through time. In G. Szmukler, C. Dare, & J. Treasure (Eds.), *Handbook of eating disorders: Theory, treatment and research.* Chichester, England: Wiley.

Russell, R. J., & Hulson, B. (1992). Physical and psychological abuse of heterosexual partners. *Pers. Individ. Diff., 13*(4), 457–473.

Russell, R. M., et al. (1992). In K. Halmi (Ed.), *Psychobiology and treatment of anorexia nervosa and bulimia nervosa.* Washington, DC: American Psychiatric Press.

Rychtarik, R. G., Connors, G. J., Whitney, R. B., McGillicuddy, N. B., Fitterling, J. M., & Wirtz, P. W. (2000). Treatment settings for persons with alcoholism: Evidence for matching clients to inpatient versus outpatient care. *J. Cons. Clin. Psychol., 68*(2), 277–289.

SAMHSA (Substance Abuse and Mental Health Services Administration). (1996). *Advance report number 17: Preliminary estimates from the drug abuse warning network.* Washington, DC: U. S. Department of Health and Human Services.

SAMHSA (1996). *National Household Survey on Drug Abuse, 1994 and 1995.* Office of Applied Studies.

SAMHSA News. (1993, Spring). *Agencies improve mental health services in jails* (Vol. 1, No. 2.). U.S. Dept. of Health and Human Services.

Saarinen, P. I., Viinamaeki, H., Hintikka, J., Lehtonen, J., & Koennqvist, J. (1999). Psychological symptoms of close relatives of suicide victims. *Eur. J. Psychiat., 13*(1), 33–39.

Sachs, R. G. (1986). The adjunctive role of social support systems. In B. G. Braun (Ed.), *The treatment of multiple personality disorder.* Washington, DC: American Psychiatric Press.

Sackeim, H. A. (1988). Mechanisms of action of electroconvulsive therapy. In A. J. Frances & R. E. Hales (Eds.), *American Psychiatric Press review of psychiatry* (Vol. 7). Washington, DC: American Psychiatric Press.

Sacks, O. (2000, May). *An anthropologist on Mars: Some personal perspectives on autism.* Keynote address. Eden Institute Foundation's Sixth Annual Princeton Lecture Series on Autism. Princeton, NJ.

Safer, D. (1994). The impact of recent lawsuits on methylphenidates sales. *Clin. Pediatr., 33*(3), 166–168.

Safer, D., & Krager, J. (1992). Effect of a media blitz and a threatened lawsuit on stimulant treatment. *JAMA, 268*(8), 1004–1007.

Safer, D., & Krager, J. (1993). Reply to "Treatment of ADHD" (Letter). *JAMA, 269*(18), 2369.

Safren, S. A., Heimberg, R. G., Horner, K. J., Juster, H. R., Schneier, F. R., & Liebowitz, M. R. (1999). Factor structure of social fears: The Liebowitz Social Anxiety Scale. *J. Anx. Dis., 13*(3), 253–270.

Saftig, P., Hartmann, D., & De Strooper, B. (1999). The function of presenilin-1 in amyloid beta-peptide generation and brain development. *Eur. Arch. Psychiat. Clin. Neurosci., 249*(6), 271–279.

Sagawa, K., Kawakatsu, S., Shibuya, I., Oiji, A., et al. (1990). Correlation of regional cerebral blood flow with performance on neuropsychological tests in schizophrenic patients. *Schizo. Res., 3*(4), 241–246.

Sakado, K., Sato, T., Uehara, T., Sakado, M., & Someya, T. (1999). Perceived parenting pattern and response to antidepressants in patients with major depression. *J. Affect. Disorders, 52*(1–3), 59–66.

Sakheim, D. K., Hess, E. P., & Chivas, A. (1988). General principles for short-term inpatient work with multiple personality-disorder patients. *Psychotherapy, 24,* 117–124.

Sakurai, S. (1998). Hypnotic approaches to a college female student with personality disorder suffering from somatization disorder. *Jap. J. Hyp., 43*(1), 11–19.

Salama, A. A. (1988). The antisocial personality (the sociopathic personality). *Psychiat. J. Univ. Ottawa, 13*(3), 149–151.

Sales, E., Baum, M., & Shore, B. (1984). Victim readjustment following assault. *J. Soc. Issues, 40*(1), 117–136.

Salkovskis, P. M. (1985). Obsessional-compulsive problems: A cognitive-behavioural analysis. *Behav. Res. Ther., 23,* 571–584.

Salkovskis, P. M. (1989). Cognitive-behavioural factors and the persistence of intrusive thoughts in obsessional problems. *Behav. Res. Ther., 27,* 677–682.

Salkovskis, P. M. (1999). Understanding and treating obsessive-compulsive disorder. *Behav. Res. Ther., 37*(Suppl. 1), S29–S52.

Salkovskis, P. M., & Westbrook, D. (1989). Behaviour therapy and obsessional ruminations: Can failure be turned into success? *Behav. Res. Ther., 27,* 149–160.

Salkovskis, P. M., Atha, C., & Storer, D. (1990). Cognitive behavioural problem solving in the treatment of patients who repeatedly attempt suicide: A controlled trial. *Brit. J. Psychiat., 157,* 871–876.

Sallee, F. R., Vrindavanam, N. S., Deas-Nesmith, D., Carson, S. W., & Sethuraman, G. (1997). Pulse intravenous clomiparamine for depressed adolescents: Double-blind, controlled trial. *Amer. J. Psychiat., 154*(5), 668–673.

Salzman, C. (1998). ECT, research, and profesional ambivalence. *Amer. J. Psychiat., 155*(1), 1–2.

Salzman, C. (1999). Treatment of the suicidal patient with psychotropic drugs and ECT. In D.G. Jacobs (Ed.), *The Harvard Medical School guide to suicide assessment and intervention.* San Francisco: Jossey-Bass.

Salzman, C., Vaccaro, B., Lieff, J., & Weiner, A. (1995). Clozapine in older patients with psychosis and behavioral disruption. *Amer. J. Ger. Psychiat., 3*(1), 26–33..

Salzman, L. (1980). *Psychotherapy of the obsessive personality.* New York: Jason Aronson.

Salzman, L. (1985). Psychotherapeutic management of obsessive-compulsive patients. *Amer. J. Psychother., 39*(3), 323–330.

Salzman, L. (1989). Compulsive personality disorder. In *Treatments of psychiatric disorders.* Washington, DC: American Psychiatric Press.

Sampath, G., Shah, A., Kraska, J., & Soni, S. D. (1992). Neuroleptic discontinuation in the very stable schizophrenic patient: Relapse rates and serum neuroleptic levels. *Human Psychopharmacol. Clin. Exp., 7*(4), 255–264.

Sanchez-Canovas, J., Botella-Arbona, C., Ballestin, G. P., & Soriano-Pastor, J. (1991). Intervencion comportamental y analisis ipsativo normativo en un trastorno de ansiedad. [Behavioral intervention and ipsative-normative analysis in an anxiety disorder]. *Anal. Modif. Conducta, 17*(51), 115–151.

Sandelowski, M. (1995). Sample size in qualitative research. *Res. Nursing Hlth., 18*(2), 179–183.

Sanders, S. K., & Shekhar, A. (1995). Anxiolytic effects of chlordiazepoxide blocked by injection of GABA-sub(A) and benzodiazepine receptor antagonists in the region of the anterior basolateral amygdala of rats. *Biol. Psychiat., 37*(7), 473–476.

Sanders, S. K., & Shekhar, A. (1995). Regulation of anxiety by GABAA receptors in the rat amygdala. *Pharmacol. Biochem. Behav., 52*(4), 701–706.

Sanderson, R. E., Campbell, D., & Laverty, S. G. (1963). An investigation of a new aversive conditioning treatment for alcoholism. *Quart. J. Stud. Alcohol., 24,* 261–275.

Sandler, M. (1990). Monoamine oxidase inhibitors in depression: History and mythology. *J. Psychopharmacol., 4*(3), 136–139.

Sanftner, J. L., & Crowther, J. H. (1998). Variability in self-esteem, moods, shame, and guilt in women who binge. *Inter. J. Eat. Disorders, 23*(4), 391–397.

Sanftner, J. L., Barlow, D. H., Marschall, D. E., & Tangney, J. P. (1995). The relation of shame and guilt to eating disorder symptomatology. *J. Soc. Clin. Psychol., 14*(4), 315–324.

Sansone, R. A., Fine, M. A., & Dennis, A. B. (1991). Treatment impressions and termination experiences with borderline patients. *Amer. J. Psychother., 45*(2), 173–180.

Sansone, R.A., Wiederman, M., & Sansone, L.A. (2000). Medically self-harming behavior and its relationship to borderline personality symptoms and somatic preoccupation among internal medicine patients. *J. Nerv. Ment. Dis., 188*(1), 45–47.

Santa Mina, E. E., & Gallop, R. M. (1998). Childhood sexual and physical abuse and adult self-harm and suicidal behaviour: A literature review. *Canad. J. Psychiat., 43*(8), 793–800.

Satir, V. (1964). *Conjoint family therapy: A guide to therapy and technique.* Palo Alto, CA: Science & Behavior Books.

Satir, V. (1967). *Conjoint family therapy* (rev. ed.). Palo Alto, CA: Science & Behavior Books.

Satir, V. (1987). Going behind the obvious: The psychotherapeutic journey. In J. K. Zeig (Ed.), *The evolution of psychotherapy.* New York: Brunner/Mazel.

Sato, T., Sakado, K., Uehara, T., Nichioka, K., & Kasahara, Y. (1997). Perceived parental styles in a Japanese sample of depressive disorders. A replication outside Western culture. *Brit. J. Psychiat., 170,* 173–175..

Saudino, J. J., Pedersen, N. L., Lichenstein, P., McClearn, G. E., & Plomin, R. (1997). Can personality explain genetic influence on life events? *J. Pers. Soc. Psychol., 72*(1), 196–206.

Saunders, D. G. (1992). A typology of men who batter: Three types derived from cluster analysis. *Amer. J. Orthopsychiat., 62*(2), 264–275.

Saunders, J. B., & Lee, N. K. (2000). Hazardous alcohol use: Its delineation as a subthreshold disorder, and approaches to its diagnosis and management. *Comprehen. Psychiat., 41*(2, Suppl 1), 95–103.

Saxena, S., Brody, A. L., Maidment, K. M., Dunkin, J. J., Colgan, M., Alborzian, S., Phelps, M. E., & Baxter, L. R., Jr. (1999). Localized orbitofrontal and subcortical metabolic changes and predictors of response to paroxetine treatment in obsessive-compulsive disorder. *Neuropsychopharmacology, 21*(6), 683–693.

Scarf, M. (1996, June 10). The mind of the Unabomber. *New Republic,* pp. 20–23.

Scarpa, A., Luscher, K. A., Smalley, K. J., Pilkonis, P. A., Kim, Y., & Williams, W. C. (1999). Screening for personality disorders in a nonclinical population. *J. Pers. Disorders, 13*(4), 345–360.

Scarr, S., Phillips, D., & McCartney, K. (1989). Working mothers and their families. *Amer. Psychologist, 44*(11), 1402–1409.

Scarr, S., Phillips, D., & McCartney, K. (1990). Working mothers and their families. *Annual Progress in Child Psychiatry and Child Development,* 261–278.

Schachar, R. J., & Wachsmuth, R. (1990). Hyperactivity and parental psychopathology. *J. Child Psychol. Psychiat. Allied Disc., 31,* 381– 392.

Schacter, D. L. (1989). Autobiographical memory in a case of multiple personality disorder. *J. Abnorm. Psychol., 98*(4), 508–514.

Schacter, D. L. (1999). The seven sins of memory: Insights from psychology and cognitive neuroscience. *Amer. Psychologist, 54*(3), 182–203.

Schacter, D. L., Glisky, E. L., & McGlynn, S. M. (1990). Impact of memory disorder on everyday life: Awareness of deficits and return to work. In D. Tupper & K. Cicerone (Eds.), *The neuropsychology of everyday life: Vol. 1. Theories and basic competencies.* Boston: Martinus Nijhoff.

Schatzberg, A. T., et al. (1982). Toward a biochemical classification of depressive disorders: V. Heterogeneity of unipolar depressions. *Amer. J. Psychiat., 130*(4), 471–475.

Schechter, D., Singer, T. M., Kuperman, J., & Endicott, J. (1998). Selection of "normal" control subjects for psychiatric research: Update on a model for centralized recruitment. *Psychiat. Res., 79*(2), 175–185.

Scheel, K. R. (2000). The empirical basis of dialectical behavior therapy: Summary, critique, and implications. *Clin. Psychol.: Sci. Prac., 7*(1), 68–86.

Scheff, T. J. (1975). *Labeling madness.* Englewood Cliffs, NJ: Prentice Hall.

Scheff, T. J. (1999). *Being mentally ill: A sociological theory.* Hawthorne, NY: Aldine de Gruyter.

Schiavi, R. C., Stimmel, B. B., Mandeli, J., Schreiner-Engel, P., et al. (1995). Diabetes, psychological function and male sexuality. *J. Psychosom. Res., 39*(3), 305–314.

Schiavi, R. C., White, D., Mandeli, J., & Schreiner-Engel, P. (1993). Hormones and nocturnal penile tumescence in healthy aging men. *Arch. Sex. Behav., 22*(2), 207–216.

Schildkraut, J. J. (1965). The catecholamine hypothesis of affective disorders: A review of supporting evidence. *Amer. J. Psychiat., 122*(5), 509–522.

Schleifer, J. S., Keller, S. E., Bartlett, J. A., Eckholdt, H. M., & Delaney, B. R. (1996). Immunity in young adults with major depressive disorder. *Amer. J. Psychiat., 153,* 477–482.

Schleifer, S. J., Keller, S. E., & Bartlett, J. A. (1999). Depression and immunity: Clinical factors and therapeutic course. *Psychiat. Res., 85*(1), 63–69.

Schlenger, W. E., Fairbank, J. A., Jordan, B. K., & Caddell, J. M. (1998). Combat-related posttraumatic stress disorder: Prevalence, risk factors, and comorbidity. In P. A. Saigh, J. D. Bremner, et al. (Eds.), *Posttraumatic stress disorder: A comprehensive text.* Boston: Allyn & Bacon.

Schlesinger, M., Dorwart, R., Hoover, C., & Epstein, S. (1997). Competition, ownership, and access to hospital services: Evidence from psychiatric hospitals. *Medical Care, 35*(9), 974–992.

Schlundt, O. G., & Johnson, W. G. (1990). *Eating disorders: Assessment and treatment.* Boston: Allyn & Bacon.

Schmidt, L.G., Dufeu, P., Kuhn, S., Smolka, M., & Rommelspacher, H. (2000). Transition to alcohol dependence: Clinical and neurobiological considerations. *Comprehen. Psychiat., 41*(2, Suppl 1), 90–94.

Schmidt, N. B. (1999). Panic disorder: Cognitive behavioral and pharmacological treatment strategies. *J. Clin. Psychol. Med. Settings 6*(1), 89–111.

Schmidt, U., Tiller, J., & Treasure, J. (1993). Psychosocial factors in the origins of bulimia nervosa. *Inter. Rev. Psychiat., 5*(1), 51–59.

Schmidt, U., Tiller, J., Treasure, J. (1993). Self-treatment of bulimia nervosa: A pilot study. *Inter. J. Eat. Disorders, 13*(3), 273–277.

Schmidtke, A., & Häfner, H. (1988). The *Werther* effect after television films: New evidence for an old hypothesis. *Psychol. Med., 18,* 665–676.

Schmidtke, A., Weinacker, B., Apter, A., Batt, A., Berman, A., Bille-Brahe, U., Botsis, A., DeLeo, D., Doneux, A., Goldney, R., Grad, O., Haring, C., Hawton, K., Hjelmeland, H., Kelleher, M., Kerkhof, A., Leenaars, A., Lonnqvist, J., Michel, K., Ostamo, A., Salander-Renberg, E., Sayil, I., Takahashi, Y., Van Heeringen, C., Varnik, A., & Wasserman, D. (1999). Suicide rates in the world: Update. *Arch. Suic. Res., 5,* 81–89.

Schmidtke, A., Weinacker, B., Stack, S., & Lester, D. (1999). The impact of the reunification of Germany on the suicide rate. *Arch. Suic. Res., 5*(3), 233–239.

Schneider, K. J. (1998). Existential processes. In L. S. Greenberg, J. C. Watson, et al. (Eds.), *Handbook of experiential psychotherapy.* New York: Guilford.

Schneider, L. S. (1996). Overview of generalized anxiety disorder in the elderly. *J. Clin. Psychiat., 57*(Suppl. 7), 34–45.

Schneider, R. H., Alexander, C. N., & Wallace, R. K. (1992). In search of an optimal behavioral treatment for hypertension: A review and focus on transcendental meditation. In E. H. Johnson, W. D. Gentry, & S. Julius (Eds.), *Personality, elevated blood pressure, and essential hypertension.* Washington, DC: Hemisphere.

Schneiderman, L., & Baum, A. (1992). Acute and chronic stress and the immune system. In N. Schneiderman, P. McCabe, & A. Baum (Eds.), *Perspectives in behavioral medicine: Stress and disease processes.* Hillsdale, NJ: Erlbaum.

Schneiderman, N. (1999). Behavioral medicine and the management of HIV/AIDS. *Inter. J. Behav. Med., 6*(1), 3–12.

Schneidman, E. S. (1998). Perspectives on suicidology: Further reflections on suicide and psychache. *Suic. Life-Threat. Behav., 28*(3), 245–250.

Schnurr, P. P., & Spiro, A., III. (1999). Combat disorder, posttraumatic stress disorder symptoms, and health behaviors as predictors of self-reported physical health in older veterans. *J. Nerv. Ment. Dis., 187*(6), 353–359.

Schnurr, P. P., & Vielhauer, M. J. (1999). Personality as a risk factor for PTSD. In R. Yehuda et al. (Eds.), *Risk factors for posttraumatic stress disorder.* Washington, DC: American Psychiatric Press.

Schnyder, U., Valach, L., Bichsel, K., & Michel, K. (1999). Attempted suicide: Do we understand the patients' reasons? *Gen. Hosp. Psychiat., 21*(1), 62–69.

Scholing, A., & Emmelkamp, P. M. G. (1996). Treatment of generalized social phobia: Results at long-term follow-up. *Behav. Res. Ther., 34*(5/6), 447–452.

Scholing, A., & Emmelkamp, P. M. (1999). Prediction of treatment outcome in social phobia: A cross-validation. *Behav. Res. Ther., 37*(7), 659–670.

Schooler, J. W. (1994). Seeking the core: The issues and evidence surrounding recovered accounts of sexual trauma. *Consciousness Cog., 3,* 452–269.

Schooler, J. W. (1996). Seeking the core: The issues and evidence surrounding recovered accounts of sexual trauma. In K. Pezdek & W. P. Banks (Eds.), *The recovered memory/false memory debate.* San Diego: Academic Press.

Schorr, E. C., & Arnason, B. G. W. (1999). Interactions between the sympathetic nervous system and the immune system. *Brain Behav. Immun., 13*(4), 271–278.

Schott, R. L. (1999). Managers and mental health: Mental illness and the workplace. *Public Pers. Manag., 28*(2), 161–183.

Schou, M. (1997). Forty years of lithium treatment. *Arch. Gen. Psychiat., 54,* 9–13..

Schover, L. R., & LoPiccolo, J. (1982). Treatment effectiveness for dysfunctions of sexual desires. *J. Sex Marital Ther., 8*(3), 179–197.

Schrader, E. (2000). Equivalence of St. John's wort extract (Ze 117) and fluoxetine: A randomized, controlled study in mild-moderate depression. *Inter. Clin. Psychopharmacology, 15*(2), 61–68.

Schreiber, F. R. (1973). *Sybil.* Chicago: Regnery.

Schuckit, M. (1999). Cited in C. Ginther, Schuckit addresses state-of-the-art addiction treatments. *Psychiatr. Times, XVI*(4).

Schuckit, M. (2000). *Drug and alcohol abuse: A clinical guide to diagnosis and treatment* (5th ed.). New York: Kluwer Academic/Plenum Publishers.

Schuldberg, D., French, C., Stone, B. L., & Heberle, J. (1988). Creativity and schizotypal traits: Creativity test scores and perceptual aberration, magical ideation, and impulsive nonconformity. *J. Nerv. Ment. Dis., 176*(11), 648–657.

Schultz, R., & Heckhausen, J. (1996). A life span model of successful aging. *Amer. Psychologist, 51*(7), 702–714.

Schultz, S. C. (2000). New antipsychotic medications: More than old wine and new bottles. *Bull. Menninger Clin., 64*(1), 60–75.

Schultz, S. K., Miller, D. D., Arndt, S., Ziebell, S., Gupta, S., & Andreasen, N. (1995). Withdrawal-emergent dyskinesia in patients with schizophrenia during antipsychotic discontinuation. *Biol. Psychiat., 38,* 713–719.

Schulz, P. M., et al. (1986). Diagnoses of the relatives of schizotypal outpatients. *J. Nerv. Ment. Dis., 174*(8), 457–463.

Schwalb, M. (1999). Interviewed in M. S. Baum, Autism: Locked in a solitary world. *HealthState, 17*(2), 18–22.

Schwartz, G. (1977). College students as contingency managers for adolescents in a program to develop reading skills. *J. Appl. Behav. Anal., 10,* 645–655.

Schwartz, G. E. (1977). Psychosomatic disorders and biofeedback: A psychobiological model of disregulation. In J. D. Maser & M. E. P. Seligman (Eds.), *Psychopathology: Experimental models.* San Francisco: W. H. Freeman.

Schwartz, G. E. (1982). Testing the biopsychosocial model: The ultimate challenge facing behavioral medicine? *J. Cons. Clin. Psychol., 50*(6), 1040–1053.

Schwartz, J. M., Stoessel, P. W., Baxter, L. R., Jr., Martin, K. M., & Phelps, M. E. (1996). Systematic changes in cerebral glucose metabolic rate after successful behavior modification treatment of obsessive-compulsive disorder. *Arch. Gen. Psychiat., 53,* 109–113.

Schwartz, S. (1993). *Classic studies in abnormal psychology.* Mountain View, CA: Mayfield Publishing.

Schwartz, S. (1999). Biological approaches to psychiatric disorders. In A. V. Horwitz & T. L. Scheid (Eds.), *A handbook for the study of mental health: Social contexts, theories, and systems.* Cambridge, England: Cambridge University Press.

Schwartz, S., & Johnson, J. J. (1985). *Psychopathology of childhood.* New York: PergamonPress.

Schwarz, K., Harding, R., Harrington, D., & Farr, B. (1993). Hospital management of a patient with intractable factitious disorder. *Psychosomatics, 34*(3), 265–267.

Schwarz, N. (1999). Self-reports: How the questions shape the answers. *Amer. Psychologist, 54*(2), 93–105.

Schweizer, E. S., & Rickels, K. (1997). Strategies for treatment of generalized anxiety in the primary care setting. *J. Clin. Psychiat., 58*(Suppl. 3), 27–31.

Scola, P. S. (1991). Classification and social status. In J. L. Matson & J. A. Mulick (Eds.), *Handbook of mental retardation.* New York: Pergamon Press.

Scott, A. (1995). "Reclaimed once more by the realities of life": Hysteria and the location of memory. *Brit. J. Psychother., 11*(3), 398–405.

Scott, J. (1990, Jul. 25). Vertigo, not madness, may have tormented Van Gogh. *Los Angeles Times,* p. A14.

Scott, J. (1995). Psychotherapy for bipolar disorder. *Brit. J. Psychiat., 167*(5), 581–588.

Scott, J., & Wright, J. H. (1997). Cognitive therapy for chronic and severe mental disorders. In L. J. Dickstein, M. B. Riba, & J. M. Oldham (Eds.), *Review of psychiatry* (Vol. 16). Washington, DC: American Psychiatric Press.

Scott, J. E., & Dixon, L. B. (1995). Assertive community treatment and case management for schizophrenia. *Schizo. Bull., 21*(4), 657–668.

Scott, J. E., & Dixon, L. B. (1995). Psychological interventions for schizophrenia. *Schizo. Bull., 21*(4), 621–630.

Scott, R. D., Fagin, L., & Winter, D. (1993). The importance of the role of the patient in the outcome of schizophrenia. *Brit. J. Psychiat., 163,* 62–68.

Scourfield, J., Soldan, J., Gray, J., Houlihan, G., & Harper, P. S. (1997). Huntington's disease: Psychiatric practice in molecular genetic prediction and diagnosis. *Brit. J. Psychiat., 170,* 146–149.

Seale, C., & Addington-Hall, J. (1995a). Euthanasia: The role of good care. *Soc. Sci. Med., 40*(5), 581–587.

Seale, C., & Addington-Hall, J. (1995b). Dying at the best time. *Soc. Sci. Med., 40*(5), 589–595.

Searleman, A., & Herrmann, D. (1994). *Memory from a broader perspective.* New York: McGraw-Hall.

Sechrest, L., McKnight, P., & McKnight, K. (1996). Calibration of measures for psychotherapy outcome studies. *Amer. Psychologist, 51*(10), 1065–1071.

Sederer, L. I. (1992). Brief hospitalization. In A. Tasman & M. B. Riba (Eds.), *Review of psychiatry* (Vol. 11). Washington, DC: American Psychiatric Press.

Sedvall, G. (1990). Monoamines and schizophrenia. International Symposium: Development of a new antipsychotic: Remoxipride. *Acta Psychiatr. Scandin., 82*(Suppl. 358), 7–13.

Sedvall, G. (1990). PET imaging of dopamine receptors in human basal ganglia: Relevance to mental illness. *Trends Neurosci., 13*(7), 302–308.

Seeman, M. (1982). Gender differences in schizophrenia. *Canad. J. Psychiat., 27,* 108–111.

Seeman, P., Lee, T., Chau Wong, M., & Wong, K. (1976). Antipsychotic drug doses and neuroleptic/dopamine receptors. *Nature, 281*(5582), 717–718.

Segal, Z. V., Gemar, M., & Williams, S. (1999). Differential cognitive response to a mood challenge following successful cognitive therapy or pharmacotherapy for unipolar depression. *J. Abnorm. Psychol., 108*(1), 3–10.

Segraves, K. B., & Segraves, R. T. (1991). Hypoactive sexual desire disorder: Prevalence and comorbidity in 906 subjects. *J. Sex Marital Ther., 17,* 55–58.

Segraves, R. T. (1993). Treatment-emergent sexual dysfunction in affective disorder: A review and management strategies. *J. Clin. Psychiat., Monogr. Ser., 11,* 7–63.

Segraves, R. T. (1995). Psychopharmacological influences on human sexual behavior. In J. M. Oldham & M. B. Riba (Eds.), *American Psychiatric Press review of psychiatry* (Vol. 14). Washington, DC: American Psychiatric Press.

Segraves, R. T. (1998). Antidepressant-induced sexual dysfunction. *J. Clin. Psychiat., 59*(Suppl. 4), 48–54.

Segrin, C. (2000). Social skills deficits associated with depression. *Clin. Psychol. Rev., 20*(3), 379–403.

Seidman, L. J. (1990). The neuropsychology of schizophrenia: A neurodevelopmental and case study approach. *J. Neuropsych. Clin. Neurosci., 2*(3), 301–312.

Seligman, M. E. P. (1971). Phobias and preparedness. *Behav. Ther., 2,* 307–320.

Seligman, M. E. P. (1975). *Helplessness.* San Francisco: W. H. Freeman.

Seligman, M. E. P. (1992). Wednesday's children. *Psychol. Today, 25*(1), 61.

Seligman, M. E. P. (1995). The effectiveness of psychotherapy. The *Consumer Reports* study. *Amer. Psychologist, 50*(12), 965–974.

Seligman, M. E. P., Castellon, C., Cacciola, J., Schulman, P., et al. (1988). Explanatory style change during cognitive therapy for unipolar depression. *J. Abnorm. Psychol., 97*(1), 13–18.

Selkoe, D. J. (1991). Amyloid protein and Alzheimer's disease. *Scientif. Amer., 265,* 68–78.

Selkoe, D. J. (1992). Alzheimer's disease: New insights into an emerging epidemic. *J. Geriat. Psychiat., 25*(2), 211–227.

Selkoe, D. J. (1998). The cell biology of beta-amyloid precursor protein and presenilin in

Alzheimer's disease. *Trends Cell Biol., 8*(11), 447–453.

Selkoe, D. J. (1999). Translating cell biology into therapeutic advances in Alzheimer's disease. *Nature, 399*(Suppl. 6738), A23–31.

Selkoe, D. J. (2000). The origins of Alzheimer disease: A is for amyloid. *JAMA, 283*(12), 1615–1617.

Selkoe, D. J., Yamazaki, T., Citron, M., Podlisny, M. B., Koo, E. H., Teplow, D. B., & Haass, C. (1996). The role of APP processing and trafficking pathways in the formation of amyloid B-protein. In R. J. Wurtman, S. Corkin, J. H. Growdon, & R. M. Nitsch (Eds.), *The neurobiology of Alzheimer's disease.* New York: New York Academy of Sciences.

Selling, L. S. (1940). *Men against madness.* New York: Greenberg.

Selye, H. (1974). *Stress without distress.* Philadelphia: Lippincott.

Selye, H. (1976). *Stress in health and disease.* Woburn, MA: Butterworth.

Semans, J. H. (1956). Premature ejaculation: A new approach. *South. Med. J., 49,* 353–357.

Seppa, N. (1996). Bullies spend less time with adults. *APA Monitor, 27*(10), 41.

Seppa, N. (1996). Helping people identify and cope with anxieties. *APA Monitor, 27*(6), 24.

Seppa, N. (1996). Psychologist testifies on handling disasters. *APA Monitor, 27*(11), 38.

Sereno, A. B., & Holzman, P. S. (1995). Antisaccades and smooth pursuit eye movements in schizophrenia. *Biol. Psychiat. 37*(6), 394–401.

Seto, M. C., Khattar, N. A., Lalumière, & Quinsey, V. L. (1997). Deception and sexual strategy in psychopathy. *Pers. Individ. Diff., 22*(3), 301–307.

Shadlen, M. F., & Larson, E. B. (1999). What's new in Alzheimer's disease treatment? Reasons for optimism about future pharmacologic options. *Postgrad. Med. J., 105*(1), 109–118.

Shaffer, D., & Craft, L. (1999). Methods of adolescent suicide prevention. *J. Clin. Psychiat., 60*(Suppl. 2), 70–74.

Shafii, M., Carrigan, S., Whittinghill, J. R., & Derrick, A. (1985). Psychological autopsy of completed suicide in children and adolescents. *Amer. J. Psychiat., 142*(9), 1061–1064.

Shah, R., & Waller, G. (2000). Parental style and vulnerability to depression: The role of core beliefs. *J. Nerv. Ment. Dis., 188*(1), 19–25.

Shain, M. (1994). Alternatives to drug testing: Employee assistance and health promotion programs. In S. Macdonald & P. Roman (Eds.), *Research advances in alcohol and drug problems: Vol. 11. Drug testing in the workplace.* New York: Plenum Press.

Shalev, A. Y. (1999). Psychophysiological and expression of risk factors for PTSD. In R. Yehuda (Ed.), *Risk factors for posttraumatic stress disorder.* Washington, DC: American Psychiatric Press.

Shalev, A. Y., Bonne, O., & Eth, S. (1996). Treatment of posttraumatic stress disorder: A review. *Psychosom. Med., 58,* 165–182.

Shalev, A. Y., Peri, T., Canetti, L., & Schreiber, S. (1996). Predictors of PTSD in injured trauma survivors: A prospective study. *Amer. J. Psychiat., 153,* 219–225.

Shaner, A., Khalsa, M., Roberts, L., Wilkins, J., Anglin, D., & Hsieh, S. (1993). Unrecognized cocaine use among schizophrenic patients. *Amer. J. Psychiat., 150*(5), 758–762.

Shapiro, D. A. (1982). Overview: Clinical and physiological comparison of meditation with other self-control strategies. *Amer. J. Psychiat., 139*(3), 267–274.

Shapiro, L. (1996, January 22). To your health? *Newsweek,* pp. 52–53.

Sharp, C. W., & Freeman, C. P. L. (1993). The medical complications of anorexia nervosa. *Brit. J. Psychiat., 162,* 452–462.

Shaw, B. F. (1976). A systematic investigation of two psychological treatments of depression. *Dissertation Abstr. Inter., 36*(8-B), 4179–4180.

Shaw, B. F. (1977). Comparison of cognitive therapy and behavior therapy in the treatment of depression. *J. Clin. Psychol., 45,* 543–551.

Shaw, B. F., & Segal, Z. V. (1999). Efficacy, indications, and mechanisms of action of cognitive therapy of depression. In D. S. Janowsky et al. (Eds.), *Psychotherapy indications and outcomes.* Washington, DC: American Psychiatric Press.

Shay, J., & Munroe, J. (1999). Group and milieu therapy for veterans with complex posttraumatic stress disorder. In P. A. Saigh, J. D. Bremner, et al. (Eds.), *Posttraumatic stress disorder: A comprehensive text.* Boston: Allyn & Bacon.

Shea, S. (1990). Contemporary psychiatric interviewing: Integration of DSM-III-R, psychodynamic concerns and mental status. In G. Goldstein & M. Hersen (Eds.), *Handbook of psychological assessment* (2nd ed.). New York: Pergamon Press.

Shea, T., Elkin, L., Imber, S., Sotsky, S., Watkins, J., Collins, J., et al. (1992). Course of depressive symptoms over follow-up: Findings from the National Institute of Mental Health treatment of depression collaborative research program. *Arch. Gen. Psychiat., 49,* 782–787.

Shear, M. K., & Beidel, D. C. (1998). Psychotherapy in the overall management strategy for social anxiety disorder. *J. Clin Psychiat., 59*(Suppl. 17), 39–46.

Shear, M. K., Brown, T. A., Barlow, D. H., Money, R., Sholomskas, D. E., Woods, S. W., Gorman, J. M., & Papp, L. A. (1997). Multicenter collaborative panic disorder severity scale. *Amer. J. Psychiat., 154,* 1571–1575.

Shedler, J., & Block, J. (1990). Adolescent drug use and psychological health: A longitudinal inquiry. *Amer. Psychologist, 45*(5), 612–630.

Shedler, J., Mayman, M., & Manis, M. (1993). The illusion of mental health. *Amer. Psychologist, 48*(11), 1117–1131.

Shellenbarger, S. (1998, September 28). Workers are taking more "mental health" days off. *Star Tribune,* p. 10D.

Shelton, R. C. (1999). Mood-stabilizing drugs in depression. *J. Clin. Psychiat., 60*(Suppl. 5), 37–40.

Shelton, R. C., Davidson, J., Yonkers, K. A., Koran, L., et al. (1997). The undertreatment of dysthymia. *J. Clin. Psychiat., 58*(2), 59–65.

Shemberg, K. M., & Doherty, M. E. (1999). Is diagnostic judgment influenced by a bias to see pathology? *J. Clin Psychol., 55*(4), 513–518.

Sher, K. J., & Trull, T. J. (1994). Personality and disinhibitry psychopathology: Alcoholism and antisocial personality disorder. *J. Abnorm. Psychol., 103*(1), 92–102.

Sheras, P., & Worchel, S. (1979). *Clinical psychology: A social psychological approach.* New York: Van Nostrand.

Sherbourne, C. D., Hays, R. D., & Wells, K. B. (1995). Personal and psychosocial risk factors for physical and mental health outcomes and course of depression among depressed patients. *J. Cons. Clin. Psychol., 63*(3), 345–355.

Sherbourne, C. D., Jackson, C. A., Meredith, L. S., Camp, P., & Wells, K. B. (1996). Prevalence of comorbid anxiety disorders in primary care outpatients. *Arch. Fam. Med., 5*(1), 27–34.

Sherlock, R. (1933). Suicide and public policy: A critique of the "new consensus." *J. Bioethics, 4,* 58–70.

Sherman, C. (1993). Behind closed doors: Therapist-client sex. *Psychol. Today, 26*(3), 64–72.

Sherman, D. K., McGue, M. K., & Iacono, W. G. (1997). Twin concordance for attention deficit hyperactivity disorder: A comparison of teachers' and mothers' reports. *Amer. J. Psychiat., 154*(4), 532–535.

Sherman, R., & Thompson, R. (1990). *Bulimia: A guide for family and friends.* Lexington, MA: Lexington Books.

Shi, J. M., Benowitz, N., Denaro, C., & Sheiner, L. (1993). Pharmacokinetic-pharmacodynamic modeling of caffeine: Tolerance to pressor effects. *Clin. Pharmacol. Ther., 53*(1), 6–15.

Shi, J. M., O'Connor, P. G., Constantino, J. A., et al. (1993). Three methods of ambulatory opiate detoxification. In L. S. Harris (Ed.), *Preliminary results of a randomized clinical trial* (NIDA Res. Monograph Series No. 132, NIH Publication No. 93–3505). Washington, DC: U. S. Government Printing Office.

Shipherd, J. C., & Beck, J. G. (1999). The effects of suppressing trauma-related thoughts on women with rape-related posttraumatic stress disorder. *Behav. Res. Ther., 37*(2), 99–112.

Shisslak, C. M., Crago, M., McKnight, K. M., Estes, L. S., Gray, G., & Parnaby, O. G. (1998). Potential risk factors associated with weight control behaviors in elementary and middle school girls. *J. Psychosom. Res., 44*(3/4), 301–313.

Shnayerson, M. (1996, July). Natural opponents. *Vanity Fair,* pp. 98–105.

Shneidman, E. S. (1963). Orientations toward death: Subintentioned death and indirect suicide. In R. W. White (Ed.), *The study of lives.* New York: Atherton.

Shneidman, E. S. (1973). Suicide notes reconsidered. *Psychiatry, 36,* 379–394.

Shneidman, E. S. (1979). An overview: Personality, motivation, and behavior theories. In L. D. Hankoff & B. Einsidler (Eds.), *Suicide: Theory and clinical aspects.* Littleton, MA: PSG Publishing.

Shneidman, E. S. (1981). Suicide. *Suic. Life-Threat. Behav., 11*(4), 198–220.

Shneidman, E. S. (1985). *Definition of suicide.* New York: Wiley.

Shneidman, E. S. (1987, March). At the point of no return. *Psychol. Today.*

Shneidman, E. S. (1991). *The key to suicide.* In personal correspondence.

Shneidman, E. S. (1993). *Suicide as psychache: A clinical approach to self-destructive behavior.* Northvale, NJ: Jason Aronson.

Shneidman, E. S. (1999). Perturbation and lethality: A psychological approach to assessment and intervention. In D. G. Jacobs et al. (Eds.). *The Harvard Medical School guide to suicide assessment and intervention.* San Francisco: Jossey-Bass.

Shneidman, E. S., & Farberow, N. (1968). The Suicide Prevention Center of Los Angeles. In H. L. P. Resnick (Ed.), *Suicidal behaviors: Diagnosis and management.* Boston: Little, Brown.

Shotton, M. A. (1998). *Caught in the net: How to recognize the signs of Internet addiction and a winning strategy for recovery.* New York: Wiley.

Shrivastava, R. K., Shrivastava, S., Overweg, N., & Schmitt, M. (1995). Amantadine in the treatment of sexual dysfunction associated with selective serotonin reuptake inhibitors. *J. Clin. Psychopharmacol., 15*(1), 83–84.

Shtasel, D. L., Gur, R. E., Gallacher, F., Heimburg, C., et al. (1992). Gender differences in the clinical expression of schizophrenia. *Schizo. Res., 7*(3), 225–231.

Shucksmith, J., Glendinning, A., & Hendry, L. (1997). Adolescent drinking behaviour and the role of family life: A Scottish perspective. *J. Adolescence, 20,* 85–101.

Shuller, D. Y., & McNamara, J. R. (1980). The use of information derived from norms and from a credible source to counter expectancy effects in behavioral assessment. *Behav. Assess., 2,* 183–196.

Shultis, C. L. (1999). Music therapy for inpatient psychiatric care in the 1990s. *Psychiatr. Times, XVI*(2).

Siegel, J. M. (1990). Stressful life events and use of physician services among the elderly: The moderating role of pet ownership. *J. Pers. Soc. Psychol., 58*(6), 1081–1086.

Siegel, R. K. (1990). In J. Sherlock, Getting high—Animals do it, too. *USA Today,* p. 1A.

Siegert, R. J. (1999). Some thoughts about reasoning in clinical neuropsychology. *Behav. Change, 16*(1), 37–48.

Siever, L. J. (1992). Schizophrenia spectrum personality disorders. In A. Tasman & M. B. Riba (Eds.), *American Psychiatric Press review of psychiatry* (Vol. 11). Washington, DC: American Psychiatric Press.

Siever, L. J., & Davis, K. L. (1991). A psychobiological perspective on the personality disorders. *Amer. J. Psychiat., 148*(12), 1647–1658.

Siever, L. J., Davis, K. L., & Gorman, L. K. (1991). Pathogenesis of mood disorders. In K. Davis, H. Klar, & J. T. Coyle (Eds.), *Foundations of psychiatry.* Philadelphia: Saunders.

Sifneos, P. E. (1987). *Short term dynamic psychotherapy evaluation and technique* (2nd ed.). New York: Plenum Press.

Sifneos, P. E. (1992). *Short-term anxiety-provoking psychotherapy: A treatment manual.* New York: Basic Books.

Sigal, J. J., Paris, J., Kardos, M., Zimmerman, G., & Buonvino, M. (1999). Evaluation of some criteria used to select patients for brief psychodynamic therapy. *Psychotherapy and Psychosomatics, 68*(4), 193–198.

Sigerist, H. E. (1943). *Civilization and disease.* Ithaca, NY: Cornell University Press.

Sigmon, S. T. (1995). Ethical practices and beliefs of psychopathology researchers. *Ethics Behav., 5*(4), 295–309.

Silberman, E. K. (1999). Pharmacotherapy. In M. Hersen & A. S. Bellack (Eds.), *Handbook of comparative interventions for adult disorders* (2nd ed.). New York: Wiley.

Silbersweig, D. A., Stern, E., Frith, C., Cahill, C., et al. (1995). A functional neuroanatomy of hallucinations in schizophrenia. *Nature, 378*(6553), 176–179.

Silva, J. A., Derecho, D. V., Leong, G. B., & Ferrari, M.M. (2000). Stalking behavior in delusional jealousy. *J. Forensic Sci., 45*(1), 77–82.

Silver, E. (1995). Punishment or treatment? Comparing the lengths of confinement of successful and unsuccessful insanity defendants. *Law Human Behav., 19*(4), 375–388.

Silver, H., Geraisy, N., & Schwartz, M. (1995). No difference in the effect of biperiden and amantadine on parkinsonian- and tardive dyskinesia-type involuntary movements: A double-blind crossover, placebo-controlled study in medicated chronic schizophrenic patients. *J. Clin. Psychiat., 56*(4), 167–170.

Silverman, K., Evans, S. M., Strain, E. C., & Griffiths, R. R. (1992). Withdrawal syndrome after the double-blind cessation of caffeine consumption. *N. Engl. J. Med., 327*(16), 1109–1114.

Silverman, M. M., Meyer, P. M., Sloane, F., Raffel, M., & Pratt, D. (1997). The Big Ten Student Suicide Study: A 10-year study of suicides on midwestern university campuses. *Suic. Life-Threat. Behav., 27*(3), 285–303.

Silverman, P. (1992). An introduction to self-help groups. In B. J. White & E. J. Madara (Eds.), *The self-help sourcebook: Finding & forming mutual aid self-help groups.* Denville, NJ: St. Clares-Riverside Medical Center.

Silverman, W. K., & Ginsburg, G. S. (1998). Anxiety disorders. In T. H. Ollendick, M. Hersen, et al. (Eds.), *Handbook of child psychopathology* (3rd ed.). New York: Plenum Press.

Silverman, W. K., La Greca, A. M., & Wasserstein, S. (1995). What do children worry about? Worries and their relation to anxiety. *Child Dev., 66,* 671–686.

Silverstein, B. (1999). Gender differences in the prevalence of clinical depression: The role played by depression associated with somatic symptoms. *Amer. J. Psychiat., 156*(3), 480–482.

Silverstone, P. H. (1990). Low self-esteem in eating disordered patients in the absence of depression. *Psychol. Rep., 67*(1), 276–278.

Silverstone, T., & Hunt, N. (1992). Symptoms and assessment of mania. In E. S. Paykel (Ed.), *Handbook of affective disorders.* New York: Guilford.

Simeon, J. G., Ferguson, H. B., Knott, V., Roberts, N., et al (1992). Clinical, cognitive, and neurophysiological effects of alprazolam in children and adolescents with overanxious and avoidant disorders. Special section: New developments in pediatric psychopharmacology. *J. Amer. Acad. Child Adol. Psychiat., 31*(1), 29–33.

Simeonsson, N., Lorimer, M., Shelley, B., & Sturtz, J. L. (1995). Asthma: New information for the early interventionist. *Topics Early Childhood Spec. Ed., 15*(1), 32–43.

Simmon (1990). Media and market study. In skin deep: Our national obsession with looks. *Psychol. Today, 26*(3), 96.

Simon, G. E. (1998). Management of somatoform and factitious disorders. In P. E. Nathan, J. M. Gorman, et al. (Eds.), *A guide to treatments that work.* New York: Oxford University Press.

Simon, G. E., & Gureje, O. (1999). Stability of somatization disorder and somatization symptoms among primary care patients. *Arch. Gen. Psychiat., 56*(1), 90–95.

Simon, G. E., & Katzelnick, D. J. (1997). Depression, use of medical services and cost-offset effects. *J. Psychosom. Res., 42*(4), 333–344.

Simon, N. (2000). Autism's home in the brain. *Neurology, 54*(1), 269.

Simonsick, E. M., Wallace, R. B., Blazer, D. G., & Berkman, L. F. (1995). Depressive symptomatology and hypertension-associated morbidity and mortality in older adults. *Psychosom. Med., 57*(5), 427–435.

Simpson, C. J., Hyde, C. E., & Faragher, E. B. (1989). The chronically mentally ill in community facilities: A study of quality of life. *Brit. J. Psychiat., 154,* 77–82.

Simpson, R. L., & Sasso, G. M. (1992). Full inclusion of students with autism in general education settings: Values versus science. *Focus Autistic Behav., 7*(3), 1–13.

Simpson, R. O., & Halpin, G. (1986). Agreement between parents and teachers in using the Revised Behavior Problem Checklist to identify deviant behavior in children. *Behav. Disorders, 12*(1), 54–58.

Simpson, S. G. (1996, January 17). Cited in W. Leary, As fellow traveler of other illness, depression often goes in disguise. *New York Times,*. p. C9.

Simpson, S. G., & Jamison, K. R. (1999). The risk of suicide in patients with bipolar disorders. *J. Clin. Psychiat., 60*(Suppl. 2), 53–56.

Sines, L. K. (1959). The relative contribution of four kinds of data to accuracy in personality assessment. *J. Cons. Psychol., 23,* 483–495..

Siomopoulos, V. (1988). Narcissistic personality disorder: Clinical features. *Amer. J. Psychother., 42*(2), 240–253.

Sirey, J. A., Meyers, B. S., Bruce, M. L., Alexopoulos, G. S., Perlick, D. A., & Raue, P. (1999). Predictors of antidepressant prescription and early use among depressed outpatients. *Amer. J. Psychiat., 156*(5), 690–696.

Sizemore, C. C., & Huber, R. J. (1988). The twenty-two faces of Eve. *Individ. Psychol. J. Adlerian Theory Res. Prac., 44*(1), 53–62.

Skau, K., & Mouridsen, S. (1995). Munchausen syndrome by proxy: A review. *Acta Paediatr., 84,* 977–982.

Skodol, A. E., Stout, R. L., McGlashan, T. H., Grilo, C. M., Gunderson, J. G., Shea, M. T., Morey, L. C., Zanarini, M. C., Dyck, I. R., & Oldham, J. M. (1999). Co-occurrence of mood and personality disorders: A report from the Collaborative Longitudinal Personality Disorders Study (CLPS). *Depress. Anx., 10*(4), 175–182.

Slade, P. (1995). Prospects for prevention. In G. Szmukler, C. Dare, & J. Treasure (Eds.), *Handbook of eating disorders: Theory, treatment and research.* Chichester, England: Wiley.

Slater, E., & Shields, J. (1969). Genetical aspects of anxiety. Special Publication No. 3. M. H. Lader (Ed.). *Brit. J. Psychiat.,* pp. 62–71.

Sleek, S. (1995). Online therapy services raise ethical questions. *APA Monitor, 26*(11), 9.

Sleek, S. (1995). Rallying the troops inside our bodies. *APA Monitor, 26*(12), 1, 24.

Sleek, S. (1996). AIDS therapy: Patchwork of pain, hope. *APA Monitor, 27*(6), 1, 31.

Sleek, S. (1996). Practitioners will eventually have to meet steeper criteria to practice geropsychology, experts predict. *APA Monitor, 27*(10), 17.

Sleek, S. (1997). Disaster victims need most long-term care, report says. *APA Monitor, 28*(10), 18.

Sleek, S. (1997). Novel approach offers hope for treating severe disorders. *APA Monitor, 28*(12), 23.

Sleek, S. (1997). Treating people who live life on the borderline. *APA Monitory, 28*(7), 20–21.

Slife, B. D., & Weaver, C. A., III. (1992). Depression, cognitive skill, and metacognitive skill in problem solving. *Cog. Emot., 6*(1), 1–22.

Sloan, E. P., Natarajan, M., Baker, B., Dorian, P., Mironov, D., Barr, A., Newman, D. M., & Shapiro, C. M. (1999). Nocturnal and daytime panic attacks—Comparison of sleep architecture, heart rate variability, and response to sodium lactate challenge. *Biol. Psychiat., 45*(10), 1313–1320.

Slome, L. R., Mitchell, T. F., Charlebois, E., Benevedes, J. M., & Abrams, D. I. (1997). Physician-assisted suicide and patients with human immunodeficiency virus disease. *N. Engl. J. Med., 336*(6), 417–421.

Slovenko, R. (1992). Is diminished capacity really dead? *Psychiat. Ann., 22*(11), 566–570.

Slovenko, R. (1995). *Psychiatry and criminal culpability.* New York: Wiley-Interscience Publications.

Slutske, W. S., Heath, A. C., Dinwiddie, S. H., Madden, P. A. F., et al. (1997). Modeling genetic and environmental influences in the etiology of conduct disorder: A study of 2,682 adult twin pairs. *J. Abnorm. Psychol., 106*(2), 266–279.

Small, G. W., Mazziotta, J. C., Collins, M. T., Baxter, W. R., et al. (1995). Apolipoprotein E type 4 allele and cerebral glucose metabolism in relatives at risk for familial Alzheimer disease. *JAMA, 273*(12), 942–947.

Small, J. A., Kemper, S., & Lyon, K. (1997). Sentence comprehension in Alzheimer's disease: Effects of grammatical complexity, speech rate, and repetition. *Psychol. Aging, 12*(1), 3–11.

Small, M. A. (1992). The legal context of mentally disordered sex offender (MDSO) treatment programs. *Criminal Justice Behav., 19*(2), 127–142.

Small, S. A., Perera, G. M., DeLaPaz, R., Mayeus, R., & Stern, Y. (1999). Differential regional dysfunction of the hippocampal formation among elderly with memory decline and Alzheimer's disease. *Ann. Neurol., 45*(4), 466–472.

Small, S. A., et al. (1999, January 17). *Diagnosing early stage Alzheimer's disease.* Paper presented at American Academy of Neurology 51st Annual Meeting, Toronto.

Smart, R. G., & Mann, R. E. (2000). The impact of programs for high-risk drinkers on population levels of alcohol problems. *Addiction, 95*(1), 37–52.

Smith, A. L., & Weissman, M. M. (1992). Epidemiology. In E. S. Paykel (Ed.), *Handbook of affective disorders.* New York: Guilford.

Smith, B. L. (1998). The impossible takes a little longer: The role of theory in teaching psychological assessment. In L. Handler, M. J. Hilsenroth, et al. (Eds.), *Teaching and learning personality assessment.* The LEA series in personality and clinical psychology. Mahwah, NJ: Erlbaum.

Smith, E., North, C., & Spitznagel, E. (1993). Alcohol, drugs, and psychiatric comorbidity among homeless women: An epidemiologic study. *J. Clin. Psychiat., 54*(3), 82–87.

Smith, G. R., Rost, K., & Kashner, T. M. (1995). A trial of the effect of a standardized psychiatric consultation on health outcomes and costs in somatizing patients. *Arch. Gen. Psychiat., 52*(3), 238–243.

Smith, K. (1991). Comments on "Teen suicide and changing cause-of-death certification, 1953–1987." *Suic. Life-Threat. Behav., 21*(3), 260–262.

Smith, K., & Killam, P. (1994). Munchausen syndrome by proxy. *MCN, 19,* 214–221.

Smith, K. A., Fairburn, C. G., & Cowen, P. J. (1999). Symptomatic repalse in bulimia nervosa following acute tryptophan depletion. *Arch. Gen. Psychiat., 56*(2), 171–176.

Smith, M. J., Brebion, G., Banquet, J. P., & Cohen, L. (1995). Retardation of mentation in depressives: Posner's covert orientation of visual attention test. *J. Affect. Disorders, 35,* 107–115.

Smith, M. L., & Glass, G. V. (1977). Meta-analysis of psychotherapy outcome studies. *Amer. Psychologist, 32*(9), 752–760.

Smith, M. L., Glass, G. V., & Miller, T. I. (1980). *The benefits of psychotherapy.* Baltimore: Johns Hopkins University Press.

Smith, R. E. (1988). The logic and design of case study research. *Sport Psychologist, 2*(1), 1–12.

Smith, S. (1991). Mental health malpractice in the 1990s. *Houston Law Rev., 28,* 209–283.

Smith, W. H. (1993). Incorporating hypnosis into the psychotherapy of patients with multiple personality disorder. *Bull. Menninger Clin., 57*(3), 344–354.

Smith-Bell, M., & Winslade, W. J. (1994). Privacy, confidentiality, and privilege in psychotherapeutic relationships. *Amer. J. Orthopsychiat., 64,* 180–193.

Smolan, R., Moffitt, P., & Naythons, M. (1990). *The power to heal: Ancient arts & modern medicine.* New York: Prentice Hall.

Smyer, M. A. (1989). Nursing homes as a setting for psychological practice: Public policy perspectives. *Amer. Psychologist, 44*(10), 1307–1314.

Smyth, J. M. (1998). Written emotional expression: Effect sizes, outcome types, and moderating variables. *J. Cons. Clin. Psychol., 66*(1), 174–184.

Smyth, J. M., Stone, A. A., Hurewitz, A., & Kaell, A. (1999). Effects of writing about stressful experiences on symptom reduction in patients with asthma or rheumatoid arthritis: A randomized trial. *JAMA, 281*(14), 1304–1309.

Snow, E. (1976, December). In the snow. *Texas Monthly Magazine.*

Snowden, P. (1997). Practical aspects of clinical risk assessment and management. *Brit. J. Psychiat., 170*(Suppl.32), 32–34.

Snyder, D. K., Wills, R. M., & Grady-Fletcher, A. (1991). Risks and challenges of long-term psychotherapy outcome research: Reply to Jacobson. *J. Cons. Clin. Psychol., 59*(1), 146–149.

Snyder, S. (1976). Dopamine and schizophrenia. *Psychiatr. Ann., 8*(1), 53–84.

Snyder, S. (1976). The dopamine hypotheses of schizophrenia: Focus on the dopamine receptor. *Amer. J. Psychiat., 133*(2), 197–202.

Snyder, S. (1980). *Biological aspects of mental disorder.* New York: Oxford University Press.

Snyder, S. (1986). *Drugs and the brain.* New York: Scientific American Library.

Snyder, S. (1991). Drugs, neurotransmitters, and the brain. In P. Corsi (Ed.), *The enchanted loom: Chapters in the history of neuroscience.* New York: Oxford University Press.

Snyder, W. V. (1947). *Casebook of non-directive counseling,* Boston: Houghton Mifflin.

Soares, J. C., Mallinger, A. G., Dippold, C. S., Frank, E., & Kupfer, D. J. (1999). Platelet membrane phospholipids in euthymic bipolar disorder patients: Are they affected by lithium treatment? *Biol. Psychiat., 45*(4), 453–457.

Sobell, M. B., & Sobell, L. C. (1973). Individualized behavior therapy for alcoholics. *Behav. Ther., 4*(1), 49–72.

Sobell, M. B., & Sobell, L. C. (1976). Second year treatment outcome of alcoholics treated by individualized behavior therapy: Results. *Behav. Res. Ther., 14*(3), 195–215.

Sobell, M. B., & Sobell, L. C. (1984). The aftermath of heresy: A response to Pendery et al.'s (1982) critique of "Individualized Behavior Therapy for Alcoholics." *Behav. Res. Ther., 22*(4), 413–440.

Sobell, M. B., & Sobell, L. C. (1984). Under the microscope yet again: A commentary on Walker and Roach's critique of the Dickens Committee's enquiry into our research. *Brit. J. Addic., 79*(2), 157–168.

Sobin, C., & Sackeim, H. A. (1997). Psychomotor symptoms of depression. *Amer. J. Psychiat., 154,* 4–17.

Sobin, C., Blundell, M., Weiller, F., Gavigan, C., Haiman, C., & Karayiorgou, M. (1999). Phenotypic characteristics of obsessive-compulsive disorder ascertained in adulthood. *J. Psychiat. Res., 33*(3), 265–273.

Sobo, S. (1999). The inadequacy of 15–minute med checks as standard psychiatric practice. *Psychiatr. Times, XVI*(4).

Sohlberg, S., & Norring, C. (1992). A three-year prospective study of life events and course for adults with anorexia nervosa/bulimia nervosa. *Psychosom. Med., 54*(1), 59–70.

Solomon, D. A., Keitner, G. I., Miller, I. W., Shea, M. T., & Keller, M. B. (1995). Course of illness and maintenance treatments for patients with bipolar disorder. *J. Clin. Psychiat., 56*(1), 5–13.

Solomon, R. L. (1980). The opponent-process theory of acquired motivation: The costs of pleasure and the benefits of pain. *Amer. Psychologist, 35,* 691–712.

Somasundaram, D. J., & Rajadurai, S. (1995). War and suicide in northern Sri Lanka. *Acta Psychiatr. Scandin., 91*(1), 1–4.

Somer, E. (1995). Biofeedback-aided hypnotherapy for intractable phobic anxiety. *Amer. J. Clin. Hypnother., 37*(3), 54–64.

Sorbi, S., Nacmias, B., Tedde, A., et al. (1998). 5–HT2A promoter polymorphism in anorexia nervosa [letter]. *Lancet, 351,* 1785.

Sorensen, J. L., & Copeland, A. L. (2000). Drug abuse treatment as an HIV prevention strategy: A review. *Drug Alc. Rev., 59*(1) 17–31.

Soric, I. (1999). Anxiety and coping in the context of a school examination. *Soc. Behav. Pers., 27*(3), 319–330.

Sorokin, J. E., Giordani, B., Mohs, R. C., Losonczy, M. F., et al. (1988). Memory impairment in schizophrenic patients with tardive dyskinesia. *Biol. Psychiat., 23*(2), 129–135.

Spalter, A. R., Gwirtsman, H. E., Demitrack, M. A., & Gold, P. W. (1993). Thyroid function in bulimia nervosa. *Biol. Psychiat., 33,* 408–414.

Spangenberg, J. J., & Theron, J. C. (1999). Stress and coping strategies in spouses of depressed patients. *J. Psychol., 133*(3), 253–262.

Spanier, C., Shiffman, S., Maurer, A., Reynolds, W., & Quick, D. (1996). Rebound following failure to quit smoking: The effects of attributions and self-efficacy. *Exp. Clin. Psychopharmacol., 4*(2), 191–197.

Spanier, C. A., Frank, E., McEachran, A. B., Grochocinski, V. J., & Kupfer, D. J. (1999). Maintenance interpersonal psychotherapy for recurrent depression: Biological and clinical correlates and future directions. In D. S. Janowsky et al. (Eds.), *Psychotherapy indications and outcomes.* Washington, DC: American Psychiatric Press.

Spanos, N. P., & Coe, W. C. (1992). A social-psychological approach to hypnosis. In E. Fromm & M. R. Nash (Eds.), *Contemporary hypnosis research.* New York: Guilford.

Spanos, N. P., Burgess, C. A., DuBreuil, S. C., Liddy, S., et al. (1995). The effects of simulation and expectancy instructions on responses to cognitive skill training for enhancing hypnotizability. [Special Issue: To the memory of Nicholas Spanos.] *Contemp. Hyp., 12*(1), 1–11.

Sparks, G., & Cantor, J. (1998, October 30). Cited in V. Andrews, Heart-stopping fear: Why the body keeps coming back for more. *HealthScout.*

Sparks, G. G., Pellechia, M., & Irvine, C. (1999). The repressive coping style and fright reactions to mass media. *Communic. Res., 26*(2), 176–192.

Sparr, L. F., Boehnlein, J. K., & Cooney, T. G. (1986). The medical management of the paranoid patient. *Gen. Hosp. Psychiat., 8*(1), 49–55.

Speakman, M. T., & Kloner, R. A. (1999). Viagra and cardiovascular disease. *J. Cardiovasc. Pharmacol. Ther., 4*(4), 259–267.

Spector, I. P., & Carey, M. P. (1990). Incidence and prevalence of sexual dysfunctions: A critical review of the empirical literature. *Arch. Sex. Behav., 19*(4), 389–408.

Spencer, T., Biederman, J., & Wilens, T. (1999). Attention-deficit/hyperactivity disorder and comorbidity. *Pediatr. Clin. N. Amer., 46*(5), 915–927.

Spencer, T., Biederman, J., & Wilens, T. (2000). Pharmacotherapy of attention deficit hyperactivity disorder. *Child Adol. Psychiat. Clin. N. Amer., 9*(1), 77–97.

Spiegel, D., & Classen, C. (2000). *Group therapy for cancer patients: A research-based handbook of psychosocial care.* New York: Basic Books.

Spiegel, D., Bloom, J. R., Kraemer, H. C., & Gottheil, E. (1989). The beneficial effect of psychosocial treatment on survival of metastatic breast cancer patients: A randomized prospective outcome study. *Lancet, 2,* 888.

Spiegel, D., Bloom, J., Kraemer, H. C., & Gottheil, E. (1989). Effect of psychosocial treatment on survival of patients with metastic breast cancer. *Lancet, 2*(8668), 888–891.

Spielberger, C. D. (1966). Theory and research on anxiety. In C. D. Spielberger (Ed.), *Anxiety and behavior.* New York: Academic Press.

Spielberger, C. D. (1972). Anxiety as an emotional state. In C. D. Spielberger (Ed.), *Anxiety: Current trends in theory and research* (Vol. 1). New York: Academic Press.

Spielberger, C. D. (1972). Conceptual and method-ological issues in anxiety research. In C. D. Spielberger (Ed.), *Anxiety: Current trends in theory and research* (Vol. 2). New York: Academic Press.

Spielberger, C. D. (1985). Anxiety, cognition, and affect: A state-trait perspective. In A. H. Tuma & J. Maser (Eds.), *Anxiety and the anxiety disorders*. Hillsdale, NJ: Erlbaum.

Spielrein, S. (1995). [On the psychological content of a case of schizophrenia (dementia praecox).] *Evolution Psychiatr., 60*(1), 69–95. [French.]

Spignesi, S. J. (1994). *The odd index*. New York: Penguin.

Spitz, H. H. (1994). Lewis Carroll's formula for cal-endar calculating. *Amer. J. Ment. Retard., 98*(5), 601–606.

Spitz, R. A. (1945). Hospitalization: An inquiry into the genesis of psychiatric conditions of early childhood. In R. S. Eissler, A. Freud, H. Hartman, & E. Kris (Eds.), *The psychoanalytic study of the child* (Vol. 1). New York: International Universities Press.

Spitz, R. A. (1946). *Anaclitic depression. The psycho-analytic study of the child* (Vol. 2). New York: International Universities Press.

Spitzer, J. (1990). On treating patients diagnosed with narcissistic personality disorder: The induc-tion phase. *Issues Ego Psychol., 13*(1), 54–65.

Spitzer, R. L., Devlin, M. J., Walsh, B. T., & Hasin, D. (1992). Binge eating disorder: A multi-site field trial of the diagnostic criteria. *Inter. J. Eat. Disorders, 11*, 191–203.

Spitzer, R. L., Gibbon, M., Skodol, A. E., Williams, J. B. W., & First, M. B. (Eds.) (1994). *DSM-IV casebook: A learning companion to the diagnostic and statistical manual of mental disor-ders* (4th ed.). Washington, DC: American Psychiatric Press.

Spitzer, R. L., Skodol, A., Gibbon, M., & Williams, J. B. W. (1981). *DSM-III case book* (1st ed.). Washington, DC: American Psychiatric Press.

Spitzer, R. L., Skodol, A., Gibbon, M., & Williams, J. B. W. (1983). *Psychopathology: A case book*. New York: McGraw-Hill.

Sponheim, S. R., Iacono, W. G., Clementz, B. A., & Beiser, M. (1997). Season of birth and elec-troencephalogram power abnormalities in schizo-phrenia. *Biol. Psychiat., 41*, 1020–1027.

Spoont, M. R. (1996). Emotional instability. In C. G. Costello (Ed.), *Personality characteristics of the personality disordered*. New York: Wiley.

Spoov, J., Suominen, J. Y., Lahdelma, R. L., Katila, H., Kymalainen, O., Isometsa, E., Liukko, H., & Auvinen, J. (1993). Do reversed depressive symptoms occur together as a syn-drome? *J. Affect. Disorders, 27*, 131–134.

Sporer, K. A. (1999). Acute heroin overdose. *Ann. Internal Med., 130*(7), 584–590.

Squire, L. R. (1977). ECT and memory loss. *Amer. J. Psychiat., 134*, 997–1001.

Squire, L. R., & Slater, P. C. (1983). Electroconvulsive therapy and complaints of memory dysfunction: A prospective three-year fol-low-up study. *Brit. J. Psychiat., 142*, 1–8.

Squires, R. F., & Braestrup, C. (1977). Benzodiazepine receptors in rat brain. *Nature, 266*(5604), 732–734.

Stacey, J. (1996, February 12). Family life: A chang-ing national portrait. *USA Today*, p. 6D.

Stack, S. (1981). Comparative analysis of immigra-tion and suicide. *Psychol. Rep., 49*(2), 509–510.

Stack, S. (1987). Celebrities and suicide: A taxono-my and analysis, 1948–1983. *Amer. Sociol. Rev., 52*, 401–412.

Stack, S. (1998). Heavy metal, religiosity, and sui-cide acceptability. *Suic. Life-Threat. Behav., 28*(4), 388–394.

Stack, S. (1998). Research on controlling suicide: Methodological issues. *Arch. Suic. Res., 4*(1), 95–99.

Stack, S. (1998). The relationship of female labor force participation to suicide: A comparative analysis. *Arch. Suic. Res., 4*(3), 249–261.

Stader, S. R., & Hokanson, J. E. (1998). Psychosocial antecendents of depressive symp-toms: An evaluation using daily experiences methodology. *J. Abnorm. Psychol., 107*(1), 17–26.

Stahl, S. M. (1998). Basic psychopharmacology of antidepressants, Part 1: Antidepressants have seven distinct mechanisms of action. *J. Clin. Psychiat., 59*(Suppl. 4), 5–14.

Stahl, S. M. (1998). How psychiatrists can build new therapies for impotence. *J. Clin. Psychiat., 59*(2), 47–48.

Stahl, S. M., & Soefje, S. (1995). Panic attacks and panic disorder: The great neurologic imposters. *Sem. in Neurol., 15*(2), 126–132.

Stahmer, A. C., & Schreibman, L. (1992). Teaching children with autism appropriate play in unsupervised environments using a self-manage-ment treatment package. *J. Appl. Behav. Anal., 25*(2), 447–459.

Stallard, P., Velleman, R., & Baldwin, S. (1998). Prospective study of post-traumatic stress disorder in children involved in road traffic accidents. *Brit. Med. J., 317*(7173), 1619–1623.

Stanley, B., Molcho, A., Stanley, M., Winchel, R., Gameroff, M. J., Parsons, B., & Mann, J. J. (2000). Association of aggressive behavior with altered serotonergic function in patients who are not suicidal. *Amer. J. Psychiat., 157*(4), 609–614.

Stanley, M., Stanley, B., Traskman-Bendz, L., Mann, J. J., & Meyendorff, E. (1986). Neurochemical findings in suicide completers and suicide attempters. In R. W. Maris (Ed.), *Biology of Suicide*. New York: Guilford.

Stanley, M., Virgilio, J., & Gershon, S. (1982). Tritiated imipramine binding sites are decreased in the frontal cortex of suicides. *Science, 216*, 1337–1339.

Stanley, M. A., & Averill, P. M. (1999). Strategies for treating generalized anxiety in the elderly. In M. Duffy (Ed.), *Handbook of counseling and psy-chotherapy with older adults*. New York: Wiley.

Stark, K. D., Bronik, M. D., Wong, S., Wells, G., & Ostrander, R. (2000). Depressive disorders. In M. Hersen, R. T. Ammerman, et al. (Eds.), *Advanced abnormal child psychology* (2nd ed.) Mahwah, NJ: Erlbaum.

Stark-Adamek, C. (1992). Sexism in research: The limits of academic freedom. *Women Ther., 12*(4), 103–111.

Statham, D. J., Heath, A. C., Madden, P. A. F., Bucholz, K. K., Bierut, L., Dinwiddie, S. H., Slutske, W. S., Dunne, M. P., & Martin, N. G. (1998). Suicidal behaviour: An epidemiological and genetic study. *Psychol. Med., 28*(4), 839–855.

Staub, E. (1996). Cultural-societal roots of violence. The examples of genocidal violence and of con-temporary youth violence in the United States. *Amer. Psychologist, 51*(2), 117–132.

Steadman, H., Monahan, J., Hartstone, E., Davis, S., & Robbins, P. (1982). Mentally diusordered offenders: A national survey of patients and facili-ties. *Law Human Behav., 6*, 31–38.

Steadman, H. J., Mulvey, E. P., Monahan, J., Robbins, P. C., Appelbaum, P. S., Grisso, T., Roth, L. H., & Silver, E. (1998). Violence by people discarded from acute psychiatric inpatient facilities and by others in the same neighbor-hoods. *Arch. Gen. Psychiat., 55*(5), 393–401.

Steckler, M.A. (1998). The effects of music on heal-ing. *Journal of Long Term Home Health Care: The Pride Institute Journal, 17*(1), 42–48.

Steege, J. F., & Ling, F. W. (1993). Dyspareunia: A special type of chronic pelvic pain. *Obstetrics and Gynecology Clinics of North America, 20*, 779–793.

Steen, S. N., Oppliger, R. A., & Brownell, K. D. (1988). Metabolic effects of repeated weight loss and regain in adolescent wrestlers. *JAMA, 260*, 47–50.

Steffens, D. C., & Blazer, D. G. (1999). Suicide in the elderly. In D. G. Jacobs et al. (Eds.), *The Harvard Medical School guide to suicide assessment and intervention*. San Francisco: Jossey-Bass.

Stein, D. J., Apter, A., Ratzoni, G., Har-Even, D., & Avidan, G. (1998). Association between multi-ple suicide attempts and negative affects in adoles-cents. *J. Amer. Acad. Child Adol. Psychiat., 37*(5), 488–494.

Stein, D. J., Christenson, G. A., & Hollander, E. (Eds). (1999). *Trichotillomania*. Washington, DC: American Psychiatric Press, Inc.

Stein, D. J., Hollander, E., & Liebowitz, M. R. (1993). Neurobiology of impulsivity and the impulse control disorders. *J. Neuropsych. Clin. Neurosci., 5*(1), 9–17.

Stein, L. I. (1993). A system approach to reducing relapse in schizophrenia. *J. Clin. Psychiat., 54*(3 Suppl.), 7–12.

Stein, M. B., & Rapee, R. M. (1999). Biological aspects of anxiety sensitivity: Is it all in the head? In S. Taylor, et al. (Eds.), *Anxiety sensitivity: Theory, research, and treatment of the fear of anxiety*. The LEA series in personality and clinical psychol-ogy. Mahwah, NJ: Erlbaum.

Stein, M. B., & Uhde, T. W. (1995). In A. F. Schatzberg & C. B. Nemeroff (Eds.), *The American Psychiatric Press textbook of psychopharmacology*. Washington, DC: American Psychiatric Press.

Stein, M. B., Fyer, A. J., Davidson, J. R. T., Pollack, M. H., & Wiita, B. (1999). Fluvoxamine treatment of social phobia (social anxiety disorder): A double-blind, placebo-con-trolled study. *Amer. J. Psychiat., 156*(5), 756–760.

Stein, M. B., Jang, K. L., & Livesley, W. J. (1999). Heritability of anxiety sensitivity: A twin study. *Amer. J. Psychiat., 156*(2), 246–251.

Stein, M. B., Liebowitz, M. R., Lydiard, R. B., Pitts, C. D., Bushnell, W., & Gergel, I. (1998). Paroxetine treatment of generalized social phobia (social anxiety disorder): A randomized controlled trial. *JAMA, 280*(8), 708–713.

Stein, M. B., McQuaid, J. R., Laffaye, C., & McCahill, M. E. (1999). Social phobia in the pri-mary care medical setting. *J. Fam. Prac., 48*(7), 514–519.

Stein, M. B., Walker, J. R., Anderson, G., Hazen, A. L., et al. (1996). Childhood physical and sexu-al abuse in patients with anxiety disorders and in a community sample. *Amer. J. Psychiat., 153*(2), 275–277.

Stein, M. B., Walker, J. R., & Forde, D. R. (1994). Setting diagnostic thresholds for social phobia: Considerations from a community survey of social anxiety. *Amer. J. Psychiat., 151*(3), 408–412.

Stein, Z., Susser, M., Saenger, G., & Marolla, F. (1972). Nutrition and mental performance. *Science, 178*, 708–713.

Steinberg, J. (1996, March 17). Implant to help dog get over post-neutering trauma. *Fresno Bee*, p. B1.

Steinberg, M., & Hall, P. (1997). The SCID-D diag-nostic interview and treatment planning in disso-ciative disorders. *Bull. Menninger Clin., 61*(1), 108–120.

Steinbrook, R. (1992). The polygraph test: A flawed diagnostic method. *N. Engl. J. Med., 327*(2), 122–123.

Steiner, H., & Wilson, J. (1999). Conduct disorder. In R. L. Hendren (Ed.), *Disruptive behavior disor-ders in children and adolescents*. Review of psychia-try series. Washington, DC: American Psychiatric Press.

Steiner, H., Smith, C., Rosenkranz, R. T., & Litt, I. (1991). The early care and feeding of anorexics. *Child Psychiat. Human Dev., 21*(3), 163–167.

Steiner, M., & Tam, W. Y. K. (1999). Postpartum depression in relation to other psychiatric disorders. In L. J. Miller, et al. (Eds.), *Postpartum mood disorders.* Washington, DC: American Psychiatric Press.

Steiner-Adair, C. (1986). The body politic: Normal female adolescent development and the development of eating disorders. *J. Amer. Acad. Psychoanal., 14*(1), 95–114.

Steinhausen, H. C. (1997). Annotation: Outcome of anorexia nervosa in the younger patient. *J. Child Psychol. Psychiat., 38*(3), 271–276.

Steinhausen, H. C., Boyadjieva, S., Grigoroiu-Serbanescu, M., Seidel, R., & Winkler-Metzke, C. (2000). A transcultural outcome study of adolescent eating disorders. *Acta Psychiat. Scandin., 101*(1), 60–66.

Steketee, G. (1990). Personality traits and disorders in obsessive-compulsives. *J. Anx. Dis., 4*(4), 351–364.

Steketee, G., Chambless, D. L., Tran, G. Q., Worden, H., & Gillis, M. M. (1996). Behavioral avoidance test for obsessive compulsive disorder. *Behav. Res. Ther., 34*(1), 73–83.

Stephens, R. S., & Curtin, L. (1995). Alcohol and depression: Effects on mood and biased processing of self-relevant information. *Psychol. Addict. Behav., 9*(4), 211–222.

Stern, T. A., & Cremens, M. C. (1998). Factitious pheochromocytoma: One patient history and literature review. *Psychosomatics, 39*(3), 283–287.

Sternbach, L. H. (1982). The discovery of CNS active 1,4-benzodiazepines (chemistry). In E. Usdin, P. Skolnick, J. F. Tallman, Jr., et al. (Eds.), *Pharmacology of benzodiazepines.* London: Macmillan.

Sternberg, E. M., & Gold, P. W. (1997). The mind-body interaction in disease. *Scientif. Amer.* [Special issue: Mysteries of the Mind.] pp. 8–15.

Sternberg, S. (1996). Human version of mad cow disease? *Sci. News, 149,* 228.

Sternberg, S. (1996). Of mad cows and Englishmen. *Sci. News, 150,* 238–239.

Stewart, J. W., Mercier, M. A., Agosti, V., Guardino, M., & Quitkin, F. M. (1993). Imipramine is effective after unsuccessful cognitive therapy: Sequential use of cognitive therapy and imipramine in depressed outpatients. *J. Clin. Psychopharmacol., 13,* 114–119.

St. George-Hyslop, P. H. (2000). Molecular genetics of Alzheimer's disease. *Biol. Psychiat., 47*(3), 183–199.

Stillion, J. M. (1985). *Death and the sexes: An examination of differential longevity, attitudes, behaviors, and coping skills.* Washington, DC: Hemisphere.

Stillion, J. M. (1995). Through a glass darkly: Women and attitudes toward suicidal behavior. In S. S. Canetto & D. Lester (Eds.), *Women and suicidal behavior.* New York: Springer.

Stillion, J. M., & McDowell, E. E. (1996). *Suicide across the life span: Premature exits* (2nd ed.) Washington, DC: Taylor & Francis.

Stimming, M. T., & Stimming, M. (Eds.). (1999). *Before their time: Adult children's experiences of parental suicide.* Philadelphia: Temple University Press.

St. Lawrence, J. S., & Madakasira, S. (1992). Evaluation and treatment of premature ejaculation: A critical review. *Inter. J. Psychiat. Med., 22,* 77–97.

Stock, W. (1993). Inhibited female orgasm. In W. O'Donohue & J. Geer (Eds.), *Handbook of sexual dysfunctions.* Boston: Allyn & Bacon.

Stodghill, R., II. (1999, March 12). Where'd you learn that? *Time.*

Stokes, T. E., & Osnes, P. G. (1989). An operant pursuit of generalization. *Behav. Ther., 20*(3), 337–355.

Stolerman, I., & Jarvis, M. (1995). The scientific case that nicotine is addictive. *Psychopharmacology, 117*(1), 2–10.

Stoline, A. M., & Sharfstein, S. S. (1996). Practice in the eye of a hurricane, or how does the psychiatrist survive in an era of change? In L. J. Dickstein, M. B. Riba, & J. M. Oldham (Eds.), *Review of psychiatry* (Vol. 15). Washington, DC: American Psychiatric Press.

Stone, M. H. (1989). Schizoid personality disorder. In American Psychiatric Association (Eds.), *Treatments of psychiatric disorders: A task force report of the American Psychiatric Association.* Washington, DC: American Psychiatric Press.

Stone, M. H. (2000). Clinical guidelines for psychotherapy for patients with. *Psychiat. Clin. N. Amer., 23*(1), 193–210.

Stoppard, J. M. (2000). *Understanding depression: Feminist social constructionist approaches.* New York: Routledge.

Stores, G. (1996). Practitioner review: Assessment and treatment of sleep disorders in children and adolescents. *J. Child Psychol. Psychiat., 37*(8), 907–925.

Stowe, Z., Casarella, J., Landry, J., & Nemeroff, C. (1995). Sertraline in the treatment of women with postpartum major depression. *Depression, 3,* 49–55.

Stoyva, J. M., & Budzynski, T. H. (1993). Biofeedback methods in the treatment of anxiety and stress disorders. In P. M. Lehrer & R. L. Woolfolk (Eds.), *Principles and practice of stress management* (2nd ed.). New York: Guilford.

Strain, E. C., Bigelow, G. E., Liebson, I. A., & Stitzer, M. L. (1999). Moderate vs. high-dose methadone in the treatment of opioid dependence: A randomized trial. *JAMA, 281*(11), 1000–1005.

Strange, P. G. (1992). *Brain biochemistry and brain disorders.* New York: Oxford University Press.

Strassberg, D. S., Kelly, M. P., Carroll, C., & Kircher, J. C. (1987). The psychophysiological nature of premature ejaculation. *Arch. Sex. Behav., 16*(4), 327–336.

Strassberg, D. S., Mahoney, J. M., Schaugaard, M., & Hale, V. E. (1990). The role of anxiety in premature ejaculation: A psychophysiological model. *Arch. Sex. Behav., 15*(4), 251–157.

Stratton, V. N., & Zalanowski, A. H. (1994). Affective impact of music vs. lyrics. *Empir. Stud. Arts, 12*(2), 173–184.

Stratton, V., & Zalanowski, A. (1999). *Study on music and emotion.* Papaer presented at annual meeting of Eastern Psychological Association.

Strauss, J., & Ryan, R. (1987). Autonomy disturbances in subtypes of anorexia nervosa. *J. Abnorm. Psychol., 96*(3), 254–258.

Stravynski, A., & Greenberg, D. (1992). The psychological management of depression. *Acta Psychiatr. Scandin., 85*(6), 407–414.

Stravynski, A., Gaudette, G., Lesage, A., Arbel, N., et al. (1997). The treatment of sexually dysfunctional men without partners: A controlled study of three behavioural group approaches. *Brit. J. Psychiat., 170,* 338–344.

Stravynski, A., Grey, S., & Elie, R. (1987). Outline of the therapeutic process in social skills training with socially dysfunctional patients. *J. Cons. Clin. Psychol., 55*(2), 224–228.

Streiner, D. L. (1999). Placebo-controlled trials: When are they needed? *Schizo. Res., 35*(3), 201–210.

Stricker, G., & Trierweiler, S. J. (1995). The local clinical scientist. A bridge between science and practice. *Amer. Psychologist, 50*(12), 995–1002.

Strickland, B. R., Hale, W. D., & Anderson, L. K. (1975). Effect of induced mood states on activity and self-reported affect. *J. Cons. Clin. Psychol., 43*(4), 587.

Strickland, C. J. (1997). Suicide among American Indian, Alaskan Native, and Canadian Aboriginal youth: Advancing the research agenda. *Inter. J. Ment. Hlth., 25*(4), 11–32.

Striegel-Moore, R. H., & Smolak, L. (2000). The influence of ethnicity on eating disorders in women. In R. M. Eisler, M. Hersen, et al. (Eds.), *Handbook of gender, culture, and health.* Mahwah, NJ: Erlbaum.

Striegel-Moore, R. H., Silberstein, L. R., & Rodin, J. (1986). Toward an understanding of risk factors for bulimia. *Amer. Psychologist, 41*(3), 246–263.

Striegel-Moore, R. H., Silberstein, L. R., & Rodin, J. (1993). The social self in bulimia nervosa: Public self-consciousness, social anxiety, and perceived fraudulence. *J. Abnorm. Psychol., 102*(2), 297–303.

Strier, F. (1999). Whither trial consulting: Issues and projections. *Law Human Behav., 23*(1), 93–115.

Strober, M., & Humphrey, L. L. (1987). Familial contributions to the etiology and course of anorexia nervosa and bulimia. [Special Issue: Eating disorders.] *J. Cons. Clin. Psychol., 55*(5), 654–659.

Strober, M., & Yager, J. (1985). A developmental perspective on the treatment of anorexia nervosa in adolescents. In D. M. Garner & P. E. Garfinkel (Eds.), *Handbook of psychotherapy for anorexia nervosa and bulimia.* New York: Guilford.

Strober, M., Freeman, R., & Morrell, W. (1997). The long-term course of severe anorexia nervosa in adolescents: Survival analysis of recovery, relapse, and outcome predictors over 10–15 years in a prospective study. *Inter. J. Eat. Disorders, 22*(4), 339–360.

Strober, M., Freeman, R., Lampert, C., Diamond, J., & Kaye, W. (2000). Controlled family study of anorexia nervosa and bulimia nervosa: Evidence of shared liability and transmission of partial syndromes. *Amer. J. Psychiat., 157*(3), 393–401.

Stroebe, M., Gergen, M. M., Gergen, K. J., & Stroebe, W. (1992). Broken hearts or broken bonds: Love and death in historical perspectives. *Amer. Psychologist, 47*(10), 1205–1212.

Stroebe, M., van Son, M., Stroebe, W., Kleber, R., Schut, H., & van den Bout, J. (2000). On the classification and diagnosis of pathological grief. *Clin. Psychol. Rev., 20*(1), 57–75.

Stromme, P., & Magnus, P. (2000). Correlations between socioeconomic status, IQ and aetiology in mental retardation: A population-based study of Norwegian children. *Soc. Psychiatr. Psychiatr. Epidemiol., 35*(1), 12–18.

Stronks, D. L., Tulen, J. H., Pepplinkhuizen, L., Verheij, R., Mantel, G. W., Spinhoven, P., & Passchier, J. (1999). Personality traits and psychological reactions to mental stress of female migraine patients. *Cephalalgia, 19*(6), 566–574.

Strupp, H. H. (1989). Psychotherapy: Can the practitioner learn from the researcher? *Amer. Psychologist, 44,* 717–724.

Strupp, H. H. (1996). The tripartite model and the *Consumer Reports* study. *Amer. Psychologist, 51*(10), 1017–1024.

Stuart, S. P. (1999). Interpersonal psychotherapy for postpartum depression. In L. J. Miller et al. (Eds.), *Postpartum mood disorders.* Washington, DC: American Psychiatric Press.

Stuart, S., & Noyes, R., Jr. (1999). Attachment and interpersonal communication in somatization. *Psychosomatics, 40*(1), 34–43.

Stuart, S., & O'Hara, M. W. (1995). Interpersonal psychotherapy for postpartum depression: A treatment program. *J. Psychother. Prac.. Res., 4*(1), 18–29.

Stuhr, U., & Meyer, A. E. (1991). Hamburg short psychotherapy comparison experiment. In M. Crago & L. Beutler (Eds.), *Psychotherapy research: An international review of programmatic studies.* Washington, DC: American Psychological Association.

Stunkard, A. J. (1975). From explanation to action in psychosomatic medicine: The case of obesity. *Psychosom. Med., 37,* 195–236.

Stunkard, A. J., Sorenson, T. I. A., Hanis, C., Teasdale, T. W., et al. (1986). An adoption study of human obesity. *N. Engl. J. Med., 314,* 193–198.

Sturgeon, V., & Taylor, J. (1980). Report of a five-year follow-up study of mentally disordered sex offenders released from Atascadero State Hospital in 1973. Criminal Justice *J. Western S. Univ., San Diego, 4,* 31–64.

Styron, W. (1990). *Darkness visible: A memoir of madness.* New York: Random House.

Sudhalter, V., Cohen, I. L., Silverman, W., & Wolf-Schein, E. G. (1990). Conversational analyses of males with fragile X, Down syndrome, and autism: Comparison of the emergence of deviant language. *Amer. J. Ment. Retard., 94,* 431–441.

Sue, S. (1991). Ethnicity and culture in psychological research and practice. In L. Garnets, J. M. Jones, D. Kimmel, S. Sue, & C. Tavris (Eds.), *Psychological perspectives on human diversity in America.* Washington, DC: American Psychological Association.

Sue, S. (1999). Science, ethnicity, and bias: Where have we gone wrong? *Amer. Psychologist, 54*(12), 1070–1077.

Sue, S., Zane, N., & Young, K. (1994). Research on psychotherapy with culturally diverse populations. In A. E. Bergin & S. L. Garfield (Eds.), *Handbook of psychotherapy and behavior change.* New York: Wiley.

Sugar, M. (1995). A clinical approach to childhood gender identity disorder. *Amer. J. Psychother., 49*(2), 260–281.

Sugarman, A., & Kanner, K. (2000). The contribution of psychoanalytic theory to psychological testing. *Psychoanal. Psychol., 17*(1), 1–21.

Suh, E., Diener, E., & Fujita, F. (1996). Events and subjective well-being: Only recent events matter. *J. Pers. Soc. Psychol., 70*(5), 1091–1102.

Sullivan, C. M., Tan, C., Basta, J., Rumptz, M., et al. (1992). An advocacy intervention program for women with abusive partners: Initial evaluation. *Amer. J. Comm. Psych., 20*(3), 309–332.

Sullivan, H. S. (1953). *The interpersonal theory of psychiatry.* New York: Norton.

Sullivan, H. S. (1962). *Schizophrenia as a human process.* New York: Norton.

Summers, M. (1996, December 9). Mister clean. *People,* pp. 139–140.

Sundbom, E., Binzer, M., & Kullgren, G. (1999). Psychological defense strategies according to the Defense Mechanism Test among patients with severe conversion disorder. *Psychother. Res., 9*(2), 184–198.

Suokas, J., & Lonnqvist, J. (1995). Suicide attempts in which alcohol is involved: A special group in general hospital emergency rooms. *Acta Psychiatr. Scandin., 91*(1), 36–40.

Suppes, T., Baldessarini, R. J., Faedda, G. L., & Tohen, M. (1991). Risk of recurrence following discontinuation of lithium treatment in bipolar disorder. *Arch. Gen. Psychiat., 48*(12), 1082–1088.

Susnick, L. C., & Belcher, J. R. (1995). Why are they homeless?: The chronically mentally ill in Washington, DC. *Inter. J. Ment. Hlth., 24*(4), 70–84.

Susser, E., Miller, M., Valencia, E., Colson, P., et al. (1996). Injection drug use and risk of HIV transmission among homeless men with mental illness. *Amer. J. Psychiat., 153*(6), 794–798.

Susser, E., Neugebauer, R., Hoek, H. W., Brown, A. S., Lin, S., Labovitz, D., & Gorman, J. M. (1996). Schizophrenia after prenatal famine. *Arch. Gen. Psychiat., 53*(1), 25–31.

Sutherland, G. (1999, February 4). Regarding definitions of love and of psycho-analyst. *The Times* (London).

Suzuki, L. A., & Valencia, R. R. (1997). Race-ethnicity and measured intelligence. *Amer. Psychologist, 52*(10), 1103–1114.

Svartberg, M., & Stiles, T. C. (1991). Comparative effects of short-term psychodynamic psychotherapy: A meta-analysis. *J. Cons. Clin. Psychol., 59,* 704–714.

Svensson, B., Hansson, L., & Nyman, K. (2000). Stability of outcome in a comprehensive, cognitive therapy based treatment programme for long-term mentally ill patients. A 2-year follow-up study. *J. Ment. Hlth UK, 9*(1), 51–61.

Svrakic, D. M. (1987). Pessimistic mood in narcissistic decompensation. *Amer. J. Psychoanal., 47*(1), 58–71.

Svrakic, D. M. (1989). Narcissistic personality disorder: A new clinical systematics. *Eur. J. Psychiat., 3*(4), 199–213.

Svrakic, D. M. (1990). The functional dynamics of the narcissistic personality. *Amer. J. Psychother., 44*(2), 189–203.

Svrakic, D. M. (1990). Pessimism and depression: Clinical and phenomenological distinction. *Eur. J. Psychiat., 4*(3), 139–145.

Swanson, J., Holzer, C., Ganju, V., & Jono, R. (1990). Violence and psychiatric disorder in the community: Evidence from the Epidemiological Catchment Area Surveys. *Hosp. Comm. Psychiat., 41,* 761–770.

Swartz, H. A. (1999). Interpersonal psychotherapy. In M. Hersen & A. S. Bellack (Eds.), *Handbook of comparative interventions for adult disorders* (2nd ed.). New York: Wiley.

Swayze, V. W. (1995). Frontal leukotomy and related psychosurgical procedures in the era before antipsychotics (1935–1954): A historical overview. *Amer. J. Psychiat., 152*(4), 505–515.

Swedo, S. E., Pietrini, P., Leonard, H. L., Schapiro, M. B., et al. (1992). Cerebral glucose metabolism in childhood-onset obsessive-compulsive disorder: Revisualization during pharmacotherapy. *Arch. Gen. Psychiat., 49*(9), 690–694.

Swendsen, J. D., & Mazure, C. M. (2000). Life stress as a risk factor for postpartum depression: Current research and methodology. *Clin. Psychol.: Sci. Prac., 7*(1), 17–31.

Swendsen, J. D., & Merikangas, K. R. (2000). The comorbidity of depression and substance use disorders. *Clin. Psychol. Rev., 20*(2), 173–189.

Swerdlow, J. L. (1995). Quiet miracles of the brain. *Natl. Geogr., 187*(6), 12–13.

Swonger, A. K., & Constantine, L. L. (1983). *Drugs and therapy: A handbook of psychotropic drugs* (2nd ed.). Boston: Little, Brown.

Szanto, K., Reynolds, C. F., III, Conwell, Y., Begley, A. E., & Houck, P. (1998). High levels of hopelessness persist in geriatric patients with remitted depression and a history of attempted suicide. *J. Amer. Ger. Soc., 46*(11), 1401–1406.

Szasz, T. S. (1961). *The myth of mental illness: Foundations of a theory of personal conduct.* New York: Harper (Hoeber).

Szasz, T. S. (1963). *Law, liberty, and psychiatry.* Englewood Cliffs, NJ: Prentice Hall.

Szasz, T. S. (1963). *The manufacture of madness.* New York: Harper & Row.

Szasz, T. S. (1977). *Psychiatric slavery.* New York: Free Press.

Szasz, T. S. (1987). Justifying coercion through theology and therapy. In J. K. Zeig (Ed.), *The evolution of psychotherapy.* New York: Brunner/Mazel.

Szasz, T. S. (1991). The medicalization of sex. *J. Human. Psychol., 31*(3), 34–42.

Szasz, T. (1997). The healing word: Its past, present, and future. In J. K. Zeig (Ed.), *The evolution of psychotherapy: The third conference.* New York: Brunner/Mazel.

Szmukler, G. I., & Patton, G. (1995). Sociocultural models of eating disorders. In G. Szmukler, C. Dare, & J. Treasure (Eds.), *Handbook of eating disorders: Theory, treatment and research.* Chichester, England: Wiley.

Szymanski, S., Cannon, T. D., Gallacher, F., Erwin, R. J., & Gur, R. E. (1996). Course of treatment response in first-episode and chronic schizophrenia. *Amer. J. Psychiat., 153*(4), 519–525.

Szymanski, S., Lieberman, J., Alvir, J. M., Mayerhoff, D., et al. (1995). Gender differences in onset of illness, treatment response, course, and biologic indexes in first-episode schizophrenic patients. *Amer. J. Psychiat., 152*(5), 698–703.

Szymanski, S., Lieberman, J., Pollack, S., Kane, J. M., Safferman, A., Munne, R., Umbricht, D., Woerner, M., Masiar, S., & Kronig, M. (1996). Gender differences in neuroleptic nonresponsive clozapine-treated schizophrenics. *Biol. Psychiat., 39,* 249–254.

Taft, C. T., Stern, A. S., King, L. A., & King, D. W. (1999). Modeling physical health and functional health status: The role of combat exposure, posttraumatic stress disorder and personal resource attributes. *J. Traum. Stress, 12*(1), 3–23.

Takahashi, Y. (1998). Suicide in Japan: What are the problems? In R. J. Kosky, H. S. Eshkevari, & R. Hassan (Eds.), *Suicide prevention: The global context.* New York: Plenum Press.

Takanishi, R. (1993). The opportunities of adolescence—Research, interventions, and policy. *Amer. Psychologist, 48*(2), 85–87.

Takano, Y., Tsukahara, T., Suzuki, T., Hara, T., et al. (1995). The improvement of psychiatric symptoms of schizophrenic patients during day care treatment. *Seishin Igaku (Clin. Psychiat.), 37*(4), 369–376.

Takei, N., van Os, J., & Murray, R. M. (1995). Maternal exposure to influenza and risk of schizophrenia: A 22 year study from the Netherlands. *J. Psychiat. Res., 29*(6), 435–445.

Takeuchi, D. T., Uehara, E., & Maramba, G. (1999). Cultural diversity and mental health treatment. In A. V. Horwitz & T. L. Scheid (Eds.), *A handbook for the study of mental health: Social contexts, theories, and systems.* Cambridge, England: Cambridge University Press.

Tallis, F. (1996). Compulsive washing in the absence of phobia and illness anxiety. *Behav. Res. Ther., 34*(4), 361–362.

Tam, W. C. C., & Sewell, K. W. (1995). Seasonality of birth in schizophrenia in Taiwan. *Schizo. Bull., 21*(1), 117–127.

Tambs, K., Harris, J. R., & Magnus, P. (1995). Sex-specific causal factors and effects of common environment for symptoms of anxiety and depression in twins. *Behav. Genet., 25*(1), 33–44.

Tamplin, A., Goodyer, I. M., & Herbert, J. (1998). Family functioning and parent general health in families of adolescents with major depressive disorder. *J. Affect. Disorders, 48,* 1–13.

Tan, S. Y., & Dong, N. J. (2000). Psychotherapy with members of Asian American churches and spiritual traditions. In P. S. Richards, A. E. Bergin, et al. (Eds.), *Handbook of psychotherapy and religious diversity*. Washington, DC: American Psychological Association.

Tanay, E. (1992). The verdict with two names. *Psychiatr. Ann., 22*(11), 571-573.

Tanzi, R. C., St. George Hyslop, P. H., & Gusella, J. T. (1989). Molecular genetic approaches to Alzheimer's disease. *Trends Neurosci., 12*(4), 152-158.

Tariot, P. N., Erb, R., Podgorski, C. A., Cox, C., Patel, S., Jakimovich, L., & Irvine, C. (1998). Efficacy and tolerability of carbamazepine for agitation and aggression in dementia. *Amer. J. Psychiat., 155*(1), 54-61.

Tartaglia, L. A., Dembski, M., Weng, X., Deng, N., et al. (1995). Identification and expression cloning of a leptin receptor, OB-R. *Cell, 83*, 1263-1271.

Tataranni, P. A., Gautier, J. F., Chen, K., Uecker, A., Bandy, D., Salbe, A. D., Pratley, R. E., Lawson, M., Reiman, E. M., & Ravussin, E. (1999). Neuroanatomical correlates of hunger and satiation in humans using positron emission tomography. *Proc. Natl. Acad. Sci. USA, 96*(8), 4569-4574.

Tate, D. C., Reppucci, N. D., & Mulvey, E. P. (1995). Violent juvenile delinquents. *Amer. Psychologist, 50*(9), 777-781.

Taube, C. A. (1990). Funding and expenditures for mental illness. In R. W. Manderscheid & M. A. Sonnenschein (Eds.), *Mental health, United States, 1990*. (DHHS Publication No. ADM 90-1708). Washington, DC: U. S. Department of Health and Human Services.

Tavris, C. (1993). Beware the incest-survivor machine. *New York Times Book Review*.

Taylor, B., Miller, E., Farrington, C. P., Petropoulos, M. C., Favot-Mayaud, I., Li, J., & Waight, P. A. (1999). Autism and measles, mumps, and rubella vaccine: No epidemiological evidence for a causal association. *Lancet, 353*, 2026-2029.

Taylor, C. B., Farquhar, J. W., Nelson, E., & Agras, S. (1977). Relaxation therapy and high blood pressure. *Arch. Gen. Psychiat., 34*, 339-342.

Taylor, E. A., & Stansfeld, S. A. (1984). Children who poison themselves. *Brit. J. Psychiat., 145*, 127-135.

Taylor, E. R., Amodei, N., & Mangos, R. (1996). The presence of psychiatric disorders in HIV-infected women. *J. Couns. Dev., 74*, 345-351.

Taylor, J. R., & Carroll, J. L. (1987). Current issues in electroconvulsive therapy. *Psychol. Rep., 60*(3, Pt. 1).

Taylor, P. J., & Gunn, J. (1999). Homicides by people with mental illness: Myth and reality. *Brit. J. Psychiat., 174*, 9-14.

Taylor, P. J., Leese, M., Williams, D., Butwell, M., Daly, R., & Larkin, E. (1998). Mental disorder and violence: A special (high security) hospital study. *Brit. J. Psychiat., 172*, 218-226.

Taylor, R. (1975). *Electroconvulsive treatment (ECT): The control of therapeutic power*. Exchange.

Taylor, R. E., & Mann, A. H. (1999). Somatization in primary care. *J. Psychosom. Res., 47*(1), 61-66.

Taylor, S. (1995). Anxiety sensitivity: Theoretical perspectives and recent findings. *Behav. Res. Ther., 33*(3), 243-258.

Taylor, S., Koch, W. J., & McNally, R. J. (1992). How does anxiety sensitivity vary across the anxiety disorders? *J. Anx. Dis., 6*(3), 249-259.

Taylor, S., Kuch, K., Koch, W. J., Crockett, D. J., & Passey, G. (1998). The structure of posttraumatic stress symptoms. *J. Abnorm. Psychol., 107*(1), 154-160.

Taylor, S., Woody, S., Koch, W. J., McLeon, P. D., & Anderson, K. W. (1996). Suffocation false alarms and efficacy of cognitive behavioral therapy for panic disorder. *Behav. Ther., 27*, 115-126.

Taylor, S. E., Kemeny, M. E., Reed, G. M., Bower, J. E., & Gruenewald, T. L. (2000). Psychological resources, positive illusions, and health. *Amer. Psychologist, 55*(1), 99-109.

Taylor, V. (1999). Gender and social movements: Gender processes in women's self-help movements. *Gender Soc., 13*(1), 8-33.

Teare, M., Fristad, M. A., Weller, E. B., Weller, R. A., & Salmon, P. (1998). Study I: Development and criterion validity of the Children's Interview for Psychiatric Syndromes (ChIPS). *J. Child Adol. Psychopharmacol., 8*(4), 205-211.

Teichman, Y., Bar-El, Z., Shor, H., Sirota, P., et al. (1995). A comparison of two modalities of cognitive therapy (individual and marital) in treating depression. *Psychiat. Interpers. Biol. Process., 58*(2), 136-148.

Telch, C. F., & Agras, W. S. (1993). The effects of a very low calorie diet on binge eating. *Behav. Ther., 24*, 177-193.

Teller, V., & Dahl, H. (1995). What psychoanalysis needs is more empirical research. In T. Shapiro & R. N. Emde (Eds.), *Research in psychoanalysis: Process, development, outcome*. Madison, CT: International Universities Press.

Telner, J. I., Lapierre, Y. D., Horn, E., & Browne, M. (1986). Rapid reduction of mania by means of reserpine therapy. *Amer. J. Psychiat., 143*(8), 1058.

Temes, R. (Ed.). (1999). *Medical hypnosis: An introduction and clinical guide*. New York: Churchill Livingstone.

Ten Kate, N. (1998, February). The marketplace for medicine. *American Demographics*.

Teng, C. T., Akerman, D., Cordas, T. A., Kasper, S., et al. (1995). Seasonal affective disorder in a tropical country: A case report. *Psychiatr. Res., 56*(1), 11-15.

Tennant, C. (1988). Psychological causes of duodenal ulcer. *Austral. N. Zeal. J. Psychiat., 22*(2), 195-202.

Teplin, L. A., Abram, K. M., & McClelland, G. M. (1994). Does psychiatric disorder predict violent crime among released jail detainees? *Amer. Psychologist, 49*(4), 335-342.

Teri, L., & Lewinsohn, P. M. (1986). Individual and group treatment of unipolar depression: Comparison of treatment outcome and identification of predictors of successful treatment outcome. *Behav. Ther., 17*(3), 215-228.

Terp, I. M., Engholm, G., Moller, H., & Mortensen, P. B. (1999). A follow-up study of postpartum psychoses: Prognosis and risk factors for readmission. *Acta Psychiatr. Scandin., 1000*(1), 40-46.

Terr, L. (1988). What happens to early memories of trauma? A study of twenty children under age five at the time of documented traumatic events. Annual Meeting of the American Psychiatry Association. *J. Amer. Acad. Child Adol. Psychiat., 27*(1), 96-104.

Terry, D., Mayocchi, L., & Hynes, G. (1996). Depressive symptomatology in new mothers: A stress and coping perspective. *J. Abnorm. Psychol., 105*(2), 220-231.

Thalen, B. E., Kjellman, B. F., Morkrid, L., Wibom, R., et al. (1995). Light treatment in seasonal and nonseasonal depression. *Acta Psychiatr. Scandin., 91*(5), 352-360.

Thapar, A., Davies, G., Jones, T., & Rivett, M. (1992). Treatment of childhood encopresis: A review. *Child Care. Hlth. Dev., 18*(6), 343-353.

Thase, M. E. (1998). Depression, sleep, and antidepressants. *J. Clin. Psychiat., 59*(Suppl. 4), 55-65.

Thase, M. E., Buysse, D. J., Frank, E., Cherry, C. R., et al. (1997). Which depressed patients will respond to interpersonal psychotherapy? The role of abnormal EEG sleep profiles. *Amer. J. Psychiat., 154*(4), 502-509.

Thase, M. E., Kupfer, D. J., Buysse, D. J., Frank, E., et al. (1995). Electroencephalographic sleep profiles in single-episode and recurrent unipolar forms of major depression: I. Comparison during acute depressive states. *Biol. Psychiat., 38*, 506-515.

Thase, M. E., Kupfer, D. J., Fasiczka, A. J., Buysse, D. J., et al. (1997). Identifying an abnormal electroencephalographic sleep profile to characterize major depressive disorder. *Biol. Psychiat., 41*, 964-973.

Thase, M. E., Trivedi, M. H., & Rush, A. J. (1995). MAOIs in the contemporary treatment of depression. *Neuropsychopharmacology, 12*(3), 185-219.

Theander, S. (1970) Anorexia nervosa. *Acta Psychiatr. Scandin.*, [Suppl.], pp. 1-194.

Thielman, S. B. (1998). Reflections on the role of religion in the history of psychiatry. In H.G. Koenig et al.. (Eds.), *Handbook of religion and mental health*. San Diego: Academic Press.

Thigpen, C. H., & Cleckley, H. M. (1957). *The three faces of Eve*. New York: McGraw-Hill.

Thoits, P. A. (1999). Sociological approaches to mental illness. In A. V. Horwitz & T. L. Scheid (Eds.), *A handbook for the study of mental health: Social contexts, theories, and systems*. Cambridge, England: Cambridge University Press.

Thomas, E. (1996, April 15). What the unabomber did to me. *Newsweek*, pp. 40-41.

Thompson, J. W., Belcher, J. R., DeForge, B. R., Myers, C. P., et al. (1995). Trends in the inpatient care of persons with schizophrenia. *Schizo. Bull., 21*(1), 75-85.

Thompson, M. P., & Kingree, J. B. (1998). Brief report: The frequency and impact of violent trauma among pregnant substance abusers. *Addic. Behav., 23*(2), 257-262.

Thompson, M. P., Kaslow, N. J., Kingree, J. B., Puett, R., Thompson, N. J., & Meadows, L. (1999). Partner abuse and posttraumatic stress disorder as risk factors for suicide attempts in a sample of low-income, inner-city women. *J. Traum. Stress, 12*(1), 59-72.

Thompson, P. M., Gillin, J. C., Golshan, S., & Irwin, M. (1995). Polygraphic sleep measures differentiate alcoholics and stimulant abusers during short-term abstinence. *Biol. Psychiat., 38*, 831-836.

Thompson, R. A., & Sherman, R. T. (1993). *Helping athletes with eating disorders*. Champaign, IL: Human Kinetics.

Thompson, R. A., & Sherman, R. T. (1999). "Good athlete" traits and characteristics of anorexia nervosa: Are they similar? *Eat. Disord.: J. Treat. Prev., 7*(3), 181-190.

Thorn, B. E., Shealy, R. C., & Briggs, S. D. (1993). Sexual misconduct in psychotherapy: Reactions to a consumer-oriented brochure. *Profess. Psychol.: Res. Pract., 24*(1), 75-82.

Thorne, B., & Lambers, E. (Eds.) (1998). *Person-centered therapy: A European perspective*. London: Sage.

Thorpe, L. U. (1999). Psychiatric disorders. In M. P. Janicki & A. P. Dalton (Eds.), *Dementia, aging, and intellectual disabilities: A handbook*. Philadelphia: Brunner/Mazel.

Thorpe, S. J., & Salkozskis, P. M. (1995). Phobia beliefs: Do cognitive factors play a role in specific phobias? *Behav. Res. Ther., 33*(7), 805-816.

Thulesius, H., & Hakansson, A. (1999). Screening of posttraumatic stress disorder symptoms among Bosnian refugees. *J. Traum. Stress, 12*(1), 167-174.

Thyer, B. A. (1999). Cognitive behavioral group therapy and phenelzine both effects in social phobia.

Tiggeman, M., & Wilson-Barrett, E. (1998). Children's figure ratings: Relationship to self-esteem and negative stereotyping. *Inter. J. Eat. Disorders, 23,* 83–88.

Tiihonen, J., Kuikka, J., Viinamaki, H., Lehtonen, J., et al. (1995). Altered cerebral blood flow during hysterical paresthesia. *Biol. Psychiat., 37*(2), 134–135.

Tiller, J. W. G., Bouwer, C., Behnke, K., et al. (1999). Moclobemide and fluoxetine for panic disorder. *Eur. Arch. Psychiat. Clin. Neurosci., 249*(Suppl. 1), S7–S10.

Tillich, P. (1952, December). Anxiety, religion, and medicine. *Pastoral Psychol., 3,* 11–17.

Time. (1998, Oct. 12). Numbers.

Time/CNN Poll. (1998). From what sources do teenagers today mainly learn about sex? In R. Stodghill, II. (1999, March 12). Where'd you learn that? *Time, 151*(23).

Time/CNN Poll. (1999, June 7). *Time, 153*(22), 56.

Tishler, C. L., McKenry, P. C., & Morgan, K. C. (1981). Adolescent suicide attempts: Some significant factors. *Suic. Life-Threat. Behav., 11*(2), 86–92.

Tkachuk, G. A., & Martin, G. L. (1999). Exercise therapy for patients with psychiatric disorders: Research and clinical implications. *Profess. Psychol.: Res. Pract., 30*(3), 275–282.

Tobin, D. L. (2000). *Coping strategies therapy for bulimia nervosa.* Washington, DC: American Psychological Association.

Todd, R. D., Geller, B., Neuman, R., Fox, L. W., et al. (1996). Increased prevalence of alcoholism in relatives of depressed and bipolar children. *J. Amer. Acad. Child Adol. Psychiat., 35*(6), 716–724.

Todd, R. D., Reich, W., Petti, T., Joshi, P., et al. (1996). Psychiatric diagnoses in the child and adolescent members of extended families identified through adult bipolar affective disorder probands. *J. Amer. Acad. Child Adol. Psychiat., 35*(5), 664–671.

Todd, T. C., & Stanton, M. D. (1983). Research on marital and family therapy: Answers, issues, and recommendations for the future. In B. B. Wolman & G. Stricker (Eds.), *Handbook of family and marital therapy.* New York: Plenum Press.

Tohen, M., & Grundy, S. (1999). Management of acute mania. *J. Clin. Psychiat., 60*(Suppl. 5), 31–34.

Tolbert, H. A. (1996). Psychoses in children and adolescents: A review. *J. Clin. Psychiat., 57*(Suppl. 3), 4–8.

Tomasson, K., Kent, D., & Coryell, W. (1991). Somatization and conversion disorders: Comorbidity and demographics at presentation. *Acta Psychiatr. Scandin., 84*(3), 288–293.

Tomchek, L. B., Gordon, R., Arnold, M., & Handleman, J. (1992). Teaching preschool children with autism and their normally developing peers: Meeting the challenges of integrated education. *Focus Autistic Behav., 7*(2), 1–17.

Torgersen, S. (1983). Genetic factors in anxiety disorders. *Arch. Gen. Psychiat., 40,* 1085–1089.

Torgersen, S. (1983). Genetics of neurosis: The effects of sampling variation upon the twin concordance ratio. *Brit. J. Psychiat., 142,* 126–132.

Torgersen, S. (1984). Genetic and nosological aspects of schizotypal and borderline personality disorders: A twin study. *Arch. Gen. Psychiat., 41,* 546–554.

Torgersen, S. (1990). Comorbidity of major depression and anxiety disorders in twin pairs. *Amer. J. Psychiat., 147,* 1199–1202.

Torgersen, S. (2000). Genetics of patients with borderline personality disorder. *Psychiat. Clin. N. Amer., 23*(1), 1–9.

Torrey, E. F. (1988). *Nowhere to go: The tragic odyssey of the homeless mentally ill.* New York: Harper & Row.

Torrey, E. F. (1991). A viral-anatomical explanation of schizophrenia. *Schizo. Bull., 17*(1), 15–18.

Torrey, E. F. (1992). Are we overestimating the genetic contribution to schizophrenia? *Schizo. Bull., 18*(2), 159–170.

Torrey, E. F. (1997). *Out of the shadows: Confronting America's mental illness crisis.* New York: Wiley.

Torrey, E. F. (1999, April 16). Interviewed in J. Lang, Local jails dumping grounds for mentally ill: 700,000 acutely ill held yearly. *Detroit News.*

Torrey, E. F., Bowler, A. E., Rawlings, R., & Terrazas, A. (1993). Seasonality of schizophrenia and stillbirths. *Schizo. Bull., 19*(3), 557–562.

Torrey, E. F., Bowler, A. E., Taylor, E. H., & Gottesman, I. I. (1994). *Schizophrenia and manic-depressive disorder.* New York: Basic Books.

Torrey, E. F., Miller, J., Rawlings, R., & Yolken, R. H. (1997). Seasonality of births in schizophrenia and bipolar disorder: A review of the literature. *Schizo. Res., 28*(1), 1–38.

Torrey, E. F., Wolfe, S. M., & Flynn, L. M. (1988). *Care of the seriously mentally ill: A rating of state programs* (2nd ed.). Washington, DC: Public Citizen Health Research Group and National Alliance for the Mentally Ill.

Travis, J. (1996, March 23). AIDS update '96: New drugs, new tests, new optimism mark recent AIDS research. *Science News, 149,* pp. 184–186.

Treaster, J. B. (1992, September 20). After hurricane, Floridians show symptoms seen in war. *New York Times.*

Treasure, J., & Szmukler, G. I. (1995). Medical complications of chronic anorexia nervosa. In G. I. Szmukler, C. Dare, & J. Treasure (Eds.), *Handbook on eating disorders: Theory, treatment and research.* Chichester, England: Wiley.

Treasure, J., Todd, G., & Szmukler, G. (1995). The inpatient treatment of anorexia nervosa. In G. Szmukler, C. Dare, & J. Treasure (Eds.), *Handbook of eating disorders: Theory, treatment and research.* Chichester, England: Wiley.

Treatment Advocacy Center. (1999, April 16). Cited in J. Lang, Local jails dumping grounds for mentally ill: 700,000 acutely ill held yearly. *Detroit News.*

Treffert, D. A. (1989). *Extraordinary people: Understanding savant syndrome.* New York: Ballantine Books.

Trestman, R. L., Horvath, T., Kalus, O., Peterson, A. E., et al. (1996). Event-related potentials in schizotypal personality disorder. *J. Neuropsych. Clin. Neurosci., 8,* 33–40.

Troiano, R. P., Frongillo, E. A., Sobal, J., & Levitsky, D. A. (1996). The relationship between body weight and mortality: A quantitative analysis of combined information from existing studies. *Inter. J. Obesity, 20,* 63–75.

Trollor, J. N. (1999). Attention deficit hyperactivity disorder in adults: Conceptual and clinical issues. *Med. J. Austral., 171*(8), 421–425.

Tross, S., & Hirsch, D. A. (1988). Psychological distress and neuropsychological complications of HIV infection and AIDS. *Amer. Psychologist, 43*(11), 929–934.

Trotter, R. J. (1985, November). Geschwind's syndrome: Van Gogh's malady. *Psychol. Today,* p. 46.

True, W. R., & Lyons, M. J. (1999). Genetic risk factors for PTSD: A twin study. In R. Yehuda et al. Eds.), *Risk factors for posttraumatic stress disorder.* Washington, DC: American Psychiatric Press.

True, W. R., Heath, A. C., Scherrer, J. F., Xian, H., Lin, N., Eisen, S. A., Lyons, M. J., Goldberg, J., & Tsuang, M. T. (1999). Interrelationship of genetic and environmental influences on conduct disorder and alcohol and marijuana dependence symptoms. *Amer. J. Med. Genet., 88*(4), 391–397.

True, W., Rice, L., Eisen, S. A., et al. (1993). A twin study of genetic and environmental contributions to the liability for posttraumatic stress symptoms. *Arch. Gen. Psychiat., 50,* 257–264.

Trujillo, A. (2000). Psychotherapy with Native Americans: A view into the role of religion and spirituality. In P. S. Richards, A. E. Bergin, et al. (Eds.), *Handbook of psychotherapy and religious diversity.* Washington, DC: American Psychological Association.

Trujillo, K. A., & Akil, H. (1991). The NMDA receptor antagonist MK-801 increases morphine catalepsy and lethality. *Pharmacol. Biochem. Behav., 38*(3), 673–675.

Trull, T. J., Sher, K. J., Minks-Brown, C., Durbin, J., & Burr, R. (2000). Borderline personality disorder and substance use disorders: A review and integration. *Clin. Psychol. Rev., 20*(2), 235–253.

Tryon, G. (1987). *Profess. Psychol., 17,* 357–363.

Tsai, L. Y. (1999). Psychopharmacology in autism. *Psychosom. Med., 61*(5), 651–665.

Tsoi, W. F. (1992). Male and female transsexuals: a comparison. *Singapore Med. J., 33*(2), 182–185.

Tsuang, M. (2000). Schizophrenia: Genes and environment. *Biol. Psychiat., 47*(3), 210–220.

Tsuang, M. T., Fleming, J. A., & Simpson, J. C. (1999). Suicide and schizophrenia. In D.G. Jacobs (Ed.), *The Harvard Medical School guide to suicide assessment and intervention.* San Francisco: Jossey-Bass.

Tucker, G. J. (1998). Putting DSM-IV in perspective. *Amer. J. Psychiat., 155*(2), 159–161.

Tucker, P. (1999, February 18). Health is hot online: Depression is No. 1 topic. *HealthScount.*

Turek, F. (1996). Melatonin hype hard to swallow. *Nature, 379,* 295–296.

Turk, C. L., Fresco, D. M., & Heimberg, R. G. (1999). Cognitive behavior therapy. In M. Hersen & A.S. Bellack (Eds.), *Handbook of comparative interventions for adult disorders* (2nd ed.). New York: Wiley.

Turkat, I. D., Keane, S. P., & Thompson-Pope, S. K. (1990). Social processing errors among paranoid personalities. *J. Psychopathol. Behav. Assess., 12*(3), 263–269.

Turner, E., Ewing, J., Shilling, P., Smith, T., Irwin, M., Schuckit, M., & Kelsoe, J. (1992). Lack of association between an RFLP near the D2 dopamine receptor gene and severe alcoholism. *Biol. Psychiat., 31*(3), 285–290.

Turner, J., Batik, M., Palmer, L. J., Forbes, D., & McDermott, B. M. (2000). Detection and importance of laxative use in adolescents with anorexia nervosa. *J. Amer. Acad. Child Adol. Psychiat., 39*(3), 378–385.

Turner, L. A., Althof, S. E., Levine, S. B., Bodner, D. R., Kursh, E. D., & Resnick, M. I. (1991). External vacuum devices in the treatment of erectile dysfunction: A one-year study of sexual and psychosocial impact. *J. Sex Marital Ther., 17*(2), 81–93.

Turner, R. J., & Lloyd, D. A. (1995, December). Lifetime traumas and mental health: The significance of cumulative adversity. *J. Hlth. Soc. Behav., 36,* 360–376.

Turner, S. M., Beidel, D. C., Borden, J. W., Stanley, M. A., et al. (1991). Social phobia: Axis I and II correlates. *J. Abnorm. Psychol., 100*(1), 102–106.

Turner, S. M., Beidel, D. C., Dancu, C. V., & Keys, D. J. (1986). Psychopathology of social phobia and comparison to avoidant personality disorder. *J. Abnorm. Psychol., 95*(4), 389–394.

Turner, S. M., Beidel, D. C., Long, P. J., & Greenhouse, J. (1992). Reduction of fear in social phobics: An examination of extinction patterns. *Behav. Ther.*, 23(3), 389–403.

Turner, S. M., Hersen, M., & Bellack, A. S. (1977). Effects of social disruption, stimulus interference, and aversive conditioning on auditory hallucinations. *Behav. Mod.*, 1(2), 249–258.

Turner, W. J. (1995). Homosexuality, Type 1: An Xq28 phenomenon. *Arch. Sex. Behav.*, 24(2), 109–134.

Turton, M. D., O'Shea, D., Gunn, I., Beak, S. A., et al. (1996, January 4). A role for glucagon-like peptide-1 in the central regulation of feeding. *Nature*, 379, 69–72.

Twain, M. (1885). *The adventures of Huckleberry Finn.*

Tweed, J. L., Schoenbach, V. J., & George, L. K. (1989). The effects of childhood parental death and divorce on six-month history of anxiety disorders. *Brit. J. Psychiat.*, 154, 823–828.

Tyrer, P. (1992). Anxiolytics not acting at the benzodiazepine receptor: Beta blockers. *Prog. Neuropsychopharmacol. Biol. Psychiat.*, 16(1), 17–26.

UNINCB (United Nations International Narcotics Control Board) Report. (1996). Cited in J. Roberts, Behavioral disorders are over-diagnosed in U.S., *Brit. Med. J.*, 312, 657.

UTMB (University of Texas Medical Branch at Galveston). (1999, May 14). *Mania drugs cut hospitalization costs.* Study presented at meeting of American Psychiatric Association, May 17, 1999.

Uchino, B. N., & Garvey, T. S. (1997). The availability of social support reduces cardiovascular reactivity to acute psychological stress. *J. Behav. Med.*, 20(1), 15–27.

Uchoa, D. D. (1985). Narcissistic transference? *Rev. Bras. Psicanal.*, 19(1), 87–96.

Uhlenhuth, E. H., Balter, M. B., Ban, T. A., & Yang, K. (1995). International study of expert judgment on therapeutic use of benzodiazepines and other psychotherapeutic medications: III. Clinical features affecting experts' therapeutic recommendations in anxiety disorders. *Psychopharmacol. Bull.*, 31(2), 289–296.

Uhlenhuth, E. H., Balter, M. B., Ban, T. A., & Yang, K. (1999). Trends in recommendations for the pharmacotherapy of anxiety disorders by an international expert panel, 1992–1997. *Eur. Neuropsychopharmacology*, 9(Suppl. 6), S393–S398.

Uhlig, R. (1996, October 31). Prosthetics improve a dog's life. *Electronic Telegraph*, Issue 526.

Ullmann, L. P., & Krasner, L. (1975). *A psychological approach to abnormal behavior* (2nd ed.). Englewood Cliffs, NJ: Prentice Hall.

Ulrich, R. S. (1984). View from a window may influence recovery from surgery. *Science*, 224, 420–421.

Ungvarski, P. J., & Trzcianowska, H. (2000). Neurocognitive disorders seen in HIV disease. *Issues Ment. Hlth. Nurs.*, 21(1), 51–70.

Uniform Crime Reports. (1997). *Crime in the United States: 1996 Uniform Crime Reports.* Washington, DC: FBI.

Uretsky, S. (1999, June 25). Clear as mud: They call it informed consent. *HealthScout.*

Uretsky, S. (1999, June 28). Mate in two: Ideas of perfection vary. *HealthScout.*

Ursano, R. J., Boydstun, J. A., & Wheatley, R. D. (1981). Psychiatric illness in U. S. Air Force Vietnam prisoners of war: A five-year follow-up. *Amer. J. Psychiat.*, 138(3), 310–314.

Ursano, R. J., Fullerton, C. S., Epstein, R. S., Crowley, B., Kao, T. C., Vance, K., Craig, K. J., Dougall, A. L., & Baum, A. (1999). Acute and chronic posttraumatic stress disorder in motor vehicle accident victims. *Amer. J. Psychiat.*, 156(4), 589–595.

Ursano, R. J., Fullerton, C. S., Vance, K., & Kao, T. C. (1999). Posttraumatic stress disorder and identification in disaster workers. *Amer. J. Psychiat.*, 156(3), 353–359.

U.S. Bureau of the Census. (1990). *Statistical abstract of the United States.* Washington, DC: U. S. Government Printing Office.

U.S. Dept. of Justice/Bureau of Justice Statistics. (1994). *Violence between inmates: Domestic violence.* Anapolis Junction, MD: Bureau of Justice Statistics Clearinghouse.

U.S. Dept. of Justice/Bureau of Justice Statistics. (1995). *Violence against women: Estimates from the redesigned National Crime Victimization Survey.* Anapolis Junction, MD: Bureau of Justice Statistics Clearinghouse.

U.S. Department of Justice. (1997, September 6). Cited in T. Daunt, Jails must alter care of mentally ill. *Los Angeles Times*, Part B, p. 1.

U.S. Public Health Service. (1999, April 16). Report. Cited in J. Lang, Local jails dumping grounds for mentally ill: 700,000 acutely ill held yearly. *Detroit News.*

Vacc, N. A., & Juhnke, G. A. (1997). The use of structured clinical interviews for assessment in counseling. *J. Couns. Dev.*, 75(6), 470–480.

Vaillant, G. E. (1983). Natural history of male alcoholism: V. Is alcoholism the cart or the horse to sociopathy? *Brit. J. Addic.*, 78(3), 317–326.

Vaillant, G. E. (1993). *The wisdom of the ego.* Cambridge, MA: Harvard University Press.

Vaillant, G. E. (1994). Ego mechanisms of defense and personality psychopathology. *J. Abnorm. Psychol.*, 103(1), 44–50.

Vaillant, G. E., & Milofsky, E. S. (1982). Natural history of male alcoholism: IV. Paths to recovery. *Arch. Gen. Psychiat.*, 39, 127–133.

Vaillant, G. E., & Perry, J. C. (1985). Personality disorders. In H. I. Kaplan & B. J. Sadock (Eds.), *Comprehensive textbook of psychiatry* (4th ed.). Baltimore: Williams & Wilkins.

Vaillant, P. M., & Antonowicz, D. H. (1992). Rapists, incest offenders, and child molesters in treatment: Cognitive and social skills training. *Inter. J. Offend. Ther. Compar. Crimin.*, 36(3), 221–230.

Valdisseri, E.V., Carroll, K. R., & Hartl, A. J. (1986). A study of offenses committed by psychotic inmates in a county jail. *Hosp. Comm. Psychiat.*, 37, 163–165.

Valenstein, E. S. (1986). *Great and desperate cures.* New York: Basic Books.

Valente, S. M., & Saunders, J. M. (1995). Women, physical illness and suicidal behavior. In S. S. Canetto & D. Lester (Eds.), *Women and suicidal behavior.* New York: Springer.

Valenti-Hein, D. C., Yarnold, P. R., & Mueser, K. T. (1994). Evaluation of the dating skills program for improving heterosocial interactions in people with mental retardation. *Behav. Mod.*, 18(1), 32–46.

Vanathy, S., Sharma, P. S. V. N., & Kumar, K. B. (1998). The efficacy of alpha and theta neurofeedback training in treatment of generalized anxiety disorder. *Indian J. Clin Psychol.*, 25(2), 136–143.

van Bommel, H. (1992). *Dying for care: Hospice care or euthanasia.* Toronto: NC Press.

Van Bourgondien, M. E., & Schopler, E. (1990). Critical issues in the residential care of people with autism. *J. Autism Dev. Disorders*, 20(3), 391–399.

Van de Castle, R. (1993). Content of dreams. In M. A. Carskadon (Ed.), *Encyclopedia of sleep and dreams.* New York: Macmillan.

VandenBos, G. R. (1996). Outcome assessment of psychotherapy. *Amer. Psychologist*, 51(10), 1005–1006.

Vandereycken, W. (1994). Parental rearing behaviour and eating disorders. In C. Perris, W. A. Arrindell, & M. Eisemann (Eds.), *Parenting and psychopathology.* Chichester, England: Wiley.

Van der Ham, T., Meulman, J. J., Van Strien, D. C., & Van Engeland, H. (1997). Empirically based subgrouping of eating disorders in adolescents: A longitudinal perspective. *Brit. J. Psychiat.*, 170, 363–368.

van der Hart, O., Brown, P., & Graafland, M. (1999). Trauma-induced dissociative amnesia in World war I combat soldiers. *Austral. New Zeal. J. Psychiat.*, 33(1), 37–46.

van der Kolk, B. A., McFarlane, A. C., van der Hart, O., & Rice-Smith, E. (1999). Treatment of posttraumatic stress disorder and other trauma-related disorders. In D. Spiegel et al., (Eds.), *Efficacy and cost-effectiveness of psychotherapy. Clinical practice.* Washington, DC: American Psychiatric Association.

Van der Molen, H. T., Nijenhuis, J. T., & Keen, G. (1995). The effects of intelligence test preparation. *Eur. J. Pers.*, 9(1), 43–56.

VanGent, E. M., & Zwart, F. M. (1991). Psychoeducation of partners of bipolar-manic patients. *J. Affect. Disorders*, 21(1), 15–18.

Van Hasselt, V., Null, J., Kempton, T., & Buckstein, O. (1993). Social skills and depression in adolescent substance abusers. *Addic. Behav.*, 18, 9–18.

van Os, J., Fañanas, L., Cannon, M., Macdonald, A., & Murray, R. (1997). Dermatoglyphic abnormalities in psychosis: A twin study. *Biol. Psychiat.*, 41, 624–626.

Van Praag, H. M. (1983). CSF 5-HIAA and suicide in non-depressed schizophrenics. *Lancet*, 2, 977–978.

Van Praag, H. M. (1983). In search of the action mechanism of antidepressants. 5-HTP/tyrosine mixtures in depression. *Neuropharmacology*, 22, 433–440.

Van Praag, H. M. (1986). Affective disorders and aggression disorders: Evidence for a common biological mechanism. In R. W. Maris (Ed.), *Biology of suicide.* New York: Guilford.

Vatz, R., & Weinberg, L. (1993, January 10). Keno krazy? *Washington Post*, p. C5.

Vaughan, K., Doyle, M., McConaghy, N., & Blaszcznski, A. (1992). The relationship between relative's expressed emotion and schizophrenic relapse: An Australian replication. *Soc. Psychiat. Psychiat. Epidemiol.*, 27(1), 10–15.

Velamoor, V. R., Norman, R. M., & Caroff, S. N., et al (1994). Progression of symptoms in neuroleptic malignant syndrome. *J. Nerv. Ment. Dis.*, 182, 168–173.

Velleman, R., & Orford, J. (1993). The adult adjustment of offspring of parents with drinking problems. *Brit. J. Psychiat.*, 162, 503–516.

Velligan, D. I., Funderburg, L. G., Giesecke, S. L., & Miller, A. L. (1995). Longitudinal analysis of communication deviance in the families of schizophrenic patients. *Psychiat. Interpers. Biol. Process.*, 58(1), 6–19.

Velting, D. M., Shaffer, D., Gould, M. S., Garfinkel, R., Fisher, P., & Davies, M. (1998). Parent-victim agreement in adolescent suicide research. *J. Amer. Acad. Child Adol. Psychiat.*, 37(11), 1161–1166.

Venditti, E., Wing, R., Jakicic, J., Butler, B., & Marcus, M. (1996). Weight cycling, psychological health, and binge eating in obese women. *J. Cons. Clin. Psychol.*, 64(2), 400–405.

Verburg, K., Griez, E., Meijer, J., & Pols, H. (1995). Respiratory disorders as a possible predisposing factor for panic disorder. *J. Affect Disorders,* 33(2), 129–134.

Verfaellie, M., Cermak, L. S., Blackford, S. P., et al. (1990). Strategic and automatic priming of semantic memory in alcoholic Korsakoff patients. *Brain Cog.,* 13(2), 178–192.

Vernberg, E. M., La Greca, A. M., Silverman, W. K., & Prinstein, M. J. (1996). Prediction of posttraumatic stress symptoms in children after Hurricane Andrew. *J. Abnorm. Psychol.,* 105(2), 237–248.

Vertosick, F. T., Jr. (1997, October). Lobotomy's back. *Discover,* pp. 66–71.

Vetter, H. J. (1969). *Language behavior and psychopathology.* Chicago: Rand McNally.

Vieira, C. (1993). Nudity in dreams. In M. A. Carskadon (Ed.), *Encyclopedia of sleep and dreams.* New York: Macmillan.

Viguera, A. C., Nonacs, R., Cohen, L. S., Tondo, L., Murray, A., & Baldessarini, R. J. (2000). Risk of recurrence of bipolar disorder in pregnant and nonpregnant women after discontinuing lithium maintenance. *Amer. J. Psychiat.,* 157(2), 179–184.

Vinogradov, S., & Yalom, I. D. (1994). Group therapy. In R. E. Hales, S. C. Yudofsky, & J. A. Talbott, (Eds.), *The American Psychiatric Press textbook of psychiatry* (2nd ed.). Washington, DC: American Psychiatric Press.

Vinson, D. (1994). Therapy for attention-deficit hyperactivity disorder. *Arch. Fam. Med.,* 3, 445–451.

Visser, P. J., Krabbendam, L., Verhey, F. R., Hofman, P. A., Verhoeven, W. M., Tuinier, S., Wester, A., Den Berg, Y. W., Goessens, L. F., Werf, Y. D., & Jolles, J. (1999). Brain correlates of memory dysfunction in alcoholic Korsakoff's syndrome. *J. Neurol. Neurosurg. Psychiat.,* 67(6), 774–778.

Vitousek, K., & Manke, F. (1994). Personality variables and disorders in anorexia nervosa and bulimia nervosa. *J. Abnorm. Psychol.,* 103(1), 137–147.

Vlaeyen, J. W. S., Haazen, I. W. C. J., Schuerman, J. A., Kole-Snijders, A. M. J., et al. (1995). Behavioural rehabilitation of chronic low back pain: Comparison of an operant treatment, an operant-cognitive treatment and an operant-respondent treatment. *Brit. J. Clin. Psychol.,* 34(1), 95–118.

Vogele, C., & Steptoe, A. (1993). Anger inhibition and family history as modulators of cardiovascular responses to mental stress in adolescent boys. *J. Psychosom. Res.,* 37(5), 503–514.

Vogeltanz, N. D., Wilsnack, S. C., Harris, T. R., Wilsnack, R. W., Wonderlich, S. A., & Kristjanson, A. F. (1999). Prevalence and risk factors for childhood sexual abuse in women: National survey findings. *Child Abuse Negl.,* 23(6), 579–592.

Volavka, J. (1995). *Neurobiology of violence.* Washington, DC: American Psychiatric Press.

Volkmar, F. R., Carter, A., Sparrow, S. S., & Cicchetti, D. V. (1993). Quantifying social development in autism. *J. Amer. Acad. Child Adol. Psychiat.,* 32(3), 627–632.

Volkow, N. D., & Fowler, J. S. (2000). Addiction, a disease of compulsion and drive: Involvement of the orbitofrontal cortex. *Cerebral Cortex,* 10(3), 318–325.

Volkow, N. D., Fowler, J. S., & Wang, G. J. (1999). Imaging studies on the role of dopamine in cocaine reinforcement and addiction in humans. *J. Psychopharmacol.,* 13(4), 337–345.

Volkow, N. D., Gillespie, H., Tancredi, L., & Hollister, L. (1995). The effects of marijuana in the human brain measured with regional brain glucose metabolism. In A. Biegon & N. D. Volkow

(Eds.), *Sites of drug action in the human brain.* Boca Raton, FL: CRC Press.

Volkow, N. D., Wang, G. J., Fowler, J. S., Logan, J., Gatley, S. J., Hitzemann, R., Chen, A. D., Dewey, S. L., & Pappas, N. (1997). Decreased striatal dopaminergic responsiveness in detoxified cocaine-dependent subjects. *Nature,* 386(6627), 830–833.

Volkow, N. D., Wang, G. J., Fowler, J. S., Logan, J., Gatley, S. J., Wong, C., Hiutzemann, R., & Pappas, N. R. (1999). Reinforcing effects of psychostimulants in humans are associated with increases in brain dopamine and occupancy of D$_2$ receptors. *J. Pharmacol. Exp. Ther.,* 291(1), 409–415.

Volpe, B. T., & Hirst, W. (1983). The characterization of an amnestic syndrome following hypoxic ischemic injury. *Arch. Neurol.,* 40, 436–440.

Volpicelli, J., Alterman, A., Hayashida, M., & O'Brien, C. (1992). Naltrexone in the treatment of alcohol dependence. *Arch. Gen. Psychiat.,* 49, 876–880.

Volz, H. P., & Laux, P. (2000). Potential treatment for subthreshold and mild depression: A comparison of St. John's wort extracts and fluoxetine. *Comprehen. Psychiat.,* 41(2, Suppl. 1), 133–137.

Von Burg, M., & Hibbard, R. (1995). Munchausen syndrome by proxy: A different kind of child abuse. *Indiana Med.,* 88(5), 378–382.

Vonnegut, M. (1974, April). Why I want to bite R. D. Laing. *Harper's,* 248(1478), 80–92.

Vostanis, P., Feehan, C., Grattan, E., & Bickerton, W.-L. (1996). A randomised controlled out-patient trial of cognitive-behavioural treatment for children and adolescents with depression: 9-month follow-up. *J. Affect. Disorders,* 40, 105–116.

Vredenburg, K., Flett, G. L., & Krames, L. (1993). Analogue versus clinical depression: A critical reappraisal. *Psychol. Bull.,* 113(2), 327–344.

WHO (World Health Organization). (1992). *World health statistics annual.* Geneva: Author.

Wadden, T. A., & Anderton, C. H. (1982). The clinical use of hypnosis. *Psychol. Bull.,* 91(2), 215–243.

Wade, T. D., Bulik, C. M., Neale, M., & Kendler, K. S. (2000). Anorexia nervosa and major depression: Shared genetic and environmental risk factors. *Amer. J. Psychiat.,* 157(3), 469–471.

Wagenaar, A. C., Murray, D. M., & Toomey, T. L. (2000). Communities mobilizing for change on alcohol (CMCA): Effects of a randomized trial on arrests and traffic crashes. *Addiction,* 95(2), 209–217.

Wahl, O. F., & Hunter, J. (1992). Are gender effects being neglected in schizophrenia research? *Schizo. Bull.,* 18(2), 313–318.

Wahlberg, K.-E., Wynne, L. C., Oja, H., Keskitalo, P., et al. (1997). Gene-environment interaction in vulnerability to schizophrenia: Findings from the Finnish Adoptive Family Study of Schizophrenia. *Amer. J. Psychiat.,* 154(3), 355–362.

Waikar, S. V., & Craske, M. G. (1997). Cognitive correlates of anxious and depressive symptomatology: An examination of the helplessness/hopelessness model. *J. Anx. Dis.,* 11(1), 1–16.

Wakefield, J. C. (1999). The measurement of mental disorder. In A. V. Horwitz & T. L. Scheid (Eds.), *A handbook for the study of mental health: Social contexts, theories, and systems.* Cambridge, England: Cambridge University Press.

Wakeling, A. (1995). Physical treatments. In G. Szmukler, C. Dare, & J. Treasure (Eds.), *Handbook of eating disorders: Theory, treatment and research.* Chichester, England: Wiley.

Walker, E., & Young, T. D., (1986). *A killing cure.* New York: Henry Holt.

Walker, E. A., Gelfand, A., Katon, W. J., Koss, M. P., Von Korff, M., Bernstein, D., & Russo, J. (1999). Adult health status of women with histories of childhood abuse and neglect. *Amer. J. Med.,* 107(4), 332–339.

Walker, L. E. (1979). *The battered woman.* New York: Harper & Row.

Walker, L. E. (1984). *The battered woman syndrome.* New York: Springer.

Walker, L. E. (1984). Battered women, psychology, and public policy. *Amer. Psychologist,* 39(10), 1178–1182.

Walker, L. E. (1999). Psychology and domestic violence around the world. *Amer. Psychologist,* 54(1), 21–29.

Walker, R. D., Howard, M. O., Walker, P. S., Lambert, M. D., Maloy, F., & Suchinsky, R. T. (1996). Essential and reactive alcoholism: A review. *J. Clin. Psychol.,* 52(1), 80–95.

Wallace, S. E. (1981). The right to live and the right to die. In S. E. Wallace & A. Eser (Eds.), *Suicide and euthanasia: The rights of personhood.* Knoxville: University of Tennessee Press.

Walsh, B. T., Wilson, G. R., Loeb, K. L., Devlin, M. J., et al. (1997). Medication and psychotherapy in the treatment of bulimia nervosa. *Amer. J. Psychiat.,* 154, 523–531.

Walters, E. E., & Kendler, K. S. (1995). Anorexia nervosa and anorexia-like syndromes in a population based female twin sample. *Amer. J. Psychiat.,* 152, 64–71.

Walton, J. W., Johnson, S. B., & Algina, J. (1999). Mother and child perceptions of child anxiety: Effects of race, health status, and stress. *Journal of Pediatric Psychology,* 24(1), 29–39.

Wanck, B. (1984). Two decades of involuntary hospitalization legislation. *Amer. J. Psychiat.,* 41, 33–38.

Wang, H. Y., Markowitz, P., Levinson, D., Undie, A. S., & Friedman, E. (1999). Increased membrane-associated protein kinase C activity and translocation in blood platelets from bipolar affective disorder patients. *J. Psychiat. Res.,* 33(2), 171–179.

Wang, S., Sun, C., Walczak, C. A., Ziegle, J. S., et al. (1995, May). Evidence for a susceptibility locus for schizophrenia on chromosome 6pter-p22. *Nature Genetics,* 10, 41–46.

Ward, A., Brown, N., & Treasure, J. (1996). Persistent osteopenia after recovery from anorexia nervosa. *Inter. J. Eat. Disorders,* 22, 71–75.

Warga, C. (1988, September). You are what you think. *Psychol. Today,* pp. 54–58.

Waring, M., & Ricks, D. (1965). Family patterns of children who become adult schizophrenics. *J. Nerv. Ment. Dis.,* 140(5), 351–364.

Warner, G. (1999, January 29). Spitzer seeks law on medication for the mentally ill. *Buffalo News,* p. 1C.

Warnock, J. K., Bundren, J. C., & Morris, D. W. (1997). Female hypoactive sexual desire disorder due to androgen deficiency: Clinical and psychometric issues. *Psychopharmacol. Bull.,* 33(4), 761–766.

Warnock, J. K., Bundren, J. C., & Morris, D. W. (1999). Female hypoactive sexual disorder: Case studies of physiologic androgen replacement. *J. Sex Marital Ther.,* 25(3), 175–182.

Warren, G., & Sampson, G. (1995). Medical audit of an assessment clinic for male erectile dysfunction. *J. Sex. Marital Ther.,* 10(1), 39–46.

Warren, L. W., & Ostrom, J. C. (1988). Pack rats: World-class savers. *Psychol. Today,* 22(2), 58–62.

Warren, R. (1997). REBT and generalized anxiety disorder. In J. Yankura, W. Dryden, et al. (Eds.), *Using REBT with common psychological problems: A therapist's casebook.* New York: Springer.

Washton, A. M., & Gold, M. S. (1984). Chronic cocaine abuse: Evidence for adverse effects on health and functioning. *Psychiatr. Ann., 14*(10), 733–743.

Wasik, J.F. (1999). The truth about herbal supplements. *Consumer Digest, 38*(4), 75–82.

Wasserman, I. M. (1992). The impact of epidemic, war, prohibition and media on suicide: United States, 1910–1920. *Suic. Life-Threat. Behav., 22*(2), 240–254.

Wasserman, I. M., & Stack, S. (2000). The relationship between occupation and suicide among African American males: Ohio, 1989–1991. In R. W. Maris, S. S. Canetto, et al. (Eds.), *Review of suicidology, 2000.* New York: Guilford.

Waters, L. (1990). Reinforcing the empty fortress: An examination of recent research into the treatment of autism. *Educ. Studies, 16*(1), 3–16.

Watkins, C. E., Jr., & Campbell, V. L., (Eds.). (2000). *Testing and assessment in counseling practice* (2nd ed.). Mahwah, NJ: Erlbaum.

Watson, C. G. (1987). Recidivism in "controlled drinker" alcoholics: A longitudinal study. *J. Clin. Psychol., 43*(3), 404–412.

Watson, C. G., Hancock, M., Gearhart, L. P. Mendez, C. M., et al. (1997). A comparative outcome study of frequent, moderate, occasional, and nonattenders of Alcoholics Anonymous. *J. Clin. Psychol., 53*(3), 209–214.

Watson, D., Clark, L. A., & Harkness, A. R. (1994). Structures of personality and their relevance to psychopathology. *J. Abnorm. Psychol., 103*(1), 18–31.

Watson, J. B., & Rayner, R. (1920). Conditioned emotional reaction. *J. Exp. Psychol., 3,* 1–14.

Watson Wyatt Worldwide. (1995, July, 26). Job satisfaction survey. Cited in M. Reinemer, Work happy. *American Demographics.*

Watten, R. G., Vassend, O., Myhrer, T., & Syversen, J.-L. (1997). Personality factors and somatic symptoms. *Eur. J. Pers., 11*(1), 57–68.

Waxweiler, R. J., et al. (1995). Monitoring the impact of traumatic brain injury: A review and update. *J. Neurotrauma, 12*(4).

Wechsler, H., & Isaac, N. (1992). "Binge" drinkers at Massachusetts colleges: Prevalence, drinking styles, time trends, and associated problems. *JAMA, 267,* 2929–2931.

Wechsler, H., Davenport, A., Dowdall, G., Moeykens, B., & Castillo, S. (1994). Health and behavioral consequences of binge drinking in college. *JAMA, 272*(21), 1672–1677.

Wechsler, H., Dowdell, G. W., Davenport, A., & Castllo, S. (1995). Correlates of college student binge drinking. *Amer. J. Pub. Hlth., 85*(7), 921–926.

Wechsler, H., Dowdell, G. W., Davenport, A., & Rimm, E. (1995). A gender-specific measure of binge drinking among college students. *Amer. J. Pub. Hlth., 85*(7), 982–935.

Wechsler, H., et. al. (1997). Survey on college binge drinking. Reported by Harvard University School of Public Health.

Weeks, D., & James, J. (1995). *Eccentrics: A study of sanity and strangeness.* New York: Villard.

Wehmeyer, M. L. (1992). Self-determination and the education of students with mental retardation. *Educ. Training Ment. Retard., 27*(4), 302–314.

Weiner, H. (1977). *Psychobiology and human disease.* New York: Elsevier.

Weiner, H., Thaler, M., Reiser, M. F., & Mirsky, I. A. (1957). Etiology of duodenal ulcer: I. Relation of specific psychological characteristics to rate of gastric secretion (serum pepsinogen). *Psychosom. Med., 19,* 1–10.

Weiner, I. B. (1995). Methodological considerations in Rorschach research [Special issue: Methodological issues in psychological assessment research.] *Psychol. Assess., 7*(3), 330–337.

Weiner, I. B. (1998). Teaching the Rorschach comprehensive system. In L. Handler, M. J. Hilsenroth, et al. (Eds.), *Teaching and learning personality assessment.* The LEA series in personality and clinical psychology. Mahwah, NJ: Erlbaum.

Weiner, I. B. (1999). Contemporary perspectives on Rorschach assessment. *Eur. J. Psychol. Assess., 15*(1), 78–86.

Weiner, I. W. (1969). The effectiveness of suicide prevention programs. *Ment. Hyg., 53,* 357–373.

Weingarten, S. M. (1999). Psychosurgery. In B. L. Miller, J. L. Cummings, et al. (Eds.), *The human frontal lobes: Functions and disorders.* The science and practice of neuropsychology series. New York: Guilford.

Weinstock, L. S. (1999). Gender differences in the presentation and management of social anxiety disorder. *J. Clin. Psychiat., 60*(Suppl. 9), 9–13.

Weintraub, M., Segal, R. M., & Beck, A. T. (1974). An investigation of cognition and affect in the depressive experience of normal men. *J. Cons. Clin. Psychol., 42,* 911.

Weir, R. F. (1992). The morality of physician-assisted suicide. *Law, Med. Hlth. Care, 20*(1–2), 116–126.

Weishaar, M. E. (2000). Cognitive risk factors in suicide. In R. W. Maris, S. S. Canetto, et al. (Eds.), *Review of suicidology, 2000.* New York: Guilford.

Weisheit, R. A. (1990). Domestic marijuana growers: Mainstreaming deviance. *Deviant Behav., 11*(2), 107–129

Weiss, D. E. (1991). *The great divide.* New York: Poseidon Press/Simon & Schuster.

Weiss, D. S., Marmar, C. R., Schlenger, W. E., & Fairback, J. A., et al. (1992). The prevalence of lifetime and partial posttraumatic stress disorder in Vietnam theater veterans. *J. Traum. Stress, 5*(3), 365–376.

Weiss, R. (1997, January 3). Study takes a new tack on asthma. *Philadelphia Inquirer,* pp. A1, A22.

Weiss, R. D., & Hufford, M. R. (1999). Substance abuse and suicide. In D.G. Jacobs (Ed.), *The Harvard Medical School guide to suicide assessment and intervention.* San Francisco: Jossey-Bass.

Weissman, M. M. (1993, Spring). The epidemiology of personality disorders. A 1990 update. *J. Pers. Disorders* (Suppl.), pp. 44–62.

Weissman, M. M. (1995). The epidemiology of psychiatric disorders: Past, present, and future generations. [Special issue: Festschfirt for Ben Z. Locke, MSPH.] *Inter. J. Methods Psychiatr. Res., 5*(2), 69–78.

Weissman, M. M. (2000). Social functioning and the treatment of depression. *J. Clin. Psychiat., 61*(Suppl.), 33–38.

Weissman, M. M., & Boyd, J. H. (1984). The epidemiology of mental disorders. In R. M. Post & J. C. Ballenger (Eds.), *Neurobiology of mood disorders.* Baltimore: Williams & Wilkins.

Weissman, M. M., & Olfson, M. (1995). Depression in women: Implications for health care research. *Science, 269*(5225), 799–801.

Weissman, M. M., Livingston Bruce, M., Leaf, P. J., Florio, L. P., & Holzer, C., III. (1991). Affective disorders. In L. N. Robins & D. A. Regier (eds.), *Psychiatric disorders in America: The Epidemiologic Catchment Area Study.* New York: Free Press.

Weissman, M. M., Myers, J. K., & Harding, P. S. (1978). Psychiatric disorders in a U. S. urban community. *Amer. J. Psychiat., 135,* 459–462.

Weissman, M. M., et al. (1992). The changing rate of major depression: Cross-national comparisons. *JAMA, 268*(21), 3098–3105.

Weissman, M. M., Bland, R. C., Canino, G. J., Faravelli, C., Greenwald, S., Hwu, H. G., Joyce, P. R., Karam, E. G., Lee, C., Lellouch, J., Lepine, J. P., Newman, S. C., Oakley-Browne, M. A., Rubio-Stipec, M., Wells, J. E., Wickramaratne, P. J., Wittchen, H. U., & Yeh, E. K. (1997). The cross-national epidemiology of panic disorder. *Arch. Gen. Psychiat., 54*(4), 305–309.

Weissman, M. M., Bland, R. C., Canino, G. J., Greenwald, S., Hwu, H. G., Joyce, P. R., Karam, E. G., Lee, C. K., Lellouch, J., Lepine, J. P., Newman, S. C., Rubio-Stipec, M., Wells, J. E., Wickramaratne, P. J., Wittchen, H. U., & Yeh, E. K. (1999). Prevalence of suicide ideation and suicide attempts in nine countries. *Psychol. Med., 29*(1), 9–17.

Weissman, R. X. (1999, February). Getting bigger all the time. Americans say they're dieting and exercising, but the bathroom scale tells a different story. *American Demographics.*

Weissman, R. X. (1999, July). Head's up! *American Demographics.*

Welch, S., & Fairburn, C. (1994). Sexual abuse and bulimia nervosa: Three integrated case control comparisons. 11th National Conference on Eating Disorders (1992, Columbus Ohio). *Amer. J. Psychiat., 151,* 402–407.

Welch, S., & Fairburn, C. (1996). Childhood sexual and physical abuse as risk factors for the development of bulimia nervosa: A community-based case control study. *Child Abuse Negl., 20,* 633–642.

Wells, A. (1998). Cognitive therapy of social phobia. In N. Tarrier, A. Wells, et al. (Eds.), *Treating complex cases: The cognitive behavioural therapy approach.* Wiley series in clinical psychology. Chichester, England: American Ethnological Press.

Wells, A., Clark, M. D., Salkovskis, P., Ludgate, J., et al. (1995). Social phobia: The role of in-situation safety behaviors in maintaining anxiety and negative beliefs. *Behav. Ther., 26*(1), 153–161.

Wells, E. A., Peterson, P. L., Gainey, R. R., Hawkins, J. D., & Catalano, R. F. (1994). Outpatient treatment for cocaine abuse: A controlled comparison of relapse prevention and twelve-step approaches. *Amer. J. Drug Alc. Abuse, 20,* 1–17.

Wells, G. L., Small, M., Penrod, S., Malpass, R. S., Fulero, S. M., & Brimacombe, C. A. E. (1998). Eyewitness identification procedures: Recommendations for lineups and photospreads. *Law Human Behav., 22*(6), 603–647.

Wells, M. E., & Hinkle, J. S. (1990). Elimination of childhood encopresis: A family systems approach. *J. Ment. Hlth. Couns., 12*(4), 520–526.

Wender, P. H., Kety, S. S., Rosenthal, D., Schulsinger, F., Ortmann, J., & Lunde, I. (1986). Psychiatric disorders in the biological and adoptive families of adopted individuals with affective disorders. *Arch. Gen. Psychiat., 43,* 923–929.

Werder, S. F. (1995). An update on the diagnosis and treatment of mania in bipolar disorder. *Amer. Fam. Physician, 51*(5), 1126–1136.

Werth, J. (1995). Rational suicide reconsidered: AIDS as an impetus for change. Annual Conference of the Association for Death Education & Counseling. *Death Stud., 19*(1), 65–80.

Werth, J. (1996). Rational suicide? Implications for mental health professionals. Washington, DC: Taylor & Francis.

Werth, J. L., Jr. (Ed.) (1999). *Contemporary perspectives on rational suicide.* Philadelphia, PA: Brunner/Mazel.

Werth, J.L., Jr. (1999). Introduction to the issue of rational suicide. In J. L. Werth, Jr. (Ed.), *Contemporary perspectives on rational suicide.* Philadelphia: Brunner/Mazel.

Werth, J. L., Jr. (2000). Recent developments in the debate over physician-assisted death. In R. W. Maris, S. S. Canetto, et al. (Eds.), *Review of suicidology, 2000*. New York: Guilford.

Wertheim, E. H., Paxton, S. J., Schutz, H. K., & Muir, S. L. (1997). Why do adolescent girls watch their weight? An interview study examining sociocultural pressures to be thin. *J. Psychosom. Med., 42*(4), 345–355.

Westen, D. (1991). Cognitive-behavioral interventions in the psychoanalytic psychotherapy of borderline personality disorders. *Clin. Psychol. Rev., 11*(3), 211–230.

Westen, D., & Shedler, J. (2000). "Theoretical clinical empirical approach to classifying Axis II disorders": Reply. *Amer. J. Psychiat., 157*(2), 309.

Westen, D., Feit, A., & Zittel, C. (1999). Focus chapter: Methodological issues in research using projective methods. In P. C. Kendall, J. N. Butcher, et al. (Eds.), *Handbook of research methods in clinical psychology* (2nd ed.). New York: Wiley.

Weston, S. C., & Siever, L. J. (1993, Spring). Biological correlates of personality disorders. *J. Pers. Disorders,* (Suppl.), pp. 129–148.

Wetterberg, L. (1999). Melatonin and clinical application. *Reprod. Nutr. Dev., 39*(3), 367–382.

Wettstein, R. M. (1988). Psychiatry and the law. In J. A. Talbott, R. E. Hales, & S. C. Yudofsky (Eds.), *American Psychiatric Press textbook of psychiatry*. Washington, DC: American Psychiatric Press.

Wettstein, R. M. (1989). Psychiatric malpractice. In A. Tasman, R. E. Hales, & A. J. Frances (Eds.), *American Psychiatric Press review of psychiatry* (Vol. 8). Washington, DC: American Psychiatric Press.

Wettstein, R. M. (1999). The right to refuse psychiatric treatment. *Psychiat. Clin. N. Amer., 22*(1), 173–182.

Wexler, D. B. (1983). The structure of civil commitment. *Law Human Behav., 7*, 1–18.

Wexler, D. B. (1999). The broken mirror: A self psychological treatment perspective for relationship violence. *J. Psychother. Prac. Res., 8*(2), 129–141.

Whaley, A. L. (1998, January). Racism in the provision of mental health services: A social-cognitive analysis. *Amer. J. Orthopsychiat., 68*(1), 48–59.

Whelan, J. P., & Houts, A. C. (1990). Effects of a waking schedule on primary enuretic children treated with full-spectrum home training. *Hlth. Psychol., 9*, 164–176.

Whipple, E. E., Webster, S. C., & Stratton, C. (1991). The role of parental stress in physically abusive families. *Child Abuse Neglect: Inter. J., 15*(3), 279.

Whisman, M. A., & McGarvey, A. L. (1995). Attachment, depressotypic cognitions, and dysphoria. *Cog. Ther. Res., 19*(6), 633–650.

Whitacre, C. C., Cummings, S. O., & Griffin, A. C. (1994). The effects of stress on autoimmune disease. In R. Glaser & J. K. Kiecolt-Glaser (Eds.), *Handbook of human stress and immunity*. San Diego: Academic Press.

Whitaker, R. (1998, November 17). Lure of riches fuels testing—Doing Harm: Research on the mentally ill. *Boston Globe*, p. A1.

Whitby, P. (1996). Spider phobia control (Spider PC). *Behav. Res. Methods Instru. Computers, 28*(1), 131–133.

Whitehead, W. E., Crowell, M. D., Heller, B. R., Robinson, J. C., et al. (1994). Modeling and reinforcement of the sick role during childhood predicts adult illness behavior. *Psychosom. Med., 56*, 541–550.

Whitehorn, J. C., & Betz, B. J. (1975). *Effective psychotherapy with the schizophrenic patient*. New York: Jason Aronson.

Whitely, J. S. (1994). In pursuit of the elusive category. *Brit. J. Psychiat. Rev. Books, 7*, 14–17.

Whiteside, M. (1983, September 12). A bedeviling new hysteria. *Newsweek*.

Whiting, J. W., et al. (1966). *I. Field guide for a study of socialization.* Six cultures series. New York: Wiley.

Whooley, M. A., & Browner, W. S. (1998). Association between depressive symptoms and mortality in older women. Study of Osteoporotic Fractures Research Group. *Arch. Internal Med., 158*(19), 2129–2135.

Whorley, L. W. (1996). Cognitive therapy techniques in continuing care planning with substance-dependent patients. *Addic. Behav., 21*(2), 223–231.

Whybrow, P. (1994). Of the muse and moods mundane. *Amer. J. Psychiat., 151*(4), 477–479.

Wichniak, A., Riemann, D., Kiemen, A., Voderholzer, U., & Jernajczyk, W. (2000). Comparison between eye movement latency and REM sleep parameters in major depression. *Eur. Arch. Psychiat Clin. Neurosci., 250*(1), 48–52.

Wichstrom, L. (1999). The emergence of gender difference in depressed mood during adolescence: The role of intensified gender socialization. *Dev. Psychol., 35*(1), 232–245.

Widiger, T. A. (1992). Categorical versus dimensional classification: Implications from and for research. *J. Pers. Disorders, 6*, 287–300.

Widiger, T. A. (1993). The DSM-III-R categorical personality disorder diagnoses: A critique and an alternative. *Psychological Inquiry, 4*, 75–90.

Widiger, T. A., & Costa, P. T. (1994). Personality and personality disorders. *J. Abnorm. Psychol., 103*(1), 78–91.

Widiger, T. A., Corbitt, E. M., & Millon, T. (1992). Antisocial personality disorder. In A. Tasman & M. B. Riba (Eds.), *American Psychiatric Press review of psychiatry* (Vol. 11). Washington, DC: American Psychiatric Press.

Widom, C. S. (1989). The cycle of violence. *Science, 244*, 160–166.

Widom, C. S. (1991, February). Presentation. Washington, DC: American Association for the Advancement of Science.

Wiederman, M. W., & Pryor, T. (1996). Substance use and impulsive behaviors among adolescents with eating disorders. *Addic. Behav., 21*(2), 269–272.

Wiederman, M. W., & Pryor, T. L. (2000). Body dissatisfaction, bulimia, and depression among women: The mediating role of drive for thinness. *Inter. J. Eat. Disorders, 27*(1), 90–95.

Wiegner, K. (1995, April 19). Shrink software. *The New York Times*, p. D5.

Wierzbicki, M., & Pekarik, G. (1993). A meta-analysis of psychotherapy dropout. *Profess. Psychol.: Res. Pract., 24*(2), 190–195.

Wiggins, J. S., & Trobst, K. K. (1997). Prospects for the assessment of normal and abnormal interpersonal behavior. *J. Pers. Assess., 68*(1), 110–126.

Wikan, U. (1991). *Managing turbulent hearts*. Chicago: University of Chicago Press.

Wilbur, C. B. (1984). Treatment of multiple personality. *Psychiatr. Ann., 14*, 27–31.

Wilcock, M., Mackenzie, I., & Bolt, J. (1999). Country-wide survey of the repeat prescription of hypnotics. *Brit. J. Psychiat., 174*, 277.

Wilcox, J. A. (1990). Fluoxetine and bulimia. *J. Psychoactive Drugs, 22*(1), 81–82.

Wilde, E. J., Kienhorst, I. C. W. M., Diekstra, R. F. W., & Wolters, W. H. G. (1992). The relationship between adolescent suicidal behavior and life events in childhood and adolescence. *Amer. J. Psychiat, 149*, 45–51.

Wilfley, D. E., & Cohen, L. R. (1997). Psychological treatment of bulimia nervosa and binge-eating disorder. *Psychopharmacol. Bull., 33*(3), 437–454.

Wilfley, D. E., Agras, W. S., Telch, C. F., Rossiter, E. M., Schneider, J. A., Cole, A. G., Sifford, L., & Raeburn, S. D. (1993). Group cognitive-behavioral therapy and group interpersonal psychotherapy for the nonpurging bulimic individual: A controlled comparison. *J. Cons. Clin. Psychol., 61*(2), 296–305.

Wilhelm, S., Otto, M. W., Lohr, B., & Deckersbach, T. (1999). Cognitive behavior group therapy for body dysmorphic disorder: A case series. *Behav. Res. Ther., 37*(1), 71–75.

Will, O. A. (1961). Paranoid development and the concept of self: Psychotherapeutic intervention. *Psychiatry, 24*(2), 16–530.

Will, O. A. (1967). Psychological treatment of schizophrenia. In A. M. Freedman & H. I. Kaplan (Eds.), *Comprehensive textbook of psychiatry*. Baltimore: Williams & Wilkins.

Willard, W. (1979). American Indians. In L. D. Hankoff & B. Einsidler (Eds.), *Suicide: Theory and clinical aspects*. Littleton, MA: PSG Publishing.

Willershausen, B., Azrak, A., & Wilms, S. (1999). Fear of dental treatment and its possible effects on oral health. *Eur. J. Med. Res., 4*(2), 72–77.

Williams, C. C. (1983). The mental foxhole: The Viet Nam veterans' search for meaning. *Amer. J. Orthopsychiat., 53*(1), 4–17.

Williams, R. (1999). Personality and post-traumatic stress disorder. In W. Yule et al. (Eds.), *Post-traumatic stress disorders: Concepts and therapy*. Wiley series in clinical psychology. Chichester, England: Wiley.

Williams, R. B. (1989). Biological mechanisms mediating the relationship between behavior and coronary heart disease. In A. W. Siegman & T. M. Dembroski (Eds.), *In search of coronary behavior*. Hillsdale, NJ: Erlbaum.

Williams, R. B. (1989). *The trusting heart: Great news about Type A behavior*. New York: Times Books.

Williams, S. L., Kinney, P. J., Harap, S. T., & Liebmann, M. (1997). Thoughts of agoraphobic people during scary tasks. *J. Abnorm. Psychol., 106*(4), 511–520.

Williams, S. S., Michela, J. L., Contento, I. R., Gladis, M. M., & Pierce, N. T. (1996). Restrained eating among adolescents: Dieters are not always bingers and bingers are not always dieters. *Hlth. Psychol., 15*(3), 176–184.

Williamson, D. A., Netemeyer, R. G., Jackman, L. P., Anderson, D. A., et al. (1995). Structural equation modeling of risk factors for the development of eating disorder symptoms in female athletes. *Inter. J. Eat. Disorders, 17*(4), 387–393.

Williamson, L. (1998). Eating disorders and the cultural forces behind the drive for thinness: Are African American women really protected? *Soc. Work Hlth. Care, 28*(1), 61–73.

Willick, M. S., Milrod, D., & Karush, R. K. (1998). Psychoanalysis and the psychoses. In M. Furer, E. Nersessian, et al. (Eds.), *Controversies in contemporary psychoanalysis: Lectures from the faculty of the New York Psychoanalytic Institute*. Madison, CT: International Universities Press.

Willing, R. (1998, November 19). Survey doubles rape estimate. Researchers say assaults exceed 876,000 in a year. *USA Today*, p. 3A.

Wills, T. A., McNamara, G., Vaccaro, D., & Hirky, A. E. (1996). Escalated substance use: A longitudinal grouping analysis from early to middle adolescence. *J. Abnorm. Psychol., 105*(2), 166–180.

Wilmer, H. A. (1996). The healing nightmare: War dreams of Vietnam veterans. In D. Barrett (Ed.), *Trauma and dreams*. Cambridge, MA: Harvard University Press.

Wilsnack, R. W., Vogeltanz, N. D., Wilsnack, S. C., & Harris, T. R. (2000). Gender differences in alcohol consumption and adverse drinking consequences: Cross-cultural patterns. *Addiction, 95*(2), 251–265.

Wilson, G. T. (1993). Psychological and pharmacological treatments of bulimia nervosa: A research update. *Appl. Prev. Psychol., 2,* 35–42.

Wilson, G. T. (1994). Behavioral treatment of obesity: Thirty years and counting. *Adv. Behav. Res. Ther., 16,* 31–75.

Wilson, G. T., Rossiter, E., Kleifield, E. I., & Lindholm, L. (1986). Cognitive-behavioral treatment of bulimia nervosa: A controlled evaluation. *Behav. Res. Ther., 24*(3), 277–288.

Wilson, J. M., & Marcotte, A. C. (1996). Psychosocial adjustment and educational outcome in adolescents with a childhood diagnosis of attention deficit disorder. *J. Amer. Acad. Child Adol. Psychiat., 35*(5), 579–587.

Wilson, K. A., & Chambless, D. L. (1999). Inflated perceptions of responsibility and obsessive-compulsive symptoms. *Behav. Res. Ther., 37*(4), 325–335.

Wilson, K. G., Hayes, S. C., & Gifford, E. V. (1997). Cognition in behavior therapy: Agreements and differences. *J. Behav. Ther. Exp. Psychiat., 28*(1), 53–63.

Wilson, W. M. (1992). The Stanford-Binet: Fourth Edition and Form L-M in assessment of young children with mental retardation. *Ment. Retard., 30*(2), 81–84.

Wincze, J. P., & Lange, J. D. (1981). Assessment of sexual behavior. In D. H. Barlow (Ed.), *Behavioral assessment of adult disorders.* New York: Guilford.

Wincze, J. P., Richards, J., Parsons, J., & Bailey, S. (1996). A comparative survey of therapist sexual misconduct between an American state and an Australian state. *Profess. Psychol:. Res. Pract., 27*(3), 289–294.

Wing, L. (1976). *Early childhood autism.* Oxford, England: Pergamon Press.

Wing, L., & Wing, J. K. (1971). Multiple impairments in early childhood autism. *J. Autism Child. Schizo., 1,* 256–266.

Winick, B. J. (1983). Incompetency to stand trial: Developments in the law. In J. Monahan & H. J. Steadman (Eds.), *Mentally disorded offenders.* New York: Plenum Press.

Winick, B. J. (1995). The side effects of incompetency labeling and the implications for mental health law. *Psychology, Public Policy, and Law, I,* 6–42.

Winick, M., Meyer, K., & Harris, R. C. (1975). Malnutrition and environmental enrichment by early adoption. *Science,* pp. 1173–1175.

Wink, P. (1996). Narcissism. In C. G. Costello (Ed.), *Personality characteristics of the personality disordered.* New York: Wiley.

Winslade, W. J. (1983). *The insanity plea.* New York: Scribner's.

Winter, L. B., Steer, R. A., Jones-Hicks, L., & Beck, A. T. (1999). Screening for major depression disorders in adolescent medical outpatients with the Beck Depression Inventory for Primary Care. *J. Adol. Hlth., 24*(6), 389–394.

Wirz-Justice, A., & Van den Hoofdakker, R. H. (1999). Sleep deprivation in depression: What do we know, where do we go? *Biol. Psychiat., 46*(4), 445–453.

Wirz-Justice, A., Graw, P., Kräuchi, K., Sarrafzadeh, A., et al. (1996). "Natural" light treatment of seasonal affective disorder. *J. Affect. Disorders, 37,* 109–120.

Wise, R. A. (1996). Neurobiology of addiction. *Curr. Opin. Neurobiol., 6,* 243–251.

Wise, T. N. (1985). Fetishism—Etiology and treatment: A review from multiple perspectives. *Comprehen. Psychiat., 26,* 249–257.

Wiseman, C. V., Gray, J. J., Mosimann, J. E., & Ahrens, A. H. (1992). Cultural expectations of thinness in women: An update. *Inter. J. Eat. Disorders, 11*(1), 85–89.

Witteman, C., & Koele, P. (1999). Explaining treatment decisions. *Psychother. Res., 9*(1), 100–114.

Wittrock, D. A., & Blanchard, E. B. (1992). Thermal biofeedback treatment of mild hypertension: A comparison of effects on conventional and ambulatory blood pressure measures. *Behav. Mod., 16*(3), 283–304.

Wittrock, D. A., Blanchard, E. B., McCoy, G. C., McCaffrey, R. J., et al. (1995). The relationship of expectancies to outcome in stress management treatment of essential hypertensions: Results from the joint USSR-USA Behavioral Hypertension Project. *Biofeed. Self-Reg., 20*(1), 51–68.

Wlazlo, Z., Schroeder-Hartwig, K., Hand, I., Kaiser, G., & Munchau, N. (1990). Exposure in vivo vs. social skills training for social phobia: Long term outcome and differential effects. *Behav. Res. Ther., 28,* 131–193.

Wolberg, L. R. (1967). *The technique of psychotherapy.* New York: Grune & Stratton.

Wolfe, D. A., Edwards, B., Manion, I., & Koverola, C. (1988). Early intervention for parents at risk for child abuse and neglect: A preliminary investigation. *J. Cons. Clin. Psychol., 56,* 40–47.

Wolfe, J. K. L., & Fodor, I. G. (1977). Modifying assertive behavior in women: Comparison of three approaches. *Behav. Ther., 8,* 567–574.

Wolfe, J. L., & Russianoff, P. (1997). Overcoming self-negation in women. *J. Rat.-Emot., & Cog.-Behav. Ther., 15*(1), 81–92.

Wolfe, S. M., Fugate, L., Hulstrand, E. P., & Kamimoto, L. E. (1988). *Worst pills best pills: The older adult's guide to avoiding drug-induced death or illness.* Washington, DC: Public Citizen Health Research Group.

Wolfensberger, W. (1972). *The principle of normalization in human services.* Toronto: National Institute on Mental Retardation.

Wolff, N., Helminiak, T. W., Morse, G. A., Calsyn, R. J., et al. (1997). Cost-effectiveness evaluation of three approaches to case management for homeless mentally ill clients. *Amer. J. Psychiat., 154*(3), 341–348.

Wolff, S. (1991). Schizoid personality in childhood and adult life I: The vagaries of diagnostic labeling. *Brit. J. Psychiat., 159,* 615–620.

Wolpe, J. (1958). *Psychotherapy by reciprocal inhibition.* Stanford, CA: Stanford University Press.

Wolpe, J. (1969). *The practice of behavior therapy.* Oxford, England: Pergamon Press.

Wolpe, J. (1987). The promotion of scientific psychotherapy: A long voyage. In J. K. Zeig (Ed.), *The evolution of psychotherapy.* New York: Brunner/Mazel.

Wolpe, J. (1990). *The practice of behavior therapy* (4th ed.). Elmsford, NY: Pergamon Press.

Wolpe, J. (1997). From psychoanalytic to behavioral methods in anxiety disorders: A continuing evolution. In J. K. Zeig (Ed.), *The evolution of psychotherapy: The third conference.* New York: Brunner/Mazel.

Wolpe, J. The case of Mrs. Schmidt [Transcript and record]. Nashville, TN: Counselor Recording and Tests.

Wolpe, J., & Plaud, J. J. (1997). Pavlov's contributions to behavior therapy. *Amer. Psychologist, 52*(9), 966–972.

Woo, S. M., Goldstein, M. J., & Nuechterlein, K. H. (1997). Relatives' expressed emotion and nonverbal signs of subclinical psychopathology in schizophrenic patients. *Brit. J. Psychiat., 170,* 58–61.

Wood, J. M., Nezworski, M. T., & Stejskal, W. J. (1996). The comprehensive system for the Rorschach: A critical examination. *Psychol. Sci., 7*(1), 3–10

Woodside, M. R., & Legg, B. H. (1990). Patient advocacy: A mental health perspective. *J. Ment. Hlth. Couns., 12*(1), 38–50.

Woodward, B., Duckworth, K. S., & Gutheil, T. G. (1993). The pharmacotherapist-psychotherapist collaboration. In J. M. Oldham, M. B. Riba, & A. Tasman (Eds.), *Review of psychiatry* (Vol. 12). Washington, DC: American Psychiatric Press.

Woodward, S. H., Drescher, K. D., Murphy, R. T., Ruzek, J. I., et al. (1997). Heart rate during group flooding therapy for PTSD. *Integ. Physiol. Eehav. Sci., 32*(1), 19–30.

Woody, G. E., McLellan, A. T., & Bedrick, J. (1995). Dual diagnosis. In J. M. Oldham & M. B. Riba (Eds.), *American Psychiatric Press review of psychiatry* (Vol. 14). Washington, DC: American Psychiatric Press.

Woody, G. E., McLellan, A. T., Luborsky, L., & O'Brien, C. P. (1998). Psychotherapy with opioid-dependent patients. *Psychiat. Times., XV*(11).

Woody, S. R., Chambless, D. L., & Glass, C. R. (1997). Self-focused attention in the treatment of social phobia. *Behav. Res. Ther., 35*(2), 117–129.

Wooley, S. C., & Wooley, O. W. (1985). Intensive outpatient and residential treatment for bulimia. In D. M. Garner & P. E. Garfinkel (Eds.), *Handbook of psychotherapy for anorexia nervosa and bulimia.* New York: Guilford.

Woolfolk, R. L., Carr-Kaffashan, L., McNulty, T. F., & Lehrer, P. M. (1976). Meditation training as a treatment for insomnia. *Behav. Ther. 7*(3), 359–365.

World Health Organization. (1948). World Health Organization constitution. In *Basic documents.* Geneva: Author.

Worrel, J. A., Marken, P. A., Beckman, S. E., & Ruehter, V. L. (2000). Atypical antipsychotic agents: A critical review. *Amer. J. Hlth. Sys. Pharmacol, 57*(3), 238–255.

Wragg, M., Hutton, M., Talbot, C., & Alzheimer's Disease Collaborative Group. (1996). Genetic association between intronic polymorphism in presenilin-1 gene and late-onset Alzheimer's disease. *Lancet, 347,* 509–512.

Wright, I. C., Rabe, H. S., Woodruff, P. W. R., David, A. S., Murray, R. M., & Bullmore, E. T. (2000). Meta-analysis of regional brain volumes in schizophrenia. *Amer. J. Psychiat., 157*(1), 16–25.

Wright, J. (1984). EAP: An important supervisory tool. *Supervisory Management, 29*(12), 16–17.

Wright, S. (2000). Group work. In B. Lask, R. Bryant-Waugh, et al. (Eds.), *Anorexia nervosa and related eating disorders in childhood and adolescence* (2nd ed.). Hove, England: Psychology Press/Taylor & Francis.

Wrobleski, A. (1999). "Rational suicide": A contradiction in terms. In J. L. Werth, Jr., et al. (Eds.), *Contemporary perspectives on rational suicide.* Series in death, dying, and bereavement. Philadelphia: Brunner/Mazel.

Wu, X., & DeMaris, A. (1996). Gender and marital status differences in depression: The effects of chronic strains. *Sex Roles, 34*(5–6), 299–319.

Wu, J., Kramer, G. L., Kram, M., Steciuk, M., Crawford, I. L., & Petty, F. (1999). Serotonin and learned helplessness: A regional study of 5-HT-sub(1A), 5-HT-sub(2A) receptors and the serotonin transport site in rat brain. *J. Psychiat. Res., 33*(1), 17–22.

Wulsin, L., Bachop, M., & Hoffman, D. (1988). Group therapy in manic-depressive illness. *Amer. J. Psychother., 42,* 263–271.

Wulsin, L. R., Vaillant, G. E., & Wells, V. E. (1999). A systematic review of the mortality of depression. *Psychosom. Med., 61*(1), 6–17.

Wunderlich, U., Bronisch, T., & Wittchen, H. U. (1998). Comorbidity patterns in adolescents and young adults with suicide attempts. *Eur. Arch. Psychiat. Clin. Neurosci., 248*(2), 87–95.

Wurtele, S. K., & Schmitt, A. (1992). Child care workers' knowledge about reporting suspected child sexual abuse. *Child Abuse Negl., 16*(3) 385–390.

Wurtman, J. J. (1987). Disorders of food intake: Excessive carbohydrate snack intake among a class of obese people. *Annals of the New York Academy of Sciences, 499,* 197–202.

Wurtman, R. (1995, October 17). Interview cited in Roan., S., Super pill. *Los Angeles Times,* pp. E1–E5.

Wyatt, R. J. (1995). Risks of withdawing antipsychotic medications. *Arch. Gen. Psychiat., 52*(3), 205–208.

Wysoker, A. (1999). Thoughts for the millenium: The rights of the mentally ill. *J. Amer. Psychiat. Nurs. Assoc., 5*(6), 197–200.

Yabe, K., Tsukahar, R., Mita, K., & Aoki, H. (1985). Developmental trends of jumping reaction time by means of EMG in mentally retarded children. *J. Ment. Def. Res., 29*(2), 137–145.

Yager, J. (1985). The outpatient treatment of bulimia. *Bull. Menninger Clin., 49*(3), 203–226.

Yager, J., Rorty M., & Rossoto E. (1995). Coping styles differ between recovered and nonrecovered women with bulimia nervosa, but not between recovered women and non-eating-disordered control subjects. *J. Nerv. Ment. Dis., 183*(2), 86–94.

Yalom, I. D. (1985). *The theory and practice of group psychotherapy* (3rd ed.). New York: Basic Books.

Yang, B., & Lester, D. (1995). Suicidal behavior and employment. In S. S. Canetto & D. Lester (Eds.) *Women and suicidal behavior.* New York: Springer.

Yang, B., Stack, S., & Lester, D. (1992). Suicide and unemployment: Predicting the smoothed trend and yearly fluctuations. *J. Socioecon., 21*(1), 39–41.

Yank, G. R., Bentley, K. J., & Hargrove, D. S. (1993). The vulnerability-stress model of schizophrenia: Advances in psychosocial treatment. *Amer. J. Orthopsychiat., 63*(1), 55–69.

Yankelovich Youth Monitor. (1994). Survey: What children fear. Cited in *Newsweek,* January 10, 1994, p. 50.

Yehuda, R., Giller, E. L., Southwick, S. M., et al. (1994). The relationship between catecholamine excretion and PTSD symptoms in Vietnam combat veterans and Holocaust survivors. In M. M. Marburg, (Ed.), *Catecholamine function in posttraumatic stress disorder.* Washington, DC: American Psychiatric Press.

Yehuda, R., Kahana, B., Binder-Brynes, K., Southwick, S. M., et al. (1995). Low urinary cortisol excretion in Holocaust survivors with posttraumatic stress disorder. *Amer. J. Psychiat., 152*(7), 982–986.

Yehuda, R., McFarlane, A. C., & Shalev, A. Y. (1998). Predicting the development of posttraumatic stress disorder from the acute response to a traumatic event. *Biol. Psychiat., 44*(12), 1305–1313.

Yeung, W. J. (1999). Interviewed in Reuters Health, *Dads spending more time with kids,* June 11, 1999.

Yoder, K. A., Hoyt, D. R., & Whitbeck, L. B. (1998). Suicidal behavior among homeless and runaway adolescents. *J. Youth Adolescence, 27*(6), 753–771.

Yontef, G. (1998). Dialogic gestalt therapy. In L. S. Greenberg, J. C. Watson, et al. (Eds.), *Handbook of experiential psychotherapy.* New York: Guilford.

Yost, E., Beutler, L., Corbishley, A. M., & Allender, J. (1986). *Group cognitive therapy: A treatment approach for depressed older adults.* New York: Pergamon Press.

Young, E., & Korszun, A. (1999). Women, stress, and depression: Sex differences in hypothalamic-pituitary-adrenal axis regulation. In E. Leibenluft et al. (Eds.), *Gender differences in mood and anxiety disorders: From bench to bedside.* Review of psychiatry series, Vol. 18, No. 3. Washington, DC: American Psychiatric Press.

Young, E. A., Abelson, J. L., Curtis, G. C., & Nesse, R. M. (1997). Childhood adversity and vulnerability to mood and anxiety disorders. *Depres. Anx., 5,* 66–72.

Young, J. E., Beck, A. T., & Weinberger, A. (1993). Depression. In D. H. Barlow (Ed.), *Clinical handbook of psychological disorders: A step-by-step treatment manual* (2nd ed.). New York: Guilford.

Young, K. S. (1996). Cited in Middle-aged women are more at risk for Internet addiction. *APA Monitor, 27*(10), 10.

Young, K. S. (1996). Psychology of computer use: XL. Addictive use of the Internet: A case that breaks the stereotype. *Psych. Rep., 79*(3, Pt 1), 899–902.

Young, M., Benjamin, B., & Wallis, C. (1963). Mortality of widowers. *Lancet, 2,* 454–456.

Young, T. J. (1991). Suicide and homicide among Native Americans: Anomie or social learning? *Psychol. Rep., 68*(3, Pt. 2), 1137–1138.

Young, W. C., Young, L. J., & Lehl, K. (1991). Restraints in the treatment of dissociative disorders: A follow-up of twenty patients. *Dissociat. Prog. Dissociat. Disorders, 4*(2), 74–78.

Youngren, M. A., & Lewinsohn, P. M. (1980). The functional relation between depression and problematic interpersonal behavior. *J. Abnorm. Psychol., 89*(3), 333–341.

Youngstrom, N. (1990). Six offender types are identified. *APA Monitor, 21*(10), 21.

Youngstrom, N. (1992). Grim news from national study of rape. *APA Monitor, 23*(7), 38.

Youngstrom, N. (1992). Psychology helps a shattered L. A. *APA Monitor, 23*(7), 1, 12.

Yudofsky, S., Silver, J., & Hales, R. (1993). Cocaine and aggressive behavior: Neurobiological and clinical perspectives. *Bull. Menninger Clin., 57*(2), 218–226.

Yutzy, S. H., Cloninger, C. R., Guze, S. B., Pribor, E. F., et al. (1995). DSM-IV field trial: Testing a new proposal for somatization disorder. *Amer. J. Psychiat., 152*(1), 97–101.

Yuwiler, A., Shih, J. C., Chen, C., & Ritvo, E. R. (1992). Hyperserotoninemia and antiserotonin antibodies in autism and other disorders. *J. Autism Dev. Disorders., 22*(1), 33–45.

Zacharakis, C. A., Madianos, M. G., Papadimitriou, G. N., & Stefanis, C. N. (1998). Suicide in Greece 1980–1995: Patterns and social factors. *Soc. Psychiat. Psychiat. Epidemiol., 33*(10), 471–476.

Zajecka, J. (1997). Importance of establishing the diagnosis of persistent anxiety. *J. Clin. Psychiat., 58*(Suppl 3), 9–13.

Zal, H. M. (1999). Agitation in the elderly. *Psychiat. Times, XVI*(1).

Zaleman, S. (Ed.). (1995). Neural basis of psychopathology. In S. H. Koslow, D. L. Meinecke, I. Lederhendler, H. Khachaturian, R. K. Nakamura, D. Karp, L. Vitkovic, D. L. Glanzman, & S. Zaleman (Eds.), *The neuroscience of mental health: II. A report on neuroscience research—Status and potential for mental health and mental illness.* Rockville, MD: National Institutes of Health, National Institute of Mental Health.

Zamichow, N. (1993, February 15). The dark corner of psychology. *Los Angeles Times,* p. A1.

Zarin, D. A., Pincus, H. A., Peterson, B. D., West, J. C., Suarez, A. P., Marcus, S. C., & McIntyre, J. S. (1998). Characterizing psychiatry with findings from the 1996 national survey of psychiatric practice. *Amer. J. Psychiat., 155*(3), 397–404.

Zaubler, T. S., & Katon, W. (1998). Panic disorder in the general medical setting. *J. Psychosom. Res., 44*(1), 25–42.

Zax, M., & Cowen, E. L. (1969). Research on early detection and prevention of emotional dysfunction in young school children. In C. D. Speilberger (Ed.), *Current topics in clinical and community psychology* (Vol. 1). New York: Academic Press.

Zax, M., & Cowen, E. L. (1976). *Abnormal psychology: Changing conceptions.* New York: Holt, Rinehart & Winston.

Zemishlany, Z., Alexander, G. E., Prohovnik, I., Goldman, R. G., Mukherjee, S., & Sackeim, H. (1996). Cortical blood flow and negative symptoms in schizophrenia. *Neuropsychobiology, 33,* 127–131.

Zerbe, K. J. (1990). Through the storm: Psychoanalytic theory in the psychotherapy of the anxiety disorders. *Bull. Menninger Clin., 54*(2), 171–183.

Zerbe, K. J. (1993). Whose body is it anyway? Understanding and treating psychosomatic aspects of eating disorders. *Bull. Menninger Clin., 57*(2), 161–177.

Zerssen, D., et al. (1985). Circadian rhythms in endogenous depression. *Psychiat. Res., 16,* 51–63.

Zhang, M., He, Y., Gittelman, M., Wong, Z., & Yan, H. (1998). Group psychoeducation of relatives of schizophrenic patients: Two-year experiences. *Psychiat. Clin. Neurosci., 52*(Suppl.), S344–S347.

Zhou, J.-N., Hofman, M. A., Gooren, L. J. G., & Swaab, D. F. (1995). A sex difference in the human brain and its relation to transsexuality. *Nature, 378,* 68–70.

Ziedonis, D., Williams, J., Corrigan, P., & Smelson, D. (2000). Management of substance abuse in schizophrenia. *Psychiatr. Ann., 30*(1), 67–75.

Zigler, E., & Hodapp, R. M. (1991). Behavioral functioning in individuals with mental retardation. *Annu. Rev. Psychol., 42,* 29–50.

Zigler, E., Taussig, C., & Black, K. (1992). Early childhood intervention: A promising preventative for juvenile delinquency. *Amer. Psychologist, 47*(8), 997–1006.

Zigman, W. B., Schupf, N., Sersen, E., & Silverman, W. (1995). Prevalence of dementia in adults with and without Down syndrome. *Amer. J. Ment. Retard., 100*(4), 403–412.

Zilbergeld, B. (1978). *Male sexuality.* Boston: Little, Brown.

Zilboorg, G., & Henry, G. W. (1941). *A history of medical psychology.* New York: Norton.

Zill, N., & Schoenborn, C. A. (1990, November). *Developmental, learning, and emotional problems: Health of our nation's children, United States, 1988* (No. 190). Advance Data: National Center for Health Statistics.

Zima, B. T., Wells, K. B., Benjamin, B., & Duan, N. (1996). Mental health problems among homeless mothers. *Arch. Gen. Psychiat., 53,* 332–338.

Zimbardo, P. (1976). *Rational paths to madness.* Presentation at Princeton University, Princeton, NJ.

Zimmerman, M. (1994). Diagnosing personality disorders: A review of issues and research methods. *Arch. Gen. Psychiat., 51,* 225-245.

Zimmerman, M., & Coryell, W. (1989). DSM-III personality disorder diagnoses in a nonpatient sample: Demographic correlates and comorbidity. *Arch. Gen. Psychiat., 46*(8), 682-689.

Zito, J. M., Safer, D. J., dos Reis, S., Gardner, J. F., Boles, M., & Lynch, F. (2000). Trends in prescribing of psychotropic medications to preschoolers. *JAMA, 283*(8), 1025-1030.

Zohar, J., & Pato, M. T. (1991). Diagnostic considerations. In M. T. Pato & J. Zohar (Eds.), *Current treatments of obsessive-compulsive disorder.* Washington, DC: American Psychiatric Press.

Zucker, K. J., Bradley, S. J., & Sullivan, C. B. L. (1996). Traits of separation anxiety in boys with gender identity disorder. *J. Amer. Acad. Child Adol. Psychiat., 35*(6), 791-798.

Zucker, K. J., Bradley, S. J., & Sullivan, C. B. L. (1996, April 7). Probing the mind of a killer. *Newsweek,* pp. 30-42.

Zucker, K. J., Bradley, S. J., & Sullivan, C. B. L. (1996, April 15). The mad bomber. *U. S. News & World Report,* pp. 29-36.

Zuckerman, M. (1978). Sensation seeking and psychopathy. In R. D. Hare & D. Schalling (Eds.), *Psychopathic behavior: Approaches to research.* New York: Wiley.

Zuckerman, M. (1989). Personality in the third dimension: A psychobiological approach. *Pers. Individ. Diff., 10,* 391-418.

Zuckerman, M. (1996). Sensation seeking. In C. G. Costello (Ed.), *Personality characteristics of the personality disordered.* New York: Wiley.

Zuger, A. (1993, July). The Baron strikes again. *Discover,* pp. 28-30.

Zuravin, S. J., & Fontanella, C. (1999). The relationship between child sexual abuse and major depression among low-income women: A function of growing up experiences? *Child Maltreat.: J. Amer. Profess. Soc. Abuse Child., 4*(1), 3-12.

Zwaigenbaum, L., Szatmari, P., Boyle, M. H., & Offord, D. R. (1999). Highly somatizing young adolescents and the risk of depression. *Pediatrics, 103*(6) 1203-1209.

Zwilling, B. S., Brown, D., Feng, N., Sheridan, J., & Pearl, D. (1993). The effect of adrenalectomy on the restraint stress induced suppression of MHC class II expression by murine peritoneal macrophages. *Brain Behav. Immun., 7,* 29-35.

illustration credits

CHAPTER 1, 2: Carol Beckwith; **3:** Patrick Gardin Stringer/AP; **4:** Catherine Allemande/Gamma Liaison; **6:** Gamma Liaison; **8:** R. Benali/S. Ferry for Life Magazine/Gamma Liason; **9:** John W. Verano; **10(l):** Zentralbibliothek, Zurich; **10(r):** Zentralbibliothek, Zurich; **11(t):** Corbis-Bettmann; **11(b):** Gamma Liaison; **12(l):** The Granger Collection; **12:** Bettmann Archives; **13:** George Wesley Bellows, *Dance in a Madhouse*, 1907. Black crayon, charcoal, pen and ink on wove paper, 48 x 62.5 cm. Charles H. and Mary F. S. Worcester Collection, 1936.223. Photograph © 1997 The Art Institute of Chicago. All rights reserved.; **14(b):** Judy Griesedieck, Minneapolis; **14(t):** Mark Marten/US National Library of Medicine/Photo Researchers; **15:** Jerry Cooke/Photo Researchers; **18:** Corbis-Bettman; **19:** Bob Daemmrich/The Image Works; **20(r):** Ron Phillips/The Everett Collection; **20(l):** Everett Collection; **CHAPTER 2, 26:** PhotoEdit; **29:** courtesy of Edna Morlok; **30:** The Everett Collection; **32:** James Aronovski/Picture Group; **33:** Joel Gordon, New York, NY; **35:** Aaron Haupt/Stock Boston; **36:** Joel Gordon, New York, NY; **38:** Christopher Brown/Stock Boston; **39:** Michael Nichols/National Geographic Image Collection; **41:** Victoria Arocho/AP Photo; **CHAPTER 3, 49:** Thomas A. Kelly/Gail Mooney/Corbis; **50:** Ou Neakiry/AP Photo; **51:** courtesy of the Dr. J. H. Kellogg Discovery Center, Battlecreek, Michigan; **52:** Ohio Historical Society; **53:** Sigmund Freud Copyrights/Everett Collection; **55:** Laura Dwight, New York, NY; **56:** Catherine Karnow/Woodfin Camp & Associates; **58:** Ursula Edelmann, Frankfurt; **59:** Bill Horsman/Stock Boston; **60(t):** A. Bandura, Stanford University; **60(b):** A. Bandura, Stanford University; **61:** Robert Allison/Contact Press Images; **62(t):** Joseph Wolpe; **62(b):** Margaret Norton, Ho/AP Photo; **64:** Leif Skoogsfor/Woodfin Camp & Associates; **67:** David Burnett/Contact Press Images; **69:** Leif Skoogfors/Woodfin Camp & Associates; **71:** Chuck Fishman/Woodfin Camp & Associates; **72:** Donna Ferrato/Domestic Abuse Awareness Project, NYC, from the book *Living with the Enemy*, Aperature.; **73:** James Nachtwey/Magnum Photos; **74:** Alon Reininger/Contact Press Images; **76(c):** Richard Nowitz/Photo Researchers; **77:** Sergei Karpukhin/AP Photo; **78:** Alon Reininger/Woodfin Camp & Associates; **CHAPTER 4, 84:** Courtesty of the Fogg Art Museum, Harvard University Art Museums, Bequest from the Collection of Maurice Wertheim, Class of 1906/David Matthews/President and Fellows of Harvard College; **85(l):** Washington University School of Medicine; **85(r):** *The Palm Beach Post*, photo by Mark Mirko; **90(b):** Rick Friedman/Black Star; **91(l):** Louis Wain; **91(r):** Louis Wain; **95:** Richard Nowitz/Photo Researchers; **96:** Joe McNally/Sygma; **98(t):** Marcus E. Raichle, MD, Washington University School of Medicine, St. Louis, Missouri; **98(b):** Roger Ressmeyer/Corbis; **99:** Travis Amos; **100:** Jeff Greenberg/PhotoEdit; **102:** Francis G. Mayer/Corbis; **106:** Elizabeth Eckert, Middletown, NY. From L. Gamwell and N. Tomes, *Madness in America*, 1995, Cornell University Press.; **107:** Tasso Taraboulsi/SABA; **CHAPTER 5, 118:** Museum of Modern Art Film Stills Archive; **121(l):** Adam Nadel/AP Photo;

121(r): Wesley Hitt/Liason International; **130:** The Everett Collection; **131:** Jim Harrison/Stock Boston; **134:** Julie Newdoll, Computer Graphics Laboratory, UCSF; **135:** University of Wisconsin Primate Laboratory, Madison; **136(t):** Bella C Laudauer Collection of Business and Advertising Art, The New-York Historical Society; **136(b):** Torin Boyd Photo, Tokyo, Japan; **140:** Michael Melford; **142:** Paulo Fridman/Gamma Liaison; **144:** The Everett Collection; **148:** Andrew Sacks/Black Star; **150(t):** Albert Ellis Institute, New York, NY; **CHAPTER 6, 156:** George Tooker, *The Subway*, 1950. Egg tempera on composition board. 18 x 36 inches. Collection of Whitney Museum of American Art. Juliana Force Purchase 50-23. Photograph copyright © 1997: Whitney Museum of Art, New York.; **160:** Nick Didlick/Reuters-Bettmann Archives; **164:** *Ahab and Moby Dick*, etching by I.W. Taber, in Herman Melville, *Moby Dick* , New York, 1899 edition. Department of Rare Books and Special Collections, Princeton University Libraries; **165:** Steve Labadessa/Outline; **168:** Philip Gould/Corbis; **170:** Philadelphia Museum of Art: William L. Helfand Collection; **172:** Bettman/Corbis; **173:** Vickie Lewis/People Weekly; **175:** Peter Turnley/Black Star; **176:** National Archives; **178:** Alain Keler/Sygma; **179(b):** Michael Schumann/SABA; **179(t):** Eyal Warshavsky/AP Photo; **181:** Mark Burnett/Stock Boston; **183:** J.P. Laffont/Sygma; **185:** Charles H. Porter IV/Sygma; **186:** Paul Connor/AP Photo; **CHAPTER 7, 192(r):** Archive Photos; **192(l):** Rick Maiman/Sygma; **195(l):** George P. A. Healy, 1887, The National Portrait Gallery, Smithsonian Institution; **195(r):** Manfred Reiner/Black Star; **197:** Greg Gibson/AP/Worldwide; **199(l):** Julie Newdoll, Computer Graphics Laboratory, UCSF; **199(r):** Julie Newdoll, Computer Graphics Laboratory, UCSF; **201:** Mark S. Wexler, Chicago; **202:** Homer Sykes/Woodfin Camp & Associates; **203:** Barry Jarvinen/AP/Wide World Photos; **204:** University of Wisconsin Primate Laboratory, Madison; **205:** Mark Lennihan/AP Worldwide Photos; **207:** Dorothea Lange, February 1936, Farm Security Administration, Library of Congress; **209:** Sideny Harris; **210:** Mimi Forsyth/Monkmeyer; **211:** Edvard Munch, *Melancholia, Laura*, 1899, Oslo kommunes kunstsamlinger Munch-Museet; **213:** Corbis; **214:** Myrleen Ferguson/Tony Stone Worldwide; **218:** Jerry Irwin; **CHAPTER 8, 226:** Joel Gordon, New York, NY; **227:** David Brauchli/AP/Wideworld Photos; **228:** Rick Rickman/Matrix; **231:** Tom Moran; **233:** Corbis; **234:** Will McIntyre/Photo Researchers; **236:** Roger Ressmeyer/Corbis; **239:** Renee Lynn/Photo Researchers; **240(b):** Robert Nickelsberg/The Image Works; **241:** Corbis; **242:** Patrick Johns/Corbis; **245:** Phil Huber/Black Star; **246:** Theo Westenberger/Gamma Liaison; **CHAPTER 9, 252:** Dr. Andrew C. Mason, Section of Neurobiology & Behavior, Cornell Univesity; **253(l):** Karsh/Woodfin Camp & Associates; **253(r):** Marc C. Biggins/Gamma Liaison; **255:** Pressenbild/Adventure; **256:** UPI/Bettmann; **257:** Grant Haller, *Seattle Post Intelligencer*/Sygma; **260:** David Woo, *Dallas Morning News*/Sygma; **262:** Everett Collection; **264(t):** Peter Cosgrove/AP Photo; **264(b):** CBS Photo

Archive; **266:** Alex Colville, *Target Pistol and Man*, 1988. Acrylic on wood particle board. 60 x 60 cm. Alex Colville, A.C. Fine Art, Inc., Wolfville, N.S., Canada; **267(t):** John Kaplan/Media Alliance; **267(b):** Adrian Arbib/Corbis; **268:** H. Yamaguchi/Gamma Liaison; **272:** Jeff Isaac Greenberg/Photo Researchers; **274:** Lawrence Migdale; **275:** The Lilly Library, Indiana University, Bloomington; **276:** Steve Nickerson/Black Star; **279:** Rob Sollett/*Staten Island Advance*; **280(t):** Nick Ut/AP/Wide World Photos; **CHAPTER 10, 288:** Frank Holl, *Convalescent*, Christopher Wood Gallery, London, Bridgeman/Art Resource, NY; **292:** John Gaps III/AP Photo; **294:** Torlin Boyd Photo, Tokyo, Japan; **296(t):** Mary Evans Picture Library/Sigmund Freud Copyrights; **296(b):** Young-Wolff/PhotoEdit; **297:** Steve McCurry/Magnum Photos; **298:** M. Siluk/The Image Works; **300:** Lester Sloan/Woodfin Camp & Associates; **301:** Jeff Greenberg/Visuals Unlimited; **302:** George Rooker/Christie's Images; **304:** Lionel Cihes/AP/Wide World Photos; **307:** Bruce Plotkin/Liason International; **309(t):** Lennart Nilsson/Boehringer Ingelheim International GmbH; **309(b):** Ted Spiegel/Black Star; **310:** Frank Fournier/Woodfin Camp & Associates; **312:** Karin Daher/Gamma press images; **313:** Rick Rickman/Matrix; **314:** Louis Psihoyos/Matrix; **315:** Tom Sobolik/Black Star; **316:** Joe McNally, *Life* © Time Warner, Inc; **317:** Peter Serling, New York, NY; **324(inset):** Steve Schapiro/Sygma; **324(l):** B. Schiffman/Gamma Liaison; **CHAPTER 11, 324(r):** David Garner; **325:** J. Polleross/The Stock Market; **328(t):** Richard Howard © 1991 *Discover*; **328(b):** Les Stone/Sygma; **330:** Donna Terek, *Michigan* magazine, *The Detroit News/Free Press*; **331:** Wallace Kirkland, *Life* © Time Warner, Inc; **332:** Claus Meyer/Black Star; **333:** Bruce McBroom/Everett Collection; **334:** Pierre August Renoir, *Seated Bather*, 1903-1906, Detroit Institute of the Arts, bequest of Robert H. Tannahill; **335:** Mary Kate Denny/PhotoEdit; **337(l):** John Annerino, Tucson; **337(r):** John Annerino, Tucson; **338:** Will Hart/PhotoEdit; **339:** Marcus/Sipa Press; **342:** Lara Jo Regan/The Gamma Liason Network; **343:** Ilene Perlman/Impact Visuals; **344:** Rosario Esposito/AP Photo; **345:** Yvonne Hemsey/Gamma Liaison; **CHAPTER 12, 350:** Liam Longman/Miramax/The Kobal Collection; **352(l):** Currier & Ives, *Washington's Farewell to the Officers of His Army*, 1848. The Museum of the City of New York. Gift of Gerald Levino.; **352(r):** Currier & Ives, *Washington's Farewell to the Officers of His Army*, 1876. The Museum of the City of New York. Gift of Gerald Levino; **356:** Kevin & Betty Collins/Visuals Unlimited; **358:** Rodolfo Valtierra/Corbis Sygma; **359:** Tony O'Brian/Picture Group; **360:** The Granger Collection; **362:** Charlie Steiner/JB Pictures; **363:** Brooks Kraft/Sygma; **364:** Michele McDonald, Arlington, Massachusetts; **366:** E.T. Archives; **367:** Vaughan Fleming/Science Photo Library/Photo Researchers; **368:** Dusan Vranic/AP Photo; **369:** Elaine Thompson/AP Photo; **370(l):** Richard E. Aaron/Sygma; **370(r):** The Everett Collection; **372:** Corbis; **374:** Jeff Mermelstein, New York, NY; **375:** C/B Productions/The Stock Market; **377:** Nick Ut/AP Photo; **379(b):** J. Pozarik/Liason; **379(t):** *The Best of Photo-*

name index

Subject Index

hallucinogens in, 366–369
mood disorders and, 374
operant conditioning and, 373–374
opponent-process theory and, 374
polysubstance abuse and, 370–371
prevalence of, 351
psychodynamic therapy for, 376–377
psychodynamic view of, 372–373
psychotic episodes in, 437t
relapse-prevention training for, 378
residential treatment centers for, 381
reward-deficiency syndrome and, 376
in schizophrenia, 466, 467b
sedative-hypnotic drugs in, 357–358
self-help programs for, 381–382
sociocultural therapy for, 381–382
sociocultural view of, 371–372
stimulants in, 360–365
substances used in, 351
suicide and, 261–263, 262t
therapeutic communities for, 381
tolerance in, 350, 375–376
treatment of, 376–382
withdrawal in, 350
    behavioral view of, 374
    biochemical factors in, 375–376
Substance abuse personality, 372
Substance dependence, 350
    diagnostic criteria for, 351t
Substance-related disorders, in DSM-IV,
    105t
Suicide, 251–282
    abuse and, 260
    age and, 259, 270–275
    alcohol and, 261–263, 262t
    altruistic, 267
    anomic, 267–268
    assisted, 276b–277b
    biological view of, 268–270
    case histories of, 253–254
    celebrity, 263–265
    by children, 254, 255, 270–271
    contagion of, 263–265
    by death darers, 255
    by death ignorers, 255
    by death initiators, 255
    by death seekers, 255
    definition of, 253
    depression and, 262t, 262–263, 265–266,
        269–270
    egotistic, 266
    by elderly, 273–275
    explanations for, 264–270
    failed attempts at, 252
    familial factors in, 253b, 268–270
    gender and, 257, 258, 259, 261, 278b
    genetic factors in, 268–270
    group, 280
    hopelessness and, 261
    illness and, 259–260, 263
    in Japan, 268b
    loss and, 258
    marital status and, 257
    modeling of, 263–265
    mood and thought changes in, 261
    motives for, 255, 256b, 281

occupational stress and, 260–261
patterns of, 257–258
post-attempt treatment for, 275–276
predictors of, 262t
prevalence of, 252, 252t
prevention of, 276–281
by prisoners, 260
psychodynamic view of, 265–266
psychological abnormalities and, 262t,
    262–263
publicity of, 263–264
race and, 258, 259
rates of, 257–258, 259
religious beliefs and, 257
retrospective analysis of, 255–257, 256b
right to, 276b–277b
schizophrenia and, 262, 262t, 263, 264b
serotonin and, 269–270
social context for, 257–258
sociocultural view of, 266–270, 281–282
stress and, 258–261
studies of, 255–257
subintentional death and, 255
substance abuse and, 261–263, 262t
survivors of, studies of, 257
victimization and, 260
Suicide education programs, 281
Suicide hot lines, 277–278
Suicide notes, 256b
Suicide prevention programs, 277–281
Superego, 55
Support groups
    for families of schizophrenics, 465
    for physical disorders, 316
Surgery, brain, memory impairment and,
    498
Survivor guilt, 184
Symbolic loss, 202
Sympathetic nervous system, stress and,
    120, 120–121, 305
Symptom-exacerbation studies, 41b
Synapse, 48, 48
Syndromes, 15, 103
Synergistic effects, in polysubstance abuse,
    370
Syphilis, 15
Systematic desensitization, 62, 146–147

Tacrine (Cognex), 503–504
Tarantism, 10
*Tarasoff v. Regents of the University of
    California*, 603
Tardive dyskinesia, 459–460
Tay-Sachs disease, 570
T cells, killer, 308, 309
Tease technique, 404
Teenagers. *See* Adolescents
Tegretol (carbamazepine), for bipolar
    disorder, 243
Temporal lobe, in memory, 494
Tension headaches, 301
Tertiary prevention, 78
Testosterone, sexual desire and, 391
Test-retest reliability, 85
Tests, 88–99

battery of, 96–97, 114
bias in, 90, 93, 99
criterion keying for, 91
neurological, 94–97, 95b, 96–99
neuropsychological, 96–99
personality, 91–94
projective, 88–91
psychophysiological, 94–97, 95b
response inventories, 94, 94t
Tetrahydrocannabinol (THC), 367, 369
Thalamus, 47, 47
    in memory, 494
    in obsessive-compulsive disorder, 171
Thematic Apperception Test, 89–90
Theory of mind, 561
Therapeutic communities, 454
    for substance abuse, 381
Therapists. *See* Psychologists
Thunderstorm phobia, 139
Tip-of-the-tongue phenomenon, 489b
Tobacco, nicotine addiction and, 364b
Tofranil (imipramine), 236
    suicide and, 269
Token economy
    for mentally retarded, 572
    for schizophrenics, 454–456
Tolerance, drug, 350, 375–376
Touching compulsions, 165. *See also*
    Obsessive-compulsive disorder
Trait anxiety, 121
Tranquilizers, 51
Transcranial magnetic stimulation, 235
Transference, 56
Transsexualism, 416–419, 417t
Transvestism, 410–411
Treatment, 5–6, 109–114. *See also specific
    therapies*
    combined approaches in, 113
    community mental health approach in,
        18–19
    current trends in, 17–22
    decision-making in, 109–110
    definition of, 6
    demonological, 10–11
    in early 20th century, 15–17
    economic issues in, 606–607
    effectiveness of, 110–113
    essential features of, 6
    in Greco-Roman period, 9–10
    historical perspective on, 8–17
    hospitalization in. *See* Hospitalization
    insurance coverage for, 19
    in Middle Ages, 10–11
    for moderate illness, 19–20
    moral, 13–15
    in 19th century, 13–15
    on-line, 66b
    outcome studies for, 111
    outpatient, 17, 18–20
    pharmacologic, 17–18
    placebo, 37
    in prehistoric times, 8–10
    providers of, 20–21, 21t
    rapprochement movement in, 112–113
    reform movement in, 13
    in Renaissance, 11–13

DSM-IV CLASSIFICATION

From the American Psychiatric Association: *Diagnostic and Statistical Manual of Mental Disorders, Fourth Edition,* Washington, DC, American Psychiatric Association, 1994. Reprinted by permission.

(All categories are on Axis I except those indicated otherwise.)

Disorders Usually First Diagnosed in Infancy, Childhood, or Adolescence

Mental Retardation

Note: These are coded on Axis II.
Mild mental retardation
Moderate mental retardation
Severe mental retardation
Profound mental retardation
Mental retardation, severity unspecified

Learning Disorders

Reading disorder
Mathematics disorder
Disorder of written expression
Learning disorder NOS*

Motor Skills Disorder

Developmental coordination disorder

Communication Disorders

Expressive language disorder
Mixed receptive-expressive language disorder
Phonological disorder
Stuttering
Communication disorder NOS*

Pervasive Developmental Disorders

Autistic disorder
Rett's disorder
Childhood disintegrative disorder
Asperger's disorder
Pervasive development disorder NOS*

Attention-Deficit and Disruptive Behavior Disorders

Attention-deficit/hyperactivity disorder
    Combined type
    Predominantly inattentive type
    Predominantly hyperactive-impulsive type
Attention-deficit/hyperactivity disorder NOS*
Conduct disorder
Oppositional defiant disorder
Disruptive behavior disorder NOS*

Feeding and Eating Disorders of Infancy or Early Childhood

Pica
Rumination disorder
Feeding disorder of infancy or early childhood

Tic Disorders

Tourette's disorder
Chronic motor or vocal tic disorder
Transient tic disorder
Tic disorder NOS*

*NOS= Not otherwise specified

Elimination Disorders

Encopresis
    With constipation and overflow incontinence
    Without constipation and overflow incontinence
Enuresis (not due to a general medical condition)

Other Disorders of Infancy, Childhood, or Adolescence

Separation anxiety disorder
Selective mutism
Reactive attachment disorder of infancy or early childhood
Stereotypic movement disorder
Disorder of infancy, childhood, or adolescence NOS*

Delirium, Dementia, and Amnestic and Other Cognitive Disorders

Delirium

Delirium due to . . . (*indicate the general medical condition*)
Substance intoxication delirium
Substance withdrawal delirium
Delirium due to multiple etiologies
Delirium NOS*

Dementia

Dementia of the Alzheimer's type, with early onset
Dementia of the Alzheimer's type, with late onset
Vascular dementia

Dementia Due to Other General Medical Conditions

Dementia due to HIV disease
Dementia due to head trauma
Dementia due to Parkinson's disease
Dementia due to Huntington's disease
Dementia due to Pick's disease
Dementia due to Creutzfeldt-Jakob disease
Dementia due to . . . (*indicate the general medical condition not listed above*)
Substance-induced persisting dementia
Dementia due to multiple etiologies
Dementia NOS*

Amnestic Disorders

Amnestic disorders due to . . . (*indicate the general medical condition*)
Substance-induced persisting amnestic disorder
Amnestic disorder NOS*

Other Cognitive Disorders

Cognitive disorder NOS*

Mental Disorders Due to a General Medical Condition Not Elsewhere Classified

Catatonic disorder due to . . . (*indicate the general medical condition*)
Personality change due to . . . (*indicate the general medical condition*)
Mental disorder NOS* due to . . . (*indicate the general medical condition*)

Substance-Related Disorders
[Alcohol; Amphetamine; Caffeine; Cannabis; Cocaine; Hallucinogen; Inhalant; Nicotine; Opioid; Phencyclidine; Sedative, Hypnotic, or Anxiolytic; Polysubstance; Other]

Substance Use Disorders

Substance dependence
Substance abuse

Substance-Induced Disorders

Substance intoxication
Substance withdrawal
Substance intoxication delirium
Substance withdrawal delirium
Substance-induced persisting dementia
Substance-induced persisting amnestic disorder
Substance-induced psychotic disorder
Substance-induced mood disorder
Substance-induced anxiety disorder
Substance-induced sexual dysfunction
Substance-induced sleep disorder
Substance-related disorder NOS*

Schizophrenia and Other Psychotic Disorders

Schizophrenia
    Paranoid type
    Disorganized type
    Catatonic type
    Undifferentiated type
    Residual type
Schizophreniform disorder
Schizoaffective disorder
Delusional disorder
Brief psychotic disorder
Shared psychotic disorder
Psychotic disorder due to . . . (*indicate the general medical condition*)
Substance-induced psychotic disorder
Psychotic disorder NOS*

Mood Disorders

Depressive Disorders

Major depressive disorder
Dysthymic disorder
Depressive disorder NOS*

Bipolar Disorders

Bipolar I disorder
Bipolar II disorder
Cyclothymic disorder
Bipolar disorder NOS*
Mood disorder due to . . . (*indicate the general medical condition*)
Substance-induced mood disorder
Mood disorder NOS*

Anxiety Disorders

Panic disorder without agoraphobia
Panic disorder with agoraphobia
Agoraphobia without history of panic disorder
Specific phobia
Social phobia
Obsessive-compulsive disorder
Posttraumatic stress disorder

DSM-IV CLASSIFICATION

From the American Psychiatric Association: *Diagnostic and Statistical Manual of Mental Disorders, Fourth Edition,* Washington, DC, American Psychiatric Association, 1994. Reprinted by permission.

(All categories are on Axis I except those indicated otherwise.)

Disorders Usually First Diagnosed in Infancy, Childhood, or Adolescence

Mental Retardation
Note: These are coded on Axis II.
Mild mental retardation
Moderate mental retardation
Severe mental retardation
Profound mental retardation
Mental retardation, severity unspecified

Learning Disorders
Reading disorder
Mathematics disorder
Disorder of written expression
Learning disorder NOS*

Motor Skills Disorder
Developmental coordination disorder

Communication Disorders
Expressive language disorder
Mixed receptive-expressive language disorder
Phonological disorder
Stuttering
Communication disorder NOS*

Pervasive Developmental Disorders
Autistic disorder
Rett's disorder
Childhood disintegrative disorder
Asperger's disorder
Pervasive development disorder NOS*

Attention-Deficit and Disruptive Behavior Disorders
Attention-deficit/hyperactivity disorder
    Combined type
    Predominantly inattentive type
    Predominantly hyperactive-impulsive type
Attention-deficit/hyperactivity disorder NOS*
Conduct disorder
Oppositional defiant disorder
Disruptive behavior disorder NOS*

Feeding and Eating Disorders of Infancy or Early Childhood
Pica
Rumination disorder
Feeding disorder of infancy or early childhood

Tic Disorders
Tourette's disorder
Chronic motor or vocal tic disorder
Transient tic disorder
Tic disorder NOS*

Elimination Disorders
Encopresis
    With constipation and overflow incontinence
    Without constipation and overflow incontinence
Enuresis (not due to a general medical condition)

Other Disorders of Infancy, Childhood, or Adolescence
Separation anxiety disorder
Selective mutism
Reactive attachment disorder of infancy or early childhood
Stereotypic movement disorder
Disorder of infancy, childhood, or adolescence NOS*

Delirium, Dementia, and Amnestic and Other Cognitive Disorders

Delirium
Delirium due to . . . *(indicate the general medical condition)*
Substance intoxication delirium
Substance withdrawal delirium
Delirium due to multiple etiologies
Delirium NOS*

Dementia
Dementia of the Alzheimer's type, with early onset
Dementia of the Alzheimer's type, with late onset
Vascular dementia

Dementia Due to Other General Medical Conditions
Dementia due to HIV disease
Dementia due to head trauma
Dementia due to Parkinson's disease
Dementia due to Huntington's disease
Dementia due to Pick's disease
Dementia due to Creutzfeldt-Jakob disease
Dementia due to . . . *(indicate the general medical condition not listed above)*
Substance-induced persisting dementia
Dementia due to multiple etiologies
Dementia NOS*

Amnestic Disorders
Amnestic disorders due to . . . *(indicate the general medical condition)*
Substance-induced persisting amnestic disorder
Amnestic disorder NOS*

Other Cognitive Disorders
Cognitive disorder NOS*

Mental Disorders Due to a General Medical Condition Not Elsewhere Classified
Catatonic disorder due to . . . *(indicate the general medical condition)*
Personality change due to . . . *(indicate the general medical condition)*
Mental disorder NOS* due to . . . *(indicate the general medical condition)*

Substance-Related Disorders
[Alcohol; Amphetamine; Caffeine; Cannabis; Cocaine; Hallucinogen; Inhalant; Nicotine; Opioid; Phencyclidine; Sedative, Hypnotic, or Anxiolytic; Polysubstance; Other]

Substance Use Disorders
Substance dependence
Substance abuse

Substance-Induced Disorders
Substance intoxication
Substance withdrawal
Substance intoxication delirium
Substance withdrawal delirium
Substance-induced persisting dementia
Substance-induced persisting amnestic disorder
Substance-induced psychotic disorder
Substance-induced mood disorder
Substance-induced anxiety disorder
Substance-induced sexual dysfunction
Substance-induced sleep disorder
Substance-related disorder NOS*

Schizophrenia and Other Psychotic Disorders
Schizophrenia
    Paranoid type
    Disorganized type
    Catatonic type
    Undifferentiated type
    Residual type
Schizophreniform disorder
Schizoaffective disorder
Delusional disorder
Brief psychotic disorder
Shared psychotic disorder
Psychotic disorder due to . . . *(indicate the general medical condition)*
Substance-induced psychotic disorder
Psychotic disorder NOS*

Mood Disorders

Depressive Disorders
Major depressive disorder
Dysthymic disorder
Depressive disorder NOS*

Bipolar Disorders
Bipolar I disorder
Bipolar II disorder
Cyclothymic disorder
Bipolar disorder NOS*
Mood disorder due to . . . *(indicate the general medical condition)*
Substance-induced mood disorder
Mood disorder NOS*

Anxiety Disorders
Panic disorder without agoraphobia
Panic disorder with agoraphobia
Agoraphobia without history of panic disorder
Specific phobia
Social phobia
Obsessive-compulsive disorder
Posttraumatic stress disorder

*NOS= Not otherwise specified